Psychology of Women

Recent Titles in
Women's Psychology

"Intimate" Violence against Women: When Spouses, Partners, or Lovers Attack
Paula K. Lundberg-Love and Shelly L. Marmion, editors

Daughters of Madness: Growing Up and Older with a Mentally Ill Mother
Susan Nathiel

Psychology of Women: A Handbook of Issues and Theories

Second Edition

Edited by Florence L. Denmark and Michele A. Paludi

Foreword by Bernice Lott

Westport, Connecticut
London

Library of Congress Cataloging-in-Publication Data

Denmark, Florence.
  Psychology of women : A handbook of issues and theories /
Florence L. Denmark and Michele A. Paludi. — 2nd ed.
    p. cm. — (Women's Psychology, ISSN 1931-0021)
  Includes bibliographical references and index.
  ISBN 978-0-275-99162-3 (alk. paper)
  1. Women—Psychology. 2. Feminist psychology. I. Paludi, Michele Antoinette.
II. Title.
  HQ1206.P747 2008
  155.6′33—dc22   2007028011

British Library Cataloguing in Publication Data is available.

Library of Congress Catalog Card Number: 2007028011
ISBN: 978-0-275-99162-3
ISSN: 1931-0021

First published in 2008

Praeger Publishers, 88 Post Road West, Westport, CT 06881
An imprint of Greenwood Publishing Group, Inc.
www.praeger.com

Printed in the United States of America

The paper used in this book complies with the Permanent Paper Standard issued by the National Information Standards Organization (Z39.48-1984).

10 9 8 7 6 5 4 3 2 1

In memory of the first generation of women psychologists, we dedicate this handbook to future scholars in the psychology of women.

Contents

List of Illustrations

FIGURES

TABLES

Foreword

Bernice Lott

In rereading the epilogue that I wrote for the first edition of Denmark and Paludi's *Psychology of Women*, I found myself wanting very much to say again some of what I wrote over a decade ago.

> The theoretical and research literature on the psychology of women that continues to grow and enrich our discipline is a source of great pride.... [W]e have succeeded ... in making mainstream psychology sit up and take notice. We have raised cogent and sophisticated arguments in our critiques of traditional psychological assumptions, theories, questions, topics, and methods.... [Our] feminist agenda ... asks new questions, proposes new relationships among personal and social variables, focuses on women's lives and experiences, is sensitive to the implications of our research for social policy and social change, and assumes that science is always done in a cultural/historical/political context. (Lott, 1993, p. 721)

This new Handbook, like the first one, contributes significantly to the advancement of this agenda. It presents, to students, teachers, researchers, and practitioners, discussions of the very latest in methods, research, and theory in the psychology of women. The reader will find chapters on multiple aspects of women's lives and on issues of particular concern to women.

Most of the new contributions to scholarship on women's lives will be seen to be associated with a feminist perspective or with feminist psychology. Central to this perspective is the empirically supported proposition that women have been, and continue to be, oppressed or denied full social equality with men. The perspective goes further in affirming that some form of transformation in our institutions is needed to change this historical and contemporary state of affairs. Within this central core, there are variations in analyses regarding the agents and processes that maintain inequality; in preferred methods of inquiry; and in the significance of such social categories as class, ethnicity, age, and sexual preference as they interact with gender. There are variations in suggested routes to social and political equality and to full access to social resources. There are also variations in answers to the question of how "essential" or heterogeneous women's experiences are across cultures, generations, and across historical periods.

To a large extent, however, that "the personal is political"—a phrase first introduced into the literature in 1969 by Carol Hanisch (1975)—remains as a salient and dominant theme within our research and theory. Hanisch wrote that it is "a political action to tell it like it is" instead of what women have "been told to say" (p. 204). Through the years, additional meanings have emerged to reflect the belief that women's lives, development, and experiences are always to be examined in a context of social structure and power relationships. And that context, almost everywhere, is one of lesser access to resources, stereotyped beliefs, and cultural prescriptions and proscriptions. This context is apparent in all aspects of life—childhood, education, family, sexuality, close relationships, work, health, art, commerce, politics, and government.

Baker (2006), in her 2005 presidential address to the Society for the Psychology of Women (Division 35 of the American Psychological Association), illustrates the continued meaning and strength of the concepts of personal and political. She explores the link between them thirty years after the idea of their interdependence was first introduced into our literature, and asserts that "the personal is political because there is no personal outside the structures of society" (p. 2). Because the role played by social structures in shaping experience is recognized by those who study the psychology of women, analyses of sexism, oppression, and power are, of necessity, incorporated into their work. It is our understanding of power that provides important parallels between feminist psychology and multicultural psychology and offers a bridge that is apparent in shared values and a similar commitment to social justice (e.g., see Reynolds & Constantine, 2004). As noted by Brown (2006), we must "say clearly that 'feminist' is a word that means committed to social justice, starting with gender equality" but not stopping there (p. 23).

Among the most significant contributions of the psychological study of women within a feminist perspective is the recognition that it is not just women's lives that need to be examined in a political context, but men's as well. Thus, as noted by Stewart & McDermott (2004), gender is understood to be "an analytical tool" (p. 518), not just an empirical category, and it signifies "a set of power relations rather than merely characteristics or features of individuals" (p. 528). Men researching "masculinity" have been influenced by feminist theory and research and by the proposition that "humans are gendered beings" (Smiler, 2004, p. 15), whose gender deeply affects lives and experiences.

The new research on gender has uncovered the data needed to question prevalent and powerful old myths. Spelke (2005), for example, examined more than forty years of research on sex differences in aptitude for mathematics and science and found that persons of both genders share the same cognitive capacities and have "equal talent" (p. 950). Further, the data do not support the supposed truism that women surpass men in verbal ability while men surpass women in spatial ability. She comes to this remarkable conclusion: explanations for "the preponderance of men on academic faculties of mathematics and science" (p. 956) will not be found in gender studies of differences in cognitive development. In a similar vein, Baker (2006) urges us to "shift the discussion from endless debates about the existence or shape of male-female differences to discussion of the purposes of such a focus" (p. 5). I have argued (Lott, 1997) that one purpose of such a focus is to support the status quo, keeping attention away from a serious examination of the conditions that our society links to gender and of the behaviors linked to those conditions. Shifting attention away from such an examination is a useful means of maintaining unequal power and gender stereotypes.

Of course, change is always occurring in both the context and specifics of our experience—at different rates in different communities and societies. One area in which change seems pitifully slow in contemporary U.S. society, however, is the deeply held assumption that when children are born, it is the mother who assumes primary responsibility for their rearing and for their health and welfare as young children. A current debate, similar to older debates, is whether motherhood responsibilities take precedence over a career (for educated middle-class women). The media have been particularly eager to write stories about women who opt out of the workforce for "the comforts of home and family" (see Goldin, 2006; Conniff, 2006). A new media tack was introduced by an article arguing that professional/career women are less likely to be happy wives and mothers—more likely, in other words, to be the source of a "rocky marriage" (Noer, 2006). But still primarily absent from such articles and narratives is attention to the role of fathers, husbands, and male partners. We are reminded of this in a counterpoint to Noer's article (Corcoran, 2006). Also typically absent is attention to the interrelationships among parenthood, work, social class, and ethnicity.

Another area of slow change in the United States is women's relative absence from positions of political power, an absence some might argue is not unrelated to the still prevalent debate of home versus family. Hahn (2006) reminds us that in 2005 women constituted just 15 percent of Congress and 22 percent of membership in state legislatures, with one lone woman in the Supreme Court. A woman serving as secretary of state in the Bush administration is a striking exception.

In this wonderful, inclusive volume that you now have before you will be found a collection of papers that examine how recent changes have impacted women's lives. There are chapters on researching and teaching about women, developmental periods in women's lives, health issues, and relationship and work issues. The reader will find papers that are heterogeneous in style, level of analysis, methodology, and specific focus area. All, however, present incisive analyses that advance our store of knowledge. Some go further and provide guidance with respect to how this knowledge can be applied to arguments and policies for social change.

REFERENCES

Baker, N. L. (2006). Feminist psychology in the service of women: Staying engaged without getting married. *Psychology of Women Quarterly, 30,* 1–14.

Brown, L. S. (2006). Still subversive after all these years: The relevance of feminist therapy in the age of evidence-based practice. *Psychology of Women Quarterly, 30,* 15–24.

Conniff, R. (2006). Stop feeding the work monster. *The Progressive,* March 23.

Corcoran, E. (2006). Counterpoint: Don't marry a lazy man. *Forbes.com,* August 23.

Goldin, C. (2006). Working it out. *New York Times,* March 16.

Hahn, C. (2006). Wanted: Women in the House (and Senate). *Ms.,* Winter, 16.

Hanisch, C. (1975). The personal is political. In *Redstockings of the Women's Liberation Movement: Feminist revolution* (pp. 204–205). New York: Random House. Reprinted from *Notes from the second year: Women's liberation; major writings of the radical feminists.* New York: Radical Feminism, 1970.

Lott, B. (1993). Epilogue. In F. L. Denmark & M. A. Paludi (Eds.), *The psychology of women: A handbook of issues and theories* (p. 721). Westport, CT: Greenwood Press.

Lott, B. (1997). The personal and social correlates of a gender difference ideology. *Journal of Social Issues, 53,* 279–298.

Noer, M. (2006). Point: Don't marry career women. *Forbes.com,* August 23.

Reynolds, A. L., & Constantine, M. G. (2004). Feminism and multiculturalism: Parallels and intersections. *Journal of Multicultural Counseling and Development, 32,* 346–357.

Smiler, A. P. (2004). Thirty years after the discovery of gender: Psychological concepts and measures of masculinity. *Sex Roles, 50,* 15–26.

Spelke, E. S. (2005). Sex differences in intrinsic aptitude for mathematics and science? *American Psychologist, 60,* 950–958.

Stewart, A. J., & McDermott, C. (2004). Gender in psychology. *Annual Review of Psychology, 55,* 519–544.

Acknowledgments

Florence L. Denmark and Michele A. Paludi extend our appreciation to Debbie Carvalko for her support and encouragement of us to edit a second edition of this handbook. We also thank the contributors to this volume for their collaboration, dedication to the field of the psychology of women, and patience with all stages of the production of this handbook.

We thank our family, friends, and colleagues for sharing their ideas with us and supporting us throughout this process: Presha Neidermeyer, Paula Lundberg Love, and Robert Wesner. We especially thank Maria Klara and Erika Baron, graduate students at Pace University, who performed numerous tasks whenever needed. We'd also like to thank Steve Salbod for his technical help.

Lastly, we acknowledge the researchers and instructors in the field of the psychology of women who have made this handbook become a reality.

CHAPTER 5

The research for this chapter was supported by National Science Foundation grant REC 0635444 to Janet Hyde and by NIH grant NIMH NRSA F32MH079171-01 to Shelly Grabe.

CHAPTER 7

The authors thank Martin Ruck for helpful comments on this chapter. We also thank Elizabeth Kachur and Amy Moors for their assistance in locating research articles.

CHAPTER 14

We would like to express appreciation to Allen Meyer for his comments on the manuscript. This chapter updates N. F. Russo & B. L. Green, "Women and Mental Health," pp. 379–436 in F. L. Denmark & M. A. Paludi (Eds.), *Psychology of Women: A Handbook of Issues and Theories* (Westport: Greenwood Press, 1993), and although the literature reported here has little overlap with that previously reported, we would like to recognize Beth Green's contributions to the conceptualization of the previous chapter, which is reflected in the approach to this new work.

CHAPTER 20

We would like to express appreciation to Allen Meyer for his comments on the manuscript and to Melissa LeBlanc for assistance in typing references. This chapter updates Green and Russo's chapter "Work and Family: Selected Issues" in the 1993 edition of this book, and although the literature reported here has little overlap with that previously reported, we would like to recognize Beth Green's contributions to the conceptualization of the previous chapter, which is reflected in the approach to this new work.

Introduction

Florence L. Denmark and Michele A. Paludi

> *The question has been asked, "What is a woman?" A woman is a person who makes choices. A woman is a dreamer. A woman is a planner. A woman is a maker, and a molder. A woman is a person who makes choices. A woman builds bridges. A woman makes children and makes cars. A woman writes poetry and songs. A woman is a person who makes choices. You cannot even simply become a mother anymore. You must choose motherhood. Will you choose change? Can you become its vanguard?*
>
> —*Eleanor Holmes Norton*

Eleanor Holmes Norton's sentiment is expressed throughout this second edition of *Psychology of Women: A Handbook of Issues and Theories.* Women are portrayed in terms of the choices we make in our careers, achievement, leadership capacity, friendships and romantic relationships, and education. Women are portrayed as being multidimensional, for example, in the ways we integrate work and family roles. Furthermore, a non-Eurocentric perspective on women is presented. New to this edition, we have included a chapter devoted to women of color and another on the international psychology of women. The chapters are also balanced for sexual orientation, class, and ethnicity. Thus, women are portrayed in terms of our culture.

Albert (1988) described advantages in placing culture prominently in the psychology curriculum. We have found these advantages to be especially useful in the psychology of women:

- We can obtain information that is not available in our own culture.
- We can obtain information about the incidence of a psychological issue in a different culture.
- Values that are common to a certain cultural group can be discussed.

- The generalizability of psychological research can be assessed by looking at research from several cultures.

In addition to the new chapters on women of color and international psychology of women (chapters 2 and 3, respectively), we have also included the following new chapters: women and leadership (chapter 21), courses in the psychology of women (chapter 6), and lesbian relationships (chapter 15). These chapters make this handbook stronger: They offer new insight into the question, What is a woman?

As in the first edition, the chapters in this handbook are guided by the following feminist frameworks:

1. Effective human behavior in social interactions and within social systems is related to understanding the relationship between the personal and political.
2. The psychology of women should treat women as the norm.
3. The subjective, personal experience of women is valid and important.
4. The psychology of women should identify the women of psychology; contributions by historical and contemporary women psychologists should be noted.
5. The information in the psychology of women should encourage individuals to critically analyze all subareas in psychology for the portrayal of women. (adapted from Lord, 1982)

Mary Roth Walsh (1985) suggested that the psychology of women serves as a "catalyst of change" by revealing serious deficiencies in psychological research and theories relevant to women. Our goal for this edition is the same as we had for the first: to have this handbook be a catalyst for change and a stimulant for further research and advocacy on the psychology of women. Thus, our goal is to have readers do as Eleanor Holmes Norton asked: to choose change, to become its vanguard.

REFERENCES

Albert, R. (1988). The place of culture in modern psychology. In P. Bronstein & K. Quina (Eds.), *Teaching a psychology of people: Resources for gender and sociocultural awareness*, 12–18. Washington, DC: American Psychological Association.

Lord, S. (1982). Research on teaching the psychology of women. *Psychology of Women Quarterly, 7*, 96–104.

Walsh, M. (1985). The psychology of women course: A continuing catalyst for change. *Teaching of Psychology, 12*, 198–203.

PART I

Foundations

Chapter 1

Historical Development of the Psychology of Women

Florence L. Denmark
Maria Klara
Erika Baron
Linda Cambareri-Fernandez

In studying the history of psychology, as is true for other disciplines, the majority of the influential work and theory has been constructed by men and for men. As Gerda Lerner (1979), an American historian, pointed out:

> Traditional history has been written and interpreted by men in an androcentric frame of reference; it might quite properly be described as the history of men. The very term "Women's History" calls attention to the fact that something is missing from historical scholarship. (p. xiv)

Due to the biased social structure and inherent sexism that was predominant from the time of the ancient Greeks until recently, women and psychology had been separated from one another, and psychology was not considered to be a field "appropriate" for women. As Agnes O'Connell and Nancy Russo (1991) noted, psychology's history has been a social construction by and for male psychologists. This was the case with the exception of the past few decades. Although women made significant contributions to psychology, they largely remained invisible (Russo & Denmark, 1987; O'Connell & Russo, 1991). However, with the advent of the women's movement, women fought and increasingly became a valuable part of the discipline. They not only took positions in research, as clinicians, and teachers but also made many significant contributions in each of these respective fields.

It is the purpose of this chapter to discuss the history of women and psychology and to give credit to some of the notable women who have worked and studied in psychology and who deserve long-overdue recognition.

How to Study Women in History

Before specifically discussing the history of women and psychology, it will be helpful to understand how women have been characterized in history in general and what methods have been used to study this subject. Lerner (1992) postulated that the traditional approach to women's history is that of "compensatory history," where only women who were noteworthy or accomplished were recognized. Using this framework to examine this history of the women in psychology would entail studying such early female psychologists as Mary Calkins, Margaret Floy Washburn, and Christine Ladd-Franklin. In other words, this approach is characterized by an examination of those who were noteworthy or whose achievements distinguished them in a field primarily comprised of men.

The next level of conceptualizing women's history can be characterized as "contribution history." Here, women are noted as important because of the contributions they made to certain fields, to reform movements, to political action, and so on. This would support an examination of how women contributed to the ongoing development of psychology and would entail, for example, an analysis of the repercussions of the Women's Movement, the advent of feminist thought, and so forth.

However, Lerner (1992) feels that there is also another way of judging and conceptualizing women's contributions throughout history: "transitional women's history." In this framework, women are not seen in one-dimensional parameters where they are studied in specific time frames or within the boundaries of definite contributions. Rather, it is a way of examining women in relation to specific categories and how women contribute, respond, develop, and react to them. Psychological issues such as sexuality, reproduction, the link between motherhood and raising children, roles of women, sexual values, sexual myths, ethnicity, race, class, and religion would all be taken into consideration as a multidirectional matrix when examining the history of women in psychology. Therefore, unilateral conclusions or examinations are not made, but rather an in-depth analysis of the role of women and the factors contributing to their lives would be sought.

Defining the Psychology of Women

The psychology of women is an area of scientific investigation that can trace its roots back to early studies of so-called sex differences;

however, the field encompasses much more than this variation. Indeed, the emphasis on difference has an implicit assumption of a myriad of differences other than biological sex. While the psychology of gender comparisons is a more apt title, it still leaves out the many topics of investigation that encompass experiences unique to women, such as pregnancy, breast-feeding, and menstruation. The term *feminist psychology* seems to invoke too many connotations and has a varied meaning among different feminists. How, then, can we best define the psychology of women?

Mednick (1976) defined the field as "the study of variations within a group and across time of the female experience." Henley (1974) favors "psychology and women" as a descriptive term. However, Mednick believes this is too broad.

We believe that Russo's definition of the psychology of women, as the study of behavior (not excluding male gender-role behavior) mediated by the variable of female sex, is one of the most useful. In the past, psychology studied behavior, but it was not mediated by the variable of female sex. Thus, the psychology of women is also defined as that which includes all psychological issues pertaining to women and their experiences (Denmark, 1977). In defining the psychology of women in this manner, it is also productive to use Lerner's (1992) "transitional history" lens (i.e., one where women's experiences are examined through their multiple layers of understanding).

Women in Psychological Research

In order to understand the contributions that women have made in the field of psychology, one must understand the status of women in psychology prior to this change. Feminists have long argued that the social sciences overlook and distort the study of women in a systematic manner that results favorably to men (Riger, 2002). The inclusion of the variables of sex and gender can be examined in three separate time frames and conceptualizations, according to Jeanne Marecek, Ellen Kimmel, Mary Crawford, and Rachel Hare-Mustin (2003):

1. Woman as problem
2. Female-male differences and similarities
3. Feminist study of women's lives

When one examines the psychological research from Wundt's 1874 establishment of the domain of psychology up to recent times, psychology appeared to focus almost exclusively on the behavior of men or male animals. In other words, the first method of examining woman was to categorize them as lacking. Much early research that included female subjects came to the conclusion that women were inferior in some way. Additionally, if females were included in the sample, neither sex nor gender differences were reported, which discounted the influence of these factors and, in essence, was an indication of the belief that men were the norm when considering various psychological factors. And again, if women were included in the studies, biased results indicated that women were by nature inferior. For instance, Sir Francis Galton's work in the 19th century focused on individual differences and concluded that "women tend in all their capacities to be inferior to men" (cited in Lewin & Wild, 1991, p. 582).

However, generally speaking, most early research never investigated comparisons between women and men at all (Schwabacher, 1972). Wendy McKenna and Suzanne Kessler (1976) reported that over 95 percent of all early research did not examine female-male comparisons, therefore ignoring any possible differences due to sex and gender. Prior to the 1970s, almost all research on women had been relegated to the periphery of psychology rather than integrated into its main body. Although the definition of psychology has undergone a metamorphosis over time, one fact remains increasingly clear—women and women's issues have still not been adequately examined.

In the decades preceding the second wave of feminism, Marecek and colleagues' (2003) second approach to studying women was employed; at this stage, much psychological research assumed profound differences between women and men. This consensus supported male superiority and domination, a societal structure very much in place at the time. Some male researchers studied sex differences and largely interpreted them to demonstrate female inferiority (Shields, 1975). In contrast, Leta Hollingworth's work in the early 1900s revealed no evidence of female-male differences in variability. In 1944, one of Freud's students, Helene Deutsch, wrote the first book entitled *The Psychology of Women*. Although agreeing with her mentor that women had more delicate psychic structures than men, she did discuss the important role of motherhood and eroticism in her book (Unger, 2001).

Psychology has often been defined as the science of behavior, both human and animal. Yet it was a common practice of researchers to include only white male humans or male animals in their research samples. This is especially ironic because even then every undergraduate statistics book stressed the basic premise that for any study to be generalizable, it had to have a representative, not a skewed, sample. Nevertheless, the idea of "male as representative of the norm" was so strong that even well-trained psychologists did not realize that they were excluding at least 50 percent of the population. What they fostered was not psychology the science of behavior, but psychology the science of white male behavior.

The third method to approach gender research—that which utilizes a feminist perspective (Marecek et al., 2003)—is more often being employed today. History is now viewed as contextual and is sensitive to gender as well as culture. When research is conducted, various factors embedded in this contextual approach should be examined. Feminist researchers are concerned with the particulars of women's experiences—how and why women come to act, think, and feel the way that they do. Although not an easy answer, it is giving credence to the perspective of woman as a multidimensional and complex being.

TWO THREADS IN THE HISTORY OF THE PSYCHOLOGY OF WOMEN

In the study of the history of the psychology of women, two main threads must be examined, as they had profound consequences and promoted new directions in the field. The first of these was Charles Darwin's 1859 publication *On the Origin of Species*, and the second was the work of Sigmund Freud. The common element between these two historical figures was their debased and inferior perception of women; ultimately they constructed their theories to support this view. Women were plagued by an inferior evolutionary code as well as a weaker psyche, according to these men. However, the response to these theories and the effort to discount them brought about a tremendous reaction and amount of research that helped to solidify and strengthen the fight of women toward equality.

Myths of Social Darwinism

Social Darwinism was based on the social theories that arose as a result of the publication of Darwin's *Origin of Species*. In an attempt to explain individual variability and variability among different species, Darwin posited theories of natural and sexual selection. He noted that while all members of a species had the possibility of producing many progeny, the population of any species remained fairly constant over time. Thus, he concluded that individuals within a species compete with each other in their "struggle for existence." In addition, he also observed that all organisms vary. Combining these thoughts, Darwin posited the theory of natural selection, popularly known as the "survival of the fittest." Individuals that had favorable variations survived and reproduced, thus transmitting the favorable traits to their offspring. In this manner, "genetic housecleaning" was performed, with natural selection eliminating unfavorable traits, since those who had them did not survive long enough to reproduce and pass the unfavorable traits to their offspring.

Darwin also observed that not all variability seemed essential to individual survival. He attempted to account for this nonessential individual variability with his theory of sexual selection. Briefly, sexual selection was similar to natural selection in that it depended on a struggle, this one "not a struggle for existence but on a struggle between males for possession of the females" (Darwin, 1871, p. 575). Unsuccessful traits resulted not in "death to the unsuccessful competitor, but in few or no offspring" (Darwin, 1859, p. 100).

Darwin believed that most traits were inherited, but he did differentiate between "transmission of character" and the "development of character." This differentiation was important in the development of sexual differences. Sexual selection theory encompassed an associated law of partial inheritance, which stated that the law of equal transmission (that is, the transmission of certain characteristics to both sexes) was not always equal; sometimes transmission was only to the same-sex offspring. Darwin stated that he was unsure as to why the inheritability of some traits seemed to be governed by the law of equal transmission, while other traits' inheritability seemed to be governed by the law of partial inheritance.

Darwin's further observations led him to believe that physical traits such as size were inherited via natural selection and equally transmitted to both sexes, but not always developed in both sexes. Other traits, such as intelligence and reason, he believed, were acquired through sexual selection and seemed to be governed by the law of partial inheritance and same-sex transmission. Now, here's the rub. It appeared to Darwin that since females did not compete for males, they did not have the same evolutionary opportunity to develop the same intelligence, perseverance, and courage as males. Thus for Darwin, the result of natural and sexual selection was that men were "superior" to women. This is the central myth of social Darwinism.

Herbert Spencer based his theories on Darwin's views and expanded them to include the interaction effects of function on biological modification. According to Spencer, since women were the primary child-rearers in society, such traits as maternal instinct and nurturing ability would have been acquired as a result of their function, that is, daily care of children. Over time, according to Spencer, these traits became fixed in biological structures; in other words, there would be a "constitutional modification produced by excess of function" (Spencer, 1864, p. 252). In addition, in his book *The Principles of Biology*, Spencer also applied Hermann Helmholtz's conservation-of-energy theory to human growth. Spencer believed that human beings had a finite fund of energy ("vital force") that could be applied either to one's individual growth or to reproduction. He also believed that the female reproductive system obviously required more "vital force" than the male's reproductive system. So, simply put, women had less available vital force or energy for their individual mental and physical growth than men did. Women's reproductive systems demanded a great supply of energy, and any requirement of energy demand for mental activity or "brain-work," particularly during adolescence, was thought by Spencer to lead to reproductive disorders, inability to breast-feed, or even infertility.

Refutation of the Myth

Given the ramifications of Darwin's theory and the consequences that this theory had for women, many early women in the field sought to prove Darwin wrong through systematic studies and alternative theories. Although no such separate field as the psychology of women existed prior to the 1970s, there were early scientists whose research impacted on the field. Leta Hollingworth was a leading harbinger of the psychology of women; she was adamant that psychology apply vigorous scientific stringency to research on women. Hollingworth was one of many early scholars, along with Helen Thompson, Mary Calkins, and Mary Putnam Jacobi, who responded to the trends of social Darwinism of her time with myth-refuting, solid empirical evidence.

Leta Hollingworth

Leta Stetter Hollingworth was one of the early researchers who concentrated on research issues that would later become relevant to the psychology of women. She investigated areas of well-established bias in psychology, such as women's social role, the mental and physical performance during the menstrual cycle, and the variability hypothesis. While a graduate student at Columbia Teachers College, she was under the tutelage of Edward Thorndike, who was himself a strong supporter of the variability hypothesis.

One of Hollingworth's contributions was her research on physical and mental performance during the menstrual cycle, which demonstrated that changes in performance were unrelated to cyclical phases. Her doctoral dissertation was titled "Functional Periodicity: An Experimental Study of the Mental and Motor Abilities of Women during Menstruation" (Hollingworth, 1914). Through her research, she found no evidence to support the variability hypothesis, which mistakenly concluded that the higher status of males was based upon their greater variability. In 1914, with Helen Montague, Hollingworth examined the birth records of 1,000 male and 1,000 female neonates. When birth weight and length were noted, the researchers found that if variability "favored" any sex, it was the female sex (Montague & Hollingworth, 1914).

Also in 1914, Hollingworth responded to social Darwinist myths by critiquing the incorrect assumptions on which they were based. For example, greater (male, of course) variability was considered to suggest greater range also. This inference is appropriate only if the distribution is Gaussian, however, which had not been proven. In short, Darwin may have had some romantic notion of greater male variability due to the "noble and intellectually enriching" male competition for females, but in reality, no greater male variability had been demonstrated. Further, even if there *had* been greater physical male variability, it would indicate nothing about greater male *intellectual* variability. Greater male intellectual variability had also not been proven, and, even if it had been, it would not mean an innately greater intellectual variability among males. Rather, Hollingworth suggested that in order for the social sciences to examine adequately the cause of seemingly lesser female achievement, social scientists also needed to examine the interaction of social constraints and cultural barriers to female achievement.

To Hollingworth and many later feminists, the essence of the problem was that throughout history, women bore children and were their caretakers. She stated that she did not intend this issue to be interpreted as an attack on motherhood, but rather a more plausible explanation than lack of "vital force" or "lack of variability." Hollingworth fostered the examination of social and cultural factors that mediate female achievement.

It is important to note that Hollingworth refuted myth with research. In 1916, she and an eminent anthropologist, Robert Lowie, reviewed the scientific literature of their day. They found when cross-cultural, biological, and psychological studies were examined, the objective evidence did not support the notion of innate female inferiority (Lowie & Hollingworth, 1916). Lowie and Hollingworth were quick to note that "every sex difference that has been discovered or alleged has been interpreted to show the superiority of males" (p. 284). For example, the higher number of males who were institutionalized was often interpreted as proof of greater male variability. If there had been a greater number of females in prisons and asylums, they wondered, would not that fact have been interpreted as evidence of general female inferiority? In summary, Hollingworth was one of the most prolific early feminist researchers, whose myth-refuting empirical evidence and logical mind did much to pave the way for what was later to become the psychology of women.

Mary Putnam Jacobi and Mary Bissell

Mary Putnam Jacobi (1877) in her book, *The Question of Rest for Women during Menstruation,* argued against the widespread belief of her time that menstruation was so debilitating that women should refrain from physical activity. In addition, she asserted, mental activity did not lead to a greater incidence or probability of pain or infertility. Jacobi's research found that exercise and higher level of education correlated with less discomfort during menstruation.

Another early researcher was Mary Bissell, who argued against the popular notion that in females emotional fragility was the norm and therefore part of femininity (Bissell, 1985). She was one of the early researchers who also pointed out the social factors that accounted for some of the emotional "fragility" of women. She recommended young women be allowed to develop their physical, as well as their intellectual, potential strength by outdoor play and the pursuit of mentally stimulating activities to eliminate boredom.

Helen Thompson and Mary Calkins

Other early researchers who responded to social Darwinism were Helen Thompson and Mary Calkins. Thompson's psychological research challenged the social mores and cultural assumptions of her time. For her doctoral thesis (H. Thompson, 1903), she studied sex differences in mental ability. Often she found similarities rather than differences between female and male subjects. When differences did occur, she was able to show how experience and environment, rather than biology alone, would account for them.

Like Hollingworth, Calkins (1896) also disputed the popular social Darwinist myth that women's mental capabilities were less varied than men's. She was a forerunner in the psychology of women, as she traversed through a field that did not readily recognize her many accomplishments. She is most known for becoming the first president of the American Psychological Association (APA) in 1905, and her achievements during this year brought her many honors. However, she is also known for being denied her doctorate from Harvard University even though she completed all of the degree requirements. The president and Fellows at Harvard in 1894 reviewed her request and refused it on the basis that she was a woman and therefore officially unable to receive a degree from Harvard. To this day, Harvard has not issued any degree in honor of Mary Whiton Calkins.

FREUD AND OTHER PSYCHOANALYTIC INFLUENCES ON THE PSYCHOLOGY OF WOMEN

In addition to the reaction to social Darwinism, another thread in the development of the psychology of women was based on reaction to Sigmund Freud. Freud, a 19th-century Viennese medical doctor who practiced neurology, founded the psychoanalytic school of psychology. Freud constructed his personality theory based on his own self-analysis and his analysis of individual case studies. When evaluating the validity and generalizability of Freudian results, one must take into account the limitations of his methodology.

Freud believed sexual drives were very important in the personality growth of both men and women. Successful satisfaction of sexual drives resulted in healthy development, whereas failure to obtain drive satisfaction would result in neurosis. Thus, a healthy individual is one who manages to obtain gratification of drives while remaining within societal norms and physiological capability. The disturbed individual would be someone who is unable to obtain gratification within the bounds of social and biological reality.

According to Freud's theory of psychosexual development, at birth there is little psychological difference between the male and female, with infants of both sexes viewing the mother as their primary love object. (In 19th-century Vienna, the mother was the expected caretaker, and in fairness to Freud, we must take into account the limitations of 19th-century Viennese cultural norms.) Psychosexual development is similar for boys and girls in the "oral" and "anal" stages, up until the "phallic" stage. At approximately three years of age, the boy's sexual impulses become centered around the penis and the girl's around the clitoris. Both boys and girls are said to have "active" or "masculine" sexual aims. By labeling these sexual aims that occur in both sexes as "masculine," rather than using a less biased term, Freud implies that such active sexual aims are somehow not appropriate for females and begins to focus on males.

Just as early experimental psychology had used mostly male subjects and focused on male behavior, the earliest psychoanalytic writings focused on male psychic development. Very briefly, one cornerstone of Freudian theory is that of the Oedipus complex, in which the boy feels rivalry and hostility toward the father and desires his mother for himself. At the same time, he fears his father's retaliation and thus fears castration by the father. These fears of castration are made worse when, according to Freudian theory, he observes females and concludes that they have been castrated and that the same thing could happen to him. This complex is resolved by identifying with the father (identification with the aggressor). In this way, the boy gives up his mother as his love object with the expectation that he will later find a substitute who will not arouse the wrath of his father. The boy thereafter identifies with the father and incorporates the father's moral values, along with those of society for which the male moral value is seen as representative. This internalization of paternal/societal male moral standards results in the formation of a *superego*, or what is often called the conscience. Male psychosexual development contains both conflict and compromise. However, in males, the conflict resolution manages to preserve the "active" sexual aims present during the phallic period, thus leaving the males active in attaining their satisfaction.

Females, according to Freud, do not have the same constellation, because when they discover they do not have a penis, they envy little boys and blame their mothers for what they are lacking (a penis). Little girls switch their affectional cathexis from the mother to the father, hoping to obtain a penis, but there is no identification with the aggressor and thus no internalization of that parent's moral code. Thus, in females, according to Freud, superego development is stunted. The girl perceives her anatomical inferiority and blames her mother, but does not identify with her "fellow castrati." Curiously, she does not identify with her father, either. According to Freudian theory, in time the "normal" female realizes that she cannot have a penis, so she wishes instead for a baby. She also renounces the clitoris as the seat of sexual satisfaction. Her sexual aims, which had been "active, masculine" aims during the phallic stage, are now transformed into passive feminine receptivity.

For Freud, a "masculine" woman has not adjusted to her anatomy. A tripartite bridge is formed in Freudian theory among anatomy, active versus passive sexuality, and feminine personality. The anatomical differences are perceived as causal factors in psychological and social differences. Thus, for the Freudians, the healthy woman renounces the active sexual satisfaction of the clitoris, has passive sexual aims, with her primary motivation being her wish for a baby, and does not socially engage in aggressive or achievement-oriented behaviors. Narcissism and vanity are essentially the "feminine" compensatory consequences of castration. In addition, jealousy, feelings of inferiority, and shame are more direct expressions of female genital dissatisfaction, since the female is less motivated to identify with the same-sex parent during the Oedipal conflict. The boy is motivated because he still has a penis and fears castration; the girl feels that she is already castrated and thus is not motivated. Therefore, women are less likely to internalize the moral codes and cultural ideals than men.

The social and political implications of Freudian theory are vast. Quite simply, by virtue of their anatomy, women are destined to be less morally mature and less acculturated than men. They are also destined to exhibit more unsatisfactory personality characteristics.

According to Freudian theory, anatomical differences and the resulting differences in sexual functions are viewed as being the causal factors in the development of psychological differences. Here, body creates psyche, and the phrase "biology is destiny" is formed. The biologically "healthy" woman has passive sexual aims, is motivated by motherhood, and spurns achievement-related behaviors. Thus, biological differences are instrumental in the creation of psychological differences, which, in turn, explain social behavior and serve to maintain the status quo.

Helene Deutsch

Helene Deutsch, a psychoanalyst who was trained by Freud, extended Freudian theory in her 1946 book, coincidentally also titled *The Psychology of Women.* In her book, Deutsch posited that personality traits such as narcissism, passivity, and masochism are the result of "feminine" biology. In response to Freudian theory, Deutsch views women as being masochistic since they are biologically bound to childbirth and menstruation, which contain both pleasure and pain. The fact that all living organisms (including men) experience both pleasure and pain is overlooked by Deutsch, who goes on to posit that masochism is therefore an adaptive formation for females. The "healthy" female is not masochistic to the point of total self-annihilation, but she does renounce her "self" in that she denies her own needs in order to obtain "love," that is, by becoming a wife and mother. Both clitoral sexuality and active vaginal pleasure are viewed by Deutsch as deviating from "normal" femininity. "Normal" female sexuality is operationally defined as female passivity, which Deutsch refers to as "receptive readiness." In addition, she also posits the circular logic that women possess a predisposition for compensatory narcissism that attempts to make up for their lack of a penis and to balance out their masochism, which is also the result of not having a penis.

Pleasure and pain, childbirth, and menstruation are facts of life. At the present time, a biological fact is that women have greater life expectancy than men, and behaviorally men tend to exhibit greater alcohol and narcotic abuse than do women. However, present-day Freudians would not conclude that man's lack of a vagina leads to greater self-destructive tendencies and earlier death. It is interesting to note that when this "biology is destiny" thinking is applied to men, the leaps in logic are glaring, yet the same leaps have long gone unnoticed as they apply to women.

REFUTATION OF FREUD'S THEORY

Alfred Adler and Carl Jung

Two of the early defectors from Freud's inner circle who served to broaden the base of the biologically centered psychoanalytic theory were Alfred Adler and Carl Jung. Adler recognized sociocultural factors in psychic development and noted the constraining contradictions of a culture that simultaneously encouraged women to adopt "feminine" characteristics while admiring and placing a higher value (economic and social) on actions and attributes characterized as "masculine." Thus, Adler was a harbinger of social psychological theories that emphasize the social context as an underlying determinant of behavior.

Rather than following Freud's emphasis on sexual motivations, Jung stressed the individual's struggle to achieve psychic harmony via the reconciliation of what is masculine and feminine in each individual. Jung believed that the experience of each individual was influenced by the experience of all of humanity, which is transmitted to each successive generation and constitutes what he termed the "collective unconscious." These memories of all of human experience, so-called racial memories, take the form of "archetypes" that unconsciously influence each individual.

Two archetypes that Jung used to explain masculinity and femininity are the *animus* and *anima*. The animus is the masculine archetype, which Jung believed was present in the female's unconscious, and the anima is the feminine archetype in the male's unconscious. While the Jungian ideal of psychic harmony would encompass the integration of one's masculine and feminine traits (which is consistent with some modern feminist thinking), he still believed that personality was formed not only from one's individual socialization experience, which is subject to change, but also by a collective historical experience, which cannot be changed. Thus for Jung, gender-role differentiation is the inevitable result of sex-linked masculine and feminine polarities. Females were seen only from a male point of view.

Karen Horney

Karen Horney (1926) in her book *Flight from Womanhood* was the first to question this bias in the psychoanalytic literature: "Almost all of those who have developed his ideas have been men. It is only right and reasonable that they should evolve more easily a masculine psychology and understand more of the development of men than of women" (p. 59). After years of analyzing male and female patients, Horney was struck by strong male "envy of pregnancy, childbirth and motherhood, as well as breasts and the act of sucking" (p. 60). Horney believes that little boys encounter "womb envy" and states that there is an unconscious male desire to deprecate women and their ability to give birth. Penis envy is a way to shift the focus away from women's childbearing ability and focus instead on male anatomy. According to Horney,

> this (male) depreciation would run as follows: In reality woman do simply desire the penis, when all is said and done motherhood is only a burden that makes the struggle for existence harder, and men may be glad that they have not to bear it. (p. 61)

In a paper titled "Inhibited Femininity," Horney (1967) regarded "frigidity as an illness" and not "the normal sexual attitude of civilized woman." She was also first to point out the social and cultural factors that impact on psychic development.

Horney was the first of Freud's students to break from him on the issue of pre-Oedipal injury resulting in neurosis. Horney believed in the possibility of pre-Oedipal injury and was also the first psychoanalyst to speak about the "real self." Pre-Oedipal injury, according to Horney, results when a child perceives herself or himself as being helpless in a hostile environment; "instead of developing a basic confidence in self and others the child develops basic anxiety" (Horney, 1950, p. 366). The child puts a check on spontaneous feelings because of a need to relieve basic anxiety. Above all, there exists a need to feel safe. This is the beginning of what Horney calls the "alienation from self."

> Not only is his *real self prevented* from a straight growth, but in addition his need to evolve artificial strategic ways to cope with others has forced him to override his genuine feelings.... It does not matter what he feels if only he feels safe. (Horney, 1950, p. 21)

The child seeks to feel safe in a hostile environment. Solutions may be based on the appeal of love (moving toward), the appeal of mastery (moving against), or the appeal of freedom (moving away). In short, the child will attempt to change the environment by loving it, by fighting it, or by leaving it (Horney, 1950).

Healthy people love, fight, and leave at appropriate times. Since the neurotic puts a check on spontaneous feelings, however, he or she does not know which solution is appropriate at different times.

> The three moves toward, against, and away from others therefore constitute a conflict, his *basic conflict.* In time, he tries to solve it by making one of these moves consistently predominant—he tries to make his prevailing attitude one of compliance, or aggressiveness, or aloofness. (Horney, 1950, p. 19)

Horney's reaction to Freud influenced others and is part of one of the threads to what would later become the psychology of women. As Hollingworth and others were able to do in the area of experimental psychology, Horney was able to apply strict scrutiny to psychoanalytic theory and to refute androcentrism and sexist bias. By taking the focus of psychoanalysis away from the androcentric Oedipus complex, she was able to pave the way for the "psychology of the self," so crucial to our present understanding of borderline and narcissistic personality disorders.

Horney suggests that Freud's observation of the female's wish for a penis may be no more important than the young male's frequently observed wish for breasts. Attributes with which Freud composed the constellation of the "masculinity complex," that is, desire for power, envy, and egocentric ambition, and which he ascribed to penis envy were noted by Horney as characteristics exhibited by neurotic men as well as neurotic women. She posits that the characteristics of the "masculinity complex" are the result of feelings of inferiority that are present in both neurotic men and neurotic women and are multiply determined. She also looks at the social and cultural factors involved in the development of feelings of inferiority, such as the cultural restrictions of women's potential.

Horney (1939) differs from Deutsch in her interpretation of masochism in that she views it as an empowering device used to promote well-being in life through influencing others by emphasizing one's frailty and pain. Masochism is not viewed by Horney as a biologically based adaptive behavior incorporating pleasure and pain as bound to feminine physiology, but rather as a social, often economically based, attitude. Our society tends to idealize the maternal woman who puts the needs of others before her own, and it tends to pay women less than men. Horney posits that these factors better account for masochistic tendencies in women than do physiological differences. She believes that, rather than being fueled by a symbolic desire to possess a penis, both normal and neurotic women tend to "overvalue love" as the result of their economic and social dependence on men due to cultural constraints on women's direct access to security, prestige, and power. By stressing the social and cultural factors as determinants of "feminine" psychology, Horney leaves room for the possibility of remediation of undesirable personality traits via the process of social change. Changes in economic opportunity as well as changes in socialization of women are presumed to impact on the female personality constellation. Conversely, when "feminine" psychology is attributed to penis envy and pain inherent in childbirth, societal changes are presumed to be psychologically inconsequential, and psychological changes in personality are deemed to be impossible.

Clara Thompson

Another psychologist who responded to Freudian orthodoxy by walking out of the New York Psychoanalytic Institute with Horney was Clara Thompson. Both Horney and Thompson stressed the importance of experience, environment, and social influences that impact personality development. Like Horney, Thompson responded to androcentric Freudian psychosexual etiology of female personality development (1941, 1942, 1943, 1964a, 1964b). Her alternative theory also stressed the impact of social and cultural factors on personality development. Thompson posits that the discovery of the vagina, rather than the penis, in and of itself need not necessarily represent psychic trauma for a female. However, it can be traumatic if the presence of a vagina, rather than a penis, is associated with lower status (both social and economic) within the family constellation. Our historical obsession with primogeniture, a system that confers the highest status on the eldest male, serves to reinforce the association of "feminine" with lower status.

As children reach the phallic stage of development (at approximately three to five years of age), both sexes struggle for autonomy and seek independence from their primary caretaker. If one assumes the primary caretaker is the mother, Thompson posits that the mother often will respond differently to her son's and daughter's attempts at autonomy, with female children being given less overt encouragement to express independence and, instead, given more rewards for remaining within the confines of the home. Often with the onset of puberty, previously tolerated tomboyish activities are no longer accepted in the adolescent girl. She is pressured by society to become "attractive" and rewarded with marriage and motherhood. Rather than the renunciation of active aims for passivity, Thompson views behavioral changes in teenage girls and differences in sexual experimentation as the result of multiple societal pressures. Thompson views female psychology as an attempt to adjust to the existing social realities; she finds women who choose to find pleasure in a life of self-sacrifice not so much seeking pain (masochistic), but rather seeking a positive adaptation to a limiting status quo.

Freudian theory also viewed women as morally inferior to men, since they did not benefit from the internalization of a superego as a result of the resolution of the Oedipus complex via identification with the aggressor and since they did not have a penis and were "already castrated." Freud further observed that many women simply mimic the views of their male companions. Thompson posits that if this view is true, it is a function of females' lower status rather than female failure to develop a conscience. People who are in a lower-status situation, one in which they are dependent upon, and subject to, the moods and authority of a more powerful other, do "try harder" to get along with the more powerful other even to the extent of entertaining the same opinions. Social psychological research on the behavior of blacks and whites, that is, "integration" behavior (Jones, 1964), provides empirical support for Thompson's position, in that the higher the status of an individual, the more successful such an individual would be in influencing others and the less vulnerable to being influenced by a lower-status individual.

Social psychological data indicate that gender differences in interactional behavior follow status differences; males are more successful than females in their influence on others and less apt to change their positions than females. Within gender, status differences simply cannot be attributed to penis envy, castration anxiety, or the failure to identify with the aggressor and internalize a superego. The real differences between men's and women's power and status appear to be a more parsimonious explanation of the behavioral differences that Freud observed.

The work of Horney and Thompson has had somewhat limited impact on psychoanalytic theory, and until recently, Deutsch's book *The*

Psychology of Women was viewed as the classic psychoanalytic view of female personality development. However, the development of the psychology of women brought other work into the forefront. Horney and Thompson have now been recognized for their contributions.

Additionally, the debate is still ongoing as to whether Freud's theories have any place in feminist discussion (see the Chehrazi [1987] and Lerman [1987] debate on the question: Is psychoanalytic theory relevant to the psychology of women?; see also Dimen [1995] and Rosen [1996]). On one hand, many feminists, as was stated above, worked to disprove Freud's theories and yet in doing so, improved and built upon his theories.

FROM THE TURN OF THE CENTURY TO THE 1950S

In 1906, psychologist James McKeen Cattell published *American Men of Science* (*AMS*), a comprehensive biographical directory of scientists in North America (Furumoto, 1987). Out of the four thousand scientists listed in this directory, 186 identified themselves as psychologists, and 22 of these were women (Cattell, 1906). These women shared with the men the position of being pioneers in the field of psychology. Among them were Mary Whiton Calkins, Margaret Floy Washburn, Christine Ladd-Franklin, Helen Thompson Woolley, and Ethel Puffer Howes. These women joined APA soon after it was organized in 1892 and presented papers at its annual meeting thereafter. However, one should not be under the assumption that this was easy or that women were readily invited into the field with open arms. On the contrary, the earliest women psychologists fought and defended their position. In 1910 Woolley stated, "There is perhaps no field aspiring to be scientific where flagrant personal bias, logic martyred in the cause of supporting a prejudice, unfounded assertions, and even sentimental rot and drivel have run riot to such an extent as here" (p. 340).

Although these 22 women were noted in the directory, they were obviously the exception rather than the rule. And even among the 22, by comparison to men psychologists of that time, their lives were not equal. In 1906, whereas 65 percent of men were college or university presidents or full, associate, or assistant professors, this was the case for only 50 percent of the women in the directory. Additionally, 15 years later, for these psychologists who were in the directory the difference was even greater: 68 percent for men and 46 percent for women (Furumoto, 1987).

Christine Ladd-Franklin

Christine Ladd-Franklin was another pioneer psychologist whose work enabled women to become a more prominent force in psychology. Throughout her life, she campaigned for equal work, equal wages, women's acceptance in institutions of higher learning, and economic independence for women. Ladd-Franklin entered Vassar College in 1866 and completed her degree in 1869, with primary interests in science and mathematics. Soon after Johns Hopkins University opened, she applied for admission there to take advanced work in mathematics, but administrators were reluctant to open their doors to women. She was, however, granted permission to attend certain lectures, which she did. It was there that she proved herself, her commitment, and her superior intellectual abilities and therefore was granted permission to attend other classes at the university. Although Ladd-Franklin completed all of the requirements for a Ph.D. in mathematics and logic by 1882, she was not granted the doctoral degree then due to her gender. Only years later was she granted her degree, in 1926.

Ladd-Franklin entered psychology in 1887, writing her initial paper and theory on binocular vision. She went on to develop her own theory on color vision, which was the basis of much of her work for the rest of her life.

It was not until Ladd-Franklin was in her mid-60s that she took up her campaign against "the Experimentalists" for excluding women in the group. This group, comprised of only male psychologists, refused to accept women into its circle, finding it impossible to view women as genuine colleagues and scholars. Led by Edward Bradford Titchener, the group banned women from its beginning in 1904. In response, many women of the time resorted to hiding under tables or behind doors to see what transpired at the meetings.

Ladd-Franklin began a regular correspondence with Titchener, explaining her case, advocating for the rights of women, and confronting him directly in regard to his views. Her personal correspondence with Titchener did not alter the group's policy, which remained in effect until it was reorganized in 1929, after Titchener's death, and was renamed the Society of Experimental Psychologists. However, what it did accomplish was bringing to the forefront the campaign for the inclusion of women into a male-dominated field. For instance, she was the second woman elected to the prestigious National Academy of Sciences. Ladd-Franklin proved tirelessly throughout her life her worthiness in academic and psychological pursuits and contributed greatly to the field (Scarborough & Furumoto, 1987).

Margaret Floy Washburn

The child of Francis Washburn and Elizabeth Floy Davis, Margaret Floy Washburn distinguished herself at an early age as someone with keen intellect and a passion for achievement. Her family background and support, educational path, and strong motivation all contributed to her outstanding accomplishments in the field.

Born in 1871 in New York, Washburn grew up with strong and outstanding female role models on both sides of her family. Her paternal aunt was a principal of a New York City public school, and her maternal aunt was a Vassar College graduate and someone who eventually earned her M.D. degree. Washburn was always an insatiable reader and took her studies seriously in private school. It was her dream to attend Vassar, and she did so, studying psychology and ethics in her senior year. She began studying psychology immediately after graduating from Vassar, later recalling, "I had two dominant intellectual interests, science and philosophy. They seemed to be combined in what I heard of the wonderful new science of experimental psychology" (Washburn, 1930, p. 338).

Washburn's plan was to attend Columbia University for graduate school and continue her studies in experimental psychology. However, the policy of Columbia at the time was to exclude women, resulting in Washburn auditing her classes, one of them being James McKeen Cattell's. After encouragement to apply for a graduate scholarship at Cornell University and equal treatment by this eminent psychologist, Washburn decided to apply. She in fact was awarded the Susan Lynn Sage Fellowship in Philosophy and Ethics at Cornell. It was here that she met E. B. Titchener, who had been trained under Wundt in Leipzig and was the only experimental psychologist on the Cornell faculty. Although he was her advisor, Titchener was never held in high regard personally by Washburn. She began studying at Cornell and completed the degree in two years, graduating in June 1894, the first woman ever to receive the doctorate in psychology.

In this same year, Washburn was elected a member of APA, making three women in total as members of the association. She served on committees and was also chair of some of these committees; this work culminated in her being elected president of APA in 1921. She was the second woman president of APA and, through her intellect and her respect and dedication to the field, gained respect for her experimental work (Scarborough & Furumoto, 1987).

Until the middle of the 20th century, there was little research carried out by women or by having women serve as participants in research. Very few women were faculty members in departments of psychology. Over time, women became concentrated in fields of psychology that reflected stereotypes of the "women's sphere" (Russo & Denmark, 1987). Thus, most women psychologists served in clinics, child guidance settings, and other mental health clinics, and some were involved with mental testing. June Etta Downey and Florence Goodenough were two women noted for their contributions to testing instruments.

In the 1930s, many women psychologists came from Europe to the United States to escape Nazism. Among these European Jewish contributors to psychology were Therese Benedek, Else Frenkel-Brunswich, Marie Jahoda, and Margaret Mahler (Russo & Denmark, 1992). In the

United States, very few ethnic minority women received higher degrees in psychology at this time. Ruth Howard (Beckham) was the first black woman to receive a Ph.D. in psychology and child development, in 1934 from the University of Minnesota. She worked as a psychologist in Chicago's Provident Hospital School of Nursing, consulted with several schools, and maintained a private practice.

Mamie Phipps Clark

Another notable African-American psychologist, Mamie Phipps Clark, was one of the first minority women who entered the field of psychology. She attended Howard University, where her chosen field of study was mathematics. It was actually her future husband, Kenneth B. Clark, who encouraged her to enter psychology. While pursuing her master's degree at Howard University, Clark's interest in developmental psychology intensified. She later pursed research with Ruth and Eugene Horowitz, who were conducting research and developmental studies with preschoolers and developed newer methods of a coloring test and the doll's test, which was very exciting to her. A fellowship she was awarded based on this research helped her gain admittance to the doctoral psychology program at Columbia University. In 1943 she obtained the Ph.D. degree in clinical psychology and was completing research on identity in Negro children. The major findings of the research indicated that Negro children become aware of their racial identity around the age of three and simultaneously acquire a negative self-image. This research was instrumental in the 1954 Supreme Court ruling to desegregate schools in the United States.

Clark, a black female psychologist, had difficulty finding employment, and it was only through a professor at City College of New York that she secured a position in an agency that analyzed research data about the nursing profession. However, soon afterward Clark accepted a position to administer psychological tests at an agency whose population was black, homeless girls. It was here that the lack of services for black and minority children in New York City became apparent. She and her husband Kenneth Clark, worked to bring services to this population, eventually founding and opening the Northside Center for Child Development in March 1946. This center offered psychological and psychiatric services to the community in Harlem and became very well known.

Clark was a pioneer in psychology, especially since she carried the challenge of being both a woman and a minority. She worked hard and persevered throughout her career to contribute in a discipline that did not welcome her with open arms (O'Connell & Russo, 2001).

In the 1940s, women psychologists were excluded from participating in an Emergency Committee in Psychology that had been created by

APA. In response, a group of women psychologists from New York organized the National Council of Women Psychologists (NCWP). One of the founders of this organization was Dr. Theodora Abel, who much later at age 90 was a recipient of the 1997 Public Interest Gold Medal awarded by APA. The NCWP evolved into the International Council of Women Psychologists and ultimately became the International Council of Psychologists.

THE 1950S AND THE 1960S

Questions regarding inherited versus environmentally induced behaviors as the causal factors of gender differences began to be raised during the 1950s and '60s. After responding to Darwin and to Freud, the development of the psychology of women proceeded to examine the nature-nurture controversy as it applied to female-male differences. Prior to the development of the psychology of women and of psychology overall, Judeo-Christian tradition designated quite rigid gender-specific behaviors. Both Darwinian and Freudian theories aligned with the Judeo-Christian tradition and served the evolution of clear-cut gender stereotypes.

Viola Klein

Viola Klein contributed to the field's growth with her description of the female stereotype. In short, she pointed out our cultural tendency to note a wide variety of differences in male ability, character, and disposition while trying to summarize women as a homogeneous psychological type. Overall, a stereotype is a false, quick-fix oversimplification of a complex social reality that tends to evoke a strong emotional response. Since they typically embody a negative emotional response, it is indicative of stereotypes that they be projected outward, that is, applied not to "us" but to "them." Klein (1950) finds it no surprise that within a largely man-made system, male researchers generally note the individual differences of men ("us") but tend to view women as a distinct psychological type ("them"). Thus, stereotypes function to provide a quick explanation of a potpourri of individual woman's behavior:

> Whether she is strong-willed or meek, single-minded or hesitant, gentle or quarrelsome—she is supposed to possess a particular version of whatever trait she manifests and her stubbornness or submissiveness, her capriciousness or lack of humor will be found "typically feminine." (Klein, 1950, p. 4)

In addition, stereotypes serve to reflect back to oneself a view of how "one is seen by others," thus contributing to an internalization of societal values. Traditionally, women were viewed as either of two feminine types, that is, "good women" or "bad women," "madonnas" or "courtesans." Both types were viewed solely in terms of their sexual relations with men. For the "madonna," sex is primarily a means of reproduction; the "courtesan" engages in sex primarily for her own pleasure. Nevertheless, both types revolve around men.

Although some articles appeared in the 1950s that were relevant to the psychology of women, they were few and far between. During the 1960s, one of the authors of this chapter (Florence L. Denmark) continued a study on women and leadership that she began as an undergraduate and later completed and published (Denmark & Diggory, 1966). This study found that women were less authoritarian than male leaders and that women followers did not conform any more than their male counterparts to their leaders' viewpoints. During the mid-1960s, these findings were unexpected and contrary to the predicted outcome.

Also, in the mid-1960s, Florence Denmark and Marcia Guttentag examined the effect of college attendance on mature women by measuring changes in their self-concept and their evaluation of the student role (Denmark & Guttentag, 1966, 1967). They found that college attendance resulted in a decrease in the perception of the ideal self, along with a decrease in the discrepancy between present self and ideal self. A possible explanation Denmark and Guttentag offered was that perhaps the rigors of college work served to reduce dissonance by releasing the student from the need to strive for unrealistically lofty aims and permitting her to be more accepting of her present self. These results contrasted with the warning of G. Stanley Hall, the founder of APA, in the early 1900s of the dangers to females if they became too educated.

Although Klein, Denmark, Diggory, and Guttentag contributed research during the 1950s and 1960s that would be relevant to the psychology of women, it was not until the late 1960s that the women's liberation movement brought its issues to the forefront of psychology. College campuses witnessed the presence of feminists who worked to give rise to women's centers and women studies programs and courses in the psychology of women.

The first Latina to receive a doctorate was Martha Bernal, who earned her Ph.D. in 1962 in clinical psychology from Indiana University. She had a distinguished career and received many awards, including the APA Award for Distinguished Contributions to the Public Interest several weeks before her death in 2002.

THE 1970S AND 1980S

In 1971, Naomi Weisstein concluded that much of psychology had been the "fantasy life of the male psychologist." During the decade of the 1970s, much work was done to challenge that reality. As one of the authors of this paper noted (Denmark, 1977), during the 1970s an increase in the research on women reflected a rapidly growing interest in them, their psychology, and their issues. This occurred concurrently with the women's liberation movement. The increasing interest in the psychology of women beginning during the late 1960s and continuing to the present time can be shown by many indicators of growth, such as papers presented at regional meetings, dissertation topics, journal articles, and books published.

The 1969 program of APA listed one symposium that specifically pertained to women. The total portion of the 1969 programs that dealt with women amounted to seven papers, four participants, and two discussants. To measure our growth, contrast this with the annual APA Convention in 2006, where there were 4 addresses, 12 symposia, 5 cosponsored symposia, 3 roundtable discussions, 2 poster sessions with numerous posters, 4 social events, and 3 business meetings sponsored by Division 35.

By the 1970s, books finally began to appear in the psychology of women. Judith Bardwick (1970) published the first book titled *The Psychology of Women*, soon followed by Julia Sherman's (1971) in-depth analysis *On the Psychology of Women* and H. Baer and Carolyn Sherif's (1974) *A Topical Bibliography on the Psychology of Women*. In mid-decade, Rhoda Unger and Florence L. Denmark (1975) edited the first issue-oriented reader in the field, containing original as well as reprinted articles. Also, in 1975, Martha Mednick and Hilda Weissman (1975) noted the growth of the psychology of women by reviewing pertinent topics in the *Annual Review of Psychology*. In 1976, a volume of reprinted articles that was totally focused on women appeared (Denmark, 1976). In 1978 Sherman and Denmark coedited a book based on a 1975 conference, "New Directions in Research," the first research conference on the psychology of women.

The appearance of several new journals, such as *Sex Roles* and *Signs* in 1975 and *The Psychology of Women Quarterly* in 1976, indicated further growth of the field. These journals continue to flourish. Overall, the percentage of articles related to the psychology of women in APA journals has increased significantly and continues to grow.

There has been a great increase in the number of dissertations in the field on the topic of women. In the July 1970 *Dissertation Abstracts International*, there were only 11 dissertations that even contained the word *woman* or *women* in the title. In 2006, the number of dissertation abstracts with one of these keywords in the title was 459. In spite of the crudeness of this indicator, the rise in the number of dissertations with topics relevant to the psychology of women is still another sign of growth of the field.

However, there was still much more to be done. Although women were emerging in the field, there certainly was not equality. Ludy

Benjamin (1974) reported that in a 1974 review of autobiographies and biographies of individuals contributing to psychology, only 33 out of 700 references were to women psychologists. Similarly, he and Kathryn L. Heider found that in 1976, only 9 textbooks out of 255 dealt with women's lives and contributions—a mere 3 percent (Benjamin and Heider, 1976).

Still, women were beginning to become more of a presence in professional organizations and as recipients of awards. For instance, two women, Leona E. Tyler and Anne Anastasi, were elected presidents of APA in 1972 and 1973, respectively. Both of these female psychologists also were recipients of the American Psychological Foundation's Gold Medal Awards in the 1980s. These gold medals are given in recognition of distinguished careers and enduring contributions to psychology in one of four areas: Lifetime Achievement in Application, Practice, or Science of Psychology, or Psychology in the Public Interest. Pauline Sears (along with her husband, Robert) was the first female psychologist to receive the Gold Medal Award in 1980.

Division 35

An official indication of the acceptance of the psychology of women as a legitimate field of study within psychology came in 1973, when the Division of the Psychology of Women was established as Division 35 of the American Psychological Association. However, rather than simply a political movement, the psychology of women represents a legitimate area of scientific investigation that can be traced back to the early 1900s.

The origins of Division 35 can be traced back to the 1969 APA convention, at which members of the Association for Women in Psychology (AWP) overtly attacked the discriminatory hiring practices of APA's own employment center. At that time women, but not men, were routinely asked about their marital status, spousal employment status, and intention to have children. AWP members protested these unfair procedures, and the APA Council of Representatives responded in 1970 by creating an active task force to study the status of women in psychology. The goal of the task force was "furthering the major purpose of APA, to advance psychology as a science and as a means of promoting human welfare—by making recommendations to insure that women be accepted as fully enfranchised members of the profession" (Task force report on the status of women in psychology, 1973).

The task force examined the status of female faculty and students in graduate psychology departments and gave recommendations to APA. In particular, it had concerns about graduate curricula: "Colleges and universities should offer general education courses and programs that inquire into the psychology of women, and an opportunity for in-depth study at both undergraduate and graduate levels of the psychology of women" (Task force report, 1973). The task force realized that knowledge of women needed to be expanded and that the generalizability of much research was questionable because women had not been included in the sample. Many people believed that a new division within APA would better meet the needs of women in psychology.

The APA Council of Representatives responded by approving the Division 35 petition, signed by 800 members who indicated interest in joining the new division in September 1973. The purpose of Division 35 was "to promote the research and study of women ... to encourage the integration of this information about women with the current psychological knowledge and beliefs in order to apply the gained knowledge to the society and its institutions" (Article 1.2, Division 35 Bylaws). Martha Mednick (1978) reports that in a 1973 APA *Monitor* article, she was quoted as saying, "The new division would not be a political organization." Rather than being a political organization, Mednick stressed the division's role of expanding knowledge about women. One of the ways in which knowledge about women has been expanded is through Division 35's journal, *The Psychology of Women Quarterly*.

By 1977, Division 35 had grown to be one of the larger APA divisions, with close to 1,500 members and affiliates. As of 1992, the division had 2,526 members, with 96.5 percent of them being women. Division 35 membership had diverse interests, with members in every other division of APA. Most of its members had (and have) doctorates in counseling, clinical, developmental, and social psychology.

After Division 35 was formed, three of its Fellows served as president of APA in the 1980s: Denmark in 1980, Janet T. Spence in 1984, and Bonnie R. Strickland in 1987 (George Albee, another Division 35 Fellow, was APA president in 1970). The psychology of women therefore had a recognized voice in the formal and informal decision making of APA. Brief biographies of these three women follow.

In 1975, the APA task force provided *Guidelines for the Non-sexist Use of Language* (American Psychological Association, 1983), and in 1977 the APA, in the third edition of the *Publication Manual*, set guidelines to avoid sexist language specific to journal articles. In 1988 the APA Council of Representatives unanimously endorsed "Guidelines for Avoiding Sexism in Psychological Research" (Denmark, Russo, Frieze, & Sechzer, 1988). APA's nonsexist guidelines have opened the way for nonsexist guidelines in other countries as well as the preparation of nonracist, nonageist, and nonheterosexist guidelines.

As Division 35 grew, it functioned to provide a forum for the development of an in-depth focus on understanding both the psychological and social realities of women. The Committee on Black Women's Concerns was formed in 1977 as part of the division. This group became a section of the division in 1984. Committees on Hispanic women and Asian American women were also established by Division 35. Thus the growth of the psychology of women has fostered growth in the areas of minority concerns.

The impact of the growth of the psychology of women was seen in the United States and internationally as well. The first International Interdisciplinary Congress on Women was held in Haifa, Israel, in 1981. This congress was organized by two psychologists, Marilyn Safir and Martha Mednick, whose biographies also follow.

During the period of the 1970s and 1980s, the psychology of women also blossomed into an interdisciplinary field—women's studies. Courses in the psychology of women began to be taught in many countries, including Israel, Ireland, the Netherlands, and Argentina as well as the United States. The cross-fertilization of women's studies and psychology resulted in an increased awareness of class and racial issues, as well as gender issues. Michele Paludi (1987) noted that the model of female development had grown from that of white, middle-class women to one encompassing women of color. The psychology of women continued to give rise to feminist pedagogy, which fostered the development of feminist identity, shared leadership during the learning process, and integration of emotional and factual learning, resulting in greater overall congruence and enhanced self-esteem. Thus, feminist pedagogy based on the psychology of women has made an invaluable contribution to the teaching of any subject.

Florence L. Denmark

Florence L. Denmark is an internationally recognized scholar, researcher, and policy maker. She received her Ph.D. from the University of Pennsylvania in social psychology and has four honorary degrees. Denmark is currently the Robert Scott Pace Distinguished Research Professor of Psychology at Pace University in New York.

A past president of the New York State Psychological Association (NYSPA) as well as APA, Denmark holds fellowship status in APA and the American Psychological Society. She is also a member of the Society for Experimental Social Psychology (SESP) and a Fellow of the New York Academy of Sciences. She has received three Divisional Awards from NYSPA, as well as NYSPA's highest award, the Allen V. Williams Sr. Memorial Award. She has received numerous national and international awards for her contributions to psychology, including the 2004 American Psychological Foundation Gold Medal for Lifetime Achievement in the Public Interest. In 2005, Denmark received the Ernest R. Hilgard Award for her career contribution to general psychology, and in 2007, she received the Raymond B. Fowler award for outstanding contributions to APA.

Denmark's most significant research and extensive publications have emphasized women's leadership and leadership styles, the interaction of status and gender, aging women in cross-cultural perspective, and the contributions of women to psychology. Denmark is the main nongovernmental organization (NGO) representative to the United Nations for the International Council of Psychologists and is also the main NGO representative for APA. She is currently chair of the New York NGO Committee on Ageing and a member of APA's Committee on Aging.

Janet T. Spence

Janet Taylor Spence began her career in psychology at Oberlin College and graduated in 1945. She took up graduate work at Yale and then transferred to the University of Iowa, the school from which she graduated with an M.A. and Ph.D. in psychology. Afterward, she took a position as a psychology instructor at Northwestern University. Spence was the first female faculty member and eventually was promoted to chair, although her promotion was slow because she was female.

Spence's research interests have always been anxiety and gender. She has held many prestigious positions within the field, the most noteworthy being her 1984 presidency of APA. Additionally, in 1989, she became the founding president of the American Psychological Society. She was also on the Governing Board of APA from 1976 to 1978 and joined the Governing Board of the Psychonomic Society in 1978. Spence has had a long and prestigious career. She has contributed greatly to the field in general and to literature on gender research specifically (http://www.webster.edu/~woolflm/spence.html).

Bonnie R. Strickland

Bonnie R. Strickland has been working and publishing in the field since she received her doctorate in 1962. Her work has primarily focused on personality variables and the need for approval. Then, in 1970, she began writing on the area of locus of control, and later, on the topic of the behavior of social activities. One of Strickland's most notable achievements was being elected president of APA in 1987. During her presidential year, she spoke in the U.S. Senate and House of Representatives. In 1988, she was appointed to the National Advisory Council of the National Institute of Mental Health (NIMH). Strickland is also past president of Division 1 (http://www.webster.edu/~woolflm/strickland.html).

Marilyn Safir

Marilyn Safir is professor emerita of the Department of Psychology at Haifa University (specializing in clinical and social psychology). She also serves as the director of Project Kidma, the Project for the Advancement of Women, which, in addition to programs for women from disadvantaged communities and villages, runs workshops for leadership training for multicultural and mixed socioeconomic groups. Safir is the founder and former director (1983–1993) of the University of Haifa Women's Studies Program. She is also a founding member of the Executive Committee and first president (1998–2002) of the Israel Association for Feminist and Gender Studies (IAFGS).

In 1968, after completing her Ph.D. in clinical psychology and research methodology at Syracuse University, Safir moved to Israel. She was a pioneer of Israel's new Women's Movement, which began in Haifa in 1970. Professor Safir is a founder and served three terms as a member of the Executive Board of the Israel Women's Network and is active in a range of women's advocacy organizations. She served as director of the National Commission on the Advancement for the Status of Women from 1986 to 1991. Safir founded and chaired the First International Interdisciplinary Congress on Women: Women's Worlds in Haifa in 1981. This was the first major international feminist women's studies congress, as a result of which an international network of feminist women's studies scholars and activist was formed, enabling a series of nine additional congresses held in various countries around the world.

Safir is a Fellow of APA and was the first recipient of the association's Division for International Psychology (52) Distinguished Visiting Professorship (August 2005–August 2006). She was also the first recipient of the Florence Denmark and Gori Gunvald Award for Research on Women and Gender, International Council of Psychologists, 2002.

Martha Mednick

Martha Mednick received her doctorate from Northwestern University in 1955 in clinical psychology. For many years until her retirement, she was a professor at Howard University in Washington, D.C. She has been a researcher and published extensively in the field of the psychology of women for many years. The social issues journal *New Perspectives on Women*, edited by Mednick and Sandra Schwartz Tangri in 1972, was an important influence on the establishment of Division 35. Mednick was one of the founders of that division as well as serving on the APA Committee on the Status of Women. She is a past president of Division 35 and has been awarded the APA Committee on Women in Psychology Leadership Award, along with the Carolyn Wood Sherif Memorial Award for feminist scholarship.

THE 1990S TO THE PRESENT

Overall, the psychology of women has continued to flourish. It impacts on all of psychology by highlighting the former methodological biases and by reexamining issues with representative samples to yield generalizable data. The psychology of women should continue to be integrated into general psychology as well as specific content areas such as abnormal, developmental, and social psychology courses (Denmark & Fernandez, 1984). In addition, the psychology of women should continue to examine issues unique to women, such as menstruation, pregnancy, and breast-feeding.

Division 35 continues to grow as well. The Division was renamed in 1999 as the Society for the Psychology of Women. Membership is strong and in the end of 2003, there were 2,511 members in the division, 97 percent of whom were women (www.apa.org). The division continues to publish a successful journal quarterly, the *Psychology of Women Quarterly*, and a newsletter, the *Feminist Psychologist*, which is issued quarterly as well.

In the 1990s to the present, the prevalence, visibility, and contributions of women have all increased strongly. There have been four more women presidents of APA.

Dorothy Cantor

Dorothy Cantor was the 105th president of the American Psychological Association in 1996–1997 and has dedicated her career to focusing on women's issues and advocacy. In her extensive career, she has organized and chaired both the APA Committee on Urban Initiatives and the Task Force on the Changing Gender Composition in Psychology. She is also a cofounder of Women in Psychology for Legislative Action. Cantor has published numerous articles and books about gender and psychology including *Finding Your Voice: A Woman's Guide to Using Self-Talk for Fulfilling Relationships, Work and Life*, *The Psychology of Today's Woman: New Psychoanalytic Visions*, *Women as Therapists: A Multitheoretical Casebook*, and *Women in Power: The Secrets of Leadership*. She is currently president of the American Psychological Foundation (http://drdorothycantor.com).

Norine Johnson

Norine Johnson was born in 1935 into a family that stressed the importance of education. She attended DePauw University in Greencastle, Indiana, where, contrary to its reputation of being an outstanding liberal arts school, she found the policies fraught with sexism. In 1964, she enrolled in Wayne State University in Detroit in the clinical psychology program and received her Ph.D. in 1972. Afterward, she worked in clinics and then took a position as the director of psychology at Kennedy Memorial Hospital for Children in Boston. She now runs a successful independent practice and a therapeutic and consultative service for families and educational systems in Boston.

In 2001, Johnson was elected president of APA, only the ninth woman president. One of the main priorities of her presidency was to provide a better future for psychology students and graduates. She considers Division 35, the Psychology of Women Division, to be her "home" at APA. According to O'Connell (1988), Johnson believes that throughout her career, she has focused on strengths and using the feminist process to bring in new frameworks for treating children, adolescent girls, and women (www.webster.edu/~woolflm/johnsonh.html).

Diane F. Halpern

Diane F. Halpern completed her undergraduate work at the University of Pennsylvania and then received a Ph.D. in psychology at the University of Cincinnati. She is currently the director of the Berger Institute for Work, Family, and Children and also is chair of the Department of Psychology of Claremont McKenna College. In 1999–2000, she was president of the Western Psychological Association, and in 2004, she served as president of APA. Much of Halpern's research centers around gender, critical thinking, learning, and work-family interaction. She was the recipient of the 1999–2000 Wang Family Excellence Award, the American Foundation Award for Distinguished Teaching, and the Distinguished Career Contributions to Education and Training Award (http://academic.claremontmckenna.edu/faculty/profile.asp?Fac+302).

Sharon Stephens Brehm

Sharon Stephens Brehm is a professor of psychology in the Clinical Science and Social Psychology programs at Indiana University in Bloomington. She received both her undergraduate and graduate degrees from Duke University. Brehm is highly regarded in the field and has published extensively on gender research, developmental psychology, and social psychology. She was elected president of APA for 2007. Previously, Brehm served four terms on the Executive Committee of the Society for Personality and Social Psychology (APA Division 8). She is also a Fellow of Division 8 and was inducted into the University of Kansas Women's Hall of Fame (http://sharon.brehm.socialpsychology.org).

Gold Medal Awardees

The American Psychological Foundation gives awards for lifetime achievement in either Science, Practice, Public Interest, or Applications in Psychology. This is one of the highest awards given in psychology. In the 1990s and 2000s, Bernice L. Neugarten (Public Interest), Frances K. Graham (Science), Eleanor Emmons Maccoby (Science), Theodora

M. Abel (Practice), Mary D. Ainsworth (Science), Mathilda B. Canter (Practice), Ethel Tobach (Public Interest), Florence L. Denmark (Public Interest), Janet Taylor Spence (Science), and Rhoda Unger (Public Interest) all were awarded Gold Medals. The number of these awards, 10, was more than three times the number of women who had received the award from its inception in 1956 through 1990. From 1990 to the present, many women also received APA awards far exceeding the number who received such awards in earlier years.

PSYCHOLOGY AND WOMEN TODAY

> We find it curious that thought is still heavily influenced by such nineteenth century theorists as Darwin, Marx, and Freud. As products of their era, they were primarily supportive of the status quo, of upper-class White male privilege with its limited knowledge of and marginal concern for women. If they were alive today, they would be astonished: What? You are still using those old books? Throw them away. (Hare-Mustin & Marecek, 1990)

The psychology of women that has been outlined above continues to grow and develop. There have been major steps taken toward making the psychology of women a legitimate field of study, but there is still much to be done. The history of the psychology of women is not a finished tale. Numerous talented and insightful women are continuing to make strides in the field in research and gender equality.

Feminist psychology has moved beyond finding fault in previous research to conducting sound research in its own right. Today it is a multifaceted enterprise that has its place in virtually every specialization area as well as encompassing many research studies (Marecek et al., 2003). It has produced a great deal of valid and important research and continues to create such research as well.

There needs to be a continuation of feminist research that builds upon existing theoretical conceptualizations that focus on critical issues in the field of the psychology of women. To do this, there are a few methods that can be employed. The *feminist positivist empiricist* and *contextual* approaches to understanding the needs of women help restructure and more thoroughly analyze gender roles and women's issues.

A *positivist empiricist approach* utilizes conventional scientific methods to produce "factual" knowledge about a particular question related to something observable and measurable in the external world (Wilkinson, 2001). Thus, feminist empiricists proposed that the problem of gender bias in research can possibly be solved by advocating strict adherence to science (Riger, 2002). This is beneficial in that it provides concrete evidence that informs the influence that sex and gender have on research. However, one limitation is that it is only applicable to scientifically measurable concepts.

Maureen McHugh, Randi Koeske, and Irene Frieze (1986) established a set of guidelines for eliminating bias in research. Among the many suggestions they noted are:

- delineating the circumstances in which gender differences are found
- assessing experimental tasks for their sex neutrality
- examining the effect of a study's female-male composition as well as the sex similarities and differences that are present

If this framework is implemented, experiments will neither make unfounded assumptions nor overlook important gender differences that exist.

A *contextual approach* looks at the psychology of women within a multidimensional framework that takes into account sociological and cultural factors when creating research questions (Wilkinson, 2001). Compared to the empiricist approach previously discussed, an epistemological (or contextual) approach focuses on the whole of women's lives (Riger, 2002). Therefore, this method encourages feminist psychologists to view women as whole beings or people who exist in a bidirectional relationship with the environment in which they live. As Jeanne Maracek (1989) stated, "What we know and how we know depend on who we are, that is, on the knower's historical locus and his or her position in the social hierarchy" (p. 372). Maracek et al. (2003) also called for methodological pluralism, which promotes the use of new modes of inquiry such as case studies, focus groups, content analysis, observational techniques, participant-observation, and field research that allow for the study of phenomena outside the laboratory.

APA's Council of Representatives adopted a Resolution on Cultural and Gender Awareness on July 28, 2004, that emphasizes various aspects of the contextual approach. The following excerpt delineates the goals of the resolution:

(1) advocate for more research on the role that cultural ideologies have in the experience of women and men across and within countries on the basis of sex, gender identity, gender expression, ethnicity, social class, age, disabilities, and religion.

(2) advocate for more collaborative research partnerships with colleagues from diverse cultures and countries leading to mutually beneficial dialogues and learning opportunities.

(3) advocate for critical research that analyzes how cultural, economic, and geopolitical perspectives may be embedded within US psychological research and practice.

(4) encourage more attention to a critical examination of international cultural, gender, gender identity, age, and disability perspectives in psychological theory, practice, and research at all levels of psychological education and training curricula.

(5) encourage psychologists to gain an understanding of the experiences of individuals in diverse cultures, and their points of view and to value pluralistic world views, ways of knowing, organizing, functioning, and standpoints.

(6) encourage psychologists to become aware of and understand how systems of power hierarchies may influence the privileges, advantages, and rewards that usually accrue by virtue of placement and power.

(7) encourage psychologists to understand how power hierarchies may influence the production and dissemination of knowledge in psychology internationally and to alter their practices according to the ethical insights that emerge from this understanding.

(8) encourage psychologists to appreciate the multiple dilemmas and contradictions inherent in valuing culture and actual cultural practices when they are oppressive to women, but congruent with the practices of diverse ethnic groups.

(9) advocate for cross national research that analyzes and supports the elimination of cultural, gender, gender identity, age, and disability discrimination in all arenas—economic, social, educational, and political.

(10) support public policy that supports global change toward egalitarian relationships and the elimination of practices and conditions oppressive to women. (American Psychological Association, 2004)

Regardless of the approach utilized, there is still much exploration required for the further development of theory and practice that will ultimately add to the contributions women make to the field and to the history of the psychology of women. Although the large "gender gap" has slowly begun to close, upon closer inspection, there still exists a large divide. For instance, in 2004, when membership statistics from APA indicated that 48 percent of the members were men and 52 percent were women, the Fellows of APA were 74 percent men and 26 percent women, indicating a great disparity between men and women in positions of prestige. This suggests that there is much work to be done along the path of establishing a more equitable environment for women.

Critical issues to be explored in the future include changing the negative, inaccurate, and harmful images of women, as well as removing occupational barriers for women who are entering male-dominated fields. The culture of masculinity and its negative impact on both men and women also needs to be redefined. In order to accomplish these goals, we should recognize the importance of qualitative as well as quantitative research methods. Furthermore, integrating both qualitative and quantitative perspectives might be the best approach to operationalizing theoretical concepts and accurately answering the resulting research questions (Denmark, Rabinowitz, & Sechzer, 2005).

It's also important to reiterate that the psychology of women is not limited to the United States. We live in a multicultural world where inclusion of global perspectives and information is critical in conceptualizing women.

Although many view history as occurring exclusively in the past, it is important to remember that history itself is an ongoing process. Therefore, we must rely on feminists to help shape the history of psychology, to draw attention to critical issues in the field of psychology of women, and to continue elucidating the important role that women play in various fields. Those who teach psychology courses should always include a discussion of the role that women have played in that particular subfield and encourage students to point out the contributions of women wherever appropriate in their courses.

The early years of the 21st century represent a time of rapid social change with profound implications for modifying gender roles. The future is filled with novel challenges that women will have to deal with, as well as opportunities they will be able to explore. It is these obstacles and prospects that will be reflected in the ongoing history of the psychology of women.

REFERENCES

American Psychological Association. (1983). Guidelines for nonsexist language in APA journals. In *Publication Manual of the American Psychological Association* (3rd ed.) (pp. 45–49). Washington, D.C.: American Psychological Association.

American Psychological Association. (2004). Resolution on Cultural and Gender Awareness in International Psychology. Retrieved April 20, 2007, from http://www.apa.org/international/resolutiongender.html.

Baer, H., & Sherif, C. (1974). A topical bibliography (selectively annotated) on the psychology of women. *Catalogue of Selected Documents in psychology, 4,* 42.

Bardwick, J. (1970). *The psychology of women: A study of bio-cultural conflicts.* New York: Harper & Row.

Benjamin, L. T. (1974). Prominent psychologists: A selected bibliography of biographical sources. *JSAS Catalog Selected Documents in Psychology, 4,* MS. 535.

Benjamin, L. T., & Heider, K. L. (1976). The history of psychology in biography. *JSAS Catalog Selected Documents in Psychology, 6,* MS. 1276.

Bissell, M. T. (1985). Emotions versus health in women. In L. M. Newman (Ed.), *Men's ideas/women's realities* (pp. 48–53). Elmsford, NY: Pergamon Press. (Original work published in 1888.)

Calkins, M. W. (1896). Community of ideas of men and women. *Psychological Review, 3,* 426–430.

Cattell, J. (1906). American men of science: A biographical directory. New York: Science Press.

Chehrazi, S. (1987). Female psychology: A review. In M. Roth Walsh (Ed.). *The psychology of women: Ongoing debates* (pp. 22–38). New Haven, CT: Yale University Press.

Darwin, C. (1859). *On the origin of species by means of natural selection.* London: John Murray.

Darwin, C. (1871). *Descent of man.* London: John Murray.

Denmark, F. L. (Ed.). (1976). *Women: Volume I.* New York: Psychological Dimensions.

Denmark, F. L. (1977). The psychology of women: An overview of an emerging field. *Personality and Social Psychology Bulletin, 3,* 356–367.

Denmark, F. L., & Diggory, J. (1966). Sex differences in attitudes toward leaders' display of authoritarian behavior. *Psychological Reports, 18,* 863–872.

Denmark, F. L., & Fernandez, L. (1984). Integrating information about the psychology of women into social psychology. In F. L. Denmark (Ed.), *Social/ecological psychology and the psychology of women* (pp. 355–368). Proceedings of the 23rd International Congress of Psychology. Amsterdam: Elsevier Science.

Denmark, F. L., & Guttentag, M. (1966). The effect of college attendance on mature women: Changes in self-concept and evaluation of student role. *Journal of Social Psychology, 69,* 155–158.

Denmark, F. L., & Guttentag, M. (1967). Dissonance in the self and educational concepts of college and non-college oriented women. *Journal of Counseling Psychology, 14,* 113–115.

Denmark, F. L., Rabinowitz, J. C., & Sechzer, J. A. (2005). *Engendering psychology: Women and gender revisited.* New York: Pearson Education.

Denmark, F. L., Russo, N., Frieze, I., & Sechzer, J. A. (1988). Guidelines for avoiding sexism in psychological research. *American Psychologist, 43*(7), 582–585.

Deutsch, H. (1946). *The psychology of women.* New York: Grune & Stratton.

Dimen, M. (1995). The third step: Freud, the feminists, and postmodernism. *American Journal of Psychoanalysis, 55,* 303–319.

Furumoto, L. (1987). On the margins: Woman and the professionalization of psychology in the United States, 1890–1940. In M. Ash & W. Woodward (Eds.), *Psychology in twentieth-century thought and society* (pp. 93–113). Cambridge: Cambridge University Press.

Hacker, H. M. (1951). Women as a minority group. *Social Forces, 30,* 60–69.

Hare-Mustin, R. T., & Marecek, J. (1990). Gender and the meaning of difference: Postmodernism and psychology. In R. T. Hare-Mustin & J. Marecek (Eds), *Making a difference: Psychology and the construction of gender.* New Haven, CT: Yale University Press.

Hebb, D. O. (1953). Heredity and environment in mammalian behavior. *British Journal of Animal Behavior, 1,* 43–47.

Henley, N. (1974). Resources for the study of psychology and women. *Journal of Radical Therapy, 4,* 20–21.

Hollingworth, L. S. (1914). Functional periodicity: An experimental study of the mental and motor abilities of women during menstruation. *Teachers College Contributions to Education, 69.*

Horney, K. (1926). The flight from womanhood: The masculinity complex in women as viewed by men and by women. *International Journal of Psychoanalysis, 7,* 324–339.

Horney, K. (1939). *New ways in psychoanalysis.* New York: W. W. Norton.

Horney, K. (1950). *Neurosis and human growth: The struggle toward self realization.* New York: W. W. Norton.

Horney, K. (1967). Inhibited femininity: Psychoanalytical contribution to the problem of frigidity. In H. Kelman (Ed.), *Feminine psychology* (pp. 71–83). New York: W. W. Norton. (Original work published in 1926.)

Jacobi, M. (1877). *The question of rest for women during menstruation.* New York: G. P. Putnam & Sons.

Jones, E. (1964). *Ingratiation: A social psychological analysis.* New York: Appleton-Century-Crofts.

Klein, V. (1950). The stereotype of femininity. *Journal of Social Issues, 6,* 3–12.

Lowie, R., & Hollingworth, L. S. (1916). Science and feminism. *Scientific Monthly, 3,* 277–284.

Lerman, H. (1987). From Freud to feminist personality theory: Getting here from there. In M. Roth Walsh (Ed.), *The psychology of women: Ongoing debates* (pp. 39–58). New Haven, CT: Yale University Press.

Lerner, G. (1979). *The majority finds its past: Placing women in history.* New York: Oxford University Press.

Lerner, G. (1992). Placing women in history: Definitions and challenges. In (Eds.), *Re-placing women in psychology: Readings toward a more inclusive history* (pp. 31–43).

Lewin, M., & Wild, C. L. (1991). The impact of the feminist critique on tests, assessment, and methodology. *Psychology of Women Quarterly, 15,* 581–596.

Lowie, R., & Hollingworth, L. (1916). Science and feminism. *Scientific Monthly, 3,* 277–284.

Maracek, J. (1989). Introduction: Theory and method in feminist psychology. *Psychology of Women Quarterly, 13* [special issue], 399–413.

Marecek, J., Kimmel, E. B., Crawford, M., & Hare-Mustin, R. (2003). Psychology of women and gender. In D. K. Freedheim & I. B. Weiner (Eds.), *Handbook of psychology* (vol. 1, pp. 249–268). New York: John Wiley & Sons.

McHugh, M., Koeske, R., & Frieze, I. (1986). Issues to consider in conducting nonsexist psychological research: A guide for researchers. *American Psychologist, 41,* 879–890.

McKenna, W., & Kessler, S. (1976). Experimental design as a source of sex bias in social psychology. *Sex Roles: A Journal of Research.*

Mednick, M. (1976). Some thoughts on the psychology of women. *Signs, 1,* 774.

Mednick, M. (1978). Now we are four: What should we be when we grow up? *Psychology of Women Quarterly, 3,* 123–138.

Mednick, M., & Weissman, H. (1975). The psychology of women: Selected topics. *Annual Review of Psychology, 26,* 1–18.

Montague, H., & Hollingworth, L. S. (1914). The comparative variability of the sexes at birth. *American Journal of Sociology, 20,* 335–370.

O'Connell, A. (1988). *Models of achievement: Reflections of eminent women in psychology.* Mahwah, NJ: Lawrence Erlbaum Associates.

O'Connell, A., & Russo, N. (1991). Overview: Women's heritage in psychology: Origins, development, and future directions. *Psychology of Women Quarterly, 15,* 495–504.

O'Connell, A., & Russo, N. (2001). *Models of achievement: Reflections of eminent women in psychology.* New York: Columbia University Press.

Paludi, M. A. (1987). *Teaching the psychology of women: Developmental considerations.* Paper presented at the meeting of the Association for Women in Psychology, Denver, CO.

Riger, S. (2002). Epistemological debates, feminist voices: Science, social values, and the study of women. In W. Pickren & D. Dewsbury (Eds.), *Evolving perspectives on the history of psychology.* Washington, DC: American Psychological Association.

Rosen, H. (1996). Feminist psychoanalytic theory: American and French reactions to Freud. *Journal of the American Psychoanalytic Association, 44,* 71–92.

Russo, N. F., & Denmark, F. L. (1987). Contributions of women in psychology. *Annual Review of Psychology, 38,* 279–298.

Scarborough, E., & Furumoto, L. (1987). *Untold lives: The first generation of American women psychologists.* New York: Columbia University Press.

Schwabacher, S. (1972). Male vs. female representation in psychological research: An examination of the *Journal of Personality and Social Psychology. JSAS Catalogues of Selected Documents in Psychology, 2,* 20.

Sherman, J. (1971). *On the psychology of women.* Springfield, IL: Charles C. Thomas.

Sherman, J., & Denmark, F. L. (1978). *The psychology of women: Future directions of research.* New York: Psychological Dimensions.

Shields, S. (1975). Functionalism, Darwinism, and the psychology of women. A study in social myth. *American Psychologist, 30,* 739–754.

Spencer, H. (1864). *The principles of biology.* New York: Appleton.

Task force report on the status of women in psychology. (1973). *American Psychologist, 28,* 611–616.

Thompson, C. (1941). The role of women in this culture. *Psychiatry, 4,* 1–8.

Thompson, C. (1942). Cultural pressures in the psychology of women. *Psychiatry, 5,* 331–339.

Thompson, C. (1943). Penis envy in women. *Psychiatry, 6,* 123–125.

Thompson, C. (1964a). *Interpersonal psychoanalysis* (M. R. Green, ed.). New York: Basic Books.

Thompson, C. (1964b). *On women.* New York: New American Library.

Thompson, H. (1903). *The mental traits of sex.* Chicago: University of Chicago Press.

Unger, R., & Denmark, F. L. (1975). *Woman: Dependent or independent variable?* New York: Psychological Dimensions.

Unger, Rhoda. (2001). Women as subjects, actors, and agents in the history of psychology. In R. K. Unger (Ed.), *Handbook of the psychology of women and gender* (pp. 3–16). Hoboken, NJ: John Wiley & Sons.

Washburn, M. (1930). Margaret Flow Washburn. In C. Murchinson (Ed.), *History of Psychology in Autobiography* (pp. 333–358). Worcester, MA: Clark University Press.

Wilkinson, S. (2001). Theoretical perspectives on women and gender. In R. K. Unger (Ed.), *Handbook of the psychology of women and gender* (pp. 17–27). Hoboken, NJ: John Wiley & Sons.

Chapter 2

Women of Color: Perspectives on "Multiple Identities" in Psychological Theory, Research, and Practice

June Chisholm
Beverly Greene

> *Some of us come from the poorest locales in the nation; some of us from very privileged backgrounds. Some of us are biracial or multiracial; some of us are disabled; some of us are lesbians or bisexuals. We come from all different ethnic, cultural, and spiritual traditions. We are immigrants, some of us. We are mothers, some of us. We are beauties, inner and outer. We are heroines. We are winners, every one of us. We are poets. We are the present. And, make no mistake, we are the future.*
>
> —*Iris Jacob (biracial), age 18*

In the 21st century, when one person of color asks another, "Where are you from?" it no longer means, "What Southern state in the U.S.A. are your people from?" Black people can no longer assume that another black person is "African American" (Black, Negro, or Colored, depending upon one's temporal/psychosociopolitical frame of reference). The question now acknowledges the potential for international origins of any person of color and leads to the question, "What country are you from?" The question reflects the changing demographics of immigrant groups in the United States, especially in urban cities, and is one effect of globalization on our society. Globalization leads us to question our assumptions about what issues are important for "women" when we do not know where in the world the women in question come from.

Clearly the meaning of gender is derived from a cultural context and what is important to women in one cultural context may not be salient at all in another.

American psychology as a cultural institution is also being influenced by globalization. The preparadigmatic "givens" of the major content areas within the field as well as the research methodology and scope of practice are being challenged to incorporate non-Western and alternative views about the human condition. The authors of this chapter contend that American psychology must out of necessity include in meaningful ways the human dimensions of race/ethnicity, gender, religion, age, sexual orientation, socioeconomic class, and disability in all psychological literature on theories, research, and the practice of the profession.

Comas-Diaz (2001) speculates that this incorporation of non-Western paradigms and imperatives will advance the field's depth and breath of knowledge about the complexities of the human condition. Developmental imperatives and cognitive patterns such as independence, separation, locus of control, and self-efficacy will be reexamined in the face of non-Western cultural alternatives such as interdependence, *amae* (a Japanese concept of filial dependence and parental indulgence), the role of destiny, fate, karma, and the reality of external social systems.

The shift within psychology toward addressing the issues raised by the human differences previously mentioned (ethnicity, gender, sexual orientation, age, disability, and so forth), as well as the way they are interrelated in the United States, has begun, albeit slowly. For example, chapters focusing on these issues are now seen in texts devoted to conventional content areas in psychology. Also, we see a rise in the number of journals focused on different aspects of diversity and the use of supplemental texts to complement traditional texts in content areas listed in course syllabi to address the shortcomings of the latter, which continue to omit or exclude analysis of these facets of human existence. While these efforts point out the limitations and misconceptions that persist within the traditional, mainstream approaches within psychological discourse, they do little to reform the enterprise that produces them.

The *multicultural perspective* in psychology emerged as some tried to grapple with how group differences with respect to culture, ethnicity, and race should be addressed and included into theoretical discourse and research that recognizes the integrity of the group and views diversity as a resource rather than a social problem. According to the American Psychological Association (2003), integrating ethnoracial/ethnocultural identity into the discipline is just beginning, as psychologists pay greater attention to the differential effects of historical, economic, and sociopolitical influences on individuals' behavior and perceptions. In time, the discipline will have a deeper awareness of ethnoracial/

ethnocultural identity in psychological constructs and will more actively integrate this material into all applications of psychology.

The goals of the multicultural perspective are persuasive. However, the discipline lacks a perspective that can account for other ways in which difference among people leads to categorizations that support the continued use of stereotypes. For example, in medicine, some physicians fail to diagnose certain diseases in individuals because their information or misinformation about different social groups leads them to consider only the possibilities that are consistent with their preconceived beliefs about that group's members. The recent findings in the medical literature identifying gender differences in the prodromal signs of an imminent heart attack suggest that many women with the condition have been and, for some time into the near future, will continue to be misdiagnosed and untreated because the standard symptom profile is based on the symptoms observed in men and taken as the norm. Here we see how a physician's stereotypic "understanding" of race/ethnicity, sexual orientation, social class, and gender prevents him or her from "seeing" the symptoms of a disease (Graves, 2001).

Similarly, within the social sciences in general, and American psychology in particular, the practitioner/researcher's perspectives about different social groups reflect the broader societal biases and misconceptions stemming from a sociopolitical system structured to protect the domination and power of certain groups while ensuring the subordination and powerlessness of others—that is, hegemony. Indeed by using the U.S. Census Bureau categories for all nonwhite people deemed "minority" and classifying individuals into the following groups: Hispanic or Latino, Black or African American, Asian, Native Hawaiian and other Pacific Islanders, and American Indian and Alaska Natives, psychological research perpetuates and helps maintain the status quo. The assumption underlying this classification scheme of "minorities"—that within a minority group, one can expect homogeneity, and that between groups, one can expect heterogeneity—is flawed and inaccurate.

The extensive body of findings based on flawed methodology lacks rigor, reflects the bias of the researchers, and supports the socially constructed "truths" about the "races" and "ethnicities" studied (Abreu, 2001; American Psychological Association, 2003; Betancourt & Opez, 1993; Graham, 1992; Helms & Talleyrand, 1997). Bond's (1959) classic parody, "Talent—and Toilets" of psychologists' historical preoccupation with RDI (race differences in intelligence) underscores how the "objective" methods of scientific inquiry serve the zeitgeist of the times. In a study he conducted, he found that National Merit Scholarship winners could more easily be identified by "more toilets, more talent; fewer toilets, less talent; lowest percentage of toilets, no talent at all" (Bond, 1959, p. 5). The premise is relevant today, in that the number of toilets continues to symbolize the occupational stature and socioeconomic success of one's family and one's access to opportunities.

Feminist perspectives present an alternative view to mainstream psychological thought, but until recently have also been narrowly focused on the meaning of gender, unwittingly excluding analyses of distinctions in class, race/ethnicity, and sexual orientation. Espin (1994) acknowledges the shortsightedness of some feminists in psychology and agrees with several feminists of color (Anzaldua, 1990; Combahee River Collective, 1979; hooks, 1984; Lorde, 1984) who point out that the experiences of women of color are not only relevant but necessary for understanding the commonalities, as well as the differences, among women, thus improving the scope and practice of the field.

Race, ethnicity, and gender are but three of several dimensions deemed important in Western culture to account for the variability in psychological functioning in various domains (e.g., academic achievement, motivation, etc.) as well as discord between individuals and groups. Other dimensions include age, ableness, class, and sexual orientation. It is not the group difference that explains differences in behavior and performance alone, it is the meaning that those differences are endowed with that creates variations in behavior and social tension. Race and ethnicity, gender, sexual orientation, disability, age, socioeconomic class, and religious or spiritual orientations have little meaning in and of themselves. The social context in which these dimensions are perceived, experienced, understood, and defined is what makes them salient. Their salience is determined by how much of a difference these differences actually make in peoples' lives, at a given time and what they mean. It is the social context that helps to define social differences, thus giving them meaning. What does it mean to share group membership? What does it mean when individuals do not share that membership? What does it mean to share multiple memberships in some contexts and not in others?

Our challenge is to make sense of these questions, as well as appreciating the complexity of these issues in the education of psychologists and training of human services professionals. Indeed, Ijima Hall (1997) admonishes that psychology must make substantive changes in its curriculum, training, research, and practice to keep abreast of the changing demographics occurring in the United States or else risk professional, ethical, and economic problems because the profession will no longer be a viable resource to the majority of the U.S. population.

Diversity is a socially constructed concept indicating the mere presence of differences. However, we are challenged to understand the meaning of the difference, not simply to acknowledge its presence. Human beings differ from one another along a range of dimensions and in innumerable ways. The groups that the authors discuss are clearly different from one another on many dimensions, just as they are similar on other dimensions. When placed on a spectrum, some of those differences are highly visible on one extreme while others are completely invisible at the other extreme. However, aside from describing the groups, what makes these differences important? It is clear that some differences are deemed extremely salient, while other kinds of differences, even though highly visible, are deemed inconsequential. The question we are left to investigate, if we are to understand the tension that often occurs when we directly experience or anticipate differences between ourselves and others, is which differences make a difference. Why are some characteristics, beliefs, or behaviors of people given great importance while others are not? In our attempts to understand the underpinnings of social inequity in our clients' lives, it is essential to gauge why differences matter, how they make a difference in the client's life, to whom they matter most, who benefits from them, and who decides *which* differences make a difference?

Johnson (2001) points out that fear of the unknown is usually given as the reason people fear and distrust those who are not like them. It would seem logical that fear of difference would be normative. Johnson, however, argues that our fears are not based on what we do not know, but rather on what we *think* we *do* know. When we personally encounter for the first time someone from a different ethnic group, someone who is lesbian, gay, or bisexual, someone from a different religion, or someone with a disability, it is really not the first encounter. It represents the culmination of a series of previous symbolic encounters that have taken place whenever a piece of information was formally or informally communicated about that group or when its members have been conspicuously omitted as if they were invisible.

Symbolic encounters occur when we overhear conversations of adults as children or watch movies or television. They are perhaps most insidious when there is no discussion about what has been said or about the feeling of tension that permeates the communication. The visceral negative reaction to the mention or presence of some group or its member among adults may leave a child who witnesses those encounters with a level of discomfort that comes to be associated with members of that group. These negative associations may linger into adulthood, when the presence of the different group members elicits discomfort for reasons that you would be hard-pressed to explain other than as a "feeling." These symbolic encounters also occur when we read, watch, or hear the news and its contents reveal who and what is considered worthy and who is not. Some of our information may come directly from peers, as well as from loved ones and trusted figures who tell us what they *know* about members of different groups based on information that they may have garnered only secondhand as well.

Such encounters may be particularly problematic if we encounter people who belong to marginalized groups only when they are in roles that are subservient to ours, when we are dominant and they are subordinate. What we think explains someone else's position in the social hierarchy relative to our own in some ways explains what we think it tells us about ourselves.

This collection of impressions serves as the body of what we *think* we *know* about people whom we do not really know at all. The information we have accumulated is shaped by many complex sociopolitical and economic variables that may have little to do with the reality of who "those" people really are. Descriptions of "them" that reflect stereotypes are not designed to accurately describe "them" and inform us; rather, they may be designed and used to serve other purposes in a larger system of hierarchical relationships. Distortions of groups often represent the way that it has become convenient or comfortable to see or perceive them. All of these things constitute what we *think* we know about people who are different long before we ever actually have direct relationships with them.

AMERICAN CULTURE

In the United States, the distinction among groups based on cultural heritage exists within a hierarchical stratification in which one group is the "dominant" culture, peopled with "a majority," and there are a variety of "subcultures" of "minority" groups that are subordinate. The dominant culture:

- owns and controls the means of production and commerce
- has the power to grant and take away livelihoods
- owns and controls the channels of communication in the society
- decides what, how, and who gets addressed in the media
- promotes in the media those aspects of culture that are considered valuable
- excludes, denigrates, or makes invisible those aspects of culture it considers inferior or of less value

The people identified as being members of the dominant culture are afforded privileges denied to those deemed nonmembers because of real or perceived differences that impact the quality of life for both the dominant and subordinate groups.

Subordinates can and have coped with the power imbalance between them and the dominants through "horizontal hostility" (Pharr, 1988), that is, members of a subordinate group expressing hostility in a horizontal direction toward one's own kind. Consequently, there may be infighting among members of a subordinate group. According to Pharr (1988), "We may see people destroying their own neighborhoods, displaying violence and crime toward their own kind, while respecting the power of those that make up the norm" (p. 61). Self-hatred is often the result of the internalization of the dominant group's beliefs that those who are subordinates are substandard, defective, and inferior.

The form self-hatred takes varies from subordinate group to subordinate group, based in part on that group's experience of oppressive forces. For example, among African Americans, both men and women, the preference for light skin and devaluation of dark skin indicates negative views about the self based on a history of stereotypes. One of our patients takes great pride in the fact that she comes from a town in a Southern state known for its single, light-skinned African American women. These women are sought out by African American men who are interested in either maintaining or improving their social status and seek to marry a light-skinned African American woman.

Another patient, who is Puerto Rican, recalled with great sadness a conference on Latina women she attended. According to her, the Latina women present seemed to divide and splinter off into antagonistic groups in which inclusion or exclusion was seemingly determined by fluency in Spanish and degree of accentedness in English.

An important factor contributing to the assimilation and acculturation of the ethnic minority group is whether the group's immigration was "voluntary" or "involuntary." Ogbu (1994) states that voluntary or immigrant minorities are people (and their descendants) who have voluntarily come to the United States because they believe that the move will ultimately lead to more economic opportunities and greater political freedom. These expectations continue to influence the way the immigrants perceive and respond to obstacles confronting them in American society (e.g., discrimination). Voluntary minorities do relatively well in education and employment, especially after mastering the language. What is important is that they apparently do not interpret their presence and reception in the United States in terms of having been forced on them by Euro-Americans.

On the other hand, involuntary minorities are people and their descendants who were originally forced against their will by Euro-Americans through slavery, conquest, or colonization to marginally participate in American society. They tend to define themselves and their cultures in opposition to cultural values of the majority.

Examples of these two types include people of color from the Caribbean (e.g., Jamaican Americans) and African Americans, respectively. While both experience oppressive racism and sexism, West Indian Americans tend to be more successful than their African American counterparts and are more optimistic about their success as well (Brice, 1982).

Featherston (1994) makes the point that women of color "live theater of the absurd" daily in their efforts to counter negative assumptions imposed from without and to create internal frames of reference that facilitate authentic self-awareness and expression. She quoted Toni Morrison (on a segment of Bill Moyers's television series *World of*

Ideas), who observed that European immigrants from different countries often had little connection to one another before leaving Europe. Once in the United States, they could unite around their whiteness against blacks. According to Morrison, it was no coincidence that "the second thing every immigrant learns when he gets off the boat is the word *nigger*." Morrison observed that, in that way, immigrants established oneness, solidarity, and union with the country. She argues that newcomers were frightened coming to a strange country in need of a job, friends, and allies, having cut their bridges to their home country. Facing chaos in a new and strange place, it became important for immigrants to belong to something larger than themselves. There is a yearning to belong to what is deemed the "large idea" that is America.

For those who are not people of color, their whiteness is the passkey for membership in the larger and more powerful force (Featherston, 1994). Roediger's (2005) review of race and labor in American history expands on the notion of immigrants becoming "white" in America by distinguishing among those immigrants who are WOA (White On Arrival) and those who were WBC (White Before Coming); the latter, RTBC (Racial Thinkers Before Coming), seemingly have a pattern of racial thinking prior to coming to America that facilitates their rapidly learning the American racial system.

Social Privilege Defined

The *Merriam-Webster Dictionary* (1996) defines *privilege* as a special advantage, immunity, or benefit granted to or enjoyed by an individual, class, or caste that people come to feel they have a right to hold. West (1994) refers to it as an "undeserved gift." While privilege is often granted for capricious reasons, once people have it, they become convinced that they must have earned it and deserve it and that they have a preemptive right to continue to have it to the exclusion of others who may want it. Social privilege facilitates the optimal development of an individual, increases access to societal opportunities, or simply makes life easier, but is not acquired by virtue of merit or personal effort. It is gained simply by being a member of the group that is privileged. It is important to understand the nature of privilege as something that is not merit-based to fully grasp the reluctance of many people to acknowledge that they may have it.

Wildman (1996), McIntosh (1988), and Johnson (2001) analyze white-skin privilege as one form of social advantage, and each discusses the ways that they and other white Americans benefit from having white skin in a racist society. In its essence, having white-skin privilege makes life easier. In her examination of race privilege, Wildman defines key elements of privilege as the systemic conferral of benefit and advantage. She argues that the characteristics of people who are members of privileged groups come to define societal norms, not surprisingly to the benefit of the people who establish the norms. Members of other groups are measured against the characteristics that are held by the privileged, usually most dominant, members of a society and are found to be wanting in some way. The privileged characteristic is legitimized as the norm, and those who stand outside of it are considered deviant, deficient, or defective. These are important concepts in mental health. Overall, "they" are seen as deserving of their lot in life.

Social disadvantage stands on the opposite end of the conceptual continuum of privilege. Frye (1996) observes that it is important to make a distinction between social disadvantage and human misery. In her analysis of social oppression, she observes that people can suffer, experience pain, and be miserable without being socially disadvantaged, that privileged status does not always protect one from the experience of human suffering or failure. To be socially disadvantaged is to have your life confined and shaped by forces and barriers that are not accidental or occasional and hence avoidable, but are systematically related to each other in such a way as to catch one between and among them and restrict or penalize motion in any direction. It is the systematic, unavoidable barriers restricting freedom of expression that can and do cause suffering and pain.

Achievements by members of privileged groups are usually attributed to individual efforts, and rewards for those efforts are seen as having been earned and deserved. Jordan observes that a myth of "earned power" and "meritocracy" was developed by the members of the dominant culture to justify their right to discriminate against and limit social opportunities for people who were different. When these myths are accepted, people are viewed as getting whatever they deserve. People who are in positions of power are seen as deserving of privilege. People who are powerless, disadvantaged, vulnerable, and exploited are presumed to be getting what they deserve as well, which includes blame, punishment, and contempt for their condition (Greene, 2000).

Members of socially disadvantaged groups would not simply go along with this arrangement unless they were convinced that the social system distributed opportunities fairly and that their subordinate place in the social hierarchy was a function of their own failings. When members of disenfranchised groups blame themselves, they do not look at the structural nature of privilege and disadvantage and protest their maltreatment. When they accept the myth of meritocracy, they may even blame themselves. This form of self-blame is expressed in *internalized* racism, sexism, abilism, classism, heterosexism, and so forth. The person of color who *believes* that white people are superior and that they are inferior has internalized racism. Believing the negative stereotypes about some aspect of your identity is a form of internalized oppression. Hence, the systemic determinants of social privilege and disadvantage are usually invisible and, if materialized, are denied by those who are in power and who benefit from them. Needless to say, members of both socially privileged and socially disadvantaged groups will have feelings about their social status relative to one another and those feelings that will affect the way they experience encounters with one another.

Hines and Boyd-Franklin write that, in the course of their work training mental health professionals, it is usually acceptable and sometimes even welcome to discuss cultural differences between various societal groups. There is general agreement that many people will differ from the human services professional and that it is incumbent on that professional to know something about the values, beliefs, and behaviors that characterize people who are different from us. These discussions about cultural specifics often evoke interest, and most people agree that a working knowledge of these differences is crucial to doing culturally competent, sensitive work with clients from culturally diverse groups. However, when the discussion shifts to explore the systemic realities of belonging to certain groups—racism, as opposed to race; heterosexism, as opposed to lesbian or gay sexual orientation; classism as opposed to class status; abilism; ageism; and so on—the mood changes. Members of the audience, who had been previously receptive, polite, and accepting become defensive, angry, attacking, and sometimes absorbed in their own guilt. This response can serve as a metaphor for what people who are members of socially disadvantaged groups report as a part of their experience when they attempt to talk about the ways they face societal discrimination or to express their anger and pain about it in the presence of members of dominant groups. Their comments evoke reactions that are often hostile.

Blaine observes that colorblindness—the belief that everyone has experienced some form of oppression, making everyone the same—and other forms of denial of differences are designed to avoid confronting the reality of social injustice. Johnson (2001) argues that privilege is not a problem just for those who do *not* have it but for those who have it as well because of its relational nature. When someone is unfairly disadvantaged by social systems and fails to get something they deserve, someone else is unfairly privileged and gains something they do not deserve. The latter, however, is harder to acknowledge.

Most people do not want to be considered racist, heterosexist, classist, sexist, and the like, but they spend more of their time seeking to avoid those *labels* than exploring their behavior and the ways that they benefit from or have participated in systems of interrelated privilege and oppression, intended or not. It is unlikely that, in a society that is racist, sexist, classist, and heterosexist and discriminates systemically on other levels, one can have privileged characteristics and not have benefited from them. But what does that mean? In a heterosexist society, a heterosexual person has the social rights that are accorded heterosexual persons and denied to GLB persons. In this example, they do not have to actively do anything to acquire the benefits of heterosexuality. Similarly, in a racist society, individuals who have white skin derive the benefits of white-skin privileges simply because they possess that characteristic. What is derived is based on the presence of privileged characteristics, not effort, ability, or merit. The rationales for doing this are built into the rules and institutions of our society. The inability of an individual to point to, remember, or name the specific events or times when they benefited from a privileged characteristic does not determine the degree to which they have benefited in some ways.

Concept of "Multiple Identities"

All people have more than one identity. Hierarchies of privilege and disadvantage exist within privileged and disadvantaged groups just as they exist between them. Some of their identities may be privileged, while others may be disadvantaged. Most, however, are more comfortable expressing the ways they are disadvantaged than the ways they are privileged. We are all nevertheless responsible for acknowledging the presence of social privilege in our own lives, and the ways we benefit from it. It is impossible to grapple with the complexity of difference if we do not acknowledge the social context of privilege and disadvantage within which salient human differences are embedded. We are not personally responsible for the existence of these systems of privilege and disadvantage, but we move within them all the time in some role or roles.

Frye (1996) observed that the presence of a privilege does not eradicate the struggles an individual encounters when those struggles are defined outside the realm of their locus of privilege. When individuals have multiple identities, some of those identities or characteristics may place them in privileged groups while simultaneously others place them in disparaged groups. Some forms of privilege may mitigate or positively moderate some forms of disadvantage, while other privileges may not mitigate them at all. Similarly, membership in some disadvantaged groups can compound the negative effects of simultaneous membership in another disadvantaged group or groups (e.g., a person of color with a disability, a poor woman with a disability, lesbians and gay men of color, poor white or poor older men and women, etc.)

Institutional privilege is conferred by interlocking social systems as a reward for the possession of characteristics valued by those who are dominant. It is indeed a matter of luck but fortuitous to be born heterosexual in a heterosexist society; white in a racist society; financially well off in a classist society; male in a sexist and patriarchal society; young in an ageist society; and able-bodied in an ableist society.

Possession of those desired characteristics does not make one a better person, despite the fact that superior value is attributed to them as a rationale for the discrepancy in social power attendant to them; still, possessing those characteristics makes life easier. Membership in those categories is a function of the luck of the draw. People do not control their ethnicity, the presence of a disability, their sex, sexual orientation, age, or the economic status of their parents; they are simply born into those statuses. For that reason, the benefits accrued as a function of these characteristics are privileges.

Values associated with white-male supremacy and white privilege predominate in American value systems, worldview, and social institutions (Bullivant, 1984; McIntosh, 1988; McLemore, 1991; Triandis, 1994). Wise (2002) states:

> That which keeps people of color off-balance in a racist society is that which keeps whites in control: a truism that must be discussed if whites are to understand our responsibility to work for change. Each thing with which "they" have to contend as they navigate the waters of American life is one less thing whites have to sweat: and that makes everything easier, from finding jobs, to getting loans, to attending college. (p. 107)

GENDER

One of the earliest and most pervasive tasks of childhood is learning to be a "psychological" male or female, a task that is generally accomplished by the age of three (Bussey & Bandura, 1984; Libby & Aries, 1989). According to Miller (1976), the preferred roles in the culture are reserved for men, the *dominants*, who, having the power and social privilege, delegate to women, the *subordinates*, the roles and services the dominants do not want to perform. Boys are raised to be independent, self-reliant, aggressive, and achievement-oriented to a greater extent than are girls. Low (1989) found that sexual restraint and industriousness were instilled in girls in about 40 cultures, while boys received such training in less than five.

Chodorow (1979) proposed that the female identity is based on attachment to the mother, whereas the male's is based on detachment. The individual's relationship to the mother in childhood is then posited to give rise to a specific style of thinking and behavior in adulthood. For the female, this style is person-centered or relational and characteristic of subordinates, that is, the social context influences thinking and problem solving, while for the male, the cognitive style is object-centered or nonrelational and characteristic of the dominants. Feminist theorists argue that the relational behavior identified by many to be female is more properly understood as a method of oppression designed by men, for women (Hogg & Frank, 1992). It is suggested to be a mechanism of social control for the purpose of excluding one gender from attaining equal access to the social power resources of the other (Hare-Mustin & Marecek, 1988).

The impact of the migration of women from the Third World to do "women's work" in America has not generated much psychological research (Ehrenreich and Hochschild, 2004). Designing empirical studies to examine how the current migration patterns of many women who leave their children behind to be cared for by relatives while they travel abroad to care for other children who are different from them along a number of dimensions may shed new light on the developmental processes Chodorow (1979) describes. For example, knowing the complex interactions of an adult caregiver and child where differences in class, culture, native language, and race or ethnicity influence the experiences of both, and the meanings attached to these differences, may contribute to our understanding of gender identity.

GENDER-ROLE INEQUALITY AND ABUSE

The general pattern around the world is that men have higher status and more power than women, but this difference is not the same across cultures (Rosaldo & Lamphere, 1974). Cultures differ in the degree of gender inequality. *Inequality* in this context is meant to convey more than "unequal treatment." It includes the heuristic view that the functions ascribed to women, and hence women themselves, are subordinate in status to men. In some cultures, this subordinate status involves a pejorative devaluation of women and women's work, which creates a diminished quality of life for them, and can be a cause of mental health problems or, in extreme cases, threatens their very lives.

The underlying ideology of this unequal treatment has been called "hostile sexism" in the psychological literature (Glick & Fiske, 2001). *Hostile sexism* resembles other forms of prejudice typically directed toward groups who are seen as threats to the in-group's status and power. In contrast, *benevolent sexism*, despite its oxymoronic quality, is a subjectively favorable, chivalrous ideology that offers protection and affection to women who embrace conventional roles—roles, however, that perpetuate their inequality in a patriarchal society. In some ways, its effects are more pernicious than hostile sexism because men and women, but especially women, embrace this ideology; thus, women tend to be more tolerant of sexist behavior and its consequences on their "inferior" status because they perceive the motivation for the behavior as being protective (Glick & Fiske, 2001).

Even in cultures where an ideal of gender equality is stated explicitly, as in Mao's China, the practice is inconsistent with the ideal. In band societies, there is often male–female reciprocity and complementarity rather than hierarchy (Triandis, 1994). In stratified societies, socioeconomic and gender inequalities are often correlated. In Africa, for example, in the non-Muslim areas, the status of women was fairly equal to the status of men until the colonial powers took over (Etienne & Leacock, 1980). Under colonization, economic exploitation occurred and gender inequality increased.

One index of gender inequality is the percentage of illiterates who are women. In general, it is desirable to have an equal number of men and women who are literate, as is the case in Scandinavia and Switzerland. In many of the developing countries, however, far more women than men are illiterate. Even in the United States, women did not match the education levels of men until the late 1970s (Triandis, 1994).

A second index of gender inequality is the gender/earnings ratio, which indicates how much women earn as a percentage of what men earn. In general, women continue to earn less than men.

Indices of gender abuse include the prevalence of wife abuse, genital mutilation of girls and young women, acid throwing, infanticide, and elder abuse (the majority of whom are women). Although husbands can no longer legally beat their wives in the United States, and wives in the United States can legally sue their husbands for damages, domestic violence remains a reality for far too many women and their families. In India, the phenomenon of bride burning has increased in the past 20 years.

An Islamic court in Nigeria overturned an earlier decision that had condemned a divorced mother, Amina Lawal, who had given birth to a child conceived outside of marriage, to be stoned to death. Her case received worldwide attention, drawing sharp criticism from the Nigerian president and the international community. Some hailed the court's decision as a triumph for Islamic justice, while others, who are seen as being conservative, adamantly denounced the ruling, claiming that there was no justice (*New York Times*, 2003). What is important to note in this discussion about gender-role inequality and abuse is that the man who allegedly was sexually involved with Lawal and was the father of her child was not charged because he had three witnesses who testified that he had not been involved with Lawal; that "evidence" was sufficient according to the law. Men in the United States, prior to the second wave of the feminist movement in the 1960s and developments in the field of DNA testing, used similar defenses when accused of having sexual relations with a woman and impregnating her.

Clitordiction and infibulation (technical terms for what is more commonly called "female genital mutilation") of girls are practiced in many parts of Africa and the Middle East. According to the World Health Organization, more than 80 million females have been subjected to genital mutilation in Africa, ranging from the removal of the foreskin of the clitoris to removal of the clitoris and labia—often with unsterilized equipment and without anesthesia—and having the two sides of the vulva sewn together. The practice reflects tribal customs and societal values and is considered a significant aspect of a woman's identity. Some men, believing that women's sexual organs are unclean and clitordiction/infibulation "purifies" women, will not marry women who have not undergone the procedure (Heise et al., 1994).

What is so inconceivable to those outside of the cultures in which these practices are condoned is that they are performed by women and are viewed as a rite of passage. The plight of 19-year-old Fauziya Kasinga, who sought asylum in the United States after fleeing Togo when she was 16 to escape having a tribal member "scrape my woman parts off," drew international attention and condemnation of this type of gender abuse. The collective outcry from Westerners was garnered by focusing on the medical health hazards for these girls and young women rather than blatantly challenging the belief systems that condone the practice. Apropos of this, legislators in several states, responding to reports that the practice of genital mutilation is occurring in the United States by immigrants from those countries in which the practice is tradition, modeled bills based on a federal bill introduced by Rep. Pat Schroeder (D-CO), which made genital mutilation illegal in the United States.

Although one may fail to comprehend the actions of some women from different cultures that adversely affect not only themselves but also other women in their culture, it undoubtedly is much more difficult to examine the beliefs and practices in one's own culture that, to outsiders, may be equally incomprehensible and perceived to be abusive to women. An example from American history is illustrative. It is noteworthy that in the 19th century, doctors in England and the United States performed clitoridectomies on women as a viable treatment for masturbation, nymphomania, and psychological problems (Abusharaf, 1998).

The recent medical practice in the United States of discharging a mother and her newborn child within 48 hours of delivery and, more recently, discharging within 48 hours of surgery women who have had mastectomies, prompted legislation to stop these practices that seem, at best, insensitive to the emotional and physical vulnerability of women at these times and, at worst, dangerous to their health and the health of the newborn. The policy for early discharge apparently stemmed from guidelines established by third-party payers (insurance companies) based on greed, albeit couched in terms of cost-effective treatment. The meteoric rise in cosmetic procedures and surgeries (breast enlargement, liposuction, Botox injections, use of steroids and growth hormones, etc.) for women of all ages, but most notably among adolescent females, to improve their appearance and enhance their emotional sense of well-being may be another illustration of culturally-sanctioned gender-based abuse in the 21st century in America.

In some parts of the world, most notably China, South Korea, India, and Nepal, studies have shown that girls often receive inferior medical care and education and less food than their brothers (Landes, Foster, & Cessna, 1995). In India and China, many women use sonograms and amniocentesis to learn if they are carrying a girl; if they are, the fetus is frequently aborted (Heise, 1994).

RACE IN AMERICA

Race matters in America. To the nonwhite person in America, race is the most important defining factor in all aspects of their life (West, 1994). It is one of the most "visible" identity membership indicators based on visual cues enabling one to quickly categorize the "other" (e.g., as a black woman, an Asian man, etc.). Historically, race was viewed as a biological category. Recent genetic analysis of different "racial groups" disputes this view and instead shows greater genetic variation within a racial group than across racial groups (Barbujani et al., 1997). Race, now viewed as a social construction, takes on a cultural significance as a result of the social processes that sustain majority/minority status (Pinderhughes, 1989).

The subordinate status assigned to persons with given physical traits and the projections made upon them are used to justify exclusion or inclusion within the society. The responses of both those who are dominant, and therefore exclude, and the victims who are subordinate, and therefore are excluded, become part of their cultural adaptation. The meaning assigned to racial categorization is determined by the dynamics of stratification and stereotyping. Hopps (1982) suggests that true understanding of minority status requires understanding of the various levels of oppression endured by the group. While discrimination and exclusion have existed in this country for a number of groups classified as "minorities," oppression has been the most severe, deeply rooted, persistent, and intractable for people of color (Hopps, 1982). Surveys on the attitudes of the majority (whites) concerning minorities show that attitudes do change often within one generation, especially during periods of social upheaval. Also, research suggests that more progress toward equality was made during the 1950s and 1960s than in the last 20 years of the 20th century; this trend is termed "symbolic racism," as it reflects subtler forms of prejudice in which race is not directly expressed but nonetheless is the subtext for opposition to policy changes and issues related to race relations (Bobo, 1999).

Apropos of contemporary forms of covert institutionalized and symbolic racism, Patricia Williams, a law professor (and a woman of color), recounted her experience with the "new rhetoric of racism" when she was in the market to buy a new home in another state. The transaction with the bank (conducted by telephone) to obtain a mortgage had gone smoothly (e.g., she met all of the criteria) up until the bank received her "corrected" contract by mail (the loan officer at the bank had, in error, checked off "white" in the box on the fair housing form and Williams had crossed it out). The attitude of the bank changed dramatically (e.g., requests for more money, more points, and a higher interest rate). "Race" was never mentioned as a reason for the stalled process; instead, the bank cited increased "economic risk." Translated, this means they were concerned about "white flight" and decreased property values in the area, which theretofore had been protected by redlining. Williams threatened to sue and was able to procure the loan based on the original terms (Williams, 1997).

The labeling and grouping of people into categories of "dominant" and "subordinate" racial and ethnic groups (e.g., White [Euro-American], Black/African American, American Indian/Alaska Native, Native Hawaiian/Other Pacific Islander, Asian, Some Other Race) by governmental agencies, policy makers, and social scientists reflects the psychosociopolitical landscape of group relations in contemporary American society, tends to obscure rather than illuminate meaningful commonalities and differences among groups, and serves to maintain the societal processes and structures of stratification of people.

In contemporary American society, the designation "black," for some, acknowledges the solidarity with people of the Black Diaspora, that is, people dispersed throughout the world whose ancestors are of African descent (Landrine, 1995). For others, it is a racial designation in which race is viewed either as a biological or genetic fact or as a social construction with scientific, sociopolitical, moral, and economic ramifications. For example, a person of African descent (i.e., whose parents are African immigrants) who was born in the United States but whose ancestors were not slaves in America would not readily identify with being called an African American, which is an ethnocultural group, not a racial group, because the term refers to African ancestors who were slaves during the slavery period in American history. However, they might be more inclined to identify with being "black," as does Sen. Barack Obama (D-IL), one of the Democratic candidates running for president in 2008, whose father is African and mother is white from Kansas, because his experience in America—that is, the response of the dominant group toward him, a "minority," despite his heritage—is that of being a black person.

ETHNICITY

In anthropological terms, an ethnic group is generally understood to designate a population that is largely self-perpetuating; shares fundamental cultural values, realized in overt unity in cultural forms; makes up a field of communication and interaction; and has a membership that identifies itself, and is identified by others, as constituting a category distinguishable from other categories of the same order (Narroll, 1964). Barth (1969) stresses that ethnic groups are categories of ascription and identification by the actors themselves, and thus have the characteristic of organizing interaction between people. When someone is identified as being a member of an ethnic group, that individual supposedly shares with that group many complex characteristics such as language, customs, traditions, physical characteristics, religion, and ancestral origin.

Ethnicity is a key aspect of one's identity. Erikson (1950) developed a framework for understanding how the individual is linked to the ethnic group and society. He viewed identity as a process located in the core of the individual, and yet also in the core of his or her communal culture. Ethnic identity may remain hidden and outside of awareness. Its effects on feelings, thoughts, perceptions, expectations, and actions of people toward others are not readily understood; nonetheless, it is maintained by a boundary (Barth, 1969). The following self-descriptions offered by two individuals during a workshop on cultural sensitivity are illustrations:

1. "I'm Syrian and Italian—pure on each side. To belong to both of these ethnic groups where I grew up meant being inferior. I have mixed feelings about my ethnic background because Italians are associated not only with food but with the underground and I have had to be connected with that emotionally. In the Syrian aspect of my life, they have not had a good historical reputation and are considered sort of sleazy—so you might say I come from a kind of underground sleaze."
2. "I now realize my father taught us to hate being Black. We couldn't go out of the house until we straightened our hair—he was ashamed of being Black, and I used to envy kids whose fathers taught them to feel proud. I have to work hard to overcome this—even now." (Pinderhughes, 1989, p. 41)

For some individuals and groups (e.g., some English-speaking whites and some ethnic minorities), ethnicity as a defining characteristic of personality and group identity at the conscious and unconscious levels may no longer retain its salience. Symbolic ethnicity, involved with the more visible aspects of ethnic heritage (e.g., acknowledging ceremonial holidays, eating ethnic food, wearing ethnic clothing on ceremonial occasions) does not bind the individual to adhere to the shared customs and traditions of the past. In other words, the term suggests that ethnicity has shifted from the center of identity to the peripheral, that other identities may have more of an impact on what one does, how one thinks, and with whom one chooses to affiliate (Schaefer, 2001; Gans, 1979).

African Americans and many individuals from the Asian and Hispanic populations are often reluctant to give up ethnic customs and traditions learned early in life in favor of Eurocentric middle-class American values and lifestyles, which may be contrary to their beliefs. African Americans have fought to overcome cultural dominance and discrimination and, through efforts such as the civil rights movement, have sought to understand and maintain our cultural heritage.

In 1994, the Bureau of the Census began hearings to consider adding new categories to the present census choices. They found that Arab Americans, for example, are unhappy with their official designation of "White, non-European." Many Native Hawaiians want to be redesignated as American Indians rather than Pacific Islanders, reflecting historical accuracy. Some Hispanics want the Census Bureau to classify them in terms of race, not ethnic origin, and to replace the category "Hispanic" with "Latino." For those with this view, the term *Hispanic* recalls the colonization of Latin America by Spain and Portugal and has become as offensive as the term *Negro* became for African Americans. Survey results show that people would prefer to be identified as Puerto Rican, Colombian, Cuban, and so on.

About one in three black Americans would like the census bureau to adopt the term *African American*. People from the Caribbean, however, tend to prefer being labeled by their country of origin, such as Jamaican or Haitian American. Africans who are not American also find the term inaccurate. It is imperative that the rich diversity in individual differences that exists within each of these groups not be overlooked.

GENDER, RACE, AND ETHNIC IDENTITIES

Gender stereotypes affect how women and men think of themselves and how they evaluate their own behavior, as well as the behavior of others; these stereotypes are learned early. The term *prostitot* refers to a stereotype perpetrated on young girls and teenagers who are brainwashed by the media, fashion, and toy industries to think of themselves as sex objects and to dress in scanty, provocative clothing, like a prostitute. Bratz dolls illustrate this stereotype, which when internalized by youth, both males and females, contributes to a young girl or adolescent's lower self-esteem and the distorted, damaging image of what it means to be male vis-à-vis female. The girl Bratz doll uses lots of makeup (message: one's natural state is ugly), wears less clothing, and shows plenty of skin. The style of dress is sexually provocative, like a prostitute, suggesting that a girl must see herself as a sex object or sex toy to be accepted and liked. In contrast, the boy Bratz doll is well dressed and often has books or a backpack, showing that he is smart and ambitious.

The need to recognize the differences as well as the common experiences women share involving race and gender can be seen when one considers the different stereotypes about women of color that are based not only on their gender but also on their ethnic/racial designation. For women of color, stress is often the result of significant role strain as we try to accommodate to different cultural expectations and values and reject stereotypes about us based not only on our gender but also on our racial/ethnic identity. Stereotypes about women of color are more than racist and sexist—we propose the term *rasexism* to capture the complexity of the impact of these prejudices.

African American women have been stereotyped as "Aunt Jemima," "Mammy," "Sapphire," "whore," and "Super Woman" (Greene, 1992; Young, 1989), as "matriarchies," and as the prototypical welfare recipient (e.g., a lazy, morally loose, single woman who continues to have children out of wedlock for a larger welfare check). The recent debacle in which radio shock jock Don Imus, on the air, called the predominantly African American women's basketball team from Rutgers University "nappy headed hos" thrust into the mainstream the pernicious denigration of women, especially African American women, prevalent in segments of the black community and music industry (e.g., gangsta rap).

The American Indian woman has been stereotyped as the "squaw," a term that became synonymous with "drudge" or "prostitute" (Witt, 1976). The newer exotified image of the American Indian woman from Hollywood is an American Indian princess, Pocahontas. Hispanic American women have been variously stereotyped as the passive, submissive, male-dominated, all-suffering woman or as a loud, histrionic, hot-tempered "Carmen Miranda type" (Rivers, 1995). The predominant stereotypic image for the Asian American woman is one of sexual/exotic attractiveness, reserve, passivity, and, paradoxically, martial arts warrior who defers to males, elders, and authority figures (Fujitomi and Wong, 1976; Chan, 1987).

These different stereotypes of women share a common theme, but their differences reflect conscious and unconscious operations in the collective psyche of Americans about gender, race, and ethnicity. In some way, each set of stereotypes serves as a justification for the sexual exploitation of the women who belong to that group.

For example, one of the authors met with a young Korean man for a psychological consultation. He had been in the United States for several years and is the father of two young children, a son and a daughter, who were born in the United States. He was experiencing emotional conflict about the best way to raise his children, who have never been to Korea and are not acquainted with traditional Korean customs. He had been raising his children the "American way," because they are Americans and he wants them to be successful here. In contrast to traditional Korean childrearing practices, his childrearing methods apparently involve much less discipline and less emphasis on honor, self-sacrifice, and respect for self and others. While expressing concern for both his children, he was more troubled by his fears for his daughter because he really doesn't like what he perceives to be the acceptable and desirable attitudes and behaviors for women in American society; he commented on media images of young girls that he finds shameful because of their lack of self-respect and modesty reflected in their style of dress and manner of speaking. In short, this man's conflict reflects his ambivalence and uncertainty about how to raise his children to become "good" Koreans able to make it as Americans in this society.

CLASS

Classism or class oppression in America is noteworthy for the degree to which its existence is denied. That denial is reflected in the meritocracy myth, which suggests that everyone has equal opportunities for success. It is also reflected in America's dim view of poor people. Newitz and Wray (1997) write that Americans love to hate the poor and that to be labeled "poor" does not generally elicit sympathy. Instead, being poor may elicit hostility and disgust from others and trigger a sense of shame in oneself. Economic impoverishment is often associated with negative character traits such as having inadequate or improper values, ineptitude, laziness, or outright stupidity (O'Hare, 1992; Newitz & Wray, 1997). Poor people are also characterized as refusing to work, living in female-headed households, living in inner-city ghettos, and living off welfare (O'Hare, 1986). Even if it were not for these direct negative characterizations, our feelings about the poor are reflected in our definitions of lower- and middle-class values and behaviors and of the word *class* itself.

In psychology, class is discussed in terms of socioeconomic status of the individual or group, which signifies, among other things, one's degree of success in achieving a quality of life, standard of living, and lifestyle idealized in the "American Dream." Presumably, the higher the socioeconomic level, the better the quality of life and the more successful are those who attain it. Conversely, the lower the socioeconomic status, the less successful the individual is in attaining a desirable standard of living, which, according to democratic ideals, is possible for all. Class, defined by income, education, and power and analyzed solely in terms of its relationship with various psychological constructs such as intelligence, locus of control, achievement motivation, and mental health, obscures the vulnerabilities of designated "minorities" who are "barred" from participating as equal players in the capitalistic marketplace of the United States. When gender, race, ethnicity, and more recently sexual orientation, age, and disability are included in discussions on class, the politics of deeply institutionalized policies and practices of discrimination become apparent.

The *Merriam-Webster Dictionary* (1996) defines *class* as high social rank, elegance, high quality, and a rating based on grade or quality. Wyche (1996) tells us that when we say that someone has "no class," we do not mean this literally. Instead, we mean that they have lower- or working-class values and are behaving like poor or working-class people. The demeaning implication is that to have lower-class values is the same as having no class at all. Consistent with Webster's definition, being of lower class equates to lacking elegance and having no or low quality or low social rank.

Middle-class values are generally deemed to include the presence of upwardly mobile striving, valuing an education, possessing the ability to delay gratification, and being willing to save and work hard. By defining middle-class values in this manner, the implication is that people who are middle class acquired that status because they have the correct values and good moral character, failing to include the role of social opportunity (jobs, education, etc.) as a pathway to solvency. This fails to address in any significant way the critical role of class oppression reflected in differential access to opportunities such as education, at one time trade union membership, and many jobs or careers that have been closed to LGB people, physically challenged individuals, ethnic minority group members, women, and others. These opportunities serve as gateways to upward mobility and middle-class status, and they are not equally distributed nor are they distributed on the basis of merit in this society.

Poor people are blamed for their circumstances with the assumption that they did not work hard enough or take advantage of available opportunities, and they are exhorted to feel ashamed of themselves and their circumstances. The pervasive and incorrect assumption is that sufficient opportunities are equally available to everyone. Blaming the poor for their plight serves to further obscure the reality of class oppression in this society. This is reflected poignantly in the lyrics of Billie Holiday's jazz classic, "God Bless the Child": "Them that's got, shall have; them that's not, shall lose" (Holiday & Herzog, 1941).

Sidel's (1993) assessment of poverty in the United States highlights just how devastating the effects of poverty are on women and ethnic minority families. Single mothers are more likely to be poor than any other demographic group, not only affecting their psychological well-being and physical health but also exposing their children to stress associated with poverty. The "feminization of poverty," a phrase originally coined by sociologist Diana Pearce (Sidel, 1993), refers to social and economic factors resulting in the increased percentage of poor women and children. These include the rapid growth of female-headed families, a labor market that continues to discriminate against female workers, and unpaid domestic responsibilities traditionally reserved for women (e.g., child care).

Rothenberg (1988) writes that she grew up with an obliviousness to her race but an acute awareness of her gender and her Jewish, upper-middle-class standing. She recalls being aware that her family was much better off than most people and that she felt sorry for those who were not as well off. Still, she acknowledges believing with absolute certainty that poor people must deserve to be poor because they either failed "to work hard enough, study hard enough, or save enough" (p. 38).

SEXUAL ORIENTATION

In *Engendered Lives*, Ellyn Kaschak (1992) writes:

> The consensual reality of western culture has held that gender is a given, contained in or identical with the sex of the newborn. Gender and gender linked attributes are viewed as natural rather than as socially and psychologically constructed. Paradoxically, then, all children must be taught what is natural ... and those who do not learn their lessons well are viewed as unnatural. (p. 39)

Kaschak's incisive analysis draws our attention to an important but frequently overlooked subtlety in this design, revealing its flaws. If specific gendered behaviors are natural outgrowths of biological sex, and if heterosexual sexual orientation is natural for everyone, why would it be necessary to so assiduously teach that which is innate and natural? Furthermore, why would that which is deemed unnatural require such strong prohibitions and stigmatizing to prevent its occurrence? It would seem that natural behavior would just naturally evolve. It is precisely because traditional gender-roles, which include heterosexual sexual orientation as the normative sexual orientation, are not ubiquitously natural or normative; they do not naturally evolve in everyone.

In fact, a natural evolution is not allowed to take place. A culture's gender-roles are socially constructed, assigned, agreed on, and change over time. It is precisely because of these factors that they require enforcing rather than simply allowing them to naturally evolve. And still, lesbian and gay sexual orientations evolve in individuals in spite of explicit prohibitions, opposition, and punitive responses to them.

Kaschak (1992) observes that it is particularly shameful not to fit neatly into a gender category. This is reflected in the shame and embarrassment that people feel when their gender is mistaken or cannot be quickly discerned. It is as if they have done something wrong, are "queer," or "peculiar" or as if something is seriously wrong with them. She adds that when methods of enforcing traditional gender-roles and categories fail, or as a result of the damage caused by them, the person in question may be deemed ill and in need of psychotherapy.

Despite many significant advances in GLB (gay, lesbian, and bisexual) psychology in the last several decades, the next century confronts us with many new challenges in the need to explore the more complex nuances and varied meanings of sexual orientation, as well as the many ways it is interrelated to other aspects of human identity. It is also necessary to conduct similar explorations of heterosexism and its connection to other forms of social oppression.

Heterosexism is not a singular or isolated experience or event. As such, heterosexism cannot be disconnected from the broader context of an individual's development or existence any more than sexism, for example, can be understood apart from the context of a woman's ethnicity, socioeconomic class, religion, or other significant aspects of her life. An exclusive focus on heterosexism as the primary locus of oppression for all lesbians and gay men presumes that it is experienced in the same way for all group members and that it has the same meaning and consequences for them. The core of this assumption is common in the psychological literature as well as in practice.

AGEISM

Unlike ethnicity and other variables, the aged represent a group with permeable group boundaries that, if we live long enough, will permit everyone entry. Unlike people with disabilities, a group which potentially any of us *could* belong to, or specific ethnic groups, to whom we cannot belong unless we are born into them, all human beings go from not belonging to this group to belonging to it (Gatz & Cotten, 1996). Because the aged come from all social groups, the degree of disadvantage due to ageism may vary across the group.

Ageing has different meanings across ethnic groups and different implications for men versus women. Ehrenberg (1996) reports that older gay men may be more vulnerable to isolation than older lesbians. Owing to the longer life span of women, lesbians may be more likely to have surviving mates and peers and are less biased (than gay men) against older partners. Older gay men were observed to be more concerned about physical appearance than older lesbians, perhaps owing to the preference for younger partners among older gay men (Ehrenberg, 1996).

Within many subgroups of people of color, older family members are considered elders, and are valued for their life's accumulated wisdom and accorded respect. In some Asian and East Indian cultural groups, adult children are expected to consult and in some instances conform to the wishes of their parents regarding career choices and when and whom to marry, in ways that Western cultures do not formally expect (although many Western ethnic groups do have this informal expectation). The status of elders in different cultures differs depending on gender, as well. In Western or mainstream American cultures, older people are often viewed as if they are no longer as useful as younger persons. This perception of older persons is confounded if they are no longer producing capital.

Older people, like persons with disabilities, are frequently regarded as if they were asexual. There may be the assumption that older persons do not miss or desire the presence of a romantic partner or companion, are not interested in a date, or do not care about being sexually active.

ABLENESS/DISABILITY

Fine and Asch (1988) observe that in research on disability, factors of sexual orientation, gender, race, and class seem to be regarded as irrelevant, suggesting that having a disability overshadows all other dimensions of social experience. They suggest that disability (as opposed to the mere presence of physical challenges), like gender, sexual orientation, ethnicity, and so forth, is a social construct. Solomon (1993) writes that it is the interaction between the presence of physical challenges or biological impairments and social, environmental, and cultural factors and social prejudice that determines whether or not the physical challenge becomes a disability. According to Fine and Asch (1988):

> no data on the numbers of lesbians with disabilities or on their acceptance by nondisabled lesbians as partners, but comments made by many disabled lesbians indicate that within the community of lesbians the disabled woman is still in search of love. (p. 3)

Despite reports from men and women with disabilities that social factors influence their sexual experiences more profoundly than physiological factors, social factors are rarely discussed in the psychological literature (Linton, 1998). As in other forms of oppression, Davis (1997, p. 9) observes that the problem is not the person with disabilities; the problem is the way that normalcy is socially constructed to create the problem of the disabled. Most people have been acculturated to stigmatize those whose bodies or other aspects of their person are deemed aberrant. Linton (1998) argues that people with disabilities need to be contextualized in contexts of human variation—as a political category, as an oppressed minority, as a cultural group.

Linton (1998) observes that people with disabilities share an important commonality with lesbians and gay men: Both groups share the experience of growing up in families with other members who do not share their minority status. Members of both groups learn about what it means to be a member of their minority group outside of their families, rather than from their own family members. This sometimes occurs in the proximity of other peers and mentors, but not always. Linton (1998) highlights difficulties in the development of group cohesion, culture, and identity when there is no consistent intergenerational transmission of culture, as is true for lesbians and gay men as well (p. 93).

MARGINALIZATION AND MARGINALITY

There is a connection between the need to establish clear boundaries among groups differing in ethnicity, class, sexual orientation, and so forth in our society and the existence of privilege and social disadvantage. The socially constructed boundaries between heterosexuals and lesbians/gay men, men and women, lower and upper socioeconomic classes, people of color and white Americans, and other groups are not needed to provide accurate descriptive information about them. These boundaries are in place to maintain and justify the system of social privilege and disadvantage associated with those characteristics. The ultimate goal is to make sure that the privileged maintain their privileges while others do not gain similar access and instead are marginalized.

The ill effects of oppression and discrimination are evident among women and men who report experiencing a sense of marginality or invisibility as a function of one or more of their "minority identities" (Comas-Diaz & Greene, 1994; Chisholm, 1996). By "marginality," we mean to suggest that many individuals experience a profound schism between their public and private presentations of self, which reflects an awareness of how the dominant Other perceives (or rather misperceives by "not seeing," stereotyping, etc.) them in those social contexts in which the minority identity or identities may be salient (e.g., family, school, work, relationships, etc.) and in which there is a dynamic interplay between designated "majority" and "minority" status. The "not seeing" results in a sense of invisibility despite the fact that the individual may be highly visible—that is, they may be invisible in terms of influence while being visible in terms of tokenism. The individual experiencing marginality exists uncomfortably in both the worlds of the dominant Other and of the minority group and is perceived and treated differently in each. In the world of work, for example, the person, marginalized because of her or his ethnicity/race, is defined by ethnicity/race and gender as well as competence. In their personal life, they often feel set apart from family and friends, who experience their "successes"—whatever may be, as determined by the dominant group—as a moving away from the minority group, sometimes literally, as in leaving the old neighborhood, or emotionally.

The psychological literature has begun to explore what has been common knowledge among those identified as being "different," "ethnic," or "a minority": individuals have multiple identities, any of which may be "majority" or "minority"—the social context determines the salience of the one(s) operating at any given time (Sedikides & Brewer, 2001; Hornsey & Hogg, 2000). As identity represents an interaction between the social and internal world, some of our identities or differences in group membership are private and some are public; some are visible, some invisible. When conducting psychological research, it is important to ascertain the salience of the identity in question to the individual when that characteristic of the individual is a variable in a study. Failure to do so may lead to a sampling error where homogeneity among the participants is assumed but in fact is nonexistent. Cole (1986) captures the dilemma facing scientists and practitioners who strive for competency with respect to race/ethnicity, gender, religion, age, sexual orientation, socioeconomic class, and disability:

> That which US women have in common must always be viewed in relation to the particularities of a group, for even when we narrow our focus to one particular group of women it is possible for differences within that group to challenge the primacy of what is shared in common. For example, what have we said and what have we failed to say when we speak of "Asian American women"?

When the external, social world distorts one's identity and imposes barriers to opportunities based on that identity, the groundwork has been laid for a distorted image of one's self and sense of self-worth and a distorted perception of others. These are fertile conditions for the development of mental health problems. Mental health interventions may assist women of color who confront this dilemma, but if mental health practitioners are not sensitive to social marginalization as a contextual factor, it may also harm them.

REFERENCES

Abreu, J. M. (2001). Theory and research on stereotypes and perceptual bias: A resource guide for multicultural counseling trainers. *Counseling psychologist, 29*, 487–512.

Abusharaf, R. (1998). Unmasking tradition. *Sciences,* March/April, 22–27.

American Psychological Association. (2003). Guidelines on multicultural education, training, research, practice, and organizational change for psychologists. *American Psychologist, 58*, 377–402.

Anzaldua, G. (Ed.). (1990). *Making face, making soul—Haciendo caras: Creative and critical perspectives by feminists of color.* San Francisco: Aunt Lute Foundation.

Barbujani, G., Magagni, A., Minch, E., Cavalli-Sforza, L. (1997). An apportionment of human DNA diversity. Proceedings of the National Academy of Sciences, *94*, 4516–4519.

Barth, F. (1969). *Ethnic groups and boundaries.* Boston: Little, Brown.

Betancourt, H., and Lopez, S. R. (1993). The study of culture, ethnicity, and race in American psychology. *American Psychologist, 48,* 629–637.

Bobo, L. (1999). Prejudice as group position: Microfoundations of a sociological approach to racism and race relations. *Journal of Social Issues, 55,* 445.

Bond, H. (1959). Talent—and toilets. *Journal of Negro Education, 28,* 3–14.

Brice, J. (1982). West Indians. In M. McGoldrick., J. K. Pearce, and J. Giordano (Eds.), *Ethnicity and family therapy* (pp. 123–133). New York: Guilford Press.

Bullivant, M. (1984). *Cultural maintenance and evolution.* Clevedon, England: Multilingual Matters.

Bussey, K., & Bandura, A. (1984). Influence of gender constancy and social power on sex-linked modeling. *Journal of Personality and Social Psychology, 47,* 1292–1302.

Chan, C. S. (1987). Asian American women: Psychological responses to sexual exploitation and cultural stereotypes. *Women & Therapy, 6,* 33–38.

Chisholm, J. F. (1996). Mental health issues in African-American Women. *New York Academy of Sciences.*

Chodorow, N. (1979). Feminism and difference: Gender, relation and difference in psychoanalytic perspective. *Socialist Review, 9*(4), 51–70.

Cole, J. B. (Ed.). (1986). *All American women: Lines that divide, ties that bind.* New York: Free Press.

Comas-Diaz, L. (2001). Hispanics, Latinos, or Americanos: The evolution of identity. *Cultural Diversity and Ethnic Minority Psychology, 7*(2), 115–120.

Comas-Diaz, L., & Greene, B. (Eds.). (1994). *Women of color: Integrating ethnic and gender identities in psychotherapy.* New York: Guilford Press.

Combahee River Collective. (1979). A black feminist statement. In Z. Eisenstein (Ed.), *Capitalist patriarchy and the case for socialist feminism* (pp. 135–139). New York: Monthly Review Press.

Davis, L. (1997). *The disability studies reader.* New York: Routledge.

Ehrenberg, M. (1996). Aging and mental health: Issues in the gay and lesbian community, in *Global Women.* Ehrenreich, B. and Hochschild, A. (Eds). (2004). New York: Owl Books.

Erikson, E. (1950). *Childhood and society.* New York: W. W. Norton.

Espin, O. M. (1994). Feminist approaches. In Comas-Diaz & Greene, 1994, pp. 265–286.

Etienne, M., & Leacock, E. (1980). *Women and colonization: Anthropological perspectives.* New York: Praeger.

Featherston, E. (Ed.). (1994). *Skin deep: Women writing on color, culture and identity.* Freedom, CA: Crossing Press.

Fine, M., and Asch, A. (1988). Disability beyond stigma: Social interaction, discrimination, and activism. *Journal of Social Issues, 44,* 3–21.

Frye, M. (1996). The necessity of differences: Constructing a positive category of women. *Signs, 21,* 991–1010.

Fujitomi, S., and Wong, D. (1976). The new Asian American woman. In S. Cox (Ed.), *Female psychology: The emerging self* (pp. 236–248). Chicago: Science Research Associates.

Gans, H. J. (1979). Symbolic ethnicity: The future of ethnic groups and cultures in America. *Ethnic and Racial Studies, 2* (January), pp. 1–20.

Glick, P., & Fiske, S. (2001). An ambivalent alliance: Hostile and benevolent sexism as complementary justifications for gender inequality. *American Psychologist, 56,* 109–118.

Graham, S. (1992). Most of the subjects were white and middle class. *American Psychologist, 47*(5), 629–639.

Graves, J. L., Jr. (2001). *The emperor's new clothes: Biological theories of race at the millennium.* New Brunswick, NJ: Rutgers University Press.

Greene, B. (1992). Black feminist psychotherapy. In E. Wright (Ed.), *Feminism and psychoanalysis.* Oxford, England: Blackwell.

Greene, R. (2000). *48 laws of power.* New York: Penguin.

Hare-Mustin, R., & Marecek, J. (1988). The meaning of difference: Gender theory, postmodernism, and psychology. *American Psychologist, 43*(6), 455–464.

Heise, L. (1994). Violence against women: The hidden health burden. World Bank Discussion Papers. In Landes, Foster, & Cessna, 1995.

Helms, J. E., & Talleyrand, R. M. (1997). Race is not ethnicity. *American Psychologist, 52,* 1246–1247.

Hogg, J., & Frank, M. (1992). Toward an interpersonal model of codependence and contradependence. *Journal of Counseling & Development, 70,* 371–375.

hooks, b. (1984). *Feminist theory: From margin to center.* Boston: South End Press.

Hopps, J. (1982). Oppression based on color. *Social Work, 27*(1), 3–5.

Hornsey, M., & Hogg, M. (2000). Assimilation and diversity: An integrative model of subgroup relations. *Personality and Social Psychology Review, 4,* 143–156.

Ijima Hall, C. (1997). Cultural malpractice: The growing obsolescence of psychology with the changing U.S. population. *American Psychologist, 52*(6), 642–651.

Kaschak, E. (1992). *Engendered lives: A new psychology of women's experience.* New York: Basic Books.

Landes, A., Foster, C., & Cessna, C. (Eds.). (1995). *Violent relationships: Battering and abuse among adults.* Wylie, TX: Information Plus.

Landrine, H. (Ed.). (1995). *Bringing cultural diversity to feminist psychology: Theory, research, and practice.* Washington, DC: American Psychological Association.

Libby, M. N., & Aries, E. (1989). Gender differences in preschool children's narrative fantasy. *Psychology of Women Quarterly, 13,* 293–306.

Linton, S. (1998). *Claiming disability: Knowledge and identity.* New York: New York University Press.

Lorde, A. (1984). *Sister outsider.* Freedom, CA: Crossing Press.

Low, B. S. (1989). Cross-cultural patterns in the training of children: An evolutionary perspective. *Journal of Comparative Psychology, 103,* 311–319.

McIntosh, P. (1988). White privilege: Unpacking the invisible knapsack. In P. S. Rothenberg (Ed.), *White privilege: Essential readings on the other side of racism* (pp. 97–101). New York: Worth, 2002.

McLemore, S. D. (1991). *Racial and ethnic relations in America.* Boston: Allyn & Bacon.

Miller, J. (1976). *Toward a new psychology of women.* Boston: Beacon Press.

Narroll, R. (1964). Ethnic unit classification. *Current Anthropology, 5*(4).

Newitz, A. and Wray, M. (1997). What is "white trash"? Stereotypes and economic conditions of poor whites in the U.S. In M. Hill (Ed.), *Whiteness: A critical period* (pp. 168–184): New York: New York University Press.

Ogbu, J. (1994). From cultural differences to differences in cultural frame of reference. In P. Greenfield & R. Cocking (Eds.), *Cross-cultural roots of minority child development* (pp. 365–391). Hillsdale, NJ: Erlbaum.

O'Hare, W. P. (1992). America's minorities: The demographics of diversity. *Population Bulletin, 47*(4), 1–47.

Pharr, S. (1988). *Homophobia: A weapon of sexism.* Inverness, CA: Chardon Press.

Pinderhughes, E. (1989). *Understanding race, ethnicity, and power: The key to efficacy in clinical practice.* New York: Free Press.

Rivers, R. (1995). Clinical issues and interventions with ethnic minority women. In J. Aponte, R. Rivers, and J. Wohl (Eds.), *Psychological interventions and cultural diversity* (pp. 181–198). Boston: Allyn & Bacon.

Rosaldo, M. Z., & Lamphere, L. (1974). *Woman, culture and society.* Stanford, CA: Stanford University Press.

Rothenberg, P. (1988). *Race, class and gender in the U.S.: An integrated study.* New York: Worth.

Schaefer, R. T. (2001). *Race and ethnicity in the United States.* Upper Saddle River, NJ: Prentice Hall.

Sedikides, C., & Brewer, M. (2001). *Individual self, relational self, collective self.* Philadelphia: Brunner-Routledge.

Sidel, R. (1993). Who are the poor? In V. Cyrus (Ed.), *Experiencing race, class, and gender in the United States* (pp. 123–128). Mountain View, CA: Mayfield.

Triandis, H. C. (1994). *Culture and social behavior.* New York: McGraw-Hill.

West, C. (1994). *Race matters.* New York: Random House.

Williams, P. (1997). Of race and risk. *Nation,* December 29.

Wise, T. (2002). Membership has its privileges: Thoughts on acknowledging and challenging whiteness. In P. S. Rothenberg (Ed.), *White privilege: Essential readings on the other side of racism* (pp. 107–111). New York: Worth, 2002.

Witt, S. H. (1976). Native women today: Sexism and the Indian woman. In S. Cox (Ed.), *Female psychology: The emerging self* (pp. 249–259). Chicago: Science Research Associates.

Wyche, K. (1996). Conceptualizations of social class in African-American women: Congruence of client and therapist definitions. *Women and Therapy, 16,* 35–44.

Young, C. (1989). Psychodynamics of coping and survival of the African American female in a changing world. *Journal of Black Studies, 20,* 208–223.

Chapter 3

International Aspects of the Development of the Psychology of Women and Gender

Marilyn P. Safir
Kareen Hill

Women are more visible today than ever before. While this development occurred as a result of many interacting factors, research on and the study of the psychology of women and gender has made a significant and major impact on this phenomenon. This field has had an international impact such that there is no continent that has not been influenced by this development. This chapter traces the international evolution and development of this field.

We follow the developments presented in chapter 1 with the beginning of the Women's Liberation Movement of the 1960s and '70s, which influenced, and was influenced by, the many feminist psychologists and academics. These feminists (primarily women) set about changing the face of research and teaching by establishing this new scholarship and creating women's studies programs.

We also focus on the American Psychological Association (APA) and the changes brought about by its members who were feminist activists, such as the establishment of the independent Association for Women in Psychology, which then went on to create Division 35 (now the Association for the Psychology of Women), the Committee on Women in Psychology, and more. Members of these and other feminist professional organizations established channels such as meetings, newsletters, and journals that enabled outreach (in part through the International Council of Psychologists) to international colleagues.

We then discuss the impact of Women's Worlds, the series of the international interdisciplinary congresses that were born through the efforts of the Executive Committee of Division 35 on the further internationalization of our field of interest. We also discuss the impact of the Internet, which continues to increase its worldwide impact on a daily basis. Where possible, we will follow a time line of these developments even when we must switch between topics.

As Denmark and Cambareri-Fernandez have aptly demonstrated in chapter 1, there were women pioneers who focused on women's psychology by the end of the 19th and beginning of the 20th centuries. However, their numbers were few and their impact muted, because women were actively discouraged or prevented from participating in the field. It took the early feminists of the 1950s and '60s and women's liberation movements of the late 1960s and '70s to raise consciousness about prejudice toward and stereotyping of women in psychology. By the late 1960s, feminist activism of both faculty and students in the social sciences and humanities created the fertile atmosphere that enabled focus on research and teaching about women. Individual courses evolved into women's studies programs, and courses on the psychology of women were often in the earliest courses taught (see chapter 1).

The *Association for Women in Psychology* (AWP) was the first national feminist psychological organization. It was established in 1969 as an independent organization at the APA's annual convention. By 1970, AWP members had presented APA with a list of 52 resolutions encompassing

> employment, education, child and health care facilities, psychological theories and practice, conventions, equity in decision making, and the general status of women. Ultimately, these resolutions became the driving force behind the establishment of the Task Force on the Status of Women in Psychology in 1970, an Ad Hoc Committee on the Status of Women in Psychology in 1972, and ultimately in 1973 the Committee on Women in Psychology. (Committee on Women in Psychology, 2004)

The AWP was also responsible for creating Division 35, the Division of the Psychology of Women of APA, in 1973.

The goal of AWP's founders was to establish a scientific and educational feminist organization so as to spotlight the impact of psychology and mental health on women's lives. The organization focused on encouraging and developing "new treatments, research and practice for women and gender, as well as reassessing those established in the past." As we can see, the AWP was a significant influence in causing momentous changes in APA. AWP's international influence increased further as a result of its inclusion as an official nongovernmental organization (NGO) for the United Nations in 1976.

The AWP newsletter, published triannually, was designed to provide information on AWP's activities and goals to all interested individuals and organizations. The organization has expanded outreach with the establishment of an e-mail list, POWR-L (http://www.awpsych.org/powrl.htm), which is cosponsored by Division 35. This is a nonmonitored e-mail list that permits its subscribers to share information. POWR-L also posts relevant events, publications of interest, and more.

Division 35, the *Association for the Psychology of Women*, was established in 1973 by members of AWP as new division of the APA.

> It was established as an APA division to give an organized voice to all who were interested in researching, teaching and practicing in psychology of women.... This division emphasizes the importance of improving women's and girl's lives by education and research and to empower women in the community.... The division produces a number of publications; among them are the journal *Psychology of Women's Quarterly* and the newsletter *Feminist Psychologist*. (Society for the Psychology of Women, 2006)

The APA's *Women's Programs Office* (WPO) is an organization devoted to the status and well-being of women psychologists and consumers. "WPO provides staff support for the Committee on Women in Psychology (CWP), it is also a source base for information regarding women's issues" (Women's Programs Office, 2006a). The WPO also has a women's psychology e-newsletter that publishes news of concern to women.

The *Committee on Women in Psychology* (CWP) was established in 1973 to monitor the progress of women's advancement and equality of women in psychology. The committee's mandate was to maintain "an active interaction with relevant organizations such as the division of psychology of women, Association for Women in Psychology and more. Division 35 was established due to a recommendation of CWP following the input of AWP" (Women's Programs Office, 2006b).

The *International Council of Psychologists* (ICP) should be mentioned at this point. This organization evolved from the *National Council of Women Psychologists* (NCWP), which had been established in the United States in 1941 as a means to improve the status of women in psychology. Its original goal was to provide access for women psychologists to positions from which women were excluded on the basis of sex during World War II. This council was the first women's psychological organization to agitate to improve women's status. However, the group decided to open membership internationally to all psychologists in 1958. This change in focus prevented NCWP from continuing in the forefront of our field. In fact, the organization changed its name to International Council of Psychologists in 1964 (Russo & Denmark, 1987).

In 1981, ICP was recognized as an NGO by the UN, where it serves as a consultative body. Today ICP's major purpose is to advance psychology and research on various issues of psychology around the world and to enable communication among psychologists. ICP in 1995 began publishing the journal *World Psychology*. In keeping with original goals of the NCWP to improve the status of women in psychology, a very active group of members continues to focus on topics relevant to women and gender. However, presentations at the annual conferences on the psychology of women and gender parallel those of the APA conferences and began appearing in the early 1970s.

Mention here should also be made of the *National Women's Studies Association* (NWSA), which was established in 1977, at a time when women's studies was expanding and flourishing. NWSA is located in the University of Maryland. Its major goal is to promote and advance feminist teaching, research, and practice in the community and in academia. Like most of the organizations we are presenting here, NWSA publishes a newsmagazine twice a year, *NWSAction*, and a scholarly publication, *NWSA Journal* (National Women's Studies Association, 2005a).

The establishment of professional journals and newsletters that focused on issues relevant to the psychology of women also helped to internationalize our field. In this context, Feminist Press deserves a special mention. From its beginnings, it has had an international outlook in terms of topics and authors and outreach to the international women's studies community that it also help to create. Feminist Press was founded by a women's collective in 1970 in order to reprint early but out-of-print feminist writings and remedy the situation—out of print, out of mind. It began publishing the *Women's Studies Newsletter* in 1972, which was converted into the journal *Women's Studies Quarterly* (*WSQ*) in 1981, to which we will return later in this chapter.

Feminist Press's current mission is to publish the most important women's voices from all eras and from the world over. By its 37th year, Feminist Press had published more than 350 books, a number of which have been professionally printed for the first time or reissued after having been overlooked or ignored by male publishers and historians. As a result of its efforts, the Press has expanded our knowledge of "herstory" and restored our knowledge of women's contributions that had been overlooked or not reported over the ages (Feminist Press, 2006a). Feminist Press has a very impressive website (www.feminist press.org). It has been a significant factor in the internationalization of women's studies, as a result of its journal and its list of international authors that can be found on its book list.

We turn now to a presentation of the earliest relevant journals. These hard-copy journals were published in the United States but were accessible beyond U.S. borders. While we have no research to cite as to how widely these journals were read abroad, they did help to acquaint readers with this blossoming field. In fact, many if not most, of these journals posted notices of meetings and, in particular, were responsible for much of the publicity regarding the first and subsequent Women's Worlds congresses discussed below.

The first such newsletter we encountered was published by the Association for Women in Science (AWIS), an organization "dedicated to achieving equity and full participation for women in science, mathematics, engineering, and technology. We are a Network, a Resource, and a Voice" (Association for Women in Science, 2005b). The *AWIS Newsletter* was founded in 1971 and published stories on policy issues and career development. In 1991, AWIS began publishing *AWIS Magazine*, and so the publication of the newsletter ceased. "Each *AWIS Magazine* focuses on issues relevant to women scientists. Examples of topics covered are career advancement, the two-spouse problem, academia, working in industry, acquiring tenure, overcoming prejudice, and creating a diverse work environment" (Association for Women in Science, 2005a).

The second publication we uncovered was *Feminist Studies*, which was first published in 1972. It was founded by a coalition of women from Columbia University's Women's Liberation Group, students in a women's studies course at Sarah Lawrence College, and feminist activists from New York City. They, in turn, established a wide network of feminists committed to creating a scholarly journal with high standards and community relevance. This feminist network believed that the women's movement needed an analytic forum to engage the issues raised by the movement. Another of their goals was to showcase contributions of both feminist activists and scholars. The title, *Feminist Studies*, was chosen to indicate that the content of the journal would be both scholarly and political and would focus on women as a social group and gender as a category of analysis. However, only three volumes were published between 1972 and 1977. Today, the University of Maryland at College Park is the home of this journal, through the Department of Women's Studies. The journal is self-published, self-supported, and independent of the university or any other institution (*Feminist Studies*, 2006).

Women's Studies Quarterly was also established in 1972.

> This journal was the first U.S. journal devoted to teaching about women. This journal offers a broad range of information for high school and post-secondary faculty who sought to transform school curriculum to include women's contributions and to address women's issues. This journal was an educational project of The Feminist Press of The City University of New York in cooperation with Rochester Institute of Technology. (International Studies Association, 2006)

WSQ was founded to establish an international forum for the exchange of ideas on women's issues and the most recent scholarship in women's studies. It "publishes articles on women's and gender studies, pedagogical materials, and resources for feminist research and practice through thematic issues that blur the boundaries between forms of academic inquiry" (Feminist Press, 2006b).

As our community grew more open and eager to learn about women's psychology and women's studies, more journals were established. *Sex Roles: A Journal of Research* was founded in 1974 by Phyllis Katz (a Division 35 Fellow and former president), who was also that journal's first editor. *Sex Roles*

> is an interdisciplinary, behavioral science journal with a feminist perspective. It publishes original research reports and theoretical and review articles that illuminate the underlying processes and consequences of gender role socialization, gendered perceptions and behaviors, and gender stereotypes. Topics include developmental, cognitive, social, and personality factors in gender role development, child rearing practices, and family organization; social influences (e.g., media, schools, peers, community); the acquisition, maintenance, and impact of stereotypes; effects of contemporary social change (socio-cultural as well as economic, legal, and political systems); gendered physical and mental health concerns; gender issues in employment and work environments; interpersonal relationships; sexual preference and identity; victimization; and methodological issues in gender research. (SpringerLink, n.d.)

Signs: A Journal of Women in Culture and Society was founded in 1975 and is probably one of the first journals to focus on what now called cultural studies.

> *Signs* publishes articles from a wide range of disciplines with a variety of perspectives—from articles engaging gender, race, culture, class, sexuality, and/or nation. The focus of its essays ranges from cross-disciplinary theorizing and methodologies to specific disciplinary issues, framed to enter conversations of interest across disciplines. (University of Chicago Press, Journals Division, 2006)

Another journal that is extremely relevant to our field is the *Psychology of Women Quarterly* (1976), which is published on behalf of the Association for the Psychology of Women and APA's Division 35. It is "a feminist journal that primarily publishes qualitative and quantitative research with substantive and theoretical merit, along with critical reviews, theoretical articles, and invited book reviews related to the psychology of women and gender" (Blackwell Publishing, 2006).

A further example from across the northern border is the Canadian journal *Atlantis: A Women's Studies Journal (Revue d'études sur les femmes)*, published "since 1975 by a group of women from Acadia University." This journal was transformed to

> meet the needs of a worldwide audience of scholars in the field of Women's Studies. It is a relevant resource for feminist knowledge and the theory and practice of modern feminism, prepared to become the first choice of reference for women's studies research. It is published the Institute for the Study of Women, Mount Saint Vincent University, Halifax, Nova Scotia, Canada. (Mount Saint Vincent University, 2004)

As we have seen, most of these journals viewed international outreach as a major goal. The first specifically designed international women's studies journal we found was *the Women's Studies International Forum*, originally *Women's Studies International Quarterly*, which began in 1978. It is a bimonthly journal that was established

> to aid the distribution and exchange of feminist research in the multidisciplinary, international area of women's studies and in feminist research in other disciplines. The policy of the journal is to establish a feminist forum for discussion and debate ... [and] to critique and reconceptualize existing knowledge, to examine and re-evaluate the manner in which knowledge is produced and distributed, and to assess the implications this has for women's lives. (Elsevier, 2006)

This is an interdisciplinary journal that publishes "feminist research [from] inside or outside formal educational institutions ... [and] papers geared toward action-oriented research as well as those which address theoretical methodological issues" (Elsevier, 2006).

Most of the earlier journals focusing on women's issues examined gender from a feminist perspective, focusing primarily on women. However as interest in this field expanded, gender studies began to focus on both men and women from a feminist perspective. An excellent example is the journal *Gender Issues*, formerly known as *Feminist Issues* (1980). The aim of this journal is to provide

> basic and applied research on the relationships between men and women; on similarities and differences in socialization, personality, and behavior; and on the changing aspirations, roles, and statuses of women in industrial, urban societies as well as in developing nations. (Ryerson University, 2006)

There has been an enormous international expansion of women's studies journals. The majority of them began to appear around the 1990s and later. For example, although the NWSA was established in 1977, it didn't begin to publish the *NWSA Journal* until 1988. This journal deals with interdisciplinary, multicultural feminist scholarship linking feminist theory with teaching and activism (National Women's Studies Association, 2005b).

We have seen that many, if not most, journals are published by women's studies associations. The aim and scope of these associations and their publications were to encourage the development of women's studies, within their particular countries and to exchange with and integrate the international knowledge base. Some publications are published in English to acquaint the international community with the status of the field within and beyond the borders of the host country. We will return to this topic after we examine the impact of what have become major international conferences, as some of the organizations we will continue to discuss, were created through the opportunities to meet colleagues at international meetings that we describe below.

An important factor in the internationalization of the psychology of women and gender, and women's studies in general, was the creation of the Women's Worlds congresses. As one of the authors (Marilyn P. Safir) was involved with the creation of these congresses, and since feminist psychologists were in the forefront of their establishment, we will delve into this issue in great detail. The First International Interdisciplinary Congress on Women: "Women's Worlds, the New Scholarship" was held at the University of Haifa in Israel from December 27, 1981, to January 1, 1982. Marilyn Safir was the cofounder and cochair, along with Martha Mednick (Howard University) and Dafna Izraeli (Tel Aviv University).

Mednick had been on sabbatical in Israel in 1972 to study kibbutz women when she read a newspaper article about the first women's liberation group in Israel and initiated a meeting with its members (Safir attended this meeting as she was one of the founders of this group). Mednick reported about the new feminist scholarship taking hold in the United States, planting the idea of women's studies in fertile ground.

Being in the public eye due to her feminist activism, Safir started to receive requests from Israeli colleagues in other fields about existing feminist research that was unfamiliar to them. It became obvious that interdisciplinary communication was lacking. Safir discovered that feminist scholars worked in isolation and were unaware of each other's work, because of the absence of a national network. In discussions with Mednick, it was apparent that lack of interdisciplinary communication was a problem in the United States as well.

Mednick mentored Safir and had encouraged her to join APA and Division 35, as well as ICP. They continually discussed the need for an international, interdisciplinary congress that would focus on the scholarship on women. Finally, in 1979, Safir and Mednick proposed holding such a congress under the auspices of the APA's Division 35's Executive Council. They also suggested holding this congress in Israel in order to awaken Israeli universities and faculties and to create the groundwork to establish women's studies programs. The congress seemed to be a way to bring the message of the importance and developing stature of the new scholarship, as well as to create both Israeli and international network.

Division 35 agreed to cosponsor the event, but could only offer enthusiastic support and the mailing lists of the organization. Since no budget was available, it was stressed that other organizations had to be solicited to cosponsor the congress. This was an opportune time, as the president of Division 35 was Carolyn Sherrif and members of the Executive Committee included Florence Denmark, who was the president-elect of APA, and Nancy Felipe Russo, the president of the Federation of Organizations of Professional Women (FOPW). The FOPW, composed of 110 organizations, "was an umbrella group for Committees on Women in scientific and professional associations (e.g., APA, AAAS, etc.) plus women's professional associations (Association for Women in Science, Society for Women Engineers, Association for Women in Psychology). Some had international members (e.g., APA, AAAS). (Nancy Felipe Russo, personal communication, February 14, 2007). Russo proposed that the Federation become a cosponsor. Internationally known sociologist Jessie Bernard also joined the congress board, and she and Dafna Izraeli invited Sociologists for Women in Society (SWS) to be another cosponsor. By the time of the congress, 12 organizations agreed to be cosponsors.

When congress names were discussed, it was decided that the "New Scholarship" would be the code word for feminist scholarship. Mednick suggested that congress be called "Women's Worlds" in honor of Bernard's newest book, which was about to be published. It is difficult to imagine the hardships of communication in Israel in 1979, both nationally and internationally, because of poor postal service and postal strikes. To telephone internationally, a caller had to reach an operator and place the call—often waiting two to three hours for the call to go through: No direct dialing, no faxes, and no Internet. This was the low-tech framework from which we had to work both in planning the congress and then in communicating with potential participants. When we received no response, we had to assume it might be because the person never received our correspondence. Many letters were sent two or three times.

An International Organizing Committee (with major fundraising activities in New York City and Washington, D.C.) was formed, and Mariam Chamberlain, then of the Ford Foundation, granted seed money that enabled us to "get the ball rolling." The U.S. National Science Foundation awarded $25,000 to be used for travel funds for young American scholars. As powerful women joined the International Organizing Committee, they helped the organizing process by soliciting a large group of organizational cosponsors. Division 35, SWS, and FOPW took the lead, the latter in particular providing a home and serving as a funding conduit. Many of FOPW's worldwide organizations were very active in publishing information about the congress in their respective newsletters.

Open calls for papers appeared in professional and interdisciplinary journals throughout the world. More than 2,000 inquiries were received, and over 400 abstracts were submitted to the Program Committee. When the congress finally took place, there were a total of 90 sessions, at which 258 papers were presented; 623 participants from 36 countries attended. The congress's directory of participants, along with the names and addresses of all the people who had ever corresponded with the congress organizers, formed the basis for the new international network. In fact, the letters or envelopes that were sent to the Israeli organizing committee were packed in a suitcase and hand-delivered to Christine Classon, the chair of the Second Congress in the Netherlands.

The First Congress was unique in a number of ways. Historically, it was the first worldwide interdisciplinary congress to focus on research on women and to be open to all interested researchers and grassroots activists. There was no one organization sponsoring and running the meetings. Rather, it was an informal collection of individuals and professional organizations, joined together for the sole purpose of organizing the event. It was a feminist congress, not only in its scholarship but also in its very conception and development. The Program Committee agreed at the outset to hold a nonelitist conference so as to reach the widest range of potential participants. We looked at the congress as a socializing experience for aspiring researchers; consequently, no abstract was rejected outright. Whenever the criteria for acceptance were not met, reviewers asked for improvement or clarification, with an option to resubmit. The committee was rewarded for its efforts. In the majority of cases, the abstracts were resubmitted and integrated into the program. This extra effort had the effect of allowing many students and young scholars to participate. An attempt was also made to keep every session interdisciplinary and international.

Several specific international networks (i.e., Women in Management) were established at the First Congress as offshoots of the international network that was created. The University of Haifa made rooms available for ad hoc meetings that enabled groups of participants to meet, thus facilitating the formation of these networks and groups of researchers. Another first was inviting grassroots groups to present their projects in "poster sessions" to enable them and academics to network. While causing some difficulties to the organizers, registration fees were charged on a sliding scale to enable participants from the developing world, students, and volunteers to attend. To enable participation of community women and people of limited funds, Haifa residents provided free lodging in their homes to many participants who could not afford to pay hotel fees. Tours were offered to all the grassroots projects in and around Haifa for interested participants. Many Haifa residents invited participants to their homes for a social evening, as well.

The First Congress had an international impact. There were glowing news articles on the front page of the *New York Times,* in *Time* magazine, and in newspapers in most of the participants' home countries. The Israeli organizers were sent articles from Japan, Greece, France, Spain, Latin America, Africa, and elsewhere. This increased the impact in Israel. The Israeli media were flooded with reports, interviews, and photos.

The congress also had specific impact on the development of feminist scholarship in Israel. In 1982, Hebrew University began a program on "Sex Differences in Society." The next year, the University of Haifa inaugurated the first Women's Studies program, and in 1984, Project Kidma for the Advancement of Women, an outreach program for community women, was founded. Also in 1984, the Israel Sociological Association established a section on Sex and Gender. An Israeli contingent has continued to attend all the subsequent congresses.

On the congress's final day, Matti Kubrick Gershenfeld, another Division 35 Executive Committee member, called a general meeting to evaluate the congress and discuss the future. More than a hundred people attended. All enthusiastically agreed that this should be the first in a series of congresses. Some suggested that an international organization be formed to take responsibility for and sponsorship of continuation of the congress. However, the general feeling was that to maintain the momentum created in this first event, another university should take responsibility for organizing the next one. Donna Shalala, at that time president of Hunter College, immediately offered her college's facilities. However, there was general agreement that it was too soon to take the congress to the United States if the goal was to continue to encourage and develop an international flavor. It was agreed to hold the congress only in countries that would give visas to all participants worldwide. A call for bids went out, and of the four bids received, the University of Groningen, in the Netherlands, was chosen by a committee composed of the congress chair, cochairs, and members of the First Congress's International Congress board from several countries. The time to create an international organization would come much latter and develop in two stages—first, a European organization created in 1987 at the Third Congress, and then a truly worldwide organization at the Seventh Congress in 1997.

The Second Congress, held in 1983, was cochaired by Christine Classon and the University of Groningen's Helen Hootsman. This congress's theme was "Strategies and Empowerment." Close to 800 participants attended.

As there had been strong Irish involvement in organizing the First Congress, there was interest in holding a congress in Dublin. Trinity College made the bid that was accepted for the Third Congress in 1987. This congress was organized by a collective: Mary Cullen, Audrey Dickson, Margaret Fine-Davis, Sylvia Meehan, and Geraldine Maone. Its theme was "Visions and Revisions." The number of attendees jumped. The organizers were able to attract approximately 2,000 grassroots participants and about 1,400 academics.

Hunter College in New York City became the Fourth Congress's venue in 1990, with its theme "Realities and Choice." It was chaired by Florence Denmark and Susan Lees. This was another huge congress with similar number of participants to the Dublin congress. However, New York City swallowed the congress, and there was much less local impact.

From there, the Fifth Congress in 1993 went to the University of Costa Rica in San José, where it was chaired by Mirta Gonzalez-Saurez. Its theme was "Search, Participation, Change." There were more than a thousand participants, with a large contingent from South and Central America. The congress and the international participants again had a strong impact on the host city.

The University of Adelaide, Australia, hosted the Sixth Congress in 1996, "Think Global, Act Local," which was chaired by Susan Magarey and was again attended by more than a thousand. This was the first congress that relied heavily on electronic correspondence.

The Seventh Congress, whose theme was "Genderations," was chaired by Gerd Bjorhovde at University of Tromsø, Norway, in 1999. The presence of its 1,100 participants could be felt all over the city. This congress was the first that created a well-developed website.

The Eighth Congress was held at Makerere University in Kampala, Uganda, in 2002 to discuss "Gendered Worlds: Gains and Challenges" and was chaired by Grace Bantebya Kyomuhendo. The organizers also set up an excellent website. Registration far outnumbered expectations, even after taking into account the earlier success and new option of online registration, with more than 3,000 participants coming from 94 countries. Excitement was generated throughout Africa, and participants came from 54 countries on that continent.

Holding the next meeting in Asia became a priority, in part because few participants from Asia had managed to attend earlier conferences—even the meeting in Australia, where a large Asian presence had been anticipated. The Ninth Congress was held in Seoul, South Korea, with the theme "Globalization from Women's Perspectives." It was hosted by the Korean Association of Women's Studies and Ewha Womans University in cooperation with Sogang, Yonsei, and Sookyung universities and the Korean Women's Development Institute. The congress chair was

Pilwha Chang and the coordinator was Eun Shil Kim. This congress's very attractive website (www.ww05.org/english2/index.htm) is still online with a slide show of pictures taken during the congress and reports in congress newspapers that may be downloaded and read. This event hosted more than 500 sessions and over 3,000 participants from all sections of Asia and the world (Safir, 2005).

Ewha Womans University, the congress site, has been at the forefront of Asian women's studies. The *Asian Journal of Women's Studies* (*AJWS*) has been published since 1995 by Ewha Womans University and the Korea Research Foundation.

> It is an interdisciplinary feminist journal that offers articles with theoretical focus, country reports providing valuable information on specific subjects and countries, research notes, and book reviews containing information on recent publications on women in Asia and elsewhere. *AJWS* aims to share and disseminate information and scholarly ideas about women's issues in Asia and all over the world, with a vision to develop women's studies in Asia and expand the horizon of western centered women's studies. (Ewha Women's Studies, 2006)

This extensive background certainly paved the way for the most exciting congress to date.

The University of Madrid has been chosen as the site for the Tenth Congress in 2008.

It is important to mention that the first truly worldwide congress on women was held under the auspices of the United Nations during the UN's International Women's Year in 1975 in Mexico City. The UN's Division for the Advancement of Women (DAW) was responsible for the preparation of four conferences. DAW was actually established as early as 1946 as a section in the UN's Human Rights Division on the Status of Women. The International Women's Year and the conference were created to focus on the continuing discrimination against women and to mandate proposal to correct the situation. The second of these conferences was held in Copenhagen in 1980, the third in Nairobi in 1985. DAW served as the secretariat for the 1995 conference in Beijing, the largest conference held under the UN auspices (Division for the Advancement of Women, 2006).

These were official UN conferences, and each participating country sent an official delegation. There were 133 member-state delegations at the first conference in 1975. More interesting for our purposes was the formation of parallel conferences organized by women who represented women's and feminist NGOs. The Nairobi Conference in 1985 is significant in this respect, as it provided a venue for feminist academics, some of whom had met at previous Women's Worlds congresses, to plan an international women's studies association that could become a sponsor of future Women's Worlds congresses.

As mentioned above, the time and facilities at the first Women's Worlds congress were not right to form an international organization to plan future congresses. First, it was not obvious that there would be a second congress. The hundred participants who stayed on to discuss another congress were enthusiastic in their desire not just to hold a second congress but also to establish a series of future conferences. Because there was no central international organization, it was decided that working to establish such an organization might actually interfere with organizing additional congresses.

However, by 1985 the time was right for the concept, and access to the Internet and World Wide Web facilitated the development of a worldwide association of women's studies organizations. This concept was presented at the NGO Forum of the United Nations Decade of Women in 1985 in Kenya. Both Tobe Levin and Erna Kas raised the idea at different NGO meetings in Nairobi. At a breakfast meeting, Levin met with Jalna Hanmer, Maitreyi Krishna-Raj, Gloria Bonder, and Peggy McIntosh and discussed the importance of such an international organization. However, a decision was made that the first step would be the formation of a European women's studies association, which would latter become *Women's International Studies Europe* (WISE). A follow-up meeting in 1987 at the Third Congress in Dublin gave further impetus to the establishment of WISE, as did grants in 1988 and 1989 from the European Union. Because of this funding, membership was originally limited to women's studies associations from EU member states. In 1990 WISE launched its publication, the *European Journal of Women's Studies,* "to explore the meaning and impact of gender within the changing concept of Europe, and to present women's studies research and theory" (Sage Publications, 2006a).

Judith Ezekiel, the list owner of WISE's nonmonitored e-mail list, pushed for the inclusion of non-EU membership. She began lobbying for the creation of a worldwide women's studies organization at the Vienna preparatory conference for the Beijing Conference. She also suggested the name *Worldwide Organization of Women's Studies* (WOWS). At the NGO meetings in Beijing in 1995, WISE, joined by the U.S.-based National Women's Studies Association, proposed the establishment of this global organization. Ezekiel and Erna Kas of WISE and Claire Moses of NWSA organized a series of workshops, and 165 women from 43 countries joined hands to endorse the creation of a worldwide organization of feminist/women's studies associations.

As the Beijing sessions were such a smashing success, it was decided to have an official founding meeting at the Sixth International Interdisciplinary Congress on Women in Adelaide, and WOWS was officially launched at this Congress. (The above discussion on WISE and WOWS are based on personal communications from Judith Ezekiel and Erna Kas [both July 15, 2002] and on Levin, 1992).

An additional international women's studies organization was established at the Seventh Congress in Tromsø in 1997: *The Feminist Knowledge Network.* This organization was created by editors of women's studies journals in order to form a network for discussions about difficulties in feminist research issues. They wanted to create an easy source of communication, promoting women's journals especially in parts of the world where communication is difficult by e-mail and Internet. The organization started an e-mail list and now has 27 journal members from 21 countries, among them are: *Asian Journal of Women's Studies, Pakistan Journal of Women's Studies, Atlantis: A women's studies journal* and more. (Memorial University, 2006)

The Tromsø congress hosted the first General Assembly meeting of WOWS. Now the time had come: rather than the organizers of the Women's Worlds congresses and the individual universities that served as hosts deciding on the venue for the next congress, WOWS formed a site-selection committee. After the congress, WOWS sent out a call for proposals to organize the next conference, and Makerere University was chosen for the 2002 congress site.

From the mid-1980s, the Internet has become more and more important in the dissemination of information of these and other congresses, conferences, and meetings, both within local areas and internationally. It can easily be seen how important the Internet has been in the preparation of this chapter. When we began our research, on August 8, 2006, we entered the term "psychology of women" into the Google search engine; within 0.31 seconds, Google had found 106 million entries. These include journals, books, articles, listings, syllabi, information about courses, programs, lecturers, and more. It should be obvious that we had to be very selective in choosing the items presented here.

One very important electronic forum website, WMST-L (www.umbc.edu/wmst/forums.html) was established by Joan Korenman at the University of Maryland in 1991.

> It is a large international forum conducted by e-mail. The forum conducts interactions about issues like women's studies, research and programs. Now the WMST-L offers accessibility to various file on topics of concern to women, such as academia, feminism, books, sexuality, and many more. It also provides many important links like applying for an academic job, body image and young girls, feminism and social change. (Korenman, 2006a)

Korenman has informed me that there are now approximately 4,900 subscribers (personal communication, December 5, 2006), including 1,000 with non-U.S. addresses. (She retrieved this information from the Listserv, which does not necessarily indicate the subscriber's nationality, just where they've subscribed from. This is also true for those with U.S. addresses: not all are Americans, but they subscribe from a U.S.

address.) Korenman called to our attention one very important WMST-L resource—the WMST-L File Collection (www.umbc.edu/wmst/wmsttoc.html). "It currently contains about 270 files," she said. "Most are discussions that took place on WMST-L, though it also includes some essays, bibliographies, etc., contributed by WMST-L subscribers. It's really a goldmine of information for professors, researchers, and students. The files are organized into 18 categories."

We employed the WMST-L in order to determine how many women's studies programs countries exist outside the United States. We found that Australia has 22 women's studies programs, Austria 6, Barbados 1, Belarus 1, Belgium 3, Brazil 1, Canada 47, Chile 4, China 2, Colombia 1, Costa Rica 3, Croatia 1, Cyprus 1, Czech Republic 3, Denmark 4, Egypt 2, Estonia 2, Finland 6, France 3, Germany 11, Greece 2, Hong Kong 4, Hungary 3, India 6, Ireland 9, Israel 7, Italy 3, Japan 2, Korea 18, Lebanon 1, Lithuania 1, Malaysia 1, Mexico 2, Mongolia 1, the Netherlands 6, New Zealand 12, Norway 6, Palestine 1, Peru 1, Poland 1, Romania 2, Russia 1, Slovakia 1, South Africa 5, Spain 4, Sri Lanka 1, Sudan 1, Sweden 10, Switzerland 5, Thailand 3, Turkey 2, Uganda 1, Ukraine 1, the United Kingdom 59, and Venezuela 1 (Korenman, 2006b).

Korenman also suggested some additional links within WMST-L, including "Women's Studies/Women's Issues Resource Sites" and "Gender-Related Electronic Forums." Links to these and a few others can be found at www.umbc.edu/wmst/. Korenman (1999) reported that there were more than 500 lists focusing on women's issues.

Returning to some of the newer and important international organizations, we will start with *Feminist Majority Foundation* (FMF), which was founded in 1987. While it was established as a North American organization, its website contains much international information and is designed for international access. The main objectives are to improve knowledge of women's health, prevent violence toward women and within the family, and promote equality. FMF proposes that, by research and action, it can empower women in all aspects of life, so the foundation conducts seminars, forums, and educational programs in order to achieve that goal (Feminist Majority Foundation, 2006). The Feminist Majority newsletter assesses issues of current concern to women. One of the links in the FMF website (www.feminist.org) allows the visitor to explore women's studies programs around the world, although we found the link in the WMST-L site above to be more inclusive and up-to-date.

A major international association is the *National Alliance of Women's Organizations* (NAWO), which was established in 1989 in the United Kingdom. This is a conglomerate of organizations composed of more than a hundred groups. NAWO aims to ensure that women's voices are heard both nationally and internationally, that gender issues are on government agendas, and that discrimination against women is eliminated (National Alliance of Women's Organizations, 2006a). NAWO has two publications: a newsletter that focuses on issues of concern such as women's rights, gender issues, and more; and a monthly e-bulletin (National Alliance of Women's Organizations, 2006b).

A smaller union is the *Feminist & Women's Studies Association (UK & Ireland)* (FWSA). This is another organization that is devoted to promoting "feminist research and teaching, and women's studies nationally and internationally." It has links with NAWO and Athena (see below) (Feminist & Women's Studies Association, 2006).

Feminism & Psychology: An International Journal was conceived by psychologists Sue Wilkinson and Celia Kitzinger of the United Kingdom. As their goal was to establish an international journal, they set up a very international editorial board. The first issue was released in 1991 with the goal of "encouraging development of feminist theory and practice in psychology. The journal presents women's concerns across a broad range of contexts spanning the academic/applied 'divide'" (Sage Publications, 2006b). An additional goal has been to present cutting-edge feminist research and debate in, and beyond, psychology. The editors are interested in creating debates and dialogues vis-à-vis the interface of feminism and psychology. They are also interested in broaching the academic-practitioner divide to represent a wide range of feminist voices, including those underrepresented in psychology journals (Sage Publications, 2006b).

The Nordic Council of Ministers created the *Nordic Institute for Women's Studies and Gender Research* (NIKK) in 1995. NIKK "is a transnational resource- and information centre on gender research and gender equality policies in the Nordic countries. NIKK is currently located at the University of Oslo in Norway" (Nordic Institute for Women's Studies and Gender Research, 2006) It has many electronic and hard-copy publications, including *Nora: Nordic Journal of Women's Studies.* This journal was established in 2003.

> Nora is an interdisciplinary journal of gender and women's studies, as well as a channel for high-quality research from all disciplines. Emphasis is placed on giving a Nordic profile to feminist research, with regard to both contents and theoretical and methodological approaches. Nora aims to discuss and examine the realities and myths of women's and men's lives in the Nordic countries, historically and today. (Taylor & Francis, 2006)

NIKK also began publishing a journal on men's studies in 2006.

Athena is another international organization, composed of 80 universities, research institutions, and documentation centers throughout Europe. It was established in 1996 by the Association of Institutions for

Feminist Education and Research in Europe (AOIFE). Athena is based in the University of Utrecht, the Netherlands. It was established:

1. To implement the recommendations of the European Subject Area Evaluation in Women's Studies (1994/95) and build on activities, aims, and objectives developed at European level and to spread and implement the findings by producing reports, articles, teaching books, and manuals.
2. To further develop and increase the exchange of ideas, expertise, and insights across national borders in order to promote effective discussion and comparison of curricula, methods, and material in Women's Studies teaching.
3. To contribute an added value to the partner institutions, since a large number will be able to use and profit from the expertise of former small scale European co-operation projects. The participating institutions will profit from pooling their expertise in their respective areas and thus allow for transferal of knowledge and good practice. The broader field of Women's Studies, and beyond, will profit through the channels of dissemination of activities, through co-operation with the participating documentation centers and international networks such as WITEC, as well as through the interdisciplinary focus.
4. To develop competence in feminist education and research in order to contribute to the knowledge and good practices needed for the mainstreaming of European policies on science, technology, and higher education, with regard to equal opportunities.
5. To contribute to equal opportunities policies and practices—in keeping with the European Commission's commitment to equal work—equal pay—as well as to social and economic development. (Universiteit Utrecht, 2003)

Athena carries out its agenda by a wide distribution of its publications and translation of important additional publications, organizing seminars and advertising results in their website.

We have traced the international evolution and development of the psychology of women and gender and women's studies. We began by examining the effects of activism within psychology departments and within profession organizations, in particular APA, as well as on university campuses in North America, to the rapid growth of research and teaching in women's studies programs. The interest and excitement generated led to the rapid expansion of our field. Outreach via printed journals and books, international news reports, and meetings enabled the spread of interest across continents. As travel became more manageable between countries, visits among feminist academics initiated the beginnings of an international network. The international congresses furthered this development by creating an exciting venue for women's studies scholars to meet in varying parts of the world, creating a truly international network of scholars. The creation of congress's websites was a significant addition to the accessibility to information and international registration.

Expanding accessibility of the Internet, which provides both easy and speedy international communication, should result in even more rapid expansion in the near future. The world is truly becoming a global village, where feminist scholars can communicate and further their interests with ease. This should allow greater collaboration among researchers internationally and increased understanding of the intersections of sex and gender with culture and social class. While many international venues are included within this global community, we must keep in mind those who are still excluded, their voices remaining silent in the productive clamor of our age.

REFERENCES

Association for Women in Science. (2005a). AWIS Magazine. Retrieved September 25, 2006, from http://www.awis.org/pubs/mag.html.

Association for Women in Science. (2005b). AWIS missions & goals. Retrieved September 25, 2006, from http://www.awis.org/about/missions.html.

Blackwell Publishing. (2006). *Psychology of Women Quarterly*. Retrieved November 5, 2006, from http://www.blackwellpublishing.com/journal.asp?ref=0361-6843&site=1.

Committee on Women in Psychology. (2004). Fifty-two resolutions and motions regarding the status of women in psychology: Chronicling 30 years of passion and progress. Retrieved September 9, 2006, from http://www.apa.org/pi/wpo/52resolutions_motions.pdf.

Division for the Advancement of Women. (2006). About the division. Retrieved December 15, 2006, from http://www.un.org/womenwatch/daw/daw/.

Elsevier. (2006). *Women's Studies International Forum*. Retrieved October 1, 2006, from http://www.elsevier.com/wps/find/journaldescription.cws_home/361/description/.

Ewha Women's Studies. (2006). *Asian Journal of Women's Studies*. Retrieved December 8, 2006, from http://ewhawoman.or.kr/acwseng/frameset4.htm.

Feminist & Women's Studies Association. (2006). The FWSA. Retrieved December 6, 2006, from http://www.fwsa.org.uk/fwsa.htm.

Feminist Majority Foundation. (2006). About the Feminist Majority Foundation. Retrieved December 9, 2006, from http://www.feminist.org/welcome/.

Feminist Press. (2006). About the Feminist Press. Retrieved September 25, 2006, from http://www.feministpress.org/about/.

Feminist Press. (2006b). *Women's Studies Quarterly*. Retrieved September 9, 2006, from http://www.feministpress.org/wsq/.

Feminist Studies. (2006). About us. Retrieved December 4, 2006, from http://www.feministstudies.org/aboutfs/history.html.

International Studies Association. (2006). *Women's Studies Quarterly*. Retrieved September 9, 2006, from http://www.isanet.org/news/wsq.html.

Korenman, J. (1999). Email forums and women's studies: The example of WMST-L. In S. Hawthorne & R. Klein (Eds.), *Cyberfeminism: Connectivity, critique, creativity* (pp. 80–97). North Melbourne, Australia: Spinifex Press, 1999.

Korenman, J. (2006a). WMST-L File Collection. Retrieved December 10, 2006, from http://research.umbc.edu/~korenman/wmst/wmsttoc.html.

Korenman, J. (2006b). Women's studies programs, departments, and research centers. Retrieved December 10, 2006, from http://research.umbc.edu/~korenman/wmst/programs.html.

Levin, T. (1992). *Women's Studies Quarterly, 3–4,* 153–162.

Memorial University. (2006). The Feminist Knowledge Network. Retrieved December 6, 2006, from http://www.mun.ca/fkn/intro.htm.

Mount Saint Vincent University. (2004). *Atlantis: A Women's Studies Journal.* Retrieved November 5, 2006, from http://www.msvu.ca/atlantis/frame/home.htm.

National Alliance of Women's Organizations. (2006a). About us. Retrieved December 10, 2006, from http://www.nawo.org.uk/index.asp?page=4.

National Alliance of Women's Organizations. (2006b). Newletters. Retrieved December 10, 2006, from http://www.nawo.org.uk/newsletter.

National Women's Studies Association. (2005a). About the National Women's Studies Association. Retrieved November 6, 2006, from http://www.nwsa.org/about.php.

National Women's Studies Association. (2005b). NWSA journal. Retrieved December 4, 2006, from http://www.nwsa.org/journal.php.

Nordic Institute for Women's Studies and Gender Research. (2006). This is NIKK. Retrieved December 6, 2006, http://www.nikk.uio.no/om/index_e.html.

Russo, N. F., & Denmark, F. L. (1987). Contributions of women to psychology. *Annual Review of Psychology*, 38, 279–298.

Ryerson University. (2006). *Gender Issues.* Retrieved December 4, 2006, from http://www.ryerson.ca/library/subjects/sexdiv/periodicals.html.

Safir, M. P. (2005). How it all began: The founding of Women's Worlds congress and international network. *Proceedings of Ninth International Congress on Women, Seoul, Korea June 19th–24th.*

Sage Publications. (2006a). *European Journal of Women's Studies.* Retrieved September 12, 2006, from http://www.sagepub.com/journalsProdAims.nav?prodId=Journal200932.

Sage Publications. (2006b). *Feminism & Psychology: An International Journal.* Retrieved October 20, 2006, from http://www.sagepub.com/journalsProdDesc.nav?prodId=Journal200868.

Society for the Psychology of Women. (2006). Division 35 of the American Psychological Association. Retrieved December 5, 2006, from http://www.apa.org/divisions/div35/.

SpringerLink. (n.d.). *Sex Roles.* Retrieved November 4, 2006, from http://www.springerlink.com/content/wk5774683436105q/.

Taylor & Francis. (2006). *Nora: Nordic Journal of Women's Studies.* Retrieved December 6, 2006, from http://www.tandf.co.uk/journals/titles/08038740.asp.

Universiteit Utrecht. (2003). What is Athena. Retrieved December 12, 2006, from http://www.let.uu.nl/womens_studies/athena/what.html.

University of Chicago Press, Journals Division. (2006). *Signs:* About the journal. Retrieved November 4, 2006, from http://www.journals.uchicago.edu/Signs/.

Women's Programs Office (2006a). About us. Retrieved December 9, 2006, from http://www.apa.org/pi/wpo/aboutus.html.

Women's Programs Office (2006b). Committee on Women in Psychology (CWP). Retrieved October 13, 2006, from http://www.apa.org/pi/wpo/cwp/cwphomepage.html.

PART II

Research and Teaching in the Psychology of Women

Chapter 4

Feminist Perspectives on Research Methods

Jeri Sechzer
Vita Carulli Rabinowitz

Editors' note: In 1993, when the first edition of the *Handbook of the Psychology of Women* was published, Vita Rabinowitz and Jeri Sechzer presented a feminist perspective on the research process and provided a framework with which to develop gender-fair research projects. Despite advances in conducting research in a gender-equitable fashion, emphasis on continually reevaluating the research methods and conclusions to ensure the minimization of bias is necessary. Because these core issues are still salient, we have decided to reproduce this chapter in its entirety, with an update at the end. *Florence L. Denmark and Michele A. Paludi*

The major goal of this chapter is to offer a feminist perspective on the research process from its inception to its completion—from problem selection to the analysis and interpretation of results. We begin our analysis with a brief review of past feminist critiques of scientific psychology, focusing in particular on three interdependent areas of special concern to feminists: the role of values in science, issues embedded in the language and conduct of science, and a general comparison of qualitative and quantitative modes of research.

Next, we use the stages of the research process to organize feminist scholarship and perspectives on such methodological issues as question formulation, integrative reviews of previous research, descriptions of researchers, sample selection, research designs, operationalizations of independent and dependent variables, and data analysis and interpretation. We conclude by considering the implications of our analyses for the teaching of research methods in psychology.

Our general view of research methods, expressed in various forms throughout the chapter, is that no research method is inherently feminist or sexist and that no scientific research method is inherently superior or inferior to another. There are, of course, highly biased research questions and applications of methods, inappropriate matches between research questions and the designs, materials, research participants, and operations used to probe them, and biased or otherwise mistaken analyses, interpretations, and uses of research data. We hope to make the point that the careful consideration of the research question—not preconceived notions of what constitutes accepted practice in one's area—should be the ultimate arbiter of which research strategies are used.

FEMINIST ASSESSMENTS OF MAINSTREAM PSYCHOLOGY

The past two decades have witnessed several fundamental challenges to traditional psychological research. Scientific psychology has been criticized repeatedly for theories and research practices that are fraught with biases of many types (Bronfenbrenner, 1977; Ellsworth, 1977) and are now considered essentially faddish, dated, trivial, or meaningless (cf. Gergen, 1973; Koch, 1981). Disenchantment with certain subfields of psychology, particularly the social, personality, and developmental areas, has reached "crisis" proportions, according to some observers (Gergen, 1973).

Some of the most pervasive and persistent attacks on mainstream psychology have been written by feminist psychologists, who have long documented the existence of blatantly sexist (and racist, ethnocentric, ageist, and classist) assumptions, theories, research methods, and interpretations (Shields, 1975a, 1975b; Grady, 1981; Jacklin, 1983; McHugh, Koeske, & Frieze, 1986; Sherif, 1987). Indeed, feminists have been criticizing academic psychology in so many outlets on so many grounds for so long, that recent reviews have commenced by considering why these earlier messages have gone unheeded (Sherif, 1987; Unger, 1981; Wallston & Grady, 1985). As a group, feminist critics argue that the quality and integrity of psychology's contribution to science and society are at stake.

Feminist critiques of psychological research can be roughly divided into two overlapping categories. In the first category are those that essentially argue that the pervasive male bias in psychology has created bodies of knowledge that are scientifically flawed—that are inaccurate for, or irrelevant to, half the human race. Within this category, the reviews vary widely in the depth and extent of their criticisms. On one end of the continuum are relatively early reviews that call on psychology to "add women" to existing, male-dominated research. Examples of such reviews are those that note the preponderance of men as subjects in single-sex designs (Carlson & Carlson,

1960), the effects of sex of the experimenter on the respondents' performance (Harris, 1971), and the fallacy of generalizing from male samples to people generally (Denmark, Russo, Frieze & Sechzer, 1988; Gannon et al., 1992). At the other end of this spectrum are those that locate the operation of white, middle-class male bias at virtually every decision point in the research process, from the identification of what topics are worthy of study, through the choice of a research design, the selection of research participants, the operationalization of independent variables, the choice of dependent measures, the types of analyses performed, to the interpretation and generalization of results (Grady, 1981; Wallston, 1983; Lott, 1985; Wallston & Grady, 1985; Denmark et al., 1988). The more sweeping of these criticisms call for more sensitivity to the ways in which a sexist society generally and a sexist profession specifically distort the research process and the products of research. They take academic psychology to task for failing on its own terms—for not following the scientific method—and for using data-gathering techniques, research materials, and designs in ways that have compromised the interpretability of data.

The second, more radical, type of critique challenges the use or overuse of the scientific method in psychology (Keller, 1974; Sherif, 1987; Unger, 1983; Fine & Gordon, 1989). One of the central themes in this view is that science has historically been inhospitable to women and may be inherently so. One of the most prominent proponents of this viewpoint, physicist Keller (1974) wrote:

> To the extent that analytic thought is conceived as "male" thought, to the extent that we characterize the natural sciences as the "hard sciences," to the extent that the procedure of science is to "attack" problems, and its goal, since Bacon, has been to "conquer" or "master" nature, a woman in science must in some way feel alien. (p. 18)

This view sees as intrinsically masculine and distorted the emphasis in science of studying events out of context, separating and compartmentalizing processes into their most basic elements. It argues for a more "feminine" approach of studying events as they occur naturally in their historical, cultural, and organizational contexts. Within psychology, Sherif (1987) and Unger (1983) have forcefully articulated this view. Sherif (1987) noted that psychology from its earliest days aped the forms and procedures of the natural sciences to gain prestige and respectability, even though the subject matter of psychology did not lend itself to these modes of inquiry. She wrote:

> Psychologists, in their strivings to gain status with other scientists did not pause long on issues raised by the differences between studying a rock, a chemical compound, or an animal, on [the] one hand, and a human individual, on the other. (Sherif 1987, p. 43)

The most severe judgments are often reserved for the laboratory experiment and its characteristic features of manipulation of variables, high experimenter control, contrived contexts, deception of respondents, and so on. On the topic of experimental methods, Unger (1983) said: "The logic of these methods (and even their language) prescribes prediction and control. It is difficult for one who is trained in such a conceptual framework to step beyond it and ask what kind of person such a methodology presupposes" (p. 11).

Rarely do feminists who challenge the dominance of the scientific method in psychology actually call for its wholesale abandonment; but most do argue for a vastly increased use of already existing nonexperimental, naturalistic research methods in psychology and the development of new unobtrusive methods to be used along with "sex-fair" experimental techniques (McHugh et al., 1986; Wallston & Grady, 1985; Wittig, 1985). All research methods have distinct advantages and disadvantages, and for this reason, multiple methods should be employed within any program of research—an approach known as "triangulation" (Wallston & Grady, 1985). The chief differences among feminists who pose a radical challenge to psychology lie in the extent to which they endorse the use of nonscientific modes of data gathering, like unstructured interviews or observations, and their willingness to regard nonexperimental or nonscientific ways of gathering information as distinctly "feminist" (Fine & Gordon, 1989).

Despite some important differences among them, feminist psychologists generally are bound by a deep concern with current research practices in psychology. A consensus is building on a number of key issues:

- Science is not, and cannot be, value-free. Values affect all phases of a research project from the choice of what to study to the conclusions drawn from the results. The effects of researchers' values on the works produced are by no means necessarily negative. Indeed, values motivate and enrich all of science. Because scientists' values cannot be obliterated any more than their gender, race, class, and social or educational background, they serve science best when they are acknowledged, examined, and counterbalanced when possible. This position is not an open invitation to indulge biases, wallow in subjectivity, or advocate political causes in the name of science. It simply acknowledges the nature and limits of science and psychological knowledge.
- Although "sex differences" have been studied in psychology since its inception, it is not clear precisely what it is that has been studied. Terms like *sex, male, female, masculine,* and *feminine* have been used too loosely and inclusively to describe everything from the biological sex of participants to social or situational factors considered appropriate to males and females. The term *gender* has been proposed to refer to the complex of biological, social, psychological, and cultural factors braided with the labels "male" and "female" (Unger, 1979). In this formulation, the term *sex* is

now largely reserved for biological aspects of males and females. This chapter observes Unger's distinctions.

- Many long-established "sex differences," upon reexamination, do not appear to be main effects that will endure over time (Deaux, 1984; Unger, 1979). Even those few gender differences that have withstood scrutiny tend to be very small and of little social significance (Maccoby & Jacklin, 1974).
- The conventional focus on "sex differences" in sex-role research obscures the many ways in which males and females are similar. A number of biases exist in selecting what findings are reported, published, and cited. Historically, in virtually all cases, this bias has worked in the direction of reporting, publishing, citing, and dramatizing gender differences and overlooking similarities.
- There is a tendency for sex-related differences on many dimensions to be interpreted as originating in innate biological differences, even in the absence of any evidence for biological causation. When gender differences are being explained, all plausible rival explanatory factors must be explored: the biological (e.g., genetic, hormonal, and physiological) and the sociocultural (e.g., familial, peer, economic, and situational), even if all these factors were not explicitly investigated in the study (McHugh et al., 1986).

We believe that psychology, to progress as a science, will continue to rely primarily on quantitative techniques and experimental methods, even as it expands the range of "respectable" techniques and methods to include qualitative and nonexperimental ones. As we hope to demonstrate, quantitative and experimental methods have already made substantial contributions to the psychology of gender and still have much to offer. Like many other feminist psychologists, we believe that the study of gender and psychology generally will benefit by becoming more, and not less, "scientific." But experiments are just one of many scientific methods worth using. As we pose more varied kinds of research questions, we must have available a much wider range of scientific methods.

Before offering a step-by-step guide to the conduct of sex-fair research, we would like to consider three overlapping issues that have concerned feminist critics of mainstream psychology: (1) the role of values in science, (2) a comparison of qualitative and quantitative modes of research, and (3) ethical issues imbedded in the language and conduct of science and research.

The Role of Values in Science

Objectivity is considered a hallmark of science, but it is perhaps most accurately viewed as a retrospective virtue. Science is presented in classrooms and textbooks as the accumulation of dispassionate fact, and teachers and students alike may come to see it that way. But practicing scientists know that it originates with people inspired by ordinary human passions, like ambition, pride, and greed, and constrained by ordinary human limitations imposed by ignorance and prejudice.

At the same time, many scientists possess some extraordinary traits as well. They passionately want to learn the truth about the object of their study. Most are highly committed to the theories they test, the research methods they use, and the conclusions they draw. Without this emotional commitment, it would be difficult to sustain the considerable effort required to receive professional training and launch professional careers in science. Largely because of pervasive beliefs about the objectivity of science and the literary conventions of scientific reporting in fields like psychology, researchers feel compelled to appear completely detached and present their efforts as only the rational exercise of intellect. The fact is, scientists vary considerably in their styles of conceptualizing problems and applying research techniques. There are many different approaches to the pursuit of knowledge using scientific methods. The standardized way of reporting research sanctioned by the American Psychological Association, known as "APA style," which seems to spring from some universally shared approach to problem solving, may obscure some important differences in practice and impose a false unanimity on research reports.

Given what is now known about "experimenter effects" in research and increasing publicity about the incidence of scientific fraud, there are probably very few psychologists today who would argue that perfect objectivity in science is possible. Most would concede that, explicitly or implicitly, every published report unavoidably expresses, to some degree, a point of view or value judgment.

But even those psychologists who reject simplistic notions of value-free science nonetheless seem to embrace more refined versions of the doctrine of objectivity (Schlenker, 1974). If it is impossible to avoid a point of view entirely, most scientific psychologists often do their best to ignore, hide, or downplay its role in research. Researchers who have been forthright about their values, as many feminist psychologists have been, are often dismissed as "advocacy" psychologists (Unger, 1982). There appears to be a widespread, if unspoken, fear among academic psychologists that for a scientist to express values openly or call attention to personal characteristics or values of the scientist in a research report is to compromise the integrity of the research. As Wittig (1985) noted: "One criticism of advocacy in psychology is that when researchers function simultaneously as advocates, their ability to discern facts is compromised and their 'evidence' serves primarily to justify already held beliefs" (p. 804).

It should be recognized that all scientists are, to greater or lesser extents, advocates as well as scholars. The tension between scholarship and advocacy is inevitable and requires constant vigilance on the part of the scientist and surveillance by the scientific community. In this way, the "forced choice" between advocacy and scholarship can be avoided. D. T. Campbell's (1969) views about the role for advocacy in applied research may well serve as a guide to the basic researcher, particularly those who work in socially relevant or politically sensitive areas like gender. Campbell saw a role for advocacy in social science research so long as the commitment of the researcher was to explore an issue or help to solve a problem, rather than to advance a particular view of the problem or impose a particular solution. The overarching commitment of all scientists must be to the truth. The distortion of the truth for political or social reasons undermines scientists' trust in the literature and the peer review system. Of course, once revealed, fraud and distortion also undermine the public's trust in science. This trust is essential to the smooth process of science. The personal values of scientists are best expressed by their choices of what is worth studying, the questions worth asking, and the best methods available to probe these questions.

Qualitative versus Quantitative Knowing

Scientists and philosophers have long recognized that there are many critical questions that science cannot address quantitatively, concerning, for example, issues of faith, morality, values, or culture. But even in the cases of questions that are potentially answerable by science, people frequently rely on nonscientific modes of gathering information. People gain a great deal by accepting the conclusions of others rather than by checking or verifying such conclusions by systematic observation. There are many things we could never experience directly, and even for those that we can, our own observations may be less reliable or insightful than those of others. In fact, culture can be viewed as a device for transmitting to people information about events that they have never experienced and may never experience themselves.

Thus, despite the clear advantage of the scientific method of data gathering, there are other ways of knowing besides scientific knowing. According to Buchler (1955), the philosopher Charles Peirce held that there are four ways of obtaining knowledge, or, as he put it, "fixing belief." The first is the method of tenacity, by which people know things to be true because they have always believed them to be true. The second method is the method of authority, whereby information is accepted as true because it has the weight of tradition, expert opinion, or public sanction. The a priori method is the third way of knowing. A priori assumptions are ones that appear to be self-evident or reasonable. The fourth way is the scientific method, whose fundamental hypothesis is that there are "real things whose characters are entirely independent of our opinions about them" (Buchler, 1955, p. 18). According to Peirce, the scientific method has characteristics that no other method of obtaining knowledge possesses: mechanisms of self-correction, objectivity, and appeals to evidence.

Just as there are other ways of knowing besides scientific knowing, there are different ways of scientific knowing. While it can probably be said that there is one scientific approach to problems—one general paradigm of scientific inquiry—there are a number of different research designs and data-gathering techniques that scientists can and do use.

The research design is the overall plan or structure of an investigation. Its purpose is to provide a model of the relationships of the variables of a study and to control variance. Research designs, which will be discussed in detail below, can be classified along a continuum with true or randomized experiments and nonexperimental approaches at the poles. True experiments are characterized by the manipulation of antecedent conditions to create at least two different treatment groups, random assignment of respondents to treatments, constraints upon respondents' behaviors, and the control of extraneous variables. Nonexperimental research designs involve less direct manipulation of antecedent conditions, little control over the assignment of respondents to conditions, fewer constraints on the responses of research participants, and less control over extraneous variables. Case studies, ex post facto studies, and passive and participant-observational methods exemplify nonexperimental approaches.

Along with choosing a research design, investigators must select strategies for observing respondents or collecting data. It is usually, but not necessarily, the case that experimental research designs are accompanied by quantitative modes of data gathering, and nonexperimental designs by qualitative modes. The distinction between quantitative and qualitative measures is not as clear-cut as those labels imply. The fact is that most observations, from thoughts and feelings to personal and societal products like diaries and documents, can probably be collected systematically and ordered logically on some dimensions and thus quantified. But some kinds of observations are more easily quantified than others. For example, questionnaires with fixed-choice alternatives yield data that lend themselves to categorization and quantification more easily than unstructured interviews. In general, unstructured interviews, sociogram analyses, mappings, many unobtrusive measures, documents, photographs, essays, and casual conversations are examples of what have come to be known as qualitative modes of data gathering.

As many reviewers have noted, both experimental/quantitative and nonexperimental/qualitative approaches to research have advantages and disadvantages, and each has its place in a program of research. Many feminist critics have attempted to increase awareness of lesser-known and little-used research methods, particularly nonexperimental and qualitative ones, and to encourage "triangulation" or "converging operations"—the use of as many different modes of operationalization and measurement of variables as possible within a program of research—as well as replication of studies to establish the reliability and generality of phenomena (Wallston, 1983; Wallston & Grady, 1985).

Like feminist psychologists, European psychologists have taken a broader perspective on the use of research methods than their American counterparts and have been critical of American psychology for its rejection of qualitative modes of knowing. Hall (1990), in his recent description of his impressions of the First European Congress of Psychology, was struck by the common European view that the word *science* has much too narrow a meaning for American psychologists. He paraphrased the keynote address of the eminent Dutch psychologist, Adrian de Groot, who opened the congress this way:

> Psychology as a natural science on the model of physics, with an insistence on the sole use of empirical methods as a means of knowing, is an American view.... In contrast, the European view of science does not exclude the academic study of the humanities, nor does it consider methods such as anecdotal evidence and reasoning necessarily non- or pre-scientific. (p. 987)

According to Hall, the focus of European criticisms of American psychology involved three fundamental concerns: narrow methodology and topic selection, lack of real concern for theory development and orientation, and an apparent unconcern for the cultural and historical context for understanding human behavior that is characteristic of research in the United States.

Hall also noted that most of the research presented at the congress was data-based, empirical studies, much like research in the United States, with the following subtle differences: wider use of nonexperimental methods, investigation of research topics not often studied in the United States, and more careful consideration given to the theoretical context of studies. He came away from the congress with the view that American psychology, with its many virtues and accomplishments, has much to learn from contemporary European psychology.

In the United States, where experimental and quantitative modes clearly predominate, the issues surrounding choices between nonexperimental/qualitative and experimental/quantitative modes have been hotly debated in some feminist circles. Some feminists have called for the alignment of feminist research with nonexperimental/qualitative methods (Carlson, 1972; Fine & Gordon, 1989). More typically, feminist critics have argued that no type of method is inherently superior to another and that each makes a unique contribution to the progress of science (Wallston & Grady, 1985). On the whole, though, feminist critics have been highly critical of widely used experimental/quantitative methods on a number of grounds and quite receptive to alternative nonexperimental/qualitative approaches.

Quantitative and experimental methods generally employ a variety of controls to remove or balance extraneous factors, determine which research participants receive which treatments at which times, and limit the possibility of invalid inference. These controls have come under fire from some feminists who regard them as by-products of sexism in science and society and often as unethical, unnatural, stifling, and undermining (Unger, 1983; McHugh et al., 1986). These critics of the quantitative/experimental research paradigm tend to be well grounded in experimental methodology and able to generate a litany of methodologically sound criticisms. About independent variables, they note that the possible and permissible range of manipulated variables like fear, grief, anger, or guilt is restricted to very low levels in an experiment; the time constraints of an experiment, especially in the laboratory, often impose other serious restrictions on independent variables, so that only acute or reactive forms of some variables, like self-esteem, can be studied. On the dependent variable side, it is by now well established that respondents who know that they are being observed by psychologists are motivated to appear better adjusted and less deviant, more tolerant and rational, more likely to turn the other cheek than retaliate when provoked and to judge others as they themselves would be judged. Psychologists now take it for granted that hypotheses involving antisocial behavior or socially undesirable behavior should be tested outside the laboratory, ideally when respondents do not know that they are being observed (Ellsworth, 1977).

All of these criticisms are true enough, often enough, to encourage feminist psychologists and others to search for alternatives to quantitative and experimental methods. They have warned against the dangers of ignoring relevant qualitative contextual evidence and overrelying on a few quantified abstractions to the neglect of contradictory or supplementary qualitative evidence (Sherif, 1987; Unger, 1983). But qualitative and quantitative methods are not interchangeable; they yield different kinds of information, and the substitution of qualitative techniques for quantitative ones does not seem promising. Quantitative and experimental methods are superior to naturalistic ones for answering causal questions. Of course, not all questions of interest are causal questions, and many important causal questions cannot be probed experimentally due to ethical or practical constraints. Moreover, before relevant variables have been identified and precise causal questions can be formulated in a research area, experimental and quantitative methods may be premature and may even foreclose promising areas of exploration. This said, it remains the case that many of the most important questions that we will ask as scientists or concerned citizens are causal questions. The best way to investigate causal laws is by conducting true or randomized experiments involving manipulated variables in controlled settings. The naturalistic observation of events cannot permit causal inference because of the ubiquitous confounding of selection and treatment. Of necessity, any effort to reduce this inherent equivocality will have the effect of increasing the investigator's control and making conditions more contrived and artificial—that is, more "experimental." Qualitative, quantitative, nonexperimental, and experimental modes of knowing may be best viewed as noninterchangeable but as compatible and complementary.

Despite the chilly climate so many women have encountered in the halls of science generally and the psychological laboratory particularly, many feminist critics recognize that it would be a great mistake for feminists to forsake quantitative and experimental methods or the laboratory for context-rich, confound-laden qualitative and nonexperimental methods. It is undisputed that gender differences are larger and more prevalent in the field than the laboratory (Deaux, 1984). As Unger (1979) noted, far more self-report surveys of sex differences exist than do reports of such differences when actual behavior is observed by others. This finding suggests that many studies of gender differences have not planned well in advance for the sophisticated analysis of those differences and/or their replication. Often, it is only after the painstaking unconfounding of variables that so often covary in naturalistic settings—like gender and status—that we can illuminate how similar the sexes are. It is in the laboratory that much of the work has been done illustrating that many behavioral differences between men and women are the results of conscious self-presentational strategies rather than of different potentials or repertoires (Deaux, 1984), status differences between men and women (Unger, 1979), or differences in how familiar men and women are with experimental stimuli (Eagly, 1978). Time after time, in studies of aggression, influencibility, self-confidence, and helping, to name a few areas, carefully controlled experimental research has been critical in successfully refuting pernicious, long-standing myths about the differences between the genders or about women. The discrete "findings" that have accumulated to form the bodies of literature in psychological studies—the contents of psychology—have often been sexist. But, as Grady (1981) has pointed out, the methods of scientific psychology are valuable to feminists and revolutionaries of all types, as they contain within them the means for challenging the status quo.

Ethical Issues Embedded in the Language and Conduct of Science

It has long been noted that the language of science is itself deeply male-oriented and sexist (Keller, 1974; Sherif, 1987; Unger, 1983) and contributes greatly to the disaffection that some feminists feel from the sciences, including psychology. It is not difficult to generate a list of scientific terms that seem to suggest a preoccupation with power and domination. Thus, we "manipulate" fear and "control" for sex. We "intervene" in field settings and "attack" problems. "Subjects" are "assigned" to treatments and "deceived." Scientists accumulate "hard" facts, and so on. The issues raised by the language of science, like those raised by the literary conventions of the scientific report, are by no means trivial. Language not only reflects but also shapes scientific thought and practice.

At least three different issues are raised by the feminist critique of the language of experimentation. The first issue concerns the perceived adversarial relationship between the experiment and the real world—between the false and contrived and the real and natural, between the distortions of science and the truth of the real world. As noted earlier, it is not clear that anything is gained by conceptualizing science and nature as dichotomies or that feminism should seek to align itself with the "natural" as opposed to the "scientific." The second and related issue concerns the labeling of the objective, rational, and interventionist in science and scientific language as "masculine." Given the apparent human fondness for dualisms and dichotomies, the effect of calling the language of experimentation and quantitative methods "masculine" is to cast the language of subjective, intuitive, and passive observational methods as "feminine." It is not clear that such classifications should be encouraged. Bleier (1984), cited in Lott (1985), has argued, "Science need not be permitted to define objectivity and creativity as that which the male mind does and subjectivity and emotionality as that which the female mind is" (p. 162). Lott goes on to say that the terms *masculinity* and *femininity* are simply cognitive constructs with no independent existence in nature. Statements that tie human characteristics like a "preoccupation with control and dominance" to gender, in Lott's words, "deny the abundance of contradictory evidence and what we know about situational variation in behavior" (p. 162).

The third concern embedded in the feminist response to the language of science is the status differential inherent in the traditional relationship between researchers, especially experimenters, and their research participants and the potential and real abuses of power that flow from this inequity. Perhaps the essence of that differential is captured in the increasingly discredited label "subjects" for research participants. Many feminist researchers seem profoundly uncomfortable with this inequity, which they view as another by-product of sexism in science. Summarizing the point of view of many feminists, McHugh et al. (1986) wrote:

> They have suggested that eliciting subjective viewpoints may be one way to "get behind" the inequality and the limited self-presentation potentially inherent in all researcher-participant interactions. Both the

> appropriateness and scientific utility of the experimenter's being neutral, disinterested, and nondisclosing have been challenged, especially when the experimenter desires to have participants behave naturally and honestly. (p. 880)

Clearly, the feminist call is for a more respectful, interactive, and "honest" relationship between researchers and research participants. Two implications of this call are that respondents should be consulted about their responses to the experiment and that researchers should disclose to respondents the purposes of the research, or at least refrain from deceiving respondents. There is a growing body of evidence in the psychology of women to suggest that it is essential on scientific as well as moral grounds to elicit the meaning of various aspects of a study from the research participants' point of view. Research situations differ in their salience, familiarity, relevance, and meanings for males and females, as well as for members of different racial and ethnic groups (Richardson & Kaufman, 1983; McHugh et al., 1986). As Richardson and Kaufman (1983) stated, gender-by-situation interactions are more the rule than the exception in psychological research, and the failure to explore and specify the meanings that research participants attach to stimuli constitutes a blight on our research literatures.

It is difficult to argue against any of the welcome trends championed by feminist critics that protect the rights and dignity of research participants and make researchers aware of the responsibilities they have to treat participants with respect and caring. Obviously, the gratuitous and uncritical practice of deceiving research participants is completely unwarranted. But there is in fact not good evidence to suggest that research participants feel harmed, violated, or diminished by today's research practices of deception or nondisclosure of the methods and purposes of the research (Abramson, 1977; Mannucci, 1977). As Smith (1983) noted, empirical research on the effects of deception seem to suggest that most respondents regard deception in a scientific context as justifiable and not unethical, especially if respondents have been thoroughly debriefed. According to Smith, respondents view research with deception more favorably than research that is trivial, uninteresting, stressful, or harmful. Mannucci (1977) pointed out that when respondents are presented with a research situation that is not what it seems, they do not always regard themselves as having been "deceived." Of course, the fact that most respondents feel that deception is justifiable does not mean that all respondents feel that way or that respondents would feel that way under all circumstances. Nonetheless, reports of negative attitudes toward research using deception, even where these attitudes were actively solicited, are rare (Smith, 1983).

Aside from respondents' attitudes toward deception, there is the issue of its actual effects on research participants. Again, research on the effects of deception on respondents suggests that there is little, if any, evidence of harm of any kind, including negative effects of inflicted self-knowledge and damage to trust in scientific research or research scientists (West & Gunn, 1978; Reynolds, 1979).

From a scientific standpoint, there is not as yet any evidence to suggest that research participants behave more naturally or honestly when they are aware of the methods and purposes of the research. Smith (1983) reviews a substantial body of evidence that indicates that respondents in fact behave less honestly when they know that they are being observed, when they are asked to take on the roles of those who face moral dilemmas, or when they know the purposes of research. Obviously, even the most vigorous defenders of deception recognize that there are clear limits to its use (Elms, 1982). We need to continue the debate about the extent to which deception-free methods like self-report, role-playing, and simulations can be used in place of deception and to continue the development and testing of alternatives to deception.

Feminist critiques of scientific psychology have also been in the forefront of efforts to protect the rights and dignity of research participants, to guard against violations of trust, and to value the totality of respondents' contributions to research. Characteristically, feminist research assigns a high priority to eliciting respondents' viewpoints and explaining fully the meaning and purposes of research at the point of debriefing. These practices have proved to be scientifically, as well as ethically, sound. Feminist research also seeks to avoid or minimize the use of deception and reminds us that there are more important values in society even than the advancement of knowledge. However, it appears that some of the concern about the use of deception and nondisclosure may be exaggerated and that these practices, when carefully monitored and scrupulously implemented, may not be as morally or methodologically problematic as once feared.

A GUIDE TO GENDER-FAIR RESEARCH

We are now prepared to consider each of the stages of the research process, with an eye to noting the pervasive white, middle-class, male bias that has distorted this process. Issues pertaining to formulating research questions, conducting integrative reviews of previous research, choosing research participants and research designs, operationalizing variables, and analyzing and interpreting results will be discussed from a feminist perspective. This orientation owes much to the excellent pioneering work of Kay Deaux, Florence Denmark, Alice Eagly, Irene Hanson Frieze, Kathleen Grady, Randi Daimon Koeske, Maureen McHugh, Rhoda Unger, and Barbara Strudler Wallston, all of whom have helped to set the standards for the conduct of gender-fair research.

Question Formulation

In recent years, researchers have begun to turn their attention to understudied and undervalued areas—hypothesis generation and question formulation. Traditionally, it has been assumed that research hypotheses are logically derived from theory. Clearly, much of what is described as basic research is derived from theoretical models. But where do these theories come from, and what are, or could be, other sources of our research?

Psychological theories, from the most formal, sweeping, and influential ones like Freud's theory of personality and Piaget's theory of cognitive development to far less ambitious ones are often derived from the experiences and observations of the theorists. The overwhelming majority of these theorists in psychology have been men. Some, like Piaget, Kohlberg, and Erikson, have tended to promote standards of healthy behavior based on the experiences of males alone and, like Freud, to depict women more negatively than men. As many feminist psychologists have argued (Sherif, 1987; Unger, 1983; Harding, 1987), up until now, traditional psychology has begun its analysis from men's experience, particularly the experience of white, middle-class males, who have dominated academic psychology. This means that psychology has posed questions about individual and social processes that men find problematic or that men want answered—questions of men, by men, for men. To be sure, many of the traditional topics studied by psychologists have been of great interest to women, and women have been the primary object of study in some lines of research. But asking questions about one sex that could and should be applied to both sexes is sexist. For instance, reports of a relationship between monthly fluctuations in female sex hormones and a woman's ability to perform certain cognitive tasks have recently received widespread attention (Blakeslee, 1988). The daily fluctuations in key male hormones, on the other hand, have not been correlated with male thinking skills. Similarly, the prenatal sexual responsiveness of males but not females has been explored (Brody, 1989). Obviously, the focus on females in the first instance and males in the second lends scientific respectability to stereotypes about female cognitive impairment and male sexual potency that might have been refuted had both genders been studied.

Topics of primary interest to women (e.g., family relationships, female alcoholism, victimization by rape, wife battering) and questions about women that women want answered (e.g., How can corporations change so that women with children can pursue careers at the same time that they raise their families?) have received far less attention than topics of primary interest to men (e.g., work outside the home, male alcoholism, aggression of men toward men, impaired male sexual response) and questions about women that men want answered (e.g., How can women's symptoms of depression and anxiety be treated medically?).

In psychology, we have devoted considerable research attention to the topics of aggression, conflict, achievement, and cognitive processes and less attention to the topics of affiliation, cooperation, and emotional processes. We have studied moral development as it pertains to applying rules and upholding rights in hypothetical situations, not as it pertains to taking care of others and fulfilling responsibilities in actual situations. While no topic or approach is inherently "masculine or "feminine," superior or inferior, the preponderance of topics and approaches studied appears to reflect a masculine bias. More importantly, they reflect a strikingly narrow and distorted view of human behavior.

We are well on our way toward developing a psychology of abstract concepts like "aggression" that lend themselves rather easily to experimental tests in the laboratory. But we have made little progress in developing the psychology of human concerns. It is remarkable that academic psychology has devoted so little attention to the phenomena that occupy people in their daily lives—relating to family and friends, making a living, saving and spending money, educating themselves, and enjoying leisure time, to name a few. We have hardly begun to understand the effects on people of being married or committed to a mate, having close friends, believing in God, losing a job, or losing a loved one. We have only recently started studying how climate, geography, crossing time zones, housing and space, and other aspects of the environment affect behavior. The complex relationships between physical health and psychological well-being are only now beginning to receive the attention they deserve from scientific psychologists. Many of the richest, most influential psychological variables we know of—gender, race, ethnicity, age, and educational background—have been given short shrift by psychologists, in part because there may be considerable professional risk involved in studying them.

Some of these areas have been ignored by scientific psychologists because they are regarded as "applied" or "clinical." Applied research is by definition regarded as less generalizable, less important, less prestigious, and more specialized than "basic" or "pure" research. As other investigators have noted, research on topics of particular interest to males is more likely to be regarded as basic, and research of particular interest to females, as applied (McHugh et al., 1986). The psychology of gender and the psychology of women suffer from this classification. Research published in feminist journals like *Psychology of Women Quarterly* and *Sex Roles* is not often cited in mainstream journals in the field as they are seen as specialized and thus of limited interest.

Another reason for avoiding these areas is that they are very difficult to study, particularly with conventional research methods. People cannot be randomly assigned to a belief in God, a Harvard education, or the loss of a loved one. So many variables are confounded with gender and age that interpreting their effects becomes treacherous, especially when one considers the social and political implications of those interpretations.

The "crisis in social psychology" is due in part to the recognition that psychologists have systematically ignored many of the most interesting, important, and pressing questions about nature and social life. Those outside the academic mainstream have not been impressed with the arguments that such questions are only of applied or limited interest or are too difficult to probe with cherished traditional research tools. For one thing, there is increasing evidence that the distinction between basic and applied research is blurring, as applied research becomes more theory-relevant and methodologically rigorous. In fact, scientific psychologists as eminent as Harvard's Howard Gardner see psychology flourishing much more as an applied than a basic field in the future (Blakeslee, 1988). To be sure, new questions do require new assumptions, models, hypotheses, and purposes of inquiry. What we need are new ways of applying scientific techniques of gathering evidence, many of which are seldom used or used mainly in other disciplines. To investigate questions of interest to them, feminist researchers can use any and all of the methods that traditional scientists have used, but use them in different ways to observe behaviors and gain perspectives not previously thought significant.

As an essential corrective to pervasive male bias, the experiences, observations, concerns, and problems of women need to be integrated into psychology. Further, we need to recognize that gender experiences vary across categories of class, race, and culture. As Harding (1987) noted, "Women come only in different classes, races, and cultures; there is no 'woman' and no 'woman's experience'" (p. 7).

Integrative Reviews of Previous Research

Despite the obvious importance of theory, experience, and observation in influencing research questions, most basic researchers probably get their specific ideas from studying other people's research—from the professional literature in a narrow and well-defined area. There are several obvious reasons, including the very obvious practical consideration of fitting one's research into an already existing body of knowledge and having one's contribution recognized as valuable. The problems with this approach from a feminist perspective should be equally obvious. Many bodies of literature in psychology are so tainted by sexist assumptions and research practices that they are unreliable guides for feminist research. How can we review research in such a way that exposes past androcentric biases and enriches future gender-fair research?

All research reports begin with a review of relevant research. Given how influential and ubiquitous they are, it is truly surprising that there are no standards for conducting such reviews. Jackson (1983) explained this by suggesting that, in the past, neither reviewers or editors attached a great deal of importance to the thoroughness or accuracy of reviews, with the result that most reviews are quite flawed.

Jackson (1983) proposed three components to the process of analyzing previous research in an area: (1) identifying and locating the known universe of relevant studies, (2) noting the systematic methodological strengths and weaknesses of past studies, and (3) judging the implications of these biases and considering how varying characteristics of research participants, treatments, and measures might affect the phenomena of interest. As we consider each component, it should be clear how androcentric biases emerge at each stage of the process.

For most researchers, the universe of relevant studies is strikingly narrow, consisting of the professional literature in a very few scholarly journals. As noted above, to the extent that the professional literature has been dominated by white, middle-class, male theorists and researchers, the literature reflects the values, interests, and concerns of this group. But bias does not exist simply because males have served as the crafters of the research agenda and the gatekeepers of the journals. Bias also exists because sex differences are much more likely to be reported in the mainstream literature than sex similarities, regardless of how unexpected or meaningless they are, because the finding of no differences is not regarded as interpretable. Thus, there is no literature that seeks to integrate the innumerable studies in which no differences are found.

There are only partial correctives for the problem of locating the relevant literature outside the mainstream in areas like the psychology of gender. One remedy lies in expanding the search for studies beyond the small number of mainstream journals with their predictable biases. Relevant journals within the discipline that may have different biases should be sought out, regardless of their circulation or prestige, as should relevant journals from different social science disciplines. Aside from scholarly journals, books, monographs, unpublished doctoral dissertations, and government and other "in-house" publications should also be sought. Papers presented at conventions might be included in the search. Special efforts must be made to incorporate the perspectives of other disciplines, social classes, and cultures representing varying philosophical and political viewpoints. Even this is not enough to redress the imbalance. Aside from deliberately and vigorously expanding the literature search, the reviewer needs to report fully the dimensions of the search strategy so that others may assess its thoroughness, adequacy, and likely sources of bias. Clearly, these prescriptions add significantly to our responsibilities as reviewers, but they are critical if we are ever to strike an essential balance in our efforts to explore complex variables like gender and race.

The second component of the integrative review, according to Jacklin (1983), is the identification of systematic methodological weaknesses and strengths in the bodies of knowledge. A number of feminists have offered cogent criticisms of the research on gender differences and the psychology of women by pointing to pervasive methodological flaws that have systematically distorted results. Jacklin, who has herself conducted some of the most ambitious and well-regarded reviews in these areas, has pointed to some of the most common problems. Although these will be discussed in more detail later, it will suffice here to note briefly the methodological flaws that exist when there are a number of variables confounded with gender, such as status or self-confidence, or when the experimenter's gender produces an effect that interacts with the gender of the respondent, but that interaction is not measured. Another confound exists when the data are obtained by filling out self-reports. There is a well-documented gender difference in the willingness or ability to disclose thoughts and feelings, in the direction of females being more disclosing, and thus there is a concern for researchers in interpreting gender differences obtained with these kinds of measures.

Exploring the implications of methodological biases and speculating about how different research participants, treatments, designs, and measures might affect conclusions are the final component of Jacklin's analyses. Thoughtful critics have already demonstrated what such analyses might yield. For instance, it has been noted that more and larger gender differences have emerged in the field than the laboratory (cf. Unger, 1979) and that the more methodologically controlled the design, the less likely it is that gender differences will emerge (Jacklin, 1983). Unger (1979) has noted that the appearance of gender differences depends upon the age, social class, and cultural background of the respondents. She has also pointed out that males and females ordinarily do not differ in how they respond to stimulus materials used in psychological research, but are especially alike in the stereotypes they have regarding the sexes and how the sexes differ (Unger, 1979). She concluded, then, that gender-of-respondent effects are not nearly as common as gender-of-stimuli effects.

Most feminist psychologists have chosen to regard the psychological literature as a legitimate source of knowledge and have attempted to counteract the many biases of omission and commission from within the discipline (Fine & Gordon, 1989). Feminists need to take a critical stance toward the biases that exist in the psychological literature, biases that necessarily place an extra burden on their integrative reviews. Many feminists have expressed great interest in the alternative to narrative discussions of research studies known as meta-analysis

(Glass, 1976; Eagly & Carli, 1981). This approach involves transforming the results of individual studies to some common metric, like significance levels or effect size, and coding various characteristics of the studies. Then, by using conventional statistical procedures, the reviewer can determine whether there are overall effects, subsample effects, and relationships among characteristics of the studies (e.g., use of a correlational design) and the findings of the bodies of literature.

The virtues of this technique from a feminist perspective are significant. Meta-analysis is a systematic and replicable approach. It can accommodate studies with a variety of methodologies and can control for biased findings due to systematic methodological flaws. It can provide estimates of population parameters and permit simultaneous investigation of the relationships among research methods, participants, scope of operationalizations, and the duration of treatment. In probing the extensive, diverse, often contradictory literature on sex-related differences and the psychology of gender, feminists have painstakingly demonstrated how well-established findings on the effects of gender must be qualified by taking into account such variables as task characteristics, response modes, gender of the experimenter, self-presentational strategies, and perceiver's stereotypes about sex-linked behavior, to name a few.

As promising as meta-analytic techniques are and as appealing as they have been to feminist reviewers, we do not mean to suggest that they solve all of the problems of traditional narrative reviews or are themselves without controversy. Some meta-analysts have been criticized for the liberal standards they tend to use in including studies in meta-analysis. The issues of whether and how to exclude studies of poor methodological quality have not been resolved. Of course, not all studies on a given topic can be retrieved for inclusion, and those that cannot are likely to differ systematically on some important characteristics from those that can. For example, retrievable studies are more likely to report differences between treatment conditions and to be published in journals than those that are not retrievable.

Combining effect sizes or significance levels is problematic as a way of estimating treatment effects unless the studies involved used the same or highly similar independent variables. The issue of how broad categories of independent and dependent variables should be has been called the "apples and oranges" problem in meta-analysis (Cook & Leviton, 1980). According to Cook and Leviton (1980), the greater the breadth of the categories used, the more likely the chances that important interaction effects will become impossible to detect and too much confidence will be placed in conclusions about main effects.

Meta-analytic techniques can aid the reviewer in analyzing, categorizing, and weighting past research and promise further clarifications in understanding the effects of gender and related variables. But they do not free the meta-analyst from the responsibility to exercise the same kinds of judgment that has always been expected of traditional reviewers.

Description of Researchers

Because they openly acknowledge the roles of background and values in research, many feminist research methodologists have proposed that researchers make these explicit in their reports (cf. Harding, 1987; Wallston & Grady, 1985). Harding (1987) wrote: "The best feminist analysis insists that the inquirer her/himself be placed in the same critical plane as the overt subject matter, thereby recovering the entire research process for scrutiny in the results of the research" (p. 9).

There is ample evidence from a wide variety of areas within psychology that the personal attributes, background, and values of researchers distort results. Eagly and Carli (1981) found in their meta-analytic study of conformity and persuasion that the gender of researcher was a determinant of the gender difference in influenceability. Male authors reported larger sex differences than female authors, in the direction of greater persuasibility and conformity among women. Sherwood and Nataupsky (reported in Unger, 1983) found that the conclusions that investigators reached about whether blacks were innately inferior to whites in intelligence could be predicted from biological information about the investigators, including birth order, educational level, birthplace of their parents, and scholastic standing. Psychotherapy outcome studies conducted by researchers who are affiliated with a particular form of psychotherapy and are not blind to treatment condition demonstrate an overwhelming tendency to find that the form of psychotherapy favored by the researcher works best (Kayne & Alloy, 1988). In contrast, when well-controlled comparison experiments are conducted by unbiased assessors, there are usually no differences between the therapies compared.

Many questions arise when we consider the idea of including descriptions of experimenters in research reports. What kinds of information should be included and excluded? How much information is necessary? Where and how should this information be incorporated into the report? Will something be lost when the researcher is no longer portrayed as an invisible, anonymous voice of authority, but as a real, historical, bounded individual?

Obviously, the kind and amount of information that experimenters should include will vary with the research topic and methods. To some extent, the question of what to include is an empirical one. We know, for instance, that gender of the experimenter so often produces an effect that interacts with gender of subject, regardless of the research topic, that gender of experimenter should probably always be noted. If a researcher is comparing forms of treatments, his or her theoretical orientation and affiliation with the treatments under study are of obvious interest to readers. As with descriptions of respondents, the information to be reported reflects the researchers' (or others') "best guess" about which variables other than those directly under study may affect the outcome of the research. Depending upon the research topic, aside from gender, the researchers' ethnic background, subarea, professional socialization, theoretical orientation, and a brief description of research experience are likely candidates for consideration.

To underscore the point that the attributes, background, and beliefs of the researcher are part of the empirical evidence for (or against) the claims advanced in the discussion, the description of the researchers may be inserted in the methods section of the report, alongside the description of respondents. Where this is not possible due to editorial policy, the material should be included in a footnote.

Because of the tendencies within our discipline to minimize the roles of values in science and embrace the "objectivist" stance, we can expect great reluctance among mainstream psychologists to "uncover" the experimenter, as this opens the investigator's perspective to critical scrutiny and may seem to limit or compromise the validity of the research. Given the growing body of evidence that experimenters' beliefs and characteristics affect results, there are solid scientific grounds to argue that this information should be open to scrutiny no less than what has been conventionally defined as relevant information. As Harding (1987) noted: "Introducing the 'subjective element' into the analysis in fact increases the objectivity of the research and decreases the 'objectivism' which hides this kind of evidence from the public" (p. 9).

Sample Selection

Issues and problems related to the selection of research participants have received much attention from psychologists who are interested in gender differences and gender-fair research. Wallston and Grady (1985) point out that, however perfunctory, brief, and inadequate they are, descriptions of respondents in psychological reports almost always include the gender of the respondents. While the routine inclusion of gender is largely due to mere convention, it also reflects pervasive assumptions that gender is a variable that might influence the outcome of research.

Despite widespread beliefs within the discipline that the gender of respondents has the potential to affect the results of a study, psychologists have long recognized the problems with conceptualizing gender as an independent variable. For one thing, gender is a descriptive, rather than a conceptual, variable, with obvious biological (genetic, hormonal, and physiological) and sociocultural (relating to socialization and social, economic, educational, and familial status) components (McHugh et al., 1986). If males and females differ on the dependent variable, it is hardly clear which of the innumerable variables confounded with biological sex actually "caused" the effect.

Psychologists have crafted a number of solutions to the problems associated with the use of gender as an independent variable. Perhaps the most common solution is drawing the same number of males and females from a single setting, specifying the sex composition of the sample, and declaring that one has "controlled for sex." As Wallston and Grady (1985) note, males and females are never randomly assigned to gender and thus are never "equivalent" prior to an intervention. For this reason, studies that compare males and females are in fact quasi-experiments rather than true experiments. As such, any gender comparisons are vulnerable to a variety of threats to internal validity, as we discuss in the section on quasi-experiments below, and inferences based on such comparisons are indeed difficult to support.

It is often overlooked that the samples of males and females available in a given setting are often actually drawn from quite different populations with respect to factors that affect the dependent variables. When the sample is comprised of males and females from different populations, the researcher is essentially "creating" rather than "uncovering" a gender difference. For example, a study of gender differences in marital attitudes using husbands and wives would be quite compromised if the men in the sample were significantly older, better educated, and better paid than the women, even though husbands and wives would presumably be quite similar on a number of other dimensions. Similarly, increasing attention has been paid in recent years to how males and females differ in lifespan activities (McHugh et al., 1986; Paludi, 1986). Thus, whereas males and females of the same age may be engaged in very different pursuits and express different values and attitudes, males and females engaged in a particular activity or found in the same setting may be at very different ages.

With college students, probably the most common respondent population studied in our discipline, a number of considerations arise. Studies of gender differences may be distorted if the proportions of males and females available are quite different or if one gender is more difficult to recruit or less likely to comply with the requirements of the study. Depending on the research topic, the special characteristics of the males and females who attend a school, choose a major, or enroll in a course should be taken into account. For example, a recent study of the achievement motivation and college enrollment patterns of Italian-American students in the City University of New York (CUNY) suggested that Italian-American women were significantly more achievement oriented than their male peers and were enrolled in college in greater numbers (Sterzi, 1988). However, subsequent analyses revealed that a strikingly high proportion of the male siblings of female students in the sample were enrolled in or had attended private colleges. Sterzi reasoned that Italian-American parents might be more likely to finance their sons' private college education than their daughters'. Thus, the Italian-American population at a relatively inexpensive public university like CUNY would contain proportionately more achievement-oriented, academically successful Italian-American women than men.

Another historically popular solution to the problems posed by gender-of-respondent effects is the use of single-gender designs. As we noted earlier, traditionally, males have appeared more often as respondents, although there is some evidence that this trend is changing and even reversing itself. There are many reasons given for the choice of studying only one gender. Some are quite practical, as when the investigator points to the need to limit the sample size or avoid costly attempts to recruit the less available gender. Less commonly, the researcher may express a preference for one gender because of beliefs about that gender's reliability in honoring research commitments or ability to endure a treatment. Many researchers use one gender to avoid having to study the vast, murky literature on gender differences, test for gender differences, and interpret any differences that might emerge.

Some investigators offer conceptual reasons for the focus on one gender (Denmark et al., 1988). These reasons are based on the assumption that the research topic is only relevant to one gender. Thus, studies on infant attachment, parental employment effects on children, interpersonal attraction, and the effects of hormonal fluctuations on cognitive ability have tended to use women and girls as respondents, whereas research on aggression, parental absence, homosexuality, antisocial behavior, sexual dysfunction, and sexual responsiveness in infancy have tended to use males.

While often unstated, the assumptions underlying the choice of males in critical theory-building studies appear to be that males are more important, function at higher levels, and behave in ways closer to the "ideal adult" than females. Thus, as we have shown, it is much more common that studies using males are generalized to females than that studies using females are generalized to males (McHugh et al., 1986; Denmark et al., 1988). No major theory of human behavior has gained acceptance within psychology after being tested exclusively on female samples, and yet major theories on achievement motivation and moral development have relied almost exclusively on research with males for their support. Similarly, in animal studies, more theories or evidence for physiological or neurobiological mechanisms have relied almost exclusively on male subjects and are then likely to be generalized to females.

Obviously, as we noted earlier, the use of single-sex designs is sometimes justifiable on theoretical grounds. In a given study, practical considerations may override others in the choice of single-sex designs, so long as the limitations of the design are clearly acknowledged. But overall, the widespread, unexamined practice of studying one sex has been costly to psychology. It has led to the development of theories that were intended to describe both sexes but are relevant only to one, and it has consistently failed to challenge sexist assumptions about the differences in behaviors, interests, and abilities between males and females.

Like the choice of treatment groups, the choice of control groups reflects hypotheses about what variables may affect the dependent variable. As many methodologists recognize, the choice of control groups is not a minor methodological consideration but a major determinant of the interpretability and validity of the study. This choice takes on special significance in the study of gender differences, because males and females are nonequivalent groups and differ on those many variables that are confounded with biological sex. The report by Denmark et al. (1988) on studies of gender differences in job turnover illustrates this point. These studies consistently suggest that women have higher rates of turnover than men. However, it was noted that turnover is correlated with job status, with those in lower-status jobs quitting more often than those in high-status positions. In these studies, gender has been confounded with job status, as women were more likely to hold low-status positions than men. When the appropriate comparison group was selected to control for job status, no gender differences in job turnover emerged.

It should be noted that controlling for variables that are confounded with gender may not be enough (Campbell, 1983). Some variables are themselves quite biased, such as socioeconomic status, which may use a husband's or father's occupational level or income to determine the woman's status.

A further problem with studying variables like socioeconomic level or occupational level along with gender is that occupations that have a higher proportion of women than men, like elementary school teaching, nursing, and stenography, are frequently less lucrative than occupations that employ more men than women, like plumbing or automobile mechanics, but require higher educational levels. It is important to determine precisely how levels of these variables are determined.

A final, often overlooked issue to be considered in selecting a sample is sample size. Whenever gender is treated as an independent variable, past research suggests that males and females are highly heterogeneous with respect to virtually all dependent variables. Thus, with so many uncontrolled variables present, gender groups might well be comprised of a number of different subgroups that should be considered separately. Under these conditions, only relatively small gender differences can be expected and large samples of males and females may be needed to detect differences. Of course, the larger the sample, the more likely it is that statistically significant differences will be attained. For these reasons, measures of the magnitude of effects should be calculated more regularly in research on gender differences (to be discussed further below), and the practical and social significance of the findings needs to be assessed quite apart from statistical significance.

Research Design

Due to space constraints, the sheer amount of material available on these topics, and the number of excellent treatments elsewhere (Cook & Campbell, 1979; Wallston & Grady, 1985; Wallston, 1983; Richardson & Kaufman, 1983), this treatment of research designs will be relatively brief. It will focus on how feminist concerns affect the choice of research designs and design issues of interest to feminists in the conduct of research rather than on how to implement these designs.

True Experiments

As we have already noted, true or randomized experiments are ones in which respondents are randomly assigned to experimental and control groups. They provide the strongest evidence of all research designs that a treatment causes an effect. When the conditions for experimentation are favorable, true experiments have considerable advantages over other designs in probing causal questions.

Many feminist methodologists who acknowledge the advantages of true experiments have also been quite critical of them in recent years, finding them more "time-consuming, laborious, and costly" than other designs (cf. Wallston, 1983). While this perception is fairly widespread, as Cook and Campbell (1979) note, there is no inherent reason this should be so, and little evidence that this is in fact the case. Random assignment to treatment per se usually adds little or nothing to the expenditure of time, labor, or money by the researcher, administrators, or research participants. Even in cases where random assignment is more costly than other modes of selection to treatment, its advantages over other modes of assignment often outweigh any minor inconvenience that its implementation might entail.

Nonetheless, there are many real impediments to conducting true experiments, especially in the field, some disadvantages to them, and many instances in which they are less appropriate than other designs. Obstacles to conducting true experiments may be ethical or practical in nature. Fortunately for humane and ethical reasons, psychologists will never assign people at random to some of life's most powerful and affecting treatments like loss of a loved one, becoming a parent, surviving a catastrophe, or receiving a formal education. In fact, most potent treatments, those that may conceivably cause participants any stress, embarrassment, discomfort, or inconvenience, are no longer permissible under current federal regulations that govern the actions of Institutional Review Boards (IRBs) for the protection of human subjects for research, as well as the guidelines of the American Psychological Association (APA). For these reasons, especially in the laboratory, typical treatments are trivial, short-lived, and unlikely to have large or lasting impacts on participants.

In real-world settings, where important, long-term treatments are more feasible, it may be difficult to justify withholding seemingly beneficial or appealing treatments from control groups or administering treatments to groups that vary greatly in perceived attractiveness. Other practical considerations may preclude the conduct of true experiments in the field. Often, these are the result of the investigator's relative lack of control over field settings. Frequently, investigators fail to make the case for random assignment to harried administrators who are mainly concerned about its effects on their constituents and bureaucracy and skeptical about its importance. Even those administrators who appreciate the value of random assignment on scientific grounds may reject it due to the inconvenience, displacement, or resistance that it might cause.

True experiments are ideal when the state of knowledge in an area is advanced enough to permit the experimenter to identify a limited number of important independent variables, specify the relevant levels of those variables, operationalize them adequately, and measure specific effects of those variables with sensitivity and precision. Under the best of conditions, only a small number of independent and dependent variables can be studied in any one experiment, affording true experiments limited opportunity to detect interaction effects, measure the effects of variables at extreme levels, or capture the richness and complexity of a real-world setting. Wallston (1981, 1983) has pointed to some of the problems that arise when experiments are performed prematurely: the choice of variables or levels of variables may be arbitrary, operationalizations may be inadequate, and experimental situations may be so unlikely and contrived as to yield misleading findings.

Despite their considerable advantages in establishing the existence of causal relationships (high internal validity and statistical validity), true experiments sometimes compromise the investigator's abilities to generalize to, and across, other operationalizations (construct validity) and other places, people, and times (external validity) due to their artificiality, obtrusiveness, or overreliance on certain kinds of manipulations, measures, research participants, or settings. Thus, while true experiments best equip researchers to probe the question, Does the treatment cause the effect? they are often less helpful in suggesting what it is that the treatment and effect should be labeled in theory-relevant terms and whether that cause-effect relationship would hold in other settings and times or with other participants.

Problems determining how the treatments and effects should be labeled conceptually—construct validity concerns—are particularly interesting and troubling to psychologists. It is a well-established finding in social science research that when people know that they are being observed, they behave differently than they would otherwise. It is also well documented that when research participants estimate that a particular response is more socially desirable than others, they tend to favor that response over others to present themselves in a more positive light. In this way, demand characteristics—extraneous features of the experimental setting that cue participants about how they should respond—are more likely to operate in true experiments conducted in laboratory settings than in nonexperimental research in the field. Demand characteristics undoubtedly contribute to the finding that gender-of-stimuli effects are more common in the literature than gender-of-respondent effects. Unger (1979) has summarized how demand characteristics may operate when gender-of-stimuli is studied:

> Using no stimulus materials other than the label male or female, investigators have found that the sex-of-stimulus person alters people's criteria for mental health, affects their evaluation of the goodness and badness of performance, leads them to make differential attributions about the causes of someone's behavior and induces differential perceptions about the values of others. (p. 1090)

As problematic as it has been to interpret the meaning of gender-of-stimuli effects in true experiments, attempts to study gender-of-subject effects in true experimental designs have posed even greater difficulties. As Wallston (1983) has pointed out, people cannot be randomly assigned to gender, so that cross-gender comparisons always render a design quasi-experimental and vulnerable to threats to internal validity. This will be discussed below.

Most research psychologists have been far more extensively trained in experimental methods than in alternative designs and have been professionally socialized to revere the true experiment. True experiments have been quite useful to feminist researchers in exploring the effects of gender and exposing sexist myths and will surely continue to serve feminist scientists well. But the limitations of true experiments are increasingly obvious in the study of gender and other variables. Often the choice for researchers is between exploring critical variables like gender, race, age, and central life experiences with nonexperimental methods and avoiding them entirely. Where true experiments are used to study these topics, the information they supply should be supplemented with data gathered using different designs with different assets and shortcomings.

Quasi-Experiments

Quasi-experiments are similar to true experiments in that they are composed of treatment and no-treatment comparison groups. But unlike true experiments, in quasi-experiments assignment to group is not random, and thus groups are nonequivalent at the outset. When experimental groups are different even before the treatment is administered, any differences that emerge among groups at the posttest period cannot be attributed to the treatment in any simple way. Instead, a host of plausible hypotheses that rival the one that the treatment caused the effect must be painstakingly eliminated before a causal relationship can be said to exist between the treatment and the effect. When gender of respondent is studied as an "independent" variable, it is incumbent upon the investigator to adduce established scientific laws, research evidence, logic, and common sense to make the case that gender, and not any of the ubiquitous factors to be discussed below, "caused" the effect.

Cook and Campbell (1979), guided by their own extensive research experience and substantive readings in social science and philosophy, have compiled the following list of plausible factors, other than the independent variables, that can affect dependent measures. All of the following major threats to the internal validity of an experiment are eliminated when random assignment to conditions is correctly carried out and maintained throughout the experiment; they may, however, operate to reduce the interpretability of many quasi-experiments, including all studies that compare males and females:

- *History.* This is a threat when an effect might be due to an event that takes place between the pretest and posttest other than the treatment. These extraneous events are much more likely to occur in field research than in laboratory settings.
- *Maturation.* This is a threat when an effect might be due to respondents growing older, wiser, more experienced, and so on between the pretest and the posttest periods, when this development is not the variable of interest.
- *Testing.* This is a threat when the effect might be the result of repeated testing. Respondents may become more proficient over time as they become more familiar with the test.
- *Instrumentation.* This is a threat when an effect might be due to a change in the measuring instrument or data-gathering technique between pretest and posttest and not to the treatment.

- *Regression to the mean.* This is a threat due to a particular statistical artifact rather than to the treatment. The statistical artifact is most likely to operate when respondents are selected on the basis of extremely high or low pretest scores. Extreme scores are likely to contain more error than scores closer to the mean and are thus more likely than other scores to "regress" to the mean in a subsequent test. This regression can appear to be a treatment effect.
- *Selection.* This is the most pervasive threat of all to valid inference in quasi-experiments. It operates when an effect may be due to preexisting differences among groups rather than the treatment.
- *Mortality.* This is a threat when an effect may be due to different rates of attrition in treatment and control groups.

"Interactions with selection" threaten validity when any of the foregoing factors interact with selection to produce forces that might spuriously appear as treatment effects.

Males and females are inherently nonequivalent groups that can be expected to differ considerably on life experiences, rates of development, familiarity with stimuli, pretest scores, and so on. Thus, these threats to internal validity commonly operate in studies where males and females are compared and make it difficult to conclude that it was gender alone (leaving aside the issue of identifying what aspect of gender it was) that caused the effect.

Generally, the interpretability of quasi-experimental designs depends upon two factors: how the treatment and control groups are selected and the pattern of the results.

In general, the closer the selection process is to random assignment—the more haphazard the selection process—the stronger the interpretability of the design.

When treatment groups are formed using preexisting, intact groups or, more troublesome still, when respondents are permitted to select themselves into or out of treatment groups, the chances are good that variations among respondents other than the treatment account for posttest differences. The pattern of results, especially when interaction effects are studied, enables the investigator to rule out many of the threats to internal validity that may seem implausible given known features of the sample or well-established scientific laws concerning, for instance, the effects of maturation, statistical regression, and so on.

Two of the most common quasi-experimental designs—and potentially the strongest—are the multiple time-series design and the nonequivalent control group design with pretest and posttest periods. In the nonequivalent control group design, the existence of pretests enables the investigator to identify and address the probable preexisting differences between groups. The inclusion of a well-chosen comparison group can help rule out many threats to internal validity. The multiple time-series design is highly similar to the nonequivalent control group design but improves upon it by featuring many pretest and posttest measures for both the treatment and comparison groups. These added observations help investigators assess and rule out threats like history, maturation, statistical regression, and testing with greater confidence than they would have if only a single pretest and posttest measure were available.

If true experiments reign in the laboratory, quasi-experiments are often carried out in real-world settings where the investigator does not have full control over the means of assignment to treatment conditions, the implementation of the treatment, or the collection of the data. Clearly, quasi-experiments often represent a compromise between the investigator's desire to exercise control over the independent and dependent variables and the practical constraints of the external environment. Despite their methodological disadvantages relative to true experiments in achieving high internal validity, quasi-experiments are often less contrived, obtrusive, and reactive than true experiments and may possess higher construct and external validity.

However appealing the relative "naturalness" of quasi-experiments is to many feminist researchers, it bears remembering that more evidence in support of sex-role stereotypes and gender differences has been found in field settings than in the laboratory, where confounded variables can be teased apart. Even the strongest quasi-experiments, those that employ similar comparison groups and feature pretests and posttests, require tremendous caution in their interpretation.

Passive Observational Methods

Passive observational methods, sometimes known as correlational designs, are ones in which the investigator neither designs nor controls the "treatment" but merely measures it. Without any control over the independent variable, a potentially limitless number of factors may vary with the variable of interest. As deficient as these designs generally are for probing causal questions, they undeniably have their place in the social sciences for generating research hypotheses and, in their more recent, sophisticated forms, can shed some light on causal relationships.

Passive observational methods are most appropriate when the variables of interest profoundly affect people—for example, unemployment, bereavement, alcoholism, home ownership, or inheriting a fortune. Clearly, it is unthinkable on ethical and practical grounds for a researcher to manipulate such events. Further, when exploring a new area of study, passive observation can generate rich hypotheses for future research. Many programs of research are launched with correlational designs that suggest what variables and levels of variables and interactions will be useful to probe in future investigations. These techniques are also indicated when the researcher seeks to establish a relationship among variables and intends to measure the strength of that relationship but is relatively unconcerned with demonstrating a causal connection among variables, as in certain kinds of forecasting.

The measurement techniques used within observational designs are not necessarily different from those that are featured in more controlled designs. There is a tendency for observational studies to rely more heavily than experimental designs on data-gathering techniques like category selection, self-report measures like surveys, interviews, and questionnaires, and the use of historical and archival records.

Feminist methodologists have long recognized and publicized how impressive the range and quality of information gathered through passive observational methods can be (Wallston & Grady, 1985, Sherif, 1987; Fine & Gordon, 1989; Gilligan, 1983). More sophisticated observational designs like cross-lagged panel and path-analytical techniques permit the investigator to probe questions beyond the simple standards in correlational analyses: Is there any kind of relationship between variables? How strong is the relationship? How well can we predict the value of one variable from the value of the other?

Regression approaches enable researchers to ask more complex questions of information gathered using nonexperimental designs: Can a simple rule be formulated for predicting one variable from a combination of others? If so, how good is the rule? Regression analyses are especially useful in applied research, where researchers need to predict future behavior or outcomes based on current available information.

Through the correlational technique of factor analysis, the investigator who is faced with a multitude of items that measure various aspects of a behavior, feeling, attitude, or belief can determine which items are highly intercorrelated and represent a single underlying construct. Factor analyses can be quite helpful to basic researchers who are interested in establishing the discriminant and concomitant validity of their theoretical constructs and to applied researchers working in such areas as survey and questionnaire construction, consumer psychology, and personnel selection who need to isolate the factors that underlie people's perceptions, attitudes, abilities, and so on.

Very recently, methodologists have shown how passive observational methods may be employed for the purpose of causal inference (Cook & Campbell, 1979; Boruch, 1983). The opportunity for exploring the direction of causality between variables exists when there are repeated measures of the same two variables over time. Sophisticated modes of analyses such as path analysis, causal modeling, and cross-lagged panel correlation can be applied to observational data when an adequate number of observations are available, and help the researcher infer which of all possible causal relationships among variables are more or less likely.

Operationalizations

Experimental Stimuli and Tasks

Males and females throughout the life span differ in the ideas, objects, and events to which they are exposed, the behaviors they are able to practice, and the reinforcements they receive in the real world. For these reasons, we can expect them to enter any experimental situation with different orientations, attitudes, perceptions, expectations, and skills. There is a growing body of literature suggesting that males and females in fact do respond to objectively "identical" stimuli differently, at least in part because the stimuli are more familiar, salient, relevant, or meaningful to one gender than the other (Jacklin, 1983). In most cases, the tasks and stimuli employed in psychological studies have tended to favor males and have served to reinforce sexist stereotypes.

One classic example of how differential experience with experimental stimuli can distort findings is provided by Sistrunk and McDavid (1971). They demonstrated that the research indicating that females are more conforming than males was systematically flawed because it was based on experimental tasks that were more relevant and familiar to males than females. Another is the reinterpretation of the literature on short-term persuasion and suggestion by Eagly (1983), who found no evidence for the widely cited finding that females are generally more suggestible than males. Eagly performed an extensive meta-analysis of the experimental literature in these areas and concluded that gender differences are largely due to formal status inequities by which men are more likely than women to have high-status roles.

Perhaps the most dramatic illustration of how differing interpretations of experimental stimuli by males and females can distort results was furnished by Gilligan (1982). She argued that the traditional conceptualizations of moral development offered by Piaget and Kohlberg reflect male experience and thought. Using a variety of research methods, she has shown that females perceive moral dilemmas quite differently from males and respond to different cues in making moral judgments. Her work seriously challenged the assumption underlying the tests of moral reasoning by Piaget and Kohlberg that there is a universal standard of development and a single scale of measurement along which differences can be designated as "higher" or "lower" in the moral sphere.

In this connection, Unger (1979) has written persuasively about the importance of ascertaining the meaning of experimental stimuli and tasks to respondents and the dangers of assuming that all respondents share the investigator's perceptions and assumptions.

As noted above, in the past decade the literature on sex-role research has forced a distinction between gender-of-stimuli effects and gender-of-subject effects. Up until recently, it was not uncommon that "male" versions of a test were offered to men and boys, and "female" versions to women and girls (Jacklin, 1983). Erroneous conclusions about gender differences were commonly deduced from these investigations. When different stimuli are presented to males and females, gender-of-respondents is confounded with gender-of-stimuli. Feminist methodologists have made the point that if the genders are to be compared, identical stimuli must be presented to both genders.

Gender of the Experimenter and Confederates

A common complaint among psychological researchers is that methods sections are typically so sketchily drawn that they rarely contain enough information about the study's materials, procedure, and context to permit replication or even a clear understanding of how extraneous variables may have affected the results. Among the information typically omitted in research reports are the gender of the experimenter and confederates and the gender composition of the sample as a whole or relevant subgroups of the sample. In this manner, researchers themselves refuse or fail to consider that these variables may affect the dependent variables, and they prevent others from making an independent evaluation of the operation of these variables. Such omissions seriously threaten the interpretability and generalizability of the research, as there is strong evidence that the gender of the investigator, confederates, and others in the experimental situation differentially affects the responses of males and females (McHugh et al., 1986). Whenever possible, multiple experimenters and confederates and varied, mixed-gender samples should be employed. In all cases, information on the gender of all participants in the research should be specified.

Single-Gender Designs

In their extensive review of the literature in the areas of aggression and attraction, McKenna and Kessler (1977) found strong evidence for gender bias in the operationalization of variables in single-gender designs. In aggression studies, for example, they found that male respondents were more often exposed to active or direct manipulations than female respondents. Whereas male respondents were frustrated, threatened, or treated in a hostile way in the experimental situation, females more often read vignettes that manipulated aggression less directly.

Dependent Measures

A pervasive gender bias in tests and measures has had a significant impact on entire areas of research. P. B. Campbell (1983) has indicated how sex differences can be created or eliminated through the selection of test items with certain forms and contents. After reviewing the research on gender differences in achievement and aptitude testing, Campbell concluded that girls do better than boys on problems with a stereotypically female orientation, like those dealing with human relationships. Boys, on the other hand, tend to do better than girls on problems with a stereotypically male orientation, like those on the topics of science and economics. Aside from item content, test format also affects the performance of males and females. Females tend to score higher on essay and fill-in-the-blank items than they do on multiple-choice items, whereas males do better on multiple-choice questions than they do on essay and fill-in-the-blank questions.

When data about feelings, attitudes, beliefs, social or moral judgments, or behaviors are obtained through self-report measures, it must be considered that males and females may differ on their willingness or ability to be candid (Campbell, 1983). P. B. Campbell (1983) has found that males are more defensive and less disclosing than females. Richardson and Kaufman (1983) note that males tend to present themselves as confident and self-assured when evaluating or predicting their ability, performance, or self-worth, whereas females tend to be self-effacing in these situations. These differences in response styles, which probably reflect gender-role expectations, strongly suggest that comparisons based on self-report measures should be cautiously interpreted and supplemented with comparisons based on other kinds of measures.

Data Analysis and Interpretation

Traditionally, whenever both genders are studied together, analyses of gender differences tend to be made—whether or not such differences are hypothesized or interpretable. In part because group differences are more interpretable and publishable than findings of no difference and partially because gender differences are more dramatic than similarities, gender differences are more likely to be reported, explained, and integrated into the literature than gender similarities. We have a large and lively literature on "sex differences" in psychology, but, as Unger (1979) notes, there is no parallel literature of "sex similarities" that seeks to integrate the innumerable studies in which no differences between males and females are found.

In fact, the most thorough, all-inclusive review of the cross-cultural literature on gender differences ever conducted has found strong evidence for very few gender differences (Maccoby & Jacklin, 1974). The work of Maccoby and Jacklin has gone far to dispel many popular myths about gender that have permeated bodies of literatures in psychology and to warn psychologists about the dangers of overgeneralizing gender differences.

Jacklin's (1983) vast experience in evaluating the extensive literature on gender differences has informed her perspective on a number of issues relevant to data interpretation. One concerns the meaning of the word *difference* and how misleading it can be. She notes that one of the largest gender differences to emerge in any body of literature is in the tendency to engage in rough-and-tumble play. Even in this case, 85 percent of boys are indistinguishable from 85 percent of girls. This finding speaks to the issue of the size and meaning of gender differences. With a large enough sample, virtually any mean difference between groups will achieve statistical significance. Even the few gender differences that appear to be durable over different peoples, places, and times rarely account for more than 5 percent of the variance (Deaux, 1984). These findings suggest that there is more variability within gender than between gender, how weak gender of respondent is as a determinant of behavior, and how important it is that researchers report the size of the effect along with comparison tests. Denmark et al. (1988) have cautioned psychologists against exaggerating the size of gender differences or drawing misleading implications from the results of comparison tests in their conclusions. These errors occur when it is suggested, for example, that females should be discouraged from careers in architecture or engineering because they tend to score slightly lower on average than males in tests of spatial ability or that females are less stable or rational than males when subtle performance variations occur with hormonal fluctuations. Other common errors in data interpretation occur when results based on one gender are generalized to both sexes. As noted earlier, this is routine practice with animal research, where, for example, threshold measurements in shock sensitivity for rats have been standardized for males only but are often generalized to both sexes (Denmark et al., 1988). A similar mistake is made when an investigator generalizes from a within-gender difference to a between-gender difference. For instance, if a significant correlation between two variables has been found for one gender but not the other, it cannot be concluded that a gender difference has been found (Jacklin, 1983).

Many feminist methodologists regard the number of variables confounded with gender as the most pervasive problem in interpreting gender differences (Unger, 1979; Deaux, 1984; Wallston & Grady, 1985; Eagly, 1987). As noted above, because males and females are "nonequivalent" at the outset of every experiment, any gender difference that may emerge at the end of the study cannot be attributed to gender per se without tremendous, explicit effort to rule out numerous plausible alternate explanations. In many cases, the males and females sampled in a particular study are drawn from very different populations with respect to the variables under study, especially when volunteers comprise the sample.

Even where gender differences exist, they have frequently been mislabeled in the literature. Many feminist writers have noted the tendency of researchers to assume that gender differences are biologically caused and immutable, although no evidence for either biological origins or inevitability may be presented (Unger, 1979; McHugh et al., 1986; Denmark et al., 1988). They argue that some gender differences may indeed be biologically determined but that the majority of studies offering such interpretations do not specify or measure the presumed causal genetic, hormonal, or physiological mechanisms involved. Frequently such studies rely in their interpretations of differences on "commonsense" notions of gender differences that incorporate popular myths, stereotypes, and prescientific notions of the origins of personality and abilities. Research reports that offer biological explanations for gender differences in the absence of solid evidence also tend to adopt simplistic models of human behavior, based on single factor causation. McHugh et al. (1986) note that most present-day researchers appear to believe that sex-related behaviors originate and are sustained in a context of interactions among biological, social, cultural, and situational factors. Behavior is multiply determined, and it is necessary on scientific as well as moral grounds to consider all possible causal factors—biological, social, cultural, and situational—even though not all variables can be explored in any one study and many are quite difficult to study using currently available research methods.

Among possible causal factors, the special status of biological variables and explanations of gender differences based on them cannot be ignored. Unger (1981) has noted that biological variables are regarded as having unalterable and pervasive effects on behavior, whereas social and cultural variables are seen as having more fleeting and limited effects. Because of the presumed prepotency of biology, those who attribute gender differences to biological factors bear the special burden of seeing their findings overapplied and misapplied over a broad range of social policy issues. Oversimplified conclusions regarding gender differences drawn from such studies can provide "scientific" justification for discriminatory policies that can seriously restrict individual opportunity throughout society. If we can conclude anything from the vast literatures on "sex differences," it is that males and females are more alike on virtually every dimension than they are different. Broad generalizations about gender differences bolstered by the simplistic notion that "biology is destiny" are simply unwarranted.

Finally, when gender differences are reported, value judgments are frequently made about the directions of the differences. Thus, male "rationality" is contrasted with female "emotionality," male "dominance" against female "submissiveness," male "independence" against female "dependence," and male "universal sense of justice" with female "amorality" or "particularity." In most instances, labels with such pejorative connotations are applied to females in the absence of any independent evidence that the behavior or trait being described actually exists or, if it does exist, that it is in any way dysfunctional, pathological, or problematic. The unspoken assumption underlying such evaluations appears to be that if the response is more often associated with females than males, there must be something wrong with it. There is much evidence to suggest that stereotypically male behaviors, attitudes, and values are more highly prized than their presumed female counterparts (Denmark et al., 1988). For example, high mathematical ability, which is regarded as a male strength, is valued more than high verbal proficiency, a traditional area of female superiority. The "male tendency" to control or hide one's emotions is widely seen as more adaptive than the corresponding "female tendency" to express one's feelings, despite the recent work in health psychology suggesting the health dangers of suppressing many emotions and the health benefits of ventilating one's feelings. Instead of permitting sexist or other biased assumptions about the value of behaviors to color their conclusions, researchers would do well to consider the adaptive features of behaviors or traits that have traditionally been viewed with disfavor.

Ironically, females whose responses are closer to the means of males in the sample than females are more often derogated for their nontraditional behavior than lauded for their similarity to the male ideal. Identical performances by males and females will earn males evaluations like "assertive" or "active" and females the more dubious labels of "aggressive" or "deviant" (McHugh et al., 1986). Perhaps one of the most misleading effects of these evaluative labels is that they encourage people to view males and females as poles apart on dimensions along which they hardly differ at all. Value judgments like these also ignore the complexity of human behavior and the context in which behavior takes place and have the effect of diminishing the responses of both men and women.

There continues to be a lively debate among feminist researchers about whether and how to analyze and report gender differences. Some champion routine testing for gender differences and reporting of findings, including failures to detect differences (Eagly, 1987; Rothblum, 1988). On the other hand, some (Baumeister, 1988) favor a gender-neutral psychology that neither studies nor reports gender differences. As Gannon et al. (1992) demonstrate, there is a growing trend within social and developmental subfields not to identify respondents' gender, let alone report on gender differences. Whatever one's position on the issue of the analysis and reporting of gender differences, or gender-neutral psychology, it seems to us that, at the minimum, the gender composition of the sample should always be identified. This will enable future scientists to use that information as they see fit.

IMPLICATIONS OF FEMINIST CONCERNS FOR THE TEACHING OF RESEARCH METHODS

The variable that divides people into males and females is surely one of the most fascinating and important, if enigmatic, that we will ever probe in psychology. As chronicled here and elsewhere, there are so many difficulties in attempting to study gender—and similar factors like race, age, and ethnicity—that most mainstream psychologists have chosen to ignore the study of gender differences and many even disparage efforts to do so (Unger, 1979, 1981). But it is difficult to imagine that an understanding of human behavior will progress when the most central psychological variables are systematically avoided. The kinds of questions raised in probing variables like gender, issues such as the role of values in science, and weighing the advantages of differing research methods will not disappear because they are difficult to address.

Just as many academic psychologists today avoid epistemological issues in their own research and writing, they tend to give short shrift to these topics when they train future scientists. The preponderance of time in courses on research methods and statistical analyses is spent teaching the nuts and bolts of conducting, analyzing, and reporting on simple true experiments in the laboratory. Almost no attention is devoted to the relationship between conceptual frameworks and research methods. When alternatives to true experiments, like passive observational methods, are discussed at all, they are generally compared unfavorably with the more tightly controlled approaches and portrayed as methods of last resort.

Many feminist psychologists have become increasingly concerned about the narrowly focused and distorted training available to students and young psychologists at both the graduate and undergraduate levels (Quina, 1986). Not only have they changed their own modes of considering problems and conducting research, but they have also changed how they instruct their students on the topics of epistemology, research methods, and statistical design. Central to their efforts is the notion that sexism, racism, and other conceptual biases have hobbled psychologists' understanding of the human experience. To that end, they attempt to foster students' awareness of their own everyday assumptions about the nature of reality and help them generate alternative and testable conceptualizations.

Paludi is a feminist psychologist who has successfully restructured graduate and undergraduate statistics and research methods courses along these lines (Bronstein & Paludi, 1988). She has altered both the form and the content of her courses to convey better the range of perspectives and methodologies available to scientists. We will draw extensively from her work to illustrate what alternative courses might look like.

Even on the most superficial levels, alternative methods courses look quite different in their structure from conventional counterparts. Students may, for example, be seated in discussion rather than lecture formats, and instructors may function more as discussion leaders or facilitators than as lecturers. Because few textbooks in these areas have been written from feminist perspectives, feminist instructors often opt to assemble their own lists of readings to supplement or supplant standard texts in these areas. Reading lists for courses like these often consist of numerous primary sources, representing a much broader range of topics and perspectives than is ordinarily offered to students in more traditional courses. For example, in a research methods course, journal articles on the nature and limits of psychological knowledge, ethics and values in science, and the differences between qualitative and quantitative ways of knowing may appear on reading lists alongside more conventional offerings on how to write the method section of a research report. Such articles can be analyzed in a discussion group where students take on the roles of advocates or critics of the various points of view.

To enhance students' understanding of some knotty methodological issues, a series of classroom or homework exercises or small research projects can be designed. In-class exercises can give students a first-hand sense of how variables like gender of experimenter, gender of stimuli, or others discussed here can operate to affect results. Students can be asked to respond to vignettes like those developed by Bronstein and Paludi (1988), in which the gender (race, age, level of disability, and so on) of the target person is varied, providing students with a clear demonstration of their own stereotypes and encouraging them to acknowledge their own biases. Gender-of-stimuli manipulations can be contrasted with parallel gender-of-respondent manipulations to illustrate the effects of gender role expectations. Similarly, the effects of other demand characteristics as they operate in laboratory (and some field) settings can be demonstrated in classroom exercises.

In statistics courses, an illuminating assignment requires students to vary the ways in which they report a set of data, to see how mode of presentation influences how results are interpreted. Encouraging students to present results in multiple modes—in graphs, tables, and words—and to apply more than one statistical test to the same numbers can help put a data set in perspective. These exercises can fuel the debate on whether statistics do in fact "lie." P. B. Campbell (1988) shows how easy it is to generate data sets where observers are apt to "see" gender differences in a table, but not in a graph, even when the numbers involved are exactly the same. Similarly, one can readily demonstrate how the type of statistical analysis used creates or obscures a difference. For example, applying an analysis of variance to a set of data supplied by males and females, students may find that a statistically significant gender difference emerges. If a regression analysis is applied to the same set of numbers, it will be revealed that respondents' gender accounts for less than 1 percent of the variance. Another way of helping students explore the meaning of similarities and differences is to induce them to consider the degree or percentage of overlap in the scores of two groups. Assigning students the task of graphing actual gender differences in skill competencies, for example, can demonstrate that the area of overlap—which is at least 90 percent even in cases of the largest gender differences—is far greater than the area representing group differences (Campbell, 1988). Most students who complete this assignment readily grasp the point that effect sizes are needed along with exact probability levels for readers to evaluate the real-world significance of any difference found.

For the laboratory sections of such courses, instead of focusing exclusively on the design and reporting of a number of true experiments in the laboratory, students might receive a wider range of assignments that introduce them to different research methods. One alternate assignment might be to conduct an unobtrusive observation of a gender, race, or age-relevant interaction. These observations might occur in a real-world setting like a restaurant, supermarket, sports arena, or bus. In another assignment, students might be asked to conduct a content analysis of some aspect of popular culture like television commercials, comic books, and magazine ads for gender, race, or age-relevant material (Bronstein & Paludi, 1988).

Instructors who seek to integrate feminist and cross-cultural perspectives into methods courses have also given consideration to modes of evaluating and grading students other than traditional multiple-choice tests, which may offer a distorted view of what some students know. In her quest to fit the type of assessment to the material and the student, Paludi, for example, administers what she calls "problem sets" to students in methods courses. After a unit on a particular topic is completed, students are asked a number of long and short essay questions that may, depending upon the topic covered, require them to analyze journal articles as to the biases, ethical violations, and threats to internal, external, construct, and statistical conclusion validity or to comment critically upon justifications of the research hypotheses, research conclusions, and so on contained therein. These problem sets may be quite lengthy and assigned as take-home exercises, or shorter versions can be administered in class. Students may be assigned the reports to be analyzed or may choose research articles on their own, including their own work. In one problem set, Paludi asks students to outline and prepare lectures for their class on topics like the issues involved in follow-up and replication studies or the place of statistics in psychology. These thought-provoking and sophisticated assignments appear to have great educational value and engage the students in ways that more typical assignments clearly do not and may lead to the creative use of statistics as well as the kind of reflective psychology that so many of us seek.

This chapter, along with some others in this volume, may provide some sense of the content that alternative methods courses might offer. One of the major departures from conventional methods courses is the expanded perspective on the research process. Instead of concentrating so heavily on true experimental designs and a few quantitative modes of data gathering, alternative courses attend to all stages of the research process: the role of theory, the review of relevant literature, the formulation of the research question and hypotheses, the selection of a research design that is well suited to the question, the selection of research participants, data analysis, interpretation of the results, publication of the results, and their incorporation into the scientific literature. The sources of bias and error that can enter into the research process at all stages are discussed, guided by Unger's critical point that methodological biases can be traced to conceptual biases such as ideology, political loyalty, values, convention, and personal background.

It is important to stress here that instructors who take a feminist perspective do not disparage or overlook traditional experimental methods or seek to replace them with less methodologically rigorous designs. The unique virtues of the true experiment for probing causal questions guarantee it a central place in any methods course in psychology, regardless of who teaches the course or how it is taught. Nor do such instructors aim to convert methods courses to "psychology of women" courses by focusing only on gender-relevant issues. One of the great contributions of feminist methodologists has been to demonstrate how concerns about gender studies have illuminated many critical and unresolved issues for all social scientists, regardless of their subject areas.

It is also necessary to acknowledge that these approaches to teaching research methods are not always easy to implement. Many feminist instructors who attempt to make alterations in central departmental offerings like statistics or experimental psychology can expect to meet with departmental resistance. Even if they are granted the academic freedom to teach their courses as they wish, they will not readily find the materials, resources, or guidelines that can help them organize their courses. Instructors of alternative courses may spend more time in consultation with students than those in conventional classes because of the "accessible atmosphere" that so many exercises, demonstrations, discussions, and debates can create.

Many questions arise when we consider these and related changes in methods courses. Will students exposed to so many perspectives, techniques, and methods be overwhelmed and confused? If time is spent on such topics as formulating research questions and conducting literature reviews, will students be able to develop the skills to conduct true experiments? If methods other than experiments are taught, will students fail to develop the proper respect for the unique virtues of experiments? Of course, these and similar questions are empirical and should be addressed by research. It may well be the case, for instance, that students need more, as well as different, kinds of methods courses to grasp the kinds of issues raised here.

As difficult as it may be for many of us to contemplate major changes in core courses, there is evidence of increasing concern among educators that the conventional curriculum in psychology is failing our students (Hall & Sandler, 1982). Many of us who have taught traditional research methods courses are well aware of how poorly they prepare most students to conduct or analyze even the simplest experiments and what little enthusiasm most students have for performing experiments or pursuing research careers. We do not mean to suggest that traditional experimental courses are invariably sexist, ineffective, or unappealing to students or that methods courses taught from a feminist perspective have ready solutions to the many problems inherent in training psychologists. Rather, we maintain that if psychologists are determined to eliminate sexism in their research and teaching, acknowledge feminist perspectives, or integrate the new scholarship on women into the appropriate literatures, they must begin by changing the way they conceptualize, use, and teach research methods. Feminist instructors have made some intriguing and worthwhile suggestions along these lines.

We are unaware of any formal evaluations of what or how much students learn about statistical and research methods when they are taught in a nontraditional fashion or how students taught in alternative ways differ in their knowledge, skills, or attitudes from students taught in more conventional ways. We urge that such evaluations take place soon so that they may contribute to the debate on these issues. Meanwhile, our strong, if informal, impression, based on the unsystematic observation of students in nontraditional classes, is that such varied perspectives and pedagogical techniques may be uncommonly effective at engaging students in the research process: getting them to think creatively about research problems, building their confidence to criticize scholarly articles, and exciting them about the prospects of designing their own studies. Perhaps most importantly, these perspectives and techniques offer them far better prospects of conducting research that captures the authenticity and totality of their own experience.

CONCLUSIONS

In our extensive review we have attempted to provide a foundation for designing gender-fair research projects. We began our analysis with a brief review of past feminist critiques of scientific psychology and focused especially on three interdependent areas that have become of concern to feminists: (1) the role of values in science, (2) issues embedded in the language and conduct of science, and (3) a comparison of qualitative and quantitative methods of research. Our general view of research methods has been expressed in various forms throughout this chapter. That is, unbiased consideration of the research questions posed should be the ultimate arbiter of which methods and research strategies should be used.

Throughout this chapter we have referred constantly to the work of Denmark et al. (1988)—*Guidelines for Avoiding Sexism in Psychological Research.* This document encompasses the issues and problems in gender-fair research presented here. It provides specific examples of common avoidable situations and suggestions for minimizing and eliminating such bias. We hope that the guidelines will be seriously considered along with the information provided in this chapter in conjunction with planning research projects.

Finally, the major goal of this chapter was to offer a feminist perspective on the research process, from problem selection to the analysis and interpretation of results. Feminist methodologists will surely continue to challenge the nature of the truths we seek as well as our modes of pursuit. In so doing, they hold forth the promise of a more morally and scientifically sound discipline. We hope that the perspectives we have offered here will sustain this challenge and help to provide a psychology for all people.

ADDENDUM BY *FLORENCE L. DENMARK* AND *MICHELE A. PALUDI*

In a brief postscript to the above chapter, we will explore the progression toward gender-fair research in the 21st century. New references after the publication of the Rabinowitz and Sechzer chapter in 1993 continue to emphasize the need for theorists and experimenters to evaluate various aspects of the research process, including question formulation, literature reviews, measurement tools and techniques, sample selection, and research designs, as well as data analysis and interpretation. The guidelines offered by McHugh, Koeske, and Frieze (1986); Denmark, Russo, Frieze, and Sechzer (1988); Landrine, Klonoff, and Brown-Collins (1995); and Halpern (1995) have paved the way for an alternative approach to the study of human behavior and other related fields such as biomedicine and health.

Indeed, psychologists have improved their research practices in response to such criticisms. Specifically, there has been an increase in the prevalence of female researchers and a decrease in the number of all-male samples, and research is more likely to be reported using nonsexist language (Denmark, Rabinowitz, & Sechzer, 2005). Despite this progress, there is still much room for significant improvement with regard to the conduct of nonsexist research in various fields.

Some feminist researchers propose that the utilization of more innovative research methodologies will aid in establishing a less gender-biased arena in the field of psychology. One example proposed by Kimmel and Crawford (2001) involves moving away from tightly controlled laboratory experiments that manipulate independent variables to determine changes in dependent variables, emphasize objectification and dehumanization, and often fail to study people in their natural environments. Several feminist researchers propose the following alternatives (Tolman & Szalacha, 1999):

1. Devote specific attention to women's issues.
2. Conduct research that focuses on and empowers women thereby eliminating inequities.
3. Observe individuals in their natural environment in an attempt to understand how they experience their everyday lives as an alternative to manipulating people or conditions.
4. Avoid thinking simplistically in terms of the causal relationship between two variables and conceptualize the relationship in an interactive, mutually influential way.
5. Consider innovative methods for studying human behavior.

With regard to innovative methods, Kimmel and Crawford (2001) suggest the use of focus groups whereby women gather to discuss a predetermined topic. This would create an opportunity for researchers to evaluate the social context in which women make meaning of their experiences and gather data based on the information that is revealed. Another example involves the use of qualitative methods that include semistructured interviews in which participants respond to open-ended questions that are tape-recorded and transcribed. It is important to note that feminist research and gender-fair research diverge on several issues, but the former can inform researchers on how to achieve the latter.

A primary focus in the progression toward gender-fair research is the exploration of topics that are of interest to or influence women. On the psychological forefront, topics such as emotional intelligence and female victimization (i.e., intimate partner violence, rape, and sexual exploitation) have received significantly more attention in the past decade. In the medicinal field, the implementation of the Women's Health Equity Act in 1990 mandated the use of women in clinical trials and called for the establishment of the Office of Research on Women's Health. This legislation spurred the development of the first scientific journal dedicated to gender-based medicine in 1992 (the *Journal of Women's Health and Gender-Based Medicine*), which focuses on clinical care for women, as well as on research into medical conditions that hold greater risk for and are more prevalent among women (Society for Women's Health Research, n.d.). Specifically, the research on heart disease and breast cancer (which represent the leading causes of death for women in the United States) has increased dramatically in the past decade (Women and heart diseases, 2002). Overall, to foster the growth of gender-fair research in various fields, it will be important to continue devoting energy to investigating important topics that pertain to women's lives.

REFERENCES

Abramson, P. R. (1977). Ethical requirements for research on human sexual behavior: From the perspective of participating subjects. *Journal of Social Issues, 33,* 184–189.

Baumeister, R. F. (1988). Should we stop studying sex differences altogether? *American Psychologist, 43,* 1092–1095.

Blakeslee, S. (1988). Female sex hormone is tied to ability to perform tasks. *New York Times,* November 18, p. A1.

Bleier, R. (1984). *Science and gender: A critique of biology and its theories on women.* New York: Pergamon Press.

Boruch, R. F. (1983). Causal models: Their import and their triviality. In B. L. Richardson & J. Wirtenberg (Eds.), *Sex role research: Measuring social change* (pp. 215–248). New York: Praeger.

Brody, J. E. (1989). Personal health: Childhood sexual expression. *New York Times,* January 26, p. B9.

Bronfenbrenner, U. (1977). Toward an experimental ecology of human development. *American Psychologist, 32,* 513–531.

Bronstein, P., & Paludi, M. A. (1988). The introductory psychology course from a broader human perspective. In P. Bronstein & K. Quina (Eds.), *Teaching the psychology of people: Resources for gender and sociocultural awareness* (pp. 21–36). Washington, DC: American Psychological Association.

Buchler, J. (1955). *Philosophical Writings of Charles Peirce.* New York: Dover.

Campbell, D. T. (1969). Reforms as experiments. *American Psychologist, 24,* 409–429.

Campbell, P. B. (1983). The impact of societal biases on research methods. In J. Wirtenberg and B. L. Richardson (Eds.), *Methodological issues in sex roles and social change* (pp. 197–214). New York: Praeger.

Campbell, P. B. (1988). *Who's better? Who's worse? Research and the search for differences.* Washington, DC: U.S. Department of Education.

Carlson, E. R., & Carlson, R. (1960). Male and female subjects in personality research. *Journal of Abnormal and Social Psychology, 61*(3), 482–483.

Carlson, R. (1972). Understanding women: Implications for personality theory and research. *Journal of Social Issues, 28*(2), 17–32.

Cook, T. D., & Campbell, D. T. (1979). *Quasi-experimentation: Design and analysis issues for field settings.* Chicago: Rand-McNally.

Cook, T. D., & Leviton, B. F. (1980). Effects of suspiciousness of deception and perceived legitimacy of deception on task performance in an attitude change experiment. *Journal of Personality, 39,* 204–220.

Deaux, K. (1984). From individual differences to social categories: Analysis of a decade's research on gender. *American Psychologist, 39,* 105–116.

Denmark, F., Rabinowitz, V., & Sechzer, J. (2005). *Engendering psychology: Women and gender revisited* (2nd ed.). Boston: Pearson.

Denmark, F. L., Russo, N. F., Frieze, I. H., & Sechzer, J. A. (1988). Guidelines for avoiding sexism in psychological research: A report of the APA Ad Hoc Committee on Nonsexist Research. *American Psychologist, 43,* 582–585.

Eagly, A. H. (1978). Sex differences in influencability. *Psychological Bulletin, 85,* 86–116.

Eagly, A. H. (1983). Gender and social influence: A social psychological analysis. *American Psychologist, 38,* 971–982.

Eagly, A. H. (1987). Reporting sex differences. *American Psychologist, 42,* 876–879.

Eagly, A. H., & Carli, L. L. (1981). Sex researchers and sex-typed communication as determination of sex differences in influencability: A meta-analysis of social influence studies. *Psychological Bulletin, 90,* 1–20.

Ellsworth, P. C. (1977). From abstract ideas to concrete instances: Some guidelines for choosing natural research settings. *American Psychologist, 32,* 604–615.

Elms, A. C. (1982). Keeping deception honest: Justifying conditions for social scientific research strategems. In T. L. Beauchamp, R. R. Faden, R. J. Wallace Jr., & L. Walters (Eds.), *Ethical issues in social science research* (pp. 232–245). Baltimore: Johns Hopkins University Press.

Fine, M., & Gordon, S. M. (1989). Feminist transformations of/despite psychology. In M. Crawford (Ed.), *Gender and thought* (pp. 146–174). New York: SpringerVerlag.

Gannon, L., Luchetta, T., Rhodes, K., Pardie, L., & Segrist, D. (1992). Sex bias in psychological research: Progress or complacency? *American Psychologist, 47,* 389–396.

Gergen, K. J. (1973). Social psychology as history. *Journal of Personality and Social Psychology, 26,* 309–320.

Gilligan, C. (1982). *In a different voice: Psychological theory and women's development.* Cambridge, MA: Harvard University Press.

Gilligan, C. (1983). New ways of development: New visions of maturity. In J. Wirtenberg & B. L. Richardson (Eds.), *Methodological issues in sex roles and social change* (pp. 17–32). New York: Praeger.

Glass, G. V. (1976). Primary, secondary, and meta-analysis research. *Educational Researcher, 5,* 3–8.

Grady, K. E. (1981). Sex bias in research design. *Psychology of Women Quarterly, 5,* 628–636.

Hall, J. P. (1990). Lessons from the First European Congress of Psychology. *American Psychologist, 45*(8), 978–980.

Hall, R. M., & Sandler, B. R. (1982). *The classroom climate: A chilly one for women.* Washington, DC: Project on the Status of Women and the Association of American Colleges.

Halpern, D. (1995). Cognitive gender differences: Why diversity is a critical research issue. In H. Landrine (Ed.), *Bringing cultural diversity to feminist psychology.* Washington, DC: American Psychological Association.

Harding, S. (1987). Is there a feminist method? In S. Harding (Ed.), *Feminism and methodology* (pp. 1–17). Bloomington: Indiana University Press.

Harris, S. (1971). Influence of subject and experimenter sex in psychological research. *Journal of Consulting and Clinical Psychology, 37,* 291–294.

Jacklin, C. N. (1983). Methodological issues in the study of sex-related differences. In J. Wirtenberg and B. L. Richardson (Eds.), *Methodological issues in sex roles and social change* (pp. 93–100). New York: Praeger.

Jackson, G. B. (1983). Methods for integrative views. In J. Wirtenberg & B. L. Richardson (Eds.), *Methodological issues in sex roles and social change* (pp. 173–196). New York: Praeger.

Kayne, N. T., & Alloy, L. B. (1988). Clinician and patient as aberrent actuaries: Expectation-based distortions in assessment of covariation. In L. Y. Abramson (Ed.), *Social cognition and clinical psychology* (pp. 295–365). New York: Guilford Press.

Keller, E. F. (1974). Women in science: An analysis of a social problem. *Harvard Magazine,* October, 14–19.

Kimmel, E. B., & Crawford, M. (2001). Methods for studying gender. In J. Worell (Ed.), *Encyclopedia for women and gender* (pp. 749–758). San Diego: Academic Press.

Koch, S. (1981). The nature and limits of psychology and knowledge: Lessons of a century qua 'science.' *American Psychologist, 36,* 257–269.

Landrine, H., Klonoff, E., & Brown-Collins, A. (1995). Cultural diversity and methodology in feminist psychology: Critique, proposal, empirical example. In H. Landrine (Ed.), *Bringing cultural diversity to feminist psychology.* Washington, DC: American Psychological Association.

Lott, B. (1985). The potential enrichment of social/personality psychology through feminist research and vice versa. *American Psychologist, 40,* 155–164.

Maccoby, E. E., & Jacklin, C. N. (1974). *The psychology of sex differences.* Stanford, CA: Stanford University Press.

Mannucci, E. (1977). Potential subjects view psychology experiments. (Doctoral dissertation, City University of New York, 1978). *Dissertation Abstracts International, 38,* 3958B–3959B (University Microfilms, No. DDK 77–32059).

McHugh, M. C., Koeske, R. D., & Frieze, I. H. (1986). Issues to consider in conducting nonsexual psychological research: A guide for researchers. *American Psychologist, 41,* 879–890.

McKenna, W., & Kessler, S. J. (1977). Experimental design as a source of sex bias in social psychology. *Sex Roles, 3,* 117–128.

Paludi, M. A. (1986). Teaching the psychology of gender roles: Some life stage considerations. *Teaching of Psychology, 13,* 133–138.

Quina, K. (1986). Teaching research methods: A multidimensional feminist curricular transformation plan. Working paper No. 164. Wellesley, MA: Wellesley College Center for Research on Women.

Reynolds, P. D. (1979). *Ethical dilemmas and social science research.* San Francisco: Jossey-Bass.

Richardson, B. L., & Kaufman, D. R. (1983). Social science inquiries into female achievement: Recurrent methodological problems. In J. Wirtenberg & B. L. Richardson (Eds.), *Methodological issues in sex roles and social change* (pp. 33–48). New York: Praeger.

Rothblum, E. D. (1988). More on reporting sex differences. *American Psychologist, 43,* 1095.

Schlenker, B. R. (1974). Social psychology as a science. *Journal of Personality and Social Psychology, 29,* 1–15.

Sherif, C. W. (1987). Bias in psychology. In S. Harding (Ed.), *Feminism and methodology: Social science issues* (pp. 37–56). Bloomington: Indiana University Press.

Shields, S. A. (1975a). Functionalism, Darwinism, and the psychology of women: A study in social myth. *American Psychologist, 30,* 739–754.

Shields, S. A. (1975b). Ms. Pilgrims Progress: The contributions of Leta Stetter Hollingworth to the psychology of women. *American Psychologist, 30,* 852–857.

Sistrunk, F., & McDavid, J. W. (1971). Sex variable in conforming behavior. *Journal of Personality and Social Psychology, 17,* 200–207.

Smith, C. P. (1983). Ethical issues: Research on deception, informed consent, and debriefing. In *Review of personality and social psychology,* vol. 4 (pp. 297–328). Beverly Hills, CA: Sage.

Society for Women's Health Research (n.d.). Advocacy accomplishments. Retrieved January 15, 2007, from http://www.womenshealthresearch.org/site/PageServer?pagename=accomplishments.

Sterzi, G. (1988). Ethnicity, socialization, and academic achievement of Italian-American college students at the City University of New York. (Doctoral dissertation, City University of New York, 1988).

Tolman, D. L, & Szalacha, L. A. (1999). Dimensions of desire: Bridging qualitative and quantitative methods in a study of female adolescent sexuality. *Psychology of Women Quarterly, 23,* 7–40.

Unger, R. (1979). Toward a redefinition of sex and gender. *American Psychologist, 34,* 1085–1094.

Unger, R. (1981). Sex as a social reality: Field and laboratory research. *Psychology of Women Quarterly, 5,* 645–653.

Unger, R. (1982). Advocacy versus scholarship revisited: Issues in the psychology of women. *Psychology of Women Quarterly, 7,* 5–17.

Unger, R. (1983). Through the looking glass: No wonderland yet! *Psychology of Women Quarterly, 8,* 9–32.

Wallston, B. S. (1981). What are the questions in the psychology of women: A feminist approach to research. *Psychology of Women Quarterly, 5,* 597–617.

Wallston, B. S. (1983). Overview of research methods in sex roles and social change. In J. Wirtenberg and B. L. Richardson (Eds.), *Methodological issues in sex roles and social change* (pp. 51–76). New York: Praeger.

Wallston, B. S., & Grady, K. E. (1985). Integrating the feminist critique and the crisis in social psychology: Another look at research methods. In V. E. O'Leary, R. K. Unger, & B. S. Wallston (Eds.), *Women, gender, and social psychology* (pp. 7–33). Hillsdale, NJ: Erlbaum.

West, S. C., & Gunn, S. P. (1978). Some issues of ethics and social psychology. *American Psychologist, 33,* 30–38.

Wittig, M. A. (1985). Metatheoretical dilemmas in the psychology of gender. *American Psychologist, 40,* 800–811.

Women and heart diseases. (2002). *Journal of the American Medical Association, 287,* 3230.

Chapter 5

Meta-Analysis in the Psychology of Women

Janet Shibley Hyde
Shelly Grabe

The tradition of gender differences research has a long history in psychology, much of it predating the modern feminist movement and some of it clearly antifeminist in nature. In the late 1800s, for example, there was great interest in differences in the size of male and female brains and how they might account for the assumed lesser intelligence of women (Hyde, 1990; Shields, 1975). In the last several decades, the mass media and the general public have continued to be captivated by findings of gender differences. For example, John Gray's book *Men Are from Mars, Women Are from Venus* (1992), which argues for enormous psychological differences between women and men, has sold more than 30 million copies and has been translated into 40 languages (Gray, 2007). Deborah Tannen's book *You Just Don't Understand: Women and Men in Conversation* (1991) argues for the different-cultures hypothesis: that men's and women's patterns of speaking are so fundamentally different that they essentially belong to different linguistic communities or cultures. That book was on the *New York Times* best-seller list for nearly four years and has been translated into 24 languages (AnnOnline, 2007). Both works and dozens of others like them argue that males and females are, psychologically, vastly different. Yet as early as 1910, feminist researchers such as Helen Thompson Woolley wrote well-reasoned criticisms of the prevailing research.

A watershed book on psychological gender differences was Maccoby and Jacklin's *The Psychology of Sex Differences* (1974). Having reviewed more than a thousand studies, they concluded that the following differences were fairly well established:

1. Girls have greater verbal ability than boys.
2. Boys outperform girls in spatial ability.
3. Boys perform better than girls on tests of mathematical ability.
4. Males are more aggressive.

They also challenged the long-standing traditional emphasis on gender differences and concluded that some beliefs in gender differences were unfounded, including such beliefs as:

1. Girls are more social than boys.
2. Girls are more suggestible (imitating and conforming).
3. Girls have lower self-esteem.
4. Girls are better at low-level cognitive tasks, boys at higher-level cognitive tasks.
5. Boys are more analytic.
6. Girls are more affected by heredity, boys by environment.
7. Girls have less achievement motivation.
8. Girls are more responsive to auditory stimuli, boys to visual stimuli.

That is, they noted many gender similarities. In the past several decades, feminist psychologists have become increasingly critical of the gender-differences tradition in psychological research. For example, some have argued that the emphasis on gender differences blinds us to gender similarities (Hyde, 1985; 2005).

In an important theoretical paper, Hare-Mustin and Marecek (1988) distinguished between "alpha bias" and "beta bias" in research and conceptualizations in the psychology of gender. *Alpha bias* refers to the exaggeration of gender differences. *Beta bias,* in contrast, refers to the minimizing of gender differences. From a feminist point of view, either can be problematic. If differences are exaggerated, for example, the research may serve as a basis for discrimination against women, who are "different." If real differences are minimized or ignored there are dangers, too; for example, if the large differences in men's and women's wages are ignored, divorce settlements might not provide adequate or equitable support for women and children (Weitzman, 1985).

Shortly after Maccoby and Jacklin's groundbreaking work in gender differences appeared, the statistical method of meta-analysis was developed (e.g., Glass, McGaw, & Smith, 1981; Hedges & Olkin, 1985; Rosenthal, 1991). This method revolutionized the study of psychological gender differences. Meta-analysis is a statistical technique that allows the researcher to synthesize results from numerous studies, and thus it is an especially appropriate tool to apply to questions of gender differences. Moreover, because it yields quantitative results—that is, it provides a measure of the magnitude of the gender difference—it can overcome problems of both alpha and beta bias. Modern techniques of meta-analysis also provide a highly nuanced view of gender differences, detecting, for example, those situations in which gender differences are more or less likely to be found. This chapter reviews existing meta-analyses of psychological gender differences. Following an introduction to the methods of meta-analysis, we review gender differences in cognitive performance, social behaviors, and motor behaviors.

META-ANALYTIC TECHNIQUES AND METHODOLOGICAL ISSUES

Traditional literature reviews—what might be called *narrative reviews*—are subject to several criticisms. They are nonquantitative, unsystematic, and subjective, and the task of reviewing 100 or more studies simply exceeds the information-processing capacities of the human reviewer (Hunter, Schmidt, & Jackson, 1982).

The review by Maccoby and Jacklin (1974) represented an advance because it made use of systematic vote counting. That is, Maccoby and Jacklin tabled all available studies of gender differences for a particular behavior, permitting the authors and the reader to count the number of studies finding a difference favoring females, the number finding a difference favoring males, and the number finding no difference.

The method of vote counting, unfortunately, also has flaws (Hedges & Olkin, 1985; Hunter et al., 1982). Statisticians have pointed out that vote counting can lead the reviewer to false conclusions (Hunter et al., 1982). For example, if there is a true gender difference in the population but the studies reviewed have poor statistical power (perhaps because of small sample sizes), the reviewer is likely to conclude that there is no effect because a majority of the studies may find no significant gender difference (for a detailed numerical example of this problem, see Hyde, 1986).

Statistical Methods in Meta-Analysis

Meta-analysis has been defined as the application of "quantitative methods to combining evidence from different studies" (Hedges & Olkin, 1985, p. 13). Essentially, then, it is a quantitative or statistical method for doing a literature review.

A meta-analysis proceeds in several steps. First, the researchers locate as many studies as they can on the particular question of interest. Computerized database searches are very useful in this phase. In the area of psychological gender differences, researchers can often obtain a very large sample of studies. For example, for a meta-analysis of gender differences in verbal ability, we were able to locate 165 studies reporting relevant data (Hyde & Linn, 1988).

Second, the researchers perform a statistical analysis of the statistics reported in each article. Crucial to meta-analysis is the concept of effect size, which measures the magnitude of an effect—in this case, the magnitude of gender difference. In gender meta-analyses, the measure of effect size typically is *d* (Cohen, 1988):

$$d = \frac{M_M - M_F}{S_w},$$

where M_M is the mean score for males, M_F is the mean score for females, and S_w is the average within-sex standard deviation. That is, *d* measures how far apart the male and female means are, in standardized units. Using this formula, negative values indicate higher average scores for females and positive values indicate higher average scores for males.

In meta-analysis, the effect sizes computed from all individual studies are then averaged to obtain an overall effect size reflecting the magnitude of gender differences across all studies. From a feminist point of view, one of the virtues of the *d* statistic is that it takes into account not only gender differences (the difference between male and female means), but also female variability and male variability (*s*, the standard deviation). That is, it recognizes that each sex is not homogenous.

If means and standard deviations for each sex are not available, *d* can be computed from other statistics, such as a *t*-test or *F*-test for gender differences. When the dependent variable is dichotomous (e.g., child fights or doesn't) and nonparametric statistics are used, they too can be converted to the effect size *d*. (For an excellent introduction to statistical methods in meta-analysis, see Lipsey & Wilson, 2001.)

In the third stage of the meta-analysis, the researchers average *d* values obtained from all studies. They can then reach conclusions such as: "Based on 165 studies that reported data on gender differences in verbal ability, the weighted mean effect size (*d*) was −0.11, indicating a slight female superiority in performance."

Meta-analytic methods make it possible to proceed one step further, to analyzing variations in values of *d*, that is, in the magnitude of the gender difference, according to various features of the studies (Lipsey & Wilson, 2001). This step is called *homogeneity analysis* because it analyzes the extent to which the values of *d* in the set are uniform or homogeneous. If there are large variations in the values of *d* across studies (and there invariably are), these variations reflect inconsistencies among the studies, and it is the task of the meta-analyst to account for the inconsistencies.

The meta-analysis then proceeds to a model-fitting stage. Either categorical or continuous models can be used. If a *categorical* model is used, the meta-analyst groups the studies into subsets or categories based on some logical, theoretically informed classification system. Statistically, the goal is to find a classification scheme that yields relatively homogenous values of *d* within each subset of studies. For example, in an analysis of gender differences in mathematics performance, one would compute an average value of *d* for studies that measured computation and another value of *d* for studies that measured mathematical problem solving. Thus investigators can determine whether the gender difference is large for some kinds of mathematics performance and close to zero for others, or even if the direction of the gender difference depends on the kinds of mathematics performance assessed—perhaps females perform better on some measures and males on others.

If a *continuous* model is used in the model-fitting stage, the meta-analyst uses a continuous variable, e.g., age, to account for variations among studies in the effect size, *d*. Eventually, a regression model is fitted in which the effect size is the criterion variable and some relevant continuous variable or variables are the predictors. For example, in studies of aggression, age may be a good predictor of the magnitude of the gender difference (Hyde, 1984).

METHODOLOGICAL ISSUES

A number of methodological issues in meta-analysis have been raised. Certainly chief among these is an issue of interpretation: When is an effect size large? Because of the way *d* is computed, it is a statistic much like *z*, and values can exceed 1. Thus it is impossible to say, in any absolute sense, that a value of 0.90, or any other value, is large. However, Cohen (1969) offered the following guidelines: a value of $d = 0.20$ is small, a value of 0.50 is moderate, and a value of 0.80 is large.

Rosenthal and Rubin (1982) introduced another scheme for deciding when an effect size is large. They used the Pearson correlation, *r*, rather than *d*, but the two can easily be translated using the approximation formula $d = 2r$ (or the exact formula

$$d = 2r\sqrt{(1-r^2)}.$$

To assess the magnitude of an effect size, they use the binomial effect size display (BESD). It displays the change in success rate (e.g., recovery from cancer due to treatment with a particular drug compared with an untreated control group) as a function of the effect size. For example, an *r* of 0.30 ($d = 0.60$) translates into an improvement in survival from 35 percent to 65 percent. Thus, according to Rosenthal and Rubin, effect sizes that appear only small to moderate may represent impressively large effects.

We would argue, however, that impressive effects in curing cancer do not necessarily transfer logically to the study of gender differences. In the latter case, the binomial effect size display can tell us something like the following: An effect size of $d = 0.40$ means that approximately 40 percent of one sex falls above the median (40 percent are above average) and 60 percent of the other sex falls above the median.

Another approach to interpreting the magnitude of an effect size is to compare it with effect sizes that have been obtained in other meta-analyses, either for related studies in the same field or for studies in other fields. One could compare the effect size for gender differences in mathematics performance with the effect size for gender differences in spatial ability, for example. Or one might compare the effect size for social class or ethnic differences in math performance. Table 5.1 provides effect sizes for gender differences documented in numerous meta-analyses.

Another major methodological issue in meta-analysis concerns the sampling of studies and the potential for sampling bias. Ideally, the sampling procedure should be well defined, systematic, and exhaustive. A poor sampling procedure will produce misleading, if not useless, results. Even with good sampling procedures, however, problems can arise because studies that found significant effects are more likely to be published than those that did not. This biases the published results in the direction of larger effect sizes. In addition, investigators may not publish data that show large and significant effects that run counter to the zeitgeist, a tendency that would serve to maintain a status quo in the literature. One way of guarding against sample bias is to seek out unpublished studies. Doctoral dissertations and major national data sets such as the National Longitudinal Survey of Youth (NLSY) or National Assessment of Educational Progress (NAEP) are perhaps the best sources of unpublished data that may show nonsignificant effects or failures to replicate.

A final issue concerns the validity of meta-analytic research on gender differences. As Eagly (1986) points out, both the construct and external validities of the aggregated results of a meta-analysis are probably greater than those of most individual studies. However, threats to that greater validity do exist and cannot be ignored. To the extent that studies in the sample rely on similar measurement instruments or have other features in common, validity may be compromised. Examples are stimulus materials that inadvertently favor one gender over the other, samples that are unrepresentative of the population, and a preponderance of laboratory, as opposed to field, studies. Eagly (1986) recommended using meta-analytic techniques to assess the effects of those study characteristics.

Table 5.1.
Major meta-analyses of research on psychological gender differences

Study	Variable	Age	Number of Reports	*d*
Cognitive Variables				
Hyde, Fennema, & Lamon (1990)	Mathematics computation	All ages	45	−0.14
	Mathematics concepts	All ages	41	−0.03
	Mathematics problem solving	All ages	48	+0.08
Hedges & Nowell (1995)	Reading comprehension	Adolescents	5*	−0.09
	Vocabulary	Adolescents	4*	+0.06
	Mathematics	Adolescents	6*	+0.16
	Perceptual speed	Adolescents	4*	−0.28
	Science	Adolescents	4*	+0.32
	Spatial ability	Adolescents	2*	+0.19
Hyde, Fennema, Ryan, et al. (1990)	Mathematics self-confidence	All ages	56	+0.16
	Mathematics anxiety	All ages	53	−0.15
Feingold (1988)	DAT Spelling	Adolescents	5*	−0.45
	DAT Language	Adolescents	5*	−0.40
	DAT Verbal reasoning	Adolescents	5*	−0.02
	DAT Abstract reasoning	Adolescents	5*	−0.04
	DAT Numerical ability	Adolescents	5*	−0.10
	DAT Perceptual speed	Adolescents	5*	−0.34

	DAT Mechanical reasoning	Adolescents	5*	+0.76
	DAT Space relations	Adolescents	5*	+0.15
Hyde & Linn (1988)	Vocabulary	All ages	40	−0.02
	Reading comprehension	All ages	18	−0.03
	Speech production	All ages	12	−0.33
Linn & Petersen (1985)	Spatial perception	All ages	62	+0.44
	Mental rotation	All ages	29	+0.73
	Spatial visualization	All ages	81	+0.13
Voyer et al. (1995)	Spatial perception	All ages	92	+0.44
	Mental rotation	All ages	78	+0.56
	Spatial visualization	All ages	116	+0.19
Lynn & Irwing (2004)	Progressive matrices	6–14 years	15	+0.02
		15–19 years	23	+0.16
		Adults	10	+0.30
Whitley et al. (1986)	Attribution of success to ability	All ages	29	+0.13
	Attribution of success to effort	All ages	29	−0.04
	Attribution of success to task	All ages	29	−0.01
	Attribution of success to luck	All ages	29	−0.07
	Attribution of failure to ability	All ages	29	+0.16
	Attribution of failure to effort	All ages	29	+0.15
	Attribution of failure to task	All ages	29	−0.08
	Attribution of failure to luck	All ages	29	−0.15
Rosenthal & Rubin (1982)	Verbal ability	11 years and older	12	−0.30

(Continued)

Table 5.1.
Major meta-analyses of research on psychological gender differences (*Continued*)

Study	Variable	Age	Number of Reports	d
	Quantitative ability	11 years and older	7	+0.35
	Visual-spatial ability	11 years and older	7	+0.50
	Field articulation	11 years and older	14	+0.51
Communication				
Anderson & Leaper (1998)	Interruptions in conversation	Adults	53	+0.15
	Intrusive interruptions	Adults	17	+0.33
Leaper & Smith (2004)	Talkativeness	Children	73	−0.11
	Affiliative speech	Children	46	−0.26
	Assertive speech	Children	75	+0.11
Dindia & Allen (1992)	Self-disclosure, all studies	Not reported	205	−0.18
	Self-disclosure to stranger	Not reported	99	−0.07
	Self-disclosure to friend	Not reported	50	−0.28
LaFrance et al. (2003)	Smiling	Adolescents and adults	418	−0.40
	Smiling: Aware of being observed	Adolescents and adults	295	−0.46
	Smiling: Not aware of being observed	Adolescents and adults	31	−0.19
McClure (2000)	Facial expression processing	Infants	29	−0.18 to −0.92
	Facial expression processing	Children and adolescents	89	−0.13 to −0.18

Hall & Halberstadt (1986)	Social smiling	Children	5	+0.04
	Social smiling	Adults	15	−0.42
	Social gazing	Children	11	−0.48
	Social gazing	Adults	30	−0.69
Stier & Hall (1984)	Initiate touch	All ages	6	−0.09
	Receive touch	All ages	5	+0.02
Social Variables				
Hyde (1984, 1986)	Aggression (all types)	All ages	69	+0.50
	Physical aggression	All ages	26	+0.60
	Verbal aggression	All ages	6	+0.43
Eagly & Steffen (1986)	Aggression	Adults	50	+0.29
	Physical aggression	Adults	30	+0.40
	Psychological aggression	Adults	20	+0.18
Knight et al. (2002)	Physical aggression	All ages	41	+0.59
	Verbal aggression	All ages	22	+0.28
	Aggression in low emotional arousal context	All ages	40	+0.30
	Aggression in emotional arousal context	All ages	83	+0.56
Bettencourt & Miller (1996)	Aggression under provocation	Adults	57	+0.17
	Aggression under neutral conditions	Adults	50	+0.33
Archer (2004)	Aggression in real-world settings	All ages	75	+0.30 to +0.63

(*Continued*)

Table 5.1.
Major meta-analyses of research on psychological gender differences (*Continued*)

Study	Variable	Age	Number of Reports	d
	Physical aggression	All ages	111	+0.33 to +0.84
	Verbal aggression	All ages	68	+0.09 to +0.55
	Indirect aggression	All ages	40	−0.74 to +0.05
Stuhlmacher & Walters (1999)	Negotiation outcomes	Adults	53	+0.09
Walters et al. (1998)	Negotiator competitiveness	Adults	79	+0.07
Eagly & Crowley (1986)	Helping behavior	Adults	99	+0.13
	Helping: Surveillance context	Adults	16	+0.74
	Helping: No surveillance	Adults	41	−0.02
Oliver & Hyde (1993)	Sexuality: Masturbation	All ages	26	+0.96
	Sexuality: Attitudes about casual sex	All ages	10	+0.81
	Sexual satisfaction	All ages	15	−0.06
	Attitudes about extramarital sex	All ages	17	+0.29
Murnen & Stockton (1997)	Arousal to sexual stimuli	Adults	62	+0.31
Eagly & Johnson (1990)	Leadership: Interpersonal style	Adults	153	−0.04 to −0.07
	Leadership: Task style	Adults	154	0.00 to −0.09

	Leadership: Democratic vs. autocratic	Adults	28	+0.22 to +0.34
Eagly et al. (1992)	Leadership: Evaluation	Adults	114	+0.05
Eagly et al. (1995)	Leadership effectiveness	Adults	76	−0.02
Eagly et al. (2003)	Leadership: Transformational	Adults	44	−0.10
	Leadership: Transactional	Adults	51	−0.13 to +0.27
	Leadership: Laissez-faire	Adults	16	+0.16
Feingold (1994)	Neuroticism: Anxiety	Adolescents and adults	13*	−0.32
	Neuroticism: Impulsiveness	Adolescents and adults	6*	−0.01
	Extraversion: Gregariousness	Adolescents and adults	10*	−0.07
	Extraversion: Assertiveness	Adolescents and adults	10*	+0.51
	Extraversion: Activity	Adolescents and adults	5	+0.08
	Openness	Adolescents and adults	4*	+0.19
	Agreeableness: Trust	Adolescents and adults	4*	−0.35
	Agreeableness: Tendermindedness	Adolescents and adults	10*	−0.91
	Conscientiousness	Adolescents and adults	4	−0.18
Wood (1987)	Individual performance	Adults		+0.38
Psychological Well-Being				
Kling et al. (1998) Analysis I	Self-esteem	All ages	216	+0.21
Kling et al. (1998) Analysis II	Self-esteem	Adolescents	15*	+0.04 to +0.16
Major (1999)	Self-esteem	All ages	226	+0.14
Feingold & Mazzella (1998)	Body esteem	All ages	NA	+0.58

(*Continued*)

Table 5.1.
Major meta-analyses of research on psychological gender differences (*Continued*)

Study	Variable	Age	Number of Reports	d
Twenge & Nolen-Hoeksema (2002)	Depression symptoms	8–16 years	310	+0.02
Wood et al. (1989)	Life satisfaction	Adults	17	−0.03
	Happiness	Adults	22	−0.07
Pinquart & Sörensen (2001)	Life satisfaction	Elderly	176	+0.08
	Self-esteem	Elderly	59	+0.08
	Happiness	Elderly	56	−0.06
Tamres et al. (2002)	Coping: Problem-focused	All ages	22	−0.13
	Coping: Rumination	All ages	10	−0.19
Motor Behaviors				
Thomas & French (1985)	Balance	3–20 years	67	+0.09
	Grip strength	3–20 years	37	+0.66
	Throw velocity	3–20 years	12	+2.18
	Throw distance	3–20 years	47	+1.98
	Vertical jump	3–20 years	20	+0.18
	Sprinting	3–20 years	66	+0.63
	Flexibility	5–10 years	13	−0.29
Eaton & Enns (1986)	Activity level	All ages	127	+0.49
Miscellaneous				
Thoma (1986)	Moral reasoning: Stage	Adolescents and adults	56	−0.21

Jaffee & Hyde (2000)	Moral reasoning: Justice orientation	All ages	95	+0.19
	Moral reasoning: Care orientation	All ages	160	−0.28
Silverman (2003)	Delay of gratification	All ages	38	−0.12
Whitley et al. (1999)	Cheating behavior	All ages	36	+0.17
	Cheating attitudes	All ages	14	+0.35
Whitley (1997)	Computer use: Current	All ages	18	+0.33
	Computer self-efficacy	All ages	29	+0.41
Konrad et al. (2000)	Job attribute preferences:			
	Earnings	Adults	207	+0.12
	Security	Adults	182	−0.02
	Challenge	Adults	63	+0.05
	Physical work environment	Adults	96	−0.13
	Power	Adults	68	+0.04

Note: Positive values of *d* represent higher scores for males. NA means not available; article did not provide this information clearly. DAT means Differential Aptitude Test. *Based on major, large national samples.

Source: J. S. Hyde, 2005. The gender similarities hypothesis. *American Psychologist, 60*, 581–592. Reprinted with permission.

META-ANALYSIS AND GENDER DIFFERENCES IN COGNITIVE PERFORMANCE

Verbal Abilities

One supposed gender difference is in verbal ability. Hyde and Linn (1988) meta-analyzed 165 reports of gender differences in verbal ability, 120 of which reported data adequate for effect size computations. Three-fourths of the *d* values were negative, and the mean value was −0.11, indicating a slight female superiority. Homogeneity analyses revealed that *d* varied with type of verbal ability (mean *d* was −0.02 for vocabulary, 0.16 for analogies, −0.03 for reading comprehension, −0.33 for speech production, −0.09 for essay writing, −0.22 for anagrams, and −0.20 for general verbal ability). In light of these findings, Hyde and Linn concluded that the magnitude of the gender difference in verbal ability is "effectively zero" (p. 64).

Spatial, Science, and Quantitative Abilities

Linn and Petersen (1985) focused on spatial ability in their meta-analysis. They culled 172 independent effect sizes from their sample and assigned each of them to one of three categories of spatial ability. For spatial perception (defined as the ability to determine spatial relationships with respect to one's own orientation), they found a mean effect size of 0.44, indicating better male performance. For mental rotation, the value was 0.73. For spatial visualization (defined as the ability to perform complex, multistep spatial manipulations), it was 0.13. These heterogeneous results render as inappropriate all global statements about gender differences in spatial ability.

Linn and Petersen analyzed their data for age trends in the magnitude of the effect sizes. They wanted to assess the evidence for the argument that gender differences in spatial ability are biologically based because they emerge in adolescence. Their results did not support this hypothesis. For example, the mean *d* for studies of spatial perception in persons under the age of 13 was the same as the mean *d* for the studies of spatial perception in persons between the ages of 13 and 18 (in each case, mean $d = 0.37$). Of course, these results do not resolve the issue of the origin of gender differences in spatial ability because not all biological explanations posit a pubertal onset.

In a more recent meta-analysis of gender differences in spatial abilities Voyer, Voyer, and Bryden (1995) analyzed 286 effect sizes and reported an overall mean weighted *d* of 0.37, demonstrating gender differences in overall spatial abilities that favor males. Homogeneity analyses using the same categories employed by Linn and Peterson (1985) indicated that mean effect sizes for spatial perception ($d = 0.44$), mental rotation ($d = 0.56$), and spatial visualization ($d = 0.19$) were comparable or smaller. Voyer et al. further demonstrated that the reported gender differences were moderated by age. Specifically, effect size magnitude increased with age for each outcome: spatial perception ($d = 0.33$, under 13 years; $d = 0.43$, 13–18 years; and $d = 0.48$, over 18 years), mental rotation ($d = 0.33$, under 13 years; $d = 0.45$, 13–18 years; and $d = 0.66$, over 18 years), and spatial visualization ($d = 0.02$, under 13 years; $d = 0.18$, 13–18 years; and $d = 0.23$, over 18 years).

Hyde, Fennema, and Lamon (1990) meta-analyzed 100 studies of mathematics performance, assessing the evidence for the effects of gender, task, and age. Across studies of samples of the general population, they obtained an average value of −0.05, indicating a negligible female advantage. An analysis of age trends revealed that females outperform males in computation in both elementary ($d = -0.20$) and middle school ($d = -0.22$) and that males outperform females in problem solving in high school ($d = 0.29$) and college ($d = 0.32$). Hyde and colleagues also found an effect for sample selectivity, in that studies of highly selective or precocious populations produced the largest gender differences. Finally, they provided evidence that cognitive gender differences are getting smaller: the mean effect size for studies published before 1974 was 0.31, whereas the mean *d* value for later studies was 0.14. Hyde et al. argued that Maccoby and Jacklin's (1974) conclusion that "boys excel in mathematical ability" (p. 352) is oversimplified and is by now outdated. This meta-analysis used mathematics performance on standardized tests as the measure. If one looks instead at math grades in school, girls perform better than boys at all grade levels (Kimball, 1989).

Mathematics Attitudes and Affect

Hyde and her colleagues (Hyde, Fennema, Ryan, Frost, & Hopp, 1990) examined 70 reports of gender differences in mathematics attitudes and affect. The dependent variables included mathematics anxiety, mathematics self-concept, parental attitudes toward the child's participation in mathematics, and mathematics success and failure attributions. The effects on *d* of the age of the children, the year of publication, and the selectivity of the sample were evaluated.

Hyde and colleagues found mostly small effect sizes (more than half were one-tenth of a standard deviation or less) for all age groups combined. The one exception to this pattern was the stereotyping of math as a male domain. It yielded a large effect size (mean $d = -0.90$), indicating that males stereotype mathematics as a masculine activity more than females do. Homogeneity analyses revealed that this gender difference in stereotyping—as well as gender differences (that favored boys) in parents' and teachers' attitudes toward the subject's participation in mathematics—peaks in the high school years. The size of the gender difference in mathematics anxiety was associated with the selectivity of the sample: it was lowest in the highly selected, precocious samples (mean $d = 0.09$) and highest in the remedial and math anxiety classes (mean $d = 0.30$).

Regression analyses showed that male students reported more positive parental and teacher attitudes in the 1970s but that female students reported more positive attitudes in the 1980s and that the gender difference in stereotyping of mathematics as a male domain has decreased somewhat over time. The authors urged caution in interpreting the former result, however, because one cannot tell from the data whether the attitudes of significant adults had become more positive toward girls or more negative toward boys.

Overall, Hyde et al. concluded that gender differences in mathematics attitudes and affect are small—too small to account for women's underrepresentation in mathematics-related occupations (thus urging us to look elsewhere for an explanation), but not so small that they can be ignored (the cumulative effect of many small disadvantages for females may still be a powerful one).

META-ANALYSES OF GENDER DIFFERENCES IN SOCIAL BEHAVIOR

Aggression

Hyde (1984, 1986) meta-analyzed a set of 143 studies of gender differences in aggression. A mean d value of 0.50 was obtained for 69 general samples. Hyde found a significant age trend in the data, indicating that the gender difference in aggression varied inversely with the average age of subjects in the study. That is, gender differences in aggression were larger among preschoolers (median $d = 0.58$) and smaller among college students (median $d = 0.27$).

Using Hedges's (1982a, 1982b) homogeneity statistics, Hyde found that type of research design (i.e., experimental versus naturalistic), method of measurement (e.g., direct observation, self-report, parent or teacher report), and type of aggression sampled (e.g., physical, verbal) all produced significant between-category differences. The naturalistic/correlational studies yielded significantly larger gender differences in aggression than did the experimental studies (mean $d = 0.56$ versus mean $d = 0.29$). However, she did not find significant differences between studies of physical aggression and studies of verbal aggression.

At about the same time that Hyde's work appeared, Eagly and Steffen (1986) published a meta-analysis of gender differences in aggression that had been reported in the experimental social psychological literature. They restricted their sample to studies of persons 14 years of age and older (most were college-age samples) and to studies in which the dependent variable was a behavioral measure of aggression toward another person. These restrictions resulted in a fairly homogeneous group of laboratory and field studies in which relatively brief encounters with strangers were assessed.

The sample of 63 studies yielded 50 independent effect sizes for analysis. Across all 50 values, the mean weighted effect size was 0.29, indicating greater male aggressiveness. However, heterogeneity analyses revealed that the mean *d* was greater for the laboratory (0.35) than for the field studies (0.21) and greater for studies of physical (0.40) than psychological (0.18) aggression. They also found that the gender difference was larger for semiprivate than for public experimental settings (0.38 versus 0.17). Also of note is the fact that every mean effect size calculated was positive, indicating great consistency in the direction of the gender difference (even though there is clearly great inconsistency in its size).

As part of their effort to fit continuous models to their effect size data, Eagly and Steffen had 200 undergraduates rate brief descriptions of the aggressive behaviors described in the studies in their sample for (1) harmfulness to the target, (2) anxiety/guilt for the respondent, and (3) dangerousness for the respondent. The participants were also asked how likely they thought it to be that (1) they, (2) the average woman, and (3) the average man would enact the aggressive behavior. The group's responses to these six questions, scored for gender differences, were included in the set of predictor variables used in the regression-type analysis. The gender difference in the undergraduate respondents' assessment of how much anxiety/guilt and danger they would feel had they perpetrated such an act of aggression predicted the magnitude of gender differences. That is, to the extent that the women respondents reported that they would feel more anxiety/guilt and danger in that situation than the men reported they would feel, *d* was large. The results of this set of analyses were, by and large, interpretable within the framework of Eagly's (1986) social role theory.

Although the Hyde et al. and Eagly and Steffen meta-analyses have shown gender differences that are moderate in magnitude, the gender difference in physical aggression is more reliable and larger than the gender difference in verbal aggression. Based on a later meta-analysis of gender differences in aggression, Archer (2004) reported that indirect or relational aggression showed an effect size for gender differences of −0.45 when measured by direct observation (just 3 studies), but was only −0.19 for peer ratings (14 studies), −0.02 for self-reports (40 studies), and −0.13 for teacher reports (8 studies). Therefore, evidence is ambiguous regarding the magnitude of the gender difference in relational aggression.

Helping Behaviors

A meta-analysis of research on gender differences in helping behavior was performed by Eagly and Crowley (1986) that is as deeply rooted in social theory as is Eagly and Steffen's (1986) work on gender differences in aggression. Eagly and Crowley were able to cull 99 effect sizes from the 172 studies they found. The mean weighted effect size was 0.34, indicating greater helping behavior among men. This result seems, at first, counterintuitive, because helping is central to the female role. However, it is exactly what social role theory predicts. The key to understanding this result is an appreciation of the dynamics of the typical social psychological study of helping behavior (which was the only type of study Eagly and Crowley included in their sample). The studies examined relatively brief encounters with strangers, encounters that call for "chivalrous acts and nonroutine acts of rescuing" (p. 300). As Eagly and Crowley argued convincingly, these are exactly the types of helping behaviors that the male role fosters. The female role, in contrast, fosters caretaking and helping behaviors primarily in the context of ongoing close relationships, which are not assessed in psychologists' typical research.

The results indicated that the gender difference in helping behavior was larger (in the male direction) in off-campus settings than in the laboratory, when there were other people around to witness the act than when there were not, when other helpers were available than when there were not, and when the appeal for help was a presentation of a need rather than a direct request. The results indicated that larger effect sizes (again, in the male direction) were associated with gender differences in the undergraduate raters' reports of how competent, comfortable, and endangered they would feel performing the helping behavior. In other words, to the extent that the male undergraduate raters said they would be more likely to perform the helping behavior and feel more competent, more comfortable, and less endangered doing it than did the female, the behavior was associated with a larger gender difference.

As mentioned earlier, Eagly and Crowley also analyzed the target—or requester—gender effects. Across 36 values, the mean weighted effect size was −0.46, indicating that women received more help than men did. The correlation between the effect size for the target's gender and the effect size for the participant's gender was negative and significant, $r = -0.40$. Thus, not surprisingly, the study characteristics that related significantly to subject gender effect size (i.e., setting surveillance, availability of helpers, type of request) were also related to target gender effect size, though in the opposite direction. Further analysis of these data revealed that men were more likely to help women than men, but received help from men and women about the same; whereas women were equally likely to help men and women, but more often received help from men than from women.

Small Group Behavior

Wood (1987) focused her meta-analysis on gender differences in group productivity. She restricted her review to laboratory studies in which an objective measure of performance on the assigned task was used. The 52 studies she found were coded for whether group members worked on the task individually or together, how it was scored (for creativity, number of solutions, time to completion, number of errors, and so on), and whether it required task-oriented or social activity for better performance. Wood found that men outperformed women when working individually in same-sex groups (mean effect size of 0.38 across 19 values). She found no evidence of a gender difference in individual performance while working in mixed-sex groups (5 studies) and only a significant tendency for mixed groups to outperform single-sex groups of either gender (8 studies).

Wood's categorical model-fitting analyses (done only on the same-sex data) yielded just two significant effects. First, for the dependent measure of number of solutions, there was better male performance when group members worked alone (mean $d = 0.78$), but not when they worked together (mean $d = -0.05$). That is, men generated more solutions than did women when they worked alone in same-sex groups, but the two sexes generated equal numbers of solutions when they worked in groups together with other members of their own gender. Second, on tasks that require task-oriented behavior for good performance, men outperformed women whether they were working individually (mean $d = 0.25$) or together (mean $d = 0.34$), whereas on tasks that require social behavior for good performance, women performed slightly better (mean $d = -0.11$). Study variables that accounted for small, but significant, portions of the variance in gender effect size were male authorship and more recent year of publication: a greater percentage of male authors and more recent year of publication were associated with larger effects. Wood called for greater appreciation, in the workplace, of the specific facilitative effects of women's interaction style on group productivity.

Leadership Behavior

Eagly and colleagues, across several meta-analyses, have thoroughly reviewed the leadership literature. Eagly and Johnson (1990) evaluated gender difference in autocratic versus democratic (also known as directive versus participative) leadership style, as well as in task versus interpersonal orientation. The 144 studies in their analysis included laboratory experiments, assessment studies, and field studies in organizational settings. Because of their belief that, in real-life settings, male and female leaders are selected according to the same criteria, Eagly and Johnson predicted that they would find smaller gender differences in the field studies than in the other two types of reports. Their prediction was supported by their results.

Across all 329 effect sizes, Eagly and Johnson obtained a mean values of 0.03, indicating virtually no gender difference. They found similarly near-zero mean effect sizes across gender comparisons on interpersonal style measures, task style measures, and bipolar measures that assessed the two styles simultaneously. However, they found a more substantial gender difference for democratic versus autocratic style (mean $d = -0.22$), a finding that suggests women are more democratic than men in their leadership style.

When they looked at the three types of studies (organizational, assessment, laboratory) in their sample separately, Eagly and Johnson found strong support for their major prediction regarding field studies, as well as consistent evidence for a gender difference in democratic versus autocratic style. More specifically, across the effect sizes computed from the 269 organizational studies, they obtained mean values of 0.01, −0.02, 0.03, and −0.21 for interpersonal style, task style, interpersonal style versus task style, and democratic versus autocratic style, respectively. The analogous values for the 43 assessment studies were −0.25, 0.08, 0.04, and −0.29; and the values for the 17 laboratory studies were −0.37, 0.19, −0.12, and −0.20. Thus, with the exception of democratic versus autocratic style, larger gender differences were obtained in studies of persons who do not actually occupy leadership positions and who are evaluated in artificial and contrived settings. In these studies, men behave in a more task-oriented fashion and women, in a more interpersonally oriented one.

The tendency for women to lead in a more democratic way and men to do so in a more autocratic way, in contrast, is found across all types of studies. Indeed, the authors found that 92 percent of the gender comparisons on this dimension were in the stereotypic direction. Eagly and Johnson suggested that female and male leaders bring to their leadership positions a wealth of gender-based experience. Consequently, though they may be selected according to the same criteria, they are not equivalent persons. Eagly and Johnson also suggested that female leaders may attempt to placate their coworkers by asking for their input, in order to cope with continued institutional hostility toward women leaders. Lastly, although Eagly and Johsnon did not argue for the greater effectiveness of a participative leadership style, they did note the current trend away from rigid, hierarchical management practices, a trend presumably guided by that belief.

In a more recent meta-analysis examining contemporary leadership styles, Eagly, Johannesen-Schmidt, and van Engen (2003) reviewed research that compared women and men on transformational, transactional, and laissez-faire leadership styles. The meta-analysis of 45 studies found that, on average, female leaders were slightly more transformational than male leaders in their leadership ($d = -0.10$). Predicted gender-related differences were also found when the transformational and transactional scales of the Multifactor Leadership Questionnaire were broken down into their respective subscales. For example, it was found that women scored higher than men on the transformational subscale of Individualized Consideration ($d = -0.23$). Men scored higher than women on one of the transactional subscales, Management by Exception-Passive ($d = 0.27$), whereas women scored slightly higher on the Contingent Reward subscale ($d = -0.13$). Men also scored higher on laissez-faire leadership ($d = 0.16$). The overall comparisons on transformational leadership, as well as its subscales, show significantly higher scores among women than men, whereas men obtained significantly higher scores on management by exception and laissez-faire styles.

Interestingly, the authors found that the reported gender differences in leadership style were moderated by setting and publication year. In particular, the authors found the smallest differences in business settings ($d = -0.07$), as opposed to governmental ($d = -0.11$) or educational ($d = -0.21$) settings. Furthermore, when publication year was taken into account, findings revealed that the gender difference reported in transformational style has gone more strongly in the female direction in recent years. Over time, perhaps women have perceived less pressure to conform to a traditionally masculine style of leadership and have experienced more freedom to lead in a manner that they are comfortable with. However, the small effects suggest that although there are differences in leadership styles between women and men, they are not large.

Another rich area of research that examines gender-related differences in leadership is the investigation of the relative effectiveness of men and women who occupy leadership roles in groups or organizations. Eagly, Karau, and Makhijani (1995) reviewed 76 studies that compared women and men managers, supervisors, officers, department heads, and coaches. Effectiveness was measured by subjective ratings anchored by *poor* leader and *outstanding* leader. When all studies in the literature were aggregated, female and male leaders did not differ in effectiveness ($d = -0.02$). However, although the overall finding indicated men and women were equivalent in effectiveness, that generalization was not appropriate in all organizational contexts. In particular, follow-up analyses indicated that findings from studies that investigated military organizations differed from the rest. When military organizations were excluded from analyses, the weighted mean effect size indicated that female leaders were rated as slightly more effective than male leaders ($d = -0.12$).

The magnitude of the overall effect size also was moderated by the traditional masculinity of the role and the sex of the subordinates. Comparisons of leader effectiveness favored men more and women less to the extent that the leadership role was male-dominated and that the subordinates were male. Recall that if military studies are included there was no overall gender difference. The remaining small and insignificant difference is important because it suggests that despite barriers and possible challenges in leadership, the women who serve as leaders are in general succeeding as well as their male counterparts. Similarly, despite the meta-analytic findings reviewed earlier that suggest that female leaders appear to behave somewhat differently than male leaders, these findings suggest that they appear to be equally effective. Furthermore, even though the data suggest that men may excel in some areas and women may excel in others, there appears no empirical reason to believe that either gender possesses an overall advantage in effectiveness.

Because gender stereotypes may cause behavior to be interpreted differently for female leaders, the issue of leadership evaluation is also important. Eagly, Makhijani, and Klonsky's (1992) synthesis of 147 experiments that examined evaluations of female and male leaders whose behavior had been made equivalent by the researchers found that evaluations were less favorable for female than for male leaders, but the effect size ($d = 0.05$) was so small that a conclusion of no effect seems reasonable. However, the bias for female leaders to be devalued was larger in specific contexts. Female leaders were devalued relative to their male counterparts when they adopted equivalent leadership styles that were stereotypically masculine (i.e., an autocratic and directive style) as well as when their evaluators were men. In contrast, female and male leaders were evaluated favorably when they adopted equivalent leadership styles that were traditionally feminine (i.e., democratic or interpersonally oriented). The finding that devaluation of women in leadership roles was stronger when leaders occupied male-dominated roles and when their evaluators were men suggests that women's occupancy of highly male-dominated leadership roles produces a violation of people's expectancies about women. Male evaluators may experience female leaders as a more threatening intrusion because leadership is traditionally a male domain.

The authors also found that the tendency to favor men over women was larger when the dependent variable was the leader's competence or rater's satisfaction with the leader rather than the perception of leadership style. Thus, the measures that were more purely *evaluative* (i.e., competence or satisfaction) yielded stronger evidence of the devaluation of women's leadership. When specific leadership style was the moderator, two of three styles examined (interpersonal orientation and potency) did not produce gender differences. However, women were perceived as more task-oriented than men. This perception, contrary to what would be expected, may reflect a tendency to view women's behavior as more extreme when it conflicts with the female stereotype. The autocratic leadership style produced significantly more favorable evaluations of male than female leaders ($d = 0.30$), but only trivial differences were found for roles occupied mainly by men ($d = 0.09$) than for those occupied equally by men and women ($d = -0.06$). There was a greater tendency to favor male leaders in male-dominated leadership positions of business and manufacturing than in organizational contexts not involving business or manufacturing. These results highlight that men's styles may be less consequential in that their leadership is not questioned and they therefore enjoy greater latitude to carry out leadership in a variety of styles.

Nonverbal Communication

Stier and Hall (1984) reviewed 43 observational studies of gender differences in touch and obtained a complex and somewhat ambiguous pattern of results. Looking first at the direction of the findings, they found that 63 percent of the studies reported more female-to-male than male-to-female touching, 71 percent reported more female-to-female than male-to-male touching, 64 percent reported more touch initiated by females, and 61 percent reported more touch received by females. However, the average effect sizes associated with each of these four variables were all near zero (0.02, 0.00, −0.09, and 0.02, respectively). Stier and Hall also reported that the majority of studies found that females react more favorably to touch than do males, although they did not include an average effect size. Their failure to find clear-cut evidence for an asymmetry in touching behavior in opposite-gender dyads forced Stier and Hall to conclude that Henley's (1977) power hypothesis did not have a strong empirical base. They did, however, suggest a modification. Drawing on Goldstein and Jefford's (1981) finding that lower-status legislators touched higher-status legislators more often than the other way around, Stier and Hall speculated that touching may be more consistent with lower, rather than higher, status and reflect the individual's "strong desire either to redress the status imbalance or to establish a bond of solidarity" (p. 456).

In her review of the literature on gender differences in nonverbal communicative behaviors, Hall (1984) devoted a chapter to each of the following topics, quantifying the evidence wherever possible: interpersonal sensitivity and judgment accuracy, expression accuracy, facial behavior, gaze, interpersonal distance and orientation, touch, body movement and position, and voice. In her concluding chapter, she provided a table (table 11.1, p. 142) in which the average point-biserial correlations between gender and performance for 21 nonverbal behaviors are displayed. (To obtain a rough comparability of statistics, $d = 2r$.) Each average effect size is based on at least five independent studies, and, where they exist, separate results are reported for infants, children, and adolescents. The data indicate that women are better at decoding nonverbal communication ($r = -0.21$), recognizing faces ($r = -0.17$), and expressing emotions nonverbally ($r = -0.25$); that they have more expressive faces ($r = -0.45$), smile ($r = -0.30$) and gaze ($r = -0.32$) more, receive more gaze ($r = -0.32$), approach ($r = -0.27$) and are approached by others more closely ($r = -0.43$), and make fewer speech errors ($r = 0.33$) and filled pauses ($r = 0.51$); and that their body movements are less restless ($r = 0.34$), less expansive ($r = 0.46$), more involved ($r = -0.16$), more expressive ($r = -0.28$), and more self-conscious ($r = -0.22$). Surely it was this set of results that led Hall and Halberstadt (1986) to comment, two years later, "In sum, based on a literature of hundreds of studies, it appears that women occupy a more nonverbally conscious, positive, and interpersonally engaged world than men do" (p. 137).

In a recent meta-analysis of research on gender differences in smiling, LaFrance, Hecht, and Paluck (2003) analyzed 418 samples and found a moderate difference ($d = -0.41$), with girls and women smiling more. However, the authors reported that the observed gender difference was highly dependent on context: if participants had a clear awareness that they were being observed, the gender difference was larger ($d = -0.46$) than if they were not aware of being observed ($d = -0.19$). The magnitude of the gender difference also depended on age and culture. Gender differences were largest among adolescents ($d = -0.56$, 13–17 years), smaller among young adults ($d = -0.45$, 18–23 years), small during adulthood ($d = -0.30$, 24–64 years), and near zero after age 65 ($d = -0.11$). Interestingly, gender differences were largest among Caucasian samples ($d = -0.43$) and smaller and comparable among African American, Native American, Indian, Asian, Australian Aboriginal, or "mixed" samples ($d = -0.25$, -0.27, -0.37, -0.30, -0.22, and -0.34, respectively).

META-ANALYSIS AND GENDER DIFFERENCES IN PSYCHOLOGICAL WELL-BEING

Taylor and Hall (1982) conducted a meta-analytic review of 107 reports of the effects of masculinity and femininity on self-esteem, adjustment, ego development, and other measures of mental health. They carried out their analysis in the context of a theoretical reconceptualization of androgyny within the framework of a two-way analysis of variance. According to this approach, Bem's (1974) model of androgyny predicts a significant interaction, whereas Spence, Helmreich, and Stapp's (1974) model predicts significant main effects for both masculinity and femininity.

Across all 107 reports, Taylor and Hall found that the strength of the association between masculinity and mental health was stronger than that between femininity and mental health, both for each gender and for each type of dependent measure. For example, the average correlation between masculinity and adjustment was 0.53 for men and 0.31 for women, whereas the average correlation between femininity and adjustment was 0.05 for men and 0.04 for women. In addition, Taylor and Hall found that, of the results that addressed the issue, about half favored psychologically balanced individuals and half favored sex-typed individuals. Taylor and Hall concluded that the traditional notion that feminine women and masculine men embody psychological health clearly must be rejected and that the balance model of androgyny has minimal and inconsistent empirical support. Rather, they argued, for each gender, "it is primarily masculinity that pays off" (p. 362).

Wood, Rhodes, and Whelan (1989) conducted a meta-analytic review of 93 studies of gender differences in life satisfaction and well-being. They were particularly interested in the effects associated with marriage, which they predicted would be especially salutary for women. Because studies of life satisfaction tend to be done disproportionately on elderly and disabled persons, Wood et al. ran validation analyses on a subset of 18 studies with samples that were representative of the U.S. population. Across the 85 effect sizes that could be computed, Wood et al. obtained a nonsignficant mean value of −0.01. The mean effect size for the 18 representative samples was −0.05, again indicating gender similarities in well-being. Effect size varied with type of measure, but all were close to zero.

To assess the effect of marital status, Wood et al. used the percentage of the respondents in the sample who were married as a predictor variable in a regression-type analysis. The effect was significant and indicated that studies with a higher percentage of married persons obtained larger effect sizes favoring women. The validation analysis yielded the same result, and the general finding held for each type of dependent measure. Additional analyses revealed that marriage is associated with enhanced well-being for both men and women, but that this difference tends to be greater for women. Wood et al. accounted for this result within the framework of social role theory. They argued that women's social role is associated with greater emotional sensitivity, expressiveness, and skillfulness and that marriage and family life provide women with greater opportunities to fulfill their gender role of "emotional specialist."

Kling, Hyde, Showers, and Buswell (1999) used a developmental approach in their meta-analysis of studies of gender differences in self-esteem, based on the assertion of prominent authors such as Pipher (1994) that girls' self-esteem takes a nosedive at the beginning of adolescence. Kling et al. found that the magnitude of the gender difference did grow larger from childhood to adolescence: in childhood (ages 7–10), d was 0.16; for early adolescence (ages 11–14), it was 0.23; and for the high school years (ages 15–18), 0.33. However, the gender difference did not suddenly become large in early adolescence and, even in high school, the difference was still not large. Moreover, the gender difference was smaller in older samples; for example, for ages 23 to 59, *d* was 0.10.

Kling and colleagues also analyzed the magnitude of gender differences as a function of ethnicity. For whites, *d* was 0.20, whereas for blacks, it was −0.04. Therefore, the gender difference in self-esteem, which is small among whites, is nonexistent among blacks, calling into question supposedly well-known psychological "facts" that are based on white samples. In this meta-analysis, too few studies reporting data on self-esteem in other ethnic groups were available for analysis.

To assess gender differences in childhood depression Twenge and Nolen-Hoeksema (2002) examined 310 studies that assessed depression with the Childhood Depression Inventory (CDI; Kovacs, 1985, 1992) among children between the ages of 8 and 16. Moderator analyses suggested that the overall effect size of 0.02 was significantly moderated by age. Specifically, there were no gender differences in CDI scores between the ages of 8 and 12 ($d = -0.04$ with 86 studies); however, girls scored higher on the CDI starting at age 13 ($d = 0.08$). At ages 14 and 15, the differences reached 0.22 and remained significantly different at age 16 ($d = 0.18$). The authors further demonstrated that when all samples for ages 13 to 16 were combined (49 studies) the overall effect size was 0.16, suggesting that while gender differences in depression were not apparent during childhood, they were significant during adolescence. The finding that boys' depression remains relatively stable between the ages of 8 and 16, whereas girls' depression begins to steadily increase after age 12 supports the notion that gender differences in depression emerge during adolescence.

META-ANALYSIS AND GENDER DIFFERENCES IN MOTOR ACTIVITY LEVEL AND MOTOR PERFORMANCE

Motor activity level has been defined as an "individual's customary level of energy expenditure through movement" (Eaton & Enns, 1986, p. 19). It is conceived of as an important component of temperament and can even be measured prenatally (e.g., Robertson, Dierker, Sorokin, & Rosen, 1982). The single meta-analysis performed to date on gender differences in motor activity level was done by Eaton and Enns (1986). They evaluated 127 independent effect sizes taken from 90 different research reports and examined the effects of developmental factors, situational factors, measurement factors, and investigator factors on the size of *d*. It is important to note that in 90 percent of the studies included in the analysis, the mean age of the sample was 15 years or less. Consequently, the results of the Eaton and Enns work are not necessarily applicable to older persons.

Across all studies, Eaton and Enns obtained an average effect size of 0.49, indicating a higher activity level for males. However, they found small and significant correlations between d and subjects' age ($r = 0.26$), the restrictiveness of the setting where the measurements were taken (e.g., playground versus classroom; $r = -0.22$), and the inclusiveness of the measurement instrument used (e.g., a low-inclusive instrument would be one that measured arm movements, whereas a high-inclusive instrument would be one that measured whole-body movements and general activity level; $r = -0.28$). A multiple regression analysis indicated that larger effect sizes were found in studies of older (i.e., preadolescent and adolescent) youths whose behavior was assessed in nonstressful, unrestrictive settings and in the presence of peers.

Thomas and French (1985) performed a meta-analysis on 64 studies of gender differences in motor performance, from which they computed 702 effect sizes. Of the 20 motor tasks included in the analysis, 12 were found to yield age-related effect size curves. For eight of these tasks (balancing, catching, grip strength, pursuit rotor, shuttle run, tapping, throw velocity, and vertical jump), the relationship between age and d was a positive linear one; for the remaining four (dash, long jump, sit-ups, and throw distance), the relationship was a quadratic one (U-shaped). The eight tasks that did not yield age-related gender differences were agility, anticipation timing, arm hang, fine eye-motor, flexibility, reaction time, throw accuracy, and wall volley. For 18 of the 20 tasks, the mean effect size across studies was positive, indicating better performance by males. Most of these values ranged between 0.01 and 0.66, with the mean effect sizes for throw velocity and throw distance being much larger (2.18 and 1.98, respectively). Only the fine eye-motor and flexibility tasks yielded negative mean effect sizes (−0.21 and −0.29, respectively), indicating better female performance.

Thomas and French concluded that the data "do not support the notion of uniform development of gender differences in motor performance across childhood and adolescence" (p. 273). They argued that before puberty, the performance differences between girls and boys are typically small to moderate (d values of 0.20–0.50), meaning that many girls are outperforming boys. They further argued that these prepubertal differences are most likely the result of environmental factors (e.g., parent and teacher expectations and encouragement, practice opportunities, and so on) and not biological ones. Then, at puberty, the greater increase in boys' size and muscle development—combined with the continued and perhaps intensified environmental influences—results in a greater gender gap in motor performance that continues through adolescence. Evidence that female Olympic athletes have continued to close the gender-related performance gap on both the 100-meter dash and 100-meter freestyle swimming events suggests that gender differences in motor performance are highly responsive to environmental forces such as training and need not persist into adulthood (Linn & Hyde, 1989).

CONCLUSION

We believe that meta-analysis is a useful tool that can advance the study of gender differences and similarities, for several reasons:

1. Meta-analysis indicates not only whether there is a significant gender difference but also how large the difference is. Therefore, it can be used to determine which psychological gender differences are large and which are small or trivial.
2. Meta-analysis represents an advance over years of psychological doctrine stating that one could never accept the null hypothesis. We believe that some effect sizes obtained through meta-analysis are so small that the null hypothesis of no gender difference can be accepted (Hyde & Linn, 1988). We recommend that any effect size less than 0.10 be interpreted as no difference. This in turn will allow researchers to lay to rest some persisting rumors of psychological gender differences that are simply unfounded.
3. One of the most important trends in gender research today is the investigation of gender x situation interactions; meta-analysis permits some powerful analyses of this sort. Eagly's report of the situations that promote different patterns of gender differences in helping behaviors is an excellent example (Eagly & Crowley, 1986).
4. Meta-analysis can be a powerful tool to analyze issues other than gender differences. Examples include analyses of the role of androgyny and masculinity or ethnicity in women's psychological well-being (e.g., Bassoff & Glass, 1982; Grabe & Hyde, 2006). As a further example, feminist psychologists are increasingly interested in investigating the joint effects of gender and ethnicity; meta-analysis can be used here as well. For example, Hyde, Fennema, and Lamon (1990) examined gender differences in math performance as a function of ethnicity and found mean d values of −0.02, 0.00, −0.09, 0.13, for blacks, Latinos, Asian Americans, and whites, respectively.
5. Meta-analyses can be theory grounded and can be used to test theories of gender. Good examples are Eagly's application of social role theory in predicting patterns of gender differences in aggression and in helping behaviors (Eagly & Crowley, 1986; Eagly & Steffen, 1986).
6. Finally, meta-analysis can be used to test the Gender Similarities Hypothesis, which stands in stark contrast to the differences model that holds that men and women, and boys and girls, are vastly difference psychologically. The Gender Similarities Hypothesis states, instead, that males and females are alike on most—but not all—psychological variables (Hyde, 2005).

REFERENCES

AnnOnline (2007). Biography: Deborah Tannen. Retrieved February 14, 2007, from http://www.annonline.com/interviews/990310/biography.html.

Archer, J. (2004). Sex differences in aggression in real-world setting: A meta-analytic review. *Review of General Psychology, 8,* 291–322.

Bassoff, B. S., & Glass, G. V. (1982). The relationship between sex roles and mental health: A meta-analysis of 26 studies. *Counseling Psychologist, 10,* 105–112.

Bem, S. L. (1974). The measurement of psychological androgyny. *Journal of Consulting and Clinical Psychology, 42,* 155–162.

Cohen, J. (1969). *Statistical power analysis for the behavioral sciences.* New York: Academic Press.

Cohen, J. (1988). *Statistical power analysis for the behavioral sciences* (2nd ed.). Hillsdale, NJ: Erlbaum.

Eagly, A. H. (1986). Some meta-analytic approaches to examining the validity of gender difference research. In J. S. Hyde & M. C. Linn (Eds.), *The psychology of gender: Advances through meta-analysis* (pp. 159–177). Baltimore: Johns Hopkins University Press.

Eagly, A. H., & Crowley, M. (1986). Gender and helping behavior: A meta-analytic review of the social psychological literature. *Psychological Bulletin, 100,* 283–308.

Eagly, A. H., Johannesen-Schmidt, M. C., & van Engen, M. L. (2003). Transformational, transactional, and laissez-faire leadership styles: A meta-analysis comparing women and men. *Psychological Bulletin, 129,* 569–591.

Eagly, A. H. & Johnson, B. T. (1990). Gender and leadership style: A meta-analysis. *Psychological Bulletin, 108,* 233–256.

Eagly, A. H., Karau, S. J., & Makhijani, M. G. (1995). Gender and effectiveness of leaders: A meta-analysis. *Psychological Bulletin, 117,* 125–145.

Eagly, A. H., Makhijani, M. G., & Klonsky, B. G. (1992). Gender and evaluation of leaders: A meta-analysis. *Psychological Bulletin, 111,* 3–22.

Eagly, A. H., & Steffen, V. J. (1986). Gender and aggressive behavior: A meta-analytic review of the social psychological literature. *Psychological Bulletin, 100,* 309–330.

Eaton, W. O. & Enns, L. R. (1986). Sex differences in human motor activity level. *Psychological Bulletin, 100,* 19–28.

Glass, G. V., McGaw, B., & Smith, M. L. (1981). *Meta-analysis in social research.* Beverly Hills, CA: Sage.

Goldstein, A. G. & Jeffords, J. (1981). Status and touching behavior. *Bulletin of Psychonomic Society, 17,* 79–81.

Grabe, S., & Hyde, J. S. (2006). Ethnicity and body dissatisfaction among women in the United States: A meta-analysis. *Psychological Bulletin, 132,* 622–640.

Gray, J. (1992). *Men are from Mars, women are from Venus.* New York: HarperCollins.

Gray, J. (2007). *John Gray, Ph.D. is the best-selling relationship author of all time.* Retrieved February 14, 2007, from http://www.marsvenus.com/john-gray.php.

Hall, J. A. (1984). *Nonverbal sex differences: Communication accuracy and expressive style.* Baltimore: Johns Hopkins University Press.

Hall, J. A., & Halberstadt, A. G. (1986). Smiling and gazing. In J. S. Hyde & M. C. Linn (Eds.), *The psychology of gender: Advances through meta-analysis* (pp. 136–158). Baltimore: Johns Hopkins University Press.

Hare-Mustin, R. T., & Marecek, J. (1988). The meaning of difference: Gender, theory, postmodernism, and psychology. *American Psychologist, 43,* 455–464.

Hedges, L. V. (1982a). Fitting categorical models to effect sizes from a series of experiments. *Journal of Educational Statistics, 7,* 119–137.

Hedges, L. V. (1982b). Fitting continuous models to effect size data. *Journal of Educational Statistics, 7,* 245–270.

Hedges, L. V., & Olkin, I. (1985). *Statistical methods for meta-analysis.* New York: Academic Press.

Henley, N. M. (1977). *Body politics: Power, sex, and nonverbal communication.* Englewood Cliffs, NJ: Prentice-Hall.

Hunter, J. E., Schmidt, F. L., & Jackson, G. B. (1982). *Meta-analysis: Cumulating research findings across studies.* Beverly Hills, CA: Sage.

Hyde, J. S. (1984). How large are gender differences in aggression? A developmental meta-analysis. *Developmental Psychology, 20,* 722–736.

Hyde, J. S. (1985). *Half the human experience: The psychology of women* (3rd ed.). Lexington, MA: D. C. Heath.

Hyde, J. S. (1986). Introduction: Meta-analysis and the psychology of gender. In J. S. Hyde & M. C. Linn (Eds.), *The psychology of gender: Advances through meta-analysis* (pp. 1–13). Baltimore: Johns Hopkins University Press.

Hyde, J. S. (1990). Review essay: Meta-analysis and the psychology of gender differences. *Signs, 16,* 55–73.

Hyde, J. S. (2005). The gender similarities hypothesis. *American Psychologist, 60,* 581–592.

Hyde, J. S., Fennema, E., & Lamon, S. (1990). Gender differences in mathematics performance: A meta-analysis. *Psychological Bulletin, 107,* 139–155.

Hyde, J. S., Fennema, E., Ryan, M., Frost, L. A., & Hopp, C. (1990). Gender comparisons of mathematics attitudes and affect: A meta-analysis. *Psychology of Women Quarterly, 14,* 299–324.

Hyde, J. S., & Linn, M. C. (1988). Gender differences in verbal ability: A meta-analysis. *Psychological Bulletin, 104,* 53–69.

Kimball, M. M. (1989). A new perspective on women's math achievement. *Psychological Bulletin, 105,* 198–214.

Kling, K. C., Hyde, J. S., Showers, C., & Buswell, B. (1999). Gender differences in self-esteem: A meta-analysis. *Psychological Bulletin, 125,* 470–500.

Kovacs, M. (1985). The Children's Depression Inventory (CDI). *Psychopharmacology Bulletin, 21,* 995–998.

Kovacs, M. (1992). *Children's Depression Inventory Manual.* North Tonawanda, NY: Multi-Health Systems.

LaFrance, M., Hecht, M. A., & Paluck, E. L. (2003). The contingent smile: A meta-analysis of sex differences in smiling. *Psychological Bulletin, 129,* 305–334.

Linn, M. C., & Hyde, J. S. (1989). Gender, mathematics, and science. *Educational Researcher, 18,* 17–27.

Linn, M. C., & Petersen, A. C. (1985). Emergence and characterization of sex differences in spatial ability: A meta-analysis. *Child Development, 56,* 1479–1498.

Lipsey, M. W., & Wilson, D. B. (2001). *Practical meta-analysis.* Thousand Oaks, CA: Sage.

Maccoby, E. E., & Jacklin, C. N. (1974). *The psychology of sex differences.* Stanford, CA: Stanford University Press.

Pipher, M. (1994). *Reviving Ophelia: Saving the selves of adolescent girls.* New York: Ballantine.

Robertson, S. S., Dierker, L. J., Sorokin, Y., & Rosen, M. G. (1982). Human fetal movement: Spontaneous oscillations near one cycle per minute. *Science, 218,* 1327–1330.

Rosenthal, R. (1991). *Meta-analytic procedures for social research* (rev. ed.). Newbury Park, CA: Sage.

Rosenthal, R., & Rubin, D. B. (1982). A simple, general purpose display of magnitude of experimental effect. *Journal of Educational Psychology, 74,* 166–169.

Shields, S. A. (1975). Functionalism, Darwinism, and the psychology of women: A study in social myth. *American Psychologist, 30,* 739–754.

Spence, J. T., Helmreich, R., & Stapp, J. (1974). The Personal Attributes Questionnaire: A measure of sex-role stereotypes and masculinity-femininity. *JSAS Catalog of Selected Documents in Psychology, 4,* 43 (Ms. No. 617).

Stier, D. S., & Hall, J. A. (1984). Gender differences in touch: An empirical and theoretical review. *Journal of Personality and Social Psychology, 47,* 440–459.

Tannen, D. (1991). *You just don't understand: Women and men in conversation.* New York: Ballantine.

Taylor, M. C., & Hall, J. A. (1982). Psychological androgyny: Theories, methods, and conclusions. *Psychological Bulletin, 92,* 347–366.

Thomas, J. R., & French, K. E. (1985). Gender differences across age in motor performance: A meta-analysis. *Psychological Bulletin, 98,* 260–282.

Twenge, J. M., & Nolen-Hoeksema, S. (2002). Age, gender, race, socioeconomic status, and birth cohort differences on the Children's Depression Inventory: A meta-analysis. *Journal of Abnormal Psychology, 111,* 578–588.

Voyer, D., Voyer, S., & Bryden, M. P. (1995). Magnitude of sex differences in spatial abilities: A meta-analysis and consideration of critical variables. *Psychological Bulletin, 117,* 250–270.

Weitzman, L. J. (1985). *The divorce revolution: The unexpected social and economic consequences for women and children in America.* New York: Free Press.

Wood, W. (1987). Meta-analytic review of sex differences in group performance. *Psychological Bulletin, 102,* 53–71.

Wood, W., Rhodes, N., & Whelan, M. (1989). Sex differences in positive well-being: A consideration of emotional style and marital status. *Psychological Bulletin, 106,* 249–264.

Chapter 6

Courses in the Psychology of Women: Catalysts for Change

Michele A. Paludi
Linda Dillon
Tina Stern
Jennifer Martin
Darlene DeFour
Christa White

> *It seemed pure waste of time to consult those gentlemen who specialize in woman and her effect on whatever it may be—politics, children, wages, morality—numerous and learned as they are. One might as well leave their books unopened.*
>
> —*Virginia Woolf*

Virginia Woolf's sentiment about British universities in the 1930s can be used to describe the need for courses in the psychology of women in the United States: the discipline of psychology, like the academy itself, has been androcentric, focusing on men and coming from a male perspective. As Stimpson (1971) noted with regard to women, there have been three kinds of problems in the curriculum: omissions, distortions, and trivializations. For example, women's contributions to psychology have been hidden from view and devalued (Furumoto & Scarborough, 1986; Scarborough & Furumoto, 1987). Mary Calkins, for example, founded the psychological laboratory at Wellesley College in 1891, invented the paired associate technique, and created a theoretical perspective of self-psychology that brought her recognition in psychology and philosophy (Furumoto, 1980). Calkins was also the first woman president of the American Psychological Association in 1905. Nevertheless, her contributions have been essentially omitted (and trivialized) in the history of psychology. According to Stevens and Gardner (1982):

> Mary Whiton Calkins was a great psychologist; one of the few women recognized a such, and one who has been poorly treated by history.... Her major contribution to her science ... her invention of the experimental procedure she called the method of right associates, is now credited to someone else and even appears in textbooks under a different name than the one she has bestowed upon it. Her general theory of psychology, which she developed over so many years and which was so controversial then, is dismissed today as unscientific, inconsequential, or unoriginal. (p. 88)

Denmark's (1994) survey of psychology textbooks for their treatment of women and gender-related issues (e.g., feminist therapy, women and leadership) indicated the absence of citation of women psychologists in 20 texts. The number of students who aspire to a career in psychology and therefore take introductory courses is quite large. Psychology is among the top 10 most popular majors (Princeton Review, 2000). These courses are the critical points at which students explore basic vocabulary and concepts in psychology. If women psychologists' contributions and gender-related topics are omitted from such entry-level courses, women and gender-related concerns may not be subsequently questioned. Therefore, they will remain marginal, not central, to the field of psychology. As Denmark (1994) noted:

> Much of the psychology curriculum being taught is without a gender-balanced perspective.... I believe it is important that we present our students with material that is not biased in order that they may obtain an accurate view of the world and come to appreciate that society has been shaped by both women and men.... Part of our role as instructors is to make our students careful consumers of information, so that traditional female and male stereotypes can be eliminated. (p. 331)

Women's contributions to psychology have also been trivialized. Women psychologists have traditionally preferred person-oriented and service-oriented subfields of psychology rather than perception, learning, and motivation. These latter subfields, however, have been traditionally viewed as more prestigious than applied psychology. The androcentric privileging of specialties that are seen to fall in the "hard" sciences stems from the belief that experimental psychology requires greater intelligence and competence than social, clinical, school, or developmental psychology. This stereotype exists to this day. Courses in social psychology, developmental psychology, educational psychology, and the psychology of women are not typically viewed to be as rigorous as courses in learning, experimental psychology, and statistics.

Feminist scholars have found different topics worthy of study in psychology, as well as studying the more common topics differently. They have provided answers to a set of research problems that did not come to light in traditional androcentric disciplines and could not be solved by the androcentric paradigm, including rape, sexual harassment, battered women, sexism in health research, and sexism in psychotherapy. Feminist scholarship is generated by examining the disparities between individual experiences or perceptions and existing theory.

Feminist education is defined by the values reflected in the questions asked. Boneparth (1977) summarized the criteria used by the women's studies program at San Jose State University, which we can relate to courses in the psychology of women: Psychology courses need to look at new and old research about women, raise new questions that are relevant to women, question the silence of traditional disciplines about women, question the androcentric bias of traditional fields, raise questions about gender-role relationships, question basic assumptions about society, and encourage students and faculty to do research on women and to share it with others. Thus, a course in the psychology of women can help shift viewing the world from revolving around men to revolving around men and women jointly.

The Psychology of Women course proposes that the rules of the discipline of psychology be changed in order to correct the omissions, distortions, and trivializations of women and women's lives. The Psychology of Women course, like the field of the psychology of women, does not merely consist of a set of political biases. Courses in the psychology of women, like other women's studies courses, have been the academic arm of the women's liberation movement. As such, its goal has been both academic and political. We view the Psychology of Women course as a tool that seeks to inquire into the evaluation of concepts such as power, division of labor, and mental health that divide our world in two.

In this chapter, we discuss these goals of the Psychology of Women course, including incorporating emotional/personal learning, teaching traditional students, the inclusion of women of color, men students in the Psychology of Women course, and stages of feminist identity development expressed in the Psychology of Women course. We also discuss how the psychology of women can be integrated into other courses in the psychology curriculum. Our view complements that offered by Walsh (1985), who asserted that the Psychology of Women course is a continuing catalyst for individual, organizational, and societal change. We also share Lord's (1982) teaching-learning model that contains assumptions consistent with our learning objectives, our assumptions about how learning occurs, and our philosophy of women's optimal development. According to Lord:

- The course should be a laboratory of feminist principles.
- The traditional patriarchal teaching-learning model is dysfunctional in the development of healthy women and men.
- Every individual in the class is a potential teaching resource.
- Integration is imperative for the development of healthy, whole women and men. Therefore the course should foster mind/body integration as well as the integration of ideas and behavior, and thoughts and feelings.
- Effective human behavior in social interactions and within social systems is related to understanding the relationship between the personal and political.
- A Psychology of Women course should deal with women only and treat women as the norm.
- If at all possible, the primary coordinators of the course should be women.
- The subjective, personal experience of women and men is valid and important.
- The student should ultimately assume responsibility for her or his own learning and growth.
- Cooperation among students in pursuing learning objectives creates a more positive learning climate than does competition; cooperative learning is fostered through the use of criterion-referenced rather than a norm-references evaluation system.
- Providing vehicles outside the class through which students can deal with personal feelings and frustrations such as journals, dyads, assertiveness training, and growth groups enhances the quality of class discussions.
- The generic use of terms such as woman the female pronouns to refer to humans is an effective teaching-learning tool.
- Both men and women should be exposed to and have an understanding of the course material. However, a structure must be provided which allows women to meet with women and men with men for a significant portion of the time.

THE ACADEMIC CONTEXT: SUPPORTIVE FEATURES

While some of the challenges involved in teaching the psychology of women have been present since the course's introduction on college campuses in the 1970s, the context in which the course is taught has not remained static. Changes in the academic environment in the 21st century have added new dimensions to existing issues and goals in Psychology of Women courses. As compared to earlier decades, some changes have resulted in an academic atmosphere that is friendlier to the goals of psychology of women, while others have fostered a more hostile climate. Some current student-centered movements in higher education embrace and promote many of the goals that Psychology of Women courses and feminist pedagogy have espoused for decades. Such overlapping goals include centralizing diversity, embracing the affective as well as the cognitive, valuing students' experiences, and encouraging participatory learning.

It is significant that these movements differ from feminist pedagogy in their political and philosophical orientation in that feminist pedagogy specifically focuses on gender and power and these movements do not. However, insofar as an institution endorses or participates in these educational trends, Psychology of Women courses can capitalize on these movements to gain institutional support for their pedagogical approaches and, at the same time, they can help meet institutional goals.

The *Greater Expectations National Panel Report* (Association of American Colleges and Universities, 2002) called for reshaping the academy itself such that there is a change in emphasis toward being more student centered than teacher centered, empowering students, promoting student involvement in social justice, valuing cooperative education, and emphasizing diversity. Another initiative of the Association of American Colleges and Universities, "Making Excellence Inclusive," developed multiple reports (e.g., Milem, Chang, & Antonio, 2005) that focus on making the integration of diversity on campuses a core goal of institutional functioning.

The service learning movement also shares some of the goals of the Psychology of Women course. Service learning, which is now an option on most campuses, provides service opportunities for students. The movement, which distinguishes itself from volunteerism, recognizes that service and engagement are a valid source of learning, and faculty have the option of integrating a service learning component in their courses and awarding course credit for these experiences. The goal of engagement, participation, incorporating knowledge into students' lives, cooperative learning, and social action can all be addressed by students' participation in service learning (Wells & Grabert, 2004). Inclusion of a service learning component in the Psychology of Women course can help to meet the feminist goals of activism and student engagement.

As Washington (2002) stated:

> While community-based service learning is an effective tool for enhancing student learning in a setting, it is particularly useful for overcoming student resistance to feminism in general, and specifically to a feminism grounded in the theory of intersectionality. Well-designed and structured service-learning projects with community organizations whose missions are aligned to course objectives allow students to integrate theory with application, often with the result that students unlearn stereotypes and

> misinformation, gain new levels of social consciousness, and even develop a burgeoning sense of civic responsibility. (p. 181)

Based in the student-centered learning movement, another initiative focuses on students' emotional response to the material they learn, the affective side of learning. The cognitive-affective learning movement also supports feminist pedagogy and the aims of the Psychology of Women course (Ott, 2004). It supports diversity in that it values ways of knowing that are often neglected or denigrated by traditional pedagogy. Its focus is on holistic, active, constructive approaches to learning that move students away from passivity and from overvaluing the cognitive and rational.

THE ACADEMIC CONTEXT: OBSTACLES

While the movements described above support some of the goals of feminist pedagogy and the Psychology of Women course, other conditions in academia create challenges. Students have become increasingly conservative, less political, and more materialistic than in previous generations (Crawford & Suckle, 1999). They are individualistic and may fail to see the relevance of feminism to them and their lives. In addition, because of the assimilation of women's and gender courses into the curriculum, many students take the course not out of a feminist sensibility, but to meet a requirement (Crawford & Suckle, 1999). The result is that many students who lack interest in or support for feminist classes' values are present in courses like Psychology of Women. The increasingly conservative student body is living in an increasingly conservative political climate and learning in an increasingly conservative academic environment. The mood in academia can be hostile to courses like Psychology of Women (Crabtree & Sapp, 2003).

The backlash against feminist and multicultural courses and those who teach them include dismissive accusations of "political correctness" and, worse, allegations of control of academia itself by "left-wing professors." Such arguments have reached an apogee with recent events, including a newly released book entitled *The Professors: The 101 Most Dangerous Academics in America* (Horowitz, 2006). The inside cover reads:

> Coming to a Campus Near You: Terrorists, racists, and communists—you know them as The Professors. We all know that left-wing radicals from the 1960s have hung around academia and hired people like themselves. But if you thought they were all harmless, antiquated hippies, you'd be wrong.

A related development is the movement in several state legislatures to pass an "academic bills of rights." These bills are based on the publicized allegation that progressive, liberal faculty members are requiring students to agree with their ideology and are punishing students who hold different opinions from themselves. Such bills are intended to have a chilling effect on courses taught from feminist and multicultural perspectives. Faculty members who teach such courses risk disapproval from students, colleagues, administrators, and now, state legislators. Mild consequences for those teaching courses like Psychology of Women can include faculty isolation; extreme outcomes can include pay, rank, and tenure being jeopardized (Crabtree & Sapp, 2003).

This may be of particular concern for women of color faculty members. Their dual status in two undervalued groups may make them particularly vulnerable to both the mild and extreme outcomes. For example, African American women faculty are tenured and promoted less rapidly than white women and African American men. They are more concentrated in nontenure track jobs and lower ranks. Teaching "controversial" topics may put their careers are risk.

Finally, the very hierarchical nature of academia itself can complicate the teaching of Psychology of Women courses in a nonhierarchical fashion. Efforts to empower students and to reduce the power differences between students and teachers can be antithetical to the traditional classroom and the institution's expectations of the role of the teacher.

STAGES OF FEMINIST IDENTITY DEVELOPMENT IN THE PSYCHOLOGY OF WOMEN COURSE

Downing and Rousch (1985) suggested that students typically proceed through five stages when confronted with feminist issues: passive acceptance, revelation, embeddedness/emanation, synthesis, and active commitment. In the passive acceptance stage of development in the course, students may find themselves and others saying that discrimination is no longer present in politics, economics, the family, or education. They may believe that traditional gender roles are advantageous.

Student resistance has been widely discussed in the literature from many standpoints. Some feminists reject the notion of resistance as simply a different manifestation of teacher authority, since it is generally applied only to students who do not agree with the teacher (Lindquist, 1994). Others have developed models of resistance, identified its components, and hypothesized about its causes (Rhoades, 1999; Markowitz, 2005). Many of the approaches that address student resistance also meet other goals of the feminist classroom. While preventing or reducing student resistance, these techniques can also help create a learning community, equalize power in the classroom, legitimatize individual's experiences, and help students connect course content to their lives.

Students have many ways of resisting information that challenges their preconceived ideas and their privileged status. Kimmell (1999) identified numerous types of resistance and faculty responses to it. Types of resistance include silence, anger, denial, defensiveness, disagreement over teacher's role, acting out, victim blaming, lack of empathy, embarrassment, feeling dismissed, avoiding complexity, confusion, and giving low faculty evaluations. Some of the numerous faculty responses to it include focusing on classroom dynamics, turning challenges back on the questioner, setting ground rules for discussions, and encouraging students to tell their stories.

Stake and Malkin's research (2003) focuses on the role of alliances and cohesion in the classroom and reaffirms that relationships matter, even in the classroom. They found that a strong alliance between the teacher and student and high levels of class cohesion among students were strong predictors of student satisfaction in women's and gender studies courses. The absence of perceived student alliance with teachers related to perceptions of teachers as intolerant and biased, one of the often-cited criticisms of the feminist classroom and a source of resistance. Low levels of class cohesion were related to perceptions of other students as intolerant. The development of alliances with students and cohesion among them is a good preventative against resistance.

Crawford and Suckle (1999) asserted that resistance develops when students perceive that ideas are being imposed on them. Using collaborative teaching and learning processes allows students to become participants in the development of meaning and reduces resistance to the experience of imposed knowledge. Participatory learning is seen as a way to reduce resistance. Enns and Forrest (2005) recommend the use of student-generated discussion questions based on readings or experiences.

Crawford and Suckle (1999) utilized a student check-in system during the first quarter of the semester. They set aside time to discuss questions about process. Such questions ask about whether students feel heard, how they perceive interactions among students, and whether speaking time is shared or is dominated by a few students. They ask students to anonymously write one comment on a note card, then shuffle the cards and redistribute them to be read by other students. They also suggest weekly check-ins that ask students to respond to questions about topics students had trouble understanding, topics they agreed and disagreed with, and topics they would like to have discussed in class. Checking in with students builds rapport among students, empowers them, and alerts the teacher to strong reactions to material (Crawford & Suckle, 1999).

Some authors suggested that addressing students' expectations, preconceived ideas, myths, and stereotypes about feminism and the psychology of women reduces resistance. Rhoades (1999) asserts that resistance increases because students perceive feminism as antifeminine or unfeminine. Identifying the origins of such beliefs and their implications can help reduce resistance. In addition, making explicit the goals and expectations for the course—particularly the value of discussion, reflection, developing a community, including everyone, valuing student experiences, empowerment, valuing of feelings, and normalizing discomfort—can help reduce anxiety and resistance. Rhoades (1999) suggests that resistance is associated with negative or disturbing feelings such as these. Dealing with emotions and affect through student-generated discussions can help reduce resistance. Fisher (2001) defined feminist pedagogy as "teaching that engages students in political discussion of gender injustice ... to understand and challenge oppressive power relations and question the meaning for differently situated women of oppression and liberation" (p. 44).

Markowitz (2005) identified a relationship between simplistic, dichotomous thinking and student resistance. Emphasizing the constructed nature of knowledge, participatory learning, and the legitimization of personal experience can help to reduce students' use of simplistic moral dichotomies by giving them more ways to understand complex phenomena.

Some of the topics traditionally taught at the beginning of a Psychology of Women course (e.g., bias in research, the first generation of American women psychologists) prompt students to question these assumptions. They may never change their opinions about men and women, but they may start to question why they have held onto certain ideas for a long time in the face of contrary evidence.

Discussing issues related to women's lives commonly transitions students into the revelation stage. They begin to remember how they have been discriminated against because of their sex, race, age, or sexual orientation. Students start also to recall viewing magazine and television advertisements that connote women as sex objects. During this revelation stage, students may become angry with themselves because they hadn't previously noticed the sexism and racism in advertisements until the class lecture/discussion.

When students share their anger about these issues in class, they find themselves wanting to spend time with peers, sharing their experiences, asking how they have dealt with the sexism, and so on. This stage is referred to as the embeddedness/emanation stage. Students make comments in class that suggest they recognize the power imbalance between the sexes in the United States and in other cultures. Consequently, students will notice themselves in the active commitment stage. They want to take more feminist courses, conduct research on women's issues, and volunteer at battered women's shelters and rape crisis centers.

Thus, the content of the Psychology of Women course presents challenges to students. The course challenges students' long-standing beliefs and perceptions (Burn, Aboud, & Moyles, 2000). It asks that students question fundamental beliefs about science, truth, and value neutrality. Students are taught that knowledge is constructed and to question scientific methods, claims, and received knowledge. That science and history, as well as sociology and psychology, have developed within a context that is not value neutral is a novel and disturbing idea for many students (Paludi, 1996). As one woman student stated: "Women's studies opens up with question, and so ... that clicked for me.... That's really the biggest difference in women's studies and any other courses I've taken.... You question all the time, all the time" (Paludi & Tronto, 1992).

Learning information that is often missing from the media and their education, and questioning the "truth" of other long-held beliefs, can have many consequences for a student. Learning about some of the specific outcomes of sexism (e.g., the wage gap, economic discrepancies for educational achievements, gender discrepancies in housework, rates of and attitudes about sexual abuse) can be disheartening and discouraging; self-protective illusions may be shattered.

The content of the Psychology of Women course challenges students' beliefs that gender inequalities are a thing of the past, that received knowledge may not be as true or secure as they would like to believe, or that their realities may be a result of privilege rather than simple merit. How are students to integrate such information into their existing cognitive schemata and lives? Such information may separate them from friends and family or may cause them to feel they must make changes in their lives that they feel unprepared to or do not want to make. They may not be ready to relinquish the benefits of privileged status. They may become more cognizant of racism and sexism in their lives and in themselves. This knowledge can be profoundly disturbing.

While many of these outcomes are desirable insofar as they increase critical thinking and analysis, they also complicate the lives of students. Often students report feeling angry, sad, or overwhelmed when they begin to see more clearly and in greater detail the inequities in society. When some long-held beliefs or ideals are challenged, students can feel confused and betrayed. Dealing with these emotions and learning about empowerment can help address some of these reactions. However, first exposure to this material is often disturbing.

In addition to raising internal conflicts or confusion, disturbing emotional reactions to the material can occur between students. Such encounters can be disturbing to both students and teachers. A faculty member's preparation for and comfort level in handling such dialogues is crucial to the development of a positive class climate and to the progress of the course (Goodman, 1995; Paludi, 1996).

Teaching the psychology of women presents challenges that are numerous, complex, and difficult. While there are few certain answers and solutions, there are many offerings of suggestions, possibilities, guides, and a growing body of empirical evidence for addressing the challenges. The resources now available are numerous and substantive.

An especially important goal for the Psychology of Women course is to provide students with hope and empowerment. Classroom dynamics can be painful, the inequalities of reality disheartening, and the removal of self-protective illusions frightening. As Crawford and Suckle (1999) state: "Most simply, we can teach that change is possible.... We can offer a vision of *collective* change" (p. 165).

This certainly was illustrated by Martin (2005), who conducted an 18-week intervention with high school girls that was planned around feminist pedagogy, including discussing sexist language and violence against women. According to Martin:

> I observed at the start of the intervention that the young women were inherently negative to women. They embraced symbols that are degrading to women such as the Playboy bunny symbol and used words such as "bitch" and "ho" to describe themselves and other women.... Their relationships with males were more important to them than were their relationships with females and the perspectives they chose; or the eyes through which they saw the world justified stereotypically male norms at the expense of female autonomy.

As one of Martin's students noted:

> I think a lot of women can't be friends because of men. For example, if I caught my boyfriend with another girl it wouldn't be his fault, it would be her fault. Don't ask me why, but that's the way it is. We are all so used to degrading other women we never have time to stop and think about what we are saying. I think women should try to get along because if we do then maybe we can get more respect from everybody else.

Another said:

> Women could be friends if they weren't as petty, judgmental, or comparative. When girls see each other they automatically look to see if the other girls are prettier than them. Nine out of ten times they won't want to be their friend. It's all about image, body language and self-esteem. Truth is, girls check each other out more than guys, not in a sexual way, they basically inventory all other girls.

Martin also noted that as the women began monitoring their language and using language affirmative to women, they started to view themselves more positively. As one woman stated:

> I really like the class. I get along with all the girls a lot better than I ever did. It brought us all together and helped us understand each other in many ways, whether it be positive or negative. Somehow we found a way to make it through and I now understand females more than I ever did. It feels great to know that we went from hating each other to becoming more understanding with friendship.

Another of the students added:

> I tried to use this class in my personal life. Like when my boyfriend would say something that was negative toward me. If he called me the B word or something just joking around, when he does do that I stop him and say "You don't call me that because it bothers me." And now he doesn't do it no more. Even if he's joking around, I told him that's offensive to me and he just doesn't do it no more. But I try to use it. If one of my friends is talking bad about somebody and they're like "Oh, she's a slut or a ho," I'm like "Well, you can't just base that on how she's dressed or how she's acting. It doesn't really matter who she's been with or not or the way she's dressing or her appearance." I try to keep "ho" and "slut" out of my vocabulary even though it's kind of hard but I try.

CRITICAL THINKING

One goal that is considered a central tenet of liberal arts education is helping students learn to think critically (Wheeler & Dember, 1979). Critical thinking involves several components: it requires empowerment, knowledge of tools of analysis, and comprehended knowledge (Sinacore & Boatwright, 2005). Paludi and Steuernagel (1990) outlined several ways faculty can teach the introductory course in women's studies as a way to facilitate students learning several foundations for a feminist restructuring of the academic disciplines. The goal of their approach is to have students critically question the treatment of women and gender (i.e., trivialization, omission, distortion) in courses they subsequently take in their undergraduate curriculum. McTighe Musil (1992) also outlined several pedagogical techniques (e.g., discussion questions, experiential exercises) and course requirements to meet this goal of critical thinking among students who major in women's studies. Elliot (1993) reported using debates as a pedagogical technique to encourage critical thinking in the Psychology of Women course.

Paludi (1996) noted that helping students learn to think critically is one goal of the Psychology of Women course as well. Critical thinking skills permit women students to see themselves as capable of critical analysis, to incorporate statistical methodologies in their analyses, and to possess sufficient knowledge and perspective to engage in substantive critical analyses. Critical thinking also encourages an opportunity for students to talk in the first person, to value their opinions and analyses. Paludi offered several pedagogical techniques for faculty to use in guiding students' critical thinking skills, including experiential exercises, popular books, and essay/discussion questions. These techniques provide students with an opportunity to reflect a broad range of knowledge and the need to define, qualify, and dispute commonly heard overgeneralizations about women's lives and behavior.

An example of an experiential exercise suggested by Paludi to encourage critical thinking is the following:

> Select a journal article describing one or a series of empirical studies. Sample journals include: *Developmental Psychology, Journal of Personality and Social Psychology, Psychology of Women Quarterly, Journal of Black Psychology, Journal of Cross Cultural Psychology*. Critically read the article, taking into account the issues of research design and research bias. Answer the following questions:
>
> 1. Is the purpose of the research clear? Explain.
> 2. Has the author been careful to cite prior reports contrary to the current hypothesis?
> 3. Is the research hypothesis correctly derived from the literature and theory that has been cited? Or, are there some important steps missing and left to the speculation of the reader?
> 4. Are there possible biases in the sampling procedure used? For example, were volunteers used? Was there a differential attrition rate among potential participants?
> 5. Are there experimental biases?
> 6. Is information presented about the sex and race of the research participants?
> 7. Were the variables of sex and race used in the statistical analyses?
> 8. Were the conclusions drawn by the author consistent with the results obtained?
> 9. In what ways do you think the biases of the author distorted the methodology, results, and interpretation?
> 10. What follow up studies do you think are needed? Why?
> 11. Were tests of effect size performed?

Paludi finds this approach to critical thinking to be empowering for students, especially for reentry women students who may have been silenced in their life experiences as well as in other courses. Critical thinking thus instills in students confidence and a positive sense of self—two important outcomes that should be expected in the Psychology of Women course.

INTERSECTIONALITY AMONG RACE, CLASS, GENDER, AND SEXUAL ORIENTATION

Boxer (1982) noted that the feminist goal for education is that it should be about and for all women, not only free from sexism but also from prejudice and discrimination based on race, class, age, sexual orientation, and other oppressive biases. Dissatisfaction with the treatment of women of color has been a source of conflict since the early 1970s and continues to plague women's studies programs and Psychology of Women courses today.

Brown, Goodwin, Hall, and Jackson-Lowman (1985) reviewed 28 textbooks on the psychology of women and found that 18 offered either minor or no reference to African American women. Asian women, Native American women, and Latinas received even less attention. They identified four definitive steps to be followed to rectify this problem:

> 1. Psychology of women writers must confront the racism, ethnocentrism, and classism manifested in the exclusion and limited treatment throughout their works of Third World, non-middle-class women.
> 2. In-depth research and study must be undertaken, as well as research programs that specifically seek to reveal the impact of culture, race, and social class on the psychological development of Third World Women.
> 3. Course offerings on Afro-American, Native American, Hispanic, Asian-American, and other Third World Women must be added to the curriculum of Women's Studies and given the same status as other required psychology of women courses.
> 4. Efforts to develop a comprehensive and integrative study of the psychology of women must be pursued. Model construction and theory development must reflect the importance of culture, racial, and social-class variables on female development. (p. 37)

Santos de Barona and Reid (1992) also noted that women of color must be central to a Psychology of Women course for two major reasons: (1) White women represent a small proportion of women in the world and (2) sex cannot be discussed independently from class, race, and ethnicity. They recommended several topics to discuss in the Psychology of Women course to make women of color central, including family relationships among ethnic groups and differential impact of employed mothers. According to Santos deBarona and Reid:

> Efforts to include ethnic issues in ongoing discussions of gender must continue. It is important to include topics for which ethnic data and theoretical perspectives are available. However, course content involving ethnic concerns should not be limited to these areas but should be expanded to promote discussion of the beliefs and stereotypes about women of all classes and ethnicities.

DeFour and Paludi (1991) also described the necessity for instructors of courses on the psychology of women to integrate the scholarship on race, class, and ethnicity into their curriculum. They offered examples of films, experiential exercises, popular books, and course topics to assist instructors in providing more of an understanding of the psychology of all women. DeFour and Paludi made three recommendations for instructors. First, it is important to avoid the use of value-laden references so as not to legitimize negative stereotypes of women of color. Second, women's experiences are extremely diverse, yet most researchers describe women of color collectively. This approach engenders the same error that occurs when one collectively describes any group: women of color are as varied and differ as much among themselves as do white women. Third, the use of the term *women of color* should also address socioeconomic class stratification.

Goodwin, McHugh, and Touster (2005) suggested several strategies for making diversity central, including:

- avoiding studying women from marginalized groups only in comparison to women in the dominant group
- incorporating scholarship by women from marginalized groups into the course
- integrating diversity throughout the course rather than the "add and stir" approach of relegating it to a separate section of the syllabus
- addressing issues of privilege and oppression

Another important issue related to teaching diversity is the notion that students and teachers have multiple, intersecting social identities that have varying degrees of importance in different contexts. Enns and Forrest (2005) indicate that "the goal, then, of a multicultural feminist pedagogy is to explore the intersections, borders, and boundaries among identities" (p. 20). This perspective recognizes that a person's reality is complex and is generally not defined by a single identity, but is instead shaped and influenced by many identities.

Each of these identities may be associated with different degrees of privilege, power, and oppression that are dynamic depending on the context. To further complicate this issue, it is, of course, not only the student who has multiple social identities, but also the teacher. The multiple identities of the students and the teacher interact with one another, complicating efforts to equalize power in the classroom. Ways to address this include helping students become aware of their multiple social identities, their positionalities and social locations inside and outside the classroom, and how these affect experiences of power and oppression. Crawford and Suckle (1999) have proposed exercises that deconstruct stereotypes and recognize the complexity of identities, including rewriting fairy tales and examining the roles and plots of romance novels. Having students describe their various identities, roles, and expectations or engaging in role-play from various positions and points of view can help students recognize the impact and intersection of multiple identities.

A safe, supportive, and inclusive classroom environment is an important condition for dealing with issues of diversity. Feminist pedagogy recognizes that some students, those from the dominant culture who bring their privilege into the classroom, will have an easier time feeling safe than those from marginalized positions. Students from marginalized groups need support from the teacher to take risks in what may have been an unsafe environment in other academic contexts (Sinacore & Enns, 2005a). Characteristics of the teacher also contribute to the perception of safety (Enns & Forrest, 2005; Sinacore & Enns, 2005b). Young (2005) suggests that when a course has a multicultural perspective, a diverse student population, and instructor-student difference in race ethnicity, gender, or sexual orientation, the conditions increase for the likelihood of a difficult dialogue. Central to the creation of a safe environment is teacher comfort with, and preparation for, handling intense emotions and "difficult dialogues," yet faculty often report feeling ill equipped and unprepared to handle such dialogues, and so they attempt to avoid them (Byars-Winston et al., 2005; Goodman, 1995; Young, 2005).

Goodman (1995) suggested that faculty can increase their comfort and preparation level by increasing their knowledge about various groups and developing awareness about themselves and their own prejudices and misinformation. The greater their knowledge, the more comfort they can have when addressing students' stereotypes. Other methods for creating a favorable climate for difficult discussions include having and enforcing discussion guidelines, helping students understand that it is difficult to avoid learning stereotypes and prejudice when one is raised in a society with sexism and racism, using examples from the teacher's life, and encouraging personal stories about experiences with discrimination.

Young (2005) identified four conditions for dealing with difficult dialogues: creating a climate for inquiry, focusing on cognitive inquiry, focusing on emotional inquiry, and developing mindful listening. One of the goals of this model is to integrate the cognitive and affective responses.

Using the pedagogical approaches of self-study and collaboration can be helpful in promoting culturally responsive teaching. Culturally responsive teaching, as defined by Gay and Kirkland (2003), involves the following three propositions:

> Multicultural education and educational equity and excellence are deeply interconnected.... Teacher accountability involves being more self-conscious, critical, and analytical of one's own teaching beliefs and behaviors.... Teachers need to develop deeper knowledge and consciousness about what is to be taught, how, and to whom (p. 181)

Gay and Kirkland stress that critical consciousness of racial and cultural issues should be examined in a self-reflective manner.

When training teachers and/or teacher leaders, it is not enough that students be asked to engage in conversations about social injustice—they need also to examine their own beliefs, biases, and the system of cultural hegemony that holds these ideas in place. These conversations can be done as "participatory spaces" (hooks, 1994), where students take part in dialoguing with one another in a safe environment.

DEVELOPMENTAL ISSUES

Multigenerational inclusivity is a challenge in the Psychology of Women course. Young women often feel that there is no longer a need for feminism since equality has been achieved (Crawford & Suckle, 1999). Two explanations have been offered for this conservatism and anti-intellectualism: first, that it is part of the much larger wave of conservative politics and a retreat from liberalism in the United States; and second, that it signals the beginning of the next stage of feminism: college women may embrace feminist values, but do not accept the collective efforts of the women's movement as a means to achieve their individual goals (Komarovsky, 1985).

Young women may reject earlier visions of feminism and feminists while subscribing to many of its principles (Zalk, described in Paludi, 1992). They may perceive an expectation that they conform to beliefs and behavior that are not part of their experience. Crucial to overcoming this belief is making the material relevant to the lives of young women. Using collaborative teaching approaches, having students identify discussion questions for class, relating course content to personal experiences, developing experiential activities, and including popular films, television shows, and novels can help students find relevance in the course material (Freedman, Golub, & Krauss, 1982; Paludi, 1991; Riger, 1979; Sholley, 1986).

Young women who identify themselves as feminists, or third-wave feminists, often identify themselves and their feminism in opposition to the previous generation of feminists (Sinacore & Enns, 2005a). Several recent studies on feminist identification suggest that women are hesitant to self-identify as feminists in large part because of the negative connotation associated with the term. Some researchers indicate that young women tend to express feminist ideas without labeling themselves as such (Percy & Kremer, 1995; Renzetti, 1987). Burn, Aboud, and Moyles (2000) found that although both women and men may agree with the goals of feminism, they may also avoid self-identification with the term for fear of being associated with the stigmatized label.

One of the authors of this chapter (J. Martin) notes that in her own observation as a high school teacher, she found that many young women today are quicker to accept negative reclamation—to self-identify with traditionally negative terms used to refer to women such as *bitch*—than they are to embrace a term such as *feminist*. She has seen that most high school–age women express one of the following three sentiments: either they have little understanding of feminism, they feel feminism is a negative term and disassociate with it, or they feel that feminism is no longer necessary.

Aronson (2003) found that feminist identification can be classified on a continuum, for example, ranging from "I'm a feminist" to "I'm a feminist, but . . . ," "I'm not a feminist, but . . . ," "I'm a fence-sitter," and "I've never thought about feminism." This qualification often stems from this need to male-identify, as in "I'm a feminist, but I don't hate men," "I agree with many feminist causes, but I'm not a prude," "I would be a feminist, but I'm not that uptight," and so on. According to Aronson, most women are fence-sitters. Some researchers believe that this ambivalence toward feminism can be cultivated into active support for the feminist movement (Aronson, 2003; Martin, 2006).

Some of the features that distinguish third-wave feminism from second-wave feminism are a more flexible attitude about what it means to be feminist, a greater tolerance for ambiguities and contradictions, and being able to define for oneself the meaning of feminism (Sinacore & Enns, 2005a). As with cultural diversity, putting generational issues at the center of the discussion can illuminate the experiences, perceptions, concerns, needs, and problems of young women, their multiple identities, and their positionality in the educational, social, occupational systems with which they interact.

Paludi (1991) offered a life-cycle developmental psychology perspective that emphasizes that individual, cultural, and historical conditions affect each person's development. She focused on the following life stages: infancy and childhood, adolescence and young adulthood, middle age, and later adulthood. Paludi stresses the continuity in psychological processes during different stages of development, such as separation. Dealing with separation is a developmental task for early childhood (e.g., separation from mothers who return to employment), during adolescence (e.g., when a young woman leaves home to attend college), and in adulthood (e.g., when a woman's child leaves home to continue with her or his own adult life).

The study of girls as a group is a relatively new phenomenon. Gilligan began her research on the psychology of women as specifically different from that of the predominant "male universal" in the 1970s. Since then, a study of girls as a group slowly began to develop within psychology and education with women like Gilligan and organizations such as the American Association of University Women leading the way. In sum, the fields of psychology and education turned to an examination of girls as the next logical step.

The history of girls' studies is not very long or comprehensive. Beginning in the 1970s, scholars such as Brown and Gilligan sought to rectify the omission of girls from the discipline of psychology and from within feminism's second wave by adding the voices of girls to the literature of adolescence (Dohrn, 2004). Many of the first studies on girls focused on their victim status or on the problems young females across racial and class lines faced living in a patriarchal society. There were studies on sexual harassment, on adolescent females' loss of voice in a patriarchal society, and ultimately on the socially constructed notion that girls' lived experiences are just different from that of boys. Such studies were necessary in explaining the experiences of American girls in a variety of cultures, to indicate that girls had more to overcome when achieving success because of the obstacles they faced living in a sexist society (Gilligan, 1982; Peterson, 1988).

This victim-based "girl" literature of the 1990s has sparked the creation of various school-based and nonprofit organizations to tackle issues faced by girls (Sprague, 2003). Girls Inc. and Girls International Forum are just two examples of national organizations that strive for the health and educational well-being of American girls today.

MEN, WOMEN, SEX, AND POWER

Virginia Woolf wrote:

> How little can a man know even of [a woman's life] when he observes it through the black or rosy spectacles which sex puts upon his nose. Hence, perhaps, the peculiar nature of woman in fiction; the astonishing extremes of her beauty and horror; her alternations between heavenly goodness and hellish depravity—for so a lover would see her as his love rose or sank, was prosperous or unhappy.

Her statement suggests that women have been always viewed in light of men and their needs (Langland, 1990).

Worell (1990) suggested that personality theories may be described as "traditional" when they reflect the following themes in their conception of human behavior: androcentrism, gendercentrism, ethnocentrism, and heterosexism. Worrell noted that personality theories mostly use boys and men as the prototype of humankind, and girls and women as variants on this dominant theme (*androcentrism*). Also, psychological theories often discuss separate paths of lifespan development for women and men as a result of the biological differences between them (*gendercentrism*). *Ethnocentrism* refers to personality theories assuming that development is identical for all individuals across all racial, ethnic, and class groups. Finally, Worell noted that personality theories assume that a heterosexual orientation is normative, while a lesbian, gay, bi, or transgendered orientation is deviant and changeworthy.

The Psychology of Women course, as recommended by Lord (1982), needs to treat girls and women as the norm, recognize racial, class, and ethnic similarities and differences among women, and treat sexual orientation in a respectful manner, noting lesbian, bi, and transgendered orientations. Treating girls and women as the norm, however, may make male students interpret this as "man hating." Women have this perception, too, and can resist this as well. It is important to discuss how thinking only in a dichotomous way is faulty. Valuing women does not mean devaluing men.

This is but one of many challenges for the participation of men in Psychology of Women courses. There are challenges for the man himself, for the faculty member, for women in the class, and for the class dynamics. Men who enroll in the course do so for various reasons. Increasingly they may be fulfilling a course requirement (Orr, 1993). Alternatively, they may endorse the goals and values of feminist courses, may come to the course as a provocateur with an opposing political agenda, or may be naïve about the nature of the course content and therefore believe they will learn about how or why their girlfriends behave the way they do. The Psychology of Women course may be their first encounter with feminist principles.

For faculty teaching a Psychology of Women course, the challenges and considerations related to teaching men are numerous and include dealing with resistance, the perception that the course content (and perhaps the professor) is "man hating" or "male bashing," provocative behavior intended to ridicule or incite, and guilt and anger in response to discussions of privilege, power and dominance issues, being in a decentralized role in the class, and their reaction to feminist pedagogy (Crawford & Suckle, 1999; Orr, 1993). Orr (1993) concluded that "resistant students cannot learn effectively themselves and may seriously hamper the learning of their fellow students" (p. 240). She cited the failure of both feminist pedagogy and critical educational theory in dealing adequately with "male students as gendered subjects" (p. 252).

In addition, Orr (1993) described the psychological benefits of using a specific critical theoretical framework to understand both masculinity and resistance of men. The framework she described allows the feminist teacher to address male resistance in three ways. First, it enables the teacher to respond to male resistance with a "more adequate and useful emotional relationship" (p. 246). Understanding resistance in terms of the critical framework allows the teacher to engage in a proactive, instead of a reactive, response to some of the frustration and anger that resistant male students can generate. Second, in addition to assisting with her own reaction to student behavior, this framework helps the feminist teacher understand student behavior in a way that "can see in it the energy and desire for emancipation" (p. 257). Finally, the framework can be used as a pedagogical strategy to help male students see themselves not only as the oppressor but also as the oppressed with respect to patriarchical social, political, and economic systems—to recognize their privilege while at the same time understanding that masculinity is in opposition to their own real interests. According to Orr, this approach can reduce the male experience of threat and guilt and help men relate issues in the class to their own experiences.

Sinacore and Boatwright (2005) report that, although female students respond more favorably to feminist pedagogical strategies than male students do, some research (Ferguson, 1992) found that most men and women preferred strategies associated with feminist pedagogy. Several studies have found that male and female students have benefited similarly from feminist classes (Stake & Gerner, 1987; Stake & Malkin, 2003). Sinacore and Boatwright (2005) urged further research on which feminist strategies work best with which types of students in which types of settings.

Both men and women stand to benefit from the participation of men in Psychology of Women courses. Since women are often in relationships with men, and since many of the issues affecting women involve men, it is crucial that women not be the only ones to understand the effects of privilege, power, androcentrism, and patriarchy. Finding an effective way to address the challenges and to teach male students this content is a worthwhile endeavor.

INTEGRATION OF THE PSYCHOLOGY OF WOMEN INTO THE PSYCHOLOGY CURRICULUM

That it is important and necessary for psychology to move from its male Euro-American origins and emphasis toward becoming a discipline that includes more of humanity is obvious. A discipline whose objective is to understand people should not have to defend their inclusion. Further, given the changing demographics of the United States, and of students in higher education and in psychology courses, Hall's (1997) warning that "American psychology may become 'culturally obsolete' unless revised to reflect a multicultural perspective" (p. 1063) was echoed by Sue, Binham, Porche-Burke, and Vasquez (1999).

Many changes are occurring, as evidenced by the plethora of research, journals, and psychological organizations dedicated to the study of women and other groups not previously represented in traditional psychology. While many psychologists support the goal of becoming a more diverse discipline, integration of corresponding content has not necessarily found its way into standard psychology courses and textbooks (Madden & Hyde, 1999). Hence, many students who take a wide array of standard psychology courses continue to be taught primarily (or exclusively) theories and research based on a small segment of humanity. Madden and Hyde (1999) concluded that while psychology has become more inclusive, the psychology curriculum does not yet adequately include gender and ethnicity, textbooks do not portray women well, and women of color are not represented in psychology textbooks at all.

Copeland (1982) identified four approaches for integrating multicultural content into courses, which can be extrapolated to include content about women and gender. They are the separate course model, the area of concentration model, the interdisciplinary model, and the integration model.

Psychology of Women courses are an example of the separate course model, and there are advantages and disadvantages to this approach. Quina and Bronstein (2003) suggest that the separate course model can "ghetto-ize" and devalue scholarship in these areas by suggesting that they are "special topics," variations from the requisite course content, and will not be covered in standard psychology classes (Denmark, 2003). Another disadvantage is that the information is not widely disseminated; only the students who take these classes gain exposure to the material.

The preferred model is the integration model, which advocates the inclusion of content from multicultural and gender perspectives into all courses (Sue et al., 1999). Integrating multicultural and gender into all courses has numerous advantages. The primary advantages are that courses become relevant to all students and that a greater number of students have exposure to a more accurate reflection of human reality (Denmark, 2003; Madden & Hyde, 1998; Sue, 2003). The integration model advocated by most researchers in this area refers to curricular transformation, rather than simply taking an existing course and adding facts or information about a particular group—the "mix and stir" approach (Madden & Hyde, 1999). Sue et al. (1999) go further and state that widespread systemic changes to the educational system are necessary to create a multicultural psychology.

Alternatively, the separate course model need not be in opposition to the integration model. There are many topics in psychology that are addressed and included in standard courses, then elaborated in a course that is more focused and specialized. Quina and Bronstein (2003) point out that while it is essential to integrate multiculturalism and gender perspectives into all psychology courses, "there is a place in the curriculum for special foci" (p. 4). These courses are supported by the development of new course materials and new scholarship that focuses on individual groups, multicultural and cross-cultural psychology, and the psychology of gender.

Many obstacles have been identified to a full integration of gender and multiculturalism in psychology courses. Some of the obstacles recapitulate problems identified in teaching the Psychology of Women course. Specifically, many faculty members may:

- feel uncomfortable or embarrassed or have other negative emotions about addressing topics of race and gender in their classes (Sue et al., 1999; Quina & Bronstein, 2003)

- feel unprepared for dealing with the difficult discussions that can result from addressing these topics (Sue et al., 1999)
- feel uncertain about their own expertise in these areas (Sue et al., 1999; Quina & Bronstein, 2003)
- feel unprepared to challenge the existing Euro-American assumptions by using new models (Sue et al., 1999)
- fear revealing their own biases or may feel they are exposing themselves to criticism (Quina & Bronstein, 2003)
- feel they do not have the time to add any additional content to their courses (Madden & Hyde, 1999)
- not have a clear idea of how to determine which groups to cover and which groups to leave out (Madden & Hyde, 1999)

As psychology recognizes the importance of integrating gender and multiculturalism into the curriculum, numerous books, articles, journals, associations, and guidelines have been developed to facilitate this goal. The importance of selecting textbooks that are inclusive is an agreed-upon starting point (Hyde & Madden, 1999; Quina & Bronstein, 2003; Sue, 2003; Denmark, 2003). Textbooks are crucial because they often determine what will be taught in the course. In addition, there are numerous resources available for helping faculty to integrate gender and multiculturalism in courses (Bronstein & Quina, 2003). The American Psychological Association (2002) has published guidelines for teaching about gender and multiculturalism.

Integration of the psychology of women into the broader psychology curriculum requires more than a series of techniques. Madden and Hyde (1999) and Quina and Bronstein (2003) emphasize the importance of developing a framework as well as strategies for integrating gender and multiculturalism into a broad range of classes. These frameworks must include ways to understand race, class, gender, and sexuality and for dealing with difference in ways that are not simply comparative to the majority culture.

As Makosky and Paludi (1990) summarized, with respect to women's studies courses (of which the Psychology of Women course is one):

> Deciding whether women's studies should be mainstreamed into the curriculum and/or maintained as a separate program in a women's studies department is a values decision made in the context of the history and mission of a particular institution and of the faculty involved. There are dangers in establishing a single model for women's studies, similar to the danger in having a single strain of corn: with uniformity, you have uniform susceptibility and weakness. We have already seen that the strengths of mainstreaming are often the weaknesses of separationism, and vice versa. Stimpson (1977) discusses the diversity in education,

social, and political circumstances that have given rise to the diversity of styles, methods, and goals in women's studies and concludes that all programs must work out their own destiny, and that all women's studies programs need to be seen as a multiplicity of intersection activities. (p. 34)

Giroux (2001) commented:

> Public schools don't need standardized curriculum and testing. On the contrary, they need curricular justice—forms of teaching that are inclusive, caring, respectful, economically equitable, and whose aim, in part, is to undermine those repressive modes of education that produce social hierarchies and legitimate in equality while simultaneously providing students with the knowledge and skills needed to become well-rounded critical actors and social agents. . . .
>
> At the very least, radical pedagogical work proposes that education is a form of political intervention in the world and is capable of creating the possibilities for social transformation. Rather than viewing teaching as technical practice, radical pedagogy in the broadest terms is a moral and political practice premised on the assumption that learning is not about processing received knowledge but actually transforming it as part of a more expansive struggle for individual rights and social justice. (pp. xxvi–xxvii)

REFERENCES

American Psychological Association. (2002). *Guidelines on multicultural education, training, research, practice, and organizational change for psychologists.* Retrieved December 27, 2006, from http://www.apa.org/pi/multiculturalguidelines.pdf.

Aronson, P. (2003). Feminists or "postfeminists"? Young women's attitudes toward feminism and gender elations. *Gender & Society, 17,* 903–922.

Association of American Colleges and Universities. (2002). *Greater expectations national panel report.* Washington, DC: Association of American Colleges and Universities.

Boneparth, E. (1977). Evaluating women's studies: Academic theory and practice. *Social Science Journal, 14,* 23–31.

Boxer, M. (1982). For and about women: The theory and practice of women's studies in the U.S. *Signs, 7,* 661–695.

Bronstein, P., & Quina, K. (Eds.). (2003). *Teaching gender and multicultural awareness: Resources for the psychology classroom.* Washington, DC: American Psychological Association.

Brown, A., Goodwin, B., Hall, B., & Jackson-Lowman, H. (1985). A review of psychology of women textbooks: Focus on the Afro-American woman. *Psychology of Women Quarterly, 9,* 29–38.

Burn, S., Aboud, R., & Moyles, C. (2000). The relationship between gender social identity and support for feminism. *Sex Roles, 42,* 1081–1089.

Byars-Winston, A., Akcali, O., Tao, K., Nepomuceno, C., Anctil, T., Acevedo, V., Banally, N., & Wilton, G. (2005). The challenges, impact, and implementation of critical multicultural pedagogies. In Enns & Sinacore, 2005, 125–141.

Copeland, E. (1982). Minority populations and traditional counseling programs: Some alternatives. *Counselor Education and Supervision, 21,* 187–193.

Crabtree, R., & Sapp, D. (2003). Theoretical, political, and pedagogical challenges in the feminist classroom. *College Teaching, 51,* 131–140.

Crawford, M., & Suckle, J. (1999). Overcoming resistance to feminism in the classroom. In S. Davis, M. Crawford, & J. Sebrechts (Eds.). *Coming into her own: Educational success in girls and women,* 155–170. San Francisco: Jossey-Bass.

DeFour, D. C., & Paludi, M. A. (1991). Integrating the scholarship on ethnicity into the Psychology of Women course. *Teaching of Psychology, 18,* 85–90.

Denmark, F. (1994). Engendering psychology. *American Psychologist, 49,* 329–334.

Denmark, F. (2003). Introduction: Creating a psychology of all people. In Bronstein & Quina, 2003.

Dohrn, B. (2004). All ellas: Girls locked up. *Feminist Studies, 30,* 402–324.

Downing, N., & Rousch, K. (1985). From passive acceptance to active commitment. *Counseling Psychologist, 13,* 695–709.

Elliot, L. (1993) Using debates to teach the Psychology of Women. *Teaching of Psychology, 20,* 35–38.

Enns, C., & Forrest, L. (2005). Toward defining and integrating multicultural and feminist pedagogies. In Enns & Sinacore, 2005, 3–23.

Enns, C., & Sinacore, A. (Eds.). (2005). *Teaching and social justice: Integrating multicultural and feminist theories in the classroom.* Washington, DC: American Psychological Association.

Ferguson, M. (1992). Is the classroom still a chilly climate for women? *College Student Journal, 26,* 507–511.

Fisher, B. (2001). *No angel in the classroom: Teaching through feminist discourse.* Lanham, MD: Rowman & Littlefield.

Freedman, R., Golub, S., & Krauss, B. (1982). Mainstreaming the psychology of women into the core curriculum. *Teaching of Psychology, 9,* 165–168.

Furumoto, L. (1980). Mary Whiton Calkins (1863–1930). *Psychology of Women Quarterly, 5,* 55–67.

Furumoto, L., & Scarborough, E. (1986). Placing women in the history of psychology: The first American woman psychologists. *American Psychologist, 41,* 35–42.

Gay, G., & Kirkland, K. (2003). Developing cultural critical consciousness and self-reflection in preservice teacher education. *Theory into Practice, 42,* 181–187.

Gilligan, C. (1982). *In a different voice: Psychological theory of women's development.* Cambridge, MA: Harvard University Press.

Giroux, H. (2001). *Theory and resistance in education: Towards a pedagogy for the opposition.* Westport, CT: Bergin & Garvey.

Goodman, D. (1995). Difficult dialogues: Enhancing discussions about diversity. *College Teaching, 43,* 47–51.

Goodwin, B., McHugh, M., & Touster, L. (2003). Who is the woman in the psychology of women? In Bronstein & Quina, 2003.

Hall, C. (1997). Cultural malpractice: The growing obsolesence of psychology with the changing U.S. population. *American Psychologist, 52,* 642–651.

hooks, b. (1994). *Teaching to transgress: Education as the practice of freedom.* London: Routledge.

Horowitz, D. (2006). *The professors: The 101 most dangerous academics in America.* Washington, DC: Regnery.

Kimmell, E. (1999). Feminist teaching, an emergent practice. In S. Davis, M. Crawford, & J. Sebrechts (Eds.), *Coming into her own: Educational success in girls and women,* 57–76. San Francisco: Jossey-Bass.

Komarovsky, M. (1985). *Women in college.* New York: Basic Books.

Langland, E. (1990). Images of women: A literature perspective. In Paludi & Steuernagel, 1990, 69–97.

Lindquist, B. (1994). Beyond student resistance: A pedagogy of possibility. *Teaching Education, 6,* 1–8.

Lord, S. (1982). Teaching the psychology of women: Examination of a teaching-learning model. *Psychology of Women Quarterly, 7,* 70–80.

Madden, M., & Hyde, J. (1998). Integrating gender and ethnicity into psychology courses. *Psychology of Women Quarterly, 22,* 1–12.

Makosky, V., & Paludi, M. (1990). Feminism and women's studies in the academy. In Paludi & Steuernagel, 1990, 1–37.

Markowitz, L. (2005). Unmasking moral dichotomies: Can feminist pedagogy overcome student resistance? *Gender and Education, 17,* 39–55.

Martin, J. (2005). Peer sexual harassment: Finding voice, changing culture. Paper presented at the American Educational Research Association, Toronto, April.

Martin, J. (2006). "Ho no mo": A qualitative investigation of female language usage, reclamation and rejection. Paper presented at the American Educational Research Association, San Francisco, April.

McTighe Musil, C. (Ed.). (1992). *The courage to question: Women's studies and student learning.* Washington, DC: Association of American Colleges.

Milem, J., Chang, M., & Antonio, A. (2005). *Making diversity work on campus: A research-based perspective.* Washington, DC: Association of American Colleges and Universities.

Orr, D. (1993). Toward a critical rethinking of feminist pedagogical praxis and resistant male students. *Canadian Journal of Education, 18,* 239–254.

Ott, T. (2004). Community colleges and cognitive-affective learning: Fulfilling the promise of a mission. *Journal of Cognitive Affective Learning, 1.* Available at http://www.jcal.emory.edu//viewarticle.php?id=29&layout-html.

Paludi, M. (1991). Value of a life-cycle developmental perspective in teaching the psychology of women. *Teaching of Psychology, 18,* 37–40.

Paludi, M. (1992). *Psychology of women.* Upper Saddle River, NJ: Prentice Hall.

Paludi, M. (1996). *Exploring/teaching the psychology of women: A manual of resources.* Albany: State University of New York Press.

Paludi, M., & Steuernagel, G. (Eds.). (1990). *Foundations for a feminist restructuring of the academic disciplines.* New York: Haworth.

Paludi, M., & Tronto, J. (1992). Feminist education. In McTighe Musil, 1992.

Percy, C., & Kremer, J. (1995). Feminist identification in a troubled society. *Feminism and Psychology, 5,* 201–222.

Peterson, A. (1988). Adolescent development. *Annual Review of Psychology, 39,* 583–607.

Princeton Review (2000). Top 10 most popular majors. Retrieved May 29, 2007, from http://www.princetonreview.com/college/research/articles/majors/popular.asp.

Quina, K., & Bronstein, P. (2003). Gender and multiculturalism in psychology: Transformations and new directions. In Bronstein & Quina, 2003.

Renzetti, C. (1987). New wave or second stage? Attitudes of college women toward feminism. *Sex Roles, 16,* 265–277.

Rhoades, K. (1999). Border zones: Identification, resistance, and transgressive teaching in introductory women's studies courses. In B. Winkler & C. DiPalma (Eds.), *Teaching introduction to women's studies.* Westport, CT: Bergin & Garvey.

Riger, S. (1979). On teaching the psychology of women. *Teaching of Psychology, 6,* 113–114.

Santos de Barona, M., & Reid, P. (1992). Ethnic issues in teaching the psychology of women. *Teaching of Psychology, 19.*

Scarborough, E., & Furumoto, L. (1987). *Untold lives: The first generation of American women psychologists.* New York: Columbia University Press.

Sholley, B. (1986). Value of good discussions in a Psychology of Women course. *Teaching of Psychology, 13,* 151–153.

Sinacore, A., & Boatwright, K. (2005). The feminist classroom: Feminist strategies and student responses. In Enns & Sinacore, 2005, 109–124.

Sinacore, A., & Enns, C. (2005a). Diversity feminisms: Postmodern, women-of-color, antiracist, lesbian, third-wave, and global perspectives. In Enns & Sinacore, 2005, 41–68.

Sinacore, A., & Enns, C. (2005b). Multicultural and feminist literatures: Themes, dimensions, and variations. In Enns & Sinacore, 2005, 99–107.

Sprague, M. (2003). An academy for Ophelia? *The Clearing House, 76,* 178–184.

Stake, J., & Gerner, M. (1987). The women's studies experience: Personal and professional gains for women and men. *Psychology of Women Quarterly, 11,* 277–284.

Stake, J., & Malkin, C. (2003). Students' quality of experience and perceptions of intolerance and bias in the women's and gender studies classroom. *Psychology of Women Quarterly, 27,* 174–185.

Stevens, G., & Gardner, S. (1982). *The women of psychology: Pioneers and innovators.* Cambridge, MA: Schenkman.

Stimpson, C. (1971). Thy neighbor's wife, they neighbor's servants: Women's liberation and black civil rights. In V. Gornick & B. Moran (Eds.), *Woman in sexist society: Studies in power and powerlessness.* New York: Basic Books.

Sue, D. (2003). Foreword: The richness of human realities. In Bronstein & Quina, 2003.

Sue, D., Binham, R., Porche-Burke, L., & Masquz, M. (1999). The diversification of psychology: A multicultural revolution. *American Psychologist, 54*(12), 1061–1069.

Walsh, M. R. (1985). The Psychology of Women course: A continuing catalyst for change. *Teaching of Psychology, 12,* 198–203.

Washington, P. (2002). The individual and collective rewards of community-based service learning. In N. Naples & K. Bojar (Eds.), *Teaching feminist activism: Strategies from the field*, 166–182. New York: Routledge.

Wells, C., & Grabert, C. (2004). Service-learning and mentoring: Effective pedagogical strategies. *College Student Journal, 38,* 573–578.

Wheeler, D., & Dember, W. (Eds.). (1979). *A practicum in thinking*. Cincinnati: University of Cincinnati Psychology Department.

Worell, J. (1990). Images of women in psychology. In Paludi & Steuernagel, 1990, 185–224.

Young, G. (2005). Dealing with difficult classroom dialogue. In Bronstein & Quina, 2003.

PART III

Women's Social and Personality Development

Chapter 7

Gender Stereotypes

Mary E. Kite
Kay Deaux
Elizabeth L. Haines

> The subtle influence of sex upon a person's perceptions may vary with each observer and play both an unconscious and conscious role in influencing actions taken. (Gesell, 1990, p. 9)

Judge Gerhard Gesell of the U.S. Court of Appeals wrote those words in his precedent-setting decision awarding a partnership to a woman who had been discriminated against on the basis of gender. In 1982, Ann Hopkins had been denied promotion to partner at the accounting firm of Price Waterhouse, despite a strong record of performance. She was the only woman considered for partnership that year; at the time, the company had only seven women among its 662 partners. Hopkins was not told to work harder. Rather, she was given advice that focused on her makeup, her jewelry, and her style of walk and talk. Hopkins then sued the firm and won, and she continued to win as the case was appealed, heard by the Supreme Court, and returned to the court of appeals (on a legal issue of burden of proof), where Judge Gesell made his decision awarding her a partnership.

The 1989 case of *Price Waterhouse v. Hopkins* (490 U.S. 228) marked a rite of passage for research on gender stereotypes. The empirical and theoretical literature of social scientists was an integral part of the process, first represented at the lower court in expert witness testimony (Fiske, 1989) and later in an amicus brief filed with the Supreme Court (Fiske, Bersoff, Borgida, Deaux, & Heilman, 1991). At each level of decision, the courts recognized the role that gender stereotypes had played in the evaluation of Hopkins.

Yet the prevalence of gender stereotyping and the consequences of such stereotypes for other women and men have not been noticeably altered by the decision in this single case. Indeed, discrimination against women continues to make the news, as evidenced by the recently settled case against Morgan Stanley, brought by the U.S. Equal Employment Opportunity Commission. Allison Schieffelin, lead plaintiff for the case, claimed that less-qualified men received promotions while she did not and, further, that her complaint about this situation led to her firing (Ackman, 2004). The case was settled out of court, apparently because the company wished to avoid testimony from other female employees.

Echoes of Ann Hopkins's experiences also are evident in a class action suit against Wal-Mart brought on behalf of more than 1.6 million women who have worked for this corporation since December 1998. The suit alleges that Wal-Mart's predominately female workforce is disproportionately assigned to lower-paying jobs with fewer opportunities for advancement; moreover, those women who have advanced are paid significantly less than their male counterparts. At this writing, this case is still in the courts and, therefore, the legal validity of these allegations has not yet been determined. However, the testimony of these women indicates that Wal-Mart's actions are rooted in gender stereotypic beliefs, such as the idea that higher salaries should be reserved for men with children to support and that women who complain about discrimination are "whiners" (Armour, 2004).

"We have met the enemy ... and he is us," Walt Kelly's comic-strip character Pogo famously said, and so it is with stereotyping, a ubiquitous process to which we all succumb. In this chapter, we will consider why that is the case, what conditions support stereotypes, and what functions they serve. We will review both theoretical analyses and empirical findings as they relate to the content of gender stereotypes and subtypes, how this content is assessed, the development of stereotypes, and how stereotypes are transmitted. Finally, we will consider possibilities for change, both in cultural endorsement and individual usage.

THE CONTENT AND STRUCTURE OF GENDER STEREOTYPES

Stereotypes are not simply labels, but are assumptions about traits and behaviors that people in the labeled categories are thought to possess. In this section, we describe the characteristics that are typically associated with women and men. For descriptive purposes, we treat these characteristics as distinct from the affective beliefs about women and men, although we recognize that doing so is to some extent artificial. We address the questions of whether women and men are likable and whether their behaviors are viewed negatively or positively in a later section of this chapter. Context is critical to such questions, an issue to which we also return later.

The Content of Gender Stereotypes

Gender stereotypes have a familiar quality, and most people would readily recognize the list of traits commonly identified as descriptive of women and men. These traits have been the focus of decades of research on gender-based stereotypes (Broverman, Vogel, Broverman, Clarkson, & Rosenkrantz, 1972; Rosenkrantz, Vogel, Bee, Broverman, & Broverman, 1968; Spence, Helmreich, & Stapp, 1974). Early researchers identified two principal dimensions: beliefs that women are concerned with the welfare of other people (labeled *expressive* or *communal*) and beliefs that men are assertive and controlling (labeled *instrumental* or *agentic*).

More recent research verifies that these constellations of personality traits remain strongly associated with women and men (see Deaux & LaFrance, 1998, for a review). Women, for example, are viewed as more emotional, gentle, understanding, and devoted, whereas men are seen as more active, competitive, independent, and self-confident. The association between gender and these traits is remarkably consistent across respondent age, geographic region, and respondent sex. Williams and Best (1990), for example, asked citizens of 30 countries to identify the traits associated with women and men; results showed considerable consensus with previous research on U.S. populations. Even so, research in this area has traditionally relied on respondents who are white and middle class; only rarely have researchers explicitly examined whether gender-based stereotypes differ when raters describe women and men of different racial or ethnic groups or of different social classes.

Researchers have expanded our understanding of gender-based stereotypes by identifying other dimensions that perceivers use to categorize women and men. Men and women are thought to occupy distinct societal roles, for example. Men are viewed as leaders, financial providers, and heads of households, while women are seen as caregivers who shop, tend the house, and provide emotional support (Cejka & Eagly, 1999; Deaux & Lewis, 1984). People report that men are good at abstract thinking and problem solving, whereas women excel in artistic and verbal reasoning (Cejka & Eagly, 1999). Popular descriptions reflect marked differences in gender stereotypes about women's and men's physical appearance: women's physical attributes include dainty, pretty, soft-voiced, and graceful; men's include athletic, brawny, broad-shouldered, and physically strong (Cejka & Eagly, 1999; Deaux & Lewis, 1984).

Finally, emotions are believed to be at once gender-segregated and more firmly associated with femininity. That is, women are believed to both experience and express a broader range of emotions than are men, although two emotions—anger and pride—are more strongly associated with men (Plant, Hyde, Keltner, & Devine, 2000). Moreover, when women do express anger, perceivers infer that this expression is a combination of anger and sadness, whereas they believe men's expression of anger represents only that emotion. Interestingly, strongly expressed emotions are viewed more negatively when the emotion is gender stereotypic. Men whose anger suggests an overreaction to an event are viewed negatively, and so are women who express excessive happiness (Huston-Comeaux & Kelly, 2002). In reality, sex differences in emotion are more evident in expression than in emotional experience and are far less prevalent than the stereotypes would lead us to believe (Fischer, 2000; LaFrance & Banaji, 1992). Nonetheless, it is testimony to the power of stereotypes that belief in the "emotional woman" persist.

Across these categories, an overarching belief in gender polarization is evident—that is, an assumption that gender-associated characteristics are bipolar (Bem, 1993). If people know, for example, that a woman has a stereotypically feminine appearance, they also expect that she will have feminine traits and occupy feminine gender roles (Deaux & Lewis, 1984). People also appear to be more certain about this consistency for male-associated characteristics, which may be related to the perceived power and status of male gender role (Conway, Mount, & Pizzamiglio, 1996; McCreary, 1994). Such beliefs have implications for how perceivers use gender-linked information; we discuss this more fully in the next section. Finally, gender-stereotypic beliefs serve both descriptive and prescriptive functions: they inform us about what women and men are *like* and also lay ground rules for how men and women *should be*.

There is no question that women's and men's social roles have changed over time. To use just one indicator, women's enrollment in undergraduate institutions has increased since 1970 at a higher rate than men's and a higher percentage of women than men earn degrees at all educational levels (National Center for Education Statistics, 2006). In the United States, 47 percent of all workers are women (U.S. Bureau of Labor Statistics, 2002b), and women now occupy 51 percent of executive, administrative, and managerial positions, up from 41 percent in 1983 (U.S. Bureau of Labor Statistics, 2002a). Most assuredly, these gains tell only part of the story. White men, for example, dominate at the highest professional levels (e.g., Fortune 500 corporate executives and members of the U.S. House of Representatives; see Fassinger, 2001), and women, on average, earn just 77 percent of what men earn (National Committee on Pay Equity, 2004). Even so, women's gains are evident and changes in gender-stereotypic beliefs reflect this advancement.

As we will discuss in more detail later, there is considerable overlap between the characteristics associated with men and the characteristics associated with high-level positions such as executive or leader. Specifically, occupants of both roles are believed to have agentic characteristics (Eagly & Karau, 2002). If societal changes in gender roles reflect women's movement into the traditional male roles, it follows that changes in gender-stereotypic beliefs would likely be evidenced in women's and men's perceived agency and not necessarily in their perceived communion. Research supports this hypothesis. Diekman and Eagly (2000) asked people to describe the gender-associated characteristics of women and men in the past (1950s), present, and future (2050). Across all time periods, the belief that women are more communal than men and that men are more agentic than women persisted. Even so, results showed a clear narrowing of the gap for agency, with smaller perceived differences in the present compared with the past and with projections that those differences would continue to shrink. Put another way, people saw stability in men's agency and women's communion over time, but also perceived an increase in women's agency (and no change in men's level of communion) that they expected to continue into the future.

Interestingly, today's women are more likely to describe their own personality as agentic than were women of 20 years ago, but women's self-reported communion has not changed over that same time period (Twenge, 1997). More generally, people's self-reported agency and communion mirror the gender stereotypic beliefs reported in this chapter; to some extent, then, gender stereotypes contain a "kernel of truth," a point to which we return later.

Subtypes

Stereotypes of women and men are very general categories. In theory, each gender stereotype refers to approximately half of the world's population. Although the distinction between male and female appears to be a primary line of demarcation (Fiske, 1998; Vonk & Ashmore, 2003), having only two global, superordinate categories often proves unsatisfactory, lacking discriminatory power in daily usage. As a consequence, people develop subcategories about particular kinds of women and men that they encounter, typically endowing these more specific stereotypes with greater detail and often more vivid imagery.

People's propensity to form these more specific categories is evidenced by the identification of more than 200 gender-associated subtypes (Vonk & Ashmore, 2003; see also Deaux, Winton, Crowley & Lewis, 1985; Eckes, 1994). This impressively large number of gender subtypes can generally be reduced, however, into a smaller set of primary categories that includes occupations (e.g., career woman, businessman), family roles (e.g., housewife, breadwinner), ideologies (e.g., feminist), physical features and activities (e.g., athlete), and sexuality-related terms (e.g., sexy woman, macho man), as Carpenter and Trentman (1998) have shown. Each of these subtype categories is associated with a distinctive set of characteristics. The career woman, for example, is described as intelligent, determined, knowledgeable, and goal-oriented, terms that do not overlap with the characterization of a sexy woman as flirtatious and seductive (Noseworthy & Lott, 1984).

Some evidence indicates that people have more sharply articulated subtypes of women than of men (Ashmore, Del Boca & Titus, 1984; Deaux et al., 1985). Moreover, it is clear that the content of stereotypes can differ quite sharply even when the labels attached to a male and female subtype appear the same. Gender stereotypes associated with being homosexual are one example, where men and women tend to be characterized in diametrically opposite, gender-reversing terms (Eliason, Donelan, & Randall, 1992; Kite & Deaux, 1987). Thus, lesbians are stereotyped with traditionally masculine characteristics, such as being athletic and wearing masculine clothing, whereas gay men are characterized by traditionally feminine traits, such as wearing jewelry and having high-pitched voices. In the Deaux et al. (1985) study, people had more articulated images of mothers than of fathers. Other research has shown that working mothers and working fathers are viewed differently: working mothers gain in competence but lose the warmth associated with being a nonworking mother, whereas working fathers are seen as successfully combining traits of warmth and competence (Cuddy, Fiske, & Glick, 2004).

Gender subtypes vary in their evaluative tone as well, although the patterns are not always consistent. In the case of the ideologically based subtype of feminist, for example, Twenge and Zucker (1999) found that feminists were seen as serious, intelligent, knowledgeable, productive, and modern. At the same time, on a less positive note, feminists also were believed to be opinionated and outspoken, and when asked to write a description of a feminist, 36 percent of their respondents included negative statements. More generally, subtypes defined as traditional are preferred to subtypes defined as modern (Haddock & Zanna, 1994; Kite & Branscombe, 1998).

Research on stereotypes has shown the predominance of two distinct dimensions, one concerned with perceived competence and the other with perceived warmth (Fiske, Xu, Cuddy, & Glick, 1999; Fiske, Cuddy, Glick, & Xu, 2002; Fiske, 2004). Often groups are characterized as being high on one of the dimensions but low on the other. For example, Eckes (2002) reported that although feminists are believed to be high on competence but low on warmth, housewives were rated just the opposite—high on warmth but low on competence. The pattern seems to be that people who fill roles requiring male-associated characteristics, such as competence, are not necessarily liked, whereas people who fill roles requiring female-associated characteristics, such as warmth, are not necessarily respected. Employment status serves as one cue to perceived competence, as suggested earlier. Even the distinction between full-time and part-time work influences competence judgments, such that the former are seen as more agentic than the latter (Eagly & Steffen, 1986). Jost and Kay (2005) also have demonstrated the complementary nature of gender stereotypes such that both positive and negative qualities (e.g., women as communal but incompetent) underlie gender stereotypes. These complementary stereotypes are endorsed by both men and women, and they appear to enhance the legitimacy and stability of the status quo.

Investigators have tended to assume that gender stereotypes are not limited to any particular ethnic group or social class. Yet there is evidence that the well-established stereotypes of women and men are limited in both respects. Landrine (1985) varied race (black and white) and class (middle and lower) information in asking people to evaluate the category of women. Her results suggested that both factors made a difference. Black women were believed, for example, to be more hostile and more superstitious than white women; white women were thought to be more dependent and more emotional. Dimensions on which social class made a difference included impulsivity and responsibility. More importantly, the ratings of white women were much more similar to the standard findings for the stereotype of "woman" than were the ratings of black women, suggesting that race is an implicit but unrecognized variable in much stereotype research. This use of white as the standard finds a parallel in Eagly and Kite's (1987) research on national stereotypes. In that case, males were the standard used in forming stereotypes of nations, and the female stereotypes were often quite divergent. Certainly more research on target variation is needed in multicultural societies such as the United States and Canada.

MEASUREMENT OF GENDER STEREOTYPES AND GENDER ROLE ATTITUDES

As we have described, there appears to be remarkable consistency in people's perceptions of what women and men are like. Yet when considering these results, it is important to recognize that the ways in which gender stereotypes are assessed plays a role in this consistency. Assessments that rely on perceivers' reports of their perceptions provide different information than do implicit measures. Moreover, descriptions can be value-neutral; people may know cultural stereotypes, but may not themselves endorse them. We turn now to a discussion of such measurement issues.

The degree to which people overgeneralize the characteristics of men and women and the valenced attitudes they hold for gender and gender role are two main strategies for assessing perceptions of gender. Researchers may directly ask participants to report on their gender beliefs and attitudes using the *self-report method* (an explicit measure).

In addition, indirect or *implicit measures* have gained in prominence over the last decade to complement the self-report measures. These implicit measures typically use response latencies to determine the degree of association between social categories and attributes. Researchers are increasingly using both explicit and implicit measures of gender stereotypes and attitudes.

Self-Report Measures: Evaluating Stereotypes

Gender stereotype researchers have traditionally relied on direct, self-report measures, such as the Ratio Measure of Sex Stereotyping developed by McCauley and Stitt (1978). These authors asked respondents to estimate the percentage of women and the percentage of men who possess instrumental, expressive, and neutral attributes. These estimates yield a ratio score that indicates the extent to which the person believes men and women differ from one another (e.g., percentage of men who are aggressive divided by percentage of women who are aggressive); with men in the numerator, higher ratios indicate that men are perceived as having more of the trait. In comparing stereotype scores obtained on this measure to group norms, Martin (1987) found that the stereotyped beliefs about differences between women and men were more extreme than the distributions of self-reported differences, suggesting that stereotypes are exaggerations of reality. In a more recent use of the ratio approach, Krueger, Hassman, Acevedo, and Villano (2003) confirm that raters accentuate gender differences and that the source of that exaggeration is from overlearning associations between characteristics and gender groups, rather than from mere categorization of women and men into groups.

In self-report measures, the researcher typically generates the instrument's content, and respondents then indicate the extent to which they believe that content describes, for example, the average man or a typical businesswoman. A limitation of such measures is that they may not capture the idiosyncratic stereotypic perceptions that some raters might have. Although this weakness can be overcome by asking respondents to generate their own content, these free-response measures can produce results that are difficult to analyze and synthesize. Eagly and Mladinic (1989) proposed a solution that addressed both limitations by examining individual differences in gender stereotypic beliefs through a two-step process. Respondents first listed five characteristics of their assigned target person. They then rated the percentage of people in the target group who have that characteristic and reported their evaluation of the characteristic on a good/bad rating scale (see also Eagly, Mladinic, & Otto, 1991). A score for each person was created following Fishbein and Ajzen's (1975; Ajzen & Fishbein, 1980) Expectancy X Value method of aggregating evaluative beliefs. Thus, these measures can assess individual differences in stereotype content and can be used to predict stereotyped behaviors and attitudes.

Self-Report Measures: Evaluating Attitudes

Many instruments have been developed to assess attitudes toward equal rights, traditional roles, and the appropriate responsibilities for women and men (Beere, 1990). Perhaps the most widely used measure is the Attitudes toward Women Scale (AWS) developed by Spence and Helmreich (1972). Early on, it was not totally clear how these measures of attitudes toward specific domains of male and female involvement related to trait-based stereotypes. On the one hand, Spence and her colleagues reported substantial correlations between trait stereotype ratings and AWS scores (Spence, Helmreich, & Stapp, 1975). On the other hand, Eagly and Mladinic (1989) found no association between scores on the AWS and attitudes toward women as assessed on an evaluative semantic differential measure. These latter authors suggested that there is an important distinction between beliefs about the rights and responsibilities of women and attitudes toward the general category of women. In fact, attitudes toward rights and responsibilities can probably not be considered as a single dimension, as the work of A. J. Martin (1990) and Glick and Fiske (1996) have demonstrated.

Another concern with traditional measures, such as the AWS, is that significant numbers of respondents now indicate support for nontraditional sex roles, producing a ceiling effect on scores (Spence & Hahn, 1997; Twenge, 1997). Such results certainly indicate progress, particularly in overt acceptance of women's changing gender roles. However, research on subtle sexism suggests that this optimistic interpretation has its limitations.

Subtle sexism is assessed by instruments such as the Ambivalent Sexism Inventory (ASI; Glick & Fiske, 1996; see also *Modern Sexism*: Swim, Aikin, Hall, & Hunter, 1995). On these measures, respondents report their degree of endorsement for negative as well as positive attitudes toward women. *Hostile Sexism* evaluates the extent to which raters perceive women as usurping the rights and roles of men and assesses negative sentiment regarding women gaining equality and power. *Benevolent Sexism* captures the paternalistic stereotypes of women, such as the belief that women are pure, weak, and in need of protection. Although these dimensions assess negative and positive attitudes toward women, hostile and benevolent sexism are positively correlated with one another; the correlation is most likely driven by the underlying perception that men and women are different from each other. In addition, the Ambivalence toward Men Inventory (AMI; Glick & Fiske, 1999) is strongly related to the ASI, but the AMI can differentiate between subjective positive and negative attitudes toward men.

Implicit Measures

Implicit measures of stereotyping such as the Implicit Association Test (IAT; Greenwald, McGhee, & Schwartz, 1998) and semantic priming (e.g., Fazio, Jackson, Dunton, & Williams, 1995) are indirect methods for assessing stereotypes. These measures have advantages over traditional self-report measures because they are less prone to intentional (e.g., social desirability concerns) or unintentional (e.g., lack of introspective access) measurement error of gender stereotypes and sexism. The IAT has been widely used because of its flexibility in assessing implicit cognition. For example, the IAT has been used to evaluate gender stereotypes (e.g., women–math association), gender identity (e.g., women–self association), and gender attitudes (e.g., women–positivity association) (Greenwald et al., 2002). Examinations of specific implicit stereotypes indicate that both men and women associate men with math and career and women with liberal arts and home (Nosek, Banaji, & Greenwald, 2002).

The discrepancy between implicit and explicit gender stereotyping depends on several factors including (1) self-presentational concerns, (2) attitude strength, (3) the structure of the attitude (bipolar or unipolar), and (4) the distinctiveness of one's attitudes from the attitudes of others (Nosek, 2005; Nosek & Smyth, 2005). Implicit–explicit discrepancies are most likely to occur for gender stereotypes that are more traditional, but perhaps unfashionable to endorse. Implicit gender attitudes have a distinctive relation to gender discrimination. Rudman and Glick (2001), for example, showed that an implicit men-agentic/women-communal stereotype predicted discrimination against a female job applicant, whereas a self-report measure did not.

Indirect measures have been debated on grounds of their construct validity. It is unclear, for example, if implicit gender stereotypes represent a person's endorsement of these stereotypes, cultural knowledge about the stereotypes, or both. A comprehensive analysis of the divergence or convergence between implicit and explicit measures reveals that implicit attitudes relate to, but are distinct from, explicit attitudes (Nosek & Smyth, 2005). Despite these debates, routine use of implicit measures of stereotyping and sexism, together with self-report, can offer converging evidence on the presence of gender stereotyping, as well as informing researchers about implicit–explicit distinctions in measurement.

Evaluating Stereotype Accuracy

Whether implicit, explicit, or both types of measures are used to evaluate stereotypes, how researchers evaluate stereotype accuracy is an important methodological and theoretical issue (Ryan, 2003). Cognitive theorists propose that stereotypes are based on a kernel of truth and are thus oversimplifications and overgeneralizations of what is true for only some members of the group. In stereotype accuracy research, researchers attempt to examine the difference between perceptions and reality.

Defining (in)accuracy and determining accuracy criteria, however, can prove difficult if stereotypical perceptions are gathered from self-report data. For example, stereotype accuracy estimates generated from self-reports of men's and women's characteristics (as the benchmark for what is true in a group) may reflect social desirability bias, because many men and women may believe that they *should* have the gender-appropriate traits and because there are social penalties for behaving in gender-atypical ways. Thus, many people may under- or overreport the extent to which they have gender-typical traits. This self-report bias exaggerates stereotype accuracy estimates because the truth estimates were originally inflated. Gender researchers are mindful of these limitations and have examined stereotype accuracy and inaccuracy by comparing stereotypic gender differences to those documented by meta-analyses and by documenting a shifting standard in evaluations of gender-related traits and behaviors.

In the first of these strategies, stereotype accuracy is examined using meta-analytic procedures, comparing measured gender differences on stereotypic measures (as the criteria for accuracy) and others' stereotypic perceptions about those gender-related traits, abilities, and behaviors. Using this method, Swim (1994) showed that people do not automatically overestimate the frequencies of gender differences; their stereotypic perceptions correlated with the effect sizes estimating gender differences. In other words, when assessed gender differences were larger, people were more likely to hold stereotypes about that particular trait or behavior.

Using a similar approach, Hall and Carter (1999) correlated perceived ratings of gender differences on 77 traits in five categories (nonverbal communication, cognitive performance, cognitive attitudes, personality, organizational behavior and other attitudes and behavior) with results of meta-analytic studies of those gender differences. As a group, participants' ratings correlated strongly ($r = 0.70$) with effect sizes; when individual accuracy was examined, however, the correlation was lower ($r = 0.43$) and varied substantially among individuals (−0.20 to +0.67). Individual skill in accuracy was related to participants' skill and motivation in social perception and a less rigid cognitive style. From these results, it appears that individual assessments of gender differences may be less accurate than what groups believe overall.

Despite some evidence for accuracy, these evaluations may still reflect stereotyping because perceptions of gender-related traits and abilities are affected by context. Emerging research on shifting standards (Biernat, 2003; Biernat & Kobrynowicz, 1997; Biernat & Manis, 1994; Biernat, Manis, & Nelson, 1991) demonstrates that, in social perception and more particularly for stereotyping, raters shift or change the standard for evaluation according to the implied comparison. As a result, a person's perceptions of traits will be affected by who is being perceived (e.g., man or woman), what the trait expectations are for the group (e.g., agency or expressiveness), and the method of evaluation (e.g., subjective or objective).

Biernat and Kobrynowicz (1997), for example, showed that a job candidate was preferred when there was a match between gender typing of the position and the applicant's gender (women were preferred as secretaries and men preferred as chiefs of staff) and when these measurements were made using an objective judgment (e.g., percentile score on standardized test). When subjective judgments (a general assessment of low to high) were used, however, the outcome was reversed: The female chief-of-staff applicant was evaluated *more* positively than the male applicant and the male executive secretary was evaluated *more* positively than the female applicant. This research indicates that context is key: evaluations of gender-related traits and behaviors are affected by expectations, social comparisons, and method of measurement. This research also explains leniency biases in evaluation, such as perceiving a father to be more hirable than other types of workers with identical credentials (e.g., Fuegen, Biernat, Haines, & Deaux, 2004).

STEREOTYPE DEVELOPMENT

To simplify and understand the social world, perceivers create categories based on a variety of characteristics, the most basic of which are race, age, and gender (Macrae & Bodenhausen, 2000). These basic categories have privileged status for two important reasons (see Fiske, Lin, & Neuberg, 1999). First, categorization is based on information that is readily available to perceivers; often this information is conveyed by physical appearance cues such as dress, hairstyle, or size. Second, this information has important cultural meaning that is reinforced in a variety of ways, for example, by explicit gender labeling or gender-stereotypic statements, through observations of boys and girls and women and men in everyday life, or by implicit information about the appropriate characteristics and roles for category members (Arthur, Bigler, Liben, Gelman, & Ruble, 2008).

We consider next how information processing influences both children's and adults' gender stereotype acquisition and then go on to describe sources of gender-stereotypic information.

Stereotype Acquisition

There is little doubt that, early in life, children learn to categorize on the basis of gender and, in doing so, acquire the building blocks for gender-based stereotyping. Research suggests that by between the ages of 3 and 12 months children have acquired the ability to visually discriminate between males and females (Leinbach & Fagot, 1993); this ability develops well before the ability to verbalize such distinctions (Fagan & Singer, 1979). Evidence for visual discrimination comes from studies of infants' habituation to stimuli. In this procedure, infants are shown pictures of one gender until it is no longer novel; then the original picture is paired with a new picture and the time spent attending to both pictures is assessed. The assumption is that if infants spend more time looking at the novel face, they have successfully discriminated between the two categories. Because this technique is based on nonverbal responses, however, there are limitations to the conclusions that can be drawn. Infants, for example, may not be attending to the biological characteristics that differentiate the sexes, but rather to a series of cues that co-occur with sex, such as clothing and hairstyle (see Arthur et al., 2008). Whatever the bases of this discrimination, it seems clear that the categories "male" and "female" are implemented at an early age.

Category use is affected by women's and men's representations in various social roles. Although women and men are approximately equally represented in the general population, the sexes are not evenly distributed across specific social roles. This uneven distribution is readily apparent in a variety of social roles, but is particularly noticeable in occupational roles (Arthur et al., 2008). Caregivers, for example, are primarily women; hence, children's experience leads them to associate "woman" with the characteristics of "caregiver." Interactions with men typically take place in discriminably different situations, leading children to draw different conclusions about what men are like.

Although it does not specifically address children's stereotype acquisition, *social role theory* is based on the premise that people's beliefs about social groups stem from observing their social world (Eagly, 1987; Eagly, Wood, & Diekman, 2000). According to this theory, when people observe others, they pay attention to the social roles others occupy, such as their occupations. In doing so, they come to associate the characteristics of the role with the individuals who occupy it. People's propensity to do so is linked to a more general tendency to misjudge how situational factors influence others' behavior, a tendency labeled the *correspondence bias* (Ross, 1977). When observing a man in a leadership role, for example, people are likely to conclude that his actions stem from his stable personality and are less likely to decide that his actions were due to the situational requirements of the leadership role (Eagly & Karau, 2002). Over time, these observations develop into stereotypic beliefs.

Consider the well-documented belief that women are communal and men are agentic. Social role theory proposes that these gender stereotypes can be explained by a consideration of women's and men's occupational roles. Women are traditionally in lower-status roles, such as homemaker, and men in higher-status ones, such as breadwinner. Women, then, are disproportionately represented in roles requiring communal traits, such as kindness and concern for others, and men disproportionately in roles requiring agentic traits, such as self-confidence and assertiveness. Observers of these different representations associate the traits required by the social role with the people who occupy that role, and thus conclude that women are helpful and warm whereas men are independent and in charge.

Social role theory has been supported by research in a number of areas, including perceptions of leadership ability, beliefs about nationalities, predictions about occupational success, and age-based stereotypes (see Eagly et al., 2000, for a review). Although, to our knowledge, this theory has not been directly tested with children, the premise that children's development of gender stereotypes stems from their experiences in the social world is certainly consistent with this perspective.

Stereotype development also is influenced by the social rewards or punishments associated with our own and others' actions (Bandura, 1986). Consistent with *social learning theory,* reinforcement is often direct, as when parents encourage children to play with gender-appropriate toys or explicitly discourage an interest in counterstereotypic behavior (Bigler & Liben, 1999). Evidence suggests that adults verbally convey information about gender stereotypes and its importance to our culture. In doing so, they increase the psychological salience of gender; the result is an increased readiness for children to stereotype on the basis of gender (see, e.g., Arthur et al., 2008; Bem, 1993). Studies of adults' verbal labeling show that parents often explicitly refer to an actor's gender in conversations with their children, even when it is not necessary to do so (Gelman, Taylor, & Nguyen, 2004).

Learning about gender stereotypes also occurs indirectly, as when children observe others being rewarded for gender-appropriate behavior (Bandura, 1986). A central prediction of social learning theory is that future behavior is patterned after those actions that have previously been positively or negatively reinforced; rewarded behaviors are chosen, and punished or ignored behaviors eschewed. Importantly, reinforcements are associated with the basic categories children have developed (such as gender), leading to beliefs about the appropriate characteristics and roles for each gender.

Ample evidence shows that children follow adults' cues. By approximately two years of age, for example, most children can correctly identify and verbalize an actor's gender (e.g., Campbell, Shirley, & Caygill, 2002; Gelman et al., 2004). Additional evidence comes from research showing that, by around 18 months, children prefer gender-stereotyped toys and can associate those toys with the "appropriate" sex, such as trucks with boys' faces (Serbin, Poulin-Dubois, Colburne, Sen, & Eichstedt, 2001). Research suggests that children learn first about gender differences in adults' attributes and physical appearance and later, especially in the elementary years, expand their knowledge to the occupations and school tasks associated with women and men and boys and girls (see Ruble, Martin, & Berenbaum, 2006). As children develop, they become more flexible in their gender-stereotypic beliefs. Young children, for example, are likely to base judgments strictly on biological sex, but by around age nine, they begin to process information about gender-related activities and interests as well (see Martin, 1989, for a review).

One lesson enforced by parents, teachers, and even peers is the importance of gender-role conformity (see Martin, 1989, for a review). Studies demonstrate that preschoolers well understand its importance, and children as young as age three reinforce gender-appropriate behavior in their peers (Lamb, Easterbrooks, & Holden, 1980; Lamb & Roopnarine, 1979). Evidence also suggests that violations of societal gender norms are noticed more readily and taken more seriously for boys than for girls. Young boys who exhibit feminine behaviors are more frequently criticized than are girls who exhibit masculine behaviors (Fagot, 1977; 1985), and boys' perceptions about a potential male friend are negatively influenced by that boy's feminine behavior (Zucker, Wilson-Smith, Kurita, & Stein, 1995).

Unwillingness to accept boys' cross-sex behavior may be rooted in a general rejection of femininity for males (Herek & Glunt, 1993) and the not-unrelated belief that showing signs of femininity indicates a gay sexual orientation (e.g., C. L. Martin, 1990; McCreary, 1994). Another factor that likely comes into play is the societal perception that the male gender role is of higher status than the female gender role (Conway et al., 1996; Feinman, 1984). Boys simply have more to lose by leaving the preferred gender role. Whatever the cause, from a young age both boys and girls are aware of the appropriate gender roles and the consequences of violating those roles.

Stereotype Transmission

Society is generous in providing information about gender. Few institutions or socializing agents can be ignored when we try to determine just how children learn about gender and its associated stereotypes. Recognizing the multiplicity of these influences is important; parceling out the relative contribution of the various agents is more challenging, given the co-occurrence of these influences in everyday life. In fact, from a multilevel systems approach (e.g. Bronfenbrenner, 1977), we accept the reality of both macrolevel and microlevel processes that mutually support a system of cultural norms. Here we limit our focus, however, considering three of the more proximal sources of socialization: family, schools and peer groups, and media. Each has been shown to be fertile ground for the promotion of gender stereotypes.

Family

The family is a concept more easily used than precisely defined. Although researchers tend to restrict their consideration of family influences to the mother and father (and far more often to the mother), family dynamics are typically much broader in their operation, including not only siblings but often extended networks of grandparents, aunts and uncles, cousins, and even biologically unrelated caretakers. Often the messages coming from these various sources are inconsistent, and thus the researcher is faced with yet another challenge when trying to assess the impact of socialization sources on the acquisition of gender stereotypes. Recognizing these difficulties, we must nonetheless rely on the available literature, which does show clear evidence of parental influence on stereotype acquisition.

As noted earlier, parents can use both direct and indirect means to teach gender stereotypes to their children: they can be explicit in saying that girls and boys have different traits, or they can implicitly convey the same message in their choice of presents or activities. Even the parents' choice of colors and room decorations in a child's early years can encourage the development of sex-differentiated concepts (Pomerleau, Bolduc, Malcuit, & Cossette, 1990). Numerous studies show that parents themselves have stereotypic beliefs about boys and girls, for example, with regard to their possession of motor skills (Mondschein, Adolph, & Tamis-Le Monda, 2002). Further research has shown that parents who more strongly endorse gender stereotypes convey their beliefs with specific expectations about their children's performance in relevant domains (e.g., English versus math). More significantly, these expectations are realized in the actual performance of their children and in their children's self-perceptions of competence (with ability level controlled; Fredricks & Eccles, 2002).

Parents, of course, vary in the degree and type of stereotypic information they convey. Mothers who are employed, for example, are less likely to have stereotyped beliefs than are mothers who work only in the home, but even this relationship appears to be moderated by other factors, including socioeconomic status and father's involvement in childrearing (Ruble et al., 2006).

Schools and Peer Groups

Parents are often the major influence on a child's socialization in the preschool years (Lytton & Romney, 1991). As children get older, however, peer influence comes to play a larger role, as do teachers and other agents in the school system. (Indeed, it is a recognition of this influence that has led many parents to opt for home-schooling, eliminating the potential influence of both of these socializing sources.) Within the schools, particularly in the early school years, segregation of boys and girls is common, even on tasks for which gender is irrelevant (Bigler, 1995; Stanworth, 1983), and research suggests that when this segregation is more obvious, children are more likely to stereotype on the basis of gender (Bigler, 1995; Bigler, Jones, & Lobliner, 1997). Specific gender-related knowledge is also learned from teachers, from classmates, and from the instructional materials used (Meece, 1987).

Children themselves show a strong preference for gender segregation; in most Western cultures, the preference for interacting with one's own sex has been observed as early as ages 2–3 years and increases steadily as children get older (LaFreniere, Strayer, & Gauthier, 1984; Maccoby, 1998). By middle childhood, only 15 percent of children report having other-sex friends (Kovacs, Parker, & Hoffman, 1996). It seems likely that this gender homogeneity reinforces the notion of separate categories and increases the likelihood that distinctive stereotypic traits will be associated with each category. Significantly, this is also the age by which preschoolers exhibit clear evidence of gender-based prejudice (Bussey & Bandura, 1992; Martin, 1989).

Media

The media have long been recognized as important sources of gender-related information. Early studies focused primarily on the potential influence of television and films; more recently, investigators have broadened their analyses to include music, video games, and the Internet. The vast majority of these studies show extensive stereotyping of both gender and ethnicity, with only slight evidence of changes over time (Signorelli, 1993, 2001). Examples are abundant. In advertisements, for example, men are more often portrayed as the voice of authority and shown in professional roles, while women are still frequently seen engaged in home-centered behaviors such as laundry and cooking (Furnham & Mak, 1999).

Television programs directed at children are substantially more stereotypic than is adult programming (Ruble et al., 2006). Video games often portray women as sex objects (Dietz, 1998). And in the classic children's fare, Walt Disney films, gender stereotypes are also in high profile (Lippi-Green, 1997). The vast majority of female characters are shown only in the home or in traditional female jobs, such as nurses or waitresses, whereas men are typically depicted in high-prestige and exciting occupations.

Although evidence for the presence of gender stereotyping in the media is ubiquitous, it is more difficult to show the causal link between exposure and endorsement of gender stereotypes. Simply viewing television, for example, does not assure that attention is being paid and the representations incorporated. It is also possible that children who spend more time watching television or surfing the Internet are initially more prone to accept gender stereotypes. One-time experimental studies are often questioned for their generalizability, and longer-term correlational studies can not definitively establish causation. Nonetheless, evidence seems to be increasingly supportive of the position that frequent television viewing is associated with stronger beliefs in gender stereotypes (Huston et al., 1992; Morgan & Shanahan, 1997).

In analyzing the impact of any of these socialization agents, we realize that the messages are multifaceted and the impact uneven. Further, it is important to recognize the role of both the individual and the specific context. As suggested above, attention to stereotypic input and subsequent storage of those messages are critical processes, ones likely to vary among children who are exposed to identical material.

Whether children use the stereotypes that they have learned is also an issue that merits further research. Some recent studies, for example, show that the context in which people are asked to describe males and females can affect what stereotypes emerge (Sami, Bennett, Mullally, & MacPherson, 2003). Further, it is important to learn more about the degree to which both children and adults believe that gender-stereotypic qualities are fixed or susceptible to change (e.g., Bigler & Liben, 1999, Martin & Parker, 1995).

STEREOTYPE USE AND CHANGE

If the learning of stereotypes is inevitable, must their persistence be assumed as well? One purpose of this next section is to explore how and when stereotypes are used. That is, what sets the stage for stereotypical thinking about men and women? A second purpose is to highlight the factors leading to stereotype change. This section ends with an exploration of how stereotyping research may be used in cases of discrimination and the challenges and promises this research holds for changing society. We also address how stereotypes may be more resistant to change in the public sphere than in private or personal areas and the possibilities for reducing stereotyping in both domains.

Automaticity and Cues for Control

It would seem plausible to assume that people who are most likely to hold and endorse stereotypes also would be the ones most likely to act in stereotypical ways. However, emerging research indicates that stereotypes do not have to be personally endorsed to affect stereotypical thought and behavior (e.g., Bargh, Chen, & Burrows, 1996). Jost and Kay (2005), for example, showed that simply asking participants about their gendered attitudes (indicating endorsement) was as effective as exposing participants to gender attitude statements (proofreading gender attitude statements) on the degree to which they thought that differences between men and women were acceptable and inevitable. In other words, stereotype use can occur even in the absence of belief in those stereotypes.

This research, along with other findings in social cognition, suggests that stereotyping operates in an automatic manner (Bargh & Chartrand, 1999). Automatic gender stereotyping does not equate with inevitable gender stereotyping, however. It is possible for us to break the stereotype habit (Devine, Plant, & Buswell, 2000), either by developing cues for control (e.g., Monteith, Ashburn-Nardo, Voils, & Czopp, 2002) or by formulating chronic egalitarian goals (e.g., Moskowitz, Gollwitzer, Wasel, & Schall, 1999). Acknowledging that gender stereotypes exist and then reminding oneself of how gender shapes interactions may be one way to foster a cue for control. Developing such cues or goals may prove difficult, however, as many women and men embrace flattering gender stereotypes about themselves because these boost their self-esteem. When an equality goal is pitted against a self-esteem goal, the need for self-esteem may override the need for equality, and hence gender stereotypes will continue to be used. Understanding how gender stereotypes contribute to personal identity and self-esteem may be critical in understanding the conditions under which stereotypes are changed.

Individuating Information

Perceivers have goals in mind when they attempt to form impressions of other people. Students want to understand how demanding or lax their professor is so that they can pitch their level of work accordingly. Job candidates may manage their self-presentation based on whether an employer seeks a conscientious conformer or an extroverted initiator. How we form impressions of others can be viewed on a continuum from category based (i.e., stereotyped) to individuated (Fiske & Neuberg, 1990). Greater use of individuated information is associated with less stereotyping.

People are more likely to have accuracy goals when they are outcome dependent, such as when they are in a position of low power (Fiske, 1993). Individuals with little power are more likely to use individuating information and less likely to stereotype than are individuals who have more power. To the extent that power differences underlie men's and women's interactions at home, in the workplace, and in society, many opportunities exist to reinforce stereotypical thought and behavior and for power differences to intensify stereotyping between men and women.

The transformational nature of individuating information on stereotypes for both high- and low-power people should not be understated, however. Kunda and Thagard (1996) note that individuating information has four times the impact on person perception than does simple stereotype knowledge. Motivating people to attend to counterstereotypical behavior, therefore, would seem helpful in overriding gender stereotypes. Unfortunately, things are not so simple; individuating information is highly context and content dependent (see, e.g., Kunda & Sherman-Williams, 1993; Kunda & Oleson, 1995; Kunda and Thagard, 1996). Individuating information can even *increase* stereotyping when the person perceived is atypical of the category and the individuating information is not related to the stereotype (Kunda & Oleson, 1995).

Characteristics of the perceiver are also relevant. People who are highly prejudiced apply individuating information in ways that reinforce stereotypes (Sherman, Stroessner, Conrey, & Azam 2005); high-prejudice people are likely to explain away gender-inconsistent information as due to situational causes.

Clearly, attending to and using individuating information does not have a direct effect on stereotype reduction; aspects of the perceiver, the perceived, the impression formation goals, and the content and context of the information have intricate effects. A model that accounted for these factors would greatly improve our understanding of how people use specific information when overriding their gender stereotypes to form judgments of men and women.

Behavioral Confirmation

Stereotypes are not internal to the perceiver or the perceived, but are created by social interaction. Research on the self-fulfilling nature of stereotypes (Geis, 1993; Jussim, 1986; Snyder, Tanke, & Berscheid, 1977) demonstrates that preexisting beliefs about a target's characteristics compel perceivers to behave in ways that elicit the stereotyped traits in their targets. Behavioral confirmation occurs at the final stages of the stereotype loop: when people act in the anticipated stereotypical ways, their behavior reconfirms their initial stereotypes that set the behavioral sequence into motion. A math teacher's belief that "women are not good at math," for example, may compel that teacher to ignore a female student in class, giving her less praise or encouragement for math performance, or not giving her the benefit of the doubt (such as not awarding partial credit) when grading her work. The student's confidence and performance may then suffer as a result of this treatment bias, thus reconfirming the stereotype in both teacher and student.

Research examples of behavioral confirmation abound. Cameron and Trope (2004) showed that people ask leading questions to confirm their stereotypes—evidence of confirmation bias. The researchers conclude that biases in how people remember and retrieve information are critical components to triggering behavioral confirmation. Chen and

Bargh (1997) demonstrated that much of this process occurs below conscious awareness, having its strongest effects when subtle nonverbal behaviors encode praise or discouragement to guide others' behavior. A potential and harmful consequence of behavioral confirmation is that the stereotyped group member appears to provide "evidence" for the stereotype herself as if she were alone in the stereotype process.

Stereotype threat (Steele, 1997) extends our understanding of how stigma can recreate stereotyping; it also outlines several promises for breaking the cycle of stereotyping between perceivers and perceived. Stereotype threat occurs when a member of a stereotyped group experiences anxiety about confirming his or her group stereotype; in turn, this anxiety interferes with performance in the stereotyped domain. For example, when women are reminded of gender-based math stereotypes ("women perform more poorly in math than men"), they do in fact perform more poorly than when no stereotypes are mentioned—even women who are highly identified with the domain of math (Spencer, Steele & Quinn, 1999). Stereotype threat seems to be intensified by a woman's solo or *token* status (Sekaquaptewa & Thompson, 2003).

In spite of these performance differences, stereotype threat is not inevitable, and slight modifications to the performance context will reduce stereotype threat effects. When women are told that a math test does not produce a gender difference, their performance is comparable to that of men (Spencer, Steele, & Quinn, 1999). Reading about the professional achievements of other women (i.e., role modeling) has reduced stereotype threat for women in mathematics (McIntyre, Paulson & Lord, 2003), and exposure to women in high-status roles enhances women's career (relative to homemaking) aspirations (Geis, Brown, Jennings, & Porter, 1984).

Davies, Spencer, and Steele (2005) argue that this kind of reframing creates an "identity-safe" environment for women. Davies et al. (2005) reduced stereotype-based choices (women preferring subordinate roles to leader roles) when they told women that there was no clear evidence for gender differences in leadership ability. Because anxiety—and its consequent effects on working memory—may be at the root of stereotype threat, the anxiety-reducing effects of role models and identity-safe environments appear to be causal in breaking the stereotype cycle (Schmader & Johns, 2003).

Role Congruity and Lack-of-Fit Models

One reason why women may experience discomfort when occupying traditionally male roles is that people who do not conform to gender roles are often evaluated negatively. *Role congruity theory* (Eagly & Karau, 2002) and the Lack-of-Fit Model (Heilman, 1983) help explain when stereotypes contribute to biased evaluations and negative reactions—especially those situations in which women compete in the workforce and other public domains. These research models propose that there is a perceived lack of fit between the agentic characteristics required of the traditional male roles and women's supposed communal/expressive characteristics, and that this disjunction plays a role in perceptual and evaluative bias. One form of bias, the "backlash effect" (Rudman, 1998), confirms that agentic women are evaluated negatively when they violate the tacit cultural assumption that they be communal. Rudman and Glick (2001) further show that implicit attitudes linking women and communal traits underlie this type of discrimination.

Although these findings highlight barriers for *attaining* employment, lack-of-fit bias also may underlie *advancement* at work—that is, the "glass ceiling." Lyness and Heilman (2006) demonstrated that the perceived lack of fit between job characteristics ("women are not suited for assembly-line jobs") appears to be driven by a stricter standard held to women (i.e., a shifting standard). Conversely, some evidence suggests that a "glass elevator" advances men in traditionally female occupations (Williams, 1992). One explanation for this gender bias operating favorably for men is that people may feel uncomfortable with a man in a "woman's job," and advancing a man to a position that complements his alleged leadership characteristics is a method for attaining gender-job fit. A male elementary school teacher might be given more consideration for the position of principal than would an equally qualified female teacher because of the status and authority associated with the principal role relative to the teacher role. Still, less attention has been paid to how lack of fit affects men in caregiving roles, such as stay-at-home father or caretaker to an ailing parent. Gender equality may only be realized when both men and women assume responsibility for caregiving roles without social penalties for either sex.

To summarize, increases and decreases in stereotyping come from variety of sources. First, stereotypes may be activated and applied automatically, even when individual endorsement of stereotype beliefs is low. Developing egalitarian goals and cues for control can be first steps in interrupting the automatic processes in stereotyping. Second, the effects of individuating information depend on characteristics of the perceived, the perceiver, and the context. The status of the perceiver also has effects, with high-status individuals more likely to engage in stereotypical thinking than those of lower status. Third, the self-fulfilling nature of stereotypes and stereotype threat appear to verify initial stereotypical thought. Providing role models and identifying safe tactics can decrease the effect of stereotypes on performance. Fourth, lack-of-fit biases may explain why equally qualified women have difficulty attaining and advancing in professions; an examination of lack-of-fit biases—for both men and women—is critical to achieving equality.

IMPLICATIONS OF STEREOTYPE USE AND CHANGE

Given what we know about the use of gender stereotypes, what are the possibilities for change? Stereotype change is possible when there is legislation that holds people accountable for their actions. Thus, we might consider it a goal to increase the application of stereotyping research to cases of discrimination. Such cases are tricky to prosecute for two reasons, however. First, if stereotypes are activated and even applied without awareness, can defendants be held responsible for their stereotyped behavior? The answer is yes. Using the same standard for responsibility as applied to other chargeable offenses (e.g., theft), one could argue that it is an individual's responsibility to know the causes and consequences of stereotyping as *common knowledge*. Here it is imperative to increase general knowledge about the conditions of activation (e.g., sexualized images of women that increase categorical thinking) so that this understanding is widespread. Moreover, it is equally important to educate people about the forces that reduce the negative effects of stereotyping, such as role modeling and egalitarian norms. By doing this, a plea of ignorance will be less effective as a defense.

A second and related challenge concerns the nature of aggregate data when they are applied to a particular case. Most research on gender stereotypes is done at the group level of analysis, and attempts to apply group data to a particular individual can prove difficult. Stereotype research may be most helpful in describing the environments that are fertile ground for prejudice but less useful in determining whether a particular person's stereotyped view of women has caused discrimination. Measures of gender stereotyping, such as the Implicit Association Test, can assess aspects of the individual, the testing context, or the larger social culture (Karpinski & Hilton, 2001), thus making it difficult to determine if a particular manager has a stereotyped view of women that contributed to his or her behavior. In this way, assessing individual differences in stereotyping may be neither appropriate nor accurate. Stereotype research used in class-action lawsuits that are directed at the nature of the organizational culture, rather than individuals per se, may be the best use. Prosecuting a context, rather than an individual, also has the added benefit of organizational examination and alteration of the whole, rather than a dismissal of a deviant few.

Although it may be possible to mold and change stereotypes in the public sphere, the private domain, such as family structure, can pose even greater challenges. As noted before, stereotypes that are flattering (i.e., benevolent sexism) or that are based in romantic fantasies (e.g., a "glass slipper effect"; Rudman & Heppen, 2003), may be particularly resistant to transformation. Furthermore, men's voluntary surrender of high-status, privileged roles in favor of lower-status, communal roles is clearly slower in coming—not surprisingly, as people do not readily relinquish control and status. Nonetheless, some potential for change may spill over from the reduced use of stereotypes in workplaces and organizational structure. If the workplace allows men and women to freely occupy roles without discrimination, then the perceived characteristics of men and women should reflect this change. With increased behavioral role and economic equality between women and men, changes in the personal sphere may follow at last.

REFERENCES

Ackman, D. (2004). Morgan Stanley: Big bucks for bias. Retrieved May 30, 2007, from http://www.forbes.com/services/2004/07/13/cx_da_0713topnews.html.

Ajzen, I., & Fishbein, M. (1980). *Understanding attitudes and predicting social behavior*. Englewood Cliffs, NJ: Prentice-Hall.

Armour, S. (2004). Wal-Mart is "rife" with discrimination, lawsuit plaintiffs say. *USA Today*, June 24, p. B3.

Arthur, A. E., Bigler, R. S., Liben, L. S., Gelman, S. A., & Ruble, D. N. (2008). Gender stereotyping and prejudice in young children: A developmental intergroup perspective. In S. Levy & M. Killen (Eds.), *Intergroup relations: An integrative developmental and social psychological perspective.* New York: Oxford University Press.

Ashmore, R. D., Del Boca, F. K., & Titus, D. (1984). Types of women and men: Yours, mine, and ours. Paper presented at the meeting of the American Psychological Association, Toronto.

Bandura, A. (1986). *Social foundations of thought and action*. Upper Saddle River, NJ: Prentice Hall.

Bargh, J. A., & Chartrand, T. L. (1999). The unbearable automaticity of being. *American Psychologist, 54,* 462–479.

Bargh, J. A., Chen, M., & Burrows, L. (1996). Automaticity of social behavior: Direct effects of trait construct and stereotype priming on action. *Journal of Personality and Social Psychology, 71,* 230–244.

Beere, C. A. (1990). *Gender roles: A handbook of tests and measures*. New York: Greenwood.

Bem, S. L. (1993). *The lenses of gender: Transforming the debate on sexual inequality*. New Haven, CT: Yale University Press.

Biernat, M. (2003). Toward a broader view of social stereotyping. *American Psychologist, 58,* 1019–1027.

Biernat, M., & Kobrynowicz, D. (1997). Gender- and race-based standards of competence: Lower minimum standards but higher ability standards for devalued groups. *Journal of Personality and Social Psychology, 72,* 544–557.

Biernat, M., & Manis, M. (1994). Shifting standards and stereotype-based judgments. *Journal of Personality and Social Psychology, 66,* 5–20.

Biernat, M., Manis, M., & Nelson, T. (1991). Stereotypes and standards of judgment. *Journal of Personality and Social Psychology, 60,* 485–499.

Bigler, R. S. (1995). The role of classification skills in moderating environmental effects on children's gender stereotyping: A study of the functional use of gender in the classroom. *Child Development, 66,* 1072–1087.

Bigler, R. S., Jones, L. C., & Lobliner, D. B. (1997). Social categorization and the formation of intergroup attitudes in children. *Child Development, 68,* 530–543.

Bigler, R. S., & Liben, L. S. (1999). Cognitive mechanism in children's gender stereotyping: Theoretical and educational implications of a cognitive-based intervention. *Child Development, 63,* 1351–1363.

Bronfenbrenner, U. (1977). Toward an experimental ecology of human development. *American Psychologist, 32,* 513–531.

Broverman, I. K., Vogel, S. R., Broverman, D. M., Clarkson, F. E., & Rosenkrantz, P. S. (1972). Sex-role stereotypes: A current appraisal. *Journal of Social Issues, 28*(2), 59–78.

Bussey, K., & Bandura, A. (1992). Self-regulatory mechanisms governing gender development. *Child Development, 63,* 1236–1250.

Cameron, J. A., & Trope, Y. (2004). Stereotype-biased search and processing of information about group members. *Social Cognition, 22,* 650–672.

Campbell, A., Shirley, L., & Caygill, L. (2002). Sex-typed preferences in three domains: Do two-year-olds need cognitive variables? *British Journal of Psychology, 93,* 203–217.

Carpenter, S., & Trentman, S. (1998). Subtypes of women and men: A new taxonomy and an exploratory analysis. *Journal of Social Behavior and Personality, 13,* 679–696.

Cejka, M. A., & Eagly, A. H. (1999). Gender-stereotypic images of occupations correspond to the sex segregation of employment. *Personality and Social Psychology Bulletin, 25,* 413–423.

Chen, M., & Bargh, J. A. (1997). Nonconscious behavioral confirmation processes: The self-fulfilling nature of automatically-activated stereotypes. *Journal of Experimental Social Psychology, 33,* 541–560.

Conway, M., Mount, L., & Pizzamiglio, M. T. (1996). Status, community, and agency: Implications for stereotypes of gender and other groups. *Journal of Personality and Social Psychology, 71,* 25–38.

Cuddy, A. J. C., Fiske, S. T., & Glick, P. (2004). When professionals become mothers, warmth doesn't cut the ice. *Journal of Social Issues, 60*(4), 701–718.

Davies, P. G., Spencer, S. J., & Steele, C. M. (2005). Clearing the air: Identity safety moderates the effects of stereotype threat on women's leadership aspirations. *Journal of Personality and Social Psychology, 88,* 276–287.

Deaux, K., & LaFrance, M. (1998). Gender. In D. T. Gilbert, S. T. Fiske, & G. Lindzey (Eds.), *Handbook of social psychology* (4th ed., vol. 1, pp. 788–827). Boston: McGraw-Hill.

Deaux, K., & Lewis, L. L. (1984). The structure of gender stereotypes: Interrelationship among components and gender label. *Journal of Personality and Social Psychology, 46,* 991–1004.

Deaux, K., Winton, W., Crowley, M., & Lewis, L. L. (1985). Level of categorization and content of gender stereotypes. *Social Cognition, 3,* 145–167.

Devine, P. G., Plant, E. A., & Buswell, B. N. (2000). Breaking the prejudice habit: Progress and obstacles. In S. Oskamp (Ed.), *Reducing prejudice and discrimination* (pp. 185–208). Thousand Oaks, CA: Sage.

Diekman, A. B., & Eagly, A. H. (2000). Stereotypes as dynamic constructs: Women and men of the past, present, and future. *Personality and Social Psychology Bulletin, 26,* 1171–1188.

Dietz, T. L. (1998). An examination of violence and gender role portrayals in video games: Implications for gender socialization and aggressive behavior. *Sex Roles, 38,* 425–442.

Eagly, A. H. (1987). *Sex differences in social behavior: A social-role interpretation.* Hillsdale, NJ: Erlbaum.

Eagly, A. H., & Karau, S. J. (2002). Role congruity theory of prejudice toward female leaders. *Psychological Review, 109,* 573–598.

Eagly, A. H., & Kite, M. E. (1987). Are stereotypes of nationalities applied to both women and men? *Journal of Personality and Social Psychology, 53,* 451–462.

Eagly, A. H., & Mladinic, A. (1989). Gender stereotypes and attitudes toward women and men. *Personality and Social Psychology Bulletin, 15,* 543–558.

Eagly, A. H., Mladinic, A., & Otto, S. (1991). Are women evaluated more favorably than men? An analysis of attitudes, beliefs, and emotions. *Psychology of Women Quarterly, 15,* 203–216.

Eagly, A. H., & Steffen, V. J. (1986). Gender stereotypes, occupational roles, and beliefs about part-time employees. *Psychology of Women Quarterly, 10,* 252–262.

Eagly, A. H., Wood, W., & Diekman, A. B. (2000). Social role theory of sex differences and similarities: A current appraisal. In T. Eckes (Ed.). *The developmental social psychology of gender* (pp. 123–174). Mahwah, NJ: Erlbaum.

Eckes, T. (1994). Features of men, features of women: Assessing stereotypic beliefs about gender subtypes. *British Journal of Social Psychology, 33,* 107–123.

Eckes, T. (2002). Paternalistic and envious gender stereotypes: Testing predictions from the stereotype content model. *Sex Roles, 47,* 99–114.

Eliason, M., Donelan, C., & Randall, C. (1992). Lesbian stereotypes. *Health Care for Women International, 13,* 131–144.

Fagan, J. F., & Singer, L. T. (1979). The role of simple feature difference in infants' recognition of faces. *Infant Behavior and Development, 2,* 39–45.

Fagot, B. I. (1977). Consequences of moderate cross-gender behavior in preschool children. *Child Development, 48,* 902–907.

Fagot, B. I. (1985). Beyond the reinforcement principle: Another step toward understanding sex role development. *Developmental Psychology, 21,* 1097–1104.

Fassinger, R. E. (2001). Women in nontraditional occupational fields. In J. Worell (Ed.), *The encyclopedia of women and gender: Sex similarities and the impact of society on gender* (vol. 2, pp. 1169–1180). New York: Academic Press.

Fazio, R. H., Jackson, J. R., Dunton, B. C., & Williams, C. J. (1995). Variability in automatic activation as an unobstrusive measure of racial attitudes: A bona fide pipeline? *Journal of Personality and Social Psychology, 69,* 1013–1027.

Feinman, S. (1984). A status theory of the evaluation of sex-role and age-role behavior. *Sex Roles, 10,* 445–456.

Fischer, A. H. (2000). *Gender and emotion: Social psychological perspectives.* Cambridge: Cambridge University Press.

Fishbein, M., & Ajzen, I. (1975). *Belief, attitude, intention and behavior: An introduction to theory and research.* Reading, MA: Addison-Wesley.

Fiske, S. T. (1989). Interdependence and stereotyping: From the laboratory to the Supreme Court (and back). Paper presented at the meeting of the American Psychological Association, New Orleans, August.

Fiske, S. T. (1993). Controlling other people: The impact of power on stereotyping. *American Psychologist, 48,* 621–628.

Fiske, S. T. (1998). Stereotyping, prejudice, and discrimination. In D. T. Gilbert, S. T. Fiske, & G. Lindzey (Eds.), *The handbook of social psychology* (vol. 2, pp. 357–411). Boston: McGraw-Hill.

Fiske, S. T. (2004). *Social beings: A core motives approach to social psychology.* Hoboken, NJ: Wiley.

Fiske, S. T., Bersoff, D. N., Borgida, E., Deaux, K., & Heilman, M. E. (1991). Social science research on trial: The use of stereotype research in *Price Waterhouse v. Hopkins. American Psychologist, 46,* 1058–1069.

Fiske, S. T., Cuddy, A. J. C., Glick, P., & Xu, J. (2002). A model of (often mixed) stereotype content: Competence and warmth respectively follow from perceived status and competition. *Journal of Personality and Social Psychology, 82,* 878–902.

Fiske, S. T., Lin, M., & Neuberg, S. L. (1999). The continuum model: Ten years later. In S. Chaiken & Y. Trope (Eds.), *Dual-process theories in social psychology* (pp. 231–254). New York: Guilford.

Fiske, S. T., & Neuberg, S. L. (1990). A continuum model of impression formation, from category based to individuating processes: Influence of information and motivation on attention and interpretation. In M. P. Zanna (Ed.), *Advances in experimental social psychology* (vol. 23, pp. 1–74). New York: Academic Press.

Fiske, S. T., Xu, J., Cuddy, A. C., & Glick, P. (1999). (Dis)respecting versus (dis)liking: Status and interdependence predict ambivalent stereotypes of competence and warmth. *Journal of Personality and Social Psychology, 55,* 473–489.

Fredricks, J., & Eccles, J. S. (2002). Children's competence and value beliefs from childhood through adolescence: Growth trajectories in two male-sex-typed domains. *Developmental Psychology, 38,* 519–533.

Fuegen, K., Biernat, M., Haines, E., & Deaux, K. (2004). Mothers and fathers in the workplace: How gender and parental status influence judgments of job-related competence. *Journal of Social Issues, 60*(4), 737–754.

Furham, A., & Mak, T. (1999). Sex-role stereotyping in television commercials: A review and comparison of 14 studies done on five continents over 25 years. *Sex Roles, 41,* 413–437.

Geis, F. L. (1993). Self-fulfilling prophesies: A social psychological view of gender. In A. E. Beall & R. J. Sternberg (Eds.), *The psychology of gender* (pp. 9–54). New York: Guilford.

Geis, F. L., Brown, V., Jennings (Walstedt), J., & Porter, N. (1984). TV commercials as achievement scripts for women. *Sex Roles, 10,* 513–525.

Gelman, S. A., Taylor, M. G., & Nguyen, S. P. (2004). Mother-child conversations about gender. *Monographs of the Society for Research in Child Development, 69,* 1–127.

Gesell, G. (1990). Findings of fact and conclusions on law of remand. Court Action 84-3040, *Ann B. Hopkins v. Price Waterhouse.*

Glick, P., & Fiske, S. T. (1996). The Ambivalent Sexism Inventory: Differentiating hostile and benevolent sexism. *Journal of Personality and Social Psychology, 70,* 491–512.

Glick, P., & Fiske, S. T. (1999). The Ambivalence toward Men Inventory: Differentiating hostile and benevolent beliefs about men. *Psychology of Women Quarterly, 23,* 519–536.

Greenwald, A. G., Banaji, M. R., Rudman, L. A., Farnham, S. D., Nosek, B. A., & Mellott, D. S. (2002). A unified theory of implicit attitudes, stereotypes, self-esteem, and self-concept. *Psychological Review, 109,* 3–25.

Greenwald, A. G., McGhee, D. E., & Schwartz, J. L. K. (1998). Measuring individual difference in implicit cognition. *Journal of Personality and Social Psychology, 74,* 1464–1480.

Haddock, G., & Zanna, M. P. (1994). Preferring "housewives" to "feminists." *Psychology of Women Quarterly, 18,* 25–52.

Hall, J. A., & Carter, J. D. (1999). Gender-stereotype accuracy as an individual difference. *Journal of Personality and Social Psychology, 77,* 350–359.

Heilman, M. E. (1983). Sex bias in work settings: The lack of fit model. *Research in Organizational Behavior, 5,* 269–298.

Herek, G. M., & Glunt, E. K. (1993). Interpersonal contact and heterosexuals' attitudes toward gay men: Results from a national survey. *Journal of Sex Research, 32,* 95–105.

Huston, A. C., Donnerstein, E., Fairchild, H., Feshbach, N. D., Katz, P. A., Murray, P., et al. (1992). *Big world, small screen: The role of television in American Society.* Lincoln: University of Nebraska Press.

Huston-Comeauz, S. L., & Kelly, J. R. (2002). Gender stereotypes of emotional reactions: How we judge an emotion as valid. *Sex Roles, 47,* 1–10.

Jost, J. T., & Kay, A. C. (2005). Exposure to benevolent sexism and complementary gender stereotypes: Consequences for specific and diffuse forms of system justification. *Journal of Personality and Social Psychology, 88,* 498–509.

Jussim, L. (1986). Self-fulfilling prophecies: A theoretical and integrative review. *Psychological Review, 93,* 429–445.

Karpinski, A., & Hilton, J. L. (2001). Attitudes and the Implicit Association Test. *Journal of Personality and Social Psychology, 81,* 774–788.

Kite, M. E., & Branscombe, N. R. (1998). *Evaluations of subtypes of women and men.* Unpublished, Ball State University, Muncie, IN.

Kite, M. E., & Deaux, K. (1987). Gender belief systems: Homosexuality and the implicit inversion theory. *Psychology of Women Quarterly, 11,* 83–96.

Kovacs, D. M., Parker, J. G., & Hoffman, L. W. (1996). Behavioral, affective, and social correlates of involvement in cross-sex friendship in elementary school. *Child Development, 67,* 2269–2286.

Krueger, J. I., Hasman, J. F., Acevedo, M., & Villano, P. (2003). Perceptions of trait typicality in gender stereotypes: Examining the role of attribution and categorization processes. *Personality and Social Psychology Bulletin, 29,* 108–116.

Kunda, Z., & Oleson, K. C. (1995). Maintaining stereotypes in the face of disconfirmation: Constructing grounds for subtyping deviants. *Journal of Personality and Social Psychology, 68,* 565–579.

Kunda, Z., & Sherman-Williams, B. (1993). Stereotypes and the construal of individuating information. *Personality and Social Psychology Bulletin, 19*(1), 90–99.

Kunda, Z., & Thagard, P. (1996). Forming impressions from stereotypes, traits, and behaviors: A parallel constraint-satisfaction theory. *Psychological Review, 103,* 284–308.

LaFrance, M., & Banaji, M. (1992). Toward a reconsideration of the gender-emotion relationship. In M. S. Clark (Ed.), *Emotion and social behavior* (pp. 178–201). Newbury Park, CA: Sage.

LaFreniere, P., Strayer, F. F., & Gauthier, R. (1984). The emergence of same-sex preferences among preschool peers: A developmental ethological perspective. *Child Development, 55,* 1958–1965.

Lamb, M. E., Easterbrooks, M. A., & Holden, G. W. (1980). Reinforcement and punishment among preschoolers: Characteristics, effects and correlates. *Child Development, 51,* 1230–1236.

Lamb, M. E., & Roopnarine, J. L. (1979). Peer influences on sex-role development in preschoolers. *Child Development, 50,* 1219–1222.

Landrine, H. (1985). Race × class stereotypes of women. *Sex Roles, 13,* 65–75.

Leinbach, M. D., & Fagot, B. I. (1993). Categorical habituation to male and female faces: Gender schematic processing in infancy. *Infant Behavior and Development, 16,* 317–332.

Lippi-Green, R. (1997). *English with an accent: Language, ideology, and discrimination in the United States.* London: Routledge.

Lyness, K. S., & Heilman, M. E. (2006). When fit is fundamental: Performance evaluations and promotions of upper-level female and male managers. *Journal of Applied Psychology, 91,* 777–785.

Lytton, H., & Romney, D. M. (1991). Parents' differential socialization of boys and girls: A meta-analysis. *Psychological Bulletin, 189,* 267–296.

Maccoby, E. E. (1998). *The two sexes: Growing apart and coming together.* Cambridge, MA: Harvard University Press.

Macrae, C. N., & Bodenhausen, G. V. (2000). Social cognition: Thinking categorically about others. *Annual Review of Psychology, 51,* 93–120.

Martin, A. J. (1990). Men's ambivalence toward women: Implications for evaluations or rape victims. (Doctoral dissertation, City University of New York, 1990).

Martin, C. L. (1987). A ratio measure of sex stereotyping. *Journal of Personality and Social Psychology, 52,* 489–499.

Martin, C. L. (1989). Children's use of gender-related information in making social judgments. *Developmental Psychology, 25,* 80–88.

Martin, C. L. (1990). Attitudes and expectations about children with nontraditional and traditional gender roles. *Sex Roles, 22,* 151–165.

Martin, C. L., & Parker, S. (1995). Folk theories about sex and race differences. *Personality and Social Psychology Bulletin, 21,* 45–57.

McCauley, C. R., & Stitt, C. L. (1978). An individual and quantitative measure of stereotypes. *Journal of Personality and Social Psychology, 36,* 929–940.

McCreary, D. R. (1994). The male role and avoiding femininity. *Sex Roles, 31,* 517–531.

McIntyre, R. B., Paulson, R. M., & Lord, C. G. (2003). Alleviating women's mathematics stereotype threat thought salience of positive group achievements. *Journal of Experimental Social Psychology, 39,* 83–90.

Meece, J. L. (1987). The influence of school experiences on the development of gender schemata. In L. S. Liben & M. L. Signorella (Eds.), *Children's gender schemata* (pp. 57–73). San Francisco: Jossey-Bass.

Mondschein, L. R., Adolph, K. E., & Tamis-LeMonde, C. S. (2000). Gender bias in mothers' expectations about infant crawling. *Journal of Experimental Child Psychology, 17,* 304–316.

Monteith, M. J., Ashburn-Nardo, L., Voils, C. I., & Czopp, A. M. (2002). Putting the brakes on prejudice: On the development and operation of cues for control. *Journal of Personality and Social Psychology, 83,* 1029–1050.

Morgan, M., & Shanahan, J. (1997). Two decades of cultivation research: An appraisal and meta-analysis. In B. R. Burleson (Ed.), *Communication yearbook* (vol. 20, pp. 1–46). Thousand Oaks, CA: Sage.

Moskowitz, G. B., Gollwitzer, P. M., Wasel, W., & Schaal, B. (1999). Preconscious control of stereotype activation through chronic egalitarian goals. *Journal of Personality and Social Psychology, 77*, 167–184.

National Center for Education Statistics (2006). *Participation in Education*. Retrieved September 4, 2006, http://www.nces.ed.gov/programs/coe/2006/section1.

National Committee on Pay Equity (2004). Women of color in the workplace. Retrieved July 13, 2004, from http://www.pay-equity.org/info-race.html.

Nosek, B. A. (2005). Moderators of the relationship between implicit and explicit evaluation. *Journal of Experimental Psychology: General, 134*, 565–584.

Nosek, B. A., Banaji, M. R., & Greenwald, A. G. (2002). Math = Male, Me = Female, therefore Math ≠ Me. *Journal of Personality and Social Psychology, 83*(1), 44–59.

Nosek, B. A., & Smyth, F. L. (2005). A multitrait-multimethod validation of the Implicit Association Test: Implicit and explicit attitudes are related but distinct constructs. *Journal of Experimental Psychology: General, 134*, 565–584.

Noseworthy, C. M., & Lott, A. J. (1984). The cognitive organization of gender-stereotypic categories. *Personality and Social Psychology Bulletin, 10*, 474–481.

Plant, E. A., Hyde, J. S., Keltner, D., & Devine, P. G. (2000). The gender stereotyping of emotions. *Psychology of Women Quarterly, 24*, 81–92.

Pomerleau, Q., Bolduc, D., Malcuit, G., & Cossette, L. (1990). Pink or blue: Environmental gender stereotypes in the first 2 years of life. *Sex Roles, 22*, 359–367.

Rosenkrantz, P. S., Vogel, H., Bee, I., Broverman, I., & Broverman, D. V. (1968). Sex-role stereotypes and self-concepts in college students. *Journal of Consulting and Clinical Psychology, 32*, 286–295.

Ross, L. (1977). The intuitive psychologist and his shortcomings: Distortions in the attribution process. *Advances in Experimental Social Psychology, 10*, 174–221.

Ruble, D. N., Martin, C. L., & Berenbaum, S. A. (2006). Gender development, pp. 858–932.

Rudman, L. A. (1998). Self-promotion as a risk factor for women: The costs and benefits of counter-stereotypical impression management. *Journal of Personality and Social Psychology, 74*, 629–645.

Rudman, L. A., & Glick, P. (2001). Prescriptive gender stereotypes and backlash toward agentic women. *Journal of Social Issues, 57*, 743–762.

Rudman, L. A., & Heppen, J. (2003). Implicit romantic fantasies and women's interest in personal power: A glass slipper effect? *Personality and Social Psychology Bulletin, 29*, 1357–1370.

Ryan, C. S. (2003). Stereotype accuracy. *European Review of Social Psychology, 13*, 75–109.

Sami, F., Bennett, M., Mallally, S., & MacPherson, J. (2003). On the assumption of fixity in children's stereotypes: A reappraisal. *British Journal of Developmental Psychology, 99*, 113–124.

Schmader, T., & Johns, M. (2003). Converging evidence that stereotype threat reduces working memory capacity. *Journal of Personality and Social Psychology, 85, 440–452.*

Sekaquaptewa, D., & Thompson, M. (2003). Solo status, stereotype threat, and performance expectancies: Their effects on women's performance. *Journal of Experimental Social Psychology, 39,* 68–74.

Serbin, L. A., Poulin-Dubois, D., Colburne, K. A., Sen, M. G., & Eichstedt, J. A. (2001). Gender stereotyping in infancy: Visual preference for and knowledge of gender-stereotyped toys in the second year. *International Journal of Behavioral Development, 25,* 7–15.

Sherman, J. W., Stroessner, S. J., Conrey, F. R., & Azam, O. A. (2005). Prejudice and stereotype maintenance processes: Attention, attribution, and individuation. *Journal of Personality and Social Psychology, 89,* 607–622.

Signorielli, N. (1993). Television, the portrayal of women, and children's attitudes. In G. L. Berry & J. K. Asamen (Eds.), *Children and television: Images in a changing sociocultural world* (pp. 229–242). Newbury Park, CA: Sage.

Signorelli, N. (2001). Television's gender role images and contribution to stereotyping: Past, present, future. In D. Singer & J. Singer (Eds.), *Handbook of children and the media* (pp. 341–358). Thousand Oaks, CA: Sage.

Snyder, M., Tanke, E. D., & Berscheid, E. (1977). Social perception and interpersonal behavior: On the self-fulfilling nature of stereotypes. *Journal of Personality and Social Psychology, 35,* 656–666.

Spence, J. T., & Hahn, E. D. (1997). The Attitudes toward Women Scale and attitude change in college students. *Psychology of Women Quarterly, 21,* 17–34.

Spence, J. T., & Helmreich, R. (1972). The Attitudes toward Women Scale: An objective instrument to measure attitudes toward the rights and roles of women in contemporary society. *JSAS Catalog of Selected Documents in Psychology, 2,* 66.

Spence, J. T., Helmreich, R., & Stapp, J. (1974). The personality attributes questionnaire: A measure of sex-role stereotypes and masculinity/femininity. *JSAS Catalog of Selected Documents in Psychology, 4,* 43.

Spence, J. T., Helmreich, R., & Stapp, J. (1975). Ratings of self and peers on sex role attributes and their relation to self-esteem and conceptions of masculinity and femininity. *Journal of Personality and Social Psychology, 32,* 29–39.

Spencer, S. J., Steele, C. M., & Quinn, D. M. (1999). Stereotype threat and women's math performance. *Journal of Experimental Social Psychology, 35,* 4–28.

Stanworth, M. (1992). *Gender and schooling.* London: Hutchinson.

Steele, C. M. (1997). A threat in the air: How stereotypes shape the intellectual identities and performance of women and African Americans. *American Psychologist, 52,* 613–629.

Swim, J. K. (1994). Perceived versus meta-analytic effect sizes: An assessment of the accuracy of gender stereotypes. *Journal of Personality and Social Psychology, 23,* 601–631.

Swim, J. K., Aikin, K. J., Hall, W. S., & Hunter, B. A. (1995). Sexism and racism: Old-fashioned and modern prejudices. *Journal of Personality and Social Psychology, 68,* 199–214.

Twenge, J. M. (1997). Changes in masculine and feminine traits over time: A meta-analysis. *Sex Roles, 35,* 461–488.

Twenge, J. M., & Zucker, A. N. (1999). What is a feminist? Evaluations and stereotypes in closed- and open-ended responses. *Psychology of Women Quarterly, 23,* 591–605.

U.S. Bureau of Labor Statistics (2002a). Employed persons by major occupation and sex, 1983 and 2002 annual averages (table 10). Retrieved September 27, 2004, from www.bls.gov.

U.S. Bureau of Labor Statistics (2002b). Employment status of the civilian non-institutional population 16 years and over by sex (table 2). Retrieved September 24, 2004, from www.bls.gov.

Vonk, R., & Ashmore, R. D. (2003). Thinking about gender types: Cognitive organization of female and male types. *British Journal of Social Psychology, 42,* 257–280.

Williams, C. L. (1992) The glass escalator: Hidden advantages for men in the "female" professions. *Social Problems, 39,* 253–267.

Williams, J., & Best, D. L. (1990). *Measuring sex stereotypes: A thirty-nation study.* Newbury Park, CA: Sage.

Zucker, K. J., Wilson-Smith, D. N., Kurita, J. A., & Stern, A. (1995). Children's appraisals of sex-typed behavior in their peers. *Sex Roles, 33,* 703–725.

Chapter 8

Girls to Women: Developmental Theory, Research, and Issues

Pamela Trotman Reid
Shauna M. Cooper
Kira Hudson Banks

How do girls become women? We believe that any response to this question must explain more than a change in size and physical maturation over time. We are not merely asking how girls mature, but how girls come to have different expectations, specific family and social roles, and characteristic interpersonal styles. Further, we consider to what extent they behave differently based on gender, and how can we explain the changes across the early life span. Our goal in this chapter is to examine the theories, research, and issues relevant to girls' development. We present a relatively comprehensive, although not exhaustive, perspective of the conditions and circumstances that influence the gender-specific development of girls from infancy through adolescence. During this examination, we particularly focus on the diversity among girls and how development evolves in different cultural and social contexts.

In virtually every society, there is a process through which female children pass on their way to mature womanhood. While we recognize the importance of genetic predisposition and physical growth, the metamorphosis also involves emotional, psychological, and social domains. In our fast-paced modern world, the complexity of growing up female has been heightened by changing definitions regarding the female role and the conflicting expectations of society. The primarily biological aspects of female behavior we will refer to as "sex"-related, that is, genetic or innate. However, we view much of female development as a socially manipulated and environmentally influenced, that is, we adopt a social-constructivist perspective, and therefore socially determined aspects are referred to as "gender"-related.

Knaak (2004) argued that gender is actually a multidimensional construct with subjective dimensions about the meaning that have yet to be fully explored. She further suggested that gender includes organizational and cultural components that are inseparable in our understanding and explanations. This is consistent with Thorne's thesis (2001), which describes gender boundaries as flexible and specific to individual contexts. We plan to consider gender interactions and intersections as we take a developmental approach.

MAJOR DEVELOPMENTAL ISSUES

At the basic level, *development* can be defined as a combination of quantitative and qualitative growth that occurs over time. We see growth as a young girl's body grows into that of a woman's. We see the results of development in her increasing grasp of language and social skills and in greater intellectual achievements. Development is also obvious in the young woman's increasing recognition of societal expectations and her possible acceptance of limits on her future behavior and aspirations.

Developmental Approach

The developmental approach to studying behavior is an attempt to establish the rules for the changes that may be observed over time (Newman & Newman, 1987). Much of developmental theory may be found to revolve about a core set of issues. Our examination of girls' development begins by addressing these traditional issues that provide a context for examining girls' changing status. We ask to what extent nature and nurture influence development; we also ask about gender constancy, and to what extent children are active in defining their role. These questions help frame our understanding of the various factors moving girls from infancy toward adulthood.

Nature and Nurture

The question of whether female development and stereotypic female behavior occurs due to the forces of nature (genetic, biological, and inherited factors) or nurture (learned, experiential, and environmental factors) provided the basis of much of developmental research through the early decades of child study. Early developmental investigators posed the issue as an either/or question. Today, most psychologists accept the belief that an understanding of both the biological concomitants of behavior and the external influences on that behavior is necessary for a psychology of women that is accurate and complete (Baumeister, 2000).

A decision to accept the interactivity of both inherited and environmental influences can have far-reaching impact. For example, in discussing the role of women in the workplace, a recently fought court case hinged on testimony from researchers claiming, on behalf of the company, that women were not interested in or suited for the higher-paying jobs because of the skills required, while other social scientists, on behalf of the female plaintiffs, presented facts suggesting that women were discouraged from pursuing the lucrative posts (Nelson & Bridges, 1999). Even for school-age girls, arguments continue about girls' aptitude and interest in science, mathematics, technological subjects, and sports. The beliefs and expectations of parents, teachers, and peers may, indeed, shape the opportunities for a girl's future role (Frome & Eccles, 1998; Howes, Phillipsen, Peisner-Feingberg, 2000).

Gender Constancy, Behavior, or Salience

Cognitive-developmental theorists and researchers, such as Piaget (1947) and Kohlberg (1976), suggested that children actively engage the environment to understand the roles of male and female. The focus on constructing understanding of gender is described as important for the child to sustain constancy in her understanding of what it means to be a girl so that she can behave in accordance with her beliefs. Social-learning theorists, on the other hand, proposed that situations and actions lead to consistent gender behaviors (Bandura & Walters, 1963). This more passive view of children's development suggests that that rewards and patterns of support shape the beliefs and gender view that children hold. More recently, gender schema theorists have studied the salience of gender roles for children's lives and proposed that this dimension has greatest impact on development (Thorne & Luria, 2003). In one effort to clarify the relationship among these three domains of gender development (i.e., constancy beliefs, consistent behaviors, and saliency), researchers studied preschool children and found that gender salience and gender-typed behavior were strongly related and predicted children's masculinity or femininity, whereas understanding of gender constancy was not a predictor of behavior (Levy, Barth, & Zimmerman, 1998).

Critical Periods versus Plasticity

Developmental research has traditionally raised the question of whether there are critical times during which a particular developmental change should occur for optimal results. The importance of determining when one set of changes influences another may be illustrated by recent environmental changes shown to affect girls' biological development. For example, until recent years the onset of menstruation and physical changes of puberty were expected to occur in the early teen years. Now, girls as young as eight years old may manifest signs of pubescence. Some researchers have attributed early onset of puberty to hormonal supplements to food sources and changes in diet (Phinney, Jensen, & Olson, 1990). This premature maturation appears to upset social and psychological development in ways we are just beginning to understand.

SOCIETAL EXPECTATIONS AND GENDER-ROLE PRESCRIPTIONS

Female roles are prescribed in every society with clear and distinct behavioral expectations for girls and women (Bem, 1981). The behavior our society accepts as appropriate for young girls and women has been defined and carefully socialized into our consciousness through a variety of sources, both personal and institutional. While there are some cultural and ethnic differences, there is a surprisingly strong consensus across groups as to what constitutes gender-appropriate behaviors for girls and women (Lott, 1987). For instance, girls are expected to be gentle, obedient, caring, and nurturing. An important notion underlying these societal expectations is that relationships and interconnectedness with others is an important aspect in the lives of girls and women (Taylor, Gilligan, & Sullivan, 1995). Although these societal expectations and gender-role prescriptions are still prevalent in today's society, now there is much more flexibility in the ways women and girls can define themselves.

Scholars have focused on the ways in which girls prepare themselves to negotiate these gender roles. While psychological theory has promoted the notion that "feminine" and "masculine" characteristics are both necessary and complementary components of a well-adjusted adult (Bem, 1983), some people have been resistant to relinquishing the notion that gender-role-related characteristics are opposite and contradictory to one another. Girls, at an early age, are able to recognize and distinguish these societal expectations and gender-role prescriptions (Martin & Ruble, 2004). Given that young girls can comprehend these societal expectations and gender-role prescriptions, it is safe to say that they can have a major impact on their growth and development. Thus, to fully understand the impact of these societal expectations on girls, we should acknowledge that gender-role-related information emanates from many sources. In the section below, we will highlight the two most influential contexts for the gender development of girls: home and school. Additionally, this section highlights the influence of the media as well as culture influences on gender development.

Influence of Parents

Undoubtedly, parents play an important role in the shaping of a girl's development of gender-role-appropriate behaviors and ideas (Lanvers, 2004; Martin, 2000). Surveys and discussions with parents of young children demonstrate a general consensus that girls are expected to be verbal, compliant, physically weak, quiet, and clean (Basow, 1992). For newborns, both parents, but fathers especially, perceive their daughters as smaller, more delicate, less active, and weaker than they perceive sons (Delk, Madden, Livingston, & Ryan, 1986). In a recent study, Peterson (2004) found that both mothers and fathers were more descriptive of their daughters' injuries than sons; the author speculated that this increased discourse surrounding the details of the injury may be related to parents' endorsement of gender roles, particularly the fragility of their daughters.

These views and beliefs about femininity, which may be held by parents, can materialize in many ways. For example, parents may encourage gender-role-appropriate activities and behaviors by providing children with sex-typed clothing and toys (Fisher-Thompson, Sausa, & Wright, 1995). At a young age, girls are dressed in ways that clearly communicate their gender status (e.g., pink, dresses).

The same pattern of gender-distinctive treatment has been found in studies regarding toy selection. Typically, these studies have found that while girls are given dolls, dollhouses, and miniature household appliances (Etaugh & Liss, 1992), boys are provided with building blocks, sports equipment, models of vehicles, and animals. In a recent study, Blakemore and Centers (2005) found that girls' toys were associated with more feminine characteristics, such as physical attractiveness and nurturance, and that boys' toys were associated with more masculine-stereotyped characteristics, such as violence and competitiveness.

Studies have also found that parents exhibit gender-typed behaviors in play activities (Gelman, Taylor, & Nguyen, 2004; Idle, Wood, & Desmarais, 1993). These findings suggest that parents may communicate their beliefs and views about gender-appropriate behaviors to their daughters at an early age. Moreover, some studies have found that young children also endorse these gender-typed norms through their own toy and clothing preferences (Blakemore, 2003). However, other investigations indicate that girls exhibit more flexibility in toy and clothing selection, leading researchers to conclude that there may be less emphasis placed upon the traditional views of femininity now compared to years past (Wood, Desmarais, & Gugula, 2002).

Parents' gender-stereotyped perceptions may also influence how parents behave in daily interactions with their daughters and sons. For instance, parents were observed to engage in more "rescuing" behavior with girls, that is, assisting and accompanying girls more often than necessary (Marmion & Lundberg-Love, 2004) than with boys. Additionally, parents, particularly mothers, appear to engage in more supportive and encouraging discussions with their daughters than with sons (Leaper, Anderson, & Sanders, 1998). Fathers, on the other hand, are found to be less involved with their daughters than sons (Stright & Bales, 2003).

Given parents' awareness of gender stereotypes, we assume that parents also hold different views of their daughters. This appears true with respect to parental expectations. The literature has suggested that parents hold different expectations for their daughters compared to their sons (Eccles, Freedman-Doan, Frome, Jacobs, & Yoon, 2000). For instance, parents hold more stereotypical beliefs about the academic abilities of their daughters (Eccles, 1993; Herbert & Stipek, 2005). In fact, Tiedemann (2000) found that, while parents had higher ratings of their daughters' language and literacy-related abilities, they had lower ratings of their mathematical abilities.

In some instances, even parents' willingness to help girls may communicate their gendered beliefs about girls' intellectual abilities in areas that have been traditionally defined as "male" (e.g., mathematics and science). For example, Bhanot & Jovanovic (2005) indicated that, although boys received more intrusive homework support, girls were more susceptible to negative effects when parents exhibited more intrusive behaviors. The authors also suggest that these intrusive helping behaviors conveyed the parents' stereotypic beliefs about boys performing better in math than girls.

These gender-role beliefs may ultimately have an indirect influence on the school performance of girls; parents' beliefs about their daughters, in turn, influence the daughters' own academic self-perceptions in negative ways (Jacobs, 1991). Additional studies have found that the association between parents and the child's self-perceptions strengthen with age, suggesting that girls may internalize their parents' gender-stereotype views of girls' abilities (cf. Tiedemann, 2000; Wigfield et al., 1997).

While there has been some consistency of findings regarding parental influences on gender-typed behaviors and activities, we should note that most studies have focused primarily on middle-class, European-American families. Thus, the extent to which these socialization patterns and strategies are exhibited in families of various ethnic and class backgrounds remains an important question. However, there is some evidence that parental responses may vary considerably based on both ethnicity and social class (Hill, 2002).

The preponderance of the literature examining gender in families of various racial and ethnic backgrounds has focused on these processes in African American families. In particular, theorists have suggested that these differences in gender-role expectations and related behaviors can be attributed to the sociohistorical context of African Americans. Specifically, scholars have suggested that, due to slavery, both African American men and women were unable to assume traditional gender roles (Collins, 1998; Hill, 2002).

Although previous studies found few differences in gender-role expectations in African American families (Nobles, 1985; Romer & Cherry, 1980), more recent investigations suggest that some ethnic-related differences do exist in gender-role-related expectations (Hill, 2002; Reid, Tate, & Berman, 1989; Reid & Trotter, 1993). Reid and Trotter (1993), for example, found that, when asked to interact with an infant, white children exhibited clear sex differences, while African American children did not. Other researchers also have suggested that there are more egalitarian gender roles in African American households (cf. McLoyd, Cauce, Takeuchi, & Wilson, 2000) and gender differences in the socialization practices of African American families (Hill, 2002; McLoyd et al., 2000). Taken together, these findings suggest that ethnicity and gender, conjunctively, may influence the gender-role expectations and behaviors of African American parents.

To date, few empirical data exist on gender-role expectations for other ethnic groups. However, the existing literature suggests that Asian American and Hispanic American parents also may expect their daughters to engage in more traditional gender-typed behaviors (Brooker & Ha, 2005; Dasgupta, 1998; Ginorio, Gutiérrez, Cauce, & Acosta, 1995). Some studies have even found that there may be less flexibility in gender-typed behaviors in Asian and Hispanic families (Denner & Dunbar, 2004; Talbani & Halsani, 2000). Furthermore, these gender-role expectations may be a great source of conflict within these families, given the differences between their expectations and those of the dominant society.

It is important to assert that other family characteristics, such as social class, religion, lifestyle, and so forth, may also influence gender-typed behaviors and activities. However, most studies have not examined how these factors may influence gender-typed parenting. There is some indication that socialization of feminine gender-role behavior does vary with social class and that this socialization would impact directly the achievement behavior exhibited by girls. Carr and Mednick's (1988) study of African American preschool children supported this contention. In particular, they found that girls with greater nontraditional gender-role training were higher in achievement. Other studies also have found class differences among African American families that suggest that working-class girls will have fewer gender-role constraints (Romer & Cherry, 1980). However, Higginbotham and Weber (1992) and Hill (1999) suggested that middle-class families had higher academic and career expectations as well as greater involvement in the education-related activities of their daughters than working-class families. Although there have been few studies that have taken an intersectional approach, several scholars have asserted the importance of examining how race, gender, and social class interact to influence the gender development of girls (Collins, 1998; Denner & Dunbar, 2004; Hill, 2002; Reid et al., 1989).

Ethnicity and social class are important influences in the gender development of girls, but it is also important to mention other parenting characteristics that influence gender roles. One area of focus has been mothers' employment status and its role in girls' development (Dundas & Kaufman, 2000; Marmion & Lundberg-Love, 2004). There is some evidence that daughters of employed mothers may be more likely to perceive women's roles as involving freedom of choice and satisfaction (Baruch & Barnett, 1986).

Another area for study is mothers' sexual orientation. Hill (1988) noted that lesbian mothers perceived their daughters and their sons to be more similar in characteristics than did heterosexual mothers. Lesbian mothers held less stereotypic ideas relating to the feminine role and encouraged more traditionally masculine role expectations of their daughters (Perlesz & McNair, 2004). Empirical evidence also suggested that roles within lesbian families may be less gender-stereotyped than in more traditional families (Dalton & Bielby, 2000; Sullivan, 1996). Thus, it is presumable that children within these households may engage in less gender-stereotyped behaviors.

Although parents have an important role in the gender development of their children, it is not the *sole* factor. We note that children's own characteristics also influence gender-role-related expectations and behaviors. In particular, research has indicated that parents appear to modify their gendered expectations and treatment of their children as they become older (van Wel, ter Bogt, & Raaijmakers, 2002). Research data also show how various characteristics of children, such as temperament, activity-level, and responsiveness, have also been found to influence the expectations parents may hold for their daughters (Karraker & Coleman, 2005). Thus, daughters' characteristics may serve as important moderators for parents' gender-typed behaviors and expectations for them.

Influences of School

Just as parents cannot be considered the sole agent of gender-role typing, we must recognize that their influence is not constant across childhood. Researchers suggest that parental influence on children's attitudes become less prominent as children transition into adolescence (Baruch & Barnett, 1986; Basow & Rubin, 1999). We must, therefore, consider other socialization agents if we are to understand fully the influences on gender-role development.

In our society, as children mature, they are particularly exposed to societal expectations in school settings. Both teachers and peers have been found to serve as strong agents for appropriate gender-role-related behaviors (Maccoby, 1998). Some studies have suggested that teachers are more open to explore gender roles with girls than boys (Cahill & Adams, 1997). Yet, much of the literature has found that, like parents, teachers reinforce gender-typed behaviors and activities. For example, teachers report more dependency in their relationships with female students (Halliday, McNaughton & Glynn, 1985; Howes et al., 2000). Also, in a recent observational study of preschool children, Chick, Heilman-Houser, and Hunter (2003) found that teachers engage in multiple gender-typed behaviors in the classroom, including girls receiving less teacher attention, girls receiving comments about their appearance and ability to help others, teachers expressing more emotion in communication with girls, and use of gender-typed toys and classroom activities. Teachers have also been found to hold gender stereotypes regarding their students. For instance, teachers have been found to perceive higher ability for girls in verbal ability and to perceive that males have higher ability in math (Eccles, 1993; Frome & Eccles, 1998; Herbert & Stipek, 2005).

In addition to teacher influences on gender-typed behaviors, some scholars have suggested that the overall school culture influences the gender development of girls (Meece & Scantlebury, 2006). Ruble and Martin (1998) suggest that schools have a "hidden curriculum" that reinforces gender-appropriate behaviors for girls. Also, the division of labor in schools may also communicate gender-typed behaviors to girls. For example, while women dominate the teaching field at the preschool and elementary levels, the majority of school principals are men (NCES, 2004). These men represent both authority and masculinity. Girls grow to expect that these characteristics belong together. As children progress through school, it becomes increasingly clear that women are also not expected to develop interests in math or science. Given that girls spend much of their time in school, school and teacher endorsement of these behaviors may have important implications for their gender development.

As youth enter school, interactions with peers become increasingly important in shaping and reinforcing the gender-typed behaviors of girls (Witt, 2000). Gender roles are clearly present in the peer interactions of girls, particularly behaviors that reinforce female gender stereotypes (Galambos, 2004; Marmion & Lundberg-Love, 2004). Although research findings are somewhat equivocal on this point, there is some indication that girls engage in more female gender-typed behaviors in peer interactions, exhibiting more collaboration (Hops, Alpert, & Davis, 1997; Phelps, 2001), more nurturing behavior (Jarvinen & Nicholls, 1996), and more self-disclosure in their friendships (Lansford & Parker,

1999) compared to boys. These gender-typed characteristics are also encouraged by both male and female peers. For instance, peers' popularity ratings of girls have been found to be based on common female gender-stereotyped characteristics, such as physical appearance and social skills (Adler, Kless, & Adler, 1992). Thus, those girls who are designated as most popular by their male and female peers often exhibit traditionally female gender-typed characteristics and behaviors.

In their interactions with male peers, girls often exhibit more subordinate behaviors. Specifically, the literature has suggested that girls accept subordinate positions even when they may possess superior knowledge and expertise (Lockheed & Hall, 1976; Mathews, 1975). Although girls may exert influence over same-sex peers' behaviors, they do not appear to exert the same influence within cross-sex friendships (Gaughan, 2006). Thus, even at an early age, female-stereotyped behaviors that emphasize passivity and submissiveness in exchanges with males are reinforced through their interactions with male peers. As girls mature, peers become more flexible with respect to gender-typed behaviors (McHale, Kim, Whiteman, & Crouter, 2004; Ruble & Martin, 1998). However, by that time, these gender-role-related behaviors and beliefs may be deeply entrenched. Thus, these behaviors that are reinforced through their peer interactions have important implications for the growth and development of girls.

Media Images and Influences

In today's highly technological world, mass media images appear ubiquitous, and the characters presented seem accepted as role models, as well as representatives of gender-role expectation. Experimental and anecdotal evidence suggest that images from print, film, and television influence girls in a number of ways: gender-role development, body satisfaction, and attitudes and behaviors related to sexual relationships. Exposure to stereotyped behavior (e.g., limited options and stereotype inflexibility) can be correlated with more stereotypical beliefs about the sexes (Ward & Harrison, 2005). On the other hand, research in the area of sexual attitudes has found that increased media exposure is related to increased levels of sexual experience, support for premarital sex, and an assumption that peers are sexually active (Ward & Rivadeneyra, 1999). Therefore, girls' interest in activities and careers, as well as their behavior and attitudes, can be influenced by the range of opportunities to which they are exposed.

For the most part, reviews of research indicated that the overwhelming majority of media images of girls and women conform to both racial and gender stereotypes (Gordon, 2004; Towbin, Haddock, & Zimmerman, 2003). Particularly in the past, popular literature and children's schoolbooks portrayed females as neat, compliant, and passive (McArthur & Eisen, 1976). Girls and women of color were rarely represented, but even when they were, it was also in very stereotypic ways (Dickerson, 1982).

Current portrayals attempt to move beyond the limited gender images to expose girls to new vistas and inspire them with the new successes and opportunities available to girls and women (Ward, 2004). Even with the nontraditional models, however, stereotypic behaviors may prevail. Through stereotyped characters, girls may receive confirmation of societal expectations that girls do not take risks, accomplish exciting feats, or leave the security of their homes and the protection of men. One young girl reflected on the messages she learned from the cartoons and movies she watched. She learned that as a girl, she needed to be helpless, in need of rescue, and pretty, while waiting for the prince (Johnson, 2003; Gordon, 2004; Towbin et al., 2003). These messages influenced her to give up tomboy tendencies to perfect the art of being weak, helpless, and boring despite her feeling that these attributes did not fit her. In time, she learned to be critical of these images she had so easily swallowed. This ability to critically analyze those messages is the basis of media literacy that can perhaps buffer some of the deleterious affects of media exposure.

Adolescents ages 8–18 consume approximately eight hours of media daily (Roberts, Foehr, & Rideout, 2005). While other forms of media are influential, television is particularly powerful, given that virtually every household in America has a television set and adolescents have been found to devote three to four hours daily to watching. Television, too, presents stereotyped images of girls and women. Sternglanz and Serbin (1974), in an early study of children's television programs, found that girls and women were depicted as nurturing, succorant, relatively inactive, and ineffective.

Preschool girls have been shown to make sex-typed choices based on the television characters they observe (Ruble et al., 1981), and even identification with characters depends on their traditional gender-role-related portrayal (McGhee & Frueh, 1980). Interestingly, girls are found to model verbal labeling rather than the active behaviors modeled by boys after observing televised characters. Even the limited presence or absence of girls and women models conveys a message that the group is not important enough to be represented. The omission could give such an impression to girls who are Chicanas, Puerto Ricans, Native Americans, or Asians, for it is rare indeed when characters from these groups are depicted in a significant way in any national media (Reid, 1979; Gordon, 2004; Towbin et al., 2003). This trend changed little over the past decades until the advent of Spanish television networks. Now, major networks and movies are integrating Spanish-speaking characters into their programs to some extent. Still the stereotyping persists in both majority and minority venues!

Research with Latinas found that adolescent girls who watched more English-language programming expressed more traditional gender attitudes (Rivadeneyra & Ward, 2005). The same relationship was present with Spanish-language programming, but this relationship diminished when acculturation was taken into account. Analysis of television programs suggests that African Americans are portrayed as more passive and lazy compared to other ethnic groups (Mastro & Greenberg, 2000) and African American female characters on television were even more stereotyped than African American males (Reid, 1979).

Stereotypes about women's and men's behavior are also clearly observable in music videos (Freudinger & Almquist, 1978; Ward, Hansbrough, & Walker, 2005). Viewing videos has become a common pastime for many adolescents, with numerous television stations dedicated to music videos, in addition to websites that allow on-demand viewing of videos. In these videos, girls and women are depicted as hypersexualized, emotional, deceitful, illogical, frivolous, dependent, and passive. Boys and men are portrayed as sexually aggressive, rational, demanding, and adventuresome. Arnett (2002) describes the typical music video as including women who are seen more as props than characters, with minimal clothes writhing around male performers. Rock music videos frequently depict gratuitous violence against women and women as sex objects (Towbin et al., 2003).

Frequent exposure to rock music videos increases the probability that subsequent women's and men's behavior will be appraised in the context of the gender-role stereotypic schemata, even for preschool and young children (Waite & Paludi, 1987). More recent research has found that increased video viewing is correlated with greater gender stereotyping, but that prime-time dramas, comedies, and movies were unrelated (Ward, Hansbrough, & Walker, 2005). Within the same study, an experimental design reiterated how the viewing of videos with stereotypical content is influential in shaping beliefs about how men and women should behave.

Along with stereotypes about gender-specific behavior, expectations, and stereotypes, the thin ideal is one of the major concepts perpetuated by the media. Some investigators have shown that the body size of models decreased significantly during the 1980s and 1990s, while the tendency to portray entire bodies of models compared to only their face or torso increased (Sypeck, Gray, & Ahrens, 2004). Others note that up to 83 percent of adolescent girls read fashion magazines, which often perpetuate the ideal of thinness (Levine & Smolak, 1996). Therefore girls are seeing more flesh of thinner models today compared to 25 years ago.

Sociocultural theory suggests that disordered eating and body image disturbance in girls is exacerbated by transmitting the idea of a thin ideal, which becomes internalized and pursued through sometimes unhealthy means (Engeln-Maddox, 2005; Groesz, Levine, & Muren, 2002; Thompson & Stice, 2001; Tiggemann, 2006). There is evidence that exposure to mass media is related to body concerns and disturbed eating, but the causal nature of the relationship is less clear. It is important to note that longitudinal studies have elucidated a reciprocal relationship between media exposure and body image concerns; that is, while exposure to media may increase body image concerns, those who develop body image issues also seek increased media content (Tiggemann, 2006). The Tiggemann (2006) study also found decreased body image was associated with the reading of fashion magazines, but unrelated to television exposure, although watching soap operas was related to increased internalization of the thin ideal. Correlational research has continued to find exposure to the thin ideal related to increased body dissatisfaction, disordered eating, and decreased self-esteem (Hawkins, Richards, Granley, & Stein, 2004; Thompson & Stice, 2001).

Another longitudinal study randomly assigned adolescent girls to receive a 15-month subscription to a teen magazine (Stice, Sprangler, & Agra, 2001). While no main effect was found for increased magazine exposure correlating with body dissatisfaction, the study did find that social support was a moderator. Subscription to the magazine led to increased body dissatisfaction among girls who had lower social support. While correlations exist, evidence remains unclear as to a direct causal effect of media exposure on body image.

Puberty poses a developmental dilemma for adolescent girls' physical self-image. It is a time when self-consciousness is heightened; cultural ideals suggest attention to weight gain, and at the same time, adolescent development moves girls away from the thin ideal. Research suggests that, since body image stabilizes around the beginning of high school (Stice et al., 2001; Tiggemann, 2006), one way we can help protect girls from the influence of mass media is to limit their intake during childhood and adolescence. Investigators found that those not yet in college are more adversely affected by the thin ideal (Groesz et al., 2002). Further empirical findings indicate that girls age 13–14 are more likely to compare themselves to thin models, compared to girls age 9–10, and those that report body dissatisfaction seek out thin ideal stimuli (Martin & Gentry, 1997). More research is needed to understand at what stages and in what states (e.g., already engaged in disordered eating, expressing body dissatisfaction) girls are most susceptible to the thin ideal.

Social comparison theory might also be important for future research. Interventions that utilize a social comparison approach report increases in body dissatisfaction; in other words, girls feel more dissatisfaction when in a position of comparison to others (Engeln-Maddox,

2005; Martin & Gentry, 1997). We should note, however, that the social comparison factor seems not to apply to African American girls. Indeed, race has been found to be a protective factor when considering the impact of media images; perhaps the negative comparisons have been so unrelenting that African American girls no longer see the images as applicable to them. While this seems to be the case for African American girls, it does not necessarily apply to Latinas. African American female adolescents have been found to be less affected by mainstream images of the thin ideal compared to white female adolescents (Schooler, Ward, Merriwether, & Caruthers, 2004). In addition, viewing predominantly African American media was found to be protective of African American girls' self-esteem, in spite of the gender stereotypes. Research has also found that for African American youth, strong identification with their race and religiosity have been found to buffer negative affects of the media (Ward, 2004) and discrimination (Neblett, Shelton, & Sellers, 2004; Operario & Fiske, 2001; Sellers, Caldwell, Schmeelk-Cone, & Zimmerman, 2003). It is unclear what mechanisms underlie these dynamics, but findings suggest that girls who feel positive about being a member of their racial or ethnic group might have a buffer against deleterious effects. For all girls, we should consider the usefulness of media literacy, education about gender-typed messages, and having open discussions to critique the portrayals of women as strategies to minimizing media effects.

Influences of Race, Culture, and Social Class

Race and Culture

Race and culture, as experienced within the United States, are oftentimes intersecting constructs. Several researchers have warned us to avoid the practice of using race in research as an explanatory variable, since it is often meant to be a proxy for culture (Helms, Jernigan & Mascher, 2005; Reid & Paludi, 1993). It is often assumed that, when we find race differences, there are underlying mechanisms at work that affect such results. In fact, race and ethnicity are both cultural contexts, in that they consist of beliefs, customs, and traditions (McLoyd, 1990). Although we focus in this section on research that has found differences across races and cultures, we will also consider within-group studies and note that the comparison of groups is not always necessary to understand varied experiences.

Since gender-typed experiences for racial groups often appear similar to those of majority groups, little explicit research has unpacked gender by ethnicity or racial group experiences. We know that, in the main, African American parents attempt to prepare their children for the realities of a racialized society by being honest and truthful about possible barriers yet also aiming to build character (Ward, 1996). It may be that African American children make more life decisions, have more freedom, or have personal responsibilities thrust on them earlier than other groups of children. Whatever the cause, one of the major issues facing African American adolescents is their involvement in risky sexual behavior. African American girls, as well as boys, are more sexually active than their peers of other groups (Brener, Kann, Lowry, Wechsler, & Romero, 2006). Since sexually transmitted diseases, including HIV, are usually contracted during adolescence (the symptoms of AIDS emerge later in life), attention to the sexual practices of adolescent girls is of great importance, affecting as it does their well-being and that of any children they might bear.

For Latinas, the challenge of adolescence is the struggle to balance the collective spirit found within the family with the individualism of U.S. society (Denner & Guzman, 2006; Taylor, 1996). It can be a delicate dance to meet the expectations of parents and family while also navigating their own social world, that is, the challenges of creating an identity in school and among peers. Much has been written about Latinas in crisis, but few investigations have actually established an understanding of normative family life for Latina adolescents.

Similarly, Native American youth also have to balance the interdependence promoted within the family with the independence expected in mainstream society. Exposure to alcohol has been a major focus of recent research, since American Indian youth have been found to engage in alcohol use earlier than other racial and ethnic groups (Kulis, Okamoto, Rayle, & Sen, 2006).

Asian American youth often experience a great deal of pressure to be the model minority (Wong & Hanglin, 2006). This pressure can keep youth who have talents outside of traditional math and science areas from expressing their skills and shame those who do not excel in those areas. Multiracial youth are a growing segment of the population and are often faced with being objectified as exotic (Root, 2004).

All young people must struggle with developing an identity and understanding themselves and how they fit into society. However, girls of color must also negotiate how race factors into their identity and how to make sense of experiences in that light. This process is called *racial identity development*. Racial identity is conceptualized as the significance and meaning African Americans place on race and being a member of that group (Sellers, Smith, Shelton, Rowley, & Chavous, 1998). With rapidly changing demographics in the United States, white American youth increasingly have to face diversity in school, the workplace, and their neighborhoods. These changes will require them to engage in the process of racial identity development, too—understanding what it means to be white, something that up until recent years has easily been avoided.

Social Class

Recent research has urged the community to reframe how we think about affluence and poverty. We more clearly recognize that social class denotes not merely more resources but also substantial differences in how individuals interpret their world. We suggest that social class is accompanied by values, expectations, and differences in responding to experiences. Still, expectations about the challenges faced by adolescents may be underestimated or misunderstood. For example, low-income youth are traditionally considered high-risk, while high-income, or affluent, youth are considered low-risk. Yet empirical findings suggest that affluent youth are at risk for a number of behaviors, including substance abuse, anxiety, and depression (Luthar & Latendresse, 2005). Research has found that suburban youth engage in use of cigarettes, alcohol, marijuana, and hard drugs at higher levels compared to inner-city youth (Luthar & D'Avanzo, 1999). Specifically, suburban girls were three times more likely to report clinical levels of depressive symptoms. While the life of affluent adolescents often provides privileges that the less affluent can only dream about, wealth does not ensure good parenting or a contented home.

Clearly, low-income adolescents also may experience a wide range of social difficulties stemming from a lack of resources, low political capital, and less respect from others. Adolescents of color are more likely to face poor academic offerings, neglected neighborhoods, and racism. For low-income girls, adolescent challenges may include social stigmatization, as well as physical and sexual abuse, witnessing violence (Vera, Reese, Paikoff, & Jarrett, 1996), or early motherhood (Murry, 1996). While we are more likely to see affluent girls struggle with anorexia, obesity—also a pressing issue for many youth in the United States—appears linked to low socioeconomic status (Stunkard & Sorenson, 1993). Risk factors for obesity include lack of knowledge about healthy foods; a tendency to buy high-fat, low-cost foods; and stress. Of course, the trajectory of experiences for individuals of any specific group will vary, but the relationships and trends are worth further investigation.

PHYSICAL DEVELOPMENT

Despite the recent focus on the integration of multiple perspectives (e.g., biopsychosocial models) and environmental influences on development, physical development and biological events remain important throughout the life span. With an understanding of how females develop through childhood and adolescence, it is important to examine the interaction between internal and external factors (Reid & Paludi, 1993). We will discuss the physical changes that occur and related social trends.

Childhood Development

The first two years of life is one of the periods, along with adolescence, where the most rapid growth occurs. During this time, girls are generally smaller in size compared with boys, but girls have more advanced skeletal and neurological systems and greater sensitivity to auditory stimuli (Paludi, 1985). In early childhood, girls have an advantage in fine motor skills and those gross motor skills that require balance, compared to boys (Thomas & French, 1985).

Research has not revealed consistent sex differences in the area of early learning, but much research has focused on physical activity. While findings have been mixed at this stage, research on physical changes during childhood and adolescence has suggested sex differences. Sports-related skills are greater among young boys, and this gap increases around adolescence (Malina & Bouchard, 1991). What is important to note is that this difference is most likely not only due to differences in muscle development. While girls' involvement in sports has increased over the past decades, boys still outnumber girls in team sports, and girls are in general less physically active, in part because boys have traditionally received more encouragement for developing sports-related skills (Centers for Disease Control and Prevention, 1999).

Consistent with research, it appears that sex differences can be interpreted not only as biological but also as a reflection of the interaction between social environment and biology (Bem, 1981; Tobach, 2004). It is not that girls are biologically inferior; in fact, girls' language acquisition is quite rapid and typically surpasses that of boys through grade school. Rather, it is the interaction of low expectations and lack of rewards for physical performance that contribute to girls' lower performance in areas that have been traditionally defined as more appropriate for boys. Whatever genetic differences might exist are exacerbated by socially constructed norms. Culturally prescribed characteristics of femininity are congruent with the lack of physical prowess.

It seems more difficult for society to focus on the physical achievements of female athletes. For example, African American tennis champions Venus and Serena Williams have been discussed in the media for their grunts during play, wardrobe, and experiences with poverty, with such commentary often overshadowing their athletic dominance on the court. Similarly, several Eastern European female tennis players are widely recognized for their physical attractiveness. A recent advertisement juxtaposed Maria Sharapova's athletic prowess with the song "I Feel Pretty." Research has investigated how cultural expectations can exert themselves through atmosphere and social pressure in unspoken and unmarked ways in the sports arena (Douglas, 2005). The message continues to be that women athletes are still judged by stereotypic norms, not by their sports-related achievements.

Adolescent Development

Puberty, another period of rapid growth, marks the beginning of adolescence and involves hormonal and bodily changes. The hypothalamus, pituitary gland, and gonads play key roles in this process. The hypothalamus signals the pituitary gland to release the hormone known as gonadotropin, which can occur during adolescents' sleep a year or so before any of the physical changes associated with puberty appear (Schowalter & Anyan, 1981). Estrogens are the dominant hormone related to female development and increase during puberty. Estradiol is an estrogen that influences breast development, uterine development, and skeletal changes. Despite the known biological links, social factors, behavior, and mood can also affect hormones and subsequently adolescent development (Brooks-Gunn & Warren, 1989; Paikoff, Buchanan, & Brooks-Gunn, 1991).

Data indicate that in most cultures the age at which girls begin to menstruate has been dropping steadily for the last several centuries. In the United States, the age when puberty is reached has steadily decreased, with the trend now leveling off. On average, most girls experience a height spurt, breast growth, and growth of pubic hair around age 10, and experience menarche, or first menstruation, around 13 years of age (Reid & Paludi, 1993). Girls typically mature on the average of two years earlier than boys. In the United States, menarche is considered in the normal range between the ages of 9 and 15. One of the contributing factors to early puberty is obesity, possibly explained by the finding that fat cells stimulate the production of sex hormones. These linkages could explain why breast and pubic hair growth and menarche occur earlier for heavy and obese girls (Must & Strauss, 1999).

In general, adolescent girls are less satisfied with their bodies and have more negative body images compared to boys (Brooks-Gunn & Paikoff, 1993). Girls who matured early had more negative feelings about menstruation compared to average or late maturing girls. Early-maturing girls have also been found to be vulnerable to problem behaviors (e.g., smoking, drinking, eating disorders; Dick, Rose, Viken, & Kaprio, 2000; Petersen, 1993). These girls often feel pressure of sexual responsibilities that they are not emotionally prepared to accept. Some suggest that the late-maturing girls are more satisfied with their body image since they more closely model the ideal of being tall and thin.

It is important to note that the effects of puberty are numerous and complex. There is not one course of events that occurs for early-, average-, or late-maturing girls. Qualitative research suggests that girls who were prepared for the change of menarche were better able to accept the body changes (Teitelman, 2004). In general, it seems that numerous socialization agents, including parents, peers, and media, among others, contribute to adolescent girls' perception of their bodies and puberty. Further, gendered socialization from these agents, particularly parents and other significant others intensifies during this time (Galambos, 2004).

COGNITIVE DEVELOPMENT

There are few differences in the areas of cognitive abilities for girls compared to boys, or women compared to men. While some scholars have suggested that males and females are innately different with respect to cognitive ability, others have asserted that males and females exhibit more similarities than dissimilarities on cognitive variables (Hyde, 2005; see also Walsh, 1997). Given this difference of opinion, the debate continues as researchers examine and attempt to explain the role of gender in cognitive ability. For males and females, cognitive development, memory, language, spatial understanding, facial recognition, numerical comprehension, and other cognitive skills proceed along similar timelines. Developmentally, girls typically advance faster through infancy. However, individual differences offer a broad array of environmental factors (including birth order and family practices) that play a role in development. Meta-analyses of research on a variety of abilities demonstrated few consistent findings linking gender to cognitive traits (Jacklin, 1989; Maccoby & Jacklin, 1987). Still, interest in examining gender–cognitive relationships continues to be high.

The earliest efforts to uncover gender differences focused on defining women as inferior based on biological traits (e.g., smaller brains, ignoring the body–brain ratio); such investigations created considerable wariness of even the most scientifically conducted studies (Shields, 1975). Thus, conclusions that suggest the cognitive abilities of girls and women are due to purely biological factors are routinely challenged (Safir, 1986), even as researchers provide clear evidence of biological forces (Resnick, Gottesman, Berenbaum, & Bouchard, 1986). In the section that follows, we discuss the state of the literature as it relates to gender differences in verbal, spatial, and mathematical ability. Additionally, we also identify major criticisms of the existing literature.

Language Ability

An area of clear distinction for girls is language ability. Girls have been found to outperform boys on verbal and language tasks (Bornstein, Haynes, Painter, & Genevro, 2000; Galsworthy, Dionne, Dale, & Plomin, 2000; Haden, Haine, & Fivush, 1997). On average, girls begin to vocalize at an earlier age than boys, are more responsive to their mothers' speech, and demonstrate more adeptness at verbal tasks (Hyde, Fennema, & Lamon, 1990; Hyde & McKinley, 1997). Studies have also demonstrated that girls exhibit more word-fluency than boys

(Halpern & Wright, 1996). These findings have been replicated in more recent studies (Lawton & Hatcher, 2005). In particular, studies have indicated that girls acquire language more quickly than boys (Haden et al., 1997). Additionally, studies have found that girls had better memory recall than boys, particularly when recalling words (Geffen, Moar, O'Hanlan, Clark, & Geffen, 1990). In support of these findings, the literature has suggested that boys are also more likely to be diagnosed with reading disabilities and speech disorders than girls (Liederman, Kantrowitz, & Flannery, 2005; Rutter et al., 2004).

Although these studies may support assumptions about gender differences in cognitive abilities, several investigations have indicated that there is more complexity than "girls are better in verbal tasks" (Hyde & McKinley, 1997; Hyde, Fennema, & Lamon, 1990). In particular, although girls had better performance on verbal tasks, particularly in the early years, a number of studies found that boys had higher scores on verbal standardized tests (Hyde & McKinley, 1997; Kramer, Kaplan, Delis, O'Donnell, & Prifitera, 1997; Morisset, Barnars, & Booth, 1995). These findings are even further complicated given that girls have been consistently found to have higher levels of academic achievement in language and writing courses compared to their male counterparts (American Association of University Women Educational Foundation, 1998; Willingham & Cole, 1997).

Mathematical Reasoning and Visual-Spatial Skills

Mathematical reasoning is the ability to apply verbal information in the process of reaching a mathematical conclusion, that is, word-problem solving. *Visual-spatial skills* can be globally defined as the "ability to discern the relationship between shapes and objects" and include special perception, mental rotation, and spatial visualization as important components (Halpern, 2000, p. 98). Both mathematical reasoning and visual-spatial skills are utilized in a variety of scientific, technological, engineering, and mathematical (STEM) fields (Halpern, 2000, p. 100). Considerable discussion has been focused on how gender differences in these areas may explain the underrepresentation of women in engineering and architectural careers.

Studies investigating gender differences in visual-spatial reasoning have consistently found that boys perform better on spatial tasks than girls (Lawton & Hatcher, 2005; Levine, Huttenlocher, Taylor, & Langrock, 1999; McGuinness & Morley, 1991). Both Halpern (2000) and Hedges and Nowell (1995) found that boys performed better on visual-spatial tasks than girls did. The conclusions of a meta-analysis by Voyer, Voyer, and Bryden (1995) concurred, and in particular suggested that gender differences in spatial perception and mental rotation represented significant and meaningful variances in abilities.

Because spatial ability is an integral component of mathematical reasoning, much of the gender difference debate has also focused on mathematical ability. In this area, as in the other, similar patterns have been found. For example, with a sample of mathematically precocious kindergarteners and first-graders, Robinson, Abbott, Berninger, and Busse (1996) found gender differences favoring males in mathematical reasoning. Other studies have supported this finding (Geary, 1994; Hyde, Fennema, & Lamon, 1990). Additionally, males have been found to perform better on mathematical standardized tests than females (Gallagher & Kaufman, 2005). When girls have been found to receive higher grades in math courses than their male counterparts, researchers scramble to explain it variously as merely computational skill, not mathematical reasoning (Spelke, 2005). The extent to which the lack of social support for girls in science, the classroom approach to teaching mathematics and sciences, or other factors impede girls' performance in STEM areas continues to be a matter for examination (Reid & Roberts, 2006).

Criticisms of Verbal and Mathematical Gender Findings

Although many studies investigate and report gender differences in cognitive abilities, the statistical effects of gender have been small to moderate (Casey, Nuttall, Pezaris, & Benbow, 1995; Hyde, Fennema, & Lamon, 1990). Indeed, Hyde and her colleagues have suggested that the attempt to determine cognitive abilities for an individual should best be conducted on that individual and not for the group (Hyde, Fenema & Lamon, 1990). Meta-analytic reviews have also found that gender alone accounts for little variance in verbal ability. More recent confirmation of these results by Hedges and Nowell (1995) similarly found gender differences in verbal tasks and mathematical reasoning with very little variance explained by gender. Thus, the results of group data may be totally inappropriate when applied to any individual girl.

Much of this literature, however, has found gender differences in both mathematical and cognitive populations. Thus, early gender differences in the literature have not been fully documented. Spelke (2005) addressed this limitation by acknowledging the few studies that have found early gender differences in mathematical and spatial reasoning. Although studies have documented that infants can perform simple arithmetic, there have been virtually no studies that have found gender differences among infants (cf. Spelke, 2005). Similarly, studies have asserted that gender differences in verbal ability favoring girls emerge in the late elementary school years and become more evident during middle school and high school (Benbow & Stanley, 1983; Leahey & Guo, 2001). Willingham & Cole (1997) found that girls became increasingly more skilled at verbal tasks, while boys become more increasingly proficient in mathematical reasoning and tasks. Overall, these findings suggest that early gender differences have not been fully documented, suggesting that there may not be biological predispositions to these verbal or mathematical abilities and also highlighting the ever-important role of socialization in understanding these differences.

Physical-Cognitive Functions

There are a number of physical functions with cognitive connections that researchers have evaluated in terms of gender. For example, studies have suggested that girls are more sensitive to touch than boys (Reinisch & Sanders, 1992). Shaffer (1989) reviewed a number of studies focused on complex cognitive functioning and found that girls were more responsive to infants, less demanding, and more likely to respond to parents' social overtures. Similarly, research by McClure (2000) also supports the idea that girls are more responsive to others' facial expressions than boys. Investigations of emotional expressiveness suggested that girls are more emotionally expressive and are also more in tune to social cues than boys are (Cervantes & Callahan, 1998). Interestingly, whether these myriad differences are due to biological underpinnings or differential socialization practices for boys and girls has not been determined.

Social Influences on Cognitive Development

Although researchers are still exploring sex differences in cognitive abilities, the literature has now began to focus on how both biological and environment factors may explain girls' superior performance on verbal tasks and boys' superior performance on mathematical and spatial tasks (Van Hulle, Goldsmith, & Lemery, 2004). Some scholars have suggested that these gender differences in cognitive ability may have biological explanations, but that they are also cultivated through socialization (Eccles et al., 2000; Maccoby, 1998). Investigations also suggest that disadvantageous circumstances in environment or experience may affect attitudes toward learning and styles of interacting with other people (Rutter, 1985).

Extrapolating from these general findings to understand the development of girls' cognitive skills leads us to expect that there will be an interaction of cognitive functioning with socialization experiences in ways that are not yet fully understood. For example, studies have found that girls' perceptions of their mathematical ability may be heightened by intervention programs (Reid & Roberts, 2006). Thus, discussions of ability on cognitive tasks should be centered on gender-role prescriptions, as well as on how girls and women are socialized in our society.

Adolescent Thought

Childhood egocentrism is defined as the inability to take another's perspective, but for adolescents, egocentrism is self-focus related to interest. Elkind (1967) notes that adolescents assume that other people are as interested in, and fascinated by, them and their behavior as they are themselves. There is, thus, a failure to distinguish between their personal concerns and the opinions of others. Some researchers have asserted that, during adolescence, youth are also more likely to define themselves based on their relation and connections to others (Labouvie-Vief, Chiodo, Goguen, Diehl, & Orwoll, 1995). Such connections appear to be of greater importance for girls and women compared to boys and men (Rycek, Stuhr, McDermott, Benker, & Schwartz, 1998). Studies that have investigated this perspective, however, have not fully proven that egocentric thought is entirely characteristic of adolescence.

Adolescence also ushers in more complex cognitive-processing and reasoning skills for youth (Piaget, 1947). In particular, this developmental period brings the ability to integrate their experiences and the experiences of others (Quintana, 1998). Deductive and conditional reasoning also emerge in adolescence (Muller, Overton, & Reene, 2001; Ward & Overton, 1990). Given that gender-role socialization may intensify during adolescence, these cognitive-processing skills may now allow girls to recognize and interpret conveyed gender-typed behaviors and expectations. It is safe to presume that this ability to interpret these behaviors and expectations also may influence the worldviews of adolescent girls. Further, adolescent girls may be more equipped to communicate these newly developed worldviews with important others in their lives (Reich, Oser, & Valentin, 1994).

In addition to the expansion of cognitive-processing skills, adolescence ushers in the exploration of identities for many female youths. During this time, adolescents begin to think about the identities that are most important to them. Quintana (1998) suggests that adolescence brings the ability to integrate one's own experiences as well as the experiences of others. Similarly, Ericksonian theory suggests that adolescence is a critical period in which social affirmations begin to accrue (Stewart & McDermott, 2004). This may be particularly important for adolescent girls, in that adolescence may bring more exploration of important social identities, including their gender identity. In developing these identities, adolescent girls may interpret and integrate their experiences and the experiences of others into overall assessments of the self. Further, adolescent girls may become more aware of themselves as women in addition to others' expectations and views of themselves as young women.

Cultural Concerns and Issues

Girls' and women's development must be viewed as taking place within a well-defined cultural and social context. During the past few decades, increasing attention has been given to identifying and understanding these contexts. Thus, a concerted effort has been undertaken to extend understanding of female experiences beyond the limits of white, middle-class contexts. Investigations have begun to examine gender-role definitions as they operate within Asian, black, and Hispanic American communities (Chow, Wilinson, & Zinn, 1996; Denner & Guzman, 2006; Jordan, 1997). Researchers seek to identify normative patterns of behavior within a variety of social class conditions. These many worlds of girls and women are important for consideration if a complete understanding of the factors that influence developmental processes is to be established.

An important concern of researchers interested in understanding the processes that lead to gender-role development in girls is the use of the assumption of universality. Study after study repeats the fatal flaw by issuing conclusions about developmental processes that influence "girls or women," when in fact only one group, white girls or women, has been observed. Serious consideration is certainly due the suggestion that there are often significant differences in the socialization experiences of ethnic minority girls. The choice to ignore the differences and to pretend that universality is the rule appears increasingly unacceptable.

On the other hand, a total rejection of applicability of findings across cultural or racial groups is also unsound. A reasonable solution may be found in the recognition that various degrees of duality exist in the socialization process for ethnic minority girls. Minority group girls, like white girls in our society, are socialized to accept various expectations and roles for which parents, community institutions, and others prepare them (Lott, 1987; Reid, 1981). Girls, regardless of race, are expected to be interested in babies, to develop verbal skills, and to be more nurturing, quieter, and more disciplined than boys. While these and many other similarities in girls' experiences may be identified, we must also recognize the differences for children in ethnic communities. The recognition includes understanding that the differences profoundly impact the way the lives of girls evolve.

REFERENCES

Adler, P. A., Kless, S. J., & Adler, P. (1992). Socialization to gender roles: Popularity among elementary school boys and girls. *Sociology of Education, 65,* 169–187.

American Association of University Women (AAUW) Educational Foundation (1998). Gender gaps: Where schools still fail our children. Washington, DC: AAUW.

Arnett, J. J. (2002). The sounds of sex: Sex in teens' music and music videos. In J. Brown, K. Walsh-Childers, & J. Steele (Eds.), *Sexual teens, sexual media* (pp. 253–264). Hillsdale, NJ: Erlbaum.

Bandura, A., & Walters, R. (1963). *Social learning and personality development*. New York: Holt, Rinehart, & Winston.

Baruch, G. K., & Barnett, R. C. (1986). Fathers' participation in family work and children's sex-role attitudes. *Child Development, 57,* 1210–1223.

Basow, S. (1992). *Gender stereotypes and roles* (3rd ed.). Pacific Grove, CA: Brooks/Cole.

Basow, S. A., & Rubin, L. R. (1999). Gender influences on adolescent development. In N. G. Johnson & M. C. Roberts (Eds.), *Beyond appearance: A new look at adolescent girls* (pp. 25–52). Washington, DC: American Psychological Association.

Baumeister, R. F. (2000). Gender differences in erotic plasticity: The female sex drive as socially flexible and responsive. *Psychological Bulletin, 126,* 347–374.

Bem, S. L. (1981). Gender schema theory: A cognitive account of sex typing. *Psychological Review, 88,* 354–364.

Bem, S. L. (1983). Gender schema theory and its implications for child development: Raising gender-aschematic children in a gender-schematic society. *Signs, 8,* 598–616.

Benbow, C. P., & Stanley, J. C. (1983). Sex differences in mathematical reasoning: More facts. *Science, 222,* 1029–1031.

Bhanot, R., & Jovanovic, J. (2005). Do parents' academic gender stereotypes influence whether they intrude on their children's homework? *Sex Roles, 52*(9/10), 597–607.

Blakemore, J. E. (2003). Children's beliefs about violating gender norms: Boys shouldn't look like girls and girls shouldn't act like boys. *Sex Roles, 48*(9/10), 411–419.

Blakemore, J. E., & Centers (2005). Characteristics of boys and girls toys. *Sex Roles, 53*(9/10), 619–633.

Bornstein, M. H., Haynes, M., Painter, K. M., & Genevro, J. L. (2000). Child language with mother and with stranger at home and in the laboratory: A methodological study. *Journal of Child Language, 27,* 407–420.

Brener, N., Kann, L., Lowry, R., Wechsler, H., & Romero, L. (2006). Trends in HIV-related risk behaviors among high school students: United States, 1991–1995. *Morbidity and Mortality Weekly Report, 55*(31), 851–854.

Brooker, L., & Ha, S. J. (2005). The cooking teacher: Investigating gender stereotypes in a Korean kindergarten. *Early Years, 25*(1), 17–30.

Brooks-Gunn, J., & Paikoff, R. L. (1993). "Sex is a gamble, kissing is a game": Adolescent sexuality and health promotion. In S. G. Millstein, A. C. Petersen, & E. O. Nightingale (Eds.), *Promoting the health of adolescents.* New York: Oxford University Press.

Brooks-Gunn, J., & Warren, M. P. (1989). The psychological significance of secondary sexual characteristics in 9- to 11-year-old girls. *Child Development, 59,* 161–169.

Cahill, B., & Adams, E. (1997). An exploratory study of early childhood teachers' attitudes toward gender roles. *Sex Roles, 36,* 517–529.

Carr, P. G., & Mednick, M. T. (1988). Sex role socialization and the development of achievement motivation in black preschool children. *Sex Roles, 18,* 169–180.

Casey, M. B., Nuttall, R., Pezaris, E. & Benbow, C. P. (1995). The influence of spatial ability on gender differences in math college entrance test scores across diverse samples. *Developmental Psychology, 31,* 697–705.

Centers for Disease Control and Prevention. (1999). Physical activity and health: Adolescents and young adults. Retrieved August 2, 2006, from http://www.cdc.gov/nccdphp/sgr/adoles.htm.

Cervantes, C. A., & Callahan, M. A. (1998). Labels and explanations in mother-child emotion talk: Age and gender differentiation. *Developmental Psychology, 34,* 88–98.

Chick, K., Heilman-Houser, R., & Hunter, M. (2003). The impact of child care on gender role development and gender stereotypes. *Early Childhood Education Journal, 29*(3), 149–154.

Collins, P. H. (1998). Intersections of race, class, gender, and nation: Some implications for black family studies. *Journal of Comparative Family Studies, 29,* 27–36.

Dalton, S. E., & Bielby, D. D. (2000). "That's our kind of constellation": Lesbian mothers negotiate institutionalized understandings of gender within the family. *Gender & Society, 14,* 36–61.

Dasgupta, S. D. (1998). Gender roles and cultural continuity in the Asian Indian immigrant community in the US. *Sex Roles, 38,* 953–974.

Delk, J. L., Madden, R., Livingston, M., & Ryan, T. T. (1986). Adult perceptions of the infant as a function of gender labeling and observer gender. *Sex Roles, 15,* 527–534.

Denner, J., & Dunbar, N. (2004). Negotiating femininity: Power and strategies of Mexican American girls. *Sex Roles, 50,* 301–314.

Denner, J., & Guzman, B. L. (2006). *Voices of adolescent strength in the United States.* New York: New York University Press.

Dick, D. M., Rose, R. J., Viken, R. J., & Kaprio, J. (2000). Pubertal timing and substance use: Association between and within families across late adolescence. *Developmental Psychology, 36,* 180–189.

Dickerson, D. P. (1982). The role of black females in selected children's fiction. Unpublished, Howard University, Washington, DC.

Douglas, D. D. (2005). Venus, Serena, and the Women's Tennis Association: When and where. *Sociology of Sport Journal, 22*(3), 256–282.

Dundas, S., & Kaufman, M. (2000). *Journal of Homosexuality, 40,* 65–79.

Eccles, J. S. (1993). School and family effects on the ontogeny of children's interests, self-perceptions, and activity choices. In J. E. Jacobs (Ed.), *Nebraska Symposium on Motivation*, vol. 40, *Developmental perspectives on motivation* (pp. 97–123). Lincoln: University of Nebraska Press.

Eccles, J. S., Freedman-Doan, C., Frome, P., Jacobs, J., & Yoon, K. S. (2000). Gender-role socialization in the family: A longitudinal approach. In T. Eckes and H. M. Trautner (Eds.), *The developmental social psychology of gender* (pp. 333–360). Mahwah, NJ: Erlbaum.

Elkind, D. (1967). Egocentrism in adolescence. *Child Development, 38,* 1025–1034.

Engeln-Maddox, R. (2005). Cognitive responses to idealized media images of women: The relationship of social comparison and critical processing to body image disturbance in college women. *Journal of Social and Clinical Psychology, 24*(8), 1114–1138.

Etaugh, C., & Liss, M. B. (1992). Home, school, and playroom: Training grounds for adult gender roles. *Sex Roles, 26,* 129–147.

Fisher-Thompson, D., Sausa, A. D., & Wright, T. F. (1995). Toy selection for children: Personality and toy request influences. *Sex Roles, 33*(3/4), 239–255.

Freudinger, P., & Almquist, E. (1978). Male and female roles in the lyrics of three genres of contemporary music. *Sex Roles, 4,* 51–65.

Frome, P. M., & Eccles, J. S. (1998). Parents' influence on children's achievement-related perceptions. *Journal of Personality and Social Psychology, 74,* 435–452.

Galambos, N. L. (2004). Gender and gender role development in adolescence. In R. M. Lerner (Ed.), *Handbook of adolescence psychology* (pp. 233–262). Hoboken, NJ: Wiley.

Gallagher, A. M., & Kaufman, J. C. (2005). Gender differences in mathematics: An integrative psychological approach. New York: Cambridge University Press.

Galsworthy, M. J., Dionne, G., Dale, P. S., & Plomin, R. (2000). Sex differences in early verbal and non-verbal cognitive development. *Developmental Science, 3*(2), 206–215.

Gaughan, M. (2006). The gender structure of adolescent peer influence on drinking. *Journal of Health and Social Behavior, 47*(1), 47–61.

Geary, D. C. (1994). Children's mathematical development: Research and practical applications. Washington, DC: American Psychological Association.

Geffen, G., Moar, K. J., O'Hanlon, C. R., Clark, C. R., & Geffen, L. B. (1990). Performance measures of 16- to 86-year-old males and females on the auditory verbal learning test. *Clinical Neuropsychologist, 4,* 45–63.

Gelman, S. A., Taylor, M. G., & Nguyen, S. P. (2004). Mother-child conversations about gender. *Monographs of the Society for Research in Child Development, 69*(1), ii–127.

Ginorio, A. B., Gutiérrez, L., Cauce, A. M., & Acosta, M. (1995). Psychological issues for Latinas. In H. Landrine (Ed.), *Bringing cultural diversity to feminist psychology: Theory, research, and practice* (pp. 241–263). Washington, DC: American Psychological Association.

Gordon, M. K. (2004). Media images of women and African American girls' sense of self. (Dissertation). *Dissertation Abstracts International, 65,* 3197B.

Groesz, L. M., Levine, M. P., & Muren, S. K. (2002). The effect of experimental presentation of thin media images on body satisfaction: A meta-analytic review. *International Journal of Eating Disorders, 31,* 1–16.

Haden, C. A., Haine, R. A., & Fivush, R. (1997). Developing narrative structure in parent-child reminiscing across the preschool years. *Developmental Psychology, 33,* 295–307.

Halliday, J., McNaughton, S., & Glynn, T. (1985). Influencing children's choice of play activities at kindergarten through teacher participation. *New Zealand Journal of Educational Studies, 20,* 48–58.

Halpern, D. F. (2000). *Sex differences in cognitive abilities* (3rd ed.). Hillsdale, NJ: Erlbaum.

Halpern, D. F., & Wright, T. M. (1996). A process-oriented model of cognitive sex differences. *Learning and Individual Differences, 8*(1), 3–24.

Hawkins, N., Richards, P. S., Granley, H. M., & Stein, D. M. (2004). The impact of exposure to the thin-ideal media image on women. *Eating Disorders, 12,* 35–50.

Helms, J. E., Jernigan, M., & Mascher, J. (2005). The meaning of race in psychology and how to change it: A methodological perspective. *American Psychologist, 60*(10), 27–36.

Herbert, J., & Stipek, D. (2005). The emergence of gender differences in children's perceptions of their academic competence. *Journal of Applied Developmental Psychology, 26*(3), 276–295.

Higginbotham, E. & Weber, L. (1992). Moving up with kin and community: Upward social mobility for black and white women. *Gender and Society, 6,* 416–440.

Hill, M. (1998). Child rearing attitudes of black lesbian mothers. In Boston Lesbian Psychologies Collective (Eds.), *Lesbian psychologies: Explorations and challenges*. Urbana: University of Illinois Press.

Hill, S. (1999). Parenting in black and white families: The interaction of gender with race and class. *Gender & Society, 13*(4), 480–502.

Hill, S. A. (2002). Teaching and doing gender in African American families. *Sex Roles, 47*(11/12), 493–506.

Hops, H., Alpert, A., & Davis, B. (1997). The development of same- and opposite-sex social relations among adolescents: An analogue study. *Social Development, 6,* 165–183.

Howes, C., Phillipson, L. C., & Peisner-Feinberg, E. (2000). The consistency of perceived teacher-child relationships between preschool and kindergarten. *Journal of School Psychology, 38,* 113–132.

Hyde, J. S. (2005). The gender similarities hypothesis. *American Psychologist, 60,* 581–592.

Hyde, J. S., Fennema, E., & Lamon, S. J. (1990). Gender differences in mathematics performance: A meta-analysis. *Psychological Bulletin, 107,* 139–155.

Hyde, J. S., & McKinley, N. M. (1997). Gender differences in cognition: Results from meta-analysis. In P. A. Caplan, M. Crawford, J. S. Hyde, & J. T. E. Richardson (Eds.), *Gender differences in human cognition* (pp. 30–51). New York: Oxford University Press.

Idle, T., Wood, E., & Desmarais, S. (1993). Gender role socialization in toy play situations: Mothers and fathers with their sons and daughters. *Sex Roles, 28,* 679–691.

Jacklin, C. N. (1989). Female and male: Issues of gender. *American Psychologist, 44,* 127–133.

Jacobs, J. E. (1991). The influence of gender stereotypes on parent and child mathematics attitudes. *Journal of Educational Psychology, 83,* 518–527.

Jarvinen, D. W., & Nicholls, J. G. (1996). Adolescents' social goals, beliefs about the causes of social success, and satisfaction in peer relations. *Developmental Psychology, 32,* 435–441.

Johnson, L. (2003). Looking pretty, waiting for the prince. Retrieved August 2, 2006, from http://www.rethinkingschools.org/publication/rsr/rsr_stud2.shtml.

Karraker, K. H., & Coleman, P. K. (2005). The effects of child characteristics on parenting. In T. Luster and L. Okagaki (Eds.), *Parenting: An ecological perspective* (2nd ed.; pp. 147–176). Mahwah, NJ: Erlbaum.

Knaak, S. (2004). On the reconceptualizing of gender: Implications for research design. *Sociological Inquiry, 74,* 302–317.

Kohlberg, L. (1976). Moral stages and moralization: The cognitive-development approach. In T. Lickona (Ed.), *Moral development and behavior*. New York: Holt, Rinehart, & Winston.

Kramer, J. H., Kaplan, E., Delis, D. C., O'Donnell, L., & Prifitera, A. (1997). Developmental sex differences in verbal learning. *Neuropsychology, 11,* 577–584.

Kulis, S., Okamoto, S. K., Rayle, A. D., & Sen, S. (2006). Social contexts of drug offers among American Indian youth and their relationship to substance use: An exploratory study. *Cultural Diversity and Ethnic Minority Psychology, 12*(1), 30–44.

Labouvie-Vief, G., Chiodo, L. M., Goguen, L. A., Diehl, M., & Orwoll, L. (1995). Representations of self across the life span. *Psychology and Aging, 10,* 404–415.

Lansford, J. E., & Parker, J. G. (1999). Children's interactions in triads: Behavioral profiles and effects of gender and patterns of friendships among members. *Developmental Psychology, 35,* 80–93.

Lanvers, U. (2004). Gender in discourse behaviour in parent-child dyads: A literature review. *Child: Care, Health, and Development, 30*(5), 481–493.

Lawton, C. A., & Hatcher, D. W. (2005). Gender differences in integration of images in visuospatial memory. *Sex Roles, 53*(9/10), 717–725.

Leahey, E., & Guo, G. (2000). Gender differences in mathematical trajectories. *Social Forces, 80,* 713–732.

Leaper, C., Anderson, K. J., & Sanders, P. (1998). Moderators of gender effects on parents' talk to their children: A meta-analysis. *Developmental Psychology, 34,* 3–27.

Levine, M. P., & Smolak, L. (1996). Media as a context for the development of disordered eating. In L. Smolak & M. P. Levine (Eds.), *The developmental psychopathology of eating disorders: Implications for research, prevention, and treatment* (pp. 235–257). Hillsdale, NJ: Erlbaum.

Levine, S. C., Huttenlocher, J., Taylor, A., & Langrock, A. (1999). Early sex differences in spatial skill. *Developmental Psychology, 35,* 940–949.

Levy, G. D., Barth, J. M., & Zimmerman, B. J. (1998). Associations among cognitive and behavioral aspects of preschoolers' gender role development. *Journal of Genetic Psychology, 159,* 121–126.

Liederman, J., Kantrowitz, L., & Flannery, K. (2005). Male vulnerability to reading disability is not likely a myth: A call for new data. *Journal of Learning Disabilities, 38*(2), 109–129.

Lockheed, M. E., & Hall, K. P. (1976). Conceptualizing sex as a status characteristic and applications to leadership training strategies. *Journal of Social Issues, 32,* 111–124.

Lott, B. (1987). *Women's lives: Themes and variations in gender learning*. Monterey, CA: Brooks/Cole.

Luthar, S. S., & D'Avanzo, K. (1999). Contextual factors in substance use: A study of suburban and inner-city adolescents. *Development and Psychopathology, 11,* 845–867.

Luthar, S. S., & Latendresse, S. J. (2005). Children of the affluent: Challenges to well-being. *Current Directions in Psychological Science, 14*(1), 49–53.

Maccoby, E. E. (1990). Gender and relationships: A developmental account. *American Psychologist, 45,* 513–520.

Maccoby, E. E. (1998). The two sexes: Growing up apart and coming together. Cambridge, MA: Belknap Press.

Maccoby, E. E., & Jacklin, C. N. (1987). Gender segregation in childhood. In W. R. Hayne (Ed.), *Advances in child development and behavior* (vol. 20, pp. 239–287). Orlando, FL: Academic Press.

Malina, R. M., & Bouchard, C. (1991). *Growth, maturation, and physical activity.* Champaign, IL: Human Kinetics.

Marmion, S., & Lundberg-Love, P. (2004). Learning masculinity and femininity: Gender socialization from parents and peers across the life span. In M. Paludi (Ed.), *Praeger guide to the psychology of gender* (pp. 1–26). Westport, CT: Praeger.

Martin, C. L. (2000). Cognitive theories of gender development. In T. Eckes & H. M. Trautner (Eds.), *The developmental social psychology of gender* (pp. 91–121). Mahwah, NJ: Erlbaum.

Martin, C. L., & Ruble, D. N. (2004). Children's search for gender cues: Cognitive perspectives on gender development. *Current Directions in Psychological Science, 13*(2), 67–70.

Martin, M. C., & Gentry, J. W. (1997). Stuck in the model trap: The effects of beautiful models in ads on female pre-adolescents and adolescents. *Journal of Advertising, 26,* 19–33.

Mastro, D. E., & Greenberg, B. S. (2000). The portrayal of racial minorities on prime time television. *Journal of Broadcasting & Electronic Media, 44,* 490–703.

McArthur, L. Z., & Eisen, S. V. (1976). Achievements of male and female storybook characters as determinants of achievement behavior by boys and girls. *Journal of Personality and Social Psychology, 33,* 467–473.

McClure, E. B. (2000). A meta-analytic review of sex differences in facial expression processing and their development in infants, children, and adolescents. *Psychological Bulletin, 126,* 424–453.

McGhee, P. E., & Frueh, T. (1980). Television viewing and the learning of sex-role stereotypes. *Sex Roles, 6,* 179–188.

McGuinness, D., & Morley, C. (1991). Sex differences in the development of visuo-spatial ability in pre-school children. *Journal of Mental Imagery, J5,* 143–150.

McHale, S. M., Kim, J., Whiteman, S., & Crouter, A. C. (2004). Links between sex-typed time use in middle childhood and gender development in early adolescence. *Developmental Psychology, 40*(5), 868–881.

McLoyd, V. C. (1990). The impact of economic hardship on black families and children: Psychological distress, parenting and socioemotional development. *Child Development, 61,* 311–346.

McLoyd, V. C., Cauce, A. M., Takeuchi, D., & Wilson, L. (2000). Marital processes and parental socialization in families of color: A decade review of research. *Journal of Marriage and the Family, 62,* 1070–1093.

Meece, J. L., & Scantlebury, K. (2006). Gender and schooling: Progress and persistent barriers. In J. Worell & C. Goodheart (Eds.), *Handbook of girls' and women's psychological health: Gender and well-being across the lifespan* (pp. 283–291). New York: Oxford University Press.

Müller, U., Overtoil, W. F., & Reene, K. (2001). Development of conditional reasoning: A longitudinal study. *Journal of Cognition and Development, 2,* 27–49.

Murry, V. M. (1996). Inner-city girls of color: Unmarried, sexually active nonmothers. In B. J. R. Leadbeater & N. Way (Eds.), *Urban girls.* New York: New York University Press.

Must, A., & Strauss, R. S. (1999). Risks and consequences of childhood and adolescent obesity. *International Journal of Obesity, 23,* S4–S12.

Neblett, E. W., Shelton, J. N., & Sellers, R. M. (2004). The role of racial identity in managing daily racial hassles. In G. Philogene (Ed.), *Racial identity in context: The legacy of Kenneth Clark* (pp. 77–90). Washington, DC: American Psychological Association.

Nelson, R. L., & Bridges, W. (1999). *Legalizing gender inequality: Courts, markets, and unequal pay for women in America*. Cambridge: Cambridge University Press.

Newman, B. M., & Newman, P. R. (1987). *Development through life*. Homewood, IL: Dorsey.

Nobles, W. (1985). *Africanity and the black family: The development of a theoretical model*. Oakland, CA: Institute for the Advanced Study of Black Family Life and Culture.

Nowell, A., & Hedges, L. V. (1998). Trends in gender differences in academic achievement from 1960–1994: An analysis of differences in mean, variance, and extreme scores. *Sex Roles, 39*, 21–43.

Operario, D., & Fiske, S. (2001). Ethnic identity moderates perceptions of prejudice: Judgments of personal versus group discrimination and subtle versus blatant bias. *Personality and Social Psychology Bulletin, 27*(5), 30–37.

Paikoff, R. L., Buchanan, C. M., & Brooks-Gunn, J. (1991). Hormone-behavior links at puberty, methodological links in the study of. In R. M. Lerner, A. C. Petersen, & J. Brooks-Gunn (Eds.), *Encyclopedia of adolescence*. New York: Garland.

Paludi, M. A. (1985). Sex and gender similarities and differences and the development of the young child. In C. McLouglin & D. F. Gullo (Eds.), *Young children in context: Impact of self, family, and society in development*. Springfield, MA: Charles C. Thomas.

Perlesz, A., & McNair, R. (2004). Lesbian parenting: Insiders' voices. *Australian and New Zealand Journal of Family Therapy, 25*, 129–140.

Petersen, A. C. (1993). Creating adolescents: The role of context and process in developmental trajectories. *Journal of Research on Adolescence, 3*, 1–18.

Phelps, C. E. R. (2001). Children's responses to overt and relational aggression. *Journal of Clinical Child Psychology, 30*, 240–252.

Phinney, V. G., Jensen, L. C., & Olsen, J. A. (1990). The relationship between early development and psychosexual behaviors in adolescent females. *Adolescence, 25*, 321–332.

Piaget, J. (1947). *The psychology of intelligence*. London: Routledge & Kegan Paul.

Quintana, S. M. (1998). Children's developmental understanding of ethnicity and race. *Applied & Preventive Psychology, 7*, 27–45.

Reich, K. H., Oser, F. K., & Valentin, P. (1994). Knowing why I now know better: Children's and youth's explanations of their world view changes. *Journal of Research on Adolescence, 4*, 151–173.

Reid, P. T. (1979). Racial stereotyping on television. A comparison of the behavior of both black and white television characters. *Journal of Applied Psychology, 64*, 465–471.

Reid, P. T., & Paludi, M. (1993). Developmental psychology of women: Conception to adolescence. In F. L. Denmark & M. A. Paludi (Eds.), *Psychology of women: A handbook of issues and theories*. Westport, CT: Greenwood.

Reid, P. T., & Roberts, S. K. (2006). Gaining options: A mathematics program for potentially talented at-risk adolescent girls. *Merrill-Palmer Quarterly, 52*, 118–134.

Reid, P. T., Tate, C. S., & Berman, P. W. (1989). Preschool children's self-presentations in situations with infants: Effects of sex and race. *Child Development, 60*, 710–714.

Reid, P. T., & Trotter, K. H. (1993). Children's self-preceptions with infants: Gender and ethnic comparisons. *Sex Roles, 29*, 171–181.

Reinisch, J. M., & Sanders, S. A. (1992). Prenatal hormonal contributions to sex differences in human cognitive and personality development. In A. Gerall, H. Moltz, & I. L. Ward (Eds.), *Sexual differentiation* (pp. 221–243). New York: Plenum.

Resnick, S. M., Gottesman, I. I., Berenbaum, S. A., & Bouchard, T. J. (1986). Early hormonal influences on cognitive functioning in congenital adrenal hyperplasia. *Developmental Psychology, 22,* 191–198.

Rivadeneyra, R., & Ward, L. M. (2005). From *Ally McBeal* to *Sabado Gigante*: Contributions of television viewing to the gender role attitudes of Latino adolescents. *Journal of Adolescent Research, 20*(4), 453–475.

Roberts, D., Foehr, U., & Rideout, V. (2005). *Generation M: Media in the lives of 8–18 year olds.* Menlo Park, CA: Henry J. Kaiser Family Foundation.

Robinson. N. M., Abbott, R. D., Berninger, V. W., & Busse, J. (1996). The structure of abilities in math-precocious young children: Gender similarities and differeces. *Journal of Educational Psychology, 88,* 341–352.

Romer, N., & Cherry, D. (1980). Ethnic and social class differences in children's sex-role concepts. *Sex Roles, 6,* 245–263.

Root, M. P. P. (2004). From exotic to a dime a dozen. *Women & Therapy, 27*(1–2), 19–31.

Ruble, D. N., & Martin, C. (1998). Gender development. In N. Eisenberg (Ed.), *Handbook of child psychology,* vol. 3, *Personality and social development* (pp. 933–1016). New York: Wiley.

Rutter, M. (1985). Family and school influences on cognitive development. *Journal of Child Psychology and Psychiatry, 26,* 683–704.

Rutter, M., Caspi, A., Fergusson, D., Horwood, L. J., Goodman, R., Maughan, B., et al. (2004). Sex differences in developmental reading disability: New findings from 4 epidemiological studies. *Journal of the American Medical Association, 291,* 2007–2012.

Rycek, R. F., Stuhr, S. L., McDermott, J., Benker, J., & Schwartz, M. D. (1998). Adolescent egocentrism and cognitive functioning during late adolescence. *Adolescence, 33,* 745–749.

Safir, M. P. (1986). The effects of nature or of nurture on sex differences in intellectual functioning: Israeli findings. *Sex Roles, 14,* 581–590.

Schooler, D., Ward, L. M., Merriwether, A., & Caruthers, A. (2004). Who's that girl? Television's role in the body image development of young white and black women. *Psychology of Women Quarterly, 28,* 38–47.

Schowalter, J., & Anyan, W. (1981). *Family handbook of adolescence.* New York: Knopf.

Sellers, R. M., Caldwell, C. H., Schmeelk-Cone, K., & Zimmerman, M. A. (2003). The role of racial identity and racial discrimination in the mental health of African American young adults. *Journal of Health and Social Behavior, 44*(3), 302–317.

Sellers, R. M., Smith, M., Shelton, N. J., Rowley, S. J., & Chavous, T. M. (1998). Multidimensional model of racial identity: A reconceptualization of African American racial identity. *Personality and Social Psychology Review, 2,* 18–39.

Shaffer, D. R. (1989). *Developmental psychology: Childhood and adolescence* (2nd ed.). Pacific Grove, CA: Brooks/Cole.

Shields, S. (1975). Functionalism, Darwinism, and the psychology of women: A study in social myth. *American Psychologist, 30,* 739–754.

Spelke, E. S. (2005). Sex differences in intrinsic aptitude for mathematics and science? A critical review. *American Psychologist, 60*(9), 950–958.

Sternglanz, S. H., & Serbin, L. (1974). Sex role stereotyping in children's television programs. *Developmental Psychology, 10,* 710–715.

Stewart, A. J., & McDermott, C. (2004). Gender in psychology. *Annual Review of Psychology, 55,* 519–544.

Stice, E., Sprangler, D., & Agras, W. S. (2001). Exposure to media-portrayed thin-ideal images adversely affects vulnerable girls: A longitudinal experience. *Journal of Social and Clinical Psychology, 20,* 270–288.

Stright, A. D., & Bales, S. S. (2003). Coparenting quality: Contributions of child and parent characteristics. *Family Relations, 52,* 232–240.

Stunkard, A., & Sorenson, T. I. (1993). Obesity and socioeconomic status: A complex relation. *New England Journal of Medicine, 329*(14), 1036–1037.

Sullivan, M. (1996). Rozzie and Harriet? Gender and family patterns of lesbian coparents. *Gender and Society, 10,* 747–767.

Sypeck, M. F., Gray, J. J., & Ahrens, A. H. (2004). No longer just a pretty face: Fashion magazines' depictions of ideal female beauty from 1959 to 1999. *International Journal of Eating Disorders, 36,* 342–347.

Talbani, A., & Hasanali, P. (2000). Adolescent females between tradition and modernity: Gender role socialization in South Asian immigrant families. *Journal of Adolescence, 23,* 615–627.

Taylor, J., Gilligan, C., & Sullivan, A. (1995). *Between voice and silence: Women and girls, race and relationship.* Cambridge, MA: Harvard University Press.

Taylor, J. M. (1996). Cultural stories: Latina and Portuguese daughters and mothers. In B. J. R. Leadbeater & N. Way (Eds.), *Urban girls.* New York: New York University Press.

Teitelman, A. M. (2004). Adolescent girls' perspective of family interactions related to menarche and sexual health. *Qualitative Health Research, 14*(9), 1292–1308.

Thomas, J. R., & French, K. E. (1985). Gender differences across age in motor performance: A meta-analysis. *Psychological Bulletin, 98,* 260–282.

Thompson, J. K., & Stice, E. (2001). Thin-ideal internalization: Mounting evidence for a new risk factor for body image disturbance and eating pathology. *Current Directions in Psychological Science, 10,* 181–183.

Thorne, B. (2001). Girls and boys together ... but mostly apart: Gender arrangements in elementary schools. In Satow, R. (Ed.), *Gender and social life* (pp. 153–166).

Thorne, B., & Luria, Z. (2003). Putting boundaries around the sexes: Sexuality and gender in children's daily worlds. In Henslin, J. (Ed.), *Down to earth sociology: Introductory readings* (12th ed.; pp. 162–174). New York: Free Press.

Tiedemann, J. (2000). Parents' gender stereotypes and teachers' beliefs as predictors of children's concept of the mathematical ability in elementary school. *Educational Psychology, 92*(1), 144–151.

Tiggemann, M. (2006). The role of media exposure in adolescent girls' body dissatisfaction and drive for thinness: Prospective results. *Journal of Social and Clinical Psychology, 25*(5), 523–541.

Tobach, E. (2004). Development of sex and gender: Biochemistry, physiology, and experience. In M. A. Paludi (Ed.), *Praeger guide to the psychology of gender,* 239–270. Westport, CT: Greenwood.

Towbin, M. A., Haddock, S. A., & Zimmerman, T. S. (2003). Images of gender, race, age, and sexual orientation in Disney feature-length animated films. *Journal of Feminist Family Therapy, 15,* 19–44.

Van Hulle, C. A., Goldsmith, H. H., & Lemery, K. S. (2004). Genetic, environmental, and gender effects on individual differences in toddler expressive language. *Journal of Speech, Language, and Hearing Research, 47*(4), 904–912.

Van Wel, R., ter Bogt, T., & Raaijmakers, Q. (2002). Changes in the parental bond and the well-being of adolescents and young adults. *Adolescence, 37,* 317–334.

Vera, E. M., Reese, L. E., Paikoff, R. L., & Jarrett, R. L. (1996). Contextual factors of sexual risk-taking in urban African American preadolescent children. In B. J. R. Leadbeater & N. Way (Eds.), *Urban girls.* New York: New York University Press.

Voyer, D., Voyer, S., & Bryden, M. P. (1995). Magnitude of sex differences in spatial abilities: A meta-analysis and consideration of critical variables. *Psychological Bulletin, 117,* 250–270.

Waite, B., & Paludi, M. A. (1987). Gender role stereotypes present in rock music videos. Paper presented to the Midwestern Psychological Association, Chicago.

Walsh, M. R. (Ed.). (1997). *Women, men, and gender: Ongoing debates.* New Haven, CT: Yale University Press.

Ward, J. V. (1996). Raising resisters: The role of truth telling in the psychological development of African American girls. In B. J. R. Leadbeater & N. Way (Eds.), *Urban girls.* New York: New York University Press.

Ward, L. M. (2004). Wading through the stereotypes: Positive and negative associations between media use and black adolescents' conceptions of self. *Developmental Psychology, 40*(2), 284–294.

Ward, L. M., Hansbrough, E., & Walker, E. (2005). Contributions of music video exposure to black adolescents' gender and sexual schema. *Journal of Adolescent Research, 20,* 143–166.

Ward, L. M., & Harrison, K. (2005). The impact of media use on girls' beliefs about gender roles, their bodies, and sexual relationships: A research synthesis. In E. Cole & H. Daniel (Eds.), *Featuring females: Feminist analysis of media* (pp. 3–24). Washington, DC: American Psychological Association.

Ward, L. M., & Rivadeneyra, R. (1999). Contributions of entertainment television to adolescents' sexual attitudes and expectations: The role of viewing amount versus viewer involvement. *Journal of Sex Research, 36,* 237–249.

Ward, S. L., Byrnes, J. P., & Overton, W. F. (1990). Organization of knowledge and conditional reasoning. *Journal of Educational Psychology, 82,* 832–837.

Wigfield, A., Eccles, J. S., Yoon, K. S., Harold, R. D., Arbreton, A. J., Freedman-Doan.

Wong, F., & Halgin, R. (2006). The "model minority": Bane or blessing for Asian Americans? *Journal of Multicultural Counseling and Development, 34*(1), 38–49.

Wood, E., Desmarais, S., & Gugula, S. (2002). The impact of parenting experience on gender stereotyped toy play of children. *Sex Roles, 47*(1/2), 39–49.

Chapter 9

Women in the Middle and Later Years

Claire Etaugh

This chapter examines the major characteristics and experiences of middle-aged and older women. To do so, we should first define what is meant by "middle age" and "old age." In fact, there is no firm consensus. Clearly, the boundaries of the middle and later years are quite flexible. No one biological or psychological event signals the beginning of middle or old age. Rather, individuals typically experience a number of life events and role transitions during these years, including those related to physical appearance and health, sexuality, marital status, parenting, grandparenting, caring for aging family members, employment, and retirement. These events are not experienced by everyone, nor do they occur at the same age or in the same sequence.

Fundamental changes in social attitudes regarding gender roles over the past several decades have begun to broaden the opportunities available to women in midlife as well as in other life stages. Important to understanding the impact of role transitions in the middle and later years is the timing or degree of predictability of these changes. For example, having the last child leave home and becoming a grandparent are frequently expected and welcome role transitions, whereas divorce, death of a spouse or partner, and providing care for ailing parents are often unplanned and stressful changes.

PHYSICAL APPEARANCE

Physical appearance begins to change in midlife (Etaugh & Bridges, 2006). The hair becomes thinner and grayer. Weight increases until about age 50 and declines somewhat after that. Fat becomes redistributed, decreasing in the face, legs, and lower arms and increasing in the abdomen, buttocks, and upper arms. Starting at about age 40, the discs between the spinal vertebrae begin to compress, resulting in an eventual loss in height of one to two inches. Bones become thinner, brittle, and more porous, especially in women, sometimes resulting in painful and crippling fractures of the hip or vertebrae. The skin becomes drier and, along with the muscles, blood vessels, and other tissues, begins to lose its elasticity. Wrinkles appear, and age spots may develop.

In our youth-oriented society, the prospect of getting older generally is not relished by either sex. For women, however, the stigma of aging is greater than it is for men, a phenomenon labeled the "double standard of aging" (Sontag, 1979). A woman's most socially valued qualities—her ability to provide sex and attractive companionship and to have children—are associated with the physical beauty and fertility of youth. As a woman ages, she is seen as less attractive because her years of social usefulness as childbearer are behind her. Men, on the other hand, are seen as possessing qualities—competence, autonomy, and self-control—that are not associated with youth but rather increase with age. Thus, the same wrinkles and gray hair that may enhance the perceived status and attractiveness of an older man may be seen as diminishing the attractiveness and desirability of an older woman. Given these societal views, it is not surprising that middle-aged women are much more dissatisfied with their appearance than are midlife men (Halliwell & Dittmar, 2003) and use more age-concealment techniques (Noonan & Adler, 2002).

The most distinct physiological change for most midlife women is menopause, the cessation of menses. In Western societies, menopause is often viewed in terms of loss of reproductive capability and decline in sexual functioning. Menopause continues to be defined in medical and psychological literature by a long list of negative symptoms and terms such as "estrogen deprivation" and "total ovarian failure." The popular press reinforces the notion of menopause as a condition of disease and deterioration that requires treatment by drugs (Derry, 2002).

Most middle-aged North American women minimize the significance of menopause, viewing it as only a temporary inconvenience and feeling relief when their menstrual periods stop (Ayubi-Moak & Parry, 2002). Postmenopausal women have more positive attitudes toward menopause than younger midlife women, with young women holding the most negative views of all (Sommer et al., 1999). Women in other cultures often have menopausal experiences and attitudes very different from those reported by Western women, indicating that menopausal symptoms are at least in part socially constructed. For example, women of high social castes in India report very few negative symptoms, and hot flashes are virtually unknown among Mayan women.

Similarly, Japanese women are much less likely than U.S. and Canadian women to report hot flashes (Etaugh & Bridges, 2006).

HEALTH

The female–male mortality gap begins before birth. While 115 males are conceived for every 100 females, the rate of miscarriage and stillbirth is higher for males. Although about 105 live males are born for every 100 live females, more male babies die in infancy (Arias, 2004) and thereafter throughout life. Starting with the 30-to-34 age group, women outnumber men. Between ages 65 and 69, only 84 males survive for every 100 females. At age 85 and beyond, women outnumber men more than two to one (U.S. Census Bureau, 2005). At the turn of the 20th century, life expectancy in the United States was about 51 years for women and 48 years for men. Since then, the gender gap has widened. Life expectancy at birth now is about 80 for women and 5½ years less for men. The gender gap exists for both blacks and whites. White women tend to outlive white men by five years (80.5 versus 75.4), and black women, on average, outlive black men by nearly seven years (76.1 versus 69.2) (Hoyert, Kung, & Smith, 2005).

Both biological and lifestyle explanations have been proposed to account for the sex difference in longevity. One biological explanation for women's greater longevity is that their second X chromosome protects them against certain potentially lethal diseases such as hemophilia and some forms of muscular dystrophy that are more apt to occur in individuals (men) who have only one X chromosome. Another biological reason for women's greater life spans may be their higher estrogen level, which, prior to menopause, may provide protection against heart disease (Gaylord, 2001).

Differences in the lifestyles of women and men also influence sex differences in longevity. Men are more likely to engage in risky behaviors such as aggression, risk-taking, smoking, and alcohol consumption, which contributes to their higher incidence of deaths resulting from homicide, accidents, lung cancer, and cirrhosis of the liver. Men also are overrepresented in dangerous occupations. On the other hand, women are more likely than men to be overweight and physically inactive. These factors contribute to a host of medical conditions, including heart disease, many kinds of cancer, and stroke—the three leading causes of death for both women and men. Also, while the frequency of men's smoking has declined, that of women's has increased. The result is that smoking-related deaths from cancer, including lung cancer, has increased for women while decreasing for men (Centers for Disease Control and Prevention, 2002). Women, however, make greater use of preventive health services and are more likely to seek medical treatment when they are ill. This may help explain why women live longer than men after the diagnosis of a potentially fatal disease. Women also are more likely than men to have extensive social support networks of family and friends, another factor related to living longer (Etaugh & Bridges, 2006).

Around the world, woman and men with higher incomes and more education have longer life expectancies and better health (Mannheim Research Institute for the Economics of Aging, 2005; Schneiderman, 2004). Some of this difference can be accounted for by a higher incidence of risk factors such as smoking, obesity, high blood pressure, and physical inactivity among the poor and working class. Additionally, people with lower incomes are less able to afford decent medical care or even adequate food, and they experience higher levels of chronic stress as a result of such experiences as financial difficulties and job loss. The combination of all these factors shortens life expectancy and increases rates of illness and disease (Chen, 2004; Schneiderman, 2004). Differences in mortality rates for women of different ethnic groups are related to their economic status. Blacks and Native Americans, for example, have both higher mortality rates and lower lifetime family incomes than Asian Americans (Torrez, 2001).

Although advances have taken place in recent years in the understanding of women's health issues, inequalities still exist in the assessment, treatment, access to care, and research on health topics relevant to women in general and to older women in particular (Etaugh & Bridges, 2006). One example is that older women are less likely than younger women to receive Pap smears or mammograms. In 2000, for instance, 43 percent of women age 75 and over had not had a Pap smear within the past two years and 39 percent had not had a mammogram during that time period. The corresponding figures for women in their 50s and early 60s were 16 percent and 21 percent, respectively (National Center for Health Statistics, 2004).

Another example is the diagnosis and treatment of older women with HIV infection. Since older women are generally viewed as sexually disinterested and inactive, they are less likely to be given information about safer sex practices (Levy, Ory, & Crystal, 2003). Today, however, more than 16,000 cases of AIDS among women age 50 and older have been diagnosed, and the number of new cases per year is growing steadily (National Center for Health Statistics, 2004). In the mid-1980s, most AIDS cases among women at that age group were caused by blood transfusions. Now, heterosexual contact is the leading cause (McNeil, 2004). One factor putting older women at increased risk during heterosexual contact is the increased thinning of the vaginal tissues and the decrease in lubrication after menopause. These conditions can lead to small skin tears or abrasions during sexual activity that increase the chance of HIV entering the bloodstream (Levy et al., 2003). Another factor in the rise of HIV in the elderly is the increase in sexual activity fueled by Viagra and similar drugs, but without a corresponding increase in condom use (Zablotsky & Kennedy, 2003).

Older women who have HIV infection may have a harder time than infected younger women in obtaining a correct diagnosis and treatment. Because physicians do not expect to see AIDS in older women, they are more likely to make a late diagnosis or a misdiagnosis. Symptoms of AIDS resemble those of various age-related diseases including Alzheimer's, which is one of the most common misdiagnoses (McNeil, 2004). Older women are also less likely to think of themselves as being at risk for AIDS, and so they may not think to ask for an HIV test (Zablotsky & Kennedy, 2003). Failure to diagnose HIV early can have serious consequences at any age since it is harder to arrest the disease as it advances. But older adults with HIV are even more likely to deteriorate rapidly because of their already weakened immune systems (Levy et al., 2003).

Women spend 64 of their years in good health and free of disability, compared with only 59 years for men. But because women live longer than men, it is women who more often live many years with chronic, often disabling illnesses (Crimmins, Kim, & Hagedorn, 2002). This phenomenon, known as the gender paradox, can be summed up in the saying: "Women are sicker; men die quicker." The gender paradox is found in every country in which these statistics have been gathered (Beers & Jones, 2004; Mannheim Research Institute, 2005). Women have higher rates of chronic fatigue syndrome, fibromyalgia, thyroid conditions, migraine headaches, anemia, urinary incontinence, and more than 80 autoimmune disorders such as rheumatoid arthritis, Crohn's disease, multiple sclerosis, and lupus (Carlson, Eisenstat, & Ziporyn, 2004; Fairweather & Rose, 2004; National Institutes of Health, 2004).

A person may have one or more chronic diseases without being disabled. The key issue is whether the chronic condition restricts daily life or reduces the ability to take care of oneself. As one might expect, the chance of developing a disability increases with age. About 18 percent of women ages 16 to 64, but 43 percent of women aged 65 and over, have at least one functional limitation ("Women and Disability," 2004). The degree of disability resulting from chronic conditions is assessed by measuring how well individuals can carry out two groups of activities:

1. *activities of daily living* (ADLs), which include basic self-caring activities such as feeding, bathing, toileting, walking, and getting in and out of a bed or chair
2. *instrumental activities of daily living* (IADLs), which go beyond personal care to include preparing meals, doing housework, shopping, doing laundry, attending social activities, using the telephone, taking medication, and managing money (Unger & Seeman, 2000)

Older women are more likely than older men to have some difficulty with both ADLs and IADLs (National Center for Health Statistics, 2004). African American women are more likely than other women to report chronic and/or disabling conditions, followed by Native American, white, and Latina women. Asian American women are only half as likely as other women to suffer from disabilities (Canetto, 2003; Carlson et al., 2004; Kelley-Moore & Ferraro, 2004).

Life satisfaction is often lower for women who have serious health problems. More than 40 percent of women with disabilities report lower life satisfaction, compared with 18 percent of women with fair or poor health and 6 percent of all women (Commonwealth Fund, 1993). But chronic illness need not prevent a woman from enjoying her life. In the Women's Health and Aging Study, 35 percent of women with moderate to severe disabilities reported a high sense of happiness and personal mastery and low levels of anxiety and depression (Unger & Seeman, 2000).

MENTAL HEALTH

Older women, compared to older men, experience more frequent negative emotions and a lower sense of well-being (Canetto, 2001). However, the psychological health of women tends to improve as they get older (Jones & Meredith, 2000). For example, in one study of African Americans, Chinese Americans, Norwegians, and American nuns (Gross et al., 1997), older women showed fewer negative emotions and more emotional control than younger women. Gender differences in depression decline or even disappear by age 80 because men's depression rates increase sharply after age 60, while those of women remain the same or decrease (Barefoot et al., 2001; Canetto, 2001; Kasen, Cohen, Chen, & Castille, 2003). Similarly, women's neurotic tendencies decline as they age, but this is not the case for men (Srivastava, John, Gosling, & Potter, 2003).

SEXUALITY

Menopausal changes in sexual physiology and hormone levels may affect sexual activity in the middle years (Burgess, 2004; Henig, 2004). Decline in the production of estrogen is responsible for many of these changes. The vaginal walls become less elastic, thinner, and more easily irritated, causing pain and bleeding during intercourse. Decreases in vaginal lubrication can also lead to painful intercourse. Normal acidic vaginal secretions become less acidic, increasing the likelihood of yeast infections. Paradoxically, one of the best remedies is to have more sex. Sexual activity increases blood flow to the vagina, which makes the tissues fuller, and also triggers lubrication (Morris, 2004).

Signs of sexual arousal—clitoral, labial, and breast engorgement and nipple erection—become less intense in midlife, and sexual arousal is slower. Most menopausal women, however, experience little or no change in *subjective* arousal. Although the number and intensity of orgasmic contractions are reduced, few women either notice or complain about these changes. Furthermore, slower arousal time for both women and men may lengthen the time of pleasurable sexual activity (Etaugh & Bridges, 2006).

While some midlife women report a decline in sexual interest and the capacity for orgasm during these years, others report the opposite pattern (Mansfield, Koch, & Voda, 1998; Rice, 2001). Many postmenopausal women find that their sexual interest and pleasure are heightened. Possible reasons for this include freedom from worries about pregnancy, and the increase in marital satisfaction which often develops during the postparental ("empty nest") years (Etaugh & Bridges, 2006). The extent of sexual activity in middle-aged women is strongly influenced by past sexual enjoyment and experience. Years of sexual experience can more than make up for any decrease in physical responsiveness. Women who have been sexually responsive during young adulthood are most likely to be sexually active as they get older (Etaugh & Bridges, 2006). In addition, both heterosexual and lesbian women who communicate openly with their partners and make changes in their sexual activities to adapt to menopausal changes are more likely than other women to report active and satisfying sex lives (Winterich, 2003).

Sexual activity and contentment during middle and later life are more likely to diminish for individuals who have lost their partners (Henig, 2004). For example, in one nationally representative study of sexuality in Americans age 45 and over, just over half of those polled, but two-thirds of those with sexual partners, were satisfied with their sex lives (AARP, 1999b). While women in their 40s and 50s are nearly as likely as men to have a sexual partner (78 percent compared to 84 percent), the "partner gap" between women and men grows in the later years. Among individuals age 75 and older, 58 percent of men but only 21 percent of women have a partner.

Unfortunately, there are a number of myths and stereotypes about sexuality in later life. Most of today's older Americans grew up at a time when attitudes toward sexuality were more restrictive than they are today, particularly for women (Leiblum & Sachs, 2002; Mares & Fitzpatrick, 2004). Unlike men, many women were taught that they should not enjoy sex and should not initiate it. In addition to this "double standard" of sexuality for women, older women are subjected to the double standard of aging discussed earlier; that is, compared to older men, women in their later years are perceived as sexually inactive and sexually unattractive (Tariq & Morley, 2003). Not surprisingly, then, men tend to choose younger women or women who look young as their sexual partners and mates (Daniluk, 1998). Many older women themselves are self-conscious about their aging bodies (Henig, 2004) and thus may avoid sexual activity with a partner or decide not to seek a new partner if they become widowed or divorced (Burgess, 2004).

Still, interest in sexual activity remains fairly high throughout adult life, declining only gradually in the later years (Burgess, 2004). In one study of older women and men, 90 percent of those over age 70 expressed a desire for sexual intimacy at least once a week (Wiley & Bortz, 1996). In a Duke University longitudinal study of adults ages 60 to 94, 50 percent of individuals 80 years and older reported still having sexual desires (Leitner & Leitner, 2004). In fact, some women find sex more satisfying and their attitudes toward sex more positive and open in later life than in their middle years. In one nationwide survey of Americans over age 60, 70 percent of sexually active women said they were as satisfied, or even more satisfied, with their sex lives than they were in their 40s (Leary, 1998). Some elderly individuals desire to be more sexually active than they are currently. In the Leary (1998) survey, nearly 40 percent of older women and men wished they had sex more frequently. One reason for this discrepancy between interest and activity, particularly among women, is the lack of a partner (Kilborn, 2004a).

MIDLIFE: CRISIS OR PRIME OF LIFE?

Contrary to popular literature's depiction of middle age as a time of crisis, turmoil, and self-doubt, empirical evidence shows that midlife women consider this period to be one of vibrancy and opportunity for growth. Mitchell and Helson (1990) characterize the early postparental period as women's "prime of life." Others describe midlife as a period of "postmenopausal zest," in which women have an increased determination, energy, and ability to fulfill their dreams and gain control over their lives. Freedom from reproductive concerns, a sense of accomplishment accompanying the successful launching of children, and an increase in available time enable women to focus more on their self-development and on their partner, job, and community (Etaugh & Bridges, 2006).

MIDLIFE ROLE TRANSITIONS

Although few women experience a midlife crisis, many go through a process of life review, an intensive self-evaluation of numerous aspects of their lives. One characteristic theme in the life reviews of current midlife women is the search for an independent identity. Helson (1992) notes that for many women, the need to rewrite the life story in middle age is related to the lessening of the dependence and restriction associated with marriage and motherhood as children grow up. Thus, many women attempt to affirm their own being, independent of their family, through graduate education, beginning a career, or switching careers.

For many midlife women, paid work is a significant predictor of psychological well-being. Middle-aged women who are involved in either beginning or building their career are both psychologically and physically healthier than women who are maintaining or reducing their career involvement (Etaugh & Bridges, 2006). Also, women who have attained the occupational goals they set for themselves in young adulthood have a greater sense of life purpose and are less depressed in midlife than those who fall short of their expectations (Carr, 1997). Furthermore, satisfaction with work predicts a general sense of well-being: the more satisfied women are with their jobs, the better they feel in general (McQuaide, 1998).

For other women, being a full-time homemaker or student can be associated with the same degree of psychological well-being as that experienced by women who are employed. Midlife homemakers whose life goal was this domestic role have a comparable sense of purpose in life as women who aspired toward and achieved an occupational role. Not surprisingly, however, women who are involuntarily out of the workforce, owing to forced early retirement or layoff, are not as satisfied with midlife as women with a chosen role (Etaugh & Bridges, 2006). Thus, there are multiple routes to well-being in midlife, and it appears that a key factor influencing midlife role evaluation is not a woman's *role* per se but fulfillment of her *preferred role.*

Although some midlife women are satisfied with traditional roles, others are disturbed about missed educational or occupational opportunities. Some middle-class women who, as young adults, devoted themselves solely to marriage and motherhood, voice regrets in midlife about earlier traditional decisions. Stewart and Vandewater (1999) examined regrets experienced by women who graduated from college in the mid-1960s. The concerns reported by these women centered on disappointments about not pursuing a more prestigious career, marrying before establishing a career, and not returning to work after having children. The women who acknowledged their regrets and made modifications based on these feelings experienced greater psychological well-being at midlife than did those who had regrets but did not use them as a basis for altering their life direction.

SPOUSAL ROLE TRANSITIONS

Experiences with marriage, divorce, widowhood, and remarriage during the middle and later years vary for women and men. Men in the

United States are more likely than women to be married during midlife, especially during the years from 55 to 64, when 79 percent of men but only 67 percent of women are still married (U.S. Census Bureau, 2005). Marital disruption is more common among African American women, poor women, and women with disabilities than among white, more affluent, and able-bodied women (Etaugh & Bridges, 2006).

Divorce

Approximately 40 percent of all American marriages end in divorce, although divorce rates have decreased somewhat in recent years (Hurley, 2005). While divorce occurs throughout the population, divorce rates vary across ethnic groups and educational levels. Asian Americans have the lowest divorce rates in the United States, and Native Americans have the highest. Black and Latina women are more likely to be separated than other women (Kreider & Simmons, 2003.) In addition, college-educated individuals are less likely to divorce than those without college degrees (Hurley, 2005).

Women with disabilities are more likely than nondisabled women or men with disabilities to be divorced (Asch, Perkins, Fine, & Rousso, 2001; Kilborn, 1999). Not surprisingly, both financial pressure and interpersonal problems can be contributing factors. Consistent with the social construction of females as caregivers and the resultant socialization of girls to be responsive to the emotional needs within a relationship, wives are less likely than husbands to leave a spouse who has a disability (Kilborn, 1999).

Although divorced mothers view themselves as better parents than do mothers in high-conflict marriages, single parenting after a divorce can be highly stressful (Hetherington & Kelly, 2002). The breakup of a marriage produces numerous stressors for custodial parents and their children. Not only must both deal with strong emotional reactions, such as grief, anger, and guilt, but also their daily routines often involve major adjustment. Financial pressures can require the mother to begin or extend her employment, there can be major modifications in household responsibilities, and the family may have to change residence.

Given these and other stressors associated with parental divorce, children tend to experience a variety of emotional and behavioral problems in the immediate aftermath (Hetherington & Kelly, 2002), but most rebound within two years and are as psychologically healthy as children from two-parent homes. A recent meta-analysis found that children in joint-custody arrangements following divorce are as well adjusted as children in two-parent families (Bauserman, 2002).

Divorced women also experience initial problems followed by satisfactory adjustment. Immediately following the breakup, it is common for divorced women to experience higher levels of depression and distress than married women. These negative reactions are greatest in the first few years after the divorce and decline somewhat over time (Lasswell, 2002), with few long-term effects on women's psychological adjustment (Amato & Keith, 1991; Thabes, 1997). Not surprisingly, other life conditions can affect a woman's adjustment to divorce. For example, studies suggest that Latinas experience more distress than white women, perhaps due to the triple burdens stemming from racism, sexism, and economic hardship (Parra, Arkowitz, Hannah, & Vasquez, 1995). However, black mothers show a greater sense of personal mastery following divorce than white mothers (McKelvey & McKenry, 2000), possibly because African American culture provides these women with greater coping skills to deal with the adversities of divorce.

Many women experience a dramatic decline in family income after divorce, which places them in a significantly worse financial situation than divorced men (Kilborn, 2004b). Divorced mothers are nearly twice as likely as divorced fathers to live in poverty. Fewer than two-thirds of divorced mothers with children under 21 are awarded child support, and less than half of these receive full child support on a regular basis (U.S. Census Bureau, 2003). White mothers are more likely than other groups to receive child support and other assets (Steil, 2001), but regardless of ethnicity, divorced women with low income and low occupational status are at risk for distress and depression (Keyes & Shapiro, 2004).

Despite the problems resulting from a breakup, divorce can represent a positive means of reacting to a neglectful, conflict-ridden, or abusive relationship, and women do not feel more upset after a divorce than they did in their high-conflict marriages. Although initially they experience depression and distress, women tend to be happier two years postdivorce than they were during the last year of their marriage. Furthermore, divorced women are likely to be less depressed than women in unhappy marriages (Hetherington & Kelly, 2002).

In addition to relief from leaving a conflict-laden marriage, many women report a variety of positive psychological outcomes—greater feelings of independence and freedom, the ability to meet the challenges of living without a spouse and to function as a single parent, which can produce a new sense of competence (Hetherington & Kelly, 2002). Moreover, they report greater life satisfaction than women who have never married (Frazier, Arikian, Benson, Losoff, & Maurer, 1996). Employment can facilitate adjustment following divorce, because it provides an identity outside of women's marital role (Bisagni & Eckenrode, 1995). Social support from family and friends is also vitally important in helping divorced women cope (Pinquart, 2003). Women who have a social network of friends and relatives to help them deal with the ramifications of divorce are less depressed in the years following the marital breakup (Jenkins, 2003; Thabes, 1997).

Widowhood and Loss of a Partner

Despite the increasing divorce rate, most marriages are terminated not by divorce but by the death of a spouse. In most countries of the world, women are much more likely to become widowed than men, since women not only have a longer life expectancy but also tend to marry men older than themselves (Kinsella & Velkoff, 2001). As of 2004, there were 11.1 million widows but only 2.6 million widowers in the United States, a ratio of more than four to one. About 59 percent of women over the age of 75, but only 22 percent of men the same age, are widowed (U.S. Census Bureau, 2005).

Remarriage rates are much higher for widowers than for widows in many parts of the world (Kinsella & Velkoff, 2001). In the United States, for example, by two years after the death of a spouse, 61 percent of men are in a new romantic relationship and 25 percent are remarried. The figures for women, on the other hand, are only 19 percent and 5 percent, respectively (Wortman, Wolff, & Bonanno, 2004). Consequently, elderly women are three times as likely to live alone as are elderly men (Fields, 2004).

One reason for the much lower remarriage rate of women is that unmarried older women greatly outnumber unmarried older men. In the United States, unmarried women age 65 and over outnumber unmarried men of that age by more than three to one (U.S. Census Bureau, 2005). Furthermore, since men tend to marry women younger than themselves, the pool of potential mates expands for an older man but shrinks for an older woman. In addition, widowed women are much less likely than widowed men to be interested in forming a new relationship. Many widows value their independence and are not eager to resume the domestic responsibilities of a long-term relationship. Some do not relish the idea of becoming a caregiver for an older man, having already experienced the stresses of caring for a terminally ill partner (Beers & Jones, 2004; Wortman et al., 2004).

Widowhood is one of the most stressful of all life events. During the first year after their husband's death, widows show poorer mental and physical health than longer-term widows (Wilcox, Evenson, Aragaki, Mouton, Wassertheil-Smoller, & Loevinger, 2003). Most elderly widowed individuals adjust to their spouse's death within two to four years, although feelings of loneliness, yearning, missing their partner, and lowered life satisfaction remain for extended periods of time (Cutter, 1999; Lucas, Clark, Georgellis, & Diener, 2003). As many as 10 to 20 percent of widows, however, experience long-term problems, including clinical depression, abuse of alcohol or prescription drugs, and increased susceptibility to physical illness. Among these are women with a prior history of depression, those whose marriages were less satisfactory, those whose husbands' deaths followed the deaths of other close relatives and friends, and those who depended on their husbands for most social contact (Cutter, 1999).

Other factors—age, the degree of forewarning of the spouse's death, and financial, social, and personal resources—also affect a woman's reaction to widowhood (Bradsher, 2001; Michael, Crowther, Schmid, & Allen, 2003). Studies comparing the mental and physical health of older widows and older married women generally have not found any differences between these groups (O'Bryant & Hansson, 1995). Younger widows, on the other hand, initially experience greater difficulties in coping with their situation (Michael et al., 2003). One reason for the greater distress experienced by young widows may be the greater likelihood that the husband's death was unexpected. Although younger individuals experience greater distress following their partner's death, the length of recovery is greater for older people (Michael et al., 2003).

Widowhood often results in a substantial reduction in financial resources for women, not only because the husband's income ceases but also because considerable expenses may be incurred during the husband's final illness (Hungerford, 2001; McGarry & Schoeni, 2003). Elderly women, especially those living alone, are more likely than elderly men to live in poverty (Jenkins, 2003).

Loneliness is another problem faced by widows. About 70 percent of elderly widows live alone (Fields & Casper, 2001). Having the social support of family, friends, and neighbors to stave off loneliness helps to alleviate the psychological and physical effects of loss-related stress (Jenkins, 2003; Pinquart, 2003; Zettel & Rook, 2004). Women friends who are themselves widowed can be particularly supportive (Belsky, 1999). Interestingly, research has found more loneliness among women who have lived with a spouse for many years than among women who live alone (Cohler & Nakamura, 1996).

The death of a spouse takes a heavier toll on men than on women. Widowed men suffer more psychological depression, psychiatric disorders, and physical illnesses and have higher death rates and suicide rates than widowed women (Canetto, 2003; Wisocki & Skowron, 2000). This may be due to the fact that women are more apt than men to admit a need for social support, to benefit from that support, and to have broad social networks with relatives and friends, including other widows (Nagourney, Reich, & Newsom, 2004).

Keep in mind that our knowledge of widows has been obtained primarily from older women, most of whom had traditional marriages. When the young women of today become widows, they will have had a different set of life experiences than the current population of widows, including a college education and a job or career, that will likely better prepare them for a healthy adjustment to widowhood (Etaugh & Bridges, 2006).

Lesbians and gay men may encounter unique problems when their partner dies. They may not be eligible for survivor benefits, and in the absence of a will, they may have no claim to the partner's estate that they have helped to build (Peplau & Beals, 2001). Loss of a same-sex partner is especially stressful if the relationship was not publicly acknowledged, but even when the relationship is open, friends, family, and work colleagues may not comprehend the severity and nature of the loss (Fullmer, Shenk, & Eastland, 1999; Walter, 2003).

Singlehood

Approximately 3.8 percent of women and 3.6 percent of men in the United States age 75 and over have never married (U.S. Census Bureau, 2005). Women with disabilities are more likely than nondisabled women or men with disabilities to remain single (Asch et al., 2001; Hanna & Rogovsky, 1992).

Today there is more acceptance of and support for single lifestyles than in the past. Still, single women continue to be portrayed negatively in the media and are widely perceived as odd, social outcasts who lead barren, disappointing lives (Fraser, 2002; Hoban, 2002; Israel, 2002). Many never-married heterosexual women are ambivalent about their marital status. On the one hand, they miss the benefits of steady companionship and feel sad about growing old alone, but at the same time, they enjoy their freedom, independence, and opportunities for self-development (AARP, 2003; Reynolds & Wetherell, 2003). Increasing numbers of single women are signing up for housewarming and birthday registries, having decided not to wait for marriage to request the china, crystal, and appliances they wish to own (Zernike, 2003). Others are not only purchasing a home instead of renting but are also buying a second, vacation home (Cohen, 2003).

The absence of a marital partner does not mean that single women are lacking social relationships. Some date (AARP, 2003) or are in committed romantic relationships, and many spend considerable time with nonromantic significant others, such as relatives, friends, and neighbors (Pinquart, 2003; Zernike, 2003). Moreover, an increasing number of middle-aged single women are choosing to become mothers via sperm donors or adoption (Hertz, 2006).

Never-married women typically have developed skills in independent living and in building support systems that stand them in good stead as they get older (Gottlieb, 1989; Newtson & Keith, 2001). Compared with married women, the never-married older woman is better educated, is in better health, places a great deal of importance on her job, is less likely to be depressed or commit suicide, values her freedom and autonomy, and has close connections with both siblings and other interpersonal supports (Gottlieb, 1989). The workplace is a significant source of friends for single women, and in retirement these women go on to form new friendships with neighbors or members of organizations to which they belong (Doress-Worters & Siegal, 1994). Single older women have also learned to cope in their earlier years with the "stigma" of not being married and so are better able to deal with the effects of ageism in their later years. Most older, single women are satisfied with their lives and seem at least as happy as married women (Newtson & Keith, 2001; Paradise, 1993).

PARENTAL ROLE TRANSITIONS

The fertility rate (that is, the average number of births a woman will have in her lifetime) declined in the United States throughout the early 20th century, reaching a low point of 2.2 births during the Depression years of the late 1930s. The "Baby Boom" following World War II peaked in the late 1950s, when the fertility rate reached 3.7. By the mid-1970s, the rate had dropped to 1.8, and it is now about 2.0. Hispanic women have the highest fertility rate, followed in descending order by black, white, and Asian women (Dye, 2005).

Women not only are having fewer children but also are having them later. Among 40- to 44-year-olds, who are near the end of their childbearing years, 19 percent had had no children in 2004, compared with only 10 percent in 1976 (Dye, 2005). However, a growing number of women are having children after the age of 40. In 2003, more than 100,000 U.S. women between 40 and 44, and nearly 6,000 women between 45 and 49, gave birth, a record high (Hamilton, Martin, & Sutton, 2004). But because fertility begins to decline after age 27, older women have a harder time conceiving. Among women over 40, half will require medical assistance in order to conceive (Brody, 2004). About 15 to 20 percent of women age 40 to 42 can become pregnant using their own eggs, compared with fewer than 3 percent of women over 44, as an increasing proportion of their eggs become abnormal (Gibbs, 2002; St. John, 2002). Women over 40 have more miscarriages than younger women; more preterm, low-birth-weight, and stillborn babies; higher levels of complications during pregnancy; and more chromosomal abnormalities (such as Down syndrome), and they are more likely to have cesarean sections (Brody, 2004; Jacobsson, Ladfors, & Milsom, 2004). The good news is that almost all older mothers, like their younger counterparts, have healthy babies, and that infant mortality rates are comparable for the two groups.

A lesser-known fact about midlife pregnancy is that about half of the pregnancies of women over 40 are unintended—a rate second only to teenagers. During perimenopause, the years prior to the end of menstruation, women may grow lax about birth control because they think there is little risk of pregnancy and may believe they have reached menopause. However, a woman's menstrual cycle becomes less regular in perimenopause, and she may go several months without a period before having one (Goldberg, 2003).

Not only have more women decided to postpone motherhood but also to remain childless. The decision not to have children is facilitated by the availability and legality of effective forms of birth control, the women's movement's emphasis on women's right to make choices in their lives, and the wider participation of women in the labor force (Caplan, 2001; Gillespie, 2003). However, the decision not to have children—to be childless or "child-free"—goes against the traditional gender norms of almost all cultures. Women who make this choice are often criticized as shallow, selfish, deviant, and unfeminine (Gillespie, 2003; Taylor & Taylor, 2003). They may be marginalized, given unsolicited advice, and pressured by others to have children (Daniluk, 1999; Letherby & Williams, 1999).

Women choose not to have children for a number of reasons. Interviews with intentionally child-free women between 40 and 78 years old found that the women wanted autonomy, self-expression, education, economic independence, and opportunities for a better life (Morell, 1993). Other women simply do not enjoy children, believe that they would not make good parents, or want a flexible lifestyle that would be hampered by children (Dierbeck, 2003). Still others perceive motherhood to be a sacrifice and a burden, involving loss of time, energy, and ultimately identity (Gillespie, 2003).

Despite the fact that more women are deciding not to have children, the majority do become mothers (Dye, 2005). Motherhood still is considered to be a central component of a woman's life, a concept that has been labeled the "motherhood mandate" (Russo & Vaz, 2001). In middle age, some mothers are still chasing toddlers around the house, whereas others, who had children in their teen years, have already launched their children into young adulthood. For most midlife mothers, however, a major event is the departure of their children from the home.

Similar to common folklore characterizing midlife as a time of crisis, this postparental period is popularly but inaccurately viewed as an unhappy "empty nest" stage of life for most women. Women generally describe the postparental years in positive rather than negative terms. Because children can be a source of tension in any marriage, women report higher marital satisfaction once their children have left home (Etaugh & Bridges, 2006). Furthermore, the departure of the last child from the home is an opportunity to begin or expand the development of a personal identity independent of family roles. For many women, as we have seen, this event marks the beginning of a midlife review period when they evaluate their lives and consider other options such as pursuing new careers, furthering their education, or providing service to their communities. However, the significant redefinition of their parenting responsibilities and the end to their identity as a child caregiver can be somewhat problematic for women whose primary identity has been that of mother. Mothers who are employed during the childrearing years and establish an identity additional to their mother role find it easier to relinquish their childcare responsibilities when their children leave home than do women who have identified primarily with their role as mother (Lippert, 1997).

Of course, mothers do not stop being parents when their children move out, but rather remain involved in their children's lives in somewhat different ways. While their contacts are generally less frequent, they continue to offer advice and encouragement and sometimes provide goal-directed help, such as financial assistance (Etaugh & Bridges, 2006). Closeness between mothers and daughters typically increases once the daughter leaves home to attend college (Smetana, Metzger, & Campione-Barr, 2004), and mother–daughter relationships often remain enormously satisfying throughout life (Blieszner, Vista, & Mancine, 1996; Lefkowitz & Fingerman, 2003).

Although most mothers experience the departure of their children at some point during midlife, there are variations in children's age of departure, and a significant number return home for some period of time after leaving, for financial reasons or following divorce. Nearly half of middle-aged parents with children over the age of 18 have an adult child living with them. Parents' reaction to their children's return is related to the degree to which the return is characterized by a continued dependence on the parents. Parents experience greater parent–child strain the greater the children's financial dependency and the lower their educational attainment. Furthermore, parents' satisfaction with the living arrangement is positively related to their child's self-esteem, possibly because low self-esteem signals difficulty in assuming independent adult roles. These findings suggest that parents are most satisfied with the parent–child relationship and experience the highest degree of well-being when they perceive their children as assuming the normative roles of adulthood (Etaugh & Bridges, 2006).

CAREGIVER ROLE TRANSITIONS

Middle-aged adults are often referred to as the "caught" or "squeeze" generation because of the responsibilities that they assume for their adolescent and young adult children on the one hand and for their aging parents on the other (Etaugh & Bridges, 2006). Women are described as the family "kinkeepers," maintaining the bonds between and within generations. Typically, it is the middle-aged woman who carries out most of the caregiving and support functions for her elderly parents and in-laws (Katz, Kabeto, & Langa, 2000; Usdansky, 2000). Demographic changes in recent years have increased these parent-care responsibilities of middle-aged women. More parents are living well into old age, and their caregiving children themselves are becoming old. Furthermore, as the birthrate declines, there are fewer siblings to share the burden of the care. Because middle-aged women are increasingly likely to be employed, caring for elderly relatives adds to their list of competing roles and responsibilities (Etaugh & Bridges, 2006).

In some cases, older persons who require care move in with family members. Nearly one in ten elderly men and two in ten elderly women reside with their adult children, siblings, or other relatives (AARP, 1999a), usually because of increasing infirmity. Living with an adult child is more prevalent among ethnic minority elderly than among whites in the United States, and this living arrangement is also common in developing countries (Bongaarts & Zimmer, 2002; Kinsella & Velkoff, 2001). In the United States, older Asian Americans are most likely to live with their children. Blacks and Latinas/Latinos are less likely to live with their children than Asian Americans are, and whites are least likely to do so (Armstrong, 2001).

GRANDPARENTAL ROLE TRANSITIONS

The stereotyped portrayal of a grandmother is often that of an elderly, white-haired woman providing treats for her young grandchildren. However, grandmothers do not fit into any one pattern. While more than 75 percent of Americans over age 65 are grandparents, some people become grandparents as early as their late 20s. About half of women experience this event by age 47 and some spend half their lives as grandmothers (Etaugh & Bridges, 2006). Many middle-aged grandmothers are in the labor force and, as we have seen, may also have responsibilities for caring for their elderly parents (Velkoff & Lawson, 1998). Thus, they may have less time to devote to grandparenting activities.

As noted earlier, the ties between family generations are maintained largely by women. Affectional ties across generations are much stronger for mothers than fathers. As one example, maternal compared to paternal grandmothers are more involved with their grandchildren (Bianchi, 2006). In some parts of the world, the presence of a maternal grandmother literally spells the difference between life and death. Research in rural Gambia, for example, has found that the presence of a maternal grandmother doubles the survival rate of her toddler grandchildren (Angier, 2002).

During their grandchildren's infancy and preschool years, nearly half of grandmothers in the United States provide the children's parents with considerable emotional support, help with child care and household chores, and economic support (Baydar & Brooks-Gunn, 1998). This supportive role tends to be more pervasive in ethnic minority groups than among whites. For example, Asian American grandparents are more likely than other groups to care for their grandchildren whose mothers are employed (Smith, 2002). Latina women are the most influential and important source of social support for their young adult daughters with children (Ginorio, Gutiérrez, Cauce, & Acosta, 1995). Both Native American and black grandmothers are significant figures in the stability and continuity of the family (John, Blanchard, & Hennessy, 2001). In one study of low-income multiracial Hawaiian children who had an absent or incapacitated parent, the nurturance and guidance of grandparents was a key factor in the children's well-being as they grew to adulthood (Werner, 2004).

For some children, grandparents are part of the family household. The number of grandparents living in homes with grandchildren has doubled since 1970 to 5.8 million in 2002, including 8 percent of black, Native American, and Latina/Latino adults, 6.4 percent of Asian American adults, and 2.5 percent of white adults (U.S. Census Bureau, 2004; Simmons & Dye, 2003). Some of the increase results from an uncertain economy and the growing number of single mothers, which has sent young adults and their children back to the parental nest. New immigrants with a tradition of multigenerational households have also swelled the number of such living arrangements (Lugaila & Overturf, 2004).

Increasing numbers of grandparents now find themselves raising their grandchildren on their own. Of the 5.8 million grandparents living in a household with a grandchild, more than 40 percent are raising their grandchildren without a parent present. About two-thirds of these "skip-generation parents" are grandmothers. Grandparents become full-time caregivers for their grandchildren for a number of reasons: parental illness, child abuse, substance abuse, and psychological or financial problems (Sanchez-Hucles, 2003; Waldrop, 2004). In some developing countries, parents migrate to urban areas to work, while grandparents remain behind and raise the grandchildren (Yardley, 2004). The AIDS epidemic has also increased the number of grandparents who are raising their grandchildren in many nations, including the United States (Knodel, Watkins, & VanLandingham, 2003; UNAIDS, 2004). The belief that caregiving grandmothers are primarily poor ethnic women of color is a myth. Parenting grandmothers can be found across racial and socioeconomic lines (Harm, 2001). About half the grandparents raising grandchildren are white, 29 percent are black, 17 percent are Latina/Latino, 3 percent are Asian American, and 2 percent are Native American.

Rearing a grandchild is full of both rewards and challenges (Waldrop, 2004). While parenting a grandchild is an emotionally fulfilling experience, there are psychological, health, and economic costs. Grandparents primarily responsible for rearing grandchildren are more likely than other grandparents to suffer from a variety of health problems, including depression, diabetes, high blood pressure, heart disease, and a decline in self-rated physical and emotional health. Furthermore, they tend to delay seeking help for their own medical problems (Gibbons & Jones, 2003; Lee, Colditz, Berkman, & Kawachi, 2003; Ruiz, Zhu, & Crowther, 2003).

LABOR FORCE TRANSITIONS

Labor force participation of middle-aged and older women has increased sharply over the past three decades. Two-thirds of married women and 71 percent of single women age 45 to 64 now are in the U.S. labor force. During the same 30-year period, by contrast, men have been retiring earlier. By 2004, only 83 percent of 45- to 64-year-old married men were in the workforce, compared to 91 percent in 1970. As a consequence of these changes, which hold across all ethnic groups, the proportion of paid workers 45 and over who are women is higher than ever before (U.S. Census Bureau, 2005).

Many midlife and older women have been employed throughout adulthood. For some working-class women, women of color, and single women, economic necessity has been the driving force. But for many women, a more typical pattern has been movement in and out of the labor force in response to changing family roles and responsibilities. Some women decide to reenter the labor force after their children are grown or following divorce or the death of their spouse (Etaugh & Bridges, 2006).

Older women work for most of the same reasons as younger women. Economic necessity is a key factor at all ages. In addition, feeling challenged and productive and meeting new coworkers and friends give women a sense of personal satisfaction and recognition outside the family (Choi, 2000). Active involvement in work and outside interests in women's middle and later years appear to promote physical and psychological well-being. Work-centered women broaden their interests as they grow older and become more satisfied with their lives. Employed older women have higher morale than women retirees, whereas women who have never been employed outside the home have the lowest.

As women get older, they also confront age discrimination in the workplace. While women's complaints filed with the Equal Employment Opportunity Commission primarily concern hiring, promotion, wages, and fringe benefits, men more often file on the basis of job termination and involuntary retirement. Women also experience age discrimination at a younger age than men (Rife, 2001). This is another example of the double standard of aging, with women seen as becoming older at an earlier age than men.

RETIREMENT

Much of what we know about the effects of retirement is based on studies of men, despite that steady increase in women in the workplace over the past 60 years. This bias reflects the assumption that retirement is a less critical event for women than for men because of women's lesser participation in the labor force and their greater involvement in family roles. But almost half of workers now are women, and retirement has equally important consequences for them (Kim & Moen, 2001b).

The decision to retire depends upon many factors, including health, income, occupational characteristics, and marital and family situations (Choi, 2000). When men retire, they are leaving a role that has typically dominated their adult years. They are more likely than women to retire for involuntary reasons, such as mandatory retirement, poor health, or age. Women, on the other hand, are more apt to retire for voluntary, family-related reasons, such as the retirement of their husband or the ill health of a relative (Canetto, 2003; Hyde, 2003).

Compared to men, women arrive at the threshold of retirement with a different work and family history, less planning for retirement, and fewer financial resources (Butrica & Uccello, 2004; Carp, 2001; Kim & Moen, 2001a, 2001b). Because women typically experience greater job discontinuity, they may have had fewer opportunities to obtain personal career goals and may therefore be more reluctant to retire. Given their more discontinuous employment history and their employment in lower-paid jobs, women are not as likely as men to be covered by pension plans, and their Social Security benefits are lower (Bethel, 2005). Many older women workers with low salaries may not be able to afford the luxury of retirement because of economic pressures, such as inadequate retirement income or sudden loss of a spouse. Widowed and divorced women are more apt than married women to report plans for postponed retirement or plans not to retire at all (Duenwald & Stamler, 2004). A growing number of women continue to work after their husbands retire. In 2000, 11 percent of all couples involving a man 55 or over consisted of a retired husband and an employed wife (Leland, 2004).

In addition, women who have strong work identities have more negative attitudes toward retiring than those with weaker work identities. Professional women and those who are self-employed, who presumably have strong work identities, are less likely than other women to retire early. Older professional women often do not make systematic plans for their retirement, nor do they wish to do so (Etaugh & Bridges, 2006; Heyl, 2004). Working-class women and men, on the other hand, are more likely to view retirement as a welcome relief from exhausting or boring labor (Gross, 2004).

While some women delay their retirement, others retire early. Poor health is one of the major reasons. Since aging black women and men tend to be in poorer health than aging whites, they are likely to retire earlier (Bound, Schoenbaum, & Waidmann, 1996). Health is a more important factor in the retirement decision for men than for women—especially unmarried women—among both blacks and whites (Hatch & Thompson, 1992; Honig, 1996). This gender difference may result from the fact that, unlike married men, married women in poor health may withdraw early from the labor force or do not enter it in the first place. Early withdrawal or nonparticipation in the workforce is enabled by having a provider husband and by societal expectations that employment is optional for women.

Women's role as primary caregiver is another factor contributing to their early retirement. Of the 2.2 million people who provide unpaid home care to frail elderly individuals, nearly three-quarters are women (Canetto, 2001). Eldercare responsibilities often result in increased tardiness and absenteeism at work, as well as health problems for the caregiver (Mor-Barak & Tynan, 1995). Because most businesses do not offer work flexibility or support to workers who care for elderly relatives, more than 20 percent of women caregivers reduce their hours or take time off without pay. Of those who continue to work, more than 8 percent are forced to retire earlier than planned (Perkins, 1992). Also, women whose husbands are in poor health are more likely to retire than women whose husbands enjoy good health (Talaga & Beehr, 1995).

Retirement has long been seen as an individual—primary male—transition. But now, couples must increasingly deal with two retirements, according to Moen, Kim, and Hofmeister (2001). In their study of 534 retired couples, these researchers found that retirement was a happy time for the couples. But the transition to retirement, defined as the first two years after leaving a job, was a time of marital conflict for both women and men. Wives and husbands who retired at the same time were happier than couples in which the spouses retired at different times. Marital conflict was highest when husbands retired first, perhaps because of uneasiness with the role-reversal of a working wife and stay-at-home husband. Not only does the situation pose a potential threat to the husband's role as provider but it can also lead to disagreements over the division of household labor (Mares & Fitzpatrick, 2004).

Although both women and men typically adjust well to retirement, women may take longer to get adjusted (Etaugh & Bridges, 2006). Newly retired women report lower morale and greater depression than newly retired men (Moen et al., 2001). Men seem to enjoy the freedom from work pressure when they retire, whereas women appear to experience the retirement transition as a loss of roles. Because women are not under the same socially prescribed pressures to be employed as are men, those who *do* work, whether out of financial need or commitment to their job, may find it more difficult to stop working (Szinovacz, 1991).

For both men and women, a high level of life satisfaction in retirement is associated with having good health, adequate income, and a high activity level (Fitzpatrick & Vinick, 2005; Kim & Moen, 2001a,

2001b). Financial factors may account for the fact that black retirees have lower levels of life satisfaction than white retirees and that black women are less satisfied than black men (Krause, 1993). Marital status is a contributing factor as well. Married people have more positive retirement attitudes and higher retirement satisfaction than unmarried retirees. Retired women, particularly unmarried ones, are more involved with friends, family, organizations, and volunteer work than are retired men or lifelong housewives (Carp, 2001; Dorfman, 1995; Etaugh & Bridges, 2006). These social contacts are important for the life satisfaction of retired women, particularly those who are unmarried (Dorfman & Rubenstein, 1993; Reeves & Darville, 1994).

FUTURE DIRECTIONS

It is important to remember that as each generation of women matures and grows older, it encounters a different set of conditions and experiences. Our current information about women in the middle and later years is based on the lives of women who grew up in circumstances very different from those of today's young women. If current trends involving family life, sexuality, reproductive freedom, and labor force participation continue, older women of the future are likely to increase their occupational prestige and economic independence, as well as to enhance their opportunities for a variety of rewarding interpersonal relationships.

One cautionary note is that most of the research on women's middle and later years has been done with white, highly educated, middle-class Western women. The midlife experiences of women of color, less-educated women, poor women, and those in non-Western cultures remain almost completely unexplored.

REFERENCES

AARP. (1999a). *A profile of older Americans, 1999.* Washington, DC: AARP.

AARP. (1999b). *Sex—What's age got to do with it?* Washington, DC: AARP.

AARP. (2003). *Lifestyles, dating and romance: A study of midlife singles.* Washington, DC: AARP.

Amato, P. A., & Keith, B. (1991). Parental divorce and adult well-being: A meta-analysis. *Journal of Marriage and the Family, 53,* 43–58.

Angier, N. (2002). The importance of grandma. *New York Times,* November 5, pp. D1, D4.

Arias, E. (2004). *United States life tables, 2002.* National Vital Statistics Reports, 53. Hyattsville, MD: National Center for Health Statistics.

Armstrong, M. J. (2001). Ethnic minority women as they age. In J. D. Garner & S. O. Mercer (Eds.), *Women as they age* (2nd ed.; pp. 97–114). New York: Haworth.

Asch, A., Perkins, T. S., Fine, M., & Rousso, H. (2001). Disabilities and women: Deconstructing myths and reconstructing realities. In J. Worell (Ed.), *Encyclopedia of women and gender* (pp. 345–354). San Diego: Academic Press.

Ayubi-Moak, I., & Parry, B. L. (2002). Psychiatric aspects of menopause: Depression. In S. G. Kornstein & A. H. Clayton (Eds.), *Women in mental health: A comprehensive textbook* (pp. 132–143). New York: Guilford.

Barefoot, J. C., et al. (2001). A longitudinal study of gender differences in depressive symptoms from age 50 to 80. *Psychology and Aging, 16,* 342–345.

Bauserman, R. (2002). Child adjustment in joint-custody versus sole-custody arrangements: A meta-analytic review. *Journal of Family Psychology, 16,* 91–102.

Baydar, N., & Brooks-Gunn, J. (1998). Profiles of grandmothers who help care for their grandchildren in the United States. *Family Relations, 47,* 385–393.

Beers, M. H., & Jones, T. V. (2004). *The Merck manual of health and aging.* Whitehouse Station, NJ: Merck Research Laboratories.

Belsky, J. K. (1999). *The psychology of aging: Theory, research and interventions.* Pacific Grove, CA: Brooks/Cole.

Bethell, T. N. (2005). The gender gyp. *AARP,* July–August 11.

Bianchi, S. M. (2006). Mothers and daughters "do," fathers "don't do" family: Gender and generational bonds. *Journal of Marriage and Family, 68,* 812–816.

Bisagni, G. M., & Eckenrode, J. (1995). The role of work identity in women's adjustments to divorce. *American Journal of Orthopsychiatry, 65,* 574–583.

Blieszner, R., Vista, P. M., & Mancine, J. A. (1996). Diversity and dynamics in late-life mother–daughter relationships. *Journal of Women and Aging, 8*(3/4), 5–24.

Bongaarts, J., & Zimmer, Z. (2002). Living arrangements of older adults in the developing world: An analysis of demographic and health survey household surveys. *Journals of Gerontology Services B: Psychological Sciences and Social Sciences, 57,* S145–S157.

Bound, J., Schoenbaum, M., & Waidmann, T. (1996). Race differences in labor force attachment and disability status. *Gerontologist, 36,* 311–321.

Bradsher, J. E. (2001). Older women and widowhood. In J. M. Coyle (Ed.), *Handbook on women and aging* (pp. 112–128). Westport, CT: Greenwood.

Brody, J. E. (2004). The risks and demands of pregnancy after 20. *New York Times,* May 11, p. D8.

Burgess, E. O. (2004). Sexuality in midlife and later life couples. In J. H. Harvey, A. Wenzel, & S. Sprecher (Eds.), *The handbook of sexuality in close relationships* (pp. 437–454). Mahwah, NJ: Erlbaum.

Butrica, B., & Uccello, C. (2004). *How will boomers fare at retirement?* Washington, DC: AARP.

Canetto, S. S. (2001). Older adult women: Issues, resources, and challenges. In R. K. Unger (Ed.), *Handbook of the psychology of women and gender* (pp. 183–197). New York: Wiley.

Canetto, S. S. (2003). Older adulthood. In L. Slater, J. H. Daniel, & A. E. Banks (Eds.), *The complete guide to mental health for women* (pp. 56–64). Boston: Beacon Press.

Caplan, P. J. (2001). Motherhood: Its changing face. In J. Worell (Ed.), *Encyclopedia of women and gender* (pp. 783–794). San Diego: Academic Press.

Carlson, K. J., Eisenstat, S. A., & Ziporyn, T. (2004). *The new Harvard guide to women's health.* Cambridge, MA: Harvard University Press.

Carp, F. M. (2001). Retirement and women. In J. M. Coyle (Ed.), *Handbook on women and aging* (pp. 112–128). Westport, CT: Greenwood.

Carr, D. (1997). The fulfillment of career dreams at midlife: Does it matter for women's mental health? *Journal of Health and Social Behavior, 38,* 331–344.

Centers for Disease Control and Prevention. (2002). Women and smoking: A report of the surgeon general. *Morbidity and Mortality Weekly Report, 51*(RR-12).

Chen, E. (2004). Why socioeconomic status affects the health of children: A psychosocial perspective. *Current Directions in Psychological Science, 13,* 112–115.

Choi, N. G. (2000). Determinants of engagement in paid work following Social Security benefit receipt among older women. *Journal of Women & Aging, 12,* 133–154.

Cohen, J. (2003). A home of their own. *New York Times,* September 19, pp. D1, D6.

Cohler, B. J., & Nakamura, J. E. (1996). Self and experience across the second half of life. In J. Sadavoy, L. W. Lawrence, L. F. Jarvik, & G. T. Grossberg (Eds.), *Comprehensive review of geriatric psychiatry—II* (2nd ed.; pp. 153–194). Washington, DC: American Psychiatric Press.

Commonwealth Fund. (1993). *The Commonwealth Fund survey of women's health.* New York: Commonwealth Fund.

Crimmins, E. M., Kim, J. K., & Hagedorn, A. (2002). Life with and without disease. *Journal of Women & Aging, 14,* 47–59.

Cutter, J. A. (1999). Coming to terms with grief after a longtime partner dies. *New York Times,* June 13, p. WH10.

Daniluk, J. C. (1998). *Women's sexuality across the life span: Challenging myths, creating meanings.* New York: Guilford.

Daniluk, J. C. (1999). When biology isn't destiny: Implications for the sexuality of women without children. *Canadian Journal of Counseling, 33,* 79–94.

Derry, P. S. (2002). What do we mean by "The biology of menopause"? *Sex Roles, 46,* 13–23.

Dierbeck, L. (2003). Choosing childlessness. In L. Slater, J. H. Daniel, & A. E. Banks (Eds.), *The complete guide to mental health for women* (pp. 40–47). Boston: Beacon Press.

Doress-Worters, P. B., & Siegal, D. L. (1994). *The new ourselves growing older.* New York: Simon & Schuster.

Dorfman, L. T. (1995). Health, financial status, and social participation of retired rural men and women: Implications for educational intervention. *Educational Gerontology, 21,* 653–669.

Dorfman, L. T., & Rubenstein, L. M. (1993). Paid and unpaid activities and retirement satisfaction among rural seniors. *Physical & Occupational Therapy in Geriatrics, 12,* 45–63.

Duenwald, M., & Stamler, B. (2004). On their own, in the same boat. *New York Times,* April 13, pp. E1, E13.

Dye, J. L. (2005). *Fertility of American women: June 2004.* Current Population Reports, P20-555. Washington, DC: U.S. Census Bureau.

Etaugh, C. A., & Bridges, J. S. (2006). *Women's lives: A topical approach.* Boston: Allyn & Bacon.

Fairweather, D., & Rose, N. R. (2004). Women and autoimmune diseases. *Emerging Infectious Diseases, 10,* 2005–2011.

Fields, J. (2004). *America's families and living arrangements, 2003.* Current Population Reports, P20-553. Washington, DC: U.S. Census Bureau.

Fields, J., & Casper, L. M. (2001). *America's families and living arrangements: March 2000.* Current Population Reports, P20-537, Washington, DC: U.S. Census Bureau.

Fitzpatrick, T. R., & Vinick, B. (2005). The impact of husbands' retirement on wives' marital quality. *Journal of Family Social Work, 7,* 83–90.

Fraser, M. B. (2002). *Solitaire: The intimate lives of single women.* New York: MacFarlane, Walter & Ross.

Frazier, P., Arikian, N., Benson, S., Losoff, A., & Maurer, S. (1996). Desire for marriage and life satisfaction among unmarried heterosexual adults. *Journal of Social and Personal Relationships, 13,* 225–239.

Fullmer, E. M., Shenk, D., & Eastland, L. J. (1999). Negating identity: A feminist analysis of the social invisibility of older lesbians. *Journal of Women & Aging, 11*(2/3), 131–148.

Gaylord, S. (2001). Women and aging: A psychological perspective. In J. D. Garner & S. O. Mercer (Eds.), *Women as they age* (2nd ed.; pp. 49–68). New York: Haworth.

Gibbons, C., & Jones, T. C. (2003). Kinship care: Health profile of grandparents raising their grandchildren. *Journal of Family Social Work, 7*(1), 1–14.

Gibbs, N. (2002). Making time for a baby. *Time,* April 15, pp. 49–54.

Gillespie, R. (2003). Childfree and feminine: Understanding the gender identity of voluntarily childless women. *Gender & Society, 17*(February), 122–136.

Ginorio, A. B., Gutiérrez, L., Cauce, A. M., & Acosta, M. (1995). Psychological issues for Latinas. In H. Landrine (Ed.), *Bringing cultural diversity to feminist psychology: Theory, research and practice* (pp. 241–263). Washington, DC: American Psychological Association.

Goldberg, C. (2003). Unexpectedly expecting: Pregnant after 40. *Boston Globe,* September 30.

Gottlieb, N. (1989). Families, work and the lives of older women. In J. D. Garner & S. O. Mercer (Eds.), *Women as they age: Challenge, opportunity, and triumph* (pp. 217–244). Binghamton, NY: Haworth.

Gross, J. (2004). Last hurdle for trailblazing women: The gold watch; Like men before them, professionals facing retirement ask what's next. *New York Times,* April 23, p. A19.

Gross, J. J., et al. (1997). Emotion and aging: Experience expression, and control. *Psychology and Aging, 12,* 590–599.

Halliwell, E., & Dittman, H. (2003). A qualitative investigation of women's and men's body image concerns and their attitudes toward aging. *Sex Roles, 49,* 675–684.

Hamilton, B. E., Martin, J. A., & Sutton, P. D. (2004). *Births: Preliminary data for 2003.* National Vital Statistics Reports, 53, no. 9. Hyattsville, MD: National Center for Health Statistics.

Hanna, W. J., & Rogovsky, E. (1992). On the situation of African-American women with physical disabilities. *Journal of Applied Rehabilitation Counseling, 23,* 39–45.

Harm, N. J. (2001). Grandmothers raising grandchildren: Parenting the second time around. In J. D. Garner & S. O. Mercer (Eds.), *Women as they age* (2nd ed.; pp. 131–146). New York: Haworth.

Hatch, L. R., & Thompson, A. (1992). Family responsibilities and women's retirement. In M. Szinovacz, D. J. Ekerdt, & B. H. Vinick (Eds.), *Families and retirement* (pp. 99–113). Newbury Park, CA: Sage.

Helson, R. (1992). Women's difficult times and the rewriting of the life story. *Psychology of Women Quarterly, 16,* 331–347.

Henig, R. M. (2004). Sex without estrogen: Remedies for the midlife mind and body. *New York Times,* June 6, p. WH12.

Hertz, R. (2006). *Single by chance, mothers by choice: How women are choosing parenthood without marriage and creating the new American family.* New York: Oxford University Press.

Hetherington, E. M., & Kelly, J. (2002). *For better or for worse: Divorce reconsidered.* New York: Norton.

Heyl, A. R. (2004). The transition from career to retirement: Focus on well-being and financial considerations. *Journal of the American Medical Women's Association, 59,* 235–237.

Hoban, P. (2002). Single girls: Sex but still no respect. *New York Times,* October 12, pp. A19, A21.

Honig, M. (1996). Retirement expectations: Differences by race, ethnicity, and gender. *Gerontologist, 36,* 373–382.

Hoyert, D. L., Kung, H. C., & Smith, B. L. (2005). *Deaths: Preliminary data for 2003.* National Vital Statistics Reports, 53, no. 15. Hyattsville, MD: National Center for Health Statistics.

Hungerford, T. L. (2001). The economic consequences of widowhood on elderly women in the United States and Germany. *Gerontologist, 41,* 103–110.

Hurley, D. (2005). Divorce rate: It's not as high as you think. *New York Times,* April 19, p. D7.

Hyde, J. S. (2003). Issues for women in middle age. In L. Slater, J. H. Daniel, & A. E. Banks (Eds.), *The complete guide to mental health for women* (pp. 48–50). Boston: Beacon Press.

Israel, B. (2002). *Bachelor girl: The secret history of single women in the twentieth century.* New York: William Morrow.

Jacobsson, B., Ladfors, L., & Milsom, I. (2004). Advanced maternal age and adverse perinatal outcome. *Obstetrics & Gynecology, 104,* 727–733.

Jenkins, C. L. (2003). Widows and divorcees in later life. *Journal of Women & Aging, 15,* 1–6.

John, R., Blanchard, P. H., & Hennessy, C. H. (2001). In J. M. Coyle (Ed.), *Handbook on women and aging* (pp. 290–325). Westport, CT: Greenwood.

Jones, C. J., & Meredith, W. (2000). Developmental paths of psychological health from early adolescence to later adulthood. *Psychology and Aging, 15,* 351–360.

Kasen, S., Cohen, P., Chen, H., & Castille, D. (2003). Depression in adult women: Age changes and cohort effects. *American Journal of Public Health, 93,* 2061–2066.

Katz, S. J., Kabeto, M., & Langa, K. M. (2000). Gender disparities in the receipt of home care for elderly people with disability in the United States. *Journal of the American Medical Association, 284,* 3022–3027.

Kelley-Moore, J. A., & Ferraro, K. F. (2004). The black/white disability gap: Persistent inequality in later life? *Journals of Gerontology, 59,* S34–S43.

Keyes, C. L. M., & Shapiro, A. D. (2004). Social well-being in the United States: A descriptive epidemiology. In O. G. Brim, C. D. Ryff, & R. C. Kessler

(Eds.), *How healthy are we? A national study of well-being at midlife* (pp. 350–372). Chicago: University of Chicago Press.

Kilborn, P. T. (1999). Disabled spouses increasingly face a life alone and a loss of income. *New York Times,* May 31, p. A8.

Kilborn, P. T. (2004a). Alive, well and on the prowl, it's the geriatric mating game. *Scottsdale Journal,* March 7, p. YT12.

Kilborn, P. T. (2004b). An all-American town, a sky-high divorce rate: Economic woes strain Roanoke's marriages. *New York Times,* May 2, p. YT20.

Kim, J. E., & Moen, P. (2001a). Is retirement good or bad for subjective well-being? *Current Directions in Psychological Science, 10,* 83–36.

Kim, J. E., & Moen, P. (2001b). Moving into retirement: Preparation and transitions in late midlife. In M. Lachman (Ed.), *Handbook of midlife development* (pp. 487–527). New York: Wiley.

Kinsella, K., & Velkoff, V. A. (2001). *An aging world, 2001.* U.S. Census Bureau, Series P95/01-1. Washington, DC: GPO.

Knodel, J., Watkins, S., & VanLandingham, M. (2003). AIDS and older persons: An international perspective. *Journal of Acquired Immune Deficiency Syndromes, 33,* S153–S165.

Krause, N. (1993). Race differences in life satisfaction among aged men and women. *Journal of Gerontology: Social Sciences, 48,* S235–S244.

Kreider, R. M., & Simmons, T. (2003). *Marital status, 2000.* Census 2000 Brief. Washington, DC: U.S. Census Bureau.

Lasswell, M. (2002). Marriage and family. In S. G. Kornstein & A. H. Clayton (Eds.), *Women's mental health: A comprehensive textbook* (pp. 515–526). New York: Guilford.

Leary, W. E. (1998). Older people enjoy sex, survey says. *New York Times,* September 29, p. B16.

Lee, S., Colditz, G., Berkman, L., & Kawachi, I. (2003). Caregiving to children and grandchildren and risk of coronary heart disease in women. *American Journal of Public Health, 93,* 1939–1944.

Lefkowitz, E. S., & Fingerman, K. L. (2003). Positive and negative emotional feelings and behaviors in mother–daughter ties in late life. *Journal of Family Psychology, 17*(4), 607–617.

Leiblum, S., & Sachs, J. (2002). *Getting the sex you want: A woman's guide to becoming proud, passionate, and pleased in bed.* New York: Crown.

Leitner, M. J., & Leitner, S. F. (2004). *Leisure in later life* (3rd ed.). Binghamton, NY: Haworth.

Leland, J. (2004). He's retired, she's working, they're not happy. *New York Times,* March 23, pp. A1, A18.

Letherby, G., & Williams, C. (1999). Non-motherhood: Ambivalent autobiographies. *Feminist Studies, 25,* 719–729.

Levy, J. A., Ory, M. G., & Crystal, S. (2003). HIV/AIDS interventions for midlife and older adults: Current status and challenges. *Journal of Acquired Immune Deficiency Syndromes, 33*(June 1), S59–S67.

Lippert, L. (1997). Women at midlife: Implications for theories of women's adult development. *Journal of Counseling & Development, 76,* 16–22.

Lucas, R. E., Clark, A. E., Georgellis, Y., & Diener, E. (2003). Reexamining adaptation and the set point model of happiness: Reactions to changes in marital status. *Journal of Personality and Social Psychology, 84,* 527–539.

Lugaila, T., & Overturf, J. (2004). *Children and the households they live in, 2000.* Census 2000 Special Reports. Washington, DC: U.S. Census Bureau.

Mannheim Research Institute for the Economics of Aging. (2005). *Health, aging, and retirement in Europe.* Mannheim, Germany: Mannheim Research Institute.

Mansfield, P. K., Koch, P. B., & Voda, A. M. (1998). Qualities midlife women desire in their sexual relationships and their changing sexual response. *Psychology of Women Quarterly, 22,* 285–303.

Mares, M.-L., & Fitzpatrick, M. A. (2004). Communication in close relationships of older people. In J. F. Nussbaum & J. Coupland (Eds.), *Handbook of communication and aging research* (2nd ed.; pp. 231–250). Mahwah, NJ: Erlbaum.

McGarry, K., & Schoeni, R. F. (2003). Widow poverty and out-of-pocket medical expenditures at the end of life. PSC Research Report no. 03–547. Population Studies Center at the Institute for Social Research, University of Michigan.

McKelvey, M. W., & McKenry, P. C. (2000). The psychosocial well-being of black and white mothers following marital dissolution. *Psychology of Women Quarterly, 24,* 4–14.

McNeil, D. G., Jr. (2004). Facing middle age and AIDS. *New York Times,* August 17, pp. D1, D6.

McQuaide, S. (1998). Women at midlife. *Social Work, 43,* 21–31.

Michael, S. T., Crowther, M. R., Schmid, B., & Allen, R. S. (2003). Widowhood and spirituality: Coping responses. *Journal of Women & Aging, 15,* 145–166.

Mitchell, V., & Helson, R. (1990). Women's prime of life: Is it the 50s? *Psychology of Women Quarterly, 14,* 451–470.

Moen, P., Kim, J. E., & Hofmeister, H. (2001). Couples' work/retirement transitions, gender, and mental quality. *Social Psychology Quarterly, 64,* 55–71.

Mor-Barak, M. E., & Tynan, M. (1995). Older workers and the workplace. In F. J. Turner (Ed.), *Differential diagnosis and treatment in social work* (4th ed.; pp. 59–73). New York: Free Press.

Morell, C. (1993). Intentionally childless women: Another view of women's development. *Affilia: Journal of Women & Social Work, 8,* 300–317.

Morris, B. R. (2004). Fighting dryness, with pills, gels and rings. *New York Times,* June 6, p. WH12.

Nagourney, A. J., Reich, J. W., & Newsom, J. T. (2004). Gender moderates the effects of independence and dependence desires during the social support process. *Psychology and Aging, 19,* 215–218.

National Center for Health Statistics. (2004). *Health, United States, 2004 with chartbook on trends in the health of Americans.* Hyattsville, MD: National Center for Health Statistics.

National Institutes of Health. (2004). *Women's health in the U.S.: Research on health issues affecting women.* NIH Publication no. 04-4697, pp. 1–29. Washington, DC: U.S. Department of Health and Human Services.

Newtson, R. L., & Keith, P. M. (2001). Single women in later life. In J. M. Coyle (Ed.), *Handbook on women and aging* (pp. 385–399). Westport, CT: Greenwood.

Noonan, D., & Adler, J. (2002). The Botox boom. *Newsweek,* May 13, pp. 50–58.

O'Bryant, S. L., & Hansson, R. O. (1995). Widowhood. In R. Blieszner & V. H. Bedford (Eds.), *Handbook of aging and the family* (pp. 440–458). Westport, CT: Greenwood.

O'Neil, J. (1999). Happy endings after difficult journeys. *New York Times,* February 2, p. D7.

Paradise, S. A. (1993). Older never married women: A cross cultural investigation. In N. D. Davis, E. Cole, & E. Rothblum (Eds.), *Faces of women and aging* (pp. 129–139). New York: Harrington Park Press.

Parra, E. B., Arkowitz, H., Hannah, M. T., & Vasquez, A. M. (1995). Coping strategies and emotional reactions to separation and divorce in Anglo, Chicana, and Mexicana women. *Journal of Divorce & Remarriage, 23,* 117–129.

Peplau, L. A., & Beals, C. P. (2001). Lesbians, gay men, and bisexuals in relationships. In J. Worell (Ed.), *Encyclopedia of women and gender* (pp. 657–666). San Diego: Academic Press.

Perkins, K. P. (1992). Psychosocial implications of women and retirement. *Social Work, 37,* 526–532.

Pinquart, M. (2003). Loneliness in married, widowed, divorced, and never-married older adults. *Journal of Social and Personal Relationships, 20,* 31–53.

Reeves, J. B., & Darville, R. L. (1994). Social contact patterns and satisfaction with retirement of women in dual-career/earner families. *International Journal of Aging and Human Development, 39,* 163–175.

Reynolds, J., & Wetherell, M. (2003). The discursive climate of singleness: The consequences of women's negotiation of a single identity. *Feminism & Psychology, 13,* 489–510.

Rice, S. (2001). Sexuality and intimacy for aging women: A changing perspective. In J. D. Garner & S. O. Mercer (Eds.), *Women as they age* (2nd ed.; pp. 147–164). New York: Haworth.

Rife, J. C. (2001). Middle-aged and older women in the work force. In J. M. Coyle (Ed.), *Handbook on women and aging* (pp. 93–111). Westport, CT: Greenwood.

Ruiz, D. S., Zhu, C. W., & Crowther, M. R. (2003). *Not* on their own again: Psychological, social, and health characteristics of custodial African American grandmothers. *Journal of Women & Aging, 15,* 167–184.

Russo, N. F., & Vaz, K. (2001). Overview: Roles, fertility and the motherhood mandate. *Psychology of Women Quarterly, 4,* 7–15.

St. John, W. (2002). The talk of the book world still can't sell. *New York Times,* May 20, pp. A1, A16.

Sanchez-Hucles, J. V. (2003). Intimate relationships. In L. Slater, J. H. Daniel, & A. E. Banks (Eds.), *The complete guide to mental health for women* (pp. 104–210). Boston: Beacon Press.

Schneiderman, N. (2004). Psychosocial, behavioral, and biological aspects of chronic diseases. *Current Directions in Psychological Science, 13,* 247–251.

Simmons, T., & Dye, J. L. (2003). *Grandparents living with grandchildren, 2000.* Census 2000 Brief. Washington, DC: U.S. Census Bureau.

Smetana, J. G., Metzger, A., & Campione-Barr, N. (2004). African American late adolescents' relationships with parents: Developmental transitions and longitudinal patterns. *Child Development, 75,* 932–947.

Smith, K. (2002). *Who's minding the kids? Child care arrangements, Spring 1997.* Current Population Reports, P70-86. Washington, DC: U.S. Census Bureau.

Sommer, B., Avis, N., Meyer, P., Ory, M., Madden, T., Kagawa-Senger, M., et al. (1999). Attitudes toward menopause and aging across ethnic/racial groups. *Psychosomatic Medicine, 61*(6), 868–875.

Sontag, S. (1979). The double standard of aging. In J. H. Williams (Ed.), *Psychology of women: Selected readings* (pp. 462–478). New York: Norton.

Srivastava, S., John, O. P., Gosling, S. D., & Potter, J. (2003). Development of personality in early and middle adulthood: Set like plaster or persistent change? *Journal of Personality and Social Psychology, 84,* 1041–1053.

Steil, J. M. (2001). Family forms and member well-being: A research agenda for the decade of behavior. *Psychology of Women Quarterly, 25,* 344–363.

Stewart, A. J., & Vandewater, E. A. (1999). "If I had it to do over again": Midlife review, midcourse corrections, and women's well-being in midlife. *Journal of Personality and Social Psychology, 76,* 270–283.

Szinovacz, M. (1991). Women and retirement. In B. B. Hess & E. W. Markson (Eds.), *Growing old in America* (4th ed.; pp. 293–303). New Brunswick, NJ: Transaction.

Talaga, J. A., & Beehr, T. A. (1995). Are there gender differences in predicting retirement decisions? *Journal of Applied Psychology, 80,* 16–28.

Tariq, S. H., & Morley, J. E. (2003). Maintaining sexual function in older women: Physical impediments and psychosocial issues. *Women's Health in Primary Care, 6,* 157–162.

Taylor, M., & Taylor L. (2003). *What are children for?* London: Short Books.

Thabes, V. (1997). A survey analysis of women's long-term, postdivorce adjustment. *Journal of Divorce & Remarriage, 27,* 163–175.

Torrez, D. J. (2001). The health of older women: A diverse experience. In J. M. Coyle (Ed.), *Handbook on women and aging* (pp. 131–148). Westport, CT: Greenwood.

UNAIDS. (2004) *2004 report on the global AIDS epidemic.* Geneva: UNAIDS.

Unger, J. B., & Seeman, T. E. (2000). Successful aging. In M. B. Goldman & M. C. Hatch (Eds.), *Women & health* (pp. 1238–1251). New York: Academic Press.

U.S. Census Bureau. (2003). *Custodial mothers and fathers and their child support, 2001.* Current Population Reports, pp. 60–225. Washington, DC: U.S. Census Bureau.

U.S. Census Bureau. (2004). *Grandparents Day 2004: Sept. 12.* CB04-FF.15.

U.S. Census Bureau. (2005). *Statistical abstract of the United States, 2006* (125th ed.). Washington, DC: GPO.

Usdansky, M. L. (2000). Numbers show families growing closer as they pull apart. *New York Times,* March 8, p. 10.

Velkoff, V. A., & Lawson, V. A. (1998). *Gender and aging: Caregiving.* 1B/98-3. Washington, DC: U.S. Bureau of the Census.

Waldrop, D. P. (2004). Caregiving issues for grandmothers raising their grandchildren. *Journal of Human Behavior in the Social Environment, 7,* 201–223.

Walter, C. A. (2003). *The loss of a life partner: Narratives of the bereaved.* New York: Columbia University Press.

Werner, E. E. (2004). What can we learn about resilience from large-scale longitudinal studies? In S. Goldstein & R. Brooks (Eds.), *Handbook of resilience in children,* chapter 7. New York: Kluwer.

Wilcox, S., Evenson, K., Aragaki, A., Mouton, C., Wassertheil-Smoller, & Loevinger, B (2003). The effects of widowhood on physical and mental health, health behaviors, and health outcomes: The women's health initiative. *Health Psychology, 22,* 513–522.

Wiley, D., & Bortz, W. M., II. (1996). Sexuality and aging—Usual and successful. *Journal of Gerontology: Medical Science, 51A*(3), M142–M146.

Wisocki, P. A., & Skowron, J. (2000). The effects of gender and culture on adjustment to widowhood. In R. M. Eisler & M. Hersen (Eds.), *Handbook of gender, culture, and health* (pp. 429–448). Mahwah, NJ: Erlbaum.

Women and disability. (2004). *Women's Psych-E, 3*(5).

Wortman, C. M., Wolff, K., & Bonanno, G. A. (2004). Loss of an intimate partner through death. In D. J. Mashek & A. Aron (Eds.), *Handbook of closeness and intimacy* (pp. 305–320). Mahwah, NJ: Erlbaum.

Yardley, J. (2004). Rural exodus for work fractures Chinese family. *New York Times,* December 21, pp. A1, A8.

Zablotsky, D., & Kennedy, M. (2003). Risk factors and HIV transmission to midlife and older women: Knowledge, options, and the initiation of safer sexual practices. *Journal of Acquired Immune Deficiency Syndromes, 33*(June 1), S122–S130.

Zernike, K. (2003). Just saying no to the dating industry. *New York Times,* November 30, pp. ST1, ST12.

Zettel, L. A., & Rook, K. S. (2004). Substitution and compensation in the social networks of older widowed women. *Psychology and Aging, 19,* 433–443.

Chapter 10

Theories of Female Personality

Phyllis A. Katz

They told the story the other way around (Adam forfeits ribs: Eve is born)—Obvious irony. Everyone knew that women do the bearing; men are born.

—*Erica Jong*

Equality is valued nearly everywhere but practiced almost nowhere.

—*Catharine MacKinnon*

Assume that you are in a small theater watching a strange pantomime between two people. The actors are wearing hoods, masks, and costumes that make them completely unrecognizable to the audience. One is somewhat shorter and moves gracefully. The other is larger, moves more vigorously and occupies more space on the stage. At one point the two sit down upon a bench and begin interacting. The taller one sits down first, occupying more than half the bench while the other tries to find space to sit down. The shorter one tries to initiate communication (nonverbally, so we get no voice cues). With each attempt, however, the taller one either looks away or interrupts.

As a spectator, do you think these two actors just differ in personality or might you be willing to conclude that these differences may be attributable to factors other than individual differences? They might differ in age (the shorter one being older), or in nationality, but the most likely assumption that most observers would make is that they differ in gender.

Why? The only distinguishing cues mentioned in the hypothetical scene were the heights, types of movement, and interaction styles of the two individuals. Other possible visual or auditory differences (such as voice or speech style) were not attributed. Nevertheless, most spectators would still conclude (1) that the characters differ in gender, (2) that the shorter one is female, and (3) that whatever personality differences are exhibited within this brief episode are probably attributable to the assumed gender differences. This is because our expectations are that people will act in accordance with our gender stereotypes, that is, that women will be more deferential, men more assertive, and so forth. Such assumptions and attributions are far from atypical in our everyday lives, whether or not we proclaim ourselves personality theorists. This example demonstrates the pervasiveness of gender in our construction and interpretation of social reality.

As scientists, we are trained to understand the overlap in statistical distributions of traits. Nevertheless, we also manifest strong biases to perceive and magnify sex differences (what Hare-Mustin & Maracek, 1988, have labeled "alpha bias") even when they have not been substantiated. Despite enormous gender similarities (e.g., Hyde, 2005), the focus of most scientists (together with the lay public) has been on differences.

It is worth considering why this is the case. In an earlier theoretical article about the development of children's racial biases, we suggested that they were facilitated by young children's propensity to employ transductive reasoning (Katz, 1979). Unlike *inductive* (from particular to general) or *deductive* (from general to particular) reasoning, *transductive* reasoning goes from particular to particular. Thus, it leads the thinker to assume that if two things are different in one respect, that they would differ in many other respects as well. While such thinking is characteristic of preschool children, it is clearly not absent in adults. If males and females look so different, the expectation is that their attributes and behavior should differ as well.

Early personality theorists were not immune to such biases and dealt with them in a variety of ways. For some, the bias was so strong that gender attributions were treated as not requiring additional explanation. Others, however, regarded perceived gender differences as "noise" in their theories, an annoying variability. Consequently, many focused only on males and assumed that female behavior represented relatively minor variations from a supposedly universal male norm. Still others assumed that female behavior, which differed too much from the male norm, was essentially deviant, a function of irrationality or other negative attributions. Males were viewed as central, and females as "other" (see Beauvoir, 1952, for an elegant elaboration of this argument). Early theories about achievement motivation (McClelland, Atkinson, Clark, & Lowell, 1953) were a prime example of how women were ignored. Human nature was essentially male nature.

The major purpose of this chapter is to consider how women have been conceptualized by personality theorists and to trace these trends historically. In so doing, we will attempt to demonstrate how political concepts about women and gender differences have played a major role in what earlier theorists regarded as a simple, objective, scientific enterprise. The political influences are particularly apparent when popular personality theories of psychology are examined in terms of whether they originated before or after the Women's Movement.

The 1970s was a watermark of change with regard to both the assumptions made about gender and the influx of women into research and theory about personality. In a classic paper by Carlson (1972), for example, demonstrating the frustration women were beginning to express about male domination in psychology, she called for "some long overdue changes in psychology's construction of human nature" (p. 17) and for greater attention to what she refers to as "distinctinctly feminine" concerns and experiences such as love, altruism, and intimacy. There have clearly been dramatic changes in the field since Carlson's paper in terms of gender research, but less in the area of theories of personality than one might expect.

This chapter is a revision of an earlier one completed in the late 1980s. Although there has been a vast amount of empirical research about gender in the intervening years, there has been very little new material on personality theory. Where relevant, some updates have been made. For the most part, however, our earlier observations about the field are still relevant.

There have been and remain numerous controversies about what constitutes an appropriate designation of the construct of "personality" (e.g., Engler, 1991). For the purposes of the present chapter, it is defined rather broadly and inclusively. *Personality* refers to those global patterns of behavior that are organized, learned, and relatively stable, that are most apparent in the social and affective domains, and that appear to distinguish individuals. The construct is a complex one, involving multiple observations and interactions. The learning of patterns over time is often referred to as the "socialization" process. Theorists have often categorized these observations in terms of more specific constructs such as personality structure, dynamics, and content. The role of gender may well differentially impact these various subcategories of personality as well.

Psychological theory serves a variety of functions, including global goals such as the understanding and prediction of individual behavior and explanations of a variety of group phenomena. Of the theories employed in psychology, personality theories have often been the most all-encompassing in their attempts to explain complex human behavior. These theories have also been influential in guiding research. Perhaps even more significantly, they have influenced generations of clinical practitioners in their treatment of males and females, an influence that has been decisive even in the absence of acceptable scientific evidence. Irrespective of whether or not these theories are susceptible to scientific test, they provide clinicians with conceptual categories, values about what constitutes healthy functioning, and preferred modes of intervention (Barlow, 1981; Giorgi, 1970; Mahrer, 1978; Frank, 2000). This is one of the reasons we chose to focus this chapter on the political implications of personality theories. As the reader will see, values clearly played a role in personality theory construction.

There may be some readers who question why a specific focus on female personality is needed at all. Isn't an emphasis on human personality sufficient? Indeed, a cursory glance at the table of contents of most undergraduate textbooks about personality theory might suggest that there is common agreement about this. Gender is rarely mentioned. We, together with other feminist theorists, do not agree with this stance. Unfortunately the term *human* has been too often synonymous with *male*. Whether particular theories are, in fact, equally applicable to both sexes appears to be essentially an empirical issue. Interestingly, evidence for such generalizability has not been forthcoming for theories that have focused upon males as the human prototype. Lest the reader think that this issue is only of historical interest, recent discussions concerning the future of personality theory in psychology in the *American Psychologist*, a journal addressed to all members of the American Psychological Association (e.g., Mayer, 2005; Maddi, 2006) make no mention of gender at all, thereby at least implicitly assuming that the same theories are equally relevant to both sexes.

There are two related general empirical questions concerning gender and personality: whether gender is important, and if so, how it manifests itself.

Is gender important in personality? There appears to be a peculiar schism in how importantly gender is viewed between many personality theorists and those in other areas of psychology. The pervasiveness and significance of gender has been widely recognized in human development, social psychology, and psychopathology. Frank (2000), for example, notes that "gender influences the ways in which our brains develop" and that "gender and gender role appear to be key determinants of the kinds of psychosocial experiences we have." According to this view, its influence could not be more significant. Despite this, however, as noted above, one has to look long and hard for any mention of gender in many textbooks about personality theory. Our answer to this question is yes, it is important—but it is not always clear how.

How then might gender manifest itself in personality structure and development? There appear to be at least three possible answers to this question.

The first possibility is that the major personality theorists are correct: the basic mechanisms underlying personality development are essentially similar for males and females. As previously noted, however, we believe that this view requires empirical justification, which has been lacking. Moreover, this assumption is certainly at odds with the vast amount of effort that has gone into demonstrating gender differences. Nevertheless, it might accord with mounting evidence of gender similarity (e.g., Hyde, 2005).

A second possibility is that there are some commonalities in underlying mechanisms that determine male and female personalities and some significant differences. Once again, it would be an empirical issue to tease out what these are, and what the distribution might be.

A third possibility is that entirely different theories may be needed to account for male and female personality (and possibly more, if one wishes to take into account other variables such as race and demographic variables). It could be argued that in an ideal and equal world, separate theories might not be necessary, but in the one in which we live, the socialization processes are so different that this might be the most parsimonious way to begin. This possibility does not necessarily imply that boys and girls differ so much at birth, but rather that their subsequent lives take such different paths that it is necessary to explore them separately so as to better understand the patterns that emerge. While developmental psychologists within the United States have often concluded that the socialization experiences of boys and girls are exceedingly different (e.g., Maccoby & Jacklin, 1974), this conclusion does not seem to generalize to females on a global scale. In a recent article in the *New York Times*, for example, Herbert (2006) describes how "women, by the millions, are systematically targeted for attack because they are women." His article was based upon a recent report released by the United Nations describing bride burnings, honor killings, female infanticide, genital mutilation, sex trafficking, and mass rape as a weapon of war, affecting hundreds of millions of girls and women. This backdrop of pervasive violence is not something that men are exposed to, but must certainly affect female personality.

Based upon these possibilities, let us consider what kinds of theoretical models are possible in terms of how gender is dealt with. Let us assume that we starting from scratch. Let us also assume that we consider three basic categories of variables to be the foundations of personality development:

1. socialization variables
2. social structure factors
3. biological factors (including genetic factors and biosocial variables)

Biosocial variables have biological foundations but take into consideration how the social environment responds to such variables.

The first kind of theoretical model (Type I), then, can be schematized as shown in figure 10.1. Type I is the Equality Model, since it assumes that all determinants affect males and females equally.

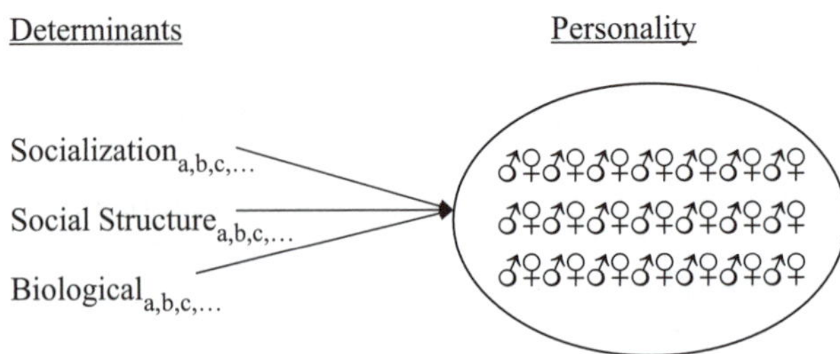

Figure 10.1. Equality Model

A second kind (Type II), similar to the first, can be schematized as in figure 10.2. This Type II model, the most common one historically, is the Male-Oriented Equality Model, wherein males are regarded as representative of humans and are the major focus of the (generally male) theorist. It is assumed that the variables postulated will affect females in the same way.

A third type of model (Type III), at the other end of the continuum, can be schematized as in figure 10.3. Type III is the Completely Different Model, which assumes that the particular variables that form the foundation for male and female personality are completely unlike one another.

Finally, a fourth type of theoretical model is possible (Type IV): the Interactive Model, as depicted in figure 10.4. The schematic drawing of the Type IV model depicts a situation in which the foundation variables are the same, but interact differentially with gender. The diagram depicts a totally interactive model, but various subsets are possible as well, in which only one or two categories of inputs interact with gender rather all three. Further complexity is possible, since certain variables within each category may interact with gender, whereas other do not. Ideally, of course, the theorist should specify the nature of these interactions.

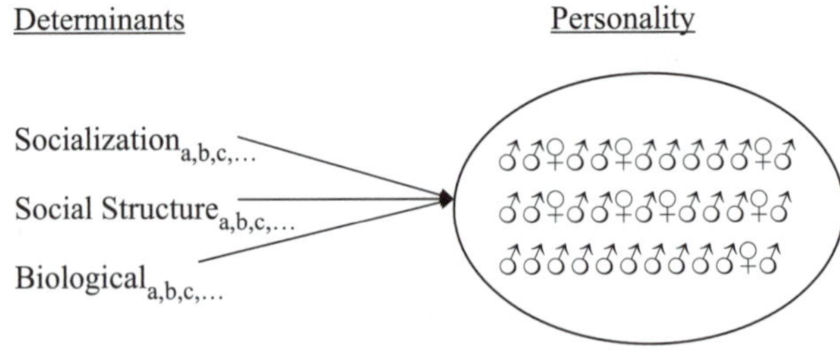

Figure 10.2. Male-Oriented Equality Model

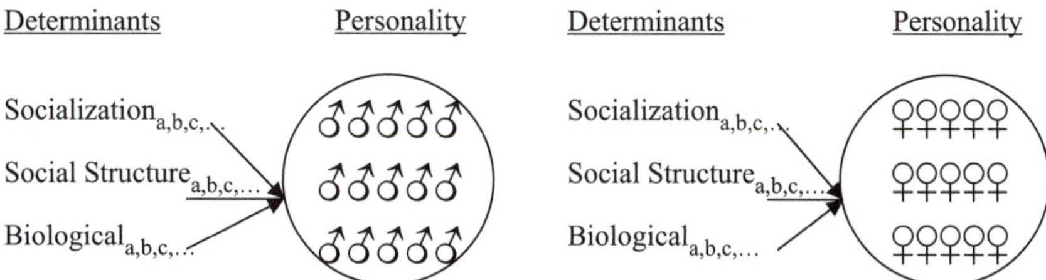

Figure 10.3. Completely Different Model

This chapter will selectively review how various personality theories have constructed female personality in the context of these issues and models. An exhaustive review would require a volume of its own. In our review, the discussion will deal with four questions that would seem quite simple if it were not for the complicated role of biases and values. These questions are:

1. Do the personalities of males and females differ in significant and meaningful ways?
2. What are the major dimensions of personality involved in these differences?
3. What factors may account for observed personality differences of males and females? (As noted above, biology, socialization, and sexism are the three most frequently discussed.)
4. What are the implications of these differences for research, treatment, and further development of theory?

HISTORY AND SUMMARY OF GENDER DIFFERENCE RESEARCH

Any concern with the implications of different theoretical approaches about gender differences requires an initial consideration of the data, the raw material used for theoretical construction. It is well beyond our

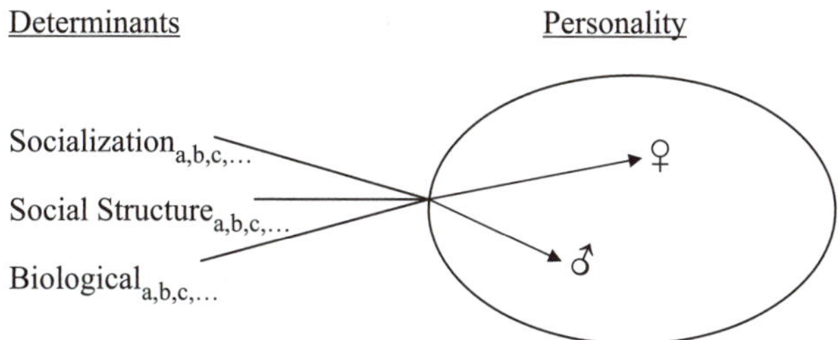

Figure 10.4. Interactive Model

present task to fully review the thousands of studies in this area, but we will attempt to highlight a few of the major ones and to indicate some of the salient historical trends. The general issues surrounding the question of gender differences concern their consistency, their magnitude, and their interpretation.

Gender Differences in Intellectual Functioning

While differences in intellectual functioning may not be considered critical to an understanding of personality differences per se, any empirical work or cultural stereotypes affirming the relative superiority of one gender's intellectual functioning over the other's may be expected to form a backdrop that differentially influences factors that have traditionally been within the domain of personality. These include self-esteem, feelings of competence, need to dominate, feelings of deference, and the general milieu of social expectations that confront males and females.

The history of this field demonstrates the vagaries of trying to establish sex differences, and there are some interesting parallels to personality theory construction as well. Early demonstrations of gender differences in intelligence were frequently published in the late 19th and early 20th centuries as male psychologists concluded that women were inferior to men in intellectual functioning (Deaux & Kite, 1987). In contrast, however, female researchers who subsequently investigated these claims (by surveying the same relevant literature) concluded that unadulterated bias and/or poor methodology had accounted for these earlier incorrect conclusions (Woolley, 1910). Subsequent scrutiny of differences in performance across a wide variety of intellectual tasks led Hollingsworth (1918) to conclude that any gender differences obtained were random and meaningless. Consequently, subsequent work in this area was guided by the assumption that there were no gender differences in intellectual functioning (or at least no differences favoring females). Perhaps this perspective prompted the decision made by Binet and Terman to eliminate questions on which females as a group scored higher than males in the development of their famous intelligence test. Yet, as Jacklin (1987) has pointed out, one wonders if the same procedure would have ensued had males scored higher.

Although contemporary researchers have concurred with the conclusion that no viable evidence exists documenting gender differences in general intellectual functioning, more recent research has focused on potential gender differences in more circumscribed cognitive abilities. Thirty years ago, the evidence suggested that boys were superior in mathematical and spatial ability, whereas girls were superior in verbal skills (Maccoby & Jacklin, 1974). Much research has been conducted since then, and these differences appear to be diminishing. In addition to a number of meta-analyses (e.g., Linn & Hyde, 1988), there has been a burgeoning of interest in an area called "stereotype threat," initiated by Claude Steele and his associates. This research has demonstrated that intellectual behavior is often determined by stereotypes that people hold about the groups in which they are categorized. Female college students, for example, performed better on a test when it was not labeled as an assessment of their mathematical ability than when it was. Thus, what we categorize as "intellectual" may have many social influences as well, and may well be affected by personality.

Sex Differences in Selected Social Behavior

As with intellectual functioning, there have been multiple studies of social behavior with a view toward establishing sex differences. Most of these have been laboratory based. Reviews of these studies suggest that there are at least four areas where sex differences have been reliably and consistently obtained:

1. aggression
2. sensitivity to nonverbal cues
3. conformity
4. helping behaviors

With regard to aggression, meta-analyses have indicated that, not surprisingly, men behave more aggressively than women do, and these differences are greater for physical than for verbal aggression (e.g., Eagly & Steffen, 1986; Eagly, 1987). These gender differences are even more pronounced in children (Hyde, 1986). While overall differences are relatively small in laboratory-based studies, males are vastly overrepresented on indices of aggression in crime statistics regarding homicides and other violent crimes, so this difference seems to be very clear-cut.

With regard to sensitivity to nonverbal cues, females show greater sensitivity. They are also better at decoding nonverbal messages than males are (see, e.g., Hall, 1978, 1984). Perhaps as a result, females also demonstrate greater ability to empathize and to communicate emotional support to others (Reisman, 1990). Such gender differences in communication and relationship style have also been noted in the domain of marital and family relationships (e.g., Markman & Kraft, 1989) and may be one of the most significant dimensions of female personality.

Females appear to be more conforming and easily influenced than males are (Eagly & Carli, 1981). While this has been frequently been interpreted as a negative quality, particularly by male researchers, it could also be interpreted as another instance of their greater sensitivity to social cues (Langer, 1989), which may be adaptive in certain circumstances but not in others.

Findings on helping behavior have been somewhat counterintuitive in that males are more likely to provide help to others than females (Eagly, 1986). Meta-analyses of this research have summarized studies in which strangers are the recipients of short-term assistance. In some instances, particularly where potential physical danger is involved, helping behavior is in accordance with prescribed male gender-role as the chivalrous or heroic one. When helping is defined as long-term nurturing behavior, however, the gender patterns are clearly different. Sociological research on families, for example, demonstrates that it is most often daughters, rather than sons, who care for aging parents (e.g., Brody, 1986), and child development literature substantiates commonsense notions that mothers typically provide more nurturance to their children than do fathers (e.g., Lamb & Lamb, 1976). Thus, there appears to be a disparity between results from laboratory-based research and real-world situations.

Gender Differences in Personality Traits

As one might expect, males attribute traits to themselves that are regarded as more normative and desirable for males, whereas females describe themselves, on average, with traits regarded as feminine. Several decades ago, new paradigms and measuring devices were offered that allowed these masculine and feminine traits to be assessed independently, instead of using methods of viewing masculinity and femininity as opposite poles of a continuum (e.g., Spence, Helmreich, & Stapp, 1974; Bem, 1974). A considerable body of research was subsequently conducted assessing the construct of androgyny, utilizing various ways of combining such independently measured male and female traits. The construct of androgyny appears to be a widely accepted one now, and research interest in it has dwindled considerably.

While androgyny allowed for greater freedom in self-descriptions, and variability was related to a number of other variables, the main effect of gender on self-descriptions still appears to be robust across cultures. Different characteristics are ascribed to males and females, largely in accordance with gender stereotypes (see, e.g., Williams & Best, 1982, 1990). Males generally perceive themselves as more dominant, autonomous, aggressive, and active, whereas females describe themselves as more nurturant, affiliative, and deferential. Interpretations of these differences have varied. Some investigators, for example, have attributed such gender differences to differential social roles (e.g., Eagly, 1995). Despite varying interpretations, however, these findings are consistent and strong.

A more recent cross-cultural review by Costa, Terracciano, & McCrae (2001) reached similar conclusions, but is of interest because the traits investigated were broader than the earlier studies cited above.

Their review focused upon 30 traits of the Revised NEO Personality Inventory, based upon a Five-Factor Model (Feingold, 1994). The factors discussed in the review were neuroticism, extroversion, openness to experience, conscientiousness, and psychoticism. Females score higher on items in the neuroticism scale (described as a broad domain of negative affect), whereas men score higher on psychoticism. No overall consistent gender differences were found on the extroversion and openness-to-experience factors, but different patterns were obtained. With regard to Factor O (openness to experience), for example, women had higher scores on openness to aesthetics, feelings, and actions, but lower ones in openness to ideas. Conscientiousness was not associated with significant gender differences in the articles reviewed.

It is important to recall that these findings are based entirely upon self-descriptions and not on behaviors observed by others. This does not mean that self-perceptions may not be a significant factor in personality, but it is clearly not the whole picture when it comes to the assessment of gender differences. This is an area where social desirability and self-presentation factors play a very important role in how people respond to questionnaires.

Gender Differences in Psychopathology

Gender differences obtained in psychological symptoms are even more impressive than in the areas previously discussed. Marked differences have been found in both the frequency and content of maladjustment for both children and adults. The gender trends obtained depend largely on age.

The developmental literature suggests that between infancy and adolescence, boys are considerably more at risk for displaying psychopathology than are girls (Erne, 1979), whereas the reverse gender difference appears in adulthood (Regier et al., 1988; Silvern & Katz, 1986). At the grade-school level, for example, the preponderance of children in special classes for those with emotional problems are boys, and a majority of these exhibit "acting out" types of symptoms—poor impulse control, physical aggressiveness, very short attention span, and so on (Achenbach, 1982; Achenbach & Edelbrock, 1981). Silvern & Katz (1986) found that gender-role patterns were also predictive of the types of mental health problems exhibited—and not just gender itself. In that study, externalizing or conduct disorder problems were associated with boys who held very stereotypically masculine self-concepts. For girls, higher levels of internalizing personality problems, such as excessive shyness and anxiety, were associated with highly stereotyped feminine self-concepts.

Sex roles appear to play a part in adult psychopathology as well, and both masculinity and femininity have their hazards. Acting-out behavior continues to predominate in males over the life span, as attested by gender differences in rates of violent crimes, antisocial personality disorders, and substance abuse, whereas women have higher rates of affective and somatization disorders (Regier et al., 1988). While it is beyond the scope of the present review, it should also be noted that psychiatric diagnosis itself may be influenced by sex bias (Strickland, 1988) so that the same behaviors may be differentially diagnosed in men and women.

There have been widely differing interpretations of these gender differences. Let us take as an example the frequently documented finding that women are twice as likely to suffer from depression as men (Dusek, 1987). Almost every imaginable type of explanation has been offered for this gender difference, ranging from the hormonal predisposition theory (Akiskal, 1979) or other biochemical differences, long accepted by physicians (better to treat with pharmaceuticals), to the possibility that the phenomenon is an artifact attributable either to women's greater verbalization about these symptoms or to clinicians' bias in diagnosis (Phillips & Segal, 1969). The fact that women have less power than males has also been suggested as an explanation for the high rate of depression in women (Nolen-Hoeksema, 1987; Herschfield & Cross, 1982). An interesting finding that has not been as widely popularized as differences in depression rates is that men have a higher incidence of successful suicides (Strickland, 1988). Achievement-oriented instrumentality is not invariably positive.

None of the various explanations for gender differences in feelings of depression has yet received unambiguous support, but considerable research continues in this area. It is somewhat ironic to note that despite discussions about possible artifacts and incomplete experimental designs (e.g., Ingram, Cruet, Johnson, & Wisnicki, 1988; Dusek, 1987), published gender differences are generally interpreted as a masculine advantage. Assertiveness and self-confidence are often taken as the criteria of psychological health, just as such masculine strengths are valued culturally. In most research concerning adults, factors such as nurturance, emotional expressiveness, and intimate communication skills are ignored as health indices, just as criminality and conduct disorder are ignored as indices of pathology in favor of depression and low self-esteem. The emphasis is particularly paradoxical in this instance, because of the long tradition of psychodynamic theory that suggests that it is healthier to express than repress. Nevertheless, if the women are the affect expressers, they are deemed less healthy.

Summary

This section has summarized findings of gender differences in a number of areas related to personality. The review is far from complete, but it is apparent that a number of gender differences have been obtained, although in many cases the effect sizes are relatively small. What it all means for personality theory is, at the very least, that gender can not be ignored, and for this reason, subsequent sections will discuss only those theories that have considered gender.

THEORETICAL MODELS USED TO INTERPRET GENDER DIFFERENCES IN PERSONALITY

There have been three major types of theories that have focused on why males and females may differ in personality patterns. They roughly, but not completely, correspond to the independent variables outlined in the introductory section. The first type has emphasized the role of biological factors. Whereas we have attempted to differentiate biosocial factors from genetic effects, these have generally been combined, and biologically focused theories have discussed the possible behavioral effects of genetic, hormonal, and morphological factors. The second type has emphasized the significance of differential socialization for boys and girls as they mature and/or an adult milieu that maintains differential expectations and treatment in a wide variety of areas. A third type, emerging more recently, has studied the role of the social structure, and particularly sexism, as the major underlying factor involved in sex differences in personality. Although this last type of theory could be subsumed under the category of socialization, its emphasis is sufficiently different to warrant separate discussion. Its focus has been on the structural aspects of society, which, in turn, influence both individual socialization and most adult activity.

Biologically Based Theories

Theories emphasizing biological factors have long been and continue to be espoused. In one sense, beliefs that behavioral differences are attributable to biological causes appear to flow quite naturally from a gender category system defined by a biological dichotomy, even when this dichotomy itself is open to question (cf. Lorber, 2005). As previously noted, unsupported generalizations from anatomical differences to behavioral ones are illogical and typical of preschool reasoning (Piaget, 1928), but are common in adults, nevertheless. We are not suggesting here that there may not be meaningful, biologically based gender differences that underlie some of the previously discussed personality differences—these are empirical questions—but only that the logic involved in formulating such hypotheses is flawed without supporting empirical data, which are rarely presented.

There are political issues with biological positions, as well. To the lay public, biological causes appear to be more fundamental and unchangeable than psychological ones. Thus, feminists may be justifiably concerned that biological findings may be used against women, much in the way that such findings historically have hindered the cause of racial equality. Often, as was illustrated in earlier sections, it is not only the accuracy of a documented difference but both the interpretation and the power of the interpreter that can be potentially damaging.

Take the case of hormonal differences between men and women. Women's greater variability has been used to buttress charges of emotional instability. Of course, men are also affected by hormones. One former president of the American Psychological Association went so far as to suggest that antitestosterone pills be taken by male leaders to reduce war (Clark, 1971). If men were to be found to be more hormonally variable than women, however, it would probably be argued that this flexibility would make them better suited to fill important leadership positions, whereas interpretations of an opposite trend suggest that women are more emotionally labile and therefore unsuited. If it were simply an issue of the difference itself, why hasn't it been proposed, for instance, that women are more suitable for elective office because their greater longevity makes it less likely that they will die while in office?

The best-known advocate of a biological approach to personality is, of course, Sigmund Freud. His oft-cited dictum that "anatomy is destiny" may be the most global statement of a biological personality theory (Freud, 1964). While anatomy may well be destiny in a society that practices female infanticide, most contemporary theorists assume that this position, at the very least, needs further elaboration and documentation. With regard to the types of models discussed at the outset, Freud's position is an example of the Type III model, that is, separate variables leading to distinctly different personalities for males and females.

Freud postulated that genital differences were the primary determinant of personality differences in females and males. His theory of psychosexual development hypothesized that all children went through several stages. During the first two, the oral stage (first year of life) and the anal stage (approximately ages 1–3), boys and girls did not differ. Major differences occurred, however, during the Oedipal stage, the third stage of development, when genital differences were observed. Freud assumed that when girls compared their anatomy to boys, they experienced castration anxiety and developed penis envy. Both of these were assumed by Freud to have long-lasting and significant personality implications for females, including feelings of inferiority, greater vanity, weaker superegos (with corresponding tendencies toward less ethical behavior), and weaker gender identity than their male counterparts. The superego differences were attributed to girls' weaker anxiety about future castration than boys, thus having less to lose from impulsive or taboo behavior. Similarly, he viewed girls as identifying more ambivalently with their own gender and sometimes seeking to take on male characteristics. Androgyny was not in fashion then. Moreover, girls' incomplete resolution of the Oedipal stage, which was itself due to anatomy, was thought to have even further consequences. Without a sufficiently mature resolution, women were presumed to be more likely to manifest the wishes associated with pre-Oedipal stages. Such wishes would include greater dependency, which Freud linked to expressions of infantile oral stage drives.

This classical Oedipal explanation of gender differences has been dismissed in many critiques (Chodorow, 1978; Horney, 1967; Shafer, 1974), and these ideas have been sufficiently discussed that they need not be pursued here in great detail. It is worth noting, however, that in the not-too-distant past, such concepts provided the theoretical structure through which therapists interpreted patients' ambitions and marital dissatisfactions as signs of penis envy and immaturity. It is also worth noting that female contemporaries of Freud such as Karen Horney had alternative views of children's reactions to the same biological differences, suggesting that "womb envy" might be at least as important as penis envy (Horney, 1967).

Even apart from which aspect of an anatomical difference might be important, and for whom, there is still the issue of how to interpret it, that is, the biosocial aspect. The meaning of a perceptual difference inevitably reflects social context and values. In this regard, it is useful to examine the contrast between Freud's and Chodorow's (1974, 1978) psychoanalytic versions of gender differences in personality because both give importance to anatomy. While Chodorow basically agreed with Freud that many (but not necessarily all) girls experience penis envy, some ambivalence and less rigidity in gender identity, and more pre-Oedipal wishes, her interpretation of the importance of these variables is vastly different than her predecessor. Of course, she was writing in a very different social context.

Chodorow argued that penis envy symbolizes frustration with the disadvantages of being female in this society. According to her, girls first develop a secure sense of femaleness, then experience restrictions, and finally, during the Oedipal stage, the anatomical difference comes to symbolize her dissatisfaction with the powerlessness of the female sex role. Chodorow's position would predict that such envy would not be common in a social context that presented more equal gender roles. How nice it would be to find such a place to do this study.

Interestingly, instead of focusing on female inferiority, Chodorow argues that it is boys who have more difficulty establishing gender identity. According to her, the biological similarity of mothers and daughters makes gender identity easier for girls, a process that is emotionally compatible with maintaining the emphatic, preverbal attachment to mother as the primary caretaker. Young boys, however, must reassure themselves of their difference from the caretaker in order to affirm their masculinity. Thus, masculinity is initially experienced through identifying oneself as different than and separate from the mother. Empirical evidence supports males' greater concern with maintaining gender-role distinctions (e.g., Silvern & Katz, 1986; Maccoby & Jacklin, 1974; Johnson, 1975).

Thus, Chorodow suggests that males are more likely than females to become excessively restricted in their insistence of gender-consistent behavior, due to the biological difference between themselves and their early caretakers. In dramatic contrast to Freud, Chodorow views this as a disadvantage to males, not female immaturity. This disadvantage is further evidenced at later ages because access to empathy and dependency feelings may become too dangerous a reminder of earlier feelings (a loss for them) as their focus upon an autonomous self becomes dominant. Thus, Chodorow's theory reverses Freud's position. A male's more complete suppression of "pre-Oedipal" longings and memories is not viewed as more mature but as unfortunate, depriving him of a more richly empathic and interdependent relationship between a fully differentiated self and others. Again, it is because of social arrangements that give mothers the dominant role in early childrearing that boys' and girls' anatomies produce different destinies. Note that this is a social structure variable, not a biological one.

There are no other global personality theories based on biological factors. There has been, however, increasing research interest in biological factors that may be associated with gender differences in behavior. One area concerns studies of individuals who were abnormally exposed to gonadal hormones in utero, either because of genetic defects or medications taken during pregnancy. A second area of burgeoning interest is in differences in brain functions. These studies have been reviewed elsewhere (e.g., Hines, 1982; Hood, Draper, Crockett, & Petersen, 1987; Brizedine, 2006) and will not be reviewed in this chapter. Some differences have been found with prenatal hormone exposure and spatial functions, but they are generally small and inconsistent.

Brizedine's book *The Female Brain* (2006) does present some interesting findings regarding what she considers to be the effects of sex hormones on brain structure. Women, for example, have 11 percent more neurons than men, with more abundant brain cells in the hippocampal region, the center of emotion and memory formation, and enlarged verbal areas. Men have larger amygdalas (associated with anger, aggression, and decoding threatening stimuli) and bigger sex-related centers. So in some ways, the newly emerging brain research, based on neuropsychological methodology confirms some of the earlier described gender differences.

While these results are interesting, there is one overriding problem with such research: in studies of humans, the biological aspects of gender are completely confounded with its social and psychological factors. There are consistent and pervasive environmental differences for boys and girls as they mature (Katz, 1983), which may themselves influence brain development, so it is difficult to disentangle which came first. Since the process of physical sex differentiation clearly involves genes and hormones, however, biological factors may well play an important role in personality development, one that future research will undoubtedly help to unravel.

Socialization Theories

Considerably more psychological attention has been devoted to positions that have espoused the significance of socialization in gender differences in personality.

Children are profoundly affected by how they are treated and responded to by the adults in their environment. At the youngest ages, it is of course the parents that are largely responsible for their early socialization, but later, the children's social environment comes to include teachers and peers and often siblings who take on increasing importance (Katz, 1979). General theories about socialization have emphasized either reinforcement factors or modeling behaviors (e.g., Bandura, 1986), and these general theories have not specifically addressed gender, although their views clearly contain the possibility of differential reinforcement or differential modeling for girls and boys.

As noted previously, there has been disagreement about how distinctively boys and girls are socialized, with earlier investigators (Maccoby & Jacklin, 1974) arguing that there were few such differences. In recent years, however, there has been considerably more focus on such differences and their importance (e.g., Ruble, 1988), and we are of the opinion that these earlier conclusions of "no difference" were incorrect, particularly when it comes to variables that are significant in personality development.

Gender stereotypes are so strong in adults that even within the first 24 hours of a child's life, parents see their sons as more alert and stronger than their daughters, whereas their daughters are perceived to be softer, more finely featured, and less attentive than boys (Rubin, Provenzano, & Luria, 1974). Infants are also treated differently by strangers as a consequence of an experimentally assigned gender label (Seavy, Katz, & Zalk, 1975). In a recently completed longitudinal study (Katz), it was found that parental behaviors have more impact on children's sex roles than did their questionnaire responses. Children who were very masculine and feminine in their toy choices and behavior at age five had had very sex-typed rooms since infancy. Even in Maccoby & Jacklin's (1974) review, they cite evidence that fathers and mothers differ with regard to how they engage their children in play, and that fathers offer more gender-stereotypic toys to their children. More rewards are associated with sex-appropriate behavior (Fagot, 1978), and boys receive more pressure in this area, particularly from their fathers (Ruble, 1988).

So, in both broad and subtle ways, parents exert a great deal of influence in (1) maintaining differential gender roles and (2) treating their male and female children differently, thereby contributing to differing personality patterns. These findings correspond to a Type IV type of theory—the variables (e.g., reinforcement) may be similar, but the behaviors reinforced are quite different, as are the results.

Some socialization theories have focused more on adult behaviors than on developmental origins. Based on an impressive array of studies, Eagly (1987) has developed a theory termed *social role theory*. This theory considers the major determinant of male and female differential social behavior to be compliance to gender-role expectations. These prescribed social roles stem from family life and occupational settings that produce the content of gender-role behaviors. Differences in male and female personality would, according to social role theory, be attributable to the distinctly different functions and responsibilities that men and women have in the home and in the workplace (see, e.g., Eccles & Hoffman, 1984; Ruble, Cohen, & Ruble, 1984). According to Eagly, these adult social roles are more directly relevant to gender differences than are prior socialization experiences or biological factors. If this were the case, then it could be argued that societal change could attenuate gender differences, despite earlier socialization.

One change that has been dramatic over the past three decades has been the entry of women into the workforce. Could this be enough to effect such a change? Perhaps to some extent, yes, at least to the degree that women's roles now frequently include working outside of the home. This is reflected in children's responses to the question, "What do you you want to be when you grow up?" In our research, we now get a variety of responses, rather than just repetitions of "A mother," the most typical response that girls gave in the 1960s and 1970s. But the variety of vocational responses obtained still reflects the gendered nature of the workplace—teachers and nurses are far more common than college professor or astronaut.

Moreover, differences in family gender roles have lagged even further behind. In terms of the models discussed at the outset, Eagly's social role theory is a complex subset of a Type IV theory. She does not argue that all the variables differentially affect males and females, only that the social structure does. Of course, that is the primary one in this paradigm.

A third theory to be discussed is the *self-in-relation theory* of Miller (1984), which is not likely to be found in texts about personality theory.

This theory is similar to social role theory in that it posits that early socialization experiences account for gender-related characteristics. It differs, however, in that it assumes that the relational self is the core self-structure in women. In this sense, it exemplifies the Type III model, assuming different personality structures in men and women.

The relational self that Miller posits differs from the self construct elaborated by psychoanalytic and traditional developmental theories. These theorists have emphasized the critical importance of separation from the mother and others in order to form a mature, separate idently (e.g., Erikson, 1963; Mahler, Pine, & Berman, 1975). According to Erikson (1963), independence and autonomy are necessary for true intimacy and relational trust to be experienced. In contrast, the self-in-relation theory assumes that relatedness is the primary and basic goal. Autonomy is assumed to develop only within the context of a capacity for relating. Thus, the self as an autonomous being is subsumed by and dependent on relational competence.

Within this perspective, the infant is seen as developing an internal representation of self that reflects a relationship with its caretakers. The formation of this self and a sense of well-being is presumed to occur as the infant and caretaker move dynamically in an emotional relationship that promotes positive emotional interplay between self and caretaker. Not only does the caretaker attend to the infant, but the infant has an effect on both the caretaker and the dynamics of their emotional relationship. There is reciprocity.

The primary thrust of this theory, then, is the importance of early emotional interactions that form the underpinnings of all subsequent emotional relationships and connections with others. Proponents of the theory do not believe that these early interactions produce fusion or a sense of merger with the other, as some psychoanalytic theorists have suggested, but that they produce a healthy sense of self, including heightened empathic competence. While the development of the self is part of development for both males and females, Miller believes that females are more apt to be encouraged to "feel as the other feels" (1984, p. 3), whereas boys are discouraged in this activity. This is where the sexes part company, although it is not entirely clear why. As development progresses, females are consequently motivated to feel related and connected to others and are less threatened by closeness. For females, self-esteem itself is assumed to be derived from feelings that they are part of relationships and play a nurturing role in them. Moreover, a feminine sense of effectiveness and competence often is based on the quality of emotional connectedness.

It is interesting to note that the socialization emphases placed on females to maintain relationships and to be emotionally attuned others (see, e.g., Surrey, 1985) have typically been negatively perceived as leading to dependency, deference, or acquiescence. The devaluation of this central orientation of women may well put them at greater risk for depression, since an integral part of their identity is often devalued. Miller and her colleagues have cast a more positive light on this and thus may provide a fruitful pathway for researchers. Moreover, applications of her theoretical assumptions to clinical practice may produce dramatically different outcomes. It is interesting to note that anthropologists have applied similar concepts to societies, labeling some as being more cooperative (i.e., more relationship-oriented) and others as more competitive (stressing autonomy). Perhaps the basic problem in ours is that we have both models, but they are often associated with different genders.

In summary, the socialization theories described above clearly point to pressure on males and females over the life span to behave in sex-appropriate ways. Theoretical and empirical analyses of the social role perspective and socialization practices suggest that the prescription of agency for males and communal qualities for females is alive and well. Yet what is heartening about recent theorizing is that there is a burgeoning amount of research concerned with the maintenance of relatedness, a cluster of characteristics previously devalued but indirectly related to all of the female social behaviors described in this chapter.

Social Structure Models: Sexism as a Theoretical Focus

Feminist researchers have brought yet a different perspective to the realm of female personality theory, both in critiquing and reconstructing earlier writing and in attending more to previously neglected or under-investigated variables that are more strongly associated with women (Fine, 1985). Feminist theorists have also been inclined to attribute most previously obtained gender differences to a political, economic, and social system that has discriminated against women for centuries. It has been argued (e.g., Schaef, 1981) that much of what seems distinctive about women is shared by other low-status groups. This would include such traits as greater sensitivity to social cues, less expressed aggression, higher deference, and better knowledge and understanding of the group in power than that group has of them. Thus, according to many recent feminist theorists, gender differences in personality are most explainable in terms of deep structural organizations of a society that has systematically condoned and practiced sexism.

Psychology is only one of many areas that are being changed by feminist thought. Feminist historians, for example, have noted the distortions and omissions that have occurred in our understanding of the past because of male historians essentially ignoring the world of women (Eisler, 1987). The law as a bastion of male power and privilege is slowly changing (MacKinnon, 2005). A burgeoning field of women's studies has demonstrated comparable trends in almost all known academic fields in the humanities and social sciences.

Within the social sciences, the formation of journals such as *Sex Roles* in 1975, the *Psychology of Women* in 1976, and *Gender and Society* in 1987 has given researchers new forums in which to publish and consolidate research in the field. Much of this research has been feminist oriented, in that attention has been given to research areas seldom seen before in other traditional journals, such as menstruation, menopause, sexual harassment, and other fairly unique aspects of the female experience.

Another aspect of feminist theory that has differed from more traditional views about gender is its contextual approach, that is, the recognition that traditional laboratory research is often inaccurate because it ignores the very contexts that are most psychologically relevant for women.

According to some feminists (e.g., MacKinnon, 1987, 2005), one of the primary reasons for women behaving differently than men has to do with male dominance and, particularly, living under the constant shadow of physical assault and sexual exploitation, as was evidenced in the United Nations report cited in the introductory section of this chapter. MacKinnon, a law professor, believes that even feminists have not yet fully appreciated the degree of misogyny and sexual sadism that underlie gender inequality. Gender in her view is primarily "an inequality of power, a social status based on who is permitted to do what to whom.... Inequality comes first; differences come after" (1987, p. 8). Feminist lawyers have adopted such views because of the seeming ineffectiveness of sex equality laws to obtain for most women decent job opportunities, reasonable physical security, and dignity. The commonalities in women's personalities, then, would be attributable to their similar social status.

The threat of exposure to violence has led to a relatively new area of research focusing on victimization. Given that violence can profoundly influence social, emotional, and cognitive development, it would seem appropriate to ask whether some gender differences in personality could be associated with gender differences in incidence of victimization.

Although all methods for studying incidence rates of violence are flawed to some extent (Gelles, 1987; Widom. 1988), it is obvious from multiple studies that women are victimized more often than men are and that large numbers of women are affected (Dobash & Dobash 1979; Finkelhor, 1984; Gelles, 1987). One difference that has occurred since the earlier version of this chapter was written is a much greater awareness of this factor, and greater monitoring of its incidence, including by governmental agencies such as the Centers for Disease Control and Prevention (CDC). Unfortunately, where the statistics have changed over the past 20 years, the change has been in an upward direction, perhaps because of better reporting.

For example, estimates of sexual abuse against girls cluster between 12 percent and 19 percent (Finkelhor, 1984), and 25 percent of women report being raped at some time during their lives. These estimates are undoubtedly low; the Department of Justice (2003) estimates that only 39 percent of rapes and sexual assaults are reported to law enforcement officials. Victims of sexual violence face both immediate and long-term psychological consequences and physical consequences (Faravelli, Giughi, Salvatori, & Ricca, 2004; Ystgaard, Hestetun, Loeb, & Mehlum, 2004) and greater risk of sexually transmitted diseases (Wingood, DiClemente, & Raj, 2000).

Domestic violence is widespread. At least one in every three women around the world has been beaten or coerced into sex or otherwise abused during her lifetime (Heise, Ellsberg, & Gottemoeller, 1999). Nearly one-third of American women report being physically or sexually abused (Straus, Gelles, & Steinmetz, 1980; Commonwealth Fund, 1999). Marital violence results in injury almost exclusively to women (Greenblat, 1983); the much less frequent wife-to-husband violence is usually retaliatory or in self-defense (Saunders, 1986). Abuse often begins before marriage, with 38 percent of college women reporting battering by dates (Cate, Henton, Koval, Christopher, & Lloyd, 1982). Startlingly, when all forms of rape, sexual abuse, and battering are combined, as they were in one study, only 8 percent of women reported having *never* been assaulted (Russell, 1986). Moreover, in many instances, children have witnessed hundreds of thousands of acts of domestic violence, as well as having been abused themselves.

These figures are staggering, and hard to fathom. While increasing attention is being devoted to this problem, particularly in Western countries, one can't help but feel that if there were something that accounted for a greater incidence of male injuries than occurred in war or automobile accidents, there would be more resources available to solve the problem.

The consequences of violence to personality are difficult to study with precision. It is difficult to disentangle other confounding environmental influences, and different studies employ diverse methods and measures. There do appear to be certain areas of consensus, however. Effects that are widely agreed on include low self-esteem, clinical levels of depression, compliance or lack of assertiveness, feelings of low control or helplessness, strong fear reactions to threatening situations, vulnerability to medical illness, and a sense of needing to hold one's aggressiveness in check because of a fear of being overwhelmed. The eerie thing about this list is its considerable overlap with personality traits, already discussed, that have been the focus of studies about gender differences in personality or that are intrinsic to gender-role stereotypes.

A particular irony should be mentioned: Child abuse may have a special relationship to the development of dissociative disorders (Briere, 1984). These disorders are exactly the sort that Freud focused on in his women patients. Freud's early "seduction hypothesis" may have been completely accurate in attributing the problems that these women had to the sexual abuse to which girls were frequently subjected during his time. When Freud later rejected the seduction hypothesis, he attributed the peculiarities of these women to their own wish-fulfilling, irrational fantasies (i.e., the theory of "infantile sexuality"), and he turned to hypotheses about women's biologically based inferiority, in part to explain women's psychological disturbance. By critically deemphasizing the importance of victimization, Freud introduced a tradition of theorizing about female personality while ignoring what was done to women.

It is puzzling, however, as to why the literature on violence has not been better integrated with the literature on gender differences in personality. This may be due to a general societal denial of the extent and importance of violence. It may also be as disquieting now as it was in Freud's time to inquire into whether certain female characteristics represent an accommodation to maltreatment.

There is little question that the sexism-feminist perspective has contributed, and continues to contribute, much to our knowledge base about women.

SUMMARY AND IMPLICATIONS

We have focused the previous discussion on possible gender differences in the structure and components of personality. This focus was not determined by a belief that gender is necessarily the most significant influence upon personality, but rather because the gender construct has been and continues to be intertwined both theoretically and politically with personality theory.

Personality theory has served an important function in psychology and psychiatry, as noted earlier in this chapter. These theories have suggested which areas are worthy of scientific attention and which are not. In the clinical area, such theories have served to define pathology and to influence therapeutic interpretations and modification of behavior. In view of this, it is quite disheartening to note that a perusal of theories promulgated prior to the mid-1960s shows that most either ignored or devalued women. Except for a few investigators (Chodorow 1974, 1978; Horney, 1967), theorists of the psychodynamic persuasion posited views that suggested women were generally inferior to men in their level of development, their morality, their strength, and their sexuality and were more prone to pathology.

While adhering to a biological explanation of gender differences, most early analytic writers focused primarily on children's perceptions of, and responses to, the superiority of male genitalia. A biological view that was not misogynist could just as readily have focused upon the role of female expectancies concerning pregnancy and birth. This issue goes beyond the "womb envy" posited by a few early female theorists. Anticipation of maternity is a uniquely female experience that may well have extremely significant ramifications for female personality. Except for Erikson's (1963) ideas about "inner space," however, almost no research attention has been devoted to such variables. Clinically, Freud could understand a woman's desire for children only by transforming it into male terms, that is, a desire for a penis. This is somewhat analgous to the creation story of a woman coming from a man's body.

Our reading of the empirical work attempting to substantiate gender differences in personality suggests that it is necessary to proceed with caution. The use of improved statistical techniques such as meta-analyses appears to have had a conservative influence on acceptance of gender differences. Many findings cited several years ago have not held up under more sophisticated statistical scrutiny. Even when they have, differences appear smaller than earlier investigators assumed. Moreover, the advent of more female investigators has been associated with a much broader range of interpretations regarding the meaning of obtained differences.

Despite these provisos, we believe that the findings suggest that there are some meaningful differences in a few enduring dimensions intrinsic to personality. It was noted even in Aristotle's time that women are more compassionate (Book 9 of the *History of Animals*, chapter 1, cited in Miles, 1935, p. 700). Women as a group do appear to be more nurturant, more interested in intimacy and connectedness, more expressive, and more empathic and responsive to others. These traits and behaviors can be conceptualized as forming a cluster labeled "relatedness." However, for a number of reasons previously alluded to, this constellation has been either neglected in research or negatively valued. These traits have often, for example, been viewed (negatively) as "dependency" or as contributing to the underpinning of psychopathology.

It has only been since women have found their voice that the valence and importance of these factors have been changing. We hope that continuing concern with the development and maintenance of relatedness will be extended to males as well, so that the various voices will be in better harmony.

Our emphasis on gender differences was not intended to obscure the very considerable variability that exists among women and girls. Gender-role socialization practices differ with socioeconomic level, race, ethnicity, and culture (Katz, 1987). Gender differences are never absent. It is because of this pervasiveness that it becomes extremely difficult to disentangle biological, social, and structural explanations. Redundancy abounds in all areas.

We feel that feminist-oriented theories of personality hold the most promise for the near future. One of their strengths is the focus upon previously neglected variables that may help us to better understand female personality. They are also helping us to reanalyze and reinterpret a multitude of older findings, as well as to develop new research paradigms designed to better illuminate the female experience.

REFERENCES

Achenbach, T. M. (1982). *Developmental psychopathology.* New York: Wiley.

Achenbach, T. M., & Edelbrock, C. S. (1981). Behavioral problems and competencies reported by parents of normal and disturbed children aged four through sixteen. *Monographs for the Society for Research in Child Development, 46*(1), serial no. 188.

Akiskal, H. S. (1979). A biobehavioral approach to depression. In R. A. Depue (Ed.), *The psychobiology of the depressive disorders: Implications for the effects of stress* (pp. 409–437). New York: Academic Press.

Bandura, A. (1986). *Social foundations of thought and action: A social cognitive theory.* Englewood Cliffs, NJ: Prentice-Hall.

Barlow, D. H. (1981). On the relation of clinical research to clinical practice: Current issues, new directions. *Journal of Consulting and Clinical Psychology, 49,* 147–155.

Beauvoir, S. de. (1952). *The second sex.* New York: Random House.

Bem, S. L. (1974). The measurement of psychological androgyny. *Journal of Consulting and Clinical Psychology, 42,* 155–162.

Briere, J. (1984). The effects of childhood sexual abuse on later psychological functioning: Defining a post-sexual abuse syndrome. Paper presented at the Third National Conference on Sexual Victimization of Children, Washington, DC.

Brizedine, L. (2006). *The female brain.* New York: Morgan Road.

Brody, E. M. (1986). Parent care as a normative family stress. Donald P. Kent Memorial Lecture. *Gerontologist, 25,* 19–29.

Carlson, R. (1972). Understanding women: Implications for personality theory and research. *Journal of Social Issues, 28*(2), 17–32.

Cate, R. M., Henton, J. M., Koval, J., Christopher, F. S., & Lloyd, S. (1982). Premarital abuse: A social psychological perspective. *Journal of Family Issues, 3,* 79–80.

Chodorow, N. (1974). Family structure and feminine personality. In M. S. Rosaldo & L. Lamphere (Eds.), *Woman, culture & society* (pp. 43–66). Stanford, CA: Stanford University Press.

Chodorow, N. (1978). *The reproduction of mothering: Psychoanalysis and the sociology of gender.* Berkeley: University of California Press.

Clark, K. B. (1971). Pathos of power: A psychological perspective. *American Psychologist, 26,* 1047–1057.

Commonwealth Fund. (1999). Health concerns across a woman's lifespan. *1998 Survey of Women's Health.*

Costa, P. T., Terracciano, A., & McCrae, R. R. (2001). Gender differences in personality traits across cultures: Robust and surprising findings. *Journal of Personality and Social Psychology, 81*(2), 322–331.

Deaux, K., & Kite, M. E. (1987). Thinking about gender. In B. B. Hess & M. M. Ferree (Eds.), *Analyzing gender: A handbook of social science research.* Newbury Park, CA: Sage.

Department of Justice (2003). Criminal victimization, 2002. Publication no. NCJ 199994. Washington, DC: GPO.

Dobash, R. E., & Dobash, R. (1979). *Violence against wives.* New York: Free Press.

Dusek, J. B. (1987). Sex roles and adjustment. In D. B. Carter (Ed.), *Current conceptions of sex roles and sex typing* (pp. 211–222). New York: Praeger.

Eagly, A. H. (1986). Some meta-analytic approaches to examining the validity of gender-difference research. In J. Hyde & M. C. Linn (Eds.), *The psychology of gender: Advances through meta-analysis* (pp. 159–177). Baltimore: Johns Hopkins University Press.

Eagly, A. H. (1987). *Sex differences in social behavior: A social-role interpretation.* Hillside, NJ: Erlbaum.

Eagly, A. H. (1995). The science and politics of comparing men and women. *American Psychologist, 50,* 145–158.

Eagly, A. H., & Carli, L. L. (1981). Sex of researchers and sex-typed communications as determinants of sex differences in influenceability: A meta-analysis of social influence studies. *Psychological Bulletin, 90,* 1–20.

Eagly, A. H., & Steffen, V. J. (1986). Gender and aggressive behavior: A meta-analytic review of the social psychological literature. *Psychological Bulletin, 100,* 309–330.

Eccles, J. S., & Hoffman, L. W. (1984). Socialization and the maintenance of a sex segregated labor market. In H. W. Stevenson & A. E. Siegel (Eds.), *Research in child development and social policy* (vol. 1). Chicago: University of Chicago Press.

Eisler, R. (1987). *The Chalice and the Blade: Our history, our future.* Cambridge, MA: Harper & Row.

Engler, B. (1991). *Personality theories, an introduction* (3rd ed.). Boston: Houghton Mifflin.

Erikson, E. (1963). *Childhood and society.* New York: W. W. Norton.

Erne, R. F. (1979). Sex differences in childhood psychopathology. *Psychological Bulletin, 86,* 574–593.

Fagot, B. I. (1978). The influence of sex of child on parental reactions to toddler children. *Child Development, 49,* 459–465.

Faravelli, C., Giughi, A., Salvatori, S., & Ricca, V. (2004). Psychopathology after rape. *American Journal of Psychiatry, 161*(8), 1483–1485.

Feingold, A. (1994). Gender differences in personality: A meta-analysis. *Psychological Bulletin, 116,* 429–456.

Fine, M. (1985). Reflections on a feminist psychology of women: Paradoxes and prospects. *Psychology of Women Quarterly, 9,* 167–183.

Finkelhor, D. (1984). *Child sexual abuse.* New York: Free Press.

Frank, E. (Ed.) (2000). *Gender and its effects on psychopathology*. Washington, DC: American Psychiatric Press.

Freud, S. (1964). Some psychical consequences of the anatomical distinction between the sexes. In J. Strackey (Ed. & Trans.), *The standard edition of the complete psychological works of Sigmund Freud* (pp. 243–260). London: Hogarth Press. (Original work published 1925.)

Gelles, R. J. (1987). *Family violence.* Beverly Hills, CA: Sage.

Giorgi, A. (1970). *Psychology as a human science.* New York: Harper & Row.

Greenblat, C. (1983). Physical force by any other name ... : Quantitative data and the politics of family violence research. In D. Finkelhor, R. J. Gelles, G.

T. Holating, & M. Straus (Eds.), *The dark side of families: Current family violence research.* Beverly Hills, CA: Sage.

Hall, J. A. (1978). Gender effects in decoding nonverbal cues. *Psychological Bulletin, 85,* 845–875.

Hall, J. A. (1984). *Nonverbal sex differences: Communication, accuracy and expressive style.* Baltimore: Johns Hopkins University Press.

Hare-Mustin, R. T., & Maracek, J. (1988). The meaning of difference. *American Psychologist, 43*(6), 455–464.

Heise, L., Ellsberg, M., and Gottemoeller, M. (1999). Ending violence against women. *Population Reports,* series L, no. 11.

Herbert, B. (2006). Punished for being female. *New York Times,* November 2, p. A27.

Herschfield, R. M., & Cross, C. K. (1982). Epidemiology of affective disorders. *Archives of General Psychiatry, 39,* 35–46.

Hines, M. (1982). Prenatal gonadal hormones and sex differences in human behavior. *Psychological Bulletin, 92*(1), 56–80.

Hollingworth, L. S. (1918). Comparison of the sexes in mental traits. *Psychological Bulletin, 15,* 427–432.

Hood, K. E., Draper, P., Crockett, L. J., & Petersen, A. C. (1987). The ontogeny and phylogeny of sex differences in development: A biopsychosocial synthesis. In D. B. Carter (Ed.), *Current conceptions of sex roles and sex typing: Theory and research* (pp. 49–77). New York: Praeger.

Horney, K. (1967). Inhibited femininity: Psychoanalytical contribution to the problem of frigidity. In H. Kelman (Ed.), *Feminine psychology* (pp. 71–83). New York: W. W. Norton. (Original work published 1926.)

Hyde, J. S. (1986). Gender differences in aggression. In J. S. Hyde & M. C. Linn (Eds.), *The psychology of gender: Advances through meta-analysis* (pp. 51–66). Baltimore: Johns Hopkins University Press.

Hyde, J. S. (2005). The gender similarities hypothesis. *American Psychologist, 60,* 581–592.

Ingram, R. E., Cruet, D., Johnson, B. R., & Wisnicki, K. S. (1988). Self-focused attention, gender, gender role, and vulnerability to negative affect. *Journal of Personality and Social Psychology, 55*(6), 967–978.

Jacklin, C. N. (1987). Feminist research and psychology. In C. Farnham (Ed.), *The impact of feminist research in the academy* (pp. 95–107). Bloomington: Indiana University Press.

Johnson, M. (1975). Fathers, mothers, and sex-typing. *Sociological Inquiry, 45,* 15–26.

Katz, P. A. (1979). The development of female identity. *Sex Roles, 5,* 155–178.

Katz, P. A. (1983). Development of racial and sex-role attitudes. In R. L. Leahy (Ed.), *The child's construction of social inequality* (pp. 41–78). New York: Academic Press.

Katz, P. A. (1987). Variations in family constellation: Effects on gender schemata. In L. S. Liben & M. Signorella (Eds.), *Children's gender concepts: New directions in child development* (pp. 39–56). San Francisco: Jossey-Bass.

Lamb, M., & Lamb, V. (1976). The nature and importance of the father–infant relationship. *Family Coordinator, 25,* 379–385.

Langer, E. (1989). *Mindfulness.* Reading, MA: Addison-Wesley.

Linn, M., & Hyde, J. (1988). Gender mathematics and science. Paper presented at the symposium "Sex-Related Differences in Spatial Ability: Recent

Meta-analyses and Future Directions'' at the convention of the Society for Research in Child Development, Baltimore, 1988.

Lorber, J. (2005). *Breaking the bowls: Degendering and feminist change.* New York: W. W. Norton.

Maccoby, E. E., & Jacklin, C. N. (1974). *The psychology of sex differences.* Stanford, CA: Stanford University Press.

MacKinnon, C. (1987). *Feminism unmodified: Discourses on life and law.* Cambridge, MA: Harvard University Press.

MacKinnon, C. (2005). *Women's lives, men's laws.* Cambridge, MA: Belknap Press of Harvard University Press.

Maddi, S. R. (2006). Taking the theorizing in personality theories seriously [review of the article ''The New Vision: Identifying and Studying Personality'']. *American Psychologist, 61*(4), 330–339.

Mahler, M., Pine, F., & Berman, A. (1975). *The psychological birth of the human infant: Symbiosis and individuation.* New York: Basic Books.

Mahrer, A. B. (1978). *Experiencing: A humanistic theory of psychology and psychiatry.* New York: Brunner/Mazel.

Markman, H., & Kraft, S. A. (1989). Dealing with gender differences in marital therapy. *Behavior Therapist, 12,* 51–56.

Mayer, J. D. (2005). A tale of two visions: Can a new view help integrate psychology? *American Psychologist, 60*(4), 294–307.

McClelland, D. C., Atkinson, J. W., Clark, R. A., & Lowell, E. L. (1953). *The achievement motive.* New York: Appleton-Century-Crofts.

Miles, C. (1935). Sex in social psychology. In C. Murchinson (Ed.), *Handbook of social psychology* (pp. 683–797). Worcester, MA: Clark University Press.

Miller, J. B. (1984). The development of women's sense of self. *Work in progress,* no. 12. Stone Center Working Papers Series. Wellesley, MA.

Nolen-Hoeksema, S. (1987). Sex differences in unipolar depression: Evidence and theory. *Psychological Bulletin, 101*(2), 259–282.

Phillips, D., & Sepal, B. (1969). Sexual status and psychiatric symptoms. *American Sociological Review, 34,* 58–72.

Piaget, J. (1928). *Judgment and reasoning in the child.* New York: Harcourt, Brace.

Regier, D. A., Boyd, J. H., Burke, J. D., Rae, D. S., Myers, J. K., Kramer, M., et al. (1988). One-month prevalence of mental disorders in the United States. *Archives of General Psychiatry, 45,* 977–986.

Reisman, J. M. (1990). Intimacy in same-sex friendships. *Sex Roles, 23,* 65–72.

Rubin, J. S., Provenzano. F. J., & Luria Z. (1974). The eye of the beholder: Parents' views on sex of newborns. *American Journal of Orthopsychiatry, 5,* 353–363.

Ruble, D. N. (1988). Sex-role development. In M. H. Bornstein & M. E. Lamb (Eds.), *Developmental psychology: An advanced textbook* (pp. 411–460). Hillsdale, NJ: Erlbaum.

Ruble, T. L., Cohen, R., & Ruble, D. N. (1984). Sex stereotypes: Occupational barriers for women. *American Behavioral Scientist, 27,* 339–356.

Russell, D. (1986). *The secret trauma: Incest in the lives of girls and women 20–37.* New York: Basic Books.

Saunders, D. G. (1986). When battered women use violence: Husband abuse or self-defense? *Violence and Victims, 1,* 47–60.

Schaef, A. W. (1981). *Women's realities: An emerging female system in a white male society.* New York: Harper & Row.

Seavy, C. A., Katz, P. A., & Zelk, S. R. (1975). Baby X: The effect of gender labels on adult responses to infants. *Sex Roles, 1*(2), 103–109.

Shafer, R. (1974). Problems in Freud's psychology of women. *American Psychoanalytic Association Journal, 22,* 469–485.

Silvern, L., & Katz, P. A. (1986). Gender roles and adjustment in elementary-school children: A multidimensional approach. *Sex Roles, 14*(3/4), 181–202.

Spence, J. T., Helmreich, R., & Stapp, J. (1974). The Personal Attributes Questionnaire: A measure of sex-role stereotypes and masculinity-femininity. MS No. 617. *JSAS Catalog of Selected Documents in Psychology, 4,* 43.

Straus, M. A., Gelles, R. J., & Steinmetz, S. K. (1980). *Behind closed doors: Violence in the American family.* Garden City, NY: Anchor/Doubleday.

Strickland, B. R. (1988). Sex-related differences in health and illness. *Psychology of Women Quarterly, 12,* 381–399.

Surrey, J. L. (1985). Self-in-relation: A theory of women's development. *Work in Progress.* Stone Center Working Paper Series. Wellesley, MA.

Widom, C. (1988). Sampling biases and implications for child abuse research. *American Journal of Orthopsychiatry, 58*(2), 260–270.

Williams, J. E., & Best, D. L. (1982). *Measuring sex stereotypes: A thirty-nation study.* Newbury Park, CA: Sage.

Williams, J. E., & Best, D. L. (1990). *Sex and psyche: Gender and self viewed cross-culturally.* Newbury Park, CA: Sage.

Wingood, G., DiClemente, R., & Raj, A. (2000). Adverse consequences of intimate partner abuse among women in non-urban domestic violence shelters. *American Journal of Preventative Medicine, 19,* 270–275.

Woolley, H. T. (1910). A review of the recent literature on the psychology of sex. *Psychological Bulletin, 7,* 335–342.

Ystgaard, M., Hestetun, I., Loeb, M., & Mehlum, L. (2004). Is there a specific relationship between childhood sexual abuse and repeated suicidal behavior? *Child Abuse and Neglect, 28*(8), 863–875.

Chapter 11

Women's Friendships and Romantic Relationships

Donna Castañeda
Alyson L. Burns-Glover

As social beings, we have a strong need to be around and interact with other people, and to establish relationships with them (Baumeister & Leary, 1995; Harlow, 1958; Fisher, 2004). The term *relationship* implies something more than a transitory interaction or superficial feeling for another, and it is in our relationships with friends and romantic partners that we often experience our deepest emotional connections.

Although both women and men need and seek out close relationships, several theories propose that relationships may be particularly important in women's lives. For example, differential gender socialization may promote a greater interest in and concern for relationships among women than among men (Cancian, 1987; Maccoby, 1998). Object relations (Chodorow, 1978; Jordan & Surrey, 1986) and self-in-relation theory (Jordan & Surrey, 1986; Surrey, 1993) posit that relationships are more central to women's sense of self than to men's. The centrality of relationships for women is thought to stem from differing developmental experiences and pathways, that is, the continuity of women's identification with mothers from early infancy, contrasted with men's emotional and psychic separation from mothers in early infancy, thought to be necessary for men to establish a masculine identity.

Our aim here is not to debate the merits or limitations of these theories, but taken together, they point to the important role that relationships play in women's lives. In this chapter, we review research on women's friendships and romantic relationships. Regarding friendships, we discuss historical perspectives on women's friendships, characteristics of women's friendships with each other, Internet friendships, and how women's friendships can be a form of resistance to oppression. Our emphasis is on women's friendships with each other, but we also examine their friendships with men in order to present a comprehensive picture of women's friendship experiences. We then turn to the topic of women's romantic relationships, where we discuss dating, sexuality, power, and violence in romantic relationships, as well as relationship satisfaction. Within both friendships and romantic relationships, we integrate issues of culture, diversity, and sexual orientation. Important to note is that we bring to this chapter not only a scholarly and feminist perspective to women's friendships and romantic relationships but also our personal history of these relationships and, most especially, the fact of our being friends for a quarter-century. Inevitably, our interpretations of the research literature are filtered through these experiences.

HISTORICAL PERSPECTIVE ON WOMEN'S FRIENDSHIPS

Although strong, affectionate, and enduring relationships between women have existed throughout history, women's close relationships with each other have historically been viewed as less important than men's relationships with men, and this devaluation has been reflected, up until recently, in the invisibility of the study of women's friendships in the research literature (O'Connor, 1992). At least in the Western world, friendship has been conceptualized primarily in terms of men's experience of this relationship and has included notions of bravery, duty, honor, loyalty, and a depth of feeling not necessarily expressed except at moments of extreme danger or death (Easterling, 1989; Nardi, 1992; Neve, 1989). Male friendships were a coming together of equals for pleasant conversation, camaraderie, and even the expression of affection (Easterling, 1989; Hansen, 1992). In fact, prior to the late nineteenth century, when same-gender close relationships began to be medicalized and stigmatized as inner "perversions," both women and men were allowed a range of physical and emotional expression in their same-gender friendships, although the notion of emotional self-reliance in relationships was still more an expectation of men than women (Faderman, 1981; Hansen, 1992; Rotundo, 1989).

Social conventions prohibited women, for the most part, from frequenting the public gathering places in which men were able to develop and carry out friendships, such as cafés, pubs, taverns, fraternal clubs, markets, barbershops, and street corners; therefore, women's friendships took place primarily in the private realm (Wellman, 1992). Women's relationships with each other were also, and to some extent still are, considered secondary to those with their spouses, children, and relatives. Thus, women, whose relationships with each other were replete with expression of emotions and needs and with physical demonstrativeness and were lived out within the mundane confines of daily domestic life, were believed incapable of development of true friendships with each other.

Beginning in the early 1900s, changes in the structure, meaning, and role of women's friendships with each other began to emerge. This is not to say that friendships were reduced in importance within individual women's lives or that the centrality of support, intimate exchange, and companionship did not continue to exist, but these changes reflect a shift to a modern conceptualization of women's friendships (see Faderman, 1981; Smith-Rosenberg, 1985). Particularly after 1920, a new emotional culture arose where emotion management, rather than the florid sentimentality of the Victorian period, was valued. This modern emotional culture deemphasized the intense and fervent self-disclosure characteristic of women's friendships in the previous century. At the same time, at least for middle-class women, an increasing cultural emphasis on the heterosexual imperative and companionate marriage emerged, detracting from the centrality of women's friendships with each other. Women began to interact more and more in the context of organizations, clubs, and work as their roles and options outside the home increased. These transformations imposed an instrumental and superficial quality on some women's friendships. Greater geographic and social mobility also reduced the degree of face-to-face visiting and lengthy correspondence that women in the previous century used to maintain their friendships. Finally, growing societal concerns about homosexuality in the early 20th century resulted in disapproval of intensely intimate relationships between women and continue today to affect what is considered appropriate emotional expressiveness between women (Rosenzweig, 1999).

Over the course of the 20th century, friendship evolved into a private experience divorced from the larger, public domain of work and institutions, so that today ideal friendship is characterized by the qualities of intimate self-disclosure, bonding, and closeness (Oliker, 1998). In the latter part of the century, friendships, and close relationships in general, came to be viewed not just as arenas for intimacy development but also as the significant avenues for individual self-development (Cancian, 1990). Most recently, efforts have been made to situate women's friendships within the larger social, economic, cultural, and political contexts in which they live (Adams & Allan, 1998; O'Connor, 1998; Oliker, 1998), thereby mirroring the increased focus on contextual understandings of women's experiences generally.

An especially significant historical factor related to women's friendships was the rise of the women's movement in the 1960s and into the 1970s. In contrast to the up-to-then prevailing cultural images of women's friendships with each other as superficial, fraught with envy and competition for male attention, and secondary to relationships with men, in the women's movement, friendships between women were considered primary. Its liberal ideology of sisterhood legitimated women's relationships with each other and encouraged solidarity between women. In fact, uniting at both the personal and political levels was considered the avenue toward overcoming oppression in a sexist society (Morgan, 1970).

Subsequent interrogation of the ideology of sisterhood has exposed its shortcomings—for example, it ignored inequalities between women based upon social class, ethnicity/race, and sexual orientation that continue to make friendships between women difficult or conflictual (Hurtado, 1996; Kilcooley, 1997; Simmonds, 1997). Women do not necessarily gravitate toward each other just because they are women, nor are friendships, even close and long-lasting ones, safe harbors from larger social divisions. A legacy of the women's movement, however, is that it demonstrates how women's relationships with each other not only are a source of individual affirmation and strength but also have the potential to initiate social change and challenge the status quo surrounding gender relations in the larger society (Morgan, 1970; O'Connor, 1998; Rose & Roades, 1987).

CHARACTERISTICS OF WOMEN'S FRIENDSHIPS

Friendships constitute some of the most important relationships women establish in their lifetime. They provide women with social support (Aronson, 1998; Lu & Argyle, 1992; Mays, 1985; Nyamathi, Bennett, Leake, & Chen, 1995; Severance, 2005), opportunities for companionship and enjoyable social interaction (Fehr, 1996; Severance, 2005), intimacy (Fehr, 2004; Parks & Floyd, 1996b; Sapadin, 1988), and instrumental assistance (Nyamathi et al., 1995; Patterson & Bettini, 1993; Walker, 1995), and they contribute to our social and personal identities (Johnson & Aries, 1983).

Despite the many important contributions of friendship to women's lives, its essence is difficult to capture. As Fehr (1996) says, "Everyone knows what friendship is—until asked to define it" (p. 5). Women's friendships with each other have often been portrayed as idyllic, where cooperation, sharing, and support-giving dominate. The negative side of these relationships has also been caricatured, where envy, competition, and jealousy prevail, often related to access to the attentions of a powerful male. Although neither picture is particularly accurate, they hint at the complexity and contradictions of women's relationships with each other (see Rind, 2002).

Implicitly, or sometimes explicitly, definitions of friendship include the notion that they are entered into and maintained voluntarily and that, unlike other significant relationships, friendships in Western cultures are not formalized through familial or societal structures or obligations (Fehr, 1996; Stein, 1993). In fact, the imposition of rigid role structures may be viewed as antithetical to formation of true friendship bonds (Bell & Coleman, 1999).

On the other hand, some researchers remind us that friendships may not be completely voluntary. We are most likely to become friends with those who are of the same gender; similar in age, social class, sexual orientation, and race/ethnicity; and who live in the same geographic area (Rose, 1995). Immigrant women may be further limited in their friendship choices by language, the ethnic/racial diversity of the communities they live in, and the degree of emphasis on family versus nonfamily social network development (Serafica, Weng, & Kim, 2000). Among Latinas, friendships with women family members are emphasized and may be especially close (Hurtado, 2003).

Lesbian women are more likely than heterosexual women to develop friendships with other lesbian women through intentionally constructed situations, such as through mutual acquaintances, private parties, gay rights events, and so forth, than through chance encounters (O'Boyle & Thomas, 1996). Bisexual women are more likely than lesbian or heterosexual women to experience cross-sexual orientation friendships (with either lesbian or heterosexual women) (Galupo, Sailer, & St. John, 2004).

Among working-class women, friendships with family members are also more common than among middle-class women, and working-class women tend to actually interact more frequently with their friends than middle-class women (Walker, 1995). In addition, class differences are seen in the types of activities working- and middle-class women engage in—for example, working-class women place more emphasis on same-gender socializing and are more likely to engage in "girls' night out" activities with their women friends, while middle-class women are more likely engage in mixed-gender socializing activities (Walker, 1995). Policy itself may contribute to or constrain women's friendships—for example, women of color who are poor may be especially subject to housing policies that ignore women's social network and emotional needs (Cook, Bruin, & Crull, 2000).

While friendships may be entered into and ended more easily than other social relationships, behavior in friendships is guided by rules that, if broken, can lead to conflict and even the dissolution of a friendship (Argyle & Henderson, 1984, 1985; Wiseman, 1986; Wright, 2006). These rules include helping a friend in times of need, mutual self-disclosure, respecting private information told in confidence, not criticizing a friend in public, and so on, and women endorse these rules to the same extent as men (Argyle & Henderson, 1984, 1985). A problematic aspect of friendships is that these rules are often assumed, rather than articulated. The supposed "naturalness" of friendship formation can inhibit women from explicit discussion of expectations from each other and the friendship. Without the formal societal mechanisms in place to support friendships as there are for other relationships (e.g., marital counseling, workplace mediation), friendships can easily disintegrate (Wiseman, 1986). In light of this, that women's friendships may entail contradictions and complexities is not surprising. The question then becomes not why women's friendships may fail, but why they can be quite durable and strong (Finchum, 2005).

Another unspoken rule that influences women's friendships is that competitiveness should not be a part of these relationships (Rind, 2002). For women, if friendships are arenas of nurturance, care, and liking, the presence of competition can lead to feelings of ambivalence and discomfort (Rind, 2002). In a series of interviews with women specifically about their best friends, Rind (2002) found that three major themes emerged, including knowing and understanding, neediness and dependence, but also competition between women. In this case, competition between women friends took place over jobs, academic performance, and social standing, among other arenas, but all the participants experienced competition negatively.

Part of the difficulty with competition may stem from women's socialization surrounding competition. Women are not necessarily socialized to deal forthrightly with competition; while girls' play activities certainly include achievement, they are not necessarily at the expense of other girls—for example, jump rope or hopscotch (Lever, 1976). Competition is more prevalent in boy's play activities than those of girls, and boys learn early on to negotiate competition in their playtime so that the activities can continue (Maccoby, 1998). Boys' activities are also more rule governed than relationship governed. Thus, when disputes develop among girls, they are more likely to dissolve their play activities than are boys (Maccoby, 1998). These interaction patterns may continue into adulthood and affect how women respond to competition in their friendships with women.

Another assumption about women's friendships is that they are, or should be, egalitarian, although this assumption may not be correct. In a sample of young adults, Veniegas and Peplau (1997) found that 60 percent of their sample was involved in an unequal power friendship, thus countering the notion that friendships are always egalitarian. They found no differences in the proportion of women and men who reported power inequalities in their friendships; they did find, however, that friendship quality was related to the distribution of power. Both women and men rated equal-power friendships greater in relationship quality (e.g., emotionally close, satisfying, disclosing, etc.) than unequal-power friendships. In this case, the effects of power on friendship quality were greater than the effects of gender.

The assumption of equality in friendship relationships often ignores relationships between women that can be quite meaningful, yet are inherently unequal and may not conform either in narrative or in actuality to Western conceptions of friendship (Barcellos Rezende, 1999). In some societies, social hierarchies may be more entrenched and friendships between women may be more likely to include unequal status. This is most obvious in work situations where hierarchical relationships between women may be long-lasting and deep and where asymmetry in power, and in the benefits of the relationship, is accepted (Barcellos Rezende, 1999; Berman, West, & Richter, 2002).

This assumption may also underplay needs women may have—that friendships can fulfill—for power, status recognition, and ego support. In a study of women of women age 14 through 80, for instance, three functions of friendship that were important to women across age groups were identified (Candy, Troll, & Levy, 1981). Along with intimacy-assistance, which includes the notion of intimacy and mutual assistance, this study also identified status, which implies that friends may provide recognition and self-esteem, and power, which includes the notion of influence or control over others. One of the few gender differences in evaluation of the quality of same-sex friendships found by Veniegas and Peplau (1997) was that women rated their friendships higher than men in ego support—that their women friends more often noticed and appreciated their abilities and congratulated them on their good fortune. Bank and Hansford (2000) found that the concept of status orientation, the degree that a friendship provided respect, influence, and prestige for the other, contributed positively to intimate friendships. They also found that it was more important to women than to men that this element be a component of their friendships. These studies highlight the expressive qualities that women's friendships include, such as closeness and intimacy, but they also demonstrate the nonreciprocal qualities of friendship, such as power and recognition, that in a culture where gender inequality is a persistent reality may also be important aspects of women's friendships.

Related to the notion of relationship rules is that the cultural scripts surrounding women's friendships, and the theories and research derived from these scripts, have been guided by assumptions of heterosexual norms (Rose, 2000; Weinstock & Rothblum, 1996). Research on lesbian friendships provides a picture of some of the diverse and alternative forms that friendships between women can take and may challenge narrower views of this relationship currently available in the research literature. For example, sexuality is always thought to be potentially present in cross-sex friendships (Bleske & Buss, 2000; Kaplan & Keys, 1997; Sapadin, 1988), but research on the role of sexuality in friendships between heterosexual women, or its developmental importance among heterosexual adolescent girls, is virtually unheard of (Diamond, 2000). Other research shows that, among lesbian women, friendships may be less distinctly separated from romantic relationships, and lesbian women appear to be more likely to remain close friends with their ex-lovers than are heterosexual women (see Kitzinger, 1996; Kitzinger & Perkins, 1993; Weinstock, 2004).

An overriding feature of women's friendships is intimacy. Intimacy is often estimated from the extent of self-disclosure, or self-revealing talk, that occurs between two persons and results in each feeling known and validated by the other (Altman & Taylor, 1973; Clark & Reis, 1988; Mark & Alper, 1985). Even though both women and men recognize the importance of talk for developing deep intimacy (Fehr, 2004; Radmacher & Azmitia, 2006), women engage in this talk more than men in their friendships (Adam, Blieszner, & De Vries, 2000; Hays, 1985), and this is true across age groups among women (Goldman, Cooper, Ahern, & Corsini, 1981). This may be a reason that, when friendship quality ratings are compared, men's friendships with each other usually rank lowest in quality (Elkins & Peterson, 1993) or strength (Wright & Scanlon, 1991) compared to women's same-sex and cross-sex friendships. Even friendships maintained exclusively online, those between women, or between women and men, show greater intimacy after two years than those between men (Cheng, Chan, & Tong, 2006).

Other research contests this gender dichotomy in expressiveness and intimacy in friendships and suggests that the reported gender differences are either very small or nonexistent (Duck & Wright, 1993; Wright, 1982). What differences do exist are not necessarily due to women and men defining intimacy differently, for example, that men define intimacy as shared activities and women as self-disclosure. In fact, when women-centered activities are the focus of investigation, women's ability to create enduring and strong intimate bonds through shared activities is readily seen (Piercy & Cheek, 2004). These differences are also not due to women and men having different developmental pathways to intimacy (Radmacher & Azmatia, 2006). Men may be just as able, and even prefer, to have greater intimacy in their friendships with men; they may also understand that openness and expressions of caring and support contribute to this. Recent research suggests that men choose to be less expressive primarily because they anticipate that their overtures will be negatively received by other men (Bank & Hansford, 2000; Fehr, 1996, 2004).

In addition to gender differences in intimacy, variations to this pattern may also be seen when social class, ethnicity/race, and culture are considered. Professional middle-class women may be less likely to self-disclose to their women friends than working-class women (Walker, 1994). This may be due to the greater geographic and occupational mobility middle-class professional women experience compared to working-class women and to the workplace competition they perceive with women coworkers. Walker's (1994) research points to how conceptualization of gender as an ongoing social construction within specific contexts, rather than a result of socialization or psychoanalytic processes, may be more useful in understanding gender differences in expressiveness.

In Western societies where an independent construction of self exists, intimacy and self-disclosure between friends are much more likely to occur, whereas in societies where an interdependent construction of self predominates, these processes may be less pronounced or may occur along with other culturally important processes. In West African societies, for instance, the notion of enemyship, that others may be a source of harm, is a more marked aspect of social reality—thus, cautious ambivalence surrounding closeness and intimacy in social relationships is more prevalent than in North American social relationships (Adams, Anderson, & Adonu, 2004).

Due to the strength of family ties and cultural constraints on strong emotional expression, students in Asian countries may engage in less intimate sharing in their friendships. For instance, compared to university students in the United States, Chinese university students self-disclose less across various topics (work, opinions, personality, etc.) and target persons (intimate friends, parents, acquaintances, etc.) (Chen, 1995). Among Korean and American university students, women engage in intimate exchanges with their friends more than men in these two groups, but overall, Korean students do this less than American students (Yoo & Malley-Morrison, 2000).

Again, although women university students in Russia and the United States engage in more intimate conversation in their friendships than do men in these countries, overall, Russian women and men do this less than American women and men (Sheets & Lugar, 2005). Friendships among Russian university students tend to be more activity focused than intimacy focused compared to those in the United States. These differences can be interpreted as cultural differences, but they may also be related to the greater need for discretion that developed under two generations of Communist rule; greater communal and crowded living conditions that increase the need to control revelation of self-relevant information; and the greater social and economic flux in Russian society recently where doing things with and for each other emerges as a more important process in friendships than self-disclosure.

To date, a considerable amount of research has been done to explore and explain gender differences in friendship intimacy (see Monsour, 2002)—attesting to the cultural primacy given to women's relationships with men that we mentioned earlier. But from a feminist perspective, a more important question is, How might the social construction of these differences support and reinforce gender inequalities? Women's friendships may be valorized for their greater intimacy than those of men, but women still have less access to important resources, and they continue to occupy a secondary status in relation to men in society. In the work world, access to power, influence, and upward mobility continue to be more available to men.

Intimacy and expressiveness in relationships are resources that women have in greater abundance than men do, but these resources do not obtain for them greater mobility in the highest echelons of economic and political power. In fact, the qualities of caring, closeness, and intimacy that women may be more adept at in their social relationships continue to be devalued in the larger culture (Taylor, 2002). Despite the emergence of a feminized version of friendship that is now considered the standard by which both women and men's friendships are evaluated, and the idea that men's friendships might even be seen as deficient in comparison to women's friendships (Cancian, 1990), this in no way alters patriarchal cultural, political, or institutional structures in society (O'Connor, 1998; Rose, 1995).

WOMEN'S FRIENDSHIPS ONLINE

Electronically mediated communication, such as e-mail, chat rooms, news rooms, instant messaging, and so on, provide a newer social context for development of friendships and other close relationships. Up until recently, men have been the predominant users of the Internet, but today women and men are almost equally likely to use it (Pew Internet and American Life Project, 2005). Furthermore, women are just as likely, and sometimes even more likely, to develop friendships online with either women or men (Parks & Floyd, 1996a; Parks & Roberts, 1998). Why women may be more likely than men to form online relationships is not clear—possibly more women are looking for friends, they may be more willing to label their online contacts as relationships, or they may be more sought after on the Internet (Parks & Floyd, 1996a).

Contrary to what is generally believed, online relationships can be similar in strength, quality, and degree of self-disclosure to offline relationships, although offline relationships may be of longer duration than those that are online (see McKenna & Bargh, 2000; Parks & Roberts, 1998). Furthermore, a significant proportion of online relationship partners go on to meet each other in person (McCown, Fischer, Page, & Homant, 2001; Parks & Roberts, 1998), suggesting that the boundaries between online and offline relationships are not highly defined.

Consistent with research on face-to-face relationships, women more than men use the Internet for interpersonal communication, such as chatting online and sending e-mail (Weiser, 2000). Women, more than men, use it to maintain contact with distant (as opposed to local) friends, and they are more likely to send e-mail to parents and other extended family members (Pew Internet and American Life Project, 2005). Although men use the Internet more intensely, that is, they log on more often and spend more time online, women include a wider array of topics in their online communications and are more satisfied with the role e-mail plays in nurturing their relationships (Pew Internet and American Life Project, 2005). On the other hand, one study found that both women and men preferred to develop online relationships with friends, rather than family members or coworkers. Furthermore, the only significant predictor of preference for online communication and relationship building was extent of Internet use, in that those who were high users of the Internet had a greater preference for online communication and relationship building than those who used the Internet less (Thayer & Ray, 2006).

Women may also feel less pressure to change their communication style in the presence of men in online contexts. Interestingly, in a prostate cancer support forum, the women partners of men experiencing prostate cancer assumed a communicative style that emphasized emotional sharing and showed only slight accommodation to the instrumental style of information seeking preferred by men on that forum. On the other hand, on a breast cancer support forum, men partners of women with breast cancer also emphasized emotional sharing and concern for the emotional welfare of family members (Seale, 2006). In this case, greater accommodation in communication style was seen among men rather than women.

A newer online phenomenon whose use has increased dramatically in the last five years is social networking websites (Pew Internet and American Life Project, 2007). A social networking website is an online place where a user can create a profile and build a personal network that connects her to other users. Adolescent girls age 15–17 are more likely than boys in that age group to have used an online social network, and they are also more likely to have created an online profile. The primary reason for use of these websites for both girls and boys is management of current friendships, but older adolescent girls and boys emphasize different processes in this friendship management. Older adolescent girls use these sites to maintain their friendships, particularly with friends they rarely see. Older adolescent boys are more likely than girls to use these sites to make new friends and to use these sites for flirting, although the overall amount of flirting activity is small (Pew Internet and American Life Project, 2007).

To date, research specifically on women's Internet friendships is rare, and the implications of technology for women's friendships are not yet fully understood. As women increase the amount and diversity of their online communication, we are likely to continue to see gender variation in friendship preferences, formation, and functions. In some cases, use of online communication may reinforce current gender expectations and patterns surrounding communication, support giving and receiving, and relationship development, while in others these expectations and patterns may be destabilized (Pew Internet and American Life Project, 2007; Seale, 2006; Thayer & Ray, 2006). An important understanding is that neither gender nor the Internet itself may be causally related to relationship formation and behavior, as compared to the motives, personalities, and identities of the persons involved (McKenna & Bargh, 2000; Peter, Valkenburg, & Schouten, 2005).

Online interactions are different from offline ones in that the former can be anonymous, without the visual cues that influence interpersonal perceptual processes, and offer the possibility of constructing multiple identities across social interactions (McKenna & Bargh, 2000). In fact, for those with identities that are marginalized in the larger society, such as those with stigmatized sexual identities, participation in online relationships can positively transform those identities and lead to the desire to more greatly express and incorporate them in real-world relationships (McKenna & Bargh, 1998; McKenna, Green, & Smith, 2001). Nonetheless, even with the democratizing and transformative potential of the Internet, other studies remind us that forces of traditional culture, ideology, politics, and economics do not disappear with technology use and these forces can insert themselves in Internet relationships as in relationships in the real world (Beetham, 2006; see Chiou & Wan, 2006).

WOMEN'S FRIENDSHIPS AS A FORM OF RESISTANCE

In psychology, women's friendships have been studied as relatively separate from the larger public world of work, politics, and social and cultural movements. Conversely, women's solidarity and sisterhood in political and social uplift work has been extensively studied (e.g., Giddings, 1985; Liss, Crawford, & Popp, 2004; Morgan, 1970), but relatively little emphasis has been placed on the role of friendship in these efforts. Women's friendships have been viewed as an aspect of the private sphere, part of each woman's domestic and emotional world. Nevertheless, it would be a mistake to ignore how women's friendships with each other can be connected to change at the larger social and cultural level—that women's friendships with each other can be viewed as "acts of resistance" (Andrew & Montague, 1998, p. 361).

Women's friendships may provide for women a location in which they can explore, redefine, and subvert their devaluation in the larger society, and friendships can form the basis for working for social change in the larger culture (Johnson & Aries, 1983). This is not a trivial consequence of friendship and can be a transformative experience for women. For example, social support, help in career advancement, and improvement in workplace atmosphere are all benefits derived from friendships at work (Berman et al., 2002), but these benefits do not accrue just to individual women—they may also empower and help women to resist male domination in a gendered workplace and beyond (Andrew & Montegue, 1998).

Even among women most at the margins of social power and prestige—working-class, ethnic/racial minority women—friendships can contribute to significant changes at the larger social and political level. Chicana cannery workers in California in the 1970s organized for better pay, promotions, and equal treatment in the workplace, and this activity grew out of the friendship networks that were already in place on the job. Although these efforts were not explicitly feminist in origin, they were inspired by the women's movement, and feminist consciousness within these groups evolved over time (Zavella, 1993). Also originally developed out of friendships with other women, Asian American women created social networks that formed the basis of the Asian American women's movement (Wei, 1993). Women's friendships are so often the unexplored backdrop of what seems to be the more important activity of political organizing and social change efforts; shifting one's focus brings to light the tremendously important role that friendships have played in these endeavors.

With this shift in focus, we also begin to see the cumulative and influential effect of women's activities that are enacted outside the traditional oppositional politics and activism characteristic of social movements. Women's resistance in oppressive marriages; caring and providing for children despite economic hardships; contending with racism, sexism, and sexual harassment in the workplace; and interacting with hostile and unresponsive institutions—in other words, the daily lives of women—can lead to social change, and all these activities are so often made possible with the help of supportive friends (Aptheker, 1989).

For instance, using the concept of positive marginality—the idea that people at the margins of society do not "necessarily internalize their exclusion but instead embrace difference as a strength and sometimes as a source of critique and action," Hall and Fine (2005, p 177) describe the friendship of two older black lesbian women. Throughout their lives, each was able to create support systems, spaces among peers free of prejudice and stereotypes, and possibilities for change despite lives marked by struggle and pain. Their friendship was a crucial element in their ability to derive strength from their experiences, rather than giving up.

Louie (2000) describes the case of an immigrant Chinese woman who worked in the garment industry under terrible conditions with low pay. Over time, women in the factory developed nurturing and supportive relationships based upon mutual empathy, practical help, and camaraderie. These relationships with other women in the factory became the foundation for self-esteem, personal strength, and validation that helped this woman surmount obstacles in her life outside the factory. Through support of her women friends, she was ultimately able to break the cycle of oppression of women in her own family by supporting her daughter, financially and emotionally, to fulfill her own educational and career plans.

Emotional and personal connection in a friendship can be empowering; it can sustain us in difficult times and provide the support to continue to struggle against oppression and inequality, not just for women but for all marginalized and oppressed people. Greater investigation of the connection between women's friendships and social change can provide models of the power of women's friendships and expand the definition and function of these relationships.

REFERENCES

Adams, G., Anderson, S. L., & Adonu, J. K. (2004). The cultural grounding of closeness and intimacy. In D. J. Mashek & A. Aron (Eds.), *Handbook of closeness and intimacy* (pp. 321–339). Mahwah, NJ: Erlbaum.

Adams, R. G., & Allan, G. (1998). *Placing friendship in context.* Cambridge: Cambridge University Press.

Adams, R. G., Blieszner, R., & De Vries, B. (2000). Definitions of friendship in the third age: Age, gender, and study location effects. *Journal of Aging Studies, 14,* 117–134.

Altman, I., & Taylor, D. A. (1973). *Social penetration: The development of interpersonal relationships.* Oxford, England: Holt, Rinehart & Winston.

Andrew, A., & Montegue, J. (1998). Women's friendship at work. *Women's Studies International Forum, 21,* 355–361.

Aptheker, B. (1989). *Tapestries of life: Women's work, women's consciousness, and the meaning of daily experience.* Amherst: University of Massachusetts Press.

Argyle, M., & Henderson, M. (1984). The rules of friendship. *Journal of Social and Personal Relationships, 1,* 211–237.

Argyle, M., & Henderson, M. (1985). *The anatomy of relationships.* London: Penguin Books.

Aronson, J. (1998). Lesbians giving and receiving care: Stretching conceptualizations of caring and community. *Women's Studies International Forum, 21,* 505–519.

Bank, B. J., & Hansford, S. L. (2000). Gender and friendships: Why are men's best same-sex friendships less intimate and supportive? *Personal Relationships, 7,* 1–23.

Barcellos Rezende, C. (1999). Building affinity through friendship. In Bell & Coleman, 1999 (pp. 79–97).

Baumeister, R. F., & Leary, M. P. (1995). The need to belong: Desire for interpersonal attachments as a fundamental human motivation. *Psychological Bulletin, 117,* 497–529.

Beetham, M. (2006). Periodicals and the new media: Women and imagined communities. *Women Studies International Forum, 29,* 231–240.

Bell, S., & Coleman, S. (1999). *The anthropology of friendship.* New York: Berg.

Berman, E. M., West, J. P., & Richter, M. N., Jr. (2002). Workplace relations: Friendship patterns and consequences (according to managers). *Public Administration Review, 62,* 217–230.

Bleske, A. L., & Buss, D. M. (2000). Can women and men be just friends? *Personal Relationships, 7,* 13–151.

Cancian, F. M. (1987). *Love in America: Gender and self-development.* Cambridge: Cambridge University Press.

Candy, S. G., Troll, L. E., & Levy, S. G. (1981). A developmental exploration of friendship functions in women. *Psychology of Women Quarterly, 5,* 456–472.

Chen, G.-M. (1995). Differences in self-disclosure patterns among Americans versus Chinese: A comparative study. *Journal of Cross-Cultural Psychology, 26,* 84–91.

Cheng, G. H. L., Chan, D. K. S., & Tong, P. Y. (2006). Qualities of online friendships with different gender compositions and durations. *CyberPsychology & Behavior, 9,* 14–21.

Chiou, W., & Wan, C. (2006). Sexual self-disclosure in cyberspace among Taiwanese adolescents: Gender differences and the interplay of cyberspace and real life. *CyberPsychology & Behavior, 9,* 46–53.

Chodorow, N. (1978). *The reproduction of mothering.* Berkeley: University of California Press.

Clark, M. S., & Reis, H. T. (1988). Interpersonal processes in close relationships. *Annual Review of Psychology, 39,* 609–672.

Cook, C., Bruin, M., & Crull, S. (2000). Manipulating constraints: Women's housing and the "metropolitan context." In K. B. Miranne & A. H. Young (Eds.), *Gendering the city: Women, boundaries, and visions of urban life* (pp. 183–207). New York: Rowman & Littlefield.

Diamond, L. M. (2000). Passionate friendships among adolescent sexual-minority women. *Journal of Research on Adolescence, 10,* 191–209.

Duck, S., & Wright, P. H. (1993). Reexamining gender differences in same-gender friendships: A close look at two kinds of data. *Sex Roles,* 28, 709–727.

Easterling, P. (1989). Friendship and the Greeks. In R. Porter & S. Tomaselli (Eds.), *The dialectics of friendship* (pp. 11–25). New York: Routledge.

Elkins, L. E., & Peterson, C. (1993). Gender differences in best friendships. *Sex Roles, 29,* 497–508.

Faderman, L. (1981). *Surpassing the love of men.* New York: Quality Paperback Book Club.

Fehr, B. (1996). *Friendship processes.* Thousand Oaks, CA: Sage.

Fehr, B. (2004). Intimacy expectations in same-sex friendships: A prototype interaction-pattern model. *Journal of Personality and Social Psychology, 86,* 265–284.

Finchum, T. D. (2005). Keeping the ball in the air: Contact in long-distance friendships. *Journal of Women & Aging, 17,* 91–106.

Fisher, J. S. (1996). *Why we love: The nature and chemistry of romantic love.* New York: Henry Holt & Co.

Galupo, M. P., Sailer, C. A., & St. John, S. C. (2004). Friendships across sexual orientations: Experiences of bisexual women in early adulthood. *Journal of Bisexuality, 4,* 37–53.

Giddings, P. (1985). *When and where I enter: The impact of black women on race and sex in America.* New York: Bantam Books.

Goldman, J. A., Cooper, P. E., Ahern, K., & Corsini, D. (1981). Continuities and discontinuities in the friendship descriptions of women at six stages in the life cycle. *Genetic Psychology Monographs, 103,* 153–167.

Hall, R. L., & Fine, M. (2005). The stories we tell: The lives of friendship of two older lesbians. *Psychology of Women Quarterly, 29,* 177–187.

Hansen, K. V. (1992). "Our eyes behold each other": Masculinity and intimate friendship in antebellum New England. In P. M. Nardi (Ed.), *Men's friendships* (pp. 35–58). Newbury Park, CA: Sage.

Harlow, H. F. (1958). The nature of love. *American Psychologist, 13,* 673–685.

Hays, R. B. (1985). A longitudinal study of friendship development. *Journal of Personality and Social Psychology, 48,* 909–924.

Hurtado, A. (1996). *The color of privilege: Three blasphemies on race and feminism.* Ann Arbor: University of Michigan Press.

Hurtado, A. (2003). *Voicing Chicana feminisms: Young women speak out on sexuality and identity.* New York: New York University Press.

Johnson, F. L., & Aries, E. J. (1983). The talk of women friends. *Women's Studies International Forum, 6,* 353–361.

Jordan, J. V., & Surrey, J. L. (1986). The self-in-relation: Empathy and the mother-daughter relationship. In T. Bernay & D. Cantor (Eds.), *The psychology of today's woman: New psychoanalytic visions* (pp. 81–104). Cambridge, MA: Harvard University Press.

Kaplan, D. L., & Keys, C. B. (1997). Sex and relationship variables as predictors of sexual attraction in cross-sex platonic friendships between young heterosexual adults. *Journal of Social and Personal Relationships, 14,* 191–206.

Kilcooley, A. (1997). Sexism, sisterhood and some dynamics of racism: A case in point. In M. Ang-Lygate, C. Corrin, & M. S. Henry (Eds.), *Desperately seeking sisterhood: Still challenging and building* (pp. 31–41). London: Taylor & Francis.

Kitzinger, C. (1996). Towards a politics of lesbian friendship. In J. S. Weinstock & E. D. Rothblum (Eds.), *Lesbian friendships: For ourselves and each other* (pp. 295–299). New York: New York University Press.

Kitzinger, C., & Perkins, R. (1993). *Changing our minds: Lesbian feminism and psychology.* New York: New York University Press.

Lever, J. (1976). Sex difference in the games children play. *Social Problems, 23,* 478–487.

Liss, M., Crawford, M., & Popp, D. (2004). Predictors and correlates of collective action. *Sex Roles, 50,* 771–779.

Louie, S. C. (2000). Interpersonal relationships: Independence versus interdependence. In J. L. Chin (Ed.), *Relationships among Asian American women* (pp. 211–222). Washington, DC: American Psychological Association.

Lu, L., & Argyle, M. (1992). Receiving and giving support: Effects on relationships and well-being. *Counseling Psychology Quarterly, 5,* 123–134.

Maccoby, E. E. (1998). *The two sexes: Growing up apart, coming together.* Cambridge, MA: Harvard University Press.

Mark, E. & Alper, T. (1985) Women, men, and intimacy motivation. *Psychology of Women Quarterly, 9,* 81–88.

Mays, V. M. (1985). Black women working together: Diversity in same sex relationships. *Women's Studies International Forum, 8,* 67–71.

McCown, J. A., Fischer, B. A., Page, R., & Homant, M. (2001). Internet relationship: People who meet people. *CyberPsychology & Behavior, 4,* 593–596.

McKenna, K. Y., & Bargh, J. A. (1998). Coming out in the age of the Internet: Identity "demarginalization" through virtual group participation. *Journal of Personality and Social Psychology, 75,* 681–694.

McKenna, K. Y., & Bargh, J. A. (2000). Plan 9 from cyberspace: The implications of the Internet for personality and social psychology. *Personality and Social Psychology Review, 4,* 57–75.

McKenna, K. Y., Green, A. S., & Smith, P. K. (2001). Demarginalizing the sexual self. *Journal of Sex Research, 38,* 302–311.

Monsour, M. (2002). *Women and men as friends: Relationships across the life span in the 21st century*. Mahwah, NJ: Erlbaum.

Morgan, R. (1970). Introduction: The women's revolution. In R. Morgan (Ed.), *Sisterhood is powerful: An anthology of writings from the Women's Liberation Movement* (pp. xv–xvi). New York: Random House.

Nardi, P. M. (1992). "Seamless souls": An introduction to men's friendships. In P. M. Nardi (Ed.), *Men's friendships* (pp. 1–14). Newbury Park, CA: Sage.

Neve, M. (1989). Male friends. In R. Porter & S. Tomaselli (Eds.), *The dialectics of friendship* (pp. 62–75). New York: Routledge.

Nyamathi, A., Bennett, C., Leake, B., & Chen, S. (1995). Social support among impoverished women. *Nursing Research, 44*, 376–378.

O'Boyle, C. G., & Thomas, M. D. (1996). Friendships between lesbian and heterosexual women. In J. S. Weinstock & E. D. Rothblum (Eds.), *Lesbian friendships: For ourselves and each other* (pp. 240–250). New York: New York University Press.

O'Connor, P. (1992). *Friendships between women*. New York: Guilford Press.

O'Connor, P. (1998). Women's friendships in a post-modern world. In Adams & Allan, 1998 (pp. 117–135).

Oliker, S. J. (1998). The modernization of friendship: Individualism, intimacy, and gender in the nineteenth century. In Adams & Allan, 1998 (pp. 18–42).

Parks, M. R., & Floyd, K. (1996a). Making friends in cyberspace. *Journal of Communications, 46*, 80–97.

Parks, M. R., & Floyd, K. (1996b). Meanings for closeness and intimacy in friendship. *Journal of Social and Personal Relationships, 13*, 85–107.

Parks, M. R., & Roberts, L. D. (1998). "Making MOOsic": The development of personal relationships on line and a comparison to their off-line counterparts. *Journal of Social and Personal Relationships, 15*, 517–537.

Patterson, B. R., & Bettini, L. A. (1993). Age, depression, and friendship: Development of a general friendship inventory. *Communication Research Reports, 10*, 161–171.

Peter, J., Valkenburg, P. M., & Schouten, A. (2005). Developing a model of adolescent friendship formation on the Internet. *CyberPsychology & Behavior, 8*, 423–430.

Pew Internet and American Life Project. (2005). How women and men use the Internet. Retrieved January 8, 2007, from http://www.pewinternet.org/ppf/r/171/report_display.asp.

Pew Internet and American Life Project. (2007). Social networking websites and teens: An overview. Retrieved January 8, 2007, from http://www.pewinternet.org/ppf/r/198/report_display.asp.

Piercy, K. W., & Cheek, C. (2004). Tending and befriending: The intertwined relationships of quilters. *Journal of Women & Aging, 6*, 17–33.

Radmacher, K., & Azmitia, M. (2006). Are there gendered pathways to intimacy in early adolescents' and emerging adults' friendships? *Journal of Adolescent Research, 21*, 415–448.

Rind, P. (2002). *Women's best friendships: Beyond Betty, Veronica, Thelma, and Louise*. New York: Haworth Press.

Rose, S. (1995). Women's friendships. In J. C. Chrisler & A. H. Hemstreet (Eds.), *Variations on a theme: Diversity and the psychology of women* (pp. 79–105). Albany: State University of New York Press.

Rose, S. (2000). Heterosexism in the study of women's romantic and friend relationships. *Journal of Social Issues, 56,* 315–328.

Rose, S., & Roades, L. (1987). Feminism and women's friendships. *Psychology of Women Quarterly, 11,* 243–254.

Rosenzweig, L. W. (1999). Introduction. In L. W. Rosenzweig, *Another self: Middle-class women and their friends in the twentieth century* (pp. 1–14). New York: New York University Press.

Rotundo, A. (1989). Romantic friendships: Male intimacy and middle-class youth in the northern United States, 1800–1900. *Journal of Social History, 23,* 1–25.

Sapadin, L. A. (1988). Friendship and gender: Perspectives of professional women. *Journal of Social and Personal Relationships, 5,* 387–403.

Seale, C. (2006). Gender accommodation in online cancer support groups. *Health: An Interdisciplinary Journal of the Social Study of Health, Illness and Medicine, 10,* 345–360.

Serafica, F. C., Weng, A., & H. K. Kim. (2000). Friendships and social networks among Asian American women. In J. L. Chin (Ed.), *Relationships among Asian American women* (pp. 151–175). Washington, DC: American Psychological Association.

Severance, T. A. (2005). "You know who you can go to": Cooperation and exchange between incarcerated women. *Prison Journal, 85,* 343–367.

Sheets, V. L., & Lugar, R. (2005). Friendship and gender in Russia and the United States. *Sex Roles, 52,* 131–140.

Simmonds, F. N. (1997). Where are the sisters? Difference, feminism, and friendship. In M. Ang-Lygate, C. Corrin, & M. S. Henry (Eds.), *Desperately seeking sisterhood: Still challenging and building* (pp. 19–30). London: Taylor & Francis.

Smith-Rosenberg, C. (1985). The female world of love and ritual: Relations between women in the nineteenth-century America. In C. Smith-Rosenberg (Ed.), *Disorderly conduct: Visions of gender in Victorian America* (pp. 53–76). New York: Knopf.

Stein, C. H. (1993). Felt obligation in adult family relationships. In S. Duck (Ed.), *Social context and relationships* (pp. 78–99). Newbury Park, CA: Sage.

Surrey, J. (1993). Self-in-relations: A theory of women's development. *Advanced Development, 5,* 1–11.

Taylor, S. (2002). *The tending instinct: How nurturing is essential for who we are and how we live.* New York: Times Books.

Thayer, S. E., & Ray, S. (2006). Online communication preferences across age, gender, and duration of internet use. *CyberPsychology & Behavior, 9,* 432–440.

Veniegas, R. C., & Peplau, L. A. (1997). Power and the quality of same-sex friendships. *Psychology of Women Quarterly, 21,* 279–297.

Walker, K. (1994). Men, women, and friendship: What they say, what they do. *Gender & Society, 8,* 246–265.

Walker, K. (1995) "Always there for me": Friendship patterns and expectations among middle- and working-class men and women. *Sociological Forum, 10,* 273–296.

Way, N., & Chen, L. (2000). Close and general friendships among African American, Latino, and Asian American adolescents from low-income families. *Journal of Adolescent Research, 15,* 274–301.

Wei, W. (1993). *The Asian American movement.* Philadelphia: Temple University Press.

Weinstock, J. S. (2004). Lesbian FLEX-ibility: Friend and/or family connections among lesbian ex-lovers. In J. S. Weinstock & E. D. Rothblum (Eds.), *Lesbian ex-lovers: The really long-term relationships* (pp. 193–238). New York: Harrington Park Press.

Weinstock, J. S., & Rothblum, E. D. (1996). What we can be together: Contemplating lesbians' friendships. In J. S. Weinstock & E. D. Rothblum (Eds.), *Lesbian friendships: For ourselves and each other* (pp. 3–30). New York: New York University Press.

Weiser, E. B. (2000). Gender differences in Internet use patterns and Internet application preferences: A two-sample comparison. *CyberPsychology & Behavior, 3,* 167–177.

Wellman, B. (1992). Men in networks: Private communities, domestic friendships. In P. M. Nardi (Ed.), *Men's friendships* (pp. 74–114). Newbury Park, CA: Sage.

Wiseman, J. P. (1986). Friendship: Bonds and binds in a voluntary relationship. *Journal of Social and Personal Relationships, 3,* 191–211.

Wright, P. H. (1982). Men's friendships, women's friendships and the alleged inferiority of the latter. *Sex Roles, 8,* 1–20.

Wright, P. H. (2006). Toward an expanded orientation to the comparative study of women's and men's same-sex friendships. In K. Dindia & D. J. Canary (Eds.), *Sex differences and similarities in communication* (pp. 37–57). Mahwah, NJ: Erlbaum.

Wright, P. H., & Scanlon, P. H. (1991). Gender role orientations and friendships: Some attenuation, but gender differences abound. *Sex Roles, 24,* 551–566.

Yoo, H. S., & Malley-Morrison, K. (2000). Young adult attachment styles and intimate relationships with close friends: A cross-cultural study of Koreans and Caucasian Americans. *Journal of Cross-Cultural Psychology, 31,* 528–534.

Zavella, P. (1993). The politics of race and gender: Organizing Chicana cannery workers in Northern California. In N. Alarcón et al. (Eds.), *Chicana critical issues* (pp. 127–153). Berkeley, CA: Third Woman Press.

PART IV

Women's Bodies and Their Minds

Chapter 12

Women's Health: Biological and Social Systems

Cheryl Brown Travis
Andrea L. Meltzer

BACKGROUND

One might begin analysis of the women's health movement in Greek antiquity with Hypatia, said to be one of the first women physicians, who disguised herself as a man in order to practice. The story may be apocryphal, but it is the case that from the time of Hippocrates, women were increasingly and systematically excluded from the practice of medicine of any sort and legally prohibited in many instances. The exclusion of women from the practice of medicine probably arose from a variety of factors, such as a general fear of and mystery regarding women's biology. Economic competition undoubtedly played a role in the diminution of women in medicine, especially as male physicians sought to enter the field of birth and family planning and midwifery was made illegal in many countries (Marieskind, 1980). Nursing gained some increased professional status under the activism of Florence Nightingale during the Crimean War of 1854. One is reminded that all the nurses were volunteers and that the Charge of the Light Brigade took place prior to morphine, antibiotics, or analgesics.

Margaret Sanger must be noted as one of the stellar figures to presage a women's health movement. She and her sister, Ethel Byrne, and another woman, Fania Mindell, opened a birth control clinic in Brooklyn, New York, in 1916, a time when it was illegal to provide even information on birth control, let alone birth control devices. Sanger and her coworkers were arrested at various times for publicly speaking and imparting information on birth control. To get a sense of the times in which she braved this monolithic opposition, it may help to recall that in 1916 women did not have the right to vote.

The contemporary women's health movement, as it emerged in the 1960s and 1970s in the United States, was situated in a sociopolitical context that saw the birth, or rebirth, of a number of social and political movements: the civil rights movement, feminist movement, and antiwar movement, along with farm workers movement and a centralization of the labor organizations in general. The first modern nationally inclusive meeting of feminists occurred in 1977, partially in response to a United Nations initiative, the Decade of Women.

Early scholars and activists in the women's health movement included Gena Corea (1977), Mary Daly (1978), Claudia Dreifus (1977), Barbara Ehrenreich and Diedre English (1973), Sheryle Ruzek (1978), Jean Marieskind (1980), Diana Scully (1980), and Peggy Sandelowski (1981). The early work of one of this chapter's authors (Travis, 1988a, 1988b) was inspired and guided by these pioneering women.

A central feature of the women's health movement has been to offer practical information and guidance directly to women regarding their own bodies. *Our Bodies, Ourselves,* first published by the Boston Women's Health Book Collective in 1970, has been one of the most widely distributed resources. Regularly updated and revised, the most recent edition (Boston Women's Health Book Collective, 2005) continues to be highly regarded.

Feminism and feminist principles favor the political, economic, and social equality of women and men and therefore favor legal and social change necessary to secure this equality (Hyde, 2006). Collectively, feminist principles serve as a framework for conceptualizing health care issues (Travis & Compton, 2001). They support work that illuminates health outcomes for girls and women and other oppressed groups, medical planning and decision making that is consensual, and exposing the hidden power and privilege within health care systems that benefit some while excluding others. Although feminism is not a homogenous philosophy, there are some general principles that seem to hold whether one assumes a liberal, socialist, cultural standpoint or postmodern perspective.

The women's health movement has centered on four broad issues. A primary issue is that traditional approaches to medicine have promoted a social construction of women, women's bodies, and women's roles that undermines the human rights of women, the safety and health of women, and the general political and social status of women. That is, the institution of medicine has actively contributed to the oppression of women.

A related issue is that the traditional physician–patient relationship reflects a traditional hierarchy and subordination of the patient and is especially onerous for women. This has been particularly grievous in the areas of gynecology, contraception, pregnancy, and birth.

A third, and related, concern is that women's voices have been trivialized and discounted in such settings, with the result that women often do not receive appropriate or timely care. In particular, women's biomedical symptoms may be discounted or reinterpreted as emotional or psychosomatic. Accounts are not rare of delayed and ponderous diagnostic processes for women with life-threatening heart conditions, painful ovarian cysts, or chronic diseases such as hypothyroidism. Conditions such as hypothyroidism (even if seemingly subclinical) may contribute to higher levels of cholesterol and subsequently to increase risk of heart disease (Michalopoulou et al. 1998). Underdiagnosis or prolonged delays in diagnosis may preclude the most effective medical interventions and necessitate more invasive procedures that are both more risky and more costly. To the extent that biomedical problems are misattributed to women's emotions or psychological distress, they also may be overmedicated with psychotropes. The problems of underdiagnosis and overmedication are compounded by the fact that many randomized clinical trials to assess diagnostic techniques or primary interventions have been developed and tested on men. The historic assumption has been that safety and effectiveness for women can be assumed if study results were favorable among men.

A fourth and continuing concern of the women's health movement has been the professional standing and opportunities for women as health care providers and administrators. Some notable improvements have evolved since 1970s, and the Health Services Resources and Services Administration reports that as of 2000, slightly more than 40 percent of students entering medical schools are women (Centers for Disease Control and Prevention, 2002).

General Feminist Principles

Historically, American society has been patriarchal, and feminist theory has had one main goal: gender equality, for women and men as well as other oppressed groups. In the health care system, giving women access to the rights and privileges they have been denied could break down this patriarchal system (Miller & Kuszelewicz, 1995). This may be achieved by providing women with additional skills and knowledge so they may further understand their rights.

Basic feminist principles may help to explain our thinking on women's health. These principles—including societal expectations and cultural context, bringing an end to patriarchal power, unity and diversity, and women's movement and activism—all play a role in reaching egalitarianism between the sexes.

Societal Expectations and Cultural Context

Our patriarchal world is shaped by societal actions and expectations. Beginning at their day of birth, boys and girls are taught how to act "masculine" and "feminine," respectively. In our society, as well as most other societies worldwide, strength, control, and domination are all associated with males (Johnson, 1997), while quietness, gentleness, and subordination are associated with females. Historically and evolutionarily, men have had power and control because they were physically stronger and bigger and were needed to protect pregnant women, in order to carry on their genes. This view may have once held strong, but it no longer is relevant to our history and advances in biology and genetics. Women are not a weaker sex and should not be treated as one.

Bringing an End to Patriarchal Power

The health care system is a male-dominated institution of social control, and there must be an end to the patriarchal power in order to gain equality between the sexes (Hercus, 2005). Women should become educated regarding their rights and privileges to ensure they receive accurate and timely care. As women empower themselves through voicing their opinion to their health care provider, this inequality begins to break down. It is also important for women to share their feelings and to build a support system (Miller & Kuszelewicz, 1995). By doing so, the minority may begin to feel less invisible and more powerful.

Unity and Diversity

Women are frequently isolated from men in many aspects of Westernized culture, including the health care system. A goal of feminism is to reduce this inequality (White, Russo, and Travis, 2001). However, one's status is marked by more than just one's sex. Other factors include race, religion, ethnicity, and sexual orientation. To create true unity for women, incorporating these other factors regarding their health, feminist theory must include multiculturalism. Progress is starting to be made in this area. For example, the American Psychological Association created Multicultural Guidelines in 2002. Unfortunately, feminist theory is only now beginning to incorporate multiculturalism (Silverstein, 2006).

Women's Movement and Activism

Feminists are ideally attempting to break down the sex inequality in the health care system in hopes to gain more opportunities for women. Women must become empowered and take action to gain this equality (White et al., 2001). However, it is important to remember that feminist activists should be represented by more than just middle-class, white women (Hutchison, 1986). Multiculturalism is an important aspect of feminism and must be incorporated to reach true equality between the sexes.

Human Rights and Women's Bodies

Women's health is a political as well as biomedical phenomenon, shaped by social, political, and economic contexts. These contexts make women's health simultaneously an aspect of human rights. In this respect, security of person and quite literally the boundaries of one's body are essential rights. As Margaret Sanger so eloquently expressed it, "No woman can call herself free who does not own and control her own body" (see Rossi, 1973, p. 533). Slavery, torture, forced marriage, genital mutilation, rape as military or political policy, sexual trafficking, forced sterilization, or forced pregnancy are all anathema to human rights. A declaration on these points is provided by the United Nations' 1948 Universal Declaration of Human Rights (UDHR), which, among its 30 articles, prohibits slavery and regulates against human cruelty and torture (United Nations, 1948).

It took nearly 30 years for a focus to emerge specifically on the status and rights of women in the first World Conference on Women, held in 1975. Simultaneously the UN created the United Nations Development Fund for Women (UNIFEM) with the goal of fostering women's empowerment and gender equality. In 1979, the UN General Assembly adopted the Convention on the Elimination of All Forms of Discrimination against Women (CEDAW), sometimes referred to as the International Bill of Rights for Women. This document defines discrimination against women and national aims to end the discrimination. The basic thesis of CEDAW is that "the full and complete development of a country, the welfare of the world and the cause of peace require the maximum participation of women on equal terms with men in all fields" (United Nations, 1979).

In an ongoing monitoring of human rights and welfare, the United Nations publishes the annual *Human Development Report* (*HDR*). The *HDR* puts forth goals that are based on three main ideas: equality for all people, the continuation of equality from one generation to the next, and the empowerment of people so that they may be included in the development process. In 1995, this report had an expanded focus on the disparity of equality between men and women (United Nations, 1995b). The UN acknowledged that men and women are unequal in every society and that strong action needs to be taken to obtain and maintain equal gender opportunities worldwide.

The 1995 *HDR* introduced the Gender-related Development Index (GDI). The GDI is a measurement of gender disparity, based on items such as life expectancy, literacy, educational attainment, and income. The UN ranked 130 countries on this scale and found that the four top-ranked countries were Sweden, Finland, Norway, and Denmark. Each of these countries has adopted gender equality as a national policy, perhaps helping to lead to less disparity. Nevertheless, the report stated even though these four countries in the Nordic Belt are high, no one society is free of gender disparity.

Also in 1995, the Beijing Declaration was promulgated at the UN Fourth World Conference on Women. This document, like the *HDR*, recognized gender inequalities everywhere and affirmed a commitment that would "ensure the full implementation of the human rights of women and of the girl child as an inalienable, integral, and indivisible part of all human rights and fundamental freedoms" (United Nations, 1995a).

The quality of women's physical and psychological health is very much shaped by these human rights of women. Despite various centers and institutes that affirm the inclusion of women's rights as fundamental to human rights, most human rights policies leave females vulnerable, especially when women's bodies are concerned. The egregious oppression and control of women by the Taliban government of Afghanistan is just one example.

Battery against women's bodies is one example of violation against human rights (Momoh, 2006). Unfortunately, in countries where customs, rituals, and tradition are highly valued, violence against women in this context is still permitted; female genital mutilation (FGM) is one example of this. It is estimated that between 100 million and 140 million women and girls worldwide have undergone FGM, and each year another two million females are at risk (World Health Organization, 2000). The prevalence remains high in approximately 28 African countries, as well as some areas in Asia and the Middle East. In addition, increasing instances are found in Europe, Australia, Canada, and the United States.

There are several deleterious health consequences of FGM, including, but not limited to, severe pain, hemorrhaging, ulceration of the genital region, possible transmission of HIV, cysts, damage to the urethra, difficulties in childbirth, and even death (Momoh, 2006). This procedure is a violation of women's physical and psychological integrity, but used to be viewed as a matter of cultural values. In such patriarchal cultures where women have relatively few resources and fewer alternatives, accepted cultural wisdom may even create meanings for such acts that seem to protect or exalt women. In a totalizing environment, some women may themselves endorse such practices. We suggest that it be viewed as oppression.

It may appear as though gender policies in distant lands are most in violation of human rights. However, many of the same issues remain problematic in the United States. For example, access to a means of safe and reliable birth control, to privacy in medical decision making, and to abortion without harassment remain areas of fatal violence in the United States. It is ironic that U.S. lawmakers might vehemently resist compulsory human papillomavirus vaccination of young girls to prevent cervical cancer as a governmental invasion of personal integrity but at the same time feel little compunction about effectively forcing a woman to maintain a pregnancy and give birth.

It is clear that internationally human rights are protected in the home, in the workplace, in the government, and elsewhere. But when it comes to the rights of women's bodies, these principles are regularly ignored, with profound impact on women's health.

EQUITY AND HEALTH CARE

Health care spending in the United States is currently measured in the trillions of dollars and will account for 17 percent of the gross domestic product by 2011 (Heffler, Smith, Won, Clemens, Keehan, & Zezza, 2002). How the delivery of health care is organized is therefore a national priority. Policy within the U.S. Department of Health and Human Services has organized health care goals for the nation in terms of prevention, protection, and promotion. *Prevention* typically deals with efforts to minimize the impact of disease and to reduce the number of individuals having impaired health. It encompasses areas such as high blood pressure control, infant health, immunizations, and sexually transmitted diseases. *Protection* goals focus on topics such as injury prevention, the control of toxic agents, and occupational health and safety. Health *promotion* is a relatively recent concept and is directed toward increasing the number of individuals who adhere to healthy lifestyles. Goals of health promotion focus on areas such as smoking cessation, the reduced misuse of alcohol and drugs, improved nutrition, physical fitness, managing stress, and reduction of violence.

In addition to the areas of prevention, protection, and promotion (the "three *P*'s"), one might conceptualize health and medical issues in terms of three *E*'s: efficacy, efficiency, and equity. *Efficacy* and *efficiency* would seem to be obvious and extremely salient features of health decision making, and researchers have been addressing these questions for more than 20 years. Efficacy and efficiency prompt researchers to ask the questions, Does it work safely? and Do the benefits outweigh the costs?

In contrast to the long-standing recognition of the relevance of efficacy and efficiency, formal policy regarding equity has only recently begun to receive the attention it deserves. *Equity* addresses the questions of barriers to individual access to care, the availability of care as a function of the organization and distribution of resources; it also pertains to variation in the quality of care across recipients. For example, studies on heart disease have found that black patients with coronary artery disease were less likely to receive revascularization than were white patients (Leatherman & McCarthy, 2002).

Equity in access and quality of care has come increasingly to the forefront of attention and, in 1999, the U.S. Congress directed the Institute of Medicine (a component of the National Academy of Sciences) to conduct a study of health care disparities. The study was designed to evaluate potential sources of racial and ethnic disparities in health care, including the role of bias, discrimination, and stereotyping at the individual (provider and patient), institutional, and health-system levels. As part of this initiative, in November 2000, President Bill Clinton signed into law an act that created a National Center on Minority Health and Health Disparities at the National Institutes of Health (NIH). However, this center gives primary focus to ethnicity as the critical distinction relevant to health care delivery and outcomes; gender is not particularly salient in the rhetoric associated with this work.

Access to Insurance and Care

Access to care and the potential effect of limited access on the national costs of health care have become major focal points for current policy and planning. Despite general economic growth over two decades, a housing boom, international trade agreements, and a stock market that has broken successive records, health care coverage was worse in 2006 than it was 20 years earlier. Results from the 2006 National Health Information Survey (Cohen & Martinez, 2006) indicate that 67 percent of the population was covered by private health insurance. In contrast to the common assumption that "things are getting better," a higher percentage of the general population had private health insurance in 1984, roughly 79 percent (National Center of Health Statistics, 1991).

There is an assumption that some government program or another safety net will provide for individuals without private insurance. Among individuals without private health insurance, Medicaid covers roughly 11 percent, and about 2 percent are covered by Medicare or military provisions (National Center for Health Statistics, 1996, 1999).[1] Current estimates by the U.S. Bureau of the Census are that approximately 15.9 percent of the U.S. population, or roughly 47 million people, lack health insurance of any sort, and another sizable percentage is underinsured (DeNavas-Walt, Proctor, & Lee, 2006). However, in 1987 only 12.9 percent of the population was uninsured (U.S. Census Bureau, 2006b). Thus, a strong argument can be made that improvements in state-of-the-art interventions and pharmaceutical breakthroughs are less available today than 20 years ago.

This increase in the percentage of uninsured cannot be dismissed as deadbeat drifters or welfare artists, because many full-time workers lack insurance. Health care for indigent and homeless individuals is only a small part of the trouble, and it cannot be solved simply by putting people to work, because most individuals below the poverty level already have one or more jobs (Travis & Compton, 2001). Those who work full-time may not escape the conundrum of how to get health care insurance. Among people ages 18–64 (and therefore not eligible for Medicare coverage) who worked full-time in 2005, 17.7 percent were uninsured (U.S. Census Bureau, 2006a).

Among those without any health coverage, more than 70 percent are people of color, even though people of color represent only about 15 percent of the general population. As illustrated in figure 12.1, Asian, black, and Hispanic individuals are much more likely to be without insurance of any kind (U.S. Census Bureau, 2006a). Women in these groups are disproportionately disadvantaged. Hispanic women, especially poor Hispanic women, consistently have the worst access to health care. These women have no regular health care providers, even for routine preventive care. They are less likely to know their blood pressure or cholesterol levels and may be more likely to have high blood pressure that is not effectively controlled by medication.

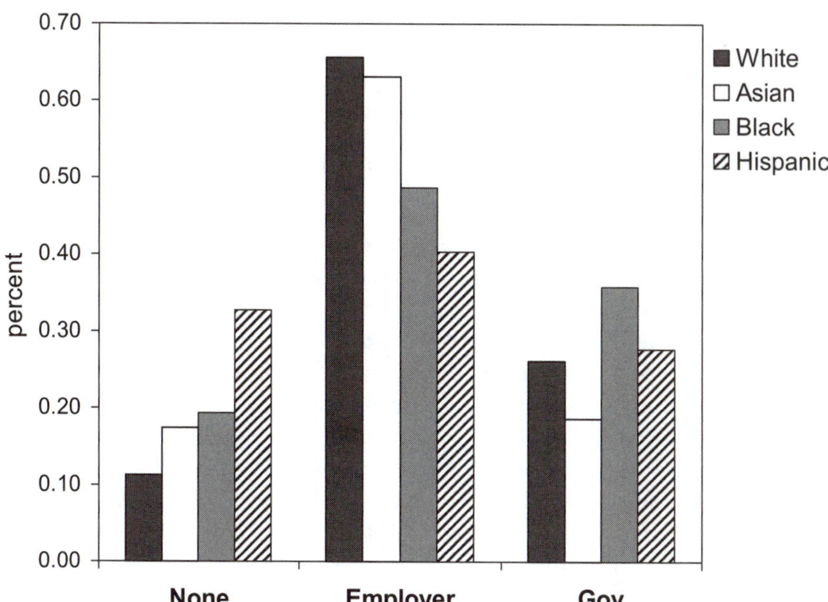

Figure 12.1. Health insurance coverage by race. *Source:* U.S. Census Bureau, 2005.

Approximately 36 percent of poor women are uninsured (National Center for Health Statistics, 1996), and this figure is even higher among Hispanic women in poverty, with approximately 45 percent having no health insurance (Pamuk, Makuc, Heck, Reuben, & Lochner, 1998).

Problems of insurance coverage and access to care are magnified for older women not yet eligible for Medicare. Women are likely to have problems in maintaining health insurance because gender roles and sexism influence individual work histories. Women are more likely to work part-time, to have interrupted work histories, and to work in settings without benefit plans. Since only about 10–15 percent of women collect pensions or annuities from private plans, their ability to maintain health insurance or to remediate problems is limited (Kirschstein & Merritt, 1985).

Medicare coverage for those over age 65 does not solve these problems. Out-of-pocket expenses (those expenses *not* covered by the main insurance program) are often higher for events experienced by older women in comparison to events common among older men. About 79 percent of expenses were covered for enlarged prostate, for example, while Medicare covers only 65 percent of expenses for breast cancer and about 48 percent of the costs for stroke (Sofaer & Abel, 1990). These financial policies impose real hardships that are likely to have a differential impact on poor and minority women. They also reflect an implicit priority for the health of men and a greater concern for providing access to care for men. Expanding analyses and evaluation to healthcare *systems*, in addition to the health behaviors of individuals, will undoubtedly reveal additional issues in women's health.

REPRODUCTIVE TECHNOLOGY, BIRTH, AND FAMILY PLANNING

One of the earliest instigating factors of the women's health movement involved the reproduction of societal patriarchy in obstetrics and gynecology. The health of lower-class women and mothers was held in thrall to a disdainful and indifferent profession of entirely male medical doctors.[2] Options for birth control were limited, and women who were poorly nourished from the beginning were weakened by repeated pregnancies and nursing. The American birth control movement, led by Margaret Sanger, developed largely in response to these conditions. The discovery and use of chloroform (just in time for the Civil War) quickly found its way to the practice of obstetrics and to an increasing norm of hospitalization for birth, medical instrumentation, and surgical births.

The overall patterns of pregnancy and birth remain major focal areas in public health and the women's movement. With advances in technology, assistance in getting pregnant has become a major industry.

Similarly, advances in technology also have brought renewed attention and choice to assistance in terminating pregnancy.

Natality and Mortality

The number and timing of pregnancies and births have a profound effect on the overall health of women and their children. These events are shaped partly by the age at marriage as well as by formal population policies, gender-roles, and cultural values. United Nations data indicate a wide variation in the number of births to women across countries: Afghanistan, 6.9; Cambodia, 5.0; China, 1.4; Egypt, 3.1; Guatemala, 4.7; Latvia, 1.1; Netherlands, 1.5; Philippines, 3.4; Rwanda, 6.0; Saudi Arabia, 5.8; Spain, 1.1; and Venezuela, 2.9 (United Nations, 2003). Women in Niger have an average of 8.0 births, perhaps the highest in the world.

Although the average U.S. woman has two births, the number of pregnancies among U.S. women is higher, due partly to pregnancy loss and to abortion. In the United States, the number of pregnancies varies significantly by race and ethnicity. A white woman will experience approximately 2.7 pregnancies in her lifetime, whereas a black, non-Hispanic woman will experience 4.5; the figure is 4.7 among Hispanic women (Ventura, Abma, & Mosher, 2003).

Although public opinion generally assumes that infant and maternal health in the United States ranks among the highest in the world, this is far from the actual standings. Infant health and mortality is a function not only of biological health but also of public health policies and access to care. With respect to infant mortality, the United States does not rank even in the top 10 countries, as indicated by table 12.1. Furthermore, within the country, there are drastic discrepancies for infant mortality among race and ethnic groups. For example, as illustrated in figure 12.2, the *best* infant mortality (Massachusetts) for black non-Hispanic women (9.5 deaths per 1,000 live births) is markedly worse than the state having the *worst* infant mortality for Asian/Pacific Islander (7.3 deaths), white non-Hispanic (7.9 deaths), or Latina (8.6 deaths) women. That is, there is a complete disjunction between rates of infant mortality among black women and rates among other ethnic and racial groups.

Interestingly, regional variations in infant mortality for race or ethnic groups do not seem to follow expectations about prevalence in the regional population. For example, the state with the best infant mortality among Native American women is New Mexico (6.8 deaths per 1,000 live births), while the worst is South Dakota (11.6 deaths), both states that have large, active Native American populations. In contrast, the state with the best infant mortality among Latina women is Virginia (4.8 deaths per 1,000 live births), while the worst is Pennsylvania (8.6 deaths), both states with relatively smaller Latina/Latino populations.

Table 12.1.
International rankings on infant mortality

Rank	Country	Rate per 1,000 births, 2002
1	Hong Kong	2.3
2	Sweden	2.8
3	Singapore	2.9
4 (tie)	Finland	3.0
4 (tie)	Japan	3.0
6	Spain	3.4
7	Norway	3.5
8 (tie)	Austria	4.1
8 (tie)	France	4.1
10	Czech Republic	4.2
27	Cuba	6.5
28	United States	7.0

Source: National Center for Health Statistics, 2005a (table 25).

The state with the worst rate for Asian or Pacific Islander women is Hawaii (7.3 deaths), a state with a high percentage of such individuals, but the state with the worst rate for black women is Wisconsin (17.9 deaths), with relatively fewer black women.

Infant mortality encompasses deaths from birth through the first year. Not infrequently infant mortality is associated with preterm delivery and low birthweight.[3] The risk of death from low birthweight is significantly higher for the infants of black women compared to white women, and the gap seems to be growing (Iyasu, Tomashek, & Barfield, 2002).

Age of the mother is another factor in infant mortality, and rates are generally higher among teenage mothers. Although recent reports have indicated a downward trend in teen pregnancy, (Guttmacher Institute, 2006b), about 84 of every 1,000 teenage girls became pregnant in 2000. There were large ethnic differences in teen pregnancies, with black and Hispanic teens having much higher pregnancy rates (Guttmacher Institute, 2006b); nevertheless, the absolute number of teen pregnancies is highest for white teenage girls.

Another factor that may contribute to low birthweight is chronic disease in the mother. For example, diabetes is more common among black women and is clearly associated with low birthweight (Martin, Hamilton, Sutton, Ventura, Menacker, & Munson, 2005). Numerous other factors have been implicated in low birthweight, but smoking (including exposure to secondhand smoke) is a serious risk (U.S.

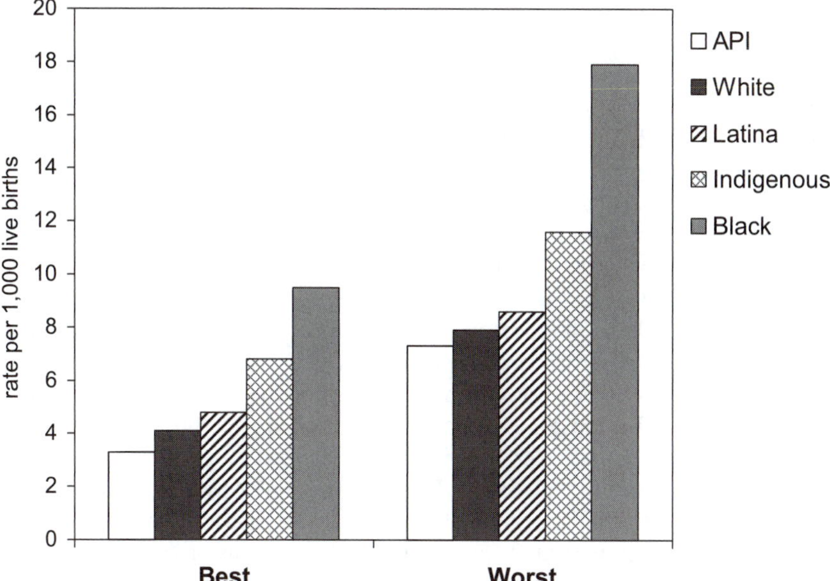

Figure 12.2. Best and worst infant mortality rates among U.S. states by race and ethnicity. *Source:* National Center for Health Statistics, 2005a (table 23, p. 177).

Department of Health and Human Services, 2004). The surgeon general's report on smoking indicates that 13–22 percent of pregnant women smoke. Smoking prevalence is clearly associated with poverty and less education, and women who do not graduate from high school are far more likely to smoke. The good news seems to be that women are about as successful as men in quitting smoking.

Reproductive Technology

Despite the four million births per year in the United States and the fact that most countries of the world are seeking to control population, there has been an increase in fertility treatment and assisted reproductive technology (ART) clinics in the United States. Fertility problems may reflect the effect of several factors, including, but not limited to, lack of egg production, low sperm production or low motility of sperm, and endometriosis, as well as difficulty in implantation of a fertilized egg in the wall of the uterus. Exposure to environmental toxins may have reproductive consequences as well. Toxins with reproductive effects are relatively common in the environment. For example, automobile exhaust contains a range of heavy metals, benzene, polycyclic aromatic hydrocarbons, and much more. Various reproductive effects associated with toxins can be direct, such as shorter gestation and lower birthweight, or indirect, such as the promotion of endometriosis that can block fallopian tubes or encase ovaries. Whatever the cause of infertility, roughly 150,000 couples seek technological assistance each year (U.S. Department of Health and Human Services, 2002).

Several forms of ART are possible. Procedures that involve hormones to stimulate ovulation or the handling only of sperm for artificial insemination are not officially designated as ART. Rather, ART involves the handling of both eggs and sperm and may be one of three different procedures. In vitro fertilization (IVF) procedures combine sperm and egg in the laboratory and insertion of the fertilized egg into the woman's uterus through the cervix, while GIFT (gamete intrafallopian transfer) transfers both sperm and unfertilized eggs to the woman's fallopian tube via a laparoscope and incision in the abdomen. The insertion of an already fertilized egg via laparoscope is termed ZIFT (zygote intrafallopian transfer). The cost is never trivial, but is relatively lower with IVF because it does not require a surgical incision, which is required for ZIFT or GIFT. Costs vary as a function of the location of the treatment center and the number of attempts or cycles involved, as well as medications and hormonal treatment; treatment for a single cycle involving either of the laparoscopic insertions is normally more than $10,000. Estimates of the costs depend on whether one is estimating the direct cost of procedures for a single cycle, the cost of producing an actual pregnancy, or the cost of producing a live birth (Garceau et al. 2002). Insurance companies differ in coverage of such procedures; for example, some will cover fertility drugs, but not procedures that involve the direct manipulation of eggs or sperm.

But does it work? The Centers for Disease Control and Prevention (CDC) report (2002) on ART indicates that of 85,826 cycles of attempted ART for women of all ages, about 34 percent led to pregnancies, but only 28 percent involved pregnancies with live births. Success rates may be shaded upward by using increasing selective baseline reference points. For example, success rate per cycle of initiated treatment will be lower than success rates calculated in reference to the number of cases where an egg was successfully retrieved. Success rates look even better when calculated only with respect to the number of cases where an egg was actually transferred. Further, the number of pregnancies per cycle will suggest a higher success rate than the number of live birth deliveries. Another consideration in contemplating reproductive technology is that roughly 12 percent of assisted reproductive pregnancies involve multiple fetuses.

Success rates vary significantly by age of the woman. Although women of all ages seek ART, the most common age is about 35. However, the success rate for an actual pregnancy via ART drops steadily after age 32 (Centers for Disease Control and Prevention, 2002). Thus, most women undergo ART when their personal likelihood of success is diminished. For example, women under age 35 have roughly a 37 percent live birth rate, compared to 21 percent for women ages 38–40. Therefore, to be fully informed on success rates with respect to pregnancy or live birth delivery, women should request information with respect to outcomes for other clients of similar age.

Emergency Contraception

Legislation and jurisprudence regulating birth control and abortion in the United States have a long history. Early laws, such as the Comstock Law of 1873, prohibited mailing lewd material, which Anthony Comstock (an inspector in the post office) took to include any mention of reproductive physiology. This remained functional law for more than 60 years, until 1936 when *United States v. One Package* (86 F.2d 737) established that registered physicians could dispense information on birth control and diaphragms. Margaret Sanger had asked that a Japanese physician ship a new type of diaphragm to her in New York, where the package was seized under the Tariff Act, which incorporated provisions of the Comstock Law. The decision of the appellate court was that the law could not be used to seize shipments originating from a doctor. This decision allowed licensed medical practitioners to dispense birth control information and devices. The authorization of other organizations like Planned Parenthood to do likewise was yet another 30 years in coming, when Planned Parenthood of Connecticut received a favorable ruling in 1965 (*Griswold v. Connecticut*, 381 U.S. 479). Access to birth control by unmarried individuals was not affirmed until 1972 (*Eisenstadt v. Baird*, 405 U.S. 438).

One might be tempted to view these as merely interesting historical tidbits having little relevance to current events. However, with the world population exceeding six billion and growing, U.S. foreign aid policy continues to impose restrictions on information about birth control, family planning, and safe means of terminating pregnancy. This is very clearly not in the spirit of the United Nations position on the status of women and family planning (United Nations, 1975, 2003). The UN reports that the majority of developing countries allow access to family planning and many would like to lower population growth in their countries. Women, who constitute most of the world's poor, are not infrequently limited in their choice of education or type of employment. They are the ultimate safety net for their children, with few options to control their reproductive lives. In fact the Beijing Declaration that arose from the UN Women's Congress holds that equal access to health care, including control of reproduction, is a fundamental aspect of human rights and the overall empowerment of women (United Nations 1995a).

Similarly, access to emergency contraception in the United States has been delayed and strictly controlled. Emergency contraception, available in a pill form in the United States, is marketed as "Plan B" and was approved in 1999 as a safe and effective means of preventing pregnancy after unprotected intercourse. It will not produce an abortion of an already-established pregnancy, but will prevent a pregnancy from occurring and functionally operates in the same way that breast-feeding suppresses ovulation. The pill provides an extra boost of progestins (levonorgestrel). The primary biological mechanism of action of emergency contraception is to inhibit or delay ovulation, and it also may have some effect on the lining that prevents implantation of a fertilized egg (Novikova, Weisberg, Stanczyk, Croxatto, & Fraser, 2007).

Initial concerns were that the availability of emergency contraception on an over-the-counter (OTC) basis might lead to generally lower vigilance in the use of contraceptives, resulting in more unwanted pregnancies and perhaps more abortions. However, monitoring of pregnancy and abortion rates in the United States and other countries has shown no change where Plan B has been available (Trussell, Ellertson, Stewart, Raymond, & Shochet, 2004). Other concerns were that young teens would be encouraged toward sexual promiscuity, which would lead to higher rates of teen pregnancy. To address this problem, Barr Pharmaceuticals, the makers of Plan B, acceded to a stipulation that Plan B be available on an OTC basis only to women over 18 years of age and by medical prescription to younger women.

Plan B may be technically legal, but readily accessing this option may be problematic. The Kaiser Family Foundation (2003) survey of physicians indicated that only about 14 percent of general practitioners discuss emergency contraception with their patients and only 6 percent had prescribed emergency contraception. Although researchers and physicians advocated OTC access to emergency contraception for a number of years (Ellertson, Trussell, Stewart, & Winikoff, 1998; Grimes, Raymond, & Scott Jones, 2001), it was not approved by the Food and Drug Administration (FDA) for OTC access until late in 2005 (see Guttmacher Institute, 2005, for a synopsis of the approval process). In fact, the FDA had recommended approval in 2003, but in 2004 reversed itself after what appears to be a top-down executive decision rather than scientific review (Wood, Drazen, & Greene, 2005). Although FDA review commissions in 2003 (two of them) had fully endorsed Plan B as safe and effective, the FDA did not grant final approval until 2005 and only after pointed inquiries from Congress and a review of the decision-making process by the Government Accountability Office (GAO). Barr Pharmaceuticals began shipping Plan B to pharmacies at the end of 2006. Even so, there is wiggle room, in that some pharmacists may refuse to provide Plan B. This may be especially problematic in states with a dispersed population and similarly dispersed options for health services.

Abortion

Each year in the United States, approximately six million women become pregnant, and about half of these are unintended (Elam-Evans et al., 2003). Of the six million pregnancies, roughly four million result in birth, and about one million involve miscarriage, with somewhat less than a million legal abortions (Ventura, Abma, Mosher, & Henshaw, 2004). The number of legal abortions in the United States has declined in recent years: there were 1,297,606 in 1980 and 1,429,577 in 1990, but just 857,475 in 2000 (the CDC publishes annual abortion surveillance summaries; see CDC, 1997, and Elam-Evans et al., 2003). A major factor in abortion involves the failure of contraceptive methods, and approximately half of all women who obtain an abortion were practicing contraception during the month they became pregnant (Guttmacher Institute, 2006a). However, abortion also varies significantly by the age and race of the mother, with higher rates among teenage girls and women over 40.

Somewhat more meaningful information on race or ethnicity and abortion makes use of ratios or abortion to live births (CDC, 2006a). The number of legal abortions obtained by minority women is necessarily smaller than the number obtained by white women, because the vast majority of women are white. Slightly over half (about 53 percent) of all abortions occur among white women, with approximately 35 percent among black women and 10 percent among other or unknown race designations.

The ratio of abortions to live births among women of a particular race or ethnicity suggests a more complex picture. Among white women, there are 165 abortions to every 1,000 live births, while among black women, the ratio is 491 to 1,000 live births. Among other[4] or unknown races, there are 347 abortions per 1,000 live births. In comparison to white women, black women are about three times as likely to seek abortion, and roughly one-third of all pregnancies among black women are terminated. Among women having a Hispanic ethnicity,[5] there were 228 abortions to 1,000 live births.

These figures are shaped to a large extent by the nature of the lives of women of differing race and ethnicity, and surveys of women for the reasons behind their choices provide some insight. Research on attitudes toward abortion that consider race indicated that black women were more likely to support abortion if they were highly invested in participation in the workforce, if they had higher education, and when racial discrimination was more salient (Dugger, 1998; Finer, Frohwirth, Dauphinee, Singh, & Moore, 2005; Siemens & Clawson, 2004). For example, Siemens and Clawson (2004) noted that a high degree of black feminist consciousness was associated with support for abortion; this was observed for black men as well as for black women.

The higher ratio of abortions to live births among black women also is likely to involve some of the same economic factors that affect the choices of white women, such as single-mother status, the presence of other children, and limited ability to financially care for another child. While there might be a strong and compelling desire to have something to love, as suggested by Lee Rainwater (1960), there are economic limits on how well this can be realized. Further, the ways in which black women actively define their own sexual interests within the context of heterosexual intimacy remains uncharted and to a large extent remains problematic for all women.

The signal Supreme Court decision on abortion was decided in 1973 in the case of *Roe v. Wade* (410 U.S. 113). This was ultimately decided on the basis that the Constitution guarantees certain areas of personal privacy, which were deemed to include decisions about abortion. This general principle has not gone unchallenged, and a large number of subsequent cases heard by the Supreme Court have involved imposing further restrictions. Subsequent to the *Roe v. Wade* decision, in 1977 Congress passed the Hyde Amendment, which allows states to limit the use of Medicaid funds for abortion services even though the same state may use Medicaid to fund expenditures for childbirth. Other Court cases have concluded that fathers may not hold veto power over their wives' choices, but that states can require delays and additional medical visits so that women may be completely informed about the procedure, and that parental notification is needed for cases involving minors (see Lewis & Shimabukuro, 2001, for a brief overview).

An important, and more recent, decision by the Supreme Court (*Planned Parenthood of Southeastern Pennsylvania v. Casey*, 505 U.S. 833 [1992]) is generally viewed as supporting the *Roe v. Wade* decision. In this decision, the Court upheld the principle that a state may not unduly burden a woman's choice of abortion by prohibiting or substantially limiting access to the means of acting upon her decision (Lewis & Shimabukuro, 2001). However, the opinion of the justices also endorsed the less compelling rationale of simply supporting precedent or letting existing law stand (Yoshino, 2007).

Public and judicial opinion, as well as federal and state statutes regarding abortion, reveal a complex and sometimes disjointed picture. The majority (62 percent) of Americans favor the availability of abortion, and very few favor a complete ban on abortion (Pew Forum on Religion and Public Life, 2005, 2006). Nevertheless, a number of state statutes have been introduced that completely ban some procedures, and in many states, half the counties are without access to an abortion provider.

Court cases, statutes, and opinions will surely shift as the medical means of terminating pregnancy offer medical as well as surgical options. Surgical options involving dilation and evacuation have been the major option for the better part of a century. However, this changed in 1996 when the Population Council submitted a new drug application to the FDA. The drug, mifepristone (known commonly as RU 486), is a method of early abortion in the first eight weeks of pregnancy. It is an antiprogestin that interferes with cell division in the fertilized egg, inhibits implantation of the egg in the uterus, and induces a sloughing of the uterine lining (Beckman & Harvey 1998). It is then followed within 48 hours by a prostaglandin[6] (misoprostol), which promotes uterine contractions. Women who have actually experienced medical abortion using mifepristone generally indicate there was less discomfort and less bleeding than they had anticipated (Beckman & Harvey 1997).

Ultimately, access to birth control and to abortion that may be accessed without undue burden or restriction is consistent with principles that value individual integrity, privacy, and self-determination for men as well as for women. Policies that, for example, forced individuals to donate blood or to donate organs would never be tolerated, despite the fact that such policies might save the lives of others. The life situation of an individual woman and her own values surely are the best basis for making these decisions.

BODY WEIGHT AND METABOLIC SYNDROME

It is well known that obesity is positively correlated with mortality, and compared to nonobese women, obese women are at greater risk of death from cardiovascular disease, diabetes, and cancer (Bender, Zeeb, Schwarz, Jockeli, & Berger, 2006). Obesity may reduce life expectancy up to 7.1 years for females who do not smoke (Peeters, Barendregt, Willekens, Mackenbach, Al Mamun, & Bonneux, 2003). Among Korean women, not only is obesity a risk factor of death, but simply being overweight (or noticeably underweight) also increases one's mortality risk (Jee et al., 2006). Current research suggests that there is a weaker association between mortality and body weight for African American women than there is for white women (McTigue et al., 2003). Nevertheless, the risk of death from four obesity-related diseases (diabetes, hypertension, coronary heart disease, and cerebrovascular disease) seems to be significantly higher for African American women than for white women, but among obese Asian American women, the risk of death is relatively higher only for diabetes (Polednak, 2004). However, it difficult to draw firm conclusions about ethnicity, obesity, and mortality because there is limited race-related data and the data available are often based on small sample sizes.

In response, health care workers have recommended healthy weights to individuals by determining their fat percentage, their waist-to-hip ratio (WHR), and their body mass index (BMI). WHR is a measure of the distribution of fat around the torso. It is obtained by dividing the circumference of the waist by the circumference of the hips. A WHR of 0.7 for women has shown to strongly correlate with general health and attractiveness (Singh, 1993). BMI, created by Adolphe Quetelet in 1853 (School of Mathematics and Statistics, 2006), is a measure of body fat based on height and weight. It is obtained by using the following equation:

$$\text{BMI} = \frac{(\text{weight in pounds})}{(\text{height in inches})^2} \times 703$$

According to recent information, BMI values can be categorized as underweight (less than 18.5), normal (between 18.5 and 24.9), overweight (between 25.0 and 29.9), or obese (more than 30) (CDC, 2006b).

Despite the growing evidence of the health burden associated with obesity, U.S. society is becoming increasingly overweight. Berg (1994) found that American adults on average weigh eight pounds more than in previous decades. Over the past four decades, the prevalence of obesity has increased from 13 percent to 31 percent in adults (McTigue et al., 2003). The National Center for Health Statistics (2005a) reports that there is a larger percentage of overweight or obese (as determined by BMI values) African American females and Mexican females than there are white females, as illustrated in figure 12.3.

Part of this current trend may be a result of an increased intake of calories and fat in the American diet. Out of convenience, the fast-food industry has soared and the "super-size" phenomenon has occurred. Historical trends documented through the National Health and Nutrition Examination Survey indicate that between 1971 and 1974, women consumed an average of 1,542 calories, but in 1999 and 2000, the average increased to 1,877 calories (Wright et al., 2004). In addition to this general increase in caloric intake, it is important to note that the percentage of calories consumed from fat is roughly 30 percent. American women are not indifferent to these trends, and more than half of the women in our society feel that their weight is unacceptable and try to do something about it. In fact, for some, the fear of becoming overweight is becoming more prevalent than actually being overweight (Huon & Brown, 1984; Schulken, Pinciaro, Sawyer, Jensen, & Hoban, 1997). Women in particular appear to fear fatness, feel fat, diet repeatedly, and try a wide variety of techniques to lose weight (Nielsen Company, 1979; Boles & Johnson, 2001).

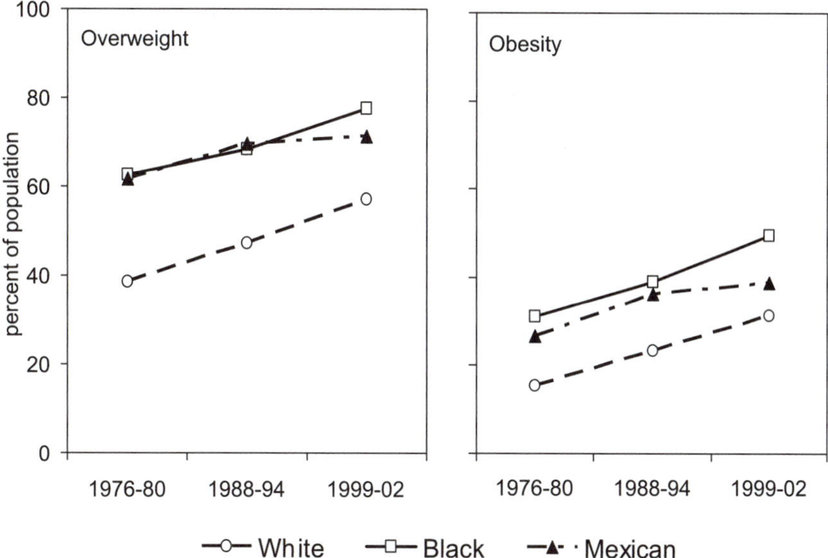

Figure 12.3. Overweight incidence and obesity among females 20 years of age and older by race and ethnicity. *Source:* National Center for Health Statistics, 2005a (table 73, p. 292).

Health Risks and Excess Weight

Increasingly, excess weight has been associated not only with a shorter life expectancy but also with general poor health. As will be discussed in more detail below, obesity is associated with an increased risk of heart disease, cerebrovascular disease, asthma, diabetes, fertility problems, and various types of cancer. In understanding the mechanisms by which various disease processes are put into action, it is important to remember that adipose tissue is not simply an inert weight but actively influences cell metabolism and can interfere with molecular communication pathways in the cell.

Obesity complicates fertility (Moran & Norman, 2004) and is a factor in adverse pregnancy outcomes. Obesity increases the risk of cesarean delivery as well as gestational diabetes (pregnant women who have never had diabetes but show high levels of blood sugar during pregnancy) and preeclampsia (dangerously high blood pressure and protein in one's urine after 20 weeks of pregnancy) (Ramos and Caughey, 2005). As with many other health conditions, these risks vary in severity as a function of ethnicity (Ramos & Caughey, 2005). For example, among pregnant women who are obese, African American women and Asian women have a higher percentage of cesarean deliveries than white women, and gestational diabetes is doubled in obese Asian and

Hispanic women. The risk of preeclampsia is increased especially high among obese Hispanic women.

Heart Disease

There has long been a general understanding that being overweight is associated with heart disease (Wilson & Kannel, 2002; Gordon, Castelli, Kjortland, Kannel, & Dawber, 1977). Excess body fat affects cardiovascular health in ways much more complex than simply requiring the heart to do more work by carrying the extra physical weight. Being overweight not only often means increased inches of localized adipose tissue but is also associated with high levels of bad, low-density cholesterol in the blood (Pietrobelli, Lee, Capristo, Deckelbaum, & Heymsfield, 1999).

Fat actively contributes to hypertension and general poor circulation by building insulin insensitivity (Löfgren et al., 2000). As will be apparent in the discussion below, insulin insensitivity has cascading effects on a number of diseases. Insulin is important to heart health because it is part of a communication pathway involved in the stiffness of arterial walls (Sengstock, Vaitkevicius, & Supiano, 2005). This might be thought of as almost a by-product of insulin insensitivity. The body senses excess sugars (glucose) in the blood and releases insulin (from the pancreas) as a messenger telling cells to take up the excess glucose. However, where there is excess body weight, insulin receptors in individual cells that might receive the insulin message have already been activated, and these cells can no longer receive the message. In response, the pancreas (for a time) insistently produces more insulin, which then affects the smooth muscle of arterial walls, making them less elastic and less capable of dilation. The inelasticity of blood vessels is a fundamental feature of atherosclerosis.

Excess body weight is also associated with generally higher levels of inflammatory activity in arterial walls, as indicated by high C-reactive protein scores (Mora, Lee, Buring, & Ridker, 2006). C-reactive protein, a marker of inflammatory activity, is now thought to be one of the most sensitive predictors of negative cardiovascular events (Cushman et al., 2005; Ridker, Cushman, Stampfer, Tracey, & Hennekens, 1997).

Asthma

Excess weight additionally is related to asthma (Luder, Ehrlich, Lou, Melnik, & Kattan, 2004). For example, early menarche, which is partly a function of higher body fat, is also associated with asthma in girls (Varraso, Siroux, Maccario, Pin, & Kauffmann, 2005). Women who gain weight after the age of 18 have a significantly increased risk of developing asthma (Camargo, Weiss, Zhang, Willett, & Speizer, 1999; Weiss & Shore, 2004). In general, individuals with poor glucose control and greater body weight also have less than optimal lung function (McKeever, Weston, Hubbard, & Fogarty, 2005).

The association of body weight, glucose tolerance, and lung function may be linked to the insulin insensitivity associated with excess weight. Since the insulin receptor pathway is hampered by excess fat, the resulting excess insulin may affect the smooth muscle of bronchi, making them more stiff and less elastic, in much the same way it affects the smooth muscle of arterial walls.

The consistent relationship between obesity and asthma suggests there is a causal relationship (Weiss, 2005). As a result, weight loss through dieting or gastric bypass surgery has shown to improve asthma-related symptoms (Stenius-Aarniala, Poussa, Kvarnstrom, Gronlund, Ylikahri, & Mustajoki, 2000), a relationship that appears to be stronger for women than for men (Weiss, 2005).

Diabetes

Given the above explanations about insulin insensitivity, it is obvious that excess body weight contributes directly to type 2 diabetes. Women with an increased amount of abdominal fat (high waist-to-hip ratios) have an increased risk for type 2 diabetes (Hu, 2003). In fact, obesity is the single most important risk factor for type 2 diabetes. Type 2 diabetes has been linked to a higher increased risk of coronary heart disease for women than for men (Manson & Spelsberg, 1996).

Risk also varies depending on ethnicity and race. Compared to African Americans and Caucasians, obese Native Americans have an increased risk for type 2 diabetes (Moore, Copeland, Parker, Burgin, & Blackett, 2006). Again, adipose tissue is not simply a passive weight: It alters genetic pathways in cell metabolism that affect inflammatory processes. The genetic mechanisms contributing to type 2 diabetes appear to be due to increased tumor necrosis factor (TNF), which may affect glucose transport in cells. This effect on glucose transport is important, because it may contribute to the insulin insensitivity that underlies type 2 diabetes (Kern, Saghizadeh, Ong, Boasch, Deem, & Simisolo, 1995; Löfgren et al., 2000).

Cancer

Cancer risk is also increased by excessive weight (Sturmer, Buring, Lee, Gaziano, & Glynn, 2006). The increased risk for cancer may have origins as early as young adulthood. For example, Okasha, McCarron, McEwen, and Smith (2002) found that women who were overweight in their college years were four times more likely to die from breast cancer than those of average weight. Evidence also suggests that adult women who gain weight, especially after menopause, have an increased risk for breast cancer (Eliassen, Colditz, Rosner, Willett, &

Hankinson, 2006); however, women who lose weight after menopause significantly decrease their risk for breast cancer.

Once again, adipose tissue is not simply an added neutral weight, but participates actively in the molecular cell biology of the body. For example, it has long been known that adipose tissue is capable of synthesizing some forms of estrogen (estrone), a process that seems to become more efficient with age (Zhao, Nicols, Bulun, Mendelson, & Simpson, 1995), and the higher breast cancer risk may be due in part to increased estrogen in overweight and obese women. This seems to be an instance where estrogen promotes increased cell division in the breast and thereby increases the likelihood of cell mutations, as well as increased numbers of any cancer cells already present (Bouchard, Taniguchi, & Viger, 2005).

Metabolic Syndrome

Metabolic syndrome refers to the constellation of metabolic pathways associated with excess weight and the associated health effects. Primary among these are insulin insensitivity, poor glucose tolerance, hypertension, hypercholestoremia, and inflammatory processes that may be associated with cancer pathways as well as with heart disease (Grundy et al., 2005). Understanding metabolic syndrome may help to explain and perhaps prevent a plethora of diseases.

The main risk factor underlying metabolic syndrome is excess weight, especially abdominal fat; other factors include physical inactivity and general aging. Unfortunately, excess weight, obesity, and metabolic syndrome seem to be increasing. Results from the Third National Health and Nutrition Examination Survey (NHANES III), conducted in 1988–1994, revealed that 47 million Americans (one out of every five people in the United States) are affected by metabolic syndrome (Ford, Giles, & Dietz, 2002). Roughly 20 percent of the general population is at risk for type 2 diabetes, and nearly half of all people over the age of 50 have some degree of insulin insensitivity. Obesity has similarly shown increases, and abdominal obesity occurs in approximately 60 percent of African American and Mexican American women and 40 percent of white women (Hu, 2003). African American women and Hispanic women have the highest prevalence of metabolic syndrome (Hall et al., 2003). This is surely a major factor in the prevalence of hypertension and diabetes in these ethnic groups.

Finding a "Healthy Weight"

With the "obesity epidemic" and the increase of eating disorders, it is important to stress the need for a "healthy weight." The cultural thinness ideal does not promote a healthy lifestyle. Not everyone can achieve the idolized size 2—or even a size 10, for that matter. In addition, it is argued that when women strive for the unobtainable goal of perfection, it feeds women's subordinate role in a patriarchal society by limiting women's participation in life in general (Allan, 1994).

Some current research is suggesting a new approach that defines a ''healthy weight'' differently. This approach is referred to as Health at Every Size (HAES) and focuses on ''living a healthy lifestyle'' as opposed to focusing on body-fat percentages, WHRs, and BMIs (Robison, 2003). The theory is that individuals who move toward a healthier lifestyle will, over time, produce a weight that is healthy. The basic framework of this approach consists of the acceptance of four things: natural diversity in body shape and size, the ineffectiveness and dangers of dieting, eating in response to internal cues, and the contribution of social, emotional, and physical factors to health and happiness.

In 2005, the Department of Health and Human Services released new recommended dietary guidelines to advise Americans on how to achieve a ''healthy weight.'' These guidelines include information regarding adequate nutrients within one's caloric needs; weight management; suggested physical activity; encouraged food groups; suggested fat, carbohydrate, sodium, potassium, alcoholic beverage intake; and food safety (U.S. Department of Health and Human Services & U.S. Department of Agriculture, 2005). The goal of these new guidelines is to promote health and reduce the risk of chronic diseases.

Maintaining a healthy weight also requires physical activity. Few adult Americans are as active as they should be. In 2005, the National Center of Health Statistics (2005a) reported that only one-third of adults are physically active (vigorously active for 20 or more minutes at least five times a week) in their leisure time (see figure 12.4). CDC and the American College of Sports Medicine recommend adults engage in at least 30 minutes of moderate-intensity physical activity most days, if not every day, of the week. These levels will help to maintain a healthy weight and reduce risk for cardiovascular disease, type 2 diabetes, cancer, and death (Centers for Disease Control and Prevention, 2005).

All in all, it is important to know that many health risks are involved with extreme weights. Being overweight or obese, or underweight as we discuss next, can have serious affects on one's health. Maintaining a healthy diet and engaging in regular exercise can assist in obtaining a healthy weight. Women should be aware of their weight, their risks, and their health and should discuss these with their health care provider.

Striving for Thinness

Although there are numerous health risks associated with excess weight and obesity, there is a high societal priority placed on women's

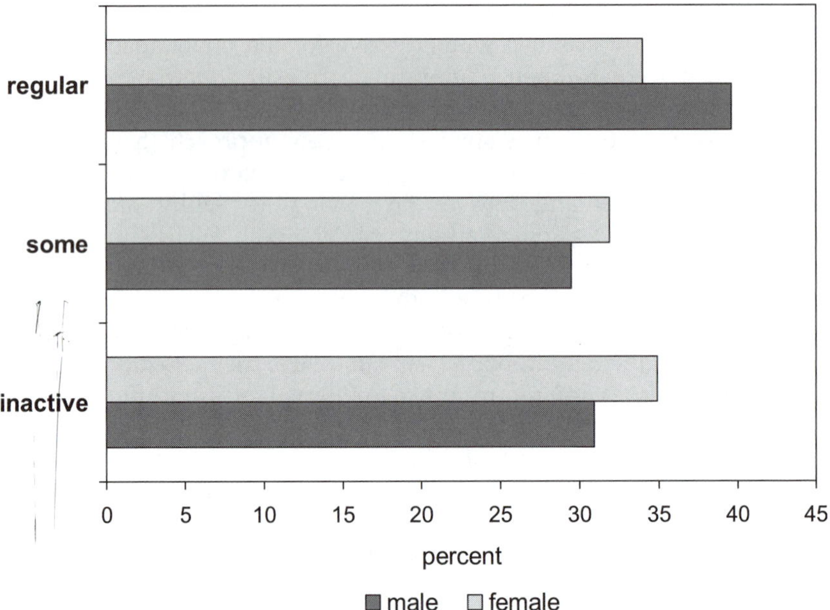

Figure 12.4. Percent reporting leisure time activity among respondents 18–44 years of age. Some leisure-time activity involved one episode of light or vigorous activity; regular activity involved vigorous activity of 20 minutes or five sessions per week. *Source:* Data are from the Health Interview Survey, National Center for Health Statistics, 2005a (table 72, p. 290).

thinness and attractiveness. Indeed, much of American culture and gender politics supports an objectification of women's bodies. Compared to men, women hold fewer professional or advanced degrees, typically have lower-prestige employment, and earn lower wages. Popular media systematically portray women as lacking authority in comparison to males and less able to control their external environments (Kilbourne, 2000). As a result, women may go to extravagant ends in hopes of gaining some control in their personal lives. Dieting and exercise may be a way to do this (Nichter, 2000). Studies of anorexia nervosa and bulimia nervosa suggest that women often alter their patterns of eating in hope of gaining a sense of control over themselves (Chesters, 1994).

Women may believe that thinness and beauty are interchangeable due to the standards that culture and society set. This can best be represented through our media. Over the years, slimness as a beauty ideal has been the subject of many advertisements, films, and books (Kilbourne, 2000). This commonality creates a cultural phenomenon in its own way. As a result, women may feel the need to transform their own appearance to meet a cultural ideal. Not surprisingly, eating disorders such as anorexia and bulimia have increased steadily over the past 30 years (Harrison & Cantor, 1997). Research suggests that the lifetime prevalence of anorexia for females is about 0.5 percent and for bulimia is 1–3 percent (American Psychiatric Association, 2000). In the United States, conservative estimates indicate that after puberty, 5 to 10 million girls and women are struggling with eating disorders, including anorexia, bulimia, binge eating disorder, or borderline conditions (Crowther, Tennenbaum, Hobfoll, & Stephens, 1992).

HEART DISEASE

For the last 50 years, heart disease has been the leading cause of death in the United States, for women as well as men, and it remains so today. That means more women die from some form of cardiovascular disease than die from all forms of cancer, liver disease, diabetes, or accidents. Common stereotypes hold that cardiovascular disease is more prevalent among men, but national data indicate that the numbers of women and of men hospitalized with cardiovascular disease have been relatively equal in recent years. Women are slightly *more* prevalent among hospital patients with any mention of heart disease, as illustrated in figure 12.5 (see annual reports of the National Hospital Discharge Survey, NHDS).

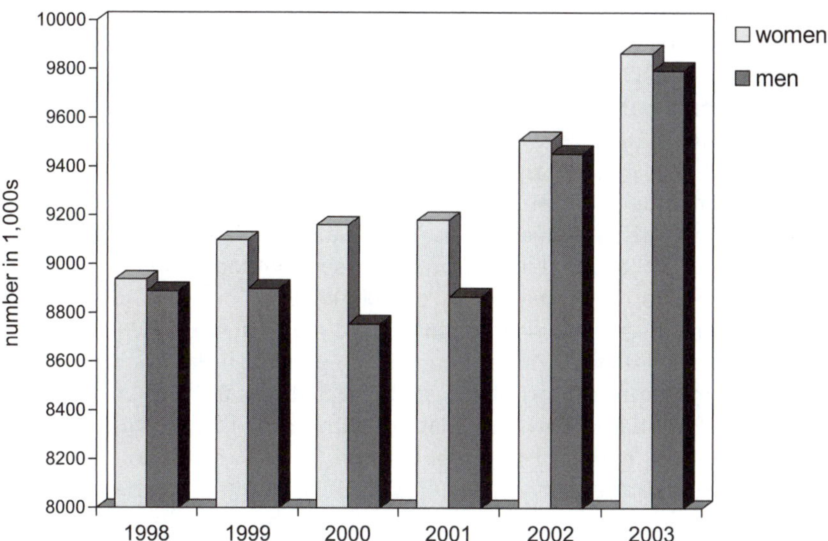

Figure 12.5. Number of hospital discharges for all listed diagnoses of heart disease by sex. *Source:* National Hospital Discharge Survey.

There is also the expectation that heart disease occurs only among older women and that relatively younger women in their 40s or 50s are not at risk. However, ischemic heart disease is the leading killer of women at all ages, with annual mortality rates that affect more women under the ages of 35, 45, and 55 years than breast cancer (Bell & Nappi, 2000). Among the 500,000 women patients hospitalized in 2000 and 2002 with a first-listed diagnosis of heart attack or acute or chronic ischemia (restricted blood flow to the heart), more than 20 percent were in their 40s or 50s.[7] Thus, relatively younger or premenopausal women may develop heart disease serious enough to require hospitalization.

A related stereotype is that heart disease among men is more serious and consequently that men are more likely to die from heart disease, whereas for women heart disease is generally milder and not as serious. However, data suggest otherwise. For example, women are less likely than men to survive hospitalization for a heart attack (acute myocardial infarction). The likelihood of death was higher for women than men among all individual patient data provided by the National Hospital Discharge Survey[8] for patients over 40 years of age admitted to hospitalizations having 300 or more beds. Among 237,000 patients hospitalized with an infarction in 2002, women had a 50 percent greater likelihood of dying than did men (OR = 1.53, CI: 1.48–1.57).

The single biggest risk factor for heart disease is smoking. Most other risk factors are also products of lifestyle. For example, eating habits that feature high-fat foods can lead to high cholesterol, and a sedentary lifestyle can contribute to hypertension. Having high-density cholesterol, often referred to as "good cholesterol," that moves fairly readily from blood into cells is not a risk factor. Bad cholesterol is low density, does not readily escape the vascular system, and is more likely to clump and adhere to the walls of blood vessels. This can occur in the microvasculature as well as in major arteries of the heart.

Diabetes is a general risk factor for heart disease and for poor outcomes of treatment. Significantly, diabetes denotes a higher risk factor among women than it does among men, and women with diabetes are twice as likely to develop heart disease compared to nondiabetic women (Centers for Disease Control, 2004).

A seldom-discussed risk factor is the tendency for women as a group to be more susceptible than men to general inflammatory conditions and autoimmune problems such as arthritis and lupus. The generalized inflammatory process that contributes to these conditions can also affect the heart and vascular system. For example, to the extent that inflammation and irregularity occur in the lining of arterial walls, cholesterol may adhere and form plaque, which gradually narrows the artery and reduces blood and oxygen flow to the heart. Such reduced blood flow and oxygen deficit is termed *ischemia*, which may be acute or chronic.[9]

Blood tests can measure C-reactive protein as an indicator of general inflammatory levels throughout the body. C-reactive is effective in predicting risk of imminent heart attack (Burke et al., 2005). Annual blood screening can assess levels of C-reactive protein, along with various types of cholesterol and levels of triglycerides. A woman's individual risk for heart attack sometime within the next 10 years can be estimated using a short questionnaire checklist that includes information about C-reactive protein (American Heart Association, 2002). The checklist is available to download for free on the World Wide Web and is a good tool to have during discussions with a physician or regular physical exam. Points are added or subtracted to a total score, depending on levels of high-density and low-density cholesterol, C-reactive protein level, age, and other factors; accompanying guidelines allow individuals to interpret their total score in terms of risk of developing heart disease or having a major cardiovascular event within the next 10 years. Treatment guidelines about possible interventions are also provided.

How to best assess and evaluate heart disease among women has been the focus of the Women's Ischemia Syndrome Evaluation (WISE) Study sponsored by the National Heart, Lung, and Blood Institute (NHLBI), and data were collected from 1996 to 1999 (Bairey Merz et al., 1999, 2006). The study was prospective,[10] involved four medical centers around the country, and enrolled a total of 944 women with chest pain or symptoms suggestive of myocardial ischemia. Thus, conclusions of the study are most relevant for women who already have been diagnosed with some type of heart disease. The women underwent complete demographic, medical, and psychosocial history, physical examination, and coronary angiography testing; about a quarter were premenopausal. A key finding of the study has been that imaging of the heart blood vessels by angiography may not reveal blockages or the full extent of disease. Among some women, plaque may line arteries in a relatively even or smooth fashion, while the entire artery stretches evenly outward to accommodate it. One suggestion emerging from the study has been the possible benefits of magnetic resonance imaging (MRI) techniques that may be more suitable for women (Bairey Merz et al., 2006; Shaw et al., 2006).

Disparities in Heart Care

Access to care, diagnostic strategies, and preferred treatments appear to differ markedly by gender (Healy, 1991; Travis, Gressley, & Phillippi, 1993; Wenger, 1985, 1987). A number of studies suggest that these gender patterns are the result of biased decision making. Tobin and colleagues (1987) reported that abnormal diagnostic findings in nuclear exercise testing resulted in significantly more referrals for cardiac catheterization for men than women with similar abnormal signs. Another study reported that women in selected Maryland and Massachusetts hospitals were less likely to undergo diagnostic angiography or coronary artery revascularization than were men (Ayanian & Epstein, 1991). A similar study of patients enrolled in the Survival and Ventricular Enlargement Study for the years 1987–1990 (1,842 men, 389 women) found that the health care history of women prior to the initial myocardial infarction indicated a less aggressive management approach than that observed for men (Steingart et al., 1991).

But aren't "things different now"? As a partial answer to this question, detailed patient diagnoses and procedures were examined for trends from 1987 to 1998 (Travis, 2005). Coronary artery bypass grafts (CABG), commonly known as bypass surgery, were one marker by which to track issues of the quality of care and medical decision making with respect to gender. As diagnostic and surgical methods have become more widely available, bypass surgery has been increasingly viewed as useful, and treatment of heart disease has become more aggressive. This is particularly true for male patients. The most frequent and key diagnostic conditions associated with bypass surgery were chronic or acute ischemia, angina, and acute myocardial infarction (heart attack).

There has never been a particularly aggressive or active surgical approach to heart disease if the patient is female, even when a woman's medical conditions are similar to those of men who receive surgical treatment. For example, in 1987 among all patients having one of the key diagnoses for bypass, about 30 percent of men versus 14 percent of women received bypass surgery. Approximately 600,000 bypass surgeries were performed in 2000, an increase of about 83 percent over the number performed in 1987. The vast majority of these have been performed on men, illustrated in figure 12.6. Among patients with key diagnoses, more than 50 percent of men versus 27 percent of women had bypass surgery. These disparities are even greater among black women. The fact that similar disparities occur among black men as well as women of all ethnicities and color indicate that the phenomenon is not due simply to gender-based differences in anatomy or physiology (Travis, 2004).

UNDERSTANDING BREAST CANCER

Cancer is the second leading cause of death in the United States, and approximately half a million deaths are attributed to cancer each year (Miniño, Heron, & Smith, 2006). However, many more people live with cancer or have had a diagnosis of cancer at some time in their life, about 15 million in any given year, or roughly 7 percent of the entire U.S. population (Lethbridge-Çejku, Rose, & Vickerie, 2004). Over

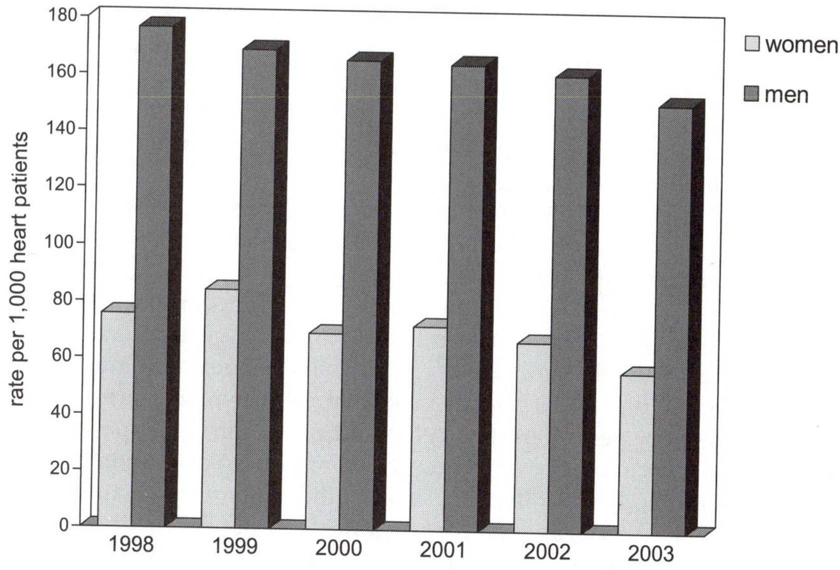

Figure 12.6. Rate of bypass surgery per 1,000 first-listed cases of heart disease by sex. *Source:* National Hospital Discharge Survey.

the course of a lifetime, a little more than a third of all women will have a diagnosis of some form of cancer (Ries et al., 2006). There is a great dread of breast cancer, partly because any diagnosis of cancer is seen as a death sentence, but in fact a high percentage of women live quite full lives despite having a diagnosis. About 88 percent of women will survive five or more years, and if the cancer is in situ[11] at the time of diagnosis, 100 percent of the women will survive five or more years (Ries et al., 2006). Treatments for breast cancer are continually developing and will not be described here. Instead we concentrate on understanding cancer biology and some of the risks.

Cancer Biology

Although one might commonly think of cancer as a single entity, such as a tumor, it is better understood as a process involving the actions of many different types of cells and messenger substances, that is, a constellation of genes, cells, and the communication pathways between them. The development of cancer (carcinogenesis) typically requires genetic changes that affect cell function. These errors may occur at several points in the genes and communication pathways. Errors early in the process might have the effect of "initiating" a cell, but these errors must accumulate before a cell becomes transformed to frankly cancerous. Changes throughout the cancer process might involve the increased frequency of cell division (proliferation), an impaired ability to repair errors, or the failure of immature (stem) cells to develop into functioning mature cells that can perform functions in an organ. Later errors in the cancer process might involve a reduced likelihood that a flawed cell will have the ability to shrink, fragment, or otherwise deactivate itself (apoptosis).

The cancer process ultimately will involve genetic mutations (mutagenesis); this is true even for individuals with no family history or genetic precursors for cancer. Genes are part of the DNA residing in the nucleus of a cell; they influence not only appearance (e.g., eye color) but also functions such as cell growth. Some gene mutations are heritable and passed from parent to child, that is, germline mutations. These germline mutations appear in special cells involved in reproduction (i.e., egg or sperm germline cells) and occur during a special type of cell division called *meiosis*. These germline mutations appear in every cell of the bodies of offspring. Many other mutations occur in general cells of the body and take place during general cell division, or *mitosis*. These general errors occur hither and thither in individual cells. Every time any cell divides, there is a window of opportunity for genetic alterations.

Mutations can take several forms (e.g., deletions, breakage, insertions of extra components or adducts, amplification of existing genes, or the translocation crossover of genetic material between chromosomes). Some genes act to suppress cell growth, while others contribute to DNA repair; changes in the function of these genes can easily contribute to cancer. Changes or errors may impair cell function or communication pathways external to the cell (e.g., hormones). Errors in a communication pathway include a cell not being able to receive needed messages, messages not being sent at all, or the wrong messages being sent. The communication pathway may be impaired because something needed to activate a gene (phosphorylate) has been blocked and can no longer attach or communicate with the cell. An example of this blocking was discussed earlier to describe insulin insensitivity.

One hypothesis suggests that individuals with an inherited (germline) mutation that is present in every cell of the body may have initiated cancer cells after only one additional mutation to any cell (Knudson, 1971).[12] This partially explains why individuals with inherited mutations are more likely to develop cancer at a younger age: They are born with one strike against them and thus start life further along a cancer pathway. Cancers without inherited germline mutations are likely to be based on a number of alterations in several different genes. It is unlikely that a single error, or even two or three errors, will produce cancer.

To a certain degree, the body has the capacity to repair or otherwise cope with errors. Some errors may be repaired through the immune system (e.g., macrophages), by removal of the sources of harmful messages (e.g., losing fat), or by deactivation of the affected cells themselves (apoptosis). However, virtually all cells divide and multiply on a regular basis, and as they do so, they replicate any errors so that new cells are also flawed. In fact, with each cell division, there is an increasing chance for initial errors to have cascading effects so that additional alterations may occur. This replication of existing errors is the second major component of the cancer process and is commonly termed *cell proliferation* or *cancer promotion*. Thus, anything that tends to increase or accelerate cell division beyond normal rates is typically correlated positively with cancer and often is termed a *cancer promoter*.

Since changes in communication pathways, in genes, and in cell activity are multifaceted and occur over time in a cascading manner, the single largest risk factor for cancer is time, that is, age. According to the Surveillance, Epidemiology, and End Results (SEER) review of cancer statistics, the majority of cancers occur in people over 50 years of age (Ries et al., 2006). Age is a major risk factor for cancer primarily because it reflects the opportunity for thousands of cell divisions and the accumulation of various glitches or errors in genes and communication pathways. In general, the types of cells that divide most frequently as part of normal bodily function are also the cells most vulnerable to cancer. For example, cells that line the colon (a type of epithelial cell) need to be replaced frequently, and cells in the colon divide and multiply accordingly.

Breast Cancer Risks

Genetic

As with almost all fatal diseases in the United States, age is the greatest risk factor for breast cancer. In addition to age, a family history that includes an inherited genetic germline mutation adds significantly to the risk. Typically a "family history" of cancer is given more weight if it involves first-degree relatives, for example, mother or sisters. More than 70 genes have been associated with the prognosis (outcome) of breast cancer. Research to assess the information value of this complex gene profile has been conducted in the Netherlands (Buyse et al., 2006) and is reported to offer a better prediction about survival without recurrence than is possible with basic clinical factors. Prognosis based solely on gross clinical factors looks at patient age, tumor size, lymph system involvement, and estrogen receptor status (Ravdin et al., 2001). The Adjuvant! computerized software tool is based on these and other clinical factors for estimating prognosis and is available online (www.adjuvantonline.com). However, most genetic research on cancer has involved research on the risk of getting cancer in the first place.

Genes associated with breast cancer susceptibility include BRCA1 (located on chromosome 17) and BRCA2 (chromosome 13).[13] The general function of these genes is still being researched, but is thought to influence DNA repair, gene stability, and overall orderly development and transition of breast stem cells to functioning cells in the breast (Foulkes, 2004; Reynolds, 2001; Starita & Parvin, 2003). The normal function of BRCA1 may be as a tumor suppressor gene that detects and promotes repair of damaged DNA (Tan, Zheng, Lee, & Boyer, 2004). Thus, having a healthy BRCA1 gene is a good thing.

Problems arise when mutations to this gene interfere with its normal function. Mutations to these genes may be inherited, but more rarely may occur by any of the random errors that occur during any cell division. Only 5–10 percent of breast cancer cases are found to have an inherited (germline) mutation in BRCA1 or BRCA2, and if one has an inherited mutation to this gene, the risk of breast cancer is more than double the risk for an average person (Antoniou et al., 2003; Malone, Daling, Thompson, O'Brien, Francisco, & Ostrander, 1998; Newman, Mu, Butler, Millikan, Moorman, & King, 1998). Women who have inherited mutations in these genes are likely to have a number of close relatives who have breast or ovarian cancer. A review of studies assessing the risk of breast cancer among women with a BRCA1 mutation suggests roughly a 65 percent risk of a diagnosis of breast cancer by age 70. The risk is elevated, but not quite as high, if there is a BRCA2 mutation (Antoniou et al., 2003). In contrast, the lifetime risk of breast cancer for all women is approximately 1 in 8 women or about 13 percent.

Age is the key to understanding the implications of "family history" as an indication of an *inherited* genetic mutation (Newman et al., 1998). Typically, when there is an inherited genetic mutation, it is more probably that cancer will have developed prior to menopause among relatives (Malone et al., 1998). Thus, family history alone is not good evidence of an inherited genetic risk of cancer. For example, if Aunt Em develops breast cancer at age 75, it has little implication about the risk for other relatives. On the other hand, if she develops breast cancer at age 35, there is more reason for concern.

Estrogen

The natural history of breast cancer is firmly linked with exposure to estrogen; this may be endogenous estrogens produced in the body, exogenous estrogens in pharmaceutical treatments, or estrogen-like substances associated with environmental toxins. The initial links between the lifetime dose of estrogen and risk of breast cancer can be seen most simply in the fact that women with early menarche (prior to age 11; Pike, Henderson, & Casagrande, 1981) or those with late menopause (after age 55; Trichopoulos, MacMahon, & Cole, 1972) have a greater exposure to estrogen over the course of their lifetimes and also have a higher incidence of breast cancer. Additionally, large-scale prospective longitudinal studies conducted through the Nurses' Health Study[14] have found that women with higher levels of estrogen in the blood are over time more likely to develop breast cancer; this is true for both postmenopausal (Missmer, Eliassen, Barbieri, & Hankinson, 2004) and premenopausal women (Eliassen et al., 2006). Women with the highest quartile of circulating sex steroids had two to three times the risk of breast cancer in comparison to women in the lowest quartile. Cancers among those women with higher levels of circulating estrogen also were more likely to be invasive rather than in situ.

Exogenous estrogens supplied through hormone replacement therapy among menopausal women have similar increased risks for breast cancer. This general association was documented a generation ago by Jick and colleagues (1980) in an epidemiological study. More recent research has continued to document an increased risk of exogenous estrogens and breast cancer. A national study known as the Women's Health Initiative and developed by the National Institutes of Health followed 16,000 women over the age of 50 for five years. Those who received replacement hormones had approximately a 25 percent greater likelihood of developing breast cancer in comparison to randomly assigned women who received only placebos (Chlebowski et al., 2003). Other recent studies have supported the increased risk (Barlow et al., 2006; McPherson, 2004; Million Women Study Collaborators, 2003; Writing Group for the Women's Health Initiative Investigators, 2002).

The biological mechanisms by which extra estrogen might induce cancer are closely related to the general biology of carcinogenesis discussed earlier. The natural role of estrogen in the body is to promote cell division and growth. This necessary component of human reproduction is part of the monthly menstrual cycle and affects breast as well as uterine tissue. Unfortunately, tissues that go through frequent cell division and growth have a greater baseline risk of incurring a series of errors in cell genes and gene-to-gene communication pathways.

The risk of uterine cancer due to replacement estrogens can be reduced to some extent by the inclusion of progestins that induce a menstrual cycle. The progestins induce menstruation, when flawed cells of the lining of the endometrium are sloughed off, but there is no similar sloughing process of flawed cells in breast tissue. Since replacement estrogen increases cell division and proliferation, it technically falls in the category of a cancer promoter. Estrogen does not necessarily *cause* errors or mutations, but it does result in an increased number of any cells that happen to have mutations, as depicted in figure 12.7.

Despite the historical and contemporary research documenting the role of estrogen in carcinogenesis, there remains a stunning promotion

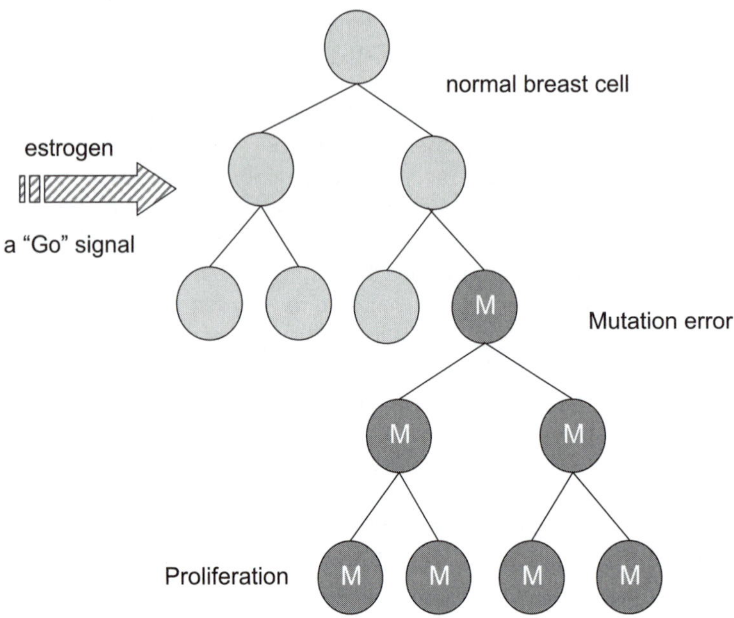

Figure 12.7. Estrogen promotion of cell division and the proliferation of cell mutations.

of the benefits and uses of estrogen supplements. The ostensible benefits of estrogen supplements for other health conditions such as Alzheimer's disease, migraines, and osteoporosis are based on mixed and conflicting studies and are seldom based on clinical trials with random assignment of participants to treatment or control groups. The touting of estrogen benefits for these other health conditions often ignores other more effective treatments that do not include estrogen. Yet, newspaper stories continue to appear with suggestions as to the potential benefits of estrogen, and general medical practitioners continue to discuss with women "safe" approaches to estrogen replacement. Typical recommendations are to use the smallest effective dose for the particular woman in order to transition through menopause and to take supplements for a "short" period of time as a way to control hot flashes and other menopausal symptoms. What women may not understand is that estrogen supplements may delay menopausal symptoms, but going off estrogen supplements is likely to provoke a return to the very symptoms they hoped to avoid. Hot flashes, sweats, flushes, and sleep disturbance are not pleasant and, if very frequent, can be disruptive. On the other hand, it would be so much more disruptive to be scheduling one's next chemotherapy or radiation treatment.

NOTES

1. Medicaid is available to individuals in poverty who are younger than age 65, while Medicare is available nationally to all individuals over age 65.

2. In 1849, Elizabeth Blackwell was the first woman to receive a doctor of medicine degree, from Geneva Medical College in New York.

3. Birthweight less than 5 pounds, 8 ounces (2.5 kilograms).

4. Asian American, American Indian, Aleut, Alaska native, and so forth.

5. Hispanic is considered an ethnicity rather than a racial designation, thus there may be Hispanic whites, non-Hispanic whites, Hispanic blacks, non-Hispanic blacks, and so on.

6. Prostaglandins occur naturally in the body and are thought to be responsible for the common experience of menstrual cramps.

7. These data are from my ongoing unpublished work on women and heart disease.

8. See Travis (2005) for more details on the individualized records of the National Hospital Discharge Survey.

9. *Ischemia* refers to any reduction in blood flow and also occurs as transient ischemia associated with minor strokes.

10. Followed the same patients for several years.

11. Meaning in a localized area without involvement of lymph nodes.

12. Knudson (1971) studied inherited retinoblastoma in children.

13. The acronyms are short for BReast CAncer 1 and 2 and usually pronounced "brack."

14. The Nurses' Health Study II was established in 1989 and recruited 116,609 female registered nurses, ages 25–42. This group has been followed biennially by questionnaire and in some cases giving blood samples.

REFERENCES

Allan, J. D. (1994). A biomedical and feminist perspective on women's experiences with weight management. *Western Journal of Nursing Research, 16,* 524–543.

American Heart Association. (2002). Adult Treatment Panel III guidelines for women. Retrieved August 20, 2006, from http://www.postgradmed.com/issues/2002/08_02/pearl_tables.htm.

American Psychiatric Association (2000). *Diagnostic and statistical manual of mental disorders* (4th ed., TR). Washington, DC: American Psychiatric Association.

Antoniou, A., Pharoah, P. D. P., Narod, S., Risch, H. A., Eyfjord, J. E., Hopper, J. L., et al. (2003). Average risks of breast and ovarian cancer associated with BRCA1 or BRCA2 mutations detected in case series unselected for family history: A combined analysis of 22 studies. *American Journal of Human Genetics, 72,* 1117–1130.

Ayanian, J. Z., & Epstein, A. M. (1991). Differences in the use of procedures between women and men hospitalized for coronary heart disease. *New England Journal of Medicine, 325(4),* 221–225.

Bairey Merz, C. N., Kelsey, S. F., Pepine, C. J., Reichek, N., Reis, S. E., Rogers, B. J., et al., for the WISE Study Group. (1999). The Women's Ischemia

Syndrome Evaluation (WISE) Study: Protocol design, methodology and feasibility report. *Journal of the American College of Cardiology, 33*, 1453–1461.

Bairey Merz, C. N., Shaw, L. J., Reis, S. E., Bittner, V., Kelsey, S. F., Olson, M., et al., for the WISE Investigators (2006). Insights from the NHLBI-sponsored Women's Ischemia Syndrome Evaluation (WISE) Study Part II: Gender differences in presentation, diagnosis, and outcome with regard to gender-based pathophysiology of atherosclerosis and macrovascular and microvascular coronary disease. *Journal of the American College of Cardiology, 47*(3) Suppl S., S21–S29.

Barlow, W. E., White, E., Ballard-Barbash, R., Vacek, P. M., Titus-Ernstoff, L., Carney, P. A., et al. (2006). Prospective breast cancer risk prediction model for women undergoing screening mammography. *Journal of the National Cancer Institute, 98*, 1204–1214.

Beckman, L. J., & Harvey, M. S. (1997). Experience and acceptability of mifepristone and misoprostol among U.S. women. *Women's Health Issues, 7*, 253–262.

Beckman, L. J., & Harvey, M. S. (1998). The acceptability of medical abortion to women. In L. J. Beckman & M. S. Harvey (Eds.), *The new civil war: The psychology, culture, and politics of abortion* (pp. 189–209). Washington, DC: American Psychological Association.

Bell, D. M., & Nappi, J. (2000). Myocardial infarction in women: A critical appraisal of gender differences in outcomes. *Pharmacotherapy, 20*, 1034–1044.

Bender, R., Zeeb, H., Schwarz, M., Jockeli, K. H., & Berger, M. (2006). Causes of death in obesity: Relevant increase in cardiovascular but not in all-cancer mortality. *Journal of Clinical Epidemiology, 59*, 1064–1071.

Berg, F. M. (1994). America gains weight. *Healthy Weight Journal, 8*, 107–110.

Boles, S. M., & Johnson, P. B. (2001). Gender, weight concerns, and adolescent smoking. *Journal of Addictive Diseases, 20*, 5–14.

Boston Women's Health Book Collective. (2005). *Our bodies, ourselves*. New York: Simon & Schuster.

Bouchard, M. F., Taniguchi, H., & Viger, R. S. (2005). Protein kinase a-dependent synergism between gata factors and the nuclear receptor, liver receptor homolog-1, regulates human aromatase (cyp19) pii promoter activity in breast cancer cells. *Endocrinology, 146*(11), 4905–4916.

Burke, G. L., Polak, J. F., Tracy, R. P., Cushman, M., Arnold, A. M., Psaty, B. M., et al. (2005). C-Reactive protein and the 10-year incidence of coronary heart disease in older men and women: The Cardiovascular Health Study. *Circulation, 112*, 25–31.

Buyse, M., Loi, S., Veer, L. V., Viale, G., Delorenzi, M., Glas, A. M., et al. (2006). Validation and clinical utility of a 70-gene prognostic signature for women with node-negative breast cancer. *Journal of the National Cancer Institute, 98*, 1183–1192.

Camargo, C. A., Weiss, S. T., Zhang, S., Willett, W. C., & Speizer, F. E. (1999). Prospective study of Body Mass Index, weight change, and risk of adult-onset asthma in women. *Archives of Internal Medicine, 159*, 2582–2588.

Centers for Disease Control and Prevention [CDC] (1997). Abortion surveillance preliminary data: United States, 1994. *Morbidity and Mortality Weekly Report, 45*(51–52), 1123–1127.

Centers for Disease Control and Prevention. (2002). Assisted reproductive technology success rates: National summary and fertility clinics reports. [Updates are posted at http://www.cdc.gov//ART/index.htm.]

Centers for Disease Control and Prevention. (2004). The burden of chronic diseases and their risk factors: National and state perspectives, 2004. Atlanta: U.S. Department of Health and Human Services. Available at http://www.cdc.gov/nccdphp/burdenbook2004.

Centers for Disease Control and Prevention. (2005). Adult participation in recommended levels of physical activity: United States, 2001 and 2003. *Morbidity and Mortality Weekly Report, 54*, 1208–1212.

Centers for Disease Control and Prevention. (2006a). Abortion surveillance: United States, 2003. *Morbidity and Mortality Weekly Report, 55*(SS-11).

Centers for Disease Control and Prevention. (2006b). About BMI for adults. Retrieved on September 4, 2006, from http://www.cdc.gov/nccdphp/dnpa/bmi/adult_BMI/about_adult_BMI.htm.

Chesters, L. (1994). Women's talk: Food, weight, and body image. *Feminism and Psychology, 4*, 449–457.

Chlebowski, R. T., Hendrix, S. L., Langer, R. D., Stefanick, M. L., Gass, M., Lane, D., et al. (2003). Influence of estrogen plus progestin on breast cancer and mammography in healthy postmenopausal women: The Women's Health Initiative randomized trial. *Journal of the American Medical Association, 289*, 3243–3253.

Cohen, R. A., & Martinez, M. E. (2006). Health insurance coverage: Early release of estimates from the National Health Interview Survey, January–June 2006. Retrieved January 21, 2007, from http://www.cdc.gov/nchs/nhis.htm.

Corea, G. (1977). *The hidden malpractice*. New York: Jove.

Crowther, J. H., Tennenbaum, D. L., Hobfoll, S. E., & Stephens, M. A. P. (1992). *The etiology of bulimia nervosa: The individual and familial context*. Washington, DC: Hemisphere.

Cushman, M., Arnold, A. M., Psaty, B. M., Manolio, T. A., Kuller, L. H., Burke, G. L., et al. (2005). C-reactive protein and the 10-year incidence of coronary heart disease in older men and women: The Cardiovascular Health Study. *Circulation, 112*(1), 25–31.

Daly, M. (1978). *Gyn/ecology*. Boston: Beacon Press.

DeNavas-Walt, C., Proctor, B. D., & Lee, C. H. (2006). *Income, poverty, and health insurance coverage in the United States: 2005*. Current Population Reports, P60-231. Washington, DC: U.S. Census Bureau.

Dreifus, C. (Ed.). (1977). *Seizing our bodies*. New York: Random House.

Dugger, K. (1998). Black women and the question of abortion. In L. J. Beckman & S. M. Harvey (Eds.), *The new civil war: The psychology, culture, and politics of abortion* (pp. 107–132). Washington, DC: American Psychological Association.

Ehrenreich, B., & English, D. (1973). *Complaints and disorders*. Glass Mountain Pamphlet No. 2. New York: Feminist Press.

Elam-Evans, L. D., Strauss, L. T., Herndon, J., Parker, W. Y., Bowens, S. V., Zane, S., et al. (2003). Abortion surveillance: United States, 2000. *Morbidity and Mortality Weekly Report, 53*(SS-12), 1–32.

Eliassen, A. H., Colditz, G. A., Rosner, B., Willett, W. C., & Hankinson, S. E. (2006). Adult weight change and risk of postmenopausal breast cancer. *Journal of the American Medical Association, 296*, 193–201.

Eliassen, A. H., Missmer, S. A., Tworoger, S. S., Spiegelman, D., Barbieri, R. L., Dowsett, M., et al. (2006). Endogenous steroid hormone concentrations and risk of breast cancer among premenopausal women. *Journal of the National Cancer Institute, 98*, 1406–1415.

Ellertson, C., Trussell, J., Stewart, F., & Winikoff, B. (1998). Should emergency contraceptive pills be available without prescription? *Journal of the American Medical Women's Association, 53*(Suppl. 2), 226–229, 232.

Finer, L. B., Frohwirth, L. F., Dauphinee, L. A., Singh, S., & Moore, A. (2005). Reasons U.S. women have abortions: Quantitative and qualitative perspectives. *Perspectives on Sexual and Reproductive Health, 37*(3), 110–118.

Ford, E. S., Giles, W. H., & Dietz, W. H. (2002). Prevalence of the metabolic syndrome among US adults: Findings from the Third National Health and Nutrition Examination Survey. *Journal of the American Medical Association, 287*, 356–359.

Foulkes, W. D. (2004). BRCA1 functions as a breast stem cell regulator. *Journal of Medical Genetics, 41*, 1–5.

Garceau, L., Henderson, J., Davis, L. J., Petrou, S., Henderson, L. R., McVeigh, E., et al. (2002). Economic implications of assisted reproductive techniques: A systematic review. *Human Reproduction, 17*(12), 3090–3109.

Gordon, T., Castelli, W. P., Kjortland, M. C., Kannel, W. B., & Dawber, T. R. (1977). Diabetes, blood lipids, and the role of obesity in coronary heart disease risk for women: The Framingham study. *Annals of Internal Medicine, 87*(4), 393–397.

Grimes, D. A., Raymond, E. G., & Scott Jones, B. (2001). Emergency contraception over-the-counter: The medical and legal imperatives. *Obstetrics and Gynecology, 98*, 151–155.

Grundy, S. M., Cleeman, J. I., Daniels, S. R., Donato, K. A., Eckel, R. H., Franklin, B. A., et al. (2005). Diagnosis and management of the metabolic syndrome: An American Heart Association/National Heart, Lung, and Blood Institute Scientific statement. *Circulation, 112*(17), 2735–2752.

Guttmacher Institute. (2005). Advocates question Plan B age restriction after FDA again delays decision. *Guttmacher Report on Public Policy, 8*(4). Retrieved January 16, 2007, from http://www.guttmacher.org/pubs/tgr/08/4/gr080412.html.

Guttmacher Institute. (2006a). Facts on induced abortion in the United States. Retrieved June 4, 2007, from http://www.guttmacher.org/pubs/fb_induced_abortion.pdf.

Guttmacher Institute. (2006b). U.S. teenage pregnancy statistics: National and state trends and trends by race and ethnicity. Retrieved June 4, 2007, from http://www.guttmacher.org/pubs/2006/09/12/USTPstats.pdf.

Hall, W. D., Clark, L. T., Wenger, N. K., Wright, J. T., Kumanyika, S. K., Watson, K., et al. (2003). The metabolic syndrome in African Americans: A review. *Ethnicity and Disease, 13*, 414–428.

Harrison, K., & Cantor, J. (1997). The relationship between media consumption and eating disorders. *Journal of Communication, 47*, 40–67.

Healy, B. (1991). The yentl syndrome. *New England Journal of Medicine, 325*, 274–276.

Heffler, S., Smith, S., Won, G., Clemens, M. K., Keehan, S., & Zezza, M. (2002). Health spending projections for 2001–2011: The latest outlook. *Health Affairs, 21*(2), 207–218.

Hercus, C. (2005). *Stepping out of line: Becoming and being feminist*. New York: Routledge.

Hu, F. B. (2003). Overweight and obesity in women: Health risks and consequences. *Journal of Women's Health, 12*, 163–172.

Huon, G., & Brown, L. B. (1984). Psychological correlates of weight control among anorexia nervosa patients and normal girls. *British Journal of Medical Psychology, 57*, 61–66.

Hutchison, L. (1986). A radical feminist perspective. In M. Bricker-Jenkins and N. R. Hooyman (Eds.), *Not for women only: Social work practice for a feminist future* (pp. 53–57). Silver Spring, MD: National Association of Social Workers.

Hyde, J. (2006). *Half the human experience.* New York: Houghton Mifflin.

Iyasu, S., Tomashek, K., & Barfield, W. (2002). Infant mortality and low birth weight among black and white infants: United States, 1980–2000, *Morbidity and Mortality Weekly Report 51*(27), 589–592.

Jee, S. H., Sull, J. W., Park, J., Lee, S. Y., Ohrr, H., Guallar, E., et al. (2006). Body-Mass Index and mortality in Korean men and women. *New England Journal of Medicine, 355*, 758–760.

Jick, H., Walker, A. M., Watkins, R. N., D'Ewart, D. C., Hunter, J. R., Danford, A., et al. (1980). Replacement estrogens and breast cancer. *American Journal of Epidemiology, 112*, 586–594.

Johnson, A. G. (1997). *The gender knot: Unraveling our patriarchal legacy*. Philadelphia: Temple University Press.

Kaiser Family Foundation. (2003). Women's health care providers experiences with emergency contraception. Retrieved January 16, 2007, from http://www.kff.org/womenshealth/3343-index.cfm.

Kern, P. A., Saghizadeh, M., Ong, J. M., Boasch, R. J., Deem, R., & Simisolo, R. B. (1995). The expression of tumor necrosis factor in human adipose tissue regulation by obesity, weight loss, and relationship to lipoprotein lipase. *Journal of Clinical Investigation, 95*, 2111–2119.

Kilbourne, J. (2000). *Killing us softly 3: Advertising's image of women*. Northampton, MA: Media Education Foundation.

Kirschstein, R. L., & Merritt, D. H. (1985). *Women's health: Report of the Public Health Service Task Force on Women's Health Issues.* Washington, DC: Public Health Service.

Knudson, A. G. (1971). Mutation and cancer: Statistical study of retinoblastoma. *Proceedings of the National Academy of Sciences, 68*, 820–823.

Leatherman, S., & McCarthy, D. (2002). *Quality of care in the United States: A chartbook*. No. 520. New York: Commonwealth Fund.

Lethbridge-Çejku, M., Rose, D., & Vickerie, J. (2004). Summary health statistics for U.S. adults: National Health Interview Survey, 2004. *Vital Health Statistics, 10*(228).

Lewis, J., & Shimabukuro, J. O. (2001) Abortion law development: A brief overview. *Almanac of Policy Issues*. Retrieved January 20, 2007, from http://www.policyalmanac.org/culture/archive/crs_abortion_overview.shtml.

Löfgren, P., van Harmelen, V., Reynisdottir, S., Näslund, E., Rydén, M., Rössner, S., et al. (2000). Secretion of tumor necrosis factor shows a strong relationship to insulin-stimulated glucose transport in human adipose tissue. *Diabetes, 49*, 688–692.

Luder, E., Ehrlich, R. I., Lou, W. Y. W., Melnik, T. A., & Kattan, M. (2004). Body Mass Index and the risk of asthma in adults. *Respiratory Medicine, 98*(1), 29–37.

Malone, K. E., Daling, J. R., Thompson, J. D., O'Brien, C. A., Francisco, L. V., & Ostrander, E. A. (1998). BRCA1 mutations and breast cancer in the general population: Analyses in women before age 35 years and in women before age 45 years with first-degree family history. *Journal of the American Medical Association, 279*(12), 922–929.

Manson, J. E., & Spelsberg, A. (1996). Risk modification in the diabetic patient. In J. E. Manson, P. M. Ridker, J. M. Gaziano, and C. H. Hennekens (Eds.), *Prevention of myocardial infarction* (pp. 241–263). New York: Oxford University Press.

Marieskind, H. (1980). *Women in the health system*. St. Louis: C. V. Mosby.

Martin, J., Hamilton, B., Sutton P., Ventura, S., Menacker, F., & Munson, M. (2005). Births: Final data for 2003. *National Vital Statistics Reports, 54*(2).

McKeever, T. M., Weston, P. J., Hubbard, R., & Fogarty, A. (2005). Lung function and glucose metabolism: An analysis of data from the third National Health and Nutrition Examination Survey. *American Journal of Epidemiology, 161*(6), 546–556.

McPherson, K. (2004). Where are we now with hormone replacement therapy? *British Medical Journal, 328*, 357–358.

McTigue, K. M., Harris, R., Hemphill, B., Lux, L., Sutton, S., Bunton, A. J., et al. (2003). Screening and interventions for obesity in adults: Summary of the evidence for the U.S. preventive services task force. *Annals of Internal Medicine, 139*, 933–949.

Michalopoulou, G., Alevizaki, M., Piperingos, G., Mitsibounas, D., Mantzos, E., Adamopoulos, P., et al. (1998). High serum cholesterol levels in persons with "high-normal" TSH levels: Should one extend the definition of subclinical hypothyroidism? *European Journal of Endocrinology, 138*, 141–145.

Miller, J., & Kuszelewicz, M. A. (1995). Women and AIDS: Feminist principles in practice. In N. Van Den Bergh (Ed.), *Feminist practice in the 21st century* (pp. 295–311). Washington, DC: NASW Press.

Million Women Study Collaborators. (2003). Breast cancer and hormone-replacement therapy in the Million Women Study. *Lancet, 362*, 419–427.

Miniño, A. M., Heron, M. P., & Smith, B. L. (2006). Deaths: Preliminary data for 2004. *National Vital Statistics Report, 154*(19).

Missmer, S. A., Eliassen, A. H., Barbieri, R. L., & Hankinson, S. E. (2004). Endogenous estrogen, androgen, and progesterone concentrations and breast cancer risk among postmenopausal women. *Journal of the National Cancer Institute, 96*, 1856–1865.

Momoh, C. (2006). *Female genital mutilation*. Oxford, England: Radcliffe.

Moore, E., Copeland, K. C., Parker, D., Burgin, C., & Blackett, P. R. (2006). Ethnic differences in fasting glucose, insulin resistance and lipid profiles in obese adolescents. *Journal of the Oklahoma State Medical Association, 99*, 439–443.

Mora, S., Lee, I. M., Buring, J. E., & Ridker, P. M. (2006). Association of physical activity and Body Mass Index with novel and traditional cardiovascular biomarkers in women. *Journal of the American Medical Association, 295*(12), 1412–1419.

Moran, L., & Norman, R. J. (2004). Understanding and managing disturbances in insulin metabolism and body weight in women with polycystic ovary syndrome: Best practices and research. *Clinical Obstetics & Gynaecology, 18*(5), 719–736.

National Center for Health Statistics. (1991). *Health, United States, 1990*. Hyattsville, MD: National Center for Health Statistics.

National Center for Health Statistics. (1996). *Health, United States, 1995*. Hyattsville, MD: National Center for Health Statistics.

National Center for Health Statistics. (1999). *Health, United States, 1999, with aging chart book*. Hyattsville, MD: National Center for Health Statistics.

National Center for Health Statistics. (2005a). *Health, United States, 2005*. Hyattsville, MD: National Center for Health Statistics.

Obesity, high blood pressure impacting many U.S. adults ages 55–64. Retrieved on October 24, 2006, from http://www.cdc.gov/nchs/pressroom/05news/hus05.htm.

Newman, B., Mu, H., Butler, L. M., Millikan, R. C., Moorman, P. G., & King, M. C. (1998). Frequency of breast cancer attributable to BRCA1 in a population-based series of American women. *Journal of the American Medical Association, 279*(12), 915–921.

Nichter, M. (2000). Fat talk: What girls and their parents say about dieting. *Psychology of Women Quarterly, 27*, 85–86.

Nielsen Company. (1979). Who is dieting and why? Chicago: A. C. Nielsen.

Novikova, N., Weisberg, E., Stanczyk, F. Z., Croxatto, H. B., & Fraser, I. S. (2007). Effectiveness of levonorgestrel emergency contraception given before or after ovulation: A pilot study. *Contraception 75*, in press.

Okasha, M., McCarron, P., McEwen, J., & Smith, D. G. (2002). Body Mass Index in young adulthood and cancer mortality: A retrospective study. *Journal of Epidemiology and Community Health, 56*, 780–784.

Pamuk, E., Makuc, D., Heck, K., Reuben, C., & Lochner, K. (1998). Socioeconomic status and health chartbook. In National Center for Health Statistics, *Health, United States, 1998*. Hyattsville, MD: National Center for Health Statistics.

Peeters, A., Barendregt, J. J., Willekens, F., Mackenbach, J. P., Al Mamun, A., & Bonneux, L. (2003). Obesity in adulthood and its consequences for life expectancy: A life-table analysis. *Annals of Internal Medicine, 138*, 24–32.

Pew Forum on Religion and Public Life. (2005). Abortion seen as most important issue for Supreme Court. Retrieved January 20, 2007, from http://pewforum.org/docs/index.php?DocID=127.

Pew Forum on Religion and Public Life. (2006). Most want middle ground on abortion: Pragmatic Americans liberal *and* conservative on social issues. Retrieved January 20, 2007, from http://pewforum.org/publications/surveys/social-issues-06.pdf.

Pietrobelli, A., Lee, R. C., Capristo, E., Deckelbaum, R. J., & Heymsfield, S. B. (1999). An independent, inverse association of high-density-lipoproteincholesterol concentration with nonadipose body mass. *American Journal Clinical Nutrition, 69*, 614–620.

Polednak, A. P. (2004). Racial differences in mortality from obesity-related chronic diseases in US women diagnosed with breast cancer. *Ethnicity and Disease, 14*, 463–468.

Rainwater, L. (1960). *And the poor get children: Sex, contraception, and family planning in the working class.* Chicago: Quadrangle Books.

Ramos, G. A., & Caughey, A. B. (2005). The interrelationship between ethnicity and obesity on obstetric outcomes. *American Journal of Obstetrics and Gynecology, 193*, 1089–1093.

Ravdin, P. M., Siminoff, L. A., Davis, G. J., Mercer, M. B., Hewlett, J., Gerson, N., et al. (2001). Computer program to assist in making decisions about adjuvant therapy for women with early breast cancer. *Journal of Clinical Oncology, 19*, 980–991.

Reynolds, T. (2001). BRCA1: Lessons learned from the breast cancer gene. *Journal of the National Cancer Institute, 93*(16), 1200–1202.

Ridker, P. M., Cushman, M., Stampfer, M. J., Tracey, R. P., & Hennekens, C. H. (1997). Inflammation, aspirin, and the risk of cardiovascular disease in apparently healthy men. *New England Journal of Medicine, 336*(14), 973–980.

Ries, L. A. G., Harkins, D., Krapcho, M., Mariotto, A., Miller, B. A., Feuer, E. J., et al. (Eds.). (2006). *SEER cancer statistics review, 1975–2003.* Bethesda, MD: National Cancer Institute. Available at http://seer.cancer.gov/csr/1975_2003/.

Robison, J. (2003). Health at every size: Antidote for the "obesity epidemic." *Healthy Weight Journal, 17*, 4–8.

Rossi, Alice S. (Ed.). (1973), *The feminist papers: From Adams to de Beauvoir.* New York: Columbia University Press.

Ruzek, S. (1978). *The women's health movement.* New York: Praeger.

Sandelowski, M. (1981). Women, health, and choice. Englewood Cliffs, NJ: Prentice-Hall.

School of Mathematics and Statistics. University of St. Andrews, Scotland. (2006). Lambert Adolphe Jacques Quetelet (1796–1874). *MacTutor History of Mathematics Archive.* Retrieved September 4, 2006, from http://www-history.mcs.st-andrews.ac.uk/Mathematicians/Quetelet.html.

Schulken, E. D., Pinciaro, P. J., Sawyer, R. G., Jensen, J. G., & Hoban, M. T. (1997). Sorority women's body size perceptions and their weight-related attitudes and behaviors. *Journal of American College Health, 46*, 69–74.

Scully, D. (1980). *Men who control women's health.* Boston: Houghton Mifflin.

Sengstock, D. M., Vaitkevicius, P. V., & Supiano, M. A. (2005). Arterial stiffness is related to insulin resistance in nondiabetic hypertensive older adults. *Journal of Clinical Endocrinology and Metabolism, 90*(5), 2823–2827.

Shaw, L. J., Bairey Merz, C. N., Pepine, C. J., Reis, S. E., Bittner, V., Kelsey, S. F., et al., for the WISE Investigators. (2006). Insights from the NHLBI-Sponsored Women's Ischemia Syndrome Evaluation (WISE) Study, part I: Gender differences in traditional and novel risk factors, symptom evaluation, and gender-optimized diagnostic strategies. *Journal of the American College of Cardiology, 47*(3) Suppl S., 4S–20S.

Siemens, E. M., & Clawson, R. A. (2004). The intersection of race and gender: An examination of black feminist consciousness, race consciousness, and policy attitudes. *Social Science Quarterly, 85*(3), 793–810.

Silverstein, L. B. (2006). Integrating feminism and multiculturalism: Scientific fact or science fiction? *Professional Psychology: Research and Practice, 37*, 21–28.

Singh, D. (1993). Adaptive significance of female physical attractiveness: Role of waist-to-hip ratio. *Journal of Personality and Social Psychology, 65*, 293–307.

Sofaer, S., & Abel, E. (1990). Older women's health and financial vulnerability: Implications of the Medicare benefit structure. *Women and Health, 16*(3/4), 47–67.

Starita, L. M, & Parvin, J. D. (2003). The multiple nuclear functions of BRCA1: Transcription, ubiquitination and DNA repair. *Current Opinion in Cell Biology, 15*, 345–350.

Steingart, R. M., Packer, M., Hamm, P., Coglianese, M. E., Gersh, B., Geltman, E. M., et al. (1991). Sex differences in the management of coronary artery disease: Survival and ventricular enlargement investigators. *New England Journal of Medicine, 325*(4), 226–230.

Stenius-Aarniala, B., Poussa, T., Kvarnstrom, J., Gronlund, E. L., Ylikahri, M., & Mustajoki, P. (2000). Immediate and long term effects of weight reduction in obese people with asthma: Randomized controlled study. *British Medical Journal (clinical research edition), 320*, 827–832.

Sturmer, T., Buring, J. E., Lee, I. M., Gaziano, J. M. & Glynn, R. J. (2006). Metabolic abnormalities and risk for colorectal cancer in the physicians' health study. *Cancer Epidemiol Biomarkers Preview, 12*, 2391–2397.

Tan, W., Zheng, L., Lee, W. H., & Boyer, T. G. (2004). Functional dissection of transcription factor ZBRK1 reveals zinc fingers with dual roles in DNA-binding and BRCA1-dependent transcriptional repression. *Journal of Biological Chemistry, 279*(8), 6576–6587.

Tobin, J. N., Wassertheil-Smoller, S., Wexler, J. P., Steingart, R. M., Budner, N., Lense, L., et al. (1987). Sex bias in considering coronary bypass surgery. *Annals of Internal Medicine, 107*, 19–25.

Travis, C. B. (1988a). *Women and health psychology: Biomedical issues*. Hillsdale, NJ: Erlbaum.

Travis, C. B. (1988b). *Women and health psychology: Mental health issues*. Hillsdale, NJ: Erlbaum.

Travis, C. B. (2004) The heart of a woman. Invited address at the annual meetings of the American Psychological Association, Honolulu, August.

Travis, C. B. (2005). Heart disease and gender inequity. *Psychology of Women Quarterly, 29*, 15–23.

Travis, C. B., & Compton, J. D. (2001). Feminism and health in the decade of behavior. *Psychology of Women Quarterly, 25*, 312–323.

Travis, C. B., Gressley, D. L., & Phillippi, R. H. (1993). Medical decision making, gender and coronary heart disease. *Journal of Women's Health, 2*(3), 269–279.

Trichopoulos, D., MacMahon, B., & Cole, P. (1972). Menopause and breast cancer risk. *Journal of the National Cancer Institute, 48*, 605.

Trussell, J., Ellertson, C., Stewart, F., Raymond, E. G., & Shochet, T. (2004). The role of emergency contraception. *American Journal of Obstetrics and Gynecology, 190*(4, Suppl. 1), S30–S38.

United Nations. (1948). Universal Declaration of Human Rights. General Assembly Resolution 217 A (III), December 10, 1948. Retrieved September 10, 2006, from http://www.un.org/Overview/rights.html.

United Nations. (1975). *Status of women and family planning*. New York: United Nations.

United Nations. (1979). Convention on the Elimination of All Forms of Discrimination against Women. Retrieved September 18, 2006, from http://www.un.org/womenwatch/daw/cedaw/cedaw.htm.

United Nations. (1995a). Fourth World Conference on Women: Beijing Declaration. Retrieved September 18, 2006, from http://www.un.org/womenwatch/daw/beijing/platform/declar.htm.

United Nations. (1995b). *Human development report, 1995.* New York: Oxford University Press.

United Nations. (2003). *World fertility report, 2003.* Retrieved August 27, 2006, from http://www.un.org/esa/population/publications/worldfertility/World_Fertility_Report.htm.

U.S. Census Bureau. (2006a). Table HI01. Health insurance coverage status and type of coverage by selected characteristics: 2005 all races. *Annual demographic survey, March supplement*. Retrieved January 21, 2007, from http://pubdb3.census.gov/macro/032006/health/h01_001.htm.

U.S. Census Bureau. (2006b). Table HI-1. Health insurance coverage status and type of coverage by sex, race and Hispanic origin: 1987 to 2005. *Historical health insurance tables*. Retrieved December 29, 2006, from http://www.census.gov/hhes/www/hlthins/historic/hihistt1.html.

U.S. Census Bureau. (2006c). Table HI08. Health insurance coverage status and type of coverage by selected characteristics for children under 18: 2005. *Annual demographic survey, March supplement*. Retrieved December 29, 2006, from http://pubdb3.census.gov/macro/032006/health/toc.htm.

U.S. Department of Health and Human Services. Health Resources and Services Administration. Maternal and Child Health Bureau. (2002). *Women's health USA, 2002*. Rockville, MD: U.S. Department of Health and Human Services. Available at http://mchb.hrsa.gov/whusa02/.

U.S. Department of Health and Human Services. (2004). *The health consequences of smoking: A report of the surgeon general, 2004.* Atlanta: Centers for Disease Control and Prevention, Office on Smoking and Health.

U.S. Department of Health and Human Services & U.S. Department of Agriculture. (2005). *Dietary guidelines for Americans, 2005* (6th ed.). Washington, DC: GPO. Available at http://www.health.gov/dietaryguidelines/.

Varraso, R., Siroux, V., Maccario, J., Pin, I., & Kauffmann, F., on behalf of the Epidemiological Study on the Gene (2005). Asthma severity is associated with Body Mass Index and early menarche in women. *American Journal of Respiratory and Critical Care Medicine, 171*(4), 334–339.

Ventura, S. J., Abma, J. C., & Mosher, W. D. (2003). Revised pregnancy rates, 1990–97, and new rates for 1998–99: United States. *National Vital Statistics Report, 52*(7).

Ventura, S. J., Abma, J. C., Mosher, W. D., & Henshaw, S. (2004). Estimated pregnancy rates for the United States, 1990–2000: An update. *National Vital Statistics Report, 52*(23).

Weiss, S. T. (2005). Obesity: Insight into the origins of asthma. *Nature Immunology, 6*, 537–539.

Weiss, S. T., & Shore, S. (2004). Obesity and asthma [NHLBI Workshop]. *American Journal of Respiratory and Critical Care Medicine, 169*, 963–968.

Wenger, N. K. (1985). Coronary disease in women. *Annual Review of Medicine, 36*, 285–294.

Wenger, N. K. (1987). Coronary heart disease in women: Clinical syndromes, prognosis, and diagnostic testing. In E. D. Eaker, B. Packard, N. R. Wenger, T. Clarkson, & H. A. Tyroler (Eds.), *Coronary heart disease in women: Proceedings of an NIH workshop* (pp. 173–186). New York: Haymarket Doyma.

White, J. W., Russo, N. F., & Travis, C. B. (2001). Feminism and the decade of behavior. *Psychology of Women Quarterly, 25*, 267–279.

Wilson, P. W., & Kannel, W. B. (2002). Obesity, diabetes, and risk of cardiovascular disease in the elderly. *American Journal of Geriatric Cardiology, 11*(2), 119–125.

Wood, A. J. J., Drazen, J. M., & Greene, M. F. (2005). A sad day for science at the FDA. *New England Journal of Medicine, 353*, 1197–1198.

World Health Organization. (2000). *Factsheet 241*. Geneva: World Health Organization.

Wright, J. D., Kennedy-Stephenson, J., Wang, C. Y., McDowell, M. A., & Johnson, C. L. (2004). Trends in intake of energy and macronutrients: United States, 1971–2000. *Morbidity and Mortality Weekly Report, 53*, 80–82.

Writing Group for the Women's Health Initiative Investigators. (2002). Risks and benefits of estrogen and progestin in healthy postmenopausal women: Principal results from the women's health initiative randomized trial. *Journal of the American Medical Association, 288*, 321–333.

Yoshino, Kenji (2007). Happy birthday, *Roe v. Wade*: On the ruling's anniversary, its fans should celebrate another case, too. *Slate*, January 18, http://www.slate.com/id/2157681/.

Zhao, Y., Nichols, J. E., Bulun, S. E., Mendelson, C. R., & Simpson, E. R. (1995). Aromatase P450 gene expression I human adipose tissue. *Journal of Biological Chemistry, 270*(27), 16449–16457.

Chapter 13

The Menstrual Cycle in a Biopsychosocial Context

Joan C. Chrisler

The menstrual cycle is a perfect example of a biopsychosocial phenomenon. It is a normal physiological process that affects and is affected by women's behavior. Women's behavior is affected by beliefs and attitudes, which are in turn affected by physiological experiences. Furthermore, women's experiences occur, our beliefs are learned, and our attitudes are formed within a cultural context. Therefore, although women around the globe share the same physiology of the menstrual cycle, we experience it differently, and these differences are caused, for the most part, by sociocultural effects on our beliefs, attitudes, and behavior.

Women who live in industrialized nations can expect to experience monthly menstrual cycles for three to four decades. The regular appearance of the menses is a sign of good health, is symbolic of our connection to other women, represents biological maturity, and signifies our ability to bear children but lets us know that we are not pregnant (Chrisler, 2004). Like other aspects of women's bodies, the menstrual cycle has become political. It provides such a clear distinction between women and men that "its correlates, concomitants, accompaniments, ramifications, and implications have become intrinsically bound up with issues of gender equality" (Sommer, 1983, p. 53).

In this chapter, you will learn about the physiological facts of the menstrual cycle and ways that these facts have been interpreted in various cultures and time periods. You will read about menstrual cycle–related changes in behavior, emotion, and cognition and why scientists have been so interested in documenting these changes. You will learn about attitudes toward menstruation and how they are influenced by, and in turn influence, popular culture. You will read about menarche, the first menstruation, and menopause, the end of menstrual cycles. You will also learn about disorders that are related to the menstrual cycle.

THE MENSTRUAL CYCLE

The menstrual cycle occurs only in primates: humans, apes, and some species of monkeys (Golub, 1992). Other mammals experience *estrus* (also referred to as "heat"); around the time of ovulation, these females are sexually active and receptive. Estrus periods are generally the only time that these females are interested in sexual behavior, and their interest is timed to coincide with fertility. The evolution from estrus cycles to menstrual cycles has allowed humans to separate ovulation from mating. Although the menstrual cycle has some effects on women's sexual desire, we are free to express our sexuality in a variety of ways at any time of the month.

The menstrual cycle is regulated primarily by the actions of four hormones: follicle-stimulating hormone (FSH), luteinizing hormone (LH), estrogen, and progesterone. The first two (FSH and LH) are gonadotropic hormones that are produced by the anterior section of the pituitary gland in order to affect the ovaries. The others (estrogen and progesterone) are ovarian hormones produced by the ovaries to affect the uterus.

The purposes of FSH are to stimulate the growth of follicles within the ovaries and to assist in the expulsion of a mature ovum. The purposes of LH are to stimulate ovulation and to promote the growth of the *corpus luteum*, that is, the "yellow body" that forms within the follicle after the ovum has been released. Estrogen, whose name comes from the Greek words that mean "to produce mad desire" (Maddux, 1975, p. 51), stimulates the growth of the uterine lining prior to ovulation, so that it will be ready to receive the implantation of the ovum should fertilization occur. Progesterone, whose name comes from the Greek words for "in favor of birth" (Maddux, 1975, p. 51), is produced by the corpus luteum to prepare the uterine lining and, if a fertilized ovum is implanted in the lining, to maintain the endometrium during pregnancy.

The average length of the menstrual cycle is 28 to 30 days; however, cycles that range in length from 21 to 40 days are still considered normal (Maddux, 1975). The typical 28-day cycle will be used to illustrate the physiological events that lead to menstruation. By convention, the first day of menstruation is considered day 1 of the menstrual cycle. This may seem counterintuitive, but even as the uterine lining is being shed during menstruation, the bottom layer of the endometrium, which is never shed, is being prepared for the next opportunity to welcome an implanted ovum. Menstruation, also known as *menses* (from the

Latin word for "month," Maddux, 1975, p. 53), usually lasts four or five days; three- to seven-day menstrual periods are considered normal, although women who use oral contraceptives may have even shorter menses. In our "typical" cycle, menstruation will cease on day 5.

The first half of the menstrual cycle is called the *follicular, preovulatory,* or *proliferative phase,* and it culminates in ovulation at around day 14. On day 1, levels of both estrogen and progesterone are low, and the uterine lining begins to shed. Also on day 1, an immature ovum in one of the two ovaries begins the process of maturation. During the weeks of the follicular phase, a new uterine lining develops. About day 14, levels of FSH, LH, and estrogen are at their highest, and the now-mature ovum is released into the fallopian tube. Some women are aware of the exact moment of ovulation because they experience a quick, sharp pain known as *mittleschmertz* (from the German words for "pain in the middle" of the cycle).

The second half of the menstrual cycle is called the *luteal, postovulatory,* or *secretory phase.* After ovulation, estrogen levels fall somewhat, then rise again as progesterone levels rise. Progesterone reaches its highest level, and estrogen is also high, about day 24. They quickly decline by day 28 if fertilization and implantation have not occurred. Their decline signals the end of the menstrual cycle. Menstruation begins, and the body returns to day 1 status.

Although the menses is often called "bleeding," blood makes up only 50–75 percent of the menstrual fluid (Maddux, 1975). Among the other elements in the fluid are endometrial tissue and cervical mucus. The amount of menstrual fluid discharged varies from woman to woman and usually from day to day in the same woman. The total amount of discharge averages 50 ml (about 3 tablespoons or less than a quarter of a cup); a range of 10 ml to 200 ml is considered normal (Gersh & Gersh, 1981). Some women discharge about the same amount of fluid daily from day 1 to day 5. Others experience a heavier flow during the first two days, which then tapers off. Still others start off lightly, then flow more heavily. There is not one correct or healthy way to menstruate; what's important for each woman to know is what is normal for her.

The menstrual cycle is a complicated series of events that is controlled by delicately balanced neuroendocrine mechanisms that involve the cerebral cortex, the hypothalamus, the pituitary gland, and the ovaries. The hormones regulate each other's actions through a complex set of negative-feedback loops. Contemplation of the system can leave one amazed at the beauty and intelligence of Nature's design of a physiological system that we take for granted will be as regular as clockwork for decades of our lives.

Still, not everyone sees it this way. The menstrual cycle, which was designed to produce life, is often described in destructive terms. Biologist Walter Heape (in 1913, as cited in Tavris, 1992, p. 159) considered menstruation to be a "severe, destructive" event that leaves in its wake "a ragged wreck of tissue, torn glands, ruptured vessels, jagged edges of stroma, and masses of blood corpuscles, which it would hardly seem possible to heal satisfactorily without the aid of surgical treatment." Heape was an antisuffrage activist (Tavris, 1992), and his anger against the uppity women of his time is evident in the exaggerated and inflammatory language he chose to describe a benign process.

Scientific objectivity is often found wanting where reproductive processes are concerned. Martin (1987) reviewed medical textbooks to see how the authors described the menstrual cycle and found that menstruation is typically described as a negative event because it represents a "failure" to conceive. Capitalist, industrialized societies are highly disapproving of systems that don't "produce," and a menstrual cycle that is not interrupted by conception can be seen as even worse than unproductive: it is "production gone awry, making products of no use, not to specification, unsalable, waste, scrap" (Martin, 1987, p. 46). Martin suggested that women who menstruate are out of men's control because they are not reproducing. Hence, male scientists described the menses as a "hemorrhage ... blood mixed with endometrial debris" (p. 45), the ovum as catastrophically disintegrating and "dying" (p. 48), and the uterus as "degenerate," "weakened," and in need of "repair" (p. 47). The most positive language is reserved for the development of the ovum, which is typically described as "maturing" or "ripening" (p. 44) within the follicle.

Martin (1987) contrasted the passive description of the development of the ova, all of which are already present in women's bodies at birth, with the active description of the development of sperm, which are not present at birth and thus must be "manufactured." One author she cited described this process as "remarkable" and noted, "Perhaps the most amazing characteristic of spermatogenesis is its sheer magnitude: the normal human male may manufacture several hundred million sperm per day" (p. 48). The man who wrote so much more enthusiastically about Nature's design of his own body than he did about women's bodies did so not only out of egocentrism or androcentrism, according to Martin, but also because of his admiration for the fact that spermatogenesis does what menstruation does not do: produce "something deemed valuable" (p. 48). Too bad he didn't consider that hundreds of millions of those sperm will be wasted every day; it takes only one to fertilize an ovum.

Cultural and Historical Perspectives

Across time and place, menstrual blood has been considered both magical and poisonous (Golub, 1992). It is easy to understand how such ideas arose. Before the physiology of the menstrual cycle was understood, it must have seemed amazing that women who were not wounded could bleed and that five days of blood loss did not kill or even seriously weaken them. Therefore, menstruation seemed magical. Because men did not have magical bleeding themselves, they must have been afraid of it, perhaps worried that close contact with it might do them some physical damage or pollute them by association with the female body. Thus, menstruation seemed poisonous. Do not dismiss these ideas as naïve or primitive; remnants of them are present today. As late as the 1920s and 1930s, scientists (see Delaney, Lupton, & Toth, 1987) were attempting to demonstrate that menstruating women exuded what were called *menotoxins* (i.e., poisonous elements) in menstrual fluid, perspiration, saliva, urine, and tears. Present-day feminists (e.g., Owen, 1993; Stepanich, 1992; Wind, 1995) who advocate the celebration of menstruation with praise to the Moon Goddess continue the idea that menses and magic are connected.

Anthropologists have reported that most societies have cultural prescriptions (i.e., rules of conduct) for menstruating women (Buckley & Gottlieb, 1988). In some societies, menstruating women were considered taboo, that is, to be avoided while "unclean." In others, menstruating women were required to refrain from some activities (e.g., cooking, cultivating crops) or to engage in certain activities to mark the onset or the end of the menses (e.g., ritual bathing). Beliefs about menstruation have no doubt been used in the past, as they are in the present, to oppress women and limit our activities. However, it may be too simple to assume that all menstrual taboos are the result of misogyny and were imposed on women by men. Feminist anthropologists (e.g., Leacock, 1978; Martin, 1988) have suggested that women who were experiencing menstrual cramps or migraines might have been glad to have a break from cooking, weeding the crops, and walking long distances to collect water, herbs, or other provisions. Similarly, the menstrual huts in which some cultures required women to stay during their menses might have been less like a prison and more like "Mom's night out." In the huts or ritual bathing places, women could relax together, talk and tell stories, and create a women's culture they kept secret from men and children. For example, in his study of the Yurok people of the Pacific Northwest, Buckley (1982) learned that the Yurok believed that menstruating women should isolate themselves because they are at the height of their spiritual power and should not have to waste attention or energy on mundane tasks. Instead women should spend the time in meditation and other spiritual pursuits. The Yurok women's isolation sounds more like a religious retreat or a spa visit than a banishment.

Nevertheless, superstitious beliefs about menstruation were (and are) common, and many have led to taboos that circumscribe menstruating women's behavior. Among the taboos described by Frazer (1951) are that drops of menstrual blood upon the ground or in a river will kill plants and animals; wells will run dry if a menstruating woman draws water from them; men will sicken or die if they are touched by or use any objects that have been touched by menstruating women; beer will turn sour if a menstruating woman enters a brewery; and beer, wine, vinegar, milk, or jam will go bad if touched by a menstruating woman. These beliefs have been reported in various places in Europe, Asia, Africa, Australia, and the Americas, and they are related to contemporary beliefs that women should not bathe, swim, wash their hair, do heavy housework, play sports, tend houseplants, or engage in sexual intercourse during the menses (see, e.g., *Tampax report*, 1981; Snow & Johnson, 1978; Williams, 1983).

The rising influence of science and the development of biomedicine in the 19th and 20th centuries produced new myths about menstruating women. Physicians of the 19th century believed that women were ill, weak, and especially dependent during their menstrual periods (Golub, 1992), and they urged their patients to rest and conserve their strength during the menses. Only middle- and upper-class women could afford to seek a doctor's advice and have household help, whose efforts made possible their employers' rest; poor and working-class women carried on their duties as usual during their menstrual periods, and no one seemed to think it odd that they were able to do so.

The foremost proponent of menstrual disability was Edward H. Clarke, a professor at Harvard Medical School. He believed that education interferes with women's health. His thesis was that the menstrual cycle requires a considerable investment of energy, and therefore any energy directed at mental activity would necessarily reduce the amount left to produce ovulation and menstruation. Furthermore, the blood flow to the brain to support studying, he thought, means less blood available to supply the ovaries and uterus for their important activities. Clarke's 1873 book *Sex in Education* went through 17 editions and was very influential with both professional and popular audiences (Bullough & Voght, 1973).

Clarke's book was published at a time when there was a movement to promote educational opportunities for women and girls. A number of women's colleges were established in the late 19th century, and it's sad to think that Clarke's influence may have caused many parents to decide against allowing their daughters to attend. Women college graduates were so rare that in 1881 a group of alumnae met to form the American Association of University Women, a national organization of women college graduates that continues today to meet in local chapters for intellectual, social, and political activities. Only 3.8 percent of American women attended college in 1910; 7.6 percent attended in 1920, and the number increased to only 10.5 percent in 1930 (Levine, 1995).

Despite several studies published around the turn of the 20th century that showed no difference in the health of women college students and women who did not attend college, "experts" continued to warn parents not to allow their daughters to engage in intellectual activities (Bullough & Voght, 1973). John Harvey Kellogg, the diet and exercise guru, wrote that many young women had permanently damaged their health by studying too much while menstruating. He also warned of the danger to menstruating women of exposure to cold, not getting enough rest, and not dressing or eating "properly." G. Stanley Hall, a very influential psychologist of the early 1900s, was a fierce opponent of coeducation. He thought that women were too frail to stand up to the rigors that men students could handle, and he urged women's colleges to provide at least four days of rest for students during their menstrual periods (Golub, 1992). It's interesting to note that, although Hall opposed coeducation, he did train several of the early women psychology graduate students in his lab at Clark University. The women remained loyal to him for the opportunity he provided them, although he did not seem to assist them later in their careers (Scarborough & Furumoto, 1987).

As late as the 1930s, textbooks continued to state that most women experienced at least some disability during menstruation and that women should limit their activities and get more rest during their periods. Today, few professionals would agree with what we might call "the debilitation hypothesis," but many professionals and the general public alike are still certain that the menstrual cycle affects women's behavior, emotions, and intellectual abilities. In 1970 physician Edgar Berman was widely quoted in the media for his comments about women politicians:

> If you had an investment in a bank, you wouldn't want the president of your bank making a loan under these raging hormonal influences at that particular period. Suppose we had a president in the White House, a menopausal woman president, who had to make the decision of the Bay of Pigs, which was, of course, a bad one, or the Russian contretemps with Cuba at that time?

In 1982, during a debate in the UN General Assembly about the war between Great Britain and Argentina over the Falkland Islands, a diplomat stated that Prime Minister Margaret Thatcher's actions were probably influenced by "the glandular system of women." Yet when men politicians declare war or make bad decisions, such as the Bay of Pigs incursion, no one ever seems to wonder what influence, if any, their physiology may have had on them.

Menstrual Cycle Effects on Behavior

Many hundreds of studies of the menstrual cycle's effects on behavior have been conducted by biomedical and behavioral scientists, and feminist scientists have had to spend their time in critiquing and refuting the results of the few studies that have concluded that menstruation has debilitating effects on women's abilities. Many of the studies on this topic are poorly designed, perhaps because they were conducted by people who had no expertise in cyclic biology, yet the researchers were able to publish their results in respectable journals—provided, of course, that their findings supported the debilitation hypothesis.

It can be difficult to publish the results of studies that do not confirm expectations, a conundrum termed "the file drawer effect" (Sommer, 1987) in reference to the unpublished papers in feminist scholars' files—many of which conclude that menstruation does not affect behavior or that women and men do not differ in some particular ability under study. The file drawer effect contributes to the waste of feminists' time as we conduct the same studies over and over again because we do not have access to the unpublished data that show the research to be unnecessary. It is also true that the one study that demonstrates a menstrual cycle effect (or a sex difference) will get much more scientific and media attention than the six studies that refute it combined.

Why are there so few good studies of menstrual cycle effects? For one thing, the menstrual cycle is complex; it represents a constantly changing biochemical process, and, because we cannot see the changes, it is not easy to know exactly what the state of the system is when measurements are taken. The only way to tell what phase of the cycle a woman is in is to do hormone assays, that is, to take a blood or urine sample and have it analyzed for hormone concentrations. If, for example, progesterone and estrogen are in high concentrations and FSH and LH are in low concentrations, then we can safely say that the woman is in the second half of the cycle—the luteal phase.

Many researchers do not use the hormone assay method of participant assignment because they cannot afford to have the lab tests done and do not have the training to do the tests themselves, or because they do not realize its importance. The next best method is the use of basal body temperature. Participants in the study are asked to take their temperature each morning when they awake and before they get out of bed. The temperatures are written in a notebook, and the researchers later plot them on a graph. Basal body temperature is typically lower in the follicular phase than in the luteal phase; it drops just prior to ovulation, then spikes up 0.4 degrees or more after ovulation occurs and continues at a higher-than-earlier level during the rest of the cycle. Although hormone levels are not confirmed in this method, they can be inferred if ovulation occurred. Women do not necessarily ovulate during every cycle, and it is important to confirm ovulation. If ovulation did not occur, the woman does not experience a "true" luteal phase; that is, her hormone level is not typical. If ovulation cannot be confirmed, the participant's data should not be included in the statistical analysis.

The least reliable way to determine cycle phase is the calendar method. In this method, the researcher asks the participant for the date of the start of her last menstrual period. On the assumption that the woman's cycle is 28 days long (an assumption that may well not be true), the researcher then uses a calendar to count the days since the reported date and estimates the participant's cycle phase. This method relies on too many assumptions: that the woman's recall of the date is accurate, that ovulation occurred, that her cycle is 28 days long. If women are using oral contraceptives, the calendar method is even more unreliable, because the pill alters hormone levels. Although the calendar method is the least reliable, it is the most popular because it is the easiest and least expensive and perhaps because the researchers who use it are ignorant about the method's defects.

Another methodological problem that makes it difficult to compare the results of studies to each other is that researchers differ in the way they divide the menstrual cycle into phases. The simple two-phase division (follicular, luteal) described earlier is insufficient for those who wish to study whether menstruation affects behavior. Therefore, some researchers define a five- or seven-day phase termed "menstrual." Others are interested in premenstrual effects on behavior, so they define a five- or seven-day phase termed "premenstrual" (occasionally the premenstrual phase is defined as 10 or even 14 days long—but more on that later). Sometimes researchers want to know if women's behavior is different around ovulation than at other times of the cycle, so they define a three- or four-day phase termed "ovulatory." So, we have various studies that define three, four, or even five different phases. Furthermore, the same phase definition is generally used for all participants in the study even though their menstrual cycles probably differ considerably in actual length, and, if the calendar method is used, we don't even know that the women were actually in the phases they were assumed to be in, anyway.

You are probably wondering why we should even discuss a body of literature that is such a methodological mess, but we must, because the results of these studies have been highly politicized. What scientists, journalists, and the general public alike know of the results of these studies influences stereotypes about women, women's beliefs and feelings about themselves and their bodies, and even classroom and labor force discrimination against women and girls.

Following from the debilitation hypothesis, a number of researchers have looked for evidence that women's academic or work performance suffers when they are menstruating. The most frequently cited study of academic performance was done by Katharina Dalton (1960a). She looked at examination scores achieved by British schoolgirls ages 11–17. Using the calendar method to assign them to cycle phases, Dalton reported that 27 percent of the students' scores were lower when they were premenstrual or menstrual than at other times in their cycles. However, she also found that 17 percent of the students' scores improved when they were menstrual or premenstrual, and the other 56 percent scored about the same whenever they took their exams. Despite the fact that the majority of Dalton's participants did not experience a decline in exam scores, the results of this study are frequently garbled in the media and even in college textbooks as evidence of a 27% drop in schoolgirls' performance around the time of menstruation.

Data from later studies (Bernstein, 1977; Sommer, 1972; Walsh, Budtz-Olsen, Leader, & Cummins, 1981), in which college or graduate students were tested every other week for several months and their scores matched to cycle phases using the calendar method, showed no evidence of any cycle-related performance decline. Nor have researchers found menstrual cycle–related effects on tests of academic abilities, such as arithmetic (Wickham, 1958; Lazarov, 1982), spelling and vocabulary (Wickham, 1958), anagrams (Golub, 1976; Rodin, 1976), or puzzles (Rodin, 1976).

Neither does women's work performance seem to be negatively affected by the menstrual cycle. Harlow (1986) reviewed a series of studies from the 1920s to the 1980s that show no diminished efficiency in women workers and no significant absenteeism due to menstrual pain. Seward's (1944) review of studies of menstrual cycle effects on women's performance and productivity on a variety of work-related tasks also concluded that there was no evidence of significant decline during menstruation. For example, no differences were found in the work performance ratings of women factory workers (Smith, 1950) or the work output of women laundry workers (Redgrove, 1971) across the menstrual cycle. Nor have researchers found cycle-related differences in physical activities, such as arm movements (Stenn & Klinge, 1972), daily walking (Chrisler & McCool, 1991; Morris & Urdry, 1970), or reaction time (Sommer, 1983), that may be related to work performance.

One would think that so many studies over such a long period of time would put to rest the idea that menstrual cycle–related changes make women less productive members of the workforce. However, one can still find occasional news stories in which "authorities" speculate that menstrual cramps and PMS (premenstrual syndrome) cost industry billions of dollars due to employee absenteeism or underperformance on the job (Tavris, 1992).

Many scientists remain so convinced that women's hormones affect our behavior that even the weight of the evidence cannot dissuade them. Instead of concluding that menstrual cycle effects are minimal or absent, some argue that they must have taken the wrong measurements, or that their measurements should be more specific than general, more molecular than molar. Thus, women have been tested across the menstrual cycle on standardized tests designed by psychologists to study cognitive and perceptual abilities and performance. No menstrual cycle effects have been found on tests of critical, creative, or abstract thinking (Chrisler, 1991; Golub, 1976; Sommer, 1972); spatial abilities (Golub, 1976; Lazarov, 1982; Wickham, 1958); speed and accuracy of cognitive performance (Rodin, 1976); speed and accuracy of visual perception (Chiarello, McMahon, & Shaefer, 1989; Compton & Levine, 1997; Rodriguez, 1999); learning and memory (Lough, 1937; Rodriguez, 1999; Sommer, 1972); or ability to recognize and label emotions accurately (Lazarov, 1982).

Women have been found to be more sensitive to (i.e., better able to perceive) faint lights and odors around the time of ovulation (Parlee, 1983; Sommer, 1983), and at least one study (Parlee, 1983) has shown women's hearing to be more acute at ovulation and at the start of the menses. Researchers (Hampson, 1990; Hampson & Kimura, 1988) have also reported that women perform better around ovulation on tests of verbal fluency, speech articulation, and manual dexterity. However, it's important to note that researchers have found evidence of sex differences that favor women in sense of smell, verbal fluency, and fine motor abilities (e.g., manual dexterity). Thus, the way to interpret the above reported findings is that women's abilities, which are always good, are even better at midcycle.

Behavioral scientists have also examined menstrual cycle effects on women's sexual behavior. Evolutionary theory predicts that the species is most likely to survive if women are most sexually active around the time of ovulation, and a number of researchers (e.g., Adams, Gold, & Burt, 1978; Morris & Urdry, 1982; Williams & Williams, 1982) have found peak sexual interest and activity at midcycle in women who were not using oral contraceptives. However, women's sexuality is complex, and researchers do not necessarily agree on what should be measured (Golub, 1992): desire, arousal, fantasies, "interest," masturbation, orgasm, self-initiated sexual activity, partner-initiated sexual activity?

In one study (Englander-Golden, 1985, as cited in Golub, 1992) in which participants were unaware of the purpose of the research, women reported three peaks in sexual arousal: at midcycle, during the premenstrual phase, and on day 4. The midcycle peak can be explained by evolutionary theory, but the others cannot. However, they can be explained socioculturally. If women live in a society that forbids or discourages sexual activity during the menses (for religious reasons—women are "unclean"—or for aesthetic reasons—it would be messy or "icky"), it makes sense to seek sexual activity just prior to the start of the menstrual taboo, and it's understandable that women would be sexually interested again as the taboo time draws to a close.

Furthermore, if women wish to avoid pregnancy, it makes sense to act on one's sexual desire at times (i.e., immediately premenstrually and postmenstrually) when pregnancy is less likely to occur. Both questionnaire and daily diary studies show considerable variability in women's sexual behavior across the menstrual cycle. Hormonal and social effects, including partner availability and even day of the week (Ripper, 1991), appear to play a role in women's sexual desires and expressions.

One thing most Americans believe they know is that the menstrual cycle affects women's moods. However, even in this case, the cycle's effects are not reliably demonstrable, and, when they appear, they are less than expected. Golub (1976) found a significant increase in anxiety and depression scores during the premenstrual phase. However, when she compared her participants' average scores to the scores of participants in other studies who took the same tests, she found that premenstrual anxiety scores were lower than anxiety scores reported during freshman orientation and during exam week; premenstrual depression scores were lower than those reported by psychiatric patients and about the same as those reported by pregnant women in the first trimester. She concluded that, although the premenstrual rise in depression and anxiety was statistically significant, it probably wasn't clinically significant. In other words, women don't "go crazy" premenstrually; the changes are just part of the normal ups and downs of life.

Other researchers, who took careful, daily mood measurements from participants who were unaware of the purpose of the studies, found that stress (Wilcoxon, Schrader, & Sherif, 1976) and day of the week (Englander-Golden, Sonleitener, Whitmore, & Corbley, 1986; Ripper, 1991; Rossi & Rossi, 1977) have a greater effect on women's mood than does the menstrual cycle and that mood fluctuates about as much in men as it does in women over the course of 28 days (Parlee, 1980; Rogers & Harding, 1981; Swandby, 1981). However, other researchers (e.g., Halbreich & Endicott, 1987; Mitchell, Woods, & Lentz, 1994) have found that women who experience depressive disorders often report that their depression is worse when they are premenstrual, a pattern that Nancy Fugate Woods and her colleagues termed "PMM"—premenstrual magnification of existing symptoms. In this case, it would not be correct to say that the premenstrual phase is the cause of women's depression, which is already present, but it appears to be the case that cyclic biochemical changes enhance the mood that already exists.

Despite the fact that daily reports do not show a pattern of menstrual cycle–related mood shifts, women do tend to report increased negative emotions, especially depression and irritability, when they are questioned retrospectively (i.e., at the conclusion of the study as opposed to daily). It may be that premenstrual mood shifts are so subtle that most psychological tests are not sensitive enough to measure them, or it may be that women have been so influenced by the stereotype of premenstrual women that we incorrectly "remember" all of our negative emotions as having occurred at that time rather than randomly throughout the month (Golub, 1992). Social psychologists refer to the latter as an "illusory correlation." Because we *expect* certain events to be related to each other (e.g., premenstrual phase and bad mood, full moon and impulsive behavior), we remember instances that confirm our expectations and forget those that do not.

Two groups of researchers (AuBouchon & Calhoun, 1985; Englander-Golden et al., 1986) designed studies to test two groups of women participants: one group was aware that the purpose of the study was to examine menstrual cycle effects on mood; the other group was unaware of the actual purpose. The "aware" groups reported a pattern of mood variability that was associated with the menstrual cycle; the "unaware" groups did not. These studies illustrate both the importance of social expectancies (i.e., we notice symptoms and behaviors that we expect will occur) and the role of experimental demand characteristics (i.e., participants who are "aware" assume that the researchers are looking for negative changes, and they try to be helpful by focusing their attention and reports on negative experiences).

Attitudes toward Menstruation

Perhaps the strongest taboo is communication about menstruation (Kissling, 1996). The majority of U.S. adults surveyed for *The Tampax Report* (1981) agreed that menstruation should not be discussed in "mixed company," and many thought it should not be discussed with the family at home. Williams (1983) found that 33 percent of the adolescent girls she surveyed would not talk about menstruation with their fathers, and nearly all of her participants agreed that one should not discuss menstruation around boys. Even psychotherapists (especially men) have reported experiencing discomfort when their clients want to discuss some aspect of menstruation (Rhinehart, 1989). When teachers separate girls and boys to view films about puberty, and when mothers arrange one-to-one "facts of life talks" with their daughters, they are conveying not only facts about menstruation but also guidelines for how to talk about it; they are marking menstruation "as a special topic, not one for ordinary conversation" (Kissling, 1996, p. 495). Exclusive talks held in privacy convey the notion that menstruation is an embarrassing event that must be concealed from others and never discussed openly.

The communication taboo is supported by the existence of dozens of euphemisms for menstruation (Ernster, 1975), and these euphemisms can be found in cultures around the world. Ernster (1976) examined a collection of American expressions in the Folklore Archives at the University of California at Berkeley, and she grouped the expressions into categories. For example, some refer to female visitors (e.g., "My friend is here," "Aunt Flo/Susie/Sylvia/Tilly is visiting me"), others to cyclicity (e.g., "It's that time again," "My time of the month/moon," "my period"), illness or distress (e.g., "the curse," "the misery," "I'm under the weather," "Lady troubles," "weeping womb," "falling off the roof"), nature (e.g., "flowers," "Mother Nature's gift"), redness or blood (e.g., "I'm wearing red shoes today," "red plague," "red moon," "bloody scourge"), or menstrual products (e.g., "on the rag," "riding the cotton pony," "using mouse mattresses" or "saddle blankets"). References to menstruation that women find particularly offensive (e.g., "on the rag" or "OTR," "her cherry's in the sherry") or that refer to the sexual taboo (e.g., "too wet to plow," "the red flag is up") are more commonly used by men and reflect especially negative attitudes toward women's bodies.

Advertisements for menstrual products are cultural artifacts that play an important role in the social construction of meaning (Merskin, 1999). Ads have contributed to the communication taboo by emphasizing secrecy, avoidance of embarrassment, freshness, and delicacy (Coutts & Berg, 1993; Delaney et al., 1987; Houppert, 1999; Merskin, 1999). Allegorical images, such as flowers and hearts, and blue liquid rather than reddish blood, have been used euphemistically to promote secrecy and delicacy (Merskin, 1999). Ads play on women's fear of being discovered as menstruating; discovery means stigma—being publicly tainted or "spoiled" (Coutts & Berg, 1993). With the invention of panty-liners, advertisers began to tell us to use their products every day so that we can feel "confident" that we can stay "fresh" and untainted (Berg & Coutts, 1994). When Oxley (1997) questioned 55 British women about their experiences with menstruation, she found that they echoed many of the themes in the ads. They felt self-conscious during their menses, preferred tampons because they are "less noticeable" than sanitary napkins, believed that menstrual blood is distasteful to self and others, and supported the sex taboo.

Advertisements are not the only form of public discourse about menstruation. Cultural attitudes are also conveyed through books, magazine and newspaper articles, jokes, and other cultural artifacts, such as "humorous" products like greeting cards and refrigerator magnets. Most of the attitudes these media convey are negative, and together they have constructed a stereotype of menstruating women, especially premenstrual women, as violent, irrational, emotionally labile, out of control, and physically or mentally ill. Over the past 20 years, my students have brought me bumper stickers (e.g., "A woman with PMS and ESP is a bitch who knows everything"), buttons (e.g., "It's not PMS, I'm always bitchy"), cartoons (e.g., In a cartoon titled "PMS Worst-case Scenario," a woman sits alone on a small desert island while a man, in the ocean surrounded by sharks, says "Somehow it feels safer out here.''), greeting cards (e.g., a picture of a cake slashed to bits and the saying ''Some special advice for the birthday girl—Never cut your cake during PMS''), a calendar of cartoons about a woman with a really bad case of PMS (e.g., ''To take her mind off her premenstrual syndrome, Melinda decides to rearrange her furniture'' by hacking it to pieces with an axe), and books (e.g., *Raging Hormones: The Unofficial PMS Survival Guide,* the cover of which pictures Joan Crawford as an axe murderer). When I share my extensive collection with my classes, students usually laugh at the first few instances, but by the time they have seen several dozen cartoons, buttons, and so on, they are usually angry and disheartened. These messages about women are sent everyday; take a walk through your local shopping mall, and you'll see them.

A content analysis (Chrisler & Levy, 1990) of 78 articles about premenstrual syndrome that were published in American magazines between 1980 and 1987 showed that writers have focused on negative stereotypes and sensational cases. The menstrual cycle was referred to as the ''cycle of misery,'' a ''hormonal roller coaster,'' ''the inner beast,'' and the ''menstrual monster'' (p. 98). The premenstrual and menstrual phases of the cycle were described as ''weeks of hell'' during which women are ''hostages to their hormones,'' and premenstrual women were described as ''cripples'' and ''raging beasts'' (p. 98). The titles of some of the articles in the analysis were ''Premenstrual Frenzy,'' ''Dr. Jekyll and Ms. Hyde,'' ''Coping with Eve's Curse,'' ''Once a Month I'm a Woman Possessed,'' and ''The Taming of the Shrew Inside of You'' (p. 97). The articles suggest that most (or all) women experience PMS.

The emphasis on violent, out-of-control women in cartoons and magazine articles could easily make us lose sight of the fact that only a small percentage of all violent crimes are committed by women. The articles described above were influenced by the newspaper coverage of two criminal prosecutions in England of women who were accused of murder (Sandie Smith) and vehicular homicide (Christine English). Dr. Katharina Dalton testified in their trials about her belief that the women had premenstrual syndrome at the time of the crimes. Smith's own lawyer described her as a ''Jekyll and Hyde'' and stated that without medical treatment the ''hidden animal'' in her would emerge (Chrisler, 2002). The trials led to an explosion of media interest in PMS, which has contributed to stereotypes about women and influenced the way that women (and men) think about women's bodies and their emotions (Chrisler, 2002).

It is not surprising that people who are exposed to the cultural influences described above would have negative attitudes toward menstruation. These attitudes are formed early and are less influenced by personal experience than one might think. Clarke and Ruble (1978) asked boys and premenarcheal girls to rate the severity of the symptoms that they believed women experience during menstruation. Boys and premenarcheal girls had well-defined beliefs and negative attitudes toward menstruation; they reported that it is accompanied by pain, emotionality, and a reduction in social and physical activities. The postmenarcheal girls did not let their own experiences guide their responses; they thought that most girls experienced more severe symptoms than they did. Similar results were found in a recent study (Chrisler, Rose, Dutch, Sklarsky, & Grant, in press) of beliefs about and experience of premenstrual symptoms, in which women college students rated their own experience of premenstrual symptoms as mild to moderate, yet believed that severe PMS is widespread and that other women's experience is significantly worse than their own.

Researchers have found that men tend to view menstruation as more debilitating than women do; women tend to rate menstruation as merely a "bothersome" event (Brooks-Gunn & Ruble, 1980, 1986; Chrisler, 1988). Men are more likely than women to describe menstruation as embarrassing, to report that their sources of information about menstruation have been negative (Brooks-Gunn & Ruble, 1986), and to associate menstruation with danger and stigma (Heard & Chrisler, 1999). People who score high on hostile sexism (Forbes, Adams-Curtis, White, & Holmgren, 2003) and women who have internalized a more sexually objectified view of their own bodies (Roberts, 2004) have been found to report more negative attitudes toward menstruation and menstruating women. Older adults (who formed their attitudes before the PMS stereotype appeared in the early 1980s) perceive menstruation as less debilitating and bothersome than do college students (Chrisler, 1988; Stubbs, 1989). Similar results have been found in Canada and Mexico (Lee, 2002; Marván, Ramírez-Esparza, Cortés-Iniestra, & Chrisler, 2006), but in other countries (e.g., India; Hoerster, Chrisler, & Rose, 2003) attitudes toward menstruation are more positive than is the case in North America.

Attitudes toward menstruation are not just an esoteric topic for academic scholars; they have a real impact on women's physical and mental health as well as our ability to attain success in our chosen pursuits. A number of studies (e.g., Levitt & Lubin, 1967; Paulson, 1961) have shown that negative attitudes toward menstruation are correlated with more painful menstrual cramps and greater incidence of other menstrual and premenstrual symptoms; however, the designs of those studies do not allow us to tell whether pain leads to negative attitudes or whether negative attitudes lead to more attention to, poorer ability to cope with, and a greater tendency to report pain. The answer probably is that it works both ways; attitudes and experience influence each other.

Negative attitudes toward menstruation and one's body in general have been correlated with a desire to forgo menstruation and an interest in trying birth control methods that suppress the menses (Johnston-Robledo, Ball, Lauta, & Zekoll, 2003), even though these methods are relatively new and their safety over long-term use is unknown. There is evidence (Roberts, 2004; Roberts & Waters, 2004) that negative attitudes toward menstruation are among the factors that that produce self-objectification, the tendency to focus on external aspects of the self over internal aspects. It is easy to see how cultural messages (e.g., the text of advertisements for menstrual hygiene products) can lead women to be ashamed of their bodies and to engage in excessive bodily surveillance, two of the signs of self-objectification. Researchers (Calogero, Davis, & Thompson, 2005; Szymanski & Henning, in press; Tylka & Hill, 2004) have shown that self-objectification predicts eating disorders, depression, and sexual problems in women.

Attitudes toward menstruation can divide women from each other by pitting those who experience severe symptoms against those who do not (Stubbs & Costos, 2004), and they affect what people think about menstruating women. For example, Forbes and his colleagues (2003) asked a group of college students to rate a set of adjectives in light of the following instruction: "Compared with the average woman, the woman during her period is..." (p. 59). Both women and men thought that a menstruating woman is more irritable, sad, and annoying, and less sexy and energized, than the average woman. In addition, men thought that a menstruating woman is more annoying and spacey, and less reasonable and nurturing, than average.

In an earlier study, Golub (1981) found that 75 percent of the male and 32 percent of the female college students she surveyed believed that menstruation affects women's thinking processes. In addition, 59 percent of the men and 51 percent of the women believed that women are less able to function when they are menstruating.

In a recent experiment by Roberts and her colleagues (Roberts, Goldenberg, Power, & Pyszczynski, 2002), their research assistant "accidentally" dropped either a tampon or a hair clip in front of the participants just before the study began. At the end of the study, the participants rated the assistant as less competent and less likable when she had dropped the tampon than they did when she had dropped the hair clip. They also exhibited a tendency to sit further away from her during the data collection when they had seen her with the tampon. If employers or coaches, for example, hold these negative attitudes and inaccurate beliefs about women, they will be less likely to hire and promote women or to provide them with opportunities to excel on the playing field.

MENSTRUAL CYCLE–RELATED TRANSITIONS AND DISORDERS

Menarche

Menarche, the first menstrual period, is a milestone in women's development and a psychologically significant event. Although it occurs relatively late in the pubertal process, as much as two years after breast buds develop (Tanner, 1991), it is menarche that provides the proof of puberty (Erchull, Chrisler, Gorman, & Johnston-Robledo, 2003). Unlike the gradual changes that accompany puberty, menarche is sudden and conspicuous (Golub, 1992), and it thus provides a rather dramatic demarcation between girlhood and womanhood. The importance of menarche is illustrated by the fact that many women have vivid and detailed memories of it that are retained over time with surprising clarity.

Given the cultural images discussed above, it is no surprise that most girls approach menarche with ambivalence. In studies of North American girls, participants typically report mixed feelings about menarche, such as proud and embarrassed or happy and frightened (Chrisler & Zittel, 1998; Koff, Rierdan, & Jocobson, 1981; Woods, Dery, & Most, 1983; Zimmerman & Chrisler, 1996). African American and Latina girls have reported less positive reactions to menarche than European American girls, and Latinas also reported the most negative beliefs about menstruation (Zimmerman & Chrisler, 1996). Interviews with British early adolescents revealed that they thought of menstruation primarily as embarrassing, shameful, and something to be hidden; they also thought of their periods as a time of illness (Burrows & Johnson, 2005).

Many girls are unprepared for menarche and do not understand what is happening to them when they experience it (Logan, 1980); this is especially likely to occur in early-maturing girls, for whom menarche appears to be more traumatic than for those who are "on time" or late (Petersen, 1983; Scott, Arthur, Panzio, & Owen, 1989). Many mothers find it difficult to talk to their daughters about menstruation and sexuality (Gillooly, 1998), so they put off having the talk as long as possible—sometimes until it is too late. When they do have "the talk," mothers often convey to their daughters the negative attitudes and inaccurate information that their own mothers told them (Britton, 1999; Costos, Ackerman, & Paradis, 2002). In one study (Scott et al., 1989) of African American girls, 27 percent of the participants said that they felt totally unprepared for menarche; this can be compared to the 10–14 percent of European American girls found in other studies (Chrisler & Zittel, 1998; Koff et al., 1981; Whisnant & Zegens, 1975).

Preparation is not everything, however, as Koff, Rierdan, and Sheingold (1982) found that even the 60 percent of their participants who rated themselves as prepared for menarche had negative feelings about the event when they actually experienced it. The films and pamphlets that girls are given to educate them about menstruation tend to use technical medical vocabularies to describe the physiological aspects of the menstrual cycle, but are otherwise vague and mysterious (Erchull et al., 2003; Havens & Swenson, 1989; Whisnant, Brett, & Zegens, 1975).

Most of these educational materials are produced by the companies that manufacture menstrual products, and they tend to present menstruation as a hygiene crisis that should be hidden from the rest of the world by following rules of careful management and concealment. The emphasis on secrecy reinforces the idea that menstruation is a negative, stigmatizing, and embarrassing event. More positive messages can be found in the following books: *Period: A Girl's Guide to Menstruation* (Loulan, Worthen, Lopez, & Dyrud, 2001), *Before She Gets Her Period: Talking to Your Daughter about Menstruation* (Gillooly, 1998), and *The Care and Feeding of You: The Body Book for Girls* (Schaefer, 1998).

Adjustment to one's new menstrual status is entwined with adjustment to thinking of oneself as a young woman. Girls are taught that menarche signals the beginning of their adult lives (Koff et al., 1982). When they experience their menstrual period for the first time, many girls are told that they are now women, and they are usually taught about the menstrual cycle in relation to reproduction (Erchull et al., 2003). Adolescents look forward to adulthood, but the average age of menarche in the United States is 12.3 years (Tanner, 1991), which is very young to be an adult.

Body image concerns often arise around the time of menarche, as girls cope with menstruation and other pubertal changes, such as weight gain and changes in body shape (Roberts & Waters, 2004). Koff, Reirdan, and Silverstone (1978) asked adolescent girls to draw pictures of a same-sex body on two occasions six months apart. The bodies drawn by postmenarcheal girls were significantly more sexually differentiated than those drawn by premenarcheal girls, and the contrast was particularly striking in the drawings of the girls whose menarcheal status changed during the course of the study. These data show the importance of menarche to the way girls organize their body image and sexual identity.

Menarche can be seen as a rite of passage to adulthood. Celebrations range from parties with the girls' friends or with other women in the family or village to rituals of cleansing or separation (Delaney et al., 1987). Celebrations of menarche are rare in Western countries (Chrisler & Zittel, 1998; Thuren, 1994), and most girls think of menstruation as too embarrassing to discuss with anyone but their mothers and close friends. Think about what a change it could make to adolescent girls' self-esteem and body image if the change in their menarcheal status was openly acknowledged with pride. (For suggestions of ways to celebrate menarche, see Chrisler & Zittel, 1998; Golub, 1992; Taylor, 1988.)

Dysmenorrhea

Dysmenorrhea is the technical term used to describe the uterine cramps, headaches, backaches, and other unpleasant symptoms that may occur during menstruation. It typically starts 2–12 hours prior to the onset of the menstrual flow and lasts 24–36 hours (Golub, 1992). Dysmenorrhea occurs only during ovulatory cycles, and it is thought that the process of ovulation triggers the production of prostaglandins, that is, hormone-like substances that cause the uterine contractions that we call menstrual cramps (Dawood, 1981; Golub, 1992). The amount of prostaglandins produced differs from woman to woman and even from cycle to cycle in the same woman; therefore, women may experience dysmenorrhea only during some cycles. Dysmenorrhea generally begins in the early teens and is most severe during the teens and early 20s; it then typically declines with age (Golub, 1992), although some women report its return prior to menopause. Almost every woman experiences menstrual cramps from time to time, and about 50 percent of women experience dysmenorrhea; about 5–10 percent of women experience symptoms severe enough to incapacitate them anywhere from an hour to three days (Golub, 1992).

Although the connection between prostaglandins and menstrual cramps was known in the mid-1960s (Pickles, Hall, Best, & Smith, 1965), prostaglandins were not generally accepted as the cause of cramps until around 1980. Prior to 1980, dysmenorrhea was commonly treated as a conversion disorder. Women who complained of severe symptoms were told that their problems were "all in their heads," advised to have a baby, or referred to a psychiatrist. Many physicians believed that only women who reject the feminine gender role would experience pain during menstruation. There is a large literature that documents the attempt by physicians and psychologists to "prove" that neuroticism causes dysmenorrhea. Many personality and attitude variables were examined, with negative or obscure results. This research area quickly became inactive with the discovery that most women were helped by anti-prostaglandin medications, and physicians and psychologists turned their attention to premenstrual syndrome. Women themselves also seemed to turn their attention to PMS, as one rarely hears complaints these days about dysmenorrhea (Chrisler & Johnston-Robledo, 2002), and self-help books for PMS commonly list cramps and other symptoms of dysmenorrhea as symptoms of PMS (Chrisler, 2003).

Today women with dysmenorrhea are advised to take an over-the-counter anti-prostaglandin medication (e.g., ibuprofen). If that does not work, they should see a gynecologist who can prescribe a stronger medication and conduct a physical examination to determine that the dysmenorrhea is indeed primary, as opposed to secondary to a more serious condition such as endometriosis or pelvic inflammatory disease. Other strategies that women find useful in coping with mild to moderate dysmenorrhea include muscle relaxation, pain control imagery, stretching exercises (e.g., yoga), warm baths, heating pads, rest, and orgasm. Systematic desensitization (Tasto & Chesney, 1974), autogenic training, and both temperature and electromyogramic biofeedback (Sedlacek & Heczey, 1977) have been used successfully in therapy to reduce menstrual pain.

Premenstrual Syndrome

Premenstrual syndrome, commonly known as PMS, refers to the experience of psychological and physiological changes in the three to five days prior to the onset of menstruation. The most frequently reported symptom of PMS is fluid retention, particularly in the breasts and abdomen. Other commonly reported symptoms include headaches, backaches, constipation, food cravings, acne, anxiety, tension, lethargy, sleep changes, irritability, and depression. More than a hundred changes have been associated with PMS in the professional and popular literature (Chrisler, 2003; Chrisler & Levy, 1990; Figert, 1996; Laws, Hey, & Eagen, 1985), including some so gendered that they would never be considered "symptoms" in men (e.g., craving for sweets, increased sexual desire). It has been suggested (Dalton, 1960a, 1960b, 1968), although there is little scientific evidence for this, that premenstrual women have difficulty concentrating, exhibit poor judgment, lack physical coordination, exhibit decreased efficiency, and perform less well at school or on the job. Women also report cognitive, behavioral, and psychological changes that they welcome and view as positive, such as bursts of energy and activity, increased creativity, increased sex drive, feelings of affection, increased personal strength or power, and feelings of connection to nature and other women (Chrisler, Johnston, Champagne, & Preston, 1994; Lee, 2002; Nichols, 1995). These premenstrual experiences are rarely mentioned in the professional or popular literature because they do not fit the conceptualization of the premenstruum as a time of illness and dysphoria.

Sometimes lists of the symptoms of PMS include some surprising items, such as seizures or convulsions, asthma attacks, and herpes. Obviously, normal luteal-phase biochemistry does not cause women to develop epilepsy, asthma, or sexually transmitted infections. However, Woods and her colleagues (Mitchell et al., 1994; Woods, Mitchell, & Lentz, 1999) have documented cases in which menstrual cycle fluctuations aggravate or magnify (PMM) existing health conditions, and they suggested that menstrual cycle–related changes are capable of triggering flare-ups of chronic conditions. Among the conditions that can flare up premenstrually are asthma, allergies, sinusitis, depression, anxiety disorders, herpes, irritable bowel syndrome, migraine headaches, and multiple sclerosis (Taylor & Colino, 2002). Symptoms of these conditions overlap with those listed above as commonly reported by women as features of PMS (e.g., fatigue, tension, sadness, anxiety, irritability, insomnia, constipation, and diarrhea). Perhaps some women who think they have PMS actually have a relapsing-remitting chronic illness that has not been diagnosed as such because some flare-ups have coincided with the premenstrual phase and thus misled the woman to dismiss them as "just PMS."

Many of the commonly listed symptoms of PMS (e.g., headaches, backaches, irritability, tension, crying, fatigue) overlap with the physical sensations associated with stress (Chrisler, 2004). A number of researchers (Beck, Gevirtz, & Mortola, 1990; Coughlin, 1990; Gallant, Popiel, Hoffman, Chahraborty, & Hamilton, 1992; Kuczmierczyk, Labrum, & Johnson, 1992; Maddocks, & Reid, 1992; Warner & Bancroft, 1990) have reported that women who describe themselves as suffering from PMS also indicate that they experience high levels of stress from such sources as workload and work monotony, financial strain, marital dissatisfaction, hectic schedules, and family conflict. Some data indicate that women who report severe symptoms of PMS do not cope as well with stress as do asymptomatic women (or those who report mild symptoms). Women who self-report PMS have been found to be more likely than other women to use coping methods such as avoidance, wishful thinking, appeasement, religion, withdrawal, and focusing on or venting emotions, and they are less likely than other women to use coping methods such as seeking social support, problem solving, and direct action (Gallant, Popiel, & Hoffman, 1994; Genther, Chrisler, & Johnston-Robledo, 1999; Ornitz & Brown, 1993).

Researchers have also reported that women who seek treatment for premenstrual symptoms exhibit higher than average trait anxiety (Giannini, Price, Loiselle, & Giannini, 1985; Halbrecht & Kas, 1977; Mira, Vizzard, & Abraham, 1985; Picone & Kirby, 1990), adhere to the traditional feminine gender role (Freeman, Sondheimer, & Rickels, 1987; Stout & Steege, 1985), and have a higher than average lifetime incidence of sexual assault and abuse (Taylor, Golding, Menard, & King, 2001) and affective disorders, especially depression and anxiety (DeJong, Rubinow, Roy-Byrne, Hoban, Griver, & Post, 1985; Dennerstein, Morse, & Varnanides, 1988; Endicott & Halbreich, 1988; Kraaimaat & Veeninga, 1995; Pearlstein, Frank, Rivera-Tovar, Thoft, Jacobs, & Mieczkowski, 1990; Warner, Bancroft, Dixson, & Hampson, 1991).

It is time to acknowledge the possibility that the stress of women's busy, overburdened lives and, in some cases, traumatic events contribute as much to the experience of PMS as does the menstrual cycle (Chrisler & Johnston-Robledo, 2002). If women's coping abilities are being strained by a history of trauma and/or affective or anxiety disorders, it makes sense that changes associated with the menstrual cycle may be perceived as the "last straw" that strains them beyond control (Chrisler & Caplan, 2002). Nor is it surprising that women who endorse the traditional feminine gender-role tend to choose indirect, passive, and self-blaming (e.g., "It's not your fault, it's my PMS") strategies for coping with stress (Chrisler & Johnston-Robledo, 2002).

Although there is a large body of literature about PMS in biomedical and psychosocial journals, there is no definitive cause of PMS (although speculations include gonadal or adrenal hormone levels, sleep disturbance, inadequate nutrition, stress, obesity, neuroticism, and self-fulfilling prophecy), nor is there a cure. Although data do indicate that women experience cyclic changes, it is difficult to know how common such changes are. Estimates of the number of women who experience premenstrual "symptoms," which depend on how the data were collected, vary from 2 percent (using the strictest criteria of a 30 percent increase in the intensity of selected emotional and physical experience charted daily over at least two menstrual cycles) to 100 percent (using the loosest criteria, e.g., "Have you ever experienced cyclic changes in your physical or emotional state?") (Chrisler, 2004). Perhaps only 5 percent of women experience symptoms severe enough to require medical attention (Rose & Abplanalp, 1983).

Despite efforts by the Society for Menstrual Cycle Research and the National Institute of Mental Health to produce a standard definition, there is little agreement on how many changes must be experienced or how severe the experience must be in order to be considered a case of PMS. So many different definitions exist in the literature that the results of studies cannot easily be compared. Even the timing of the premenstrual phase is unclear. Some researchers define it as three to five days or five to seven days prior to menstruation. Others have defined it as the time between ovulation and menstruation (about two weeks), and some self-help books suggest that the premenstrual phase can last almost three weeks (Chrisler, 2003).

The problem of prevalence estimates is made more difficult by the fact that premenstrual experience is highly variable and personal. All women do not experience the same changes; moreover, the experience of any given woman may vary from cycle to cycle. In addition, PMS has become such a part of popular culture in the past 25 years that the results of surveys have undoubtedly been affected by a response bias in the direction of the stereotype of the premenstrual woman (Chrisler, 2004). Thus, many women have diagnosed themselves with PMS.

Feminist scholars (e.g., Chrisler & Caplan, 2002; Figert, 1996; Houppert, 1999; Martin, 1988; Rittenhouse, 1991) have noted ways in which political expediency has influenced scientific and cultural interest in the premenstrual phase of the menstrual cycle. The social construction of PMS is generally agreed to have begun during the Great Depression with the publication of an article by Robert Frank (1931), an American gynecologist, who described a condition he called "premenstrual tension." He wrote that women became tense and irritable just prior to menstruation, and he expressed concerns about their tendency to engage in "foolish and ill considered actions" during that time (p. 1054). Frank's discovery added a modern veneer to the cult of invalidism and Victorian-era concerns about the ill effects that intellectual exertion might have on the menstrual cycle, and it provided a good reason why women should stay out of the workforce and leave the few jobs that were available to men.

Katharina Dalton, who coined the term *premenstrual syndrome*, published her first work on it during the 1950s, when middle-class women were being urged to become full-time homemakers and leave their jobs to veterans of World War II. Biomedical and social scientists began to pay serious attention to PMS in the 1970s, after the widespread gains of the women's liberation movement. By the mid-1980s, during the conservative antifeminist backlash in the United States and the United Kingdom, in which the British courts accepted PMS as a plea of diminished responsibility, PMS was firmly established as a cultural stereotype of women (see Chrisler, 2002). At the same time, the American Psychiatric Association devised *premenstrual dysphoric disorder* (PMDD; first termed "late luteal phase dysphoric disorder") and inserted it into the third revised edition of the *Diagnostic and Statistical Manual of Mental Disorders* (*DSM-III-R*). Thus we can see a clear pattern of professionals stepping forward to remind women each time they make gains in the public sphere that they cannot go much further due to their delicate physical and emotional health.

PMDD is defined in the *DSM-IV* (American Psychiatric Association, 1994) as requiring at least five of the following (with at least one among the first four) symptoms present during most of the week that precedes the menses:

> 1) feeling sad, hopeless, or self-deprecating; 2) feeling tense, anxious, or "on edge"; 3) marked lability of mood interspersed with frequent tearfulness; 4) persistent irritability, anger, and increased interpersonal conflicts; 5) decreased interest in usual activities, which may be associated with withdrawal from social relationships; 6) difficulty concentrating; 7) feeling fatigued, lethargic, or lacking in energy; 8) marked changes in appetite, which may be associated with binge eating or craving certain foods; 9) hypersomnia or insomnia; 10) a subjective sense of being overwhelmed or out of control; 11) physical symptoms such as breast tenderness or swelling, headaches, or sensations of "bloating" or weight gain, with tightness of clothing, shoes, or rings. There may also be joint or muscle pain ... [or] suicidal thoughts. (p. 716)

To distinguish PMDD from other forms of depression that might simply worsen at points during the menstrual cycle, the criteria state that all of the symptoms must be absent during the week after the menses. The *DSM-IV* description also includes the estimates that at least 75 percent of women report minor or isolated premenstrual changes, but only 3–5 percent experience symptoms that meet the PMDD criteria. Although it was the stated intent of the psychiatrists who developed PMDD to move away from the "kitchen sink" diagnostic criteria of PMS and define a subset of women who experienced a unique psychiatric disorder, the symptoms of PMDD overlap with those of PMS as defined by Debrovner (1982) and others, and advertisements for pharmacological treatments for PMDD have encouraged women to confuse PMS and PMDD (Chrisler & Caplan, 2002; Cosgrove & Riddle, 2003). Furthermore, no definitive evidence has ever been produced to show that PMDD is a separate entity from PMS or from other forms of depression (Chrisler & Caplan, 2002). Feminist scholars (e.g., Caplan, McCurdy-Myers, & Gans, 1992; Nash & Chrisler, 1997; Offman & Kleinplatz, 2004) have expressed concerns that the presence of PMDD in the *DSM* will result in more, not fewer, erroneous diagnoses of women's complaints and will lead to increased bias and discrimination against women. (For a discussion of the politics of the development and implementation of the psychiatric diagnosis, see Caplan, 1995, or Figert, 1996.)

An interesting new line of research consists of qualitative studies (e.g., focus groups, interviews, discourse analysis) of women's beliefs about, attitudes toward, and embrace of or resistance to the PMS label. Most of the participants in these studies have been white women, as have most of the women who have sought services at PMS clinics (Markens, 1996) and most of the women depicted in the cultural products mentioned earlier. Although African American and European American women have reported similar levels of premenstrual symptoms in community studies (Stout, Grady, Steege, Blazer, George, & Melville, 1986), African American women's apparent reluctance to seek medical services and the scarcity of articles about PMS in magazines that target black women (Markens, 1996) suggest that the resistance to the PMS label may be greater in some ethnic and socioeconomic groups than in others. Perhaps women who have experienced discrimination that is class-, race-, language-, or sexual orientation–based are less willing to call attention to their female state or less able to believe that they can expect sympathy for their condition than are women who have experienced less (or less overt) discrimination in their lives.

In a series of interviews with women patients recruited from a PMS clinic in England, Swann and Ussher (1995) found that their participants' views of PMS were very similar to those presented in popular culture. They firmly believed that PMS is biologically based, and they rejected situational attributions for their distress, which the authors described as "romantic discourse" (e.g., "everything else in my life is fine, it's just my PMS") (p. 365). Swann and Ussher's participants adopted a "dualistic discourse" (p. 364) that parallels the Jekyll and Hyde or "me/not me" discourse in self-help books for PMS (Chrisler,

2003). One of their participants spoke of herself as possessed by a sort of menstrual madness ("this thing that takes over me"; Swann & Ussher, 1995, p. 364) that causes her to lose control of her emotions and actions. In framing their premenstrual experience this way, women assert that Ms. Hyde—"not me"—is responsible for any interpersonal problems, impulsivity, or other negative outcomes that derive from actions taken during the premenstrual phase of the cycle.

In more recent studies (Cosgrove & Riddle, 2003; Lee, 2002) of community samples of women with and without PMS, there is evidence of more ambivalence and some resistance, yet beliefs similar to those expressed by the English PMS patients. Lee (2002) found that women with negative attitudes toward menstruation were more likely to consider PMS to be an appropriate label for their personal experience and to believe that women's symptoms are not taken seriously without a medical explanation. Women with more positive attitudes toward menstruation were more critical of the label PMS, even though most of them said that they did experience it to some extent. Some commented that the term disempowers women by subsuming their experiences under the umbrella of illness. A few spoke of "changes" rather than "symptoms," as many feminist writers do, in order to "own" both the problematic and the positive fluctuations they experienced.

Cosgrove and Riddle (2003) also found the frequent use of dualistic ("me/not me") discourse in their participants' accounts of their premenstrual experience. It is interesting to note that the women in their study who resisted the PMS label used biological discourse (e.g., genetics) to explain why they did not suffer from PMS (e.g., "I'm just lucky that I have good genes"). This shows how firmly the biological basis of PMS is implanted in the culture, even though the scientific evidence to sustain it is lacking.

Behavioral, nutritional, and pharmacological treatments that target individual symptoms can help women to cope with premenstrual changes. Vitamin B, aspirin, diuretics, exercise, relaxation techniques, extra sleep, and reduction of salt intake may be particularly useful (Chrisler & Johnston-Robledo, 2000). Women should also be encouraged to challenge their attributions about their premenstrual experiences. Instead of labeling their experiences as "symptoms," they could call them "changes." Women can be encouraged to think of themselves as "sensitive," rather than as "ill" or as "overreacting" (Koeske, 1983). If we lived in a society in which women wore loose clothing such as robes or saris, would we even notice water retention (Rome, 1986), much less consider it a symptom of a disorder? Why is an occasional urge to eat a candy bar or a salty snack seen as a sign of a medical condition (Chrisler, 2004)? Are there benefits to the experience of cyclic variations? Is change not preferable to stagnation (Chrisler & Johnston-Robledo, 2000)? Furthermore, women should be educated about the fact that hormones do not make people angry or irritable, although they may intensify those reactions. There are always reasons for women's anger, and it is those reasons, not hormonal levels, that should be addressed.

Menopause

Menopause refers to the cessation of reproductive capacity; it is defined as 12 months without a menstrual period. Menopause occurs as a result of age-related changes that lead to the gradual diminishing of the production of ovarian hormones. The average age of North American women at menopause is 50 years, but it can occur naturally at any age between 40 and 60 (Golub, 1992). The process that leads to menopause (known as *perimenopause*) takes about seven years to complete. Therefore, a woman who will reach menopause at age 50 will probably notice the first changes in her menstrual cycle at around age 43. Early changes are likely to include menstrual cycle irregularity, including shorter or longer cycles and heavier or lighter menstrual flow. Menopause can also occur artificially, as a result of the surgical removal of the uterus and ovaries, and women who reach menopause in this sudden way often report more severe symptoms and distress than those who approach it gradually (Voda, 1997).

Perhaps because it is associated with aging, menopause is often viewed in Western societies as a negative event. However, surveys (e.g., Huffman, Myers, Tingle, & Bond, 2005; Maoz, Dowty, Antonovsky, & Wijsenbeck, 1970; Neugarten, Wood, Kraines, & Loomis, 1968) of midlife women have typically shown that women have mixed feelings. The downside of menopause, women say, is the loss of fertility, physiological changes that accompany it, feeling less feminine, having a clear sign of aging, and a belief that it has come too soon. The upside is the end of dealing with menstrual periods, the end of contraceptive concerns, and a general sense of liberation. Older women typically have more positive attitudes toward menopause than younger women do, and they are more likely than younger women to agree that postmenopausal women feel freer, calmer, and more confident than ever. Many women find that the worst part of menopause is not knowing what to expect.

One reason why women do not know what to expect is that until recently menopause was not discussed very much; women tended to keep their experiences private. However, knowing about others' experiences does not help much in predicting one's own. Perimenopausal physiological changes and women's emotional reactions to them are highly variable. The most common menopause-related symptom is the hot flash (or flush), which, surveys show, is experienced by between 43 percent and 93 percent of women (Woods, 1982). One reason women complain about the experience of hot flashes is the concern that sweating or flushing red skin will alert other people to their perimenopausal status: the secret will be "out."

Other frequent perimenopausal complaints include sweating, vaginal dryness, headaches, vertigo, fatigue, weight gain, aches and pains, insomnia, irritability, tingling sensations, and anxiety. Some of these symptoms are undoubtedly related to each other. For example, hot flashes that occur during sleep (also known as "night sweats") can awaken women several times each night. Regular experience of sleep deprivation leaves women fatigued and irritable and may increase their anxiety as bedtime draws near. Stress is known to trigger hot flashes, and so do caffeine, alcohol, hot weather, and spicy foods (Voda, 1982). The notion that depression is linked to menopause (once known as "involutional melancholia") is not empirically supportable; data from large epidemiological surveys (e.g., McKinley, McKinley, & Brambila, 1987) indicate that women are no more likely to be depressed at midlife than they are at any other developmental stage.

Images of older women and information about menopause in the media tend to be negative (Chrisler, Torrey, & Matthes, 1999; Gannon & Stevens, 1998; Mansfield & Voda, 1993; Rostosky & Travis, 2000). The first widespread public discussion of menopause was occasioned by the publication in 1966 of Robert Wilson's book *Feminine Forever*, which championed estrogen replacement therapy. Wilson's (1966) thesis was that menopause signals the end not only of women's reproductive capacity, but also of their attractiveness, femininity, sexuality, energy, and, ultimately, health. He defined menopause as a deficiency disease and pointed to synthetic hormones as its cure. Articles in the popular press, inspired by Wilson's book, described menopausal women as "crippled castrates" and menopause as "a natural plague," "a horror of living decay," "progressive defeminization," "one of nature's mistakes," and a "serious physical and mental syndrome" that only medical treatment can "prevent" (Chrisler et al., 1999, p. 30). It seems that Tavris (1992, p. 133) was correct when she noted that "the only thing worse for women than menstruating is not menstruating."

Within 10 years of the publication of Wilson's book, the medical professionals' and the public's enthusiasm for unopposed estrogen treatment began to dim, as it became clear that it did not produce all of the effects claimed for it. Estrogen did help to reduce hot flashes, but it did not retard aging, make older women supple and graceful, or improve psychological symptoms. Furthermore, it was shown to lead to uterine cancer. Feminist theorists (MacPherson, 1981; McCrea, 1983) and women's health organizations (e.g., the Boston Women's Health Book Collective, the National Women's Health Network) urged women to think of menopause not as an illness but as a normal developmental transition (like menarche) to which one must adjust.

However, the potential to market hormone replacement therapy (HRT) to the approaching Baby Boom generation may have been too much for pharmaceutical companies to resist. They began to produce combinations of synthetic estrogen and progesterone in order to avoid uterine cancer, and soon the media were telling women that HRT would not only reduce the troublesome symptoms of perimenopause but also prevent heart disease, osteoporosis, and cognitive decline. Experts urged all perimenopausal women to begin HRT at the earliest signs of menstrual cycle–related changes and to continue it for the rest of their lives, even though Medicaid, Medicare, and many private insurance plans did not reimburse women for the cost.

In 1991 the National Institutes of Health began the Women's Health Initiative (WHI) HRT trial, which was designed to look at heart disease rates in a large-scale, double-blind, clinical trial, the type of research often referred to in medicine as the "gold standard." The WHI was stopped in 2002, several years ahead of schedule, because the results showed that the number of blood clots in women on HRT was three times higher than that in women in the control group. The data also showed increased rates of stroke and breast cancer in women on HRT. Thus, not only was HRT not the panacea its proponents had claimed, it could actually harm women's health. Women's health activists, including members of the Society for Menstrual Cycle Research, who had long expressed skepticism about the claims made for HRT and urged women not to use it over the long term in the absence of demonstrated need and safety, were both vindicated and angered by the results of the WHI. Not only had millions of women put their health at risk by following medical advice, but proponents of HRT immediately began to criticize the carefully designed WHI and to seek ways to utilize HRT "safely."

Many women who had been using HRT (or had been planning to use it) were disappointed to learn that it was no longer an option for them. Coping with physical symptoms is an important task during the menopausal transition, and there are many safe ways to do it. Good health habits at midlife, such as exercise, proper diet, and stress management, are often helpful. Vitamins E and C and herbal treatments (e.g., yams, motherwort, black cohosh) might help to control hot flashes, as would noting and then avoiding triggers of hot flashes, and many cognitive-behavioral techniques can also assist in coping. Women might try dressing in layers, carrying a fan, standing in front of an air conditioner or open refrigerator, sipping cool drinks, and using imagery (e.g., walking through a snowstorm, swimming in a mountain stream) (Golub, 1992; Greenwood, 1996; Voda, 1997). Perimenopausal women should concentrate on the positive aspects of the achievement of menopause and should remind themselves, when a symptom occurs, that this, too, shall pass. Books such as *Menopause: Me and You* (Voda,

1997) and *Mind over Menopause* (Kagan, Kessel, & Benson, 2004) contain other good advice for midlife women.

CONCLUSION

It is striking that a phenomenon as familiar as the menstrual cycle can be so misunderstood. College students in my Psychology of Women classes, who are otherwise well educated and sophisticated, tell me that they have never heard the word *menarche*. They do not understand the difference between dysmenorrhea and PMS, and they confuse "the menstrual cycle" with "the menses," or menstrual phase of the cycle. How is it possible that cultural images of stereotypical premenstrual women can be found everywhere, yet menstruation remains a taboo topic of conversation? The answer no doubt is political.

As Sommer (1983) noted, the menstrual cycle is such a clear differentiation between women and men that its very existence has become politicized and used against women—to keep them out of higher education, good jobs, and powerful roles; to keep them in their traditional places. In ancient times, men found menstruation frightening; it was mysterious because it could not be understood. Today it is women who find menstruation (and menopause, and the premenstrual phase of the cycle) frightening because they have been convinced that anything to do with the menstrual cycle signals illness that requires medical treatment. Women fear that they will lose control of their emotions and appetites when they are premenstrual; that they will be discovered, humiliated, and stigmatized when they are menstruating; that they will not be able to cope with the symptoms of menopause; and that the decline in gonadal hormone levels will leave them vulnerable to all manner of disease. Women have been taught to see their own bodies as the enemy, as shameful, disgraceful, and unmanageable, and to be preoccupied with their bodies' deficits—real or imagined. If we accept this negative and medicalized cultural framing of a benign psychophysiological process once known to earlier generations of women as "my friend," there will be no need for the powers-that-be to keep women in our "places"—we will do it ourselves.

REFERENCES

Adams, D. B., Gold, A. R., & Burt, A. D. (1978). Rise in female-initiated sexual activity at ovulation and its suppression by oral contraceptives. *New England Journal of Medicine, 229,* 1145–1150.

American Psychiatric Association. (1994). *Diagnostic and statistical manual of mental disorders* (4th ed.). Washington, DC: American Psychiatric Association.

AuBuchon, P. G., & Calhoun, K. S. (1985). Menstrual cycle symptomatology: The role of social expectancy and experimental demand characteristics. *Psychosomatic Medicine, 47,* 35–45.

Beck, L. E., Gevirtz, R., & Mortola, J. F. (1990). The predictive role of psychosocial stress on symptom severity in premenstrual syndrome. *Psychosomatic Medicine, 52,* 536–543.

Berg, D. H., & Coutts, L. B. (1994). The extended curse: Being a woman every day. *Health Care for Women International, 15,* 11–22.

Bernstein, B. E. (1977). Effects of menstruation on academic performance among college women. *Archives of Sexual Behavior, 6,* 289–296.

Britton, C. J. (1999). Learning about "the curse": An anthropological perspective on experiences of menstruation. *Women's Studies International Forum, 19,* 645–653.

Brooks-Gunn, J., & Ruble, D. N. (1980). The Menstrual Attitude Questionnaire. *Psychosomatic Medicine, 42,* 503–512.

Brooks-Gunn, J., & Ruble, D. N. (1986). Men's and women's attitudes and beliefs about the menstrual cycle. *Sex Roles, 14,* 287–299.

Buckley, T. (1982). Menstruation and the power of Yurok women: Methods in cultural reconstruction. *American Ethnologist, 9,* 47–60.

Buckley, T., & Gottlieb, A. (1988). A critical appraisal of theories of menstrual symbolism. In T. Buckley & A. Gottlieb (Eds.), *Blood magic: The anthropology of menstruation* (pp. 3–50). Berkeley: University of California Press.

Bullough, V., & Voght, M. (1973). Women, menstruation, and nineteenth century medicine. *Bulletin of the History of Medicine, 47,* 66–82.

Burrows, A., & Johnson, S. (2005). Girls' experiences of menarche and menstruation. *Journal of Reproductive and Infant Psychology, 23,* 235–249.

Calogero, R. M., Davis, W. N., & Thompson, J. K. (2005). The role of self-objectification in the experience of women with eating disorders. *Sex Roles, 52,* 43–50.

Caplan, P. (1995). *They say you're crazy: How the world's most powerful psychiatrists decide who's normal.* Reading, MA: Addison-Wesley.

Caplan, P. J., McCurdy-Myers, J., & Gans, M. (1992). Should "premenstrual syndrome" be called a psychiatric abnormality? *Feminism & Psychology, 2,* 27–44.

Chiarello, C., McMahon, M. A., & Shaefer, K. (1989). Visual cerebral lateralization over phases of the menstrual cycle. *Brain and Cognition, 11,* 18–36.

Chrisler, J. C. (1988). Age, sex-role orientation, and attitudes toward menstruation. *Psychological Reports, 63,* 827–834.

Chrisler, J. C. (1991). The effect of premenstrual symptoms on creative thinking. In D. L. Taylor & N. F. Woods (Eds.), *Menstruation, health, and illness* (pp. 73–83). Washington, DC: Hemisphere.

Chrisler, J. C. (2002). Hormone hostages: The cultural legacy of PMS as a legal defense. In L. H. Collins, M. R. Dunlap, & J. C. Chrisler (Eds.), *Charting a new course for feminist psychology* (pp. 238–252). Westport, CT: Praeger.

Chrisler, J. C. (2003). How to maintain your control and balance: The "pop" approach to PMS. Paper presented at the meeting of the Mid-Atlantic Popular Culture Association, Wilmington, DE, November.

Chrisler, J. C. (2004). PMS as a culture-bound syndrome. In J. C. Chrisler. C. Golden, & P. D. Rozee (Eds.), *Lectures on the psychology of women* (3rd ed.; pp. 110–127). Boston: McGraw-Hill.

Chrisler, J. C., & Caplan, P. (2002). The strange case of Dr. Jekyll and Ms. Hyde: How PMS became a cultural phenomenon and a psychiatric disorder. *Annual Review of Sex Research, 13,* 274–306.

Chrisler, J. C., Johnston, I. K., Champagne, N. M., & Preston, K. E. (1994). Menstrual joy: The construct and its consequences. *Psychology of Women Quarterly, 18,* 375–387.

Chrisler, J. C., & Johnston-Robledo, I. (2002). Raging hormones? Feminist perspectives on premenstrual syndrome and postpartum depression. In M. Ballou & L. S. Brown (Eds.), *Rethinking mental health and disorder: Feminist perspectives* (pp. 174–197). New York: Guilford.

Chrisler, J. C., & Levy, K. B. (1990). The media construct a menstrual monster: A content analysis of PMS articles in the popular press. *Women & Health, 16*(2), 89–104.

Chrisler, J. C., & McCool, H. R. (1991). Activity level across the menstrual cycle. *Perceptual and Motor Skills, 72,* 794.

Chrisler, J. C., Rose, J. G., Dutch, S. E., Sklarsky, K. G., & Grant, M. C. (In press). The PMS illusion: Social cognition maintains social construction. *Sex Roles.*

Chrisler, J. C., Torrey, J. W., & Matthes, M. M. (1999). Brittle bones and sagging breasts, loss of femininity and loss of sanity: The media describe the menopause. In A. M. Voda & R. Conover (Eds.), *Proceedings of the 8th conference of the Society for Menstrual Cycle Research* (pp. 23–35). Scottsdale, AZ: Society for Menstrual Cycle Research.

Chrisler, J. C., & Zittel, C. B. (1998). Menarche stories: Reminiscences of college students from Lithuania, Malaysia, Sudan, and the United States. *Health Care for Women International, 19,* 303–312.

Clarke, A. E., & Ruble, D. N. (1978). Young adolescents' beliefs concerning menstruation. *Child Development, 49,* 231–234.

Compton, R. J., & Levine, S. C. (1997). Menstrual cycle phase and mood effects on menstrual asymmetry. *Brain and Cognition, 35,* 168–183.

Cosgrove, L., & Riddle, B. (2003). Constructions of femininity and experiences of menstrual distress. *Women & Health, 38*(3), 37–58.

Costos, D., Ackerman, R., & Paradis, L. (2002). Recollections of menarche: Communication between mothers and daughters regarding menstruation. *Sex Roles, 46,* 49–59.

Coughlin, P. C. (1990). Premenstrual syndrome: How marital satisfaction and role choice affect symptom severity. *Social Work, 35,* 351–355.

Coutts, L. B., & Berg, D. H. (1993). The portrayal of the menstruating woman in menstrual product advertisements. *Health Care for Women International, 14,* 179–191.

Dalton, K. (1960a). Effects of menstruation on schoolgirls' weekly work. *British Medical Journal, 1,* 326–328.

Dalton, K. (1960b). Schoolgirls' behavior and menstruation. *British Medical Journal, 2,* 1647–1649.

Dalton, K. (1968). Menstruation and examinations. *Lancet, 2,* 1386–1388.

Dawood, M. Y. (1981). Hormones, prostaglandins, and dysmenorrhea. In M. Y. Dawood (Ed.), *Dysmenorrhea* (pp. 21–52). Baltimore: Williams & Wilkins.

DeJong, R., Rubinow, D. R., Roy-Byrne, P., Hoban, M. C., Griver, G. N., & Post, R. M. (1985). Premenstrual mood disorder and psychiatric illness. *American Journal of Psychiatry, 142,* 1359–1361.

Delaney, J., Lupton, M. J., & Toth, E. (1987). *The curse: A cultural history of menstruation* (rev. ed.). Urbana: University of Illinois Press.

Dennerstein, L., Morse, C. A., & Varnanides, K. (1988). Premenstrual tension and depression: Is there a relationship? *Journal of Psychosomatic Obstetrics and Gynecology, 18,* 45–52.

Endicott, J., & Halbreich, U. (1988). Clinical significance of premenstrual dysphoric changes. *Journal of Clinical Psychiatry, 49,* 486–489.

Englander-Golden, P. Sonleitener, F. J., Whitmore, M., & Corbley, G. (1986). Social and menstrual cycles: Methodological and substantive findings. In V. Olesen & N. F. Woods (Eds.), *Culture, society, and menstruation* (pp. 77–96). Washington, DC: Hemisphere.

Erchull, M. J., Chrisler, J. C., Gorman, J. A., & Johnston-Robledo, I. (2003). Education and advertising: A content analysis of commercially produced booklets about menstruation. *Journal of Early Adolescence, 22,* 455–474.

Ernster, V. L. (1975). American menstrual expressions. *Sex Roles, 1,* 3–13.

Figert, A. E. (1996). *Women and the ownership of PMS: The structuring of a psychiatric disorder*. New York: Aldine de Gruyter.

Forbes, G. B., Adams-Curtis, L. E., White, K. B., & Holmgren, K. M. (2003). The role of hostile and benevolent sexism in women's and men's perceptions of the menstruating woman. *Psychology of Women Quarterly, 27,* 58–63.

Frank, R. T. (1931). The hormonal causes of premenstrual tension. *Archives of Neurology and Psychiatry, 26,* 1053–1057.

Frazer, J. G. (1951). *The golden bough*. New York: Macmillan.

Freeman, E. W., Sondheimer, S. J., & Rickels, K. (1987). Effects of medical history factors on symptom severity in women meeting criteria for premenstrual syndrome. *Obstetrics and Gynecology, 72,* 236–239.

Gallant, S. J., Popiel, D. A., & Hoffman, D. M. (1994). The role of psychological variables in the experience of premenstrual symptoms. In N. F. Woods (Ed.), *Mind-body rhythmicity: A menstrual cycle perspective* (pp. 139–151). Seattle: Hamilton & Cross.

Gallant, S. J., Popiel, D. A., Hoffman, D. M., Chahraborty, P. K., & Hamilton, J. A. (1992). Using daily ratings to confirm premenstrual syndrome/late luteal phase dysphoric disorder II: What makes a real difference? *Psychosomatic Medicine, 54,* 167–181.

Gannon, L., & Stevens, J. (1998). Portraits of menopause in the media. *Women & Health, 27*(3), 1–15.

Genther, A. B., Chrisler, J. C., & Johnston-Robledo, I. (1999). Coping, locus of control, and the experience of premenstrual symptoms. Paper presented at the annual meeting of the American Psychological Association, Boston, August.

Gersh, E. S., & Gersh, I. (1981). *Biology of women*. Baltimore: University Park Press.

Giannini, A. J., Price, W. A., Loiselle, R. H., & Giannini, M. D. (1985). Pseudo cholinesterase and trait anxiety in premenstrual tension syndrome. *Journal of Clinical Psychiatry, 46,* 139–140.

Gillooly, J. B. (1998). *Before she gets her period: Talking with your daughter about menstruation*. Los Angeles: Perspective.

Golub, S. (1976). The effect of premenstrual anxiety and depression on cognitive function. *Journal of Personality and Social Psychology, 34,* 99–104.

Golub, S. (1981). Sex differences in attitudes toward and beliefs regarding menstruation. In P. Komnenich, M. McSweeney, J. A. Noack, & N. Elder (Eds.),

The menstrual cycle: Research and implications for women's health (pp. 129–134). New York: Springer.

Golub, S. (1992). *Periods: From menarche to menopause*. Newbury Park, CA: Sage.

Greenwood, S. (1996). *Menopause naturally* (4th ed.). Volcano, CA: Volcano Press.

Halbreich, U., & Endicott, J. (1987). Dysphoric premenstrual changes: Are they related to affective disorders? In B. E. Ginsburg & B. F. Carter (Eds.), *Premenstrual syndrome: Ethical and legal implications in a biomedical perspective* (pp. 351–367). New York: Plenum Press.

Halbreich, U., & Kas, D. (1977). Variations in the Taylor MAS of women with premenstrual syndrome. *Journal of Psychosomatic Research, 21,* 391–393.

Hampson, E. (1990). Estrogen-related variations in human spatial and articulatory motor skills. *Psychoneuroendocrinology, 15,* 97–111.

Hampson, E., & Kimura, D. (1988). Reciprocal effects of hormone fluctuations on human motor an perceptual-spatial skills. *Behavioral Neuroscience, 102,* 456–459.

Harlow, S. D. (1986). Function and dysfunction: A historical critique of the literature on menstruation and work. In V. L. Olesen & N. F. Woods (Eds.), *Culture, society, and menstruation* (pp. 39–50). Washington, DC: Hemisphere.

Havens, B., & Swenson, I. (1989). A content analysis of educational media about menstruation. *Adolescence, 24,* 901–907.

Heard, K. V., & Chrisler, J. C. (1999). The Stereotypic Beliefs about Menstruation Scale. In D. Berg (Ed.), *Looking forward, looking back: The place of women's every day lives in health research* (pp. 139–143). Scottsdale, AZ: Society for Menstrual Cycle Research.

Hoerster, K. D., Chrisler, J. C., & Rose, J. G. (2003). Attitudes toward and experience with menstruation in the US and India. *Women & Health, 38*(3), 77–95.

Houppert, K. (1999). *The curse: Confronting the last unmentionable taboo*. New York: Farrar, Straus, & Giroux.

Huffman, S. B., Myers, J. E., Tingle, L. R., & Bond, L. A. (2005). Menopause symptoms and attitudes of African American women: Closing the knowledge gap and expanding opportunities for counseling. *Journal of Counseling & Development, 83,* 48–56.

Johnston-Robledo, I., Ball, M., Lauta, K., & Zekoll, A. (2003). To bleed or not to bleed: Young women's attitudes toward menstrual suppression. *Women & Health, 38*(3), 59–75.

Kagan, L., Kessel, B., & Benson, H. (2004). *Mind over menopause: The complete mind/body approach to coping with menopause*. New York: Free Press.

Kissling, E. A. (1996). Bleeding out loud: Communication about menstruation. *Feminism & Psychology, 6,* 481–504.

Koeske, R. D. (1983). Lifting the curse of menstruation: Toward a feminist perspective on the menstrual cycle. *Women & Health, 8*(2/3), 1–16.

Koff, E., Reierdan, J., & Jacobson, S. (1981). The personal and interpersonal significance of menarche. *Journal of the American Academy of Child Psychiatry, 20,* 148–158.

Koff, E., Rierdan, J., & Sheingold, K. (1982). Memories of menarche: Age, preparation, and prior knowledge as determinants of initial menstrual experience. *Journal of Youth and Adolescence, 11,* 1–9.

Koff, E., Rierdan, J., & Silverstone, E. (1978). Changes in representation of body image as a function of menarcheal status. *Developmental Psychology, 14,* 635–642.

Kraaimaat, F. W., & Veeninga, A. (1995). Causal attributions in premenstrual syndrome. *Journal of Psychology and Health, 10,* 219–228.

Kuczmierczyk, A. R., Labrum, A. H., & Johnson, C. C. (1992). Perception of family and work environments in women with premenstrual syndrome. *Journal of Psychosomatic Research, 36,* 787–795.

Laws, S., Hey, V., & Eagen, A. (1985). *Seeing red: The politics of premenstrual tension.* London: Hutchinson.

Lazarov, S. (1982). The menstrual cycle and cognitive function. (Doctoral dissertation, Yeshiva University). *Dissertation Abstracts International, 43,* 280B.

Leacock, E. (1978). Women's status in egalitarian society: Implications for social evolution. *Current Anthropology, 19,* 247–255.

Lee, S. (2002). Health and sickness: The meaning of menstruation and premenstrual syndrome in women's lives. *Sex Roles, 46,* 25–35.

Levine, S. (1995). *Degrees of equality: The American Association of University Women and the challenge of twentieth-century feminism.* Philadelphia: Temple University Press.

Levitt, E. E., & Lubin, B. (1967). Some personality factors associated with menstrual complaints and menstrual distress. *Journal of Psychosomatic Research, 11,* 267–270.

Logan, D. D. (1980). The menarche experience in 23 foreign countries. *Adolescence, 15,* 247–256.

Lough, E. M. (1937). A psychological study of functional periodicity. *Journal of Comparative Psychology, 24,* 359–368.

Loulan, J., Worthen, B., Lopez, B., & Dyrud, C. W. (2001). *Period: A girl's guide to menstruation.* Minnetonka, MN: Book Peddlers.

MacPherson, K. (1981). Menopause as disease: The social construction of a metaphor. *Advances in Nursing Science, 3,* 95–113.

Maddocks, S. E., & Reid, R. L. (1992). The role of negative life stress and PMS: Some preliminary findings. In A. J. Dan & L. L. Lewis (Eds.), *Menstrual health in women's lives* (pp. 38–51). Urbana: University of Illinois Press.

Maddux, H. C. (1975). *Menstruation.* New Canaan, CT: Tobey/Dell.

Mansfield, P. K., & Voda, A. (1993). From Edith Bunker to the six o'clock news: What and how midlife women learn about menopause. *Women & Therapy, 14*(1/2), 89–104.

Maoz, B. Dowty, N., Antonovsky, A., & Wijsenbeck, H. (1970). Female attitudes toward menopause. *Social Psychiatry, 5,* 35–40.

Markens, S. (1996). The problematic of "experience": A political and cultural critique of PMS. *Gender & Society, 10,* 42–58.

Martin, E. (1987). *The woman in the body: A cultural analysis of reproduction.* Boston: Beacon Press.

Martin, E. (1988). Premenstrual syndrome: Discipline, work, and anger in late industrial societies. In T. Buckley & A. Gottlieb (Eds.), *Blood magic: The anthropology of menstruation* (pp. 161–181). Berkeley: University of California Press.

Marván, M. L., Ramírez-Esparza, D., Cortés-Iniestra, S., & Chrisler, J. C. (2006). Development of a new scale to measure beliefs about and attitudes toward menstruation (BATM): Data from Mexico and the United States. *Health Care for Women International, 27,* 453–473.

McCrea, F. B. (1983). The politics of menopause: The "discovery" of a deficiency disease. *Social Problems, 31,* 111–123.

McKinley, J. B., McKinley, S. J., & Brambilla, D. (1987). The relative contribution of endocrine changes and social circumstances to depression in mid-aged women. *Journal of Health and Social Behavior, 28,* 345–363.

Merskin, D. (1999). Adolescence, advertising, and the idea of menstruation. *Sex Roles, 40,* 941–957.

Mira, M., Vizzard, J., & Abraham, S. (1985). Personality characteristics in the menstrual cycle. *Journal of Psychosomatic Obstetrics and Gynecology, 4,* 329–334.

Mitchell, E. S., Woods, N. F., & Lentz, M. J. (1994). Differentiation of women with three perimenstrual symptom patterns. *Nursing Research, 43,* 25–30.

Morris, M. N., & Urdry, J. R. (1970). Variations in pedometer activity during the menstrual cycle. *Obstetrics and Gynecology, 35,* 199–201.

Morris, M. N., & Urdry, J. R. (1982). Epidemiological patterns of sexual behavior in the menstrual cycle. In R. C. Friedman (Ed.), *Behavior and the menstrual cycle* (pp. 129–154). New York: Marcel Dekker.

Nash, H. C., & Chrisler, J. C. (1997). Is a little (psychiatric) knowledge a dangerous thing? The impact of premenstrual dysphoric disorder on perceptions of premenstrual women. *Psychology of Women Quarterly, 21,* 315–322.

Neugarten, B. L., Wood, V., Kraines, R. J., & Loomis, B. (1968). Women's attitudes toward menopause. In B. L. Neugarten (Ed.), *Middle age and aging: A reader in social psychology* (pp. 195–200). Chicago: University of Chicago Press.

Nichols, S. (1995). Positive premenstrual experiences: Do they exist? *Feminism & Psychology, 5,* 162–169.

Offman, A., & Kleinplatz, P. J. (2004). Does PMDD belong in the *DSM?* Challenging the medicalization of women's bodies. *Canadian Journal of Human Sexuality, 13,* 17–27.

Ornitz, A. W., & Brown, M. A. (1993). Family coping and premenstrual symptomatology. *Journal of Obstetric, Gynecologic, and Neonatal Nursing, 22,* 49–55.

Owen, L. (1993). *Her blood is gold: Celebrating the power and mystery of menstruation.* San Francisco: Harper.

Oxley, T. (1997). Menstrual management: An exploratory study. *Feminism & Psychology, 8,* 185–191.

Parlee, M. B. (1980). Positive changes in moods and activation levels during the menstrual cycle in experimentally naïve subjects. In A. J. Dan, E. A. Graham, & C. P. Beecher (Eds.), *The menstrual cycle: A synthesis of interdisciplinary research* (pp. 247–263). New York: Springer.

Parlee, M. B. (1983). Menstrual rhythms in sensory processes: A review of fluctuations in vision, olfaction, audition, taste, and touch. *Psychological Bulletin, 93,* 35–48.

Paulson, M. J. (1961). Psychological concomitants of premenstrual tension. *American Journal of Obstetrics and Gynecology, 81,* 733–738.

Pearlstein, T. B., Frank, E., Rivera-Tovar, A., Thoft, J. S., Jacobs, E., & Mieczkowski, T. A. (1990). Prevalence of Axis I and Axis II disorders in women with late luteal phase dysphoric disorder. *Journal of Affective Disorders, 20,* 129–134.

Petersen, A. E. (1983). Menarche; Meaning of measures and measuring meanings. In S. Golub (Ed.), *Menarche: The transition from girl to woman* (pp. 63–76). Lexington, MA: Lexington Books.

Pickles, V. R., Hall, W. J., Best, F. A., & Smith, G. N. (1965). Prostaglandins in endometrium and menstrual fluid from normal and dysmenorrhoeic subjects. *Journal of Obstetrics and Gynecology, 72,* 185–192.

Picone, L., & Kirby, R. J. (1990). Relationship between anxiety and premenstrual syndrome. *Psychological Reports, 67,* 43–48.

Redgrove, J. A. (1971). Menstrual cycles. In W. P. Colquhoun (Ed.), *Biological rhythms and human performance* (pp. 211–240). London: Academic Press.

Rhinehart, E. D. (1989). Psychotherapists' responses to the topic of menstruation in psychotherapy. Paper presented at the meeting of the Society for Menstrual Cycle Research, Salt Lake City, UT, June.

Ripper, M. (1991). Comparison of the effect of the menstrual cycle and the social week on mood, sexual interest, and self-assessed performance. In D. L. Taylor & N. F. Woods (Eds.), *Menstruation, health, and illness* (pp. 19–32). Washington, DC: Hemisphere.

Rittenhouse, C. A. (1991). The emergence of premenstrual syndrome as a social problem. *Social Problems, 38,* 412–425.

Roberts, T.-A. (2004). Female trouble: The Menstrual Self-evaluation Scale and women's self-objectification. *Psychology of Women Quarterly, 28,* 22–26.

Roberts, T.-A., Goldenberg, J. L., Power, C., & Pyszczynzki, T. (2002). "Feminine protection": The effects of menstruation on attitudes toward women. *Psychology of Women Quarterly, 26,* 131–139.

Roberts, T.-A., & Waters, P. L. (2004). Self-objectification and that "not so fresh feeling": Feminist therapeutic interventions for healthy female embodiment. In J. C. Chrisler (Ed.), *From menarche to menopause: The female body in feminist therapy* (pp. 5–21). Binghamton, NY: Haworth.

Rodin, J. (1976). Menstruation, reattribution, and competence. *Journal of Personality and Social Psychology, 33,* 345–353.

Rogers, M. L., & Harding, S. S. (1981). Retrospective and daily menstrual distress measures using Moos' instruments (Forms A and T) and modified versions of Moss' instruments. In P. Komnenich, M. McSweeney, J. A. Noack, & N. Elder (Eds.), *The menstrual cycle: Research and implications for women's health* (pp. 71–81). New York: Springer.

Rome, E. (1986). Premenstrual syndrome through a feminist lens. In V. L. Olesen & N. F. Woods (Eds.), *Culture, society, and menstruation* (pp. 145–151). Washington, DC: Hemisphere.

Rose, R. M., & Abplanalp, J. M. (1983). The premenstrual syndrome. *Hospital Practice, 18*(6), 129–141.

Rossi, A., & Rossi, E. (1977). Body time and social time: Mood patterns by menstrual cycle and day of the week. *Social Science Research, 6,* 273–308.

Rostosky, S. S., & Travis, C. B. (2000). Menopause and sexuality: Ageism and sexism unite. In C. B. Travis & J. W. White (eds.), *Sexuality, society, and feminism* (pp. 181–210). Washington, DC: American Psychological Association.

Scarborough, E., & Furumoto, L. (1987). *Untold lives: The first generation of American women psychologists.* New York: Columbia University Press.

Schaefer, V. L. (1998). *The care and feeding of you: The body book for girls.* Middleton, WI: American Girl Library/Pleasant Company.

Scott, C. S., Arthur, D., Panzio, M. I., & Owen, R. (1989). Menarche: The black American experience. *Journal of Adolescent Health Care, 10,* 363–368.

Sedlacek, K., & Heczey, M. (1977). A specific treatment for dysmenorrhea. *Proceedings of the Biofeedback Society of America, 8,* 26.

Smith, A. J. (1950). Menstruation and industrial efficiency II: Quality and quantity of production. *Journal of Applied Psychology, 34,* 148–152.

Snow, L. F., & Johnson, S. M. (1978). Myths about menstruation: Victims of our own folklore. *Journal of Women's Studies, 1,* 64–72.

Sommer, B. (1972). Menstrual cycle changes and intellectual performance. *Psychosomatic Medicine, 34,* 263–269.

Sommer, B. (1983). How does menstruation affect cognitive competence and psychophysiological response? *Women & Health, 8*(2/3), 53–90.

Sommer. B. (1987). The file drawer effect and publication rates in menstrual cycle research. *Psychology of Women Quarterly, 11,* 233–242.

Stenn, P. G., & Klinge, V. (1972). Relationship between the menstrual cycle and bodily activity in humans. *Hormones and Behavior, 3,* 297–305.

Stepanich, K. K. (1992). *Sister moon lodge: The power and mystery of menstruation.* Woodbury, MN: Llewellyn.

Stout, A. L., Grady, T. A., Steege, J. F., Blazer, D. G., George, L. K., & Melville, M. L. (1986). Premenstrual symptoms in black and white community samples. *American Journal of Psychiatry, 143,* 1436–1439.

Stout, A. L., & Steege, J. F. (1985). Psychological assessment of women seeking treatment for premenstrual syndrome. *Journal of Psychosomatic Research, 29,* 621–629.

Stubbs, M. L. (1989). Attitudes toward menstruation across the lifespan. Paper presented at the meeting of the Society for Menstrual Cycle Research, Salt Lake City, UT, June.

Stubbs, M. L., & Costos, D. (2004). Negative attitudes toward menstruation: Implications for disconnection within girls and between women. In J. C. Chrisler (Ed.), *From menarche to menopause: The female body in feminist therapy* (pp. 37–54). Binghamton, NY: Haworth.

Swandby, J. R. (1981). A longitudinal study of daily mood self-reports and their relationship to the menstrual cycle. In P. Komnenich, M. McSweeney, J. A. Noack, & N. Elder (Eds.), *The menstrual cycle: Research and implications for women's h*ealth (pp. 93–103). New York: Springer.

Swann, C. J., & Ussher, J. M. (1995). A discourse analytic approach to women's experience of premenstrual syndrome. *Journal of Mental Health, 4,* 359–367.

Szymanski, D. M., & Henning, S. L. (In press). The role of self-objectification in women's depression: A test of objectification theory. *Sex Roles.*

The Tampax report. (1981). New York: Ruder, Finn, & Rotman.

Tanner, J. M. (1991). Secular trends in age of menarche. In R. Lerner, A. Petersen, & J. Brooks-Gunn (Eds.), *Encyclopedia of adolescence* (pp. 637–641). New York: Garland.

Tasto, D. L., & Chesney, M. A. (1974). Muscle relaxation for primary dysmenorrhea. *Behavioral Therapy, 5,* 668–672.

Tavris, C. (1992). *The mismeasure of woman.* New York: Simon & Shuster.

Taylor, D. (1988). *Red flower: Rethinking menstruation.* Freedom, CA: Crossing Press.

Taylor, D., & Colino, S. (2002). *Taking back the month.* New York: Perigree/Berkley.

Taylor, D., Golding, J., Menard, L., & King, M. (2001). Sexual assault and severe PMS: Prevalence and predictors. Paper presented at the meeting of the Society for Menstrual Cycle Research, Avon, CT, June.

Thuren, B. M. (1994). Opening doors and getting rid of shame: Experiences of first menstruation in Valencia, Spain. *Women's Studies International Forum, 17,* 217–228.

Tylka, T. L., & Hill, M. S. (2004). Objectification theory as it relates to disordered eating among college women. *Sex Roles, 51,* 719–730.

Voda, A. M. (1982). Menopausal hot flash. In A. M. Voda, M. Dinnerstein, & S. R. O'Donnell (Eds.), *Changing perspectives on menopause* (pp. 136–159). Austin: University of Texas Press.

Voda, A. M. (1997). *Menopause, me and you.* New York: Harrington Park Press.

Walsh, R. N., Budtz-Olsen, I., Leader, C., & Cummins, R. A. (1981). The menstrual cycle, personality, and academic performance. *Archives of General Psychiatry, 38,* 219–221.

Warner, P., & Bancroft, J. (1990). Factors related to self-reporting of the premenstrual syndrome. *British Journal of Psychiatry, 157,* 249–260.

Warner, P., Bancroft, J., Dixson, A., & Hampson, M. (1991). The relationship between premenstrual mood and depressive illness. *Journal of Affective Disorders, 23,* 9–23.

Whisnant, L., Brett, E., & Zegens, L. (1975). Implicit messages concerning menstruation in commercial educational materials prepared for adolescent girls. *American Journal of Psychiatry, 132,* 815–820.

Whisnant, L., & Zegens, L. (1975). A study of attitudes toward menarche in white middle-class American adolescent girls. *American Journal of Psychiatry, 132,* 809–814.

Wickham, M. (1958). The effects of the menstrual cycle on test performance. *British Journal of Psychology, 49,* 34–41.

Wilcoxon, L. A., Schrader, S. L., & Sherif, C. W. (1976). Daily reports of activities, life events, moods, and somatic changes during the menstrual cycle. *Psychosomatic Medicine, 38,* 399–417.

Williams, G. D., & Williams, A. M. (1982). Sexual behavior and the menstrual cycle. In R. C. Friedman (Ed.), *Behavior and the menstrual cycle* (pp. 155–176). New York: Marcel Dekker.

Williams, L. R. (1983). Beliefs and attitudes of young girls regarding menstruation. In S. Golub (Ed.), *Menarche: The transition from girl to woman* (pp. 139–148). Lexington, MA: Lexington Books.

Wilson, R. A. (1966). *Feminine forever.* New York: Evans.

Wind, L. H. (1995). *New moon rising: Reclaiming the sacred rites of menstruation.* Chicago: Delphi Press.

Woods, N. F. (1982). Menopausal distress: A model for epidemiological investigation. In A. M. Voda, M. Dinnerstein, & S. R. O'Donnell (Eds.), *Changing perspectives on menopause* (pp. 220–238). Austin: University of Texas Press.

Woods, N. F., Dery, G. K., & Most, A. (1983). Recollections of menarche, current menstrual attitudes, and perimenstrual symptoms. *Psychosomatic Medicine, 44,* 285–293.

Woods, N. F., Mitchell, E. S., & Lentz, M. J. (1999). Premenstrual symptoms: Delineating symptom clusters. *Journal of Women's Health and Gender-based Medicine, 8,* 1053–1062.

Zimmerman, N. S., & Chrisler, J. C. (1996). *Menstrual attitudes and beliefs in adolescent girls.* Paper presented at the meeting of the American Psychological Association, Toronto, August.

Chapter 14

Women and Mental Health

Nancy Felipe Russo
Jessica Tartaro

According to reports from the World Health Organization (WHO), an estimated 450 million people around the globe suffer from mental and behavioral disorders—one person in four will develop one or more of these disorders during their lifetime—and psychiatric conditions make up five of the 10 leading causes of disability and premature death worldwide. There are large gender differences in patterns of the rates of mental disorders, the largest gender gap being in anxiety and mood disorders (World Health Organization, 2000, 2004). Depressive disorders alone have been found to represent the fifth greatest disease burden for women, while constituting the seventh greatest burden for men across all physical and mental illnesses (Desjarlais, Eisenberg, Good, & Kleinman, 1996).

With increasing awareness of the impact of gender on mental health, the literature on women's mental health has proliferated across the disciplines in the past two decades. For example, focusing only on articles appearing in peer-reviewed journals, a PsycInfo search for the keywords *women* and either *mental health, mental disorder, depression,* or *anxiety* (the last two being the two most common diagnoses for women) identified 455 articles published in such journals from 1980 to 1989, 1,086 articles published between 1990 and 1999, and 1,953 articles published between 2000 and April 2007. This is an underestimation of the published literature, as specifying other disorders (e.g., eating disorders) would have increased the count. Further, books, book chapters, and other publication venues were not examined. In sum, at least for feminist psychologists, women's mental health is a vital and growing area in psychology and across the disciplines. Indeed, women's mental health has even emerged as a recognized field of biomedical research (Blehar, 2006).

In addition to the burgeoning peer-reviewed literature, numerous public policy reports focus on critical issues for women's mental health and document health disparities and the need for more evidence-based application of the new research findings on women in mental health research, training, and service delivery (e.g., Agency for Healthcare Research and Quality, 2005; American Psychological Association, 1996a, 1996b, 1998, 2007; Hamilton & Russo, 2006; Mazure, Keita, & Blehar (2002). Further, in addition to *Guidelines for Psychotherapy with Lesbian, Gay, and Bisexual Clients* (2000) and *Guidelines on Multicultural Education, Training, Research, Practice, and Organizational Change for Psychologists* (2003), the American Psychological Association recently approved its new *Guidelines for Psychological Practice with Girls and Women* (2006). This work is informed by new theoretical understandings of gender as well as mental health that offer innovative perspectives on women's experiences, circumstances, and development over the life cycle.

This chapter highlights new conceptualizations, methodological issues, and selected research findings related to women and mental health. We focus on the literature published in the 1990s and beyond, including reference to previous or work only when it has a special contribution to make to the point being discussed (see Russo & Green, 1993, and Maracek, 2001, for discussions of previous literature). Because of limited space and the need to narrow the scope of the chapter, and given the wide variation across cultural context, we focus on U.S. studies. We reference international studies only when the findings reveal neglected issues in need of consideration in the U.S. context.

ADVANCES IN UNDERSTANDING MENTAL HEALTH AND DISORDER AMONG WOMEN

In the United States, the biomedical research establishment has continued to focus on the role of sex hormones, seeking evidence for male–female differences in the brain and behavior. Nonetheless, the persistence of health disparities has meant that consideration of social and cultural influences cannot be avoided, and a public health perspective is increasing in influence (Blehar, 2006). Although both genetics and biological factors clearly play a role in risk and expression of mental disorder, it cannot be denied that the mental health problems of women are strongly rooted in their social conditions—conditions that vary in severity globally as well as within nations. Such conditions include hunger (affecting at least 60 percent of women in developing countries), lack of educational and economic resources (with women's work lowly paid and often under dangerous conditions), gender-based violence (including sexual abuse and partner violence), and social disruption leading to displaced populations (including migration due to insufficient economic opportunity, social conflict and war, and natural disaster) (Demyttenaere et al., 2004; Desjarlais et al., 1996).

More needs to done to explain the large variation found across study samples and the extent to which individuals develop adaptive coping skills that lower risk for adverse responses to future traumas. Specific theories explaining gender differences vary depending on the specific disorder studied; however, the more promising theories for explaining gender differences reflect a biopsychosocial perspective with a stress-and-coping perspective (e.g., Hammen, 2005; Keyes & Goodman, 2006; Taylor & Stanton, 2007).

Developmentally, the convergence of adverse experiences, including poverty, discrimination, and victimization, appears to create an "an emerging profile of vulnerability" (Alexander, 1996, p. 61) of risk for mental and addictive disorders. Although specific forms of early trauma, such as sexual abuse, physical violence and abuse, parental death, and parental psychopathology, have been linked to poor adult mental health for some time, the concept of "cumulative adversity" has begun to take hold (Hammen, 2005; Kessler & McGee, 1993; Turner & Lloyd, 1995). Support for this concept is found in the documented relationship of lifetime exposure to adverse life events and an increased risk of anxiety and depressive disorder (Turner & Lloyd, 2004). Evidence suggests that life adversity may sensitize individuals, making them more vulnerable to later negative life events and trauma (Keane, Marshall, & Taft, 2006). Given that activation of cortisol and other normal stress hormones may affect brain structures and physiology, this is an area where biopsychosocial research paradigms are needed (Bowman & Yehuda, 2004; Keane et al., 2006).

Congruent with feminist principles that have guided much of the cutting edge of the U.S. feminist literature (Worell & Johnson, 1997; White, Russo, & Travis, 2001) over the past two decades, there has been an increasing shift of theoretical focus from disorder to the resilience and empowerment of women. A common theme is the need to view mental health in its sociopolitical context, with emphasis on examining power inequities and social control mechanisms at home, at work, and in therapeutic relationships. The need to recognize the complexity of the interacting influences of other dimensions of difference, including ethnicity, class, age, sexual orientation, and disability, has been slowly but increasingly recognized (McCall, 2005; Russo & Vaz, 2001). As Stewart and McDermott (2004) have emphasized, theorizing how these multiple and interlocking dimensions of difference interact requires recognizing "(1) no social group is homogenous, (2) people must be located in terms of social structures that capture the power relations implied by those structures, and (3) there are unique, non-additive effects of identifying with more than one social group" (pp. 531–532).

At the same time that intersections of difference require more theorizing, the importance of recognizing variation within groups characterized by multiple dimensions of difference (e.g., gender and ethnicity) cannot be overemphasized. Fortunately, there are now numerous studies that focus on mental health in subpopulations of women within difference categories (e.g., African Americans, women over 65, lesbian mothers, women with fibromyalgia) and various contexts (college women, women in prison, women in residential treatment, urban women). It is not possible to consider separately all dimensions of difference in our discussion here (Greene & Sanchez-Hucles, 1997). Nonetheless, it should be kept in mind that the rates and predictors of mental disorder can vary substantially within subpopulations of difference categories. For example, analyses of the National Latino and Asian American Study (Alegria, Mulvaney-Day, Torres, Polo, Cao, & Canino, 2007) found that among the four Latina subethnic groups, women of Mexican heritage were less likely than Puerto Rican women to have a depressive disorder, and Puerto Rican women had the highest overall lifetime and past-year prevalence rates compared to other women.

Theorizing Gender and Its Relation to Mental Health

The revolutionary change in understanding of the relationship of culture to personality and the self (Lehman, Chiu, & Schaller, 2004; Triandis & Suh, 2002) and psychopathology (Lopez & Guarnaccia, 2000) has profound implications for theorizing gender's relation to mental health. Researchers have begun to "unpack" culture (Lopez & Guarnaccia, 2000, p. 573) and have shown the importance of understanding just what it is about our social worlds that affects risk for psychopathology. What is all too often neglected in both cultural and gender analyses, however, is the recognition that gender is a social construct that is a product of one's culture. Understanding gender's complex relationship to mental health requires amending traditional biomedical models of mental health, crossing interdisciplinary boundaries, and asking questions at multiple levels and from multiple perspectives, including the individual, the family, society, and culture (Hamilton & Russo, 2006).

Gender theory continues to lead research application. Today gender is not viewed as simply a personal attribute of the individual. Rather, it is theorized as a complex, multilevel cultural construct that determines the meanings of being female or male in a particular culture or context (Anderson, 2005; Deaux & Major, 1987; Frable, 1997; Hamilton & Russo, 2006; Ridgeway & Smith-Lovin, 1999; Russo & Pirlott, 2006;

Stewart & McDermott, 2004). Meanwhile, research that has examined differences in the mental health of women and men predominately equates gender with the cultural categories of male and female found in Western countries.

In Western society, gender is typically organized around the social categories of male and female and is assigned at birth based on biological sex (which may be defined anatomically or genetically, depending on the situation). The cultural package that constitutes the meaning of one's gender assignment to a category should not be confused with the category itself. Although we present findings of research studies that assume a dichotomous view of gender (male/female), it should be kept in mind that gender classifications differ across culture. Further, within Western society the transgender movement (Lev, 2004, 2007) is challenging the dichotomous view of gender as anchored in anatomical characteristics, instead proposing gender as being on a *continuum* (Ellis & Erikson, 2002). The gender continuum provides a schema for conceptualizing gender that allows for and validates the breadth of gender expression possibilities, which may or may not align with an individual's biological sex (Korell & Lorah, 2007).

Advances in understanding gender differences in psychological distress and mental disorder will require examining the cultural discourse that reifies and justifies gender differences in social and economic status, fosters destructive stereotypes and discrimination, objectifies women, and sexualizes violence. It will also require an "unpacking" of gender that includes a more sophisticated and in-depth examination of gender in relation to women's development, roles, and life circumstances. Such an examination is made more difficult by the continuing changes that are occurring in the roles, status, and life circumstances of women in the United States and around the world (see chapter 3 in this volume).

Unpacking Gender: Selected Key Concepts

Gender can be thought of as a cultural package of many interconnected elements that, separately as well as in combination, can influence mental health and well-being. These include gendered traits, emotions, values, expectations, norms, roles, environments, and institutions—all of which can change and evolve within and across cultures and over time (Bourne & Russo, 1998). Gender defines the appropriateness of behavioral, psychological, and social characteristics of males and females over the life cycle, and it shapes the way we construe ourselves and construct our identities (Cross & Madsen, 1997). Gender also functions as "master" (or meta-) status—one that transcends specific contexts—that determines position in society, a position that typically accords women with less power, privilege, and resources than men (Stewart & McDermott, 2004).

As noted above, gender intersects with other dimensions of social difference, and the effects of gender may differ depending on one's specific mix of social identities (see chapters 2 and 15 in this volume). In sexist and racist societies, when identities are associated with stigma, prejudice, and discrimination, they may be associated with increased risk for psychological distress and psychopathology (Landrine & Klonoff, 1997; Wyche, 2001). For example, the impact of the double burden of gender and ethnic discrimination in mental health and its treatment is well recognized (American Psychological Association, 2003, 2006; Brown, Abe-Kim, & Barrio, 2003; Brown & Keith, 2003; Bryant et al., 2005; Sparks, 2002; Sparks & Park, 2000; Wyche, 2001).

Age, ethnicity, race, sexual orientation, class, physical ability, and size are among the social dimensions associated with stigmatized identities that may elicit prejudice and discrimination, confer differential access to power and privilege, and converge with gender to magnify or diminish risk for experiencing negative life events (e.g., exposure to violence) and gaining access to psychological and social coping resources (e.g., collective self-esteem, social support).

Perhaps one of the most important, yet still muddled, conceptual distinctions that has significant implications for research on mental health is *sex versus gender*. In general, *sex* is recognized across the disciplines as a biological category, based on biological characteristics used to define male and female, while *gender* is defined as a social category, based on a social definition of the way males and females should differ physically, cognitively, emotionally, and behaviorally.

Problems arise, however, in the assumption that the effects of biology are solely the result of biological processes. Biological, psychological, and social processes constantly interact, and gender can be a powerful determinant of that interaction. Krieger (2003) illustrates the usefulness of distinguishing between sex and gender, while recognizing that gender has biological dimensions in predicting health outcomes, in 12 case examples that encompass situations from birth defects to mortality and include occupational and environmental disease, trauma, pregnancy, menopause, and access to health services, among others. In these, gender and sex-linked biology are singly, neither, or both relevant as independent or synergistic determinants of the selected outcomes. Taken as a whole, these examples articulate how gender relations can influence expression and interpretation of biological traits. They also show how the reverse—that is, how sex-linked biological characteristics—may contribute to or magnify gender differences in mental health.

We believe that advancing theoretical perspectives on gender's relation to mental health must consider the complex interplay among biology, the social context, gender, and social roles. Such advancement rests on:

1. recognizing that the concepts of genetics and biology, although related, are not identical
2. developing more sophisticated understandings of the relations among biological, psychological, and social processes as prelude to understanding gender's impact on those relations
3. incorporating biological considerations in conceptions of gender
4. fully appreciating the implications of the facts that gender is a social category which may have more than two units and that no trait or behavior intrinsically "belongs" to a specific gender

Conflicts and contradictions among women's gender-role expectations have implications for women's mental health and for intervention in the development of psychopathology. Chronic strains associated with female gender-roles, including reduced power, role burden, housework inequities, child-care inequities, parenting strains, and lack of affirmation in close relationships, have been found to partially mediate gender differences in depression (Nolen-Hoeksema, Larsen, & Grayson, 1999). Marital dissatisfaction is associated with higher risk for psychiatric disorders for both women and men, a finding that holds separately for groupings of anxiety, mood, and substance-use disorders. However the association is stronger for women and specific for more disorders. After controlling for age, education, and presence of other specific disorders, marital dissatisfaction has been found to be uniquely related to major depression and posttraumatic stress disorder (PTSD) for women and to dysthymia for men (Whisman, 1999).

If characteristics and behaviors associated with work and family-role expectations change (perhaps divergently) faster than gender-role socialization, coping skills may be undermined. Expectations among gender-roles may conflict—for example, women's feminine gender-role as "woman" may mandate deferent and passive behaviors towards men, while her work or mother roles may require supervising, disagreeing with, or opposing the actions of men. Such conflicts may undermine women's well-being and increase their risk for psychopathology. In particular, a woman who has a traditional conception of her feminine gender-role as woman and who has been socialized to be an obedient wife and caring mother may experience substantial distress and conflict upon finding herself married to a man who physically abuses her children. Violations of stereotypes and gender-role expectations may lead to discrimination, stigmatization, and marginalization, with implications for mental health (Hamilton & Russo, 2006). For example, the relationship of sexual orientation to mental health is profoundly affected by the stigma associated with homosexuality (Herek &

Garnets, 2007, provides a recent review of the literature on sexual orientation and mental health, including the effects of stigma).

Keeping these concepts in mind, the remainder of this chapter summarizes selected recent research related to women's mental health. We first summarize epidemiological findings on gender differences in patterns of mental disorder, with particular attention to differences in patterns by race/ethnicity and marital roles. The next section provides additional information on high-prevalence disorders for women: anxiety (with special attention to PTSD), depressive, and eating disorders. Then, using a stress-and-coping perspective, we examine risk factors and life events contributing to the gender gap in rates of psychological disorder; topics discussed include pregnancy and its resolution, sexualized objectification, and stigma, prejudice, and discrimination. We only briefly touch on women's work and family roles in these discussions, as they are considered in chapter 20 of this volume. It is hoped that this selective summary of research findings will stimulate new research as well as an improvement in psychological education, training, and practice.

THE EPIDEMIOLOGICAL PICTURE

Prevalence of Psychological Disorder

Large and complex gender differences in patterns of mental health disorder continue to be found in national and community surveys and in service delivery statistics (Kessler, Chiu, Demler, Merikangas, & Walters, 2005; Kessler et al., 1994; Levin, Blanch, & Jennings, 1998; Sachs-Ericsson & Ciarlo, 2000). Although there are substantial gender differences in patterns of mental disorder, whether or not women are at higher risk than men for mental disorder has been subject to debate (Russo, 1995). Results from the National Cormorbidity Survey (Kessler et al., 1994) found that among people age 15–54, 47.3 percent of women and 48.7 percent of men had experienced a psychiatric disorder some time in their lives, but *patterns* of disorder differed by gender: Women had higher rates of anxiety disorder and depressive disorder than men (for anxiety: 30.5% of women vs. 19.2% of men; for depressive disorder: 23.9% vs. 14.7%). The reverse pattern was found for substance-abuse disorders (35.4% of men were identified as having a substance disorder vs. 17.9% of women). Lifetime comorbidity was also higher for women, who were more likely to have experienced three or more psychiatric disorders. Consequently, how the debate is resolved continues to depend on whether or not one believes that alcohol and drug abuse should be defined as mental disorders (Gove, 1980; Russo, 1995). This section will focus on women's excess in mental disorder compared to men and will not consider alcohol and drug disorders in detail.

In discussing rates of mental disorder, two things should be kept in mind. First, simply because there is a gender difference in the rate of a disorder does not mean that the disorder does not have a significant impact on the mental health of the gender with the lower rate (Kessler et al., 2005). For example, women have lower lifetime prevalence rates of substance disorders than men (14.1% vs. 25.7%), but the percentages of women with alcohol and drug disorders (7.5% and 4.8 %, respectively) have been found to be higher than the percentages of women with obsessive-compulsive disorders (2.6%) and dysthymia (3.1%), both disorders with higher rates for women compared to men.

Second, important gender differences may be related to other aspects of a disorder than simply its rate, including developmental pathway, comorbidities, course, and relapse. For example, compared to males, female adolescents appear to progress faster to regular use of drugs than males. They are more likely than males to begin substance use with cigarettes, whereas males typically begin substance use with alcohol (Thomas, Deas, & Grindlinger, 2003).

As Kessler (2006) describes, bipolar disorder provides an interesting example of why focusing on disorder rate may lead to overlooking important gender influences on the disorder. Gender differences are not found in lifetime prevalence rates of bipolar disorder. However, among men and women with that disorder, the proportion of lifetime episodes that are depressive versus manic is significantly higher among women (Arnold, 2003). Thus, a disorder may not have a gender difference in lifetime prevalence or in general treatment response, but may still lead to more depressive episodes in women than men (Kessler, 2006).

In sum, it is clear from the data that achieving significant advances in mental health research will require understanding the relationship of gender to mental health. Understanding the complex ways that gender and its correlates affect mental health is a fundamental challenge to mental health researchers and a necessary condition for improving the mental health of the U.S. population. Its significance cannot be overstated.

Diagnosis, Treatment, and Service Delivery

Gender differences in diagnosis and treatment point to social and cultural variables as potent mental health influences. Use of treatment facilities obviously does not solely reflect prevalence and incidence of mental disorder. Gender and ethnic differences in such things as stigma, cultural beliefs, cultural norms with regard to expressing psychological distress and help-seeking, diagnostic practices, treatment accessibility, and preference for alternative forms of treatment can contribute to gender and ethnic differences in utilization statistics (Snowden & Yamada, 2005). Such differences underscore the importance of understanding the relationship of social and cultural factors to diagnosis, treatment, and delivery of mental health services to women.

Epidemiological analyses must become more detailed and sensitive to methodological limitations if they are not to be Eurocentric and misleading. Global summaries of service utilization data can mask important interactive effects of gender, ethnicity, and diagnosis. Ultimately, understanding utilization of mental health services requires sophisticated research approaches that simultaneously consider effects of gender, race/ethnicity, and other dimensions of difference in a biopsychosocial context over the life cycle.

Bias in Diagnosis and Treatment

As Russo (1995) has pointed out, interactive effects of gender, race, and age on the most frequently diagnosed types of disorders may reflect the paradoxical effects of gender stereotyping: Women are both overrepresented and underserved as a treatment population. Disorders that are congruent with gender stereotypes and society's feminine gender-role expectations (e.g., anxiety, depression) continue to show higher rates of treatment. In contrast, for disorders that are incongruent with gender stereotypes and society's feminine gender-role expectations (e.g., alcoholism), women have been invisible and neglected.

Continuing changes in gender stereotypes (see chapter 7 in this volume) means that the extent to which there is congruence between expectations about women's gender and gender-roles and definitions of mental disorder affects diagnosis and treatment judgments requires ongoing assessment. Among other things, such congruence may reflect overpathologizing (inappropriately perceiving patients whose behavior violates norms as more disturbed), overdiagnosis (inappropriately applying a diagnosis as a function of group membership), and underdiagnosis (inappropriately avoiding application of a diagnosis as a function of group membership) (Lopez, 1989).

Evidence for overpathologizing by psychologists has been in higher probability of overdiagnosis of depression (particularly by male psychiatrists) in women, according to studies of case history descriptions (Loring & Powell, 1988), but underdiagnosis of depression in men (Waisberg & Page, 1988). Underdiagnosis has been a particular concern for women who abuse alcohol and drugs (Russo, 1995).

Women receive prescriptions for psychotropic drugs at a higher rate than men, for a variety of reasons, including gender differences in age, physical illnesses, psychiatric disorders, help-seeking that leads to exposure to the medical system (which results in more prescriptions), and stressful life events (Hamilton, 1995; Hamilton, Grant, & Jensvold, 1996; Hamilton & Jensvold, 1995). Both excessive and inappropriate drug treatment continue to be major issues, particularly for older women (Russo, 1995). Waisberg and Page (1988) found that female patients were associated with stronger recommendations for drug treatment in all diagnostic categories except depression, where male patients were associated with stronger recommendations. A tendency to misdiagnose other disorders in women as depression may lead to inappropriate treatment; drugs that are appropriate to treat major depression are not necessarily effective in treating other disorders (see Yonkers & Hamilton, 1995).

Childhood physical and sexual abuse are also linked to subsequent onset of multiple mental health and substance use problems, complicating the task of diagnosis (Hiday, Swanson, Swartz, Borum, & Wagner, 2001; Horwitz, Widom, McLaughlin, & Raskin White, 2001; Kendler, Bulik, Silberg, Hettema, Myers, & Prescott, 2000; Molnar, Buka, & Kessler, 2001). Misdiagnosis of PTSD due to rape or battering as clinical depression has been of particular concern (McGrath, Keita, Strickland, & Russo, 1990; Russo & Denious, 2001).

This brief picture points to both the complexity and the psychosocial nature of the relationships among gender, ethnicity, marital status, and mental health. Gender differences in mental disorder are associated with age, race/ethnicity, marital roles, parental roles, and economic status (Alegria et al., 2007; Breslau, Aguilar-Gaxiola, Kendler, Su, Williams, & Kessler, 2005; Kessler et al., 2005; Kessler, 2006; Mowbray & Benedek, 1988; Whisman, 1999). Narrow intrapsychic or biological approaches are not sufficient to achieve understanding of the etiology, diagnosis, treatment, and prevention of mental disorders in women. Further, the overlapping of symptoms of psychopathology with gender stereotypes makes misdiagnosis a concern (McGrath et al., 1990; Russo, 1995).

HIGH-PREVALENCE DISORDERS FOR WOMEN: ANXIETY AND MOOD DISORDERS

Researchers around the globe have consistently reported higher rates of anxiety and mood disorders in women, whereas men consistently show higher rates of substance and antisocial disorders (Alonso et al., 2004; Breslau, Schultz, & Peterson, 1995; Kessler et al., 2005; Klose & Jacobi, 2004; Schoevers, Beekman, Deeg, Jonker, & van Tilburg, 2003; World Health Organization, 2000, 2001).

Measurement Issues

Hammen (2005) and Kessler (2006) provide summaries of measurement issues in research that focus on depression but apply to mental health research in general. We will not repeat them here except to note that bias in willingness to self-report symptoms does not appear to be a factor in explaining gender differences in rates of depressive disorder. Gender may affect recall bias, however. For example, women report a more chronic course of depression than men, but this has now been explained as due to differential recall (Kessler, 2006).

Cutoff scores from summary scales that assess depressive symptomatology (e.g., CESD) should not be equated with a diagnosis of depression. Anxiety and mood disorders are heterogeneous diagnostic categories in the *Diagnostic and Statistical Manual of Mental Disorders* (4th ed.; *DSM-IV*; American Psychiatric Association, 1994) that often involve overlapping symptomatology. A variety of summary scales are currently used to assess depressive symptoms such as crying, feelings of sadness and unhappiness, and eating and sleep difficulties. Interpreting results from such scales is problematic because such symptoms are associated with a variety of psychiatric disorders as well as physical conditions, including anxiety disorders (Breslau et al., 1995).

A number of researchers have suggested that the largest gender differences in such symptomatology are found for less severe symptoms (Clark, Aneshensel, Frerichs, & Morgan, 1981; Craig & Van Natta, 1979). This suggests that interpretation of gender differences found in research using summary scales should be interpreted with caution, as such scales do not separate milder forms of distress, such as sadness, from more severe psychiatric disorder (Newmann, 1984).

There is also concern that gender differences in milder forms of symptomatology may reflect gender-role expectations rather than signaling risk for depression. One study that compared the Beck Depression Inventory (BDI) and the Depression Scale (DEPS) within the same population found significant gender differences on both scales, but the differences were largely explained by the responses to the items relating to crying and loss of interest in sex. The researchers concluded that these items are psychologically and culturally related to female gender, resulting in gender-biased results from measures that include them (Salokangas, Vaahtera, Pacriev, Sohlman, & Lehtinen, 2002).

Anxiety Disorders

Community studies indicate that 31 percent of women and 19 percent of men will have an anxiety disorder during their lifetime. This gender difference in the rates emerges in childhood—one study found that by age 10, 17.9 percent of girls compared to 8.0 percent of boys had a history of anxiety disorder (Breslau et al., 1995).

Common features for anxiety disorders are symptoms of anxiety and avoidance behavior, in addition to panic disorder (with and without agoraphobia), agoraphobia (without history of panic disorder), simple phobia, social phobia, obsessive-compulsive disorder, posttraumatic stress disorder, acute stress disorder, and generalized anxiety disorder, among other categories. Related disorders include adjustment disorder with anxious mood, eating disorders, dream anxiety disorder, organic anxiety disorder, and avoidant personality disorder.

The gender difference in rate of anxiety disorder varies with type of disorder. In the National Comorbidity Survey, the lifetime prevalence rates for panic disorder were 5 percent and 2 percent, respectively, for women and men. For agoraphobia, the comparable rates were 7 percent in women and 3.5 percent in men. Anxiety disorders often occur together (e.g., panic disorder and agoraphobia are highly comorbid), as well as with other disorders (particularly depression) and medical conditions. For example, panic disorder is highly comorbid with coronary heart disease (Ginsburg, 2004).

Panic Disorder and Agoraphobia

It has been suggested that loss of social support and disruption of interpersonal relationships are risk factors for panic disorder. Weissman and colleagues (1986) found that panic disorders were higher among single mothers than among married mothers, for both black and white women. Interestingly, those researchers also reported that married mothers had higher risk than single mothers for obsessive-compulsive disorder. This was particularly true for black married mothers, whose rates exceeded those of black single mothers by nearly seven to one. The comparable figure for white mothers was nearly three to one. These findings suggest that risk factors may differ for subtypes of anxiety disorders.

Agoraphobic women have been found to exhibit extreme forms of personal attributes associated with the feminine gender-role, including helplessness, overdependency, and passivity. A discussion solely focusing on an excess in feminine gender-related attributes is incomplete, however. Lack of instrumentality (an attribute associated with the masculine gender-role) also characterizes agoraphobics.

Posttraumatic Stress Disorder

Recent findings from the National Comorbidity Survey Replication place PTSD as the fifth most common psychiatric disorder in the United States (Kessler et al., 2005). Women have higher rates of PTSD than men (Keane et al., 2006). For example, in the National Comorbidity Survey, women's lifetime prevalence rate was more than double that of men (10.4% vs. 5.0%), and about 60 percent of men, compared with 51 percent of women, were exposed to one or more traumatic events (Kessler et al., 1995).

Findings from meta-analytic research suggest that women are twice as likely to develop PTSD after a traumatic event, and traumatic symptoms for women are likely to persist four times longer than for men

(Norris, Foster & Weisshaar, 2002). Researchers concur that women's higher rates of PTSD are related to the type of trauma to which they are exposed, namely, interpersonal assaults such as rape or sexual abuse in childhood or adulthood (Olff, Langeland, Draijer, & Gersons, 2007). Cortina and Kubiak (2006) analyzed National Violence against Women Survey data from 591 survivors of partner violence and concluded that posttraumatic stress is more directly attributable to violent circumstances rather than "feminine vulnerability."

Violent circumstances encompass many forms, including childhood physical and sexual abuse, acquaintance rape, courtship violence and wife-battering, marital rape, and stalking (see chapters 16 through 18 in this volume). Analyses of the National Comorbidity Survey found that women who reported being victims of childhood sexual abuse were at higher risk for 13 of 16 subsequent lifetime anxiety, mood, and substance disorders in comparison to women who did not report such experiences (Molnar et al., 2001). Women with reported childhood sexual abuse histories were found to be at 10.2 times greater risk for PTSD, 9.1 times greater risk for manic-depressive disorder, 2.0–2.3 times greater risk for drug problems and dependence, 1.8–2.7 times greater risk for major depressive disorder and dysthymia, 1.5–2.8 times greater risk for alcohol problems, and 1.3–1.9 times greater risk for other anxiety disorders (Molnar et al., 2001). In short, violence is indicted in the development of multiple disorders beyond PTSD. Comorbidity research suggests that the effects of violence may work through an initial impact on anxiety.

Comorbidity

Anxiety is comorbid with depression, particularly for women (Breslau et al., 1995). Symptoms of anxiety disorders are correlated with other disorders, complicating diagnosis. For example, the symptoms of PTSD overlap with depression, including depressed mood, sleep and appetite disturbance, social withdrawal, lowered self-esteem, and psychomotor retardation or agitation (American Psychiatric Association, 1994). In particular, research that clarifies the origins and relationships among symptoms of anxiety and depression disorders is needed. Taken together, these symptoms constitute a large proportion of women's excess in psychopathology.

Experiencing a mix of stressors that combine danger and loss is strongly related to the development of comorbid anxiety and depression (Brown, Harris, & Eales, 1993). Comorbidity research suggests that anxiety may serve as a pathway to depression for women (Breslau et al., 1995). Anxiety disorders (generalized anxiety disorder, panic disorder, phobia) have been found to significantly predict increased risk for developing major depressive disorder in women and men

(Hettema, Prescott, & Kendler, 2003). Both anxiety and depressive diagnoses are also correlated with personality disorders (for a more complete discussion of the implications of this overlap, see McGrath et al., 1990). Misdiagnosis may account for some of that overlap, and possible misdiagnosis of PTSD in women who have experienced physical and sexual abuse, rape, or battering has been of particular concern (McGrath et al., 1990; Russo & Denious, 2001).

Depressive Disorders

Women's higher risk for depression compared to men is one of the most consistent findings in the literature (Kessler, 2006; Weissman et al., 1996). It is not explained by gender differences in willingness to report symptoms or help-seeking, but appears to be a genuine effect that may relate to differences in roles and life stress (Kuehner, 2003; Mirowsky & Ross, 1995; Nazroo, Edwards, & Brown, 1998).

As the leading cause of disease-related disability among women around the world (Murray & Lopez, 1996), depression has been considered to represent such a significant threat to women's mental health that the American Psychological Association (APA) established a President's Task Force to study risk factors and treatment issues in women's depression, followed by an APA Summit on Depression (Mazure et al., 2002). *Women and Depression: A Handbook for the Social, Behavioral, and Biomedical Sciences* (Keyes & Goodman, 2006) provides the comprehensive and up-to-date review of research findings.

Depressive disorders are classified along with "bipolar disorders" under the category "mood disorders" in the *DSM-IV* (American Psychiatric Association, 1994). Key categories recognized in the *DSM-IV* for this discussion include subtypes of major depression and dysthymic disorder, and depressive disorder not otherwise specified (NOS).

Gender differences have not been substantiated for all depressive subtypes—the gender gap is widest for major depression and dysthymia, but there is no evidence of greater risk for bipolar disorder or seasonal affective disorder (Kessler, McGonagle, Swartz, Blazer, & Nelson, 1993; Kessler et al., 2005). Thus, women's excess in mood disorder appears to be largely due to greater risk of unipolar depression.

Sets of symptoms that are persistent are defined as *depressive syndromes*, some of which have become defined as *disorders*. It should not be assumed that depression varies along a single continuum from common symptoms to major depression. Gender differences are also found in minor depression (Kessler et al., 1997) or brief recurrent depression (Angst and Merikangas, 1997).

Depressions differ in kind and severity (American Psychiatric Association, 1994). Different depressive syndromes may have different precursors (Hamilton, 1988). Psychological or pharmacological treatments that have been based on clinical trials for major depression may be totally inappropriate for treatment of depressive symptoms (Weissman & Myers, 1980; Weissman et al., 1987). Note also that some types of depression are sex specific, including postpartum depression, perimenopausal depression, and premenstrual dysphoric disorder. As Kessler (2006) points out, the extent to which these disorders may contribute to gender differences in more general types of depression is unknown.

Explaining the Gender Gap in Depression

No one theory or set of theories fully explains gender differences in depression. Current theories of women's depression span biological, psychological, social, and cultural variables (Hammen, 2005; Keyes & Goodman, 2006). Risk factors for women's depression include psychological attributes such as response styles (Mazure & Maciejewski, 2003; Nolen-Hoeksema, 1990, 2003) as well as social roles and conditions, including work and family roles, poverty, and exposure to violence, prejudice, stereotyping, and depression. Both greater exposure to stressful life events and lack of access to coping resources (personal, social, and economic) have been found to contribute to women's excess in depression (McGrath et al., 1990; Keyes & Goodman, 2006).

Rates of depressive symptoms vary cross-nationally with indicators of gender inequality, underscoring the strong relationship of women's status to risk for depression (Arrindell, Steptoe, & Wardle, 2003). Rates of depressive symptoms and the clinical syndrome also vary within nations by regions (urban versus rural) and between U.S. states as ranked according to indicators of gender inequality (Chen, Subramanian, Acevedo-Garcia, & Kawachi, 2005).

Recent data suggest that the relationship between women's marital roles and depression is complex. There is a stronger gender difference in depression among married than unmarried people, but as Kessler (2006) points out, whether married, never married, or previously married, the gender difference of first onset of major depression is similar. However, marital stability affects women differently than men. Further, life events associated with chronicity and recurrence differ for women and men. In particular, financial pressures are more depressogenic for men than women, whereas family problems are more depressogenic for women than men (Kessler and McLeod, 1985). These processes create a stronger association between gender and depression among married than unmarried people.

Prior psychiatric history appears to play a key mediating role in gender differences in depressive disorders, making understanding the mental health effects of the events of early childhood and adolescence the key to preventing women's depression in later years. There is a gender difference in depressed mood that begins in childhood and is found in adolescents and adults (Kessler, 2006). A gender gap in depression rates begins to emerge in early adolescence (Breslau et al., 1995). By age 15, a gender difference in major depression has emerged (Kessler et al., 1993; Nolen-Hoeksema & Girgus, 1994). It should be noted that gender differences in depressed mood do not necessarily reflect gender differences in clinical depression. Women are also significantly more likely than men to have depressed mood in the nonclinical range as well (Almeida & Kessler, 1998).

The emergence of a gender difference in depression during adolescence raises questions about the contribution of sex hormones to the development of depression among women. However, Kessler (2006) argues that hormonal effects are not sufficient to explain this gender difference. He recognizes that changes in depressed mood have been associated with other experiences such as menopause, use of oral contraceptives, and hormone replacement therapy. He points out, however, that rates of major depression have not been linked to these experiences. Furthermore, the emergence of a gender difference in depression varies across U.S. racial/ethnic groups (Hayward, Gotlib, Schraedley, & Litt, 1999).

The pathways to depression appear to differ for women and men in gender-stereotyped ways. Specifically, diagnoses of depression and anxiety are more likely to be found together for women, while depression and substance abuse are more likely to be paired for men. The patterns of being depressed found in women's daily experiences suggest that women may be more likely than men to experience short-term depressive episodes, possibly as a response to stressors in their lives (Kessler, 2006).

Eating Disorders

Eating disorders are characterized by gross disturbances in eating behavior. Although anorexia and bulimia nervosa are distinct diagnoses, they can be related, and they typically begin in adolescence or early adulthood. Since 1980, bulimia has been distinguished from anorexia in the *DSM* (American Psychiatric Association, 1994).

Although eating disorders are uncommon in the general population, they are comorbid with other disorders and role impairment, and they are frequently undertreated, perhaps because they are viewed as normative behavior in some subpopulations. Lifetime prevalence estimates of *DSM-IV* anorexia nervosa, bulimia nervosa, and binge-eating disorder are 0.9, 1.5, and 3.5 percent, respectively, among women, compared to 0.3, 0.5, and 2.0 percent among men. Risk of bulimia nervosa and binge-eating disorder has increased with successive birth cohorts (Hudson, Hiripi, Pope, & Kessler, 2007).

All three disorders are significantly comorbid with many other *DSM-IV* disorders, including anxiety, obsessive-compulsive disorder, depression, and substance-abuse disorder (Hinz & Williamson, 1987; Hudson et al., 2007). In particular, patients diagnosed with anorexia have been found to have strong family histories of major depression and to be themselves depressed (Winokur, March, & Mendels, 1980).

The essential features of anorexia nervosa, as defined by the *DSM*, are distorted body image, refusal to maintain body weight at a normal level, intense fear of gaining weight or becoming fat even though underweight, and, in females, amenorrhea (American Psychiatric Association, 1994. Weight loss in excess of 15 percent of normal body weight has been an arbitrary guideline for alerting professionals to anorexia in their patients.

In contrast, bulimia nervosa is characterized by a "binge-purge" cycle, in which there are recurrent episodes of consuming large amounts of food and then "purging" them by extreme methods such as self-induced vomiting, laxative and diuretic abuse, excessive exercise, or fasting. Purging may or may not be a symptom of anorexia nervosa. The typical bulimic woman is of normal body weight, although she perceives herself as being overweight.

Measurement Issues

The accuracy of prevalence estimates for eating disorders has been subject to debate. Estimates vary considerably, depending on the criteria used for diagnosis. Assessing bulimia is especially problematic, as researchers have not agreed on definitions for such central concepts as what constitutes a binge (e.g., number of calories versus duration of eating) or how to document frequency of binging and purging. Compounding these difficulties are the reluctance of many bulimic women to report their behaviors and the inaccuracy of self-report measures.

Again, distinctions between symptoms and disorders need to be made. In a discussion of methodological issues in bulimia treatment outcome research, Wilson (1987) argues that change in bulimic behavior alone is insufficient for evaluating improvement; changes in body image disturbance, feelings of self-efficacy, nutrition, and eating patterns must also be assessed. Research has provided some evidence that there are differences in pathology associated with increasing severity of the eating disorders (Mintz & Betz, 1988; Striegel-Moore et al., 1986). Research is needed that continues to address these definitional, diagnostic, and treatment issues, including the relationship of disordered eating to specific classes of stressful live events, such as sexual abuse and assault (Root, 1991).

There are class as well as gender differences in eating disorders, which typically involve women who are young, middle or upper class, and white. Some researchers have even gone so far as to call eating disorders a "culture-bound" syndrome, that is, a syndrome specific to a culture and one in which cultural factors play an important etiological role (Nasser, 1988). Many authors have pointed to Western culture's increasingly thin standards for female beauty and the accompanying stigmatization of obesity as important factors explaining the rapid increase in rates of eating disorders (Boskind-White & White, 1987; Garner & Garfinkel, 1980; Striegel-Moore et al., 1986).

Dietary restraint is considered to be a central risk factor for the development and maintenance of eating disorders (Polivy & Herman, 1985; Davis, Freeman, & Gamer, 1988). Even if dieting behaviors are the norm—which this evidence certainly suggests is true—the question remains as to why only a minority of U.S. women, mostly white women, develop clinical eating disorders in response to sociocultural pressures for thinness. In this regard, self-esteem and perceived control are once again implicated in the development of gender differences in psychological disorder (Travis, 1988). It has even been suggested that the self-esteem of females with eating disorders rests on approval of others and adherence to social ideals, with a tenuous balance between self-regard and social confirmation that results in an other-directedness so extreme that bodily needs can be more readily ignored (Travis, 1988, pp. 151–152). The fact that bulimia is more likely to be found in white women suggests that the social ideals are tied to the gender-role of white women in society, one that differs from that of black women in ways that have etiological significance.

An other-directed sense of self-esteem and locus of control in the context of a diet-oriented culture may thus be the disastrous combination for women's mental health. Bulimic women are found to be more likely to endorse such statements as "Thin is beautiful" and to have internalized these standards to a greater extent than other women (Rodin, Silberstein, & Striegel-Moore, 1985).

Furthermore, there is some evidence suggesting that bulimic women have overendorsed a stereotypical gender-role in which physical beauty, defined in white women's terms, has been a central component. In addition to examining the contribution of sociocultural factors to risk for eating disorders, a number of theories have attempted to explain eating disorders in terms of such factors as personality disturbance (Katzman & Wolcbik, 1984), social impairment (Norman & Herzog, 1984; Johnson & Berndt, 1983; Herzog et al., 1987), family systems theory, and biological disturbances (Hinz & Williamson, 1987; Lee, Rush, & Mitchell, 1985). Unfortunately, no one of these theories seems to address fully the complicated etiological questions that are central to understanding, treating, and preventing eating disorders. Further, explanations of eating disorders must not ignore the dynamics of gender-roles that appear so central to the development of pathological eating behaviors.

UNDERSTANDING WOMEN'S EXCESS IN PSYCHOLOGICAL DISTRESS AND DISORDER

Nearly three decades ago, the Subpanel on the Mental Health of Women of the President's Commission on Mental Health observed:

> Circumstances and conditions that American society has come to accept as normal or ordinary lead to profound unhappiness, anguish, and mental illness in women. Marriage, family relationships, pregnancy, child-rearing, divorce, work and aging all have a powerful impact on the well-being of women.... Compounding these ordinary events, women are also subject to some extraordinary experiences such as rape, marital violence, and incest, which leave them vulnerable to mental illness. (Subpanel on the Mental Health of Women, 1978, p. 1038)

These observations continue to be apt. In particular, they are confirmed in research that links mental health to gender-roles and gender-related life circumstances, including poverty, violence, unwanted pregnancy and abortion, and the experience of stigma, prejudice, and discrimination.

A Stress-and-Coping Perspective

Approaches to understanding women's excess in psychological distress and disorder can be placed in four categories:

1. person-centered (focuses on women's vulnerability or resistance to disorder due to biological or psychological characteristics that make women more or less responsive to stressful life events)
2. situation-centered (focuses on stressors or coping resources related to women's gender-roles and life circumstances)
3. interactionist (examines interrelationships between the first two, including women's perceptions and cognitions of events and internal and external coping resources to deal with them)
4. methodological (explains excess as an artifact of such things as measurement, sampling, lack of appropriate controls, or bias in diagnosis)

Although an interactionist research perspective is the ideal, most research has traditionally fallen into one of the first two categories.

Hopefully, future research will aim for biopsychosocial models that are interactionist in nature, controlling for methodological biases. Note that biological factors are not equal to genetic factors. Genetic factors have been directly implicated in a variety of mental disorders. However, there is little evidence that such direct action operates differently for men and women, and seeking to explain women's excess in mental disorder by genetic factors has not led to definitive conclusions, nor does it appear promising (McGrath et al., 1990). Thus, they receive little attention in this chapter.

A framework that includes both stress and coping provides a useful interactionist model for conceptualizing the conditions that contribute to increased risk for such mental disorders for women. A stress-and-coping framework considers events in context and examines the interaction of sources of stress, coping resources, coping strategies, and social support, all of which may involve biological, psychological, social, or environmental factors (Folkman & Moskowitz, 2004; Taylor & Stanton, 2007). Although we focus here on proximal life events, it must be noted that measures that typically assess "proximal" causes of distress in women's lives (e.g., life event scales) neglect the "distal" conditions that "govern the allocation of social and material resources in relation to gender" (Stoppard, 2000, p. 84).

Life Events and Life Crises

A stress-and-coping perspective reflects the broader shift in mental health research that has documented the mental health impact of daily hassles and chronic stress, as well as major negative life events (Taylor & Stanton, 2007). Negative life events and life crises are one reason for women's higher rates of distress and disorder. Conceptualizations and classifications of stressors depend on their meaning in the context of male–female power dynamics that affect appraisals of threat and coping resources. More needs to be known about how the gendered meaning of a negative life event affects its consequences. For example, a study that compared rape victims with victims of a severe, life-threatening, but nonsexual event (e.g., car accident, violent robbery, physical assault) found rape victims to have high rates of a variety of symptoms, including depressed mood, distressing dreams, and difficulty in falling asleep. The study's authors concluded that the sexual nature (we would argue "gendered meaning") of the event made the difference between groups (Faravelli, Giugni, Salvatori, & Ricca, 2004).

As we have seen above, stress has been found to precipitate anxiety and mood disorder—disorders with a clear excess for women compared with men. Research has shown consistent gender differences in the types of coping strategies used by females and males. A meta-analysis suggested that women tend to appraise stressors as more severe than men did, suggesting stress appraisal as a potential explanation for coping differences between men and women (Tamres, Janicki, & Helgeson, 2002).

Distinguishing between social and other types of stress is an advance, but the inferences of the fact that a social stressor has both immediate and long-term threat implications have yet to be fully recognized. Social stressors may be more likely to be associated with the potential for stigma and social exclusion for women, making social support a coping resource of direct relevance for dealing with the issues posed by the particular stressor, with resulting physiological benefits. Methods that assess number and quality of events are important. For example, a higher number of events associated with humiliation, entrapment, and bereavement has been found to contribute to increased risk for depression in women (Fullilove, 2002). Also, sexism, racism, and heterosexism appear to function as chronic stressors in which cognitive appraisals mediate the relationship between perceived discrimination and outcomes of discrimination-related stress (Klonoff & Landrine, 1995; Meyer, 2003)

Women's Response to Stressful Life Events

Exposure to stressors is not sufficient to produce mental disorder. Recent research has focused on identifying the variables, internal and external, that separate individuals who develop mental health problems in response to negative life events and life crises from those who do not (Taylor & Stanton, 2007). To avoid stereotyping, we prefer the tern *risk factors* rather than *vulnerability factors* to designate such variables.

A recent meta-analysis suggested that women tended to appraise stressors as being more severe than men did, suggesting stress appraisal as a potential explanation for coping differences between men and women (Tamres et al., 2002). However, Kessler, McLeod, and Wethington (1984) have reported that women's greater level of responsiveness was not found in all types of events, but generally reflected those involving "network crises that have the capacity to provoke distress through the creation of empathic concern" (Kessler et al., 1985, p. 84).

Before attributing gender differences in interpersonal behavior to personal attributes, it should be recognized that lack of power associated with gender-roles for women, combined with the normative expectation of the feminine gender-role that women should always respond to the needs of others, may play a critical role in creating such differences. It may also be that a trait (e.g., expressiveness) will not correlate with psychopathology unless a provoking agent, such as relationship loss, occurs (Brown & Harris, 1978). Another possibility is that women's orientation toward others puts them at higher risk for psychopathology due to the effects of shame (Denious, Russo, & Rubin, 2004). Wright, O'Leary, and Balkin (1989) found shame to be more strongly related to depressive symptomatology than guilt, for both women and men. Although they did not find a gender difference in levels of shame in their sample, their research was based on a college student population. The concept of shame may be very different in college women compared with women in the general population.

It has been postulated that female sex-role socialization results in the development of maladaptive personal attributes and styles of coping that contribute to risk for psychopathology in response to stress. In some of these formulations, women are seen as having a psychic "cost of caring" due to their psychological orientation toward other people (Belle, 1982; Kessler et al., 1984).

As noted below, a variety of studies has found that a sense of mastery or agency, rather than expressive traits, significantly correlates with measures of well-being or symptomatology. However, most measures of mental health used in this research have emphasized anxiety, affective, and somatoform disorders. It may be that, by definition, such disorders reflect a lack of mastery, autonomy, efficacy, or competence. Research by Huselid and Cooper (1994) suggests that the beneficial effects of expressiveness may have been overlooked in previous research due to a focus on internalizing disorders. Using an adolescent sample, they examined the extent to which gender-role ideology and attributes accounted for sex differences in internally directed psychological distress and externally directed deviant behavior. Holding traditional gender-role attitudes was positively related to externalizing problems among males, but not among females. "Masculine" instrumental attributes were associated with lower internalized distress, whereas "feminine" expressive attributes were associated with lower externalized behavior problems. These associations were similar across black and white racial groups and across age groups from 13 to 19 years.

Women's orientation toward others has also figured predominately in theories seeking to explain women's responses to stress, but the gendered analysis applied has been incomplete. In particular, new theories of gender differences in stress responses, such as the "tend-and-befriend" theory posed by Taylor, Klein, Lewis, Grunewald, Gurung, and Updegraff (2000) do not sufficiently consider that the qualities of social stressors and of the women's social context could very well underlie the tend-and-befriend response in women. Klein, Corwin, and Ceballos (2006) discuss the biology of the stress response and discuss such theories in more detail.

In considering women's inclinations to nurture or tend and befriend, one must keep in mind that caring and nurturing are central aspects of women's feminine gender-role, as well as the gender-roles of wife and mother. Are women more responsive because of a gender-related psychological trait, such as nurturance? Or are they more responsive because they are fulfilling gender-role expectations about women held by themselves or by others, for example, that women should be nurturant, warm, and caring? Or are they responding to gender-role expectations held by themselves or others related to their roles as wife, mother, daughter, sister, or aunt? Perhaps it is all of the above.

Systematic biopsychosocial research from a stress and coping perspective has potential for answering these questions, but only if the complexities of gender are kept in mind.

Mastery and Perceived Control

Mastery, perceived control, and related constructs—the obverse of powerlessness—have been positively associated with health and well-being and negatively associated with psychopathology in women and men (Taylor & Stanton, 2007). Women who are lower in mastery, instrumentality, or perceived control may also be more likely to have both helplessness expectancies (i.e., the expectation that outcomes are not controllable) and negative outcome expectancies (i.e., not being able to attain highly valued outcomes or to avoid aversive outcomes). These are postulated to combine to create hopelessness, which leads to depression in response to negative life events (Abramson, Metalsky, & Alloy, 1989).

Mastery and its related concepts are predictive of self-esteem, which is clearly an important factor in psychopathology, particularly depression. Brown, Bifulco, Harris, and Bridge (1986) offer a model with low self-esteem functioning as a predisposition for depression, with life events interacting to increase risk (e.g., lack of an intimate relationship with husband, the presence of three or more children age 14 or under at home, lack of paid employment). Assessment of the mental health outcomes of interaction of gender-related attributes with gender-role provoking agents is a promising research area.

Mueller and Major's (1989) work demonstrated the positive impact of self-efficacy (a construct related to mastery) in an experimental study evaluating a counseling intervention aimed at enhancing self-efficacy for coping and lowering self-blame for pregnancy after having an abortion. Abortion patients who received a self-efficacy intervention during a preabortion counseling session were less depressed after the abortion than women who received an attribution intervention, and both groups were less depressed than the control group, which received the standard preabortion counseling session. This study causally links perceived self-efficacy to mental health outcomes of abortion and suggests that interventions oriented to promote self-efficacy may have preventative effects.

Personal attributes such as mastery and perceived control may be most effectively conceptualized as moderating variables in an interactionist framework. As Reich and Zautra (1990) point out, however, the concept of perceived control is multidimensional, and perceived control beliefs are themselves influenced by life events, both positive and negative. They suggest, for example, that social support is differentially related to symptomatology in individuals low in internal control compared with individuals high in internal control.

These findings support the work of Hobfoll (1986), who has proposed a model of ecological congruence to predict the effectiveness of specific resources in buffering the effects of stressful life events. In Hobfoll's model, resource effectiveness is situation dependent and is related to personal and cultural values, time since the event, and stage in the individual's development, among other things.

Lazarus and Folkman (1984) also considered the fit between coping resources and situational demands, but their work had a greater focus on cognitive resources than Hobfoll's model. Because stress and coping are situation specific, study of specific types of events is needed to assess matching stressful event, resource, and situation. This model suggests that lack of congruence among gender-related attributes, attitudes, and values of the person, the meanings of the coping responses (to the person as well as the person's reference groups), and the expected consequences and meaning of coping processes may contribute to increased risk of psychopathology in women (Taylor & Stanton, 2007).

Developmental Issues

The female excess in psychopathology begins to appear in adolescence and changes developmentally in complex ways (Kessler, 2006; Nolen-Hoeksema & Girgus, 1994). Given that adolescence and young adulthood are major formative periods in the development of adult gender-role identities, adolescence is a particularly interesting developmental period for research on the origins of women's excess in psychopathology. In conceptualizing causal dynamics in the development of gender differences in psychopathology, it is important to recognize that personal attributes such as mastery, perceived control, and self-esteem may be both a cause and a consequence of stressful life events. Further, in additional to being stressful, adverse events, such as intimate violence, may undermine women's access to important psychological, social, and economic coping resources by interfering with their ability to become educated and gain employment (Koss, Bailey, Yuan, Herrera, & Lichter, 2003; Penze, Heim, & Nemeroff, 2006).

Measurement Issues

Kessler and McLeod (1985), and Taylor and Stanton (2007) discuss methodological and conceptual issues in research on life events, life stress, and life crises. Both longitudinal and experimental research designs that are based on transactional models will be needed for causal dynamics to be more fully understood. Even then, mental health problems themselves can also be both a cause and a consequence of gender-related stressful life events such as unwanted pregnancy, marital disruption, job loss, and stigma, prejudice, and discrimination.

In the above sections, we have integrated a discussion of the effects of one of the most pervasive and profound classes of gender-related life events with multiple, profound, and long-lasting effects—intimate violence (Coker et al., 2002; Dutton, Green, Kaltman, Roesch, Zeffiro, & Krause, 2006; Russo, Koss, & Ramos, 2000). We limit our remaining discussion to three clusters of events chosen for more in-depth consideration: pregnancy and its resolution; sexualized objectification; and stigma, prejudice, and discrimination.

REPRODUCTIVE-RELATED EVENTS: A FOCUS ON PREGNANCY AND ITS RESOLUTION

Reproductive life events are a normal part of women's lives and relate uniquely to women's biology. They are critical to a feminist perspective, as women's biology is so often used to justify women's disadvantaged social, economic, and political status. They also offer superb examples of the need for biopsychosocial models of stress and coping, point to the importance of distinguishing between acute and chronic sources of stress, and underscore the importance of viewing women as active agents in the stress-and-coping process.

Pregnancy and Birth

Pregnancy is associated with a low incidence of psychiatric disorders, which may reflect selection (mentally healthy women may be more likely to have partners and become pregnant), coping resources (partners may be more supportive during pregnancy), or differential diagnosis (practitioners may be less likely to label a pregnant women as having a psychiatric disorder). Hamilton and colleagues (1988) pointed out that the relative lack of psychiatric disorder during pregnancy, despite elevated levels of steroid hormones, contrasts with the changes in symptoms that sometimes occur with cyclic hormonal elevations. They suggested that these differences may reflect adaptations in gonadal steroid receptor functioning. A focus on gonadal steroids, such as androgen, which are found in both men and women, is needed to counterbalance a research bias in the literature toward steroids of primarily ovarian origin, particularly estrogen (Hamilton, 1984). Gender-comparative research is required to ascertain if there are, indeed, specific clinical correlates of biological changes at childbirth.

Hobfoll and Leiberman (1987) tested Hobfoll's stress-and-coping model to compare women's emotional response to normal delivery, miscarriage (spontaneous abortion), delivery by cesarean section, and preterm delivery, at the time of the event and three months later. Although all of these events involve acute stress, preterm delivery was also seen as involving the chronic stress of coping with a preterm infant and was thus predicted to have longer-term effects than the other three groups. Indeed, although there was no significant difference in depression among the groups at the initial time, the group-by-time interaction effect was significant. The spontaneous abortion and cesarean-section acute-stress groups decreased more on depression than the preterm chronic stress or the normal delivery (considered baseline stress) groups. This points to the importance of separating acute from chronic sources of stress involved with reproductive-related events.

High self-esteem was found to be a personal resource associated with lower depressive symptomatology at both times of measurement for all groups. Intimacy with spouse was associated with lowered symptomatology at the time of the event, but not later. Hobfoll and Leiberman suggest that high self-esteem is a transituational personal resource always available for women having it, while spouse support was viewed as dependent on situational demands and constraints.

Postpartum illness may resemble several major categories of psychiatric disorder, including depression, mania, delirium, organic syndromes, and schizophrenia. "Baby blues" (i.e., mild postpartum dysphoria) is distinguished from severe postpartum depression by the severity and frequency of symptoms, timing of the course of the disorder, and epidemiology. The illness, which is reported in between 39 percent and 85 percent of women, occurs about the third or fourth day after delivery and lasts from a day or two up to as much as two weeks. Severe postpartum depression occurs in about 10 percent of women, may occur from six weeks to four months after delivery, and can last from six months to a year (Hamilton et al., 1988a; O'Hara, Zekowski, Phillips, & Wright, 1990).

Stern and Kruckman (1983) conducted a cross-cultural study of postpartum depression that supports the conception of postpartum depression as socially constructed. They suggest that postpartum depression in the United States may reflect a lack of social support for the women's transition to her motherhood role and a lack of social structuring during the postpartum period.

Whiffen (1988) also reported that mothers' perceptions of their infants as "difficult" were positively correlated with depression. Such perceptions may be a result of depressed mood. However, research is needed to assess whether mothers who are prone to depression are more likely to have infants who cry more and are more temperamental, thus creating a source of stress that results in depressive symptomatology. Perceiving the infant as difficult was most strongly related to depression if the mother had expressed optimistic expectations about the child's behavior before birth. Lack of congruence between expectancies and outcomes may be particularly stressful for new mothers. Researchers have linked postpartum depression to stress brought on by the transition to a motherhood role (O'Hara et al., 1984), but the extent to which unwanted pregnancy underlies these findings is unknown.

Unwanted Pregnancy, Childbearing, and Abortion

The impact of childbearing on mental health depends on whether the pregnancy was wanted. Unintended and unwanted pregnancy is a stressful life event, whether terminated in birth or abortion (Russo, 1992). In 1994, 49 percent of pregnancies in the United States were unintended, the majority of them unwanted; about 54 percent of those unintended pregnancies were terminated by abortion. The highest rates of such pregnancies were found in women who were between 18 and 24 years of age, poor, unmarried, and black or Hispanic—groups already affected by social disadvantage and at higher risk for depression (Henshaw, 1998).

Pregnancies that are wanted by the woman but unwanted by the partner may be particularly stressful. For example, a study of 124 cohabiting couples experiencing an unintended first pregnancy found that pregnancies associated with the highest risk for postpartum depressive symptoms were those considered intended by females and unintended by their partners (Leathers & Kelley, 2000).

Preexisting mental health was the most powerful predictor of post-pregnancy mental health, however the pregnancy was resolved (Adler, David, Major, Roth, Russo, & Wyatt, 1992; Russo, David, Adler, & Major, 2004). This suggests that shared risk factors for depression and unintended pregnancy need to be investigated. Chief among gender-related shared risk factors is exposure to intimate violence (Russo & Denious, 1998). Unwanted pregnancies are highly correlated with exposure to intimate violence, including childhood physical and sexual abuse, rape, and partner violence (Dietz et al., 2000; Russo & Denious, 2001; Wyatt, Guthrie, & Notgrass, 1992). According to a study by the Centers for Disease Control and Prevention (CDC), 12 percent of mothers with newborns whose pregnancies had been unwanted (no births wanted at the time or in the future) reported having been "physically hurt" by their husband or partner during the 12 months before delivery, compared to 8 percent of new mothers with mistimed pregnancies and 3.2 percent of new mothers with intended pregnancies. The highest rates of injury (16.6%) were found among unmarried new mothers with unwanted pregnancies (Gazmararian et al., 1995).

In addition to increased likelihood of experiencing intimate violence, women with unintended pregnancy may experience other co-occurring negative circumstances (e.g., partner leaving in response to the pregnancy, financial strain). Although not associated with clinically significant depression, there is also the stress of being stigmatized for terminating the pregnancy (Major & Gramzow, 1999), being exposed to clinic protesters, and experiencing harassment at clinic sites (Cozzarelli & Major, 1994, 1998.

A charged political context complicates researching the relationship between unintended pregnancy and depression. Fueled by controversies over sexuality and abortion, attacks on the integrity of science have involved unprecedented attempts to manipulate scientific findings to serve a conservative social political agenda (Mooney, 2004). Conservative politicians' willingness to undermine the integrity of those federal agencies established to serve the public's health is seen in attacks on the CDC as a result of informing the public that there was no evidence that abortion causes breast cancer or that condoms, when used properly, can prevent a variety of sexually transmitted infections (Denious & Russo, 2005).

The mental health effects of abortion have become particularly controversial as "abortion damage" is now being used to justify arguments for restrictions on abortion and plays a central role in the strategy to overturn *Roe v. Wade* (Denious & Russo, 2005). Unfortunately, much of the research on emotional consequences of abortion has been based on clinical samples, conducted with inadequate methodology, and has focused on negative consequences.

Although it is argued that clinical disorder, particularly anxiety and depression, often result from abortion, this is not substantiated in the scientific literature. A review of the well-controlled empirical studies conducted in the United States documents the relatively minor risks of first-trimester abortion to women's psychological well-being, concluding that clinically significant adverse symptoms occur in a minority of women, and when they do occur, their strongest predictor was mental health before the abortion (Adler, David, Major, Roth, Russo, & Wyatt, 1990). Similarly, a meta-analysis showed that research designs comparing pre- and postabortion indicators of mental health found women to be between 0.50 and 0.60 of a standard deviation *better off* after abortion. For designs based on comparison groups, which varied in nature, results were mixed: women who had an abortion were found to range between 0.04 of a standard deviation better off and 0.08 of a standard deviation worse off in comparison to other groups of women (Posavac & Miller, 1990).

A women's emotional responses after abortion can be understood in a stress-and-coping framework. Although the abortion experience per se does not appear to be a significant risk factor for psychopathology, some women are at higher risk for emotional responses after an unwanted pregnancy that is terminated by abortion, and appraisal of the abortion experience is a key factor in determining outcome (Major, Richards, Cooper, Cozzarelli, & Zubek, 1998). Risk factors include a history of emotional disturbance, not expecting to cope well with the abortion, feeling coerced to have the abortion, difficulty in deciding to have an abortion, termination of a pregnancy that was originally wanted, abortion in the second trimester of pregnancy, self-blame for the unwanted pregnancy, and limited or no social support (Adler et al., 1990, 1992).

Adoption is sometimes proposed as an alternative to abortion for resolution of unwanted pregnancy, but little research has been conducted on the psychological consequences of adoption. As in the case of abortion, clinical and case studies do suggest that some women may be at risk for psychological and interpersonal difficulties after giving up a child for adoption, and for some people such risks persist over long periods of time (Pannor, Baron, & Sorosky, 1978). Studies of the postadoption experience suffer many of the same limitations of those of postabortion experience, however, including reliance on clinical samples and a focus on negative experiences. Although the research is scanty, it is noteworthy that risk factors that put women at higher risk of emotional responses after adoption are similar to those after abortion (Russo, 1992).

In summary, research suggests that gender-related attributes and gender-roles are related to women's risk for psychopathology after stressful reproductive-related life events. Women's responses to reproductive-related events can be understood in a stress-and-coping framework, whereby risk factors and coping resources interact to influence the relationship between stressful events and the development of psychopathology.

SEXUALIZED OBJECTIFICATION

There has been a great deal of theoretical (Burnett, Baylis, & Hamilton, 1994; Frederickson & Roberts, 1997), methodological (McKinley, 1996; McKinley & Hyde, 1996), and substantive work that has found objectification, particularly sexualized objectification, to be a powerful influence on women's thoughts, feelings, and behaviors in Western culture (Klonoff & Landrine, 1995; Landrine, Klonoff, Gibbs, Manning, & Lund, 1995; Landrine & Klonoff, 1997; Klonoff, Landrine, & Campbell, 2000). The body dissatisfaction and shame that can result from objectified body consciousness in a culture in which women's bodies play a central role in defining their worth and in which one "can never be too rich or too thin" have profound mental health implications (Joiner, Schmidt, & Wonderlich, 1997; Lin & Kulik, 2002; Denious et al., 2004; Tiggemann & Kuring, 2004). The sexualized objectification of girls, in particular, has become widely recognized as linked to a host of negative psychological, social, and behavioral outcomes (American Psychological Association, 2007).

Congruent with findings from Landrine et al. (1995), one study found the most important contributors to the effect of frequency of objectification experiences were being called degrading, gender-stereotyped names and being the target of offensive (sexualized) gestures. However, externalized self-perceptions (e.g., "I tend to judge myself by how I think other people see me") moderated this relationship. Taken as a whole, this research suggests that frequency of objectification experiences predicts depressive symptoms, with this effect moderated by the tendency to rely on the opinions and evaluations of others (Hamilton & Russo, 2006).

The stigma and resulting shame that can result from objectification experiences may explain the link of objectification experiences with depression and eating disorders (Denious et al., 2004). They argue that shame may be triggered by the stigma of not meeting cultural appearance standards. Unfortunately, research has focused on the relationship of body shame to eating disorders, and little is known about its relationship to other disorders, including depression.

In summary, basic research is needed on the processes that underlie the dynamics of stigmatization, shame, and depression fueled by objectification processes. Research on the dynamics of gender and its relationship to objectified body consciousness in a body-conscious culture is particularly needed to inform treatment and prevention efforts.

STIGMA, PREJUDICE, AND DISCRIMINATION

Stigma may be uncontrollable or controllable, hidden or visible, and may be linked to an individual characteristic or group membership. Attributes, experiences, and behaviors that are stigmatized vary with culture and over time. Stigmas label people as different and devalued by others, leading to low status and loss of power and discrimination (Link & Phelan, 2001). Stigma, particularly when attached to personal attributes such as sex, race, sexual orientation, and disability, poses a threat to one's personal and social identity. It can affect mental health through a variety of psychological and interpersonal mechanisms, including activation of stereotypes, expectancy effects, social exclusion, and other forms of negative treatment, including sexist and racist discrimination.

Research on the impact of sexism has found that the negative impact of sexist events on anxiety and mood disorders may be substantial (Klonoff & Landrine, 1995; Landrine et al., 1995; Krieger, Rowley, Herman, Avery, & Phillips, 1993). Experiencing sexist events (e.g., being treated unfairly by employer, called a sexist name like "bitch" or "cunt," being exposed to degrading sexual jokes) has been found to explain gender differences among college women and men in symptoms of anxiety, depression, and somatization (Klonoff et al., 2000).

Stigmatization may undermine mental health by interfering with perceiving or obtaining social support from others (Crocker, Major, & Steele, 1998; Major & O'Brien, 2005). Disclosing stressful life events is an important part of the coping process, and for stigmas that can be concealed, the process of concealment may increase risk for physical and psychological problems (Pennebaker, 1995). Disclosure may result in social rejection and exclusion, which have powerful negative effects as well, making management of stigma a highly stressful process.

The effects of social support on the contribution of shame to women's psychopathology are a promising area of study (Denious et al., 2004). The role of shame is particularly important to understand because of its possible implications for treatment. If guilt is contributing to the problem, sharing the information with a therapist would be expected to have cathartic effects, and an active therapeutic stance is not necessarily needed. If shame is the underlying factor, exposure of shame experiences may make the client "only feel worse" unless the therapist takes an active stance and communicates "positive regard" to the client (Wright et al., 1989, p. 229).

Stigmatization associated with stressful life events can affect women's willingness to seek help for dealing with those events, undermine their mental health, and increase risk for depression. Depending on the norms of the community, women can be stigmatized for being victims of childhood sexual abuse, being raped, losing their virginity, staying single, having more than one sexual partner, having menstrual cramps, being a lesbian, having a child when not married, being childless, being battered by their husband, being too fat, having an abortion, placing a child for adoption, working when her children are young, being a "bad" mother, and being menopausal, among other things. These are just a few examples of a variety of gender-related events associated with stigma that have implications for mental health. Basic research on both gender and stigma is needed to refine their conceptualization and measurement so that the relationships among gender, stigma, and depression can be adequately understood.

Full understanding of the gender gap in depression requires knowing both the extent to which gender shapes the events in women's lives that are stigmatized and how social inequality undermines women's ability to overcome stigmatization. However, stigma depends on power—social, political, and economic—but power dynamics are all too often overlooked in analyses of stigma. As Link and Phelan (2001) point out, "there is a tendency to focus on the attributes associated with those [stigmatizing] conditions rather than on power differences between people who have them and people who do not" (p. 375). They argue that stigma is dependent on the power to label and negatively stereotype members of stigmatized groups, lower their status, and limit their access to major life domains such as education, jobs, housing, and health care. Link and Phelan also suggest that to intervene in the stigma one must (1) produce fundamental changes in beliefs and attitudes or (2) change the power relations that enable dominant groups to act on those stigmatizing beliefs and attitudes. The potential for success of either approach will depend on knowledge of the interrelationships among gender, stigma, and mental health (Hamilton & Russo, 2006).

WOMEN'S MENTAL HEALTH: CURRENT STATUS, FUTURE PROSPECTS

This review has highlighted new conceptualizations, methodological issues, and selected research findings related to gender and mental health, including gender differences in diagnosis and treatment and patterns in rates of mental disorders. The implications of gender as a dynamic social construct for women's mental health are complex and vary across age, ethnic, and racial groups. We argue that future advances in understanding the relation of gender to women's mental health require appreciating the violence, powerlessness, and lack of access to resources associated with women's social roles and position in society.

Symptoms of mental disorders that have high prevalence for women overlap with each other, as well as with women's gender stereotypes. Misdiagnosis—of one disorder for another or of normal role behavior for psychopathology—continues to be a critical issue in women's mental health. A stress-and-coping framework that includes biological, psychological, social, and cultural variables related to gender and considers the behaviors of women in their larger context continues to hold promise for mental health research and theory. The politicization of mental health research related to contraception and abortion, however, reminds us of the importance of the larger social context to the setting of research priorities.

Also, we must remember that, despite pervasive gender differences in mental health, they were identified as a priority of the National Institute of Mental Health only when forced to do so by Congress (Russo, 1990). Today, with some minor exceptions, public concern for health disparities is what keeps attention to social factors alive in national health funding agencies. Continued monitoring of mental health funding and service delivery bodies will be needed as long as women's position in society is devalued and biomedical models continue to dominate funding for women's health research. Only when there is a true commitment to developing biopsychosocial models of mental health will gender (as opposed to sex) achieve the priority it deserves by the mental health establishment.

REFERENCES

Abramson, L. Y., Metalsky, G. I., & Alloy, L. B. (1989). Hopelessness depression: A theory-based subtype of depression. *Psychological Review, 96*, 358–372.

Adler, N., David, H. P., Major, B. N., Roth, S. H., Russo, N. F., & Wyatt, G. E. (1990). Psychological responses after abortion. *Science, 248*(April 6), 41–44.

Adler, N. E., David, H. P., Major, B. N., Roth, S., Russo, N. F., & Wyatt, G. (1992). Psychological factors in abortion: A review. *American Psychologist, 47*, 1194–1204.

Agency for Healthcare Research and Quality. (2005). *2005 National Healthcare Disparities Report*. AHRQ Publication No. 06-0018. Rockville, MD: Agency for Healthcare Research and Quality. Available at http://www.ahrq.gov/qual/nhdr05/nhdr05.htm.

Alegria, A., Mulvaney-Day, N., Torres, M., Polo, A., Cao, Z., & Canino, G. (2007). Prevalence of psychiatric disorders across Latino subgroups in the United States. *American Journal of Public Health, 97*, 68–85.

Alexander, M. J. (1996). Women with co-occurring addictive and mental disorders: An emerging profile of vulnerability. *American Journal of Orthopsychiatry, 66*, 61–70.

Almeida, D. M., & Kessler, R. C. (1998). Everyday stressors and gender differences in daily distress. *Journal of Personality and Social Psychology, 75*, 670–680.

Alonso, J., Angermeyer, M. C., Bernert, S., Bruffaerts, R., Brugha, T. S., & Bryson, H., et al. (2004). Prevalence of mental disorders in Europe: Results from the European Study of the Epidemiology of Mental Disorders (ESEMeD) project. *Acta Psychiatrica Scandinavica, Supplement*, 21–27.

American Psychiatric Association. (1994). *Diagnostic and statistical manual of mental disorders* (4th ed.). Washington, DC: American Psychiatric Association.

American Psychological Association. (1996a). *Research agenda for psychosocial and behavioral factors in women's health*. Washington, DC: American Psychological Association. Retrieved from http://www.apa.org/pi/wpo/research.html.

American Psychological Association. Presidential Task Force on Violence and the Family. (1996b). *Violence and the family: Report of the American Psychological Association Presidential Task Force on Violence and the Family*. Washington, DC: American Psychological Association.

American Psychological Association. Task Force on Women, Poverty, and Public Assistance. (1998). *Making welfare-to-work really work*. Washington, DC: American Psychological Association.

American Psychological Association. (2000). Guidelines for psychotherapy with lesbian, gay, and bisexual clients. *American Psychologist, 55*, 1440–1451.

American Psychological Association. (2003). Guidelines on multicultural education, training, research, practice, and organizational change for psychologists. *American Psychologists, 58*, 377–402.

American Psychological Association. (2006). *Guidelines for psychological practice with girls and women*. Washington, DC: American Psychological Association.

American Psychological Association. Task Force on the Sexualization of Girls. (2007). *Report of the APA Task Force on the Sexualization of Girls*. Washington, DC: American Psychological Association.

Anderson, K. L. (2005). Theorizing gender in intimate partner violence research. *Sex Roles, 52*, 853–865.

Angst, J., & Merikangas, K. (1997). The depressive spectrum: Diagnostic classification and course. *Journal of Affective Disorders, 45*, 31–39.

Arnold, L. M. (2003). Gender differences in bipolar disorder. *Psychiatric Clinics of North America, 26*, 595–620.

Arrindell, W. A., Steptoe, A., & Wardle, J. (2003). Higher levels of state depression in masculine than feminine nations. *Behavior Research and Therapy, 41*, 809–817.

Belle, D. (1982). The stress of caring: Women as providers of social support. In L. Goldberger & S. Breznitz (Eds.), *Handbook of stress: Theoretical and clinical aspects*. New York: Free Press.

Bleher, M. E. (2006). Women mental health research: Emergence of a biomedical field. *Annual Review of Clinical Psychology, 2*, 135–160.

Bourne, L. E., Jr., & Russo, N. F. (1998). *Psychology: Behavior in context*. New York: W. W. Norton.

Bowman, M. L., & Yehuda, R. (2004). Risk factors and the adversity-stress model. In G. M. Rosen (Ed.), *Posttraumatic stress disorder: Issues and controversies* (pp. 15–38). New York: Wiley.

Breslau, J., Aguilar-Gaxiola, S. Kendler, K. S., Su, M., Williams, D., & Kessler, R. C. (2005). Specifying ethnic differences in risk for psychiatric disorders in a USA national sample. *Psychological Medicine, 35*, 1–12.

Breslau, N., Schultz, L., & Peterson, E. (1995). Sex differences in depression: A role for pre-existing anxiety. *Psychiatry Research, 58*, 1–12.

Brown, C., Abe-Kim, J. S., & Barrio, C. (2003). Depression in ethnically diverse women: Implications for treatment in primary care settings. *Professional Psychology: Research and Practice, 34*, 10–19.

Brown, D. R., & Keith, V. (Eds.). (2003). *In and out of our right minds: The mental health of African American women* (pp. 83–98). New York: Columbia University Press.

Brown, G. W., Bifulco, A., Harris, T., & Bridge, L. (1986). Life stress, chronic subclinical symptoms and vulnerability to clinical depression. *Journal of Affective Disorders, 11*, 1–19.

Brown, G. W., & Harris, T. (1978). *Social origins of depression: A study of psychiatric disorder* in *women*. New York: Free Press.

Brown, G. W., Harris, T. O., & Eales, M. J. (1993). Aetiology of anxiety and depressive disorders in an inter-city population: 2. Comorbidity and adversity. *Psychological Medicine, 23*, 155–165.

Bryant, R. M., Coker, A. D., Durodoye, B. A., McCollum, V. J., Pack-Brown, S. P., Constantine, M. G., et al. (2005). Having our say: African American women, diversity, and counseling. *Journal of Counseling and Development, 83*, 313–319.

Chen, Y. Y., Subramanian, S. V., Acevedo-Garcia, D., & Kawachi, I. (2005). Women's status and depressive symptoms: A multilevel analysis. *Social Science and Medicine, 60*(1), 49–60.

Clark, V. A., Aneshensel, C. S., Frerichs, R. R., & Morgan, T. M. (1981). Analysis of effects of sex and age on response to items on the CES-D Scale. *Psychiatry Research, 5*, 171–181.

Coker, A. L., Davis, K. E., Arias, I., Desai, S., Sanderson, M., Brandt, H. M., et al. (2002). Physical and mental health effects of intimate partner violence for men and women. *American Journal of Preventive Medicine, 23*, 260–268.

Cortina, L. M., & Kubiak, S. P. (2006). Gender and posttraumatic stress: Sexual violence as an explanation for women's increased risk. *Journal of Abnormal Psychology*, 115(4):753–759.

Cozzarelli, C., & Major, B. (1998). The impact of antiabortion activities on women seeking abortions. In L. J. Beckman & S. M. Harvey (Eds.), *The new civil war: The psychology, culture, and politics of abortion* (pp. 28, 81–104). Washington, DC: American Psychological Association.

Craig, T. I., & Van Natta, P. A. (1979). Influence of demographic characteristics on two measures of depressive symptoms. *Archives of General Psychiatry, 36*, 149–154.

Cross, S. E., & Madsen, L. E. (1997). Models of the self: Self-construals and gender. *Psychological Bulletin, 122*, 5–37.

Deaux, K., & Major, B. (1987). Putting gender into context: An interactive model of gender-related behavior. *Psychological Review, 94*(3), 369–389.

Demyttenaere, K., Bruffaerts, R., Posada-Villa, J., Gasquet, I., Kovess, V., Lepine, J. P., et al. (2004). Prevalence, severity, and unmet need for treatment of mental disorders in the World Health Organization World Mental Health Surveys. *Journal of the American Medical Association, 291*, 2581–2590.

Denious, J., & Russo, N. F. (2005). Controlling birth: Science, politics, and public policy. *Journal of Social Issues, 61*, 181–191.

Denious, J., Russo, N. F., & Rubin, L. (2004). The role of shame in socio- and subcultural influences on disordered eating. In M. A. Paludi (Ed.). *Praeger Guide to the Psychology of Gender* (pp. 219–237). Westport, CT: Praeger.

Desjarlais, R., Eisenberg, L., Good, B., & Kleinman, A. (1996). *World mental health: Problems and priorities in low-income countries*. Oxford: Oxford University Press.

Dietz, P., Spitz, A. M., Anda, R. F., Williamson, D. G., McMahon, P. M., Santelli, J. S., et al. (2000). Unintended pregnancy among adult women exposed to abuse or household dysfunction during their childhood. *Journal of the American Medical Association, 282*, 1259–1364.

Dutton, M. A., Green, B., Kaltman, S. I., Roesch, D. M., Zeffiro, T. A., & Krause, E. D. (2006). Intimate partner violence, PTSD, and adverse health outcomes. *Journal of Interpersonal Violence, 21*, 955–968.

Ellis, K. M., & Erikson, K. (2002). Transsexual and transgenderist experiences and treatment options. *Family Journal: Counseling and Therapy for Couples and Families, 10*, 289–299.

Faravelli, C., Giugni, A., Salvatori, S., & Ricca., V. (2004). Psychopathology after rape. *American Journal of Psychiatry, 161*, 1483–1485.

Folkman, S., & Moskowitz, J. T. (2004). Coping: Pitfalls and promise. *Annual Review of Psychology, 55*, 745–774.

Frable, D. E. S. (1997). Gender, racial, ethnic, sexual, and class identities. *Annual Review of Psychology, 48*, 139–162.

Fullilove, M. (2002). Social and economic causes of depression. *Journal of Gender Specific Medicine, 5*(2), 38–41.

Garner, D., & Garfinkel, P. (1980). Sociocultural factors in the development of anorexia nervosa. *Psychological Medicine, 10*, 647–656.

Gazmararian, J. A., Adams, M. M., Saltzman, L. E., Johnson, C. H., Bruce, F. C., Marks, J. S., et al. (1995). The relationship between pregnancy intendedness and physical violence in mothers of newborns. *Obstetrics & Gynecology, 85*, 1031–1038.

Ginsberg, D. L. (2004). Women and anxiety disorders: Implications for diagnosis and treatment. *CNS Spectrums, 9*(9), 1–16.

Gove, W. (198?). Mental illness and psychiatric treatment among women. *Psychology of Women Quarterly, 4*, 345–362.

Greene, B., & Sanchez-Hucles, J. B. (1997). Diversity: Advancing an inclusive feminist psychology. In J. Worell & N. G. Johnson (Eds.), *Shaping the future of feminist psychology: Education, research, and practice* (pp. 173–202). Washington, DC: American Psychological Association.

Hamilton, J. (1984). Psychobiology in context: Reproductive-related events in men's and women's lives. *Contemporary Psychiatry, 3,* 12–16.

Hamilton, J. A. (1995). Sex and gender as critical variables in psychotropic drug research. In B. Brown, P. Rieker, & C. Willie (Eds.), *Racism and sexism and mental health* (pp. 297–350). Pittsburgh, PA: University of Pittsburgh Press.

Hamilton, J. A., Grant, M., & Jensvold, M. F. (1996). Sex and treatment of depressions: When does it matter? In J. A. Hamilton, M. Jensvold, E. Rothblum, & E. Cole (Eds.), *Psychopharmacology of women: Sex, gender and hormonal considerations* (pp. 241–260). Washington, DC: American Psychiatric Press.

Hamilton, J. A., & Jensvold, M. (1995). Sex and gender as critical variables in feminist psychopharmacology research and pharmacotherapy. In J. A. Hamilton, M. Jensvold, E. Rothblum, & E. Cole (Eds.), *Psychopharmacology from a feminist perspective* (pp. 9–30). Binghamton, NY: Haworth Press.

Hamilton, J. A., & Russo, N. F. (2006). Women and depression: Research, theory, and social policy. In Keyes & Goodman, 2006, pp. 479–522.

Hammen, C. (2005). Stress and depression. *Annual Review of Clinical Psychology, 1,* 293–319.

Hayward, C., Gotlib, I. H., Schraedley, P. K., & Litt, I. F. (1999). Ethnic differences in the association between pubertal status and symptoms of depression in adolescent girls. *Journal of Adolescent Health, 25,* 143–149.

Henshaw, S. K. (1998). Unintended pregnancy in the United States. *Family Planning Perspectives, 30*(1), 24–29, 46.

Herek, G. M., & Garnets, L. (2007). Sexual orientation and mental health. *Annual Review of Clinical Psychology,* 3, 353–375.

Hettema, J. M., Prescott, C. A., & Kendler, K. S. (2003). The effects of anxiety, substance use and conduct disorders on risk of major depressive disorder. *Psychological Medicine, 33,* 1423–1432.

Hiday, V. A., Swanson, J. W., Swartz, M. S., Borum, R., & Wagner, H. R. (2001). Victimization: A link between mental illness and violence? *International Journal of Law and Psychiatry, 24,* 559–572.

Hinz, L. D., & Williamson, D. A. (1987). Bulimia and depression: A review of the affective variant hypothesis. *Psychological Bulletin, 102,* 150–158.

Hobfoll, S. E. (1986). The ecology of stress and social support among women. In S. Hobfoll (Ed.), *Stress, social support and women.* (pp. 3–14). Washington, D.C.: Hemisphere.

Hobfoll, S. E., & Lieberman, J. R. (1987). Personality and social resources in immediate and continued stress resistance among women. *Journal of Personality and Social Psychology, 52,* 8–26.

Horwitz, A. V., Widom, C. S., McLaughlin, J., & Raskin White, H. (2001). The impact of childhood abuse and neglect on adult mental health: A prospective study. *Journal of Health and Social Behavior, 42,* 184–201.

Hudson, J. I., Hiripi, E., Pope, H. G., Jr., & Kessler, R. C. (2007). The prevalence and correlates of eating disorders in the National Comorbidity Survey Replication. *Biological Psychiatry, 61,* 348–358.

Huselid, B. F., & Cooper, M. L. (1994). Gender roles as mediators of sex differences in expression of pathology. *Journal of Abnormal Psychology, 103,* 595–603.

Joiner, T. E., Schmidt, N. B., & Wonderlich, S. A. (1997). Global self-esteem as contingent on body satisfaction among patients with bulimia nervosa: Lack of diagnostic specificity? *International Journal of Eating Disorders, 21*, 67–76.

Katzman, M., & Wolchik, S. (1984). Bulimia and binge eating in college women: A comparison of personality and behavioral characteristics. *Journal of Consulting and Clinical Psychology, 52*, 423–428.

Keane, T. M., Marshall, A. D., & Taft, C. T. (2006). Posttraumatic stress disorder: Etiology, epidemiology, and treatment outcome. *Annual Review of Clinical Psychology, 2*, 161–197.

Kendler, K. S., Bulik, C. M., Silberg, J., Hettema, J. M., Myers, J., & Prescott, C. A. (2000). Childhood sexual abuse and adult psychiatric and substance use disorders in women: An epidemiological and co-twin control analysis. *Archives of General Psychiatry, 57*, 953–959.

Kessler, R. C. (2006). The epidemiology of depression among women. In Keyes & Goodman.

Kessler, R., Chiu, C., Demler, W., Merikangas K., & Walters, E. (2005). Prevalence, severity, and comorbidity of 12-month *DSM-IV* disorders in the National Comorbidity Survey Replication. *Archives of General Psychology, 62*, 617–627.

Kessler, R. C., & Magee, W. (1993). Childhood adversities and adult depression: Basic patterns of association in a US national survey. *Psychological Medicine, 23*, 679–690.

Kessler, R. C., McGonagle, K. A., Swartz, M., Blazer, D. G., & Nelson, C.B. (1993). Sex and depression in the National Co-Morbidity Survey I: Lifetime prevalence, chronicity, and recurrence. *Journal of Affective Disorders, 29*, 85–96.

Kessler, R. C., McGonagle, K. A., Zhao, S., Nelson, C. B., Hughes, M., Eshleman, S., et al. (1994). Lifetime and 12-month prevalence of *DSM-III-R* psychiatric disorders in the United States: Results from the National Comorbidity Survey. *Archives of General Psychiatry, 51*, 8–19.

Kessler, R., & McLeod, J. (1985). Sex differences in vulnerability to undesirable life events. *American Sociological Review, 49*, 620–631.

Kessler, R. C., McLeod, J. D., & Wethington, E. (1984). The cost of caring: A perspective on the relationship between sex and psychological distress. In I. G. Samson & B. R. Samson (Eds.), *Social support: Theory, research and applications* (pp. 491–506). The Hague: Martinus Nijhoff.

Keyes, C. L. M., & Goodman, S. H. (Eds). (2006). *Women and depression: A handbook for the social, behavioral, and biomedical sciences.* New York: Cambridge University Press.

Klein, Corwin, and Ceballos. (2006). In Keyes & Goodman.

Klonoff, L., & Landrine, H. (1995). The Schedule of Sexist Events: A measure of lifetime and recent sexist discrimination in women's lives. *Psychology of Women Quarterly, 24*, 439–472.

Klonoff, L., Landrine, H. & Campbell, R. (2000). Sexist discrimination may account for well-known symptoms. *Psychology of Women Quarterly, 24*, 93–99.

Klose, M., & Jacobi, F. (2004). Can gender differences in the bullets of mental disorder be explained by sociodemographic factors? *Archives of Women's Mental Health, 7*(2), 133–148.

Korell, S. C., & Lorah, P. (2007). An overview of affirmative psychotherapy and counseling with transgender clients. In K. J. Bieschke, R. M. Perez, & K. A. DeBord (Eds.), *Handbook of counseling and psychotherapy with lesbian, gay, bisexual, and transgender clients*. (2nd ed.; pp. 271–288). Washington, DC: American Psychological Association.

Koss, M. P., Bailey, J., Yuan, N. P., Herrera, V. M., & Lichter, E. L. (2003). Depression and PTSD in the survivors of male violence: Research and training initiatives to facilitate recovery. *Psychology of Women Quarterly, 27*, 130–142.

Krieger, N. (2003). Genders, sexes, and health: What are the connections—and why does it matter? *International Journal of Epidemiology, 32*, 652–657.

Krieger, N., Rowley, D. L., Herman, A. A., Avery, B., & Phillips, M. T. (1993). Racism, sexism, and social class: Implications for studies of health, disease, and well-being. *American Journal of Preventive Medicine, 9*(Suppl. 2), 82–122.

Kuehner, C. (2003). Gender differences in unipolar depression: An update of epidemiological findings and possible explanations. *Acta Psychiatrica Scandinavica, 108*(3), 163–174.

Landrine, H., & Klonoff, E. A. (1997). *Discrimination against women: Prevalence, consequences, remedies*. Thousand Oaks, CA: Sage.

Landrine, H., Klonoff, E. A., Gibbs, J, Manning, V., & Lund, M. (1995). Physical and psychiatric correlates of gender discrimination: An application of the Schedule of Sexist Events. *Psychology of Women Quarterly, 19*, 473–492.

Lazarus, R. S., & Folkman, S. (1984). *Stress, appraisal, and coping.* New York: Springer.

Leathers, S. J., & Kelley, M. A. (2000). Unintended pregnancy and depressive symptoms among first-time mothers and fathers. *American Journal of Orthopsychiatry, 70*, 523–531.

Lee, N. F., Rush, A. J., & Mitchell, J. E. (1985). Bulimia and depression. *Journal of Affective Disorders, 9*, 231–238.

Lehman, D. R., Chiu, C., & Schaller, M. (2004). Psychology and culture. *Annual Review of Psychology, 55*, 689–714.

Lev, A. I. (2004). *Transgender emergence: Therapeutic guidelines for working with gender-variant people and their families*. New York: Haworth Clinical Practice Press.

Lev, A. I. (2007). Transgender communities: Developing identity through connection. In K. J. Bieschke, R. M. Perez, & K. A. DeBord (Eds.), *Handbook of counseling and psychotherapy with lesbian, gay, bisexual, and transgender clients* (2nd ed.; pp. 147–175). Washington, DC: American Psychological Association.

Levin, B. L., Blanch, A. K., & Jennings, A. (Eds.). (1998). *Women's mental health services: A public health perspective*. Thousand Oaks, CA: Sage.

Lin, L. F., & Kulik, J. A. (2002). Social comparison and women's body satisfaction. *Basic and Applied Social Psychology, 24*(2), 115–123.

Link, B. G., & Phelan, J. C. (2001). Conceptualizing stigma. *Annual Review of Sociology, 27*, 363–385.

Lopez, S. (1989). Patient variable biases in clinical judgment: Conceptual overview and methodological considerations. *Psychological Bulletin, 106*, 184–203.

Lopez, S. R., & Guarnaccia, P. J. J. (2000). Cultural psychopathology: Uncovering the social world of mental illness. *Annual Review of Psychology, 51*, 571–598.

Loring, M., & Powell, B. (1988). Gender, race and *DSM-ID*: A study of the objectivity of psychiatric diagnostic behavior. *Journal of Health and Social Behavior, 29,* 1–22.

Major, B., & Gramzow, R. H. (1999). Abortion as stigma: Cognitive and emotional implications of concealment. *Journal of Personality and Social Psychology, 77,* 735–745.

Major, B., & O'Brien, L. T. (2004). The social psychology of stigma. *Annual Review of Psychology, 56,* 1–29.

Major, B., Richards, C., Cooper, M. L., Cozzarelli, C., & Zubek, J. (1998). Personal resilience, cognitive appraisals, and coping: An integrative model of adjustment to abortion. *Journal of Personality and Social Psychology, 74,* 735–752.

Marecek, J. (2001). Disorderly constructs: Feminist frameworks for clinical psychology. In R. K. Unger (Ed.), *Handbook of the psychology of women and gender* (pp. 303–317). New York: John Wiley & Sons.

Mazure, C., Keita, G. P., & Blehar, M. C. (2002). *Summit on Women's Depression: Proceedings and recommendations*. Washington, DC: American Psychological Association Women's Programs Office.

Mazure, C. M., & Maciejewski, P. K. (2003) The interplay of stress, gender and cognitive style in depressive onset. *Archives of Women's Mental Health, 6,* 5–8.

McCall, L. (2005). The complexity of intersectionality. *Signs, 30,* 1771–1800.

McGrath, E., Keita, G. P., Strickland, B. R., & Russo, N. F. (1990). *Women and depression: Risk factors and treatment issues.* Washington, DC: American Psychological Association.

McKinley, N. M., & Hyde, J. S. (1996). The Objectified Body Consciousness Scale: Development and validation. *Psychology of Women Quarterly, 20,* 181–215.

Meyer, I. H. (2003). Prejudice, social stress, and mental health in lesbian, gay, and bisexual populations: Conceptual issues and research evidence. *Psychological Bulletin, 129,* 674–697.

Mintz, L., & Betz, N. (1988). Prevalence and correlates of eating disordered behaviors among undergraduate women. *Journal of Counseling Psychology, 35,* 463–471.

Mirowsky, J., & Ross, C. E. (1995). Sex differences in distress: Real or artifact? *American Sociological Review, 60,* 449–468.

Molnar, B. E., Buka, S. L., & Kessler, R. C. (2001). Child sexual abuse and subsequent psychopathology: Results from the National Comorbidity Survey. *American Journal of Public Health, 91,* 753–760.

Mooney, C. (2004). Research and destroy: How the religious right promotes its own "experts" to combat mainstream science. *Washington Monthly,* October. Available at http://www.washingtonmonthly.com/features/2004/0410.mooney.html.

Mueller, P., & Major, B. (1989). Self-blame, self-efficacy, and adjustment to abortion. *Journal of Personality and Social Psychology, 57,* 1059–1068.

Murray, C. J. L., & Lopez, A. D. (1996). Alternative visions of the future: Projecting mortality and disability, 1990–2020. In C. J. L. Murray & A. D. Lopez (Eds.), *The global burden of disease: A comprehensive assessment of mortality and disability from diseases, injuries, and risk factors in 1990 and projected to 2020* (pp. 321–395). Boston: Harvard University Press.

Nasser, M. (1988). Culture and weight consciousness. *Journal of Psychosomatic Research, 32*, 573–577.

Nazroo, J. Y., Edwards, A. C., and Brown, G. W. (1998). Gender differences in the prevalence of depression: Artefact, alternative disorders, biology or roles? *Sociology of Health & Illness, 20*, 312–330.

Newmann, J. P. (1984). Sex differences in symptoms of depression: Clinical disorder or normal distress? *Journal of Health and Social Behavior, 25*, 136–160.

Nolen-Hoeksema, S. (1990). *Sex differences in depression.* Stanford, CA: Stanford University Press.

Nolen-Hoeksema, S. (2003). *Women who think too much: How to break free of overthinking and reclaim your life.* New York: Henry Holt.

Nolen-Hoeksema, S., & Girgus, J. S. (1994). The emergence of gender differences in depression during adolescence. *Psychological Bulletin, 115*, 424–443.

Nolen-Hoeksema, S., Larsen, J., & Grayson, C. (1999). Explaining the gender difference in depressive symptoms. *Journal of Personality and Social Psychology, 77*, 1061–1072.

Norris, F., Foster, J., & Weisshaar, D. (2002). The epidemiology of sex differences in PTSD across developmental, societal, and research contexts. In R. Kimerling, P. Oimette, & J. Wolfe (Eds.), *Gender and PTSD* (pp. 3–42). New York: Guilford.

O'Hara, M., Neunaber, D., & Zekoski E. (1984). Prospective study of postpartum depression: Prevalence, course, and predictive factors. *Journal of Abnormal Psychology, 93*, 158–171.

Olff, M., Langeland, W., Draijer, N., & Gersons, B. (2007). Gender differences in posttraumatic stress disorder. *Psychological Bulletin, 133(2)*, 183–204.

Pannor, R., Baron, P., & Sorosky, A. (1978). Birthparents who relinquished babies for adoption revisited. *Family Child Placement Practice 17*, 329–337.

Pennebaker, J. W. (1995). *Emotion, disclosure, and health.* Washington, DC: American Psychological Association.

Penze, Heim, & Nemeroff. (2006). In Keyes & Goodman.

Posavac, E., & Miller, T. (1990). Some problems caused by not having a conceptual foundation for health research: An illustration from studies of the psychological effects of abortion. *Psychology & Health, 5*, 13–23.

Reich, J., & Zautra, A. (1990). Dispositional control beliefs and the consequences of a control-enhancing intervention. *Journal of Gerontology, 45*, 46–51.

Ridgeway, C. L., & Smith-Lovin, L. (1999). The gender system and interaction. *Annual Review of Sociology, 25*, 191–216.

Rodin, J., Silberstein, L., & Striegel-Moore, R. (1985). Women and weight: A normative discontent. In T. Sonderegger (Ed.), *Psychology and gender: Nebraska Symposium on Motivation* (pp. 267–307). Lincoln: University of Nebraska Press.

Root, M. P. (1991). Persistent disordered eating as a gender-specific, posttraumatic stress response to sexual assault. *Psychotherapy: Theory, Research, and Practice, 28*(Special Issue: *Psychotherapy with victims*), 96–102.

Russo, N. F. (1995). Women's mental health: Research agenda for the twenty-first century. In B. Brown, B. Kramer, P. Rieker, & C. Willie (Eds.), *Mental health, racism, and sexism* (pp. 373–396). Pittsburgh, PA: University of Pittsburgh Press.

Russo, N. F., & Denious, J. (1998). Understanding the relationship of violence against women to unwanted pregnancy and its resolution. In L. J. Beckman & S. M. Harvey (Eds.), *The new civil war: The psychology, culture, and politics of abortion* (pp. 211–234). Washington, DC: American Psychological Association.

Russo, N. F., & Denious, J. E. (2001). Violence in the lives of women having abortions: Implications for public policy and practice. *Professional Psychology: Research and Practice, 32*, 142–150.

Russo, N. F., & Green, B. L. (1993). Women and mental health. In F. L. Denmark & M. A. Paludi (Eds.), *Psychology of women: A handbook of issues and theories* (pp. 379–436). Westport, CT: Greenwood Press.

Russo, N. F., Koss, M. P., & Ramos, L. (2000). Rape: A global health issue. In J. Ussher (Ed.), *Women's health: Contemporary international perspectives* (pp. 129–142). London: British Psychological Society.

Russo, N. F., & Pirlott, A. (2006). Gender-based violence: Concepts, methods, and findings. *Annals of the New York Academy of Sciences, 1087*, 178–205.

Russo, N. F., & Vaz, K. (2001). Addressing diversity in the Decade of Behavior: Focus on women of color. *Psychology of Women Quarterly, 25*, 280–294.

Sachs-Ericsson, N., & Ciarlo, J. A. (2000). Gender, social roles, and mental health: An epidemiological perspective. *Sex Roles, 43*, 605–628.

Salokangas, R. K. R., Vaahtera, K., Pacriev, S., Sohlman, B., & Lehtinen, V. (2002). Gender bias in the personality disorders criteria: An investigation of five bias indicators. *Journal of Affective Disorders, 68*(2/3), 215–220.

Schoevers, R. A., Beekman, A. T. F., Deeg, D. J. H., Jonker, C., & van Tilburg, W. (2003). Comorbidity and risk-patterns of depression, generalised anxiety disorder and mixed anxiety-depression in later life: Results from the AMSTEL study. *International Journal of Geriatric Psychiatry, 18*, 994–1001.

Snowden, L. R., & Yamada, A.-M. (2005). Cultural differences in access to care. *Annual Review of Clinical Psychology, 1*, 143–166.

Sparks, E. (2002). Depression and schizophrenia in women: The intersection of gender, race/ethnicity, and class. In M. Ballou & L. S. Brown (Eds.), *Rethinking mental health and disorder: Feminist perspectives* (pp. 279–305). New York: Guilford.

Sparks, E. E., & Parks, A. H. (2000). The integration of feminism and multiculturalism: Ethical dilemmas at the border. In M. M. Brabeck (Ed.), *Practicing feminist ethics in psychology* (pp. 203–224). Washington, DC: American Psychological Association.

Stern, G., & Kruckman, L. (1983). Multi-disciplinary perspectives on post-partum depression: An anthropological critique. *Social Science and Medicine, 17*, 1027–1041.

Stewart, A., & McDermott, C. (2004). Gender in psychology. *Annual Review of Psychology, 55*, 519–544.

Stoppard, J. M. (2000). *Understanding depression: Feminist social constructionist approaches.* London: Routledge.

Striegel-Moore, R., Silberstein, L., & Rodin, J. (1986). Toward an understanding of risk factors for bulimia. *American Psychologist, 41*, 246–263.

Subpanel on the Mental Health of Women. President's Commission on Mental Health. (1978). Report of the Special Population Subpanel on Mental Health of Women. *Task Panel Report submitted to the President's Commission on Mental Health* (vol. 3). Washington, DC: GPO.

Tamres L., Janicki, D., & Helgeson, L. (2002). Sex differences in coping behavior: A meta-analytic reiew and an examination of relative coping. *Personality and Social Psychology Review, 6*, 2–30.

Taylor, S. E., Klein, L. C., Lewis, B. P., Gruenewald, T. L., Gurung, R. A. R., & Updegraff, J. A. (2000). Female responses to stress: Tend-and-befriend, not fight-or-flight. *Psychological Review, 107*, 411–429.

Taylor, S. E., & Stanton, A. (2007). Coping resources, coping processes, and mental health. *Annual Review of Clinical Psychology, 3*, 377–401.

Thomas, S. E., Deas, D., & Grindlinger, D. R. (2003). Gender differences in dependence symptoms and psychiatric severity in adolescents with substance use disorders. *Journal of Child & Adolescent Substance Abuse, 12*(4), 19–34.

Tiggemann, M., & Kuring, J. K. (2004). The role of body objectification in disordered eating and depressed mood. *British Journal of Clinical Psychology, 43*, 299–311.

Travis, C. (1998). *Women and health psychology: Biomedical issues*. Hillsdale, NJ: Erbaum.

Triandis, H. C., & Suh, E. M. (2002). Cultural influences on personality. *Annual Review of Psychology, 53*, 133–160.

Turner, R. J., & Lloyd, D. A. (1995). Lifetime traumas and mental health: The significance of cumulative adversity. *Journal of Health and Social Behavior, 36*, 360–376.

Turner, R. J., & Lloyd, D. A. (2004). Stress burden and the lifetime incidence other psychiatric disorder in young adults. *Archives of General Psychiatry, 61*, 481–488.

Waisberg, J. & Page, S. (1988). Gender role nonconformity and perception of mental illness. *Women and Health, 14*, 3–16.

Weissman, M., Bland, R. C., Canino, G. J., Faravelli, C., Greenwald, S., Hwu, H. G., et al. (1996). Cross-national epidemiology of major depression and bipolar disorder. *Journal of the American Medical Association, 276*, 293–299.

Weissman, M., Leaf, F., & Bruce, M. (1987). Single-parent women: A community study. *Social Psychiatry, 22*, 29–36.

Weissman, M., & Myers, J. (1980). The New Haven Community Survey 1967–75: Depressive symptoms and diagnosis. In S. Sells and R. Crandall (Eds.), *Human functioning in longitudinal perspective* (pp. 74–88), Baltimore: Williams & Wilkins.

Weissman, M., Myers, J., Thompson, W., & Belanger, A. (1986). Depressive symptoms as a risk factor for mortality and for major depression. In L. Erhlenmayer-Kimling & N. Miller (Eds.), *Life span research on the prediction of psychopathology* (pp. 251–260). Hillsdale, NJ: Erlbaum.

Whisman, M. A. (1999). Satisfaction and psychiatric disorders: Results from the National Comorbidity Survey. *Journal of Abnormal Psychology, 108*, 701–706.

Whiffen, V. (1988). Vulnerability to postpartum depression: A prospective multivariate study. *Journal of Abnormal Psychology, 97*, 467–474.

White, J., Russo, N. F., & Travis, C. B. (Eds.). (2001). *Feminism and the Decade of Behavior*. Oxford, England: Blackwell.

Wilson, G. (1987). Assessing treatment outcome in bulimia nervosa: A methodological note. *International Journal of Eating Disorders, 6*, 339–348.

Worell, J., & Johnson, N. (Eds.). (1997). *Feminist revisions: New directions for education and practice*. Washington, DC: American Psychological Association.

World Health Organization (2000). *Women's mental health: An evidence based review*. Geneva: World Health Organization.

World Health Organization (2001). *Putting women first: Ethical and safety recommendations for research on domestic violence against women*. Geneva: Department of Gender and Women's Health.

World Health Organization (2004). *Prevention of mental disorders: Effective interventions and policy options*. Geneva: World Health Organization, Department of Mental Health and Substance Abuse.

Wright, F., O'Leary, J., & Balkin, J. (1989). Shame, guilt, narcissism and depression: Correlates and sex differences. *Psychoanalytic Psychology, 6*, 217–230.

Wyatt, G. E., Guthrie, D., & Notgrass, C. M. (1992). Differential effects of women's child sexual abuse and subsequent sexual revictimization. *Journal of Consulting & Clinical Psychology, 60*, 167–173.

Wyche, K. F. (2001). Sociocultural issues in counseling for women of color. In R. K. Unger (Ed.), *Handbook of the psychology of women and gender* (pp. 330–340). New York: John Wiley & Sons.

Yonkers, K., & Hamilton, J. A. (1995). Psychotropic medications. In M. Weissman (Ed), *Psychiatry update: Annual review* (vol. 13, pp. 147–178). Washington, DC: American Psychiatric Press.

Chapter 15

Diverse Women's Sexualities

Ruth E. Fassinger
Julie R. Arseneau

Several years ago, an article appeared in the popular press about the viability of creating a "women's Viagra," that is, a drug that would enhance women's sexual "performance" in the same way that Viagra improves penile functioning (i.e., sustained erection) and thus performance for men. An accompanying illustration highlighted the difficulty of the scientific task by portraying the differences between men's and women's sexual response using light switches as an analogy: Men's response was presented as a simple toggle switch with on and off positions, whereas women's response was illustrated as an entire lightboard with multiple switches, dimmers, color codings, and complicated circuitry extending in all directions. Begging the question of whether this illustration accurately represents actual differences in men's and women's sexual response, we would contend that it probably *does* capture important aspects of the study of sexuality—that is, an implicit belief that proper wiring leads to predictable response, confidence that understanding the wiring allows the switch to be fixed so it works correctly, utter bafflement about why women's circuitry is so mysterious and convoluted (i.e., different from men's), and preoccupation with the properties and functionality of each individual wire.

These kinds of assumptive underpinnings in sexuality research have led to a focus on women's sexuality as homogenous and problematic (particularly as it interferes with men's access and pleasure), almost exclusive attention to biological and physiological aspects of women's sexual functioning, disregard of contextual factors and individual differences in sexual behavior and response, and the virtual invisibility of nonheterosexual women in this research (e.g., Brown, 2000; Fassinger, 2000; Fassinger & Morrow, 1995; Peplau & Garnets, 2000; Rothblum, 2000; Rust, 1997, 2000; Tavris, 1992; Tiefer, 2000). Thus, we begin with the observation that the existing empirical literature in women's sexuality is fundamentally flawed, and many of its findings and conclusions therefore are compromised. Rather than extensively reviewing these (suspect) findings, we will take an issues-driven approach, outlining some of the difficulties in the way women's sexuality is perceived, discussed, and studied and applying a feminist critical lens for interacting with this existing work—that is, offering a kind of secret decoder ring for uncovering hidden messages regarding women's sexual behavior and response embedded in popular and professional discourse. We will use specific research findings primarily to illustrate and elaborate the issues under consideration.

First, we will present a brief history and context for the chapter, deconstructing the term *women's sexuality*. Next we will discuss the limitations inherent in heteropatriarchal notions of women's sexuality and the major outcome of such assumptions, namely, the regulation of women's sexualities (including discussion of the marginalization of particular sexual behaviors). We will conclude the chapter by highlighting a few of the implications of this perspective for research, clinical practice, professional training, education, and policy. Throughout, we incorporate the experiences and issues of sexual minority women (e.g., lesbians, bisexual women) in order to provide an integrative, rather than category-driven, discussion. We also note that the concerns of this chapter are both embedded in and borrow from almost every other chapter in this volume; we refer the reader to those chapters as pertinent.

STUDYING "WOMEN'S SEXUALITY"

To understand limitations in the existing literature, it is useful to consider the history and context for the study of sexuality in the past century or so. At the heart of this legacy is the dominance of a "sexological" model of sexuality (Tiefer, 2000; Kaschak & Tiefer, 2001) in public and professional discourse. This perspective assumes the salience and universality of sexual experience—that it is an important component of identity, and that its fundamental physiological processes (stimulation, vasocongestion, orgasm) are experienced similarly across time, place, and populations. This model privileges biological and physiological factors, buttressed by decontextualized, narrowly technical definitions of bodily parts and functions. It utilizes a health rhetoric of sexuality, with the concomitant labeling of sexual thoughts (e.g., fantasies), feelings (e.g., desire), and behaviors (e.g., response to genital stimulation) as "normal" or "abnormal." This approach also highlights differences between men and women and posits heterosexuality as normative (see Tiefer, 2000, and Kaschak & Tiefer, 2001, for a detailed discussion of the sexological model).

The dominant themes in this literature evolved from an emphasis on the scientific (i.e., ''objective,'' quantitative) study of sexuality, an overreliance on extrapolations from animal research, and a modern sensibility regarding the importance of sexuality as a core component of individual identity. This paradigm is so ingrained in Western discourse regarding sexuality (e.g., in the media, in education, in family structures, and in academic and professional disciplines such as psychology) that it is invisible; like any nonconscious ideology, it is so pervasive that it assumes the mantle of truth.

However, as Tiefer (2000) and others (e.g., Brown, 2000; Fassinger & Morrow, 1995; Kaschak & Teifer, 2001; Peplau & Garnets, 2003; Rothblum, 2000; Rust, 1997, 2000; Tavris, 1992) have argued, the sexological or traditional view of women's sexuality fails to capture women's experiences adequately because it does not take into account the cultural—and political—realities of women's lives that deeply diversify their sexual experiences. Conversely, social constructionist perspectives purposefully attend to the way in which sexual experience is organized and influenced by norms and expectations that, in turn, are shaped by social trends, historical contexts, cultural locations, and individual experiences. Because sexuality is so thoroughly culturally situated, a model that pretends scientific objectivity by stripping away context cannot possibly represent women's (or even men's) experiences accurately. Unfortunately, traditional sexological study has produced research findings that reflect little more than a preponderance of ''quantitative information about frequencies of different forms of genital activity'' (Tiefer, 2000, p. 95), rather than meaningful information about the ways in which these genital (or other) activities are viewed and enacted by diverse individuals within their particular contexts.

Thus, we would be negligent in writing a chapter about ''women's sexuality'' without interrogating that term. ''Women'' are not a monolithic group but rather reflect a rich diversity of experience shaped by contextual factors, including age, sociodemographic and geographic locations, relationship status and configuration, and the political milieu. Moreover, the ''sexuality'' of these diverse women is more accurately represented as myriad sexual experiences or multiple ''sexualities'' (attitudes, beliefs, behaviors, preferences), which also are affected deeply by contextual realities.[1] As but one example of contextual influences on women's sexuality, research (Laumann, Gagnon, Michael, & Michaels, 1994) has indicated that men with college degrees are twice as likely as other men to identify as gay or bisexual, but the odds for women increase a remarkable 900 percent, suggesting that education is far more powerfully related to women's sexuality than to men's.

Social constructionist approaches to understanding diverse women's sexualities also highlight the way in which behavior and identity become conflated in the attempt to organize and categorize human experience, imbue it with meaning, and assign labels to it. Same-sex behavior, for example, has a societally determined terminology and discourse associated with it, which includes the assumption that it manifests deep internal structures of the self. Thus, the behavior (same-sex intimacy) comes to define what one *is*—a "lesbian" or "bisexual"—and the acceptance or rejection of those labels, in turn, is viewed as a reflection of important individual characteristics (e.g., maturity, mental health) or sociopolitical realities (e.g., homonegative or binegative prejudice; see Bohan, 1996; Fassinger, 2000; and Herek & Garnets, 2007, for more detailed discussion).

Disentangling the oft-conflated concepts of *sexual behavior, sexual identity,* and *sexual orientation* is essential for understanding diverse women's sexualities, because a growing body of contemporary (largely feminist) research demonstrates weak or inconsistent links between women's sexual arousal, desires, behaviors, preferences, identities, and self-labeling (Basson, 2005; Brown, 2000; Meston & Bradford, 2007; Peplau & Garnets, 2000; Rothblum, 2000; Rust, 1997, 2000). Only a small percentage of lesbians, for example, report congruence between their behavior, desire, and identity; indeed, many women experience their sexuality as fluid, dynamic, and gender inclusive (Brown, 2000; Peplau & Garnets, 2000; Rothblum, 2000; Rust, 1997, 2000). Women are more likely than men to endorse multiple sexual orientations concurrently, and studies (e.g., Chivers, Rieger, & Latty, 2004) have found that women tend to be aroused by both male and female images (whereas male arousal tends to be more gender specific). Many lesbian-identified women have been or continue to be intimately involved with men or acknowledge an ongoing possibility of heterosexual relationships, and studies have revealed small but consistent percentages of heterosexual-identified American women also reporting attractions to other women (e.g., 4.4% in Laumann et al., 1994); these numbers also probably greatly underestimate the extent of same-sex attraction among women because the stigma attached to homosexuality leads to underreporting.

Research findings also highlight the disconnect between desire and labeling, in that very small percentages (e.g., 0.5% in Laumann et al., 1994) of women who report attraction to women and men actually claim a bisexual identity, suggesting great fluidity in bisexual identification for women (Fox, 1995; Rothblum, 2000; Rust, 1997, 2000). Of course, homonegative prejudices likely combine with binegative stigma to render bisexual identification a less viable choice for many women with otherwise "bisexual" attractions or behaviors. It should be noted that the relative availability of information about women's sexualities reflects the social acceptability of individual self-identifications, with the most information available about heterosexual-identified women, a much smaller amount available about lesbians, even less about bisexual women, and virtually nothing about women whose identifications fall outside of these three categories (e.g., queer, questioning, bi-curious, or unlabeled women).

Women are less likely than men to demonstrate a match between sexual behavior and self-identification, instead utilizing self-labels that encompass "romantic, social, and political relationships with others as well as their sexual feelings and behaviors" (Rust, 2000, p. 215). Relationships between women are enacted in a wide range of behaviors, including intense intimacy that may be romantic or passionate in nature if not expressly erotic (e.g., Boston marriages, passionate friendships; see Diamond, 2002, and Rothblum & Brehony, 1993). Moreover, emotionally intense relationships appear to trigger fluidity in sexual attraction for women (Baumeister, 2000; Diamond & Savin-Williams, 2003), making women's reported attractions to women difficult to interpret. Diamond and Savin-Williams (2003) capture this problem nicely in a quotation from an adolescent woman in one of their studies, who said, "I'm not sure if I want her or want to *be* her" (p. 140).

It is important to note that women who identify as transgender, transsexual, genderqueer, androgynous, bigender, or pangender or who reject gender as a meaningful organizer of their experience are either excluded from or ignored in most sexuality research and discourse, rendering the experiences of gender-variant individuals invisible. The result of this oversight is the fostering of a view of gender that is untenable in its conceptual oversimplification (Arseneau & Fassinger, 2007; Fassinger & Arseneau, 2007). In the absence of more complex, inclusive models of gendered sexualities, we acknowledge that our own discussion of "women" in this chapter focuses primarily on individuals whose biological and social genders are concomitantly female. The difficulty in accessing the experiences of gender-variant women illustrates the limitations in using a narrow paradigm to understand women's sexualities. Unfortunately, the dominant paradigm is not only narrow, but also is grounded in (heterosexual) men's experiences, a problem that leads to much confusion and misperception in understanding women's sexualities.

HETEROPATRIARCHAL CONSTRUCTIONS OF WOMEN'S SEXUALITY

Perhaps the manifestation of the sexological model that is most deleterious to women is the foregrounding of (heterosexual) men's sexual experience. This phallocentric conceptualization of sexuality privileges genital contact, penile penetration, male pleasure, female passivity, and reproduction above all other considerations. There are a number of difficulties for women—and impediments to understanding diverse women's sexualities—that emanate from this masculinist or "heteropatriarchal" view of sexuality (i.e., simultaneously heterosexist and patriarchal; Brown, 2000).

The first problem in a heteropatriarchal view of sexuality is that it is phallocentric, in which frequency of sexual contact is prized over duration, and orgasm over intimacy. Traditionally defined, "having sex" (or, more technically, *coitus*) is a heterosexual, relatively brief encounter (typically less than 15 minutes, with nongenital, nonbreast contact averaging less than one minute), in which the chief goal is the insertion of a penis into an orifice (preferably a vagina) and which ends with ejaculation and subsequent penile flaccidity. Thus, the penis clearly defines the beginning and ending of a sexual event, and it is the frequency of these kinds of events that typically is assessed in sexuality studies.

The inappropriateness of this measure of sexual frequency for women is made clear when considering that women tend to be more relational in their sexual activity, focusing more on intimacy and less on orgasm, with a concomitant broader notion of what constitutes intimate or erotic behavior. For example, women tend to hold less permissive attitudes toward casual sex, and their sexual fantasies are likely to include a familiar partner with details capturing the setting and the affection and commitment in the relationship (Peplau & Garnets, 2003). Moreover, defining sex narrowly as coitus or penis–vagina intercourse erases a great deal of the sexual activity of women who may be engaging in oral–genital activities that they do not view as "having sex." This could be particularly true for young, unmarried heterosexual women, who may deliberately choose oral–genital behavior precisely because they do not consider it sex, and it therefore is not in violation of social scripts emphasizing chastity. What do researchers learn, for example, from asking girls about their "first" experiences of heterosexual sex, or even their first experiences of intercourse? And how do girls who are sexually active with other girls answer such questions?

In fact, for women in same-sex relationships, the absence of a live penis renders the phallocentric conception of "frequency" particularly absurd. Frye's (1992, p. 110) critique of research finding lower sexual frequency in lesbian than heterosexual couples captures this problem nicely:

> What we do ... considerably less frequently, takes on the average, considerably more than 8 minutes to do. Maybe about 30 minutes at the least. Sometimes maybe about an hour. And it is not uncommon that among these relatively uncommon occurrences, an entire afternoon or evening is given over to activities organized around doing it. The

> suspicion arises that what 85% of heterosexual married couples are doing more than once a month, and what 47% of lesbian couples are doing less than once a month are not the same thing.

The danger in defining sex and measuring sexual frequency according to phallocentric standards should not be dismissed as mere intellectual quibbling on the part of feminists, because such definitions actually exert harm on women, especially those in same-sex relationships. When two women—who have been socialized to value intimacy and emotional connection—devote hours or days to erotic activity that doesn't "count" as sex in the dominant social discourse, they may themselves come to dismiss the sexualness of that activity. If the absence of a human penis renders sexual activity invisible, then the full range of women's same-sex erotic behavior is ignored, and women in same-sex relationships may discount the sexual aspects of their intimate interactions.

This invisibility of erotic life also contributes to the myth of lesbian "bed death" (presumed lessening of sexual interest over time in lesbian relationships), a myth that has become a clinical entity even though it lacks definitional clarity and empirical validity (Iasenza, 2002). This myth obscures the fact that lesbian couples tend to report greater levels of relationship satisfaction than other (same-sex male or heterosexual) couples (Iasenza, 2002; Peplau & Fingerhut, 2007), despite their reports of less frequent sexual activity. It also disregards evidence of fewer sexual problems among lesbians than heterosexual women; one recent study, for example, found significantly fewer problems with orgasm, less trouble lubricating, less pain with vaginal entry, and less sexual guilt (Nichols, 2004). An additional problem for lesbians in defining relationships in overly sexual terms is that decreases of sexual activity may be viewed erroneously as decreases in affection and a threat to the relationship, and conversely, the loss of an important same-sex relationship may raise doubts or confusion about sexual identity.

A second problem with the heteropatriarchal model of sexuality is the pervasive assumption that female sexuality exists only in reference to men and in the service of men's needs. Gender-role socialization reinforces women's sexual responsiveness to men and men only—indeed, the mere presence of a man is presumed to spark erotic energy in women (Brown, 2000). For heterosexual women, erotic energies should be funneled only into relationships with men (i.e., attracting and maintaining male interest). Sexual pleasure is the province of men, and women are reluctant to interfere with male pleasure, even for reasons of self-protection (e.g., condom use; Wyatt & Riederle, 1994). Self-stimulation (masturbation) is prohibited, except possibly as an adjunct to stimulation by a male partner; indeed, research indicates that women often have little awareness of their own erotic patterns and needs and are more likely than men to experience, guilt, fear, and anxiety about sexual activity (Gilbert & Scher, 1999). Women's erotic and romantic fantasies are expected to have males as targets. Attractions to or sexual encounters with other women are acceptable only as sexual "turn-ons" for men. And, of course, a woman's sexual attractiveness is to be flaunted only enough to attract a male or to shore up that male's virile image to others, lest she be viewed as sexually loose or overly available, leaving her a very fine line to walk.

Female sexuality that exists in the absence of a male is either invisible or dangerous. Thus, for sexual minority (e.g., lesbian, bisexual) women, most if not all of their sexual lives are cast as incomprehensible, unpleasant, immoral, and even criminal. Brown (2000) has pointed out that a chief reason lesbians are threatening is because their very existence debunks the myth that women are not sexual—the act of claiming a lesbian identity means declaring oneself as a person to whom a sexual life and erotic preferences matter. Moreover, in addition to publicly claiming that they are sexual beings, self-identified lesbian and bisexual women also expose the fallacy that men are the only viable path for meeting women's sexual and relational needs. Combined with the popular myth that sexual minority women (and men) seek to recruit others into sexually deviant lifestyles, it is little wonder that such women are perceived as threatening, especially by heterosexual men.

This leads to a third problem with the heteropatriarchal approach to sexuality: strict heterosexuality is viewed as normative, and deviations from this expectation force public declaration, categorization and labeling, scrutiny, and continual defending. Nonheterosexual orientations are rigidly categorized into a small, manageable number (with considerable resistance to expanding the categories), and congruence across all aspects of the erotic (e.g., desire, fantasy, behavior, attraction, self-labeling) within each category is presumed. The act of claiming a non-normative sexuality in a dominant discourse of "compulsory heterosexuality" (Rich, 1994) compels the individual to declare her (or his) nonconformance, thereby making sexuality a public (vs. private) issue. This helps to explain why "coming out" is viewed as such a prominent developmental event for sexual minority individuals, and why it has been privileged in gay-affirmative discourse as the ultimate indicator of mature and comfortable acceptance of deviance (see McCarn & Fassinger, 1996, for a critique of this notion; also see Herek & Garnets, 2007). The need for public declaration of sexual nonconformity also dictates that the biological sex of the partner will be privileged as the single dimension that defines sexual orientation. This conflation of erotic, gender expression, and role preferences into one variable—the biological sex of the preferred partner—is especially constraining for women, who, as we have noted, report a broader sexual experience.

In addition, the culturally situated nature of sexuality renders discussion of sexuality a taboo in communities where sexual matters are considered highly private and personal. In these communities, coming out as an expression of any form of sexual behavior (deviant or not) means denying some of the most fundamental values of that culture (Chan, 1997; Fygetakis, 1997). Espin (1997), for example, notes that there may not be words to describe certain sexual experiences or the words may be too shameful in some languages; this is supported by her observation that many immigrant women discuss sexual matters in English rather than their native languages. Similarly, Greene (1997) contrasts "coming out" as an expression of identity to the "bringing in" of same-sex partners in some African American families and communities, a practice that underscores the acceptance of a particular relationship even in the absence of a public claiming of a sexual minority identity label. Thus, while homonegative prejudice often has been noted as a problem in nonmajority ethnic communities, it also is critically important to understand that the way in which identity management is handled in some communities need not be a manifestation of confusion, dysfunction, or self-denial, but may represent a realistic response to the desire to retain ethnic identity and values in a context of public discourse that fails to understand or honor those values (Greene, 1997).

The final problem with a heteropatriarchal perspective that rigidly categorizes sexuality and discriminates against non-normative sexual expressions is that it compels sexual minorities to essentialize the very aspects of themselves that are different or "transgressive" (see Fassinger & Arseneau, 2007) in order to wage battles over political and social change. Most civil rights legislation, for example, relies on essentialist definitions (i.e., unchangeable aspects of the self that are beyond the control of the individual) to invoke the argument for protected class status. Thus, sexual orientation must be represented as immutable, and the actual broad, fluid, dynamic expressions that characterize women's experiences of sexuality are completely erased in the service of social justice. Interestingly, there is evidence (Veniegas & Conley, 2000) that, despite increased public endorsement of biological explanations of homosexuality, sexual minority women more frequently hold views favoring at least some degree of choice in sexual identity—that they hold to a view that honors their lived experience despite the implied loss of legal protection suggests a fierce transgressive stance that merits attention.

Clearly, masculinist assumptions regarding sexuality do women an egregious disservice. Women's day-to-day experiences of sexuality can be compromised not only by the actions and misperceptions of others but also by internalized expectations that constrain their sexual expression and limit their erotic repertoire. Moreover, pervasive ideologies that are deeply embedded in social discourse regarding sexuality filter into professional discourse as well, distorting the implementation and interpretation of research and rendering much of our "knowledge" in this arena suspect. Indeed, Rothblum (2000) observed that female sexuality is an area where we don't even know most of the questions, let alone the answers. In addition, decades of social psychology research have made clear that where knowledge is limited and the potential for misunderstanding (and even fear) is high, a common human response is to attempt to exert control over the phenomenon that is creating social confusion and anxiety. In the sexuality arena, this results in direct and indirect attempts to control and regulate women's sexualities.

REGULATION OF WOMEN'S SEXUALITIES

In the dominant social discourse on sexuality, women's sexual desire and behavior—because they are poorly understood and threatening to the masculinist social order—must be regulated and controlled. The greater sexual freedom of men relative to women across most contemporary societies is so widely acknowledged as to be almost axiomatic. The regulation of women's sexualities in Western industrialized cultures manifests in many forms and is differentially localized, from macro-level legislative action to individual enactments of social scripts.

Historically, heteropatriarchal definitions of sex have been transcribed into law, and only recently has consensual sex between adults been decriminalized in the United States. The 2003 Supreme Court decision in *Lawrence v. Texas*, which found the Texas law banning "homosexual conduct" unconstitutional, effectively repealed the sodomy laws of that state and of the remaining 12 states with similar laws in effect at that time. Although individual state sodomy laws varied in their definitions of prohibited behavior, many criminalized all nonprocreative sex acts (e.g., oral and anal sexual contact), whether between same-sex or other-sex individuals. This represents a severe constriction of private life not widely recognized because of the selective enforcement of the law in regard to same-sex (especially male) couples only (American Civil Liberties Union, 2003). The recent Court decision appears to eliminate this particular heteropatriarchal regulation of sexuality. Nevertheless, existing laws criminalizing abortion as well as prostitution and other forms of "sex work" (see Farley, 2001, for a critique of this terminology) clearly converge on sexuality-related issues for women, whose very bodies remain battleground for political and legislative action.

Normative social scripts about sexuality also are used to limit, direct, and otherwise control the sexual behaviors of women. The madonna/whore bifurcation gives women two basic scripts around which to construct a sexual self, and society makes clear which is the "appropriate" choice. Any sexual activity apart from men and reproductive goals is viewed as suspect and problematic in some way, and gendered contradictions abound (e.g., young men are supposed to gain sexual experience, girls are not; men are supposed to be sexually aggressive, women are not; men are supposed to enjoy sex, women are not, except—perhaps—in the confines of marriage). Research has documented many examples of this double standard of sexual behavior; young women are judged more negatively than men, for instance, when they provide a condom for protection or engage in sexual activity outside of a committed relationship (Hynie, Lydon, & Taradash, 1997). Women are permitted to experience desire only in certain circumstances, and only in certain acceptable ways. They are expected to demonstrate ambivalence and control over sexual activity; women (and, increasingly, girls) must be "sexy" but not "sexual." It is women who carry the burden of preventing pregnancy, as men are viewed as having unbridled urges that women must monitor.

The sad irony of these social prohibitions against sexual activity in young women is that these very same women are also at high risk for sexual abuse and exploitation. Moreover, given that much abuse is perpetrated within families, young women receive confusing messages about men, power, family, marriage, and personal safety—messages that render them helpless, uncertain, and unable to develop healthy, assertive ways of enacting sexual desires and needs (see also chapters 7, 8, 16, and 17 in this volume). In addition, female sexual scripts permeate the mass media and are adopted by girls of increasingly young ages. Not only does this sexualization of girls have a negative influence on their ability to develop healthy sexual self-images and self-protective sexual behaviors, but it also has been linked to increased rates of eating disorders, depression, anxiety, poor body image, and low self-esteem (American Psychological Association, 2007).

It is important to note that many subcultures exist within the United States, as do culturally specific dictates about sexuality, some of which exaggerate even further the roles of women, men, and heterosexuality. These cultural influences may include religious, socioeconomic, racial, or ethnic norms (e.g., machismo, marianismo, silence about sexuality, clitoral mutilation, etc.). It might also be noted that, while there are ethnic group–specific stereotypes of women, most of these also fall into groupings that are either undersexualized or oversexualized. For example, Latinas have been portrayed as either sensuous or virtuous in popular media, and African American women have been presented according to "Mammy" and "Jezebel" images (Reid & Bing, 2000). Older women and women with disabilities typically are portrayed as asexual beings, when allowed to be visible at all (Crawford & Ostrove, 2003).

While social scripts related to women's sexuality may at times be covert or intangible, other aspects of the regulation of women's sexuality are highly corporeal. The high rates of sexual violence against women and girls, for example, exert inexcusable physical and psychological harm. Sexual victimization makes it likely that sexual desire will be even more compromised for women, and making sex frightening, painful, or traumatic is yet another way of dominating women and girls to maintain control over them. Given that even the most conservative estimates indicate that at least one in five women will report experiencing sexual victimization in her lifetime, much of it from partners and within families (and note that many women do not report these crimes when they occur), the significance of this means of subjugating women's sexual selves cannot be understated (see also chapters 16 and 17).

Sexual minority women occupy a particularly problematic place in this system of sexual regulation and subjugation. As we have noted, the public declaration of nonmale-dependent sexuality, implicit in coming out as a lesbian or bisexual woman, is seen as threatening. This hampers the sexual expression of sexual minority women because they are coerced into erasing the obviously erotic from their relationships in an attempt to not oversexualize themselves or "flaunt" their sexuality within a heteronormative and oppressive social context (especially to men, who exhibit the highest levels of sexual intolerance; Herek, 2003). Moreover, as virtually all sexual, intimate, romantic, and affectional behavior or verbalization may be viewed as flaunting, the otherwise vast erotic repertoire of these women becomes severely constrained. This creates considerable difficulty for intimate relationships, as constraint may lead to continual public dismissal of one's partner—what Fassinger (2003) refers to as "a thousand points of slight"—and this habitual process does not simply disappear when the couple is safely home, the door locked, and the curtains drawn. When combined with the barriers to coupling already present in the environment (e.g., lack of legal and fiscal supports, lack of protection of family structures, lack of role models, etc.), the similarity to sanctioned (i.e., heterosexual married) couples in longevity and relationship satisfaction (Kurdek, 2005; Peplau & Fingerhut, 2007) is perhaps surprising. Certainly, the commitment of female same-sex couples offers critically important perspectives about relationship strength (see chapter 11 for a more extended discussion of lesbian and bisexual women in couples and families).

An outcome of the regulation of women's sexuality and sexual behavior is the problematizing of women's sexuality and sexual functioning. The most obvious instance of this is the medicalization of normative processes in women's physical functioning, examples of which are readily available, such as controlling the "raging hormones" associated with menstruation and menopause, surgical removal of women's reproductive organs, feminine hygiene products that attempt to make healthy bodily processes invisible and "sanitary," and the like. Recently, pharmaceutical companies have developed and mass-marketed drugs that suppress menstruation, prompting debate over whether menstruation is really necessary (Scott-Jones, 2001). Despite the rhetoric of convenience—and even liberation—associated with these interventions, the problematizing of women's bodies that is inherent in medical regulation complicates women's relationships to their own bodies and their sexual selves (see also chapters 13 and 14).

The normative social discourse around regulating women's sexuality both shapes and is revealed by the codification accepted and used in psychology. The *Diagnostic and Statistical Manual of Mental Disorders* (*DSM-IV-TR*; American Psychiatric Association, 2000) has been criticized for its acontextual bias, which may be harmful to women (Becker, 2001; Caplan, 1995) and arguably to individuals occupying any marginalized sociodemographic status; its particular perspectives on sexuality also have been critiqued specifically in now-classic works deconstructing the *DSM* relative to women's socialization and sexist contexts (e.g., Caplan, 1995; Tavris, 1992; also see more recent work: Basson, 2005; Meston & Bradford, 2007).

Most relevant to the present discussion is the assertion that the categories of dysfunction outlined in the *DSM-IV-TR* derive from studies predominantly composed of men (and, of course, appear in a text compiled primarily by men). The masculinist perspective of the *DSM* reflects a decontextualized view of sexuality that is harmful to women. In this diagnostic system, social and environmental problems either are placed on the oft-ignored Axis IV or are assigned V-codes. The cultural impact on women thus is erased or downplayed, and the diagnosis of women's sexual dysfunction thereby "plucks human suffering out of its context" (Becker, 2001, p. 342). It also virtually ensures that most mental health problems faced by women will be attributed to female anatomy and physiology (Fassinger, 2000). One study (Nash & Chrisler, 1997), for example, found that participants' knowledge of the Premenstrual Dysphoric Disorder diagnosis (popularly known as PMS) increased attributions of a hypothetical woman's premenstrual difficulties, as well as the likelihood that a psychiatric diagnosis would be applied if the difficulties were believed to be related to the woman's menstrual cycle (see also chapter 12).

Much of the regulation of women's sexuality is organized around pregnancy and disease prevention, and these foci in the dominant social discourse around women's sexuality serve to maintain views of women as reproductive vessels (i.e., madonnas) or sexual miscreants (i.e., whores). For example, a human papillomavirus (HPV) vaccine has been developed and is now available (with some states fighting to make it mandatory) for young girls in the name of disease prevention, especially cervical cancer. But such a vaccine keeps the onus of responsibility for preventing the spread of HPV solely on girls, and the fervor with which this particular form of regulation of female sexuality is being pursued is perhaps not surprising given the sex-negative climate in the United States at present. Indeed, one writer observed: "Never has compulsory use of a drug been pushed with such breakneck speed ... advanced largely through political and legislative channels instead of medical authorities and public education campaigns."

Similarly, the well-documented reluctance of men to use condoms means that women bear the burden of preventing pregnancy as well as sexually transmitted infection. A recent exploratory analysis of relationships and sexual scripts among African American women illuminated the "catch-22" that these women experience related to safer-sex behaviors. The researchers found two sexual scripts broadly endorsed by their participants: men control sex; and women want to use condoms but men control condom use (Bowleg, Lucas, & Tschann, 2004).

Clearly, the dangers of illness and unwanted pregnancy for women are real (e.g., heterosexual women represent the proportionally largest increase in HIV infections in recent years; Landrine & Klonoff, 2001), and studies of menopausal women indicate increased sexual enjoyment, which has been linked to a lack of pregnancy fears (Etaugh & Bridges, 2001). While encouraging women and girls to protect themselves is important work for psychologists, it is imperative that men take more responsibility for their sexual behaviors.

The medicalization of women's sexuality often also seems to be organized around attending to the (imagined) needs of the (imagined) male partner. For example, "laser vaginal rejuvenation"—that is, surgical procedures focused on reconstructing the hymen, tightening the vagina, and altering the appearance of the labia to look more attractive—are touted as a way of enhancing women's sexual pleasure (Boodman, 2007), but it seems clear that pleasing men is the actual goal of such procedures, as they are not connected to any known paths to sexual arousal for women. As another example of the medicalization of sexuality organized around male pleasure, the physical changes associated with menopause (e.g., vaginal dryness) are publicly bemoaned and widely medically treated, but most women report little or no change in subjective arousal (Etaugh & Bridges, 2001), making clear that it is men's presumed needs that are being served by easier access to women. Moreover, lesbians as a group appear to be less concerned about menopause than heterosexual-identified women, perhaps due, in part, to less body-image concern and less self-definition based on mother and spouse roles (see Rothblum, 1994), suggesting more varied responses to this developmental milestone than simple physiological changes would imply (see also chapter 9).

In a socially and professionally endorsed system of ideologies that so severely constrains women's sexualities, any behavior or expressed desire that strays from the social script for women will seem questionable at best and wildly deviant at worst. As noted previously, much of the existing study of women's sexuality is organized around categorizing behaviors, attractions, responses, and identities as "normal" or "abnormal." Traditionally, a heteropatriarchal standard has been used for defining which aspects of sexuality are "normal"—most specifically, a heterosexual identity prizing a narrow range of behaviors culminating in vaginal intercourse between monogamously coupled (ideally, married) other-sex partners. Many other aspects of sexuality (e.g., masturbation, sexual dominance, polyamory, pornography, paraphilias) are rendered marginal through silence and invisibility or through active proscription, although it is worth noting that increased access to technology, particularly the Internet, has provided a virtual space in which individuals engaging in marginalized behaviors or occupying marginalized statuses can interact. An exhaustive discussion of "fringe" sexual practices is beyond the scope of this chapter; moreover, the very fact that these aspects of sexuality are relegated to the margins means that limited empirical or even anecdotal information is available about their role in women's sexual lives. However, we note here the example of masturbation as a sexual behavior unfortunately relegated to marginalization.

Normative sexual scripts dictate that masturbation, while considered appropriate (indeed necessary) for men, is unacceptable for women. Studies have shown that reports of frequency of masturbation are significantly higher for men than women, and these gender differences are large and persistent across racial/ethnic groups (Laumann et al., 1994). What is less clear is whether these reported differences reflect actual differences in behavior, differences in reporting, or a combination of both. Cultural differences in messages about masturbation for women likely exist, and sexual self-stimulation also may serve various purposes for women. One recent study, for example, found more frequent rates of masturbation among white women than African American women; interestingly, the authors also found a significant relationship between masturbation frequency and positive body image among white women, but no such association for African Amercian women (Shulman & Horne, 2003).

Lesbian-identified women have been found to report more frequent masturbation than heterosexual-identified women, and one recent study found that heterosexual women were significantly less likely than lesbians to report ever having masturbated (5% vs. 32%; Matthews, Hughes, & Tartaro, 2005). These findings are difficult to interpret given the stigma surrounding female masturbation, particularly for heterosexual women, whose sole source of sexual pleasure is expected to reside in a human penis; thus, these findings may simply represent greater acceptance of masturbation among lesbians and the resultant divergences in reporting trends between the two groups.

The negative consequences of marginalizing masturbation are made obvious by the fact that learning self-pleasuring (including genital self-stimulation) is a cornerstone of many approaches to sex therapy with women. Under the assumption that sex-negative feelings and self-pleasuring taboos likely prevent many women from exploring their own bodies and understanding their own sexual response patterns, therapeutic interventions seek to free women of the guilt and shame associated with masturbation and other self-pleasuring activities. It seems abundantly clear that many of women's sexual problems might be avoided or lessened by greater freedom to explore and enjoy every aspect of their own bodies.

IMPLICATIONS AND APPLICATIONS

The issues we have raised in this chapter have important implications for the way research is conceptualized and conducted, for the ways in which knowledge is applied to practice (therapy, education, professional training of psychologists), and for the ways in which knowledge is put to use in advocating for women in legislative and policy arenas. Although detailed discussion is beyond the scope of this chapter, we highlight here a few broad suggestions for further work in these professional arenas.

In research, feminists have long pointed out that the dominant social discourse dictates the kinds of questions asked, the topics studied, the methods utilized, and the inferences made from results obtained through scientific approaches. Peplau and Garnets (2003), for example, assert that sexual orientation might well have been termed "relational orientation" if women had been the basis of research and model construction, and they point out the assumptive straitjacket implicit in labeling "political lesbians" (lesbians who choose same-sex partners based on feminist political ideologies) but not "economic heterosexuals" (heterosexual women who choose—or remain with—male partners based on financial security or earning potential).

In addition to myopic development and labeling of constructs related to diverse women's sexualities, there remain innumerable critically important questions yet unasked. For example, Brown's (1989) landmark question remains unanswered by research: What if the relational experiences of sexual minority women (e.g., lesbians, bisexual women) were centralized rather than marginalized in professional discourse and research in psychology? What could be learned about women's relational capacities when they are not constrained by men or by heteropatriarchal ideas? For example, instead of viewing "lesbian merging" (see Biaggio, Coan, & Adams, 2002) as a problem in women's same-sex relationships (stemming from the idealization of autonomy in relationships based on male needs and norms), what if "deep intimacy" were perceived instead, and this standard used (rather than autonomy) as the sine qua non of a successful intimate relationship?

Similarly, rather than defining "nonmonogamy" by something it *isn't* (i.e., nonadherence to one partner only), how would relational assumptions change if it were viewed as something it *is*—an opportunity for "polyamorous" connections to several people as one potential way of enriching intimate relationships? What would be the effect on the discourse of sexuality if women breaking these boundaries were seen as admirable adventurers rather than dangerous deviants? Indeed, Tiefer (2000) noted the value in asking the unasked and finding results that counter popular notions: "Studies that effectively puncture prevailing assumptions are generally in women's interest because prevailing assumptions generally stereotype and misrepresent women's lives" (p. 101).

The implications of these issues for clinical practice are vast, but can be condensed into one simple directive: It is critically important that therapists learn how to talk about sex in therapy (Pope & Greene, 2006) and that they do so from a feminist standpoint of helping women (and men) understand the social, cultural, and political contextualization of their sexual lives. In this way, both women and men would broaden both their views about the locus of responsibility in sexual intimacy and their behavioral repertoire of pleasuring activities. Of course, practitioners are unlikely to become facile in working with sexual content in therapy unless they have been trained to work effectively with such material; thus, competent clinical practice is linked to issues of professional training.

Unless training deliberately and comprehensively debunks myths and misinformation related to women's sexuality, it is likely that psychologists (who, after all, are not immune from the internalization of pervasive societal messages about sexuality) will perpetuate the status quo in their own work. Unfortunately, there is persistent evidence that clinical and counseling psychology training programs are providing little to no education in gender or sexual orientation at the current time. Fassinger (2000) pointed out that even in counseling psychology (where diversity has been embraced publicly), current graduate training practices suggest widespread inadequacy and relatively intractable sexist and heterosexist assumptions embedded in training (Mintz, Rideout, & Bartels, 1994; Phillips & Fischer, 1998). Many if not most students fail to receive necessary formal training in either gender or sexual orientation issues, and it is probably safe to assume that even relevant coursework, when offered, likely ignores or avoids explicit attention to sexual behavior and practices. Research on gender and sexuality in training also suggests scant focus in supervision, as existing knowledge held by students is gleaned largely through individual initiative rather than programmatic expectations and resources.

Educational efforts must not be limited to the training of professional psychologists; although this might produce clinicians who are better able to ameliorate suffering that stems from sexual difficulties, it does not meet the goal of preventing such difficulties from occurring in the first place. Education about sexuality must focus more attention on offering comprehensive and accurate information to girls and women, as well as boys and men, over the life span in schools, religious institutions, and families. As sex-negative societal attitudes do not prevent sexual activity but merely prevent healthy, self-protective, planful sexual activity (Fassinger, 2000), the recent national increase in abstinence-only education programs can be viewed as ineffective at best and dangerously misguided at worst.

Moreover, the widespread invisibility of sexual minority issues from most sex education curricula virtually ensures that young sexual minority women will not receive the information and support that they need to develop healthy sexual behavior (Rofes, 1997). The combination of secrecy and shame around same-sex attraction makes it likely that acceptable dating opportunities will be limited, that role models for healthy adult same-sex relationships will be lacking, that internalization of self-denigrating attitudes will compromise sexual expression, that inadequate social resources will lead stifling of sexual desire, and that, overall, young women with same-sex attractions may have considerable difficulty successfully negotiating the developmental tasks of adolescence and young adulthood related to healthy interpersonal romantic and intimate relationships (Bohan, 1996; Ryan & Futterman, 1998).

In the policy arena, there is much work to do in addressing the policies, laws, and norms that render women's sexualities perpetually misunderstood and problematic. The American Psychological Association (APA) has issued many resolutions on issues related to women's sexualities. For example, there have been resolutions supporting reproductive choice, denouncing the antigay discrimination of defense-of-marriage initiatives in various states, and supporting same-sex parenting. Most recently, APA passed new *Guidelines for Psychotherapy with Women and Girls,* which include sexuality and sexual issues throughout the extensive and detailed document. In addition, an APA task force recently released its report on the sexualization of girls, indicating the myriad ways that the dominant social discourse regarding sexuality harms young women (American Psychological Association, 2007). All of these actions within organized psychology suggest a vibrant agenda for future advocacy work in schools, communities, workplaces, and legislative systems. It is our hope that psychologists will rise to this important challenge—first learning, and then teaching others, about diverse women's sexualities.

Note

1. Although we make an argument here for the use of the term *diverse women's sexualities* to more accurately capture the experiences under consideration in this chapter, we will use the more traditional terminology when referencing traditional views found in the literature.

REFERENCES

American Civil Liberties Union. (2003). Why sodomy laws matter. Retrieved March 2, 2007, from http://www.aclu.org/lgbt/crimjustice/11896res20030626.html.

American Psychiatric Association. (2000). *Diagnostic and statistical manual of mental disorders* (4th ed. text rev.). Arlington, VA: American Psychiatric Association.

American Psychological Association. Task Force on the Sexualization of Girls. (2007). *Report of the APA Task Force on the Sexualization of Girls.* Washington, DC: American Psychological Association.

Arseneau, J. R., & Fassinger, R. E. (2007). Challenge and promise: The study of bisexual women's friendships. *Journal of Bisexuality, 6*(3), 69–90.

Basson, R. (2005). Women's sexual dysfunction: Revised and expanded definitions. *Canadian Medical Association Journal, 172*(10), 1327–1333.

Baumeister, R. F. (2000). Gender differences in erotic plasticity: The female sex drive as socially flexible and responsive. *Psychological Bulletin, 126*(3), 347–374.

Becker, D. (2001). Diagnosis of psychological disorders. In J. Worrell (Ed.), *Encyclopedia of women and gender: Sex similarities and differences and the impact of society on gender* (pp. 333–343). San Diego: Academic Press.

Biaggiao, M., Coan, S., & Adams, W. (2002). Couples therapy for lesbians: Understanding merger and the impact of homophobia. *Journal of Lesbian Studies, 6*(1), 129–138.

Bohan, J. S. (1996). *Psychology and sexual orientation: Coming to terms.* New York: Routledge.

Bowleg, L., Lucas, K. J., & Tschann, J. M. (2004). "The ball was always in his court": An exploratory analysis of relationship scripts, sexual scripts, and condom use among African American women. *Psychology of Women Quarterly, 28*(1), 70–82.

Brown, L. S. (1989). New voices, new visions: Toward a lesbian/gay paradigm for psychology. *Psychology of Women Quarterly, 13,* 445–458.

Brown, L. S. (2000). Dangerousness, impotence, silence, and invisibility: Heterosexism in the construction of women's sexuality. In C. B. Travis & J. W. White (Eds.), *Sexuality, society and feminism* (pp. 273–298). Washington, DC: American Psychological Association.

Caplan, P. J. (1995). *They say you're crazy: How the world's most powerful psychiatrists decide who's normal.* Reading, MA: Addison-Wesley.

Chan, C. S. (1997). Don't ask, don't tell, don't know: The formation of a homosexual identity and sexual expression among Asian American lesbians. In

B. Greene (Ed.), *Ethnic and cultural diversity among lesbians and gay men* (pp. 240–248). Thousand Oaks, CA: Sage.

Chivers, M. L., Rieger, G., & Latty, E. (2004). A sex difference in the specificity of sexual arousal. *Psychological Science, 15*(11), 736–744.

Crawford, D., & Ostrove, J. M. (2003). Representations of disability and the interpersonal relationships of women with disabilities. *Women and Therapy, 26*(3–4), 179–194.

Diamond, L. M. (2002). "Having a girlfriend without knowing it": Intimate friendships among adolescent sexual-minority women. *Journal of Lesbian Studies, 6*(1), 5–16.

Diamond, L. M., & Savin-Williams, R. C. (2003). Explaining diversity in the development of same-sex sexuality among young women. In L. D. Garnets & D. C. Kimmel (Eds.), *Psychological perspectives on lesbian, gay, and bisexual experiences* (2nd ed.; pp. 130–148). New York: Columbia University Press.

Espin, O. M. (1997). Crossing borders and boundaries: The life of narratives of immigrant lesbians. In B. Greene (Ed.), *Ethnic and cultural diversity among lesbians and gay men* (pp. 191–215). Thousand Oaks, CA: Sage.

Etaugh, C. A., & Bridges, J. S. (2001). Midlife transitions. In J. Worrell (Ed.), *Encyclopedia of women and gender: Sex similarities and differences and the impact of society on gender* (pp. 879–891). San Diego: Academic Press.

Farley, M. (2001). Prostitution: The business of sexual exploitation. In J. Worrell (Ed.), *Encyclopedia of women and gender: Sex similarities and differences and the impact of society on gender* (pp. 879–891). San Diego: Academic Press.

Fassinger, R. E. (2000). Gender and sexuality in human development: Implications for prevention and advocacy in counseling psychology. In S. D. Brown & R. W. Lent (Eds.), *Handbook of counseling psychology* (3rd ed.; pp. 346–378). Hoboken, NJ: John Wiley & Sons.

Fassinger, R. E., & Arseneau, J. R. (2007). "I'd rather get wet than be under that umbrella": Differentiating the experiences and identities of lesbian, gay, bisexual, and transgender people. In K. J. Bieschke, R. M. Perez, & K. A. DeBord (Eds.), *Handbook of counseling and psychotherapy with lesbian, gay, bisexual, and transgender clients* (2nd ed.; pp. 19–49). Washington, DC: American Psychological Association.

Fassinger, R. E., & Morrow, S. L. (1995). OverCome: Repositioning lesbian sexualities. In L. Diamant & R. McAnulty (Eds.), *The psychology of sexual orientation, behavior, and identity: A handbook* (pp. 197–219). Westport, CT: Greenwood Press.

Fox, R. C. (1995). Bisexual identities. In A. R. D'Augelli & C. J. Patterson (Eds.), *Lesbian, gay, and bisexual identities over the lifespan: Psychological perspectives* (pp. 48–86). New York: Oxford University Press.

Fygetakis, L. M. (1997). Greek American lesbians: Identity odysseys of honorable good girls. In B. Greene (Ed.), *Ethnic and cultural diversity among lesbians and gay men* (pp. 152–190). Thousand Oaks, CA: Sage.

Gilbert, L. A., & Scher, M. (1999). *Gender and sex in counseling and psychotherapy.* Boston: Allyn & Bacon.

Greene, B. (1997). Ethnic minority lesbians and gay men: Mental health and treatment issues. In B. Greene (Ed.), *Ethnic and cultural diversity among lesbians and gay men* (pp. 216–239). Thousand Oaks, CA: Sage.

Herek, G. M. (2003). The psychology of sexual prejudice. In L. D. Garnets & C. C. Kimmel (Eds.), *Psychological perspectives on lesbian, gay and bisexual experiences* (pp. 157–164). New York: Columbia University Press.

Herek, G. M., & Garnets, L. D. (2007). Sexual orientation and mental health. *Annual Review of Clinical Psychology, 3,* 105–127.

Hynie, M., Lydon, J. E., & Taradash, A. (1997). Commitment, intimacy, and women's perceptions of premarital sex and contraceptive readiness. *Psychology of Women Quarterly, 21*(3), 447–464.

Iasenza, S. (2002). Beyond "lesbian bed death": The passion and play in lesbian relationships. In S. M. Rose (Ed.), *Lesbian love and relationships* (pp. 111–120). Binghamton, NY: Harrington Park Press.

Kurdek, L. A. (2005). What do we know about gay and lesbian couples? *Current Directions in Psychological Science, 14*(5), 251–254.

Landrine, H., & Klonoff, E. A. (2001). Health and health care: How gender makes women sick. In J. Worrell (Ed.), *Encyclopedia of women and gender: Sex similarities and differences and the impact of society on gender* (pp. 577–592). San Diego: Academic Press.

Laumann, E. O., Gagnon, J. H., Michael, R. T., & Michaels, S. (1994). *The social organization of sexuality: Sexual practices in the United States.* Chicago: University of Chicago Press.

Matthews, A. K., Hughes, T. L., & Tartaro, J. (2005). Sexual behavior and sexual dysfunction in a community sample of lesbian and heterosexual women. In A. M. Omoto & H. S. Kurtzman (Eds.), *Sexual orientation and mental health* (pp. 185–205). Washington, DC: American Psychological Association.

McCarn, S. R., & Fassinger, R. E. (1996). Revisioning sexual minority identity formation: A new model of lesbian identity and its implications for counseling and research. *Counseling Psychologist, 24*(3), 508–534.

Meston, C. M., & Bradford, A. (2007). Sexual dysfunctions in women. *Annual Review of Clinical Psychology, 3,* 81–104.

Mintz, L. B., Rideout, C. A., & Bartels, K. M. (1994). A national survey of interns' perceptions of their preparation for counseling women and of the atmosphere of their graduate education. *Professional Psychology: Research and Practice, 25*(3), 221–227.

Nash, H. C., & Chrisler, J. C. (1997). Is a little (psychiatric) knowledge a dangerous thing? The impact of premenstrual dysphoric disorder on perceptions of premenstrual women. *Psychology of Women Quarterly, 21*(2), 315–322.

Nichols, M. (2004). Lesbian sexuality/female sexuality: Rethinking "lesbian bed death." *Sexual and Relationship Therapy, 19*(4), 363–371.

Peplau, L. A., & Fingerhut, A. W. (2007). The close relationships of lesbians and gay men. *Annual Review of Psychology, 58,* 405–424.

Peplau, L. A., & Garnets, L. D. (2000). A new paradigm for understanding women's sexuality and sexual orientation. *Journal of Social Issues, 56*(2), 329–350.

Phillips, J. C., & Fischer, A. R. (1998). Graduate students' training experiences with lesbian, gay, and bisexual issues. *Counseling Psychologist, 26*(5), 712–734.

Reid, P. T., & Bing, V. M. (2000). Sexual roles of girls and women: An ethnocultural lifespan perspective. In C. B. Travis & J. W. White (Eds.), *Sexuality, society and feminism* (pp. 141–166). Washington, DC: American Psychological Association.

Rich, A. (1994). Compulsory heterosexuality and lesbian existence. In A. Rich, *Blood, bread, and poetry*, 23–75. New York: Norton.

Rothblum, E. D. (1994). Transforming lesbian sexuality. *Psychology of Women Quarterly, 18*, 627–641.

Rothblum, E. D. (2000). Sexual orientation and sex in women's lives: Conceptual and methodological issues. *Journal of Social Issues, 56*(2), 193–204.

Rothblum, E. D., & Brehony, K. A. (1993). *Boston marriages: Romantic but asexual relationships among contemporary lesbians.* Amherst: University of Massachusetts Press.

Rust, P. C. R. (1997). "Coming out" in the age of social constructionism: Sexual identity formation among lesbian and bisexual women. *Journal of Lesbian Studies, 1*(1), 25–54.

Rust, P. C. R. (2000). Bisexuality: A contemporary paradox for women. *Journal of Social Issues, 56*(2), 205–211.

Ryan, C., & Futterman, D. (1998). *Lesbian and gay youth: Care and counseling.* New York: Columbia University Press.

Scott-Jones, D. (2001). Reproductive technologies. In J. Worrell (Ed.), *Encyclopedia of women and gender: Sex similarities and differences and the impact of society on gender* (pp. 333–343). San Diego: Academic Press.

Shulman, J. L., & Horne, S. G. (2003). The use of self-pleasure: Masturbation and body image among African American and European American women. *Psychology of Women Quarterly, 27*(3), 262–269.

Tavris, C. (1992). *The mismeasure of woman*. New York: Touchstone.

Tiefer, L. (2000). The social construction and social effects of sex research: The sexological model of sexuality. In C. Brown Travis & J. W. White (Eds.), *Sexuality, society, and feminism* (pp. 79–107). Washington, DC: American Psychological Association.

Veniegas, R. C., & Conley, T. D. (2000). Biological research on women's sexual orientations: Evaluating the scientific evidence. *Journal of Social Issues, 56*(2), 267–282.

Wyatt, G. E., & Riederle, M. H. (1994). Reconceptualizing issues that affect women's sexual decision-making and sexual functioning. *Psychology of Women Quarterly, 18*(4), 611–625.

PART V

Victimization of Women

Chapter 16

Understanding and Preventing Rape

Courtney E. Ahrens
Karol Dean
Patricia D. Rozee
Michelle McKenzie

> *Men rape. This is Fact One, and no discussion of sexual assault should distract us from this reality. Historically, men have always denied and evaded Fact One. That is Fact Two, and no discussion of the causes of sexual assault should deflect us from this responsibility. Recognition of reality and acknowledgment of responsibility can come with great difficulty to most men. Evasions, denials, and defensiveness, however, miss the point and simply will no longer suffice.*
>
> —*Charlie Jones*

Feminist scholarship and activism have transformed the way we in the Western world conceptualize the legal, social, and personal factors concerning rape. In this chapter, we explore feminist contributions to defining and assessing the prevalence of rape, describe research on societal and individual level causes of rape, provide an overview of the psychological and physical health impact of rape, critique the institutional response to rape, and examine the efficacy of prevention programs. We conclude this chapter with a series of suggestions for continuing the fight against rape started by our feminist sisters many decades ago.

DEFINITIONS AND PREVALENCE OF RAPE

Feminist thinking has resulted in a paradigmatic shift away from viewing rape as a crime against the victim's husband or father to seeing it as a crime against the woman herself. Early 20th-century views of rape were strongly influenced by the legal backdrop of British common law that held that rape was "an accusation easily to be made and hard to be proved, and harder to be defended by the party accused, tho [*sic*] never so innocent" (p. 75; Hale, 1736; quoted in Garvey, 2005). Even though there was no empirical evidence to support this argument, these words held sway for two centuries. It was not until the second wave of the women's movement that conceptualizations of rape began to change.

The second wave of the women's movement in the 1970s saw the creation of consciousness raising (CR) groups as a method of creating female solidarity and political action by sharing life experiences with other women. CR groups put rape on the feminist agenda (Gavey, 2005). As a result of the knowledge gained in such groups, the prevalence of sexual victimization in women's lives led women to understand that "the personal is political"; in other words, rape was not an individual woman's problem, but a result of structural factors that pervade society and enable rape to occur (Gavey, 2005). The antirape movement soon developed within the organized women's movement, educating the public and advocating for legislative change. Early feminists challenged the victim-blaming attitudes embedded in the legal doctrine of rape. With the establishment of rape crisis centers in the 1970s, women began to define a woman-centered view of rape, accompanied by support, counseling, and crisis intervention services.

Alongside these activist efforts, feminist social scientists and other scholars began to examine rape. Several groundbreaking feminist studies demonstrated that rape was prevalent worldwide (Brownmiller, 1975); that rape was often hidden within the guise of "normal" dating behavior (Koss, 1985) or marriage (Russell, 1982); and that the continued prevalence of rape was based on identifiable, generally accepted myths about rape (Burt, 1980). The potentially damaging effects of rape were first described by Burgess and Holmstrom (1974) in their pioneering work on the "rape trauma syndrome." Subsequent studies have identified the clinical aspects of rape trauma syndrome and its basis in posttraumatic stress disorder discussed later in this paper.

State by state, early feminists were able to change rape laws that embodied rape myths and revictimized rape survivors. Rape activists worked to change laws that excluded rape by spouses, the so-called spousal rape exemption, but it took until 1993 before marital rape became a crime in all 50 states. Activists were also successful in broadening the definition of rape to go beyond simple penile penetration to include penetration with objects and oral and anal penetration. There have also been changes to the way that consent is assessed, removing the requirement of resistance or physical injury to prove nonconsent. For example, the U.S. Department of Justice's (2007) Office on Violence against Women now defines sexual assault as "any type of sexual contact or behavior that occurs without the explicit consent of the recipient of the unwanted sexual activity." Its definition includes vaginal or oral penetration with any object, forced oral sex, or forced masturbation.

This general definition of rape is reflected in many state laws. Although there is significant variation among state rape laws, most states include a description of physical acts such as oral, anal, and vaginal penetration. Most states also include circumstances when victims cannot consent, such as when a person is unconscious, drugged, developmentally disabled, or mentally ill.

California has a particularly detailed and inclusive definition of rape. According to a series of penal codes, rape is an act of sexual intercourse that occurs against a person's will under any of the following conditions: by means of threat or force, when a person is intoxicated and cannot resist, when a person is unconscious of the nature of the act (e.g., asleep, the act was misrepresented), through the threat of future retaliation, or through the threat of official action (e.g., incarceration, deportation) (California penal codes 261, 262). Similar codes restrict unwanted oral copulation (penal code 288a) and penetration by an object (penal code 289). In each case, any sexual act that was not fully consented to is included in the definition. According to subsection 261.6, a person must voluntarily and actively cooperate in the sexual act—if a person has not consented in word and deed, it may be considered rape.

The way rape is defined affects prevalence rates. Definitional and methodological differences may contribute to this variation (Koss, 1992). Some studies rely exclusively on legal definitions of rape, but legal definitions are relatively narrow and may not fit women's experiences (Rozee, 2005). The terminology used in prevalence surveys can also result in varying rates. Studies that define rape in behavioral terms (e.g., "Have you ever been forced to have sex against your will?") find higher rates than studies that use the word *rape* (Rozee & Koss, 2001). Screening criteria, too, can affect prevalence rates. Studies differ in the time frame about which they inquire. Some studies focus only on adult rapes (versus lifetime), but the way adulthood is defined still differs from study to study (e.g., 14 and over, 16 and over, 18 and over). The scope of the survey also makes a difference. Some studies focus exclusively on rape, while others combine rape, attempted rape, and sexual assault. Finally, recruitment strategies can affect prevalence rates. Rape has one of the lowest reporting rates for any violent crime (Kilpatrick, Edmunds, & Seymour, 1992; Rozee & Koss, 2001), so studies that rely exclusively on police reports have much lower estimates. As a result of these variations, there is great controversy about how to best assess prevalence (DeKeseredy & Schwartz, 2001; Kilpatrick, 2004; Koss, 1996).

To obtain an understanding of how common rape is, it is therefore necessary to look at the findings of multiple studies. Among the most commonly cited national-level studies is the FBI's Uniform Crime Statistics (UCR). This report includes instances of forced penile–vaginal intercourse that were actually reported to the police in a given year. The most recent statistics from the UCR indicate that 93,934 women were forcibly raped in 2005. However, most researchers estimate that reported rapes comprise only a small portion of the number of actual rapes committed each year (Kilpatrick, 2004).

The Bureau of Justice Statistics's National Crime Victimization Survey (NCVS) is more comprehensive. This survey includes any form of unwanted sexual penetration against men or women through psychological or physical coercion. The most recent statistics from the NCVS indicate that 191,670 people were victims of rape, attempted rape, or sexual assault in 2005. These statistics are still considered somewhat low by most experts, however, because the methodology used to elicit rape reports from victims does not facilitate disclosure (Kilpatrick, 2004; Koss, 1996).

To remedy these methodological problems, the National Violence Against Women Survey (NVAWS) used more behaviorally based screening questions. The NVAWS found that 302,100 women were raped in the 12 months prior to the survey (Tjaden & Thoennes, 2000) and that 18 percent of women had been raped in their lifetime. Similarly, the National Women's Study used behaviorally based questions and found that 12.65 percent of women had been raped in their lifetime (Resnick, Kilpatrick, Dansky, Saunders, & Best, 1993).

Other studies have focused on more specialized populations. An early study of rape among college students found that 15 percent of college women had been raped in their lifetime (Koss, Gidycz, & Wisniewski, 1987). More recent studies with the same population have confirmed these findings. The National College Health Risk Behavior Survey found that 20 percent of college students had been raped in their lifetime and 15 percent had been raped since the age of 15 (Brener, McMahon, Warren, & Douglas, 1999), while the National Survey of Adolescents focused on youth ages 12–17 and found that 13 percent of the girls had been sexually assaulted in their lifetime (Kilpatrick, Saunders, & Smith, 2003).

Some studies have found even higher rates. A nationally representative sample of U.S. Navy recruits found that 36 percent of the women had been raped in their lifetime (Merrill et al., 1998), and a national telephone survey found that 34 percent of married women had been threatened or forced into having unwanted sex with their spouse or previous romantic partner (Basile, 2002).

After a review of these and other prevalence studies, Rozee & Koss (2001) concluded that the rate of rape in the United States has remained at a consistent 15 percent lifetime prevalence over the last quarter-century, despite various prevention efforts. Rape is common worldwide as well. It is estimated that rape occurs in 43–90 percent of nonindustrialized societies (Rozee, 1993), and one in three women worldwide have been subjected to some form of male violence (Heise, Ellsberg, & Gottemoeller, 1999).

Rates of rape do differ by type of assailant, however. While most people envision a "real rape" scenario that involves a stranger with a gun who inflicts a high degree of injury to the victim (Estrich, 1987), stranger rapes are actually the least common type of rape. In fact, recent research suggests that less than a third of all sexual assaults are committed by strangers (Tjaden & Thoennes, 2000). Acquaintance, date, and marital rape, on the other hand, are far more common. According to the NVAWS, 76 percent of all rapes and physical assaults against women are committed by current or former husbands, cohabitating partners, or dates (Tjaden & Thoennes, 2000).

Rates of rape also differ by gender and age. The vast majority of rape cases involve male perpetrators and female victims. Of the rapes included in the 2005 NCVS, 98 percent of the rapists were male and 92 percent of victims were female. Rape is also more commonly perpetrated against young girls and women. According to the NVAWS, 21.6 percent of rapes were committed against children under the age of 12, 32.4 percent against teenagers between the ages of 12 and 17, 29.4 percent against young adults between the ages of 18 and 24, and 16.6 percent against adults over the age of 25 (Tjaden & Thoennes, 2000).

There is also some evidence that rape rates differ according to race/ethnicity. According to the 2005 NCVS, 46 percent of sexual assault victims were Caucasian, 27 percent were black/African American, and 19 percent were Hispanic/Latino (Tjaden & Thoennes, 2000). These rates are in contrast to a general population distribution of 75.1 percent white, 12.3 percent black, and 12.5 percent Hispanic (U.S. Census Bureau, 2000). The NVAWS also examined prevalence differences between ethnic groups and found that American Indian/Alaskan Native women had relatively higher rates of sexual and physical assault, while Asian American women had relatively lower rates (Tjaden & Thoennes, 2000). While this research suggests that racial/ethnic differences may exist, the paucity of research on different racial/ethnic groups makes it difficult to determine whether such differences are accurate or merely reflect differential rates of reporting.

Taken together, this research suggests that the crime of rape continues to victimize a wide range of women and children every year. Such high prevalence rates have prompted researchers to examine the causes of rape in an effort to identify individual, social, and cultural factors that could be changed to prevent rape.

CAUSES OF RAPE

There are several theorized explanations for why rape occurs. Feminist theories tend to focus at the macro level, examining the contribution of social norms, gender-roles, and structural inequities that promote and enable rape. Personality and social psychological research tends to devote more effort to the micro level, examining individual-level characteristics and conditions under which rape occurs. While this literature is often overlapping and complementary, there are some distinct differences in foci. In this section, we will explore the theoretical causes of rape proposed by each of these theories, providing a critique and synthesis throughout.

Feminist Theory

Feminist theory tends to rely on sociocultural explanations of sexually aggressive behavior. It draws on the larger cultural milieu as an explanation for the behavior of individuals. In its most basic formulation, feminist theory considers rape to be an element of oppression in a male-controlled hierarchical structure (see, for example, Brownmiller, 1975; Griffin, 1979; Russell, 1984; Stanko, 1985). Bringing a critical eye to the structure of society, feminist conceptualizations examine social norms, beliefs, and practices that promote and normalize rape.

Feminist theory begins with the premise that rape is not natural or inevitable in the realm of human sexual behavior. Sanday (1981) conducted a study of a range of societies and concluded that there were cultures that were more and less rape-prone. There were even some cultures that were considered to be rape-free. If it is possible to have cultures without rape, this suggests that cultures have a role in regulating rape, and that sexual practices that support rape are learned, not simply instinctive responses.

Following from this premise, feminist scholars have focused on a number of learned cultural beliefs and practices that enable rape to occur. One such belief is that women should be passive and dependent, while men should be dominant and in control. Men learn elements of the masculine role throughout their lives in the context of social interactions and through social learning (Bandura, 1979; Bandura, Ross & Ross, 1961). The stereotypical masculine gender-role includes the qualities of being forceful, powerful, tough, callous, competitive, and dominant. Males are also discouraged from showing vulnerability. Such gender-roles often simultaneously disempower women while teaching men that the world is theirs for the taking.

These gender-roles then intersect with sexual scripts that dictate a passive sexual role for women and a dominant one for men. Women are taught to attract men; men are taught to pursue women. Such beliefs are often reinforced by peers who share similar beliefs about violence, hostility toward women, and patriarchy (Schwartz & DeKeseredy, 1997). In fact, sexual violence often becomes normalized in groups where women are viewed as objects to be sexually conquered (Koss &

Dinero, 1988; Martin & Hummer, 1989). This may be particularly likely in fraternities and athletic teams that promote hostility and degrading treatment of women (Humphrey & Kahn, 2000).

Several empirical studies have found that members of fraternities tend to have attitudes that are associated with sexual aggression. For example, they are likely to have traditional attitudes toward women, to endorse sexual promiscuity, and to believe in male dominance and in rape myths (Koss & Dinero, 1988; Martin & Hummer, 1989; Sanday, 1981). Fraternities may actively create, or simply not challenge, hostile attitudes within their membership.

In a recent study, Bleecker and Murnen (2005) surveyed men who were and men who were not affiliated with fraternities on a college campus. They also analyzed the images of women displayed in the college dormitory rooms of both groups of men. They found that fraternity men had more images of women displayed, and these images were rated by an independent group of college women as more degrading than the images of women in the rooms of nonfraternity men. Fraternity men were also more likely to endorse rape myths.

Regardless of where such scripts are learned or how they are reinforced, sexual scripts often lead men to a view of sex as a commodity that women withhold at will, leading some men to pursue sex even when a woman says no. This is particularly true when male dominance translates to a sense of male entitlement. If a man believes that sexual access to a woman's body is a right, rape is a justifiable response to a woman who is withholding what is rightfully his (Herman, 1989). Sexual scripts are also related to the belief that sex is a form of exchange between men and women (Herman, 1989). Men expect that they will receive sexual rewards for providing affection and gifts. According to this script, the man who buys dinner for his date feels he has a right to sex, even if it is by force (Goodchilds & Zellman, 1984). Such sexual scripts can easily lead to rape. They can also make it difficult for both men and women to distinguish coerced sex from noncoerced sex because our understanding of sexuality includes male dominance even in "romantic" interactions (Gavey, 2005).

This difficulty in identifying rape also results from prevailing rape myths that our society continues to hold about what types of assaults "qualify" as rape and who should be held responsible for assaults that occur. Some of these myths have to do with the narrow definition of rape. These myths suggest that rape occurs only between strangers (Ward, 1995). In fact, feminists have suggested that our society holds a script about what constitutes "real rape" that includes the image of a stranger conducting a surprise attack at night with a weapon (Estrich, 1987). As a culture, this image of rape is so consistently understood by both men and women that it keeps women from reporting forced sex perpetrated by someone they know since they are not sure it is "real" rape. This script also protects men from acknowledging that unwanted sex with an acquaintance is rape. An acquaintance rapist believes that he could not have raped since he is not a stranger to the victim (Gavey, 2005; Herman, 1989).

Other rape myths are based on inaccurate stereotypes or assumptions that allow men and women to avoid the truth that forced sex is actually rape. These myths place the responsibility for fending off assaults on the women. Rape myths dictate that all women can prevent rape by keeping away from dangerous situations. Her action or inaction has led to the rape. Observers might ask, "Why was she out so late at night?" or "Why did she let him into her apartment?" (Medea & Thompson, 1974; Ward, 1995). Essentially, the myth is that women are responsible for their own rape, since men cannot be expected to control themselves (Donat & White, 2000; Herman, 1989). Rape myths allow men to ignore their coercive behavior, and they demand that women blame themselves for their own victimization.

Burt (1980) found that men and women who believe that there is a naturally adversarial relationship between males and females are more accepting of rape myths. Importantly, males who believe in rape myths are more likely to be sexually coercive and to report that they have committed rape than men who do not believe in rape myths. Lonsway and Fitzgerald (1995) also found that men with more hostility toward women are more likely to accept rape myths.

Our culture also enables rape through the objectification of women. Women are consistently portrayed as sexual objects in the media. Such depictions dehumanize women and promote the idea that they are less intelligent and less powerful in society (MacKinnon, 1987). This is particularly likely in pornography. Many pornographic depictions portray reward or minimal punishment for engaging in sexual aggression. When exposed to these contingencies, men learn that women enjoy rape, that men will find sexual assault pleasurable, and that rape is an appropriate way to sexually relate to women. Exposure to these depictions has been found to lead to more hostile attitudes toward women, more rape myth acceptance, and more behavioral aggression in both experimental and correlational studies (Allen, Emmers, Gebhardt, & Giery, 1995; Allen, D'Alessio, & Brezgel, 1995; Linz, Donnerstein, & Penrod, 1984; Malamuth, Addison, & Koss, 2000).

These cultural supports for rape serve a political function. Ruth (1980) describes rape as "an act of political terror" meant to keep women in their place (p. 269). By perpetuating a system in which all men keep all women in a state of fear, rape is a tool that maintains inequality by creating fear of this specific form of assault, which influences women's mobility and freedom in daily life (Gordon & Riger, 1989; Rozee, 2003). As a result of the pernicious effects of rape fear, women seek protection from some men against the risk of abuse by other men.

Personality and Social Psychological Theories

Early theories about the causes of rape focused on psychopathology of individual convicted rapists (e.g., Groth, 1979). The emerging feminist and antirape movements of the 1970s, however, opened our eyes to the extent of rape and the ways in which rape was normalized through social norms and structures. As a result, research on the personality characteristics of rapists moved away from a pathology model and began to focus on "unidentified" rapists. Researchers studying this population investigated several logical personality traits. These included: low self-esteem, impulsivity, delinquency, jealousy, aggressive/hostile personality styles, poor communication/social skills, promiscuity, need for power, depression, sociopathy, anger, and hostile attitudes toward women (see White & Koss, 1991).

Several of these variables were combined by Malamuth and his colleagues (Malamuth, Linz, Heavey, Barnes, & Acker, 1995; Malamuth, Sockloskie, Koss, & Tanaka, 1991) to form the Confluence Model of sexual aggression. The model proposes two theoretically distinct paths in the statistical prediction of sexual aggression. The "impersonal sex" path is theorized to assess "a noncommittal, game-playing orientation in sexual relations." Men identified by this path are "willing to engage in sexual relations without closeness or commitment" (Malmuth, p. 231). The impersonal sex path consists primarily of life experiences, such as experiencing family violence (as a victim or witness), higher levels of sexual experience (measured by the number of sexual partners), and nonconformity or delinquency (variables that measure the tendency to violate social rules).

In this model, the second, "hostile masculinity" path is comprised of personality and attitudinal variables. It is designed to measure "an insecure, defensive, hypersensitive, and hostile distrustful orientation ... toward women, and gratification from controlling or dominating women" (p. 231). Measured variables have typically included negative masculinity (a tendency to identify with the negative and power-based aspects of the male sex role), hostility toward women (a suspicious, blaming orientation toward women), adversarial sexual beliefs (a belief that the relationship between males and females is of necessity adversarial), and dominance motive (the consideration of dominance as a primary motive for engaging in sexual behavior). Attitude measures have included rape myth acceptance (the belief in various rape myths blaming women) and acceptance of interpersonal violence (the belief that some level of violence is normal in interpersonal relationships).

These paths have been considered to be theoretically independent. The hostile masculinity path is primarily reliant on personality factors or attitudes that are hostile toward women, while the impersonal sex path does not include these attitudes. However, risk analyses have indicated that the combination of variables from both paths produces the highest risk of sexual aggression (Dean & Malamuth, 1997).

Conceptual support for the hostile masculinity path can be found in Zurbriggen's study (2000) of the cognitive associations between power and sex. In her study, men who demonstrated a strong implicit social motive toward power and who strongly associated power and sex reported a higher frequency of engaging in sexual aggression. This emphasis on power and control is consistent with feminist conceptualizations of the motives for rape. Yost and Zurbriggen (2006) also found that men who were more willing to engage in sexual activity with multiple partners and who endorsed rape myths and negative attitudes toward women were more likely to report sexual aggression. Importantly, men with an orientation toward impersonal sex who did not have coercive attitudes toward women and sexuality were not more likely to be aggressive. Such findings have been replicated in a number of studies in both the United States (e.g., Abbey & McAuslan, 2004; Dean & Malamuth, 1997; Nagayama Hall, Sue, Narang, & Lilly, 2000; Nagayama Hall, Teten, DeGarmo, Sue, & Stephens, 2005; Wheeler, George, & Dahl, 2002) and other countries (Abrams, Viki, Masser, & Bohner, 2003).

Longitudinal studies have also supported this model (Malamuth et al., 1995). Sechrist and White (2003) analyzed the predictive ability of the primarily behavioral impersonal sex path over five data collection waves. Participants completed a survey at the beginning of their college career, reporting on their experience of sexual aggression during adolescence, and again at the end of each academic year. Men's report of experiencing physical abuse as a child, promiscuity, delinquency, and previous sexual aggression perpetration reported at earlier time points predicted sexual aggression at subsequent times.

Other longitudinal studies suggest that subtypes of aggressive men may exist, however. Abbey and McAuslan (2004) measured sexual aggression and Confluence Model variables at two time points, one year apart. They found that men who reported aggression at the first time point but not the second evidenced less hostility toward women than men who were aggressive at both time points. Furthermore, men who were aggressive at only one time point also had a stronger tendency to misperceive women's sexual intentions, were more influenced by situational factors (e.g., alcohol consumption, peer approval of sexual aggression, misperception of women's intentions) and tended to show more remorse than men who were aggressive at both time points. Based on these results, Abby and McAuslan (2004) conclude that some men (26% of the aggressive men in this sample) may utilize sexual aggression as a strategy for sexual access during adolescence, but then desist from using that strategy in future interactions.

Other studies have looked at the variable of empathy as a potential moderator of the effects of the Confluence Model predictor variables.

Dean and Malamuth (1997) measured the construct of Dominance/Nurturance. In that study, male participants were divided on the basis of their responses to the Bem Sex Role Inventory. Men who reported high scores on the Confluence Model variables were analyzed for sexual assault risk. The results indicated that men who were relatively less nurturant were substantially more likely to report that they had engaged in sexual aggression than men who were more nurturant. Similarly, Wheeler, George, and Dahl (2002) used the Interpersonal Reactivity Index (Davis, 1980) as a more direct measure of empathy. They found that including empathy with other Confluence Model variables improved the amount of variability accounted for in sexual coercion. The men at highest risk for aggression were low in empathy, but had high scores on the hostile masculinity and impersonal sex variables. Martin, Vergeles, de la Orden Acevedo, del Campo Sanchez, and Visa (2005) found that, for men who were low in empathy, the need for control and dominance in relationships with women, along with a tendency toward impersonal sex, best predicted sexual aggression.

Other researchers have focused on aspects of the social environment as predictors of aggression. Among college students, most sexual assaults occur in the context of dates or parties (Abbey, McAuslan, & Ross, 1998; Koss et al., 1987). The actual assault was found to be most likely to occur at the home of either the woman or the man, where the perpetrator may sense that he has control of the isolated environment (Abbey, McAuslan, Zawacki, Clinton, & Buck, 2001). Abbey and her colleagues (Abbey & McAuslan, 2004; Abbey et al., 1998; Abbey et al., 2001; Abbey, Zawacki, Buck, Clinton, & McAuslan, 2004; Muehlenhard & Linton, 1987) have found that alcohol use by the perpetrator or the victim occurred in about one-third to one-half of sexual assaults reported by this population. Although alcohol use may lead to a general disinhibition, the cognitive impairments associated with alcohol intoxication are believed to influence both perpetrator judgment and victim resistance (Abbey et al., 2004; Norris, Nurius, & Dimeff, 1996). Finally, sexual assault appears to be more likely when a woman does not want consensual sexual contact to escalate to sexual intercourse (Abbey et el., 2001).

Although much of the research described here has studied men who report that they have been sexually aggressive, an important line of research has examined men who indicate that they have never raped but that they have a proclivity or interest in being sexually aggressive. Men who report this pattern, termed "attraction to sexual aggression" (Malamuth, 1989), indicate that they would be interested in rape or "forcing a female to do something sexual she didn't want to" if they did not fear punishment. A surprisingly large percent of male participants, approximately 35 percent, indicate some likelihood of engaging in these behaviors (Malamuth, 1981).

The majority of the empirical psychological research conducted on explanations of rape has focused on identifying the personality characteristics and the environmental or situational concomitants of sexual aggression. However, evolutionary psychologists have also explored rape as a sex-differentiated strategy used in mating. Although this theory is frequently criticized by feminist theorists, understanding the theory and critiques of it are essential for anyone seeking a comprehensive understanding of research on rape.

Evolutionary Theory

Evolutionary theorists have described rape as an evolutionarily adaptive approach for mating (see, for example, Buss, 1994; Shields & Shields, 1983; Symons, 1979; Thornhill & Palmer, 2000; Thornhill & Thornhill, 1983). The premise of the theory is that women and men have evolved gender-differentiated adaptations in response to different biological structures and constraints in reproduction. For females, the most adaptive approach to mating is to have fewer, high-quality partners who can provide resources to assist in the care of offspring. In pursuing access to females, males can potentially utilize several strategies, including honest courtship, deceptive courtship, and forced sex. Forced sex is only employed when the conditions are beneficial to men—that is, when they cannot achieve sexual access using other strategies (perhaps because of low status or poor genetic quality) or when they perceive the potential risks (e.g., likelihood of punishment) to be low relative to the potential benefit of successful mating.

Because the evidence needed to support these theories about the evolutionary origin and primary motivation and purpose of rape is not readily accessible to researchers, theorists in this area have developed research predictions concerning specific aspects of sexual aggression. For example, Thornhill and Thornhill (1983) suggested that men with low status (and presumably less access to resources considered desirable by women) would be more likely to rape than men of high status.

Vaughan (2001, 2003) tested this prediction utilizing data from the British Prison Service, Law Reports, and Probation Probation Service about reported rapes. She found that there were fewer high-status than low-status offenders. In further analysis of the types of rape committed, she found that low-status men were more likely to rape strangers than high-status men, and that high-status men were more likely to rape partners and step-relatives than low-status men. However, as Vaughn points out, high-status men may be more likely to avoid prosecution and conviction than low-status men. In addition, the operational definition of status used in the study was occupation. This may be an oversimplified approach to categorizing resources and may be quite unrelated to the meaning of status in the early evolutionary environment in which these adaptations are theorized to have formed (Gard & Bradley, 2000).

As this example illustrates, empirical evidence for many of the predictions stemming from evolutionary theory does not provide unequivocal support for the stated hypotheses. In addition, evolutionary theory concerning rape has been criticized on the basis of several substantive issues (see Travis, 2003). First, evolutionary theorists utilize a narrow definition of rape and have excluded from the analysis, or ignored, examples or circumstances of rape that are not easily explained by the theory (e.g., homosexual rape, rape that is not for reproductive purposes, rape in the context of war) (Gard & Bradley, 2000; Poulin, 2005; Tobach & Reed, 2003). Second, a standard methodology in evolutionary theory has been to use a comparative approach, in which nonhuman animal behavior is offered as an analogue to human behavior. However, evolutionary psychology has been criticized for its failure to use this approach in a scientifically rigorous manner. For example, when Thornhill and Palmer (2000) advanced their comparative argument, they ignored low rates of rape among the closest nonhuman relatives (i.e., chimpanzees and bonobos) in favor of examples of scorpion flies (Lloyd, 2003). Finally, the insistence by some evolutionary theorists that rape is always and only focused on sexual access to females, to the exclusion of other potential motivations, oversimplifies this complex behavior in pursuit of a single explanatory factor. This pursuit damages efforts to integrate aspects of evolutionary theory with existing psychological research concerning psychopathology, personality, and social explanations (Koss, 2003; Ward & Siegert, 2002).

THE IMPACT OF SEXUAL ASSAULT ON MENTAL AND PHYSICAL HEALTH

While much of the energy of the antirape movement has been focused on identifying and transforming cultural supports for rape, concern for victimized women has always been a priority as well. Since the beginning of the movement, activists and researchers alike have sought to document the profound impact that rape can have on women's lives. The ways in which rape survivors process their assaults depend on many factors, including cognitive evaluations of the assault, physiological reactions, past victimizations, and social support. A great deal of research has documented the short-term and long-term effects of rape trauma, as well as the extensive symptoms that may be experienced. Given the nature of rape, the mental and physiological impact can be severe. Mental health conditions associated with rape include depression, posttraumatic stress disorder, generalized anxiety disorder, panic disorder, obsessive-compulsive disorder, social phobia, agoraphobia, somatization disorder, alcohol/substance abuse, and bulimia

(Boudreaux, Kilpatrick, Resnick, Best, & Saunders, 1998; Dickinson, deGruy, Dickinson, & Candib, 1999; Ullman & Brecklin, 2002b). All of these conditions, as well as physical symptoms, can have a profound influence on how survivors are able to recovei from the trauma.

Posttraumatic Stress

Sexual or physical assaults are the strongest predictors of posttraumatic stress disorder (PTSD)—more than other traumatic events such as natural disaster, serious accidents or injuries, witnessing homicide, or tragic death of a close friend or family member (Resnick et al., 1993). PTSD is one of the most common effects of rape. It is characterized by reexperiencing symptoms (such as distress caused by recurrent thoughts or dreams of the rape), avoidance symptoms (such as efforts to avoid anything associated with the rape or emotional numbing), and arousal symptoms (such as hypervigilance, sleeping problems, or irritability).

Researchers have assessed the intensity and longevity of PTSD symptoms on rape survivors and have found that, although symptoms are most severe immediately after the rape, many women still have PTSD symptoms even many years postassault. As many as 78 percent of survivors have met the criteria for PTSD from two weeks up to a year after the assault (Frazier, Conlon, & Glaser, 2001). Even several years later, more than a third of survivors still met the criteria for PTSD (Ullman & Brecklin, 2002a, 2002b, 2003) and report an average of five current PTSD symptoms; reexperiencing the rape was the most commonly reported symptom (Frazier, Steward, & Mortensen, 2004).

Sleep problems are a frequent symptom reported by rape survivors. Poor sleep quality has been linked to PTSD symptom severity and has a profound impact on daytime dysfunction and fatigue (Krakow et al., 2001). Nightmare frequency has been linked to anxiety and depression for survivors with PTSD (Krakow et al., 2002). Other stressors appear to exacerbate PTSD symptoms in rape survivors. PTSD symptoms are elevated among rape survivors who get pregnant, have an abortion, or test positive for HIV. PTSD is also related to suicidal ideation, engaging in self-hurting behaviors, and engaging in dangerous sexual behaviors (Green, Krupnick, Stockton, & Goodman, 2005). Survivors with PTSD also appear to have higher rates of drinking problems, related in part to higher tension reduction expectancies and thinking that drinking could help them cope (Ullman, Filipas, Townsend, & Starzynski, 2006).

The mental processes survivors experience in order to understand their rape can have a substantial impact on how they cope. Some cognitions increase PTSD symptom severity, including cognitive processing style during the assault, appraisal of assault-related symptoms, negative beliefs about the self and the world, and maladaptive control strategies (Dunmore, Clark, & Ehlers, 2001). Reexperiencing rape also affects PTSD severity. Women who have more than one traumatic life event, including rape, have higher rates of PTSD (Ullman & Brecklin, 2002b).

Self-Blame

Studies on rape survivors' self-blame have been growing in number. Survivors often use some form of external or internal blame to understand what they have been through. Survivors can attribute the rape to external factors, including rapist blame and social blame, or to internal factors, including perceived controllable aspects of the survivor's behavior and uncontrollable aspects of her character.

While early research suggested that behavioral self-blame might help survivors feel more in control of future rapes (Janoff-Bulman, 1989), most subsequent research has suggested that both behavioral and characterological self-blame are detrimental to survivors' health (Frazier, 1990, 2003). The discrepancy appears to lie with the notion of future control. While Janoff-Bullman (1989) assumed that blaming your own behavior would help rape survivors feel in control of future assaults, Frazier and colleagues (2004) have demonstrated that blame and control are actually separate constructs. According to Frazier et al. (2004), many survivors perceive future assaults as preventable or controllable, even if they were not able to control their past assault.

This distinction is important, because it suggests that all forms of self-blame should be avoided. Interestingly, recent research also suggests that other forms of blame such as blaming the rapist or blaming society may also be related to higher levels of emotional distress (Frazier, 2003; Koss & Figueredo, 2004a). This may be because higher levels of blame are reflective of rumination and the lack of cognitive resolution.

Fear and Anxiety

Rape survivors have significantly higher reports of anxiety within a year of the rape (Frazier, 2003) and several years postassault (Frazier, Steward, & Mortensen, 2004). Perceived life threat is a significant predictor of the severity of panic responses after an assault (Nixon, Resick, & Griffin, 2004). Survivors are three times more likely than nonvictims to have a generalized anxiety disorder or a panic disorder (Dickinson et al., 1999) and report higher levels of fear (Harris & Valentiner, 2002) and health anxiety than nonvictims (Stein, Lang, & Laffaye, 2004). Survivors who feel like they have more control over their recovery process have fewer anxiety symptoms (Frazier, Steward, & Mortensen, 2004).

Depression

The impact of rape on depression can be temporary or long-term. Rape survivors report higher immediate depression symptoms, and still report higher levels up to a year after the rape (Frazier, 2003). Rape survivors also have significantly elevated rates of suicidal ideation during the first year (Stephenson, Pena-Shaff, & Quirk, 2006). Even many years postassault, survivors report higher long-term rates of depression, including lifetime major depression and dysthymia, when compared to nonvictimized women (Dickinson et al., 1999; Frazier, Steward, & Mortensen, 2004; Harris & Valentiner, 2002; Kaukinen & DeMaris, 2005; Ullman and Brecklin, 2002a, 2003). Rape survivors also report higher levels of suicidal ideation and of attempted suicide at some point in their life, with a significantly increased risk for lifetime suicide attempts among women who experienced both childhood and adulthood sexual assault (Ullman & Brecklin, 2002a).

Social Adjustment

Many aspects of survivors' lives can be impacted by rape, including family, friends, and work. Work adjustment was impaired up to eight months postassault (Letourneau, Resnick, Kilpatrick, Dean, & Saunders, 1996). The literature is limited in findings about other aspects of survivors' lives. As far as positive life changes, survivors report having increased empathy, better relationships with family, and greater appreciation of life as soon as two weeks after the assault (Frazier et al., 2001).

Several years afterward, rape survivors report that they have a fairly high level of support and a moderate level of social conflict, perceived stress, and conflict in interpersonal relationships (Ullman & Brecklin, 2002b), and social functioning only slightly below that of nonvictims (Dickinson et al., 1999). Survivors who perceived having more control over their recovery process had better psychological adjustment and greater life satisfaction (Frazier, Steward, & Mortensen, 2004). Survivors of acquaintance rape perceived a larger risk in intimacy when compared to nonvictims (McEwan, de Man, & Simpson-Housley, 2002, 2005).

Sexual Functioning

The literature shows that the impact of rape on sexual functioning can be extensive, but the quantity of research in the area is limited. Survivors report many problems with sexual functioning, primarily related to sexual avoidance or sexual dysfunction, and as many as 90 percent of survivors report a sexual disorder within the first year of rape (Faravelli, Giugni, Salvatori, & Ricca, 2004). The absence of sexual desire is the most reported symptom experienced by survivors, followed by sexual aversion (Faravelli et al., 2004).

Rape survivors several years postassault had significantly higher scores for sexual anxiety and avoidance than nonvictims did (Harris & Valentiner, 2002). Almost half of survivors eight years after the assault had low sexual health risk, which included sexual avoidance, sexual abstinence, fewer sexual partners, increased condom usage, and decreased alcohol and/or drug usage during sex (Campbell, Sefl, & Ahrens, 2004). In contrast, one-third of survivors showed patterns of high sexual health risk, including increased sexual activity frequency, reduced condom usage, and increased alcohol and/or drug usage during sex (Campbell et al., 2004). College rape survivors report higher rates of sexual dysfunction and dangerous sexual behaviors than others in their cohort, including irresponsible sexual behaviors, potentially self-harmful behaviors, or inappropriate usage of sex to accomplish nonsexual goals (Green et al., 2005).

PHYSICAL HEALTH

Rape survivors have an increased rate of health problems throughout their lifetime. Survivors report higher levels of somatization and health anxiety (Stein et al., 2004); more health complaints and higher-intensity complaints (Conoscenti & McNally, 2006); more frequent visits to health care professionals (Stein et al., 2004; Conoscenti & McNally, 2006); and multiple sick days (Stein et al., 2004). Forty-three percent of women who were assaulted in childhood and adulthood had lifetime contact with health professionals for mental health or substance abuse problems (Ullman & Brecklin, 2003). Survivors also report more incidence of headaches, chest pains, overwhelming fatigue (Stein et al., 2004), chronic medical conditions (Ullman & Brecklin, 2003), pelvic pain, painful intercourse, rectal bleeding, vaginal bleeding or discharge, bladder infection, painful urination (Campbell, Lichty, Sturza, & Raja, 2006), pregnancy, abortion, HIV testing, and STD infection (Green et al., 2005).

With higher frequency of mental and physical health problems, rape survivors have a higher prevalence of taking prescription drugs and alcohol. Rape survivors use antidepressants, alcohol, sedatives/tranquilizers, and other prescription drugs more than nonvictimized women (Sturza & Campbell, 2005). Survivors with mental health disorders such as PTSD or depression are as much as 10 times more likely than nonvictims to use prescription drugs (Sturza & Campbell, 2005).

Despite such high levels of physical health problems, less than a third of rape survivors have a medical examination or receive medical care postassault (Monroe, Kinney, Weist, Dafeamekpor, Dantzler, & Reynolds, 2005; Resnick et al., 2000). Major injuries during rape are uncommon, with less than half of survivors sustaining injuries; minor physical injuries, involving cuts, bruises, or soreness, are more common than serious injuries (Resnick et al., 2000; Ullman et al., 2006). When survivors do seek medical care, a little more than half inform their health care providers about the rape (Resnick et al., 2000). Fear of having contracted an STD or HIV/AIDS is a major motivator to receive medical care postassault (Resnick et al., 2000). Most survivors report having some degree of fear or concern about contracting HIV from the rape (Resnick et al., 2002). Less than half of postassault medical exams included testing for gonorrhea, chlamydia, HIV, syphilis, and hepatitis (Monroe et al., 2005).

While it is clear that rape can have profoundly negative psychological and physical health consequences for survivors, the recovery process allows many survivors to identify personal or relational strengths they had not previously recognized. Although a variety of terms are used to describe this aspect of recovery (e.g., *personal growth, positive change, stress-related growth*), the most common term is *posttraumatic growth* (Tedeschi & Calhoun, 1996). Posttraumatic growth is said to occur when victims of traumatic events reassess their lives and adopt new perspectives in a number of domains, including perceiving new possibilities, relating better to others, perceiving new personal strengths, experiencing spiritual change, and experiencing a greater appreciation of life (Tedeschi & Calhoun, 1996). While posttraumatic growth can be seen as a positive outcome in its own right, it has also been linked to higher overall levels of psychological adjustment and lower levels of distress and depression (Frazier et al., 2001).

It is therefore heartening that rates of positive growth are so high. Across studies, between 50 and 60 percent of individuals who have experienced a traumatic event subsequently experience some form of positive change (Tedeschi & Calhoun, 1996). Women may be particularly likely to experience positive growth after a traumatizing situation (Park, Cohen, & Murch, 1996; Tedeschi & Calhoun, 1996) and African American women may be more likely to experience positive changes than Caucasian women (Kennedy, Davis, & Taylor, 1998). Among rape victims in particular, Frazier and colleagues (Frazier, Steward, & Mortensen, 2004) examined a number of immediate and long-term predictors of posttraumatic growth. Social support, approach coping, religious coping, and control over the recovery process were all significant predictors of posttraumatic growth two weeks post assault. Furthermore, increases in each of these variables were associated with increases in posttraumatic growth over time.

COPING WITH RAPE

The methods survivors use to cope with the rape have a substantial impact on the course of their recovery. Whereas some survivors avoid thinking about the rape and may even resort to maladaptive coping strategies such as using alcohol or drugs, others deal with their feelings directly by talking to other people and seeking help.

Avoidance Coping

Avoidance coping involves efforts to suppress or avoid thinking about the stressor or one's emotional reaction to the stressor (Roth & Cohen, 1986). In the case of rape, survivors may engage in a number of avoidance strategies such as keeping busy, isolating themselves, and suppressing thoughts about the assault (Burt & Katz, 1987; Meyer & Taylor, 1986). There is also a growing body of literature that suggests that many survivors may use drugs or alcohol to help them suppress thoughts and feelings associated with the assault (Sturza & Campbell, 2005; Miranda, Meyerson, Long, Marx, & Simpson, 2002). Survivors may also actively avoid people, places, and activities that remind them of the rape (Feuer, Nishith, & Resick, 2005). While many survivors may use avoidance coping strategies periodically, survivors with high levels of self-blame and survivors who received negative social reactions tend to use avoidance coping more frequently (Littleton & Breitkopf, 2006; Ullman, 1996**a**).

These efforts to avoid thinking about the rape may initially help survivors cope with overwhelming emotions (Cohen & Roth, 1987), but using avoidance coping as a long-term strategy has been shown to be detrimental to survivors' recovery (Arata, 1999; Frazier & Burnett, 1994; Frazier, Mortensen, & Steward, 2005; Neville, Heppner, Oh, Spanierman, & Clark, 2004; Valentiner, Foa, Riggs, & Gershuny, 1996). This is particularly true when survivors engage in cognitive avoidance that prohibits them from integrating or making meaning of the assault (Boeschen, Koss, Figueredo, & Coan, 2001; Foa & Riggs, 1995).

Approach Coping

On the opposite end of the spectrum, *approach coping* involves dealing directly with a stressor or with one's emotional reaction to the stressor (Roth & Cohen, 1986). In the case of rape, the assault itself cannot be changed, so approach coping involves dealing directly with emotional responses to the rape and the recovery process itself. Examples of approach coping include strategies such as help-seeking, cognitive reappraisal, and letting one's emotions out (Burt & Katz, 1987; Meyer & Taylor, 1986). These strategies are consistently found to be beneficial to survivors' recovery (Arata, 1999; Arata & Burkhart, 1998; Frazier & Burnett, 1994; Valentiner et al., 1996), particularly when they help survivors feel in control of the recovery process (Frazier et al., 2005).

HELPING SURVIVORS

While rape survivors' own coping strategies may help mitigate harmful outcomes and promote posttraumatic growth, there is a substantial amount that the larger community can do to assist rape survivors as well. Both formal support providers (such as legal, medical, and mental health personnel) as well as informal support providers (such as friends, family, and romantic partners) play important roles in helping survivors heal. Unfortunately, these same sources of support may also inadvertently harm survivors who turn to them for help. A growing body of research suggests that survivors receive high levels of both positive and negative social reactions when they turn to others for help (Campbell, Ahrens, Sefl, Wasco, & Barnes, 2001; Filipas & Ullman, 2001; Golding, Siegel, Sorenson, & Burnam, 1989; Ullman, 1996a). Positive social reactions include efforts such as listening, comforting, emotionally supporting survivors, and providing tangible assistance. Negative social reactions include actions such as disbelieving the survivors, holding survivors accountable, pulling away from survivors, and trying to control survivors' behaviors (Davis, Brickman, & Baker, 1991; Golding et al., 1989; Herbert & Dunkel-Schetter, 1992; Sudderth, 1998; Ullman, 2000). Overall, survivors receive more types of positive social reactions, but they receive negative social reactions more frequently (Filipas & Ullman, 2001)

As a result, many rape survivors are extremely cautious when selecting support providers to whom to disclose. While more than two-thirds of rape survivors disclose the assault to at least one person (Ahrens, Campbell, Ternier-Thames, Wasco, & Sefl, 2007; Fisher, Daigle, Cullen, & Turner, 2003; Golding et al., 1989; Ullman & Filipas, 2001a), survivors tell an average of only three different people (Ahrens, Cabral, & Abeling, under review; Filipas & Ullman, 2001). Most often, these disclosures are to informal support providers such as friends and family rather than to formal support providers such as the police or medical personnel (Campbell, Ahrens, et al., under review; 2001; Filipas & Ullman, 2001; Fisher et al., 2003; Golding et al., 1989; Ullman, 1996a). Overall, informal support providers engage in more positive social reactions and fewer negative social reactions than formal support providers (Ahrens et al., 2007; Filipas & Ullman, 2001; Golding et al., 1989), but specific relationship contexts and organizational demands affect the nature of support received. These contexts are described in greater detail below.

Friends, Family, and Romantic Partners

Research on disclosure and social reactions has consistently shown that friends are the most common disclosure recipient, are rated as more helpful than other sources of support, and appear to have a greater impact on survivors' recovery than any other support provider (Ahrens et al., 2007, under review; Davis et al., 1991; Filipas & Ullman, 2001; Littleton & Breitkopf, 2006; Ullman, 1996a, 1999). On the other hand, research on the support provided by family members and romantic partners is mixed. While many family members and romantic partners react well, both family members and romantic partners have also been found to react in extremely egocentric ways, focusing more on their own anger and frustration than on survivors' needs (Ahrens & Campbell, 2000; Emm & McKenry, 1988; Filipas & Ullman, 2001; Littleton & Breitkopf, 2006; Smith, 2005). Family members and romantic partners also appear to have a greater tendency to be overprotective and react by trying to control the survivors' decisions and behavior (Davis, Taylor, & Bench, 1995; Remer & Elliott, 1988). Some family members and partners also appear to be ashamed of what happened to the survivor, resulting in relationship problems and efforts to silence the victims so other people do not find out (Ahrens, 2006; Riggs & Kilpatrick, 1997).

Not surprisingly, such negative reactions from romantic partners have been associated with worse recovery outcomes than negative reactions from other sources (Davis et al., 1991; Filipas & Ullman, 2001; Ullman, 1996a), perhaps because of the betrayal of trust and intimacy that is involved in negative reactions from loved ones. In fact, negative social reactions received at the time of rape disclosure and low social support are related to greater PTSD symptom severity (Ullman & Filipas, 2001a). But nondisclosure appears to have its costs as well. Survivors who did not disclose their assault were found to have less satisfaction in their friendships than survivors who disclosed (Littleton & Breitkopf, 2006).

Legal System

Between 10 and 40 percent of rape survivors report the assault to the police (Campbell, Wasco, Ahrens, Sefl, & Barnes, 2001; Filipas & Ullman, 2001; Fisher et al., 2003; Golding et al., 1989; Ullman, 1996a), and very few of the cases that are reported ever result in jail time (Frazier & Haney, 1996; Phillips & Brown, 1998). One study of 861 reported rapes found that only 12 percent resulted in convictions and only 7 percent in a prison sentence for the convicted rapist (Frazier & Haney, 1996).

Such low rates of sentencing are the result of attrition at each stage of the legal process (Frazier & Haney, 1996; Lee, Lanvers, & Shaw, 2003). For example, both the patrol officers who respond to the crime and the detectives who investigate it have been known to question victims' credibility (Campbell & Johnson, 1997; Jordan, 2004) and have even been known to subject survivors to polygraph tests (Sloan, 1995) despite the fact that false claims of rape are no higher than for any other felony. These doubts affect the amount of time and effort that police put into investigating and building a case (Campbell & Johnson, 1997; Jordan, 2004), which may, in turn, affect the likelihood that a case will be accepted for prosecution. Both the amount of corroborating evidence (e.g., injuries, witnesses) and the extent to which the case matches stereotypical assumptions about rape affect whether a case will be accepted for prosecution. Only those cases that prosecutors feel they can win are ever brought to trial. This is because district attorneys are promoted based on their win–loss ratios. If prosecutors are not confident that a jury will find the defendant guilty, they tend to not prosecute cases, even if the cases meet all of the legal requirements of a crime (Frohmann, 1991, 1997, 1998; Martin & Powell, 1994).

Prosecutors are particularly concerned about how a jury will perceive a case because it is the defendant who gets to choose between a jury trial or a bench trial. Not surprisingly, most rapists choose jury trials, because defense attorneys know they can rely on the faulty beliefs held by most jurors (Bryden & Lengnick, 1997; Tetreault, 1989). This is an effective strategy for defense attorneys, since criminal trials require that the prosecutor prove ''beyond a reasonable doubt'' that the sexual act did occur, that the rapist was the one involved in the act, and that the sexual act was unwanted. Advances in forensic evidence collection techniques and DNA technology have made it harder to call the first two points into question, but defense attorneys are still able to cast doubt on issues of consent. Despite the development of rape shield laws, rape victims' past sexual history, manner of dress, risky behavior, and behavior both during and after the assault continue to be questioned during trials. Every effort is made to discredit the victim and hold her responsible for the assault (Frohmann, 1991, 1997, 1998). It is therefore not surprising that many rape survivors refer to the court process as a ''second assault'' (Campbell et al., 1999; Madigan & Gamble, 1991; Martin & Powell, 1994). This trauma is then exacerbated when defendants are found not guilty or receive only minimal sentences involving probation and community service only, an occurrence that is all too common (Frazier & Haney, 1996).

As a result of these problems with the criminal justice system, there has been a push toward considering alternative responses to rape. Two alternative approaches have received the most attention: civil remedies and restorative justice programs. Advocates of the civil court approach argue that the lower standard of proof in civil trials (''preponderance of evidence'' rather than ''beyond a reasonable doubt'') would make it easier to hold assailants responsible for their actions (Des Rosiers, Feldthusen, & Hankivsky, 1998). While civil trials do not result in criminal sentencing, victims could receive monetary compensation and the knowledge that a court of law found the assailant to be responsible for causing the victim undue harm. Advocates of this approach argue that civil trials could be more empowering for survivors than the current system (Des Rosiers et al., 1998).

Proponents of restorative justice approaches are also concerned about the empowerment of survivors. While there are many different types of restorative justice programs, the most widely touted approaches for cases of sexual assault include peacemaking and community conferencing. Emanating from indigenous practices of the Navajo and Maori peoples, these approaches bring together the survivor, the assailant, their friends and family, and other community members with expertise relevant to the process (Coker, 1999; Braithwaite & Daly, 1998). The goal of this meeting is to discuss the impact of the incident on both parties, come up with a solution to repair the damage, and ensure that further harm does not ensue (Koss, Bachar, Hopkins, & Carlson, 2004). Proponents of this approach suggest that it is beneficial for several reasons. First, this approach may be empowering for survivors because it gives them decision-making authority about acceptable solutions, allows a survivor's emotional pain to be acknowledged rather than refuted, and includes the whole community in providing support to the survivor (Koss, 2000). This approach may also be effective in creating change in the assailants' behavior by engaging the assailant's family and entire community in shaming the assailant and monitoring future behavior (Braithwaite & Daly, 1998; Koss, 2000). While the effectiveness of these approaches may hinge on the nature of the families and communities involved, these approaches have been rated quite highly by survivors and have been found to result in lower rates of recidivism (Koss, 2000; McCold & Wachtel, 2002).

Medical System

Less than half of all rape survivors disclose the assault to medical personnel (Ahrens et al., under review; Filipas & Ullman, 2001; Fisher et al., 2003; Golding et al., 1989; Ullman, 1996). Survivors who do turn to medical personnel are typically seeking sexual health-related services such as STD screening and treatment, pregnancy tests and prevention, and treatment for external and internal injuries (Osterman, Barbiaz, & Johnson, 2001; Resnick et al., 2000). Survivors who disclose the rape are also required to be given a forensic medical exam to collect evidence for prosecution. Forensic evidence collection procedures typically include the confiscation of survivors' clothes, a gynecological exam, documentation of external and internal injuries, swabs of affected orifices, and collection of specimens from survivors' hair, nails, and pubic area (Ledray, 1995). According to the Violence against Women Act of 1994, these forensic examinations should be free of charge, but in one study, only a small percentage of women were aware of this, and more than half were charged for their postassault medical exam or related medical services (Monroe et al., 2005).

While most survivors who turn to the medical system are expecting support and assistance, many survivors report feeling retraumatized by their interaction with medical personnel. In some cases, survivors appear to be retraumatized by the invasive nature of the forensic medical exam (Ahrens, 2006; Campbell, 2006; Domar, 1986), and in other cases by the cold or hostile way some medical personnel respond to them (Ahrens et al., 2007; Campbell, Sefl, Barnes, Ahrens, Wasco, & Zaragoza-Diesfeld, 1999). According to one study, many women express being disappointed, surprised, or troubled with the way in which their doctors reacted to their assault disclosure, often feeling like their doctors were uncomfortable with the disclosure and wanted to write a prescription and dismiss them as fast as possible (Sturza & Campbell, 2005). In still other cases, survivors feel retraumatized by the denial of needed medical services such as testing and treatment for STDs and pregnancy (Campbell & Bybee, 1997).

This insensitivity to rape survivors' needs is partially a result of organizational characteristics of medical settings, particularly emergency rooms. Emergency rooms are set up to handle emergent, life-threatening cases in a quick and efficient manner; they are not structured to provide counseling and support to traumatized rape survivors. This disconnect between the organizational demands of the setting and rape survivors' needs may result in inadequate care and secondary victimization, particularly when medical personnel do not consider taking time to support rape victims and conduct forensic exams to be part of their job (Martin & Powell, 1994).

As a result of drawbacks associated with traditional medical settings, rape crisis centers and hospitals across the country are increasingly teaming up to create specialized sexual assault units. Known as Sexual Assault Nurse Examiner (SANE) programs or Sexual Assault Response Teams (SART), these units provide coordinated medical services in safe, quiet settings staffed by specially trained personnel in a manner consistent with rape survivors' needs (Ahrens, Campbell, Wasco, Aponte, Grubstein, & Davidson, 2000; Campbell, Townsend, et al., 2006; Ledray, 1995). It is not surprising that such programs increase the number of services and decrease the amount of distress experienced by survivors who seek medical attention in these settings (Campbell, Patterson, & Litchy, 2005; Campbell et al., 2006).

Mental Health System

Rates of disclosure to rape crisis centers and counselors vary dramatically from study to study. While some studies have found rates of disclosure as high as 52 percent, others have found rates as low as 1 percent (Filipas & Ullman, 2001; Fisher et al., 2003; Golding et al., 1989; Ullman, 1996). There is also some discrepancy in the types of reactions that counselors and advocates have been found to engage in. While counselors and rape crisis advocates have been found to be among the most helpful support providers to whom survivors disclose (Ahrens et al., under review; Ullman, 1996), there is evidence that some counselors engage in negative social reactions toward survivors (Campbell & Raja, 1999). Such differences in survivors' experiences may hinge on the extent to which counselors have been trained in rape and on organizational philosophies about the causes and resolutions of rape, both of which may still vary considerably from counselor to counselor and agency to agency.

This variation likely emanates from the fact that the rape crisis movement is still relatively young. Emerging out of grassroots efforts to ensure equal rights for women, the first rape crisis centers emerged in the 1970s and focused primarily on social change. Although early centers also focused on the needs of current victims by providing peer support and advocacy, their guiding philosophy was embedded in notions of patriarchy, power inequities, and violence as a form of social control (Campbell & Martin, 2001; Matthews, 1994). Peer support and advocacy were therefore focused on helping victims locate their personal experiences in a larger political context and empowering women not only to overcome their own rape but also to work for changes in the larger society as well (Campbell, Baker, & Mazurek, 1998).

As funding sources increased, however, there was a push for rape crisis centers to become more institutionalized. Funding agencies began to require a more hierarchical organization, including boards of directors, executive directors, and licensed counselors (Matthews, 1994). Funding agencies also began to redirect the centers' efforts away from larger social change and toward the provision of direct counseling services. As a result, many rape crisis centers have lost their activist agenda, and some have even merged with larger agencies focused on helping crime victims more generally (Campbell et al., 1998; O'Sullivan & Carlton, 2001). Sadly, agencies that lack a specific focus on sexual assault tend to downplay the importance of social factors, focusing instead on rape victims' coping strategies and relationship patterns. Such agencies are also less likely to engage in wider community collaboration, community education, or in-service training efforts with other agencies who work with rape victims (Campbell & Ahrens, 1998; Campbell et al., 1998; O'Sullivan & Carlton, 2001).

As a result, many counselors focus almost exclusively on individualistic solutions rather than societal solutions. This tendency is exacerbated by a relative lack of training on women's issues in many graduate clinical or counseling psychology programs. Although most graduate programs address rape at some point, rape and other women's issues are not always incorporated into core courses, and programs do not always offer courses specifically about these topics (Campbell, Raja, & Grining, 1999; Mintz, Rideout, & Bartels, 1994). Counseling interns have also been found to endorse high levels of rape myths (Kassing & Prieto, 2003; McKay, 2002) and a number of misconceptions about rape in culturally diverse communities (Neville & Heppner, 2002).

PREVENTION AND RESISTANCE

Rape Prevention

Since the 1970s, rape prevention programs have been integral to empowering women and providing a safe place to discuss and address victimization experiences. Rape crisis centers, universities, and various community organizations have developed myriad rape prevention and education programs offered in multiple settings in the community.

Typically, rape *prevention* programs focus on changing the attitudes/behaviors of potential rapists, while rape *avoidance* programs focus on teaching potential victims to avoid rape. However, this distinction is not always made in the literature, leading to some confusion in interpreting this body of research. The most problematic issue is the focus of most programs on changing women's behavior and attitudes, while far fewer programs have systematically examined men's behavior. One multivariate study found that women's precautionary behavior had no preventive effects on the occurrence of subsequent crimes (Norris & Kaniasty, 1992). Yet Cahill (2001) notes that most women continue to take these precautions because they believe that the risk of rape can be significantly reduced, or even eliminated, simply by changing their own behavior. Such precautions by women must be viewed as somewhat tangential, since gender is the primary predictor of being a rape victim, and rape prevention can only be accomplished by changing men's behavior (Rozee & Koss, 2001).

Since most rape prevention programs lack published empirical studies of their effectiveness, there is very little information about how many programs exist, how they are designed and conducted, or their theoretical viewpoints (Anderson & Whiston, 2005). Researchers have found that very few programs include any kind of theoretical grounding or evaluative component (Bachar & Koss, 2001; Schewe & O'Donohue, 1993).

Most studies assessing the effectiveness of rape prevention education programs have found support for short-term change in rape-supportive attitudes, but there is little support for any impact past the immediate attitude change (Anderson & Whiston, 2005). A recent review found that most programs were aimed at mixed-sex audiences, with content related to challenging rape myths, decreasing rape-supportive attitudes, and increasing knowledge about rape (Bachar & Koss, 2000). Evaluations show small but favorable attitude change that tends to decay or regress to pretest levels in a relatively short period of time (Anderson & Whiston, 2005; Bachar & Koss, 2001). Lonsway (1996) conducted a comprehensive review of all published rape education programs targeting women and men. Nearly all programs focused on attitude change, but only half actually decreased rape-supportive attitudes. Even among these, the change did not remain in long-term follow-up.

Recent studies of programs that assessed rape reduction as an outcome measure found disheartening results. Most researchers in this area have concluded that there is no evidence for the effectiveness of current rape prevention programs on reducing the incidence of sexual victimization, rape, or attempted rape (Anderson & Whiston, 2005; Bachar & Koss, 2001; Breitenbecher & Gidycz, 1998; Breitenbecher & Scarce, 1999; Campbell & Wasco, 2005; Sochting, Fairbrother, & Koch, 2004). For example, Breitenbecher and Scarce (1999) found no reduction in the incidence of sexual assault despite an increase in knowledge about sexual assault. A later meta-analytic study of both published and unpublished empirical research concluded that there is little support for the effectiveness of current rape education efforts in reducing sexual assault, but the authors note the difficulty in obtaining accurate follow-up information on participants (Anderson & Whiston, 2005). A review of empirical studies by Sochting, Fairbrother, and Koch (2004) confirms these findings.

While the educational *content* necessary to make lasting change and long-term impact on the incidence or rape is not clear, there does seem to be consistent agreement on ways to improve the *structure* of future educational programs. Studies show that more interactive, focused interventions, of longer duration, consisting of multiple sessions, presented by professional educators, are most effective (Anderson & Whiston, 2005). There is some evidence that providing education in single-sex rather than mixed-sex groups is more effective for women, especially if the group focuses on risk reduction (Anderson & Whiston, 2005); others found single-sex groups more effective for men, as well (Brecklin & Forde, 2001).

In a recent reflection on 20 years of research, Campbell and Wasco (2005) note, "Neither community-based practitioners nor academic researchers have been able to identify models of prevention effective enough to put a dent in incidence rates" (p. 120). This conclusion was echoed by Rozee and Koss (2001), who conclude that the incidence of rape has remained at a steady 15 percent despite growing efforts at prevention.

Feminist scholars have suggested that a more effective approach to rape prevention efforts would be to target men's behavior (Rozee & Koss, 2001). Yet there are few rape prevention programs aimed at men and fewer studies targeting men's behavior, and these have been unable to identify factors critical to changing men's behavior (Campbell & Wasco, 2005). Many of these efforts have identified important proxy variables, such as modifying rape myths and creating empathy, yet have not examined reduction in sexually aggressive behavior (O'Donohue, Yeater & Fanetti, 2003). Despite an emphasis on enhancing male empathy, most programming was not effective in creating sustained empathy that affected change in sexually aggressive behavior (Anderson & Whiston, 2005; Foubert, 2000; Lobo, 2005).

Community-based programs focused on men working with men seem to have some promise for future rape prevention efforts. Such programs generally consist of support and education programs focused on improving communication between men and women, strengthening men's resistance to depictions of appropriate (aggressive) male sexual behavior, encouraging men to confront peers who engage in rape supportive beliefs and behaviors, recognizing that rape prevention is a men's issue, and encouraging men to organize, learn about rape, and speak up against male aggression, including donating time and money to rape prevention efforts.

Rape Resistance

While it is clear that efforts to reduce the prevalence of rape must ultimately change the beliefs and behavior of potential perpetrators, the fact that these programs have yet to work highlights the importance of helping potential victims remain safe. Rape avoidance training targeted at women would benefit by focusing on:

- risk reduction (Anderson & Whiston, 2005)
- identifying and repelling sexually aggressive men (Bachar & Koss, 2000; Rozee & Koss, 2001)
- predicting behaviors of aggressive men (Rozee, Bateman, & Gilmore, 1992)
- selection and approaches toward potential victims (Stevens, 1994)
- known rape tactics that may alert women to potential danger (Cleveland, Koss, & Lyons, 1999)

In addition, based on consistent evidence of the effectiveness of physical resistance strategies over passive strategies in avoiding rape (Rozee & Koss, 2001; Ullman, 1997) rape prevention programs must devote time to physical self-defense.

The importance of rape resistance is highlighted by research suggesting that women who do not resist are more likely to be raped (Clay-Warner, 2002; Furby & Fischhoff, 1986; Kleck & Sayles, 1990; Koss & Mukai, 1993; Rozee & Koss, 2001; Ullman, 1997, 1998; Ullman & Knight, 1991, 1992, 1993, 1995; Ullman & Siegel, 1993; Zoucha-Jensen & Coyne, 1993). Yet most rape prevention programs focus on risk reduction and avoidance, rather than self-defense training.

Although the empirical evidence strongly supports the efficacy of physical self-defense, it is important to note that not all women are able to physically resist, due to characteristics of the situation, the perpetrator, or the woman herself. This does not mean that the victim is at fault if she does not fight back. The woman's choice of response in the given situation must be honored and respected. We all make the best choices we can under our given circumstances. By focusing on empowerment, we do not undermine the reality of women's victimization.

The problem is that most women have been taught that to physically resist a rapist is both futile and foolish (Rozee, 2003). One common myth is that because of men's greater size and strength, it is unlikely that a woman can successfully defend herself. Research on rape resistance has consistently determined that women who fight back immediately are less likely to be raped than women who do not (Furby & Fischhoff, 1986; Ullman, 1997). Furby and Fischhoff (1986) found that these results held in both stranger and acquaintance rape situations and even in the presence of a weapon.

A second myth is that if a woman tries to fight off her attacker, she is more likely to be injured. Despite evidence that risks for serious injury are minimal, a widespread belief is that injuries are common in rape cases when the woman resists (Ryckman, Kaczor, & Thornton, 1992). In fact, injuries stemming from resistance tend to be minor, consisting mainly of cuts and bruises, with less than 3 percent suffering more serious injury such as a broken bone (Ruback & Ivie, 1988). Recent evidence clearly shows that women who fight back are no more likely to be injured than women who do not (Ullman, 1997). Ullman's (1997) research demonstrated that it is important to consider the *sequence* of events. She found that women fought back because they were being hurt; they were not hurt because they resisted. Physical self-defense often occurred in response to physical attack. Resistance is likely to prevent rape and result in no more injury than no resistance.

A further advantage of resistance is that women who do not resist are more often blamed for the rape (Ong & Ward, 1999) and get negative reactions from juries. Juries tend to assume consent in the absence of verbal or physical resistance (Warner & Hewitt, 1993). The more the victim-survivor resisted, the more certain are the observers that a rape occurred (Krulewitz & Nash, 1979). In addition, resistance may facilitate faster psychological recovery whether or not a rape occurs (Bart & O'Brien, 1985). Women who resist may blame themselves less for what happened and have more positive attitudes toward themselves because, despite the outcome, they did all they could do to prevent the rape (Furby & Fischhoff, 1986). The unfortunate truth is that many women enroll in self-defense classes only *after* they are raped (Huddleston, 1991; Brecklin, 2004).

A second line of research has examined the efficacy of participating in self-defense classes. Self-defense classes teach skills for preventing and responding to sexual violence, yet are not typically part of rape education programs. Instead, women must seek out instruction in the community, generally paying a fee for the service. McCaughey (1998) argues that one reason feminists should embrace self-defense is so that it will reach more women, much as rape education does currently.

Recognizing the importance of preventing rape on campus, many universities are now offering self-defense courses as part of their curricular offerings.

Experimental tests of the efficacy of self-defense training in reducing the incidence of future rapes are few and far between. In general, these studies have found that self-defense training may facilitate rape avoidance. A recent multivariate analysis found that women with self-defense training, compared to women without such training, were more likely to say that fighting back stopped the offender or made him less aggressive (Brecklin & Ullman, 2005). Women in this study who had self-defense training were also more likely to have experienced attempted rape versus completed rape, thus supporting the effectiveness of trained resistance.

Some researchers have pointed out that self-defense training may have other positive effects that could reduce women's risk of assault (Brecklin & Ullman, 2005). In a longitudinal study of self-defense training, Hollander (2004) found that the classes gave women more confidence in potentially dangerous situations, less fear of strangers, and more positive feelings about their bodies. Several authors have suggested that self-defense classes are life-transforming learning experiences for many women (Cermele, 2004; Hollander, 2004). Thus, while rape resistance supporters have been criticized for reinforcing the notion that women are responsible for rape prevention, the evidence is strong that rape resistance is the best stopgap measure for women until effective primary prevention programs with men are designed and implemented.

SUGGESTIONS FOR CHANGE

The preceding review suggests that rape continues to be a pandemic problem in the United States and that it has long-lasting effects on survivors and society as a whole. While our understanding of the causes of rape has increased dramatically over the past three decades, our ability to effectively intervene and prevent rape has lagged behind. Even though substantial efforts are being made to combat this problem, much remains to be done. Based on problems identified in the preceding review of the literature, this concluding section focuses on potential areas for change, in the hope that, together, we can continue to combat the problem of rape.

Preventing Rape

Although prevention programs aimed at changing simple attitudes about rape have not been effective in reducing rape incidence, feminist efforts to change sociocultural conditions are still vital to rape reduction. Continued efforts to challenge traditional gender-roles, sexual scripts, and rape myths are clearly needed. If anything, the past decade has been characterized by a backlash against such efforts. Whereas changing social norms in the 1970s and 1980s raised societal awareness of the negative effects of gender socialization, the turn of the century has been marked by highly gendered marketing and merchandise aimed at children. This retraditionalization of our children is bound to have long-lasting impacts on our society. It is also bound to affect rates of rape. Continued efforts to raise awareness of the problematic nature of gender socialization and "normal" sexual scripts are therefore essential.

The past decade has also been marked by dramatic technological advances that have substantially altered our access to information. Unfortunately, these advances have also made pornography and other degrading images of women much more accessible. Whereas the social stigma of walking into an adult bookstore or strip club may have kept some men (and certainly children) from being exposed to these images, the proliferation of pornography on the Internet has made such images almost commonplace. Enhancing the quantity of more positive and accurate images of women in mass media may counteract the potential negative effects of these images.

In addition, more research is needed to identify effective rape prevention programs. Psychological research on the causes of rape has identified points of intervention that may be further explored in terms of their ability to truly change men's behavior, but this research is not always incorporated into the design of rape prevention programs. In designing such programs, practitioners should focus on empirically supported causes of rape. They should also explore innovative ways of changing personality constructs such as hostility toward women and lack of empathy that have been identified as correlates of rape in the literature.

Prevention programs should also focus more specifically on engaging men in the fight against rape. Too often, men are resistant to the messages promoted by current rape prevention efforts. More attention needs to be paid to developing programs that give men a proactive role, allowing them to act as allies with women and role models for other men. Simply providing information about rape is not enough. To change the incidence of rape, we need to engage men in the process of changing the rape-supportive environments in which they live. There are now a number of websites by and for men on how men can work together to reduce male violence toward women, particularly sexual assault. A few of these are:

- www.stopviolence.com/domviol/menagainst.htm
- www.mencanstoprape.org/
- www.menendingrape.org/index.htm
- http://menagainstsexualviolence.org/
- www.menstoppingviolence.org/index.php

Rape prevention programs should also heed the cumulative results of evaluation studies. While the overall picture remains somewhat bleak, it is clear that specific structural aspects of prevention programs work better than others. Prevention programs that are experiential rather than didactic, that focus on one gender rather than mixed groups, that extend over a substantial period of time rather than a one-shot effort, and that are run by professionals rather than peers appear to be the most effective. At the very least, rape prevention programs should follow these structural guidelines in order to increase their chance of success. In the meantime, schools and universities, as well as communities, should also expend the resources necessary to provide self-defense training for women and girls. While such programs should by no means take the place of prevention programs targeting men, the benefits of self-defense training for women is clear.

Improving the Community Response to Rape Survivors

Most rape survivors are in need of help and assistance from both loved ones and professionals. Unfortunately, not all survivors receive the support they need. The continuing prevalence of negative social reactions toward rape survivors highlights the need for ongoing community education programs and training for community personnel. Such programs should focus proactively on how to best help rape survivors and avoid negative social reactions. Research suggests that friends, family, and romantic partners are often confused about how to best help their loved one (Ahrens & Campbell, 2000; Smith, 2005). Instruction before the fact on how to help survivors may help reduce negative reactions that stem from ignorance about how to help. The same may be true for community personnel, who may benefit from information about survivors' needs and training on how to most effectively support survivors.

Improving the community response to rape may also require a critical examination of the organizational structures of the legal, medical, and mental health systems. It is possible that strategic changes to the protocols, reward structures, and daily operations of these organizations could lead to substantial changes in how rape survivors are treated. For example, the current system rewards police officers for weeding out false claims. Imagine the changes that would occur if they were instead rewarded for thorough investigations and survivor satisfaction. Similarly, the current system rewards prosecutors for their win–loss ratios. Imagine the changes that would occur if they were instead rewarded for prosecuting every crime that meets the legal definition of rape. In the medical system, emergency room protocols are oriented for fast, efficient care that prioritizes life-threatening emergencies. Imagine the changes that would occur if medical personnel were rewarded for taking the time to emotionally support rape survivors and conduct thorough forensic examinations. And imagine the changes that would occur if counselors were required to take an entire class dedicated to working with survivors of interpersonal violence in order to be licensed.

Of course, such organizational changes would require substantial increases in funding, resources, and political will. Sadly, rape is not at the top of society's political agenda, and without public outcry, it is not likely that large-scale social change will happen soon. This highlights the importance of continued activist and social change efforts to keep rape in the forefront of the public's eye and to pressure politicians to make important changes to public policy and funding initiatives to effectively address rape. While rape crisis centers used to play a key role in such social change efforts, many centers have abandoned their social change initiatives in favor of more individualized treatment approaches. This has left a vacuum that must be filled by those of us interested in social change.

While many researchers feel that social action is beyond the scope of their training and responsibilities, increasing numbers of academics have stepped into the public policy arena and have begun to focus on conducting social action research that aims to effect substantial social change in the organizations, communities, and societies in which they work. Changing our rape culture will require the dedication and contributions of a multitude of individuals, and there are certainly important roles that students and academics can play. We encourage everyone reading this chapter to consider the role that they themselves can play and to join us in the fight against rape.

REFERENCES

Abbey, A., & McAuslan, P. (2004). A longitudinal examination of male college students' perpetration of sexual assault. *Journal of Consulting and Clinical Psychology, 72,* 747–756.

Abbey, A., McAuslan, P., & Ross, L. T. (1998). Sexual assault perpetration by college men: The role of alcohol, misperception of sexual intent, and sexual beliefs and experiences. *Journal of Social and Clinical Psychology, 17,* 167–195.

Abbey, A., McAuslan, P., Zawacki, T., Clinton, A. M., & Buck, P. O. (2001). Attitudinal, experiential, and situational predictors of sexual assault perpetration. *Journal of Interpersonal Violence, 16,* 784–807.

Abbey, A., Zawacki, T., Buck, P. O., Clinton, A. M., & McAuslan, P. (2004). Sexual assault and alcohol consumption: What do we know about their relationship and what types of research are still needed? *Aggression and Violent Behavior, 9,* 271–303.

Abrams, D., Viki, G. T., Masser, B., & Bohner, G. (2003). Perceptions of stranger and acquaintance rape: The role of benevolent and hostile sexism in victim blame and rape proclivity. *Journal of Personality and Social Psychology, 84,* 111–125.

Ahrens, C. E. (2006). Being silenced: The impact of negative social reactions on the disclosure of rape. *American Journal of Community Psychology, 38*(3), 263–274.

Ahrens, C. E., Cabral, G., & Abeling, S. (under review). Healing or hurtful: Rape survivors interpretations of social reactions from different support providers. *Psychology of Women Quarterly.*

Ahrens, C. E., & Campbell, R. (2000). Assisting rape victims as they recover from rape: The impact on friends. *Journal of Interpersonal Violence, 15*(9), 959–986.

Ahrens, C. E., Campbell, R., Ternier-Thames, N. K., Wasco, S., & Sefl, T. (2007). Deciding whom to tell: Expectations and outcomes of rape survivors first disclosures. *Psychology of Women Quarterly.*

Ahrens, C. E., Campbell, R., Wasco, S. M., Aponte, G., Grubstein, G., & Davidson, W. S. I. (2000). Sexual assault nurse examiner (SANE) programs: Alternative systems for service delivery for sexual assault victims. *Journal of Interpersonal Violence, 15*(9), 921–943.

Allen, M., D'Alessio, D., & Brezgel, K. (1995). A meta-analysis summarizing the effects of pornography: II. Aggression after exposure. *Human Communication Research, 22*(2), 258–283.

Allen, M., Emmers, T., Gebhardt, L., & Giery, M. (1995). Exposure to pornography and acceptance of rape myths. *Journal of Communication, 45*(1), 5–26.

Anderson, L. A., & Whiston, S. C. (2005). Sexual assault education programs: A meta-analytic examination of their effectiveness. *Psychology of Women Quarterly, 29,* 374–388.

Arata, C. M. (1999). Coping with rape: The roles of prior sexual abuse and attributions of blame. *Journal of Interpersonal Violence, 14*(1), 62–78.

Arata, C. M., & Burkhart, B. R. (1998). Coping appraisals and adjustment to nonstranger sexual assault. *Violence against Women, 4*(2), 224–239.

Bachar, K. J., & Koss, M. P. (2001). From prevalence to prevention: Closing the gap between what we know about rape and what we do. In C. M. Renzetti, R. K. Bergen, & J. L. Edelson (Eds.), *Sourcebook on violence against women* (pp. 117–142). Thousand Oaks, CA: Sage.

Bandura, A. (1979). The social learning perspective: Mechanisms of aggression. In H. Toch (Ed.), *Psychology of crime and criminal justice.* New York: Holt, Rinehart & Winston.

Bandura, A., Ross, D., & Ross, S. A. (1961). Transmission of aggression through imitation of aggressive models. *Journal of Abnormal and Social Psychology, 63,* 575–582.

Bart, P. B., & O'Brien, P. (1985). *Stopping rape: Successful survival strategies.* New York: Pergamon.

Basile, K. C. (2002). Prevalence of wife rape and other intimate partner sexual coercion in a nationally representative sample of women. *Violence and victims, 17*(5), 511–524.

Bleecker, E. T., & Murnen, S. K. (2005). Fraternity membership, the display of degrading sexual images of women, and rape myth acceptance. *Sex Roles, 53,* 487–493.

Boeschen, L. E., Koss, M. P., Figueredo, A. J., & Coan, J. A. (2001). Experiential avoidance and post-traumatic stress disorder: A cognitive mediational model of rape recovery. *Journal of Aggression, Maltreatment & Trauma, 4*(2), 211–245.

Boudreaux, E., Kilpatrick, D. G., Resnick, H. S., Best, C. L., & Saunders, B. E. (1998). Criminal victimization, posttraumatic stress disorder, and comorbid psychopathology among a community sample of women. *Journal of Traumatic Stress, 11,* 665–678.

Braithwaite, J., & Daly, K. (1998). Masculinities, violence, and communitarian control. In S. L. Miller (Ed.), *Crime control and women: Feminist implications of criminal justice policy* (pp. 151–172). Newbury Park, CA: Sage.

Brecklin, L. (2004). Self-defense/assertiveness training, women's victimization history, and psychological characteristics. *Violence against Women, 10*(5), 479–497.

Brecklin, L., & Forde, D. (2001). A meta-analysis of rape education programs. *Violence and Victims, 16*(3), 303–321.

Brecklin, L., & Ullman, S. (2005). Self-defense or assertiveness training and women's responses to sexual attacks. *Journal of Interpersonal Violence, 20*(6), 738–762.

Breitenbecher, K., & Gidycz, C. (1998). An empirical evaluation of a program designed to reduce the risk of multiple sexual victimization. *Journal of Interpersonal Violence, 13*(4), 472–488.

Breitenbecher, K. H., & Scarce, M. (1999). A longitudinal evaluation of the effectiveness of a sexual assault education program. *Journal of Interpersonal Violence, 14,* 459–478.

Brener, N. D., McMahon, P. M., Warren, C. W., & Douglas, K. A. (1999). Forced sexual intercourse and associated health-risk behaviors among female college students in the United States. *Journal of Consulting and Clinical Psychology, 67*(2), 252–259.

Brownmiller, S. (1975). *Against our will: Men, women, and rape.* New York: Simon & Schuster.

Bryden, D., & Lengnick, S. (1997). Rape in the criminal justice system. *Journal of Criminal Law and Criminology, 87*(4), 1385–1429.

Burgess, A., & Holmstrom, L. (1974). Rape trauma syndrome. *American Journal of Psychiatry, 131*(9), 981–986.

Burt, M. (1980). Cultural myths and supports for rape. *Journal of Personality and Social Psychology, 38*(2), 217–230.

Burt, M. R., & Katz, B. L. (1987). Dimensions of recovery from rape: Focus on growth outcomes. *Journal of Interpersonal Violence, 2*(1), 57–81.

Buss, D. M. (1994). *The evolution of desire: Strategies of human mating.* New York: Basic Books.

Cahill, A. J. (2001). *Rethinking rape.* Ithaca, NY: Cornell University Press.

Campbell, R. (2006). Rape survivors' experiences with the legal and medical systems: Do rape victim advocates make a difference? *Violence against Women, 12*(1), 30–45.

Campbell, R., & Ahrens, C. E. (1998). Innovative community services for rape victims: An application of multiple case study methodology. *American Journal of Community Psychology, 26*(4), 537–571.

Campbell, R., Ahrens, C. E., Sefl, T., Wasco, S. M., & Barnes, H. E. (2001). Social reactions to rape victims: Healing and hurtful effects on psychological and physical health outcomes. *Violence and victims, 16*(3), 287–302.

Campbell, R., Baker, C. K., & Mazurek, T. L. (1998). Remaining radical? organizational predictors of rape crisis centers' social change initiatives. *American Journal of Community Psychology, 26*(3), 457–483.

Campbell, R., & Bybee, D. (1997). Emergency medical services for rape victims: Detecting the cracks in service delivery. *Women's Health: Research on Gender, Behavior and Policy, 3,* 75–101.

Campbell, R., & Johnson, C. R. (1997). Police officers' perceptions of rape: Is there consistency between state law and individual beliefs? *Journal of Interpersonal Violence, 12*(2), 255–274.

Campbell, R., Lichty, L. F., Sturza, M., & Raja, S. (2006). Gynecological health impact of sexual assault. *Research in Nursing & Health, 29*(5), 399–413.

Campbell, R., & Martin, P. Y. (2001). Services for sexual assault survivors: The role of rape crisis centers. In C. M. Renzetti, J. L. Edleson, & R. K. Bergen (Eds.), *Sourcebook on violence against women* (pp. 227–241). Thousand Oaks, CA: Sage.

Campbell, R., Patterson, D., & Lichty, L. F. (2005). The effectiveness of sexual assault nurse examiner (SANE) programs: A review of psychological, medical, legal, and community outcomes. *Trauma, Violence, & Abuse, 6*(4), 313–329.

Campbell, R., & Raja, S. (1999). Secondary victimization of rape victims: Insights from mental health professionals who treat survivors of violence. *Violence and Victims, 14*(3), 261–275.

Campbell, R., Raja, S., & Grining, P. L. (1999). Training mental health professionals on violence against women. *Journal of Interpersonal Violence, 14*(10), 1003–1013.

Campbell, R., Sefl, T., & Ahrens, C. E. (2004). The impact of rape on women's sexual health risk behaviors. *Health Psychology, 23*(1), 67–74.

Campbell, R., Sefl, T., Barnes, H. E., Ahrens, C. E., Wasco, S. M., & Zaragoza-Diesfeld, Y. (1999). Community services for rape survivors: Enhancing psychological well-being or increasing trauma? *Journal of Consulting and Clinical Psychology, 67*(6), 847–858.

Campbell, R., Townsend, S. M., Long, S. M., Kinnison, K. E., Pulley, E. M., Adames, S. B., et al. (2006). Responding to sexual assault victims' medical and emotional needs: A national study of the services provided by SANE programs. *Research in Nursing & Health, 29*(5), 384–398.

Campbell, R., & Wasco, S. (2005). Understanding rape and sexual assault: 20 years of progress and future directions. *Journal of Interpersonal Violence, 20*(1), 127–131.

Campbell, R., Wasco, S. M., Ahrens, C. E., Sefl, T., & Barnes, H. E. (2001). Preventing the "second rape": Rape survivor's experiences with community service providers. *Journal of Interpersonal Violence, 16*(12), 1239–1259.

Cermele, J. A. (2004). Teaching resistance to teach resistance: The use of self-defense in teaching about gender violence. *Feminist Teacher, 15,* 1–15.

Clay-Warner, J. (2002). Avoiding rape: The effect of protective actions and situational factors on rape outcome. *Violence and Victims, 17*(6), 691–705.

Cleveland, H., Koss, M., & Lyons, J. (1999). Rape tactics from the survivors' perspective: Contextual dependence and within-event independence. *Journal of Interpersonal Violence, 14*(5), 532–547.

Cohen, L. J., & Roth, S. (1987). The psychological aftermath of rape: Long-term effects and individual differences in recovery. *Journal of Social & Clinical Psychology, 5*(4), 525–534.

Coker, D. (1999). Enhancing autonomy for battered women: Lessons from Navajo peacemaking. *UCLA Law Review, 47,* 1–111.

Conoscenti, L. M., & McNally, R. J. (2006). Health complaints in acknowledged and unacknowledged rape victims. *Journal of Anxiety Disorders, 20*(3), 372–379.

Davis, M. H. (1980). A multidimensional approach to individual differences in empathy. *JSAS: Catalog of Selected Documents in Psychology, 10,* 85.

Davis, R., Brickman, E., & Baker, T. (1991). Supportive and unsupportive responses of others to rape victims: Effects on concurrent victim adjustment. *American Journal of Community Psychology, 19*(3), 443–451.

Davis, R., Taylor, B., & Bench, S. (1995). Impact of sexual and nonsexual assault on secondary victims. *Violence and Victims, 10*(1), 73–84.

Dean, K. E., & Malamuth, N. M. (1997). Characteristics of men who aggress sexually and of men who imagine aggressing: Risk and moderating variables. *Journal of Personality and Social Psychology, 72,* 449–455.

DeKeseredy, W. S., & Schwartz, M. D. (2001). Definitional issues. In C. M. Renzetti, J. L. Edleson, & R. K. Bergen (Eds.), *Sourcebook on violence against women* (pp. 23–34). Thousand Oaks, CA: Sage.

Des Rosiers, N., Feldthusen, B., & Hankivsky, O. (1998). Legal compsensation for sexual violence: Therapeutic consequences and consequences for the judicial system. *Psychology, Public Policy, and the Law* 4(1/2), 433–451.

Dickinson, L. M., deGruy, F. V., III, Dickinson, W. P., & Candib, L. M. (1999). Health-related quality of life and symptom profiles of female survivors of sexual abuse. *Archives of Family Medicine, 8,* 35–43.

Domar, A. (1986) Psychological aspects of the pelvic exam: Individual needs and physician involvement. *Women and Health, 10,* 75–90.

Donat, P., & White, J. (2000). Re-examining the issue of nonconsent in acquaintance rape. In C. B. Travis and J. W. White (Eds.), *Sexuality, society, and feminism* (pp. 355–376). Washington, DC: American Psychological Association.

Dunmore, E., Clark, D. M., & Ehlers, A. (2001). A prospective investigation of the role of cognitive factors in persistent posttraumatic stress disorder (PTSD) after physical or sexual assault. *Behaviour Research and Therapy, 39*(9), 1063–1084.

Emm, D., & McKenry, P. C. (1988). Coping with victimization: The impact of rape on female survivors, male significant others, and parents. *Contemporary Family Therapy, 10*(4), 272–279.

Estrich, S. (1987). *Real rape: How the legal system victimizes women who say no.* Cambridge, MA: Harvard University Press.

Faravelli, C., Giugni, A., Salvatori, S., & Ricca, V. (2004). Psychopathology after rape. *American Journal of Psychiatry, 161*(8), 1483–1485.

Feuer, C. A., Nishith, P., & Resick, P. (2005). Prediction of numbing and effortful avoidance in female rape survivors with chronic PTSD. *Journal of Traumatic Stress, 18*(2), 165–170.

Filipas, H. H., & Ullman, S. E. (2001). Social reactions to sexual assault victims from various support sources. *Violence and Victims, 16*(6), 673–692.

Fisher, B. S., Daigle, L. E., Cullen, F. T., & Turner, M. G. (2003). Reporting sexual victimization to the police and others: Results from a national-level study of college women. *Criminal Justice and Behavior, 30*(1), 6–38.

Foa, E. B., & Riggs, D. S. (1995). Posttraumatic stress disorder following assault: Theoretical considerations and empirical findings. *Current Directions in Psychological Science, 4*(2), 61–65.

Foubert, J. (2000). The longitudinal effects of a rape-prevention program on fraternity men's attitudes, behavioral intent, and behavior. *Journal of American College Health, 48*(4), 158–163.

Frazier, P. (1990). Victim attributions and post-rape trauma. *Journal of Personality and Social Psychology, 59*(2), 298–304.

Frazier, P. (2003). Perceived control and distress following sexual assault: A longitudinal test of a new model. *Journal of Personality and Social Psychology, 84*(6), 1257–1269.

Frazier, P., Conlon, A., & Glaser, T. (2001). Positive and negative life changes following sexual assault. *Journal of Consulting and Clinical Psychology, 69*(6), 1048–1055.

Frazier, P. & Haney, B. (1996). Sexual assault cases in the legal system: Police, prosecutor, and victim perspectives. *Law & Human Behavior, 20*(6), 607–628.

Frazier, P., Steward, J., & Mortensen, H. (2004). Perceived control and adjustment to trauma: A comparison across events. *Journal of Social & Clinical Psychology*, 23(3), 303–324.

Frazier, P., Tashiro, T., Berman, M., Steger, M., & Long, J. (2004). Correlates of levels and patterns of positive life changes following sexual assault. *Journal of Consulting and Clinical Psychology, 72*(1), 19–30.

Frazier, P. A., & Burnett, J. W. (1994). Immediate coping strategies among rape victims. *Journal of Counseling & Development, 72*(6), 633–639.

Frazier, P. A., Mortensen, H., & Steward, J. (2005). Coping strategies as mediators of the relations among perceived control and distress in sexual assault survivors. *Journal of Counseling Psychology, 52*(3), 267–278.

Frohmann, L. (1991). Discrediting victims' allegations of sexual assault: Prosecutorial accounts of case rejections. *Social Problems, 38*(2), 213–226.

Frohmann, L. (1997). Convictability and discordant locales: Reproducing race, class, and gender ideologies in prosecutional decision-making. *Law and Society Review, 31*(3), 531–556.

Frohmann, L. (1998). Constituting power in sexual assault cases: Prosecutorial strategies for victim management. *Social Problems, 45*(3), 393–407.

Furby, L., & Fischhoff, B. (1986). *Rape self-defense strategies: A review of their effectiveness.* Eugene, OR: Eugene Research Institute.

Gard, M., & Bradley, B. S. (2000). Getting away with rape: Erasure of the psyche in evolutionary psychology. *Psychology, Evolution & Gender, 2,* 313–319.

Garvey, N. (2005). *Just sex? The cultural scaffolding of rape*. London: Routledge.

Golding, J. M., Siegel, J. M., Sorenson, S. B., & Burnam, M. A. (1989). Social support sources following sexual assault. *Journal of Community Psychology, 17*(1), 92–107.

Goodchilds, J., & Zellman, G. (1984). Sexual signaling and sexual aggression in adolescent relationships. In N. Malamuth & E. Donnerstein (Eds.), *Pornography and sexual aggression.* Orlando, FL: Academic Press.

Gordon, M., & Riger, S. (1989). *The female fear*. New York: Free Press.

Green, B. L., Krupnick, J. L., Stockton, P., & Goodman, L. (2005). Effects of adolescent trauma exposure on risky behavior in college women. *Psychiatry: Interpersonal and Biological Processes, 68*(4), 363–378.

Griffin, S. (1979). *Rape: The politics of consciousness.* San Francisco: Harper & Row.

Groth, A. N. (1979). *Men who rape: The psychology of the offender.* New York: Plenum.

Harris, H. N., & Valentiner, D. P. (2002). World assumptions, sexual assault, depression, and fearful attitudes toward relationships. *Journal of Interpersonal Violence, 17*(3), 286–305.

Heise, L., Ellsberg, M., & Gottemoeller, M. (1999). Ending violence against women. *Population Reports, 27,* 1–43.

Herbert, T. B., & Dunkel-Schetter, C. (1992). Negative social reactions to victims: An overview of responses and their determinants. In L. Montada, S. Filipp, & M. J. Lerner (Eds.), *Life crises and experiences of loss in adulthood* (pp. 497–518). Hillsdale, NJ: Erlbaum.

Herman, D. (1989). The rape culture. In J. Freeman (Ed.), *Women: A feminist perspective* (4th ed.; pp. 20–44). Mountain View, CA: Mayfield.

Hollander, J. A. (2004). "I can take care of myself": The impact of self-defense training on women's lives. *Violence against Women, 10*(3), 205–235.

Huddleston, S. (1991). Prior victimization experiences and subsequent self-protective behavior as evidenced by personal choice of physical activity courses. *Psychology, 28,* 47–51.

Humphrey, S., & Kahn, A. (2000). Fraternities, athletic teams, and rape: Importance of identification with a risky group. *Journal of Interpersonal Violence, 15*(12), 1313–1322.

Janoff-Bulman, R. (1989). Assumptive worlds and the stress of traumatic events: Applications of the schema construct. *Social Cognition, 7*(2), 113–136.

Jordan, J. (2004). Beyond belief? Police, rape, and women's credibility. *International Journal of Policy and Practice, 4*(1), 25–59.

Kassing, L. R., & Prieto, L. R. (2003). The rape myth and blame-based beliefs of counselors-in-training toward male victims of rape. *Journal of Counseling & Development, 81*(4), 455–461.

Kaukinen, C, & DeMaris, A. (2005). Age at first sexual assault and current substance use and depression. *Journal of Interpersonal Violence, 20*(10), 1244–1270.

Kennedy, J., Davis, R., & Taylor, B. (1998). Changes in spirituality and well-being among victims of sexual assault. *Journal for the Scientific Study of Religion, 37*(2), 322–328.

Kilpatrick, D. G. (2004). What is violence against women? Defining and measuring the problem. *Journal of Interpersonal Violence, 19*(11), 1209–1234.

Kilpatrick, D. G., Edwards, C. N., & Seymour, A. E. (1992). *Rape in America: A report to the nation.* Arlington, VA: National Crime Victims Center.

Kilpatrick, D. G., Saunders, B. E., & Smith, D. W. (2003). *Youth victimization: Prevalence and implications.* NIJ 194972. Washington, DC: National Institute of Justice.

Kleck, G., & Sayles, S. (1990). Rape and resistance. *Social Problems, 37*(2), 149–162.

Koss, M. (1985). The hidden rape victim: Personality, attitudinal, and situational characteristics. *Psychology of Women Quarterly, 9*(2), 193–212.

Koss, M. (1992). The underdetection of rape: Methodological choices influence incidence estimates. *Journal of Social Issues, 48,* 61–76.

Koss, M. (1996). The measurement of rape victimization in crime surveys. *Criminal Justice and Behavior, 23*(1), 55–69.

Koss, M. (2000). Blame, shame, and community: Justice responses to violence against women. *American Psychologist, 55*(11), 1332–1343.

Koss, M. (2003). Evolutionary models of why men rape: Acknowledging the complexities. In Travis, 2003, pp. 191–205.

Koss, M., Bachar, K. J., Hopkins, C. Q., & Carlson, C. (2004). Expanding a community's justice response to sex crimes through advocacy, prosecutorial, and public health collaboration: Introducing the RESTORE program. *Journal of Interpersonal Violence, 19*(12), 1435–1463.

Koss, M., & Dinero, T. (1988). Predictors of sexual aggression among a national sample of male college students. *Annals of the New York Academy of Sciences, 528*, 133–147.

Koss, M., & Figueredo, A. J. (2004a). Change in cognitive mediators of rape's impact on psychosocial health across 2 years of recovery. *Journal of Consulting and Clinical Psychology, 72*(6), 1063–1072.

Koss, M., & Figueredo, A. J. (2004b). Cognitive mediation of rape's mental health impact: Constructive replication of a cross-sectional model in longitudinal data. *Psychology of Women Quarterly, 28*(4), 273–286.

Koss, M., Gidycz, C. A., & Wisniewski, N. (1987). The scope of rape: Incidence and prevalence of sexual aggression and victimization in a national sample of higher education students. *Journal of Consulting and Clinical Psychology, 55*(2), 162–170.

Koss, M., & Mukai, T. (1993). Recovering ourselves: The frequency, effects, and resolution of rape. In F. L. Denmark and M. A. Paludi (Eds.), *Psychology of women: A handbook of issues and theories* (pp. 477–512). Westport, CT: Greenwood Press.

Krakow, B., Germain, A., Warner, T. D., Schrader, R., Koss, M. P., Hollifield, M., et al. (2001). The relationship of sleep quality and posttraumatic stress to potential sleep disorders in sexual assault survivors with nightmares, insomnia, and PTSD. *Journal of Traumatic Stress, 14*(4), 647–665.

Krakow, B., Schrader, R., Tandberg, D., Hollifield, M., Koss, M. P., Yau, C. L., et al. (2002). Nightmare frequency in sexual assault survivors with PTSD. *Journal of Anxiety Disorders, 16*(2), 175–190.

Krulewitz, J., & Nash, J. (1979). Effects of rape victim resistance, assault outcome, and sex of observer on attributions of rape. *Journal of Personality, 47*(4), 557–574.

Ledray, L. (1995). Sexual assault evidentiary exam and treatment protocol. *Journal of Emergency Nursing, 21*, 355–359.

Lee, S., Lanvers, U., & Shaw, S. (2003). Attrition in rape cases: Developing a profile and identifying relevant factors. *British Journal of Criminology, 43*, 583–599.

Letourneau, E., Resnick, H., Kilpatrick, D., & Saunders, B. (1996). Comorbidity of sexual problems and posttraumatic stress disorder in female crime victims. *Behavior Therapy, 27*(3), 321–336.

Linz, D., Donnerstein, E., & Penrod, S. (1984). The effects of multiple exposures to filmed violence against women. *Journal of Communication, 34*(3), 130–147.

Littleton, H., & Breitkopf, C. R. (2006). Coping with the experience of rape. *Psychology of Women Quarterly, 30*(1), 106–116.

Lloyd, E. (2003). Violence against science: Rape and evolution. In Travis, 2003, pp. 235–261.

Lobo, T. (2005). Evaluation of a sexual assault prevention program for college men: Effects on self-reported sexually aggressive behavior, social perceptions, and attitudes.

Lonsway, K. (1996). Preventing acquaintance rape through education. What do we know? *Psychology of Women Quarterly, 20*, 229–265.

Lonsway, K., & Fitzgerald, L. (1995). Attitudinal antecedents of rape myth acceptance: A theoretical and empirical reexamination. *Journal of Personality and Social Psychology, 68*(4), 704–711.

MacKinnon, C. (1987). *Feminism unmodified: Discourses on life and law*. Cambridge, MA: Harvard University Press.

Madigan, L., & Gamble, N. (1991). *The second rape: Society's continued betrayal of the victim*. New York: Lexington Books.

Malamuth, N. (1981). Rape proclivity among males. *Journal of Social Issues, 37*(4), 138–157.

Malamuth, N. (1989). The Attraction to Sexual Aggression Scale. *Journal of Sex Research, 26*(1), 26–49; *26*(3), 324–354.

Malamuth, N., Addison, T., & Koss, M. (2000). Pornography and sexual aggression: Are there reliable effects and can we understand them? *Annual Review of Sex Research, 11*, 26–91.

Malamuth, N. M., Linz, D., Heavey, C. L., Barnes, G., & Acker, M. (1995). Using the confluence model of sexual aggression to predict men's conflict with women: A 10-year follow-up study. *Journal of Personality and Social Psychology, 69*, 353–369.

Malamuth, N. M., Sockloskie, R. J., Koss, M. P., & Tanaka, J. S. (1991). Characteristics of aggressors against women: Testing a model using a national sample of college students. *Journal of Consulting and Clinical Psychology, 59*, 670–681.

Martin, A. F., Vergeles, M. R., de la Orden Acevedo, V., del Campo Sanchez, A., & Visa S. L. (2005). The involvement in sexually coercive behaviors of Spanish college men. *Journal of Interpersonal Violence, 20*, 872–891.

Martin, P. Y., & Hummer, R. A. (1989). Fraternities and rape on campus. *Gender & Society, 3*, 457–473.

Martin, P. Y., & Powell, R. (1994). Accounting for the "second assault": Legal organizations framing of rape victims. *Law and Social Inquiry, 19*, 853–890.

Matthews, N. 1994. *Confronting rape: The feminist anti-rape movement and the state*. London: Routledge.

McCaughey, M. (1998). The fighting spirit: Women's self-defense training and the discourse of sexed embodiment. *Gender & Society, 12*, 277–300.

McCold, P., & Wachtel, T. (2002). Restorative justice theory validation. In E. G. M. Weitekamp & H. J. Kerner (Eds.), *Restorative justice: Theoretical foundations* (pp. 110–142). Cullompton, Devon, England: Willan.

McEwan, S. L., de Man, A. F., & Simpson-Housley, P. (2002). Ego-identity achievement and perception of risk in intimacy in survivors of stranger and acquaintance rape. *Sex Roles, 47*(5/6), 281–287.

McEwan, S. L., de Man, A. F., & Simpson-Housley, P. (2005). Acquaintance rape, ego-identity achievement, and locus of control. *Social Behavior and Personality, 33*(6), 587–592.

McKay, K. A. (2002). Therapist responses to clients who have been raped: The effect of rape myth acceptance and ambivalent sexism on therapist perceptions of treatment responsesProQuest Information & Learning.

Medea, A., & Thompson, K. (1974). *Against rape: A survival manual for women; How to avoid entrapment and how to cope with rape physically and emotionally*. New York: Farrar, Straus & Giroux.

Merrill, L. L., Hervig, L. K., Newell, C. E., Gold, S. R., Milner, J. S., & Rosswork, S. G., et al. (1998). Prevalence of premilitary adult sexual victimization and aggression in a Navy recruit sample. *Military Medicine, 163*(4), 209–212.

Meyer, C. B., & Taylor, S. E. (1986). Adjustment to rape. *Journal of Personality and Social Psychology, 50*(6), 1226–1234.

Mintz, L. B., Rideout, C. A., & Bartels, K. M. (1994). A national survey of interns' perceptions of their preparation for counseling women and of the atmosphere of their graduate education. *Professional Psychology: Research and Practice, 25*(3), 221–227.

Miranda, R. J., Meyerson, L. A., Long, P. J., Marx, B. P., & Simpson, S. M. (2002). Sexual assault and alcohol use: Exploring the self-medication hypothesis. *Violence and Victims, 17*(2), 205–217.

Monroe, L. M., Kinney, L. M., Weist, M. D., Dafeamekpor, D. S., Dantzler, J., & Reynolds, M. W. (2005). The experience of sexual assault: Findings from a statewide victim needs assessment. *Journal of Interpersonal Violence, 20*(7), 767–776.

Muehlenhard, C. L., & Linton, M. A. (1987). Date rape and sexual aggression in dating situations: Incidence and risk factors. *Journal of Counseling Psychology, 34,* 186–196.

Nagayama Hall, G. C., Sue, S., Narang, D. S., & Lilly, R. S. (2000). Culture-specific models of men's sexual aggression: Intra- and interpersonal determinants. *Cultural Diversity and Ethnic Minority Psychology, 6,* 252–267.

Nagayama Hall, G. C., Teten, A. L., DeGarmo, D. S., Sue, S., & Stephens, K. A. (2005). Ethnicity, culture, and sexual aggression: Risk and protective factors. *Journal of Consulting and Clinical Psychology, 73,* 830–840.

Neville, H. A., & Heppner, M. J. (2002). Prevention and treatment of violence against women: An examination of sexual assault. In C. L. Juntunen & D. R. Atkinson (Eds.), *Counseling across the lifespan: Prevention and treatment* (pp. 261–277). Thousand Oaks, CA: Sage.

Neville, H. A., Heppner, M. J., Oh, E., Spanierman, L. B., & Clark, M. (2004). General and culturally specific factors influencing black and white rape survivors' self-esteem. *Psychology of Women Quarterly, 28*(1), 83–94.

Nixon, R. D. V., Resick, P. A., & Griffin, M. G. (2004). Panic following trauma: The etiology of acute posttraumatic arousal. *Journal of Anxiety Disorders, 18*(2), 193–210.

Norris, F., & Kaniasty, K. (1992). A longitudinal study of the effects of various crime prevention strategies on criminal victimization, fear of crime, and psychological distress. *American Journal of Community Psychology, 20*(5), 625–648.

Norris, J., Nurius, P. S., & Dimeff, L. A. (1996). Through her eyes: Factors affecting women's perception of and resistance to acquaintance sexual aggression threat. *Psychology of Women Quarterly, 20,* 123–145.

O'Donohue, W., Yeater, E., & Fanetti, M. (2003). Rape prevention with college males: The roles of rape myth acceptance, victim empathy, and outcome expectancies. *Journal of Interpersonal Violence, 18*(5), 513–531.

Ong, A., & Ward, C. (1999). The effects of sex and power schemas, attitudes toward women, and victim resistance on rape attributions. *Journal of Applied Social Psychology, 29*(2), 362–376.

Osterman, J. E., Barbiaz, J., & Johnson, P. (2001). Emergency interventions for rape victims. *Psychiatric Services, 52*(6), 733.

O'Sullivan, E., & Carlton, A. (2001). Victim services, community outreach, and contemporary rape crisis centers. *Journal of Interpersonal Violence, 16*(4), 343–360.

Park, C. L., Cohen, L. H., & Murch, R. L. (1996). Assessment and prediction of stress-related growth. *Journal of Personality, 64*(1), 71–105.

Phillips, C., & Brown, D. (1998). *Entry into the criminal justice system: A survey of police arrests and their outcome.* London: Home Office.

Poulin, C. (2005). The causes of rape: Understanding individual differences in male propensity for sexual aggression (review). *Canadian Psychology, 46,* 254–256.

Remer, R., & Elliott, J. E. (1988). Characteristics of secondary victims of sexual assault. *International Journal of Family Psychiatry, 9*(4), 373–387.

Resnick, H., Holmes, M. M., Kilpatrick, D. G., Clum, G., Acierno, R., Best, C. L., et al. (2000). Predictors of post-rape medical care in a national sample of women. *American Journal of Preventive Medicine, 19*(4), 214–219.

Resnick, H., Kilpatrick, D. G., Dansky, B. S., Saunders, B. E., & Best, C. L. (1993). Prevalence of civilian trauma and posttraumatic stress disorder in a representative national sample of women. *Journal of Consulting and Clinical Psychology, 61,* 984–991.

Resnick, H., Monnier, J., Seals, B., Holmes, M., Nayak, M., Walsh, J., et al. (2002). Rape-related HIV risk concerns among recent rape victims. *Journal of Interpersonal Violence, 17*(7), 746–759.

Riggs, D. S., & Kilpatrick, D. G. (1997). Families and friends: Indirect victimization by crime. In R. C. Davis, R. J. Lurigio, & W. F. Skogan (Eds.), *Victims of crime* (pp. 120–138). Thousand Oaks, CA: Sage.

Roth, S., & Cohen, L. J. (1986). Approach, avoidance, and coping with stress. *American Psychologist, 41*(7), 813–819.

Rozee, P. (1993). Forbidden or forgiven: Rape in cross-cultural perspective. *Psychology of Women Quarterly, 17,* 499–514.

Rozee, P. (2005). Rape resistance: Successes and challenges. In A. Barnes (Ed.), *The handbook of women, psychology, and the law* (pp. 265–279). San Francisco: Jossey-Bass.

Rozee, P., Bateman, P., & Gilmore, T. (1991). The personal perspective of acquaintance rape prevention: A three-tier approach. In A. Parrot & L. Bechhofer (Eds.), *Acquaintance rape: The hidden crime* (pp. 337–354). New York: John Wiley.

Rozee, P. D. (2003). Women's fear of rape: Cause, consequences and coping. In J. Chrisler, C. Golden, & P. Rozee (Eds.), *Lectures in the psychology of women.* (3rd ed.). New York: McGraw-Hill.

Rozee, P. D., & Koss, M. P. (2001). Rape: A century of resistance. *Psychology of Women Quarterly, 25*(4), 295–311.

Ruback, R., & Ivie, D. (1988). Prior relationship, resistance, and injury in rapes: An analysis of crisis center records. *Violence and Victims, 3*(2), 99–111.

Russell, D. (1982). The prevalence and incidence of forcible rape and attempted rape of females. *Victimology, 7*(1), 81–93.

Russell, D. E. (1984). *Sexual exploitation: Rape, child sexual abuse, and workplace harassment.* Beverly Hills, CA: Sage.

Ryckman, R., Kaczor, L., & Thornton, B. (1992). Traditional and nontraditional women's attributions of responsibility to physically resistive and nonresistive rape victims.

Sanday, P. (1981). The socio-cultural context of rape: A cross-cultural study. *Journal of Social Issues, 37*(4), 5–27.

Schewe, P., & O'Donohue, W. (1993). Rape prevention: Methodological problems and new directions. *Clinical Psychology Review, 13*(7), 667–682.

Schwartz, M., & DeKeseredy, W. (1997). *Sexual assault on the college campus: The role of male peer support*. Thousand Oaks, CA: Sage.

Sechrist, S. M., & White, J. W. (2003). The Confluence Model in the prediction of sexual aggression: Adolescence through college. Paper presented at Southeastern Psychological Association, New Orleans, March.

Shields, W. M., & Shields, L. M. (1983). Forcible rape: An evolutionary perspective. *Ethology and Sociobiology, 4,* 115–136.

Sloan, L. M. (1995). Revictimization by polygraph: The practice of polygraphing survivors of sexual assault. *Medicine & Law, 14*(3), 255–267.

Smith, M. E. (2005). Female sexual assault: The impact on the male significant other. *Issues in Mental Health Nursing, 26*(2), 149–167.

Sochting, N., Fairbrother, N., & Koch, W. J. (2004). Sexual assault of women: Prevention efforts and risk factors. *Violence against Women, 10*(1), 73–93.

Stanko, E. (1985). *Intimate intrusions: Women's experience of male violence.* Boston: Routledge & Kegan Paul.

Stein, M. B., Lang, A. J., & Laffaye, C. (2004). Relationship of sexual assault history to somatic symptoms and health anxiety in women. *General Hospital Psychiatry, 26*(3), 178–183.

Stephenson, H., Pena-Shaff, J., & Quirk, P. (2006). Predictors of college student suicidal ideation: Gender differences. *College Student Journal, 40*(1), 109–117.

Stevens, D. (1994). Predatory rapists and victim selection techniques. *Social Science Journal, 31*(4), 421–433.

Sturza, M. L., & Campbell, R. (2005). An exploratory study of rape survivors' prescription drug use as a means of coping with sexual assault. *Psychology of Women Quarterly, 29*(4), 353–363.

Sudderth, L. K. (1998). "It'll come right back at me": The interactional context of discussing rape with others. *Violence against Women, 4*(5), 572–594.

Symons, D. (1979). *The evolution of human sexuality*. Oxford: Oxford University Press.

Tedeschi, R. G., & Calhoun, L. G. (1996). The posttraumatic growth inventory: Measuring the positive legacy of trauma. *Journal of Traumatic Stress, 9*(3), 455–472.

Tetreault, P. A. (1989). Rape myth acceptance: A case for providing educational expert testimony in rape jury trials. *Behavioral Sciences & the Law, 7*(2), 243–257.

Thornhill, R., & Palmer, C. T. (2000). *A natural history of rape: Biological bases of sexual coercion*. Cambridge, MA: MIT Press.

Thornhill, R., & Thornhill, N. W. (1983). Human rape: An evolutionary analysis. *Ethology and Sociobiology, 4,* 137–173.

Tjaden, P., & Thoennes, N. (2000). Prevalence and consequences of male-to-female and female-to-male intimate partner violence as measured by the

National Violence against Women Survey. *Violence against Women, 6*(2), 142–161.

Tobach, E., & Reed, R. (2003). Understanding rape. In Travis, 2003, pp. 105–138.

Travis, C. B. (2003). *Evolution, gender and rape*. Cambridge, MA: MIT Press.

Ullman, S. (1998). Does offender violence escalate when rape victims fight back? *Journal of Interpersonal Violence, 13*(2), 179–192.

Ullman, S. (1999). Social support and recovery from sexual assault: A review. *Aggression and Violent Behavior, 4*(3), 343–358.

Ullman, S., & Knight, R. (1991). A multivariate model for predicting rape and physical injury outcomes during sexual assaults. *Journal of Consulting and Clinical Psychology, 59*(5), 724–731.

Ullman, S., & Knight, R. (1992). Fighting back: Women's resistance to rape. *Journal of Interpersonal Violence, 7*(1), 31–43.

Ullman, S., & Knight, R. (1993). The efficacy of women's resistance strategies in rape situations. *Psychology of Women Quarterly, 17*(1), 23–38.

Ullman, S., & Knight, R. (1995). Women's resistance strategies to different rapist types. *Criminal Justice and Behavior, 22*(3), 263–283.

Ullman, S., & Siegel, J. (1993). Victim–offender relationship and sexual assault. *Violence and Victims, 8*(2), 121–134

Ullman, S. E. (1996a). Do social reactions to sexual assault victims vary by support provider? *Violence and Victims, 11*(2), 143–157.

Ullman, S. E. (1996b). Social reactions, coping strategies, and self-blame attributions in adjustment to sexual assault. *Psychology of Women Quarterly, 20*(4), 505–526.

Ullman, S. E. (1997). Review and critique of empirical studies of rape avoidance. *Criminal Justice and Behavior, 24,* 177–204.

Ullman, S. E. (2000). Psychometric characteristics of the social reactions questionnaire: A measure of reactions to sexual assault victims. *Psychology of Women Quarterly, 24*(3), 257–271.

Ullman, S. E., & Brecklin, L. R. (2002a). Sexual assault history and suicidal behavior in a national sample of women. *Suicide and Life-Threatening Behavior, 32*(2), 117–130.

Ullman, S. E., & Brecklin, L. R. (2002b). Sexual assault history, PTSD, and mental health service seeking in a national sample of women. *Journal of Community Psychology, 30*(3), 261–279.

Ullman, S. E., & Brecklin, L. R. (2003). Sexual assault history and health-related outcomes in a national sample of women. *Psychology of Women Quarterly, 27,* pp. 46–57.

Ullman, S. E., & Filipas, H. H. (2001a). Correlates of formal and informal support seeking in sexual assaults victims. *Journal of Interpersonal Violence, 16*(10), 1028–1047.

Ullman, S. E., & Filipas, H. H. (2001b). Predictors of PTSD symptom severity and social reactions in sexual assault victims. *Journal of Traumatic Stress, 14*(2), 369–389.

Ullman, S. E., Filipas, H. H., Townsend, S. M., & Starzynski, L. L. (2006). The role of victim–offender relationship in women's sexual assault experiences. *Journal of Interpersonal Violence, 21*(6), 798–819.

U.S. Census Bureau. www.census.gov.

U.S. Department of Justice. Office on Violence against Women. (2007). About sexual assault. Retrieved June 6, 2007, from http://www.usdoj.gov/ovw/sexassault.htm.

Valentiner, D. P., Foa, E. B., Riggs, D. S., & Gershuny, B. S. (1996). Coping strategies and posttraumatic stress disorder in female victims of sexual and nonsexual assault. *Journal of Abnormal Psychology, 105*(3), 455–458.

Vaughan, A. E. (2001). The association between offender socioeconomic status and victim-offender relationship in rape offences. *Psychology, Evolution & Gender, 3,* 121–136.

Vaughan, A. E. (2003). The association between offender socioeconomic status and victim-offender relationship in rape offences—revised. *Sexualities, Evolution & Gender, 5,* 103–105.

Ward, C. (1995). *Attitudes toward rape: Feminist and social psychological perspectives.* London: Sage.

Ward, T., & Siegert, R. (2002). Rape and evolutionary psychology: A critique of Thornhill and Palmer's theory. *Aggression and Violent Behavior, 7,* 145–168.

Warner, A., & Hewitt, J. (1993). Victim resistance and judgments of victim "consensuality" in rape. *Perceptual and Motor Skills, 76*(3), 952–954.

Wheeler, J. G., George, W. H., & Dahl, B. J. (2002). Sexually aggressive college males: Empathy as a moderator in the "Confluence Model" of sexual aggression. *Personality and Individual Differences, 33,* 759–775.

White, J. W., & Koss, M. P. (1991). Adolescent sexual aggression within heterosexual relationships: Prevalence, characteristics and causes. In H. E. Barbarbee, W. L. Marshall, and D. R. Laws (Eds.), *The juvenile sexual offender* (pp. 182–202). New York: Guilford Press.

Yost, M. R., & Zurbriggen, E. L. (2006). Gender differences in the enactment of sociosexuality: An examination of implicit sexual motives, sexual fantasies, coercive sexual attitudes, and aggressive sexual behavior. *Journal of Sex Research, 43,* 163–173.

Zoucha-Jensen, J., & Coyne, A. (1993). The effects of resistance strategies on rape. *American Journal of Public Health, 83*(11), 1633–1634.

Zurbriggen, E. L. (2000). Social motives and cognitive power-sex associations: Predictors of aggressive sexual behavior. *Journal of Personality and Social Psychology, 78,* 559–581.

Chapter 17

Intimate Partner Violence: Perspectives on Research and Intervention

Maureen C. McHugh
Nicole Livingston
Irene H. Frieze

Feminist researchers in the United States and Great Britain in the 1970s and 1980s began to work with battered women and brought the problem of women being violently attacked by their husbands or boyfriends to the forefront of general awareness (Frieze, 2005b). Such work has had great impact on the public, as there is now widespread understanding of and much sympathy for the battered woman (Frieze, 2000). Comparisons of studies over the last 30 years show decreasing acceptance of men who beat or batter their female partners in the United States (e.g., Felson, 2002; Rothenberg, 2003; Simon, Anderson, Thompson, Crosby, Shelley, & Sacks, 2001; Vandello & Cohen, 2003). There is also a high awareness that couple violence does exist, as many individuals report personally knowing someone involved in such a relationship (Sorenson & Taylor, 2005).

Since the publication of our chapter "Research on Battered Women and Their Assailants" (McHugh, Frieze, & Browne, 1993) in the earlier edition of this volume, extensive changes have occurred in the research on intimate partner abuse and in our understanding of the phenomenon. Approaches to domestic violence have evolved from viewing the problem as being limited to women in severely violent marriages to recognizing the prevalence of serious levels of physical violence and psychological abuse in many types of intimate relationships. Within the research on partner violence, some topics, such as the prevalence of violence against women and the reactions of the victim, have continued to receive attention. Researchers not only have identified more types of victims but also have begun to examine patterns and types of conflict and abuse within intimate relationships, including mutual violence (McHugh & Frieze, 2006). In this review, we focus on the ways in which intimate partner violence has been conceptualized, researched, and treated.

The explosion of research on intimate violence makes it difficult to summarize the entirety of this literature in a single chapter. Here, we review this research, looking first at conceptions and measurement of violence. We examine the research on battered women and male batterers, but we also include recent research on other patterns of violence. We then examine where we are in our attempts to intervene with violent partners.

We argue for new conceptualizations of intimate partner conflict, including more complex conceptualizations of the role of gender in intimate partner violence, and contend that conceptualizations of intimate partner violence should include the sociocultural context of the conflict. We also argue for more careful selection of treatment options.

RESEARCH ON INTIMATE PARTNER VIOLENCE

Labels and Conceptualizations

Today, researchers do not agree on their conceptualization of partner violence; this is reflected in differences in terminology. Debates about definitions and labels are struggles about conceptualization and ideology (McHugh, Livingston, & Ford, 2005). For example, some researchers continue to use the terms *domestic violence*, *family violence*, and *spouse abuse*. These individuals generally view violence as gender symmetrical, that is, equally likely to be perpetrated by men or women (e.g., Straus & Gelles, 1986; Straus, 1999). Feminist researchers use terms such as *women battering* and contend that generic terms such as *domestic violence* and *spouse abuse* do not distinguish between battering and mutually combative relationships, ignore the nature and consequences of violence, and obscure the dimensions of gender and power that are fundamental to understanding the abuse of women (Breines & Gorden, 1983; Schechter, 1982). The term *woman battering* carries its own implications.

Use of the terms *battered wife*, *batterer*, and *assailant* results in an image of a severely abused woman who is beaten repeatedly by her very violent husband. Research conducted on women seeking shelter at battered women's shelters confirms the reality of this construction, at least for some women. However, as will be discussed, this is only one of several types or patterns of violence documented by the research on intimate partner violence. For example, serious ongoing violence has been reported for gay men and lesbians in committed relationships (Coleman, 1991; Renzetti, 1992, 1993). Violence in earlier stages of romantic relationships is termed *dating violence* and has been documented in both heterosexual and gay and lesbian relationships. Furthermore, research suggests that much of the violence that occurs in dating, marriages, and committed relationships is relatively low level and is often mutual or bilateral (e.g., Anderson, 2002; Archer, 2000; Frieze, 2005).

Until recently, researchers did not distinguish levels or patterns of violence. Both the terms *battering* and *domestic violence* imply or are specifically limited to physical acts of aggression. Other research argues for the importance and the impact of psychological, sexual, and emotional abuse (Jones, Davidson, Bogat, Levendosky, & von Eye, 2005; Chang, 1996; Tolman, 1992). McHugh and her colleagues (McHugh & Bartoszek, 2000; McHugh et al., 2005) argue that existing theoretical explanations are not adequate to explain the varied and extensive forms of intimate partner violence. Here we most frequently use the widely accepted term *intimate partner violence,* unless we are specifically referring to women who experience severe levels of violence from a partner; these women will be labeled as *battered women*.

As the research on battered women has matured, it has become more and more evident that, although the plight of the battered woman is very real, relationship violence and aggression is much more complex than originally envisioned, and severely battered women are only a part of relationship violence. First, it is not uncommon for couples to fight by hitting, pushing, or slapping each other. Importantly, violence, or physical aggression, is not only something that men do to women. Both women and men engage in this type of activity. However, much of this type of physical fighting, labeled "violence" by researchers, tends to be low-level violence that does not generally result in injury (Frieze, 2005a, 2005b). In order to understand relationship violence, we have to carefully consider what we mean by "violence."

Unilateral and Severe Violence: The Battered Woman

One of the patterns of partner violence first discussed in the literature is what is typically labeled *wife battering*. Wife battering has been constructed as a pattern of domination, intimidation, and coercive control (Dutton & Goodman, 2005; Pence & Paymar, 1993; Dasgupta, 2002). In the most typical pattern of this type of severe couple violence, a husband or male partner becomes extremely violent toward his wife or female partner, using physical violence as well as psychological abuse or belittling of her. In these relationships, high levels of violence become routine, with the woman living in constant fear that something she does will initiate another round of such violence.

Psychological abuse often precedes physical violence (Frieze, 2005). Continuing criticism, correcting, and humiliation undermine the woman's confidence. Increasingly she sees herself as someone who is not competent or capable enough to live independently. She is encouraged to view the world as hostile and to see others as not interested in her. Over time, the female victim develops low self-esteem after hearing so often that she deserves the physical abuse. Often, the batterer is violent to his children as well, meaning that physical child abuse is also present. It is not unusual for the batterer to abuse alcohol or drugs. These related issues may create additional complexities, making it difficult to clearly know how much the violence itself is contributing to the reactions found in battered women (Frieze, 2005).

Research on women who have experienced serious physical violence has resulted in the identification of a pattern of battering (Frieze, 2005; Pagelow, 1997; Walker, 1984). Within this type of partner violence, the physically abusive partner often physically and socially isolates his victim, perhaps even prior to the use of any physical violence. Women are often discouraged by the batterer from daily calls home or other interactions with immediate family or friends. They report that their partner criticized their friends and limited their social interactions. Sometimes the partner provided transportation to and from classes or work, thus limiting the possibilities for socializing afterward.

These relationships may develop gradually. Browne (1987) and Walker (1984) note that abused women often report that their partners were extremely attentive and affectionate early in the relationship. They showed great interest in the woman's whereabouts, a desire to be with them all the time, and intense expressions of affection and jealousy, and they wanted an early commitment to a long-term relationship. Over time, these behaviors that were initially seen as evidence of love became intrusive, controlling, and triggers to assault. The abuser's concern for the wife's whereabouts becomes a form of surveillance, and the batterers are often described as evidencing severe and delusional jealousy (Frieze, 2005; Hotaling & Sugarman, 1986).

Within this type of relationship, violence often escalates in severity and frequency over time (Pagelow, 1981, 1997). Intimate violence may end in death, and approximately 1,000 women a year are killed by partners (U.S. Department of Justice, 2006). In addition to physical injury, research indicates that battering of women by men is associated with psychosocial and mental health problems in women (e.g., Browne, 1993; Frieze, 2005; Goodman, Koss, & Russo, 1993; Janoff-Bulman & Frieze, 1983). Men's violence against women is related to depression, anxiety, and hyperreactive responses in women (Goodman et al., 1993). Women in violent relationships experience decreases in marital satisfaction (Lawrence & Bradbury, 2001) and increases in personal levels of distress (Testa & Leonard, 2001).

Other Forms of Couple Violence

The extremely violent family interactions described above are not the only type of couple violence, nor even the most common form of physical aggression in couples. Some research suggests that many family members engage in low-level, mild violence with each other. Researchers have begun to examine these less extreme forms of physical aggression recently in married couples and cohabitating same-sex and heterosexual couples (Frieze, 2000).

A meta-analysis by Archer (2000) of marital and dating violence studies found that women actually engage in more acts of physical aggression than men. Most of these studies measured partner violence with a scale called the Conflict Tactics Scale (CTS). Limitations of this scale are discussed later in this chapter. Data such as that analyzed by Archer are difficult to relate to the work on battered women, especially since there is such clear evidence of battered women being abused by partners. But further examination of these studies indicated that much of the "violence" found in many couples consists of hitting, slapping, shoving, or other relatively minor acts of physical aggression. As Archer noted, the majority of those who do suffer injury from violent behavior of a romantic partner are women. At the same time, it is clear that there are some women who can and do engage in highly violent acts toward their partners.

Another form of partner aggression is psychological abuse. This can include attempts to dominate the partner, indifference toward the partner, monitoring of the partner's behavior, attempts to undermine the partner, and isolation of the partner (Jones et al., 2005). These behaviors tend to occur together and can be found in severely violent relationships as well as less physically violent partnerships. Reactions to these nonviolent forms of aggression can be just as severe as toward acts of physical aggression (Frieze, 2005; Jones et al., 2005).

Women's Use of Violence

As reported by Archer (2000) and others, recent evidence suggests that women's participation in and even initiation of violence is higher than many researchers initially believed. The empirical data reported for studies using the CTS or other similar methods indicate that both sexes admit to using violence against their intimate partners (Frieze, 2005a; McHugh, 2005). Straus and his colleagues (e.g., Straus, Gelles, & Steinmetz, 1980) presented some of the first indications that not all relationship violence was perpetrated by men on women and that in fact some women were violent toward their husbands. Using the CTS in a nationally representative sample, Straus and colleagues (Straus & Gelles, 1986; Straus, Gelles, & Steinmetz, 1980) report that women initiate both minor and severe forms of physical violence with the same frequency as men do.

Strauss (1979) interprets their findings as indicating gender symmetry, arguing that both sexes engage in equal amounts of violence in relationships. Others (Browne, 1987; Browne & Dutton, 1990; Dobash, Dobash, Cavanagh, & Lewis, 1998) have challenged this conclusion. The interpretation that men and women are equally combative ignores the physical and economic power disparities between men and women and fails to consider injury, motive, or consequences of the aggressive acts (Johnson, 1995). In a study of women arrested for domestic violence, Hamberger (1997) found that about two-thirds of the arrested women said they were battered and had used violence to protect themselves or to retaliate. Although many of the women acknowledged initiating violence, they generally did so in the context of a relationship in which the male partner initiated violence more often and was likely to have initiated the overall pattern of violence. However, some studies have found that some women were being arrested for partner violence that was not a response to prior violence from their partners (e.g., Buzawa & Austin, 1993).

Over time, there has been more and more research and clinical evidence that women are sometimes violent toward their intimate partners. For example, in a recent analysis of a national representative sample, Anderson (2002) found that 10 percent of all couples reported some type of violence toward each other in the previous year. Looking at the patterns of violence in more detail, it was noted that in 7 percent of the couples, both were violent; for 2 percent, only the woman was violent; and for 1 percent, only the man was violent. This study shows the same general pattern of more women reporting engaging in violent acts toward their partner than men seen in results reported by Straus and his colleagues (1980). Other studies of couples living together show similar patterns (see a meta-analysis by Archer, 2000).

Williams & Frieze (2005) found similar data, again using a nationally representative sample of 3,505 men and women in stable couple relationships. Overall, 18 percent of the sample reported some violence in their relationship. To address questions raised about whether the violence was mutual and who was the more violent, the man or the women, the violence group was divided into mutual and one-sided violence relationships. About 4 percent of the sample reported that both they and their partner used severe violence, and 5 percent reported mutual low-level violence. More men than women reported being the targets of one-sided violence, and more women than men reported being the violent one in the couple. Recently, other researchers have similarly documented multiple patterns of mutual violence in heterosexual couples (Milan, Lewis, Ethier, Kershaw, & Ickovics, 2005; Weston, Temple, & Marshall, 2005). These data indicating female violence toward intimate partners cannot and should not be ignored (see McHugh, 2005). The question is how these data should be interpreted.

Feminists contend that gender and unequal distribution of power between men and women are important explanatory factors in intimate violence (e.g., Dobash & Dobash, 1979). Others have consistently argued that intimate violence is a human issue and that it is not surprising that women are as likely as men, or even more prone than men, to use physical aggression in intimate relations (McNeely & Mann, 1990). Bograd (1990) argues that the importance of gender in understanding violence is not contingent on data establishing men as the (only) batterers.

Acknowledging that women are (increasingly) violent has profound implications for both individuals and social movements (Hamberger, 1997). Even while rejecting the position of gender symmetry—the conclusion that women's violence is equivalent to men's—we may need to rethink our conceptions of gender issues in partner violence. Three recent special issues of professional psychological journals have focused on the questions raised by research documenting women's use of violence in intimate relations and the gender issues raised by this research (Frieze & McHugh, 2005; McHugh & Frieze, 2006; *Violence & Victims* special issue).

Measuring Intimate Violence

While many validated and standardized scales to measure partner mistreatment have been published (Gondolf, 1998), most of the research has relied on the use of the Conflict Tactics Scale designed by Straus (1979) and used extensively by Straus, Gelles, and their colleagues (e.g., Straus, 1979; Straus & Gelles, 1986; Straus, Gelles, & Steinmetz, 1980). Continued use of this scale allows for comparability of results but also perpetuates inadequacies in the literature. The scale asks respondents about a list of specific things they and their partner did during disagreements. Often the respondent also indicates what he or she did during the conflict or disagreement. Specific behaviors listed range from trying to discuss the issue calmly; to arguing heatedly, but short of yelling; to various violent actions such as throwing something at, pushing, grabbing, shoving, or hitting the partner. Individuals are generally given a score depending on how many of the violent actions or threats of violent actions they have carried out. In most cases, couples are classified as "violent" if they have *ever* done *any* of the violent behaviors. This means that slapping or pushing someone once results in the label *violent* being applied to this person and to the relationship. Researchers may also count up the number of violent incidents to get an overall measure of the level of violence.

By reporting any of the actions labeled as violent on the CTS, a respondent is typically labeled as an *abuser* or a *batterer* by the researcher, and the targets of the acts are classified as *victims* or as *battered*. Such labels may *not* reflect how the person sees him- or herself, however. This discrepancy between the researcher's conception of violence and the perspective of the research participants is demonstrated in a study of female employees at a large southeastern university. Women in this study were asked if they had experienced any of a list of violent actions (a procedure similar to the CTS). Then, for each of the events they experienced, they were asked if this was an instance of "physical abuse" and if they thought of themselves as a "victim of violence." They were also asked if they thought of themselves as a "battered woman." More than a third of the women did not accept any of these three types of labels for the acts they had experienced. Others accepted one or more of the labels, but not all of them (Hamby & Gray-Little, 2000).

Use of the CTS has led to confusion over the mutuality of domestic violence. The CTS does not distinguish between use of violence and initiation of violence. Because of this, women defending themselves against hostile or even deadly attacks would be classified as engaging in mutual domestic violence, based on CTS scores.

The use of the Conflict Tactics Scale has been criticized by many researchers (see Frieze, 2005a, or McHugh, 2005, for a fuller discussion of these issues). The scale does not differentiate initiated violence from acts of self-defense nor does it assess the seriousness of the injuries inflicted. The CTS does not allow for consideration of the victims' ability to repel or restrain offenders or to retaliate against them. The focus of the measure is on violent behaviors, but it does not address the meanings of those actions or the effects of these behaviors (Brush, 1990). For example, a large, strong man might slap a woman and injure her severely, whereas a small woman might slap a larger man and he hardly notices it, with no real injury at all. Using the CTS, these two actions would count equally as violence. Because of this criticism, Straus has revised his measure, calling it the CTS2 (Straus, Hamby, Boney-McCoy, & Sugarman, 1996). The CTS2 includes questions about violent actions, like the original CTS, but adds questions about how serious ones injuries are. Both the CTS and the CTS2 assume that couple violence is associated with disagreement and conflict.

Another problem inherent to the CTS is that it includes only a small number of possible violent behaviors (Marshall, 1994). The severe violence items included on the CTS are kicking, biting, hitting with a fist, hitting with an object, beating someone up, and using a knife or gun. Three items assess "minor" violence: throwing something; pushing, grabbing, or shoving; and slapping. However, there are many additional ways in which women have reported being hurt by their partners. For example, the Tolman (1989) Maltreatment of Women Scale has more than 50 items. To address this limitation in the CTS, many researchers create new items when they use it.

Partly as a result of reliance on the CTS, little research has been conducted on the effects of psychological and sexual abuse within intimate relationships. Psychological abuse has primarily been studied as an aspect of a physically abusive relationship (e.g., Tolman, 1989; Walker, 1979). There is increasingly an understanding of both the prevalence and the seriousness of psychological abuse (Chang, 1996; Tolman, 1992). More than half of women in one study reported emotional abuse as the reason for their divorce (Cleek & Pearson, 1985), and 27 percent of college women characterized at least one of their dating relationships as involving some type of physical aggression (Raymond & Brushi, 1989).

Alternative measures to the CTS have been developed (Feindler, Rathus, & Silver, 2003; Frieze, 2005b). For example, the Index of Spouse Abuse (ISA) developed by Hudson and McIntosh (1981) is recommended by Gondolf (1998). The 30 items of the ISA address psychological as well as physical abuse. This scale measures only the respondents' experience of violence by her partner. Instruments like the ISA may be administered as a follow-up to screening questions about violence. However, these scales are less likely to be used. Reliance on a single scale, the CTS, has limited our understanding of intimate partner violence (McHugh et al., 2005).

There are some limitations of all of these measures. In an effort to study those who are targets of violence, researchers generally rely on the self-reports of victims and perpetrators (White & Kowalski, 1991). This is true of the CTS as well as of most other measures. Such reports may be suspect, as they are undoubtedly affected by social desirability. The validity of self-reports is also dependent on the exactness of the participant's memory. We are presented with these difficulties any time we rely on self-reports of behavior to know what people are actually doing. But, the limitations of self-reports are a special problem in studying violence and aggression (Yllo & Bograd, 1986).

Another issue is that people reporting on past incidences of physical aggression may not report accurately. Some forms of violence may not be recognized as something memorable and are simply forgotten. In various settings and circumstances, pushing and hitting are not perceived as violence and may be quickly forgotten. Such unrecognized acts of physical aggression probably occur for much low-level violence among acquaintances and partners—it is not extreme, and no one is injured. Additionally, some researchers have investigated acts of hitting, pushing, and wrestling that are experienced as playful aggression and are not perceived by participants as acts of violence (Ryan and Mohr, 2005). There is no reason we would tend to remember this happening, and we would never consider reporting this on a crime victimization survey or to the police or to researchers asking about "violence" directly. However, some of these acts may be recorded as violence using the CTS.

Is hitting always violence, regardless of the experience and meaning it has for the participants? On the other hand, women whose clothes have been trashed may see this as more violent than a slap, and yet this act is not counted as violence in research because it is not recorded by the scales used to measure partner violence. How many times did he slap you? This may not be the most important question we need to ask about intimate conflict. McHugh, Livingston, and Ford (2005) argue that different conceptualizations of violence and abuse can contribute to a pluralistic, complex, and multilayered conception of intimate partner abuse. Reliance on a single measure that oversimplifies, reduces, or reifies our construction of violence would be viewed as problematic.

There may also be differences in the ways men recall and report their own and partner's violence and how women do (White & Kowalski, 1991). Intimate partner violence may be less salient to men than to women (Graham & Wells, 2001). In a random sample of 1,753 adults in Ontario, Canada, people were asked if they had ever been personally involved in a situation with another adult where someone was "pushing, grabbing, hitting, or being physically aggressive in any other way" in the last 12 months (Graham & Wells, 2001). Most people said no. The 9 percent who answered affirmatively were then asked more about the incident. Those who experienced such an event were more often males and more likely to be younger. It was estimated that men were 25 times more likely than women to have had these experiences.

Graham and Wells (2001) further reported that the types of aggressive experiences reported by women differed for those most reported by men. For women, the aggression more often involved someone who they considered an intimate partner and the aggression occurred in the home. It was often associated with jealousy. The aggression was upsetting for these women. For men, the acts of aggression most easily recalled often involved a male stranger and occurred in a bar or other public location. Men tended not to be upset by these incidents. Graham and Wells suggest that men may not take intimate partner violence as seriously as women and may be less likely to remember it. These findings are quite consistent with other data indicating that men are generally less likely to show strong negative psychological or emotional reactions to being assaulted, while women are more likely to have negative reactions to being assaulted (Acierno, Kilpatrick, & Resnick, 1999).

Considering Context and Respondents

One approach to understanding partner violence is the construction of theoretically or empirically based patterns to classify violent couple relationships (e.g., Frieze, 2005a; Johnson, 1995; Johnson & Leone, 2005; Williams & Frieze, 2005; Weston et al., 2005). Men and women may perform different patterns of violence, or they may experience violence victimization differently even when the violent actions are the same.

For example, Johnson and Leone (2005) posit a typology of situational couple violence and intimate terrorism to explain conflicting data on intimate abuse. The more gender-balanced violence found in community samples may fit into the pattern of situational couple violence that is typically mild in nature. The more severe, and commonly male-perpetrated, violence epitomized by the "battered woman" and evidenced in clinical samples may fit the intimate terrorism pattern. Johnson's patterns emphasize the importance of distinguishing between overlapping but divergent phenomena. Similarly, using community samples, Williams and Frieze (2005) and Weston and her colleagues (2005) have identified several patterns or types of couple violence based on frequency and severity of the violence.

As this work indicates, who we study as victims or perpetrators is a critical factor in our construction of interpersonal violence. Studying wives as victims leads to the construction of wife abuse (the idea that helpless women are victimized by abusive male partners), whereas studying lesbian partners engaged in mutual violence leads to alternative conceptualizations. Others (Hamby, 2005; Johnson, 1995; Saunders, 2000) have argued that sample differences between family conflict and violent crime studies, and between shelter and clinical samples and community samples, can at least partly explain the inconsistencies between finding unilateral "battering" versus retaliatory or mutual abuse (e.g., Johnson & Ferraro, 2000; Swan & Snow, 2003). The identification and documentation of varied types and patterns of intimate partner violence (e.g., Johnson & Leone, 2005; Weston et al., 2005; Williams & Frieze, 2005) have been suggested as a way to reconcile inconsistencies in the findings. Who we study turns out to determine our conceptualization of intimate violence. Thus, we need to carefully consider which populations of people are neglected.

The patterns of violence may be affected not only by the composition of the research sample but also by the larger sociohistorical context of the research. The respondents inhabit a unique and idiosyncratic time and place. Young people differ from older individuals not only by age but also in the sociohistorical context in which they were socialized. Age or cohort effects might account for some of the differences in findings. Female-initiated and mutual violence may be more common among younger women. One interpretation is that postfeminist young women see violence as a gender-neutral behavior. Much of the existing research on relationship violence overrepresents young adults, and the young men and women in the United States today were raised in an era of television viewing and video games that were not a part of the childhoods of people over 50. Research has documented that exposure to media violence impacts the acceptability and use of violence (e.g.,

Frieze, 2005a; Vega & Malamuth, 2007), and yet this understanding is rarely raised as a factor in the literature on relationship violence.

Moving toward New Conceptualizations of Intimate Partner Violence

Recent reviews (McHugh, 2005; Brush, 2005) suggest that despite several decades of research on intimate partner violence, we have not made substantive progress in developing widely accepted theories or models that explain men and women's use of violence in relationships. Sorenson & Taylor (2005) conclude that the question of "assailant gender in heterosexual intimate partner violence goes beyond the epidemiological questions of who does what, with what frequency, and with what outcomes?" (p. 95). The continuation or escalation of violence is evidence of our inability to prevent or intervene in couples' violence and indirectly speaks to our ability to understand intimate violence.

Gender, as a category assigned to individuals, colors general perceptions of behavior and shapes the ways we view ourselves. Gender shapes the meaning of violent acts; acts of physical aggression are viewed differently depending on the actor and target (Sorenson and Taylor, 2005; Marshal, 1992a). Violence, like other behaviors, occurs in a cultural context, and in our culture, men are accorded more resources, privileges, and power than women. Feminist theorists continue to view violence as shaped by gender-roles and status, arguing that gender-related values, beliefs, norms, and social institutions support intimate partner violence against women (e.g., Koss, Bailey, Yuan, Herrera, & Lichter, 2003; Koss, Goodman, Browne, Fitzgerald, Keita, & Russo, 1994; Russo, 2006).

A full understanding of gender-based violence requires going beyond a focus on sex differences in rates of specific acts; a gendered perspective involves the examination of how gender shapes the predictors, dynamics, and outcomes of violence for both women and men (Russo & Pirlott, 2006; McHugh et al., 2005).

Anderson (2005), Brush (2005), and McHugh and colleagues (2005) contend that explanatory models of intimate violence are restricted by the inadequacy of our understanding of gender. Anderson (2005) views the confusion about how partner assaults are gendered as a reflection of a larger theoretical confusion about what it is that we mean by gender (West & Zimmerman, 1987). She contends that even as theories of gender have changed dramatically in the past three decades, these changes have not been adopted in substantive areas within the social sciences (Alway, 1995; Ferree, Lorber, & Hess, 1999; Stacey & Thorne, 1985).

Traditionally, gender has been conceived as an individual trait. Individualist approaches to the study of gender propose that individual persons are gendered beings (Risman, 1998). Anderson (2005) points out that individualist theories presuppose that a propensity to use aggression and violence is an innate or learned characteristic of masculine persons. She explains why this individualistic approach has led to the conclusion that gender is not a particularly important predictor of intimate partner violence. However, a growing number of psychologists have challenged the gender paradigm that assumes gender is dichotomous or essential (McHugh & Cosgrove, 2004).

Anderson (2005) explains that the "sex differences" approach to gender fails to consider the complex ways in which gender operates in social interactions between people. For example, gender can be confirmed or constructed through the use of violence. Violence is one means by which men can perform masculinity (Anderson & Umberson, 2001). Individuals may be more likely to use violence against their partners as a result of gender antagonism or hostility. Men's and women's violence is perceived and evaluated differently; this has been empirically documented by the work of Sorenson and Taylor (2005) measuring the social acceptability of interpersonal violence committed by men and women. Across several studies, we see that men view women's acts of aggression directed toward them as not violent, and women who admit to committing acts of aggression do not report using violence. Similarly, Marshall (1992a, 1992b) has demonstrated that the severity of specific physical acts is rated differently depending on whether or not the perpetrator of the act is male or female.

Williams and Frieze (2005) reiterate that violence which appears to be equivalent in terms of acts may be subjectively different and may have different effects for men and women. Others (e.g., Kimmel, 2002) have similarly posited that even if men and women perform behaviors at the same frequency (as reported via objective questions), women experience more negative outcomes (e.g., lower relationship satisfaction) following partner violence than do men. In a recent study of victimization and perpetration, both Anderson (2002) and Williams and Frieze (2005) found that when both women and their partners displayed violent behaviors, women experienced more psychological problems following their victimization than the men who were victimized. However, Williams and Frieze also noted that both women and men show negative effects of violence. Regardless of the seemingly symmetrical nature of men's and women's violence, violence may in fact be gendered in the effects of violence on men and women. An arresting and consistent finding is that victimization is associated with significantly more negative psychosocial outcomes for women than men.

Anderson (2005) calls for researchers and theorists to develop more complex constructions of gender as one path to understanding violence in interpersonal relationships. Preventing intimate partner violence may depend on the development of theories that take into account the complex multifaceted aspects of gender.

Toward a Postmodern Approach

Rather than continuing to argue over whether interpersonal violence is best understood as battering of women partners by men or as men and/or women engaged in mutual combat, we can move toward an understanding of interpersonal violence that includes all the available evidence. Collectively, we can try to develop a more complex and complete picture. Some researchers have moved in this direction by positing different patterns of intimate violence (e.g., Johnson & Leone, 2005; Weston et al., 2005; Williams & Frieze, 2005). Another approach is to more carefully consider the characteristics of the violence. Furgusson and colleagues suggest that when examining intimate partner violence, certain important dimensions should be considered. These include the level of overall violence, the frequency of the violence, and the level of injury.

McHugh, Livingston, and Ford (2005) argue for use of a feminist and postmodern framework for understanding the complexities of the research findings on intimate partner abuse. Both the feminist and postmodern perspectives share appreciation for the fact that context matters, and for the fact that decontextualizing the individual frequently supports the status quo and potentially defends oppressive conditions (Cosgrove & McHugh, 2002). Consistent with both a feminist and a social constructionist perspective, McHugh and colleagues (2006) call for more careful consideration of the way we construct and research concepts such as violence, abuse, and aggression and the way we conceptualize gender.

The methods we employ, and the samples we recruit, to study violence are influenced by our starting ideological perspectives and the way we construct violence and gender. What we think we are studying and how we choose to study it subsequently influence our interpretations and explanations of violence. Rather than a positivist approach that gives researchers a privileged status, in which they are implicitly "authorized," by their status as scientists or their use of scientific methods, to uncover truths about the violence in participants' lives (Cosgrove, 2004), we argue against the conceptualization of intimate violence as a single truth, or as a debate between polarized positions. As postmodernists, we reject either/or dichotomies as simplistic and not helpful. Accepting either the view that intimate violence is unilateral—that is, men beating women—or the conclusion that interpersonal violence is gender symmetric—that is, equally and reciprocally utilized by men and women—limits our conceptual framework and results in tunnel vision. Rather, interpersonal violence is conceptualized as a complex, multifaceted, and dynamic aspect of human interaction that occurs in multiple forms and patterns. The experience and meaning of violence is viewed as connected to both the relationship and the larger context in which the violence occurs.

INTERVENTION

Psychological interventions for relationship violence are often complex and difficult, and when ineffective, the results can be dire and even lethal. Therefore, it is imperative that the clinician addressing this issue possess both the breadth of knowledge and the finely calibrated expertise necessary to treat such a multidimentional and serious problem. This section seeks to contribute to the study of intimate violence with a discussion of interventions, an evaluation of the utility of existing interventions, and suggestions for improvement. Also, the recent acknowledgment that females also perpetrate violence in their romantic relationships is a call for interpersonal violence researchers to develop interventions aimed specifically at female perpetrators. The following offers some preliminary suggestions in an effort to move in this direction.

Treating the Victim

"*Why does she stay?*" is the most often-asked question about woman abuse in class discussions, in public forums, and in the research literature. This question reveals a basic assumption about woman battering—that if the woman would leave, she wouldn't get beaten. This is indicative of one primary form of intervention, a strategy that is focused on the victim; the solution is to physically and psychologically relocate the woman. We would argue that this perspective is both victim-blaming and counterproductive. The batterer may continue to stalk or terrorize her after leaving, or he may go on to batter someone else (Frieze, 2005a).

Early research focused on the logistical reasons why some women did not leave an abusive husband. For example, the woman may have stayed due to a lack of money, transportation, or a safe place to go (Bowker, 1983; Browne & Williams, 1989). Others have suggested that social factors such as loss of social status, disapproval of family and friends, and feelings of failure or guilt for abandoning the relationship limit her options for leaving (Dobash & Dobash, 1979; Walker, 1979). Abused women's perceptions of alternatives may be influenced by societal expectations related to gender and role relationships that encourage women to be self-sacrificing and adaptive and to care for and protect those close to them regardless of the cost (Browne, 1987; Walker & Browne, 1985). Researchers have also emphasized psychological factors underlying women's decision not to leave. Walker's (1979) work suggested that battered women have learned helplessness. Chandler's (1986) phenomenological analysis of battered women's experiences suggests that overriding fear and a loss of a sense of self characterize the severely battered woman. Other research perspectives emphasize the emotional bonds that battered women form with their abusers (Browne, 1987; Dutton & Painter, 1981; Walker, 1983).

Some researchers have challenged this view of battered women as helpless and virtually imprisoned by her batterer. These critiques emphasize the help-seeking, coping mechanisms, and survival skills of battered women. For example, Gondolf and Fisher (1988) critique the learned helplessness model of wife abuse and examine the ways in which battered women in their Texas sample acted assertively and logically in response to the abuse. The women in their sample, like the women studied by Bowker (1983), persistently sought help from a wide range of sources. The more intensified and prolonged the abuse, the greater the variety and the extent of their help-seeking. These studies suggest that individuals and agencies have failed to adequately respond to battered women's requests for help. Researchers working from this perspective argue that many women return to or remain with their abusers because they lack access to community resources (Gondolf, 1988; Sullivan, Basta, Tan, & Davidson, 1992).

Other researchers point to concerns about violent reactions. Some battered women fear that their violent husbands will retaliate against them and their children if they try to leave (e.g., Ridington, 1978). Threats of kidnapping and custody battles are common tactics used by abusive partners to keep women in violent relationships. This fear of violent retaliation is a realistic one. Women who have left an abusive partner have been followed and harassed for months or even years, and some have even been killed (Browne, 1987; Mechanic, 2002). Stahly (1996) reports National Crime Survey data from the Department of Justice documenting that 70 percent of domestic violence crime doesn't occur until *after* the relationship has ended. Walker reports that women are at increased risk for severe violence and homicide after leaving the batterer. Stalking of the woman by the abuser is also quite common during breakup (Tjaden & Thoennes, 2000).

Shelters as Solutions

As a result of research documenting the prevalence and seriousness of intimate partner violence against women, a national network of shelters for battered women has been established. Over the years, these agencies have sheltered millions of women from violence. Yet, the shelters cannot accommodate all battered women and may have inadvertently limited our attempts to intervene in intimate partner violence. It has been argued that shelters have led researchers to focus on women as victims, while at the same time holding women responsible for solving intimate partner violence (e.g., Krenek, 1998). Krenek (1998) points out that now police and prosecutors may expect the battered woman to go to the shelter and to leave the abuser and the domicile. She suggests that in some localities police punish women who do not leave by arresting them. Krenek (1998) and Stahly (1996) both ask the same question: *Why should a woman and her children have to leave home to feel safe?*

Treating the Male Batterer

It is apparent that treating the female victim of severe partner violence in isolation is an inadequate and often problematic approach. This strategy may implicitly indict the victim as responsible for the violence or place the onus of executing a solution on her. Thus, some researchers and clinicians have focused on treating the perpetrator of partner violence rather than the victim (see Babcock, Green, & Robie, 2004, for a review of batterers' treatment programs). Whereas these approaches for treating the batterer possess the allure of placing less blame on the victim, they are far from ideal and plagued with their own inherent problems. Traditionally, the clinician treating the victim envisions a male client (although as previously discussed, this assumption may not always be accurate), and so the exploration of this topic begins with treating the male who uses intimate partner violence.

Babcock and her colleagues (2004) suggest that ideally the first step in treating the male who uses intimate partner violence in his relationships is to get to know the client. Understanding who the client is guides successful implementation of the intervention strategy and thus is a vital initial step. To this aim, researchers and clinicians have attempted to elucidate the profile of the male who requires such treatment.

Who are these men that batter their intimate female partners? One of the most consistent findings with regards to batterers is that they are likely to have a history of violence in their family of origin (e.g., Frieze, 2005a; Hotaling & Sugarman, 1986). Men who have witnessed parental violence and men who have been abused as children or adolescents are more likely to become batterers than those who have not (e.g., Caesar, 1988; Hastings & Hamberger, 1988; Sugarman & Hotaling, 1989). Witnessing parental violence has been found to be more predictive than experiencing abuse as a child (Tolman & Bennett, 1990). As many as three-quarters of men seeking counseling for battering witnessed abuse between their parents, whereas, in another study, half were abused as children (Fitch & Papantonio, 1983).

Although researchers have been unable to identify a unitary batterer personality profile (Hamberger & Hastings, 1988), higher rates of certain psychiatric conditions have been found among batterers (Rosenbaum, Geffner, & Benjamin, 1997). Personality disorders and characteristics such as antisocial, borderline, and narcissistic occur at higher rates among batterers (Hamberger & Hastings, 1991; Hart, Dutton, & Newlove, 1993; Hastings & Hamberger, 1988).

Generally, men who batter are more likely than nonviolent partners to be violent or aggressive in other ways and with other people. They are more likely to have a criminal history (e.g., Roberts, 1987) and to have used violence outside of the home (e.g., Shields, McCall, & Hanneke, 1988). White and Straus (1981) report that batterers are twice as likely as nonviolent husbands to have an arrest record for a serious crime, and Gayford (1975) reports that 50 percent of his sample of male batterers had spent time in prison. Somewhere between one-third (Flynn, 1977) and 46 percent of batterers (Fagen, Stewart, & Hansen, 1983) have been arrested for other violence. Batterers have consistently higher rates of committing child abuse than men who are not violent with their partners (Hotaling & Sugarman, 1986). Thus, the violence and aggression used by at least some batterers is not confined to their partner.

However, the clearest conclusion one can draw from the available literature is that batterers are a heterogeneous group. It makes sense that not all batterers are alike. There may be various types of batterers, with different etiological and abuse patterns, and with implications for diverse interventions (Dutton, 1988; Gondolf, 1988). Further, the results of a particular study may depend on how the sample was recruited. For instance, batterers who have been remanded by the courts to batterer groups may differ significantly from men in a community survey who admit to use of violence toward their partner. This inherent heterogeneity adds another kink to the puzzle of how to effectively treat the perpetrator of intimate partner violence.

Due to a shift in the understanding of interpersonal violence, including increased knowledge of the heterogeneity of male batterers and the growing acknowledgment of female perpetration, there is an amplified need to address this heterogeneity when treating male perpetrators. Traditionally, interventions for male batterers have included unstandardized combinations of punishment and treatment that are typically implemented in group settings (e.g., Babcock et al., 2004). Babcock and colleagues (2004) discuss the lack of empirical support for the efficacy of intimate violence treatment at reducing recidivism. Given the lack of treatment effectiveness for male perpetrators, it is vital to assess, as violence researchers and clinicians, where we stand currently and, more importantly, where we are heading.

Treating the Male Who Uses Interpersonal Violence

The heterogeneity of male batterers reflected in the various typologies of perpetrators is echoed in the different treatment models of intimate partner violence. However, many components of treatment are shared across approaches. The vast majority (90%) of interventions utilize a group format, whereas individual and couples' therapy is generally considered to be inappropriate (Babcock et al., 2004). The main focus of all treatment modalities is to eliminate violent, controlling, and coercive behavior by the batterer (Geffner & Rosenbaum, 1990). This is addressed through helping the batterer to accept responsibility for and understand the consequences of his violence. Other similar components of these programs include anger management skills, improving self-esteem, fostering empathy within the batterer, and teaching adaptive, nonviolent conflict resolution and aggression control. Challenging patriarchal beliefs of family roles, conveying the inadequacy of provocation as a justification for violence, and educating the batterer about the issue of control in partner violence are additional emphases of treatment programs (e.g., Geffner & Rosenbaum, 1990).

Another prominent aspect of intervention is psychoeducation. One such approach is the Duluth Domestic Abuse Intervention Program, which utilizes a feminist model (Pence & Paymar, 1993). This treatment roots domestic violence in patriarchal ideology and indicts the societal sanctioning of men's use of power and control over women. Thus, men's use of violence is viewed not as a loss of control, but rather an assertion of it. Men are viewed as using violence in order to gain control of their partners. A major aim of the Duluth model is accountability, aiding males in becoming aware of the deleterious effects of their violence (Pence & Paymar, 1993). Consciousness-raising exercises are employed to help men switch from using behaviors that involve power and control to using behaviors that incorporate equality (Babcock, Miller, & Siard, 2003). Throughout the course of treatment, these goals are achieved by stressing eight themes: nonviolence, nonthreatening behavior, respect, trust and support, honesty and accountability, sexual respect, partnership, and negotiation and fairness (Pence & Paymar, 1993).

There are many other treatment models that build on similar ideas. Cognitive-behavioral therapy is often employed in the treatment of intimate partner violence (e.g., Murphy & Eckhardt, 2005). Babcock and her colleagues (2004) suggest that in this model the emphasis is on all behavior as learned. Thus, violence is believed to be reinforced through decreasing bodily tension, achieving compliance from the victim, temporarily ending aversive situations, and giving the batterer a sense of power and control. This approach focuses on the positive and negative consequences of violence and then imparts skills such as communication, assertiveness, anger management, identification of alternatives, and social skills (Babcock et al., 2004)

As previously mentioned, treatment for batterers typically includes a combination of punishment and rehabilitation (Babcock et al., 2004). As a result, men who attend treatment rarely do so voluntarily. This affects men's motivation to change and is reflected in the attrition difficulties experienced by nearly all treatment programs (Geffner & Rosenbaum, 1990). Most men who commence treatment minimize or deny the extent of abuse and its consequences, offer justifications and excuses, and present with high levels of anger, suspiciousness, and personality disturbances (Geffner & Rosenbaum, 1990). They may also blame others or the criminal justice system for the incident that led to their being in treatment and have little motivation to remain in treatment (Eckhardt, Babcock, & Homack, 2004). Additionally, if the men are court-ordered to participate in treatment, they may have ulterior motivates for completing treatment and may not truly be invested in changing their behavior (Geffner & Rosenbaum, 1990). All of these factors pose additional barriers to developing and implementing efficacious treatment programs for partner-assaultive individuals.

A recent meta-analysis on treatment efficacy has shown that effect sizes for interventions for interpersonal violence are very small (Babcock et al., 2004). When the Duluth psychoeducation intervention, cognitive behavioral therapy, and other treatments were compared, meta-analytic review indicated no significant differences in average effect sizes between the different treatment models. The largest effect sizes were observed with a 16-week group that included retention techniques (cognitive behavioral therapy or supportive therapy groups, plus motivational interviewing techniques) and a 12-week relationship-enhancement skills training group. The researchers hypothesized that the small effect sizes were the result of clients' noninvestment and attrition. The largest effect sizes were observed when the treatment included components of relationship enhancement, interpersonal skills, empathy, communication, and identification and management of emotions. Babcock and her colleagues (2004) surmised that the higher success rates observed with these types of treatments might be a reflection of their focus on emotion rather than cognitions.

Alternative treatments have emerged from the transtheoretical model of behavior change (Prochaska, DiClemente, & Norcross, 1992) and the motivational interviewing techniques of Miller and Rollnick (1991). The transtheoretical model proposes that not all individuals come to therapy ready to change or with an awareness of their problem (Prochaska et al., 1992), and so it incorporates this truism into the intervention strategy. An individual's awareness of a problem and motivation to change ranges from precontemplation (complete lack of awareness regarding the problem and absence of desire to change) to contemplation (full awareness of the problem and readiness to change) to action (behavior directed toward change). According to this model, specific techniques to instigate change need to be tailored to the individual's stage of change (Prochaska et al., 1992). This approach offers promise for intimate partner violence as it acknowledges that some individuals may not desire change, which is commonly the case among clients who are court-ordered to treatment, and it takes active steps to address this issue. Researchers found that this approach appealed to the group facilitators of treatment groups for partner-assaultive men and also appeared to resonate with the men themselves (Eckhardt et al., 2004).

Also inherent to the treatment of intimate partner violence is the issue of attrition. Motivational interviewing techniques, which acknowledge the ubiquity of ambivalence, work to resolve ambivalence by increasing the client's intrinsic motivation to change, and thus offer a buffer against attrition (Miller & Rollnick, 1991). Indeed some researchers have shown that adding motivational interviewing techniques to existing treatment models not only improved retention rates but also reduced rates of recidivism (Taft, Murphy, Elliott, & Morrel, 2001). In light of the disappointing effect sizes Babcock and her colleagues (2004) found in their meta-analytic review of batterer treatment and their hypothesis that these low rates of success might be due in part to client's lack of investment in treatment and attrition, these findings offer concrete suggestions for how clinicians might improve treatment.

In order to learn how to better treat perpetrators of interpersonal violence, it is important to understand *when* current treatment programs work. Peluso & Kern (2002) investigated the lifestyles of batterers, especially those who completed treatment and those who did not. Those who are rule focused, dislike ambiguity, and enjoy highly structured environments are less likely to drop out of domestic violence treatment programs. Those who complete batterer treatment programs are more independent, assertive, questioning of authority, and able to see others' points of views, and are not highly defensive when they perceive criticism. These individuals also tend to be more focused on following the rules and compliant with guidelines of the treatment program. Individuals who do not complete treatment may do so because they are defensive and unwilling to admit the extent of their violent behavior, as well as intolerable of confrontation. They are averse to changing their manner of relating to their partners. Batterers who drop out of treatment tend to be overly cautious or chaotic in the way they cope with problems that mimic the tactics experienced in their families. They typically come from unpredictable, chaotic, or abusive families and develop defensive strategies of coping with unpredictability. These individuals seek control through unacceptable methods (Peluso & Kern, 2002).

Another way to improve retention rates is to incorporate a transtheoretical approach to the treatment of batterers. The transtheoretical model matches the client's processes of change to how motivated the client is to change, and how he or she defines the problem (Prochaska et al., 1992). It has been suggested that this model will enhance motivation and improve retention rates (Eckhardt et al., 2004).

Similarly, Babcock and colleagues (2003) suggest that including motivational interviewing in treatment programs can improve the current efficacy of treatment. Motivational interviewing is designed to increase a client's motivation to change and assist in therapy model (Miller & Rollnick, 1991). As previously mentioned, research has shown that adding a motivational interviewing component to the treatment of batterers appeared to improve both retention and recidivism rates (Taft et al., 2001).

Treating the Female Who Uses Interpersonal Violence

As discussed, existing interventions, which are almost exclusively designed for male batterers, are certainly an ill-fitting solution to women's perpetration of violence in their intimate relationships (e.g., Hamberger & Guse, 2002). Existing treatments implicitly or explicitly include a component on gender roles and the relationship of masculinity to violence. As already noted, the current approaches may not be effective with men, and there is even less reason to expect them to be successful with women who use violence.

One issue that people have argued differentiates male perpetration from female perpetration is that of motive. Some research has suggested that, when queried as to the reasoning behind using violence in a romantic relationship, women typically endorse different motives than men do. Generally, men's use of interpersonal violence has been conceptualized as instrumental aggression; males use aggression as a means to an end (Swan & Snow, 2003). For example, some find that women are more likely to use violence as a method of self-defense or in retaliation to a partner's attempt to control them (Swan & Snow, 2003). Obviously, this difference has important clinical implications, in that instrumental violence and retaliatory violence are animals of a different breed and must be addressed as such. This is also brings up the issue of reciprocity. A couple that is enmeshed within a cycle of violence characterized by male perpetration and female retaliation is not likely to respond to an intervention born of the traditional male batterer/female victim model. In such a cycle of behavior, each violent act is the consequence of a preceding behavior, and the continuation of violence hinges on each partner's actions. Such a pattern of interpersonal violence is not amenable to traditional treatment methods, which almost exclusively treat only one partner of the dyad in isolation (Babcock et al., 2004).

Following from this is the consideration of the female perpetrator as a victim. Not only are women perpetrators of violence likely responding to abuse from a current partner (Swan & Snow, 2003), but they are also likely to have a long-standing history of victimization (Langhinrichsen-Rohling, Neidig, & Thorn, 1995). Even though men who use violence also demonstrate a history of victimization, current treatment models do not address the issue of victimization of (male) batterers. These data have mostly been interpreted as a reflection of the intergenerational transmission of violence via learning processes. This conceptualization of the development and maintenance of violent behaviors also has important clinical implications. Individuals who have learned that performing acts of violence can achieve specific desired consequences are not likely to relinquish the use of such behaviors unless more adaptive, alternative methods are taught to them.

Differences between Males and Females Who Use Interpersonal Violence

As discussed, whereas men's use of violence against their interpersonal partners has traditionally been understood as arising out of a desire to control the partner and exert power in the relationship, many women who use violence in their relationships report self-defense and retaliation motives (Swan & Snow, 2003). This difference strongly suggests that interventions designed to treat violent men cannot simply be applied to interpersonally violent women who are acting in self-defense or retaliation. (Of course, when women are the only ones who are violent in the relationship, or when their partner is highly dependent, they may be more similar to the male batterers discussed earlier; see Olson, 2002.)

Another important difference between male and female perpetration is that of the consequences of violent behavior within intimate relationships. Although recent research has suggested that rates of violence might be equal, the consequences are generally not. For instance, some men might be severely injured as the result of intimate partner violence, but women are more likely to sustain injuries as a consequence of interpersonal violence, and these injuries are more likely to be serious (Archer, 2000; Tjaden & Thoenness, 2000). The National Violence against Women Survey found that women victimized by male partners were twice as likely to be injured as men victimized by female partners (Tjaden & Thoennes, 2000). Not only do women experience more serious injury, but research documents that women also experience more negative psychological consequences than men as a result of partner violence (Anderson, 2005). In other research, men were at least 1.5 times more likely to exert severe (including violence so severe as to be lethal) violence against their partner (Straus et al., 1980; Swan & Snow, 2002; Saunders & Browne, 2000). Thus, a clinician working with an abusive man will need to structure the therapy differently and consider these divergent consequences than when working with an abusive woman if the woman is severely injured by the violence but the man is not.

In addition to these explicit antecedents and consequences that will weigh heavily on case conceptualization and treatment, there are also some more implicit consequences of interpersonal violence that may have treatment implications as well. How violent behavior is interpreted depends, in part, on the gender of the perpetrator. Some researchers have shown that the social acceptability and attributions of responsibility for violent behavior hinged on the gender of the perpetrator (Sorenson & Taylor, 2005). These societal reactions can also have serious clinical implications. A violent woman who sees her behavior met with a dismissive societal reaction may have trouble accepting responsibility for her behavior and also struggle to take initiative to make the life changes necessary for successful therapy. Conversely, a woman who uses violence in her interpersonal relationship may experience negative emotional consequences as a result of breaking traditional gender-roles, and this may be an additional issue that merits therapeutic attention.

Similarities between Males and Females Who Use Interpersonal Violence

Although there are several important and treatment-relevant dissimilarities between male and female perpetrators, men and women who are violent in their interpersonal relationships are also similar across several dimensions. Both groups are likely to have histories of victimization and to have learned to use violence in their interpersonal interactions (White & Widom, 2003). This is an issue that also needs to be addressed in therapy, not only in the realm of treating any posttraumatic stress symptoms that might be evident but also addressing the fact that for some interpersonally violent individuals, violence is a learned behavior and must be treated as such.

Although women are more likely to report self-defense and retaliation as a motivation for using violence in their intimate relationships, male and female perpetrators do endorse some of the same motivations for violence. Hamberger, Lohr, Bonge, and Tolin (1997) asked both male and female court-referred perpetrators their motivations for domestic violence and found that, although there were some motives that were gender specific, several motivations were endorsed by both male and female abusers. These common motivations include control, anger expression, and coercive communication (Hamberger et al., 1997). In a study of men and women arrested for partner violence, Hamberger and Guse (2005) found three clusters in their analysis of the characteristics of their sample. One sample, mostly men, reported desires for control and domination as primary motives for violence. Another group, equally divided among men and women, reported that self-defense and retaliation were primary motives for violence, along with desires for control and domination.

An awareness that not all female perpetrators are responding to abuse from their partner is critical to the clinician's successful treatment of the problem. Additionally, research has suggested that women who use instrumental violence are more severely violent than women who do not (Swan, 2000). Therefore, women who use violence proactively rather than reactively must be treated as violent people. Such women are not likely to respond to therapeutic models based on the assumption that female interpersonal violence occurs only in response to their own victimization. In fact, such therapy may increase the occurrence of violent behavior if it communicates justification for such actions to the woman.

Lastly, both male and female perpetrators are likely to have common characteristics that will have serious clinical implications. These include factors such as motivation to change, resistance, and denial. As stated previously, only 40–60 percent of male batterers who attend the first session of treatment actually complete the full course (Eckhardt et al., 2004). Some researchers theorize that these high attrition rates are due to the typical batterer's lack of motivation to change and denial of responsibility for their behavior (Eckhardt et al., 2004). If many of the female perpetrators of interpersonal violence also find their way to treatment via a court order, it is probable that they, too, evidence these characteristics. Since lack of motivation, resistance, and denial will weigh so heavily on the success of treatment, it is imperative that such issues be addressed at the outset of therapy, for both men as well as women.

NEW DIRECTIONS FOR INTERVENTIONS FOR INTIMATE PARTNER ABUSE

From the research on both men's and women's use of interpersonal violence, it is apparent that easy, diagnostic categories exist for neither group. Instead, both populations are heterogeneous and must be treated as such. Despite the preponderance of male batterer typologies, there has been little empirical evidence to suggest that such groupings are clinically useful. Furthermore, there is also a lack of evidence that clinicians can accurately classify batterers into types (Langhinrichsen-Rohling, Huss, & Ramsey, 2000). In fact, in their effort to examine the clinical utility of batterer typologies by comparing empirically derived and theoretically based grouping strategies, Langhinrichsen-Rohling and her colleagues (2000) found that the two strategies resulted in divergent classification decisions and led to the predication of unique, treatment relevant variables. This suggests that different typologies alert clinicians to different batterer characteristics that may guide treatment. Therefore, fitting a client into a particular batterer type delineated by a list of specific attributes may cause the clinician to ignore other important client traits that may also influence treatment.

Such typologies ignore the importance of context as well. They often fail to consider social history, the severity and scope of previous violence, and substance abuse (White & Gondolf, 2000), which if not specifically attended to in therapy, is apt to actively interfere with any intervention the clinician attempts to implement. By fitting clients into subtypes that exclude pertinent contextual factors, clinicians may fail to treat the whole individual, and such an intervention is likely doomed, as it would only address a portion of the problem.

Whereas batterer typologies do reflect an attempt to acknowledge the heterogeneity of individuals who use violence in their intimate relationships, we assert that such approaches stop short of truly matching treatment to individual clients. Typing is still an attempt to fit individuals into existing subgroups, and such a protocol will inevitably result in the omission of unique client characteristics relevant to a complete case conceptualization and efficacious treatment plan. Such classification systems may also represent a temptation to quickly and easily group clients according to a few traits and characteristics and implement a treatment according to their membership in a particular subgroup. We assert that there are no shortcuts, and attempts to utilize such shortcuts are destined to lead to dead ends, or unintended and undesired destinations.

Further illustrating the importance of treatment–client matching, some researchers have suggested that adding components of Prochaska and colleagues' (1992) transtheoretical approach to traditional batterer interventions might decrease attrition rates, a common impediment to success, and therefore reduce recidivism rates among treatment completers (Eckhardt et al., 2004). The transtheoretical model acknowledges that individuals enter therapy in varying degrees of readiness to change and that a mismatch between the client's assumed and actual motivation to change will decrease chances for improvement (Prochaska et al., 1992).

This issue is particular salient in the area of clinical interventions for interpersonal violence, as many of the individuals who enter into therapy are not there of their own accord (Babcock et al., 2004). Therefore, approaches that acknowledge this factor and actively deal with it are likely to achieve better results than those that do not. Similarly, motivational interviewing techniques that strive to develop the client's intrinsic motivation to change by building and illustrating the discrepancy between their values and their current circumstances, instead of pushing societal values and emphasizing external motivation to change (Miller & Rollnick, 1991), also offer some promise. Evidence suggests that adding motivational interviewing techniques to interventions for intimate partner violence does decrease attrition and recidivism (Taft et al., 2001). Both the transtheoretical and motivational interviewing approaches emphasize the importance of tailoring treatment to the client, and both offer possible methods for improving existing interpersonal violence treatment programs.

In addition to matching the intervention to the client's motivation and readiness to change, a probable way to increase the success of treatment is to include more contextual factors in the assessment of individual cases. One of the places this is most evident is that of individuals' motivation to use violence in their relationships. Whereas some female perpetrators use instrumental violence, others are violent as a way of defending themselves or retaliating against abuse from their partners (Babcock et al., 2003). Individuals who use violence to achieve specific goals and individuals who use violence because it is a part of a behavioral pattern maintained by both partners in the relationship will necessitate divergent treatment approaches. It is therefore imperative that the clinician examine the violent behavior in its particular context, in order to correctly identify all the relevant factors that work to maintain the violent behavior.

Additionally, the prevailing mode of group therapy—with only one member of the couple—and the reluctance to treat dyads with couples therapy (Babcock et al., 2004) may not be appropriate for those couples enmeshed in reciprocal patterns of intimate partner violence. In fact, treating only one member of a pair that is experiencing such a pattern of behaviors is destined to fail, as it addresses only half of the problem. Of course, couples therapy is not appropriate in those cases of clear-cut, one-sided perpetration. This point further illustrates the vital importance of fully assessing the unique context in which violence occurs.

Beyond the inclusion of context, there are many individual factors that have important treatment implications. Although fitting perpetrators into typologies is of dubious utility, the research does suggest several individual characteristics that will help guide treatment. These include antisocial, psychopathic tendencies; mood disorders; and substance abuse problems (White & Gondolf, 2000). Evidence of these conditions might necessitate addressing these issues first before intervening with the violent behavior, or structuring treatment to address these additional problems concomitantly. Other important characteristics include victimization history and socialization history. If the intervention utilized is a cognitive-behavioral approach, it is then necessary to assess how violent behavior was learned and maintained for that particular individual. Lastly, it is necessary to assess the client's stage of change and motivation to change. Tailoring interventions dependent on these factors is likely to decrease attrition and therefore increase the efficacy of treatment (Babcock et al., 2004)

As evidenced by the small effect sizes observed in Babcock and her colleagues' meta-analysis and sentiments like that batterers' interventions "work a little, probably" (Levesque & Gelles, 1998), it is apparent that there is much room for improvement in this area. Moreover, with the recent and burgeoning acknowledgment of female perpetration, there is the additional difficulty of designing and implementing interventions geared toward women. Due to the lack of overwhelming evidence for the efficacy of existing treatment for males and the differences among male and female perpetration of intimate partner violence, it is obvious that the existing models cannot simply be applied to women without any modification.

Tailoring therapy to the patterns, meaning, and context of violence is an extension of the postmodern perspective that multiple forms of violence exist. Clinicians have frequently been taught a particular perspective on intimate partner abuse—for example, that men batter women, or that violence is mutual and symmetrical—and have developed a clinical approach based on that model. Just as we are arguing for the perspective that multiple forms of violence exist, we encourage clinicians not to subscribe to a single model of violence and a single "correct" intervention for intimate partner violence. We anticipate that greater treatment success will be achieved by the development of multiple treatment options and by tailoring therapy to clients. Finally, we hope that with a more complex understanding of the types and patterns of violence and abuse that occur in intimate relationships, we may eventually move to prevention of intimate partner abuse.

REFERENCES

Acierno, R., Kilpatrick, D. G., & Resnick, H. S. (1999). Posttraumatic stress disorder in adults relative to criminal victimization: Prevelance, risk factors, and comorbidity. In P. A. Saigh & J. D. Brenner (Eds.), *Posttraumatic stress disorder: A comprehensive text.* (pp. 44–68). Boston: Allyn & Bacon.

Alway, J. (1995). The trouble with gender: Tales of a still missing feminist revolution in sociological theory. *Sociological Theory, 13*(3), 209–228.

Anderson, K. L. (2002). Perpetrator or victim? Relationships between intimate partner violence and well-being. *Journal of Marriage and the Family, 64,* 851–863.

Anderson, K. L. (2005). Theorizing gender in intimate partner violence research. *Sex Roles, 52,* 853–865.

Anderson, K. L., & Umberson, D. (2001). Gendering violence: Masculinity and power in men's accounts of domestic violence. *Gender and Society, 15,* 358–380.

Archer, J. (2000). Sex differences in aggression between heterosexual partners: A meta-analytic review. *Psychological Bulletin, 126,* 651–680.

Babcock, J. C., Green, C. E., & Robie, C. (2004). Does batterers' treatment work? A meta-analytic review of domestic violence treatment. *Clinical Psychology Review, 23,* 1023–1053.

Babcock, J. C., Miller, S. A., & Siard, C. (2003). Toward a typology of abusive women: Differences between partner-only and generally-violent women in the use of violence. *Psychology of Women Quarterly, 27*(2), 153–161.

Bograd, M. (1990). Why we need gender to understand human violence. *Journal of Interpersonal Violence, 5*(1), 132–135.

Browne, A. (1987). *When battered women kill.* New York: Free Press.

Browne, A. (1993). Violence against women by male partners: Prevalence, outcomes, and policy implications, *American Psychologist, 48*(10), 1077–1087.

Browne, A., & Dutton, D. (1990). Escape from violence: Risks and alternatives for abused women. In R. Roesch, D. Dutton, & V. Sacco (Eds.), *Family violence: Perspectives in research and practice* (pp. 67–91). Simon Fraser University Press.

Browne, A., & Williams, K. R. (1989). Exploring the effect of resource availability and the likelihood of female-perpetrated homicides. *Law & Society Review, 23,* 75–94.

Brush, L. D. (1990). Violent acts and injurious outcomes in married couples: Methodological issues in the National Survey of Families and Households. *Gender & Society, 4*(1), 56–67.

Brush, L. D. (2005). Philosophical and political issues in research on women's violence and aggression. *Sex Roles, 52,* 867–873.

Buzawa, E. S., & Austin, T. (1993). Determining police response to domestic violence victims. *American Behavioural Scientist 36,* 10–623.

Caesar, P. L. (1988). Exposure to violence in the families of origin among wife-abusers and maritally nonviolent men. *Violence and Victims, 3,* 49–63.

Chandler, S. (1986). *The psychology of battered women.* Unpublished doctoral dissertation. Department of Education, University of California, Berkeley.

Chang, V. N. (1996). *I just lost myself: Psychological abuse of women in marriage.* Westport, CT: Praeger.

Cleek, M. G., & Pearson, T. A. (1985). Perceived causes of divorce: An analysis of interrelationships. *Journal of Marriage and the Family, 47*(1), 179–183.

Coleman, V. E. (1991). Violence in lesbian couples: A between groups comparison. *Dissertation Abstracts International, 51*(11-B), 5634–5635.

Cosgrove, L. (2004). Negotiating the quantitative/qualitative impasse in sexuality research on girls and women. Paper presented at the 29th Annual Association for Women on Psychology Conference, Philadelphia, February.

Cosgrove, L., & McHugh, M. C. (2002). Deconstructing difference: Conceptualizing feminist research from within the postmodern. In L. H. Collins, M. R. Dunlap, & J. C. Chrisler (Eds.), *Charting a new course for feminist psychology* (pp. 20–36). Westport, CT: Praeger.

Dasgupta, S. D. (2002). A framework for understanding women's use of non-lethal violence in intimate heterosexual relationships. *Violence against Women, 8,* 1364–1389.

Dobash, R. P., Dobash, R. E., Cavanagh, K., & Lewis, R. (1998). Separate and intersecting realities: A comparison of men's and women's accounts of violence against women. *Violence against Women, 4,* 382–414.

Dutton, D. (1988). Profiling of wife assaulters: Preliminary evidence for a trimodal analysis. *Violence and Victims, 3,* 5–30.

Dutton, D., & Painter, S. (1983). Traumatic bonding: The development of emotional attachments in battered women and other relationships of intermittent abuse. *Victimology, 6* 139–155.

Dutton, M. A., & Goodman, L. A. (2005). Coercion in intimate partner violence: Toward a new conceptualization. *Sex Roles, 52,* 743–756.

Eckhardt, C. I., Babcock, J., & Homack, S. (2004). Partner assaultive men and the stages and processes of change. *Journal of Family Violence, 19*(2), 81–93.

Feindler, E. L., Rathus, J. H., & Silver, L. B. (2003) The assessment of family violence: An overview. In E. L. Feindler, J. H. Rathus, & L. B. Silver (Eds.), *Assessment of family violence: A handbook for researchers and practitioners* (pp. 3–10). Washington, DC: American Psychological Association.

Felson, R. B. (2002). *Violence and gender reexamined.* Washington, DC: American Psychological Association.

Ferree, M. M., Lorber, J., & Hess, B. B. (Eds.). (1999). *Revisioning gender.* Thousand Oaks, CA: Sage.

Fitch, F. J., & Papantonio, A. (1983). Men who batter: Some pertinent characteristics. *Journal of Nervous and Mental Disease, 171*(3), 190–192.

Frieze, I. H. (2000). Violence in close relationships—Development of a research area: Comment on Archer (2000). *Psychological Bulletin, 126,* 681–684.

Frieze, I. H. (2005a) Female violence against intimate partners: An introduction. *Psychology of Women Quarterly, 29*(3), 229–237.

Frieze, I. H. (2005b). *Hurting the one you love: Violence in relationships.* Pacific Grove, CA: Wadsworth.

Gayford, J. J. (1975). Wife battering: A preliminary study of 100 cases. *British Medical Journal, 1,* 194–197.

Geffner, R., & Rosenbaum, A. (1990). Characteristics and treatment of batterers. *Behavioral Sciences & the Law, 8,* 131–140.

Gondolf, E. W. (1988). Who are those guys? Toward a behavioral typology of batterers. *Violence and Victims, 3,* 187–203.

Gondolf, E. W. (1998). *Assessing woman battering in women's health services.* Thousand Oaks, CA: Sage.

Gondolf, E. W., & Fisher, E. R. (1988). *Battered women as survivors: An alternative to treating learned helplessness.* Lexington, MA: Lexington Books.

Goodman, L. A., Koss, M. P., & Russo, N. F. (1993). Violence against women: Mental health effects: II. Conceptualizations of posttraumatic stress. *Applied and Preventive Psychology, 2*(3), 123–130.

Graham, K., & Wells, S. (2001). Aggression among young adults in the social context of the bar. *Addiction Research & Theory, 9*(3), 193–219.

Hamberger, L. K. (1997). Female offenders in domestic violence: A look at actions in their context. *Journal of Aggression, Maltreatment, and Trauma, 1,* 117–129.

Hamberger, L. K., & Guse, C. E. (2002). Men's and women's use of intimate partner violence in clinical samples. *Violence against Women, 8,* 1301–1331.

Hamberger, L. K., & Guse, C. E. (2005). Typology of reactions to intimate partner violence among men and women arrested for partner violence. *Violence and Victims, 20,* 303–317.

Hamberger, L. K., & Hastings, J. E. (1988). Characteristics of male spouse abusers consistent with personality disorders. *Hospital and Community Psychiatry, 39*(7), 763–770.

Hamberger, L. K., & Hastings, J. E. (1991). Personality correlates of men who batter and nonviolent men: Some continuities and discontinuities. *Journal of Family Violence, 6*(2), 131–147.

Hamberger, L. K., Lohr, J. M., Bonge, D., & Tolin, D. E. (1997). A empirical classification of motivations for domestic violence. *Violence against Women, 3,* 401–423.

Hamby, S. L. (2005). Measuring gender differences in partner violence: Implications from research on other forms of violent and socially undesirable behavior. *Sex Roles, 52,* 725–742.

Hamby, S. L., & Gray-Little, B. (2000). Labeling partner violence: When do victims differentiate among acts? *Violence and Victims, 15*(2), 173–186.

Hart, S. D., Dutton, D. G., & Newlove, T. (1993). The prevalence of personality disorders among wife assaulters. *Journal of Personality Disorders, 7,* 329–341.

Hastings, J. E., & Hamberger, L. K. (1988). Personality characteristics of spouse abusers: A controlled comparison. *Violence and Victims, 3,* 31–48.

Hotaling, G. T., & Sugarman, D. B. (1986). An analysis of risk markers in husband to wife violence: The current state of knowledge. *Violence and Victims, 1*(2), 101–124.

Hudson, W. W., & McIntosh, S. R. (1981). The assessment of spouse abuse: Two quantifiable dimensions. *Journal of Marriage & the Family, 43*(4), 873–885.

Janoff-Bulman, R., & Frieze, I. H. (1983). A theoretical perspective for understanding reactions to victimization. *Journal of Social Issues, 39*(2), 1–17.

Johnson, M. P. (1995). Patriarchal terrorism and common couple violence: Two forms of violence against women. *Journal of Marriage & the Family, 75*, 283–294.

Johnson, M. P., & Ferraro, K. J. (2000). Research on domestic violence in the 1990s: Making distinctions. *Journal of Marriage & the Family, 62*, 948–963.

Johnson, M. P., & Leone, J. M. (2005). The differential effects of intimate terrorism and situational couple violence: Findings from the National Violence against Women Survey. *Journal of Family Issues, 26*, 322–349.

Jones, S., Davidson, W. S., Bogat, G. A., Levendosky, A., & von Eye, A. (2005). Validation of the Subtle and Overt Psychological Abuse Scale: An examination of construct validity. *Violence and Victims, 20*(4), 407–416.

Kimmel, M. S. (2002). "Gender symmetry" in domestic violence: A substantive and methodological research review. *Violence against Women, 8*, 1332–1363.

Koss, M. P., Bailey, J. A., Yuan, N. P., Herrera, V. M., & Lichter, E. L. (2003). Depression and PTSD in survivors of male violence: Research and training initiatives to facilitate recovery. *Psychology of Women Quarterly, 27*, 130–142.

Koss, M. P., Goodman, L. A., Browne, A., Fitzgerald, L. F., & Keita, G. P. (1994). The culture and context of male violence against women. In M. P. Koss, L. A. Goodman, A. Browne, L. F. Fitzgerald, & G. P. Keita (Eds.). *No safe haven: Male violence against women at home, at work, and in the community* (pp. 3–17). Washington, DC: American Psychological Association.

Langhinrichsen-Rohling, J., Huss, M. T., & Ramsey S. (2000). The clinical utility of batterer typologies. *Journal of Family Violence, 15*, 37–53.

Langhinrichsen-Rohling, J., Neidig, P., & Thorn, G. (1995). Violent marriages: Gender differences in levels of current violence and past abuse. *Journal of Family Violence, 10*, 159–176.

Lawrence, E., & Bradbury, T. N. (2001). Physical aggression and marital dysfunction: A longitudinal analysis. *Journal of Family Psychology, 15*, 135–154.

Levesque, D. A., & Gelles, R. J. (1998). Does treatment reduce recidivism in men who batter? A meta-analytic evaluation of treatment outcome. Paper presented at the Program Evaluation and Family Violence Research Conference, Durham, NH, July.

Marshall, L. L. (1992a). Development of the Severity of Violence against Women Scales. *Journal of Family Violence, 7*, 103–121.

Marshall, L. L. (1992b). The Severity of Violence against Men Scales. *Journal of Family Violence, 7*, 189–203.

Marshall, L. L. (1994). Physical and psychological abuse. In W. R. Cupach & B. H. Spitzberg (Eds.), *The dark side of interpersonal communication* (pp. 281–311). Hillsdale, NJ: Erlbaum.

McHugh, M. C. (2005). Understanding gender and intimate partner abuse. *Sex Roles, 52*, 717–724.

McHugh, M. C., & Bartoszek, T. A. (2000). Intimate violence. In M. Biaggio & M. Hersen (Eds.), *Issues in the psychology of women* (pp. 115–144). New York: Plenum.

McHugh, M. C., & Cosgrove, L. (2004). Feminist research methods: Studying women and gender. In M. A. Paludi (Ed.), *Praeger guide to the psychology of gender* (pp. 155–182). Westport, CT: Praeger.

McHugh, M. C., & Frieze, I. H. (2006). Understanding gender and intimate partner violence: Theoretical and empirical approaches. *Sex Roles.*

McHugh, M. C., Frieze, I. H., & Browne, A. (1993). Research on battered women and their assailants. In F. L. Denmark & M. A. Paludi (Eds.), *Psychology of women: A handbook of issues and theories* (pp. 513–552). Westport, CT: Greenwood Press.

McHugh, M. C., Livingston, N. A., & Ford, A. E. (2005). A postmodern approach to women's use of violence: Developing multiple and complex conceptualizations. *Psychology of Women Quarterly, 29,* 323–336.

McNeely, R. L., & Mann, C. R. (1990). Domestic violence is a human issue. *Journal of Interpersonal Violence, 5*(1), 129–132.

Mechanic, M. B. (2002). Stalking victimization: Clinical implications for assessment and intervention. In K. E. Davis, I. H. Frieze, & R. D. Maiuro (Eds.), *Stalking: Perspectives on victims and perpetrators* (pp. 31–61). New York: Springer.

Milan, S., Lewis, J., Ethier, K., Kershaw, T., & Ickovics, J. R. (2005). Relationship violence among adolescent mothers: Frequency, dyadic nature, and implications for relationship dissolution and mental health. *Psychology of Women Quarterly, 29,* 302–312.

Miller, W. R., & Rollnick, S. (1991). *Motivational interviewing: Preparing people to change addictive behavior.* New York: Guilford Press.

Murphy, C. M., & Eckhardt, C. I. (2005). *Treating the abusive partner: An individualized cognitive behavioral approach.* New York: Guilford Press.

Olson, L. N. (2002). Exploring "common couple violence" in heterosexual romantic relationships. *Western Journal of Communication, 66,* 104–128.

Pagelow, M. D. (1981). Violence against wives: A case against the patriarchy. *American Journal of Sociology, 86*(6), 1475–1476.

Peluso, P. R., & Kern, R. M. (2002). An Adlerian model for assessing and treating the perpetrators of domestic violence. *Journal of Individual Psychology, 58*(1), 87–103.

Pence, E., & Paymar, M. (1993). *Education groups for men who batter: The Duluth model.* New York: Springer-Verlag.

Prochaska, J. O., DiClemente, C. C., & Norcross, J. C. (1992). In search of how people change: Applications to addictive behaviors. *American Psychologist, 47,* 1102–1114.

Raymond, B., & Brushi, I. G. (1989). Psychological abuse among college women in dating relationships. *Perceptual and Motor Skills, 69,* 1283–1297.

Renzetti, C. (1992). *Violent betrayal: Partner abuse in lesbian relationships.* Newbury Park, CA: Sage Publications.

Ridington, J. (1978). The transition process: A feminist environment as reconstitutive milieu. *Victimology,* 2(3/4), 563–575.

Risman, B. (1998). *Gender vertigo: American families in transition.* New Haven, CT: Yale University Press.

Roberts, A. R. (1987). Psychosocial characteristics of batterers: A study of 234 men charged with domestic violence offenses. *Journal of Family Violence, 2,* 81–93.

Rosenbaum, A., Geffner, R., & Benjamin, S. (1997). A biopychosocial model for understanding relationship aggression. In R. Geffner, S. B. Sorenson, and P. K. Lundberg-Love (Eds.), *Violence and sexual abuse at home: Current issues in spousal battering and child maltreatment* (pp. 57–80). New York: Haworth Press.

Rothenberg, B. (2003). "We don't have time for social change": Cultural compromise and the battered women syndrome. *Gender & Society, 17,* 771–787.

Russo, A. (2006). Framing the victim: Domestic violence, media, and social problems. *Violence against Women, 12,* 116–119.

Russo, N. F., & Pirlott, A. (2006). Gender-based violence: Concepts, methods, and findings. In F. L. Denmark, H. H. Krauss, E. Halpern, & J. A. Sechzer (Eds.), *Violence and exploitation against women and girls* (pp. 178–205). Boston: Blackwell.

Ryan, K. M., & Mohr, S. (2005). Gender differences in playful aggression during courtship in college students. *Sex Roles, 53*(7), 591–601.

Saunders, D. (2000). Are physical assaults by wives and girlfriends a major social problem? A review of the literature. *Violence against Women, 8,* 1424–1448.

Saunders, D., & Browne, A. (2000). Intimate partner homicide. In R. T. Ammerman & M. Hersen (Eds.), *Case studies in family violence* (2nd ed.; pp. 415–449). Dordrecht, Netherlands: Kluwer Academic.

Shields, N. M., McCall, G. J., & Hanneke, C. R. (1988). Patterns of family and nonfamily violence: Violent husbands and violent men. *Violence and Victims, 3,* 83–97.

Simon, T., Anderson, M., Thompson, M., Crosby, A., Shelley, G., & Sacks, J. (2001). Attitudinal acceptance of intimate partner violence among U.S. adults. *Violence and Victims, 16*(2), 115–126.

Sorenson, S. B., & Taylor, C. A. (2004). Injunctive social norms of adults regarding teen dating violence. *Journal of Adolescent Health, 3*(6), 468–479.

Sorenson, S. B., & Taylor, C. A. (2005). Female aggression toward male intimate partners: An examination of social norms in a community-based sample. *Psychology of Women Quarterly, 29,* 78–96.

Stacey, J., & Thorne, B. (1985). The missing feminist revolution in sociology. *Social Problems, 3*(4), 301–316.

Straus, M. A. (1979). Measuring intrafamily conflict and aggression: The Conflict Tactics Scale (CTS). *Journal of Marriage and the Family, 41,* 75–88.

Straus, M. A. (1999). The controversy over domestic violence by women: A methodological, theoretical, and sociology of science perspective. In X. B. Arriage & S. Oskamp (Eds.), *Violence in intimate relationships* (pp. 17–44). Thousand Oaks, CA: Sage.

Straus, M. A., & Gelles, R. J. (1986). Societal change and change in family violence from 1975 to 1985 as revealed by two national surveys. *Journal of Marriage and the Family, 48,* 465–479.

Straus, M. A., Gelles, R. J., & Steinmetz, S. K. (1980). *Behind closed doors: Violence in the American family*. Garden City, NY: Doubleday.

Straus, M. A., Hamby, S. L., Boney-McCoy, S., & Sugarman, D. B. (1996). The revised Conflict Tactics Scales (CTS2): Development and preliminary psychometric data. *Journal of Family Issues, 17*(3), 283–316.

Sugarman, D. B., & Hotaling, G. T. (1989). Violent men in intimate relationships: An analysis of risk markers. *Journal of Applied Social Psychology, 19,* 1034–1048.

Sullivan, C. M., Basta, J., Tan, C., & Davidson, W. S. (1992). After the crisis: A needs assessment of women leaving a domestic violence shelter. *Violence and Victims, 17*(3), 267–275.

Swan, S. C. (2000). Women's use of violence. Research presented at the Workshop on Gender Symmetry, sponsored by the National Institute of Justice, Violence against Women & Family Violence, Arlington, VA, November 20. Summary available online at http://www.ojp.usdoj.gov/nij/vawprog/proceed.htm.

Swan, S. C., & Snow, D. L. (2002). A typology of women's use of violence in intimate relationships. *Violence and Victims, 20,* 355–379.

Swan, S. C., & Snow, D. L. (2003). Behavioral and psychological differences among abused women who use violence in intimate relationships. *Violence against Women, 9,* 286–319.

Taft, C. T., Murphy, C. M., Elliott, J. D., & Morrel, T. M. (2001). Attendance enhancing procedures in group counseling for domestic abusers. *Journal of Counseling Psychology, 48,* 51–60.

Testa, M., & Leonard, K. E. (2001). The impact of marital aggression on women's psychological and marital functioning in a newlywed sample. *Journal of Family Violence, 16,* 115–30.

Tjaden, P., & Thoennes, N. (2000). Extent, nature, and consequences of intimate partner violence: Findings from the National Violence against Women Survey. Washington, DC: National Institute of Justice; Centers for Disease Control and Prevention.

Tolman, R. M. (1989). The development of a measure of psychological maltreatment of women by their male partners. *Violence and Victims, 4,* 159–177.

Tolman, R. M. (1992). Psychological abuse of women. In R. T. Ammerman and M. Hersen (Eds.), *Assessment of family violence: A clinical and legal sourcebook* (pp. 291–310). New York: Wiley.

Tolman, R. M., & Bennett, L. W. (1990). A review of quantitative research on men who batter. *Journal of Interpersonal Violence, 5,* 87–118.

U.S. Department of Justice. Bureau of Statistics. (2006). Homicide trends in the U.S.: Intimate homicide.

Vandello, J. A., & Cohen, D. (2003). Male honor and female fidelity: Implicit cultural scripts that perpetuate domestic violence. *Journal of Personality and Social Psychology, 84*(5), 997–1010.

Vega, V., & Malamuth, N. M. (2007). Predicting physical aggression: The role of pornography in the context of general and specific risk factors. *Aggressive Behavior, 33,* 104–117.

Walker, L. E. (1979). *The battered woman*. New York: Harper & Row.

Walker, L. E. A., & Browne, A. (1985). Gender and victimization by intimates. *Journal of Personality, 53*(2), 179–196.

West, C., & Zimmerman, D. H. (1987). Doing gender. *Gender & Society, 1,* 125–151.

Weston, R., Temple, J. R., & Marshall, L. L. (2005). Gender symmetry and asymmetry in violent relationship: Patterns of mutuality among racially diverse women. *Sex Roles, 53*(7/8), 553–571.

White, H. R., & Widom, C. S. (2003). Intimate partner violence among abused and neglected children in young adulthood: The mediating effects of early aggression, antisocial personality, hostility, and alcohol problems. *Aggressive Behavior, 29,* 332–345.

White, J. W., & Kowalski, R. M. (1991). Deconstructing the myth of the non-aggressive woman. *Psychology of Women Quarterly, 18,* 487–508.

White, R. J., & Gondolf, E. W. (2000). Implication of personality profiles for batterer treatment. *Journal of Interpersonal Violence, 15*(5), 467–488.

White, S. O., & Straus, M. A. (1981). The implications of family violence for rehabilitation strategies. In S. E. Martin, L. E. Sechrest, & R. Redner (Eds.), *New directions in the rehabilitation of criminal offenders.* Washington, DC: National Academy of Sciences.

Williams, S. L., & Frieze, I. H. (2005). Patterns of violent relationships, psychological distress, and marital satisfaction in a national sample of men and women. *Sex Roles, 52,* 771–784.

Yllo, K., & Bograd, M. (Eds.), (1988). *Feminist perspectives on wife abuse.* Newbury Park, CA: Sage.

Chapter 18

Violence against Women: International Workplace Sexual Harassment and Domestic Violence

Janet Sigal
Vidal Annan Jr.

Workplace sexual harassment is a worldwide problem that has received considerable research attention in recent years. It is difficult to assess the incidence of sexual harassment cross-culturally for a number of reasons. In some cultures, the concept does not even exist; definitions of sexual harassment vary in other cultures, and methodological issues complicate cross-national comparisons.

Domestic violence also is an international problem affecting countless women. Once again, cross-cultural incidence figures are difficult to obtain, particularly in countries where the government refuses to acknowledge that domestic violence is a problem.

Both domestic violence and workplace sexual harassment may be conceptualized as human rights violations. Sexual harassment generally is seen both as violence against women and as a form of sex discrimination that prevents women from achieving their rightful place in employment and academic settings. However, it also can be seen as interfering with human rights. Since sexual harassment victims still are predominantly women, men may attempt to use power and sexual harassment to subordinate women in the workplace.

Domestic violence clearly is a human rights issue in which victims experience severe physical and psychological consequences. Women constitute the majority of domestic violence victims. In the home setting, men use a form of more direct violence against women than with workplace sexual harassment, but the motivation is similar: to keep women in their place and under the control of men.

We propose that there are several parallels between sexual harassment and domestic violence. In both cases, the primary perpetrators are male, and the majority of victims are female. Both processes involve human rights violations. Intimate partner violence is more personal and physical because the male head of the family has more direct control over his spouse than employers have over their employees. Workplace perpetrators cannot beat or physically harm the women in their employ, so the employer attacks them sexually to maintain his power over women. In both types of behavior, the victim often feels responsible for her punishment (e.g., domestic violence victims may think, "I have not been a good wife"; sexual harassment victims may believe that they "must have given the wrong signals"), and some of the physical and psychological consequences are comparable. There also may be common characteristics of perpetrators in both types of settings. In addition, conceptually similar terms might be used to describe each setting: "hostile work environment" for workplace sexual harassment, and "hostile home environment" for domestic violence.

This chapter provides a selective review of relevant theories and cross-cultural studies designed to examine the proposed parallels in the two types of violence against women. The focus is on settings in which women are victims, since women still are the predominant victims both in the home and the workplace. Studies on same-sex domestic violence and sexual harassment are not addressed here.

THEORIES AND MODELS

We will examine cross-cultural studies on workplace sexual harassment and domestic violence through two theoretical approaches: the Integrated Model of Sexual Harassment, and feminist, sociocultural, and power models of domestic violence.

Integrated Model of Sexual Harassment

In 1995, Fitzgerald, Hulin, and Drasgow developed a theoretical model designed to predict the occurrence of sexual harassment in workplace settings. There were two essential components in this model:

1. *Organizational climate:* the attitudes among employees and managers concerning support for, or opposition to, sexual harassment behavior. Clearly, if these attitudes are supportive of sexually harassing acts and protective of harassers, then there is a greater likelihood that sexual harassment is prevalent in the organization.

2. *Job gender context:* factors such as the ratio of male to female employees, and whether or not the jobs are associated with traditional male or female role structures.

The model predicted an increase in sexual harassment behaviors in work settings that were dominated by men and where there were traditional gender-role "appropriate" positions. Several physical and mental health consequences as well as job-related attitudes followed from the sexual harassment, according to the model.

Although this model was developed to describe conditions conducive to workplace sexual harassment, it also is applicable to domestic violence. In terms of organizational climate, if a country's culture is supportive of men abusing or beating their wives, and if the culture protects and does not punish the abusers, then it is likely that domestic violence will be prevalent in that culture.

Feminist, Sociocultural, and Power Models of Domestic Violence

The basic conceptualization common to these explanations of domestic violence is that it is gender based and fostered through socialization resulting in acceptance of traditional gender-roles. In this traditional gender-role framework, the male role is to provide for the family economically, as well as to offer protection and security for the family. The female role is to raise the children and to have responsibility for providing a smooth and comfortable family life. In addition to the perception of the traditional roles that men and women should play in the family, there are associated traits that men and women are supposed to embody. For example, the man is supposed to be strong and dominating, whereas women should be weak and submissive (Sigal & Nally, 2004, pp. 27–28).

One possible consequence of the traditional gender-role assumption is that men will have more power and status than women in society, a consequence that feminist theorists interpret as the oppression of women. Patriarchal cultures, which embody traditional role structures, can be characterized as supporting dominance by men over women in all important areas of society, including familial, governmental, and economic. Men are seen as superior to women and traditional gender-roles are generally reinforced, thus producing significant gender inequality in the society. Araji and Carlson (2001) suggest that patriarchal societies may foster domestic violence because the dominant male is perceived to be "appropriately" disciplining and controlling the behavior of the subordinate females in the family.

In its extreme form, patriarchal cultures may develop into "cultures of honor." In certain cultures, the honor of the *patriarch,* or male head of a family, is dependent on the behavior of others in the family, particularly the chastity of the women. In order to maintain his honor, the patriarch must strictly control the women's behavior to keep them from "straying" (Baker, Gregware, & Cassidy, 1999). In other words, women in patriarchal and particularly in cultures of honor are almost entirely restricted to the home setting. If a woman behaves in a manner that adversely affects the honor of the patriarch, he is expected to punish her severely to restore his honor. In this manner, culture-of-honor societies are supportive of wife beating.

Although the culture-of-honor formulation applies solely to domestic violence, the concepts of power and the subordination of women also are congruent with the occurrence of sexual harassment. Particularly in countries with a patriarchal structure, but in other cultures as well, men generally are in powerful positions in the workplace and therefore would have the ability to engage in sexually harassing behaviors. In fact, Wallace (1998) makes that argument in his discussion of the sociocultural model of sexual harassment.

In the following sections of the chapter, international workplace sexual harassment and domestic violence will be discussed separately. Laws and incidence statistics will be presented and cross-cultural studies described. Some proposed categorizations of types of sexual harassers and domestic violence perpetrators will be examined, along with consequences for victims of both types of violence. Finally, a comparison of workplace sexual harassment and domestic violence in the international context will be discussed, along with methodological considerations that complicate cross-cultural comparisons.

CROSS-CULTURAL WORKPLACE SEXUAL HARASSMENT

Definitions

The U.S. Equal Employment Opportunity Commission's (2005) basic definition of workplace sexual harassment states:

> Unwelcome sexual advances, requests for sexual favors, and other verbal or physical conduct of a sexual nature constitute sexual harassment when this conduct explicitly or implicitly affects an individual's employment, unreasonably interferes with an individual's work performance, or creates an intimidating, hostile, or offensive work environment.

In effect, the EEOC is distinguishing between coercive "quid pro quo" or "sex for favors" and "hostile work environment" sexual harassment.

Recent psychological definitions have somewhat clarified and expanded the EEOC's definition. Gelfand, Fitzgerald, and Drasgow (1995) identified the following categories of sexual harassment:

1. *Gender harassment:* Disparagement of women in general, stemming from adversarial attitudes toward women, and other behaviors engaged in to distress women (in 1999, Fitzgerald, Magley, Drasgow, and Waldo

further subdivided this category into *sexist hostility*, referring to gender-based inequitable treatment or discrimination, and *sexual hostility*, a term describing persistent sexually related jokes or remarks)

2. *Unwanted sexual attention:* Continually asking someone for a date despite her refusals, but without negative consequences
3. *Sexual coercion* or "quid pro quo."

International Laws against Sexual Harassment

Workplace sexual harassment is not a problem that is specific to America or Western countries. The movement of women into traditionally male-dominated fields of employment is a global trend. As a result, issues of gender-related power and dominance are being observed in workplaces worldwide. The reaction from governments and communities to this problem has ranged from denial of its existence to criminal prosecution of perpetrators.

In 1992, the International Labor Organization (ILO) conducted one of the earliest international surveys to assess the legislative responses of 23 industrialized countries to workplace sexual harassment. All surveyed countries were found to have some kind of law on the subject in place, although the legal categories varied from equal opportunity employment statutes to labor, tort, and criminal laws. For example, Australia, Canada, Denmark, Ireland, New Zealand, Sweden, the United Kingdom, and the United States all have equal employment opportunity laws. The majority of the surveyed countries have labor laws focusing on quid pro quo sexual harassment cases in which the employee was forced to quit to avoid the offensive behavior or the employee was fired for refusing to submit to unfair labor practices. Tort law, which is defined as a legal wrong that can be remedied by court action, has been applied to sexual harassment in Japan, Switzerland, the United Kingdom, and the United States. France was the only country at the time that had passed a criminal law related to sexual harassment; however, in other countries, sexual harassment could rise to the level of criminality in extreme cases such as assault or indecent behavior. Also, only seven countries at the time of the survey had specific sexual harassment laws in place.

In less industrialized countries, the response to sexual harassment has been more gradual. For example, in Malaysia, women's groups have been pressuring the government and employers to adopt and enforce the existing code on sexual harassment. The Code of Practice on the Prevention and Eradication of Sexual Harassment in the Workplace, as it is called, is not a legally enforceable statute, although it does provide guidelines for employers to deal privately with sexual harassment issues on the job. The code lists specific acts that are construed as sexual harassment, such as leering, lewd jokes, crude sounds and gestures, and flirting. Despite political pressure, only about 1 percent of companies in the country were reported to have adopted the code by the late 1990s, thus prompting calls for stricter, more enforceable laws on the issue (McCarthy, 1997).

Aside from the ILO, which has been criticized by other world organizations such as the International Labor Rights Fund for not having a more specific convention against workplace sexual harassment (Kompipote, 2002), much of the international momentum toward addressing sexual harassment as a problem has come from the United Nations Convention on Elimination of All Forms of Discrimination Against Women (CEDAW), which was adopted in 1979 by the UN General Assembly. According to this convention, discrimination against women is defined as

> any distinction, exclusion, or restriction made on the basis of sex which has the effect or purpose of impairing or nullifying the recognition, enjoyment, or exercise by women, irrespective of their marital status, on the basis of equality of men and women, of human rights and fundamental freedoms in the political, economic, social, cultural, civil, or any other field. (United Nations, 1979, Article 1)

CEDAW has called on member states to take all appropriate measures to eliminate discrimination against women by any person, organization, or enterprise. Under general international law and specific human rights covenants, states also may be responsible for providing compensation, as well as investigating and punishing acts of violence, if they fail to act with due diligence to prevent violations of rights (United Nations, 2003). Sexual harassment is considered by CEDAW as a form of violence against women, and as a result all member states are encouraged to develop legal channels to address such cases in their countries.

A 2003 report by the special rapporteur to the Commission on Human Rights presented a detailed and extensive review of developments both within the UN system and in member countries with respect to issues of violence against women, including sexual harassment legislation (United Nations, 2003). The report showed that over the period of 1994 to 2003, several countries, including developing nations such as Kenya, Senegal, Bolivia, and Jordan, instituted specific codes and laws against sexual harassment. In other countries, such as Ghana, that do not have an explicit laws, individuals can find redress to sexual harassment by referencing more general laws on workplace discrimination or sexual assault.

In India, where it is reported that every 51 minutes, a woman is harassed (Srinivasan, 1998), a recent court decision has moved the country toward more stringent prosecution of harassment cases. The Indian Supreme Court ruled that in the absence of domestic law, international conventions could be referred to in interpreting and safeguarding women against harassment.

Cross-Cultural Studies of Workplace Sexual Harassment

A landmark article by Timmerman and Bajema (1999) reviewed a large number of sexual harassment incidence studies conducted in northwestern European countries. Although cross-national comparisons were difficult, according to the authors, due to the widely varying procedures and types of samples, the researchers concluded that generally 30–50 percent of women surveyed had experienced some form of sexual harassment. The figures ranged from less than 10 percent in one study each in Ireland, Finland, Norway, and Sweden to 90 percent in a sample of police in the United Kingdom. Additional methodological issues described by the researchers included the number of questions asked of respondents, the time frame within which respondents provided incidence figures, and whether individuals reported only about their own sexual harassment experiences or described experiences of women they had observed or heard about. The representativeness of the samples also complicated any cross-national comparisons.

In North America, Crocker and Kalemba (1999) found that more than 50 percent of Canadian women surveyed in one study reported having been sexually harassed in the prior year, and close to 80 percent had experienced sexual harassing behaviors at work sometime.

A report from Asia suggested that about 75 percent of working women in Japan and Korea, which are both patriarchal cultures, have experienced sexually harassing behaviors (International Labor Organization, 2001).

In the Middle East, Barak, Pitterman, and Yitzhak (1995) found that an average of 36 percent of the working women in Israel had experienced gender sexual harassment.

Wasti, Bergman, Glomb, and Drasgow (2000) suggested that in Turkey, which is part of both Europe and Asia and is characterized by a patriarchal culture with adherence to traditional gender-roles, the climate in organizations would be likely to condone sexual harassment, an interpretation consistent with the power and patriarchal models described earlier. They also concluded that the Fitzgerald, Hulin, and Drasgow integrated model (1995) could be applied directly to other countries. The two core concepts of the model, "organizational climate" and "job-gender context," predicted sexual harassment in Turkey as well as in the United States (Fitzgerald, Drasgow, Hulin, Gelfand, & Magley, 1997).

This selective overview of international sexual harassment studies is less extensive than the subsequent review of international domestic violence research for a few reasons. In addition, since sexual harassment is a concept that is not universally recognized or discussed in many cultures, the majority of studies have been conducted in Westernized countries. However, some of the reviewed studies are congruent with the model, which suggests that patriarchal cultures create an environment for sexual harassment.

Outcomes for Victims

The integrated model developed by Fitzgerald, Hulin, and Drasgow (1995) predicted that women who are sexually harassed would experience negative physical and mental health consequences. In a study supporting the model, Cortina, Fitzgerald, and Drasgow (2002) reported that, in their Latina sample, individuals who experienced sexual harassment in its more extreme forms had higher levels of depression and anxiety than other respondents. In another investigation, Dansky and Kilpatrick (1997) surveyed more than 3,000 participants from the United States to examine the psychological consequences of sexual harassment victimization. Using standardized diagnostic measures, the researchers found that women who had been sexually harassed were more likely to suffer from posttraumatic stress disorder (PTSD) and depression than those who had not been victimized. Once again, these results supported the integrated model.

Types of Perpetrators

In one of the earliest attempts to categorize perpetrators, Pryor (Pryor, 1987; Pryor, Lavite, & Stoller, 1993) established the Likelihood of Sexually Harassing (LSH) scale. Pryor proposed that men varied in terms of their propensity to engage in sexual harassment behavior and indicated that these individual tendencies would combine with a supportive workplace climate to facilitate the expression of these types of behavior.

More recently, Lengnick-Hall (1995) developed the following three classifications of workplace sexual harassers:

1. *Hard-core harassers:* Men who actively look for settings and situations where they can harass victims
2. *Opportunists*: Men who engage in sexual harassment only when given an opportunity
3. *Insensitive individuals:* Men do not realize that their behavior is causing discomfort

Both types 2 and 3 can be stopped from harassing women, whereas it is difficult to prevent type 1 harassers from engaging in this behavior.

Lucero, Middleton, Finch, and Valentine (2003) analyzed a large number of published arbitration cases to further identify categories of perpetrators. Based on these cases, these authors clarified the types of men who engaged in the most prevalent workplace sexual harassment as:

1. *Persistent harassers:* This category included men who harassed varying numbers of women either using extreme ("hard-core") or less extreme forms of harassment
2. *Exploitives:* These individuals were opportunists who took advantage of the situation, but also seemed to engage in more sexually related behaviors than the persistent perpetrators

Lucero and colleagues suggested that interventions be developed to match the type of harasser. One problem with this study, however, is that many victims do not report being harassed, and the majority of incidents probably do not reach the arbitration stage, thus qualifying the authors' conclusions.

Methodological Issues in Cross-Cultural Sexual Harassment Research

According to Sigal and Jacobsen (1999), several difficulties arise in cross-cultural sexual harassment incidence studies, including the lack of standardized measures, the nature of the samples—particularly in terms of how representative these samples are of workplace sexual harassment in the countries surveyed—how the samples were recruited (most often, convenience samples constitute the participant pool), varying conditions of administration of measures, and translation problems, as well as cultural appropriateness of materials.

INTERNATIONAL DOMESTIC VIOLENCE

Definitions

The American Psychological Association Task Force on Violence and the Family (American Psychological Association, 1996) defined intimate partner violence or domestic violence as "a pattern of abusive behaviors including a wide range of physical, sexual, and psychological maltreatment used by one person in an intimate relationship against another to gain power unfairly or maintain that person's misuse of power, control, and authority." A variation on this basic statement was expressed in the United Nations' definition of violence against women, which was adopted by the General Assembly in the 1993 Declaration on the Elimination of Violence against Women. The definition states that violence against women is

> any act of gender-based violence that results in, or is likely to result in, physical, sexual, or psychological harm or suffering to women, including

threats of such acts, coercion, or arbitrary deprivation of liberty, whether occurring in public or private life. (United Nations, 1993, Article 1)

Although there are commonalities in these two definitions, particularly in the specification of types of harm or maltreatment, the differences are interesting. The UN definition includes the identification of the victims as women, whereas the APA definition is basically gender neutral. In addition, the UN definition specifies that harm has to occur or be likely to occur, is applicable to any specific behavior, and doesn't mention intention. Conversely, the APA definition is related to a pattern of abusive behavior and includes the concept of abusive behaviors designed to achieve or maintain unfair power over another person. The APA definition seems to relate more specifically to the power-based theories described in an earlier section of this chapter than the UN definition does.

International Laws on Domestic Violence

The United Nations is one of the foremost international entities working toward developing legal means of addressing issues of gender-based violence. As with sexual harassment, its Convention on the Elimination of All Forms of Discrimination against Women focuses on helping UN member nations to develop legal means of dealing with domestic violence, which is deemed a violation of a basic human right. In a 2000 report, the special rapporteur to the United Nations on violence against women, Radhika Coomaraswamy, examined the issues that individual countries are facing in developing laws against domestic violence.

According to the report (Coomaraswamy, 2000), under international human rights law, states have a duty not only to avoid committing human rights violations themselves but also to prevent and respond to human rights abuses perpetrated by their citizens. CEDAW has made recommendations to states as to how they should proceed in implementing domestic violence laws. The report also presents different strategies used internationally to address domestic violence.

Types of Intimate Partner Violence

Wallace (1998) cited Walker's well-known "cycle of violence" as a significant conceptualization of the course of spouse battering. According to this cycle, the first stage is "tension building," in which the abuser becomes increasingly angry and enraged and engages in smaller acts of spouse battering. This stage is followed by the "explosion stage," in which the battering becomes extremely violent. Finally, there is a period of "calm, loving respite," with contrition and apologies on the part of the abuser, along with his promises that he will never hurt her again.

In another approach, Johnson and Ferraro (2000) identified the following four categories of partner violence:

1. *Common couple violence* occurs in the course of arguments and is unlikely to lead to abusive and violent patterns of behavior.
2. *Intimate terrorism,* according to the authors, is a pattern of behavior that is most relevant to the current presentation. It is conceptualized as a means used to control the other person and as more likely to evolve into violent attacks. It is perpetrated much more frequently by men than by women and is most likely to cause injury and be associated with emotional abuse.
3. *Violent resistance* is violence by women in response to abuse perpetrated by their partners.
4. *Mutual violent control* is unusual in that both partners engage in violence to control the other person.

Johnson and Ferraro suggest that the second form of intimate partner violence is the most relevant to domestic violence, and this chapter discusses only studies involving that type of violent interaction.

CROSS-CULTURAL STUDIES OF DOMESTIC VIOLENCE

In this section of the chapter, we will discuss international investigations of domestic violence in terms of incidence rates and also how the theories and models described earlier relate to the various studies. The international research is organized in terms of geographical regions. Once again, the section is a selective overview of recent research.

Latin America

Flake (2005) investigated domestic violence in Peru, which was identified by the investigator as a patriarchal culture. Information was obtained from a "nationally representative household survey of more than 27,000 women, aged 15 to 49" (p. 359). The final sample included 15,991 women. The survey, which requested information only on physical abuse, revealed that close to 40 percent of the sample had been physically abused. Risk factors for abuse included early marriages, low educational attainment for the woman, and violence in the natal family. Other factors focused on alcohol consumption of the abuser and the lack of marriage ties between the partners.

There were some inconsistent patterns related to the woman's status. On the one hand, higher status of the female partner seemed to be a protective factor against abuse, but on the other hand, if the male partner's status was below that of the female, abuse seemed to be more likely. This finding is congruent with the patriarchal culture interpretation of violence against women. In Latin America, the concept of *machismo* revolves around the man as the dominant partner who is expected to be "strong, sexually aggressive, and able to consume large amounts of alcohol" (Flake, 2005, p. 354). *Marianismo*, conversely, refers to expectations that the woman will be dominated by the man and should accept any treatment passively, including that of domestic abuse. The traditional Latin American conceptualization is that the woman is dominated first by her father, then by her husband, and finally by her son if she is widowed. Therefore, according to Flake, if the woman has a higher status than the man, he might attempt to reestablish his domination through physical violence.

One of the strengths of Flake's research, besides the sample (large and representative), is the presentation of domestic violence as complex and the suggestion that there are a number of risk factors that can predict intimate partner violence in Peru. In addition to describing the influence of the patriarchal society, which fits with the integrated model in terms of a culture supportive of domestic violence, Flake raises the possibility that acceptance of violence by political forces (as is the case in Peru's history) may be internalized to produce tolerance and approval by individuals in the private sphere.

Limitations of the Flake investigation include the fact that the measure of domestic violence was one question, dealing solely with physical violence, and the results were based on self-reports. As will be seen in many studies, there is a significant likelihood that respondents will underreport the incidence of intimate partner violence. Flake suggests that this study be viewed as a beginning investigation that should lead to studies with improved methodologies.

In an investigation in another Latin American country, Ceballo, Ramirez, Castillo, Caballero, and Lozoff (2004) described the results of the administration of the Conflict Tactics Scale (CTS; Straus, 1979) to measure physical and verbal domestic abuse among 215 poor mothers in Chile. Close to 80 percent of the women reported experiencing verbal abuse, and more than 30 percent had experienced physical abuse.

Ceballo and colleagues offered several explanations for the abuse described by the respondents in their study. Domestic violence in Latin America is often viewed as *la violencia privada*—violence that is kept within the family. The authors also identified Chile as a patriarchal culture with a history of political violence, which may have created an increased tolerance for wife beating. Until quite recently (1989), Chile supported the concept of a man's total control and "ownership" of his wife, which would suggest that any form of violence by the partner would be seen as an acceptable means of maintaining that control. McWhirter (1999) added to this analysis of the Chilean culture, stating that it is seen as appropriate for men to show that they love their women by physically and verbally abusing them. McWhirter also suggests that machismo and dependence on alcohol play a role in the occurrence of domestic violence in Chile. These explanations conform to both of the models or theories described earlier in the chapter.

The strengths of the Ceballo et al. (2004) study include the use of the standardized scale, the CTS, which is widely administered in cross-cultural studies of domestic violence. Participants were from the working class and generally were quite poor, a sample that is not involved in many studies and is difficult to recruit. Trained interviewers conducted the study, which is another advantage of the investigation.

The authors themselves cited several limitations of their study, including the problems that some forms of violence were not investigated and that self-report measures are subject to biases such as underreporting. In addition, the sample was selective and the results may not generalize to other women in Chile.

Middle East

Recently, researchers have begun to explore domestic violence in Middle Eastern countries. Many of these countries conform to the patriarchal culture described earlier, and some of these countries are characterized as "cultures of honor." In addition, support for domestic violence as a method of controlling female behavior and protection of abusers are strong components of the cultural climate in these nations.

In a significant investigation in Israel, Haj-Yahia (2000) surveyed 1,111 Arab women to determine the extent of domestic violence they experienced during the period of time of their engagement. In an attempt to obtain a representative sample in a sensitive manner, the author approached clergymen in the Arab community to obtain a list of names of Arab women whose engagement had been announced. The average engagement period was a little more than a year. The majority of women were Muslim, and all were going to marry partners of the same religion. The study utilized women from the respondent's community as assistants and included the administration of the self-report measure of the Revised Conflict Tactics Scale (CTS2; Straus, Hamby, Boney-McCoy, & Sugarman, 1996), which was adjusted to be culturally appropriate. Haj Yahia found that psychological abuse had been experienced most often by the engaged women (close to 75% of the women had been psychologically abused at least once), followed by smaller percentages of physical abuse (just under 20%), and then by sexual abuse (13%).

Haj Yahia's investigation had many strengths, including the use of the standardized Revised CTS, evaluated and adjusted for cultural appropriateness; the involvement of community women as research assistants to enhance the comfort and security of participants; the large return rate (close to 80%); and the sensitive manner in which the sample was recruited. Again, issues arise in terms of the use of a self-report measure, and the nature of the sample, although in this case an attempt was made to make the sample as representative as possible to ensure generalization to other Arab women in Israel. Finally, it may be questioned as to whether Arab women in Israel are comparable to Arab women residing in Arab countries.

In another study by Haj Yahia (2002) conducted in Jordan, the country is described as a patriarchal society in which traditional gender-roles are paramount and where men are considered to be dominant both according to Islam as it is interpreted (although he mentions that clearly there are other more egalitarian interpretations of the Koran) and in society and the culture. Within this framework, Haj Yahia investigated attitudes toward wife beating among more than 350 Jordanian wives, the majority of whom were Muslim. Respondents were approached in public organizational settings such as health clinics in three different locations: a city, a village on the outskirts of the city, and a refugee camp. In the study measuring female attitudes, a standardized scale, the revised Inventory of Beliefs about Wife-Beating (IBWB; Saunders, Lynch, Grayson, & Linz, 1987) and the Familial Patriarchal Beliefs Scale (FPB scale; Smith, 1990), among other measures, were administered to participants. All measures were modified to be culturally appropriate.

Haj Yahia found that a strong tendency emerged among Jordanian women in his sample to justify wife beating (from about 35% to close to 70%, depending on the described behavior of the wife), particularly if she is disobedient or does not respect her husband's family. In general, Jordanian women saw the women's behavior as being the cause of the beating and believed that the beating would help them to become better wives. These wives also tended to dismiss the violent behavior of the husbands (e.g., "They are men and that's how men are," Haj Yahia, 2002, p. 288) and failed to support punishment for abusive husbands. Haj Yahia stated that most Arab countries do not have specific laws against domestic abuse. It could be inferred that, far from seeing the abuse even as a "private family matter" as was indicated in some of the studies performed in Latin America, these respondents did not view the abuse as a problem at all, although Haj Yahia did not reach this conclusion. Patriarchal beliefs also played a role in predicting these attitudes.

This second Haj Yahia study also was a significant contribution to cross-cultural investigations of domestic abuse in part because of the standardized measures used, which were reviewed for cultural appropriateness, and for the sensitive manner in which the materials were administered. However, as Haj Yahia stated, the study still involved a convenience sample, which would limit generalization of the results, and all measures were self-reports. Most importantly, as indicated by the author, the investigator did not ask if the women had been physically or psychologically abused. However, it is an important initial attempt to describe the influence of a variety of factors on attitudes toward wife beating in Jordan. Of course, sampling men, although it would be extremely difficult, would add to the generalizability of the results.

This study certainly confirmed our view that patriarchal cultures such as Jordan would be supportive of domestic abuse and violence. Araji and Carlson (2001) described examples from Jordan, which the authors characterized as a culture of honor to further illustrate the influence of a supportive culture on violence against women. The authors suggested that "honor killings," in which a male family member, often a brother, murders a female, account for a significant proportion of the murders in Jordan. The researchers described one incident in which a 16-year-old girl was raped by her brother. When she reported the rape to her older brother, another brother was encouraged to kill his sister, which he did by stabbing her to death. Several relatives watched the killing and encouraged and cheered when the murder took place.

A recent newspaper article (Bilefsky, 2006) suggested a variation on the honor killings described by Araji and Carlson (2001). It described the dilemma of families in Turkey now that officials have begun to assign more severe penalties, such as life in prison, to male family members who kill women in their families. In the past, younger brothers were assigned the task, because they usually received lenient penalties. Since harsher sentences have begun to be imposed in Turkey, family members have started to pressure girls who have "strayed" (e.g., falling in love with a boy, wearing a short skirt, etc.) to commit suicide, which the article termed "honor suicide." Family members may hand the victim a gun or another weapon and lock her in a room until she commits suicide. In the poor, rural area of Batman in Turkey, there have been 102 suicides by women since 2000.

In the first major study of domestic violence in Syria (Zoepf, 2006), husbands and wives in approximately 1,900 families were questioned. It was revealed that about 25 percent of the married women in the sample had experienced physical spouse abuse. Although methodological details of the major study were not revealed in the article, thus preventing a critical analysis, the study was significant because, in general, domestic violence is not discussed or seen as a problem in Syria. Married women who are beaten are viewed as "being in a bad relationship" rather than victims of domestic violence.

Finally in this selective review of Middle East studies, Sa (2004) examined the data obtained from administering two questions on physical marital abuse as part of a more general survey, the 1995 Egypt Demographic and Health Survey (EDHS-95). Data from more than 6,000 married women, a part of the overall sample, revealed that close to a third of the respondents reported having experienced physical abuse or wife beating at some point during their marriage. The EDHS-95 report stated that female participants believed that wife beating was justified under some circumstances.

Sa interpreted these results in terms of the patriarchal culture of Egypt. Even though Egypt seems to be more progressive than other countries in the area, the traditional gender-role pattern prevails in the society and in the home, where the woman is viewed as inferior and the male head of the family has the power. Education is a mediating variable, resulting in a lower level of spouse battering when the husband or wife has a more advanced educational background than in other cases. Sa concluded that although spousal abuse, or violence against wives, is a serious problem in Egypt, again it is not publicized and remains "covered under the veil" (Sa, 2004, p. 14). However, the data in Sa's report have to be interpreted with caution since, as the author points out, they are based on self-report measures and most likely are biased by underreporting.

Europe

McCloskey, Treviso, Scionti, and dal Pozzo (2002) compared characteristics and risk factors of abused women in Italy with those in the United States. Thirty-two battered women were recruited from a hotline service in Rome (the author indicated that it was unclear what the response rate was for this sample), and their responses were compared with 50 women recruited from shelters in the southwest part of the United States, representing a response rate of 50 percent. The U.S. sample consisted of approximately equal numbers of Hispanic and European-American women. The researchers administered a modified version of the CTS and a measure of psychopathology (the Brief Symptom Inventory; Derogatis & Melisaratos, 1983).

All samples in the study demonstrated comparable levels of physical abuse, but American women had experienced sexual abuse more frequently than Italian women. One important difference was that Italian women generally stayed in their marriages longer than American women, which could be attributed in part to the Italian family structure, which may be more patriarchal, according to the authors, making it more difficult for the wives to leave. The researchers found that alcohol was implicated in wife beating in the United States, but not in Italy.

McCloskey et al. (2002) reviewed several limitations of their study, including the fact that the samples were self-selected and therefore generalization was limited, there was an absence of control samples of women who were not abused, the measures were all based on self-reports, and there might have been underreporting of the abuse. In addition, the numbers of respondents were small for both samples, and the Italian group was recruited from a source (hotline) that was different from the American sample, which was recruited from shelters.

An analysis of domestic violence in Russia was proposed by Horne (1999). In her article, Horne cited a number of sources that suggested the rate of domestic violence in Russia could be at least four or five times as extensive as that in other Western nations. In examining the possible causes of this increased incidence of intimate partner violence, she discussed the influence of the lowered status of women as well as the reemergence of traditional gender-roles in Russian society. Horne proposed that these factors are a more significant determination of high rates of incidence than the commonly held perceptions that the unpredictability of the changing economic and political climate, the general increase of violence in society, and the problem of alcoholism are the primary causes of increased violence against female partners. To support her contention, Horne discussed the concept of domestic violence as a family issue rather than a national social problem, as well as the difficulties that women face in the Russian legal system. Horne does suggest that the services for abused women may be improving, but the overall impression is that the Russian culture is generally condoning, if not actively supportive, of domestic violence—a concept congruent with the integrated model presented earlier in this chapter.

The final European study that will be discussed in this section was conducted by Antonopoulou (1999). In a mailed survey administered to more than 670 individuals as part of a class project, gender differences in perceptions of the equality of women and men in Greece emerged in the predicted direction; that is, men were more likely than women (50% to 33%) to think that women had societal status equal to men. Consistent with this finding, more than 70 percent of women believed that gender discrimination still existed in Greece.

Methodological evaluation of this study was almost impossible due to the paucity of details presented in the article, but the author suggested that generalization of these results was limited by the self-selective sample. In addition, it does not appear as though the questions were standardized; the gender samples were unequal, with about 50 percent more women than men; and no statistical domestic violence incidence evidence was presented.

Asia

Xu, in a study published in 1997, revealed that close to 60 percent of a sample of 586 married women in Chengdu, China, in 1986 reported spousal abuse by their husbands, with psychological abuse occurring more frequently than physical abuse. Xu identified China as embodying a patriarchal family culture similar to the Latin American and other cultures. According to the author, Confucianism requires women to obey their fathers first, then their husbands, and finally their sons. Consistent with points made earlier, Xu suggested that domestic violence is seen as an issue for the family, not for the society. In addition, the author found that frequent conflicts and poor communication were associated with increased spousal abuse.

Xu (1997) pointed to limitations of the study in terms of an inability to provide causal links between cultural aspects and spousal abuse as well as a lack of information about abusers, an important issue that also applies to several other cross-cultural studies. In addition, self-report, the lack of standardized measures, and the fact that the data were obtained so many years ago limited the conclusions that can be drawn from this study.

More recently, Xu, Zhu, O'Campo, Koenig, and Mock (2005) published another study of incidence of spousal violence in China. The randomly selected sample in this investigation consisted of 600 women who were recruited from a clinic in Fuzhou, China, in 2000. An impressive proportion of close to 90 percent of those approached agreed to participate in the study. The measures were derived from the World Health Organization (WHO) Multicultural Study on Women's Health and Life Experiences Questionnaire, a culturally appropriate measure based in part on the standardized CTS. Physical, psychological, and sexual abuse measures were administered by health care individuals in a face-to-face setting. Close to 45 percent of the respondents had experienced spousal abuse at least once during their marriage and about 25 percent in the last year, with frequent altercations being associated with the last figure. A large percentage of the women felt that if a husband found out that his wife had been having an affair, he would be justified in abusing her (with a higher percentage associated with women who had experienced abuse than those who had not). The authors suggested that, although the modern Chinese culture publicly supports equality between men and women, the society—and many women in this sample—still endorse the patriarchal society and family structure.

This study was a considerable improvement over the first reviewed investigation by Xu in terms of the time of data collection and the standardization of the measures. The response rate also was impressive. Once again, however, self-reports could have produced biased underreporting, particularly in a society where spousal abuse is not a publicly discussed issue.

In Japan, another Asian country where domestic violence has been considered a private matter and there is a patriarchal culture, Yoshihama (2005) used a focus group approach to investigate spousal abuse. Sixty-four women who had experienced physical, psychological, or sexual abuse from male partners were recruited in three different Japanese cities (Yokohama, Kobe, and Sapporo) by women's organizations. More than 50 percent of the sample were still married to the perpetrator of the abuse. Women described a pattern of physical, psychological, and sexual abuse with several specific examples of psychological abuse, for example, "Who do you think you are? You are just a woman" (p. 1244.) A variety of tactics utilized by their partners were described, including blaming the woman, denying that they had engaged in the abuse, using threats, concealing any wounds the women may have incurred by injuring them in hidden places, and preventing them from contacting support systems. Yoshihama indicated that the abuse was consistent with the patriarchal society of Japan, that the violence was a means of controlling their partners, and that in-laws either seemed to be "helpless bystanders, or at times, co-perpetrators in their son's abuse" (pp. 1253–1254). Therefore, according to Yoshihama, in-laws' behavior "constitute a key component in the patriarchal clan system that supports domestic violence" (p. 1254).

The author mentioned some difficulties with the study, in that the sample was relatively small and basically self-selected and that only self-identified abused women participated. The results may not generalize to abused women in Japan in general, and the methodology did not permit a comparison with nonabused women. In addition, the focus group approach may have affected women in a positive way (e.g., to share, understand, and talk about their experiences); however, women also may have been directly influenced in a negative way by this approach (e.g., possibly seeing the violence as more normative).

Kozu (1999) also described the Japanese patriarchal structure, particularly in the family, as contributing to the condoning of spousal abuse (e.g., the wife calls her husband *shujin*, "master," p. 51). In addition to the adherence to traditional gender-roles, cultural expectations focus on maintaining harmony in society or in the family and avoiding shame at any cost. As a result, domestic abuse would most likely remain a private matter. Kozu discussed one national study in 1992, which found that almost 80 percent of the close to 800 respondents reported having experienced domestic violence. According to Kozu, these results should be regarded with caution, however, since the survey included all volunteers and may not have been representative of Japanese women in general.

In India, Panchandeswaran and Koverola (2005) conducted interviews, including semistructured surveys, with 90 abused women seeking help in Chennai (Madras) in Tamil Nadu. The authors indicated that India is another patriarchal culture in which domestic violence is considered to be a family issue. The majority of respondents were Hindus and had been married at an early age. The participants were recruited from counseling centers and were interviewed by a social worker using the language of the community. Close to 80 percent of the sample reported being abused every day, and more than 40 percent stated that the abuse had started soon after their marriage. Although some of the respondents had experienced severe physical abuse (70% reported threats that their husbands would kill them), a higher percentage (90%) were exposed to psychological abuse. Several factors were precursors to the abuse, including "sexual jealousy," alcohol abuse by their spouses, and dowry-related issues such as considering the dowry to be insufficient. As was the case in Japan, in-laws were implicated in the abuse in many cases. Women were reluctant to seek help from the police, and many were dissatisfied with the police response. The authors stated that despite the formation of all-women police stations, the police generally were part of the patriarchal structure of the society and did not respond effectively to the abused women. The participants were most positive about their help from counseling centers.

Once again, this study had significant limitations. The authors suggested caution in generalizing the results, since the respondents were selected from counseling centers. In addition, the format and nature of the questions were not discussed in a manner thorough enough to form conclusions about the validity of the data collected. Finally, only abused women were sampled, and abusers were not involved in the study.

A second study, by Jejeebhoy (2006), focused on the same issues as the previous one, including identifying India as a patriarchal society where men exert control over women. However, this study was conducted in rural communities in northern and southern India rather than in a city. A survey of more than 1,800 women was described and approximately 40 percent reported that they had experienced intimate partner violence. However, the author reiterated the claim, which has been reported in other studies, that this figure represented underreporting. Two precipitating events that were considered significant were the wife's "disobedience" to the husband (e.g., not taking care of his dinner, or flirting with another man) and the husband's excessive drinking. The patriarchal nature of the Indian culture appears to have been internalized by the female respondents since approximately 75 percent of the women condone wife beating and believe that a "bad wife" deserves to be punished and the husband has the "right" to punish her.

One of the positive aspects of this study was the inclusion of two samples from disparate rural communities, but the study was limited in generalization to that type of setting and also was methodologically weaker because standardized measures such as the CTS were not utilized. In addition, Jejeebhoy stated that the somewhat differing results from the two communities should be interpreted with caution, since the questions were asked in a different form for respondents in each area.

Africa

Koenig et al. (2003) surveyed more than 5,000 women in a rural community in southwest Uganda (the Rakai area, where the majority of residents are of the Baganda ethnic group) in 2000–2001. The researchers stated that the predominant pattern was "patrilineal" (i.e., where women stay with their husband's clan) and a significant number of men had many wives or sexual partners. Women were questioned about domestic violence with a revised form of the CTS, and the interviewers were experienced and of the same gender as the respondents. Approximately 40 percent of the women were found to be victims of psychological or verbal violence, and a little over 30 percent experienced physical abuse. Both failure to take care of the house or the husband and disobedience by the wife were cited as common precipitants for violence, as well as excessive drinking by the male spouse. A large majority of women (and a higher percentage of men whose attitudes also were measured) condoned abuse of the female spouse in certain situations.

This study had many positive points, including the large sample, the high response rate, the inclusion of attitude measures, and the use of the basic standardized CTS. Questions that remain include whether there was underreporting of abuse and how well the results would generalize to other areas of Uganda.

In general, the studies reported in this section of the chapter supported our interpretation of domestic violence in many cultures as being due in part to both the patriarchal nature of the societies and the social climate in various countries. In particular, Latin American, Middle Eastern, and Asian studies provided the strongest confirmation of the validity of the integrated model and power theories as explanations of international intimate partner violence.

A recent analysis by Archer (2006) reached somewhat similar conclusions. The researcher reviewed studies conducted in various countries and stated that "husbands' physical aggression against wives is inversely related to women's societal power" (p. 147), an association which "clearly support[s] the link between patriarchal values and physical aggression by husbands" (p. 47). Archer also suggested that collectivist cultures, in which the welfare of the society, family, and culture is seen as more important than the needs of the individual, are associated with higher levels of spousal abuse of women than individualist cultures.

OUTCOMES FOR VICTIMS OF DOMESTIC VIOLENCE

Two studies that were reviewed earlier examined the relationship between intimate partner victimization and psychological consequences. In the first, the research by Ceballo et al. (2004) investigated domestic violence effects on female victims in Chile. Women who had experienced spousal battering showed high amounts of depression, as measured by the Center for Epidemiological Studies Depression Scale (CES-D; Radloff, 1977). There also was an association with PTSD symptoms, but the researchers cautioned that it could not definitely be determined if the spousal abuse was the cause of these symptoms.

In the second study, McClosky et al. (2002) utilized the Brief Symptom Inventory (Derogatis & Melisaratos, 1983) to measure the psychological consequences of domestic abuse in the United States and Italy. The most frequent psychological difficulty experienced by the abused women in their sample was depression. More than 40 percent of the battered women had thought about committing suicide and/or had internalized the characterization of themselves as worthless.

In a relevant review article, Fischbach and Herbert (1997) discussed several additional physical and psychological effects of wife beating, including ''dowry deaths,'' ''honor killings,'' ''bride burnings'' that are often concealed as ''accidents,'' and chronic pain, as well as psychological effects such as depression, suicide, and substance abuse. The authors point out that much of the evidence for psychological consequences of domestic violence emanates from studies in ''developed countries'' or Western nations. One of the difficulties in determining the association between spousal abuse and psychological symptoms, according to Fischbach and Herbert, is that mental illness is conceptualized differently in various cultures, and also that in many countries psychological problems are seen as stigmatizing so that there is little identification of individuals with these difficulties.

Types of Perpetrators of Domestic Violence

One of the most frequently cited classification of perpetrators was developed by Holtzworth-Munroe and Stuart (1994). This categorization identified three types of potential abusers:

1. *''Family-only'' batterers:* This type of perpetrator engages in less violent behavior and is not likely to be psychologically disturbed.
2. *Dysphoric-borderline men* engage in more violent behavior both against their wives and other people outside the family home. These abusers are psychologically disturbed, exhibit borderline personality characteristics, and may have an alcohol abuse problem.
3. *Violent antisocial abusers* are the most violent both at home and elsewhere and exhibit antisocial personality disorder characteristics.

More recently, Jacobson and Gottman (1998) used a dual classification system to identify abusers as either ''cobras,'' who were described as ''cold,'' as detected by physiological measures, even when attacking their victims, and ''pit bulls,'' who showed more physiological activation patterns when attacking their partners. Johnson and Ferraro (2000) compared the cobra category to the antisocial abusers of the above system, and the pit bulls to the dysphoric-borderline category.

Clearly it is important to understand perpetrators' behavior and characteristics so that prevention and intervention programs may be developed to eliminate domestic violence cross-culturally. Primary prevention programs are targeted to large groups of individuals, but likely would be most effective with the family-only batterers. Secondary programs developed to target at-risk abusers might be effective with the dysphoric-borderline perpetrators. However, it is possible that any prevention program would be ineffective with violent antisocial abusers.

The issue of classification of batterers and development of appropriate prevention programs cross-culturally is a significant step forward. In many countries, the issue is seen as a private one that is not discussed in public; there is cultural support for wife battering, which sometimes is internalized by battered women; or prevention programs are directed solely or primarily at domestic violence victims. It is important for societies to assign responsibility for violence to perpetrators and to develop programs to reduce spousal violence, as well as to train victims to protect themselves and to provide these battered spouses with supportive services and shelters.

Methodological Issues in International Domestic Violence Research

Two review articles provided an overview of some of the major issues that complicate cross-cultural research on domestic violence. Fischbach and Herbert (1997) emphasized the difficulty of cross-cultural comparisons because of the varying ways in which cultures identify domestic violence—if there is any public consideration of the issue in the country at all. In addition, they pointed out the problem of the underreporting of domestic violence by respondents, a difficulty emphasized by several of the studies reviewed above. Some reasons proposed by Fischbach and Herbert to explain this phenomenon included the socialization of women to accept abuse as a justified form of controlling and shaping women's behavior, particularly in cultures where there are restrictive traditional gender-roles.

The Haj Yahia studies (2000, 2002) cited earlier and other research suggested that women internalize the concept that wives who behave inappropriately deserve their punishment, which in other cultures would be seen as wrong and categorized as abuse. Cultures that support wife abuse and do not have severe penalties for abusers would fit into the model of the effect of the climate on attitudes and behaviors of spouses.

The review article by Fischbach and Herbert (1997) also suggested other motivations for the underreporting, including the woman's feelings of shame because she accepts her husband's view that she is a bad wife, and her fear that if she reports this abuse, even in a study, her husband will punish her. The wife also may be protective of her spouse, especially considering that the cycle of violence includes a stage characterized by apologies for the abuse and loving statements by the husband, and protective of her family, which might experience shame as a result of her "bad behavior."

Kishor (2005) suggested ways in which underreporting may be reduced, if not eliminated. If respondents are presented with many questions concerning varying forms of abuse, interviewers are trained to establish rapport, questions on abuse are asked later in the interview, and extensive safeguards of confidentiality and protection are provided, this issue may be less prevalent. However, in certain countries (e.g., in Pakistan, as discussed by Kamal and Tariq, 1997), it is extremely difficult even to recruit respondents; therefore even these safeguards may be insufficient to produce accurate prevalence statistics.

Another issue is the varying types of measures used in studies of domestic violence cross-culturally. The most methodologically sound approach is to use standardized measures such as the CTS-R. Kishor emphasized the advantages of the CTS-R, probably the most widely utilized domestic violence measure in cross-cultural research. The author indicated that this measure has been incorporated into a general Demographic Health Survey (DHS) as part of a series of cross-cultural projects. The CTS-R includes a series of questions about different specific incidents of domestic abuse, rather than asking respondents if they had experienced domestic abuse in general. This approach is comparable to the advantages of the Revised Sexual Experiences Questionnaire (SEQ-R; Fitzgerald, Gelfand, & Drasgow, 1995), which also asks individuals about experiences of specific types of sexual harassment. This approach yields more valid data than simply asking if individuals have experienced domestic violence, since specific behaviors can be stated comparably in diverse cultures and the term *domestic abuse* might be understood in different ways in various countries.

Kishor (2005) described other problems with cross-cultural studies, including the issue of whether the surveys or interviews ask about abuse within a recent time frame or lifetime abuse figures. The author also states that standardized quantitative measures such as the CTS-R do not investigate reasons for the abuse, nor do these measures provide data on risk factors for abuse or the consequences of intimate partner violence.

Another related problem cited by Kishor is that almost all the studies are cross-sectional, but that in order to infer causes of abuse, studies need to be longitudinal. Of course, considering the difficulties in recruiting respondents for one-time cross-sectional comparisons, realistically it would be almost impossible to obtain volunteers for a longitudinal study.

Other methodological problems, as can be ascertained from the preceding review of cross-cultural domestic violence research, relate to the types of sample; in particular, how large and how representative are the samples involved in the studies? The same issue of the sample representativeness arises in any cross-cultural comparisons. Most cross-country researchers recruit convenience samples, and the results present difficulties in generalization even to the country in question. In addition, many of the studies reviewed in this chapter were restricted to a single country and did not include cross-cultural comparisons. Even the time frame in which the varying experiments were conducted can confound any meaningful cross-country comparisons.

Another issue relates to the researchers' organization. If the research is conducted under the auspices of a university or research center, the results might be different from a study conducted by the government. Governments may restrict the release of negative information, such as high rates of domestic abuse, particularly if the government is characterized by a patriarchal structure. Also, as mentioned earlier, in several countries there is a "code of silence" that prohibits discussion or public consideration of controversial issues such as domestic abuse.

While reviewing the cross-cultural research on domestic violence, it seemed that the majority of the studies focused on prevalence of the abuse and did not focus very much on types of abusers or consequences to victims. Abuse statistics, although flawed, are important to establish, but the motives, behaviors, and attitudes of abusers, as well as physical and psychological consequences to victims, provide a more extensive and realistic picture of the problem. Obviously, as Kishor (2005) suggests, it is important to have cultures and government acknowledge the scope and nature of domestic abuse and develop governmental support, services, and programs for abused wives, but cultural attitudes (e.g., attitudes toward violence and toward women) and characteristics of abusers also should be examined.

The senior author of this chapter was amazed by doctoral students' responses to a question raised in class about how to reduce or eliminate domestic abuse. These students' responses focused entirely on services for victims and how to train women to avoid the abuse, while neglecting the issue of how to reduce or eliminate the abusers' behavior. Support for an emphasis on abusers as well as on the victims of domestic abuse echoes an article by Kilmartin (2006). He stated that domestic violence is a "men's issue" and that it is men's responsibility to stop the violence. Kilmartin recounted that the typical response from people when they learn that his research is concerned with spousal abuse is "Why does she stay with him?" rather than "Why does he hit her?" Men's negative attitudes toward women clearly have to be changed, but Kilmartin also says that men have to change their self-attitudes and conceptualizations of their gender: Instead of thinking that "boys will be boys," men should start to explore how men can learn to exert more control over their violent behavior.

COMPARISON OF INTERNATIONAL SEXUAL HARASSMENT AND DOMESTIC VIOLENCE

The broad rationale for a comparison of international domestic violence and sexual harassment is that both types of violence function as a means for men to control and limit the actions of women. As has been described earlier, sexual harassment primarily occurs in environments in which women are increasingly achieving access to power, authority, and self-determination in work and school settings. Sexual harassment can be seen as a way in which males, who have long held power in these environments, attempt to maintain their status and control. In other words, sexual harassment can be seen as a "territorial" response to the perceived threat or competition from females. Domestic violence, which may take the form of sexual, physical, or psychological abuse, can perhaps more easily be seen as a tactic by which males hold onto power in the face of perceived challenges or threats from their female partners.

Beyond these obvious similarities, our review of the relevant research seems to suggest that there are also theoretical reasons why these two types of violence can be seen as expressions of a common behavior dynamic. As outlined by the integrated model (Fitzgerald, Hulin, & Drasgow, 1995), there are two factors that govern the occurrence of sexual harassment: a climate that condones or does not limit this behavior and a male-dominated environment. According to power and sociocultural models of domestic violence, abuse occurs in environments that have strong patriarchal structures where men hold power and women are expected to be submissive.

To explain domestic violence and sexual harassment under a common model, we propose an overlap of the two theories, such that the hostile work environment, as proposed by the integrated model, is seen as representing a subsample of a larger patriarchal society, as proposed by the sociocultural models. That is to say, the work or school settings (in the case of sexual harassment) and the home environment (in the case of domestic violence) both represent environments in which men dominate women. In both of these environments, there are cultural sanctions as to what types of behaviors—in this case, violence—can be employed by males in their attempts to control women. In most patriarchal communities, the type of violence condoned in an office setting is different from what is allowable at home. In the workplace, physical violence is generally prohibited, and therefore violence in this environment is expressed through sexual inappropriateness (e.g., in quid pro quo). For example, a male worker who feels threatened or challenged by a female colleague may make off-color comments about her appearance or, in extreme cases, engage in sexual coercion. In the home environment in patriarchal societies, there are generally very few limits on men as far as what they can do to control their partners. As a result, our model predicts that the violence will take many forms, including mental, physical, and sexual abuse.

There are some limits to this particular theoretical comparison, however. Based on the integrated model, there should be higher rates of both types of violence, sexual harassment and domestic violence, against women in patriarchal societies, because of the concentration of power in men, than in nonpatriarchal societies. However, this general prediction is almost impossible to investigate because of a number of confounding factors. The most important impediment to a cross-cultural comparison of incidence rates in the two types of cultures is that statistics are almost nonexistent in many countries, particularly so in patriarchal cultures (for example, in Syria, as we discussed earlier, the first major incidence study on domestic violence was conducted only very recently). In several countries, there is a "culture of silence" (for example, in Latin America and the Middle East), resulting in almost no consideration of these types of issues in the public domain. In addition, what would be perceived as abuse in nonpatriarchal cultures might be considered to be "appropriate punishment of erring wives" in patriarchal cultures.

Another confounding factor relates to the identification of cultures as patriarchal or nonpatriarchal. In particular, in countries with diverse populations, such as the United States, Canada, England, and many European nations, classifying an entire country as patriarchal or nonpatriarchal may be inaccurate.

Another issue relates specifically to sexual harassment. Although some researchers hypothesized that patriarchal cultures might have higher rates of sexual harassment than nonpatriarchal cultures (e.g., Wasti et al., 2000; Menon & Kanekar, 1992), the very nature of the patriarchal culture suggests that women will be restricted to the home rather than joining the workforce. Therefore, sexual harassment rates might be lower in patriarchal cultures simply because there are fewer women in the workforce than in nonpatriarchal societies.

Several of the methodological issues that we raised earlier in our analysis of both international workplace sexual harassment and domestic violence also preclude any test of comparative incidence rates among various nations. In addition, even if incidence figures are available, public access to these statistics may be limited by governments attempting to protect their image.

Specific Comparisons of Workplace Sexual Harassment and Domestic Violence

Beyond the theoretical comparisons, there are other conceptual parallels that can be drawn between the two types of violence. For example, sexual harassment can be divided into two forms: quid pro quo and hostile work environment; domestic violence also can be assigned categories: physical abuse (including murder), psychological abuse, and sexual abuse. Although power and dominance issues are relevant to all categories of sexual harassment and intimate partner violence, quid pro quo can be seen as conceptually similar to physical abuse, and hostile work environment appears to be more related to psychological abuse.

Both quid pro quo and physical abuse are clearer examples of inappropriate behavior and are more difficult to misinterpret than psychological abuse and hostile work environment. In legal cases, quid pro quo harassment incidents have to happen only once to be actionable; similarly, severe physical abuse clearly can lead to arrest and convictions of the abuser. However, hostile work environment sexual harassment is much more difficult to prosecute, as is psychological domestic abuse, even though these types of behaviors probably occur more frequently than the more severe forms of violence. In each case, there has to be a pattern of behavior before action can be instituted.

The public view of psychological abuse and hostile workplace climate clearly is less negative than reactions to more severe forms of abuse. The lesser forms of abuse are seen as relatively ambiguous, and as not very serious, which can lead to legal problems in prosecution. Physical evidence is readily available in physical abuse cases, but not in psychological abuse.

Another similar aspect of both types of violence is that laws may be passed prohibiting the behavior, but enforcement of these laws lags behind the legislation in many countries, and not just in patriarchal societies. Abused wives often are discouraged and fail to report the abuse, and the same pattern is true for victims of workplace sexual harassment.

Reactions of Victims, Outcomes for Victims, and Types of Perpetrators

In both types of violent behavior, female victims often internalize blame or responsibility for their victimization (as seen, for example, in the Haj Yahia, 2002, finding that Jordanian women believe that women who are physically abused deserve this treatment because they are "bad wives"). In terms of outcomes, the clearest psychological consequence of both intimate partner violence and workplace sexual harassment is depression. The issue of whether or not PTSD is associated with these types of victimization has to be resolved through more methodologically sound studies.

Comparisons of types of perpetrators of sexually harassing behaviors and intimate partner violence are less clear-cut, primarily because there has not been sufficient research related to perpetrators. It is possible, however, to conceptually relate chronic, persistent quid pro quo sexual harassers to "hard-core" domestic abusers. In both cases, treatment would be unlikely to eliminate the harassers' behavior. Family-only batterers may be similar to opportunistic harassers—more situational perpetrators. Victims are readily accessible in the family setting, and situational factors such as frustration (e.g., financial, relatives, crying babies) may contribute to these types of spouse abusers. In a comparable sense, opportunistic harassers do not continually seek out victims, but if they are available and the workplace climate is supportive of harassment and protective of harassers, then the sexual harassment behavior may occur. Similarities between the two types of perpetrators also focus on the prediction that family-only batterers and opportunistic sexual harassers may be prevented from engaging in the negative behavior by secondary prevention programs directed toward at-risk individuals.

CONCLUSION

In this chapter, we have reviewed a number of studies on international workplace sexual harassment and domestic violence, and we generally have found support for our contention that the integrated model of sexual harassment and the power and socialization models of domestic violence are productive frameworks within which to analyze the results of these studies. In addition, we have examined a number of intersecting concepts that relate the two areas of intimate partner violence and workplace sexual harassment. Our review was selective and evaluative in terms of indicating a number of methodological difficulties that complicate cross-cultural comparisons of these behaviors. It is clear that conducting more specific comparisons across nations is important, as is increased attention to physical and psychological outcomes for victims, as well as characteristics and programs for perpetrators.

REFERENCES

American Psychological Association. (1996). *APA Presidential Task Force on Violence and the Family report*. Washington, DC: American Psychological Association.

Antonopoulou, C. (1999). Domestic violence in Greece. *American Psychologist, 54,* 63–64.

Araji, S. K., & Carlson, J. (2001). Family violence including crimes of honor in Jordan. *Violence against Women, 7,* 586–621.

Archer, J. (2006). Cross-cultural differences in physical aggression between partners: A social-role analysis. *Personality and Social Psychology Review, 10,* 133–153.

Baker, N. V., Gregware, P. R., & Cassidy, M. A. (1999). Family killing fields: Honor rationales in the murder of women. *Violence against Women, 5,* 164–184.

Barak, A., Pitterman, Y., & Yitzhak, R. (1995). An empirical test of the role of power differential in originating sexual harassment. *Basic and Applied Social Psychology, 17,* 497–517.

Bilefsky, D. (2006). How to avoid honor killings in Turkey? Honor suicide. *New York Times,* July 16, p. A3.

Ceballo, R., Ramirez, C., Castillo, M., Caballero, G. A., & Lozoff, B. (2004). Domestic violence and women's mental health in Chile. *Psychology of Women Quarterly, 28,* 298–308.

Coomaraswamy, R. (2000). Combating domestic violence: Obligations of the state. In UNICEF, *Domestic violence against women and girls* (pp. 10–11). Florence, Italy: UNICEF. Available at www.unicef-icdc.org/publications/pdf/digest6e.pdf.

Cortina, L. M., Fitzgerald, L. F., & Drasgow, F. (2002). Contextualizing Latina experiences of sexual harassment: Preliminary tests of a structural model. *Basic and Applied Social Psychology, 24,* 295–311.

Crocker, D., & Kalemba, V. (1999). The incidence and impact of women's experiences of sexual harassment in Canadian workplaces. *Canadian Review of Sociology and Anthropology, 36,* 541–558.

Dansky, B. S., & Kilpatrick, D. G. (1997). Effects of sexual harassment: Theory, research, and treatment (pp. 1152–1174). Boston: Allyn & Bacon.

Derogatis, L. R., & Melisaratos, N. (1983). Brief Symptom Inventory: An introductory report. *Psychological Medicine, 13,* 595–605.

Fischbach, R. L., & Herbert, B. (1997). Domestic violence and mental health: Correlates and conundrums within and across cultures. *Social Science Medicine, 45,* 1161–1176.

Fitzgerald, L. F., Drasgow, F., Hulin, C. L., Gelfand, M. J., & Magley, V. J. (1997). The antecedents and consequences of sexual harassment in organizations: A test of an integrated model. *Journal of Applied Psychology, 82,* 578–589.

Fitzgerald, L. F., Hulin, C. L., & Drasgow, F. (1995). The antecedents and consequences of sexual harassment in organizations. In G. Kaita & J. Hurrell Jr. (Eds.), *Job stress in a changing workforce: Investigating gender, diversity, and family issues* (pp. 55–73). Washington, DC: American Psychological Association.

Fitzgerald, L. F., Magley, V. J., Drasgow, F., & Waldo, C. K. (1999). Measuring sexual harassment in the military: The Sexual Experiences Questionnaire (SEQ-DOD). *Military Psychology, 11,* 243–263.

Flake, D. F. (2005). Individual, family, and community risk markers for domestic violence in Peru. *Violence against Women, 11,* 353–373.

Gelfand, M. J., Fitzgerald, L., & Drasgow, F. (1995). The structure of sexual harassment: A confirmatory analysis across cultures and settings. *Journal of Vocational Behavior, 47,* 64–177.

Haj-Yahia, M. M. (2000). Patterns of violence against engaged Arab women from Israel and some psychological implications. *Psychology of Women Quarterly, 24,* 209–219.

Haj-Yahia, M. M. (2002). Beliefs of Jordanian women about wife beating. *Psychology of Women Quarterly, 26,* 282–291.

Holtzworth-Munroe, A., & Stuart, G. L. (1994). Typologies of male batterers: The subtypes and the differences among them. *Psychological Bulletin, 116,* 426–497.

Horne, S. S. (1999). Domestic violence in Russia. *American Psychologist, 54,* 55–61.

International Labor Organization (1992). Combating sexual harassment at work. *Conditions of Work, 11.*

International Labor Organization (2001). Government, employer, and worker representatives gather in Penang to combat risk of sexual harassment at work. Press release, October 2. Retrieved July 27, 2003, from http://www.ilo.org/public/english/region/asro/bangkok/newsroom/pr0112.htm

Jacobson, N., & Gottman, J. (1998). *When men batter women: New insights into ending abusive relationships.* New York: Simon & Schuster.

Jejeebhoy, S. J. (1998). Wife beating in rural India: A husband's right? Evidence from survey data. *Economic and Political Weekly, 33,* 855–862.

Johnson, M. P., & Ferraro, K. J. (2000). Research on domestic violence in the 1990s, making distinctions. *Journal of Marriage and the Family, 62,* 948–963.

Kamal, A., & Tariq, N. (1997). Sexual Harassment Experience Questionnaire for workplaces of Pakistan: Development and validation. *Pakistan Journal of Psychological Research, 12,* 1–20.

Kilmartin, C. (2006). Men's violence against women. *Society for the Psychological Study of Men and Masculinity Bulletin, 10*(4). Retrieved September 16, 2006, from http:/www.apa.org/divisions/div51/div51/01.htm.

Kishor, S. (2005). Domestic violence measurement in the demographic and health surveys: The history and challenges. Paper presented at "Violence against Women: A Statistical Overview, Challenges, and Gaps in Data Collection and Methodology and Approaches for Overcoming Them," an expert group meeting organized by the UN Division for the Advancement of Women, the Economic Commission for Europe, and the World Health Organization, Geneva, Switzerland, April.

Koenig, M. A., Lutalo, T., Feng, Z., Nalugoda, F., Wabwire-Mangen, F., Kiwanuka, N., et al. (2003). Domestic violence in rural Uganda: Evidence from a community-based study. *Bulletin of World Health Organization, 81,* 53–60.

Kompipote, U. (2002). *Sexual harassment in the workplace.* Washington, DC: International Labor Rights Fund.

Kozu, J. (1999). Domestic violence in Japan. *American Psychologist, 54,* 150–154.

Lengnick-Hall, M. L. (1995). Sexual harassment research: A methodological critique. *Personnel Psychology, 48,* 841–864.

Lucero, M. A., Middleton, K. L., Finch, W. A., & Valentine, S. R. (2003). An empirical investigation of sexual harassers: Towards a perpetrator typology. *Human Relations, 56,* 1461–1483.

McCarthy, J. M. (1997). Landmark decision on sexual harassment for Malaysian women. *Journal of International and Comparative Law, 3.* Retrieved September 9, 2006, from http://www.nesl.edu/intljournal/vol3/mal.htm.

McCloskey, L. A., Treviso, M., Scionti, T., & dal Pozzo, G. (2002). A comparative study of battered women and their children in Italy and the United States. *Journal of Family Violence, 17,* 53–74.

McWhirter, P. T. (1999). La violencia privada: Domestic violence in Chile. *American Psychologist, 57,* 37–40.

Menon, S. A., & Kanekar, S. (1992). Attitudes toward sexual harassment of women in India. *Journal of Applied Social Psychology, 22,* 1940–1952.

Panchandeswaran, S., & Koverola, C. (2005). The voices of battered women in India. *Violence against Women, 11,* 736–758.

Pryor, J. B. (1987). Sexual harassment proclivities in men. *Sex Roles, 17,* 269–290.

Pryor, J. B., Lavite, C. M., & Stoller, L. M. (1993). A social psychological analysis of sexual harassment: The person-situation interaction. *Journal of Vocational Behavior, 42,* 68–83.

Radloff, L. S. (1977). The CES-D Scale: A self-report depression scale for research in the general population. *Journal of Applied Psychological Measures, 1*(3), 385–401.

Sa, Z. (2004) Women's status, marital power relations and wife beating in Egypt. Paper presented at the 2004 annual meeting of the Population Association of America, Boston, April 1–3.

Saunders, D. G., Lynch, A. B., Grayson, M., & Linz, D. (1987). The inventory of beliefs about wife beating: The construction and initial validation of a measure of beliefs and attitudes. *Violence and Victims, 2,* 39–57.

Sigal, J., & Jacobsen, H. (1999). A cross-cultural exploration of factors affecting reactions to sexual harassment: Attitudes and policies. *Psychology, Public Policy, and Law, 5,* 760–785.

Sigal, J., & Nally, M. (2004). Cultural perspectives on gender. In M. A. Paludi (Ed.), *The psychology of gender* (pp. 27–40). Westport, CT: Praeger.

Smith, M. D. (1990). Patriarchal ideology and wife beating: A test of a feminist hypothesis. *Violence and Victims, 5,* 257–274.

Srinivasan, A. (1998). Sexual harassment. *Indian Journal of Gender Studies, 5,* 115–125.

Straus, M. A. (1979). Measuring intrafamily conflict and violence: The conflict scales. *Journal of Marriage and the Family, 41,* 75–88.

Straus, M. A., Hamby, S. L., Boney-McCoy, S., & Sugarman, D. B. (1996). The revised Conflict Tactics Scales (CTS2): Development and preliminary psychometric data. *Journal of Family Issues, 17*(3), 283–316.

Timmerman, G., & Bajema, C. (1999). Sexual harassment in northwest Europe: A cross-cultural comparison. *European Journal of Women's Studies, 6,* 419–439.

United Nations. (1979). Convention on the Elimination of All Forms of Discrimination against Women. Retrieved September 11, 2006, from http://www.un.org/womenwatch/daw/cedaw/cedaw.htm.

United Nations. (1993). Declaration on the Elimination of Violence against Women. General Assembly Resolution 48/104, December 20, 1993. Retrieved September 10, 2006, from http://www.ohchr.org/english/law/eliminationvaw.htm.

United Nations. Commission on Human Rights. (2003). *Integration of the human rights of women and the gender perspective.* Geneva: United Nations.

U.S. Equal Employment Opportunity Commission. (2005). Sexual harassment. Retrieved March 12, 2006, from http://www.eeoc.gov/types/sexual_harassment.html.

Walker, L. E. (1999). Psychology and domestic violence around the world. *American Psychologist, 54,* 21–29.

Wallace, H. (1998). *Victimology: Legal, psychological and social perspectives.* Boston: Allyn & Bacon.

Wasti, S. A., Bergman, M. E., Glomb, T. M., & Drasgow, F. (2000). Test of the cross-cultural generalizability of a model of sexual harassment. *Journal of Applied Psychology, 86,* 766–778.

Xu, X. (1997). The prevalence and determination of wife abuse in urban China. *Journal of Comparative Family Studies, 28,* 280–303.

Xu, X., Zhu, F., O'Campo, P., Koenig, M. A., & Mock, V. (2005). Prevalence and risk factors for intimate partner violence in China. *American Journal of Public Health, 95,* 78–85.

Yoshihama, M. (2005). A web in the patriarchal clan system. *Violence against Women, 11,* 1236–1262.

Zoepf, K. (2006). UN finds that 25% of married Syrian women have been beaten. *New York Times,* April 11, p. A5.

PART VI

Achievement Motivation, Career Development, and Work

Chapter 19

Women and Achievement

Martha Mednick
Veronica Thomas

Scholars and laypersons alike have long been concerned about women and the why, or more often the why not, of their achievement. It was not, however, until the late 1960s, growing substantially in the 1970s, that psychologists began to take a serious look at the psychological study of women, offering new theories, methods, techniques, and innovative perspectives on women's experiences, circumstances, and development. These efforts were taking place within the larger context of the women's movement of the 1960s and the overall rediscovery of important contributions of women to various segments of American society.

In the last edition of this *Handbook*, we examined women and the psychology of achievement in terms of theory and research related to achievement motivation; the fears of success and failure; cognitive variables affecting gender and achievement; gender differences in causal attributions for success and failure; and occupational aspiration and career development of women, with special emphasis on women's achievement in mathematics and science-related fields; and methodological issues in relation to the study of women's achievement. The review, which synthesized findings through the 1980s, also summarized what the literature, although then quite limited, had to say about minority women. The current goal is to continue the story from the 1990s to the present, addressing what researchers have been trying to explain, what kinds of concepts are being studied, and how feminist perspectives continue to affect the questions being asked, conclusions drawn, and perhaps thoughts on the future.

VISIBLE CHANGES IN WOMEN AND ACHIEVEMENT: INTO THE 21ST CENTURY

Psychological theorizing and research on women and achievement have continued to develop and expand during the past two decades. The current look at women and the research in the field, however, calls for a reexamination of this issue within a context quite different from the one that existed in the 1980s. Presently, different kinds of questions are being asked related to women and achievement, and in different settings (e.g., politics, the military, and other nontraditional fields). There has been, to some extent, a change in climate about "women's place" in society, gender-roles and stereotypes, and gender "difference" research. Over the past three decades, women have made significant strides in various spheres of American life, social, economic, and political.

Women and Politics

One of the most visible achievements among women in American society since the 1980s has been in politics. A record number of women serve in the 110th Congress (Center for American Women and Politics, 2007). In 2007, women held 86, or 16.1 percent, of the 535 seats in Congress—16 (16%) of the 100 seats in the Senate and 70 (16.1%) of the 435 seats in the House of Representatives. Further, in January 2007, Nancy Pelosi (D-CA) became the first woman to serve as Speaker of the U.S. House of Representatives. She holds the highest position in the House and is third in the presidential line of succession.

Women of color have also made strides in national politics since the 1980s. For example, in 1992, Carol Moseley-Braun (D-IL) was the first African American women to win a major-party Senate nomination and the first woman of color to serve in the U.S. Senate. In 1992, Lucille Roybal-Allard (D-CA) was elected and served as the first Mexican American woman. During that same year, Nydia Velázquez (D-NY) was also elected to the House and was the first Puerto Rican woman to serve. In 2005, Condoleezza Rice, an African American woman, became U.S. secretary of state, having already served for four years as the assistant to President George W. Bush for national security affairs.

It is important to note, relative to women leadership in national politics, that the United States is markedly behind many other countries. The Inter-Parliamentary Union, the international organization of parliaments of sovereign states, ranked the United States 70th among the world's countries in terms of ratio of female representatives in the national legislature (Inter-Parliamentary Union, 2007)—lagging substantially behind Rwanda, where almost half (48.8%) of the legislative seats are held by women, China, Iraq, Afghanistan, and every country in Scandinavia.

Over the last half of the 20th century, 42 countries have had at least one woman as president or prime minister (*San Francisco Chronicle*, 2007). These include Great Britain (Margaret Thatcher), Sri Lanka (Sirimavo Bandaranaike), Ireland (Mary Robinson), Rwanda (Agathe Uwilingiyimana), Bermuda (Pamela Gordon), Jamaica (Portia Simpson Miller), Liberia (Ellen Johnson-Sirleaf), New Zealand (Helen Clark), Finland (Tarja Kaarina Halonen), India (Indira Gandhi), Israel (Golda Meir), Canada (Kim Campbell), and France (Edith Cresson). Some of these women, as well as other women country leaders, were elected; others were appointed. Some followed their husbands or fathers into political office, while others were elected or appointed based upon their own political contributions and reputation. In 2007, there were 11 women leading governments, including seven presidents, one chancellor, and three prime ministers.

While the increase in representation is welcome, the lack of women in the political pipeline remains a serious barrier to further growth of women in the upper echelons of elected officials.

Women and Postsecondary Education

Another significant change is in the area of postsecondary education in general, especially in certain fields. Women have earned more bachelor's degrees than men every year since the 1981/82 academic year and more master's degrees since 1985/86 (U.S. Department of Education, 2005). Furthermore, over the past 25 years, there has been more diversification among major fields selected by women. In 1970, for example, women earned 43 percent of the bachelor's degrees awarded in the United States, but the majors were very sex-segregated, with women particularly overrepresented in education, humanities, and some social sciences. During that same year, overall, women received only 13 percent of doctoral degrees. By 2003/04, women were receiving 57 percent of bachelor's degrees awarded, 59 percent of master's degrees, and 48 percent of doctorates (U.S. Department of Education, 2005). That year, they received 46 percent of first professional degrees.

In some fields, numbers of doctorates awarded to women have surpassed those of men. For example, doctorates in microbiology awarded to women rose from 18 percent in 1971 to 52.1 percent in 2005; in anthropology, from 26 percent to 56.3 percent; and in sociology, from 21 percent to 62 percent. Between 1971 and 2005, women's share of doctorates awarded in psychology rose from 13 percent to 42 percent, and in 2005, women received 37.7 percent of doctorates in science and engineering fields overall. Interestingly enough, computer science is the only science field to have the dubious distinction of witnessing a decline in the share of its bachelor's degrees granted to women between 1983 and 2002, with the percentage of bachelor's degrees awarded to women in the field dropping from 36 percent to 27 percent (National Science Foundation, 2006).

Scholarship on the segregation (and integration) of academic fields generally focus on explaining segregation in terms of women's, rather than men's, choices of sex-typical fields (England et al., 2003). Women's entry into male-dominated fields has been the principal cause of declines in sex segregation, while the scarcity of men in prominent female-dominated fields (e.g., education, humanities, social sciences) remains a significant obstacle to further gender integration (Jacobs, 1995). Some scholars argue that this gender "shake-up" in the academy was part of a larger change of the gender system involving women's increased continuity of employment, an organized women's movement, and a push for the federal commitment to antidiscrimination laws (England et al., 2003).

Women, Employment, Changing Gender Composition, and Desegregation of Fields

As a result of the increasing number of women receiving degrees across various majors, most of the major professions and scientific fields (e.g., accounting, law, medicine, dentistry) underwent dramatic shifts in gender composition over the past 25 years. With the shift particularly evident in the discipline of psychology, in 1991 the Board of Directors of the American Psychological Association (APA) appointed a Task Force on the Changing Gender Composition of Psychology. At that time (in 1991), psychology had the largest percentage of women in its ranks among the science and engineering disciplines.

The APA task force was charged with examining shifts in the gender composition of the discipline and identifying the implications of these shifts for psychology. As a result of an intensive case study, the task force put forth five major conclusions:

1. The representation of women has increased substantially in many other scholarly disciplines.
2. The increasing representation of women in psychology has been especially dramatic.
3. The growth in women's participation in psychology can be attributed partially to increased demands for psychological personnel and their improved access to training and employment.
4. It is likely that the growth in women's participation in psychology can also be traced to diminished numbers of men choosing to enter the discipline, particularly since the early 1980s, due to the declining status or prestige of the occupation.
5. The participation of women in the various employment sectors and work roles, along with the career advancement, has been more mixed.

The task force also concluded, consistent with the work of various occupational segregation researchers (e.g., Reskin & Roos, 1990), that it does not appear that the increased presence of women necessarily leads to their increased status and influence within that profession and the larger society.

Over the past 25 years, researchers began to consider whether men avoided entering fields when a certain level of female participation is reached. This fits with some scholars' (e.g., Williams, 1993) notion that the social construction of masculinity includes rejection of whatever is seen as female. Interestingly enough, using national data, findings from empirical research show that the higher the percentage of women obtaining degrees in a field in a given year, the fewer men that entered the field 4–7 years later (England et al., 2003). As a result, England and colleagues (2003) concluded this men's avoidance of fields as they "feminize" may impede an integrated equilibrium such that as fields increase their female population, fewer men enter them, which further increases their percentage of females, which leads even fewer men to enter.

Although women have made remarkable strides in education over the past three decades, these gains have not yet translated to full equity in pay—even for college-educated women who work full-time. Thus, a typical college-educated woman working full-time earns $46,000 a year, compared to $62,000 for college-educated male workers—a difference of $16,000 (Day & Hill, 2007). The gap, starting early, widens as time goes by, such that 10 years after graduation, women have fallen further behind, earning 69 percent of what men earn. A 12 percent gap appears even when controlling for variables such as hours, occupation, parenthood, and other factors known to directly affect earnings (Day & Hill, 2007). This also may contribute to men's seeming avoidance of fields they perceive as "female." England (1992), a sociologist, argues that if young men taking courses see women as majors, graduate students, teaching assistants, and young faculty members, they may conclude that this is a "female field" and avoid majoring in it and applying for graduate study. This may, according to England, be because they anticipate that if fields become "too female," their pay compensation will decline, as claimed by advocates of comparable worth.

PSYCHOLOGICAL RESEARCH ON ACHIEVEMENT AND GENDER

So, what can psychological theory and research now say about women and achievement since the late 1980s? In this update of the original chapter with a view from the 1990s to the present, we examine the extent of continuing interest in women and achievement in the psychological literature, explore the context of research in this area over the past 15 years, consider the kinds of questions being formulated and reformulated, and make projections for the early decades of the 21st century. As with our original chapter, our overarching questions remain: In what ways has a feminist perspective affected the questions being asked regarding women and the psychology of achievement? Have the phenomena being studied changed? If so, what is the nature of the change? Have important, useful theories or perspectives been developed? How have we dealt with integrating race, class, and ethnicity into this work?

Much of psychology's focus on achievement has centered on the concept of motivation, particularly achievement motivation and related concepts. Research often sought to answer a myriad of questions, such as:

- What is achievement motivation?
- What elicits achievement motivation in individuals?
- What enhances, sustains, and directs achievement motivation?
- How does achievement motivation vary across gender, ethnicity, and other cultural and contextual variables?

While there is some consensus regarding the definition of achievement motivation, per se, there is little agreement on how to best explain individual, contextual, and interactive differences.

An Overview of Achievement Motivation

Psychologists have long been interested in examining individual behavior that is motivated by the need for achievement. The classic way of studying achievement motivation was personified by the work of McClelland (1961) and Atkinson (1958), who defined achievement motivation as "competition with a standard of excellence." As such, achievement motivation was viewed as the desire to strive for success in situations involving a standard of excellence. In the Atkinson and Feather (1966) framework, individuals' achievement behavior is based on three factors:

1. the individual's predisposition to achievement
2. the individual's perception of the probability of success
3. the individual's perception of the value of the task

Here, it was presumed that the strength of motivation to perform some act was a multiplicative function of the strength of the motive, the expectancy (subjective probability) that the act will have as a consequence the attainment of an incentive, and the value of the incentive.

Achievement motivation researchers argue that the individual's perception of the probability of achieving the task would cause a "need to achieve" and a "fear of failure." These motives, in turn, would influence individuals' decisions on whether or not to ultimately attempt the task. The need for achievement (*nAch*), like all motives, was assumed to energize individual behavior in certain (achievement-related) situations. The originators of this achievement motivation theory had almost nothing to say about gender as a fundamental issue.

Achievement motivation was commonly measured though the use of the Thematic Apperception Test (TAT), a projective technique in which participants produced stories about a series of pictures. These pictures were considered to be portrayals of cultural situations in which behavior related to the achievement motive might be expected to occur. The underlying assumption with the TAT is that individuals will project their own motivations and interests onto the pictures. If an individual's stories consistently stress achievement, working hard, or excelling, it would be scored high for achievement motivation. In scoring TAT stories, several categories of achievement themes are considered, including an explicit statement about a desire to meet an achievement goal, action taken toward attainment of the achievement goal, thinking about reaching or failing to reach the achievement goal, blocks to meeting the goal, and assistance received in meeting the goal.

Clearly, achievement motivation has a long and robust history in the field due to the centrality of competence-relevant processes for human functioning and well-being and the broad applicability of these processes to such domains as schools, sports, and work (Elliot, Shell, Henry, & Maier, 2005). As such, achievement motivation, as formulated by McClelland and Atkinson, has spurred much research over the past 25 years. This body of work has focused, primarily, on the prediction and explanation of competence-relevant behavior.

Recent research has conceptualized achievement motivation in different ways. Three prominent constructs in contemporary research on achievement motivation are implicit theories of ability, perceived competence, and achievement goals (Cury, Elliot, Da Fonseca, & Moller, 2006). *Implicit theory of ability* includes individuals' lay conceptions of the nature of competence and ability. *Perceptions of competence* characterize individuals' beliefs about what they can and cannot accomplish in competence-relevant settings. *Achievement goals* are individuals' cognitive representations of competence-based outcomes that they strive to attain or avoid. Three types of achievement goals have been articulated:

1. *performance approach goals*, focusing on attaining competence relative to others
2. *performance avoidance goals*, focusing on avoiding incompetence relative to others
3. *mastery goals*, focusing on the development of competence itself and of task mastery

The achievement goal approach offers the link between achievement motivation and performance. Ultimately, achievement goals affect the way a person performs a task and represents a desire to show competence (Harackiewicz, Barron, Carter, Lehto, & Elliot, 1997).

Achievement Motivation and Women

A number of other psychological concepts have been studied in relation to achievement and gender (as well as ethnicity). These include task persistence, task engagement, attributions, stereotypes, expectancies, and abilities, particularly in relation to mathematics. Traditional achievement motivation theories were, for the most part, intrapersonal in nature with a focus on individual's need, beliefs (e.g., expectancies), goals, task values, and self-regulatory mechanism. Within the past 15 years, researchers have urged that theories and research related to achievement motivation pay more attention to social context (Juvonen & Wentzel, 1996; Wigfield & Eccles, 2002).

In the 1990s, there grew an increasing realization of the complexity of understanding women's achievement and other issues related to the psychology of women. In the sixth edition of *Half the Human Experience: The Psychology of Women*, Hyde (2004) notes the striking paradox in the achievement literature. Based on an extensive review of the literature, Hyde concluded that girls start out in life with good abilities, yet end up in adulthood with lower-status jobs and less recognized achievement than men. Furthermore, girls do better in school, yet in adulthood they occupied lower-status and lower-paying jobs than do men. So, the big questions posed by many other feminist psychologists are:

- Given fewer early gender differences in abilities and achievement, why is this the case by adulthood?
- How can we best explain the ability–achievement gap among women in American society?

Today, most psychologists generally acknowledge that while social structures and discrimination based upon gender (as well as ethnicity and class) account for some of the achievement outcomes for women, they do not provide a complete explanation.

Explaining Gender Differences in Achievement Motivation

Little empirical research was conducted on the achievement strivings of women prior to the 1970s. Much of the need-for-achievement research done in the 1950s and 1960s was conducted on men, most likely because McClelland, who did much of this work, was at Harvard University, which was primarily a male institution at that time. Equally important, the absence of empirical interest in women and achievement may have been due to the biased belief that achievement was important only in the lives of men—that women were not motivated for achievement, but instead were motivated by social concerns or by a need for affiliation. In other words, women were presumed to be motivated by a desire for approval from other people rather than by internalized standards of excellence (Hoffman, 1972) and, as a result, did not receive serious attention in the achievement motivation field. Over the past 25 years, increased research related to gender and achievement that focused on personality and internal factors, such as expectancies and attributions, has been conducted to help explain women's achievement-related motivation and outcomes.

Findings from studies on achievement motivation in women have been mixed. Early studies concluded that women displayed lower levels of achievement motivation than did men (Alper, 1974; Hoffman, 1972). During that time, women's lower level of achievement motivation (as measured) was thought to explain their lower levels of occupational achievement.

Hyde (2004) concluded that the ideas related to gender differences in achievement motivation need to be reassessed, given that reviews of available research found little compelling evidence for lower achievement motivation in girls and women. She noted that the meaning of research findings is complex because achievement motivation has not been consistently tested under the same conditions in various studies. Hyde reports that under the simplest case (the "neutral" or "relaxed" condition), participants are simply given the test. In this condition, women show higher level of achievement motivation than do men. Under "achievement arousal" conditions (e.g., when participants are given anagram tests which they are told measure intelligence and capacity to organize, to evaluate situations quickly and accurately, and to be a leader), the literature demonstrates that males' achievement motivation increases sharply, whereas that of women does not. Hyde concluded that research on gender and achievement motivation is muddled, but gender similarities seem to be the rule. As such, more attention is being directed to gender similarities as well as differences, and researchers are being urged to examine the effect of situation and context, race and ethnicity, social class, and disability, as well as gender, on motivation (Hyde & Kling, 2001).

Fear of Success

The concept of a motive to fear success was developed by Horner (1968, 1972), and it generated a great deal of research shortly after its appearance in the published literature. Horner created this concept in an effort to better understand the basis of gender differences in achievement motivation. She argued that the motive to avoid success is related to the perceived conflict between achievement and femininity, and the perceived connection between achievement and aggressiveness, the latter behavior (aggression) being seen as inappropriate for women. Also, Horner postulated that competition against other individuals would elicit fear of success in women because of the affiliative and interpersonal concerns of women.

From Horner's conceptualization of fear of success in the late 1960s through the mid-1980s or so, fear of success was a very appealing construct, especially in the popular literature. Following several years of enthusiasm and much research in the area, however, the construct fell under harsh criticism because many of Homer's hypotheses and findings failed the test of replication. Another major problem was the consistent inability to empirically separate the fear of success construct from other related, though supposedly theoretically distinct, constructs such as fear of failure and test anxiety (Shaver, 1976). The consistent failures in construct validation created so many intractable theoretical and technical problems that research in the fear of success area virtually ceased after its heyday in the 1970s (Piedmont, 1995).

In the second edition of her text *The Psychology of Women*, Paludi (2002) drew the following conclusions in reference to Horner's original experiment on fear of success:

- No reliable gender or age differences in fear of success have been observed.
- Fear of success has shown no consistent relationship to ability or career goals in women.
- Inconsistent data exist to support the hypothesis that fear of success is less likely among black women and more likely among white women.
- Inconsistent data exist to support a relationship between fear of success and gender-role identity.
- It is unclear whether fear of success taps a motive or a cultural stereotype.

Despite fierce criticism, limited study of fear of success continues. Some of this work focuses on measurement issues, whereas other work relates to how fear of success correlates to various behavioral outcomes. Sancho and Hewitt (1990), for example, studied the extent to which scales designed to measure fear of success may actual be measuring fear of social rejection, with findings further calling into question the measures used. In another study, Piedmont (1995) took a look at fear of success and its conceptual relatives (i.e., fear of failure, text anxiety) within the context of a comprehensive personality taxonomy in hopes of providing a structure for better understanding how these motivational constructs impacted women's performance. Rothman (1996) studied fear of success in both men and women and concluded that fear of success has risen among men because men must now compete with both women and men in the job market. Despite this conclusion, the author further noted that women still may be particularly susceptible to fear of success, since they may develop the fear from gender-role stereotyping as well as from suboptimal early environments. Similarly, in arguing that fear of success is relevant to both men and women, Fried-Buchalter (1997) investigated fear of success, fear of failure, and imposter phenomenon among male and female marketing managers. Her results demonstrated that female managers were significantly higher than male managers on fear of success, but no significant gender differences occurred on the fear of failure and imposter phenomenon variables.

Gender Considerations in Defining and Measuring Achievement Motivation

From a feminist analysis, there has been some criticism of the use and interpretation of the TAT to elicit achievement motivation in women. Feminist scholars have also criticized the interpretation of earlier findings of achievement motivation studies. Stewart and Chester (1982) argued that achievement researchers ignored data suggesting that women are not aroused by traditional achievement manipulations. Some researchers (Adams, Priest, & Prince, 1985; Spence & Helmreich, 1978) question the notion of achievement motivation as a unitary construct, instead pointing out the need to recognize and measure multidimensional aspects of achievement motivation in women and men. Doyle and Paludi (1995) stress that women might fulfill their achievement need in ways that are defined as appropriate for women and strive for excellence in a wider range of domains than do men.

Responding to a number of studies reporting lower levels of achievement motivation in women in comparison to men, increasingly feminist scholars put forth arguments that questioned measurement that they felt were skewed toward male dominance and began to articulate some motivational theories of their own. Feminist psychologists noted the sex bias and methodological flaws in traditional research on achievement motivation (Hyde & Kling, 2001) and proposed vastly improved models, such as Eccles's (1987, 2005) expectancy × value model of achievement behavior.

Cognitive Variables Affecting Gender and Achievement

Cognitive approaches to examining issues related to women and achievement have been very popular over the past few decades. These approaches consider differences and similarities in how women and men think about achievement and cognitive and affective processes that instigate, direct, and sustain human action. In this section, we review published studies (since 1990) related to self-efficacy for, stereotypes and expectancies of, and attributions for achievement. Cognitive variables have long been utilized in theory of achievement and social learning, and they continue to have prominence in explanatory efforts focusing on gender and ethnic differences in various aspects of achievement. Two concepts that gained considerable attention since our last review—self-handicapping and stereotype threat—will also be considered.

Self-Efficacy

The concept of self-efficacy, introduced by Bandura (1986), refers to the belief or confidence that one can do the behaviors necessary to achieve a designed goal. Bussey and Bandura (1999) argued that self-efficacy develops in four ways:

1. Through graded mastery experiences
2. Through social modeling, such as seeing individuals such as oneself succeed at the task
3. Through social persuasion, in which another person expresses confidence in one's ability to succeed
4. By reducing stress and depression, building physical strength, and changing misrepresentation of bodily states

Individuals with a high level of self-efficacy pursue a relatively high level of performance and are prepared to persevere when they encounter problems (Bandura, 1986; Vrugt, 1994). A great deal of research in this area focuses on how self-efficacy influences academic motivation, learning, and achievement (Schunk, 1995). Bandura, Barbaranelli, Caprara, and Pastorelli (2001) also postulated that self-efficacy beliefs play a significant role in career choice and pursuing a career.

Gender differences in self-efficacy have been the focus of considerable study of academic achievement. Researchers often report that boys and men tend to be more confident than girls and women in science, mathematics, and technology-related subjects (Wigfield, Eccles, & Pintrick, 1996). However, Schunk and Pajares (2002) argue that gender differences in self-efficacy are often confounded by a number of other factors. For example, Pajares (1996) found that gender differences are often nullified when previous achievement is held constant. Also, boys and girls tend to adopt differing stances when responding to self-efficacy instruments, with boys being more self-congratulatory in their responses, whereas girls are more modest (Wigfield et al., 1996).

Another confounding factor they suggested is related to the manner in which gender differences typically are assessed and reported. Traditionally, students are asked to provide confidence judgments that they can accomplish a particular task or that they possess certain academic skills, and differences in the average level of confidence are interpreted as gender differences in self-efficacy. The nature of gender differences varies depending on whether asking boys and girls to provide self-judgments in the traditional manner or asking them to make comparative judgments regarding their ability in comparison to other boys and girls in their class and school.

Schunk and Pajares (2002) pointed out that the nature of the self-beliefs that may be underlying gender differences must be examined. These investigators noted studies concluding that gender differences in social, personality, and academic variables may actually be a function of general orientation (or the stereotypic beliefs about gender that students hold), rather than of gender per se. Since there is little empirical evidence for gender differences in self-efficacy among elementary-age children, Schunk and Pajares also suggest that gender differences are related to developmental level. Differences often begin to emerge following children's transition to middle or junior high school, with girls typically showing a decline level of self-efficacy beliefs (Wigfield, Eccles, MacIver, Reuman, & Midgley, 1991; Wigfield et al., 1996).

Over the past 25 years, Eccles and her colleagues have been studying social and psychological factors in an attempt to better understand the occupational and educational choices of men and women, and a comprehensive theoretical model of achievement-related choices was put forth. Within this framework, gender differences and individual differences within each gender regarding educational and occupational choices are thought to be tied to differences in people's expectations for success and subjective task value (i.e., importance the individual attaches to the various options perceived by the individual as available). In Eccles's and her colleagues' model, the relationship of these beliefs to cultural norms, experiences, aptitudes, and those personal beliefs and attitudes that are commonly assumed to be associated with achievement-related activities were also specified (Eccles, 1987, 2005; Eccles, Wigfield, & Schiefele, 1998).

Eccles and colleagues, in particular, have examined the sources and consequences of achievement self-efficacy beliefs (Eccles, 1994; Eccles, Barber, & Jozefowicz, 1999. Expectation of task-related success, which stems in part from beliefs of important others, is one of the major predictors of achievement choice in their model. This predictor has been confirmed in empirical studies. For example, the endorsement of gender stereotypes by parents was found to foster beliefs that their children had sex-typed abilities in various domains, including mathematics, sports, and social activities (Jacobs & Eccles, 1992). Subsequently, parental ability beliefs predicted children's self-perceptions, which in turn predicted their mathematics performance. This predictor has held true for adults as well.

Less research has focused on ethnic differences (and similarities) in self-efficacy, and even less has examined ethnic × gender differences (and similarities). Graham (1994) reviewed 133 empirical studies examining achievement motivation, locus of control, causal attributions, expectancy of success, and self-concept of ability in samples of African Americans. Her review demonstrated that African Americans generally appear to maintain a belief in personal control, have high expectancies, and enjoy positive regard. Graham's review was guided by an intrapersonal view of motivation (individual needs, self-directed thoughts, and feelings) with little attention to the larger context in which achievement strivings unfold (Graham & Hudley, 2002). In later work, Graham and Hudley (2002) pointed out the limitation of this approach, arguing the race and gender for understanding motivation and competence requires an examination of factors, many of which are historical and structural, that are unique to the lives of people of color.

Causal Attributions for Success and Failure

For years, social psychologists have studied the attributions or the process by which individuals make judgments about the causes of events. The study of attributions or judgments about why events occur includes individuals' results attributed to ability, effort, luck, and task difficulty. Further, these attributions have been categorized as those due to internal sources, such as ability and effort, and those due to external sources, such as luck and task difficulty.

The cognitive attribution theory of achievement motivation was proposed by Weiner (1972) to explain differences between high- and low-achievement individuals. Weiner's theory states that these differences are due to the individuals' beliefs of the causes of their successes and failures. High-achievement-oriented persons attribute the cause of their success to their own ability and hard work, whereas low-achievement-oriented persons attribute their successes to external causes (e.g., luck, a mistake) and their failures to internal causes (lack of ability).

Gender and ethnic differences have been reported in individuals' causal attributions for success and failure (Birenbaum & Kraemer, 1995), although this research is mixed. The general pattern reported for women is that of greater externality for success and more internality for failure; men's success and women's failures were generally attributed to internal dispositions, while men's failures and women's successes were attributed to external or environmental factors (Betz, 1993).

Even in the early 1980s, a meta-analysis of all the available studies on gender and attribution patterns indicated that the size of the gender differences described in studies is very small and that those effects that do occur may be due to how the information was elicited (Frieze, Whitley, Hausa, & McHugh, 1982). Hyde (2004) believes that research may still uncover important gender differences in causal attributions if the study designs become more complex, particularly if attention is given to situational factors, such as the type of task that is used.

Self-Handicapping

While much recent work has emerged in the literature on this topic, self-handicapping strategies were identified in the 1970s as a way for discounting ability attributions for probable failure while augmenting ability attributions for possible success. In fact, the notion of self-handicapping was introduced in the 1970s (Berglas & Jones, 1978) to described as an individual's attempt to reduce a threat to esteem by actively seeking or creating factors that interfere with performance as a causal explanation for failure. In other words, it is the process in which an individual deliberately does the things that increase probability of failure (Trice & Bratslavsky, 2000). The goals of self-handicapping are to disregard ability as the causal factor for a poor performance and to embrace ability as the causal factor for a success.

Contrary to what some researchers originally hypothesized, findings from various studies demonstrate that men, more often than women, self-handicap (e.g., Hirt, McCrea, & Kimble, 2000; Midgley & Urdan, 1995; Rhodewalt & Hill, 1995). Interesting enough, self-handicapping behavior does not appear to reduce motivation to succeed, and in some context, it may increase it (Rhodewalt, 1990). Lucas and Lovaglia (2005) found that the idea of self-handicapping behavior is related to the desire to protect a valued status position and that minorities and women self-handicapped less often than did whites and men. They argue that white men, in particular, generally enjoy (unearned) privilege and higher status than other groups, which perhaps explains the propensity for these men to self-handicap.

Stereotype Threat

Another cognitive factor that has been recently introduced into the psychological literature to explain the underperformance of disadvantaged groups, particularly in academic settings, is that of stereotype threat. Originally introduced and tested by Steele (1992, 1997, 1998, 1999) and later examined by other investigators (e.g., Osborne, 2001; Steele, James, & Barnett, 2002; Steele & Aronson, 1995), stereotype threat emphasizes the deleterious outcome stemming from the threat of being viewed through the lens of a negative stereotype or the fear of doing something that would inadvertently confirm that stereotype. Stereotype threat is thought to result in uncomfortable feelings arising when individuals believe they are at risk of confirming a negative stereotype in the eyes of others (Spencer, Steele, & Quinn, 1999; Steele, 1997; Steele & Aronson, 1995).

In contexts in which particular stereotypes are active, Steele argues that individuals who are members of the negatively stereotyped groups will be conscious of the content of those stereotypes, and this may negatively affect their performance. For example, in the context of performance on standardized mathematics tests, women who are currently aware of gender stereotypes related to mathematics ability may experience anxiety related to the confirmation of those stereotypes, and as a result, their performance on the math tests will suffer. In other words, women fear that others will attribute their poor mathematics test performance to their gender. Steele argues that the stereotype does not necessarily have to be believed by individuals from disadvantaged group for it to have a negative effect. Instead, he stresses that stereotype threat is cued by the "mere recognition" that a negative stereotype could apply itself in a given situation.

As a test of stereotype theory, Steele, James, and Barnett (2002) investigated the perceptions of undergraduate women in male-dominated academic areas. Their results supported the notion of stereotype threat; that is, the undergraduate women participants in mathematics, science, or engineering were most likely to report feeling threatened by negative gender stereotypes that allege they are not as capable as men. The investigators noted the interesting finding that this feeling of threat was not similarly expressed by men majoring in female-dominated areas. The researchers argue that although these men are currently a minority in certain academic areas (e.g., K–12 teaching, nursing), they have not historically been negatively stereotyped or discriminated against in these domains because of their gender, and accordingly, it is not surprising that their experience differs from those described by women in male-dominated fields.

Using a sample of men and women who were highly and equally qualified, Spencer, Steele, and Quinn (1999) found that gender differences in mathematical performance could be eliminated by reducing stereotype threat. After observing gender differences in performance on a mathematics test, the investigators had participants perform the same test after being told either that the test produces gender differences or that it does not. Findings demonstrated that women who were told that the test does not produce gender differences performed as well as men, while women who were told that the test does produce differences performed significantly worse than men.

Another study, conducted by Brown and Josephs (1999), found similar results with women who had been told that the test would determine whether they were weak at mathematics (the stereotype-consistent test description). These women performed worse than the women who had been simply told that the test would indicate whether they were strong in mathematics. Subsequent research demonstrated that group identification influences the effects of stereotypes on performance. Schmader (2002) found that women for whom gender identity was important performed worse than did men on a mathematics test when they were told that the test produced gender differences, while women who placed little importance on their gender identity performed as well as men on the same test.

While Steele's theory of stereotype threat was thought to apply to any group for which there is a stereotype of intellectual inferiority, most of the psychological research done to test this theory has focused upon African American students or women in the mathematics domain, with little attention given to other disadvantaged groups (Osborne, 2001).

Gender, Mathematics, and Science: A Special Case

As an example of using cognitive concepts for predicting real-world behavior, much attention has been given to girls' and women's achievement in mathematics and science. Mathematics preparation has been seen as playing an important role in shaping individuals' careers (Betz, 1992; Meece, Wigfield, & Eccles, 1990), given that mathematics proficiency is required for entry into a wide range of college majors and occupations. Early research focused on mathematics avoidance and "math anxiety" as being detrimental to women's career development (e.g., Meece, Eccles-Parsons, Kaczala, Goff, & Futterman, 1982). There is solid evidence indicating that males have higher achievement in mathematics and higher levels of enrollment in mathematics courses (Hanna, 2003). What is a matter of dispute, however, is the extent to which these results are caused by socialization factors or innate differences.

Jordan and Nettles (1999) examined data from the National Educational Longitudinal Study of 1988 and found that girls had lower scores than boys on mathematics in the 12th grade, which is a pattern that exists in many other countries (Hanna, Kundiger, & Larouche, 1990). Given that gender differences in mathematics ability do not appear until around puberty, and that they appear in several countries, the differences have often been attributed to innate biological differences, social factors, and anxiety among females. In fact, gender differences in mathematics have long been explained as a sex-linked deficit—inferior spatial visualization among girls (Collins & Kimura, 1997) and deficits found in boys in terms of reading abilities and attention (Nass, 1993; Nordvik & Amponsah, 1998). A report by the American Association of University Women (1992), on the other hand, blames achievement differences on differential treatment of girls in the classroom, curricula that either ignore or stereotype women, and gender bias that undermines girls' self-esteem. Many psychologists and other social scientists argue that mathematics and science course differential patterns, and not biological factors, are the reason for observed gender differences in complex problem solving (Betz, 1992).

Closer inspection of the data resulted in conclusions that gender differences are negligible across most skills tapped by mathematics standardized tests (Hyde, 2005; Hyde, Fennema, & Lamon, 1990). Hyde, Fennema, and Lamon (1990), for example, reported that modest gender differences favoring boys emerge by high school and college in complex mathematical problem-solving tasks, which are viewed as critical for success in mathematics-related majors and occupations. Other explanatory factors put forth for gender differences in mathematics-related choices include internalized beliefs systems about proficiencies in mathematics (Hyde, Fennema, & Lamon, 1990), social environmental variables such as discriminatory practices, absence of social support (Betz, 1993), and how mathematics is taught (Meece et al., 1990). Recent studies show that gender differences in mathematics and science-related interests or academic choices may be partially mediated by self-efficacy (Lent, Lopez, & Bieschke, 1993). Thus, when belief about one's ability was controlled, Lent et al. (1993) found that the contribution of gender to the prediction of interest in and intention to pursue mathematics or science was either eliminated or substantially reduced, suggesting that perceived efficacy help account for men's and women's differential enrollment patterns in college mathematics courses.

Psychologists have also studied the valuing of various educational subjects and occupations as an explanation for gender differences in mathematics-related subject interest in school and subsequent career aspirations. At the elementary level, Eccles and Harold (1992) found clear evidence of gender differences in the value attached to various school subjects and activities. In their work, they found no gender difference in expectations for success in mathematics, but girls reported liking mathematics less than did the boys and rated mathematics as less useful than did boys. However, a review of the recent literature suggests that gender differences in cognitive variables such as self-efficacy may not be large enough to account for the wide disparity observed in men's and women's participation in mathematics-intensive fields. Researchers (e.g., Hyde, Fennema, Ryan, Frost, & Hopp, 1990) conclude that men's and women's differential participation in mathematics-related fields is determined by multiple factors (e.g., cognitive, expectations, social, familiar, economic) and that no one or two variables can explain all of the variance (Lent et al., 1993). Still, Hyde, Fennema, Ryan, et al., 1990 argue that, since mathematics learning is a long-term process, even small gender differences in self-beliefs about ability can have a cumulative and, ultimately, potent effect on academic and career choices.

The argument continues and has high visibility in scholarly literature. In a recent critical review article, Spelke (2005) discussed a long-standing issue related to gender disparity in the mathematics, engineering, and science faculties of U.S. universities. The author revisited the pair of longstanding claims—first, that males are more focused on objects from the beginning of life and therefore are predisposed to better learning about mechanical systems; males have a profile of spatial and numerical abilities producing greater aptitude for mathematics; and males are more variable in their cognitive abilities and therefore predominate at the upper reaches of mathematical talent. Spelke concluded that research on cognitive development in human infants, preschool children, and students at all levels fails to support these claims. Instead, she noted, the overwhelming research provides evidence that mathematical and scientific reasoning develop from a set of biological-based cognitions that both males and female share. Boys and girls harness abilities in the same ways, at the same times, to master the concepts and operations of elementary mathematics. Spelke also found, from her critical review of empirical research, that although older boys and girls show somewhat different cognitive profiles, the differences are complex and subtle and stem primarily from differing strategy choices. As a result, these capacities lead both men and women to develop equal talent for mathematics and science. In sum, Spelke concluded that the differing profiles do not add up to a male or female advantage in learning advanced mathematics and that the wealth of research on cognition and cognitive development, conducted over the past 40 years, provides no reason to believe that the gender imbalances on science faculties, or among physics majors, are a result of sex differences in aptitude.

There has been little empirical attention in the psychological literature given to understanding minority girls' and women's outcomes related mathematics-related issues. Decades of data from various reports released from the U.S. Department of Education, as well as the National Science Foundation, clearly show that individuals of color, excluding Asians, are less advantaged at every level from elementary school to graduate school onto the STEM (science, technology, engineering, mathematics) workforce. The achievement gap in mathematics is recognized as one of the most significant problems of African American students (both boys and girls) in U.S. schools, with the gap declining in the 1980s but widening in the 1990s. For example, in 1990, there was a 33-point gap reported between the scores of black and white students on the National Assessment of Educational Progress (NAEP) mathematics test at the eighth-grade level; by 2000, the gap had widened to 39 points. Similarly, in 1990 Latino students were 28 points behind their white counterparts, growing to 33 points in 2000 (U.S. Department of Education, various years, 1990–2005).

A number of factors have been offered to explain the achievement gap in mathematics between students of color and white students. Some of these factors examined include cognitive development (Cooper

& Schleser, 2004) and school-related variables (e.g., teacher quality, curriculum and instruction, classroom environment, teacher expectations), as well as factors outside of school such as socioeconomic status and parental influences (e.g., Darling-Hammond & Sykes, 2003; Ferguson, 1998; Jussim, Eccles, & Madon, 1996).

CONCLUSION

In the 1990s, some researchers called for reconsideration of what is (and is not) achievement, since "success" was generally considered within a masculine paradigm. Success was often represented by achievement in a high-level career, academic excellence, and other accomplishments typically associated with the values of middle-class men. As a result, accomplishments that were associated with women and traditional feminine characteristics received little or no attention. Doyle and Paludi (1995) called for a redefinition of achievement and achievement-related issues in a way that does not keep women's lives and realities invisible.

In a recent review of the literature on gender, competence, and achievement, Hyde and Durik (2005) pointed out three overarching issues that should frame the discourse in this field:

1. the importance of balanced consideration of gender differences and gender similarities
2. the importance of adopting a developmental approach, that is, recognizing that gendered patterns are not present at birth but, instead, emerge developmentally as a result of the culmination of experiences with parents, teachers, peers, and others
3. the importance of distinction between gender as a person variable (characteristic of the person) and gender as a stimulus variable (i.e., gender serving as a cue to others interacting with and responding to an individual)

Since the last edition of this *Handbook*, there has been more compelling evidence published to refute the "gender difference" or "gender gap" hypothesis in many areas, including various aspects of achievement (e.g., cognitive abilities, mathematics). The findings of an analysis of 46 meta-analyses that were conducted during the last two decades of the 20th century underscores that men and women are basically alike in terms of personality, cognitive ability, and leadership (Hyde, 2005). Using meta-analytical techniques that revolutionized the study of gender differences starting in the 1980s, Hyde (2005) concluded that males and females, from childhood to adulthood, are more alike than different on most psychological variables, resulting in what she calls a *gender similarities hypothesis*. With this notion, she has successfully argued for ending the apparent endless effort of psychologists (mostly male) to demonstrate female difference (i.e., generally inferiority).

Research related to women and achievement, like other research, must distinguish between research on sex differences and research on the effects of sexism. Yoder and Kahn (2003) called for adopting the strategy of treating these global categories (e.g., gender, race, ethnicity) as marker variables for factors that need to be identified. From this perspective, simply reporting gender or race/ethnic differences is meaningless. Baker (2006) stresses that once we treat these so-called "natural" or "real" categories as socially constructed explanatory labels given power by their treatment as real, it becomes important to "interrogate findings of difference to determine the factors for which the category variable, be it race or gender, serves as a marker" (p. 6).

Diversity has become the "hot issue" that encompasses consideration of the effect of multiple and interacting social categories (Russo & Vaz, 2001), and the field has certainly made considerable progress in "diversity-mindfulness." Diversity-mindfulness, from a feminist perspective, involves the process of perceiving and processing a multiplicity of differences among individuals, their social contexts, and their cultures, and it incorporates the feminist values of diversity, egalitarianism, and inclusiveness into critical analyses (Russo & Vaz, 2001). Based upon our review, there is still, however, much "diversity-mindfulness" work to be done in examining unique issues related to achievement among girls and women of color, across different socioeconomic groups, from the vantage point of the population's own social reality and not one presumed by others.

As we look at where the field as a whole stands now, we see the complexity of the discussion. Though feminist psychology has advanced considerably since the 1980s, a complete understanding of the phenomena we have looked at in this chapter is elusive and the quest is very frustrating. One central piece of most feminist analyses is a front-and-center discussion of the dynamics of power and its impact on women's outcomes. In our review of women and achievement, its glaring absence, from a conceptual and empirical perspective, was quite disappointing. Addressing power in the study of the achievement, attainment, and ability is probably essential to obtaining a clear understanding of the phenomenon.

For us, the best recent statement from a feminist psychologist on the matter was found in the work of Rhoda Unger. In her book *Resisting Gender: Twenty-Five Years of Feminist Psychology*, Unger (1998) presents a lively and compelling discourse in which she notes that, although feminism is almost synonymous with changes in power dynamics, psychologists have routinely managed to ignore the central role of power in their work. Unger goes on to note that while psychologists have not studied power dynamics from the social structural point of view, sociologists have done so. But sociologists, in turn, neglect to consider the internal side of the equation, and so results are limited in another way.

Is the personal political or the political personal? How to address this enigma is a critical issue for feminist psychology.

It has long been recognized by some that the social power structure permeates every aspect of our lives. Unger (1998) notes that the social psychologist Kenneth Clark, in 1966, discussed the dynamics in relation to black youth. Feminist psychologist Mary Henley (1995) did similar work in her programmatic studies of the meaning of touch in interpersonal relationships, and Carolyn Sherif (1976) wrote in this vein as well. These approaches, though significant for the advancement of the field, have not been translated for (and by) feminist psychology to aid in better understanding women's behavior. Many psychologists study women's behavior and still report findings in isolation of their social context. While such research tells us about the person, it says nothing about the social and cultural context of her life. The former approach is not wrong, it is just not enough.

Whether the visible success and achievements of women over the past three decades (e.g., in education, politics, employment) will succeed in changing aspirations for little girls or their mothers has yet to be seen and cannot yet be reliably be predicted. The complexity of motivation, as noted by Eccles (2005), makes clear dimensional links difficult to construct. While the fundamental question of the why, or why not, of women's achievement will likely continue to persist, it is essential that the field ask more complex questions, develop more sophisticated research designs to answer these questions, and embed research findings in a relevant cultural and contextual framework.

REFERENCES

Adams, J., Priest, R. F., & Prince, H. T. (1985). Achievement motive: Analyzing the validity of the WOFO. *Psychology of Women Quarterly, 9*(3), 357–370.

Alper, T. (1974). Achievement motivation in college women: A now-you-see-it-now-you-don't phenomenon. *American Psychologist, 29,* 194–203.

American Association of University Women. (1992). *How schools shortchange girls: A study of major findings on girls and education*. Washington, DC: AAUW Educational Foundation, Wellesley College Center for Research on Women.

Atkinson, J. W. (1958). *Motives in fantasy, action, and society*. Princeton, NJ: Van Nostrand.

Atkinson, J. W., & Feather, N. T. (1966). *A theory of achievement motivation*. New York: John Wiley & Sons.

Baker, N. L. (2006). Feminist psychology in the service of women: Staying engaged without getting married. *Psychology of Women Quarterly, 30,* 1–14.

Bandura, A. (1986). The explanatory and predictive scope of self-efficacy theory. *Journal of Social and Clinical Psychology, 4,* 359–373.

Bandura, A., Barbaranelli, C., Caprara, G., & Pastorelli, C. (2001). Self-efficacy beliefs as shapers of children's aspirations and career trajectories. *Child Development, 72,* 187–206.

Berglas, S., & Jones, E. E. (1978). Drug choice as a self-handicapping strategy in response to noncontingent success. *Journal of Personality and Social Psychology, 36,* 405–417.

Betz, N. E. (1992). Career assessment: A review of critical issues. In S. Brown & R. W. Lent (Eds.), *Handbook of counseling psychology* (2nd ed.; pp. 453–484). New York: Wiley.

Betz, N. E. (1993). Women's career development. In F. Denmark & M. Paludi (Eds.), *Psychology of Women: A handbook of issues and theories* (pp. 627–684). Westport, CT: Greenwood Press.

Birenbaum, M., & Kraemer, R. (1995). Gender and ethnic-group differences in causal attribution for success and failure in mathematics and language examinations. *Journal of Cross-Cultural Psychology, 26,* 342–359.

Brown, R. B., & Josephs, R. A. (1999). A burden of proof: Stereotype relevance and gender differences in math performance. *Journal of Personality and Social Psychology, 76*(2), 246–257.

Bussey, K., & Bandura, A. (1999). Social cognitive theory of gender development and differentiation. *Psychological Review, 106,* 676–713.

Center for American Women and Politics. (2007). Women in the U.S. Congress 2007: Fact Sheet. New Brunswick, NJ: National Information Bank on Women in Public Office, Eagleton Institute of Politics, Rutgers University.

Collins, D. W., & Kimura, D. (1997). A large sex difference on a two-dimensional mental rotation task. *Behavioral Neuroscience, 111*(4), 845–849.

Cooper, J. A., & Schleser, R. (2004). Closing the achievement gap: Examining the role of cognitive developmental level in academic achievement. *Early Childhood Education Journal, 33*(5), 301–306.

Cury, F., Elliot, A. J., Da Fonseca, D., & Moller, A. (2006). The social-cognitive model of achievement motivation and the 2 × 2 achievement goal framework. *Journal of Personality and Social Psychology, 90,* 666–679.

Darling-Hammond, L., & Sykes, G. (2003). Wanted: A national teacher supply policy for education; The right way to meet the "highly qualified teacher" challenge. *Education Policy Analysis Archives, 11*(33). Retrieved June 11, 2007, from http://epaa.asu.edu/epaa/v11n33.

Day, J. G., & Hill, C. (2007). *Behind the pay gap.* Washington, DC: American Association of University Women.

Doyle, J., & Paludi, M. (1995). *Sex and Gender: The human experience,* 3rd Ed. New York: McGraw Hill.

Eccles, J. S. (1987). Gender roles and women's achievement-related decisions. *Psychology of Women Quarterly, 11,* 135–172.

Eccles, J. S. (1994). Understanding women's educational and occupational choices: Applying the Eccles et al. model of achievement-related choices. *Psychology of Women Quarterly, 18*(4), 585–609.

Eccles, J. S. (2005). Subjective task value and the Eccles et al. model of achievement-related choices. In A. J. Elliott & C. W. Dweck (Eds.), *Handbook of competence and motivation* (pp. 105–121). New York: Guilford Press.

Eccles, J. S., Barber, B. L., & Jozefowicz, D. M. H. (1999). Linking gender to educational, occupational, and recreational choices: Applying the Eccles et al. model of achievement-related choices. In W. B. Swann, J. H. Langlois, & L. A. Gilbert (Eds.), *Sexism and stereotypes in modern society: The gender science of Janet Taylor Spence.* Washington, DC: American Psychological Association.

Eccles, J. S., & Harold, R. D. (1992). Gender differences in educational and occupational patterns among the gifted. In N. Colangelo, S. G. Assouline, & D. L. Amronson (Eds)., *Talent development: Proceedings from the 1991 Henry B. and Jocelyn Wallace National Research Symposium on Talent Development* (pp. 2–29). Unionville, NY: Trillium Press.

Eccles, J. S., Wigfield, A., & Schiefele, U. (1998). *Motivation*. In N. Eisenberg (Ed.), *Handbook of child psychology* (vol. 3, 5th ed.; pp. 1017–1095). New York: Wiley.

Elliot, A. J., Shell, M. M., Henry, B. K., & Maier, M. A. (2005). Achievement goals, performance, contingencies, and performance attainment: An experimental test. *Journal of Educational Psychology, 97*(4), 630–640.

England, P. (1992). *Comparable worth: Theories and evidence*. New York: Aldine de Gruyter.

England, P., Allison, P., Li, S., Mark, N., Thompson, J., Budig, M., et al. (2003). *Why are some academic fields tipping toward female? The sex composition of U.S. fields of doctoral degree receipt, 1971–1998.* Http://www.stanford.edu/dept/soc/people/faculty/england/Tipping.pdf.

Ferguson, R. F. (1998). Teachers' perceptions and expectations and black–white test score gap. In C. Jencks & M. Phillips (Eds.), *The black–white test score gap* (pp. 273–317). Washington, DC: Brookings Institution Press.

Fried-Buchalter, S. (1997). Fear of success, fear of failure, and imposter phenomenon among male and female marketing managers. *Sex Roles, 37,* 847–859.

Frieze, I., Whitley, B., Hanusa, B., & McHugh, M. (1982). Assessing the theoretical models for sex differences in causal attributions for success and failure. *Sex Roles, 8*, 333–343.

Graham, S. (1994). Motivation in African Americans. *Review of Educational Research, 64,* 55–117.

Graham, S., & Hudley, C. (2002). Race and ethnicity in the study of motivation and competence. In A. J. Elliot & C. S. Dweck (Eds.), *Handbook of competence and motivation* (pp. 292–413). New York: Guilford Press.

Hanna, G. (2003). Reaching gender equity in mathematics education. *Educational Forum, 67*(3), 204–214.

Hanna, G., Kundiger, E., & Larouche, C. (1990). Mathematical achievement of grade 12 girls in fifteen countries. In L. Burton (Ed.), *Gender and mathematics: An international perspective* (pp. 87–97). London: Cassell Educational.

Harackiewicz, J. M., Barron, K. E., Carter, S. M., Lehto, A. T., & Elliot, A. J. (1997). Predictors and consequences of achievement goals in the college classroom: Maintaining interest and making the grade. *Journal of Personality and Social Psychology, 73,* 1284–1295.

Henley, N. M. (1995). Ethnicity and gender issues in language. In H. Landrine (Ed.), *Bringing cultural diversity to feminist psychology* (pp. 361–396). Washington, DC: American Psychological Association.

Hirt, E. R., McCrea, S. M., & Kimble, C. E. (2000). Public self-focus and sex differences in behavioral self-handicapping: Does increasing self-threat still make it "just a man's game"? *Personality and Social Psychology Bulletin, 26,* 1131–1141.

Hoffman, L. W. (1972). Early childhood experience and women's achievement motives. *Journal of Social Issues, 28,* 129–156.

Horner, M. S. (1968). Sex differences in achievement motivation and performance in competitive and noncompetitive situations. (Doctoral dissertation, University of Michigan). *Dissertation Abstracts International, 30,* 407.

Horner, M. S. (1972). Toward an understanding of achievement related conflicts in women. *Journal of Social Issues, 28,* 157–175.

Hyde, J. S. (2004). *Half the human experience: The psychology of women* (6th ed.). Boston: Houghton Mifflin.

Hyde, J. S. (2005). The gender similarities hypothesis. *American Psychologist, 60*(6), 581–592.

Hyde, J. S., & Durik, A. M. (2005). Gender, competence, and motivation. In A. J. Elliot & C. S. Dweck (Eds.), *Handbook of competence and motivation* (pp. 375–391). New York: Guilford Press.

Hyde, J. S., Fennema, E., & Lamon, S. J. (1990). Gender differences in mathematics performance: A meta-analysis. *Psychological Bulletin, 107,* 139–155.

Hyde, J. S., Fennema, E., Ryan, M., Frost, L. A., & Hopp, C. (1990). Gender comparisons of mathematics attitudes and affect: A meta-analysis. *Psychology of Women Quarterly, 14,* 299–324.

Hyde, J. S., & Kling, K. C. (2001). Women, motivation, and achievement. *Psychology of Women Quarterly, 25,* 364–378.

Inter-Parliamentary Union. (2007). Women in national parliaments. Retrieved March 31, 2007, from http://www.ipu.org/wmn-e/classif.htm.

Jacobs, J. A. (1995). Gender and academic specialties: Trends among recipients of college degrees in the 1980s. *Sociology of Education, 68,* 81–98.

Jacobs, J. E., & Eccles, J. A. (1992). The impact of mother's gender role on mothers' and children's ability perception. *Journal of Personality and Social Psychology, 63,* 932–944.

Jordan, W. J., & Nettles, S. M. (1999). How students invest their time outside of school: Effects on school-related outcomes. *Social Psychology of Education, 3* (4), 217–243.

Jussim, L., Eccles, J., & Madon, S. (1996). Social perception, social stereotypes, and teacher expectations: Accuracy and the quest for the powerful self-fulfilling prophecy. *Advances in Experimental Social Psychology, 28,* 281–287.

Juvonen, J., & Wentzel, K. R. (1996). *Social motivation: Understanding children's school adjustment.* New York: Cambridge University Press.

Lent, R. W., Lopez, F. O., & Bieschke, K. J. (1993). Predicting mathematics-related choice and success behaviors: Test of an expanded social cognitive model. *Journal of Vocational Behavior, 42,* 223–236.

Lucas, J. W., & Lovaglia, M. J. (2005). Self-handicapping: Gender, race, and status. *Current Research in Social Psychology, 10*(16), 234–249. Available at http://www.uiowa.edu/~grpproc/crisp/crisp.10.16.html.

McClelland, D. C. (1961). *The achieving society.* Princeton, NJ: Van Nostrand.

Meece, J. L., Eccles-Parsons, J., Kaczala, C. M., Goff, S. E., & Futterman, R. (1982). Sex differences in math achievement: Toward a model of academic choice. *Psychological Bulletin, 91,* 324–348.

Meece, J. L., Wigfield, A., & Eccles, J. S. (1990). Predictors of math anxiety and its consequences for young adolescents' course enrollment intentions and performance in mathematics. *Journal of Educational Psychology, 82,* 60–70.

Midgley, C., & Urdan, T. C. (1995). Predictors of middle-school students' use of self-handicapping strategies. *Journal of Early Adolescence, 15*(4), 389–411.

Nass, R. D. (1993). Sex differences in learning abilities and disabilities. *Annals of Dyslexia, 43,* 61–78.

National Science Foundation. (2006). *Science and engineering indicators: 2006.* Arlington, VA: National Science Foundation.

Nordvik, H., & Amponsah, B. (1998). Gender differences in spatial abilities and spatial ability among university students in an egalitarian educational system. *Sex Roles, 38,* 1009–1023.

Osborne, J. W. (2001). Testing stereotype threat: Does anxiety explain race and sex differences in achievement? *Contemporary Educational Psychology, 26,* 291–310.

Paludi, M. A. (2002). *The psychology of women* (2nd ed.). Upper Saddle River, NJ: Prentice Hall.

Piedmont, R. L. (1995). Another look at fear of success, fear of failure, and text anxiety: A motivational analysis using the five-factor model. *Sex Roles, 32,* 139–157.

Reskin, B. F., & Roos, P. A. (1990). *Job queues, gender queues: Explaining women's inroads into male occupations.* Philadelphia: Temple University Press.

Rhodewalt, F. (1990). Self-handicappers: Individual differences in the preference for anticipatory, self-protective acts. In R. L. Higgins, C. R. Synder, & S. Berglas (Eds.), *Self-handicapping: The paradox that isn't* (pp. 69–106). New York: Plenum.

Rhodewalt, F., & Hill, K. S. (1995). Self-handicapping in the classroom: The effects of claimed self-handicaps on responses to academic failure. *Basic and Applied Social Psychology, 16*(4), 397–416.

Rothman, M. (1996). Fear of success among business students. *Psychological Reports, 78,* 863–869.

Russo, N. F., & Vaz, K. (2001). Addressing diversity in the decade of color. *Psychology of Women Quarterly, 25,* 280–294.

Sancho, A. M., & Hewitt, J. (1990). Questioning fear of success. *Psychological Reports, 78,* 803–806.

Schmader, T. (2002). Gender identification moderates stereotype threat effects on women's math performance. *Journal of Experimental Social Psychology, 38*(2), 194–201.

Schunk, D. H. (1995). Self-efficacy and education and instruction. In J. E. Maddux (Ed.), *Self-efficacy, adaptation, and adjustment: Theory, research, and application* (pp. 281–303). New York: Plenum Press.

Schunk, D. H., & Pajares, F. (2002). The development of academic self-efficacy. In A. Wigfield & J. Eccles (Eds.), *Development of achievement motivation.* San Diego: Academic Press.

Shaver, P. (1976). Questions concerning fear of success and its conceptual relatives. *Sex Roles, 2,* 305–320.

Sherif, C. W. (1976). Bias in psychology. In J. A. Sherman and E. T. Beck (Eds.), *The prism of sex: Essays in the sociology of knowledge* (pp. 91–133). Madison: University of Wisconsin Press.

Spelke, E. S. (2005). Sex differences in intrinsic aptitude for mathematics and science: A critical review. *American Psychologist, 60,* 950–958.

Spence, J. T., & Helmreich, R. L. (1978). *Masculinity & femininity: Their psychological dimensions, correlates, and antecedents.* Austin: University of Texas Press.

Spencer, S. J., Steele, C. M., & Quinn, D. M. (1999). Stereotype threat and women's math performance. *Journal of Experimental Social Psychology, 35*(1), 4–28.

Steele, C. (1992). Race and schooling of black Americans. *Atlantic Monthly* (April), 68–78.

Steele, C. (1997). A threat in the air: How stereotypes shape intellectual identity and performance. *American Psychologist, 52,* 613–629.

Steele, C. (1998). Stereotyping and its threat are real. *American Psychologist, 53*(6), 680–681.

Steele, C. (1999). Thin ice: "Stereotype threat" and black college students. *Atlantic Monthly* (August), 44–54.

Steele, C., & Aronson, J. (1995). Stereotype threat and the intellectual test performance of African Americans. *Journal of Personality and Social Psychology, 69,* 797–811.

Steele, J., James, J. B., & Barnett, R. C. (2002). Learning in a man's world: Examining the perceptions of undergraduate women in male-dominated academic areas. *Psychology of Women Quarterly, 26,* 46–50.

Stewart, A. J., & Chester, N. L. (1982). Sex differences in human social motives: Achievement, affiliation, and power. In A. J. Stewart (Ed.), *Motivation and society.* San Francisco: Jossey-Bass.

Trice, D. M., & Bratslavsky, E. (2000). Giving in to feel good: The place of emotion regulation in the context of general self-control. *Psychological Inquiry, 11,* 149–159.

Unger, R. K. (1998). *Resisting gender: Twenty-five years of feminist psychology.* Thousand Oaks, CA: Sage.

U.S. Department of Education. National Center for Education Progress (NAEP) (1990–2005). Mathematics assessments.

U.S. Department of Education. National Center for Education Statistics. (2005). *The condition of education.* Washington, DC: GPO.

Vrugt, A. (1994). Perceived self-efficacy, social comparison, effect reactions, and academic performance. *British Journal of Educational Psychology, 64*(3), 465–472.

Weiner, B. (1972). Attribution theory, achievement motivation, and the educational process. *Review of Educational Research, 42*(2), 203–215.

Wigfield, A., & Eccles, J. S. (2002). The development of competence beliefs, expectancies for success and achievement values from childhood through adolescence. In A. Wigfield and J. Eccles (Eds.), *Development of achievement motivation* (pp. 91–120). London: Academic Press.

Wigfield, A., Eccles, J., MacIver, D., Reuman, D., & Midgley, C. (1991). Transitions at early adolescence: Changes in children's domain-specific self-perceptions and general self-esteem across the transition to junior high school. *Development Psychology, 27,* 552–562.

Wigfield, A., Eccles, J. S., & Pintrick, P. D. (1996). Development between the ages of 11 and 25. In D. C. Berliner & R. C. Calfee (Eds.), *Handbook of educational psychology* (pp. 148–185). New York: Macmillan.

Williams, C. (1993). Psychoanalytic theory and the sociology of gender. In P. England (Ed.), *Theory on gender/feminism on theory* (pp. 131–150). New York: Aldine de Gruyter.

Yoder, J. D., & Kahn, A. S. (2003). Making gender comparisons more meaningful: A call for more attention to social context. *Psychology of Women Quarterly, 27*(4), 281–290.

Chapter 20

Work and Family Roles: Selected Issues

Julia R. Steinberg
Maren True
Nancy Felipe Russo

Multiple work and family roles are the norm for the majority of American women; the challenge for women in the 21st century has become balancing work and personal life (Frone, 2003; Gambles, Lewis, & Rapoport, 2006). According to the U.S. Department of Labor, in 2006, 59 percent of American women age 16 or older were in the labor force—66 million women. For women between the ages of 25 and 54, the figure was 72 percent. The majority (75%) of employed women worked at full-time jobs. Labor force participation rates were highest for divorced and never-married women (67% and 61%, respectively). Nonetheless, among married women, nearly 6 out of 10 (59%) combined the roles of wife and worker (the figure is similar for separated women). The proportion of married-couple families in which only the husband worked hit an all-time low: 19.8 percent. Dual-worker families, with both husband and wife employed, constituted the largest category of workers (51.8%). In 6.5 percent of married couples, only the wife worked (U.S. Bureau of Labor Statistics, 2007b).

A substantial proportion of employed women combine the roles of mother and worker, or mother, wife, and worker. The majority of mothers of young children are now members of the American workforce, and adults of both genders are assuming greater caregiving duties for aging relatives. In 2006, 67 percent of married mothers with school-age children were in the labor force; the figure was 72 percent for unmarried mothers and 56 percent for mothers with children under three years of age (U.S. Bureau of Labor Statistics, 2007b). Addressing discrimination against working mothers, characterized as the "maternal wall," has emerged as the new frontier in the struggle for women's equality in employment (Biernat, Crosby, & Williams, 2004).

These statistics are a reminder that women balance the roles of worker, wife, and mother in different combinations over the course of their lives. The numbers also suggest that changes in the world of work need to reflect an inclusive view of family that recognizes alternative family forms, including dual-worker couples and single-headed households (Steil, 2001). Beyond these statistics, a more inclusive view of family would also include lesbian, gay, and bisexual couples, cohabiting partners with and without children, and other unions involving family or home life (Fassinger, 2000). Nonetheless, the world of work has been slow to adapt to this new reality and continues to be largely organized for the traditional family breadwinner/caregiver model that assumes that mothers stay at home (American Psychological Association, 2004; Halpern, 2005).

The changing norms, expectations, and circumstances in which women perform their work and family roles present continual challenges with powerful implications for women's mental health and well-being. In particular, families that do not fit the traditional norm—single-parent families or lesbian, gay, and bisexual couples and families—must resolve work and family conflicts in a context of stigma and discrimination, compounding their difficulties (Schultheiss, 2006). Stereotyping and idealization of women's work and family roles must be replaced with an understanding of women's diverse realities, and the world of work needs to be realigned to reflect those realities (American Psychological Association, 2004).

The literature on women's mental health has proliferated across the disciplines in the past two decades. For example, focusing only on articles appearing in peer-reviewed journals, a PsycInfo search using the keywords *women, work, family*, or *multiple roles* identified 776 articles published in such journals from 1980 to 1989, 1,565 published between 1990 and 1999, and 2,503 published between 2000 and the April 2007. This is an underestimation of the published literature, as using more specific search terms (e.g., *working mothers, role conflict*) would have increased the count. In addition, books, book chapters, and other publication venues were not tallied.

This chapter highlights new conceptualizations, methodological issues, and selected research findings related to women's work and family roles. We focus on the literature published in the 1990s and beyond, including reference to previous work only when it has a special contribution to make to the point being discussed (see Green & Russo, 1993; Bianchi, Robinson, & Milkie, 2006; and Gilbert & Rader,

2001, for discussions of previous literature). Because of limited space and the need to narrow the scope of the chapter, and given the wide variation across cultural context, we focus on U.S. studies, referencing international studies only when the findings reveal neglected issues in need of consideration in the U.S. context.

After presenting a brief profile of women at work and in the family, we highlight recent literature on women's multiple roles, focusing on the implications of these roles for women's mental health. This focus on mental health is important for two reasons. First, women's mental health and well-being are important in their own right. Second—and the reason that this information is included in a chapter on women and work—"concern" about negative effects of employment on women's well-being can be used to undermine women's aspirations and to rationalize gender discrimination. We view women as actors, with the power to perform roles to their benefit. Accurate information about both benefits and problems associated with women's changing roles is a foundation for women's empowerment.

WOMEN'S EXPERIENCE AT WORK

A number of books discuss women's issues and experiences at work in greater depth (e.g., Gambles et al., 2006; Grossman & Chester, 1990; Karsten, 2006; Martin & Jurik, 2007; Powell, 1999). Here we focus on three interrelated issues—stereotyping and discrimination, gender segregation in the workplace, and employment rewards for women—that have particular implications for women's mental health and well-being.

Gender Stereotyping

Gender stereotypes and sexist discrimination are interrelated. In most instances, it is illegal in the United States to discriminate by assigning work roles on the basis of gender (although there are exceptions, such as actor and actress roles). Nonetheless, because expectations for the feminine gender-role are transituational, women take their feminine gender-role, with its concomitant gender stereotypes, into the workplace (see chapter 14 in this volume for a more complete discussion of the definitions of gender-roles used here). Kite, Deaux, and Haines, in chapter 7 of this volume, provide an in-depth discussion of stereotyping. Here we focus on concepts we believe are particularly important for understanding the effects of stereotyping on work and family life.

Women, particularly mothers, continue to be stereotyped as caretakers and nurturers and are not taken seriously as committed workers, despite the fact that women are single heads of households and the contributions of married women to their household incomes keep many families above the poverty line. Gender myths and stereotypes and women's subordinate roles and status are mutually reinforcing (Eagly & Karau, 2002; Eagly, Wood, & Dickman, 2000). Women are seen as nurturing, submissive, dependent, and accommodating, and thus are more likely to be viewed (and to view themselves) as suited to service tasks and subordinate positions (DeArmond, Tye, Chen, Krauss, Rogers, & Sintek, 2006). Stereotypes thus function to support and justify the status quo (Jost & Kay, 2005; Kay & Jost, 2003). Occupying subordinate positions reinforces the impression of nurturance, dependence, and lack of leadership ability (Eagly & Karau, 2002; Eagly et al., 2000).

Stereotypes related to warmth and competence jointly affect perceptions of admiration and liking (warm + competent), contempt (cold + incompetent), envy and disliking (cold + competent), and pity (warm + incompetent) (Cuddy, Fiske, & Glick, 2004; Fiske, Cuddy, Glick, & Xu, 2002; Fiske, Cuddy, & Glick, 2002). These dimensions of warmth and competence, which parallel the long-standing gender divide of homemaker/breadwinner, are rooted in gender myths about the essential natures of women and men that persist despite a mountain of studies documenting their similarity and showing that distributions of traits among women and men overlap and that warmth and agency are human attributes held by both women and men (Hyde, 2005).

Stereotypes can affect feelings, thoughts, and behavior at an implicit level, beyond conscious awareness and even when not consciously accepted (Devine, 1989; Greenwald & Banaji, 1995). Humor may enhance the implicit effects of stereotypes; it appears to increase tolerance for discrimination, perhaps because it generates a noncritical mindset that leaves sexist attitudes and behavior unscrutinized (Ford, 2000). Although stereotyping and evaluation biases may be subtle, they nonetheless have complex effects on how we evaluate others, such that equal performance does not necessarily bring equal rewards for women (Benokraitis, 1997; Fiske, 1998; Swim, Borgida, & Maruyama, 1989).

Stereotypes can function as double-edged swords, such that being viewed as having "feminine" traits (e.g., being gentle, warm, and helpful) can lead to perceptions of incompetence, devaluation, and exploitation (Cuddy et al., 2004), while having "masculine" traits (e.g., being forceful, assertive, having leadership abilities, strong personality) can lead to sanctions, including sexual harassment, in educational and occupational settings (Berdahl, 2007). When men accommodate others, the norm of reciprocity is engaged, and the others "owe" them favors in return. In contrast, accommodating women are taken for granted. Further, women's reasons for not accommodating are seen as less credible, and women are required to be more assertive to reach their goals than are men (Geis, Carter, & Butler, 1982).

The process of subtyping helps make stereotypes resistant to change (Park, Wolsko, & Judd, 2001). When confronted with evidence that a stereotype of a particular group (e.g., women) is inaccurate, subcategories of that group may be created as exceptions, leaving the original stereotypes of the overarching group intact. Common subtypes of women around the world include housewife, career woman, feminist/lesbian, and secretary (Eckes, 1994, 2002). Stereotypes and their subtypes can have both positive and negative elements, enabling a person to hold positive attitudes toward women while justifying sexist discrimination. For example, working mothers are subtyped as either "homemakers" or "professional women" and viewed as "warm but incompetent" or "cold but competent," respectively. When working women become mothers, they become perceived as more warm, but less competent (a tradeoff not experienced by men), which puts them at a disadvantage in work situations where competence ratings predict interest in hiring, promoting, and educating employees (Cuddy et al., 2004). Stereotypes related to the warmth and competence of mothers contribute to barriers to employment for working mothers—the aforementioned maternal wall (Biernat et al., 2004).

The fact that stereotypes have both positive and negative elements can create paradoxical effects. For example, on the one hand, there is substantial prejudice and discrimination against lesbians (Lubensky, Holland, Wiethoff, & Crosby, 2004). On the other hand, lesbians generally have higher earnings than heterosexual women with similar qualifications and positions (e.g., see Berg & Lien, 2002). Peplau and Fingerhut (2004) suggest that two factors, one related to stereotyping, underlie this paradox. First is the effect of the expectation that lesbians are financially self-sufficient on educational and occupational decision making. Second, and more relevant here, is the effect of stereotyping lesbians as more able and committed workers than heterosexual women, particularly mothers. In their study, the ratings of heterosexual and homosexual women diverged only when motherhood was considered. Among heterosexuals, mothers received lower ratings on competence and career orientation than nonmothers, but not among lesbians (Peplau & Fingerhut, 2004).

The impact of a particular stereotype on a woman can depend on its relevance to her situation (Shapiro & Neuberg, 2007). Steele and his colleagues (for a review see Steele, Spencer, & Aronson, 2002) developed the concept of *stereotype threat* to refer to a situational threat in which the target of a negative stereotype may possibly be judged, acted toward, or affected in a negative manner by a stereotype. For instance, because of the widely held stereotype that women are inferior in math ability relative to men, math settings become potential situations of stereotype threat for women. That is, situations such as taking the GRE-Quantitative, SAT-Math, or simply being in a math class may pose an extra threat to women in that that they realize others (or they themselves) may judge them or act based on the stereotype (Shapiro & Neuberg, 2007).

Gender stereotyping has long been linked to distinct employment issues for women, who must deal with evaluation bias, greater pressure on their performance, exclusion from certain jobs and promotional opportunities, differential supervision, overprotection, unprofessional sexual remarks, incivility and harassment, unequal employment rewards, and gender segregation between and within occupations. Such concerns shape self-perceptions of occupational futures in complex ways (e.g., see Chalk, 2005).

Discrimination

Over the last two decades, a variety of concepts have been offered to refine our understanding of discrimination against women. As "old-fashioned" overt sexism and racism have become illegal and increasingly socially disapproved, the "isms," including *modern sexism*, have become more covert and subtle (Benokraitis & Feagin, 1995; Benokraitis, 1997). As Meyerson and Fletcher (2000) so aptly observed:

> The women's movement [once] used radical rhetoric and legal action to drive out overt discrimination, but most of the barriers that persist today are insidious—a revolution couldn't find them to blast away. Rather, gender discrimination now is so deeply embedded in organizational life as to be virtually indiscernible. Even the women who feel its impact are often hard-pressed to know what hit them. (p. 127)

New concepts and measures have been developed to assess these "modern" forms of discrimination (Swim, Mallett, Russo-Devosa, & Stangor, 2005). These include the Modern Sexism Scale, which assesses denial of continuing discrimination, antagonism toward women's demands, and special consideration for women (Swim, Aikin, Hall, & Hunter, 1995; Swim & Cohen, 1997). The recognition that sexism can have both positive and negative elements (i.e., can reflect ambivalence) has led to examination of the relationship of stereotype content to discriminatory intentions and behavior (Cuddy et al., 2004).

This research supports a *stereotype content model* that suggests prejudice will differ depending on the relative status and interdependence (cooperative vs. competitive) among groups (Fiske et al., 2002). This research has important implications for understanding the differential treatment of subtypes of women, including career women (who are perceived as competent but not warm), housewives (perceived as warm but incompetent), and working mothers (perceived as more warm but less competent than women without children) (Cuddy et al., 2004).

Research on the effects of *ambivalent sexism* (Glick & Fiske, 1996) has distinguished between *hostile sexism* and *benevolent sexism*, which are independent clusters and attitudes that can be held in varying degrees by the same person. Hostile sexism represents negative attitudes toward women who are not stereotypically feminine or do not fulfill their gender-roles. One example is the belief that women who are not homemakers should be stigmatized. Benevolent sexism, by contrast, represents

> a set of interrelated attitudes toward women that are sexist in terms of viewing women stereotypically and in restricted roles but that are subjectively positive in feeling tone (for the perceiver) and also tend to elicit behaviors that are typically categorized as prosocial (e.g., helping) or intimacy-seeking (e.g., self-disclosure). (Glick & Fiske, 1996, p. 491)

Benevolent sexism is not benign; its consequences may be damaging to the recipient, and it functions to reinforce traditional stereotyping, masculine dominance, and female dependence. For example, commenting on a coworker's appearance may be well intentioned. Despite such intentions, such remarks can undermine a woman's feelings of being respected as a colleague and of being taken seriously in her work. Hostile and benevolent sexism work together to rationalize disparate treatment of women (Glick & Fiske, 2001).

The usefulness of distinguishing the concepts has been demonstrated in a series of studies which found that men who endorsed the hostile sexism items also attributed more negative feminine traits to women, whereas men who endorsed the benevolent sexism scale ascribed positive feminine traits to women. Generally, hostile sexist attitudes have been found to be associated with negative evaluations of women in nontraditional careers, whereas benevolent sexist attitudes are associated with positive evaluations of women in the traditional homemaker role (Franzoi, 2001; Glick, Diebold, Bailey-Werner, & Zhu, 1997; Glick, Sakalli-Ugurlu, Ferreira, & de Souza, 2002). Furthermore, women who are presented as violating traditional gender-role norms (e.g., by inviting a man back to her house for sex) or as behaving counter to the traditional feminine gender-role (e.g., being non-nurturing) are more harshly evaluated by benevolent but not hostile sexists. Finally, Masser and Abrams (2004) found that hostile, but not benevolent, sexism is related to negative attitudes toward individual women who seek to advance in the workplace.

Interpersonal Mistreatment, Incivility, and Sexual Harassment

At the same time that the "isms" have become more subtle, incivility and other forms of interpersonal mistreatment in the workplace have come to be understood as modern forms of discrimination

(Cortina, in press). Since the term "chilly climate" was introduced in the 1980s (Hall & Sandler, 1982), the negative impact of small-scale, day-to-day negative interactions ("microaggressions") on the intellectual and emotional well-being of women in educational settings has been recognized. Conceptual parallels to this work can be found in contemporary studies of interpersonal mistreatment and incivility in the workplace. Today, incivility is viewed as a manifestation of sexism and racism, and *selective incivility* is conceptualized as a modern form of discrimination that explains why gender and racial disparities persist despite concerted efforts to eliminate bias (Cortina, in press).

As Cortina (in press) observes, incivility in the workplace is an insidious and widespread form of antisocial behavior. In her groundbreaking review, she reports the rates of incivility found in a variety of studies dealing with diverse employment contexts—ranging from 64 to 79 percent (Cortina, in press). Sexual harassment, an extreme form of maltreatment, is a common and all-too-often underreported experience, particularly in male-dominated environments. For example, a meta-analysis of 71 studies found that that 58 percent of women in academia had experienced harassing behavior at work; this rate was higher than that reported by women in the private sector or nonmilitary government organizations (Ilies, Hauserman, Schwaochau, & Stibal, 2003).

Interpersonal mistreatment in the workplace has been classified into "nonsexual mistreatment" (which encompasses hostility, emotional abuse, bullying, generalized workplace abuse, and incivility) and "sexual harassment" (Cortina et al., 2002; Lim & Cortina, 2005; Miner-Rubino & Cortina, 2004). Examples of nonsexual acts include verbal aggression (e.g., swearing), disrespect (e.g., interruption, public humiliation), and isolation from important work activities. Incivility in the workplace is defined as "low intensity deviant behavior with ambiguous intent to harm the target, in violation of workplace norms for mutual respect" (Andersson & Pearson, 1999, p. 457). Although incivility may have injurious objectives, intentions of the perpetrators are ambiguous; indeed, they may even have rational, nondiscriminatory explanations for their behavior, making it difficult to challenge. Incivility can be conceptualized as a violation of personal norms of respect that may vary across and within workplaces.

Some research suggests that males and females may have different thresholds for perceiving such violations of norms for mutual respect, and these perceptions vary by congruence of gender and race of the perpetrators and targets of uncivil behavior (Montgomery et al., 2004). Rotundo, Nguyen, and Sackett (2001) conducted a meta-analysis of 62 studies of gender differences in perceptions of harassment in seven areas:

1. derogatory attitudes—impersonal
2. derogatory attitudes—personal

3. unwanted dating pressure
4. sexual propositions
5. physical sexual contact
6. physical nonsexual contact
7. sexual coercion

The first six categories represented hostile work environment harassment, and the seventh represented quid pro quo harassment. They found that women perceived a broader range of social-sexual behaviors as harassing. Furthermore, although the gender difference was not large (overall standardized mean difference = 0.30), the gender differences in perception were larger for behaviors involving hostile work environment harassment—specifically, the derogatory attitudes toward women, dating pressure, and physical sexual contact categories—compared to the differences found for sexual propositions or sexual coercion.

The distinction Rotundo and colleagues (2001) make between hostile work environment and quid pro quo harassment is important, because it has legal implications. Some courts have adopted a "reasonable woman standard," which asks whether the unwelcome behavior was so pervasive or severe as to create a hostile or abusive working environment from the viewpoint of an objective, reasonable woman (as opposed to that of a reasonable person or man). The difference between the reasonable-person standard and the reasonable-woman standard becomes an issue only in hostile work environment cases. Quid pro quo causes of action do not trigger the same "pervasive and severity" test that engages the standard. Thus, Wiener and Hurt (2000) argue that researchers who seek to influence the law should distinguish between hostile work environment cases and quid pro quo cases, and in addition should include cases of varying severity.

Bullying is another form of maltreatment that is highly stressful and underreported (Bjorkqvist, Osterman, & Hjelt-Back, 1994; Zapf & Einarsen, 2001). There is some evidence that the experience of bullying differs for women and men (Rayner & Cooper, 1997), but more needs to be known about how gender affects the frequency, forms, and effects of workplace bullying. Lewis and Orford (2005) point out that bullying has typically been conceptualized as interpersonal conflict and addressed in a variety of ways—at the individual level (focusing on personal attributes of targets and bullies, at the group level (focusing on the group process of "mobbing"), and at the organizational level (focusing on organizational culture and the role of the manager). They suggest that bullying is best conceptualized as a subtle and evolving process, with different terms needed to distinguish between uses of bullying behavior and the contexts in which it occurs. In their qualitative study of social processes in workplace bullying, Lewis and Orford found interactive relationships between disclosures of bullying, reactions of others, and psychological health of the bullying target.

Themes derived from the lived experiences reported by the women in the Lewis and Orford (2005) study suggest that if workplace bullying is to be understood and prevented, it will be important to focus on the social processes, social environments, and relationships at home and at work, rather than on the personal attributes of individuals. One of the themes, characterized as the "ripple effect," suggests that bullying may create a particularly toxic form of spillover from work to family contexts, with the stresses of workplace bullying interacting with other stresses in relationships at home, taking a toll on the psychological health of family members and making the maintenance of personal relationships more difficult. Although based on a sample of professional women in the United Kingdom, the benefits of focusing on the social environment of the workplace rather than individuals likely applies to the United States as well. We would argue that the point is also well-taken with regard to incivility and other forms of interpersonal maltreatment.

Generally, researchers have focused on sexual and nonsexual acts of interpersonal mistreatment in the workplace separately, and both have been found to have negative effects on victims (Barling, Rogers, & Kelloway, 2001). Lim and Cortina (2005) report evidence that general incivility and sexual harassment tend to co-occur, with types and combinations of mistreatment having different effects on psychological and job-related outcomes. Specifically, the highest occupational well-being and mental and physical health were found in the group that did not describe any experiences of interpersonal mistreatment and were increasingly lower in the groups that reported incivility by itself and incivility plus gendered harassment. Health and well-being were lowest in the group that reported the trifecta of incivility, gendered harassment, and sexualized harassment.

The negative impact of mistreatment and harassment of women in the workplace extends beyond effects on the women themselves. Employees who witness or learn about sexual harassment in their organization can experience *bystander stress*, which is reflected in lower levels of job satisfaction. *Ambient sexual harassment* (indirect exposure to harassment) has been found to contribute to negative outcomes even without direct exposure to sexual harassment (Glomb, Richman, Hulin, Drasgow, Schneider, & Fitzgerald, 1997; Schneider & Fitzgerald, 1997). Miner-Rubino and Cortina (2004) examined the relationship of gender and interpersonal hostility in a work environment among 289 public-sector employees who reported no personal experience of hostility at work. Their findings suggest that working in a misogynous context can undermine employee well-being, with observed incivility (i.e., rude, disrespectful behavior) toward women having negative effects on all workers regardless of gender; male-skewed workgroups reported the most negative effects.

Similarly, Settles, Cortina, Malley, and Stewart (2006) found that women scientists who experienced sexual harassment and gender discrimination reported poorer job outcomes. Personal negative experiences and perceptions of the workplace climate had negative effects on job satisfaction and productivity. After harassment and discrimination were controlled, perceptions of a generally positive, nonsexist climate, as well as effective leadership, were related to positive job outcomes, underscoring the importance of countering the formal and informal structural mechanisms that contribute to a chilly academic climate for women scientists.

The report of a four-year, participant-observer study of transit operatives by Swerdlow (1989) provides a vivid description of the challenge women's entry into nontraditional occupations presents to the men whose masculine identity is tied to an ideology of male supremacy. In her study, the men's job security was not at issue, and the most common attitudes were encouragement and support. However, women's competent performance in this nontraditional, blue-collar job setting challenged a "deeply held belief in male superiority" (Swerdlow, 1989, p. 374). Men did not attempt to remove the women from the workplace to maintain that ideology, but instead developed interpretations and practices that enabled them to reconcile women's competent performance with their chauvinistic beliefs. These practices included hostility directed at undermining feelings of competence and sexualization of the workplace and work relationships to objectify, demean, and dominate their fellow women workers. These behaviors allowed men to maintain their supremist ideology even while accepting women in the workplace. When women made errors, they were spotlighted and remembered—and interpreted as evidence of women's general incompetence. When women were competent, they received effusive praise as exceptions to the rule, and stereotypes could be safely maintained. Women were also perceived by men as not actually doing exactly the same work as men and as receiving preferential treatment.

For many men in the Swerdlow (1989) study, sexualization of women was their major accommodation strategy. As she so eloquently states:

> By forcing sexual identities into high relief, men submerge the equality inherent in the work and superimpose traditional dominant and subordinate definitions of the sexes. Men have a stake in seeing women as sexual beings because in no arena is male domination less ambiguous for working-class men than sexuality. (Swerdlow, 1989, p. 381)

Despite the fact that men persisted in regarding women as a group as sex objects, there is hope. Women did develop nonsexist, egalitarian relationships with their male work partners. Men's accommodative strategies enabled them to accept women coworkers and, over time, treat them individually as equals.

Although Swerdlow's (1989) research deals with blue-collar transit workers, her expressive portrayal of attempts to maintain female subordination may apply across occupational categories and worker classes. It points to the need for researchers to examine strategies to maintain male gender-role supremacy in the presence of egalitarian changes in other roles in the workplace and in the family. It also demonstrates how the sexualized objectification of women can be used to undermine women's authority and power in a work setting. This work underscores the importance of research that articulates how sexualized objectification of women functions to undermine female authority, power, advancement, and well-being in the workplace.

Gender Segregation

Although women are found in every occupation, gender segregation in the workforce continues to be an issue for women in the 21st century (Browne, 2006; Padavic & Reskin, 2002; Reskin, 1984). Patterns of segregation reflect both the individual choices of women as well as interpersonal and institutional sexism. Betz (see chapter 22 in this volume) and Fouad (2007) review the career choice literature, so we will not discuss it in depth here except to say that is still not well understood why women tend to go into one field of work rather than another, and there may be more than one answer, depending on the particular field and employment context. For example, stereotype threat may contribute to the gender segregation seen in science, technology, engineering, and mathematics (STEM) fields due to persistent and widespread cultural stereotypes about women's inferiority in mathematics (Spencer, Steele, & Quinn, 1999; Steele, 1997). This stereotype threat might not be operate the same way in other occupations.

Theories of career choice and persistence have emphasized the importance of cognitive factors, such as self-efficacy, for the participation and performance of college women in traditionally male-dominated STEM fields (Lent et al., 2005; Fouad, 2007). Women who have confidence in their math ability are much more likely than those who do not to expect positive outcomes regarding math performance and to have interest in math-related fields. Confidence, outcome expectations, and interest in a domain all relate to major choice (Lent et al., 2005). This may be particularly true for women in male-dominated areas such as the STEM fields where disciplinary values mirror male gender-role stereotypes and emphasize individualistic achievement, competence, tough-mindedness, and intellectual detachment.

Recent reports by the National Science Board and National Science Council (e.g., National Science Foundation, 2004, 2007), have expressed concern about the persistent underrepresentation of women, particularly ethnic minority women, in STEM disciplines. It may be that the focus on cognitive factors needs to be broadened to encompass motivational and emotional factors affecting career choice and persistence. As Clewell and Campbell (2002) have observed, "although intervention efforts heretofore may have been successful in getting girls ... the requisite academic skills to embark on [a science and engineering] career, these efforts have not been sufficient to get girls to *want* to be scientists or engineers" (p. 277).

Many studies have investigated factors influencing women's STEM career decisions, but such research has generally emphasized cognitive rather than emotional factors. Broadening the investigation of career choice and persistence to encompass the effects of positive and negative emotions may be the step needed to break through the barriers that underlie resistance to the greater gender integration of the scientific workforce and retard the advancement of women in STEM fields. In particular, factors contributing to conflicts between work and family responsibilities and the lack of institutional action to ameliorate them continue to be a leading concern, even for women in highly skilled, highly paid professions such as science and engineering. For example, in a National Research Council study of female engineering faculty, by far the most important factor reported as having negative impact on the women's careers, identified by more than half of the respondents, was "balancing work and family responsibilities" (National Research Council, 2001a). Difficulties women face in balancing the demands of academic work and family responsibilities continue to be emphasized in national reports on women in STEM fields (e.g., National Academy of Sciences, National Academy of Engineering, & Institute of Medicine, 2006; National Research Council, 2001b; National Science Foundation, 2004, 2007).

Analysis of the progress of women in academe provides a good illustration of how institutional norms and structures shape career choices and undermine persistence. Multiple studies have demonstrated that the concentration of women in the lower-paid, lower-prestige, part-time, and temporary teaching positions is due, in large part, to the conflicts between career and family demands (Bernstein & Russo, in press). The situation is complex, reflecting the direct negative effects of outmoded practices (e.g., a rigid tenure clock) as well as the absence of positive support (e.g., child care services, job sharing), but there is insufficient translation of how these inequities operate in particular academic and disciplinary contexts. As Bronstein and colleagues aptly noted:

> Having both a family and an academic career is no simple matter. The tenure system in the United States was set up for male faculty, whose wives provided all the homemaking so that their husbands could devote

their energies solely to academic career advancement. (Bronstein, Rothblum, & Solomon, 1993)

Bailyn (2003) articulately summarized the research on barriers to women's progress in the academy:

> What this means is that the academy is anchored in assumptions about competence and success that have led to practices and norms constructed around the life experiences of men, and around a vision of masculinity as the normal, universal requirement of university life. (p. 143)

She also reminds us how easy it is to forget that venerable academic practices, such as the tenure clock, are "not God-given, but are constructed by mere men" (p. 143), underscoring the importance of challenging assumptions of academic culture and asking whether the fully autonomous expert role is a necessary condition for first-rate scholarship and whether success requires total priority given to one's work.

Gender segregation reflects job power and status. Women, particularly ethnic minority women, continue to be more likely to be found in lower-paying jobs than men, even within the same occupation (Guthrie & Roth, 1999) and to occupy lower ranks within organizations (Reskin & Roos, 1990). Although women may choose, enter, and persist in high-paying male-dominated occupations, they are still more likely to end up with lower positions and salaries or in less secure positions. For example, in academe, in 2005/06, female professors earned 81 percent of what men earned across all ranks and types of institutions (American Association of University Professors, 2006).

Similarly, Roth (2004) interviewed 15 men and 22 women who graduated from five elite graduate MBA programs in finance and began their careers in the early 1990s in securities on Wall Street. She found that five to seven years after beginning their careers, the women's median income was 60.5 percent of the men's, primarily reflecting the fact that women were concentrated in lower ranks. As another example, women who become physicians are more likely to go into family practice or general practice rather than specializing, and they tend to be found in small group practices, whereas men are more likely to specialize and be found in a solo practice or take over an established practice (Mayorova, Stevens, Scherpbier, Van der Velden, & Van der Zee, 2005).

Gender segregation of occupational fields becomes reflected in employment settings, such as academia, where variation in the proportion of women across fields is mirrored in gender variation across departments. For instance, in the top 50 research universities, women comprise about only 6.6 percent of tenure-track or tenured physicists, but one-third of tenure-track or tenured psychologists (Nelson, 2005). Women continue to be underrepresented in middle- and upper-level positions in academic administration, even when looking across all types of higher education institutions and in fields where there are similar proportions of eligible men and women (American Association of University Professors, 2006).

Gender segregation is both an outcome of and a contributor to the persistence of gender discrimination in the workplace. Insofar as the roles of women at work require behaviors that fit gender and ethnic stereotypes, supervisors may be able to behave in discriminatory ways without feeling dissonance with other egalitarian attitudes. In consequence, people do not have to monitor their behaviors, nor are they able to recognize the discriminatory outcomes of carrying out their occupational roles (Kahn & Crosby, 1985). Men may work well with women who are in subordinate positions (secretaries, administrative assistants), but become uncomfortable—if not downright threatened—by female peers or superiors, particularly in male-dominated occupational settings. As women rise in their professions, particularly in male-dominated fields, they must deal with the responses of male peers and subordinates, who may or may not welcome women's entry into previously male territory. While some men may be supportive, others may respond with hostility and harassment, including sexual harassment and refusal to teach skills and knowledge essential to job performance (Deaux, 1984).

Evidence suggests that as the proportion of women increases in a traditionally male field, the attitudes of males toward women change from neutral to resistant. By comparison, as the proportion of males in traditionally female occupations increases, women's attitudes move from being favorable to neutral. Meanwhile, problems for women who enter traditionally male occupations include those associated with having a token status. (Kanter, 1977, defined women as tokens in a group unless they were more than 15 percent of the members.) Tokens are subjected to increased scrutiny and stereotyping. If the stereotypes are negative—as they are for women and minorities—they can be inhibiting and stress-producing (Lord & Saenz, 1985).

Sexual harassment may function differently in male-dominated occupational settings compared with female-dominated ones. Some evidence suggests that in male-dominated occupations, coworkers are more likely to harass women in retaliation for perceived threats to male economic and social status. In traditionally female occupations, on the other hand, harassment is more likely to be conducted by supervisors who threaten the jobs of women who fail to comply with sexual demands. Legal protection is clearest and most effective for women who are harassed by their supervisors, because the differential power relationships are more clear and laws and policies specifically prohibit such harassment (Carothers & Crull, 1984). Such research underscores the importance of controlling for occupational context in research on the experience of women at work.

Employment Rewards

Women's increasing participation in the workforce has not been matched by similar changes in employment rewards. A gender gap persists in the earnings of full-time wage and salary workers: In 2005, with regard to median weekly earnings, women earned $585 per week compared with $722 for men (i.e., they earned 81¢ for every dollar earned by men; U.S. Bureau of Labor Statistics, 2006). In general, theories of the wage gap have either focused on gender differences in personal characteristics and qualifications (human capital theories) or emphasized gender differences in the experiences and contexts of women (discrimination theories) (Blau, Simpson, & Anderson, 1998). However, the reasons for the persistence of the wage gap between women and men continue to be inadequately understood and may not be revealed without more complex, multilevel explanatory frameworks. Prokos and Padavic (2005) examined the role of cohort effects and glass ceiling barriers on the income differences between male and female scientists and engineers. Their results indicated a continuing pay gap that was not fully explained by either factor. The gender pay gap in these fields appeared to reflect unassessed barriers that do not change in intensity as individuals age and have not diminished for recent cohorts.

Compensation goes beyond salary. Voluntary employer-paid benefits (i.e., those not legally mandated, in contrast to Social Security benefits), including pensions, insurance, vacation, and sick leave, constituted nearly 20 percent of employee compensation in 2006 (U.S. Bureau of Labor Statistics, 2007a). Women are less likely to receive pension benefits than men. In 2004, among people over 65 years of age who received pensions, the median pension income for men was $12,000, compared to $6,600 for women. Among men, white men had the highest median pension benefit ($12,492), with black men close behind ($12,000). The figure was substantially lower for Hispanic men ($8,400) compared to other men, but it was nonetheless higher than the median for women, regardless of race/ethnicity. Among women, black women had the highest median pension benefit ($7,800), followed by white women ($6,500) and Hispanic women ($6,000). The gender gap in pension benefits reflects the intersecting effects of gender and race on occupational segregation. The fact that a higher proportion of black women are former government employees than are other women is the most probable explanation for their higher median benefit (Joint Economic Committee, 2007).

Although working women's rates of job-based coverage are similar to that of men, they are less likely than men to be insured through their own job (38% vs. 50%, respectively). Being in the labor force is no guarantee of insurance coverage; only 21 percent of uninsured women are in families without workers (Henry J. Kaiser Foundation, 2007). A full analysis of factors influencing women's employment rewards would consider forms of compensation other than salaries and include a consideration of more intangible benefits, including job satisfaction.

The concentration of women in low-paying occupations is a major reason for the gender gap in wages. Research sponsored by the American Association of University Women found job and workplace characteristics explained about a third of the variation in women's wages compared to a fourth of the variation in men's wages in 2001 (Day & Hill, 2007). In general, the larger the proportion of women in an occupation, the lower the earnings in that occupation (Reskin & Bielby, 2005). Elimination of pay inequities will require analyses that go beyond occupational groupings to examine the employment settings of specific occupations. Women earn less than men in all major occupational groups, even those in which the majority of workers are women.

Another related line of research has looked at the resources and praise women receive in traditionally male domains (Vescio, Gervais, Snyder, & Hoover, 2005; Vescio, Snyder, & Butz, 2003). This research looked at the effect of the interplay of power (higher-status versus lower-status groups) and stereotypes on the behavior of members of both lower- and higher-power groups. In a series of studies, Vescio et al. (2005) found that powerful men who stereotype women in a weakness-focused manner (i.e., women are illogical and weak) in a male-dominated domain gave fewer valued resources and more praise to subordinate women. That is, women mentored by men holding stronger gender stereotypes were likely to receive more verbal praise, but fewer professional resources and opportunities, than their male peers. Their findings suggest that the same event may lead to different responses on the part of women and men. When given devalued positions by a supervisor, both men and women felt angry, but this anger predicted better performance among men and lower performance among women. These results suggest that the argument "There's no discrimination—he's equally mean to everyone" rests on an inadequate analysis of the effects of negative feedback on women and men.

Ethnicity and Earnings

The earnings gap in 2005 was greater when intersecting effects of gender and race/ethnicity are taken into account. Using the median earnings for white males for a full-time workweek—$743—as a standard of comparison, white women earned 80¢ for every dollar earned by white men; black women, 67¢; and Hispanic women, 58¢. In addition, black men earned 75¢ and Hispanic men 66¢ for every dollar earned by white men (U.S. Bureau of Labor Statistics, 2006). Addressing the complex structural, social, and psychological processes that underlie these differences is essential for closing the earnings gaps associated with gender and race/ethnicity.

Among these issues is the segregation of women of color into occupations that not only differ from white women but also differ by racial/ethnic group. For example, both black and Hispanic women are more likely to work in institutional service jobs (e.g., private household work, cleaners, typists, hospital orderlies) than Anglo women, but Hispanic women are more often found in production or service jobs than either black or Anglo women, and black women are more heavily concentrated in office and administrative support positions (National Committee on Pay Equity, 2007).

The forces that produce gender and ethnic pay differentials are complex. They are only partially explained by differences in education or training or in family responsibilities. Space precludes an in-depth discussion of differences in employment patterns by gender and ethnicity in this chapter (see U.S. Bureau of Labor Statistics, 2007b; National Committee on Pay Equity, 2007). A key point here, however, is that researchers who seek to study how work-related psychological and social variables differ by gender and ethnicity must recognize that the intersections of gender and race affect the segregation that pervades the workplace. Comparisons across gender and racial groupings must be made with care.

It must be remembered that the behavior of individuals reflects the power and status of their position. Women's actions (and reactions to them) reflect their lower status and organizational powerlessness. It is important to avoid the "fundamental attribution error" of assuming that deference, helpfulness, sensitivity, and other powerless behaviors are due to women's psychological traits. As Reid and Comas-Diaz (1990) have said so well, "Among the various characteristics which have been identified as contributors to status, gender and ethnicity are undoubtedly the most permanent, most noticeable, and have the most established attributional systems to accompany them" (p. 397).

Employment Satisfaction

Satisfaction derived from one's work is an intangible, but nonetheless important, employment reward. Interestingly, women continue to show similar levels of employment satisfaction compared with men, despite receiving lower compensation. This "paradox of the contented female worker" (Crosby, 1982) persists, even though gender discrimination is recognized as a social problem by both men and women and women are aware, aggrieved, and outraged at its continued existence. This is not explained by different job values or preferences (Major, 1987).

Crosby (1982) posits a theory of relative deprivation to explain this paradox. Relative deprivation occurs when people believe that their present condition is not as good as they both want it to be and believe they deserve it to be (Crosby, 1984a, 1984b). Reference group is the key in this framework: Women do not feel deprived when they earn less than men because they are comparing themselves with other women. Aspects of this theory have been investigated in research on factors contributing to gender differences in pay expectations, feelings of entitlement, and denial of disadvantage.

Pay Expectations

There are substantial differences in pay expectations: Men expect to be paid more than women (Major, 1993). For example, in a study of pay expectations of management interns, Major and Konar (1984) examined the contribution of five factors gender differences in pay expectations:

1. career path factors (gender differences in pay expectations may reflect differences in educational and occupational choices that lead to lower-paying occupations)
2. objective job inputs (examining the belief that women may be less qualified or have poorer performance than men)
3. perceived job inputs (women may have lower performance expectations, devalue their performance, and differ in their explanations for their performance compared with men)
4. job facet importance (women may value different facets of their job than men; specifically, they may consider money less important)
5. social comparison effects (women may use different reference group comparisons than men, and if they compare themselves to other women who as a group make less then men, they are evaluating their outcomes against a lower comparison standard)

Gender differences were found on only three of these factors: career path, job facet importance, and comparison standards. More than half of the women, compared with just 10 percent of men, chose personnel as a career specialty (a management field with a higher proportion of women than other management specialties). Women placed less importance on salary and more importance on interesting work than did men. Women also had different comparison salary expectations than men; women's estimate of the earnings of others entering their field was about $2,200 less than men's estimate. This was despite the fact that the supervisors of male and female interns did not differ in their estimates of what "typical others" would earn in the intern's field. Comparison pay estimates had the largest influence on pay expectations, accounting for 28 percent of their variance. Specialty area accounted for 15 percent of their variance; job facet importance, 5 percent. Number of years women planned to work and actual work performance as rated by supervisors did not help explain women's lower pay expectations.

Like Crosby (1982), Major and Konar (1984) suggested that one explanation for the gender difference in comparison standards is a tendency for men and women to compare themselves with others of the same sex, leading to a lower comparison standard for women. They also recognized, however, that women might use the same others for comparison, but estimate pay differently, due to differences in pay information.

Male dominance of occupations may relate to women's comparison standards in complex ways. One possibility is that male dominance of an occupation lowers performance expectations for women, in turn leading to lowered feelings of entitlement and lower pay expectations if the woman enters such an occupation. Women have lower self-efficacy and performance expectations for traditionally male occupations, and a substantial amount of research has examined the relationship of those expectations to career choice (see chapter 22).

Negotiation skills may play a role as well. Kray, Thompson, and Galinsky (2001) have investigated effects of stereotyping women as less convincing, powerful, and assertive relative to men on negotiation behaviors. Using a negotiations task among dyads of MBA students at a top business school, they found that when the task was described as indicative of negotiating skills and future success, women's negotiation performance (agreement in price between a buyer and seller) was lower than men's. In contrast, when the task was presented as a learning tool not diagnostic of ability, women and men performed equally. They suggest that negotiation skills training may help to close, but not eliminate, the gender gap observed in starting salary—a gap that is particularly detrimental, as it sets the foundation for a widening wage gap even if there is no further discrimination. One year out of college, women working full-time earn only 80 percent as much as their male peers; 10 years later, women make 69 percent as much as men earn. Even controlling for hours worked, occupation, parenthood, and other factors normally linked to compensation, college-educated women still earn less than college-educated men (American Association of University Women, 2007).

A comprehensive examination of inequities in the workplace would go beyond employment rewards to examine situations where women and men are paid equally, but where women are working harder and are more productive. Major, Vanderslice, and McFarlin (1984) provide evidence that women not only expect to be paid less but pay themselves less than men do when given the same task to accomplish. Further, when given a fixed amount of money, women work longer and are more productive and more accurate than men, particularly when their work is monitored. The focus on pay inequities has led to a knowledge gap in this area. We need to know about performance inequities as well.

Women's Reference Groups

Women do not necessarily compare themselves solely with other women, but when they do, it appears to be linked to their economic status. Zanna, Crosby, and Loewenstein (1987) examined the relationship between gender of reference group and feelings of dissatisfaction or deprivation among professional women (many in male-dominated occupations); 28 percent of the women used reference groups that were predominantly male, while 42 percent used groups that were predominantly female. Salary level, but not job prestige ratings, distinguished who used which type of reference group. Women who compared themselves with males made substantially higher salaries than women who compared themselves with females; women using mixed groups fell between the two. Unfortunately, these researchers did not attempt to examine the effects of gender segregation within the occupations of the women studied. This would require going beyond occupational prestige (although that is correlated with proportion of males in an occupation) and examining the subfields of the occupations (e.g., one might expect an industrial psychologist to have a male referent group, and a child psychologist to have a female referent group).

Interesting differences in choice of reference group and marital and parental roles were discovered, however. Women who had female reference groups were more likely to be mothers, while women with male reference groups were likely to be married but have no children. Single women were more likely to use a mixed reference group (Zanna et al., 1987). These findings suggest that the mother role has a pervasive impact on women's identity at work as well as at home and that research comparing working women with housewives must control for maternal status (Biernat et al., 2004).

Strategies to address pay inequities must go beyond a focus on the objective qualities of women's jobs and include the attitudes and reference groups of women holding those jobs. Future research also needs to go beyond salaries to include women's expectations regarding other forms of compensation, as well as access to training and promotional opportunities. Further, more needs to be known about women's reference groups, which may differ for women of diverse ethnicity. For example, working-class Chicanas who perceive themselves as having occupational mobility in jobs with little or no advancement have been found to compare themselves with local working-class reference groups of similar ethnicity (Segura, 1989).

Social comparison occurs in context. Evidence suggests that women's work satisfaction is influenced by the relationship of work and family domains. Using a meta-analysis, Ford, Heinen, and Langkamer (2007) found that substantial variability in job satisfaction is explained by family domain–specific variables. Furthermore, substantial variability in family satisfaction was explained by work domain–specific variables, with job and family stress having the strongest effects on work–family conflict and cross-domain satisfaction.

The Denial of Disadvantage

Women's failure to perceive the personal relevance of gender injustice in society contributes to the slow pace of change toward gender equality in the workplace. The "denial of individual disadvantage" (i.e., the failure to recognize that women we know face the same employment disadvantages as women in general) has been found in research in samples of heterosexual women (Crosby, 1982), lesbians (Crosby, Pufall, Snyder, O'Connell, & Whalen, 1989), blacks (Abeles, 1976), and French Canadians (Guimond & Dube-Simard, 1983). Sometimes that individual is ourselves, and the phenomenon is more aptly termed "denial of personal disadvantage" (Crosby et al., 1989, p. 81).

Crosby and her colleagues (1989) summarize emotional and cognitive mechanisms that help account for the denial of women's disadvantage on the part of both women and men, including self-protective cognitions. They point out the importance of identification with an oppressed group for discrimination to be perceived. They also document men and women's difficulty in perceiving discrimination when data are presented on a case-by-case basis, showing the need for information in aggregate form before discriminatory patterns can be revealed. They underscore that all people, whether gender-biased or not, have difficulty in perceiving gender bias in individual cases. They conclude that the need for social reform should not be measured by how concerned people are with their personal situation—people do not have a well-developed sense of their personal disadvantage. Their advice to employers:

> Do not trust your own impressions any more than you trust the impressions of the women in your organization. Women may be motivated to deny their own disadvantage; but nobody ... should trust conclusions based on unaggregated figures. Only by bringing all the data together can one see patterns. (Crosby et al., 1989, p. 97)

Strategies for Changing Women's Status in the Workplace

Women's strategies to eliminate inequity have differed in different occupations (Sacks, 1983), and there is much to be learned from each of them. These strategies include individual and class-action lawsuits;

proposing legislation; lobbying; formation of unions; collective bargaining; strikes and sit-ins; stockholder proxy fights; consumer boycotts; changing professional ethics, accreditation, and licensing criteria to prohibit discriminatory behavior; forming women-oriented businesses to compete against sexist institutions; and public ridicule. Diversity training has become routine for big business, and "diversity management" a new field of expertise (Agars & Kottke, 2004). A more nuanced and contextualized understanding of what combinations of strategies are effective for what particular problems under what conditions is now needed. In particular, more attention needs to be paid to the subtleties of modern discrimination, particularly as it is expressed in selective incivility and interpersonal maltreatment in the workplace.

The research on women's status referenced in this chapter suggests a variety of strategies for empowering women at work and eliminating inequalities in the workplace. Some of them focus on the women themselves. Workshops, networking groups, and other vehicles to help prepare women to deal with issues in the workplace, particularly when they are tokens, are one approach. Such workshops could help raise women's sense of entitlement and eliminate their denial of personal disadvantage by increasing their comparison standards and helping them understand how procedures and practices in the workplace promote gender bias in opportunities and outcomes.

Changing women's response to their treatment in the workplace is not sufficient, however. In addition to workshops designed to help women deal with issues in the workplace, the persistence of evaluation bias suggests the need for workshops targeted toward (1) eliminating stereotyping and bias on the part of evaluators and (2) educating employers about the denial of individual disadvantage. Blanchard and Crosby (1989) argue that, given that women and other disadvantaged groups minimize the level of their personal suffering from discrimination, affirmative action (which does not require members of disadvantaged groups to come forward on their own behalf) is critical for progress to occur.

Certainly effective change requires that strategies aimed at individuals must be complemented by a variety of institutional and policy-oriented efforts, including adequate compensation for "women's work" (including a decent minimum wage), paid family and medical leave, and workplace flexibility. Salary secrecy can be eliminated, and employers can be required to provide aggregate data on salaries and other forms of compensation so that bias in employment rewards can be monitored. Rewards, accolades, and other indicators of quality also play an important role in eliminating evaluation bias and discriminatory behavior. If an authority "certifies" the quality of a product by a woman, it is less likely to be perceived as unequal (Pheterson, Kiesler, & Goldberg, 1971). The purpose and criteria for rewards can be scrutinized, modified if necessary, and monitored.

Public reminders about attitudes toward, and commitments to, affirmative action before each evaluation also help to reduce discriminatory behaviors (Snyder & Swann, 1976). Larwood, Szwajkowski, and Rose (1988) have pointed out that even well-intentioned managers "rationally" make discriminatory decisions in order to impress their higher-ups. Their research has shown that, in the absence of contrary evidence, managers will discriminate against women and ethnic minorities based on their beliefs about the preferences of those having power over them. Their work suggests that individuals holding power at the top of an organization will be perceived as preferring white males unless clear evidence to the contrary is provided. Larwood and her colleagues suggest that such evidence might include appointing minorities and women to key positions, placing them in positions of authority that require others to work for them, and taking unusual steps to communicate a credible preference for equal opportunity that go beyond typical nondiscrimination pronouncements.

Progress is being made with regard to the development of "family friendly" policies. Originally conceptualized in terms of childcare benefits and parental leave, they now include alternative work arrangements such as job sharing, flexible scheduling, and telecommuting (Catalyst, www.catalyst.org, is a good source for information about adoption of diversity- and family-related policies by business). Even as we must challenge obsolete beliefs and stereotypes about women, particularly mothers, we must challenge the workaholic stereotype of the "ideal worker" and the equation of long hours with higher commitment and productivity. Best Buy provides an example of an alternative approach. In response to retention and morale issues, this company instituted a policy called ROWE (Results-Only Work Environment), whereby workers set their own schedules and are responsible for meeting performance goals. Reports suggest a positive outcome, including improved retention and productivity (Day & Hill, 2007).

WOMEN'S STATUS IN THE FAMILY

Contemporary women make substantial economic contributions to their families, continue to have the major responsibility for housework and dependent care (including children and elderly parents), and disproportionately suffer the effects of discrimination, violence, and poverty to the detriment of their mental health (Belle, 1990; Belle & Doucet, 2003; see also chapter 14). Women's economic role in the family has continued to increase. In 2004, wives' earnings contributed about 35 percent of their family incomes (U.S. Bureau of Labor Statistics, 2006). The median yearly income for husband-and-wife earner families was $77,899, compared to $51,303 for husband-only earner families. In 2004, in married-couple families in which the wife worked,

33 percent of these wives earned more than their husbands (note that this figure includes families in which the husband did not work; U.S. Bureau of Labor Statistics, 2006).

Women's economic status has both direct and indirect links to their mental health and well-being. Income has been found to be positively associated with mental health for both white and black women (Baruch & Barnett, 1987). Although employment may create difficulties for women in caring for children, it can also provide a buffer for other types of stress, particularly for low-income women. Compared with housewives, employed married women with lower incomes have been found to be more affected by stress due to childrearing but less affected by other life events. Thus, higher-income women's ability to purchase assistance to cope with time and work demands may mitigate stresses from childrearing that women with lower incomes cannot avoid (Cleary & Mechanic, 1983).

Ross, Mirowsky, and Huber (1983) found that the higher a woman's income, the more her husband was likely to share in home responsibilities (the correlation was with her income, not his). It may be that with money comes power to negotiate roles, with concomitant mental health benefits. However, women who make secondary or minimal contributions to family income may be "unable to redistribute obligations and thus will suffer continued difficulties and dissatisfaction" (Thoits, 1987, p. 19).

Education is a significant preventive against psychological distress and depression, perhaps because it may lead to an increased sense of mastery and sense of control, necessary conditions for the development of active problem-solving approaches and successful negotiation of stress and coping resources. There are also strong and complex relationships among education, work, and compensation, with educational choices setting the foundations for later occupational segregation and inequities in compensation (Day & Hill, 2007). Education also widens "possibilities for new role bargains suggested through reading, travel, and lectures by 'experts'" (Thoits, 1987, p. 18). It is a resource that leads to effectiveness in both homemaker and work roles, and it needs to be considered in research examining mental health effects of work and family resources and responsibilities.

Ethnic Minority Families

Racial and ethnic differences in psychological distress are enhanced among people with low incomes, particularly poor black women (Kessler & Neighbors, 1986). Social class is not sufficient to explain such differences; doing so will require simultaneously examining gender effects. Ethnic minority families have greater sources of stress, as well as fewer resources to deal with that stress (cf. Belle, 1990; Staples,

1987). They are also more likely to have unintended pregnancies, unwanted births, and larger family sizes (U.S. Bureau of the Census, 2000).

Different opportunity structures for the races have shaped family organization in numerous ways (Zinn, 1989). Women's marriage and divorce rates vary with race and ethnicity. The profound effect of location in the social structure on ethnic minority family organization can be seen in the large differences in the proportion of never-married women by race. Black women are much more likely never to marry than are either white or Hispanic women. For example, in 2003, 63 percent of black women 25–29 years of age had not yet married, compared with about 36 percent for white and 35 percent for Hispanic women, respectively (U.S. Bureau of the Census, 2003). Black women are also more likely to be divorced or separated than either white or Hispanic women. In 2003, among black women aged 15 years and order, 41 percent had never married, 18 percent were divorced or separated, and 31 percent were currently married. In contrast, for white women, the percentages were 23 percent never married, 13 percent divorced or separated, and 55 percent married; for Hispanic women, the respective figures were 30, 13, and 52 percent (U.S. Bureau of the Census, 2003). Any discussion of women's multiple roles must recognize that a significant proportion of contemporary women are not married—that is, they are divorced, widowed, or never married—and that generalizations about family circumstances across ethnicities should be made with care.

Female-Headed Households

Regardless of race or ethnicity, a large proportion of unmarried women are mothers who head single-parent households. The number of one-parent families went from 9.4 million in 1988 to about 18.5 million in 2005. Approximately 14 million of these families—76%—were maintained by women in 2005 (U.S. Bureau of Labor Statistics, 2007). In 2005, there were more than 17 million children in female-headed households, where financial difficulties are greatest. The median family income for female-headed households without spouses was $22,037; for male-headed households, it was $34,677 (U.S. Bureau of the Census, 2005a).

The reasons women maintain one-parent families differ by ethnic group. White women are more likely to do so because of marital dissolution; in contrast, black single mothers are more likely to have never married. As Zinn (1989) observes, race and ethnicity create "different routes to female headship, but Whites, Blacks, and Latinos are all increasingly likely to end up in this family form" (p. 78). The childcare needs of such families are considerable, and lack of access to child care has a differential impact on ethnic minority children.

This brief portrait of women's family resources and responsibilities points to the importance of examining the relationship of women's family roles to their roles in other social structures, such as the workplace and the community. The remainder of this chapter focuses on the interrelationships among women's work and family roles, with specific regard to one category of outcome: their impact on women's mental health and well-being.

MULTIPLE ROLES AND WOMEN'S MENTAL HEALTH: COMPLEX RELATIONSHIPS

Conceptualizing women's negotiation of their multiple roles in their social and cultural contexts requires understanding work and family dynamics as a complex multilevel process. The apparent lack of attention to the context of the work–family interface leaves a gap in psychologists' knowledge, which we encourage future researchers to fill. Similarly, differences in the work–family interface that are associated with socioeconomic status also have been overlooked (Allen et al., 2001). Whether or not a combination of employment, marriage, and motherhood results in mental health costs or benefits depends on a variety of factors, including personality characteristics, family variables, and job variables.

Conceptualizing Relationships among Women's Multiple Roles

As women's work and family roles have evolved, so has thinking about their interrelationships. Researchers are moving beyond the individualistic focus reflected in the "juggling" metaphor used to represent a women's attempts to balance her array of responsibilities. Today researchers are examining how various facets of their lives—related to work, family, and other roles and responsibilities—affect each other in dynamic, interactive ways, with positive as well as negative effects (Halpern & Murphy, 2004).

For example, research on multiple roles traditionally focused on the conflict between women's work and family roles. As Ford et al. (2007) describe, work and family conflict (WFC) was originally conceptualized as one-dimensional and bidirectional—that is, the influence of work on family and the influence of family on work were viewed one-dimensionally (e.g., Holahan & Gilbert, 1979). WFC antecedents were typically classified into three categories: time-based pressures, strains, and behavioral incompatibilities (Greenhaus & Beutell, 1985).

This conceptualization subsequently evolved, with measures of WFC based on a two-dimensional reciprocal model—work interference with family (WIF) and family interference with work (FIW)—becoming widely studied (Bellavia & Frone, 2005). WIF and FIW have also been operationalized in a measure assessing three subtypes: time-based conflict, strain-based conflict, and behavior-based conflict (Carlson, Kacmar, & Williams, 2000), although it has yet to be widely used.

Thus, it is now recognized that women's roles as wife and worker, mother and caretaker, can conflict or facilitate each other in a dynamic, bidirectional, reciprocal way (Demerouti, Bakker, & Bulters, 2004; Frone, 2003; Frone, Russell, & Cooper, 1997). Resources, stimulation, and social validation from one type of role may "spill over" and offset the strains of others (Frone, 2003). Both negative and positive work–family spillover can operate simultaneously (Grzywacz, 2000) and have implications for women's mental health and well-being (Frone, Russell, & Barnes, 1996; Grant-Vallone & Donaldson, 2001). Although role conflict, overload, and strain are possible, many researchers have documented beneficial effects of multiple roles for women's physical and mental health (Helson, Elliot, & Leigh, 1990; Marcussen & Piatt, 2005; Thoits, 1986; Voyandoff, 2004).

While marital status and satisfaction have long been important predictors of psychological distress, researchers have just begun to examine the psychological functions of marriage for men and women in social, economic, and political contexts. Marriage is generally more likely to be associated with mental health for men than women. Further, the quality of marriage is more strongly related to home life satisfaction for women compared with men (Gove & Zeiss, 1987). This difference may reflect gender differences in the psychological functions of marriage. Males may have more instrumental gains from marriage (e.g., in the form of services, such as housekeeping). Females, who have fewer alternatives, may invest more emotionally in their marital roles. The stronger impact of relationship quality for women compared with men may also reflect men's greater participation in employment roles that offer buffers to marital stress.

Thoits (1987) has provided a succinct and lucid summary of theory and research on the relationship of women's multiple roles and mental health. She evaluated the proposition that multiple role occupancy is harmful to women, pointing out that this approach relies on an oversocialized, deterministic view of human beings. It fails to recognize that women are active agents who can construct their own realities and who may choose not to conform to role expectations. Further, role expectations held by women and significant others may be flexible, ambiguous, or inconsistent. Feminist researchers, who assume women are active agents and seek women's empowerment, have rebutted simplistic role overload/conflict approaches (Baruch, Biener, & Barnett, 1987).

A major problem with research that has examined the relationship between paid employment and mental health for wives is the failure to separate family responsibilities associated with the role of wife from those associated with the role of mother. In general, motherhood is associated with increased psychological distress for women whether or not they work outside the home (Barnett & Baruch, 1985; Thoits, 1986). Distress appears higher when children are young (Thoits, 1986) and increases with the number of children living in the home (Brown, Bhrolchain, & Harris, 1975; Pearlin & Johnson, 1977; Radloff, 1975).

Unfortunately, whether or not the number, timing, and spacing of children were planned or the children were wanted is typically not ascertained. Yet, before the days of effective birth control, a primary rationalization for not investing in women employees was their unpredictable fertility. In addition to being a source of potential conflict between the work and mother roles, unintended pregnancies may generate stressful conflict between the wife and (anticipated) mother roles as well if they are wanted by the woman but unwanted by the partner. For example, one study found that pregnancies associated with the highest risk for postpartum depressive symptoms were those considered intended by females and unintended by their partners (Leathers & Kelley, 2000).

There is also a strong and complex relationship between intimate violence and unwanted pregnancy to consider. Unintended pregnancies are strongly correlated with exposure to intimate violence, including childhood physical and sexual abuse, rape, and partner violence (Russo & Pirlott, 2006). Advancing our understanding of the interrelationships of the mother, wife, and worker roles will require considering the intendedness of pregnancy and wantedness of births by both spouses. The pervasiveness of intimate violence in the lives of women and its contribution to risk for unintended pregnancy also needs to be considered when assessing factors that disadvantage working mothers and undermine their mental health (Hamilton & Russo, 2006).

Role Quality

Understanding when multiple roles do and do not promote mental health requires consideration of the joint and interacting effects of the qualities of those roles. Research has only recently begun to consider the interactive effects of the family and work roles. Research that does examine such effects suggests that the independent effects of marital and occupational status are not sufficient to predict well-being for all role combinations. It is necessary to look at specific role combinations and to know whether or not a specific role is perceived as stressful.

As Baruch and Barnett (1987) have observed:

> What really matters is the nature of the experiences within a role. Those concerned with women's mental health should now, therefore, turn their attention to understanding how to enhance the quality of women's experiences within each of their many roles. (p. 72)

Achieving that understanding requires more complex paradigms. It will be necessary to assess both the advantages and the disadvantages of multiple roles, using a dynamic, psychosocial approach that focuses on relevant processes or mechanisms, and to consider the psychological, family, and job characteristics of both spouses (McBride, 1990).

Psychological Factors

The assumption that women are active agents implies that personality characteristics and other psychological variables should affect the number, type, and quality of roles. In a classic study, Helson, Elliot, and Leigh (1990) analyzed data from a longitudinal study of Mills College graduates that assessed personality characteristics at age 21 and number of roles (partner, parent, and worker) at age 43. Examination of the differences among combinations of roles revealed that women with one role were less happy, content, and organized and felt greater alienation than women with multiple roles. There was no evidence that the three-role group had any more role conflict or overload than the other groups. The only difference between the three-role and two-role groups was the greater communality (feelings of being similar to others) of the former.

Those researchers affirmed that quality of roles was more important than number of roles in predicting women's psychological health. They first examined the relationship between number of multiple roles and psychological health at age 43 after antecedent personality characteristics were controlled. Measures of two dimensions of psychological health—well-being and effective functioning—were used. The number of roles was not correlated with psychological health at age 43 after controlling for such health at age 21.

Quality of roles (assessed through measures of marital satisfaction and status at work), on the other hand, did continue to predict psychological health, even after controlling for previous psychological health. Regardless of previous psychological characteristics, marital satisfaction was associated with contentment, and status at work was associated with effective functioning. Status level of work was also associated with attributes of an enhanced self-autonomy, individuality, and complexity. Unfortunately, the joint effects of marital satisfaction and work status were not explored. Further, because the study is correlational, it is difficult to separate the effects of work status on personality versus the effects of personality on work status.

The findings of Helson and her colleagues (1990) suggest an explanation for the psychological benefits of employment per se; that is, employment, even when it is stressful, may contribute to a more autonomous sense of self, thus promoting mental health. Both job satisfaction and being married have been found to be related to life satisfaction for both black and white women (Crohan, Antonucci, Adelmann, & Coleman, 1989). Russo and Tartaro (see chapter 14) consider the relationship between concepts such as mastery and women's mental health.

Marital Quality

The effects of women's employment on marital quality—that is, marital strain and marital satisfaction—appear to depend on a couple's attitudes toward the wife's employment. Perceived control over the choice to work is related to marital satisfaction in dual-career couples (Alvarez, 1985). Research on dual-worker married couples with preschool children has reported couples similar in attitudes toward women's roles to be higher in marital satisfaction levels (Cooper, Chassin, & Zeiss, 1985).

The mix of the couple's attitudes and personality characteristics has been found to be important to marital satisfaction as well. Higher levels of marital satisfaction and lower conflict surrounding domestic tasks are associated with higher combined levels of instrumental and expressive personality characteristics (Cooper et al., 1985; Gunter & Gunter, 1990). Individuals with such characteristics may have the best fit with the multiple agentic and communal qualities of work, marriage, and parenthood roles.

Ross et al. (1983) found that if a wife wanted to work but had no help from her husband with home responsibilities, her distress level increased, while his did not. Husbands' distress increased only in couples where the preference of both husband and wife was for the wife to stay at home. The lowest distress levels were found in dual-career couples who shared childcare and household responsibilities. It thus may be that difficulties in negotiation of childcare tasks can explain the finding of Gove and Zeiss (1987) that the presence of children affected whether or not congruence between employment and wife's preference for working affected her happiness. Such findings point to the importance of research on marital power, multiple roles, and mental health. Sharing of child care affects marital satisfaction for both men and women (Barnett & Baruch, 1987).

The effects of intimate violence, including battering and marital rape, are not often considered when studying the relationship of role quality, marital power, and work roles. Albaugh and Nauta (2005) investigated relationships among college women's experiences of violence from intimate partners, career decision self-efficacy, and perceived career barriers. Sexual coercion was found to be negatively correlated with three aspects of career decision self-efficacy (self-appraisal, goal selection, and problem solving) after adjusting for symptoms of depression. In contrast, negotiation (a positive conflict tactic) was positively correlated with goal-selection self-efficacy. Intimate partner abuse was generally unrelated to perceived barriers, with the exception of disability/health concerns, which were negatively related to psychological aggression, sexual coercion, and negotiation. Marital rape is associated with lowered marital quality and greater marital dissatisfaction, and most often occurs in marriages characterized by nonsexual violence. An estimated 10 to 14 percent of all married women experience marital rape, compared to an estimated 40 to 50 percent who are battered.

Marital Power

Family roles are by definition reciprocal, that is, defined in terms of rights and responsibilities toward one another. Thus, they depend on shared expectations and agreements on the tradeoffs between employment and family responsibilities. How such tradeoffs are negotiated in marriage clearly has mental health implications for women (Steil, 2001). A sense of power or influence in the relationship is related to relationship satisfaction for women in both heterosexual (Steil & Turetsky, 1987) and lesbian (Eldridge & Gilbert, 1990) couples.

Employment may enhance a wife's ability to negotiate tradeoffs to her satisfaction and mental health benefit. Employed wives have more influence over decision making in the home than nonemployed wives (Crosby, 1982). In a study of professional women, the amount a women earned relative to her husband (i.e., her income disparity) was more important than her absolute level of income in predicting her influence in family decision making. Influence was also correlated with how important a woman perceived her career to be (Steil & Turetsky, 1987).

Factors that contribute to equality in marital power appear to operate differently for women when they have children, at least among professional women (Steil, 2001). Steil and Turetsky (1987) found that for professional women without children, the women's perceived job importance was positively correlated with their influence in marital decision making. In addition, relative economic status—that is, a smaller negative or a positive income disparity relative to spouses—was associated with both greater influence in decision making and more freedom from household responsibilities for women. For mothers, however, reduced income disparity did not affect either influence in decision making or responsibility for household or childcare tasks. The only variable with an effect was psychological; the more a mother perceived her job as important, the less her responsibility for the household. Responsibility for child care was not affected by either variable.

Dominance of the husband in decision making per se did not relate to women's marital satisfaction. It was the outcome of the decision that was important. Women who had husbands who were "dominant" in decision making that resulted in shared responsibility for household tasks were satisfied as wives. The greater the sharing of household and childcare tasks, the greater the women's marital satisfaction. Shared responsibility also enhanced women's psychological well-being, especially that of mothers. The more responsibility a woman had for child care, the higher her depressive symptomatology (dysphoric mood and somatic symptoms). For nonmothers, marital equality contributed to well-being through its association with marital satisfaction. For mothers, marital equality contributed to well-being even beyond its contribution to marital satisfaction, suggesting additional relief for direct stress from burdens of household tasks (Steil & Turetsky, 1987).

The burden of those tasks on women is considerable. It has been estimated that wives spend somewhere between 30 and 60 hours per week on household labor, compared with 10 to 20 hours per week spent by husbands (Berardo, Shehan, & Leslie, 1987; Denmark, Shaw, & Ciali, 1985). Further, women's household labor involves tasks that are more time-consuming and are of more immediate necessity (Gunter & Gunter, 1990).

Women's long hours combined with gendered stressors and lack of access to resources are reflected in their rates of fatigue and tiredness (Hamilton & Russo, 2006). For example, in one study, fatigue was ranked first among their concerns by nearly 28 percent of women, and it was among the top 10 of more than 80 percent (Stewart, Abbey, Meana, & Boydell, 1998). Fatigue significantly predicts depressive symptom scores and reports of sleep dysfunction (Lavidor, Weller, & Babkoff, 2003).

The gender-related factors that contribute to women's fatigue extend beyond those associated with role overload. Hamilton and Russo (2006) suggest that the gender-related conditions that lead to fatigue and increased risk for depression for women may reflect a complex combination of factors, depending on their social and economic context, including:

- excess total hours of labor (including excess work due to poverty)
- excess of calorie-burning physical labor
- excess "emotional work" (e.g., excess nurturing and "caregiving," which can lead to "burnout" and depression)
- excess stress due to childbirth and excess work by new mothers postpartum (where much of the work could and should be done by others)
- cumulative effects of coping with chronic stressors, including those associated with poverty, sexualized objectification, intimate violence, and perceived discrimination
- sleep deprivation or insufficient sleep
- inadequate nutrition (which could reflect hunger or excessive dieting, depending on the women's situation)
- lack of *enjoyable* physical activity—a lack that is promoted by stereotypically female hobbies and leisure activities, which are too often

sedentary and typically occur in the home or other private, restricted places

- lack of health-promoting physical activity, caused by exhaustion, perceived lack of time, and the presence of children, given the gendered nature of parenting
- excess anxiety (e.g., related in part to fears of violence, which can be intensified by experiences of sexism and objectification, or due to past violence and posttraumatic stress disorder), which can impair sleep
- violence, which creates anxiety and interferes with sleep
- objectification and stigmatization, both of which can create anxiety
- the stress of "ambiguity" (e.g., as women, we continually ask ourselves: Was that a "compliment" or was that sexual harassment or bullying?), along with culturally sanctioned "mixed messages" (e.g., gendered "double-binds" and Catch-22 "behavioral scripts"), which can lead to rumination or "thinking too much" (Hamilton & Russo, 2006)

More needs to be known about the full range of demands on women's time and energy—demands that may include responsibilities beyond those associated with work and family roles. It may be that a broader conceptualization of women's activities (e.g., self-care and social and community relationships) will yield a better understanding of sources of energy renewal, as well as depletion, for women's ability to cope with life's demands.

Child Care

The individuals who take themselves out of the job market altogether to care for their children incur long-term career advancement costs, often taking whatever jobs they can get upon reentry to the job market. McDonald (2005) found that during midcareer, "reentry-level" nonsearchers (people who obtain their jobs without searching thanks to unsolicited tips about job openings) tend to be women with little work experience who have been out of the labor market taking care of family responsibilities.

The literature is in conflict about gender differences in relation to burnout and absence due to illness. Bekker, Croon, and Bressers (2005) examined the contribution of childcare obligations, job characteristics, and work attitudes to emotional exhaustion and absence in 404 male and female nurses. Contrary to expectations and current stereotypes, women did not have higher absence rates due to illness; further, men reported significantly higher levels of emotional exhaustion than women. Emotional exhaustion was associated with illness absence, childcare investment, and number of hours worked.

Mental health benefits of mothers' employment are increased when women are satisfied with their childcare arrangements (Parry, 1986; VanMeter & Agronow, 1982). Ross and Mirowsky (1988) found that a greater number of children increased depression levels for nonemployed wives, but had no relationship to husbands' depression levels. For employed mothers, however, the relationship of number of children to depression depended both on accessibility of child care and on the husband's support: if child care was accessible and husbands shared in it, depression levels were low; in contrast, employed mothers without accessible child care and with sole responsibility for it had extremely high depression levels.

Orth-Gomer and Leinweber (2005) examined the double exposure to stressors from work and family on coronary risk and depressive outcomes on 292 female coronary patients and 292 age-matched female healthy controls. In a five-year follow-up analysis, double exposure to stress from work and family was accompanied by the highest risk and the worst prognosis for females' coronary disease. In female coronary patients, depressive outcomes were frequent and linked to family stress more closely than to work stress. In the healthy female controls, both family and work stress—and most significantly their combination—led to depressive outcomes.

Poor childhood environments can also lead to a cycle of poor employment outcomes within families across generations, illuminating the importance of quality child care not only for the mental health of parents currently in the workforce and the current lived experience of their children but also for the future workforce represented by those same children. Ek, Sovio, Remes, & Järvelin (2005) found that childhood family characteristics, along with other social characteristics, predicted poor employment outcomes at age 31. Among men, lack of success on the job market was predicted by the mother's receptivity toward social aid and satisfaction with existing circumstances in early childhood, low family social status in adolescence, and low vocational training in early adulthood. Among women, poor employment outcomes were predicted by low school attainment in adolescence and low vocational training in early adulthood and were associated with having more than two children. Among both genders, having a low income, poor subjective health, and poor life satisfaction, as well as receiving little social support, was associated with poor employment outcomes in young adulthood.

Marital Equality and Ethnic Minority Women

Marcussen and Piatt (2005) found that blacks and whites reported similar experiences of role conflict and perceptions of role success and balance, but the association between these experiences and well-being varied by race and gender. The importance of examining issues of marital satisfaction and equality among diverse ethnic groups was also underscored by the findings of Golding (1990), who examined interrelationships among division of housework, household strain, and depressive symptomatology among Hispanic and non-Hispanic white men and women 18 years of age and older (the men and women were not married to each other). Although she describes her study as examining the consequences of housework, Golding's measure is actually a measure of sharing of, not level of, housework. Despite her model resting on flawed assumptions, the data are quite interesting when they are cast with labels that more accurately represent what is being measured. We present them in some detail, as they document the need to conduct research that examines the interaction of gender and ethnicity in diverse ethnic groups.

Equity in sharing four household tasks—cooking the main meal, washing dishes, doing laundry, and cleaning the house—was ascertained, with 0 indicating responsibility of spouse, 1 indicating shared responsibility, and 2 indicating responsibility of respondent. These scores were summed into a scale that ranged from 0 to 8. The distribution of tasks was bimodal, with nearly 65 percent of women having sole responsibility for housework, compared with 3 percent of men.

An interaction effect for ethnicity and gender was found in the division of household labor on these tasks. Mexican American women were most likely to have major responsibility for household tasks. Their mean rating was 7.4 on the 8-point scale, compared with non-Hispanic women, who had a mean rating of 6.4. Conversely, Mexican American men had a mean rating of 1.0, and non-Hispanic men had a mean rating of 2.2, both indicating little sharing of household tasks. Thus, Mexican American men were less likely to participate in housework than non-Hispanic men, and Mexican American women were less likely to share housework than non-Hispanic women.

The household strain measure included items assessing the presence or absence of having more household duties than one could do or should have to do, spending too many hours on housework, and housework's interference with other activities. These were summed to make a scale of 1 to 4. The level of household strain was low, but varied with gender and ethnicity. Mexican American women had the highest levels of household strain (1.3), followed by Mexican American men (0.8), non-Hispanic women (0.6), and non-Hispanic men (0.3). Whether or not the perceived household strain of Mexican American men reflects a resistance to sharing housework tasks or a larger overall level of household tasks for Mexican American families cannot be ascertained from this study.

Separate regression analyses for women and men were conducted to predict household strain. For women, being Mexican American and employed and having unequal sharing of housework predicted household strain. For men, being Mexican American predicted household strain. Lack of sharing of housework was associated with household strain for women, but not for men, perhaps because men rarely took on the responsibility for housework. The fact that inequities in housework were associated with household strain is consistent with research that inequities in division of household tasks are a source of grievance for women (Crosby, 1982).

Lack of sharing of housework was found to be associated with depressive symptomatology through its association with household strain for both Hispanic and non-Hispanic women. Household strain was associated with such symptomatology for both women and men, regardless of employment, age, and socioeconomic status. Unfortunately, the study provided no information about presence of children. Responsibility for child care was not distinguished from other forms of household responsibilities.

Lack of marital equality is associated with low education (Antill & Cotton, 1988; Rexroat & Shehan, 1987), but lack of education does not totally explain ethnic differences in marital equality. When Golding (1990) conducted her analyses on individuals with a 12th-grade education or above, the main effect for ethnicity that had been found for the entire sample disappeared, but the interaction effect for gender and ethnicity persisted.

Understanding Women's Inequality in the Family

The research reviewed in this chapter also shows that issues of women's equality in the family, as in the workplace, cross lines of ethnicity and class. We argue that understanding women's inequality in the family will require separating characteristics and behaviors mandated by masculine and feminine gender-roles from those of gendered family roles, particularly those of husband, wife, father, and mother. Masculine gender-roles may change so that performing domestic tasks may not threaten masculine gender identity, but unless the gender-roles of wife and mother change as well, inequalities in the family will persist, and women will continue to be responsible for household labor.

Evidence for this assertion is found in a study by Gunter and Gunter (1990). Those authors examined the relationship between gender-role (masculinity versus femininity as measured by the Bem Sex Role Inventory) and sharing of domestic tasks in a white, middle-class population. They found that when husbands were androgynous or undifferentiated, both husbands and wives performed the domestic tasks that were frequent, repetitious, and pressing. When a husband was sex-typed, however, women performed most tasks and husbands the least. They suggest that the gender identity of masculine males

> may be bound up not only in what they do, but equally in what they do not do. In other words, it may be as important to a sex-typed male *not* to

> dust or vacuum or change a diaper as it is to be able to change a tire or repair the plumbing. (p. 366)

Gunter and Gunter (1990) also found, however, that neither the husbands' nor the wives' gender-role orientation was related to the reasons given for performing household tasks. Women were more likely to report they did a task because it was their job or because it would not be done otherwise. Men, on the other hand, were more likely to report that domestic tasks were not their job. Perhaps research on male feelings of entitlement in the work setting (e.g., Major, 1987) may be helpful in understanding male feelings of entitlement in the family setting.

In particular, factors contributing to inequities in the family appear to differ for women who are mothers, underscoring the importance of separating effects of the gender-role of wife from that of mother. The gender-role that has least changed for women is that of mother, who still is primarily responsible for child care, whether or not she is employed, and faces the "maternal wall" of disadvantage in the workplace (Biernat et al., 2004).

CONCLUSION

This brief portrait of women's roles and status at work and in the family suggests that although great changes have occurred in women's work and family roles, gender inequalities in rewards, resources, and status persist. These inequalities are magnified for women of color and have profound impact on the mental health and well-being of all women, particularly mothers. Factors contributing to women's disadvantaged status have been discussed, and some strategies for research and action to empower women have been identified.

In the final analysis, however, it may be naïve to focus our attention on specific factors, such as gender segregation or husband–wife income disparity, currently identified as contributing to gender-based inequities at work or in the family. As myths and stereotypes are rebutted, myths are reinvented, and new rationalizations for the status quo emerge (Barnett, 2004). As Reskin (1988), quoting Lieberson (1985), pointed out, "Dominant groups remain privileged because they write the rules, and the rules they write 'enable them to continue to write the rules'" (p. 60). She focused on gender segregation, reminding us that it is but a symptom of the basic cause of the earnings gap—that is, men's desire to preserve their advantaged position. The principle goes beyond the workplace. Attempts to eliminate inequitable outcomes that fail to recognize the dominant group's stake in maintaining its superior status are incomplete (Reskin, 1988). Unless we can forge strategies that promote human equality as a superordinate goal for men and women of all races, women's disadvantaged status is unlikely to change.

REFERENCES

Abeles, R. P. (1976). Relative deprivation, rising expectations, and black militancy. *Journal of Social Issues, 32,* 119–137.

Agars, M. D., & Kottke, J. L. (2004). Models and practice of diversity management: A historical review and presentation of a new integration theory. In M. Stockdale & F. J. Crosby (Eds.), *The psychology and management of workplace diversity* (pp. 55–77). Malden, MA: Blackwell.

Albaugh, L. M. F., & Nauta, M. M. (2005). Career decision self-efficacy, career barriers, and college women's experiences of intimate partner violence. *Journal of Career Assessment, 13,* 288–306.

Allen, T. (2001). Family-supportive work environments: The role of organizational perceptions. *Journal of Vocational Behavior, 58,* 414–435.

Alvarez, W. F. (1985). The meaning of maternal employment for mothers and their perceptions of their three-year-old children. *Child Development, 56,* 350–360.

American Association of University Professors (2006). *AAUP faculty gender equity indicators.* Washington, DC: American Association of University Professors.

American Psychological Association. (2004). *The report of the APA Presidential Initiative on Work and Families: Aligning public policies, schools, and communities with the realities of contemporary families and the workplace.* Washington, DC: American Psychological Association. Available at http://www.apa.org/work-family.

Andersson, L. M., & Pearson, C. M. (1999). Tit for tat? The spiraling effect of incivility in the workplace. *Academy of Management Review, 24,* 452–471.

Antill, J. K., & Cotton, S. (1988). Factors affecting the division of labor in households. *Sex Roles, 18,* 531–553.

Bailyn, L. (2003). Academic careers and gender equity: Lessons learned from MIT. *Gender, Work and Organizations, 10*(2), 137–153.

Barling, J., Rogers, G. A., & Kelloway, E. K. (2001). Behind closed doors: In-home workers' experience of sexual harassment and workplace violence. *Journal of Occupational Health Psychology, 6,* 255–269.

Barnett, R. C. (2004). Women and work: Where are we, where did we come from, and where are we going. *Journal of Social Issues, 60,* 667–674.

Barnett, R. C., & Baruch, G. K. (1985). Women's involvement in social roles and psychological distress. *Journal of Personality and Social Psychology, 49,* 135–145.

Barnett, R. C., & Baruch, G. K. (1987). Social roles, gender, and psychological distress. In R. C. Barnett, L. Biener, & G. K. Baruch (Eds.), *Gender and stress* (pp. 122–143). New York: Free Press.

Baruch, G. K., & Barnett, R. C. (1987). Role quality and psychological well-being. In F. Crosby (Ed.), *Spouse, parent, worker: On gender and multiple roles* (pp. 63–73). New Haven, CT: Yale University Press.

Baruch, G. K., Biener, L., & Barnett, R. C. (1987). Women and gender in research on work and family stress. *American Psychologist, 42,* 130–136.

Bekker, M. H. J., Croon, M. A., & Bressers, B. (2005). Childcare involvement, job characteristics, gender and work attitudes as predictors of emotional exhaustion and sickness absence. *Work & Stress, 19,* 221–237.

Bellavia, G. M., & Frone, M. R. (2005). Work-family conflict. In J. Barling, E. K. Kelloway, & M. R. Frone (Eds.), *Handbook of work stress* (pp. 113–147). Thousand Oaks, CA: Sage.

Belle, D. (1990). Poverty and women's mental health. *American Psychologist, 45,* 385–389.

Belle, D., & Doucet, J. (2003). Poverty, inequality, and discrimination as sources of depression among U.S. women, *Psychology of Women Quarterly, 27,* 101–113.

Benokraitis, N. V. (Ed.). (1997). *Subtle sexism: Current practice and prospects for change*. Thousand Oaks, CA: Sage.

Benokraitis, N. V., & Feagin, J. R. (1995). *Modern sexism: Blatant, subtle, and covert discrimination* (2nd ed.). Englewood Cliffs, NJ: Prentice Hall.

Berardo, D. H., Shehan, C. L., & Leslie, G. R. (1987). A residue of tradition: Jobs, careers and spouses' time in housework. *Journal of Marriage and the Family, 49,* 381–390.

Berdahl, J. (2007). The sexual harassment of uppity women. *Journal of Applied Psychology, 92,* 425–437.

Berg, N., & Lien, D. (2002). Measuring the effect of sexual orientation on income: Evidence of discrimination? *Contemporary Economic Policy, 20,* 394–414.

Bernstein, B. L., & Russo, N. F. (In press). Work, life, and family imbalance: How to level the playing field. In M. Paludi (Ed.). *Career paths and family in the academy: Progress and challenges*. Thousand Oaks, CA: Sage.

Bianchi, S. M., Robinson, J. P., & Milkie, M. A. (2006). *Changing rhythms of American family life*. New York: Russell Sage Foundation.

Biernat, M., Crosby, F. J., & Williams, J. C. (2004). The maternal wall: Research and policy perspectives on discrimination against mothers. *Journal of Social Issues, 60*(4), all.

Bjorkqvist, K., Osterman, K., & Hjelt-Back, M. (1994). Aggression among university employees. *Aggressive Behaviour, 20,* 27–33.

Blanchard, F., & Crosby, F. (1989). *Affirmative action in perspective.* New York: Springer-Verlag.

Blau, F. D., Simpson, P., & Anderson, D. (1998). Continuing progress? Trends in occupational segregation in the United States over the 1970s and 1980s. *Feminist Economics,* 4(3), 29–71.

Bronstein, P., Rothblum, E. D., & Solomon, S. (1993). Ivy halls and glass walls: Barriers to academic careers for women and ethnic minorities. In R. Boice & J. Gainen (Eds.), *New directions for teaching and learning, No. 53.* San Francisco: Jossey-Bass.

Brown, G. W., Bhrolchain, M. N., & Harris T. (1975). Social class and psychiatric disturbance among women in an urban population. *Sociology, 9,* 225–254.

Browne, K. R. (2006). Evolved sex differences and occupational segregation. *Journal of Organizational Behavior, 27,* 143–162.

Carlson, Kacmar, & Williams, 2000.

Carothers, S. C., & Crull, P. (1984). Contrasting sexual harassment in female- and male-dominated occupations. In K. B. Sacks & D. Remy (Eds.), *My troubles are going to have trouble with me: Everyday trials and triumphs of women workers* (pp. 209–228). New Brunswick, NJ: Rutgers University Press.

Chalk, L. M. (2005). Occupational possible selves: Fears and aspirations of college women. *Journal of Career Assessment, 13,* 188–203.

Cleary, P. D., & Mechanic, D. (1983). Sex differences in psychological distress among married people. *Journal of Health and Social Behavior, 24,* 111–121.

Clewell, B. C., & Campbell, P. B. (2002). Taking stock: Where we've been, where we are, where we're going. *Journal of Women and Minorities in Science and Engineering,* 8 (3&4), 255–284.

Cooper, K., Chassin, L., & Zeiss, A. (1985). The relation of sex-role attitudes to the marital satisfaction and personal adjustment of dual-worker couples. *Sex Roles, 12,* 227–241.

Cortina, L. M. (In press). Unseen injustice: Incivility as modern discrimination in organizations. *Academy of Management Review.*

Cortina, L. M., Lonsway, K. A., Magley, V. J., Freeman, L. V., Collinsworth, L. L., Hunter, M., et al. (2002). What's gender got to do with it? Incivility at the workplace: Incidence and impact. *Law and Social Inquiry, 27,* 235–270.

Crohan, S., Antonucci, T., Adelmann, P., & Coleman L. (1989). Job characteristics and well-being at midlife: Ethnic and gender comparisons. *Psychology of Women Quarterly, 13,* 223–235.

Crosby, F. J. (1982). *Relative deprivation and working women.* New York: Oxford University Press.

Crosby, F. J. (1984a). The denial of personal discrimination. *American Behavioral Scientist, 27*(3), 371–386.

Crosby, F. J. (1984b). Relative deprivation in organizational settings. *Research in Organizational Behavior, 6,* 51–93.

Crosby, F. J., Pufall, A., Snyder, R. C., O'Connell, M., & Whalen, P. (1989). The denial of personal disadvantage among you, me, and all other ostriches. In M. Crawford & M. Gentry (Eds.), *Gender and thought: Psychological perspectives* (pp. 79–99). New York: Springer-Verlag.

Cuddy, A. J. C., Fiske, S. T., & Glick, P. (2004). When professionals become mothers, warmth doesn't cut the ice. *Journal of Social Issues, 60*(4), 701–718.

Day, J. G., & Hill, C. (2007). *Beyond the pay gap.* Washington DC: AAUW Educational Foundation.

DeArmond, S., Tye, M., Chen, P., Krauss, A., Rogers, A. D., & Sintek, E. (2006). Age and gender stereotypes: New challenges in a changing workplace and workforce. *Journal of Applied Social Psychology, 36,* 2184–2214.

Deaux, K. (1984). Blue-collar barriers. *American Behavioral Scientist, 27,* 287–300.

Demerouti, E., Bakker, A. B., & Bulters, A. J. (2004). The loss spiral of work pressure, work–home interference and exhaustion: Reciprocal relations in a three-wave study. *Journal of Vocational Behavior, 64,* 131–149.

Denmark, F. L., Shaw, J. S., & Ciali, S. D. (1985). The relationship between sex roles, living arrangements, and the division of household responsibilities. *Sex Roles, 12,* 617–625.

Devine, P. (1989). Stereotypes and prejudice: Their automatic and controlled components. *Journal of Personality and Social Psychology, 56,* 5–18.

Eagly, A. H., & Karau, S. J. (2002). Role congruent a theory of prejudice toward female leaders. *Psychological Review, 109,* 573–598.

Eagly, A. H., Wood, W., & Dickman, H. (2000). Social role theory of sex differences and similarities: A current appraisal. In T. Eckes & H. M. Trautner

(Eds.), *The developmental social psychology of gender* (pp. 123–174). Mahwah, NJ: Erlbaum.

Eckes, T. (1994). Explorations in gender cognition: Content and structure of female and male subtypes: *Social Cognition, 12,* 37–60.

Eckes, T. (2002). Paternalistic and envious gender stereotypes: Testing predictions from the stereotype content model. *Sex Roles, 47,* 99–114.

Ek, E., Sovio, U., Remes, J., & Järvelin, M. (2005). Social predictors of unsuccessful entrance into the labour market: A socialization process perspective. *Journal of Vocational Behavior, 66,* 471–486.

Eldridge, N. S., & Gilbert, L. A. (1990). Correlates of relationship satisfaction in lesbian couples. *Psychology of Women Quarterly, 14,* 43–62.

Fassinger, R. E. (2000). Gender and sexuality in human development: Implications for prevention and advocacy in counseling psychology. In S. D. Brown & R. W. Lent (Eds.), *Handbook of counseling psychology* (3rd ed.; pp. 346–378). New York: Wiley.

Fiske, S. T. (1998). Stereotyping, prejudice and discrimination. In D. Gilbert & S. Fiske (Eds.), *The handbook of social psychology* (vol. 2, pp. 357–411). Boston: McGraw-Hill.

Fiske, S. T., Cuddy, A. J. C., & Glick, P. (2002). Emotions up and down: Intergroup emotions result from perceived status and competition. In D. M. Mackie & E. R. Smith (Eds.), *From prejudice to intergroup emotions: Differentiated reactions to social groups* (pp. 247–264). New York: Psychology Press.

Fiske, S. T., Cuddy, A. J. C., Glick, P., & Xu, J. (2002). A model of (often mixed) stereotype content: Competence and warmth respectively follow from perceived status and competition. *Journal of Personality and Social Psychology, 82,* 878–902.

Ford, M. T., Heinen, B. A., & Langkamer, K. L. (2007). Work and family satisfaction and conflict: A meta-analysis of cross-domain relations. *Journal of Applied Psychology, 92,* 57–80.

Ford, T. E. (2000). Effects of sexist humor on tolerance of sexist events. *Personality and Social Psychology Bulletin, 26,* 1094–1107.

Fouad, N. A. (2007). Work and vocational psychology: Theory, research, and applications. *Annual Review of Psychology, 58,* 543–564.

Franzoi, S. L. (2001). Is female body esteem shaped by benevolent sexism? *Sex Roles, 44*(3–4), 177–188.

Frone, M. R. (2003). Work–family balance. In J. C. Quick & L. E. Tetrick (Eds.), *Handbook of occupational health psychology* (pp. 143–162). Washington, DC: American Psychological Association.

Frone, M. R., Russell, M., & Barnes, G. M. (1996). Work–family conflict, gender, and health-related outcomes: A study of employed parents in two community samples. *Journal of Occupational Health Psychology, 1,* 57–69.

Frone, M. R., Russell, M., & Cooper, M. L. (1997). Relation of work/family conflict to health outcomes: A four-year longitudinal study of employed parents. *Journal of Occupational & Organizational Psychology, 70,* 325–335.

Gambles, R., Lewis, S., & Rapoport, R. (2006). The myth of work–life balance: The challenges of our time for men, women, and societies. Hoboken, NJ: John Wiley & Sons.

Geis, F. L., Carter, M. R., & Butler, D. J. (1982). *Research on seeing and evaluating people.* Newark: University of Delaware.

Gilbert, L. A., & Rader, J. (2001). Current perspectives on women's adult roles: Work, family, and life. In R. K. Unger (Ed.), *Handbook of the psychology of women and gender* (pp. 156–169). New York: Wiley.

Glick, P., Diebold, J., Bailey-Werner, B., & Zhu, L. (1997). The two faces of Adam: Ambivalent sexism and polarized attitudes toward men. *Personality and Social Psychology Bulletin, 23,* 1323–1334.

Glick, P., & Fiske, S. T. (1996). The Ambivalent Sexism Inventory: Differentiating hostile and benevolent sexism. *Journal of Personality and Social Psychology, 70,* 491–512.

Glick, P., & Fiske, S. T. (2001). An ambivalent alliance: Hostile and benevolent sexism as complementary justifications for gender inequality. *American Psychologist, 56,* 109–118.

Glick, P., Sakalli-Ugurlu, N., Ferreira, M. C., & de Souza, M. A. (2002). Ambivalent sexism and attitudes toward wife abuse in Turkey and Brazil. *Psychology of Women Quarterly, 26,* 292–297.

Glomb, T. M., Richman, W. L., Hulin, C. L., Drasgow, F., Schneider, K. T., & Fitzgerald, L. F. (1997). Ambient sexual harassment: An integrated model of antecedents and consequences. *Organizational Behavior & Human Decision Processes, 71,* 1309–1328.

Golding, J. M. (1990). Division of household labor, strain, and depressive symptoms among Mexican Americans and non-Hispanic whites. *Psychology of Women Quarterly, 14,* 103–117.

Gove, W. R., & Zeiss, C. (1987). Multiple roles and happiness. In F. Crosby (Ed.), *Spouse, parent, worker: On gender and multiple roles* (pp. 125–137). New Haven, CT: Yale University Press.

Grant-Vallone, E. J., & Donaldson, S. I. (2001). Consequences of work–family conflict on employee well-being over time. *Work & Stress, 15,* 214–226.

Green, B., & Russo, N. F. (1993). Work and family: Selected issues. In F. L. Denmark & M. Paludi (Eds.), *Psychology of women: A handbook of issues and theories,* 683–719. Westport, CT: Greenwood Press.

Greenhaus, J. H., & Beutell, N. J. (1985). Sources of conflict between work and family roles. *Academy of Management Review, 10,* 76–88.

Greenwald, A. G., & Banaji, M. R. (1995). Implicit social cognition: Attitudes, self-esteem, and stereotypes. *Psychological Review, 102,* 4–27.

Grossman, H., & Chester, N. (Eds.). (1990). *The experience and meaning of work in women's lives.* Hillsdale, NJ: Erlbaum.

Grzywacz, J. G. (2000). Work–family spillover and health during midlife: Is managing conflict everything? *American Journal of Health Promotion, 14,* 236–243.

Guimond, S., & Dube-Simard, L. (1983). Relative deprivation and the Quebec nationalist movement: The cognition–emotion distinction and the personal–group deprivation issue. *Journal of Personality and Social Psychology, 44,* 526–535.

Gunter, N. C., & Gunter, B. G. (1990). Domestic division of labor among working couples: Does androgyny make a difference? *Psychology of Women Quarterly, 14,* 355–370.

Guthrie, D., & Roth, L. M. (1999). The state, courts, and equal opportunities for female CEOs in U.S. organizations: Specifying institutional mechanisms. *Social Forces, 78*(2), 511–542.

Halpern, D. F. (2005). Psychology at the intersection of work and family: Recommendations for employers, working families, and policymakers. *American Psychologist, 60,* 397–409.

Halpern, D., & Murphy, S. E. (Eds.). (2004). *Changing the metaphor: From work–family balance to work–family interaction.* Mahwah, NJ: Erlbaum.

Hamilton, J. A., & Russo, N. F. (2006). Women and depression: Research, theory, and social policy. In C. L. M. Keyes & S. H. Goodman (Eds.). *Women and depression: A handbook for the social, behavioral, and biomedical sciences* (pp. 479–522). New York: Cambridge University Press.

Helson, R., Elliot, T., & Leigh, J. (1990). Number and quality of roles: A longitudinal personality view. *Psychology of Women Quarterly, 14,* 83–101.

Henry J. Kaiser Foundation. (2007). Women's health policy facts: Women's health insurance coverage. Retrieved June 2, 2007, from http://www.kff.org/womenshealth/upload/6000_05.pdf.

Holahan, C. K., & Gilbert, L. A. (1979). Interrole conflict for working women: Careers versus jobs. *Journal of Applied Psychology, 64,* 86–90.

Hyde, J. S. (2005). The gender similarities hypothesis. *American Psychologist, 60,* 581–592.

Ilies, R., Hauserman, N., Schwaochau, S., & Stibal, J. (2003). Reported incidence rates of work-related sexual harassment in the United States: Using meta-analysis to explain reported rate disparities. *Personnel Psychology, 56,* 607–631.

Joint Economic Committee. (2007). Pension charts derived from U.S. Bureau of the Census, March Current Population Survey. Retrieved June 1, 2007, from http://jec.senate.gov/charts/pensions/pension-charts.pdf.

Jost, J. T., & Kay, A. C. (2005). Exposure to benevolent sexism and complimentary gender stereotypes. *Journal of Personality and Social Psychology, 88,* 498–509.

Kahn, W. A., & Crosby, F. (1985). Change and status: Discriminating between attitudes and discriminatory behavior. In L. Larwood, B. A. Gutek, & A. H. Shromberg (Eds.), *Women and work: An annual review* (vol. 1, pp. 215–238). Beverly Hills, CA: Sage.

Kanter, R. M. (1977). *Men and women of the corporation.* New York: Basic Books.

Karsten, M. F. (Ed.). (2006). *Gender, race, and ethnicity in the workplace: Issues and challenges for today's organizations.* Westport, CT: Praeger.

Kay, A. C., & Jost, J. T. (2003). Complementary justice: Effects of "poor but happy" and "poor but honest" stereotype exemplars on system justification and implicit activation of the justice motive. *Journal of Personality and Social Psychology, 85,* 823–837.

Kessler, R., & Neighbors, H. (1986). A new perspective on the relationships among race, social class, and psychological distress. *Journal of Health and Social Behavior, 27,* 107–115.

Kray, L. J., Thompson, L., & Galinsky, A. (2001). Battle of the sexes: Gender stereotype confirmation and reactance in negotiations. *Journal of Personality and Social Psychology, 80*(6), 942–958.

Larwood, L., Szwajkowski, E., & Rose, S. (1988). Sex and race discrimination resulting from manager–client relationships: Applying the rational bias theory of managerial discrimination. *Sex Roles, 8,* 9–29.

Lavidor, M., Weller, A., Babkoff, H. (2003). How sleep is related to fatigue? *British Journal of Health Psychology, 8,* 95–105.

Leathers, S., & Kelley, M. (2000). Unintended pregnancy and depressive symptoms among first-time mothers and fathers. *American Journal of Orthopsychiatry, 70,* 523–531.

Lent, R. W., Brown, S. D., Sheu, H. B., Schmidt, J., Brenner, B., Gloster, C. S., et al. (2005). Social cognitive predictors of academic interests and goals in engineering: Utility for women and students at historically black universities. *Journal of Counseling Psychology, 52*(1), 84–92.

Lewis, S. E., & Orford, J. (2005). Women's experiences of workplace bullying: Changes in social relationships. *Journal of Community Applied Social Psychology, 15,* 29–47.

Lieberson, S. (1985). *Making it count.* Berkeley: University of California Press.

Lim, S., & Cortina, L. M. (2005). Interpersonal mistreatment in the workplace: The interface and impact of general incivility and sexual harassment. *Journal of Applied Psychology, 90,* 483–496.

Lord, C. G., & Saenz, D. S. (1985). Memory deficits and memory surfeits: Differential cognitive consequences of tokenism for tokens and observers. *Journal of Personality and Social Psychology, 49,* 918–926.

Lubensky, M. E., Holland, S. L., Wiethoff, C., & Crosby, F. J. (2004). Diversity and sexual orientation: Including and valuing sexual minorities in the workplace. In M. Stockdale & F. J. Crosby (Eds.), *The psychology and management of diversity* (pp. 206–203). Malden, MA: Blackwell.

Major, B. (1987). Gender, justice and the psychology of entitlement. In P. Shaver & C. Hendrick (Eds.), *Sex and gender: Review of personality and social psychology* (pp. 124–148). Newbury Park, CA: Sage.

Major, B. (1993). Gender, entitlement, and the distribution of family labor. *Journal of Social Issues, 49*(3), 141–160.

Major, B., & Konar, E. (1984). An investigation of sex differences in pay expectations and their possible causes. *Academy of Management Journal, 27,* 777–792.

Major, B., Vanderslice, V., & McFarlin, D. B. (1984). Effects of pay expected on pay received: The confirmatory nature of initial expectations. *Journal of Applied Psychology, 14,* 399–412.

Marcussen, K., & Piatt, L. (2005). Race differences in the relationship between role experiences and well-being. *Health, 9,* 379–402.

Martin, S. E., & Jurik, N. C. (2007). *Doing justice, doing gender: Women in legal and criminal justice occupations.* Thousand Oaks, CA: Sage.

Masser, B. M., & Abrams, D. (2004). Reinforcing the glass ceiling: The consequences of hostile sexism for female managerial candidates. *Sex Roles, 51*(9–10), 609–615.

Mayorova, T., Stevens, F., Scherpbier, A., Van der Velden, L., & Van der Zee, J. (2005). Gender-related differences in general practice preferences: Longitudinal evidence from the Netherlands, 1982–2001. *Health Policy, 72,* 73–80.

McBride, A. B. (1990). Mental health effects of women's multiple roles. *American Psychologist, 45,* 381–384.

McDonald, S. (2005). Patterns of informal job matching across the life course: Entry-level, reentry-level, and elite non-searching. *Sociological Inquiry, 75,* 403–428.

Meyerson, D. E., & Fletcher, J. K. (2000). A modest manifesto for shattering the glass ceiling. *Harvard Business Review, 78*(1), 127–136.

Miner-Rubino, K., & Cortina, L. M. (2004). To a context of hostility toward women: Implications for employees' well-being. *Journal of Occupational Health Psychology, 9*(2), 107–122.

National Academy of Sciences, National Academy of Engineering, & Institute of Medicine (2006). *Beyond bias and barriers: Fulfilling the potential of women in academic science and engineering.* Washington, DC: National Academies Press.

National Committee on Pay Equity. (2007). Women of color in the workplace. Retrieved June 22, 2007, from http://www.pay-equity.org/info-race.html.

National Research Council. Committee on Women in Science and Engineering. (2001a). *Female engineering faculty at U.S. institutions: A data profile.* Retrieved May 2, 2007, from http://www7.nationalacademies.org/cwse/.

National Research Council. Committee on Women in Science and Engineering. (2001b). *From scarcity to visibility: Gender differences in the careers of doctoral scientists and engineers.* Washington, DC: National Research Council.

National Science Foundation. (2004). *Women, minorities, and persons with disabilities in science and engineering, 2004.* NSF 04–317. Arlington, VA: National Science Foundation.

National Science Foundation. Division of Science Resources. (2007). *Women, minorities, and persons with disabilities in science and engineering, 2007.* Arlington, VA: National Science Foundation.

Nelson, D. J. (2005). *A national analysis of diversity in science and engineering faculties at research universities.* Retrieved June 22, 2007, from http://cheminfo.ou.edu/~djn/diversity/briefings/diversity%20report%20final.pdf.

Orth-Gomer, K., & Leinweber, C. (2005). Multiple stressors and coronary disease in women: The Stockholm Female Coronary Risk Study. *Biological Psychology, 69,* 57–66.

Padavic, I., & Reskin, B. F. (2002). *Women and men at work* (2nd ed.). Thousand Oaks, CA: Pine Forge Press.

Park, B., Wolsko, C., & Judd, C. M. (2001). Measurement of subtyping in stereotype change. *Journal of Experimental Social Psychology, 37,* 325–332.

Parry, G. (1986). Paid employment, life events, social support, and mental health in working-class mothers. *Journal of Health and Social Behavior, 27,* 193–208.

Pearlin, L. I., & Johnson, J. (1977). Marital status, life-strains and depression. *American Sociological Review, 42,* 704–715.

Peplau, L. A., & Fingerhut, A. (2004). The paradox of the lesbian worker. *Journal of Social Issues, 60,* 719–736.

Pheterson, G. L., Kiesler, S. B., & Goldberg, P. A. (1971). The evaluation of the performance of women as a function of their sex, achievement, and personal history. *Journal of Personality and Social Psychology, 19,* 114–118.

Powell, G. N. (Ed.). (1999). *Handbook of gender and work.* Thousand Oaks, CA: Sage.

Prokos, A., & Padavic, I. (2005). An examination of competing explanations for the pay gap among scientists and engineers. *Gender & Society, 19,* 523–543.

Radloff, L. S. (1975). Sex difference in depression: Occupational and marital status. *Sex Roles, 1,* 249–265.

Rayner, C., & Cooper, C. (1997). Workplace bullying: Myth or reality—can we afford to ignore it? *Leadership and Organization Development Journal, 18,* 211–214.

Reid, P., & Comas-Diaz, L. (1990). Gender and ethnicity: Perspectives on dual status. *Sex Roles, 22,* 397–407.

Reskin, B. F. (Ed.). (1984). *Sex segregation in the workplace: Trends, explanations, remedies.* Washington, DC: National Academy Press.

Reskin, B. F. (1988). Bringing the men back in: Sex differentiation and the devaluation of women's work. *Gender & Society, 2,* 58–81.

Reskin, B. F., & Bielby, D. D. (2005). A sociological perspective on gender and career outcomes. *Journal of Economic Perspectives, 19*(1), 71–86.

Reskin, B. F., & Roos, P. A. (1990). *Job queues, gender queues: Explaining women's inroads into male occupations.* Philadelphia: Temple University Press.

Rexroat, C., & Shehan, C. (1987). The family life cycle and spouses' time in housework. *Journal of Marriage and the Family, 49,* 737–750.

Ross, C. E., & Mirowsky, J. (1988). Child care and emotional adjustment of wives' employment. *Journal of Health and Social Behavior.* 29(2), 127–138.

Ross, C. E., Mirowsky, J., & Huber, J. (1983). Dividing work, sharing work, and in between: Marriage patterns and depression. *American Sociological Review, 48,* 809–823.

Roth, L. M. (2004). Engendering inequality: Processes of sex-segregation on Wall Street. *Sociological Forum, 19*(2), 203–228.

Rotundo, M., Nguyen, D.-H., & Sackett, P. R. (2001). A meta-analytic review of gender differences in perceptions of sexual harassment. *Journal of Applied Psychology, 86,* 914–922.

Russo, N. F., & Pirlott, A. (2006). Gender-based violence: Concepts, methods, and findings. *Annals of the New York Academy of Sciences, 1087,* 178–205.

Sacks, K. (1983). In B. Haber (Ed.), *The women's annual* (pp. 263–283). Boston: G. K. Hall.

Sandler, B., & Hall, R. (1982). *The classroom climate: A chilly one for women?* Washington, D.C.: Project on the Status and Education of Women, Association of American Colleges.

Schneider, K. T., & Fitzgerald, L. F. (1997). Ambient sexual harassment: An integrated model of antecedents and consequences. *Organizational Behavior and Human Decision Processes, 71,* 309–328.

Schultheiss, D. E. P. (2006). The interface of work and family life. *Professional Psychology: Research and Practice, 37,* 334–341.

Segura, D. (1989). Chicana and Mexican immigrant women at work: The impact of class, race, and gender on occupational mobility. *Gender & Society, 3*(1), 37–52.

Settles, Cortina, Malley, and Stewart A. (2006). The climate for women in academic science: The good, the bad, and the changeable. *Psychology of Women Quarterly, 30,* 47–58.

Shapiro, J. R., & Neuberg, S. L. (2007). From stereotype threat to stereotype threats: Implications of a multi-threat framework for causes moderators, mediators, consequences, and interventions. *Personality and Social Psychology Review, 11,* 107–130.

Snyder, M., & Swann, W. B., Jr. (1976). When actions reflect attitudes: The politics of impression management. *Journal of Personality and Social Psychology, 34,* 1034–1042.

Spencer, S. J., Steele, C. M., & Quinn, D. M. (1999). Stereotype threat and women's math performance. *Journal of Experimental Social Psychology, 35,* 4–28.

Staples, R. (1987). Social structure in black female life. *Journal of Black Studies, 17,* 267–286.

Steele, C. M. (1997). A threat in the air: How stereotypes shape intellectual identity and performance. *American Psychologist, 52,* 613–629.

Steele, C. M., Spencer, S. J., & Aronson, J. (2002). Contending with group image: The psychology of stereotype and social identity threat. In M. P. Zanna (Ed.), *Advances in experimental social psychology* (vol. 34, pp. 379–440). San Diego: Academic Press.

Steil, J. (2001). Family forms and member well-being: A research agenda for the decade of behavior. *Psychology of Women Quarterly, 25,* 344–363.

Steil, J., & Turetsky, B. (1987). Marital influence levels and symptomatology among wives. In F. Crosby (Ed.), *Relative deprivation and working women* (pp. 74–90). New York: Oxford University Press.

Swerdlow, M. (1989). Men's accommodations to women entering a nontraditional occupation: A case of rapid transit operatives. *Gender & Society, 3,* 373–387.

Swim, J. K., Aikin, K. J., Hall, W. S., & Hunter, B. A. (1995). Sexism and racism: Old-fashioned and modern prejudices. *Journal of Personality and Social Psychology, 68,* 199–214.

Swim, J. K., Borgida, E., & Maruyama, G. (1989). Joan McKay versus John McKay: Do gender stereotypes bias evaluations? *Psychological Bulletin, 105,* 409–429.

Swim, J. K., & Cohen, L. L. (1997). Overt, covert, and subtle sexism: A comparison between the Attitudes toward Women and Modern Sexism Scales. *Psychology of Women Quarterly, 21,* 103–118.

Swim, J. K., Mallett, R., Russo-Devosa, Y., & Stangor, C. (2005). Judgments of sexism: A comparison of the subtlety of sexism measures and sources of variability in judgments of sexism. *Psychology of Women Quarterly, 29,* 406–411.

Thoits, P. A. (1986). Multiple identities: Examining gender and marital status differences in distress. *American Sociological Review, 51,* 259–272.

Thoits, P. A. (1987). Negotiating roles. In F. J. Crosby (Ed.), *Spouse, parent, worker: On gender and multiple roles* (pp. 11–22). New Haven, CT: Yale University Press.

U.S. Bureau of Labor Statistics. (2006). *Women in the labor force: A databook.* Retrieved June 22, 2007, from http://www.bls.gov/cps/wlf-databook 2006.htm.

U.S. Bureau of Labor Statistics. (2007a). Employer costs for employee compensation—December 2006. Retrieved June 1, 2007, from http://www.bls.gov/news.release/ecee.nr0.htm.

U.S. Bureau of Labor Statistics. (2007b). Employment characteristics of families in 2006. Retrieved May 10, 2007, from http://www.bls.gov/news.release/famee.nr0.htm.

U.S. Bureau of the Census. (2005). Table S2002. Median earnings in the past 12 months (in 2005 inflation-adjust dollars) of workers by sex and women's earnings as a percentage of men's earnings by selected characteristics. 2005 American Community Survey.

VanMeter, M. J., & Agronow, S. J. (1982). The stress of multiple roles: The case for role strain among married college women. *Family Relations, 33,* 131–138.

Vescio, T. K., Gervais, S. J., Snyder, M., & Hoover, A. (2005). Power and the creation of patronizing environments: The stereotype-based behaviors of the powerful and their effects on female performance in masculine domains. *Journal of Personality and Social Psychology, 88,* 658–672.

Vescio, T. K., Snyder, M., & Butz, D. A. (2003). Power in stereotypically masculine domains: A social influence strategy × stereotype match model. *Journal of Personality and Social Psychology, 85,* 1062–1078.

Voyandoff, P. (2004). Implications of work and community demands and resources for work-to-family conflict and facilitation. *Journal of Occupational Health Psychology, 9,* 275–285.

Wiener, R. L., & Hurt, L. E. (2000). How do people evaluate social sexual conduct at work? A psycholegal model. *Journal of Applied Psychology, 85,* 75–85.

Zanna, M. P., Crosby, F., & Loewenstein, G. (1987). Male reference groups and discontent among female professionals. In B. Gutek & L. Larwood (Eds.), *Women's career development* (pp. 28–41). Newbury Park, CA: Sage.

Zapf, D., & Einarsen, S. (2001). Bullying in the workplace: Recent trends in research and practice—An introduction. *European Journal of Work and Organisational Psychology, 10,* 369–373.

Zinn, M. B. (1989). Family, feminism, and race in America. *Gender & Society, 4,* 68–82.

Chapter 21

Women and Leadership

Jean Lau Chin

Interest in women's roles, women's issues, and the role of gender has grown in both the scientific literature and the popular press as the numbers of women in the workforce rise and women increasingly demand equal rights in all domains of work, community, and society. However, the study of women and leadership has been scant. Most books and studies of leadership have been about men leaders within corporations or the public eye. In the public press, being a leader typically means "having the corner office" or being the chief executive. Women as chief executives are still a relatively new phenomenon, such that they make news or the covers of *Fortune* magazine just by holding the position (e.g., Harrington & Shanley, 2003).

Leadership theories and studies about good leadership and effective leadership styles seldom distinguish characteristics related to gender. While theories and studies of leadership have typically been based on male leadership, their results are typically generalized as being universal to both men and women. In the field of the psychology of women, the study of leadership has been equally scant; this literature has focused on issues of equity, the relationship between women and society, and psychological and physiological processes of women. As women fought for an equal place at the table, bolstered by the women's movement, the push to increase the numbers of women in leadership roles has been an even more uphill battle. Indvik (2004) points to the scarcity of women in higher levels of corporate leadership. While women made up 46.6 percent of the workforce in the United States in 2002, they filled only 15.7 percent of corporate officer positions. She suggests that sex differences in worldview, socialization, and life experience may result in different mental models or "implicit theories" of leadership among women.

Studies of leadership have been largely confined to men for the simple reason that they have historically held most of the leadership roles in society and its institutions. Although there is general agreement that women face more barriers to becoming leaders than men do, especially for leader roles that are male-dominated (Eagly & Johannesen-Schmidt, 2001), there is much less agreement about *how* women actually lead. There is much to suggest that women lead differently from men, and feminist leadership styles are different and more collaborative despite significant overlap between the leadership styles of men and women. The intersection of identities across race, ethnicity, gender, class, and profession—that is, diverse women leaders—contribute additional dimensions that may influence differences in leadership styles (Chin, Lott, Rice, & Sanchez-Hucles, 2006).

Many women embrace feminist principles of inclusion, gender equity, collaboration, and social justice in their work and lifestyles. Feminist women are concerned with how differential power and oppression contribute to the unequal status of women compared to men in all realms of work, family, and social environments. As president of the Society for the Psychology of Women of the American Psychological Association during 2002–2003, I created a presidential initiative, "Feminist Visions and Diverse Voices: Leadership and Collaboration," to understand how feminist principles influenced women in their leadership and leadership styles (Chin, 2004).

A yearlong dialogue among feminist women psychologists ensued about women and leadership. Deconstructing existing theories of feminism and leadership was necessary to understand what effective leadership styles among women meant, and how they intersected with feminist principles. Telecommunications technology was used to promote scholarship through 15 Web-based discussion boards coupled with teleconferences and face-to-face meetings toward the goals of enhancing a feminist process of collaboration. We considered this approach innovative as a process to convene scholarly dialogue.

While many of the 100 feminist women participating in the initiative had already played prominent roles as advocates for women's issues and social change, that is, "getting a seat at the table"; promoting a feminist agenda, that is, feminist policy; infusing feminist principles in service, training, and research; and managing organizations, institutions, and departments, few viewed themselves as "true leaders." As the literature on feminist leadership was scarce, it became apparent that capturing the experiences of women and feminists as leaders was as important as the empirical studies of women and leadership.

DECONSTRUCTING THEORIES OF LEADERSHIP

Several trends are evident in the literature on leadership. Some approaches emphasize the characteristics residing in a leader—

leadership traits, skills, or styles—while other approaches examine the contexts of leadership, for example, situations in which leadership is exercised and the rewards and punishments of leadership. Still others emphasize the interpersonal process between leaders and who they lead, the power relationship between leader and follower.

Leadership Characteristics: Trait Approach

Early leadership studies focused on identifying those qualities that made for great leaders, that is, personality characteristics. These trait approaches suggest that individuals have special innate characteristics that make them leaders, in other words, that a person is "born to be a leader" or "a natural leader" (Northouse, 2004). Studies concentrated on those traits that differentiated leaders from followers (Bass, 1990); some traits associated with great leaders have included intelligence, dominance, confidence, and masculinity (Lord, DeVader, & Alliger, 1986).

Whereas these approaches studied men leaders and examined leadership of men within male-dominated contexts, definitions of effective leadership tended to be associated with "masculine traits" and male charisma, and hence are called "Great Man" theories. Trait approaches have been criticized for their inattention to gender and the leadership styles of great women. Moreover, the prominence of gender biases would favor the leadership of men as more effective, and their masculine traits as more expectable indicators of good leadership.

Competencies of Leadership: Skills Approach

The skills approach identifies the essential competencies of good and effective leadership and focuses on the measurement and development of those competencies. Northouse (2004) defines three competencies of leadership—problem-solving skills, social judgment skills, and knowledge—while Bennis (1984) describes four: management of attention (giving the message), management of meaning (developing the vision), management of trust (interpersonal connectedness), and management of self (knowledge of one's skills).

How do women and feminists manage these competencies? The recurring answer among the participants in the initiative was that women tend to be more collaborative. This competency was further defined as having social judgment and interpersonal connectedness, skills commonly associated with feminist relational styles. The use of a collaborative process as a skill and competency of leadership lies in women "being" feminist and using "the self" to promote an effective leadership style. In contrast to the trait approach, the skill approach is promising for women because it suggests that leadership skills are competencies that can be acquired (although some might argue that collaboration is more innate to women).

Style Approach

The style approach focuses exclusively on what leaders do (behavior) and how they act (process), where *style* is understood as relatively stable patterns of behavior. Northouse (2004) defines leadership as a process whereby an individual influences a group of individuals to achieve a common goal, emphasizing process or a transactional event over the traits or characteristics residing in the leader. Two styles of leadership have received considerable attention in the recent literature on leadership. Transformational leaders act as catalysts of change (Aviolo, 1994) and tend to be visionary (Tichy & Devanna, 1986), with a holistic picture of how the organization should look when meeting its stated goals, while transactional leaders are focused on getting things done (that is, task-oriented), act with directedness, and use rewards to achieve an organization's stated goals (Bennis, 1984; Sergiovanni, 1984).

Several studies (e.g., Bass & Avolio, 1994) found women to be more attentive than men to "the human side of enterprise" (McGregor, 1985), suggesting that female leaders tend to base judgments more on intuition and emotions than on rational calculation of the relationships between means and ends. Other studies identify women's management styles as more democratic and participatory than those typically adopted by men (Mertz & McNeely, 1997). However, a meta-analysis by Eagly and Johnson (1990) of research comparing the leadership styles of women and men found a more complex relationship of gender differences. In organizational studies of those holding leadership roles, female and male leaders did not differ in their use of an interpersonally oriented or task-oriented style. However, in laboratory experiments, women were somewhat more gender stereotypic in using an interpersonal-oriented style in leadership studies.

A meta-analysis of transformational, transactional, and laissez-faire leadership styles among women (Eagly, Johannesen-Schmidt, & van Engen, 2003) found that female leaders were more transformational than male leaders and also engaged in more of the contingent reward behaviors that are a component of transactional leadership. Male leaders were generally more likely to manifest the other aspects of transactional leadership (active and passive management by exception) and laissez-faire leadership. Although these differences were small, the implications are encouraging, because they identify areas of strength in the leadership styles of women. A transformational style is also consistent with feminist principles of inclusion, collaboration, and social advocacy.

A FRAMEWORK FOR UNDERSTANDING WOMEN AND LEADERSHIP

When we deconstruct theories of leadership, we find that several dimensions are missing to understand women and leadership. Current contexts of leadership remain male dominated and do not celebrate women's strengths in gender-equitable work environments. Moreover, current theories of leadership omit the discussion of gender; feminist values and principles are not included in evaluating leadership or leadership styles. Consequently, writings and studies of women and leadership, when they exist, are often defensive and comparative with men, as in the title of a *Fortune* magazine article: "Power: Do Women Really Want It?" (Sellers, 2003).

Some dimensions of leadership are described below that would be inclusive of women leaders and that enable us to understand their leadership styles from a strength-based perspective. These include ethics-based, contextual, collaborative, diversity, transformational, and feminist leadership.

Ethics-Based Leadership

Fine (2006) suggests that the literature on women and leadership tends to focus on how women lead. The characteristics of women's leadership that are identified, such as collaboration, participation, communication, and nurturance, are viewed in terms of their use as a means of reaching organizational ends; Fine proposes shifting that focus to the underlying *values* expressed in those means, namely, care for other people. This then is consistent with the ethic of care revealed in women's career choices and their desire to help others. In her collection of narratives, women discursively constructed leadership through a *moral discourse of leadership* that emphasized (1) leading in order to make a positive contribution in the world, (2) collaboration, (3) open communication, and (4) honesty in relationships—that is, the women imbue *each* element of their leadership with a moral dimension. This is different from other approaches to leadership.

Contextual Leadership

Studies have suggested that situational contexts influence leadership styles. Madden (2003) suggests that, since behavior occurs within a context and is influenced by the power relationships among the participants, we need to examine the contexts in which women lead—in other words, "leadership is contextual." Gender-role biases still exist and influence the appraisal and expectations of women leaders. Eagly & Karau (2002) suggest that the perceived incongruity between the female gender-role and leadership roles leads to two forms of prejudice: perceiving women less favorably than men as potential occupants of leadership roles, and evaluating behavior that fulfills the prescriptions of a leader role less favorably when it is enacted by a woman. One consequence is that attitudes are less positive toward female leaders than male leaders. Other consequences are that it is more difficult for women to become leaders and to achieve success in leadership roles.

Eagly (1987) also found that women leaders were evaluated differently than men and were expected to engage in activities and actions congruent with their culturally defined gender-roles; leadership was typically not one of them, because of stereotypes about women. Forsyth, Heiney, and Wright (1997) found that group members favor men over women when selecting and evaluating leaders, even when actual leadership behaviors are held constant in a variety of group settings. They examined this role-incongruence hypothesis in small groups led by women who adopted a relationship- or task-oriented leadership style. Group members with liberal attitudes regarding women's roles responded positively to both leadership types, while group members with conservative attitudes felt the task-oriented leader was more effective, but rated her more negatively on measures of collegiality. These results suggest that reactions to women leaders are tempered by expectations about the role of women and men in contemporary society.

The organizational culture, that is, the context in which leadership occurs, is important to understand, since much of leadership involves managing the organization and realizing its purpose. Women leaders often manage within masculinized contexts and must adapt their leadership styles accordingly. These contexts often constrain women leaders with an expectation to behave consistently with their gender-roles. Meanwhile, these same behaviors may be defined as signs of ineffective leadership. Kolb and Williams (2000) argue for a fundamental change in organizational cultures away from masculinized contexts and toward gender-equitable work environments.

Karakowsky and Siegal (1999) found that the proportional representation of men and women in a work group, along with the gender orientation of the group's task, can significantly influence the kind of leadership behavior exhibited in group activity. Using feminist principles to deconstruct principles of leadership, Fletcher (2003a, 2003b) makes the distinction between feminist attributes and feminist goals. While organizations may have feminist attributes, such as relational and collaborative processes, environments that ignore gender and power dynamics do not have feminist goals. She advocates trying to create more egalitarian environments, but suggests that organizations need to challenge the power structure and masculinized frameworks in which they operate to do so. Absent that recognition, the rhetoric may sound feminist, but the goal is not there to make it feminist. Consequently, a feminist leadership model needs to have the achievement of feminist values as its goal.

Power structures are inherent in leadership roles with the dominance of leaders to their followers such that some have questioned if a collaborative process of leadership is possible within existing contexts or organizational cultures, which tend to be hierarchical and masculinized. Indvik (2004) suggests that men's discomfort with women leaders takes many forms. Research has shown that women perceive a need to adapt their behavioral style so that men can avoid feeling intimidated (Ragins, Townsend, & Mattis, 1998), and thus a narrower range of acceptable behavior exists for female leaders than for male leaders (Eagly, Makhijani, & Klonsky, 1992). Some have attempted to transform these relationships to more egalitarian ones by redefining the relationship as one of servant leader to their followers.

Collaborative Leadership

With advances in technology and communication, businesses and corporations are increasingly engaged in an international and global economy, resulting in an examination of the transferability of leadership and management practices across cultures. Western businesses that observed high levels of productivity in collective societies and diverse ethnic cultures, for example, in Japan, began an examination of these management practices and leadership styles with the goal of importing them to Western businesses and organizations. At the same time, non-Western businesses, in a race for a place in the international marketplace, sought to import and emulate Western business management practices. This resulted in identifying dimensions of team and collaborative leadership different from that observed in the United States. More recently, non-Western businesses have shifted from merely adopting Western theories and practices to cherishing their unique social and cultural factors, while using applications from Western theories of management (Kao, Sinha, & Wilpert, 1999).

A collaborative style and process have also been viewed as essential to a feminist leadership style. Feminist principles dictate that all will be involved in planning and decision making, and consensus building is valued. The feminist literature has shown that women tend to use nurturance to engage, communicate, and lead. The use of a collaborative process is viewed as leveling the playing field between leader and follower and creating more egalitarian environments; these collaborative and egalitarian processes have been described as "shared leadership."

Collaborative leadership has emerged recently as essential to the skills and processes of the "modern" leader (Cook, 2002). Raelin (2003) introduced the "Four C's of Leaderful Practice" and says that leadership in this century needs to be concurrent, collective, collaborative, and compassionate. While he recommends a process closely akin to a feminist process, he does not view gender as essential to the process, nor does he introduce feminism as being among its principles. Feminist women have noted that women emphasize planning and organizing work using an empathic approach, while placing less emphasis on the "need to win at all costs" compared to men.

Rawlings (2000) suggests that current business trends of globalization, accelerated growth, and reengineering require more cross-functional collaboration and integrated strategies across organizations. Senior and middle management teams are being asked to work together with more interdependence, with shared accountabilities outside their own functions, and with higher levels of trust and participation. This advent of the strategic leadership team does not fit neatly with traditional beliefs about the autocratic nature of teams and team building—these differences have been dichotomized as democratic versus autocratic styles.

Looman (2003) suggests that to cope with current complex and volatile environmental and cultural trends, leaders must integrate their cognitive and emotional mental processing systems and function from a metacognitive perspective. They must turn from a profitability-at-all-costs focus toward a focus on environments that encourage development of individual minds and problem solving through humanitarian collaboration and evolutionary progress. Looman identifies important changes in the environment that call for a more reflective style of leadership and suggests internal characteristics needed by leaders who can make careful long-range plans for the future that integrate human potential rather than splinter it.

Diverse Leadership

Diverse feminist groups differ in their leadership styles, and the issues they face as leaders are influenced by and made more complex when considering race, ethnicity, ability status, and sexual orientation. For example, an African American woman may identify with the values of straightforwardness and assertiveness in her leadership style. An Asian American woman may identify more with values of respectfulness and unobtrusiveness. Others may perceive the African American woman to be intimidating and deem the Asian American woman passive (Sanchez-Hucles, 2003).

Interpretation of the behaviors of diverse women leaders may vary depending on the different ethnic and contextual perspective from which it is viewed. Women leaders having multiple identities associated with race, culture, gender, disability, and sexual orientation face additional challenges to their leadership roles as they grapple with their multiple identities and expectations. While individual differences contribute greatly to how men and women lead, the commonalities that bond the experiences of women, of racial/ethnic groups, and of disability and lesbian groups contribute to how they function in leadership roles.

Current models of leadership limit their definitions of leadership to those within corporate, management, and public office. Our initiative at the Society for the Psychology of Women, which included diverse women in leadership roles, reminded us of leadership in working for social change, social justice, and community advocacy as important motivations for women taking on leadership roles. Unlike the corporate leader who embraces charitable causes, these community leaders define the ills in their communities as their primary roles of leadership.

The diversity within these groups also results in differences in leadership styles. Morrison and von Glinow (1990) find that women and minorities face a "glass ceiling," that is, external limits and constraints on women and leadership, that limits their advancement toward top management in corporate U.S. society. We need to factor in issues of racial prejudice and discrimination, as well as contributions of culture, to understand the different leadership styles that each group may embrace. For example, confrontational and assertive styles of African American women, attempts to achieve harmony and balance among Asian American women, and Native American women "standing by their men" as they take on leadership roles may well reflect their historic experiences in U.S. society.

Historically, our definitions and views of heroes and leaders have been associated with "masculine" traits—military battle and physical valor. Kidwell, Willis, Jones-Saumty, and Bigfoot (2006) suggest that we rethink these associations of leadership, giving as examples Native American women who needed to stand by their men to survive in U.S. society as they took on roles of leadership; if we were to interpret these behaviors as ineffective, dependent, or not leadership, we would have missed the point and ignored the contexts in which these women leaders led.

CAPTURING THE EXPERIENCES OF WOMEN AS LEADERS

While deconstructing theories of leadership provides us with a framework for thinking about women and leadership, capturing the experiences of women as leaders will give additional insight to the thinking and analyses needed to understand new models of leadership that are inclusive of women leaders and the ways in which they provide effective leadership. Most of the participants in my presidential initiative were feminist leaders instrumental in the women's movement and advocates for women's rights and feminist principles; many defined themselves as leaders of thought and social change. Women leaders from diverse racial/ethnic groups gave historical accounts of women in leadership roles within their communities; their experiences and views of leadership differed from those of white women, lending credence to the intersection of identities as important dimensions. Diverse women leaders often operate in both racialized and masculinized contexts.

These experiences suggest a need to expand our notions of leadership to be inclusive of not only leadership roles that are in the public eye (e.g., national and corporate leadership) but also those in community leadership roles. These experiences challenge historic theories of leadership purporting to be genderless and highlight the fact that early leadership models were drawn primarily from the experiences of white men leading in contexts governed by male values and white middle-class norms.

These experiences emphasize that current definitions of full-time work and leadership in the corporate world do not account for women being able to take time for childrearing or childbearing. Prescribed career paths for success do not factor in discontinuities because of pregnancy and childbirth. Rather, women's time away from their careers is viewed as reflecting a lesser commitment to the job and to career growth. Leadership and leadership styles, as a result, are evaluated from a masculine perspective and compared against masculine traits.

Many women in the initiative recognized the gender-role constraints on their leadership styles, and the masculinized contexts that influenced the ways in which they led—sometimes bound by them, and other times seeking to change them. Clearly, expectations and perceptions influence how women leaders behave. As the *Fortune* magazine article (Sellers, 2003) mentioned above about powerful women in corporate leadership positions describes, many women have chosen to relinquish high-level jobs, seeking to find balance in their lives and redefining the game of corporate life, and thereby questioning if women really want the power at all costs. A look at some women leaders in the public eye is instructive. How did these women lead? How were they allowed to lead?

The first lady is by definition a leader, but only because her husband is elected president of the United States. Hillary Clinton, as first lady, was characterized alternately by her unfeminist stand-by-her-man stance in supporting her husband and by her "unfeminine" behavior, perceived as opportunistic motives for the presidency. While her health care reform proposal during her days as first lady was one of the most comprehensive and complex ever proposed, it failed, perhaps because our country was not ready to accept having its first lady advocating for substantive policy reform; nor could it accept her use of her role to further her political aspirations—yet she is now a U.S. senator. With the exception of Eleanor Roosevelt, most first ladies focused on more modest goals such as beautification projects.

Another prominent leader, Dr. Joycelyn Elders, was characterized by her controversial stands on health policy during her days as U.S. surgeon general.

> It didn't take long for Dr. Joycelyn Elders, the first black and second woman to hold the position of U.S. Surgeon General, to stir up

> controversy. In fact, this determined woman in the uniform of a three-star admiral did it less than a year into Bill Clinton's presidency, speaking out on drug legalization (she's for it) and abortion rights (she wants to keep coverage in the Clinton health plan). Elders has also been just as critical of the tobacco industry as her predecessor, a Reagan appointee, C. Everett Koop. (Motavalli, 1994)

Yet, Dr. Koop did not receive criticism anywhere near that received by Dr. Elders for speaking out on similar issues.

Both Joycelyn Elders and Hillary Clinton were limited by the expectations of how women should behave. In choosing to define policy and to be outspoken in their respective roles, they violated the norm of silent, passive, and conforming women.

Andrea Jung, described as an Asian American wonder woman (*Goldsea*, 2002) is CEO of Avon Products. Her leadership style has been described as both assertive and feminist, perhaps because the business that she leads is viewed as "feminine" (i.e., context) or because she did not behave outside the expectations of the public (i.e., perceptions). In 2003, she was named by *Fortune* for the sixth time as one the 50 most powerful women in American business.

> Jung found that ... most [businessmen] still considered women fragile vessels whose self-confidence could be shattered with a well delivered put-down and whose strength would be depleted after eight hours of high-powered deal making. Jung realized that men ... refused to recognize their own limitations, while women did all too well. Jung thought businesswomen needn't dwell in this world of delusion [and recognized that the] corporate landscape [is] sculpted by male values. "Women don't support other women as well as they should," she says. (2002)

Jung chose to remedy the situation by adopting strategies typically used by her male colleagues, while refusing to accept the limitations placed upon her by virtue of her gender. Perhaps the reasons for her success as a woman leader was her willingness to step outside her expected roles; she was not afraid to seek out mentors and heed their advice.

Women leaders face a complexity of issues that include continuing perceptions and expectations that can limit them in their roles and behaviors if they allow them to. When Democrats of the U.S. House of Representatives elected Nancy Pelosi of California as house minority leader in 2002, she became the first woman ever to head a party in either chamber of the legislature. Yet she was still described within a masculinized context; in the *Boston Globe*, McGrory (2002) wrote: "He is called the Hammer. She's a velvet hammer. He is Tom DeLay, the newly elected House majority leader, who is all coercion and threat. She is Nancy Pelosi of California, who is all persuasion and smiles."

This description of our House leaders reflects the gender bias and differential language we use describing women leaders in masculinized contexts. While the description points to Pelosi's collaborative and interpersonal strengths, it also reflects the tendency to "feminize" women leaders in ways that suggest weakness or to suggest incredulity when women behave as decisive and effective leaders.

Women leaders face additional burdens, stressors, and challenges in taking on leadership roles. Diane Halpern (2002), past president of the American Psychological Association, sums it up nicely:

> One example of what I mean by additional stressors for women leaders is the concern that I am not being "feminist" enough, especially when I don't see the benefit in finding consensus for all issues (e.g., when it means compromise to my values). I am free in this context (an on-line project on feminist leadership) to think about ways stress may vary for women and men leaders. But in other psychology-related areas, it seems as though talk about these possible differences is not compatible with being a feminist.

These examples suggest that women leaders still lead within contexts that are male dominated; definitions of women leadership are still tempered by comparisons with men; many women feel that they are often expected to behave in ways consistent with "feminine roles." This can create a no-win situation where women leaders are made to feel marginalized, diminished, or weak if they behave gender-prescribed ways (i.e., are too feminine) or are criticized if they step out of these roles (i.e., are too masculine). These gender biases and gender attributions placed on women's behaviors are constraining. All too often, "feminine" behaviors are rated negatively with respect to leadership; for example, tears signal weakness, and nurturing leadership styles are viewed as lacking in substance. Conversely, women leaders adopting "masculine" behaviors are also viewed negatively; an aggressive and direct male leader is often viewed as forthright and taking charge, while the same behavior in a female leader is viewed as overbearing and angry.

Some common negative attributions people make of "strong women leaders" are: "She's a bitch," "What a dragon lady," "She acts like a man." Equally negative attributions are often made when women leaders "act like women"; for example, sometimes characterizing a woman's leadership style as "maternal," "nurturing," or "persuasion and smiles" is used to convey weakness and ineffectual leadership.

TRANSFORMING LEADERSHIP

To understand women and leadership, we need to transform current leadership models to incorporate the relevance of gender and diversity.

Social change, advocacy, policy, and institutional transformation are strong motives for many women seeking or attaining positions of leadership. Feminist principles of collaboration, diversity, and inclusiveness are important values for many women, which they bring to their roles as leaders. Current models of leadership that focus on transformational rather than transactional leadership styles, visionary versus task-oriented characteristics, are relevant to women if we do not limit ourselves to simple dichotomies between men and women. While women, especially feminist women, are more likely to be transformational in their leadership styles, it is not as simplistic. The vision, social change principles, and feminist values they bring to their leadership may also include nurturing qualities; gender and social contexts, biases, perceptions, and expectations will continue to influence their notions of leadership and their leadership behaviors. In essence, the experiences of women and men in the same leadership roles are often different.

Iwasaki, MacKay, and Ristock (2004) explored the experiences of stress (e.g., negative and positive aspects of stress, different levels of stress, lack of sleep, pressure, financial stressors, being a manager) among both female and male managers. In addition to substantial similarities, a number of important gender differences emerged. Gender continues to be socially constructed in society; specifically, there are differing gender-role expectations and responsibilities for women and men. Female managers experienced "emotional stress," primarily because of the pressure to meet expectations of being responsible and caring for people both inside and outside of their home. In contrast, male managers tended to focus on themselves and regard other things as beyond their control or responsibility.

To study women and leadership, we need to transform leadership and leadership theories to enable them to capture the essence of leadership among women. In Chin et al. (2006), some concepts were introduced, such as coacted harmony, collaborative leadership, participatory leadership, empowerment leadership, servant leader, transformational leader, appreciative leadership, shared power, and positive marginality to do so. All were intended to reflect the contexts of leadership and the need to transform leadership models.

Women leaders more commonly lead in the context of a male advantage, that is, in masculinized contexts; they are evaluated and perceived differently from men based on our current gender-related biases. Ethnic minority women leaders are often questioned in subtle and indirect ways that question their competence or assume they got to where they did because of affirmative action, not because they can do the job.

We need to view leadership as contextual, value driven, diversity inclusive, and collaborative. We look to transform models of leadership—to identify diverse leadership styles across diverse groups, to embrace core values that motivate those in leadership roles, and to identify effective leadership styles for men and women to achieve the outcomes they envision for the organizations and institutions they lead. Transforming leadership does not mean that men cannot or should not be leaders. Rather, it means that women can and should be effective leaders *without* needing to change their essence or adopting values that are not syntonic with their gender or culture. It is about using feminist principles to promote pathways to leadership, recognizing the obstacles and drawing on its strengths. It is about measuring and identifying effective leadership styles that are not simply based on identifying the characteristics of good male leaders. It is about how issues of power, privilege, and hierarchy influence the contexts in which leadership occurs.

FEMINIST LEADERSHIP

While we examine women and leadership, we need to consider how to incorporate ethics, collaboration, contexts, diversity, and transformational concepts into a new model of feminist leadership. An important distinction from the feminist literature is that being female and being feminist are not the same. We conclude that feminist leadership is a goal—and it is a style. Feminist women who aspire to and achieve leadership positions bring to these positions values and characteristics that shape how they lead, but they are also shaped by the environments in which they find themselves. Based on feminist principles and values, it is a goal of feminist women that they apply these principles of collaboration, egalitarianism, and inclusiveness to leadership and to the positions of leadership in which they find themselves; therefore, it is a goal.

A feminist leadership perspective argues for gender-equitable environments and against masculinized contexts; it argues against women needing to act like men. A feminist leadership perspective introduces ethics, social justice, collaboration, and inclusiveness as critical to their motivations for seeking positions of leadership. For women leaders and feminist leaders, the objectives of leadership include empowering others through:

- one's stewardship of an organization's resources
- creating the vision
- social advocacy and change
- promoting feminist policy and a feminist agenda (e.g., family-oriented work environments, wage gap between men and women)
- changing organizational cultures to create gender-equitable environments

For many women, an effective leadership style is transformational.

REFERENCES

Aviolo, B. J. (1994). The alliance of total quality and the full range of leadership. In Bass & Aviolo, pp. 121–145.

Bass, B. M. (1990). *Bass & Stogdill's handbook of leadership: Theory, research, and managerial application* (3rd ed.). New York: Free Press.

Bass, B. M., & Aviolo, B. J. (Eds.). (1994). *Improving organizational effectiveness through transformational leadership*. Thousand Oaks, CA: Sage.

Bennis, W. (1984). Transformative power and leadership. In T. J. Sergiovanni & J. E. Corbally (Eds.), *Leadership and organizational culture* (pp. 64–71). Urbana: University of Illinois Press.

Chin, J. L. (2004). 2003 Division 35 presidential address: "Feminist leadership: Feminist visions and diverse voices." *Psychology of Women Quarterly, 28*(1), 1–8.

Chin, J. L., Lott, B., Rice, J., & Sanchez-Hucles, J. (Eds.). (2006). *Women and leadership: Transforming visions and diverse voices*. New York: Blackwell.

Eagly, A. H. (1987). *Sex differences in social behavior: A social-role interpretation*. Hillsdale, NJ: Erlbaum.

Eagly, A. H., & Johannesen-Schmidt, M. C. (2001). The leadership styles of women and men. *Journal of Social Issues, 57*(4), 781ff.

Eagly, A. H., Johannesen-Schmidt, M. C., and van Engen, M. L. (2003). Transformational, transactional, and laissez-faire leadership styles: A meta-analysis comparing women and men. *Psychological Bulletin, 129*(4), 569–591.

Eagly, A. H., & Johnson, B. T. (1990). Gender and leadership style: A meta-analysis. *Psychological Bulletin, 108*(2), 233–256.

Eagly, A. H., and Karau, S. J. (2002). Role congruity theory of prejudice toward female leaders. *Psychological Review, 109*(3), 573–598.

Eagly, A. H., Makhijani, M. G., and Klonsky, B. G. (1992). Gender and the evaluation of leaders: A meta-analysis. *Psychological Bulletin, 111*(1), 3–22.

Fletcher, J. (2003a). The different faces of feminist leadership. Paper presented at the annual meeting of the American Psychological Association, Toronto.

Fletcher, J. (2003b). The greatly exaggerated demise of heroic leadership: Gender, power, and the myth of the female advantage. http://www.simmons.edu/gsm/cgo/insights13.pdf.

Forsyth, D. R., Heiney, M. M., & Wright, S. S. (1997). Biases in appraisals of women leaders. *Group Dynamics, 1*(1), 98–103.

Goldsea. (2002). Asian American wonder women: Executive sweet. *Goldsea*, http://goldsea.com/WW/Jungandrea/jungandrea.html; retrieved June 12, 2007.

Halpern, D. (2002). Collaboration as a feminist process. Retrieved July 2003, from http://www.feministleadership.com.

Harrington, A., & Shanley, M. (2003). The 50 most powerful women in American business. *Fortune,* October 13, pp. 103–108.

Indvik, J. (2004). Women and leadership. In Northouse, 2004, pp. 265–299.

Iwasaki, Y., MacKay, K. J., and Ristock, J. (2004). Gender-based analyses of stress among professional managers: An exploratory qualitative study. *International Journal of Stress Management, 11*(1), 56–79.

Kao, H. S. R., Sinha, D., & Wilpert, B. (1999). *Management and cultural values: The indigenization of organizations in Asia.* Thousand Oaks, CA: Sage.

Karakowsky, L. & Siegal, J. (1999). The effects of proportional representation and gender orientation of the task of emergent leadership behaviour in mixed-sex work groups. *Journal of Applied Psychology, 34,* 620–631.

Kidwell, C. S., Willis, D. J., Jones-Saumty, D., & Bigfoot, D. S. (2006). Feminist leadership among American Indian women. In Chin, Lott, Rice, & Sanchez-Hucles, 2006.

Kolb, D., & Williams, J. (2000). *Shadow negotiation: How women can master the hidden agendas that determine bargaining success.* New York: Simon & Schuster.

Looman, M. D. (2003). Reflective leadership: Strategic planning from the heart and soul. *Consulting Psychology Journal: Practice & Research, 55*(4), 215–221.

Lord, R. G., DeVader, C. L., & Alliger, G. M. (1986). A meta-analysis of the relation between personality traits and leadership perceptions: An application of the validity generalization procedures. *Journal of Applied Psychology, 71,* 402–410.

Madden, M. (2003). Management and leadership styles. Retrieved July, 2003, from http://www.feministleadership.com.

McGregor, D. (1985). The human side of enterprise. In D. S. Pugh (Ed.), *Organization theory,* London: McGraw-Hill.

McGrory, M. (2002). Pelosi's a salve for a wounded party. *Boston Globe,* November 16, 2002.

Morrison, A. M., and von Glinow, M. A. (1990). Women and minorities in management. *American Psychologist, 45*(2), 200–208.

Motavalli, J. (1994). The voice of our Elders: The outspoken Surgeon General Jocelyn Elders is using her "bully pulpit" to take on the tobacco companies. *E Magazine, 4,* E948.

Northouse, P. G. (2004). *Leadership: Theory and practice.* Thousand Oaks, CA: Sage.

Raelin, J. A. (2003). *Creating leaderful organizations: How to bring out leadership in everyone.* San Francisco: Berrett-Koehler.

Ragins, B., Townsend, B., & Mattis, M. (1998). Gender gap in the executive suite: CEOs and female executives report on breaking the glass ceiling. *Academy of Mangement Executive, 12*(1), 28–42.

Rawlings, D. (2000). Collaborative leadership teams: Oxymoron or new paradigm? *Consulting Psychology Journal: Practice & Research, 52*(1), 36–48.

Sanchez-Hucles, J. (2003). Diversity in feminist leadership. Retrieved July, 2003, from http://www.feministleadership.com.

Sellers, P. (2003). Power: Do women really want it? *Fortune,* October 13, pp. 80–100.

Sergiovanni, T. (1984). Cultural and competing perspectives in administrative theory and practice. In T. J. Sergiovanni & J. E. Corbally (Eds.), *Leadership and organizational culture* (pp. 1–12). Urbana: University of Illinois Press.

Tichy, N., & Devanna, M. A. (1986). *The transformational leader.* New York: Wiley & Sons.

Women may make better managers—Study. (1997, April)

Chapter 22

Women's Career Development

Nancy E. Betz

The critical importance of a man's "vocation" to his societal prestige, self-esteem, and economic condition has long been a foundational assumption in society, and in the early part of the 20th century, psychologists began to study this vocation. Frank Parsons, in his classic volume *Choosing a Vocation* (1909), postulated that self-knowledge, knowledge of the world of work, and "true reasoning" to match the two were the sine qua non of satisfactory vocational choices. Although these ideas made great sense, it would be 55 years before they were thought to have any relevance to the lives of women.

As recently as 1964, the preface to Borow's volume *Man in a World at Work* stated:

> Work is the social act around which each of us establishes a meaningful and rewarding life routine. One has but to witness the lives of men without work, or of men who lack edifying work—alienated, thwarted and cutoff from the fulfillment of the most human of sentiments, a sense of usefulness and purpose—to recognize the validity of the commonly voiced doctrine that work is, indeed, a way of life. (p. xi)

In this poignant statement, there is no acknowledgment of nor concern expressed for women—it was assumed that when women "worked" (as in outside the home), it was because their labor was needed by the economy, as was the case with the Rosie the Riveters of World War II (Colman, 1995), that they were working until they could "land" a husband, or that they were that most pitiable of characters—the spinster (see, for example, Toibin, 2004).

It has only been since the 1960s that women's work has been taken seriously by at least some segments within psychology and society, and the concept of women actually having careers, vocations other than motherhood, received serious study. Today the study of women's career development is a vibrant and critically important field of psychology—we now take women's careers seriously.

Women today constitute a significant portion of the labor force, and the vast majority of U.S. women work outside the home. In 2005, of women age 25–44, 75 percent were employed (U.S. Bureau of Labor Statistics, 2005). Of women with children under 18, 71 percent are employed, and 62 percent and 57 percent of those with children under age 6 and under age 3, respectively, are employed (U.S. Bureau of Labor Statistics, 2005). The odds that a woman will work outside the home during her adult life are over 90 percent (U.S. Bureau of Labor Statistics, 2003). What this adds up to is that paid employment (versus work inside the home) is now the rule, not the exception. There is *no* category of women for whom the majority is not employed outside the home (Barnett & Hyde, 2001).

Not surprisingly, the most common family lifestyle today is the "dual-earner" family (Gilbert & Kearney, 2006). As described by Gilbert and Kearney (2006) and by Barnett and Hyde (2001), we now have "work-family convergence" (Gilbert & Kearney, 2006, p. 196), where both work and family are considered important in the lives of both women and men, and where many if not most workers prefer the two roles equally. Thus, as psychologists, educators, and counselors, it is essential to understand the issues facing women at work *and* the reality that both work and family roles are salient in the lives of contemporary women and men.

WHY CAREERS ARE IMPORTANT TO A WOMAN'S QUALITY OF LIFE

Women, like men, need a variety of major sources of satisfaction in their lives—as once stated by Freud (according to Erickson, 1950), the psychologically well-adjusted human being is able "to love and to work" effectively. Both women and men need not only the satisfactions of interpersonal relationships, with family and/or friends, but also the satisfaction of achievement in the outside world. We now have research evidence that women, like men, need to utilize their talents and abilities and that multiple roles are important for people's psychological well-being.

Utilization of Abilities

Research has shown that the fulfillment of individual potential for achievement is vitally important. Although the roles of homemaker and mother are important and often very satisfying, they do not allow most women to fulfill their unique abilities and talents. These, rather, must be fulfilled through career pursuits or volunteer and avocational activities, just as they are in men. This is not to discount the importance of childrearing, but only to point out its insufficiency as a lifelong answer to the issue of self-realization. Even if a woman spends a number of years creatively rearing children, these children inevitably grow up and begin their own lives—lives that must of necessity be increasingly independent from the parental home.

The evidence is strong that homemakers who do not have other outlets for achievement and productivity are highly susceptible to psychological distress, particularly as children grow and leave home. For example, of the women in the Terman studies of gifted children (Terman & Oden, 1959), when followed up in their 60s (Sears & Barbie, 1977), the women who reported the highest levels of life satisfaction were the employed women. Least satisfied with their lives were those who had been housewives all of their adult lives. The most psychologically distressed women were those with exceptionally high IQs (above 170) who had not worked outside the home. It seems fairly clear in the Terman study that women with genius-level IQs who had not pursued meaningful careers outside the home have suffered psychological consequences.

Kerr (1997; Kerr, Foley-Nicpon, & Zapata, 2005), in an extensive program of research on gifted girls, notes that, although the aspirations of girls are as high as are those of their gifted male counterparts, "the theme of their lives is one of declining achievement goals" (Kerr et al., 2005, p. 19). Gifted girls often experience pressure, subtle or not so subtle, to do an "about-face" (Kerr, 1997; Reis, Callahan, & Goldsmith, 1996) during adolescence—to shift their personal priorities and self-evaluations from academic achievement to the achievement of romance.

Gifted girls were also quite concerned about the effects of their giftedness on others' attitudes toward them, fearing that these attitudes would be negative (Kerr, Colangelo, & Gaeth, 1988). Not surprisingly, by the sophomore year of college, gifted young women have likely changed their majors to less challenging areas, by their senior year they have reduced the level of their career goals, and by college graduation they have given up their former career dreams altogether, all because of the pervasive "culture of romance" (Holland & Eisenhart, 1990; Kerr et al., 1988, p. 16). It does not seem unreasonable to suggest that these young women of today will experience the same eventual loss of self and the psychological problems experienced by the gifted women in the older Terman studies.

Multiple Roles

In a related vein, there is strong evidence for the beneficial effects of working outside the home on a woman's psychological adjustment, regardless of her marital status. Early research on the relationship between marital status and psychological health concluded that the healthiest individuals were the married men and the single women, whereas married women were at particularly high risk for psychological distress (Bernard, 1971). However, it does not seem to be marriage per se that is detrimental to women's psychological adjustment, but rather the lack of meaningful paid employment. In these studies, the women who were not employed accounted for the more frequent occurrence of psychological distress among the married women.

In a related vein, there is strong evidence that multiple roles, that is, those of both worker and family member, are important to women's mental and physical health (Barnett & Hyde, 2001). Most research finds that even though multiple roles are time consuming and can be stressful, they are protective against depression (Crosby, 1991) and are facilitative of positive mental health.

There are several hypotheses concerning why multiple roles are beneficial for women (Barnett & Hyde, 2001). First, when more than one role is important in one's life, stress or disappointment in one domain can be "buffered" by success or satisfaction in another role. Second, the added income of a second job/career can reduce the stress of being the sole breadwinner and can in fact provide an economic "lifeline" when one spouse or partner becomes unemployed. In difficult economic times, characterized by high unemployment and corporate downsizing or collapse, two incomes can be virtually life-saving. Third, jobs provide an additional source of social support, which increases well-being (Barrett & Hyde, 2001). For example, Greenberger and O'Neil (1993) found that although men's well-being was related most significantly to social support from their wives, women's well-being was related to support from neighbors, supervisors, and coworkers, as well as from husbands.

There is also evidence to contradict myths that a woman's career commitment will have a negative effect on her marriage and family. It seems that more equitable sharing of breadwinning may benefit marital satisfaction in both spouses, but especially husbands (Wilke, Ferree, & Ratcliff, 1998). Also interesting is data showing that the two roles are not contradictory but may in fact have a mutually catalytic effect—studies of the relationship between work commitment and family commitment show a positive correlation between the two (Marks & MacDermid, 1996).

In considering women's career development and multiple roles, it should also be noted that there are today many lifestyle alternatives. There are 12 million single parents in this country, most of them women (Gilbert, 2002). There is also an increasing number of people who choose to remain single, as well as growing numbers of committed gay and lesbian couples, many of whom are now choosing to have or adopt children. Thus, although the heterosexual dual-career marriage will be the modal lifestyle, the options of remaining single or in a committed same-sex or nonmarital partnership should also be considered viable in life planning (see Farmer, 1997). It goes without saying that the issues of combining work and parenthood are different for single people, who usually carry sole responsibility for home and parenting, and for those in same-sex partnerships, for whom there is no obvious assignment of roles and responsibilities based on gender. But regardless of the precise nature of the family unit, helping people to have and manage multiple roles will be beneficial.

INEQUITIES IN WOMEN'S LABOR FORCE PARTICIPATION

Although women now work in overwhelming numbers, their work continues to be focused in traditionally female occupations and to be less well paid than that of men (American Association of University Women, 2002). Even though women have made much progress in entering traditionally male-dominated professions such as medicine and law, where half the entering students are women, the occupational world still has many areas of extreme sex segregation. For example, more than 90 percent of preschool, kindergarten, elementary, and special education teachers; dental hygienists; secretaries; child care workers; cleaners and servants; hairdresser; occupational and speech therapists; and teacher's aids are women (U.S. Bureau of Labor Statistics, 2003). Men still comprise only 11 percent of nurses, although this percentage is up from 8 percent a few years ago.

In contrast, women remain seriously underrepresented in scientific and technical careers and in high-level positions in business, government, education, and the military. For example, women earn fewer than 20 percent of the bachelor's degrees in fields such as engineering and physics and fewer than 10 percent of the graduate degrees in engineering (Kuh, 1998). High technology is among the fastest growing and well-paid occupational fields, yet women represent only about 14 percent of engineers, 30 percent of computer systems analysts, and 25 percent of computer programmers (U.S. Bureau of Labor Statistics, 2003, 2005). Women account for 8 percent of physicists and astronomers, 7 percent of air traffic controllers, 5 percent of truck drivers, 4 percent of pilots, and 5 percent of firefighters. Women remain only a small proportion of workers in the generally well-paid skilled trades; for example, they comprise 2 percent of carpenters and electricians (U.S. Bureau of Labor Statistics, 2005). Career education programs continue to be seriously gender segregated, with 90 percent of women in training programs in traditionally female fields such as health care and office technology (American Association of University Women, 2002).

Women also continue to be paid less for full-time employment in this country. Overall, women make 77 percent as much as men when both are employed full-time (U.S. Bureau of Labor Statistics, 2005), although this constitutes an improvement over the 73 percent reported in the 2003 data. The income gap is greater for middle-aged and older workers than it is for young workers and is greater for white women compared to African American or Hispanic women, probably because the incomes of African American and Hispanic males are also depressed relative to those of white men. However, the incomes of women in nontraditional careers are 150 percent that of women in traditional careers (U.S. Bureau of Labor Statistics, 2003).

In considering women's lower income, it is essential to note that women cannot assume they will be taken care of by a husband. Today the average marriage lasts seven years (Harvey & Pauwels, 1999), and 20 percent of children live in a single-parent home—12 million single-parent households, most of them headed by women (U.S. Bureau of Labor Statistics, 2003). Women are much more likely to be widowed than men, and women represent 75 percent of the elderly poor, a percentage much greater than their representation (59%) among the elderly. The odds that a woman will have to care for herself financially during adult life are high, and failure to prepare her for this likelihood with high-quality education or training can have tragic consequences.

In summary, career pursuits will play a major role in most women's lives, so it is imperative that we develop knowledge and interventions that will help women make career choices that they find fulfilling, satisfying, and economically sustaining. Yet the data I have described suggest that a substantial number of women are still selecting a smaller range of traditionally female, lower-paid careers and are making substantially less money than men, even when employed full-time. In the next sections, I will discuss barriers to choice and barriers to equity, but following each discussion of barriers I will also discuss supportive factors. This organization follows the distinction of career barriers that originated in the writings of Farmer (1976) and Harmon (1977) in their pioneering work on women's career development (and see Farmer, 2006, for an excellent history of this work). We as psychologists can be better prepared to help girls and women make choices that can facilitate their quality of life if we understand both the barriers to and supports of women's career development.

BARRIERS TO WOMEN'S PERCEIVED CAREER OPTIONS AND CHOICES

Some barriers to career choices are socialized barriers, that is, socialized belief systems or behavior patterns that lead women themselves to avoid certain career fields. Factors that will be discussed herein are avoidance of mathematics coursework, low self-efficacy and outcome expectations, gender and occupational stereotypes, and a restricted range of vocational interests. Problems with our educational system, the concept of the null educational environment, and multiple-role concerns are other barriers to women's career development.

Math: The Critical Filter

The critical importance of a sound mathematics background for entrance to many of the best career opportunities in our society (e.g., engineering, scientific, and medical careers, computer science, business, and the skilled trades) is now generally agreed upon (Chipman & Wilson, 1985), and a lack of math background constitutes one of the major barriers to women's career development.

The classic study of the importance of math to career options was that of Sells (1973). In a study of freshmen at the University of California at Berkeley, Sells found that only 8 percent of the women, compared to 57 percent of the men, had taken four years of high school math. Four years of high school math was prerequisite to entering calculus or intermediate statistics courses required in three-fourths of the university's major fields, and the university did not provide remedial courses to allow a student to complete the prerequisites post hoc. Thus, 92 percent of the freshmen women at Berkeley were prevented by lack of math background from even considering 15 of the 20 major fields. The five remaining options were predictable—such traditionally female major areas as education, the humanities, the social sciences, librarianship, and social welfare. Thus, decisions to "choose" these majors may have in many cases been by default, through failure to qualify for any major requiring considerable math background.

Sells (1982) further elaborated the vital importance of math preparation for both career options and future earnings. Four full years of high school math are vital to surviving the standard freshman calculus course, now required for most undergraduate majors in business administration, economics, agriculture, engineering, forestry, health sciences, nutrition, food sciences, and natural, physical, and computer sciences. Only the arts and humanities do not now require a math background. Further, Sells (1982) showed a strong and direct relationship between college calculus background and both starting salaries and employers' willingness to interview students for a given job. Mathematics and science are important even for noncollege-degree technical occupations (U.S. Department of Labor, 2000). As so well stated by Sells (1982), "Mastery of mathematics and science has become essential for full participation in the world of employment in an increasingly technological society" (p. 7).

Given the importance of having an adequate math background to career options, females' tendency to avoid math coursework has been one of the most serious barriers to their career development. Further, it is fairly clear now that it is lack of math background, rather than lack of innate ability, that is to blame for females' poorer performance on quantitative aptitude and mathematics achievement tests (e.g., Chipman & Wilson, 1985; Eccles & Jacobs, 1986; National Center for Education Statistics, 2004; Spelke, 2005). Thus, a critical issue is females' avoidance of math. Educational and counseling interventions capable of helping young women to be full participants in an increasingly technological society may be among the most crucial strategies in attempts to broaden women's career choices. These issues are dealt with more extensively in the discussion of counseling implications.

Self-Efficacy Expectations

The concept of self-efficacy expectations has become one of the most important in helping to understand the career options that people consider. Self-efficacy expectations (Bandura, 1977, 1997) refer to people's beliefs that they can successfully complete specific tasks or behaviors to reach goals. For example, an individual may perceive herself as able (or unable) to solve algebraic equations, fix a flat tire, or care for an infant.

Self-efficacy expectations are postulated by Bandura (1977, 1997) to have at least three behavioral consequences:

1. approach versus avoidance behavior
2. quality of performance of behaviors in the target domain
3. persistence in the face of obstacles or disconfirming experiences

Thus, low self-efficacy expectations regarding various behavioral domains are postulated to lead to avoidance of those domains, poorer performance in them, and an increased tendency to "give up" when faced with discouragement or failure. In the context of career development, self-efficacy expectations can influence the types of courses, majors, and careers individuals feel comfortable attempting. They can influence performance on the tests necessary to complete college course work or the requirements of a job training program. Finally, the postulated effects of self-efficacy on persistence influence long-term pursuit of one's goals in the face of obstacles, occasional failures, and dissuading messages from the environment, such as gender or race-based discrimination or harassment.

In earlier work (Betz & Hackett, 1981), Gail Hackett and I postulated that the experiential antecedents leading to the development of strong self-efficacy expectations were much less available in the socialization experiences of young females than in those of young males, at least in behavioral domains in the sciences, mathematics, technology, the out-of-doors, and mechanical areas, and that this experiential impoverishment could be a significant cause of women's continued underrepresentation in careers in science and technology and the skilled trades, among others. Twenty-five years of research has supported these postulates.

In education or job-content domains, college women tend to score lower than college men on self-efficacy in domains having to do with math, science, computer science and technology, mechanical activities, and outdoor and physical activities (Betz & Hackett, 1981, 1997; Betz, Borgen, Rottinghaus, Paulsen, Halper, & Harmon, 2003; Borgen & Betz, 2007). Women tend to score higher than men on self-efficacy in social domains of activity, such as teaching and counseling. For example, we asked college women and men to report whether or not they felt themselves capable of completing various educational majors (Betz & Hackett, 1981). Even though the men and women as a group did not differ in their tested abilities, they differed significantly in their self-efficacy beliefs. These differences were especially striking toward occupations involving mathematics: 59 percent of college men versus 41 percent of college women believed themselves able to complete a degree in that field. Seventy-four percent of men, compared to 59 percent of women, believed they could be accountants. Most dramatically, 70 percent of college men but only 30 percent of comparably able women believed themselves able to complete a degree in engineering.

We also found that self-efficacy was related to the range of career options considered, and that self-efficacy for mathematics is linked to choice of a science career (Betz & Hackett, 1981, 1983). Other studies have shown that self-efficacy beliefs are related to performance and persistence. For example, Lent, Brown, and Larkin (1984, 1986) showed that efficacy beliefs regarding the educational requirements of scientific and technical occupations were related to both the performance and persistence (continuing enrollment) of students enrolled in engineering programs. And some studies (e.g., Pajares, 1996) have suggested that women tend to more accurately estimate their mathematical abilities, while men often overestimate theirs. Overestimation is postulated to lead to "approach" behavior—effort and persistence—and so may lead to skill enhancement and expansion of options, more likely therefore to characterize the efforts of young males than females.

Thus, low self-efficacy, especially in relationship to male-dominated careers or careers requiring mathematical or technical expertise, may reduce the self-perceived career options of women. Another concept in Bandura's (1997) social cognitive theory that is important for women is that of outcome expectations, the belief that desired outcomes will follow from successful behaviors. Given continuing discrimination in the workforce, it would not be surprising if women felt that competent work behavior might not be rewarded or might even be disparaged in certain contexts. Women of color may have particularly low outcome, as well as self-efficacy, expectations due to experiences with oppression and racial bias (Byars & Hackett, 1998).

Occupational and Gender Stereotypes

Gender-related stereotypes detrimentally affect the development of girls and women in at least two ways. First, stereotypes regarding gender-roles may lead girls to believe that they *should* prioritize homemaking and childrearing roles and deemphasize their own educational achievements. One manifestation of this stereotyping is a progressive decrease in the aspirations of girls. Numerous studies suggest that although boys and girls start out with equally high aspirations, girls reduce theirs over time (Farmer, 1997; Kerr, 1997). For example, in the high school valedictorian sample studied by Arnold and Denny (Arnold, 1995), the boys and girls initially aspired to relatively similar levels of career prestige, but as adults the women selected less prestigious majors and ended up in lower-level career fields. In Farmer's (1997) longitudinal study of high school students, men's persistence in science was related to high aspirations when young, while for women their youthful high aspirations often faded as they matured (Farmer, 1997). In Arnold and Denny's (Arnold, 1995) sample of high school valedictorians, the girls but not the boys showed steady decrements in aspirations and also in self-esteem after college. The stronger the home/family priorities, the more precipitous were the declines in both aspirations and self-esteem.

And as mentioned earlier, Kerr and colleagues (Kerr, 1997; Kerr et al., 2005), in their extensive program of research on gifted girls, noted the shift in adolescence in personal priorities and self-evaluations from academic achievement to the achievement of romance and the increasing worry that high achievement would be negatively perceived by their male peers and potential romantic partners. This shift in priorities cannot help but be related to the progressive decline in aspirations once girls enter college (Kerr et al., 2005).

The second way that stereotypes affect women's career choices is through stereotypes about occupations best suited for males and females. Although beliefs that some occupations are more appropriate for men than women may have lessened, they still exist, as is shown by research. In an illuminating recent study, for example, Nelson, Acke, and Manis (1996) found that college students assumed that men were majoring in engineering and women in nursing even when contrary information was provided. For example, a 20-year-old male described as having worked in a day-care center was assumed to be majoring in engineering, while a young woman who had had considerable outdoor and mechanical experience was assumed to be majoring in nursing.

Children are susceptible to these stereotypes and begin to use them to guide choice. Early studies (see Betz, 1994, for a review) showed that people consistently rate many occupations as either masculine or feminine. For example, in the classic study of gender stereotypes in occupations, Shinar (1975) showed that miner, federal judge, engineer, physicist, and heavy equipment operator were judged to be highly masculine, while nurse, receptionist, elementary school teacher, and dietician were seen as highly feminine. Children learn these stereotypes at ages as young as two to three years and begin to incorporate gender-roles into their considerations of careers at ages 6–8, grades 1 through 3 (Gottfredson, 1981).

Restricted Vocational Interests

Ability, aptitude, and vocational interest measures are extensively used in career assessment and counseling with the idea of achieving a fit or match between the person and environment. This objective can be traced back to Frank Parsons's (1909) "matching men and jobs" approach as discussed in the introduction to this chapter. Now referred to in more contemporary terms as "person–environment fit" or "trait-factor" models (Dawis, 1992, 2000), the basic assumptions of the model remain elegant in their simplicity, yet broad in their usefulness. Simply stated, the bases of this approach are that:

1. individuals differ in their job-related abilities and interests
2. job/occupational environments differ in their requirements and in the kinds of interests to which they appeal
3. congruence or "fit" between an individual's characteristics and the characteristics of the job is an important consideration in making good career choices

Among the important variables to be taken into consideration in these models are abilities and aptitudes, such as those measured by the Differential Aptitude Tests (DAT) and Armed Services Vocational Aptitude Battery (ASVAB), and vocational interests as included in Holland's theory (1997) and measured by the Strong Interest Inventory (Donnay, Morris, Schaubhut, & Thompson, 2005; see also Walsh & Betz, 2001, for a comprehensive discussion of career assessment methods). From the matching perspective, the purpose of assessment is to assist a student or adult in generating educational or career options that represent a good person–environment fit.

While the "matching model" has been supported by much empirical research, we have also come to realize that this model oversimplifies the career choice process for some groups of people. For example, research has indicated that women tend to underutilize their abilities in selecting careers (Betz & Fitzgerald, 1987). In addition, women's overrepresentation in traditionally female careers and underrepresentation in many male-dominated careers may be due partly to restrictions in how their vocational interests have developed and how they are measured.

Using Holland's (1997) vocational theory as an example, women score lower on Realistic themes and higher on Social themes than men when raw scores (simple number of items endorsed) are used to measure the Holland types (Lunneborg, 1979). The Realistic theme includes technical, outdoor, and "hands-on" activities—the kinds of skills often taught in high school "shop," electronics, and trades courses or under the tutelage of a parent comfortable with home and automobile repair. Realistic interests are part of inventory suggestions for careers in engineering, and thus lower scores on this theme constitute a significant barrier to the suggestion of this occupational field to young women. The Social theme includes social, interpersonal skills often thought important to teach girls but neglected in the teaching of boys (Tipping, 1997; Yoder, 1999).

When such measures are used, gender stereotypes tend to be perpetuated by the test materials themselves. There is strong evidence that these interest differences are in part due to stereotypic gender socialization, because boys are exposed to different types of learning opportunities growing up than are girls. Educational and career options are thus restricted because of restricted interest development. Although part of the answer to this problem is to increase the breadth of socialization experiences afforded to *both* genders, at a practical level we can also address these problems by using interest inventories that are not gender restrictive—that is, that do not perpetuate gender stereotypes. This can be done using within-gender normative scores (comparing raw scores to those of members of the same gender) and gender-balanced interest inventories (where interest scales include items familiar to both genders rather than primarily to just one). These approaches will be discussed in the last section on implications for education and interventions.

Multiple-Role Concerns

Fitzgerald, Fassinger, and Betz (1995) noted that "the history of women's traditional roles as homemaker and mother continue to influence every aspect of their career choice and adjustment" (p. 72), typically in the direction of placing limits on what can be achieved. The research of Arnold and Denney (see Arnold, 1995) following the lives of Illinois valedictorians provided a particularly vivid illustration of how the aspirations of academically gifted women, but not those of similarly gifted men, steadily decreased as they completed college and entered career fields. In her longitudinal study of midwestern high school students, Farmer (1997) noted that a large number of young women interested in science chose to pursue nursing because they thought it would fit well with having and rearing children or with being a single or divorced head of household. Men in the Farmer study made no such compromises. In Farmer's sample of women (high school students in 1980) career motivation was inversely related to homemaking commitment.

Kerr et al. (2005) noted that "a culture of romance which is virulently inimical to female achievement still thrives in coeducational colleges and universities" (p. 30), and that it leads even gifted young women to reduce their major and career aspirations, to be much more likely than their male counterparts to follow their partner to his job location, to take responsibility for child care, to give up full-time work for part-time work, and to give up leadership positions as too demanding to combine with domestic responsibilities. In essence, she takes full executive responsibility at home (Bem & Bem, 1976), so it may be perceived as an undue burden (and probably is!) to also take such responsibility at work.

Women today may not be viewing home and career as an "either/or" choice, but many *do* plan careers mindful of how they will integrate these with home and family. In contrast, many men plan their careers without needing to sacrifice levels of achievement to accommodate home and families (Farmer, 1997). Spade and Reese (1991) noted that men reconcile the demands of work and family by "reverting to the traditional definition of father as provider" (p. 319). As concluded by Gerson (1986) and discussed further by Eccles (1987), women's choices about work continue to be inextricably linked with their decisions about family, and thus family role considerations limit women's investment in the occupational world.

Although we have witnessed tremendous increases in workforce participation among women in all marital and parental categories, the relationship of marital/parental status to career attainment, commitment, and innovation is still very strong. Studies have shown inverse relationships between being married and having children and every measurable criterion of career involvement and achievement (see Betz & Fitzgerald, 1987, for a comprehensive review). This inverse relationship is not true among men. Highly achieving men are at least as likely as their less highly achieving male counterparts to be married and to have one or more children. In other words, men do not have to downscale their aspirations in order to have a home and family. Women, like men, deserve to "have it all."

Barriers in the Educational System

It is probably difficult to overestimate the importance of education to career development and achievement. The nature and level of obtained education are importantly related to subsequent career achievements and to adult socioeconomic status and lifestyle. An undergraduate degree is now a necessary minimum requirement for the pursuit of many occupations, and graduate or professional education is the only route to careers in many professions. All workers, men and women, earn more with increasing levels of education. Education is crucial for economic power (Wycott, 1996) and independence (Cardoza, 1991). In short, appropriate educational preparation is a major "gateway" to occupational entrance. Education creates options, while lack of education closes them; without options, the concept of "choice" itself has no real meaning. Thus, the decisions individuals make concerning their education, both in terms of level and major areas of study, will be among the most important career decisions they ever make. Further, success and survival in the educational programs chosen will be critical to the successful implementation of these career decisions.

Studies commissioned by the American Association of University Women (1992, 1999, 2002) and reviews done by Sadker and Sadker (1994) and Zittleman and Sadker (2003) document the continuing disadvantaged position of girls in our educational system. Researchers have concluded that girls receive less attention from teachers than do boys, that teachers have stereotyped views of the sexes, and that teaching materials such as textbooks continue to have gender-biased content or to marginalize or ignore women. For example, Siegel and Reis (1998) found that although teachers perceived gifted girls as working harder and doing better work than gifted boys, they gave the boys higher grades. In another study (Fennema et al., 1998), teachers continued to perceive that boys are better at math and that they like it better in comparison to gifted girls.

Research by Brody (1997) and others has also convincingly documented a decline in self-esteem among girls, but not boys, from elementary to middle and high school. For example, 55 percent of elementary school girls agreed with the statement "I am good at a lot of things," but this percentage declined to 29 percent in middle school and 23 percent in high school. Interestingly, girls who pursued math and science courses and who participated in sports maintained their self-esteem over this time period (American Association of University Women, 1992). Because of the combination of lack of support with outright discouragement and harassment, Sandler and Hall (1996) described our schools as providing a "chilly educational climate" for girls and women.

When girls enter college, they can expect to encounter an educational environment that may continue to be "chilly." Sexual harassment, being discouraged from classroom participation, and lack of support and mentoring can affect women in any major, but these and other subtle or direct messages that "she doesn't belong" are particularly true in male-dominated fields such as engineering and the physical sciences (see the discussion of the experiences of "token" women in the next section on barriers to equity). Ehrhart and Sandler (1987) documented other types of differential treatment of women in higher education such as disparaging women's intellectual capabilities or professional potential, using sexist humor, advising women to lower their academic and career goals, and focusing on marriage and children as a potential barrier to the career development of women but as an advantage for men.

As stated by Pearson, Shavlik, and Touchton (1988):

> The present record of higher education, in spite of some significant efforts, is not particularly good. Female students, on the whole, still experience a loss of personal and career confidence over the period they spend in higher education, even when they make very high grades. For men, the reverse is true.

One of the most basic and important concepts summarizing the difficulties faced by women in higher education is Freeman's (1979) concept of the *null educational environment.* A null environment is one that neither encourages nor discourages individuals—it simply ignores them (Betz, 1989; Freeman, 1979). Its outcome is to leave the individual at the mercy of whatever environmental or personal resources to which she or he has access.

The effects of null environments on women were first postulated by Freeman (1979) following her study of students at the University of Chicago. Students were asked to describe the sources and extent of environmental support they received for their educational and career goals. Although both male and female students reported being ignored by faculty (thus experiencing what Freeman dubbed the null educational environment), male students reported more encouragement and support from others in their environments, for example, parents, friends, relatives, and significant others.

When added to the greater occurrence of negative messages regarding women's roles and, in particular, regarding women's pursuit of careers in fields traditionally dominated by men, the effect of the faculty simply ignoring the women students was a form of passive discrimination—discrimination through failure to act. As stated by Freeman (1979), "An academic situation that neither encourages nor discourages students of either sex is inherently discriminatory against women because it fails to take into account the differentiating external environments from which women and men students come," where external environments refer to difference in familial, peer, and societal support for career pursuits (p. 221). In other words, professors do not have to overtly discourage or discriminate against female students; society has already placed countless negative marks on the female student's "ballot," so a passive approach, a laissez-faire attitude, is enough to contribute to her failure. Career-oriented female students, to survive, must do it without much support from their environments (Betz, 1989).

Discrimination can thus result from acts of omission as well as commission, and both have negative effects on females' progress and success in higher education. Leppel (2001) illustrates a phenomenon akin to the null environment, using women in nontraditional majors as an example: they may feel both more negative pressure and less positive emotional support from friends and family than women in more traditional majors, and in many cases, these students then change to traditional majors. It is not enough to avoid discriminating—positive support must be provided to counteract other negative environmental influences. Thus if we are not actively supporting and encouraging women, we are, in effect, leaving them at the mercy of gender-role and occupational stereotypes.

Eccles (1987) stated it well when she wrote: "Given the omnipresence of gender-role prescriptions regarding appropriate female life choices, there is little basis for females to develop non-traditional goals if their parents, peers, teachers, and counselors do not encourage them to consider these options" (p. 164). Failure to support her may not be an error of commission, like overt discrimination or sexual harassment, but it is an error of omission because its ultimate consequences are the same: limitations on a woman's ability to fully develop and utilize her skills and talents in educational and career pursuits.

SUPPORTS TO WOMEN'S CAREER CHOICES

Among the factors that have been found to facilitate women's career achievements, including perceiving a broader array of career options, are a number of variables which, by their absence, can serve as barriers. Just as unsupportive environments can serve as barriers, supportive environments can be very helpful. One of the most crucial areas of support is that from families, especially parents and older relatives, and this has been found true for women of all racial and ethnic groups. Studies by Fisher and Padmawidjaja (1999), Pearson and Bieschke (2001), and Juntunen, Barraclough, Broneck, Seibel, Winlow, and Morin (2001), among others, have found parental support and availability to be very important in the career aspirations and achievements of Mexican American, African American, and Native American, as well as white, women. Kitano and Perkins (1996) noted that high-achieving girls in Latino and Asian cultures are those with extra encouragement from their families.

A number of other studies have found maternal employment, particularly in nontraditional career fields, is related to daughters' higher career aspirations (e.g., Selkow, 1984). Gomez, Fassinger, Prosser, Cooke,

Mejia, and Luna (2001) found that although Latina high achievers came from families where traditional gender-roles were emphasized, most also had nontraditional female role models—for example, their mothers were often nontraditionally employed or, if homemakers, held leadership roles in community organizations. On the other hand, Hackett, Esposito, and O'Halloran (1989) and Weishaar, Green, and Craighead (1981), among others, have reported that the presence of a supportive male family member was important in girls' pursuit of nontraditional career fields. Many women pursuing nontraditional career fields relied heavily on male mentors (Betz, 2002), since no female mentors were available in their environments.

In addition to supportive family and mentors, much previous research has shown the importance of personality factors such as instrumentality, internal locus of control, high self-esteem, and a feminist orientation in women's career achievements (Betz & Fitzgerald, 1987; Fassinger, 1990). Instrumentality, one of the critical factors in Farmer's (1997) study, refers to a constellation of traits that were previously called "masculinity" but were seen eventually to reflect a collection of characteristics having to do with independence, self-sufficiency, and the feeling that one was in control of one's life. It has also been described as "agency" and has much in common with self-efficacy (Bandura, 1997).

The possession of instrumental traits does not mean that one cannot also possess the most traditionally feminine traits of nurturance and sensitivity to others. These characteristics are now referred to as "expressiveness" or "communion." Together, instrumentality and expressiveness form the "androgynous" personality style, which is thought to be desirable for both women and men. Thus, positive factors related to support and mentoring from others, along with a personality characterized by high self-esteem and self-efficacy and a sense of self-sufficiency and instrumentality, can help women reach their career goals.

WOMEN OF COLOR: CONTINUING DOUBLE JEOPARDY

Before moving to a discussion of barriers to success in the workplace, explicit attention should be paid to the status and unique concerns of women of color. Although research on women of color is also mentioned where relevant throughout this chapter (see also chapter 2 in this volume), a few more general factors should be mentioned.

The disadvantages facing women in the labor force are accentuated for women of color, who have often been described as facing the "double jeopardy" of both gender and race discrimination (Beale, 1970; see also Gomez et al., 2001). Women of color are employed in proportions comparable to that of white women, but earn less than either white women or minority men. Lesbians and physically disabled women also earn less than heterosexual white women (Yoder, 1999).

With reference to specific groups, African American women have achieved higher educational and occupational levels and have had more options compared to African American men (Jewell, 1993), but they have also often been found in menial jobs such as maids and nannies at a ratio exceeding that of white women and still make less money than do both white women or African American men (DeVaney & Hughey, 2000). Since they are the most likely group to be supporting a child or children alone, this can create a special hardship. See Bingham, Ward, and Butler (2006) for a recent review of issues in the career development and career counseling of African American women.

Latinos currently represent the largest minority group in the United States, 32.8 million or 12.5 percent of the U.S. population in the 2000 census. The achievement of Latino men and women both in terms of educational and occupational levels lags well behind that of other U.S. minorities except for Native Americans (Arbona & Novy, 1991; Flores, Navarro, & Ojeda, 2006). Mexican American women lag behind other women of Hispanic ethnicity in college completion rates (Flores et al., 2006), and adult Latinas have higher unemployment rates and lower labor-force participation rates in comparison to Latino males or white women. They also lag behind Latino men who, on the average, earned poorer grades in college. In understanding the career behavior of Latinas, Flores et al. (2006) urge the assessment of individual adherence to traditional Latino/Latina cultural values—although greater adherence may impair individual career development, counseling interventions must take an attitude of respect toward the value systems of the culture if they are to be ultimately successful.

Asian American women are somewhat more likely than other groups of women to be found in occupations emphasizing math or technology, but they are still predominately found in traditionally female fields and, like other groups of women, earn less money than men (Ali, Lewis, & Sandal, 2006).

Finally, Native American women, including Native Hawaiians, are almost absent from our literature (Bowman, 1998) and are the most occupationally disadvantaged and the most likely to be unemployed of any group of women. McCloskey and Mintz (2006) have carefully reviewed issues that must be considered in aiding the career development of Native American women. Clearly, the career development needs of women of color must receive more of our attention.

EXTERNAL BARRIERS TO EQUITY

Discrimination

The barrier of discrimination has long been discussed as crucial in women's attempt to attain equity in the workplace (see Fassinger,

2002a; Phillips & Imhoff, 1997). Although outright gender discrimination is against the law, informal discrimination continues to exist (Fitzgerald & Harmon, 2001). For example, although women may be allowed to enter a male-dominated workplace, it may be made clear to them, overtly or more subtly, that they are not welcome. Messages ranging from overt verbal harassment to simply being ignored and receiving no social support from colleagues can make a work environment very unpleasant, and less obvious forms of discrimination in pay, promotions, and perquisites of the job may exist as well (Fitzgerald & Harmon, 2001).

The importance of promotions is related to the continuing existence of the "glass ceiling," which refers to artificial barriers, based on attitudinal or organizational bias, that prevent some groups of people from advancing in an organization, and in particular keep only a very small number of women at top levels of management (Yoder, 1999). In 1995 the Department of Labor's Federal Glass Ceiling Commission concluded that there still existed a corporate ceiling, as evidenced by the fact that only 3–5 percent of senior corporate leadership positions were held by women, far fewer than their proportionate representation in the labor force. The commission reported that, although the notion of a "glass ceiling" implies subtlety, the ceiling for women of color is by no means subtle and is better depicted as a "concrete wall" (Federal Glass Ceiling Commission, 1995, pp. 68–69).

Another barrier to women in nontraditional careers is that of being a "token." First described by Kanter (1977), tokens are people who in gender or race (or both) constitute less than 15 percent of their work group. Tokens experience stress, social isolation, heightened visibility, and accusations of role violations ("you don't belong here"). Research on women of color who are double tokens, such as the African American women firefighters studied by Yoder and Aniakudo (1997) and the African American women police officers studied by Martin (1994), shows that these women faced insufficient instruction, coworker hostility, silence, overly close and punitive supervision, lack of support, and stereotyping—an unwavering message of exclusion and a hope that they would fail (Yoder & Aniakudo, 1997). These studies suggest that both race and gender are barriers to these women's satisfaction and success. As one African American firefighter put it, "being a black female—it was like two things needed to be proven" (Yoder & Aniakudo, 1997, p. 336).

Sexual Harassment

Sexual harassment also continues to be a major problem in the workplace, with serious consequences for both women and organizations. Sexual harassment is described in detail by authors such as

Fitzgerald (1993, 2003); Koss, Goodman, Browne, Fitzgerald, Keita, and Russo (1994); Mackinnon and Siegel (2003); and Norton (2002). Research now distinguishes two categories of sexual harassment, "quid pro quo" harassment and "hostile environment" harassment. Quid pro quo harassment refers to situations in which an employee is asked to give in to a supervisor's sexual demands in exchange for pay, a promotion, or continued employment, with the implied threat of loss of raise or promotion, or even loss of employment, if the employee refuses to comply. Hostile environment harassment refers to instances where the employee is subject to sexual innuendo, sexist or sexually oriented comments, physical touching, or sexually oriented posters or cartoons placed in the work area. The issue here is making women workers "sex objects" at work. Women are there to make a living and advance their careers, and sexual harassment can seriously interfere with those aims.

Although sexual harassment is not limited to men harassing women—women can harass men, and same-sex harassment can also occur—the vast majority (90%) of complaints involve men harassing women. On the basis of large-scale surveys of working women, Fitzgerald (1993) estimated that one of every two will be harassed during their work lives. Gutek (1985) reported even greater likelihoods of harassment for Hispanic and African American women. Although responses to sexual harassment are beyond the scope of this chapter, suffice it to say that this is a major barrier to women's equity in the workplace. Research has shown decreases in job satisfaction and organizational commitment, job withdrawal, increased symptoms of anxiety and depression, and higher levels of stress-related illness as responses to sexual harassment (Norton, 2002). Clearly these are mental health as well as economic issues and can seriously compromise job performance and job satisfaction.

Multiple Roles

Another of the persistent conditions affecting women's equity in the workplace, and their job satisfaction, is that, while their workforce participation has increased dramatically, their work at home has not decreased. Although multiple roles are in general positive for mental health, the picture becomes more complex when women are expected to shoulder the major burden of homemaking and child care. As well stated by Barnett and Hyde (2001), "there are upper limits to the benefits of multiple roles" (p. 789) when the number of roles becomes too great or the demands of one role become excessive—this would seem to apply to the case where the woman is now expected to cope with two full-time jobs, one outside and the other inside the home. Instead of "having it all," women are "doing it all" (Fitzgerald & Harmon, 2001, p. 215).

Research suggests that few men view parenting and homemaking as their responsibility—they are primarily available to "help out" (Farmer, 1997). Yoder (1999) summarized data showing that, on average, women in married couples do 33 hours of household chores weekly, compared to 14 for their husbands. This constitutes 70 percent of the workload for women and 30 percent for men—not including child care. Counting child care, these women are working a full-time job at home, in addition to what they are doing at their place of employment. These figures describe African American and Latina/Latino couples as well. Supreme Court Justice Ruth Bader Ginsburg noted that there can be no equity in the workplace until men assume equal sharing of homemaking and parenting roles (Farmer, 1997).

A related problem is the lack of organizational structures and support systems for employees with families. Subsidized child or elder care, paid family leave, flextime, job sharing, and telecommuting can greatly ease the burdens of managing home, family, and careers, burdens carried mostly by women (Fitzgerald & Harmon, 2001). The United States is still the only developed country in the world without a national childcare policy nor a systematic means of addressing the serious problems of elder care (Fitzgerald & Harmon, 2001).

SUPPORTS TO CAREER ACHIEVEMENT AND SATISFACTION

A useful framework for considering supports to women's career development has come from Fassinger's (2002b) series of studies on diverse groups of eminent women. Using qualitative methodologies and modified grounded theory (Strauss & Corbin, 1998), they have studied eminent African American and Caucasian women (Richie, Fassinger, Lenn, Johnson, Prosser, & Robinson, 1997), Asian American women (Prosser, Chopra, & Fassinger, 1998), lesbians (Hollingsworth, Tomlinson, & Fassinger, 1997), Latinas (Gomez et al., 2001), and women with physical and sensory disabilities (Noonan, Gallor, Hensler-McGinnis, Fassinger, Wang, & Goodman, 2004). They summarize findings of the supports that enabled these women to persist and succeed in spite of extensive experience with oppression with the words "persistence, connection, and passion" (Richie et al., 1997). These might also be viewed as strengths of women that carry them through or enable them to surmount the barriers they confront.

Persistence is critical to succeeding in the face of obstacles, and strong self-efficacy expectations for one's career, self-esteem, and sense of purpose are essential to persistence. The characteristics of instrumentality discussed previously—the sense of being in control of one's own life and destiny, of being agentic, able to act on one's own behalf—are also important to persistence.

Related to both self-efficacy and instrumentality is "coping efficacy," which plays an increasingly important role in Lent, Brown, and

Hackett's (1994, 2000) social cognitive career theory. In their words, "When confronted with adverse contextual conditions, persons with a strong sense of coping efficacy (beliefs regarding one's capabilities to negotiate particular environmental obstacles) may be more likely to persevere toward their goals" (Lent et al., 2000, p. 76). Gomez et al. (2001) found coping strategies especially important to their highly achieving Latinas, as did Richie et al. (1997) with highly achieving African Americans and white women. These strategies include

> tenacity and persistence; flexibility; creativity; reframing and redefining challenges, barriers, or mistakes; maintaining a balanced perspective in understanding how racism and sexism may affect career-related behaviors; developing support networks congruent with personal style, values, and culture; and developing bicultural skills where applicable. (Gomez et al., 2001, p. 298)

Connection refers to the essential part played by familial and peer/ friend support in facilitating persistence in one's goals. There is ample literature documenting the importance of family, including spouse and children, friends both at work and outside of work, and mentors. This importance has been shown for women of color as well as for white women. As a few examples, Gilbert (1994) and Gomez et al. (2001) discussed the crucial role of a supportive spouse in managing both career and home/family responsibilities. Gomez et al. (2001) reported that supportive families were crucial in maintaining women's career commitment after the birth of children. Richie et al. (1997) emphasized the importance of interconnectedness with others in the continuing high achievement of both African American and white women. Connection may also be facilitated by a feminist orientation, which gives women a sense of community beyond themselves. Feminist orientation has consistently been shown to be a facilitative factor in women's career achievements (Fassinger, 1990).

Finally, *passion* is, for some women, loving what they do; for others, it's feeling that they have made a difference in the world (Gomez et al., 2001). For many women, this is the sense of a life's "calling." Although not all people, women or men, are lucky enough to have such a passion in their work, helping people find careers about which they can feel passionate should be one of the goals of the psychologist.

IMPLICATIONS FOR INTERVENTIONS

The preceding sections of this chapter have emphasized the importance to women of successful career development, as well as success in their personal relationships, yet have also outlined ways in which women continue to lag behind men in both the variety of career options they consider and the subsequent success in these pursuits. Psychologists and educators may be able to help women to close these gaps. In general, suggestions for interventions can be divided into those facilitating the career choice process and those enabling the career adjustment process.

Counseling for Career Choice

Because a sexist society and stereotypic socialization have often stood in the way of women's pursuit of a full range of career options, research supports overt attempts to restore options that society has taken away. In other words, psychologists need to remain aware of the possible impact of sexism and stereotyping in concert with null environments and to accept the role of active options restorers.

The following guidelines for assisting women in the process of making educational and career decisions are derived from the literature reviewed in the first part of this chapter. They can be used by psychologists, counselors, educators, parents, and those in positions to influence public policy (see Fassinger, in press).

1. Encourage high-quality and extensive education and training. Do not overlook the importance of technical schools, two-year and community colleges, and the military for excellent training and education.
2. Adopt the rule that one cannot take too much math. Encourage young women to stay in math coursework as long as possible. Math background opens options and prevents others from being eliminated by default.
3. When in doubt, stress decisions that eliminate the fewest options, such as staying in school and continuing in math.
4. Serve as a catalyst for the creation of new learning experiences for women, so that they can fully develop all their capabilities, including those not reinforced by traditional gender stereotyping.
5. Explore a woman's outcome expectations and barriers to her goal pursuits, with the idea of helping her to develop coping mechanisms, coping self-efficacy, and barrier-surmounting sources of social support.
6. Remember that all it takes is one supportive psychologist, counselor, teacher, or parent to enrich the null environment.
7. Assess the role of culture and ethnicity in the client's career planning. Help her to make decisions that, as far as possible, integrate her individual and cultural values.
8. Integrate facilitative psychological and career theories as appropriate in counseling and educational practice.

Using Theories to Guide Practice

Several major theories of career development have particular relevance to the career choice process of women. The first of these is social cognitive theory, based originally on the theory of Albert Bandura (1997). This theory supports the idea of continuing growth through one's lifetime as a result of new learning experiences and new ideas. Below are more detailed suggestions for the uses of social cognitive and trait-factor theories in career choice counseling with women.

Social Cognitive Theory

It is important to informally or formally assess a woman's self-efficacy beliefs for career fields. Informal assessment may include general questions regarding her beliefs in her competence in domains relevant to her career decision making, performance, or advancement. For a young woman, questions might include:

- "What would you ideally like to do for a career?"
- "What is holding you back from your ideal?"
- "What career fantasies have you had and what keeps you from pursuing them?"
- "What careers would you pursue if you thought you could do *anything?*"

The purpose of these questions is to identify self-imposed limits on what she can do. It may be that these are realistic limits if the girl or woman does not actually have the aptitude for that area, but the real contribution of self-efficacy is that it focuses our attention on people who are unrealistically underestimating their capabilities. The evidence is clear that women are particularly prone to underestimate their capabilities and must accordingly have these beliefs challenged. Further probing when a young woman reports herself unable to master a specific domain of behavior should focus on the quality of her background experiences—if she dropped out of math in 10th grade because "math was for boys," then it is no wonder she lacks confidence and competence in math.

Low self-efficacy for career tasks and fields, because it leads to avoidance, can become a self-fulfilling prophecy—we avoid what we fear, so we don't learn it and never become good at it, thereby verifying our perceptions of ourselves as incompetent. Someone, perhaps a psychologist, needs to help her break this vicious circle. The psychologist should refuse to accept "I can't" for an answer unless and until the client has made a serious attempt to learn the subject and master it.

In addition to the informal assessment of self-efficacy, there is now a large number of inventories assessing self-efficacy with respect to career behaviors (see Betz & Hackett, 2006). Measures of career-decision self-efficacy (Betz, Klein, & Taylor, 1995), math self-efficacy (Lopez, Lent, Brown, & Gore, 1997), career-search self-efficacy (Solberg et al., 1994), self-efficacy for the Holland themes (Betz, Harmon, & Borgen,

1996), and self-efficacy with respect to 28 basic domains of vocational activity such as Leadership, Writing, Science, Public Speaking, and Using Technology (the Career Confidence Inventory; Borgen & Betz, 2007) are available.

Self-efficacy measures may also be used jointly with parallel vocational interest measures (Betz & Rottinghaus, 2006; Betz & Wolfe, 2005). For example, the General Occupational Themes of the Strong Interest Inventory, measuring the resemblance of the client to each of Holland's six personality types, now has parallel self-efficacy measures for the six types in the Skills Confidence Inventory (Betz et al., 1996; Betz & Rottinghaus, 2006).

Using these two measures jointly, we look for themes on which the client has both high interests and high self-efficacy—these themes represent good possibilities for career exploration. However, areas of high interest but lower efficacy can still be options if efficacy can be increased through interventions based on Bandura's (1997) theory (see Brown & Lent, 1996, for some other suggestions). Self-efficacy interventions are based on Bandura's four sources of efficacy information and should therefore ideally include performance accomplishments, vicarious learning or modeling, managing anxiety, and providing support and encouragement.

In planning for successful performance accomplishments, opportunities should be sought where success is at first virtually ensured, and only after some successful experiences (allowing a moderate degree of self-efficacy to be established) should more difficult challenges be faced. Community or technical colleges offering entry-level or remedial courses, adult education programs, and programmed-learning materials may be good sources for such experiences.

In using modeling, the counselor would need to locate people who have succeeded in the field in which the client lacks self-efficacy. It is helpful, though not essential, if these models are the same race and gender as the individual, and this may be especially true if the domain of behavior is nontraditional for that person's gender. For example, a woman teaching automobile maintenance and repair or carpentry to other women will provide helpful modeling influences because these are traditionally male domains. Similarly, a man teaching parenting to young men would provide the additional benefit of modeling a nontraditional competency. Models can be in person, on film, on television, in books, or via other media. For example, a book on the life of a female astronaut or scientist could provide useful modeling for a young girl considering these fields.

The third component of an efficacy-enhancing intervention is anxiety management. Learning new things may be associated with anxiety, particularly if these are gender-nontraditional domains. If a domain such as math has been associated with males, and if a woman has internalized the message "Girls can't do math," anxiety will likely accompany new learning efforts. Thus teaching anxiety management techniques may also be appropriate. Relaxation training and learning to consciously focus self-talk on the task at hand rather than on the self can be helpful.

Finally, the psychologist or educator can serve as the woman's "cheerleader" as she tries new things. This role includes generally encouraging her that she *can* do it, and more specifically reinforcing her efforts as she tries new things. Helping her set goals, reinforcing her when she achieves them, and helping her to try again when she has temporarily faltered are all important. Finally, the psychologist can counter beliefs (such as "Girls can't do math") that are getting in her way.

In addition to assessing self-efficacy expectations, outcome expectations should also be assessed. This is especially true for women of color, who may expect more barriers to their success than white women have. Similarly, women wishing to pursue traditionally male-dominated occupations may have concerns about the extent to which their efforts will lead to desired rewards and outcomes. Although these concerns may be realistic, helping the woman to consider coping strategies and learn about typical organizational/institutional grievance procedures may be helpful. Assertiveness training, learning to seek social support, and externalizing rather than internalizing the causes of discrimination and harassment may be useful.

Using the Matching (Trait-Factor) Model

Trait-factor theories suggest that we should help young women to fully develop their abilities, talents, and interests. Structured methods of ability and interest assessment have always been a useful part of the assessment of these individuals, but there are a few additional considerations, as well.

First, where possible, use within-gender norms to highlight directions in which a female client has developed in spite of gender-role socialization. Many aptitude and interest measures now provide same-sex norms (usually within-gender percentiles). For example, the Armed Services Vocational Aptitude Battery and the Differential Aptitude Test, two of the most widely used multiple-aptitude batteries in career counseling with high school students, both provide within-gender percentiles, as well as combined group standard scores (see Walsh & Betz, 2001) Most vocational interest inventories—for example, the Strong Interest Inventory—also now provide within-gender norms.

As with self-efficacy expectations, we should see the woman as a "work in progress," not a finished product. New learning experiences and opportunities can "open the doors" in terms of capabilities and interests, and counselors should always ask questions enabling them to assess the relative richness versus poverty of a woman's previous educational and experiential background. If she has not had a chance to learn it, then assume she can learn to do it, help her find new learning opportunities, and help convince *her* that she can do it.

Career Education and Expanding Options

Farmer (1997) noted the crucial importance of career education in the schools. Lack of guidance about how to prepare for higher education and occupations, and how to choose a career in the first place, characterize many of our schools. Farmer made suggestions for career education that can increase sex equity. For example, girls might be introduced to a wider range of careers and urged to gain information on those in science and engineering. The National Science Foundation funds Project WISE (Brookhaven National Laboratory, Upton, New York), which supports programs that involve high school women in science activities. The project produces a booklet called "The Future Is Yours—Get Ready," which describes 250 different occupations in the sciences and engineering (cf. Farmer, 1997). The Girl Scouts of America sponsors a program called Bridging the Gap, designed to help girls become involved in science and engineering (cf. Farmer, 1997). Many colleges and universities also now have programs to assist women enrolled in colleges of engineering (Fassinger & Asay, 2006). Kerr's (1997; Kerr et al., 2005) developed programs to encourage and support mathematically and scientifically talented women at Arizona State University and have made extensive and widely applicable resources available. Psychologists should be aware of these resources and encourage talented girls and women to study them.

Counseling for Career Achievement and Satisfaction

For employed women, concerns usually fall in the areas of success/performance and satisfaction. As was indicated previously, discrimination, sexual harassment, tokenism, and lack of support represent a few barriers to women's career success and satisfaction. Additionally, the overload that may be experienced from two full-time jobs, rather than one, for women taking full responsibility for family and housework can be a major cause of decrements in *both* performance and satisfaction. A few general guidelines may be useful.

1. Help women at work develop support systems.
2. Help change the system, or help young women and men change the system, as it pertains to flexible work schedules and family leave policies (which ideally allow leave for adoption as well as childbearing and for elder care, and which assume that men are as willing to be responsible for those they love as are women).

3. Help token women (especially women of color) find support, often by broadening the net that is cast to find support. For example, the lone woman faculty member in chemistry (see Fassinger, in press) may find support in a group consisting of all the faculty women in the College of Sciences.
4. Teach women to expect full participation in homemaking and childrearing from their husbands or partners. Teach men that it is their responsibility, and also to their benefit, to participate fully in home and family life and work.
5. Help women develop effective cognitive and behavioral coping strategies, as discussed earlier in the section on supports for career achievement and satisfaction.

For an adult woman considering career change or advancement, we should help her to explore areas of behavior where she feels her skills are holding her back or preventing her from pursuing desired options. In many fields, technical expertise is necessary to, but not sufficient for, the pursuit of managerial or supervisory roles—we know that women lack seriously in technical training and that this lack limits their advancement possibilities (American Association of University Women, 2002; U.S. Department of Education, 2000). If she wishes to make such a move, a woman's self-efficacy beliefs regarding her managerial/leadership skills may be highly relevant to her perceived options. Another assessment question might be, "What new skills would increase your options or satisfaction, and what is stopping you from developing these new skills?" In many cases, the counselor will hear perceived self-efficacy—self-doubts about competence and ability to move in a new direction—and should be prepared to help a woman with such self-doubts to appraise accurately the competencies and abilities she feels she is lacking.

There also may be cases where a woman is in an occupation with poor fit for her abilities or interests. In such cases, "going back to the beginning"—doing a comprehensive assessment of her abilities, interests, values, and self-perceptions may be the best place to start.

Organizational and Structural Change

We in psychology and counseling also have a responsibility to work for organizational, legal, and societal changes that will reduce sexism, stereotyping, discrimination, and harassment and create more flexible and "family-friendly" workplaces (Meara, 1997). In focusing on women's career development and what is needed in order to facilitate it, Harmon (1997) also noted that we may have shortchanged the other side of the issue—that is, how to facilitate men's development in homemaking and childrearing roles. For example, as we counselors provide support for women's working and help them gain self-efficacy for non-traditional careers, we should also support men's pursuits of nurturing roles and help them gain self-efficacy with respect to nurturing and multiple-role management. Gilbert (1994) and Harmon (1997) both suggest that it is time to develop theories that conceptualize career development and family life in a more interactive way. Such theory development would hopefully increase the satisfaction and well-being of both women and men in multiple life roles.

CONCLUSION

In summary, although women have made significant progress in their attempts to fulfill their talents and interests and to achieve equity and satisfaction in their work, there remain many barriers and inequities that continue to demand our attention. These barriers and inequities can be addressed at many levels—with the individual, in institutions such as school and colleges, in business and military organizations, and through legal, political, and societal change. As well, continuing research and study designed to examine the dynamics of choice, success and satisfaction, and the mechanisms of positive change are needed.

REFERENCES

Ali, S. R., Lewis, S. Z., & Sandal, R. (2006). Career counseling for Asian women. In W. B. Walsh & M. J. Heppner (Eds.), *Handbook of career counseling with women* (2nd ed.; pp. 241–270). Mahwah, NJ: Erlbaum.

American Association of University Women (1992). *The AAUW Report: How schools shortchange girls.* Washington, DC: American Association of University Women.

American Association of University Women (1999). *Gender gaps: Where schools still fail our children.* New York: Marlowe.

American Association of University Women (2002). *Title IX at 30: Report card on gender equity.* Washington, DC: American Association of University Women.

Arbona, C., & Novy, D. M. (1991). Career aspirations and the expectations of black, Mexican American, and white students. *Career Development Quarterly, 39,* 231–239.

Arnold, K. D. (1995). *Lives of promise: What becomes of high school valedictorians.* San Francisco: Jossey-Bass.

Bandura, A. (1977). Self-efficacy: Toward a unifying theory of behavioral change. *Psychological Review, 84,* 191–215.

Bandura, A. (1997). *Self-efficacy: The exercise of control.* New York: W. H. Freeman.

Barnett, R. C., & Hyde, J. S. (2001). Women, men, work, and family: An expansionist theory. *American Psychologist, 56,* 781–796.

Beale, F. (1970). Double jeopardy: To be black and female. In T. Cade (Ed.), *The black woman: An anthology* (pp. 90–100). New York: New American Library.

Bem, S. & Bem, D. J. (1976). Case study of a non-conscious ideology: Training the woman to know her place. In S. Cox (Ed.), *Female psychology* (pp. 180–191). Chicago: Science Research Associates.

Bernard, J. (1971). The paradox of the happy marriage. In V. Gornick & B. K. Moran (Eds.), *Women in sexist society* (pp. 145–162). New York: Mentor.

Betz, N. E. (1989). The null environment and women's career development. *Counseling Psychologist, 17,* 136–144.

Betz, N. E. (1994). Basic issues and concepts in career counseling for women. In W. B. Walsh & S. H. Osipow (Eds.), *Career counseling for women* (pp. 1–47). Hillsdale, NJ: Erlbaum.

Betz, N. E. (2002). Women's career development: Weaving personal themes and theoretical constructs. *Counseling Psychologist, 30,* 467–481.

Betz, N. E., Borgen, F., Rottinghaus, P., Paulsen, A., Halper, C., & Harmon, L. W. (2003). The Expanded Skills Confidence Inventory. *Journal of Vocational Behavior, 62,* 76–100.

Betz, N. E., & Fitzgerald, L. F. (1987). *The career psychology of women*. New York: Academic Press.

Betz, N. E., Harmon, L., & Borgen, F. (1996). The relationships of self-efficacy for the Holland themes to gender, occupational group membership, and vocational interests. *Journal of Counseling Psychology, 43,* 90–98.

Betz, N. E., & Hackett, G. (1981). The relationship of career-related self-efficacy expectations to perceived career options in college women and men. *Journal of Counseling Psychology, 28,* 399–410.

Betz, N. E., & Hackett, G. (1983). The relationship of mathematics self-efficacy expectations to the selection of science-based college majors. *Journal of Vocational Behavior, 23,* 328–345.

Betz, N. E., & Hackett, G. (1997). Applications of self-efficacy theory to the career development of women. *Journal of Career Assessment, 5,* 383–402.

Betz, N. E., & Hackett, G. (2006). Career self-efficacy theory: Back to the future. *Journal of Career Assessment, 14,* 3–11.

Betz, N. E., Klein, K., & Taylor, K. (1996). Evaluation of a short form of the Career Decision-Making Self-Efficacy scale. *Journal of Career Assessment, 4,* 47–57.

Betz, N. E., & Rottinghaus, P. (2006). Current research on parallel measures of interests and confidence for basic domains of vocational activity. *Journal of Career Assessment, 14,* 56–76

Betz, N. E., & Wolfe, J. (2005). Measuring confidence for basic domains of vocational activity in high school students. *Journal of Career Assessment, 13,* 251–270.

Bingham, R., Ward, C. M., & Butler, M. M. (2006). Career counseling with African American women. In W. B. Walsh & M. J. Heppner (Eds.), *Handbook of career counseling with women* (2nd ed.; pp. 219–240). Mahwah, NJ: Erlbaum.

Borgen, F., & Betz, N. (2007). Relating confidence to the healthy personality: The relationship of the Career Confidence Inventory and the Healthy Personality Inventory. *Journal of Career Assessment, 15.*

Borow, H. (Ed.). (1964). *Man in a world at work.* Boston: Houghton Mifflin.

Bowman, S. L. (1998). Minority women and career adjustment. *Journal of Career Assessment, 6,* 417–431.

Brody, J. E. (1997). Girls and puberty: The crisis years. *New York Times*, November 4, p. B8.

Brown, S., & Lent, R. (1996). A social cognitive framework for career choice counseling. *Career Development Quarterly, 44*, 354–366.

Byars, A., & Hackett, G. (1998). Applications of social cognitive theory to the career development of women of color. *Applied and Preventive Psychology, 7*, 266–267.

Cardoza, D. (1991). College attendance and persistence among Hispanic women: An examination of some contributing factors. *Sex Roles, 24*, 133–147.

Chipman, S. F., & Wilson, D. M. (1985). Understanding mathematics course enrollment and mathematics achievement: A synthesis of the research. In S. F. Chipman, L. R. Brush, & D. M. Wilson (Eds.), *Women and mathematics: Balancing the equation* (pp. 275–328). Hillsdale, NJ: Erlbaum.

Colman, P. (1995). *Rosie the Riveter: Women working on the home front in World War II*. New York: Random House.

Crosby, F. J. (1991). *Juggling: The unexpected advantages of balancing home and family*. New York: Free Press.

Dawis, R. V. (1992). The individual differences tradition in counseling psychology. *Journal of Counseling Psychology, 39*, 7–19.

Dawis, R. V. (2000). The person environment tradition in counseling psychology. In W. E. Martin Jr. & L. Swartz-Kustad (Eds.), *Person environment psychology and mental health* (pp. 91–111). Mahwah, NJ: Erlbaum.

DeVaney, S. B., & Hughey, A. W. (2000). Career development of ethnic minority students. In D. A. Luzzo (Ed.), *Career counseling with college students* (pp. 233–252). Washington, DC: American Psychological Association.

Donnay, D. A. C., Morris, M., Schaubhut, N., & Thompson, R. (2005). *Strong Interest Inventory manual: Research, development, and strategies for interpretation*. Mountain View, CA: CPP.

Eccles, J. (1987). Gender roles and women's achievement-related decisions. *Psychology of Women Quarterly, 11*, 135–172.

Eccles, J. S., & Jacobs, J. (1986). Social forces shape math participation. *Signs, 11*, 367–380.

Ehrhart, J. K., & Sandler, B. R. (1987). *Looking for more than a few good women in traditionally male fields*. Washington, DC: Project on the Status and Education of Women.

Erickson, E. (1950). *Childhood and society*. New York: Norton.

Farmer, H. S. (1976). What inhibits achievement and career motivation in women? *Counseling Psychologist, 6*, 12–14.

Farmer, H. S. (1997). *Diversity and women's career development*. Thousand Oaks, CA: Sage.

Farmer, H. S. (2006). History of career counseling for women. In W. B. Walsh & M. J. Heppner (Eds.), *Handbook of career counseling with women* (2nd ed.; pp. 1–44). Mahwah, NJ: Erlbaum.

Fassinger, R. E. (1990). Causal models of women's career development in two samples of college women. *Journal of Vocational Behavior, 36*, 225–240.

Fassinger, R. E. (2002a). Hitting the ceiling: Gendered barriers to occupational entry, advancement, and achievement. In L. Diamant & J. Lee (Eds.), *The psychology of sex, gender, and jobs* (pp. 21–46). Westport, CT: Praeger.

Fassinger, R. E. (2002b). Honoring women's diversity: A new, inclusive theory of career development. Paper presented at the meeting of the American Psychological Association, Chicago, August.

Fassinger, R. E., & Asay, P. A. (2006). Career counseling for women in science, technology, engineering, and mathematics fields. In W. B. Walsh & M. J. Heppner (Eds.), *Handbook of career counseling with women* (2nd ed.; pp. 427–452). Mahwah, NJ: Erlbaum.

Federal Glass Ceiling Commission. (1995). *Report on the glass ceiling for women.* Washington, DC: U.S. Department of Labor.

Fennema, E., Carpenter, T., Jacobs, V., Franke, M., & Levi, L. (1998). A longitudinal study of gender differences in young children's mathematical thinking. *Educational Researcher, 27,* 6D11. *Journal for Research in Mathematics Education, 27,* 403–434.

Fisher, T. A., & Padmawidjaja, L. (1999). Parental influences on career development perceived by African American and Mexican American college students. *Journal of Multicultural Counseling and Development, 27,* 136–152.

Fitzgerald, L. F. (1993). Sexual harassment: Violence against women in the workplace. *American Psychologist, 48,* 1070–1076.

Fitzgerald, L. F. (2003). Sexual harassment and social justice: Reflections on the distance yet to go. *American Psychologist, 58,* 915–924.

Fitzgerald, L. F., Fassinger, R. E., & Betz, N. (1995). Theoretical advances in the study of women's career development. In W. B. Walsh & S. H. Osipow (Eds.), *Handbook of vocational psychology* (2nd ed.; pp. 67–110). Mahwah, NJ: Erlbaum.

Fitzgerald, L. F., & Harmon, L. W. (2001). Women's career development: A postmodern update. In F. L. T. Leong & A. Barak (Eds.), *Contemporary models in vocational psychology* (pp. 207–230). Mahwah, NJ: Erlbaum.

Flores, L., Navarro, R., & Ojeda, L. (2006). Career counseling with Latinas. In W. B. Walsh & M. J. Heppner (Eds.), *Handbook of career counseling with women* (2nd ed.; pp. 271–314). Mahwah, NJ: Erlbaum.

Freeman, J. (1979). How to discriminate against women without really trying. In J. Freeman (Ed.), *Women: A feminist perspective* (2nd ed.; pp. 217–232). Palo Alto, CA: Mayfield.

Gerson, K. (1986). *Hard choices: How women decide about work, career, and motherhood.* Berkeley: University of California Press.

Gilbert, L. (1994). Curent perspectives on dual career families. *Current Directions in Psychological Science, 3,* 101–104.

Gilbert, L. A. (2002). Changing roles of work and family. Paper presented at the meeting of the American Psychological Association, Chicago, August.

Gilbert, L. A., & Kearney, L. K. (2006). Sex, gender, and dual earner families. In W. B. Walsh & M. J. Heppner (Eds.), *Handbook of career counseling with women* (2nd ed.; pp. 193–218). Mahwah, NJ: Erlbaum.

Gomez, M. J., Fassinger, R. E., Prosser, J., Cooke, K., Mejia, B., & Luna, J. (2001). Voices abriendo caminos (Voices forging paths): A qualitative study of the career development of notable Latinas. *Journal of Counseling Psychology, 48,* 286–300.

Gottfredson, L. S. (1981). Circumscription and compromise: A development theory of occupational aspirations. *Journal of Counseling Psychology, 28,* 545–579.

Greenberger, E., & O'Neil, R. (1993). Spouse, parent, worker: Role commitments and role-related experiences in the construction of adults' well-being. *Developmental Psychology, 29,* 181–197.

Gutek, B. (1985). *Sex and the workplace.* San Francisco: Jossey-Bass.

Hackett, G., Exposito, D., & O'Halloran, M. S. (1989). The relationship of role model influences to the career salience and educational and career plans of college women. *Journal of Vocational Behavior, 35,* 164–180.

Harmon, L. W. (1977). Career counseling of women. In E. Rawlings & D. Carter (Eds.), *Psychotherapy for women.* Springfield, IL: Charles C. Thomas.

Harmon, L. W. (1997). Do gender differences necessitate separate career development theories and measures? *Journal of Career Assessment, 5,* 463–470.

Harvey, J. H., & Pauwels, B. G. (1999). Recent developments in close relationships. *Directions in Psychological Science, 8,* 93–95.

Holland, D. C., & Eisenhart, M. A. (1990). *Educated in romance: Women, achievement, and college culture.* Chicago: University of Chicago Press.

Holland, J. L. (1997). *Making vocational choices: A theory of vocational personalities and work environments* (3rd ed.). Odessa, FL: Psychological Assessment Resources.

Hollingsworth, M. A., Tomlinson, M. J., & Fassinger, R.E. (1997). Working it "out": Career development among prominent lesbian women. Paper presented at the meeting of the American Psychological Association, Chicago, August.

Juntunen, C. L., Barraclough, D. J., Broneck, C. L. Seibel, G. A., Winlow, S. A., & Morin, P. M. (2001). American Indian perspectives on the career journey. *Journal of Counseling Psychology, 48,* 274–285.

Kanter, R. M. (1977). *Men and women of the corporation.* New York: Basic Books.

Kerr, B. (1997). *Smart girls: A new psychology of girls, women, and giftedness.* Scottsdale, AZ: Gifted Psychology Press.

Kerr, B., Colangelo, N., & Gaeth, J. (1988). Gifted adolescents' attitudes toward their giftedness. *Gifted Child Quarterly, 32,* 245–247.

Kerr, B., Foley-Nicpon, M., & Zapata, A. L. (2005). In B. Kerr, S. Kurpius, & A. Harkins (Eds.). (2005). *Handbook for counseling girls and women.* Vol. 2, *Talent development* (pp. 15–39). Mesa, AZ: Nueva Science Press.

Kitano, M. K., & Perkins, C. O. (1996). International gifted women: Developing a critical resource. *Roeper Review, 19,* 24–30.

Koss, M. P., Goodman, L. A., Browne, A., Fitzgerald, L. F., Keita, G. P., & Russo, N. F. (1994). *No safe haven: Male violence against women.* Washington, DC: American Psychological Association.

Kuh, C. V. (1998). Data on women doctoral-level scientists and universities. Paper presented at National Invitational Conference on Women in Research Universities, Harvard University and Radcliffe College.

Lent, R. W., Brown, S. D., & Hackett, G. (1994). Toward a unifying social cognitive theory of career and academic interest, choice, and performance. *Journal of Vocational Behavior, 45,* 79–122.

Lent, R. W., Brown, S. D., & Hackett, G. (2000). Contextual supports and barriers to career choice: A social cognitive analysis. *Journal of Counseling Psychology, 47,* 36–59.

Lent, R. W., Brown, S. D., & Larkin, K. (1984). Relation of self-efficacy expectations to academic achievement and persistence. *Journal of Counseling Psychology, 31,* 356–362.

Lent, R. W., Brown, S. D., & Larkin, K. (1986). Self-efficacy in the prediction of academic success and perceived career options. *Journal of Counseling Psychology, 33,* 265–269.

Leppel, K. (2001). The impact of major on college persistence among freshmen. *Higher Education, 41,* 327–342.

Lopez, F. G., Lent, R. W., Brown, S. D., & Gore, P. A., Jr. (1997). Role of social-cognitive expectations in high school student's mathematics-related interest and performance. *Journal of Counseling Psychology, 44,* 44–52.

Lunneborg, P. (1979). Service vs. technical interest—Biggest sex difference of all? *Vocational Guidance Quarterly, 28,* 146–153.

MacKinnon, C., & Siegel, R. B. (Eds.) (2003). *Directions in sexual harassment law.* New Haven, CT: Yale University Press.

Marks, S., & MacDermid, S. M. (1996). Multiple roles and the self: A theory of role balance. *Journal of Marriage and the Family, 58,* 417–432.

Martin, S. E. (1994). "Outsider within" the station house: The impact of race and gender on black women police. *Social Problems, 41,* 383–400.

McColskey, C., & Mintz, L. (2006). A culturally oriented approach for career counseling with Native American women. In W. B. Walsh & M. J. Heppner (Eds.), *Handbook of career counseling with women* (2nd ed.; pp. 315–350). Mahwah, NJ: Erlbaum.

Meara, N. M. (1997). Changing the structure of work. *Journal of Career Assessment, 5,* 471–474.

National Center for Education Statistics (2004). *The nation's report card: National assessment of educational progress.* Department of Education. Washington, DC: GPO.

Nelson, T. E., Acke, M., & Manis, M. (1996). Irrepressible stereotypes. *Journal of Experimental Social Psychology, 32,* 13–38.

Noonan, B. M., Gallor, S. M., Hensler-McGinnis, N., Fassinger, R. E., Wang, S., & Goodman, J. (2004). Challenge and success: A qualitative study of the career development of highly achieving women with physical and sensory disabilities. *Journal of Counseling Psychology, 51,* 68–80.

Norton, S. (2002). Women exposed: Sexual harassment and female vulnerability. In L. Diamant & J. Lee (Eds.), *The psychology of sex, gender, and jobs: Issues and solutions* (pp. 82–103). Westport, CT: Praeger.

Pajares, F. (1996). Self-efficacy beliefs and mathematical problem-solving in gifted adolescents. *Contemporary Educational Psychology, 21,* 325–344.

Parsons, F. (1909). *Choosing a vocation.* Boston: Houghton Mifflin.

Pearson, C., Shavlik, D., & Touchton, J. (Eds.). (1988). *Prospectus for educating the majority: How women are changing higher education.* Washington, DC: American Council on Education.

Pearson, S. M., & Bieschke, K. (2001). Succeeding against the odds: An examination of familial influences on the career development of professional African American women. *Journal of Counseling Psychology, 48,* 301–309.

Phillips, S., & Imhoff, A. (1997). Women and career development: A decade of research. *Annual Review of Psychology, 48,* 31–59.

Prosser, J., Chopra, S., & Fassinger, R. E. (1998). *A qualitative study of careers of Asian American women.* Paper presented at the annual conference of the Association of Women in Psychology, Baltimore, March.

Reis, S. M., Callahan, C. M., & Goldsmith, D. (1996). Attitudes of adolescent gifted girls and boys toward education, achievement, and the future. In K. D. Arnold, K. D. Noble, & R. F. Subotnik (Eds.), *Remarkable women: Perspectives on female talent development* (pp. 209–224). Cresskill, NJ: Hampton Press.

Richie, B. S., Fassinger, R. E., Lenn, S. G., Johnson, J., Prosser, J., & Robinson, S. (1997). Persistence, connection, and passion: A qualitative study of the career development of highly achieving African-American-black and white women. *Journal of Counseling Psychology, 44,* 133–148.

Sadker, M., & Sadker, D. (1994). *Failing at fairness: How our schools cheat girls.* New York: Touchstone.

Sandler, B. R., & Hall, R. (1996). *The chilly classroom climate: A guide to improve the education of women.* Washington, DC: National Association for Women in Education.

Sears, P. S., & Barbie, A. H. (1977). Career and life satisfaction among Terman's gifted women. In J. C. Stanley, W. George, & C. Solano (Eds.), *The gifted and creative: Fifty-year perspective* (pp. 72–106). Baltimore: Johns Hopkins University Press.

Selkow, P. (1984). Effects of maternal employment on kindergarten and first-grade children's vocational aspirations. *Sex Roles, 11,* 677–690.

Sells, L. (1973). High school mathematics as the critical filter in the job market. In *Developing opportunities for minorities in graduate education.* Proceedings of the Conference on Minority Graduate Education, University of California, Berkeley.

Sells, L. (1982). Leverage of equal opportunity through mastery of mathematics. In S. M. Humphreys (Ed.), *Women and minorities in science* (pp. 7–26). Boulder, CO: Westview Press.

Shinar, E. H. (1975). Sexual stereotypes of occupations. *Journal of Vocational Behavior, 7,* 99–111.

Siegel, D., & Reis, S. M. (1998). Gender differences in teacher and student perceptions of gifted students' ability and effort. *Gifted Children Quarterly, 42,* 39–47.

Solberg, V. S. H., Good, G., & Nord, D. (1994). Career search efficacy: Ripe for intervention and applications. *Journal of Career Development, 21,* 63–72.

Spade, J., & Reese, C. (1991). We've come a long way, maybe: College students plans for work and family. *Sex Roles, 24,* 309–321.

Spelke, E. (2005). Sex differences in intrinsic aptitude for math and science: A critical review. *American Psychologist, 60,* 950–958.

Strauss, A. L., & Corbin, J. (1998). *Basics of qualitative research: Techniques and procedures for developing grounded theory* (2nd ed.). Newbury Park, CA: Sage.

Terman, L. M., & Oden, M. H. (1959). *Genetic studies of genius.* Vol. 5, *The gifted group at midlife.* Stanford, CA: Stanford University Press.

Tipping, L. (1997). Work and family roles: Finding a new equilibrium. In H. Farmer (Ed.), *Diversity and women's career development* (pp. 243–270). Thousand Oaks, CA: Sage.

Toibin, C. (2004). *The master.* New York: Scribner.

U.S. Bureau of Labor Statistics (2003). *Facts on women workers.* Washington, DC: U.S. Department of Labor, Bureau of Labor Statistics.

U.S. Bureau of Labor Statistics (2005). *Women in the labor force: A databook.* Washington, DC: U.S. Department of Labor, Bureau of Labor Statistics.

U.S. Department of Education. National Center for Education Statistics. (2000). *Vocational education in the United States.* Washington, DC: U.S. Department of Education.

U.S. Department of Labor. (2000). *Occupational outlook handbook.* Washington, DC: GPO.

Walsh, W. B., & Betz, N. E. (2001). *Tests and assessment.* Englewood Cliffs, NJ: Prentice Hall.

Weishaar, M. E., Green, G. J., & Craighead, L. W. (1981). Primary influences of initial vocational choices for college women. *Journal of Vocational Behavior, 34,* 289–298.

Wilke, J. R., Ferree, M. M., & Ratcliff, K. (1998). Gender and fairness: Marital satisfaction in two-earner couples. *Journal of Marriage and the Family, 60,* 577–594.

Wycott, S. E. M. (1996). Academic performance of Mexican American women: Sources of support that serve as motivating variables. *Journal of Multicultural Counseling and Development, 24,* 146–155.

Yoder, J. (1999). *Women and gender: Transforming psychology.* Upper Saddle River, NJ: Prentice Hall.

Yoder, J., & Aniakudo, P. (1997). "Outsider within" the firehouse. *Gender and Society, 11,* 324–341.

Zittleman, K., & Sadker, D. (2003). The unfinished gender revolution. *Educational Leadership, 60,* 59–63.

Index

About the Editors and Contributors

EDITORS

Florence L. Denmark, Ph.D., is the Robert Scott Pace Distinguished Research Professor at Pace University in New York, where she served as chair of the psychology department for 13 years. A social psychologist who has published extensively in the psychology of women and gender, she has long been an energetic force in advancing psychology internationally, particularly as it concerns the psychology of women and human rights.

Dr. Denmark served as the 88th president of the American Psychological Association in 1980 and has been an active member of many of its boards and committees, including the Council of Representatives and Board of Directors. She is a Fellow of 13 APA divisions and served as a president of APA Divisions 1, 35, and 52. In addition, she was president of the International Council of Psychologists, Eastern Psychological Association, New York State Psychological Association, and Psi Chi and a vice president of the New York Academy of Sciences.

Denmark has four honorary doctorates and is the recipient of many regional, national, and international awards, including the American Psychological Foundation's Gold Medal for Lifetime Achievement in the Public Interest and the Ernest Hilgard Award honoring Career Contribution of General Psychology. Dr. Denmark is currently an APA and an ICP NGO representative to the UN, and she continues to teach graduate courses at Pace University.

Michele A. Paludi, Ph.D., is the author or editor of 26 college textbooks and more than 140 scholarly articles and conference presentations on psychology of women, the psychology of gender, and sexual harassment and victimization. Her book *Ivory Power: Sexual Harassment on Campus* (1990) received the 1992 Myers Center Award for Outstanding Book on Human Rights in the United States.

Dr. Paludi served as chair of the U.S. Department of Education's Subpanel on the Prevention of Violence, Sexual Harassment, and Alcohol and Other Drug Problems in Higher Education. She was one of six scholars in the United States to be selected for this subpanel. She also was a consultant to and a member of former New York governor Mario Cuomo's Task Force on Sexual Harassment.

Dr. Paludi serves as an expert witness for court proceedings and administrative hearings on sexual harassment. She has had extensive experience in conducting training programs and investigations of sexual harassment and other EEO issues for businesses and educational institutions. In addition, Dr. Paludi has held faculty positions at Franklin & Marshall College, Kent State University, Hunter College, Union College, and Union Graduate College.

CONTRIBUTORS

Courtney E. Ahrens is an assistant professor in the psychology department at California State University, Long Beach. She completed her doctoral training in community psychology at the University of Illinois at Chicago. Dr. Ahrens's research focuses on violence against women, with a particular focus on the disclosure of sexual assault and community resources for survivors. She also works closely with local rape crisis centers and domestic violence agencies to help them evaluate their services and conduct prevention programs on campus. In addition to her community-based research, Dr. Ahrens also regularly teaches psychology of women, community psychology, and a specialized class on domestic violence.

Vidal Annan Jr. received his doctoral degree in experimental psychology from Rutgers University in 2000. After working for three years as a postdoctoral fellow conducting research in cognitive science, he became interested in the theory and treatment of mental disorders. To further his knowledge in this area, he enrolled in the clinical psychology respecialization program at Fairleigh Dickinson University. He is currently completing his third year in this program and is looking forward to beginning his clinical internship.

Julie R. Arseneau, M.A., is a doctoral candidate in counseling psychology at the University of Maryland, College Park. She completed Master of Arts and Master of Education degrees in psychological counseling at Teachers College–Columbia University. Her research interests include the social construction of gender and sexuality, popular beliefs about sexual orientation and gender identity, and the career development and experiences of women in nontraditional fields.

Kira Hudson Banks is an assistant professor of psychology at Illinois Wesleyan University. She received her B.A. from Mount Holyoke College and her M.A. and Ph.D. from the University of Michigan, where she was a Rackham Merit and Ford Foundation Fellow. A clinical psychologist by training, Dr. Banks teaches courses such as abnormal psychology, psychology of racism, and seminars on racial identity and intergroup dialogue. Her research and publications involve understanding the experience of discrimination and examining the development of social justice and civic engagement attitudes among students.

Erika Baron received her B.A. in psychology from the University of Michigan. She is pursuing her Psy.D. in school-clinical child psychology at Pace University in New York City. Her research interests include the effects of body image on female adolescent personality development, as well as gender issues in a cross-cultural perspective.

Nancy E. Betz received a Ph.D. in psychology from the University of Minnesota. She is professor of psychology at the Ohio State University. Dr. Betz has authored or coauthored more than 150 articles and chapters on the topics of the career development of women, applications of Bandura's self-efficacy theory to career exploration and decision making, and issues in the use of psychological tests with women. She is the coauthor of *The Career Psychology of Women* (with Louise Fitzgerald) and *Tests and Assessment* (with Bruce Walsh). She served for six years as the editor of the *Journal of Vocational Behavior* and currently serves on the editorial boards of several scholarly journals.

Alyson L. Burns-Glover is a professor of psychology at Pacific University, Forest Grove, Oregon. She earned her B.A. at California State University, Long Beach, in research psychology and her M.A. and Ph.D. in social/personality psychology at the University of California, Davis. Her research focuses on social identity theory, minority student academic achievement, and specifically the health and well-being of Native and local Hawaiians.

Linda Cambareri-Fernandez is a graduate of Pace University's School-Community, now School-Clinical, Child Psychology doctoral program. She is in private practice in New York City.

Donna Castañeda is an associate professor in the psychology department at San Diego State University–Imperial Valley Campus. She completed her B.A. in psychology at the University of Washington and her

M.A. and Ph.D. in social psychology at the University of California, Davis. Her research focuses on gender, ethnicity, and their relationship to physical and mental health. She has investigated the impact of close relationship factors in HIV sexual risk behavior, particularly among Latinas/os; the HIV/AIDS prevention needs of women factory workers in Mexico; the close relationship context and how it affects intimate partner violence; and the relationship between marital satisfaction and mental health among wives and husbands. Another area of interest is the role of structural factors, or aspects of service delivery systems, in the provision of health and mental health services to Latina/o communities.

Jean Lau Chin, Ed.D., ABPP, is professor and dean of the Derner Institute for Advanced Psychological Studies at Adelphi University in New York. Prior to her current position, she was systemwide dean of the California School of Professional Psychology at Alliant International University. Dr. Chin is a licensed psychologist with more than 35 years of clinical, educational, and management experience in health and mental health services. She has held the positions of president, CEO Services; regional director, Massachusetts Behavioral Health Partnership; executive director, South Cove Community Health Center; and codirector, Thom Child Guidance Clinic. She was also an associate professor at Boston University School of Medicine and assistant professor at Tufts University School of Medicine.

Dr. Chin has published extensively, with nine books and more than 200 presentations in the areas of culturally competent service delivery and ethnic minority, Asian American, and women's issues in health and mental health. Her most recent books are *Women and Leadership: Transforming Visions and Diverse Voices* and *Learning from My Mother's Voice: Family Legend and the Chinese American Experience*. She serves on many national and local boards, including the Council for National Register for Health Service Providers in Psychology, and the Council of Representatives and the Board for the Advancement of Psychology in the Public Interest of the American Psychological Association.

June Chisholm is a professor of psychology at Pace University. She is a clinical psychologist who worked for many years as a senior psychologist in the Outpatient Psychiatric Department at Harlem Hospital Center, providing psychological services to an ethnically diverse, primarily poor, urban population. She has a small, part-time private practice in Manhattan. Her clinical and research interests include issues in the psychological treatment of women of color, psychological assessment of children and adults, parenting, community psychology, violence, and prejudice in the theory and practice of psychology.

Joan C. Chrisler is a professor of psychology at Connecticut College. She has published extensively on issues related to women's health and embodiment, especially on attitudes toward menstruation, premenstrual syndrome, body image, and weight. Her most recent books are *From Menarche to Menopause: The Female Body in Feminist Therapy* (2004, Haworth), *Women over 50: Psychological Perspectives* (2007, Springer), and *Lectures on the Psychology of Women* (4th ed., 2008, McGraw-Hill). She has served as president of the Society for Menstrual Cycle Research and the Society for the Psychology of Women (APA Division 35).

Shauna M. Cooper, currently a postdoctoral fellow at the University of North Carolina–Chapel Hill, received her Ph.D. in developmental psychology from the University of Michigan in 2005. She received her B.A. in psychology and communication studies from the University of North Carolina–Chapel Hill. Her research focuses on socialization practices in African American families and its role in the development of African American children and adolescents. Also, her work explores specific factors that contribute to the development of adolescent girls, particularly African American girls. She will be an assistant professor at the University of South Carolina starting in the Fall term, 2007.

Karol Dean is an associate professor of psychology at Mount Saint Mary's College in Los Angeles. She completed her doctoral training in personality psychology at the University of California, Los Angeles. Her primary research interest is in sexual aggression. Dr. Dean has conducted research on the identification of predictors of sexual aggression among college men. She teaches courses on violence against women, psychology of gender, and research methods.

Kay Deaux is Distinguished Professor of Psychology and Women's Studies at the Graduate Center of the City University of New York. Her involvement in the study of gender issues has been extensive, including basic research inside and outside the laboratory, expert witness testimony in cases of gender discrimination, and teaching courses on gender, psychology, and law. She has served as president of the Society for the Psychological Study of Social Issues and the American Psychological Society, and has been a recipient of the Carolyn Wood Sherif Award and the Heritage Research Award from Division 35 of the American Psychological Association.

Darlene DeFour, Ph.D., is a social psychologist/community psychologist. She is a graduate of Fisk University and received her doctorate from the University of Illinois at Urbana-Champaign. She is currently an associate professor of psychology at Hunter College of the City

University of New York. There she teaches such classes as social psychology, personal adjustment, psychology of women, theories of ethnic identity development, and issues in black psychology.

Dr. DeFour is currently a member of the board of directors of the new york association of black psychologists and has served on the board of directors of the national association. She is also active in several divisions of the American Psychological Association. The theme of her current research is the exploration of the various ways that violence in the form of racism and sexism as well as physical violence affects the everyday lives of adolescent and adult black females.

Linda Dillon is in human resources for the New York State Education Department. She is currently completing a certificate in human resource management at Union Graduate College.

Claire Etaugh received her Ph.D. in developmental psychology from the University of Minnesota. She is a professor of psychology at Bradley University, where she has taught psychology of women courses since 1979. A Fellow of the Society for the Psychology of Women and Developmental Psychology divisions of the American Psychological Association, she has published more than 100 articles in such journals as *Psychology of Women*, *Sex Roles*, *Child Development*, and *Developmental Psychology*. Dr. Etaugh is coauthor of *The World of Children*, *Psychology of Women: A Lifespan Perspective*, and *Women's Lives: A Topical Approach.* She has been a consulting editor for *Psychology of Women Quarterly* and *Sex Roles.*

Ruth E. Fassinger, Ph.D., is interim chair of the Department of Counseling and Personnel Services, professor of counseling psychology, and a Distinguished Scholar-Teacher at the University of Maryland, College Park. She specializes in the psychology of women and gender, sexuality and sexual orientation, the psychology of work, and advocacy and social justice issues. She is a Fellow of the American Psychological Association in several divisions, currently serves on the editorial board of the *Journal of Lesbian Studies*, and has received numerous awards for her scholarship, teaching, and professional contributions.

Irene H. Frieze is a professor of psychology and women's studies at the University of Pittsburgh. She is the author of *Hurting the One You Love: Violence in Relationships* (2005, Thompson/Wadsworth). Her research on battered women began in the 1970s and has continued ever since. She has expanded this focus on battered women to look at dating violence and stalking, as well as coercive sex. Dr. Frieze has published nearly 200 articles, books, book chapters, and reviews over her career and continues to work on violence in relationships today.

Shelly Grabe, a recipient of the Ruth L. Kirschstein National Research Service Award for her research on women's body objectification, received her Ph.D. in clinical psychology from the University of Missouri–Columbia and completed her residency at the University of Washington School of Medicine. She currently holds fellowship positions in psychology and women's studies at the University of Wisconsin–Madison. Her research interests involve how cultural objectification of women's bodies serves to keep women in a position of marginalized status via threats to their psychological well-being. Dr. Grabe is frequently involved in public action that focuses on women's psychological health and international human rights. She identifies as a scholar-activist and is committed to exploring how the scholarly study of gendered social structures can foster social change. Her work has been highlighted by the Association of Women in Psychology, *USA Today*, and CBS News.

Beverly Greene, Ph.D., ABPP, is a professor of psychology at St. John's University and a clinical psychologist in independent practice in Brooklyn, New York. She is a Fellow of seven divisions of APA (9, 12, 29, 35, 42, 44, and 45) and of the Academy of Clinical Psychology. An active participant in APA governance, she is an elected member of the APA Council of Representatives (Div. 42—Independent Practice). The recipient of numerous national awards for significant contributions to the scholarly literature, she is the 2006 recipient of the Florence Halpern Award for Distinguished Professional Contributions to Clinical Psychology (Div. 12). Forthcoming publications include *A Minyan of Women: Family Dynamics, Jewish Identity and Psychotherapy Practice* (Haworth Press) and *Phenomenal Women: Psychological Vulnerability and Resilience in Black Women.*

Elizabeth L. Haines is an assistant professor at William Paterson University in Wayne, New Jersey. Her research interests are in the area of stereotyping and prejudice with special emphasis on implicit measurement, stereotypes of parents in the workplace, women's self-concept change, and the physiological correlates of racism.

Kareen Hill began her military service in 1999, when she was drafted into the Israel Air Force, where she was responsible for logistics of equipment and supplies. In 2003, she enrolled in a B.A. program in behavioral sciences at the Max Stern Academic College of Emek Yezreel, where she majored in psychology and criminology. She graduated in 2006. During her studies, she was a research assistant to Dr. Khawla Abu Baker, whose research focused on Arab women in Israel. Hill was responsible for seeking and reviewing published literature in a variety of subjects related to women, analyzing data, editing articles prior to publication, gathering subject matter for writing books and summaries, and active participation in relevant seminars. Following her graduation, she began working as a research assistant to Prof. Marilyn P. Safir at the University of Haifa. Hill's plans for the future include beginning M.A. studies in information science at Bar Ilan University, beginning in October 2007.

Janet Shibley Hyde is Helen Thompson Woolley Professor of Psychology and Women's Studies at the University of Wisconsin. Her research, over three decades, has focused on psychological gender differences and similarities and women balancing work and family. Her current work focuses on the emergence of gender differences in depression in adolescence. Since 1990, Dr. Hyde has been codirector of the Wisconsin Study of Families and Work (www.wsfw.us). She is the author of two undergraduate textbooks, *Half the Human Experience: The Psychology of Women* and *Understanding Human Sexuality*. A Fellow of the American Psychological Association and the American Association for the Advancement of Science, Dr. Hyde has won numerous awards, including the Heritage Award from the Society for the Psychology of Women for her career contributions to research on the psychology of women. In 2002 she was listed among the top 100 psychologists in the world in terms of citations in introductory psychology textbooks.

Phyllis A. Katz is currently director of the Institute for Research on Social Problems, formerly located in Boulder, Colorado, and now located in Bal Harbour, Florida. Dr. Katz received her Ph.D. from Yale University in clinical and developmental psychology and has taught at Queens College, New York University, the Graduate Center of the City University of New York, and the University of Colorado. Her research has focused upon the development of gender-roles and racial attitudes in children, and she has published extensively in these two areas.

Dr. Katz was the founding editor of *Sex Roles*, the first publication devoted entirely to scholarly research on women's issues and was also editor of the Society for the Psychological Study of Social Issues' *Journal of Social Issues*. She has served as president of SPSSI, as well as the Society for the Psychology of Women, has been on the governing council of the APA, and has been a recipient of the Carolyn Sherif and the APA Public Interest Senior Research awards.

Her most recent book, *The Feminist Dollar: The Wise Woman's Buying Guide*, was coauthored with her daughter, Margaret Katz Cann. Dr. Katz is currently working on a book describing the results of her longitudinal study of how young children develop concepts and attitudes about race and gender, entitled *Black and White and Pink and Blue*.

Mary E. Kite is a professor of psychological science at Ball State University. Recently, she served in administrative roles at Ball State, including acting graduate dean and associate graduate dean. Throughout her career, she has maintained an active research program in the area of stereotyping and prejudice, particularly as it relates to antigay prejudice and racism. Most recently, she coauthored a textbook on stereotyping and prejudice (with Bernie Whitley). Dr. Kite is a Fellow of the Society of the Teaching of Psychology, the Society for the Psychology of Women, and the Society for the Psychological Study of Lesbian, Gay, and Bisexual Issues. In 2006, she served as president of the Society for the Teaching of Psychology. She is currently secretary-treasurer of the Midwestern Psychological Association and chairs the APA Task Force on Diversity Education Resources.

Maria Klara received her B.A. from Boston College in 1999 and her M.S. in counseling psychology from Northeastern University in 2003. She is currently pursuing her Psy.D. in school-clinical child psychology at Pace University. Her academic interests include women and gender issues, psychological assessment, and clinical work with adolescents.

Nicole Livingston is a doctoral candidate in the Clinical Psychology Program at Indiana University of Pennsylvania. She is currently conducting her dissertation research on relational aggression and recently presented this work at the 2007 Association for Women in Psychology conference. She is a coauthor (with Maureen McHugh and Amy Ford) of an article on postmodern perspectives on gender and violence published in the 2005 special issue of *Psychology of Women Quarterly*. Her clinical interests include gender issues and forensic psychology.

Bernice Lott is professor emerita of psychology and women's studies at the University of Rhode Island and is a former dean of its University College. She has taught at the University of Colorado and Kentucky State College and was a visiting scholar/professor at Brown University's Center for Research and Teaching on Women; Stanford University's Institute for Research on Women and Gender; the Department of Psychology in Waikato University, New Zealand; and the University of Hawaii–Manoa. She received the University of Rhode Island's Excellence Award for scholarly achievement, served as president of APA's Division 35 (Psychology of Women), and has been honored for scholarly, teaching, mentoring, and social policy contributions by APA's Committee on Women, Division 35, the Association for Women in Psychology, and the National Multicultural Conference and Summit. In 1999, the University of Rhode Island awarded her the honorary degree of Doctor of Humane Letters.

Dr. Lott is the author of numerous theoretical and empirical articles, chapters, and books in the areas of social learning, gender, poverty, and other social issues, and is a Fellow of APA and of Divisions 1, 8, 9, and 35. She has represented Divisions 9 and 35 on the coalition of Divisions for Social Justice. Her areas of interest are interpersonal discrimination; the intersections among gender, ethnicity, and social class; multicultural issues; the social psychology of poverty; and the social psychology of dissent. Currently, she represents Division 9 (SPSSI) on APA's Council of Representatives and is a member of an Interdivisional Minority Pipeline Project working on strategies to increase the recruitment and retention of graduate students of color.

Jennifer Martin is the department head of English at a public alternative high school for at-risk students in Michigan and holds a Ph.D. in educational leadership. She created an intervention strategy to reduce the high rate of peer sexual harassment that was occurring within her school; this became her dissertation research and was how her interest in sexual harassment began. Dr. Martin serves as a mentor to adolescent females in the alternative high school. She has also started a successful women's studies program, where students are involved in service-learning projects and have partnered with a domestic violence and sexual assault nonprofit. Teaching women's studies in high school is a political and social cause for her, as is feminist self-identification and the reasons why many young women are hesitant to identify as feminists. She is an advocate for at-risk students in general, as well.

In addition to high-school teaching, Dr. Martin is an adjunct lecturer at Oakland University, where she teaches graduate research methods and feminist methodology. Her research interests include peer sexual harassment, feminist identification, teaching for social justice, detracking, service-learning, and the at-risk student.

Maureen C. McHugh is a social psychologist and gender specialist. A professor of psychology at Indiana University of Pennsylvania, she has introduced more than 2,500 students to the psychology of women. In addition to journal articles, Dr. McHugh has published chapters in many of the edited texts for the psychology of women, including the first *Handbook on the Psychology of Women*. Her work focuses on gender differences, feminist methods, and violence against women. She and Irene Frieze received the Distinguished Publication Award from the Association for Women in Psychology (AWP) for their coedited special issue of *Psychology of Women Quarterly* on measures of gender-role attitudes. With Frieze, she coedited two additional special issues in 2005, of *Psychology of Women Quarterly* and *Sex Roles*, on gender and violence and intimate relationships. Dr. McHugh served as the president equivalent of AWP and received the Christine Ladd Franklin Award for service to AWP and feminist psychology.

Michelle McKenzie received her B.A. in French with a minor in psychology from California State University, Long Beach, followed by her M.A. in psychology from Pepperdine University. She is a rape crisis counselor and volunteer with the Sexual Assault Crisis Agency. She is also on the Speaker's Bureau for the Rape, Abuse and Incest National Network.

Martha Mednick received her doctorate from Northwestern University in 1955 in clinical psychology. For many years until her retirement, she was a professor at Howard University in Washington, D.C. She has been a researcher and has published extensively in the field of the psychology of women for many years. The social issues journal *New Perspectives on Women*, edited by Mednick and Sandra Schwartz Tangri in 1972, was an important influence on the establishment of Division 35, the Psychology of Women. Dr. Mednick was one of the founders of the division, as well as serving on the APA Committee on the Status of Women. She is a past president of Division 35 and has been awarded the APA Committee on Women in Psychology Leadership Award, as well as the Carolyn Wood Sherif Memorial Award for feminist scholarship.

Andrea L. Meltzer is a doctoral student in the experimental program of the psychology department at the University of Tennessee–Knoxville. Her recent work includes body dissatisfaction among women, sexism in the workforce, and gender disparities regarding health care issues.

Vita Carulli Rabinowitz is a professor in the department of psychology and acting provost at Hunter College of the City University of New York. She received her doctorate in social psychology at Northwestern University. Her current research and writings are in the area of sex and gender bias in behavioral and biomedical research, feminist perspectives on research methods, and gender equity, faculty development, and the advancement of women in academia. As an administrator, Dr. Rabinowitz has a particular interest in revitalizing undergraduate education and curricular reform and innovation, and in faculty development to support research, teaching, and leadership.

Pamela Trotman Reid, Ph.D., is the provost and executive vice president at Roosevelt University and a professor of psychology. She previously held administrative and professorial ranks at the University of Michigan, the City University of New York Graduate Center, and the University of Tennessee–Chattanooga. Her research interests have focused on gender and racial socialization. In particular, her more than 60 journal articles, book chapters, book reviews, and essays address the intersections of discrimination based on social class, race, sex, and related topics. Active in scholarly organizations, she has held elected positions on boards and committees of APA and other professional organizations.

Dr. Reid has been an invited speaker at scores of international, national, and regional conferences and more than two dozen colleges and universities. She is the recipient of several national awards, among them the Distinguished Leadership Award given by the APA Committee on Women in Psychology, the Distinguished Publication Award from the Association of Women in Psychology, and the Distinguished Contribution to Research Award from the Society for the Psychological Study of Ethnic Issues. She holds a B.S. from Howard University, an M.A. from Temple University, and a Ph.D. from the University of Pennsylvania.

Patricia D. Rozee is a professor of psychology and women's studies at California State University, Long Beach. She is the founding director of the Center for Community Engagement. Dr. Rozee received her Ph.D. in social psychology from the University of California, Davis, and completed a two-year postdoctoral fellowship in applied social psychology at Vanderbilt University. She has published extensively in the area of violence against women, especially sexual assault and rape resistance. Dr. Rozee has taught the psychology of women for more than 20 years. She is also a coeditor of the award-winning textbook *Lectures on the Psychology of Women*, now in its fourth edition.

Nancy Felipe Russo, Ph.D., Regents Professor of Psychology and Women and Gender Studies at Arizona State University, is a former editor of the *Psychology of Women Quarterly* and author or editor of more than 200 publications related to gender and the psychology of women. A former president of the Society for the Psychology of Women (APA Division 35), Dr. Russo is the recipient of the society's Centennial Heritage Award for Contributions to Public Policy and the Carolyn Wood Sherif Award in recognition of distinguished contributions to research, teaching, mentoring, and service to psychology and society. A Fellow of APA and APS (American Psychological Society), Russo is the recipient of APA's 1995 Award for Distinguished Contributions to Psychology in the Public Interest and the 2003 Distinguished International Psychologist Award from APA's Division of International Psychology. Dr. Russo is the current editor of the *American Journal of Orthopsychiatry*.

Marilyn P. Safir is professor emerita, department of psychology at Haifa University (specializing in clinical and social psychology). She graduated with her Ph.D. in clinical psychology and research methodology at Syracuse University in 1968 and then moved to Israel. Dr. Safir serves as the director of Project KIDMA for the Advancement of Women, which, in addition to programs for women from disadvantaged communities and villages, runs workshops for leadership training for multicultural and mixed socioeconomic groups. Dr. Safir is the founder and former director (1983–1993) of the University of Haifa's Women's Studies Program. She is also a founding member of the Executive Committee and first president of the Israel Association for Feminist and Gender Studies (1998–2002).

Jeri Sechzer is visiting professor of psychology at Pace University. She received her Ph.D. in behavioral neuroscience from the University of Pennsylvania. Dr. Sechzer's main research and publications primarily concern sex and gender issues in behavioral and biomedical science, behavioral neuroscience, bioethics, and values in science. She has recently begun to address issues of relation, psychology, and gender.

Dr. Sechzer is a Fellow of the American Psychological Association (Division 35, Psychology of Women; Division 6, Behavioral Neuroscience and Comparative Psychology; and Division 52, International Psychology), the American Association for the Advancement of Science, the New York Academy of Medicine, and the New York Academy of Sciences. She has been the recipient of many honors and awards, including the Leadership Award of the Association for Women in Science (New York Chapter) and the Wilhelm Wundt Award of the New York State Psychological Association for the scientific contributions to psychology.

Janet Sigal is a professor of psychology at Farleigh Dickinson University. She received her Ph.D. from Northwestern University. She has delivered numerous presentations and publications in the area of women's issues, including sexual harassment and domestic violence. She is a Fellow of the American Psychological Association and an APA NGO representative at the UN.

Julia R. Steinberg, M.A., is a doctoral candidate in the graduate program in social psychology at Arizona State University, where she serves as a research assistant for the university's Office of Academic Institutional and Cultural Change. Her research interests span several gender/women's issues, including body image, pregnancy outcomes and mental health, and the persistence of women in math and science fields. Her dissertation focuses on understanding the effects and moderators of stereotype threat for women who persist in engineering, math, and science fields.

Tina Stern grew up in Cleveland and has lived in Atlanta since 1987. She earned her undergraduate degree from Boston University, her master's degree from Cleveland State University, and her Ph.D. from the University of Georgia. She is a professor of psychology at Georgia

Perimeter College, where for many years she has taught courses on the psychology of women. In addition, as a licensed psychologist, Dr. Stern maintains a clinical practice. Since her days at Boston University, she has been interested in, and written about, issues related to women and in particular the psychology of women.

Jessica Tartaro, M.A., is a doctoral student in the clinical health psychology program at Arizona State University. She currently serves as the first graduate fellow of the American Orthopsychiatric Association and is editor of the *Ortho Bulletin*, the newsletter for that organization. Tartaro is the 2006 recipient of an APA Society of Clinical Psychology Student Excellence in Service Award for her work to counter violence against women and to link local issues to global concerns. Her current research focuses on spirituality among cancer patients, and her practice explores the integration of yoga in community-based mental health services.

Veronica Thomas is a professor in the department of human development and psychoeducational studies, Howard University. Her research interests include the psychology of black women, the academic and socioemotional development of youths placed at risk, and culturally responsive evaluations.

Cheryl Brown Travis is a professor in the department of psychology at the University of Tennessee–Knoxville and chair of the women's studies program. Her recent work on women and health care issues has focused on gender and race disparities in the treatment of heart disease. Her latest books include an edited volume on evolution, gender, and rape and an coedited volume on sexuality, society, and feminism.

Maren True is a doctoral student in the graduate program in social psychology at Arizona State University under the mentorship of Dr. Nancy Felipe Russo. Her research interests encompass objectification theory and women's life history decisions, including education, family, and career choices. Before graduating from Colorado College in 2003, she worked for several years as a residential treatment counselor for troubled youth and as a telephonic counselor and subsequent team leader for the Colorado, Montana, Idaho, and Ohio Tobacco Cessation Quitlines.

Christa White is completing her undergraduate degree in psychology at Union College, where she has conducted research on integrating work/life for women and the treatment at the workplace of women who are physically challenged.